Choices under Duress of the Holocaust

Benjamin Murmelstein and the Fate of Viennese Jewry

VOLUME I — VIENNA

Leonard H. Ehrlich and Edith Ehrlich

Edited by Carl S. Ehrlich

With a Foreword by Harriet Pass Freidenreich

TEXAS TECH UNIVERSITY PRESS

This book is typeset in Bauer Bodoni and New Caledonia. The paper used in this book meets the minimum requirements of ANSI/NISO Z39.48-1992 (R1997). ♾

ZukunftsFonds der Republik Österreich This book was made possible in part by the generous support of Zukunftsfonds der Republik Österreich.

Designed by Janis Owens
Cover photographs by DÖW

Library of Congress Control Number: 2018943434

ISBN 978-1-68283-034-5

Printed in the United States of America
18 19 20 21 22 23 24 25 26 / 9 8 7 6 5 4 3 2 1

Texas Tech University Press
Box 41037
Lubbock, Texas 79409-1037 USA
800.832.4042
ttup@ttu.edu
www.ttupress.org

Contents

PART II

Captivity

Foreword

THIS IMPRESSIVE VOLUME results from more than thirty years of research on the life of a very complex and controversial individual, Benjamin Murmelstein, who was one of the leading administrators of the Viennese Jewish Community after the Anschluss and later became the last head of the Council of Jewish Elders in Theresienstadt/Terezin. It is an extremely important work because it demonstrates the unbearable obstacles and limitations confronting European Jewish leaders who were trying to save the lives of their fellow Jews during World War II. *Choices under Duress* addresses many of the crucial issues raised by Holocaust research past and present. Could a righteous Jew in a prominent position have survived the Holocaust? Should all Jews appointed by Nazis to positions of authority over other Jews be considered collaborators? Does history treat Jews who survived the Holocaust more critically than those who perished?

In 1973–74, Leonard H. and Edith Ehrlich, the husband-and-wife team who co-authored this book, began investigating the role Benjamin Murmelstein played in Vienna and Theresienstadt for personal reasons. Growing up in Vienna in the 1930s, Leonard Ehrlich developed great respect for the leader of his youth services, Rabbi Murmelstein, whom he viewed as an intellectual role model and chose as the rabbi for his bar mitzvah. Together with their families, Leonhard Ehrlich, as he was then known, and Edith Schwarz, who was later to become his wife, were among the 120,000 Viennese Jews who were able to emigrate after the Anschluss with the help of the *Israelitische Kultusgemeinde* (IKG), the reconstructed Jewish communal organization headed by Joseph Löwenherz and his deputy Benjamin Murmelstein. Ehrlich never forgot his synagogal mentor and questioned the claims of survivors that Murmelstein under Nazi rule had been transformed into a monster whom they held responsible for the fate of the remaining Jews in Vienna and also of those incarcerated in the "model ghetto" of Theresienstadt. With support from his wife Edith, Leonard H. Ehrlich, by then a professor of philosophy at the University of Massachusetts, set out to gain a more balanced understanding of the actual situation in Vienna and later in Theresienstadt and the choices available to Murmelstein and other Jewish functionaries under Nazi control. They researched all the available primary sources and interviewed Murmelstein extensively. The Ehrlichs also tracked the lives and deaths of Viennese Jews after they were deported "to the East." It took over three decades for them to complete this very ambitious project.

The Ehrlichs were not the only individuals grappling with the Murmelstein story over the last thirty years or so. In 2014 a documentary entitled *The Last of the Unjust* became available for public viewing. This film, directed by well-known French cinematographer

Claude Lanzmann, was based on interviews that Lanzmann had conducted in 1975 with Benjamin Murmelstein. Unlike *Shoah*, the acclaimed documentary of Holocaust survivors also filmed in the same era but released in 1985, this more recent production received generally negative reviews. One reviewer, who labeled it "The Last of the Self-Righteous," condemned Lanzmann for presenting a sympathetic portrayal of his subject, asserting that he had not researched the topic in any depth.[1] Although the Ehrlichs do not mention Lanzmann in their work, they certainly provide the documentation that his film lacks and lay a sounder basis for the reconsideration of the reputation of Benjamin Murmelstein.

In the late 1970s, I started researching my book *Jewish Politics in Vienna, 1918–38* (Indiana University Press, 1991), which ends with the Anschluss, precisely where the Ehrlichs' study began. I had undertaken a much easier task because there was plenty of documentation available reflecting a wide variety of perspectives, including many different newspapers and publications, as well as communal records from the very extensive IKG collection at the Central Archives for the History of the Jewish People on the Givat Ram campus of the Hebrew University in Jerusalem. Like the Ehrlichs, I was initially discouraged from using these voluminous records, all of which had survived the war, but I too was fortunate enough to have received assistance from Ya'akov, the courier who brought me box after box of materials. The Ehrlichs only had access to official records that had been issued or approved by Nazi officials and scattered in many different archives, as well as various testimonies from postwar trials. During the Nazi era, few Jewish newspapers or other publications were permitted in Vienna and they, as well as all correspondence with the outside world, were censored. I, however, was able to examine the entire interwar Jewish press, whether Jewish Nationalist, Liberal, Orthodox, or Socialist, private papers in the Zionist Archives, and other published and unpublished sources both in Israel and in Vienna. I did not do any interviewing for this project because I assumed that virtually all of the IKG leaders from before 1938 were deceased and others would probably not be able to provide reliable information. The Ehrlichs, in addition to interviewing Murmelstein at great length on several occasions, also spoke with many Viennese Jews and Holocaust survivors about their memories of Murmelstein in both Vienna and Theresienstadt, but for the most part the survivors' accounts were based on rumors rather than eyewitness testimonies.

After the Nazi takeover, the *Israelitische Kultusgemeinde Wien* was a completely different entity than the one I had studied, although the name remained the same. During the interwar era, the Jewish Community in Vienna, like others in Central Europe, chose their own leadership in elections held every four years with Liberals, Jewish Nationalists, Orthodox, and Socialist parties contesting seats on the executive and in the communal council. Many inner tensions among the various political factions continued to fester in wartime Vienna. In the 1920s, the Liberal members of the Union of Austrian Jews, most of whom had migrated to the city in the mid to late nineteenth century from Hungary, Bohemia, and Moravia, dominated the organized Jewish Community, but by the mid-1930s Jewish Nationalists or Zionists, many of whom had been born in Galicia and moved to Vienna in the early twentieth century, gained a majority. The German-speaking "Western Jews," especially those who originated in Bohemia and Hungary, considered themselves superior to the "Eastern Jews" (pejoratively referred to as *Ostjuden*), who hailed from Galicia and could speak Yiddish as well as German.

After the Anschluss, the Nazis took full control of the IKG, sent many of its former leaders to Dachau, and appointed all of its top functionaries. They selected Zionists, some of whom had served in the previous administration, rather than Liberals, because Liberals considered themselves to be German-Austrians of the Jewish faith, a view that was contrary to Nazi ideology. As head of the Community, the Nazis appointed Joseph (Josef) Löwenherz, a Jewish Nationalist lawyer from Galicia, who had served as vice-president of the IKG and then became its executive director, and as his deputy they chose Benjamin Murmelstein, a brilliant young and respected scholar, also a Zionist from Galicia, who was next in line to become the chief rabbi of the Austrian capital. Both men had been resented as outsiders even before the Anschluss, albeit for different reasons. Löwenherz and Murmelstein worked directly under Adolf Eichmann and his lieutenants throughout the war but, unlike most other Nazi appointees, managed to survive. This work focuses on the grave difficulties these two men faced and analyzes the choices they made under great duress. It also compares the dire situation of the Jewish functionaries in Nazi-controlled Vienna with the similarly desperate plight of their counterparts in Berlin and Prague and later the in-fighting among them, especially in Theresienstadt.

In the aftermath of World War II, a series of trials of Nazi war criminals occurred in Germany, Czechoslovakia, Poland, the Soviet Union, and elsewhere. The Nuremberg Trials of 1946, presided over by American judges, used German documentation to convict numerous top Nazi officials, condemning many of them to death. Several less known trials and honor courts against Jews accused of collaboration with the Nazis also occurred; at times it seems as if these Jewish survivors were treated even more harshly than the Nazis themselves. Murmelstein was imprisoned in Prague immediately after the war for his supposed collaborative role in Theresienstadt, but then freed and never indicted due to lack of evidence. His testimony before a Czech court against Karl Rahm, the last Commandant of Theresienstadt in 1944, led to Rahm's conviction and his death sentence. Löwenherz, although he encountered similar challenges, was exonerated by an honor court in London in 1946. Subsequently, Murmelstein faced a Jewish court of honor in Rome, but as before he was never formally charged with any crimes or indicted. Nevertheless, although some postwar witnesses praised Murmelstein for his efforts on behalf of his fellow Jews, his reputation never recovered from all of the hateful accusations from Viennese Jews as well as Theresienstadt survivors, who blamed him for the deaths of their loved ones.

The Eichmann trial in Jerusalem in 1961, conducted by Israeli judges, turned into a show trial featuring, for the first time, public testimonies of Holocaust survivors, very few of whom had ever met Adolf Eichmann in person during the war. The two surviving Jews with the greatest amount of experience in dealing with Eichmann and his lieutenants throughout the war were unable to attend this trial, Joseph Löwenherz because he was seriously ill in New York and Benjamin Murmelstein, then living in Rome, because he was *persona non grata*, and the Israeli government refused to offer him protection. Although Murmelstein provided a written personal account of Eichmann's role in the forced emigration and deportation of Viennese Jews, his firsthand testimony was never used during the trial. Indeed, Gershon Scholem, a respected historian of Jewish mysticism who had made *aliyah* from Germany in the 1930s, argued at the time of the trial that Murmelstein deserved the death penalty but Eichmann did not! Why were Jews who worked under the direct control of Nazis, especially those trying to save Jewish lives, considered more culpable after the war than the Nazi officials themselves?

Hannah Arendt, the German-Jewish political philosopher who found refuge in the United States in 1941, wrote a scathing critique that she entitled *Eichmann in Jerusalem: The Banality of Evil*, based on her observations at that trial. In addition to characterizing the lone defendant not as a devil or a monster but as a rather bland bureaucrat, she accused the members of the *Judenräte*, Jewish councils in the ghettoes of wartime Central and Eastern Europe, of helping to facilitate the deaths of Jews sent to concentration camps. Neither a historian nor an eyewitness herself, Arendt nevertheless categorically judged all Jewish functionaries under Nazi rule to be willing or unwilling collaborators. Along similar lines, Raul Hilberg, dean of Holocaust historians, in his authoritative book *The Destruction of European Jewry* based primarily on German war records, condemned the Jewish leadership within the ghettoes for assisting the Nazi perpetrators in their systematic round-ups and killings of Jews. Only later did Isaiah Trunk, in his important study *Judenrat* that focused on Poland, provide a more nuanced portrayal of the administrators of these Jewish councils by analyzing the variety of tactics that they employed in their efforts to prolong the lives of the Jews who lived in the ghettoes. He concluded that one cannot make generalizations about the conduct of those men, each of whom faced a difficult, indeed an impossible, situation and handled it somewhat differently.[2]

Most general Holocaust histories tend to focus on Vienna only in the immediate aftermath of the Anschluss in order to demonstrate the harsh treatment of Viennese Jews and the violence and humiliation they experienced after the Nazis marched triumphantly into the Austrian capital. The sequence of anti-Jewish measures that were implemented in Germany over a five-year period came into effect almost overnight in Vienna and were carried out within one-and-a-half years through rapid forced emigration and the confiscation of Jewish property. Roughly two-thirds of Viennese Jews managed to escape before emigration was halted completely in October 1941, largely thanks to the efforts of Löwenherz, Murmelstein, and their staff within the IKG. Those Jews who remained in Vienna thereafter, most of whom were elderly, hospitalized, orphaned, or else of mixed Jewish-German parentage, have attracted less scholarly attention. Studies of the Jewish functionaries working for the IKG are even rarer, especially compared to the stories about the victims or memoirs of survivors.

The first book to examine the IKG in Vienna from 1938 to 1945 sympathetically and in some depth is Doron Rabinovici's *Eichmann's Jews*, published in English in 2011. Rabinovici aptly describes Murmelstein as "a technocrat of the administration of terror." As he phrases it, "The scholar became an administrator, the intellectual a bureaucrat, and the man of god a manager of misery."[3] Nearly all other published studies have portrayed Benjamin Murmelstein, who headed the emigration department before 1941 and was put in charge of deportations thereafter, in a very negative light. His detractors have described him disparagingly as overweight, sloppy, relentless, ambitious, calculating, cynical, arrogant, haughty, and dictatorial. His defenders, however, characterize him as loyal, gifted, hardworking, and a brilliant wordsmith who did not suffer (Jewish) fools gladly. He did not seek popularity among the Jews trapped in Vienna or incarcerated in Theresienstadt but instead instilled fear and demanded their cooperation. In his relations with Nazi officials, he could be conciliatory and tactful, without being obsequious or going beyond certain limits that he set for himself. He was capable of seeing situations from a Nazi perspective and understanding the underlying meaning behind their doubletalk. He did what he could for as long as he could to try to protect the lives of as many Jews as possible, particularly those who seemed the most vulnerable: the elderly, the sick, the handicapped, and the very young. Although he was not able to maintain his high moral standards as a rabbi, he did his best to help other Jews survive and not aggrandize himself. Shouldn't he be given credit for the lives he saved through emigration and not just be held responsible for the deaths of those deported whom he could not save?

Choices under Duress of the Holocaust addresses many important questions that Holocaust scholars have only recently begun to raise. Should all Elders or other appointed members of a *Judenrat* be considered collaborators because they worked with the Nazis? What did they know about what was going on in the outside world? When did they learn about Auschwitz and other death camps? Did they have any power of their own, and could they make their own decisions regarding life and death? Were they able to make real choices? Could they actually make a difference and save lives, or was that simply not possible in the long run? Were they themselves victims? What was it like to be the last head of a *Judenrat* or Council of Elders still alive after the war?

While Leonard and Edith Ehrlich began their exhaustive research on Benjamin Murmelstein and the IKG Vienna in the 1970s, only since 1990 have scholars like Dan Diner, Dan Michman, and Doron Rabinovici attempted to comprehend the tremendous pressure that came to bear upon the shoulders of the functionaries whom the Nazis appointed to head Jewish councils and the extremely restricted options available to them.[4] *Choices under Duress* is more than just a biographical study of Benjamin Murmelstein, a very controversial individual. Using all the available documents and other primary sources, it is a comprehensive history of the IKG of Vienna from the Anschluss to the end of World War II and of the fate of Viennese Jewry both before and after leaving the Austrian capital. It closely examines the relationships between the Nazi officials and their appointed Jewish functionaries, who felt compelled to follow their orders in the vain hope of helping their fellow Jews survive for as long as possible, and it explains the dire conditions under which the Jewish bureaucracy was forced to operate throughout the war, both in Vienna and later in Theresienstadt. Leonard and Edith Ehrlich's research methodology goes far beyond the historical data they collected to include detailed psychological and philosophical analyses of the very limited choices available to Murmelstein and his counterparts in other communities and ghettoes during the Holocaust.

Vienna served as a model for Nazi treatment of Jews in other cities and towns in Central and Eastern Europe, and the IKG proved to be the prototype for the organization of Jews in Berlin, Prague, and ghettoes in Poland and elsewhere in occupied Europe. From the

Anschluss to the end of the war, even when very few Jews remained in Vienna, the IKG continued to function with Joseph Löwenherz as its head, as did the Council of Elders in Theresienstadt from 1942 to 1945, with Benjamin Murmelstein as its chief elder in the final months of the war. This book, *Choices under Duress of the Holocaust* by Leonard and Edith Ehrlich, is likely to become the definitive study of Vienna's Jewish community and its leadership during the Holocaust, even though some historians may still disagree with its conclusions.

Harriet Pass Freidenreich
Yardley, PA
February 2015

Preface

On December 4, 2010, my late parents, Leonard H. Ehrlich and Edith Ehrlich (aka LHE and EE), emailed a brief note to their children and children-in-law. Leaving aside their signatures, the totality of their message reads as follows: "Dear children, the writing of Choices under Duress is finished." This brought to an end their active involvement in a project to which they had devoted over a third of a century. Over the next few weeks, my father worked on what would be his last conference paper, presented at the American Philosophical Association Eastern Division Annual Meeting at a session dedicated to him and my mother as founders of the Karl Jaspers Society of North America on December 27 of that year. He was working on a brief philosophical autobiography when his advancing congestive heart failure forced him to lay down his metaphorical pen a few short weeks later. He passed away on June 8, 2011.

Although my mother would in theory have been able to midwife their joint project to publication, by the time her husband and creative collaborator passed away, her advanced macular degeneration precluded her active participation in the publication project. Thus it happened that I became executor and editor of what had become my parents' *Nachlass* (literary legacy). The last two short projects my father worked on were quickly published,[1] as was a lecture he held at the Vienna Wiesenthal Institute for Holocaust Studies (*Wiener Wiesenthal Institut für Holocaust-Studien*) on the subject matter of this book.[2] Still to be tackled are my mother's memoirs: *Chapters from a Young Life: Childhood in Vienna, Refugee in England and America*. But it is this book, *Choices under Duress of the Holocaust*, with which I have primarily been concerned off and on over the past few years.

When my parents began this project, I was a teenager. By the time the draft was completed, I was in my mid-fifties. Although my parents were very active scholars primarily in the area of philosophy and published many other works during their years of labor on *Choices under Duress of the Holocaust*, it was this project that they viewed as their most important and to which they always returned. What they originally set out to do was to investigate the choices that the Jewish leadership under Nazi domination made from a philosophical perspective. Taking as their test case that of Rabbi Dr. Benjamin Murmelstein, the last surviving *Judenältester*, whom my father remembered from his childhood in Vienna, they quickly realized that they would need to contextualize their philosophical musings within a broader historical context in order to offer a fair assessment of the decision-making process available to Jewish leaders during those terrible years under Nazism. In order to do so, they minutely investigated the history of the Jewish Community of Vienna and its fate, both of those Jews in Vienna and of those interned at the "model ghetto" of Theresienstadt. The actions of the Jewish leadership under Nazi domination have oftentimes been questioned in the postwar period. However, as my parents painstakingly document, an examination of the evidence makes their actions appear much more nuanced and not as open to condemnation as first thought. What was originally planned as a three-hundred-page book expanded over the decades to become a manuscript of some two thousand pages. Once their original publication contract expired owing to the unanticipated tardiness and length of the project, they decided to wait until the project was finished before seeking another publisher. By the time they finished their work, however, they were no longer in any condition to do so. Hence, the responsibility of midwifing the book to publication fell into my lap.

While my parents had hoped to live long enough to see the publication of this, their magnum opus, neither of them was able to do so. Although my mother outlived my father by four-and-a-half years, passing away from pancreatic cancer on November 11, 2015, I expected her to live a lot longer and therefore did not push myself as hard for the publication as I now realize in retrospect I should have. One somewhat tardy expression of the desire to disseminate this work in a swifter manner that still managed to meet with my mother's approval was the decision to publish the work in two volumes not to appear simultaneously but consecutively. Thus, the first volume, focusing on Vienna, will appear before the second, encompassing Theresienstadt and the philosophical final section, the latter of which represents the aim and culmination of their massive study. The hope is that no more than two years will separate the publication of the one from that of its companion.

When I took over the publication responsibilities, I assumed that I would have to do no more than find a publisher. As it turned out, a lot more was involved, including editing the manuscript and finding illustrations. While I have ended up making thousands of small changes to the manuscript—encompassing spelling, punctuation, syntax, harmonization, clarification, assembling a bibliography and a glossary, and so on—I have made a deliberate decision not to make any substantial changes that would mute my parents' voices or convey an impression that they continued their research and writing longer than they actually did. In addition, I am painfully aware that I was unable to answer all outstanding questions arising from the manuscript or to iron out all problems with the text, partly because I had no access to their sources, partly because their system of notation was not always clear to me, and partly because this is not my area of expertise.

When my parents began this project, Holocaust studies was a new and struggling academic endeavor. By the time it was finished, the Holocaust had arguably become the most examined field of Jewish studies. This older perspective explains why my parents dedicated so much of their work to establishing some basic historical parameters. It may appear needless to convey this information today, but when their work commenced the Holocaust and the fate of Viennese Jewry were anything but common knowledge.

Taking over and publishing the work of other people is a daunting task, particularly if, as in my case, one's field of knowledge and expertise lies elsewhere. During the course of my work on getting my parents' *Choices under Duress of the Holocaust* published, I have been aided by many people without whom this work would never have seen the light of day.

*Leonard H. Ehrlich delivering a lecture about Benjamin Murmelstein at the Vienna Wiesenthal Institute for Holocaust Studies (*Wiener Wiesenthal Institut für Holocaust-Studien*) on May 13, 2008. He is flanked by Edith Ehrlich, who participated in the discussion afterward. (© CSE)*

Thanks are due to Benton M. Arnovitz, my parents' main contact at the United States Holocaust Memorial Museum (USHMM) in Washington, D.C., who put me in touch with Robert Mandel, at that time the Director of Texas Tech University (TTU) Press, to whom I am most grateful for accepting this manuscript into TTU Press's publication program. My gratitude extends to his successor, Courtney Burkholder, and to Joanna Conrad, the Assistant Director and Editor-in-Chief, for their help in seeing this project through to its completion, as well as to Nancy Benjamin, who served as the project manager in getting this volume to press.

Benton Arnovitz was also instrumental in establishing contacts for me with other departments at the USHMM. Thanks to Raye L. Farr, Neal Guthrie, Anatol Steck, and especially Brad Bauer and James Gilmore, I was able to donate my parents' voluminous research materials, including audiotaped interviews, to the USHMM, where they will be accessible to future generations of scholars.

In addition to accepting this project for publication, Robert Mandel of TTU Press made two important suggestions for this work. The first suggestion was to have an outside scholar write a foreword to this book. I am grateful to my colleague Professor Sara R. Horowitz for suggesting that I contact Professor Marsha L. Rozenblitt for suggestions; and I'm grateful to Professor Rozenblitt for putting me in touch with Professor Harriet Pass Freidenreich, an expert on Viennese Jewish history, to whom I'm indebted for supplying this volume with its important contextualizing foreword.

Mandel's second suggestion was that I break up the text with about four illustrations per chapter owing to the length of the manuscript. In order to do some preliminary investigative work along these lines, my mother and I traveled to Vienna and Terezin (Theresienstadt) in April/May 2012. Our trip to Vienna and our meetings at various archives there were facilitated and organized by Dr. Evelyn Adunka and Dr. Ingo Zechner. In addition to their aid during our Vienna visit, Drs. Adunka and Zechner were most helpful at every stage of the publication process. Without their invaluable aid and support, this book would never have been published. My gratitude to the two of them is enormous. They were also instrumental in helping to procure (and extend) a generous publication grant from the Future Fund of the Republic of Austria (*Zukunftsfonds der Republik Österreich*), to which I also express my great gratitude and thanks, as well as to its director, Professor Herwig Hösele, and to my primary correspondent there, Mag. Anita Dumfahrt.

During our visit to Vienna, my mother and I were able to visit with the following people, mainly at their respective places of employment: Dr. Elisabeth Boeckl-Klamper of the *Dokumentationsarchiv des österreichischen Widerstandes* (Documentation Centre of Austrian Resistance, aka DÖW), Mag. Angelika Shoshana Duizend-Jensen at the *Wiener Stadt- und Landesarchiv* (Vienna City and Provincial Archive), Dr. Sylvia Mattl-Wurm and Mag. Isabella Wasner-Peter of the *Wienbibliothek im Rathaus* (Vienna City Library), Mag. Gerhard Milchram at the *Wien Museum* (Vienna Museum), Dr. Hans Petschar and Mag. Michaela Pfundner of the *Bildarchiv und Grafiksammlung der Österreichischen Nationalbibliothek* (Picture Archive and Graphic Collection of the Austrian National Library), and Dr. Danielle Spera of the *Jüdisches Museum der Stadt Wien* (Vienna Jewish Museum), the latter of whom took the opportunity to interview my mother on video for their collections about growing up in prewar Vienna and working on the Murmelstein project. I would like to express my thanks to all for their help and for taking the time to meet with us. My portion of the Vienna/Theresienstadt trip was supported by a generous grant from the Israel and Golda Koschitzky Centre for Jewish Studies at York University. I am grateful to its former director, Professor Sara R. Horowitz, for helping to make this opportunity possible.

Of particular help with the procurement of pictures has been Judith Cohen, Director of the Photographic Reference Collection at the USHMM. Albert Knoll of the *KZ-Gedenkstätte Dachau* (Concentration Camp Memorial Site Dachau) kindly supplied some photos and information pertaining to the internment of Viennese Jews there. Other photographs came from the Associated Press, the Bundesarchiv in Koblenz, the Leo Baeck Institute of New York, the Museum of History and Industry in Seattle, the Österreichische Nationalbibliothek, the Wiener Library of London, and the Wiener Stadt- und Landesarchiv. I am grateful to all who were of assistance at these institutions. A small research grant from the Faculty of Liberal Arts and Professional Studies at York University has helped to cover the costs of securing publication rights to some of the illustrations used in this volume.

Thanks are also due to my former graduate assistant, Marielle S. Indar, who did some of the preliminary formatting of the first volume. As well, I would like to express my thanks to Benjamin Murmelstein's son, Dr. Wolf Murmelstein, whom I met at his home in Ladispoli north of Rome in the summer of 2014 and who shared some valuable information with me. We had met once before in the summer of 1980, when I was on a backpacking trip by train through Europe. I had contacted his father, whose name was well-known to me thanks to my parents' research, and arranged to meet the two of them at a delicious pizzeria in one of Rome's astoundingly beautiful piazzas. Although I was too shy to immortalize the meeting with a photo, an oversight I sincerely regret, even at that young age I was fully cognizant of the historical incongruity of my sitting in the sun in Rome sharing a pizza with the last surviving *Judenältester* and his son. The following day I took a bus tour of Rome, booked and paid for by a most insistent Benjamin Murmelstein, who wanted to make sure that I—a poor student—saw all the most important sites and sights of his adopted home.

Thanks also to my sister, Dr. Karin Ehrlich Adelman, who acted more or less as my parents' personal physician during their last years of decline, and to my wife, Rabbi Michal Shekel, who shouldered more than her fair share of the household burdens during the time I was oblivious to the world while sitting at my desk.

When I first assumed the responsibility for publishing my parents' work, I asked my mother to whom this book would be dedicated, since there appeared to be no dedication page in the manuscript. She replied that in all the years that she and my father had worked on this project they had never once discussed this issue. However, it seemed inconceivable to me that my father had no concrete plans for a dedication in mind. Leaving aside his many (co-)edited books, he had previously published two monographs, both of which were dedicated in memory of specific victims of the Nazis: The first[3] was dedicated in memory of his uncles Henryk Fischgrund and Dr. Leon Ehrlich, as well as of his friend and fellow frontline medic Joseph Frani; the second[4] was dedicated in memory of his childhood friends, the twins Ilse and Kurt Mezei, who appear on multiple occasions in *Choices under Duress*. The last time I saw my father, I tried to elicit from him what his plans were for dedicating this book. Unfortunately, he was no longer able to respond to the question. Thus we will never know whether he planned to dedicate *Choices under Duress* to additional victims of the Holocaust, or perhaps even to his children and/or grandchildren. Be that as it may, this book itself serves as a memorial to the Jewish community into which my parents were born and where they spent their earliest years before fleeing to a new life in the New World. In addition, it serves as a capstone of and fitting epitaph for my parents' shared life of learning.

It is now six years since the draft manuscript was completed. In the interim, both my parents have passed away without the pleasure of seeing their magnum opus in print. While this was unfortunately inevitable in the case of my father, in that of my mother it was due to my slow progress in preparing the manuscript for publication. Nonetheless, in finally delivering it, I can only echo the hope expressed in the closing words of the biblical book of Nehemiah: "O my God, remember it to my credit!" (Neh 13:31b, NJPS).

Carl S. Ehrlich
York University
Toronto, Ontario
November 30, 2016
29 Heshvan 5777 (EE's first yahrzeit)

Abbreviations

AJDC	American Jewish Joint Distribution Committee, New York (also Joint)
AN	Aktennotiz (memorandum)
CA: A/W	Central Archives for the History of the Jewish People, Jerusalem
CBF	Central British Fund
CGJ	Council for German Jewry
DAF	Deutsche Arbeitsfront (German Labor Front)
DDSG	Donaudampfschiffahrtsgesellschaft (Danube Steamship Company)
DNB	Deutsches Nachrichtenbüro (German Press Service)
DÖW	Dokumentationsarchiv des österreichischen Widerstands (Documentation Archive of the Austrian Resistance)
EE	Edith Ehrlich née Schwarz
EICH/Eich	Eichmann trial papers
Gestapa	Geheimes Staatspolizeiamt (Headquarters of the Secret State Police)
Gestapo	Geheime Staatspolizei (Secret State Police)
HIAS	Hebrew Immigrant Aid Society
HICEM	Immigration organization founded in 1927; the name is an acronym of its sponsors: HIAS, JCA, and Emigdirect
HSSPF	Höherer SS- und Polizeiführer (Higher SS and Police Leader)
HStf./HStuf.	Hauptsturmführer (Captain)
IKG	Israelitische Kultusgemeinde (Jewish Community, mainly of Vienna but also of other cities)
IZG	Institut für Zeitgeschichte, Munich
JCA	Jewish Colonization Association, registered in Britain but based in France
Joint	American Jewish Joint Distribution Committee, New York (also AJDC)
JTA	Jewish Telegraph Agency, New York
KG	Kultusgemeinde(n) ("Jewish community[-ies]") (see also IKG)
KZ	Konzentrationslager (concentration camp)
L-papers	Löwenherz Papers at the Leo Baeck Institute, New York
LBI	Leo Baeck Institute, New York
LHE	Leonard H. Ehrlich
M	Benjamin Murmelstein
MER	Mitteleuropäisches Reisebüro (Central European Travel Bureau)
MK	Member of Knesset, the Israeli Parliament
MM	Margit (Margarete) Murmelstein

M-Ms.	Murmelstein Manuscript
M-O	Mährisch-Ostrau (Moravian Ostrava)
NA	National Archives, College Park, Maryland
NKVD	the Soviet People's Commissariat for Internal Affairs, or secret police
NSDAP	Nationalsozialistische Deutsche Arbeiterpartei (National Socialist German Workers' Party)
NSKK	Nationalsozialistisches Kraftfahrkorps (National Socialist Motor Corps)
NSV	Nationalsozialistische Volkswohlfahrt (National Socialist Welfare Organization)
NYK	Nippon Yusen Kaisha Line
OKW	Oberkommando der Wehrmacht (Supreme Command of the Wehrmacht)
OStuf.	Obersturmführer (Sergeant Major)
Palamt	Palästina-Amt Wien (Palestine Office of Vienna)
RM	Reichsmark, the currency of the German Reich
RSHA	Reichssicherheitshauptamt (Reich-headquarters of the [SS] Security Service)
RV	Reichsvertretung der Deutschen Juden (National Representation of the German Jews) (until 1943) or Reichsvereinigung der Juden in Deutschland, "National Association of the German Jews/Jews in Germany" (as of 1939)
RWM	Reichswirtschaftsministerium (Reich Ministry for Economics)
SA	Sturmabteilung (Storm Troop, Nazi paramilitary corps also known as the "Brownshirts")
Schf.	Scharführer (squadron leader)
SD	Sicherheitsdienst (Security Service)
Sipo	Sicherheitspolizei (Security Police)
SS	Schutzstaffel (Protection Detachment, the dreaded Nazi paramilitary corps)
Stapo	Staatspolizei (State Police)
Stubaf.	Sturmbannführer (Major)
USchf.	Unterscharführer (junior squadron leader)
YIVO	Yidisher Visnshaftlekher Institut (Jewish Scientific Institute, founded in Vilna (Vilnius) in 1925; now YIVO Institute for Jewish Learning in New York)
YV	Yad Vashem, Jerusalem

Chapter 1

Introduction: Rush to Judgment, Lingering Doubts

How the Project Came to Be

An elderly man turns from Via Sebastiano Grandis to the Piazza di Santa Croce in Gerusalemme. It is in a neat, middle-class, residential neighborhood at the outskirts of the center of Rome, about one mile south of the Piazza dei Cinquecento and the Stazione Termini. The man stands no more than five and a half feet tall and is of stocky build; those who knew him thirty years earlier would have remembered him as being overly corpulent. But no more. He walks erect; his face is lined by the cares of a long life. His expression may seem grim, but it can change in an instant. He continues on the north side of Viale Felice, which is lined with shops and cafés. As he slowly passes by, the shopkeepers extend their friendly greetings, which he returns with a courtly gesture, in Italian accented by the languages of the places he has lived. The man is welcome and respected in his neighborhood.

Far from here, in Israel, in Vienna, in the United States, and elsewhere, he is reviled, scorned, hated, and accused of having been the tyrannical oppressor of his fellow Jews who collaborated with the Nazis in deporting them to the death camps.

Who is this man?

His name is Benjamin Murmelstein. In Vienna he was, next to Joseph (Josef) Löwenherz, the main Jewish functionary of the Jewish Community under the Nazis, until they deported him to the Theresienstadt ghetto, where he served as the Deputy Jewish Elder and, at the end, as the Chief Elder.

I (Leonard H. Ehrlich) first heard about Murmelstein's terrible reputation the year after the end of World War II, in which I had served as a frontline medic. At that time, the extent of the catastrophe that had befallen my people and my family was becoming clearer and clearer, with new revelations at the Nuremberg trials and from survivors' reports. Once my father told me about something he had read in the *Aufbau*,[1] for him a major source of information: "Your Murmelstein turned out to have been a major collaborator, and he is on trial in Prague." My father was referring to an article by the writer Max Brod, who is well known as the literary executor of Franz Kafka and whose brother had perished in Theresienstadt. On the basis of reports from former inmates of Theresienstadt, Brod claimed that Murmelstein had done the Nazis' work there, that he was being tried, and that he would surely justify himself the way Nazis on trial then did, namely, that he was merely following orders.

"*Your* Murmelstein," my father said. Why "my" Murmelstein? In Austria, during the First Republic (1919–1938), every child was required by law to receive religious instruction, which was a carryover from the time of the Austro-Hungarian Empire, when the emperor carried the title of Apostolic Majesty and had the status of a cardinal of the Roman Catholic Church. For Jewish children of school age, the Jewish Community provided Hebrew schools and Sabbath youth services scheduled at community synagogues on Saturday afternoons. The one I attended from age six until eleven or twelve was on Kluckygasse, whose rabbi was the young Dr. Murmelstein. The service of about one hour centered on the reading of part of the weekly Torah portion. Murmelstein often arranged for the participation of school-age children in the service. I particularly remember a boy named Rubin, who with his beautiful voice did a splendid job as cantor and was very popular with the other children. Rabbi Murmelstein also instituted for his youth services an innovation that was so well received that it was adopted by all the synagogues in Vienna, namely, *Kalenderblätter* (leaves from a calendar), that is, card-sized leaflets suited to the weekly Torah portion, with some verses from it, an exegetical statement taken from the Talmud, and a prayer; some even had graphic illustrations.[2] The *Kalenderblätter* were handed out by monitors, some of whom were rabbinical students, some of whom were Hebrew teachers; one of the latter was my former Hebrew teacher, Isak Herzberg. Monitors were necessary because there were many more children than seats. The synagogue was crowded, and the children tended to be unruly.

The children came in small groups to these services, usually without their parents. One time there was an unusual sight: A father came up the aisle holding a little boy by the hand. Although this father was clean-shaven, he was evidently an observant man to judge by his black suit and hat, and he was looking for a place to seat his little boy. Presently he spotted me two seats away from the aisle. I was no angel then, but I must have seemed like the sort of boy the man was looking for. He motioned me to move over to make room for his son, who was somewhat younger than I. The distinctive contours of the boy's face made an impression on me. It may also have been his set, unmoving expression. Was it grim? Sullen? Resentful? Scared? I did not know. While I chanted with the others, the boy stared at me. I disregarded him; he stared at me. The children's unruliness reached a crescendo. Upset by the inappropriate behavior of my peers, I was glad to see that Rabbi Murmelstein's patience was at an end. With an angry mien, he strode to the pulpit, faced the congregation, and put an end to the noise, at least for a while. The boy, paler even than before, stared at me. Next week the father again sought me out and seated the boy next to me. The boy's expression had not changed, and he stared at me. The father must have given up teaching the boy some religion because I did not see him again. But I never forgot his face.

Part of the youth service was a brief sermon by the officiating rabbi. Most of the time, it was given by Murmelstein and sometimes by one of the students of the rabbinical seminary. Some of the other speakers were more refined rhetoricians, some spoke in a manner that children would enjoy, some even entertained them, and in this way kept them quiet for a while. Murmelstein did not talk down to the children; with Murmelstein we were faced

Leonard H. Ehrlich with his parents, Helene Ehrlich née Fischgrund and Josef (Joseph) Ehrlich, on the SS Rotterdam *on their way to freedom in the United States (November 1939). (© CSE)*

with the challenge to grow in our capacity to understand. He skillfully related the weekly Torah portion to some moral or some point of Jewish consciousness that he wanted to put across. I appreciated the seriousness of what he presented, the clarity of his expression, and the power of his knowledge. I cannot say that I understood much of what he had to say, but I saw that there was something important to understand. I cannot deny that in those tender years Murmelstein was an example for me of what learning awaited me, not that I ever wished to become a rabbi. I admired him in a way that I never did the excellent teachers of the Jewish Gymnasium (high school) that I attended.

Therefore, "my" Murmelstein. Therefore also, my father understood when I wished to become bar-mitzvah under Rabbi Murmelstein's tutelage rather than in the synagogue my family normally attended. It took place in March 1937, about a year before the Anschluss, when Nazi Germany annexed Austria. It was the last time I saw Murmelstein, until I met him on Via Sebastiano Grandis forty years later.

I was nonplussed when in 1946 my father told me what "your Murmelstein" was accused of. It was one of many facts I had to come to terms with, now that we were on the threshold of living our lives, in my confusion and anger over the world we had inherited, over my wartime experiences, over my life as a refugee, over what had happened to my people and to my family. It would be decades before I would be in a position to tackle the question of the function and performance of the Jewish leadership under the Nazis. But one thing I carried with me all that time: The accusation against Murmelstein did not jibe with my youthful impression of him as one who arrived at informed and considered judgments, and as one who was utterly devoted to his Judaism.

■ ■ ■

The activities of the intervening years did not leave me time to pursue this topic, the two views of Murmelstein. Yet, it remained present in my mind and was furthered in a number of ways. The most pertinent was a course on philosophical problems of the destruction of European Jewry, which I began teaching in the early 1960s, mainly to honors students.

Apart from philosophical writings, the students read Raul Hilberg's *The Destruction of the European Jews* and Hannah Arendt's *Eichmann in Jerusalem*. It was interesting to note that the most intelligent students gained the impression from Hilberg's book not only that Jewish leaders did the Nazis' work but that the performance of Murmelstein and Löwenherz were the prime exemplars of such leadership, Murmelstein because of his sinister treachery, Löwenherz because of his weakness vis-à-vis the Nazis. Through discussion I had to help the students realize that Hilberg hardly attempts to adduce any evidence for this harsh judgment, and that innuendo or attribution or judgmental assertions do not constitute evidential research. As for Arendt, she left them with the view that one can gain the image of the Judenrat, the council of Jewish elders appointed by the Nazis, in general by gleaning from reports about various individuals who were in that position. Here too I had to guide the students to see that what is controversial about the Judenräte is not their function per se, nor their having to exercise it under the Nazis, but the choices they had to make in their specific situations; hence, there is no such thing as the general position of the Judenrat. It was at times difficult explaining all this to the students while upholding deserved respect for the authors and maintaining the authority of their seminal works.

The works of other authors that were available at that time, such as Rosenkranz's[3] or Gold's,[4] were hardly more useful. H. G. (Hans Günther) Adler's publications about Theresienstadt are to be highly regarded for their extensive use of the hard documentation available in the 1950s and early 1960s. Yet, his vituperative appraisal of Murmelstein as *Judenältester* (the head of the Nazi-appointed council of Jewish elders) corrupt—and his all too readily accusing Jakob (Jacob) Edelstein and his regime—make Adler's treatment of these figures suspect in works that are otherwise sound.[5]

I soon gained certain insights from these early treatments of Murmelstein's and Löwenherz's performance as leading Jewish functionaries under the Nazis, in particular their choices under the duress of those times and in their positions. First, from the beginning there has been a rush to judgment that has prevailed over the years. Yet, actions are taken within contexts; and judgments about such actions must not be rushed but must be based on a determination of the reasons they were taken. Second, such premature judgment can be confirmed or confuted only by research that goes beyond what has been so scantily adduced by even the best authors, beyond "it says here that he negotiated with the Nazis," "he did this or that," "he was in such a position," "he said so and so," "this was his character," and so on. Third, it may be arduous, time-consuming, and frustrating, but the net of research has to be cast in a wide arc in order to penetrate to some degree the duress under which choices were made, decisions were taken, actions undertaken. Only then can attempts at judgment be made, or cautiously suggested.

In light of these considerations, the topic of research was now more-or-less defined, the aim projected, and the roadmap sketched out.

- The *topic* was the choices and actions that were possible for Murmelstein and Löwenherz under the duress of their forced leadership in the extreme situation of Nazi terror and persecution.

- The *aim* was to clarify, with respect to these two men, the kind of policy they practiced, as well as the nature of responsibility, liability, and justifiability for their choices under such duress.
- The *road* thereto was to explore and clarify the complex context of their cases, to develop and apply a methodology of research and interpretation that is suitable to the cases and their attendant problems, and to bring to light the truth in view of the controversies that have surrounded them and of this kind of situation generally.

In short, the road was that of historical research, tempered by what we perceived as the failings and shortcomings of our predecessors. The philosophical questions of the evaluation of choices under duress had to be set aside to await the determination of what really happened, that is, the nature of the duress, what the Jews generally and especially the problematic protagonists actually faced, what choices were available, what choices had to be made.

Research Adventures

The first step was a negative one, a matter of housecleaning, that is, to start from scratch and enter the project as if nothing else had been written or researched. The question as to how and where to begin was complicated by my academic and professional commitments. Since it was clear that the project would be extensive and protracted and since my wife, Edith, had along the way become involved in it, it made sense to make the research, the interpretation, as well as the subsequent writing of the book a joint project. In retrospect, we often wondered whether we would have embarked on it had we had the slightest inkling of how extensive and protracted it would turn out to be. Except for the introductory chapter up to this point, and most of the chapters of Part Four (in a future volume), all the chapters are co-authored.

The next and major step was to find and to gain access to pertinent documentation about the situation, mainly in Vienna but also in Theresienstadt, as well as to the proceedings of meetings in which Murmelstein and Löwenherz had functioned in their leadership positions. The fact that both of us had experienced the first period after the Anschluss as observant teenagers—in the case of Edith Ehrlich (EE) for fourteen months, and in my (LHE's) case twenty months—was helpful but not substantive. While we did not embark on our research in a major way until our year at the University of Freiburg in 1973–74, we did try to find material before then, only to realize that there was very little available. An important turning point in our orientation occurred when we went to the YIVO Institute for Jewish Research in New York to look up and obtain copies of the papers from the War Victims Association, which Hilberg cites in connection with his sharp accusations against Löwenherz and Murmelstein. Looking at the bundle of papers at leisure at home, we came to realize that they do not at all support Hilberg's condemnations, and that he was able to present them by means of selective quotations while bracketing out significant contexts that stared the reader in the face. We treat the case of the war victims in chapter 16 of the second volume of our research. The revelation of the cavalier treatment of the matter by one whom we had learned to respect and admire left us liberated to proceed on our own authority.

Much of the documentation was in the form of memoirs or reminiscences of people who were in Vienna or in Theresienstadt at that critical period but not in a position to know about Löwenherz's or Murmelstein's exercise of their functions. Over the years we have found that in spite of the paucity of direct documentation, in spite of the ignorance of ordinary Jews who lived through those times about the actual activities of those two, it was striking how much was firmly asserted about the two of them. We met a number of people who were eager to tell what they knew about Murmelstein. When we asked, "How do you know?" it was often puzzling to the informer that his or her say-so was not sufficient. We asked, "Were you there?" The answer invariably was "no." "Then how do you know?" Answer: *"Es ist bekannt"* ("It is generally known").

The extent to which the widespread opinion of Murmelstein and Löwenherz was unreasoned, uninformed, and downright prejudicial can be seen from the following example. In Vienna we were referred to a woman who was at the time we met her the director of a foundation. After our mutual introductions, she informed us that we could not expect any funding from her foundation, news that was of complete indifference to us because we were there for another reason. In the interview she told us that she and her mother had been sent to Theresienstadt and from there to Auschwitz, where she survived but her mother perished. She blamed Murmelstein for that, saying, *"In meiner Familie gilt Murmelstein als der Mörder unserer Mutter"* ("In my family Murmelstein is considered to be our mother's murderer"). When we told her that we would soon be going to Israel, she mentioned that her brother, who had also been in Theresienstadt, lived in Israel, and she gave us his name. In Israel we had forgotten about this meeting, when two gentlemen contacted us. They had been in Vienna and in Theresienstadt and heard that we were doing research about Murmelstein. We agreed to meet them in Tel Aviv. They gave us some interesting though not vital material. Their main complaint against Löwenherz and Murmelstein was that they had "usurped" Desider Friedmann's position at the IKG (Israelitische Kultusgemeinde Wien) and that if Friedmann had remained as leader of the IKG, things would surely not have been so bad for the Jews in Vienna. By then we were able to recognize this as an example of the fact that the ordinary Jews in Vienna were in the dark regarding the power arrangements under the Nazis. Some apparently did not even know that Friedmann was kept under arrest by the Nazis as of one week after the Anschluss. This also indicated to us that even Jews who endured the whole of the seven years of those horrible times remained in ignorance of the facts that directly or remotely affected them and instead oriented themselves by facile impressions and convenient rumors, which they carried as truth during the decades following their liberation. Curiously, we found that in Israel, with all its research institutions and memorial archives, a similar ignorance is widespread about the concrete situation of the Jews under the Nazis.

Let us return to the interview. While we were talking with the two men about Theresienstadt, something dawned on us. We stopped our recording, removed the tape, inserted one of the ones from our satchel, and asked one of the men, "Do you recognize this voice?"

"It is my sister," he said. A few minutes after resuming the interview about Murmelstein in Theresienstadt, we asked, "Would you say that in your family Murmelstein is considered to be your mother's murderer?" He denied it. So much for the reliability of would-be witnesses about matters they could not have witnessed.

Not that there was no actual witness to the events, namely, Murmelstein himself. (Löwenherz had died in 1960.) We knew that he was alive and in Rome and wondered why he was not playing a role in the consideration of matters about which he was a unique witness, being one of the few major Jewish functionaries the Nazis permitted to survive, and perhaps the only one still alive. He certainly was not reluctant to write. In the YIVO archives we found a copy of Murmelstein's report about Theresienstadt, which he wrote, apparently at the request of the Czech authorities, immediately after the liberation of Theresienstadt, while he was still free there, that is, prior to his arrest in June 1945. We were impressed by the acuity of his insight about what use the ghetto had for the Nazis and the internal dynamics of the inmate population, at a time when few were informed about the full extent of the execution by the Nazis of their policy concerning the Jews. We also located a copy of his book *Terezin. Il ghetto-modello di Eichmann* (*Theresienstadt: Eichmann's Model Ghetto*) published in 1961.[6] At our request, a young colleague in the Italian Literature Department at the University of Massachusetts at Amherst had a pair of his students translate the book as a senior honors project. Since the work was done under his supervision, one could see by the quality of the translation that for all three the subject matter was beyond their comprehension. But with the aid of our smattering of Italian, the translation was sufficiently serviceable for us to realize how important it would be, in addition to our archival research, to interview Murmelstein himself.

Our intention was not to tell Murmelstein's story. Instead we thought that our main research would consist of solid archival material, that is, official documents as well as reports and testimonies of credible witnesses. The archival material was not to be used either to verify or to refute what Murmelstein would tell us. (In fact, it turned out that there was no one-to-one correlation between anything Murmelstein told us and what we found in the archives.) The plan was to obtain from the documentary research a broad image of the situation of duress and the choices made, and to see in what ways, if any, Murmelstein's narrative fits or does not fit. When we did the interviews with Murmelstein, they unexpectedly but fortuitously contained information about events of which he was a unique source. In this book we make only sparse use of this valuable material.

Establishing contact with Murmelstein as well as finding and gaining access to pertinent archival material were difficult. Both required the recommendation or the intercession of helpful and interested parties.

When we began in earnest to embark on our concerted research in 1974, we were sent to Dr. Jonny Moser. Moser was then already the main researcher on the Holocaust in Vienna, focusing on the Nisko episode (see chapter 7). He had never met Murmelstein personally but had corresponded with him. He was also in touch with Dr. Margarete Feiler in New York, who had been associated with Murmelstein at the IKG from 1938 until her emigration late in 1940. Moser had suggested to Feiler that it would please Murmelstein if she were to get in touch with him, which she did. According to Moser, Feiler was probably the only one left who could talk about Murmelstein's service at the IKG, at least in his first two years there. Before leaving, Moser gave us copies of some studies Murmelstein had written for Eichmann in 1940, which we subsequently wrote about (see chapter 10). Since the time she arrived in New York, Feiler had been employed at the New York headquarters of the American Jewish Joint Distribution Committee (the Joint). On the telephone she told us that when Dr. Joseph Schwartz was the Joint representative in Europe, he had known Murmelstein, was greatly impressed with his performance on behalf of the Jews of Vienna, and, though retired, would be prepared to meet with us. We made an appointment at the Joint office for the last week of December 1974. We were delighted to meet Dr. Feiler, a youthfully vital woman who, in her late sixties, was herself about to retire. Unfortunately Dr. Schwartz could not keep the appointment because of sudden illness. How sad and devastated we all were when we read his obituary in *The New York Times* the following day. At the Joint office, we were introduced to Mrs. Klepfisz, who was then the keeper of the archive, a survivor of the Warsaw ghetto fighters. Mrs. Klepfisz did not permit photocopies. Handwriting notes was hopelessly laborious, even with a team of four working for hours, we two and our two teenaged children. Hence, researching the valuable Joint material had to wait for a number of years.

In those early days we went to speak with persons who might give us some information or views about Murmelstein and Löwenherz. At YIVO we visited Director Isaiah Trunk soon after the publication of his book *Judenrat*.[7] He had never heard of Murmelstein, and to him Löwenherz was merely the person who forwarded the money transfers from the Joint to the major ghettos in Poland, as can be seen in his book (see our chapter 12 in the second volume).

In Vienna, Simon Wiesenthal spoke with us in his office for one and a half hours, standing. He knew nothing about Murmelstein, only that he had heard his name mentioned as *Murmelschwein* (Murmelswine). In their knowledge about the Holocaust, both Wiesenthal and Trunk were oriented toward Eastern Europe and not toward Germany, Austria, and the German Protectorate of Bohemia and Moravia. At a later time, we found some valuable material about the Protectorate in Wiesenthal's archive.

We had better luck at the Leo Baeck Institute (LBI) in New York. Thanks to the help and genuine interest of the archivist, Dr. Sybil Milton, we made good progress with our research, although at that time the LBI deposits concerning Vienna and Theresienstadt were spotty. When it became known that our research concerned Murmelstein, a lady who had been in Theresienstadt, had known Rabbi Baeck personally, and had been at the LBI from its inception sat down next to us and began a conversation. From our responses, she discerned our researcher's suspension of judgment. Finally, she said what was on her mind: "*Sagen Sie nichts gutes über Murmelstein*"—"don't say anything favorable about Murmelstein." She also referred us to Klara Caro, the widow of the last rabbi of the line deriving from the author of the *Shulhan Arukh*, who had died in Theresienstadt. We visited Mrs. Caro, who was close to 90, in her room in an old-age residence in New Jersey. She told us that Murmelstein had treated her and her husband well in Theresienstadt and that she attended the lectures he gave, which she regarded as the best she had ever heard. She served us tea in the loveliest dishes and was nonplussed when at the end of our visit she learned from us that Murmelstein was still alive and was neither convicted nor executed by the Czech authorities, as she had thought. Mrs. Caro's favorable comments about Murmelstein, even before she knew that he had survived the accusations against him, were in amusing contrast to the views of the LBI official who had sent us to her. Privileged as we felt to have met that grand old lady, we realized that we would have to be more selective in choosing interviewees. We would restrict ourselves to those who, through their own official function or through their personal contact with the persons we were investigating, had valid insights into the role they played and had to play and the duress under which they had to make choices.

Dr. Milton referred us to several contacts that would be highly valuable to us. We kept in touch with her after she became the Chief Historian and Archivist of the United States Holocaust Memorial Museum in Washington, D.C.

In those years we met many persons who volunteered what they knew about Murmelstein. In Freiburg there was a widow who had reclaimed her house after surviving Theresienstadt. She placed most of the house at the disposal of the newly formed Jewish Community as a small synagogue. Talking about Murmelstein, she became agitated and told of how terrible a person he was. "Why?" we asked. Answer: when the Nazis demanded 1,000 Jews for deportation, he said, "*Ich stelle Ihnen 2,000 zur Verfügung*" ("I am placing 2,000 at your disposal"). It struck us how widespread, especially among survivors, such absurd beliefs were as to what power a Jewish functionary possessed, and Murmelstein in particular. Murmelstein himself gave us a copy of a clipping that was forwarded to him from Israel at the time of the Eichmann trial. The item was written by a Dr. Israel Kanner and published in *Yediot Hadashot*, a German-language newspaper. It is headed "Contra a Jewish Quisling." We quote it in full in our English translation:

> When the German military marched into Vienna in March 1938, Rabbi Dr. Murmelstein placed himself at the disposal of the Gestapo from the first moment. He had free access to Gestapo Headquarters, denounced [people] by giving the SS and the SA all imaginable information, and became directly responsible for the murder of the great Zionist leaders, Dr. Desider Friedmann and *Oberbaurat* Robert Stricker. Upon the occupation of Czechoslovakia and Poland, he shifted the center of his activity to these countries. He bears the responsibility for the deportation of thousands of Jews from there to the gas chambers. At war's end he was arrested in Czechoslovakia and sentenced to prison, but he succeeded to escape and flee to Italy. Today he is a librarian at the Vatican. It is time to bring this "Jewish Eichmann" to court. My contribution [to this journal] might stimulate others to produce material about him, so that the process of his apprehension can get under way.[8]

It may be beside the point that Kanner had been a rabbinical student in Vienna who did not meet Murmelstein's strict standards and had to leave the seminary; young as he was, Murmelstein was an instructor there. But, one did not have to hold a personal grudge against Murmelstein to make such bizarre accusations against him. At war's end, Murmelstein was left with a bad reputation, which, over the years, fed on itself and grew. With the paucity of readily available relevant documentation, and in the absence of the use of such documentation for sound inquiry, it was possible to make the wildest accusations and the most bizarre claims with impunity, as the case of Kanner demonstrates. Their intensity was proportionate to the accuser's distance from any position where he might have been a witness to an actual event. And, regrettably, the few scholars who touched upon the subject of Murmelstein's performance by and large failed to pay attention to the question of the credibility of their sources.

One item in Kanner's array of claims needs to be discussed at this point, namely, Murmelstein's supposed employment in the Vatican. Why Murmelstein settled in Rome will be recounted toward the end of this book. But, the fact that it was Rome led to all sorts of allegations. He was said to have found refuge with the Pope. He was even confused with the Chief Rabbi of Rome, Israel Zolli, who toward the end of the war was converted to Roman Catholicism by Pope Pius XII. In our interview with Rabbi Forhand, we mentioned that Murmelstein lived in Rome. Right away Forhand's deliberate gestures indicated something like, "Aha, there you have it." Our wordless reaction gave him pause, and we explained that Murmelstein continued his prewar research in Judaica in the Vatican Library, which has a vast and important holding in Judaica. Forhand then retracted by showing us the Vatican Library slips from the time of his own father's research there in the 1930s.

While claims and accusations against Murmelstein could be discounted, his bad reputation could not be disregarded, and we had to consider that the reasons for it, whatever they would turn out to be, were bound to be a factor in evaluating his performance as a leading functionary under the duress of the Nazi times. Thus, while the rush to judgment about Murmelstein's performance provided the impetus, lingering doubt about it served as the methodological jumping-off point for our inquiry.

■ ■ ■

After meeting us, Dr. Feiler mentioned us in her correspondence with Murmelstein, and that we wanted to interview him in Rome. It was evidently Moser's idea for us to be appraised by Feiler and for her to make a recommendation to Murmelstein. Murmelstein permitted Feiler to make copies of his letters to her available to us, and we found them to be invaluable background for our interviews. Apparently Feiler mentioned that one of us was a professor of philosophy, and it was amusing to read his admonition that he would not approve if it were a matter of "*Individualphilosophie*," by which he probably meant Sartrean existentialism. On the basis of his readiness to receive us, we got in touch with Murmelstein directly, upon Feiler's bidding. (His letters to Feiler, to us, and to others are small but valuable items in our archive, since donated to the United States Holocaust Memorial Museum in Washington, D.C.) It took two years from our first contact with Murmelstein until he was ready to receive us—he had become that distrustful.

Our search for relevant archival material was also making progress. Moser had mentioned to us that the papers of the IKG, which had accumulated during the Nazi years, had been transferred to Jerusalem. Professor Yehudah Bauer, the internationally undisputed dean of Holocaust research, whom we met at a Holocaust conference in New York, assured us that the papers are well organized and available at an archive at the Hebrew University of Jerusalem.

Sabbatical leave granted by the University of Massachusetts at Amherst enabled us to undertake the first and major thrust of research in 1977. To gain access to the IKG papers

Leonard H. Ehrlich interviewing Benjamin Murmelstein in Rome (August 1977). (© CSE)

in Jerusalem, we had to obtain a letter of permission in Vienna, since the IKG still retained legal ownership of the archives. A cousin, who was a prominent member of the Viennese community, referred us to the IKG president, Dr. Anton Pick, who referred us to the Executive Director Karl Lazar, who provided us with the letter. Others in Vienna, who knew Murmelstein during those critical times, assured us that our journey to Rome would be in vain because Murmelstein would find a way of not receiving us. In Rome, Murmelstein actually did request that we delay our first meeting for a day or two. In time we discerned an indication that the reason for the delay was that Murmelstein's apprehension over the impending interviews affected his well-being, and he needed more time to brace himself. He also hinted that he was still recovering from a serious illness.

For the first meeting we were picked up from the hotel by Murmelstein's wife. During the streetcar ride, we were able to ascertain that this was not a second marriage and that Margit née Geyer did not divorce him at war's end, as reputed. Mrs. Caro was one of several people who had spread this false claim. The structure of the meetings was routine. We arrived in mid-afternoon and stayed about four hours. Between six and seven o'clock Mrs. Murmelstein served a simple supper, during which the tape recorder was usually turned off. At first we hesitated because the situation required that the parties not seem to be in each other's debt. However, to have refused would have been discourteous, and the repast was too modest to be an issue. We also refrained from bringing any gifts; only at the very end of the second set of interviews did we thank Mrs. Murmelstein for her hospitality by presenting her with a scarf and a simple houseplant. Nothing personal was exchanged between Murmelstein and us; neither was in debt to the other.

We always had spare blank tapes with us since we did not know how long Murmelstein would be able to speak. We signaled to him when a tape needed to be turned or replaced.

In the first set of interviews, we recorded twenty-two hours in six sessions, which took place over a period of ten days, since Fridays and Saturdays were reserved for Shabbat. At the end of the first set of interviews, Murmelstein presented us with a signed copy of his *Terezin* book. He also gave us, or sent to us, copies of documentary material that we needed.

We soon abandoned the notes of subjects we had prepared because Murmelstein was more than ready to take the lead in bringing up matters that not only were on his mind but that he wanted to cover in his own way. By doing so, he brought in nuances of matters that did not appear in the literature. In the process, we were often able to steer the proceedings in the direction of a response to our unanswered questions. We soon noticed that Murmelstein did not easily take up direct questions. While he sometimes spoke quickly and rhapsodically, even in the form of incomplete sentences and clauses, he was always extremely careful of what he said and avoided speaking about matters he wanted to take to his grave, as he at one time phrased it.

Our interviews with Murmelstein were held in German, as had been our correspondence with him. However, whereas his letters were written in flawless elegant German, in speaking with us, and especially when he got excited (which was to be expected, given the subject matter) he reverted to a special dialect spoken by the Jews of Galicia. Aware of our background, Murmelstein knew that we would understand him. This dialect is composed mainly of Austrian-inflected modern German, much Yiddish, and some Hebrew, full of special idioms and adages. Most of those who spoke and understood it died in the Holocaust, and when the last of our generation is gone, so will be this language. Thus, when it came to having the tapes transcribed by two natives of Germany, we found that there was much they could not understand; we ended up transcribing the last few tapes ourselves. Still, the efforts of Evelyn Sillmann Ehrlich and Dr. Traute Marshall were valuable and are appreciated. The preservation of the tapes is of great importance as an additional document of the loss not just of life but of a vernacular tongue.[9]

Murmelstein understood what we were doing, namely, that after the interviews we would do documentary and other research in Israel and that we would return to Rome and talk again, fortified with additional knowledge.

Between the first and second set of interviews, we spent three-and-a-half months in Israel. It was our first time in Israel. We went there by ship from Brindisi over Greece to Haifa. Harbor patrol boats were circling the ship as we lay at anchor a mile from shore. It left us time to see the first view of the land that over the centuries so many beheld who had yearned to return to the land of our fathers. Our children picked us up and, tired as we were from the journey, took us that day to Qumran and introduced us to falafel.

The next day we went to the Hebrew University and sought out Professor Bauer to direct us to the collection of the IKG papers. He asked what we were working on; and when we mentioned Murmelstein, he hesitated for a moment. Bauer was the first of many in Israel to seem surprised by our choice of topic. Bauer leaned toward us in a gesture of confidentiality and said, "Do you know that Murmelstein is still alive?" We said, "Yes, we just came from Rome, where we taped twenty-two hours of exclusive interviews with him." Bauer alerted us to some research material available in Jerusalem that might be of interest to us and directed us to the Central Archives of the Jewish People where the IKG papers were deposited, located in the basement of the same building. Half an hour later, we sat in the office of the director, Dr. Daniel Cohen. We presented our letter from IKG Director Lazar, while keeping a copy for ourselves. With Lazar's letter in front of him, Cohen was faced with the need to accommodate us. Yet, he hesitated. He asked us what we were interested in. When we told him that it was mainly Murmelstein, he sought to deflect us by leaning toward us in a gesture of confidentiality and saying, "You know the man is still alive?" We told him that in Rome we just had twenty-two hours of exclusive interviews with Murmelstein, and to Cohen's even greater astonishment we pulled out the business card Murmelstein had given us. In great agitation Cohen tried to get a hold of it and to note the address, but we retrieved it.

Subsequently we learned that the collection of papers the IKG produced in the seven years under the Nazis stretched over some 420 meters of shelf space, housed in the subbasement of the building. During the Six-Day War, the IKG boxes were used to protect the little basement windows against possible air raids, which fortunately never occurred. The collection was well catalogued by the archivist Dr. Avshalom Hodik. This facilitated our work with the overwhelming amount of material because we could be selective in choosing files that appeared to be most relevant to our research. The work was intense. We found we could do no more than four hours of uninterrupted work. We kept Yaakov, the photocopy technician, busy for all these weeks. Altogether about 100,000 items went through our hands. A goodly number of them we examined carefully enough to determine the usefulness of obtaining copies.

We alternated working at the Central Archive with research at the Yad Vashem Archive. Three days every week at the one, three days at the other. In those days, many of the staff at Yad Vashem were survivors from the camps in the East, and they were understandably attached to the material as the testimony of what they had gone through. They somehow made us feel like "American" interlopers, who would adulterate their patrimony of blood. But we respected their prerogative. Others were fellows engaged in specific research projects, who regarded the relevant material as their private preserve and would not countenance intrusion by outsiders. The fruitfulness of our research at Yad Vashem was made possible by one person, the archivist Bronka ("Bronia") Klibanski. She was ingenuously forthcoming and generous. She opened the entire archive for our use and helped us find matters of interest to us. Klibanski was a remarkable person with a remarkable history. As a teenager, she was in the resistance movement in the Białystok region in Poland. With truly singular courage, she had been an informant about the activities of the Germans. Being tall and blond, she was able to move freely between the German occupation personnel and the resistance fighters in the forests. Very little of the deposits at Yad Vashem was directly related to the core of our research, but it provided important peripheral contexts.

During our thirteen weeks of work at the two archives, we accumulated about ten thousand photocopies, enough to keep us occupied over the decades to follow. While in Israel, we also met with a number of people who were interested in our research, for example, Ruth Bondy and Ze'ev Goshen. We also conducted a number or interviews, most notably with Rabbi Dr. Elimelekh Rimalt, MK, who had been a friend of Murmelstein's in Vienna, and Ambassador Ze'ev Shek, a survivor of Theresienstadt, where, as a youth leader

Edith Ehrlich with Margit Murmelstein née Geyer in the Murmelsteins' apartment in Rome (February 1977). (© CSE)

and member of the underground, he had dealings with Murmelstein. We also attended a conference on the Judenräte at Yad Vashem, at which Gideon Hausner, Yehudah Bauer, Herbert Rosenkranz, and Raul Hilberg were among the speakers.

Back in Rome for our second set of interviews with Murmelstein, we spent five sessions with him and recorded another twenty hours. We went over a number of matters that we had covered before, but there were a significant number of new topics. In the last session, both parties were exhausted and excited, mindful of all that was yet unexplored, yet bowing to the discipline of time. Near the end, we ventured to raise a topic that Murmelstein had tended to eschew. We asked his opinion about some of the more prominent people he had to deal with, for example, Berthold Storfer and Leo Baeck. And voluble as he was at that point, he spilled some things that he had evidently intended to take to his grave. Margit Murmelstein had been present at every one of the sessions. She seldom spoke up but now did not hesitate to relate her own experience with Baeck at the time Murmelstein was arrested in June 1945.

One could not consider Murmelstein's performance in Vienna without considering that of Löwenherz. And while Löwenherz was responsible for a goodly amount of the IKG papers that we acquired, more was needed, in particular those papers on which the report was based that Wilhelm Bienenfeld prepared for the Nuremberg Military Tribunal in 1945–46. That there were such papers was also proven by the sixty pages that were copied for the Eichmann trial and are published in the collection of the trial documents. Murmelstein directed us to Löwenherz's son in New York, who had been his student at the Gymnasium where Murmelstein taught the mandatory religion classes. The papers in question were in Löwenherz's possession, and at their request he lent them to the Israeli police for the Eichmann trial. Löwenherz died soon after that, and in time the papers were returned to his widow, Sophie Löwenherz. Löwenherz's son, the musicologist Professor Siegmund Levarie, after speaking to us for a while, volunteered to lend us the papers. They consisted of some eight hundred pages of *Aktennotizen* (memoranda)—most of them written by Löwenherz, many by Murmelstein, a few by others—which were written for and had to be submitted to the Nazi authorities between May 1938 and March 1945. (We shall explain the *Aktennotizen* in time.) These papers were another major source for our research. Levarie arranged for us to meet and interview his mother, Mrs. Löwenherz, which we did in the year before she died. She also gave us additional papers, as did Levarie. In time we organized the papers and, after our exclusive use of them, Professor Levarie deposited the papers at the Leo Baeck Institute in New York at our recommendation.

With all the literature that had been written about Theresienstadt and about the Jewish leadership there, we still lacked solid material, especially concerning Murmelstein. His own writings about Theresienstadt—and there were several published and unpublished ones—were mainly interpretations of the significance of the camp itself, of events that took place there, and of persons who had played a role there. Adler's books were full of valuable documentation, but they were marred by his interpretations. Our interview with Adler in London confirmed that he had a special animus against Murmelstein. We felt that we needed documentation that would shed light on Murmelstein's views but were in some way independent of him. Murmelstein himself alerted us to the court files in Leitmeritz, where the trial of Karl Rahm, the last Nazi Commandant of Theresienstadt, took place, as well as the pretrial investigation of Murmelstein himself. But how were we to get there in the days of the Iron Curtain? We asked Dr. Sybil Milton, who referred us to *Oberstaatsanwalt* Dr. Adalbert Rückerl, the director of the German center in Ludwigsburg for the collection of documents for the use of provincial court proceedings against war criminals. We asked him for permission to do research there and to refer us to the Leitmeritz court files. In response, Rückerl wrote that he had obtained permission from the Justice Ministry for us to do research at the Ludwigsburg archive and that he had good collegial relations with the director of the Czech war crimes documentation center, and he suggested we direct ourselves to him.

We had wanted to do research in Prague for a while, but Rudolf Bunzel, who had been in the Theresienstadt administration and had a close working relation with Murmelstein, who in turn had referred us to him, cautioned us against any foolhardy attempt to go snooping as Americans in Czechoslovakia, which was then under a very strict Stalinist regime. When we nonetheless became serious about going there, he asked us how we would answer when they asked what the tendency of our research is. "Against the Nazis," we said, which met with Bunzel's approval.

We were fully aware that the trip to Czechoslovakia could be risky, even dangerous. We obtained the necessary visas in London, without divulging the purpose of the trip. Our plan was to drive to Prague, do our research, and leave for Austria after a certain number of days. In Munich, we told our relatives that if they did not receive our telephone call upon our crossing into Austria by a certain date, they should inform the U.S. consulate. We were advised not to carry newspapers or journals or any other literature with us. It was good advice. When we crossed into Czechoslovakia, after the passport clearance, a young woman inspected the contents of our luggage piece by piece. Her supervisor was standing in front of the customs building and watched the procedure. She was very friendly, even solicitous. Presently she found LHE's passport from the time he was a boy of 14. Though issued in 1938 after the Anschluss, it was still an Austrian passport. The woman was visibly shaken and truly regretted the discovery of what appeared to be an incriminating item. LHE explained that we would be leaving Czechoslovakia for Austria, and that whenever he returned to Austria he took the old passport with the red "J" (meaning *Jude*, i.e., "Jew") stamp on the first page out of protest against what happened to him in his native country. She took the passport to her superiors, and after a while she put it back without a word.

In Prague we went to the documentation center, where Dr. Kamis was expecting us. After a pleasant conversation we asked how we could get access to the needed court records in Leitmeritz (Litoměřice). Kamis pointed toward a table at his back covered with stacks of documents and said, there they are. We worked with them for a few days in the cordial atmosphere of that office, whose personnel consisted of Kamis, another lawyer, Dr. Sikora, and a cheerful secretary. One time we asked Kamis about the missing folder no. 5 of the Rahm trial record. Kamis said it is not available; he looked for the right word of what it contained, which we supplied, namely, *Urteilsbegründung*—the basis of the judgment. We could not divulge to him that we were in possession of a copy of it, given to us by Murmelstein, the original of which somehow made its way to him during the turmoil of the communist coup in 1948. On the last day we requested photocopies of most of both records—of the Rahm trial and the Murmelstein investigation—and offered prepayment. Kamis said that the Czech government would bear the cost. We did receive the boxes with some five hundred papers a few weeks later, another highly important item in our archive.

On the day of our leaving Prague, we had a brief appointment with Erich Kohn, the engineer who figured out that the construction project he was put in charge of by order of the Nazis at Theresienstadt was really a gas chamber. After that, we drove to the country villa of Jiři (Georg) Vogl, the hydrotechnical engineer in Theresienstadt, whom the Soviet army installed as the leader of the camp after its liberation. He called himself a "socialist" and was favored by the communist regime, witness the dacha he was able to build himself. For a moment Vogl was visibly furious when we told him that we were interested in Murmelstein and that he was still alive. But, though he quickly regained his composure, the matter put a damper on the proceedings. At one point, we mentioned that we had taped some of the interviews we conducted in the past. Of course, we did not dare bring a tape recorder to Czechoslovakia at that time. Nonetheless, as we were taking our leave, Vogl asked whether we had been recording our meeting with him. We assured him that we would not have done so without his prior agreement. The situation was uncanny, and we

Leonard H. Ehrlich's Austrian passport (issued August 1, 1938) with the big red "J" identifying him as a Jew (Jude). *(© CSE)*

had visions of driving away only to be intercepted by the authorities. To protect ourselves, we thought of asking Vogl on the way to the car, whether it was true that his older son was living in California, a fact that the Czech communist authorities would have frowned on. Once he had affirmed this, we felt we were even and could safely drive to the border with Austria. The inspection at the border took over an hour and included the placement of mirrors under the car. By the time we crossed the border, it was nighttime, but we soon found a telephone to assure our Munich contact that we were safe.

After the fall of the communist regime, we thought it would be easier to do research in Prague and Theresienstadt, only to find that all archival materials relevant to the Holocaust, whether in private or governmental archives, were now closed to outsiders. Tourists were welcome; others were not.

We continued to look for collateral material at various other places. At some of them we were well received and found much that fleshed out the structure of the complex edifice that was forming in our minds. Some of these places we visited multiple times over the years. One of these is DÖW, the *Dokumentationsarchiv des österreichischen Widerstands* (Documentation Archive of the Austrian Resistance). Originally, we were referred to it by Dr. Milton, who happened to be related to Professor Dr. Herbert Steiner, the founder and director of DÖW. We also spent much time at the archive of the *Institut für Zeitgeschichte* (Institute for Contemporary History) in Munich, which is Germany's main research institute for the Nazi period. We visited the Tracing Service Archive of the International Red Cross in Arolsen, Germany. The director, Dr. A. Opitz, invited us to do research there. Three years later, when we were ready to do so, Opitz had retired and the new director told us that he was bound by the German privacy protection law to deny us access.[10]

We had similar bad luck in London, where access to archival materials at Woburn House and to officials who had been there between 1938 and 1940 would have been of prime importance. In addition, no one was able to refer us to the location of the papers of the Jakob Ehrlich Society, the association of Austrian refugees in England. Before it became defunct sometime after the war, the society was the venue of the trial of Löwenherz in an honor court proceeding. We were left with the distinct impression that there was a concerted effort in London to keep out outside researchers when Dr. Josef Fraenkel, who had edited a collection of studies on *The Jews of Austria* (1967), refused to meet with us and assured us on the telephone that he had no knowledge of the Löwenherz proceedings or the whereabouts of the Ehrlich Society papers.

However, we did not have to leave London without any gain because Fraenkel informed us that Dr. Carl (Charles) Kapralik[11] was still alive and told us how to get in touch with him. Our visit with the nearly 90-year-old gentleman was the most delightful interlude during the decade of our major research. When we reached him by telephone, he told us that his wife had recently left him after fifty-eight years of marriage. As it turned out, she had died. This self-assured, self-deprecating, charming humor prevailed throughout the two hours of our conversation; a last whiff of the atmosphere of the genteel society that converged in Vienna at the end of the Empire. We traveled for an hour to reach the old pub above which he lived in a small, exquisitely furnished and appointed apartment. We seemed to be in the country but were still within the London city limits. The building stood at the bend of the Thames, and Kapralik told us how comfortable it was to have lived there for so many decades. He confirmed what he had written about the performance of Löwenherz and Murmelstein in the first year after the Anschluss. While we did not learn anything new, we would not have missed the encounter with that good man for anything.

An Overview of the Aims and Structure of This Book

From the beginning, our conception of the book reflected the original topic:

- *Method*. We would apply appropriate methods for identifying, researching, and interpreting valid documentation and for organizing and telling the results.
- *Duress*. We would characterize the duress that was determinative of the situation under which choices had to be made. As the story unfolds, we would account for the kinds of ongoing as well as changing modes and stages of duress. We would identify the instruments of duress: the persons, the control, the persecution, and the terror. We would clarify not only the immediate but also the wider contexts that defined the situation of terror: the international, the political, and the wartime situations.
- *Choice*. With respect to the duress prevailing at the time, we would describe what possible choices for action were envisaged by the Jewish leaders on behalf of the

Jews as far as this can plausibly be elicited. We would describe what choices were available and made, on the one hand, with respect to salient areas of need (such as emigration, caring for the old and the disabled, preserving assets and property, fostering the young, saving as many and whoever could be saved) and, on the other hand, with respect to carrying out the function of forced leadership and dealing with the Nazis as authors of duress.

"Duress" and "choice" are not separable topics. This means that the two are so intertwined that choices have to be understood with respect to the duress that determined the necessity for making choices. It is not enough to take up the controversial question of the choices made by the *Judenräte* while being aware that they were under duress. The question of choice always has to be taken up with respect to the *duress that was actually experienced*. Otherwise, the question of choice is separated from the consideration of duress, and awareness of the latter is reduced to ineffective lip service. Treating the two as inseparable is a distinctive mark of our study.

- *Judgment*. We knew that any critical reflections about choice under duress that would successfully counter the usual rush to judgment would have to arise from the kind of thorough and sweeping account we meant to present. Not only would we reflect critically about the consequences of these choices and their impact on those who made them, but we would also discuss the judgments that were made about these choices in the past, since their questionable nature originally impelled our inquiry. We would also critically reflect on the methods used and, most important, about the original problem of possible and permissible choices under the extreme duress of forced leadership.

In this way, even as "method" underlay the process from beginning to end, and "duress" and "choice" were intertwined like a double helix, so too "judgment" arising from it accompanied the account.

It took much of a quarter century to put this book together. The originally projected length multiplied fourfold. The basic sequence and content of the book remained the same; however, the overall configuration and the ramification of topics changed as the book grew. Over the years we revised its table of contents a dozen times. Let us explain its final form.

The largest portion of the book is primarily historical, in which we discuss duress and choice in their relevant contexts. It is, in the main, the history of the destruction of the Jewish Community of Vienna and the performance of the Jewish leadership in its dealings with the Nazis on behalf of the Jews. Following the phases of the history, this portion divides into three parts.

Part I: Amalek. Since biblical times Amalek has been the quintessential—and oftentimes metaphorical—enemy bent on destroying the Jews. In the case under consideration here, it was a real Amalek that burst upon the scene with the Anschluss, which occurred at the time of Purim in 1938 (see chapter 2). In chapter 2, we also show how, thanks to Eichmann, heretofore a minor and insignificant functionary, the Nazi regime learned how to proceed against the Jews in an organized way, which led eventually to the Nazi party's program of ridding the realm ruled by them of Jews. In chapters 3 and 4, we show how the Nazis abrogated Viennese Jewish organized life, putting in place an organization through which they could deal with the Jews. For tactical reasons, the Nazis gave the new organization the semblance of the previous IKG, the traditional Jewish community organization. Its former director, Löwenherz, was forced to lead the new organization. He would soon appoint Murmelstein as his right-hand man. Together with a large staff, they would initiate a massive emigration effort, support the increasing number of impoverished Jews, care for both elderly and children, offer retraining in practical skills to would-be emigrants, obtain financial support (from the United States and Great Britain) for all their internal tasks, and obtain greatly needed foreign currency for emigration. Above all, in a situation without precedent they devised ways of dealing with the Nazi authorities in such a way that, under the guise of carrying out or transmitting their orders, they managed to serve the interests of Jews. The procedures developed in Vienna would serve the Nazis as a paradigm first for Berlin, then Prague, and would, in radical form, appear as the system of *Judenräte* in the conquered territories. Until that time, the Nazis instigated waves of persecution and mass arrests including Kristallnacht (see chapter 5) to motivate the Jews to emigrate and to increase their disfranchisement and dispossession. As recounted in chapter 6, in the seventeen months or so covered by Part I, the Jewish leadership of Vienna facilitated the emigration of close to two-thirds of the Jews of Austria, a proportion unmatched anywhere else.

Part II: Captivity. The outbreak of World War II on September 1, 1939, sealed the Jews in captivity within the domain of Nazi rule. This phase is marked by the establishment of the first *Judenräte* in the newly conquered area of Poland and the centralization and consolidation of the Nazi apparatus dealing with the solution of the Jewish question. The phase of captivity began with the portent of subsequent deportations in the form of the Nisko episode (chapter 7). The sharpening duress was felt in the many ways dealt with in chapter 8, such as in the tightening financial stranglehold on the Jewish leadership and their valiant though largely futile resistance (see the section "Financial Stranglehold"). Tedious as this section may be for the reader, it shows the step-by-step dynamic of sustained and constantly increasing Nazi duress as well as that of the Jewish leaders' readiness to act on behalf of Jewish interests, even though the enemy held all the cards and they had nothing but their untiring vigilance and the courage to plead their case over and over again. As regards the Jewish population at large, we discuss evictions and labor camps as marks of their captivity (see the section "Marks of Captivity"). Parallel with dealing with the financial stranglehold, the Jewish leadership intensified the emigration effort that was severely hampered by the wartime situation (chapter 9). It took nothing less than a heroic effort to get an additional 12,000 Jews to overseas refuges. In this connection, we recount the baffling story of the visa stoppage imposed for six months by the U.S. State Department and its tragic consequences and the clumsy interference by well-meaning Zionist leaders that caused transports to be delayed and caught in the maw of the German occupation of Yugoslavia. This phase also saw that behind the scenes the Nazis were articulating the plans for what they would refer to as "the final solution of the Jewish question." It is evident that their articulation was furthered by some studies and position papers that they ordered the Jewish leaders to prepare and submit during the course of 1940. This is discussed in chapter 10, which brings to an end the first volume of this work.

■ ■ ■

[Note: The following is a preview of the contents of the forthcoming second volume of this project. — Ed.]

Part III. Overlapping the events of Part II are those of the *Catastrophe* that is both the main topic and the title of Part III. "A catastrophe for the Jews" is how Löwenherz referred to the deportations when he spoke with Eichmann's deputy in Berlin (chapter 11). In the chapters of this part, we give an account of the three phases of deportations from Vienna in unprecedented detail. We not only recount the deportation process and procedure that the Nazis carried out but we also lay great stress on the role of the Jewish leadership, in particular of Löwenherz and Murmelstein. Here, for the first time, is the account of what really happened with regard to that controversial matter. In chapter 12, which deals with the first phase of the deportations, we also show how the Nazis prepared the general population for the removal of the Jews from amongst their midst and how they were able to assuage the concerns of the Jewish leaders about the elderly and about the destination of the transports. Isolating the Jews from non-Jews in a city like Vienna, maintaining control over them by forbidding contact with others, and isolating them from any source of information other than what they fed them enabled the Nazis to move quickly and in an orderly manner. These restrictions of contact and information were enforced especially strictly in regard to the Jewish leadership and enabled the Nazis to proceed against the deported Jews while those left behind remained ignorant of the truth. In chapter 13, we show that behind this veil of secrecy the Nazis sent mobile killing units to the east and initiated the killing centers, known as *Aktion Reinhard*. The establishment of the Theresienstadt ghetto was part of the Nazis' attempt to assuage the concerns, on the part of the Jewish leadership in Vienna, over the care of the old and of others meriting special consideration. Theresienstadt was the destination of the third phase of deportations, which are discussed in chapter 14. Beyond the deportation phases of our retelling of the catastrophe of the Jews of Vienna, we consider in chapter 15 the special case of the war veterans, and in chapter 16 the story of the remnant of the Jewish Community of Vienna until the liberation. In continuation of chapter 14, we relate in chapter 17 Murmelstein's role in Theresienstadt (Terezin) during the critical events of 1943 and 1944, and in chapter 18 his career there as Chief Elder in the final months of the ghetto, when its existence and the lives of its inmates hung in the balance, and were saved significantly by Murmelstein's cool presence of mind. Part III closes with chapter 19, in which we recount the postwar fates of Löwenherz and Murmelstein.

Following the primarily historical first three parts is Part IV: Critical Reflections. We have indicated that both methodology and critical reflection are embedded in the first three parts, the former as underlying our research and interpretation and the latter as arising from the story of choice under duress. Both are taken up explicitly in Part IV. In chapter 20, we explain what we consider to be an appropriate methodological approach to a topic such as ours, and from that perspective we take a critical look at what some more prominent authors have done with respect to it. The main section of the final chapter (chapter 21) is a critical exploration of "Politics under Duress." It examines and appraises the choices under duress with respect to the performance of Murmelstein and Löwenherz within the constantly changing situations that they actually faced, as recounted in the first three parts. We approach the question by means of two critical subsections. In "Josephus?" we show that judgment has to be bound to specific given contexts and is invalid if undertaken from the perspective of contexts that are historically removed and substantively foreign to the situation under consideration. Similarly, the subsection "Gandhi?" shows that judgment that is not keyed to the specific given situation of duress is aberrant and, in effect, vacuous. The relevant features of duress actually suffered by the Jews of Vienna, and under which Murmelstein and Löwenherz had to make choices on their behalf, are articulated and discussed in the subsection on "The Situation: Unfolding and Unprecedented." In the subsection on "Choices beyond Morality," we give a summary overview of the choices made by the Jewish leadership on behalf of the Jews of Vienna under the duress of their forced leadership. This leads, under the heading "Politics under Duress," to a reflection on the question of the possible and permissible choices and actions under the duress of the Holocaust.

Postscripts

Retrospect

We never felt that we had completed our research, and we never made use of all the research material that we had gathered; nor have we included in our book all that we meant to. This pertains especially to the topic of Theresienstadt. While we gathered a great amount of new material and sketched out a far-ranging treatment of this very important topic over the years, we finally had to reduce it to what we present in chapters 14, 17, and 18 in the next volume. All the material we have amassed is organized, and we plan to deposit it in a suitable archive.[12] We hope it will be of use to future researchers. The material pertaining to Theresienstadt should form the basis for a thorough treatment, which has been sorely lacking up to now, especially in English. We hope that some of our archival material will be published someday, especially the interviews.

Washington, New York, London, Paris, Rome, Geneva, Ludwigsburg, Munich, Dachau, Prague, Vienna, Jerusalem, Tel Aviv, Haifa, to mention only the main locations—it was a productive but exhausting journey, protracted over years, carried on during sabbatical leaves from the university and aided by minor foundation grants as well as a larger one from the National Endowment for the Humanities (NEH), yet financed mainly by ourselves. Over the years, we did a lot of follow-up research at many of the places mentioned above. While we would never feel that we were finished with our research, after the decade of the major thrust it was time to compile our notes and drafts and sketches and, above all, to work up the overwhelming amount of documentary material into a book.

A *personal word*. One time, when the editor to whom we were assigned by our original publisher took us to task regarding the excessive amount of time it took to finish our book, we responded as follows:

> We are astonished when we reflect on how much time of the best of our mature years this project is costing us. We were naïve when, many years ago, we thought the project could be finished in a predictably short time. As we made use of the great amount of documentation, we found that more words and more time were required than could be anticipated. And especially when we elaborated the segments of chapters 8 ("Tightening Grip") and 9 ("Frantic Effort to Save 12,000 More") . . . the stressful nature of the subject matter forced us to put our work aside for a while.

The way in which our work has been affecting us has, curiously, not diminished as we passed into old age, and has, in fact, increased. Fortunately LHE had his more strictly philosophical work, which, because it is demanding, has been providing the kind of distraction that enabled him, after some weeks or even months, to resume our writing on *Choices under Duress* without the personal background coming into play. And EE had her own writing to help her recover, especially her reminiscences of her Jewish childhood in Vienna, and her youth as a Jewish refugee in England and the United States, as well as the revision of her book on *Suffering in Nietzsche: Motive and Mask*.

We pushed off writing the chapters on the deportations until they were the only ones left to do. When we finally did work on them, we realized that we had not become inured over time against being affected to the core.

Writing these chapters, we could not help but visualize the fate of friends, relatives, and other persons whom we had known in our young years in Vienna. While we were not able to dispel the visions that haunted us, we believe that we have succeeded in keeping our personal involvement with the topic out of our book. We were reminded of the praise our friend and colleague David Wyman received for the coolly "surgical" clarity with which he wrote about the relatively poor response on the part of some significant segments of American society and government to the need to rescue the Jews from the Nazi Holocaust. But we also remembered how, in an interview on national television, Wyman admitted crying when, in his research, he, the scion of generations of Christian clergy, learned about the failure of a number of churchmen to be responsive to that need. We decided that a few pages of this book need to reflect the personal note, if for no other reason than as a reminder that the duress was suffered by beings of flesh and blood. We did this in the way we began this introductory chapter by adding at the end of the book a few personal "Lasting Impressions" and by interspersing in the body of the book a few notes about people we had known and what happened to them. The latter are set off from the regular text, and their respective author identified as either EE or LHE.

Postscript 2007

Early in 2007 we were informed of the cache of IKG papers from the Holocaust period that had been found in Vienna and was in the process of being catalogued and stored in an archive established for this purpose. We have since viewed the overwhelming number of boxes and sampled some of their contents. From what we have seen, except for filling in details, by and large the archive would not provide any documentary material that would modify our account and interpretation of choices under duress of the Holocaust.

Later that year we learned of Raul Hilberg's death. The unexpected news jarred us not only because he was younger than we but also because we could no longer fulfill a promise. For decades Hilberg had been fully aware of the fact that our research caused us to disagree with his interpretation of the performance of Löwenherz and especially of Murmelstein. We spent some time together in Jerusalem at the conference on the *Judenrat* in 1977, at which he was one of the main speakers. We had just come from conducting our first set of interviews with Murmelstein and told him that we would soon return for the second set. At this point Hilberg, with a certain dismissive tone of voice, said, "*Ich lass' ihn grüssen*" ("I send him my regards"). When we told Hilberg that this is precisely the same message Murmelstein had asked to deliver to him, we all broke into laughter. Walking down the avenue commemorating the righteous gentiles at the Yad Vashem Holocaust memorial in Jerusalem, we told him that after the completion of our book but before its actual publication, we would let him see whatever criticism of his interpretation it contained, a promise we now cannot fulfill. Nevertheless, even though Hilberg can no longer respond to them, it would not be appropriate to tone them down. Nonetheless, we would like our readers to know of our high regard for Hilberg and of our friendly meetings with him.

PART I

Amalek

Chapter 2

The End of a World

Anschluss

"*Wir sagen: Ja*," said the speaker during the service ushering in the Sabbath on this Friday evening, March 11, 1938. "*Wir sagen: Ja*" ("We say: Yes")," which is to say, we shall cast a "yes" vote, in favor of an independent Austria.

As long as anyone could remember, living in Vienna meant living in stormy times, even when, with the fall of the Habsburg Empire in 1918, the city ceased to be a center of world affairs. And certainly these last few days before the German Anschluss (absorption) of Austria were stormy times in Vienna, and doubly so for its Jews. For while the regime did not regard itself as anti-Semitic, particularly in its top leadership, it was shored up by spokesmen for interests who could marshal support by appealing to one of the constants of modern popular opinion in Austria, namely, anti-Semitism. The Jews had reason to be apprehensive because plans were afoot to restrict their access to higher education and the professions. Sporadic anti-Semitic actions had been increasing in frequency and severity, and the regime was mildly yet definitely a police state. Nevertheless, the Jews also had reason to be positively involved in the sudden decision Chancellor Kurt von Schuschnigg asked the citizens of Austria to make: To vote "yes" would be an endorsement of the regime; a "no" vote would be an unthinkable act: an invitation to Nazi Germany to take over Austria.

It has often been said that the Anschluss was nothing other than the enactment of the desire of the Austrians to join in national union with Germany, a desire confirmed by plebiscite after the fall of the multinational Habsburg Empire and frustrated by the victors at Versailles, especially France. The enthusiasm with which the Austrians, and in particular the Viennese, greeted Hitler upon his triumphant return to his native soil is taken as a confirmation that for the Austrians the Anschluss was the longed-for national union. But all this seems wrong. First, most Austrians knew, at least up to March 11, that a distinction had to be drawn between a union based on national, cultural, and economic affinity on the one hand and a fascist dictatorship on the other. Almost every faction in Austria had reason to regard Anschluss to a Germany that was ruled by the National-Socialist regime as a blessing that was mixed at best: The supporters of the Engelbert Dollfuss-Kurt von Schuschnigg regime knew that Nazism was hardly in tune with Christian social virtue or with the work ethic of a society of estates that they had been trying to create. The Socialists, whose power had been cruelly broken by Dollfuss, were demoralized or seething "in the closet" or in exile; but they were in a much better position than their comrades in Germany to reorient themselves and their cause, and to plan, to hope, and to wait. The Viennese Jews certainly knew of the dismantling of the civil liberties of German Jews, of the harassment and the economic constraints imposed in Nazi Germany; and some had personal or tribal memories of such experiences from postwar Poland or prewar Russia. In comparison, Austria seemed a haven well worth supporting. And now, under unprecedented pressure and, as it turned out, in the last minute, the regime was wooing the support of all factions, including the Socialists and the Jews.

To the Jews the choice was clear. What was not clear was whether they could in so short a time be marshaled to exercise their choice. The plebiscite had been announced by Chancellor Kurt von Schuschnigg on Wednesday evening, March 9, 1938,[1] at the end of a speech he gave in Innsbruck, at a rally of precinct leaders of the Fatherland Front, purportedly a patriotic coalition, in effect the only legally permitted party and thus the political arm of the regime. He asked the people whether they wanted an Austria that was both German and independent, Christian and united, with bread and peace and equal rights for all, and announced a plebiscite for four days hence, on Sunday, March 13. The precinct leaders cheered for a long time, and the nation, glued to the radio, cheered with them for their leader, who rose to the occasion by defying Hitler's pressures. The band played the "Andreas-Hofer Song," and they, with the Chancellor, sang along. Did anyone notice that this, the most stirring and beloved of Austria's patriotic songs—about the Tyrolean peasant and innkeeper who led a band of rebels in Europe's only uprising against Napoleon—was a dirge, solemnly recalling how this popular hero, betrayed to the enemy, was bound and taken to his execution? Schuschnigg, in any case, recalled not the end but the beginning of that rebellion. He ended his speech with the words spoken in Allemanic dialect, which were Andreas Hofer's signal for the gathering of his army of mountain peasants: "*Mander, 's ischt Zeit!*" ("Men, it's time!").

But there was not much time. Even though the choice was clear for the Jews, the majority of them were not used to siding with the kind of people found in the Fatherland Front, and some may have hesitated or even been afraid to cast their vote. A good way to reach a significant number of Jews in the short time available was at the Friday evening services ushering in the Sabbath. The excitement and anxiety caused by the rapidly progressing political developments would surely bring large congregations, especially to the Great Leopoldstadt Synagogue. This "Second Temple," built in the 1850s to accommodate the burgeoning influx of Jews to Vienna, was a monument to Viennese Jewry's checkered career of emancipation. Unlike the "first" synagogue, built three decades earlier and hidden behind an ordinary house in consideration of the fact that Vienna was the official residence of a ruler who carried the title of His Apostolic Majesty, the "second" synagogue was permitted to stand free. Rebuilt after a fire of suspicious origin, it was still the largest in Vienna and one of the largest in Europe.

Tonight, on this March 11, it held at least two thousand congregants. "The atmosphere was charged as if with electricity," the speaker, Dr. Emil Lehmann, recalled four decades later.[2] He was at the time about 30 years old, a teacher of religion at a prestigious Gymnasium—not a rabbi but an effective youth leader and a gifted speaker whose services were tapped on special occasions. The post of Rabbi of the Great Synagogue had, in effect, been vacant since Dr. Israel Taglicht was called, less than half a year before, to fulfill the function of Chief Rabbi of Vienna. In this capacity he officiated at the central, "first" synagogue. Rabbi Taglicht was very old, and it was expected that whoever moved into the prestigious pulpit of the Great Synagogue would be his successor—all the more reason to be cautious about filling that vacancy. There were several rabbis in Vienna who were gifted scholars and speakers, and who could deal diplomatically with groups within and outside of the Jewish Community. But none seemed to measure up to the four great religious leaders of the Viennese Jews in the century from the 1820s until Chief Rabbi Zwi Perez Chajes's untimely death in 1927, and none seemed to have the capacity and stature which the uncertain and challenging times seemed to require, with one exception: A man of great brilliance and enormous energy, an internationally recognized scholar in several rabbinical and secular areas, as well as a pragmatic administrator, a talented teacher at all levels, and a respected rabbi since his mid-twenties. He would have been the natural candidate for the prestigious pulpit at the Great Synagogue, were it not for the seniority of all the other rabbis, and for certain faults: he was too young, too ambitious, not yet polished enough, and, to some, his appearance did not conform to the image of a rabbi. His name was Dr. Benjamin Murmelstein.

In the absence of a rabbi, someone had to be found for this important congregation on such a special occasion. Dr. Isidor Oehler, the able Inspector of the Jewish schools, had an inspiration: On Thursday, late in the evening, he called Lehmann and gave him the delicate assignment. The young man rose at five o'clock and worked on his speech. The coming Sabbath was the one before Purim, the festival commemorating the deliverance of the Jews from the threat of extermination at the hands of Haman in ancient Persia; on this Sabbath three extra verses[3] are added to the weekly reading from the Torah. These begin with the word *zakhor* (remember), hence this Sabbath is referred to as *Shabbat Zakhor*, the Sabbath of Remembrance. That it was what Amalek had done to them that the children of Israel were being admonished to remember did not need to be mentioned. That Amalek, rather than the mystical Sabbath bride, was even then standing before the gate, no one would have guessed, even then. Rather, Lehmann took the word "remember" as his cue,[4] and in a rousing speech fulfilled his assignment to tell the assembled Jews not to hesitate or be afraid, and to *remember* to make the only choice that was possible for them—to vote "yes."

The fact that Lehmann was given this assignment suggests that the leaders of the Jewish Community regarded the survival of the regime as vital to Jewish existence in Austria, such as it might be. This was by no means the only indicator. The funding of the whirlwind campaign on behalf of the plebiscite was supported by a check for 300,000 Austrian shillings, which Dr. Desider Friedmann, as the president of the IKG (*Israelitische Kultusgemeinde*), had collected on behalf of the Jews of Vienna and deposited that Friday morning at the central office of the Fatherland Front.[5]

Lehmann was not committing an indiscretion when he used the rabbi's pulpit to speak in favor of the plebiscite question. Far from advocating one side in a disputed question, he was giving expression to the surely unanimous opinion of the Jewish populace, to whom it would not have been acceptable if a rabbi had taken sides on a question of Jewish or general politics, especially since the Jews of Vienna were hotly divided in both. The issues that divided the community were many and serious: The traditional liberals, who advocated a Jewish existence patriotically tied to Austria, were opposed by the Zionists, who believed that Jewish existence meant building a national home in Palestine. Both groups bitterly opposed assimilationists, who thought they had blended into the general Austrian population and regarded their ties to Judaism as tenuous and merely historical. Standing apart from all three groups were some orthodox Jews, whose interest in the politics of Jewish existence was restricted to the question of whether the laws of the land permitted their living and educating their children in strict adherence to *halakhah* (Jewish religious law). All these rifts were now bridged as the Jews of Vienna made their—as it turned out—last political decision as Austrian citizens. In light of the available alternatives, it was a sound choice.

Those among us who like to pause to discern the symbolic significance of events may regard the choice of Vienna's Jews as emblematic of their situation in the vortex about to engulf them: the Holocaust. Their political choice was sound but vacuous; for, unbeknownst to them, they had no choice. Unbeknownst to them, that afternoon a drama was enacted that forced Austria's sudden hero, Chancellor von Schuschnigg, to "postpone" the plebiscite and to persuade the president of Austria to accept his resignation. At around the time that the congregants in the synagogue were turning to the gates to welcome the Sabbath, Schuschnigg was doing what little he could to make sure the world would know that his government and the independence of his country were ending not by free choice but by choice under duress. As Lehmann was ending with a rousing "*Wir sagen: Ja*," Schuschnigg was about to step to the microphone to tell the truth. When Lehmann returned home a short while later, he could still hear over the radio the words with which Schuschnigg took leave of his brief place in world history: "*Gott schütze Österreich!*" ("May God protect Austria!").

Schuschnigg could not protect Austria, no one could, and God did not. Yet, Austria died with style. At the main studio of the Austrian Broadcasting Service, Dr. Arthur Schuschnigg, the director of the music division, unexpectedly heard his brother speak, put a record on the turntable, and left. His choice was the adagio of Haydn's Emperor Quartet, which consists of variations on the Imperial Anthem that Haydn had composed.[6] Others put on more music that seemed appropriate, until with grim suddenness a new crew arrived.

The congregants at the Great Synagogue did not realize that while they had entered the synagogue as citizens, admittedly embattled but as free to choose as anyone in Austria, they were leaving it as outlaws, their livelihood about to be ruined, their lives about to be shattered, with no choice left but to save what could be saved, and to escape if possible. Jews who had stayed at home heard of the end of their world over the radio. Those who walked home from the synagogue in anticipation of the Sabbath meal soon had their appetites spoiled. Swastikas were beginning to appear on houses and armbands. But the real whirl of enthusiasm on the part of the Viennese masses, their regimented spontaneity, did not develop until the next day. Later that night German news broadcasts and press releases told stories of serious disturbances in Vienna. But, they were not true. No doubt there were tension and anxiety in the air, maneuverers scurrying here and there, occasional shouting matches between bunches of people, either for Schuschnigg or for Hitler. Vienna was a city in search of cathartic release. One could sense that "something was up." But aside from the members of the—until a few days before illegal—Nazi Party, and the *dramatis personae* of the government, no one really knew anything until they heard their favorite Friday evening hour of light music interrupted for a "special announcement," which to the astonishment of all was made in the familiar voice of Chancellor von Schuschnigg. The official German talk about serious disturbances that needed to be quelled corresponded more to the Nazi regime's fumbling search for pretexts than to reality. It was, after all, their first takeover of a country.

Thus, the radical change in the lives of the Austrian Jews came as a sudden, stunning blow. They had just a few hours to formulate their own versions of the questions: "What does it all mean?" and "Now what?" The stimuli to ask questions such as these and to appraise one's capacity for engaging in suitable action were not long in coming.

The scenario that Berlin had composed for the "Return of Austria to the German Reich" did not run exactly according to the text but sufficiently so to give some semblance of legality to the appointment of a Nazi puppet as Chancellor and to his "request" for the entry of German troops to "reestablish order." This happened during the night. The next day, German troops started the occupation of the country, heading toward Vienna in particular. On Sunday, soldiers started walking in pairs through neighborhoods, shirt collars outside of their field-gray tunics, no weapons in sight, mannishly cheerful and correct, altogether making a good impression. Neighbors and their children, of whom one would never have suspected it, appeared in uniforms of Nazi organizations, and Nazi flags of all sizes were waved in an infectious holiday spirit that the Jewish onlooker perceived as a shattering absurdity. Were these his fellow Viennese, the ones who only two days before had rallied to Schuschnigg for an independent Austria with a patriotic pride born of the never forgotten glory of the Habsburg Empire, and with contempt for the coarse "Prussians"? With bitter irony, many a Jew recalled the line from the anthem of the Republic written to fit the melody of Haydn's Imperial Anthem:

Deutsche Arbeit, ernst und ehrlich	German labor—earnest, honest
Deutsche Liebe, zart und weich	German love—tender, gentle

The Viennese Jew knew: He had not changed, but his world had changed overnight. In what way the world had changed for the Jews, that was yet to be revealed.

Hitler had won a fantastic victory. He was in a hurry to enter the city that a quarter-century earlier had let him know that the world had no use for a nonentity with pretensions. But, everything had to be orchestrated in accordance with totalitarian pomp. First came the provincial capital city of Linz. Those who listened to the radio on the afternoon of Saturday, March 12, could hear how the crowds in the main square were being prepared for the frenzied reception of the Führer. It had all happened so suddenly that no prior preparations could be made. But, one by one, each house on the old town square, plain but quaint and not without charm, was being decked out with festoons and flags. The waiting crowd, casually regaled with improvised haranguing, learned to chant "*Ein Volk! Ein Reich!*" and later an improved version, "*Ein Volk! Ein Reich! Ein Führer!*" The afternoon waned, and still no Hitler. Lights were turned on in the windows fronting the square. And then it came, the casual confirmation that for the Jews the world had changed. One of the stores in the central old square of Linz had Jewish owners. They held out: no festoon, no flag, no light. And the smooth-voiced master of ceremonies, an old-time, "illegal" Nazi of Linz, the proprietor of a music shop, a retired Captain Ziebland,[7] let them know that this was noticed. "We know who our friends are!" Readily, the crowds played along. Though they were under firm control, the effect of the agitation was threatening, an irresistible protest against the exposed enemy. Finally, after what under the circumstances was a heroically long time, the triumphant howl of the masses told the radio audience that lights had been turned on in the Jew's house and a flag foisted upon his choice property. The Jews who were listening knew, and just as important, so did the non-Jews, who were henceforth to be called "Aryans."

On Sunday, March 13, no one remembered the plebiscite, which would surely have brought Hitler a stunning defeat. It was the day on which Hitler, overwhelmed by the reception that the Austrians were according him, decided that this was the time for the Anschluss rather than for the projected interim measure of keeping Germany and Austria nominally independent though under the personal union of a common head of state, namely, himself. The next day, Monday, March 14, Hitler at last made his triumphant entry into Vienna. It seemed as if all of Vienna turned out for the reception. The screaming and yelling reached its high point when Hitler finally showed himself on the balcony of the Imperial Hotel. He tried to speak. For the first time in his career, he could not control a crowd—they greeted him with chaotic adulation. The Viennese! The Anschluss was, in effect, completed.

As an expression for an act of personal or political joining, the word *Anschluss* is delicately neutral; it does not as such imply "incorporation" or "absorption." Only the conduct of public affairs could bring that out, and it did.

In times of change, there occurs a gap between the departure of the old authority and the establishment of effective control by the new. Opportunistic elements of the rabble have a nose for these gaps. Scenting loot, they step forth from the crowd, rob, and disappear into the protective anonymity of the crowd, before the new authority has taken hold. So, also now the rabble turned to business. Since this was the gap of authority, the first order of business was for individuals to rob Jewish stores, especially those isolated in neighborhoods where few Jews lived, and to beat up their owners, especially if they resisted. Jews for whom the word *pogrom* was merely a part of grim folklore of tribal memory had a rude awakening when they learned that their Jewish neighbors, who had lived through pogroms in Tsarist Russia, had fully expected the robbing. To the latter, it was no news that Jews could not count on police protection and that it was the Jews, and not the perpetrators, who were arrested. The initial wave of robbing was not restricted to individuals and shops; it was extended to such institutions as synagogues. In a memoir prepared two decades later,

Dr. Leo Landau, the President of the Polish Congregation in Vienna, recalled how he was summoned to his congregation's community building early on Monday, March 14.[8] The street was swarming with people. As he was conducted into the building by troopers, the officers of the police station across the street did not lift a finger. Once inside, he was accused to no avail of being an agent of Moscow. Forced to lead the troopers to the synagogue's safe at their command, Landau noticed that the *pushkes* (collection boxes for charities) had been vandalized. After they took the money from the safe, they ordered Landau to remain in his office and not to use the telephone for two hours, and left. It soon dawned on him that the "action" had been unofficial and that the troop did not want him to notify any authorities. He was lucky to have escaped arrest at that time, but his luck ran out a few weeks later.

The reason for the confusion of Vienna's Jews is that the robbing—and, as we shall see, other severe harassment of the initial period after the Nazi takeover—was perpetrated by a special rabble, one that did not deem it necessary to retreat into the crowd, and in fact regarded itself as the new authority. The marauding rabble made its appearance in the person or under the leadership of none other than the SA (*Sturm-Abteilung*), the heretofore illegal, brown-shirted storm troopers. The two decades between the wars had witnessed the appearance of paramilitary branches of political parties; hence, in principle a uniformed troop such as the SA was not unfamiliar. What was different was its open, lawless doings, the apparent impunity with which they engaged in them, and, for their Jewish victims, the absence of any recourse. Only in retrospect, after considerable analysis on the part of political philosophers, did the world come to an understanding of what the victims were facing at first hand and for the first time: This was openly and avowedly a totalitarian movement, without any need to regard opinion outside of its sphere of influence or the consequences of its acts. It was composed of a rabble, whose most immediately visible grassroots element was the SA, a rabble of those who rightly or wrongly regarded themselves as disaffected, who were only capable of and receptive to simple definitions of their problems and prone to avail themselves of whatever solutions seemed most ready at hand. In this way anti-Semitism, which was particularly endemic to Austria, gave the onset of Nazi rule in Austria its characteristic complexion. The movement toward the "final solution" of the Jewish problem experienced with the Anschluss of Austria a thrust forward to new intensities and into new dimensions. Before the new authority could establish itself, its own rank and file showed the degree to which popular anti-Semitism provided the vigor of the Nazi movement and how ready they were to proceed with the correlative item of the agenda, the active persecution of the Jews.

The robbing spree in the initial period of the Anschluss proceeded quickly and efficiently. How it was at all possible was explained by Siegfried Kolisch in a postwar memoir. Kolisch was an architect and the proprietor of a building enterprise. He reported an incident that proves that in the years before the Anschluss there were cells of illegal Nazis among the employees in enterprises and businesses owned by Jews, whose job it was to collect information as to what the respective "Jew possesses, what he said, and a general description of him." Such information was reported to the cell leader, noted on file cards, compiled and collected, and kept in readiness for the day it would be put to use. Kolisch's business was in Kritzendorf, a suburb of Vienna. In this capacity, his company was renovating a building there, where the local illegal Nazi cell had its headquarters, about two years before the Anschluss. His workmen found a crate in the cellar, which was brought to Kolisch's office. Kolisch invited Anton Jütting, the boss of the local illegal Nazi cell, in order to ascertain whether the crate with "these file cards about Jews of the neighborhood" were the property of the cell. The cards included information on Jewish "property, jewelry, liquid and unmovable assets, and how employees are treated,"[9] and Kolisch inquired "what the purpose was of the comments on the cards." Kolisch would receive his answer through the events following the Anschluss.

Much of the open, petty robbing stopped fairly soon, for two reasons: First, it was all too obvious that the rabble was the vanguard of the new authority. The Nazi Party could ill afford a tarnishing of its image when, under its aegis, a new order was to be established. Hence, at the same time that the new authority was trying to install itself, it had to issue instructions that unauthorized confiscations, expropriations, and arrests were forbidden. For public consumption SA involvement was disclaimed by asserting that the unauthorized looting was perpetrated by communists disguised as brown-shirts.[10]

Vienna had both a larger number and a larger proportion of Jews than any city that had been under Nazi domination up to this time. As the former capital of the Habsburg Empire, it had attracted enterprising Jews from the different ethnic regions of the empire. Under the auspices of emancipation and liberalism, they were eager to participate in and contribute to what for them was, even in the center of Europe, a New World. Even though increasing anti-Semitism in the two decades after the collapse of the Empire had caused the impoverishment of an increasing number of Vienna's Jews, the assets under Jewish control must have seemed attractive booty. Pillage of such proportions required appropriate specialists and beneficiaries and could not be left to the petty thieves. And this was the second reason why the open robbing had to stop. But for the first few days these elements had their day and, as it happened, they were the vanguard of the instigators of larceny on a grander scale soon to be undertaken by official means.

Incidents such as looting businesses and bloodying their owners or any Jew at hand were heartbreaking, and in some cases soul-breaking shocks for the immediate victims. By and large, however, they could be regarded as individual and relatively petty actions. What did they signify to the Jews of Vienna? That they were to be treated as outlaws at anyone's whim? Or that the rabble got out of hand for a short time and that things would settle down soon, to a vastly and oppressively changed but orderly existence? For the time being, the Jews were thrown into confusion. This took many forms, depending on the individual: disconsolation, a wait-and-see attitude, obstinately acting as if all this would blow over, depending on good sense to prevail and order and decency to be reestablished, and so on.

We can characterize the deepening confusion into which the Jews were thrown: Ordinarily disruptions in life are suffered in contexts that provide a person with some degree of validity as a human being, where compensatory or remedial action is possible. If injured, one can seek redress; if struck with misfortune, one can rise again; if destitute, one can seek help; at the end of one's powers, there is hope. A life without such a context is unimaginable. Without a modicum of validity there is, indeed, no life. The sun still shines, the town and landscape are still in place, the faces familiar, but a darkness opens up in which there are no bearings, no outstretched hands, no resource nourishing life, no recourse justifying existence. This is the darkness that was descending upon the Jews of Europe, and in Vienna it descended first and with precipitous speed. When the Jews saw the solid Austrian patriot turning into a hailer of Hitler, the pride of a gentle culture openly looting and beating, they knew the dread that comes with the knowledge that the threads connected to one's right to life have been torn.

The looting stopped, for the most part, in time to be replaced by the massive expropriation in the guise of legality and administrative regulation. But the vigor of open persecution by the "legionnaires" of the new order, as the leaders of the regime's elite such as Reinhard Heydrich referred to them, continued. Jews were summoned from their homes, sometimes picked up on the street, and made to scrub away the slogans that had been painted on the pavements during the short-lived campaign on behalf of the aborted plebiscite. Who would have ever thought that any youngster who put on a brown uniform could arrogate unto himself the right to fetch someone for such a purpose? Who would have thought that one would go, and go without asking about the uniformed man's right to take him? But, they fetched, and they went. Who would have thought that the question of right was settled in the immediacy of mob rule and an atmosphere of terror? But, the mob was functioning, and terror prevailed. And who would have thought that the decent elements of the citizenry would not lift a finger and would in fact watch the plight of their Jewish fellows with open satisfaction? This was a revelation to the Jews subjected to the indignity, to some Austrians, who, though powerless, kept their principles and their dignity, and to foreign correspondents, who reported and commented on what they saw. Some of the Jews who suffered the abject humiliation were, understandably, shattered in their innermost soul. But who would have thought that in this first encounter with persecution most of the Jews would find within them sparks of elemental defiance? But, this was also the case. Some of the few who were crushed by the humiliation were admonished by their fellow Jews who were scrubbing alongside them. Most scrubbed as if it was the most natural thing to do, in spite of the fact that the troopers added excessive amounts of lye to the buckets, that the brushes were designed for teeth rather than pavements, that the populace was howling insulting approval and shamelessly joined the troopers and street urchins in their cruel sport. Some Jews showed their defiance in a grander manner. One Jew, the story goes, when summoned, asked for time to dress. Presently he appeared in the full-dress officer's uniform that had hung in his closet from the time of the First World War, replete with rank and combat decorations. The boys in brown uniform told him he was excused and asked him to turn back. But, he insisted, and went and performed. Another Jew, scrubbing at Hochstädtplatz, spoke to his neighbors among the watchers as if the occasion were a garden party. Turning to a family which was looking out a window, he said, "Ah, Dr. Ulsamer, are you here too? Hello! Nice evening, isn't it?"[11] Such stories made their rounds among the Jews and, coupled with their perception of the doom settling on them, they sparked the will to live, the strength to endure, the courage to escape.

The situation of many Viennese Jews quickly turned desperate. A goodly number had been leading a hand-to-mouth existence, living in one or two rooms in apartments of

Jews forced to scrub the streets of Vienna. (USHMM—03741)

people almost equally poor. Many of them had lost their livelihood, such as it was, immediately after the Anschluss. They were faced not only with starvation but, unable to pay their weekly rent, also with eviction. The needy had been receiving some support from the many charitable Jewish volunteer groups or from the organized charity of the IKG. All of a sudden, the charities were closed, their funds inaccessible, their assets frozen, their supplies unreplenished. An untold number of people were helped then and later by nameless fellow Jews. But, more and more of the desperate showed up at the IKG. They were helped in the first few days with the small amounts needed to pay the rent or buy food, without the formalities that were ordinarily required to authorize disbursements.[12] These people were soon joined by others whose situation had also become problematic through the loss of a job or a business, the arrest of a spouse, father, or son. The narrow street in the oldest part of Vienna, on which the IKG was located, became crowded with worried Jews.

The community had been large, made up of disparate elements, with a variety of needs, commitments, orientations, and agendas. The activities of the community were conducted through hundreds of organizations, large and small, only some of them branches of the official central Jewish organization (IKG), or under its supervision. Now, however, a new challenge arose for the IKG, the challenge of central leadership and of providing services on an unprecedented scale and, in large part, in unprecedented areas. But before this challenge could be articulated, much less met, the new regime closed the IKG. Thereby it deprived the Jews of Vienna of their leadership, which at that crucial time had the effect of intensifying the terror.

At the time of the Anschluss, the IKG had tried to operate in its normal way, opening as usual on Sunday, March 13. On that very day, the staff of the welfare department was beginning to face the new problems, which were to multiply and intensify in the succeeding few days. By and large, the community was left alone by the authorities, except for one inspection that a former official remembers to have taken place on March 16.[13] But on March 18, one week after the fateful Friday of the Anschluss, the new authorities from the Reich were ready to deal with the IKG. Members of the SS, the *Schutzstaffel* (protection squadron or bodyguard), appeared in full dress uniform—black suit, white gloves, gleaming boots. They were accompanied by steel-helmeted SS men in field-gray battle dress and by Heydrich's official photographer,[14] who recorded the event, starting with the assembly point in the courtyard of what until a week before was Austria's Interior Ministry. A photograph in the courtyard is of special interest. Among the groups waiting for the action to begin one can see the two SS men who would inspect the central offices of the IKG receiving tips or instructions from a Viennese civilian. Standing with another group of civilians is another young SS officer, whom we can identify as Adolf Eichmann. We surmise that he came along as an observer, having no known role in the proceedings of that day.

The SS at the former Austrian Interior Ministry. The arrow points to a young SS officer who would become infamous: Adolf Eichmann. (DÖW 2774[1] Eichmann)

One of the photographs show two vehicles parked on Seitenstettengasse, the short and narrow street on which the IKG and Central Synagogue are located. One of them is a staff bus, the other is what in Vienna was called *Überfallswagen*, an open, bus-sized, police vehicle used for raids. The photographer recorded the portal to the building, pictures on the walls of the Jewish Community's past worthies, including the paintings of Rabbi Preacher Isak Noa Mannheimer, who founded the modern Jewish Community of Vienna, and of the celebrated Cantor Salomon Sulzer, who modernized Jewish liturgical music. With all the lights turned on, the splendidly simple interior of the synagogue was also recorded. The emblematic Hebrew passage from Psalm 16:8 above the Holy Ark is prominently displayed: "God's presence is always before me." The door to Robert Stricker's office bears the legend "admittance only by appointment"; the irony was not lost on anyone, since the men came unannounced. The raid on the IKG Vienna was a new departure for the Nazis; later we shall see that they had not found a way of effectively penetrating the Jewish leadership in Berlin; in Vienna, they learned how to do so.

Why did they come? Surely not to discover new, secret protocols of the Jewish world conspiracy. Instead, they looked for evidence of the Jewish leaders' opposition to Nazism in the form of a record of their contribution to the recent campaign fund on behalf of Schuschnigg's plebiscite. Some of the photographs show the two SS men inspecting ledgers, while the diminutive but distinguished looking president of the community, Dr. Desider Friedmann, sits at his desk, visibly frustrated by not being able to indulge his chain-smoking habit. Other pictures show the tall and aristocratic-looking Dr. Josef Löwenherz, who, as the director of the Jewish Community, was its chief executive officer, sitting at his desk visibly concerned over having to deal with the officious intruders. At the same time, the different departments of the community building were subjected to inspections, duly recorded by the camera. One of the pictures shows the rabbinic court: Two elderly bearded rabbis, whose names we do not know, preside at the table; two younger ones are standing behind them, one of them Rabbi Murmelstein.[15]

At about noon, the staff was told to clear the building. It was soon evident that the synagogue complex housing the Community's offices had been closed. President Friedmann and Director Löwenherz were arrested. The raid and the arrests provided the Nazis the opportunity to grope their way toward turning the Jewish leadership into an instrument for getting rid of the Jews. To this end, Löwenherz would be released after a few weeks to direct the IKG again under new auspices. Friedmann would be one of the 151 prominent Austrians—60 of them Jews—who were in the first shipment from Vienna to the concentration camp Dachau on April 1, 1938.[16]

One of the pictures taken (see page 42) shows one of the bearded presidents of the rabbinic court being stopped as he leaves the building, long enough to be surrounded by SS men crowning a day's job well done with hilarity over the rare sight of how, according to them, a quintessential old Jew should look.

Desider Friedmann was a distinguished lawyer in Vienna, a prominent leader in the Jewish community, influential in the leading circles of Austria, and an internationally recognized proponent of the Zionist cause to establish a Jewish homeland in what was at that time the British Mandate of Palestine. His rise through the strata governing the

Dr. Josef Löwenherz, the Director of the Israelitische Kultusgemeinde Wien *(Jewish Community of Vienna), at his desk suffering the intrusion of the SS on March 18, 1938. (USHMM—37072)*

Community was a weather vane of the success in Vienna of Theodor Herzl's charge to his followers at the First Zionist Congress (1897) to secure control over the Jewish communities. His election to the presidency of the Vienna Community in January 1933 marked the fact that the combined lists of the Zionist groups had received, for the first time, the majority of the votes cast in the election of the Jewish Community Directorate.[17] In 1934 the shaky regime of postwar Austria tried to put an end to party turmoil by abolishing the democracy put in place after the establishment of the Austrian Republic in 1918. They did this by proclaiming an interim constitution with the aim to establish, in time, a Christian political system structured in accordance with estates rather than class differences. In its accommodation to nationalistic agitation, the new constitution failed to provide for adequate representation of the interests of minorities, in particular the Jews, although they were obliged to do so according to the Treaty of St. Germain-en-Laye (1919), which established the truncated borders of Austria following the dissolution of the Austro-Hungarian Empire as a consequence of World War I. Instead, it placed an exceedingly small number of Jews, namely, three, in representative bodies. The most important of these bodies was the State Council, to which Friedmann was appointed in his capacity as elected president of the largest Jewish community in Austria.[18] This appointment entitled him to advise the chancellor, though mainly at the pleasure of the latter. The manner and extent to which Friedmann represented Jewish interests—at a time when the Jews were under great economic and political pressure and at the same time serving the interests of the country, which was then politically threatened from inside and outside—will probably never be fully known. No one lived to tell, and little appears in the documents. In the apologetic account of his authoritarian regime that he wrote in his later years, the late Chancellor Schuschnigg had precious little to say, but what he says is telling:

> Friedmann tried on his own initiative to obtain . . . the aid and support of international Jewry on behalf of the Austrian struggle for independence and against Nazism; he also tried to dispel the myth of the alleged anti-Jewish position of the Austrian regime, a myth spread occasionally in Western countries for transparent political or personal reasons.[19]

Soon after his election to the presidency of the Jewish Community and right after the regime of Chancellor Dollfuss crushed the Socialists in their attempt to take over the government in February 1934, Friedmann was asked to make use of his contacts abroad to help steady the Austrian currency. A similar instability occurred when Schuschnigg, Dollfuss's successor, was rudely summoned by Hitler to Berchtesgaden in February 1938. Now it was Schuschnigg who was reported to have asked Friedmann to marshal help abroad to steady the Austrian shilling. And, as we have already learned, in the last days of the regime the secretary-general of its political arm, Dr. Guido Zernatto, asked Friedmann for a Jewish contribution to the plebiscite fund, which Friedmann collected in one day and delivered on the last day of independent Austria.[20] The SS reported in its newspaper *Das schwarze Korps* (The Black Corps) that during their search of the IKG on March 18, they had found evidence of this and of another contribution, together amounting to 800,000 shillings.[21]

Friedmann's performance on behalf of the Dollfuss-Schuschnigg regime explains his arrest by the Nazis. It also raises a question: The Jews supported the regime simply because it was in their interest. By this token, the regime had an interest in securing the support of the Jews—and, contrary to Schuschnigg's claim, it was not given by Friedmann merely "on his initiative" but was requested by the regime. For example: After his trip to see Hitler, doubts spread abroad about the stability of Austria. When the head of the Austrian house of Rothschild had to go abroad for reasons of business, Schuschnigg asked him not to, so as not to give the appearance that Austria was a sinking ship. Rothschild was also said to have contributed two million shillings in support of the plebiscite campaign. In short, in addition to having an interest in supporting the regime, the Jews of Austria had some clout, and the regime had political reasons to appreciate it. Consequently, what exaction of performance on the part of the regime was secured by the spokesmen of Jewish interests in exchange for Jewish performance? How was Jewish support used politically to protect Jewish interests? The sad fact is that Schuschnigg's choice under duress, his "yielding to might"—as he said in his last broadcast—without having his army fire a single shot, on the pious grounds that he did not want to see the "spilling of German blood," in effect abandoned the Jews to their dismal fate. The Jews owed Austria everything; but Schuschnigg, the regime, Austria, and its people did not owe its Jewish citizens a thing.

Friedmann's holding the highest post in the Jewish Community, his being the most highly placed Jew in the regime, his travel abroad at the time when doing so for the regime meant acting against Hitler, and his collecting Jewish contributions for the dreaded plebiscite—all these facts were sufficient reason for his arrest and for his being kept either in concentration camps (Dachau, Buchenwald, and Theresienstadt) or under surveillance in Vienna for over six and a half years. He could not be permitted to emigrate but was useful as a potential hostage. When, toward the end of the Nazi era, it became apparent, as in so many other cases, that his value as hostage was outweighed by his status as enemy, Friedmann, together with certain other "prominent people" was sent from Theresienstadt to his extermination in Auschwitz. He was to be on one of the last major deportation trains that left Vienna for Theresienstadt in the fall of 1942, and on one of the last major deportation trains from Theresienstadt to Auschwitz in October 1944.[22]

Another prominent Jew, who suffered a fate similar to that of Friedmann, was Robert Stricker. He was one of the two vice presidents of the Community, the one who represented the Jewish nationalists and Zionists. A versatile activist on behalf of Jewish causes, he was a vigorous proponent of Zionism and a fighter for Jewish interests in his many capacities, for example, as one of the few Jewish representatives in the parliament of the newly founded democracy after the First World War.[23] As an articulate and authoritative journalist and newspaper editor, he earned the special enmity of the Nazis by his outspoken opposition to anti-Semitism and Nazism. Arrested in the first few days, released after many months in concentration camps, he was among the last to be deported to Theresienstadt and thence to Auschwitz.[24]

A third Jew who was among the quickly arrested prominent members of the Community, Dr. Jakob Ehrlich, did not survive for a very long time.[25] Past member of the Directorate of the Jewish Community, representative of the Zionist faction, elected member of the city council of Vienna right after the First World War, later appointed to the same council under the authoritarian regime, and thus one of the regime's three ranking Jews, Ehrlich was revered as one of the most indefatigable soldiers on the postwar battlefields of Austrian Jewry. In Dachau he was subject to severe abuse, and his remains were sent to his family as early as July 1938, one of the earliest victims of the Holocaust.

Dachau

The name struck horror in all who heard it, but no one really knew why. It stood for unspeakable terror. One only knew that those who were sent there had little chance of surviving, those who were released were changed forever, and none of them told what happened there. Only after the demise of the regime did some former inmates feel free to tell. One of these was Kolisch, who was arrested and sent to Dachau concentration camp at the time of Kristallnacht. We will paraphrase selected segments from his postwar graphic description of the ordeal from arrest and detention, and transport to, reception at, sojourn in, and release from the camp.

A rabbi encounters a wall of German military men outside the IKG during the "razzia" *of March 18, 1938. (DÖW 2774[3][6])*

■ ■ ■

Arrest and Arrival. At the detention facility, a gymnastics hall formerly maintained by the Jewish Community, the inmates, no matter what age or physical condition, were forced to do strenuous exercises beyond human endurance. The SA (*Sturmabteilung*, Storm Troop, Nazi paramilitary corps also known as the Brownshirts) had free reign there and beat the prisoners mercilessly; whatever food they were given had to be provided by the IKG. In time there were selections as to who would stay in custody, who would be released, and who would go to the concentration camp. The latter prisoners were taken to the *Westbahnhof* (Vienna's Western Railway Terminal), where a company of SA awaited them. Some of them [SA] chased the Jews from the vehicles, while others formed a gauntlet that the prisoners had to run under, accompanied by blows from the howling SA men. The Jews had to jump into the freight cars that were provided with two rows of benches, on which they had to sit tightly packed without moving, while constantly looking at the light of a lamp. Each car had two guards, who threatened to shoot anyone who moved.

After a long journey the train arrived in Dachau, where a large contingent of heavily armed SS awaited them. Under continuous blows, the prisoners were marched to the camp. There they had to await their processing by standing all day from 9:00 a.m. to 6:30 p.m.

It was their fourth day without any food. They then had their hair cut to the skin and were shaved, had to undress completely, were sent to a shower with steaming hot water, and were finally given their prisoner's garb. At half past midnight, they were picked up by their *Blockälteste* (block chief), who took them to their block. There were 28 blocks in the camp, which were long rectangular buildings, each designed to house 1,000 inmates. However, at maximum capacity Dachau held 60,000 inmates. The *Blockältesten* were Aryans serving sentences for crimes; their rule over the fellow inmates was absolute. When they arrived at their block, the Jews were given their first meal in four days, consisting of "a portion of a completely cold lunch."[26] The prisoners were given a patch with their number, which they had to sew on their prison uniforms. They were also given a triangular patch, its color indicating the type of prisoner: A "Jew" wore a yellow patch.

Escape. The camp was constructed in such a way that the prisoners were constantly reminded that there was no hope of escape. Desperate prisoners would commit suicide by touching the high-voltage fence. The immediately charred body could only be removed by shutting off the electric current. This kind of event provided an opportunity for sadistic actions by the guards, resulting in many additional deaths, sometimes counting into the hundreds. After every one of the three daily roll calls, selected prisoners had to collect the dead and take them to the camp crematorium, which operated day and night.

One time an SS man came to the camp on his motorbike and left it running as he entered the office. A prisoner mounted the bike and at breakneck speed rode to freedom. Immediately there was an alarm, and the tens of thousands of prisoners had to fall into ranks, while a swarm of SS motorbikers went after the escapee. The prisoners had to remain standing until he was caught and returned. Toward evening it rained and, soaked through, they continued standing. They stood there that night, and the next day, and a second night without food. Hundreds keeled over and died. Finally, in the afternoon of the third day, the escapee was returned, beaten until he lost consciousness, and revived with buckets of water, and this was repeated until he expired. Only then could the prisoners break rank, and in the evening received some ice-cold food. The incident reduced the camp population by close to 1,000 men.[27] In Kolisch's words: "The dead fulfilled their duty; this seemed to be the camp's main purpose."

Delousing. The prisoners were assigned to "blocks," each housing 1,000. Kolisch was assigned to Block no. 28. During one of the many inspections, this one of the prisoners' shirts, a louse was said to have been found on one of them. When this was reported, the camp leadership ordered an immediate delousing of the block. To clear the barrack, the prisoners had to strip bare and pile their clothing in a heap, so as to be included in the fumigation of the barrack. Wearing only shoes, they then marched to the bathhouse. In groups of 150 they entered, bathed, were given fresh clothing, and returned outside to stand until the whole contingent finished. With the temperature at –3°C (27°F), 400 of the waiting men died of exposure. The survivors had to join the 1,000 men in Block no. 22 for a temporary sojourn. After two days, they returned to the now fumigated Block no. 28. The incident left 200 of them with cases of pneumonia, to which they succumbed after a few more days. Altogether the alleged—but never substantiated—louse cost the lives of 600 human beings.[28] As Kolisch said, "The dead fulfilled their duty; this seemed to be the camp's main purpose . . . but the operation of the camp continued unchanged, and new arrivals brought the number up to date."

Released in Silence. At 3:30 a.m., the time of the wakeup call, the block chiefs were informed of those who were to be released from the camp that day. Immediately, they were isolated from the others, so as not to receive any messages from fellow inmates to be delivered back home. After stripping off all their prison clothes, the releasees bathed and were handed sacks with the clothing they had worn when they arrived at the camp. When they were dressed and had received all the cash their loved ones had been forwarding for them, they were taken to an anteroom where they were told about what was expected from them upon their release: Immediately upon arrival in their hometown, they would have to report to the local Gestapo officer to whom they would be assigned as their probation officer, who would monitor their behavior and from whom they would receive further instruction as to periodically reporting to him. They would have to understand fully that no matter where they were, they would be within the grasp of and could not evade the arm of the Gestapo. In particular, they were most severely constrained to silence (*schwerste Schweigepflicht*) concerning anything they had seen or heard in the camp. "We shall fetch and return anyone who tells the least bit about Dachau." What would happen to those who break the silence? The releasees were taken to the next room, which was the quarter for those who broke the *Schweigepflicht*. Kolisch wrote: "The sight of this room and of its inmates was the most horrible I had seen in my life, and the inhuman impression surely fixed the duty to silence in all, so that the public learned nothing about Dachau." What the releasees saw was a roomful of men, lying in their own excrement, with no water and no food, until they died in unspeakable misery. When asked why they were there, those who still had the strength, slurred "broke silence duty."[29]

■ ■ ■

Some prominent Jews who were not active in the community were also arrested, such as Baron Louis Rothschild,[30] and members of the literary and theatrical professions.

It is by no means the case that only prominent Jews were arrested in the first period of the Nazi takeover; in fact, hundreds of ordinary Jews suffered that fate, and the number increased into the thousands during the great wave of arrests between May 20 and the end of June. Neither is it the case that all prominent Jews were arrested at that time or even all members of the Representative Directorate of the Community.

But the arrest of the main community leaders left the mass of Jews without the leadership authorized by them to function as spokesmen and representatives, a leadership that could impel the needed reorientation, articulate policy, offer guidance, and organize remedial steps. The arrest of the leaders and the closing of the Jewish Community were significant factors in the deterioration of the situation. Certain matters could not be handled without this leadership. While some representations on behalf of the Jews and even of all Jews were made, while some remedies were sought and found, the actions were sporadic and specific, and the competence and performance of those who acted was limited. The chaos caused by the lack of leadership no doubt exacerbated despair, fear, and hysteria. A population in such a state is ripe for administrative control; hence, to a regime whose aim it is to exercise this sort of control, this is a desirable state of affairs. On the other hand, it was possible that the fury of even the most popular anti-Semitism directed against these unfortunates might spend itself and turn to sympathy; hence, to bring the Jewish masses under control was, aside from being a convenience, a necessity of local governance.

In addition, the Nazis were in a hurry to institute a kind of control over the Jews of Vienna that would be suitable for the special place the Jews occupied in the ideological program of the regime. Simply put, the program called for a *policy of getting rid of the Jews*. As we will see, they would use the opportunity that the novel situation of Vienna afforded to succeed in organizing the Jewish population for this purpose, a success that they did not achieve in the *Altreich* (the "old Reich," that is, Germany without its conquests). Before they could proceed with this, the Nazis had to consolidate their authority, a task that was connected with winning a plebiscite, one which Hitler announced for April 10.

The interregnum at the IKG between March 18 and the reopening of the Community under the new auspices lasted barely six weeks. What happened to the Jews in these intervening weeks was their abandonment, the abrogation of their recourse to civil rights, the prevailing terror, and the isolation resulting from all these factors. This made the Jews ready for the new IKG, and—by establishing the situation in which its leadership was to function—it determined the IKG's new career as well as the mode of its operation.

Betrayed, Abandoned, Isolated

In the wake of the Anschluss, the Nazi regime was faced with special tasks. It had to establish and confirm its domination over the new *Volksgenossen* (fellow countrymen), the Austrians, and to derive the benefits of approbation from the old *Volksgenossen* for its bold stroke. These wholly internal tasks involved a number of activities whose common point of reference was a plebiscite set for April 10. Since actions against the Jews of Austria figured prominently in carrying out these internal tasks, we will have to characterize the Jews' new situation with reference to this context.

Externally the regime's task in this period was—as usual, as long as there was no danger of a war, for which it was not yet ready—one of diplomatic pacification coupled with propagandistic manipulation of public opinion. Diplomacy was no problem, since it soon turned out that the governments that counted as regional powers,[31] not being prepared to back any disapproval they might harbor with requisite action, found ways to acquiesce in the takeover of Austria and what it entailed. Public opinion was another matter. The foreign press reported the attendant excitement and enthusiasm, as well as the grim consequences, especially as pertains to the fate of the Jews.

Actions against the Jews in Germany at the beginning of the Nazi regime were mild by comparison with the vehemence following the Anschluss. But in 1933–1934 these actions were a novelty, which tended to give the regime a bad press at the critical time when it was first established. Sensitive to this, spokesmen of the regime propagandized against the "*Greuelpropaganda*" ("horror propaganda") and kept the development of their policy respecting the Jews at a level which, in retrospect, can be regarded as moderate. Hermann Göring had even summoned some representatives of the Jewish Community of Germany to urge them to counteract the *Greuelpropaganda* that was being spread abroad. This was in 1933. In 1938 no Nazi official at or near the highest level exposed himself to Jews. Even if Jews had been summoned and the attempt of forcing a denial had succeeded, the facts that would have put a lie to it were all too evident. The only available propaganda ploy was to face up to the facts and explain them away.

But who should do this? Perhaps Dr. Arthur Seyss-Inquart? Hardly. He was the *Statthalter* (governor) of Germany's newest province, who, a few days earlier, had been chancellor of Austria for some hours—long enough to surrender his country illegally to Nazi Germany. Or perhaps Josef Bürckel, the most highly placed of the German officials who were flooding Austria—to the dismay of the Austrian Nazis, who never dreamed that they would have to compete for positions with their "liberators"? Bürckel's position was too important for him to expose himself at this time to a matter that seemed so unimportant and with respect to which he had to maintain freedom of action. The job was left to the new mayor of the new good-old Vienna, who was Dr. Hermann Neubacher, a high-ranking member of the—until lately illegal—Austrian Nazi party.

On the sixth day of the Anschluss, Mayor Neubacher called in the foreign press, ostensibly presenting the new situation from an Austrian perspective. In his statement, he noted that never before had such a complete political reversal taken place in a more humane manner. Characterizing certain actions—he never mentioned "Jews"—as "small incidents," he attributed them to the sort of "over-zealousness" that always accompanied a revolution.

In concluding, Neubacher managed to combine smooth bureaucratese and New Order jargon with an allusion to Vienna's lighthearted theater world that had always made a press assignment to this city so attractive:

> When these days of ferment are over—and they are in the process of liquidation—we shall present the spectacle of a genuine first-rate Austrian discipline, which will not take second place to a German discipline of any kind. This we promise you.[32]

Why did the mayor of Vienna need to promise anything to the public represented by the foreign press corps? Evidently to gain acquiescence for what the regime was about. Why did the mayor need to brag about the Austrian potential for discipline second to none, not even to the German? Was it that the unprecedented vehemence of the pogrom against the Jews at the hands of the mob—the main element of which were the storm troopers—was an embarrassment to the regime? Though it was a good propaganda ploy to make it appear so, Vienna's enthusiasm for anti-Semitic actions and the scope that they could attain was hardly inopportune for the regime. Admittedly the mayor's promise to the press was neither convincing nor effective, but then the regime was at a stage when it felt free to accelerate the movement of the Nazi program and, corollarily, to be less cautious about its image and less ambitious in its foreign propaganda efforts.

As we examine how the situation of the Jews developed in Vienna, we may well keep some questions in mind that arise from the mayor's promise: How successful was the promised new Austrian discipline in the "liquidation" of the "small incidents" of the "days of ferment"? What was the true nature of the mayor's promise regarding the role that the persecutions played in disciplining the Austrians and turning them into German *Volksgenossen*? What form did the promised application of "genuine" (i.e., Nazi) discipline take to the treatment of Jews? In spite of the *démenti*, in spite of the efforts to control the individual actions against Jews and to channel them into official policies and their execution, clandestine actions continued sporadically in the form of scattered outbreaks and continued even within the framework of officially sanctioned proceedings against the Jews. A few illustrative examples of what happened to Jews of Vienna in the period following the Anschluss will suffice. Ampler accounts can be found in the literature about the period, and even there the endless litany of suffering inflicted by the Viennese, shed of the touted veneer of charm and culture, is barely accounted for.

Jewish children were systematically beaten up on the way to school. In school they were harassed by schoolmates, with the teacher's collusion of silence. Jewish proprietors were driven from their enterprises. Stores continued to be robbed. So were private dwellings. Some enterprising storm troopers were lucky enough to have girlfriends who, until the Nuremberg laws were fully instituted in Austria, were permitted to retain their positions as maids in Jewish households and could not be dismissed. The troopers used the information to which the girls were privy, as well as their authority as uniformed party members, to help themselves to the valuables of the Jews. Other Jews were driven from their homes, sometimes their possessions were appropriated together with their apartments; some Jews were brought back to their apartments, albeit to clean their toilets. Scores were settled, and a great number of more gratuitous brutalities were committed on those under arrest or detention. Jewish women who were unlucky enough to have to appear before officials were subjected to vulgar and brutish treatment. In some neighborhoods, Jewish women did not dare appear on the street for some time. Jews were forced to paint the word *Jude* (Jew) on stores owned by Jews; sometimes children and even the owners' children had to perform this task. Jewish passersby were forced to hold defamatory placards in front of Jewish stores, while doing deep knee bends until they keeled over. Torturous hours-long exercise sessions to the breaking point were reserved for the woods of Vienna's Prater park, traditionally the locale of popular recreation and amusement, for which Jewish youths were rounded up by bands of storm troopers. Synagogue services were invaded. Cars were "requisitioned," and their Jewish former owners were made to wash them, and so on.

Incidents of this nature were frequent though relatively scattered. In the first place, a goodly number of the almost one hundred and seventy thousand Jews in Vienna remained unscathed by the pogrom. Second, some were individual acts, some types of action occurred in waves, some waves were localized. Third, many, perhaps most of these actions were the result of momentary impulse by one or a band of persons, and perhaps none were the result of the kind of party decisions that show up in filed records. But, even if relatively scattered and not recorded for the historian's scrutiny as faithfully as more dramatic occurrences, these incidents did take place throughout the spring and the summer of 1938; and they did not cease when the putative crackdown was announced and the false denial was issued. The fact that those incidents could occur, the fact that most of them occurred in the open and, in any case, were a matter of common knowledge, the fact that they could—and did—occur at any time and in any place and were unhindered and unopposed, these were determinants of the radically changed political situation of the Jews, as we will see. In any case, in light of these occurrences it can hardly be said that the mayor's promise had been well kept.

Things were different in regard to the second, implied sense of Mayor Neubacher's promise. According to it, the clandestine abuse of the Jews was to have its counterpart in highly visible official actions detrimental to the Jews, and both, the unofficial and official persecutions, would be among the instruments by means of which the subordination of the Austrians—especially the Viennese—under the domination of the Nazi regime would be effected. How was this done?

Initial Persecution

The new masters of Austria faced difficult tasks in every major sector of life. Politically, opposition had to be neutralized, enemies rendered harmless, and the alignment of population segments of each major shade of opinion secured. Administratively, all levels of government had to be reorganized and subordinated to the regime, and the bureaucracy, the police, and the army incorporated into the regime's wider organs of authority. Economically, Austria had to be made to function as part of a large power with aggressive policy plans befitting an industrial society of high development and potential, moreover a society professing concern over full employment, cradle-to-grave security, and the universal distribution of modern amenities. Most important for the totalitarian regime, the skein of the Austrian Nazi party had to be rewound into strands of a larger web; at the same time, the sole and dominant authority of the party and its supreme leader had to be established and its acknowledgment assured.

There ensued a flurry of activity on all these fronts. True to the nature of this totalitarian regime, the activities moved along two or more tracks, some in competition with each other. Equally true to type, they were highly organized activities, motivated by a usually-not explicitly-expressed ideological momentum, and impelled by the relentless efforts and ubiquitous presence of party functionaries. Let us look at this activity.

The primary aim of the first few weeks of the Anschluss was the efficient and effective alignment (*Gleichschaltung*) of Austria with the national community as conceived by the Nazi movement. The activities in each of the named segments were coordinated to achieve this aim. Even the party, which had the prime responsibility for this effort, had to postpone its reorganization.

The plebiscite scheduled for April 10 served as the occasion for this effort. The Nazi regime inherited the plebiscite from Schuschnigg. But the Nazi potentates in Berlin no doubt recognized the plebiscite as a singular opportunity for a display of Austria's alignment with the *fait accompli* of the Anschluss. Yet, it was an opportunity that was not without risk; after all, one of the reasons Schuschnigg's plebiscite was unacceptable to the Nazis was that anyone could predict that it would result in a defeat for Hitler. Since nothing in this matter could be left to chance, Hitler picked a man of experience, one who not only had aligned the population of the Saar Territory with Nazi Germany but had delivered its decisive plebiscite vote with a 91 percent majority. Josef Bürckel, the man in question, had, in fact, been picked to succeed Franz von Papen as German Ambassador to Austria, and for this reason was a member of Hitler's entourage as he proceeded toward Austria on March 12, that is, before Bürckel knew that he would inherit the plebiscite, and even before he knew that the full Anschluss would be effected. However, by noon of March 13, by the time the Anschluss had become certain, Bürckel had new orders from Hitler in his pocket:

1. I charge Gauleiter [Regional Party Leader] Bürckel, of the Saarpfalz region, with the reorganization of the NSDAP [Nazi-Party] in Austria.
2. In this capacity Gauleiter Bürckel, as Commissar of the NSDAP in Austria, is entrusted with the preparation for the plebiscite.
3. I have provided Gauleiter Bürckel with the power to take or order any measure required for the responsible fulfillment of the assigned mandate.[33]

Thus, from the very beginning the connection was clear between the reorganization of the party and the organization of the plebiscite. Equally clear was that, regardless of the track of authority provided by any government that may be constituted or reconstituted in Austria, the party was to be the first and primary track of authority. This in itself meant that it was the party's ideological dispositions that determined which popular momentum was to provide the thrust of the forward movement of the party's authority.

The party's engine ran on a fuel that in Austria, and particularly in Vienna, it found in known plenitude but perhaps unsuspectedly volatile readiness: the fuel of anti-Semitism. The party strategists from Hitler on down no doubt counted on it to intensify the thrust of the Nazi movement. The speeches which his paladins gave in the propagandistic softening-up for the plebiscite did not fail to contain the sharpest attacks against the Jews, with more or less oblique references to the conditions in Vienna, as we will see.

That the opportunity for the consolidation and advancement of the movement's power afforded by the plebiscite was recognized can also be seen in the fact that the plebiscite was extended to the whole of Germany and (constitutionally illegally) attached to the dissolution of Parliament coupled with the election of a new "list." It is instructive to look at the relevant documents. The "Decree of the Führer" of March 18 "affords the German people an opportunity to commit themselves in their entirety" to the new Greater Germany and, extending the plebiscite to all of Germany, to express themselves about "the reunion of Austria with the German Reich, which was accomplished (*vollzogen*) on March 13."[34] It is presupposed that the "reunion"—itself a concept whose implied claim to historical validity is highly questionable—has been "accomplished"; what the plebiscite is about is "commitment." Almost as an afterthought, Parliament is being dissolved "in order to offer the German *Volksgenossen* in Austria representation in the Greater German Reichs-Parliament."

How a parliamentary election can be part of a plebiscite was revealed a few days later when the format of the ballot was promulgated. On it, only one brief question was asked, printed over four lines and in three sizes of print:

Do you agree to the
reunion of Austria with the German Reich
effected on March 13, 1938, and do you vote for the list of our Führer
Adolph Hitler?[35]

Centered below "Adolf Hitler" was a large circle under the word ***Ja*** (yes); off to the right, a small circle under the word *Nein* (no). On the day of the plebiscite, the officials at the polling places said to the voters, while pointing to the large circle: simply mark a cross here. In Vienna, most voters did not bother going into the voting booth because they were afraid to do so. For word had gotten around that in some polling stations the names of those who went into the booths were flagged on the lists as potential opponents. In any case, the vote of April 10 was neither the sign nor the signal for, but the result of, the alignment of Austria. And this is not surprising, for the organized effort by the party, as well as the means at its disposal, were massive and overwhelming.

The task facing the party in the campaign can be defined in a simple manner: If Schuschnigg had been permitted to go through with the plebiscite, the vast majority of Austrians would have voted for him on March 13. The Nazis gave themselves four weeks to secure the support of that majority.

In the main, the majority consisted, first, of persons whose political orientation was determined by their Roman Catholicism; these were concentrated in the rural areas and smaller towns. And second, of the Social Democrats, that is, the anti-Soviet Austro-Marxists, who were cruelly suppressed by the Dollfuss regime during the attempted insurrection of February 1934 and who were concentrated in the industrial centers, especially Vienna.

The Catholics provided the main support of the Dollfuss-Schuschnigg regime. This regime, after a fashion, with its authoritarian ways and nationalistic cant, prepared the way for the Nazis. It had capitulated to the Nazis—with no discernible protest from its erstwhile supporters. However, the spokesmen of its party organ, the Patriotic Front, had been arrested, except for a few who had managed to escape across the borders. When the arrests, which reached into the thousands, began to include the petty officials and the cadre of the Patriotic Front, Bürckel himself put a stop to them, a clever ploy to gain support. With the political structure of the defunct regime gone, the Catholics could be reached only through the Church and its hierarchy. As he had in Germany five years earlier, in Austria, too, Hitler, as the chief tactician and executor of the Nazi regime, sought the accommodation of the Church. In Germany, this accommodation had resulted in the political neutralization of the Church and in restricting the exercise of its interests. Nevertheless, in Austria, Hitler would find the Church only too willing to repeat this process, moreover in a form that suited his immediate aim of aligning Austria.

How this happened has bearing on the situation of the Jews in Vienna as regards their abandonment and their consequent isolation. The behavior of the spokesmen of the Church in Austria at that time also helps to define the nature of choice under duress. For both these reasons, we have to report the facts of this episode in the early days of the Anschluss, examine them in context, and spell out their consequences.

Huge placards in Vienna displaying Hitler's face and urging a Yes (Ja) *vote in the Austrian plebiscite. The ad on top of the streetcar proclaims: "For Greater Germany and Adolf Hitler"* ("Für Groß-Deutschland und Adolf Hitler")*. Photo taken on April 10, 1938. (© AP)*

The Bishops' Declaration

The facts are, briefly, as follows. On the day of the climax of the Anschluss, March 15, Cardinal Theodor Innitzer, who as archbishop of Vienna was primate of Austria, paid an initial courtesy call on Hitler. On the next day, the press carried a brief item to the effect that the meeting had taken place. When it failed to publish also the cardinal's call on Catholics to maintain loyal relations to the state, the cardinal complained to Bürckel. The complaint served Bürckel as a pretext to suggest the negotiation of an agreement of accommodation between the Church and the new regime, as was done in the Saar Territory, Bürckel's previous bailiwick. There it had taken quite some time to accomplish; in Vienna it took barely a week. In spite of discussions among the seven bishops of Austria, in spite of attempts at intercession on the part of the Papal Nuncio Gaetano Cicognani, the text of the "Solemn Declaration" of the Austrian bishops "in the matter of the Plebiscite" was essentially one that was drafted by Bürckel himself. The nuncio's urging that the bishops' declaration express not only their "deepest conviction" respecting the "great historical events" but also their commitment to "guarding the rights of God and the Church" was not heeded but was reflected in a "foreword" to the bishops' declaration. In this foreword, the two spokesmen of the bishops base their confidence about the rightness of releasing the declaration on Bürckel's claim to adhere to the political credo: Render unto Caesar what is Caesar's and unto God what is God's (Matthew 22:21). In a brief covering letter, Theodor Cardinal Innitzer averred that the bishops had performed their "national duty freely and without coercion," and, assured that the bishops in the old Reich would do the same, he added, in his handwriting, *Heil Hitler*, before affixing his signature.

How astonished he and his brother bishops must have been, when one week later the Party published—in various forms and media, so also in its official newspaper *Völkischer Beobachter*, which was already being published in a Viennese edition—all three documents, and huge facsimiles of them were placarded about Vienna and the provinces. A fourth frame provided an exegesis of these texts in connection with a summons to solidarity in voting "yes" in the plebiscite. The Führer's plenipotentiary for the plebiscite, Gauleiter Bürckel, was visibly identified as the "publisher." Given the position of its author in the context of the regime, the summons informs "the whole German nation" of the "joy and sincere satisfaction" with which it had "noted the united position taken by the Austrian bishops."[36]

These are the facts. Now let us look at some aspects of this episode in context.

As vice-chancellor under Hitler, Franz von Papen, a practicing as well as political Catholic, was, in 1933, the instrument of aligning the Catholic Center with the Nazi regime. At the same time, he negotiated, on behalf of the Nazi regime, the Concordat with the Vatican. Later, as plenipotentiary for matters concerning the Saar, he did what he could (1) to gain the support of the Saar Church hierarchy in order to sway the faithful toward voting in favor of rejoining the Saar to Germany; (2) to counteract popular Catholic opposition to the Nazi regime, an opposition that was not prepared to vote in favor of the Saar rejoining a Nazified Germany; and (3) to keep the Vatican neutral in the matter of the Saar plebiscite. When von Papen's function in Berlin and as Saar-Plenipotentiary was exhausted, he was replaced in the latter position by Bürckel, who wheedled a declaration from the German bishops that proved to be a decisive factor in the Nazi regime's success in the Saar plebiscite. Von Papen was sent out on new assignments as Nazi Germany's Emissary Extraordinary—including to Vienna, where he quickly made his contacts, especially among influential Catholics, who would prove useful in bringing about the Anschluss with Austria. One of his last acts before his recall from this assignment early in 1938 was to arrange the ill-fated meeting between Schuschnigg and the Führer. At the time of the Anschluss, he was in Vienna in order to pack up and say good-bye. But, his usefulness was not at an end, even after Bürckel took his place once again. Having found out, through his contacts, that Innitzer as the primate of Austria would be prepared to call on Hitler as the head of the new governing power, von Papen suggested to Hitler, at the time of the parade which climaxed the Anschluss delirium, that Austria be given proof that he recognized its Catholic tradition.[37] The very brief meeting took place two hours later.

Von Papen received Innitzer at the portal of the Imperial Hotel. The streets were filled with an immense crowd. Predictably, Nazi sympathizers shouted their obscenities at the cardinal. More significantly, when the crowd saw who was emerging from the limousine to pay obeisance to the new ruler, there were massive shouts of "*pfui*!" and a cacophony of whistles[38]—the Viennese equivalent of the Bronx cheer. It was a time, as we have noted, when ideology determined which of the conflicting popular forces provided the forward thrust of political authority. Innitzer heard both. Would the coarse expression of indignation reverberate in the recesses of his judgment when he faced Hitler a few minutes hence?

No minutes were kept of the meeting. Hitler is supposed to have said, "The Church will not have any reason to regret taking a loyal position with respect to the State. If good cooperation should ensue here in Austria, then such a religious springtime could also have its effect on the old Reich."[39] Very deftly put! The reference to the Church's loyal position vis-à-vis the state reflects Innitzer's declaration of March 12, the day following the collapse of the regime whose plebiscite he had supported on March 10 in the name of the Austrian Church. In that first post-Anschluss declaration, Innitzer—after calling on the faithful to offer a prayer of thanks for the bloodless upheaval—admonished, "Of course, all directives of the authorities must be complied with gladly and willingly."[40] And Hitler's offer of "good cooperation" is, in turn, reflected in Innitzer's covering letter to Bürckel three days later, in which the enclosed Solemn Declaration and Foreword are tendered as a basis for "good cooperation."

What did Innitzer say to Hitler? According to von Papen, Innitzer averred that the Austrians felt themselves to be Germans and attributed their late opposition to the Anschluss to "fears of Nazism's revolutionary methods."[41] He also expressed the support of the Austrian Catholic Church, not unconditionally but "in the fight against unfaith and bolshevism."[42] Brave and good words, these. But let us consider the date: March 15. By then, thousands of the supporters of the defunct regime—political executors of the Church's modern social thinking[43]—had been arrested. By then, the regime was also permitting the demonstration of a popular version of its terrorist methods in the open, though supposedly clandestine, persecution of the Jews. The seduction of "unfaith" was being played out at that very time, as it were, if not under the window of the Imperial Hotel, then under that of the archbishop's palace. "Nazism's revolutionary methods" were being employed, in large part with unprecedented furor, right here in Vienna. Also, bolshevism was never a serious issue in Austria and, under the circumstances, at best a gratuitous swipe at the utterly shattered Austro-Socialists, at worst a canard to hide the fact that the two interlocutors were poles apart in ideology as well as in access to mundane power, and one of them sorely in need of an issue both could agree on. Considering all this, Innitzer's unique chance of confronting Hitler with the moral authority of the Church and of employing the political power which—in conjunction with the Church's secular embodiment—is the inevitable consequence of that authority, seems sadly wasted.

Let us recall other facts in the sequence: The regime's official announcement of the meeting between the Führer and the cardinal appeared in the press and over the radio. Cardinal Innitzer himself issued a report of the meeting in a pastoral letter to the faithful, exhorting them, in Hitler's words, to "take a loyal position with respect to the State."[44] This letter, however, was not published in the press, although similar exhortations by leaders of other Christian confessions were. Inasmuch as nine out of ten Austrian Christians were Catholic, the omission seems strange and must have been deliberate. While it may not have been clear what the regime had to gain from denying the head of the Austrian Catholic Church access to the public media, one thing must have been very clear: The

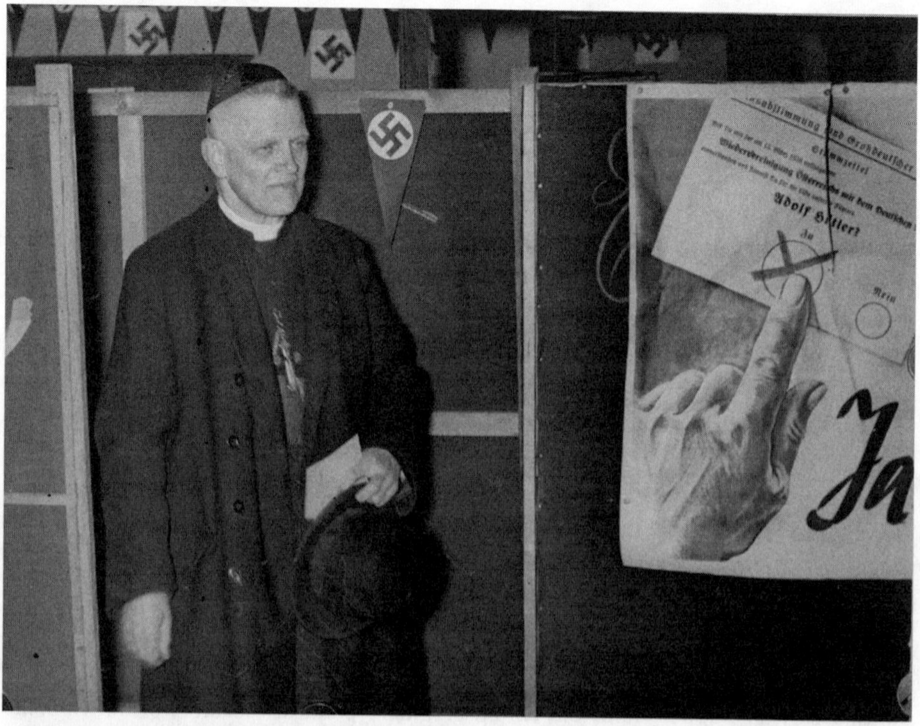

Theodor Cardinal Innitzer, the archbishop of Vienna, next to a poster supporting a yes vote for Hitler in the Austrian plebiscite. (Innitzer-HMW_141964-Wien Museum)

Church and its chief spokesman had their freedom only at the pleasure of the new masters. Innitzer sent a letter of complaint. No response followed. Instead, when Innitzer convened an urgent meeting of the bishops for March 18, Bürckel invited himself, ostensibly for the purpose of discussion. However, at the conference appeared not Bürckel but a trio of assistants, each of them professing to be a practicing Catholic. In short, with respect to whatever required discussion, Bürckel reserved for himself the freedom of deliberation but, as soon became sufficiently evident, was not prepared to grant such freedom to the bishops. True, the bishops were being maneuvered, but clearly they were needed; and that gave them courage.

Innitzer, at least, should have recalled a number of facts at this time, facts concerning the relationship between the Nazi regime and the Church in connection with what was sufficiently clearly a precedent case, that of the Saar plebiscite less than four years earlier:[45] First was the pressure the regime had placed on the German bishops to sway the faithful of the Saar in favor of rejoining Germany, to neutralize the strong Catholic movement there whose slogans were "For return to Germany, but not to Hitler Germany" and "Christ, not Hitler is our leader (*Führer*)." The second fact was Bishop Franz Rudolf Bornewasser's[46] unanswered letter of August 27, 1934, to Hitler, in which he calls the treatment of the Church (after the conclusion of the concordat!) a hindrance to the Saar's Catholic population voting in favor of reunification, and Bishop Bornewasser's refusing an invitation to see Hitler until the letter was answered. More important, the third relevant fact was the lessening of the tension between the Church and the regime in inverse proportion to the need of the bishop's support in the plebiscite. The fourth relevant fact was the quelling of the Catholic anti-Nazi movement by the Church hierarchy, which, coupled with its declaration favoring reunion with Germany, even if Nazi, were decisive moves; the hierarchy took this step fully expecting that the regime, being in debt to the Church, would settle the differences between them. And, finally, was the blatant disappointment of these expectations once the plebiscite was over and the support of the Church no longer needed.

It is obvious that this precedent did not affect the decisions made by Innitzer or his brother bishops. It is equally obvious that Bürckel was intent on using the bishops before they realized that they had an advantage and that it was incumbent upon them to make use of it. He did not have much time. Whereas the regime had had almost twenty-four months to prepare for the Saar plebiscite, the bishops now had only twenty-four days. The cries of "Christ, not Hitler, is our leader" had to be forestalled this time, and the authority of the Church hierarchy secured for the immediate task of alignment. This had to be done before the grim facts of the Jewish neighborhoods and of the prison cells had the opposite rather than the desired effect, namely, that of leading the faithful to the rueful realization of who the Christians' true leader is. Nor could Innitzer be given time to develop the idea that Hitler's cryptic statement held a promise of negotiable concessions or that the "religious springtime" would last beyond April 10 or that "cooperation" was to be taken at face value.

Bürckel's own advantages, besides being in the seat of totalitarian power, were many. At the point at which the bishops were about to start orienting themselves, he already had a scheme. He also had the element of surprise on his side—whoever heard of the highest mundane authority inviting himself to a bishops' conference; and what could be on his mind?

Also, the bishops, and in particular Innitzer, found themselves to be in a compromised, even vulnerable, position.

There was, first, Innitzer's recent support of the Schuschnigg-plebiscite. A Sudeten-German by birth, Innitzer belonged to the German-nationalist camp of Austrians, which had favored union with Germany after the breakup of the Habsburg Empire and had therefore, initially, supported National Socialism. When the anti-Christian nature of the movement became evident, he had dissociated himself from it, an act the Nazis regarded as a defection.

Second, unlike the majority of the leading clerics of Austria, Innitzer did not subscribe to ecclesiastical anti-Semitism. As a professor at the University of Vienna, he was reputed to have helped indigent Jewish students. When, during his tenure as rector, anti-Semitic students increased their attacks on Jewish students, he was prepared to close the university for a year unless the attacks stopped. In this way he aided the self-help efforts organized by Jewish veterans to protect students and synagogue assemblies from the more brutal variety of Viennese anti-Semitism, which began to surface after the establishment of the Republic. Chroniclers and historians of those times give Innitzer special due for words he spoke at a dedication ceremony of the Pauluswerk, a subsidiary mission to the Jews devoted to training Jewish converts to Catholicism:

> At a time when racial hatred and the idolization of race celebrate triumphs, it is well for us—who stand on the foundation of the old culture of our Austrian fatherland—to stress that we think otherwise. When Christ, the Lord, said they shall all be as one, his brothers among the Jews shall not be excluded. We shall keep the great watchword "Justice and Love" in mind precisely at a time—I am not saying this only for your sakes, rather it should be said more often—when Jews are denied the most basic natural right.[47]

"It should be said more often," and there are many ways of saying it and decisive situations and unique opportunities in which to say it. Be that as it may, vis-à-vis the Nazis, Innitzer can be said to have been compromised sufficiently to seek carefully ways of securing his role as chief shepherd of the faithful under the new, as yet undefined, situation before deciding on actions appropriate to his office.

Siegismund Waitz, the prince-archbishop of Salzburg[48] and spokesman for Austria's Western Church Province, was—as outspoken supporter of the Dollfuss-Schuschnigg regime—no less compromised than his superior, Cardinal Innitzer. Happily, he did not carry another of Innitzer's burdens of the recent past, namely, a charitable attitude toward the Jews. He saw in Judaism a worldwide danger, which could be exorcised only by means of mass conversion. It was this Prince-Archbishop Waitz who demonstrated how accommodating the bishops were to Bürckel's designs. Waitz was not only kept abreast of developments by Innitzer but kept in touch with the papal nuncio. He came to the meeting carrying the draft of a declaration for his brother bishops' consideration and approval in the presence of Bürckel or, as it turned out, his emissaries. In short, the bishops were to hand the regime what it desired on a silver platter.

But Bürckel was not to be outdone. After expressing regrets over Innitzer's complaints—this in lieu of an answer to his letter, the emissaries sprang the draft of Bürckel's declaration on the bishops, and Waitz kept silent about his own draft. And so it happened that, instead of the hard bargaining required where much is at stake yet where evidently each partner needs the other, there was merely accedence to a demand. Instead of a joint or mutual declaration, a declaration was issued by one side, dictated by the other. Finally, instead of using the opportunity to uphold the moral authority of the Church by assuming a firm political stand, the bishops played it safe—and thus lost the Church's authority vis-à-vis the new potentates and vis-à-vis those who depended on that authority.

Did the bishops realize what they were doing or what they were failing to do? It is said that the bishops attending the special meeting did not consider the matter of the declaration important. This is understandable. After all, regimes and the challenges they bring with them come and go, but Mother Church will last until the end of days. And so they signed the regime's report card, blanks to be filled in by the regime itself, with high marks for their economic accomplishments, particularly as it affected the poor (marks which they never would have granted freely nor ever did grant to, for example, a socialist regime), and giving their blessings to its war against bolshevism. Here are their pious words: "We are also convinced that, through the efforts of the national-socialist movement, the danger of universally destructive, godless bolshevism has been averted."[49] The specter of bolshevism had been evoked with great effect, as a last-minute campaign tactic at the time of the Saar plebiscite, in order to gain Catholic support. Evidently, Bürckel still knew what he was doing. Evidently, the bishops did not as yet. The effect, as we already know in part, was not long in coming.

According to Innitzer's covering letter, the declaration was prepared in order to facilitate "good cooperation" between the Church and the new regime.

Instead, the regime took from the Church its office—not rendered unto the Church by any Caesar—of directing itself to the faithful in its own way and in its own time on the matter of the plebiscite. The reference thereto in the declaration indicates, with sufficient clarity, that the Church meant to make a careful appeal to individual conscience. The bishops expressed their intention of declaring their commitment to the German Reich; they do not go on to say that they expect the faithful to do the same but merely "expect all faithful Christians to know what they owe their nation."[50] Perhaps an overly subtle difference, but the difference is there, and it leaves the critical opening for an appeal to the judgment of the priest and his parishioners. And of course, the Church could not do otherwise. But the statement is all Bürckel needed. What the bishops gave to Bürckel when they tendered their declaration is not what he took when he accepted it. They offered a basis for "cooperation." The regime did not need cooperation. It required domination consummated by the expressed deference thereto. The regime's calculated expectation, in wheedling the declaration from the bishops, was not to gain a grip on the Church's authority, which is, after all, magisterial, pastoral, and sacramental. Rather, the regime meant to ride on the crest of the Church's remaining authority before the wave shattered against the rock of reflection and sober interference, before its force dissipated in the safe harbor toward which the Nazi maneuver was heading, and to accomplish this before it was to meet the breakers of the regime's repressive policy against the Church.

The maneuver with the Church was the enactment of the logic inherent in the regime and its movement. This logic precluded the prospect of cooperation held out by the Church. Cooperation presupposes two wills, each valid in its own right, each recognized as such by the other, even if one is ascendant. But, validities other than its own are precisely what were denied by the nature of the movement as empowered in the regime. In its attitude to the Church, the rejection of such a basis for "cooperation" had been clear since the crude beginnings of the Nazi movement. The penultimate point of its Program of 1920 reads: "We demand freedom of all religious confessions in the State, insofar as they do not jeopardize its [the State's] status (*soweit sie nicht dessen Bestand gefährden*), or offend the customary and moral sensibility of the German race."[51] This, of course, excludes the Jews; but it also invalidates any sort of scruple a faithful Christian may entertain with respect to defining not only the humanity of man along racial lines but also the mode of moral and customary—not to speak of political and social—intercourse. The totalitarian, that is, exclusive, character of the Nazi movement was nailed down in the last of the twenty-five points of 1920: "In order to execute the foregoing, we demand: The creation of strong central Reich-power. The political central parliament's unconditional authority over the whole Reich and its organization in general."[52] Subsequent developments, in particular the treatment of the Church on the part of the Nazi regime in Germany, were to bear out the fact that this regime had no place for cooperation, neither in its ideology nor in the execution of its policy. But, perhaps the Austrian bishops and their chief spokesman, Cardinal

Innitzer, had not done their homework. Or, if Innitzer knew of the political consequences of the Concordat of 1933 between the Vatican and Nazi Germany, if he knew of the statement wheedled out of other bishops by the same Bürckel prior to the plebiscite in the Saar Territory in 1935, if he knew of the life of the Church in the five years of the Nazi regime in Germany, Innitzer failed to learn the lessons to be drawn from this. But, if he did learn them, then he failed to see their applicability to the situation in which he and his Church suddenly found themselves. Or else, in the face of the terror—such as the mass arrests, the pressure for alignment that reached into the smallest corners of the social structure, and last but not least the visible persecution of the Jews—he lost the Church's nerve, whose center he was, and sought by means of what Hilberg called "preemptive compliance" to avert whatever he imagined as the worst. Hilberg, however, had formulated this concept of "preemptive compliance" to characterize a reaction pattern on the part of Jews in the extreme situation of utter powerlessness, a situation surely not applicable to the Church, which was the only remaining authority when all else in Austria had collapsed.[53]

The declaration, the foreword, and the covering letter did not serve the purpose intended by the bishops, namely, to function as a basis for "good cooperation." Much less did it remain the Church's instrument for speaking to the faithful in the matter of the plebiscite. Plastered all over—accompanied by the regime's exegesis, it was, in fact, the regime's main propaganda ploy in the campaign, apart from its own representational pomp, propagandistic bombast, and arm twisting. To the extent that the bishops had intended the declaration to facilitate the prudent choice of a "yes" vote on the part of those who—out of motives the Church understood and fostered—harbored qualms of conscience, such intention might have been achieved if the bishops had had control over its publication. Normally, such control would consist of internal use of the declaration in connection with the pastoral care of the faithful and of its publication in the press in conjunction with an official comment by a spokesman of the Church. That the Church no longer had any uncensored access to the media of public information should have been clear to the bishops before they signed the declaration; they were forewarned when the cardinal's statement was not published on March 16, whereas the regime's announcement of his meeting with Hitler was. And whatever internal use the Church was able to make of the declaration was overshadowed by the manner of its publication by the regime. The public had no way of knowing whether the utilization of the declaration—plus foreword, covering letter, and Nazi exegesis—for massive propaganda purposes was condoned by the bishops. Neither did anyone give thought to this question. Nor did they need to. The facts of the matter precluded such a question. They showed that nothing was publicized in this regime that did not serve its purpose, and that the Church had given to the regime a declaration which it could publicize. Far from facilitating the "yes" vote on the part of the faithful, the effect of the declaration was to leave no choice to those prepared to look to the Church for moral strength. "The declaration can bring the past to a conclusion," said Bürckel's exegesis for all to see. The "past" was only a few days distant, and the regime was far from finished with their arrests and the persecution of those who had ruled in alliance with the Church. For these unfortunates and with respect to them, the evident *Gleichschaltung* (alignment) of the Church did not ease any conscience but evoked a realization of the bishops' betrayal.

And, confronted with the juxtaposition of pogrom and the bishops' declaration, and, if they read the exegesis, learning that the declaration "demonstrates that in these times—eventful for the German people and its future—the Catholic Church also wants to find its way to the new state," the Jews knew that for them there was neither a future nor a way. For them the sense of betrayal was compounded by that of abandonment.

The passersby did not need to read the placards. A casual look at them did its work. The cardinal-archbishop's covering letter carried the heading—legible from afar—"Austria's bishops wrote to Gauleiter Bürckel in favor of the plebiscite." One could also see the seal over the large letterhead: "The Archbishop of Vienna." The seal itself showed the familiar cardinal's hat with its two pyramids of tassels surrounding the escutcheon. The band across the bottom carried the motto Innitzer had chosen at his elevation to archbishop: *In caritate servire*, "to serve in charitable love." These details escaped the casual observer; he did discern, however, in the same hand as the cardinal's signature, the words "*und Heil Hitler*!" Many a passerby shook his head, if he dared, and grimly reiterated the words with which the faithful were wont to greet their burly, smiling, genuinely popular cardinal-archbishop, "*unser Innitzer!*" ("our Innitzer").

"*Inser Unnitzer*" ("our useless one") murmured many a Jew as he passed the same placard. This Yiddish alliterative reversal may have been crude, and the joke coarse, but who will begrudge the Jews their expressing, with time-honored bitter humor, that man's dignity is more intimately tied to performance than to rank and station or good intention?

This is not to say that the performance of benign acts towards Jews—that is, Jews who converted to Catholicism or who were married to Catholics—on the part of Innitzer or with his support were lacking.[54] These, in fact, did occur; and it is only fair and just that this be recorded. It is also fair and just to record that it occurred in marked contrast to the anti-Semitic proclivity of many an Austrian churchman and some of Innitzer's brother bishops, an anti-Semitic proclivity not just with respect to Jews by religion but also to converted Jews. In 1938 Innitzer, as part of the negotiations aimed at arriving at a *modus vivendi* with the regime, tried to secure special status for Jewish Catholics. While this failed, many actions were undertaken to help them, especially in regard to emigration. Most of the aid to converted Jews rendered in the first few months was given by the *Pauluswerk*, an organization devoted to missionizing among Jews and caring for Jewish converts to Catholicism, under the vigorous leadership of Innitzer's protégé Johannes (later: John) Österreicher, himself a Jewish convert to Catholicism. However, in August 1938 this organization was disbanded by the Nazi regime; and Österreicher, who had written some polemical tracts against the Nazi racist theories, was tipped off by informed friends, escaped arrest, and fled the country.[55]

In addition to Innitzer's performance on behalf of Jewish Catholics, the devastating effect of his and the other bishops' initial stance vis-à-vis the new regime on determining the new situation of the Jews should also not blind us to the Church's own new situation under that regime. Within seven months after the Anschluss, this situation had become clear. Even as Austria, especially Vienna, was the locale of a decisive intensification of the Nazi movement's Jewish policy, so Vienna was the locale of a degree of repression of the Church that had hitherto not been tried in the Altreich. The new Jewish policy aimed toward the "final solution." The new Church policy was directed against the supra-national nature of the Catholic Church and toward a national church, apparently also toward a new Nazi religion. In these months, the Church suffered serious setbacks in its role—traditional in Austria and vital to the Church for its very existence—in public and religious education.[56]

Innitzer's leadership of the Austrian bishops in their hasty issuance of a painfully unqualified endorsement of Austria's Anschluss to a Germany that was Nazi entailed the abdication of any responsibility by the Church for the dire fate of the Jews. Undoubtedly, this is why the literature takes care to mention—as we did—some of Innitzer's acts before the Anschluss that testify to what, for an Austrian churchman of those days, was an unusually benign attitude toward the Jews. One of these acts was the telegram of condolence that he sent to the Jewish Community in July 1936 on the death of his colleague, the chief rabbi of Vienna, Dr. David Feuchtwang.[57] No doubt this is to Innitzer's lasting credit, especially if one also recalls his condemnation—cited above—of Nazi racism earlier that year, and if we consider the following: There is no record of Innitzer's predecessor marking in any public manner the passing of Feuchtwang's predecessor, the great and venerated Rabbi Dr. Zwi Perez Chajes. Also, while Dr. Chajes's funeral procession in 1927 was joined by the president of the Republic, Dr. Michael Hainisch, and by the former chancellor, the then Chief of the Vienna Police Johannes Schober, the highest ranks of government were not personally represented at Feuchtwang's funeral.[58] Considering these portents of changing times, Innitzer's credit for having sent that telegram is well earned. But contexts, like circles on water, do not stand still.

On one of the days following the bishops' solemn declaration, some storm troopers forced Feuchtwang's successor as chief rabbi of Vienna, Dr. David Israel Taglicht, to put on his tallit and, like so many other Jews, to scrub the street. Taglicht was a small, frail man, and old, past seventy-five, not an inspiring presence but a man of dignity and learning. For the sport fashionable in those weeks, that of scrubbing "parties," the chief rabbi was quite a catch. The logic of Jewish testimony under mockery—as any Christian who had received the benefit of catechism and homily knows—calls for shouting abusive questions. What abuses were shouted at Taglicht is not recorded, and it does not matter; his answer is and does. It made its rounds among the sorely tried Jews. He said, "I am washing God's earth," thus uttering a gratuitous blessing upon the soil that nourished what would prove to be the most diligent breed of murderers among the Germans.

An event like this is a passing event. But when one considers whose humiliation was attempted by the brown-shirted legionnaires, the participants—the present ones and the absent ones—become representative measures of man's conscience. Heinrich Böll tried to shake the conscience of the overwhelming majority of bystanders in a book that established his rank among German authors of the postwar period. Its title is *Wo warst Du, Adam . . .* (Where were you, Adam . . .). The allusion is to God's calling to Cain after the murder of Abel, "Where is your brother Abel?" and to Cain's response to God, "Am I my brother's keeper?"[59] But in Böll's novel it is Adam, the father of all men, and thus mankind at large who is being addressed. Or else, if the Germans are addressed then not as Cain, which would be too abhorrent an allusion, and certainly not as Cain's victim, his brother Abel—

favored by the Lord—but as Adam, representing any man. Generalization into "Adam" may be a literary entrance, when the front door to conscience is closed. But, in the flow of life, it is the commission and omission by flesh and blood that functions as the posing and disposing of questions of fateful choice.

With respect to Austria's primate, this question must be asked: Where was he when the chief rabbi suffered humiliation, and in him the community of fellow Jews? Where were the words "which should be said more often" and never more urgently than when they are said outside the arena of mere words? This was the arena where forces were unleashed and powers exercised that not only test men's mettle and gauge the measure of authorities but plumb the vulnerable vessel of mundane existence for the substance of soul it may contain.

How did the cardinal and the bishops perform as regards choice under the initial duress of the Anschluss? Nothing of what in retrospect—and only in retrospect—stands out as failure was intended by the Church leaders—the failure to maintain the Church's posture as moral authority, a posture which would have been a source of strength for the faithful in the trying period ahead; the failure to represent vigorously this authority in dealing with the regime's potentates with regard to the officially condoned injustices that the Anschluss unleashed; the failure to plead for the Jews, a failure tantamount to isolating the Jews from what remained as a meager but last recourse; and the failure to use the weight of the Church's authority in exacting performance for performance.

What the churchmen did intend was an appeal to the faithful to consider national union with Germany as desirable, without thereby condoning the excesses of the regime. If success as such were a criterion of right choice, then this too ended in failure. However, here too the factor of intent arises, albeit in the following form: granting that the churchmen did not know what they were being used for, were they in a position to infer a need to be wary and circumspect? We have seen how the Nazis used their combination of tactics in dealing with the bishops: secrecy as to their intent, speed, the element of surprise, and the isolation of their opponents. And yet, though an isolated instance, there was, as we have seen, the precedent of the Saar plebiscite and, related to it, there were five years of the German Church's experience with the Nazi regime. Exoneration by virtue of ignorance cannot be applied in this case.

In the case of Schuschnigg's choice, one can at least claim impotence due, on the one hand, to the apparent abandonment of Austria by France, Great Britain, and Italy, and on the other, to the uncertainty as to whether his will to resist would be matched by his fellow Austrians' readiness to fight. The churchmen were, to be sure, not in a position where such considerations of temporal power obtain. While the kind and context of power with which and in which they operated were different, they were there and functioning. Unlike the situation for choice that was about to unfold for the Jews, the Church and its spokesmen were not captive to the absolute will of their bargaining partners.

It might be claimed that the bishops' action was not important enough to merit severe scrutiny as a paradigm of wrong choice under duress. Bürckel's purpose in obtaining the bishops' endorsement was, after all, merely to align the Catholic vote in the plebiscite. Yet, as we have seen, the fateful and symbolic import of the bishops' action extended far beyond that purpose, to the detriment not only of the Jews but of the Church's authority and, more immediately, to the benefit of the Nazi momentum in winning the plebiscite vote.

■ ■ ■

Having succeeded in obtaining the bishop's endorsement, similar endorsements to align the Socialists and others were almost routine. The high point in this effort was the publication of an interview with Dr. Karl Renner in *Neues Wiener Tagblatt*, April 2, 1938.[60] Renner had been the main force in the establishment of the Republic of Austria, having been its first chancellor and the president of the Austrian delegation to the peace conference at St. Germain. In this interview, he referred to his past advocacy of national self-determination and to the fact that from the day of the establishment of the Republic he and the Austrian Socialists had advocated national union with Germany. He did not mention that the Austrian Socialists dropped this item from their agenda when the Nazi regime was established in Germany, nor that he had also advocated a federation of sovereign national states along the Danube, that is, Austria, Czechoslovakia, and Hungary. Obviously, the Anschluss with Nazi Germany did not accord with what he and the Socialists understood by national union with Germany. Nonetheless, this is what Renner endorsed in announcing that he would vote "yes" to the Anschluss, even though the methods with which the Anschluss had been "accomplished" were not those "to which [he] subscribed."[61]

There are indications that the reason Renner publicly endorsed the Anschluss in preparation of the plebiscite was that he was urged to do so by leading Socialists in order to motivate Bürckel to release the Jewish Socialist leader Robert Danneberg, as well as the leader of the former Socialist paramilitary organization *Schutzbund*, Alexander Eifler.[62] But, it is also said that Renner had no illusions about the Nazis' readiness to reciprocate in this manner.[63] Why then did he issue the endorsement? He himself reports that the Socialist leaders realized that it would be futile to choose demonstrative defiance under the duress of absolute power and of isolation from access to any means of communication; this would only result in needless victims. It has also been suggested that Renner's motive may have been to protect his Jewish son-in-law and his half-Jewish grandchildren. One of these grandsons, Karl Deutsch-Renner, denied[64] that this was a motive.

Renner's endorsement was almost as important to the Nazis as that of the bishops. The endorsement of others was less important but diligently solicited and reported, such as that of Dr. Michael Hainisch, the aged first president of the defunct republic and a liberal, who had grown up under the influence of the liberal newspaper *Die Presse*, whose Jewish editor was the famous Dr. Josef Szeps, and some editorials of which were written—anonymously—by the ill-fated Crown Prince Rudolf. The endorsements of prominent men and women in all walks of life followed, for example, famous theater personalities such as Paula Wessely, her husband Attila Hörbiger, and his brother, the popular comic actor Paul Hörbiger.[65]

In addition to endorsements, the Nazis aligned the Viennese by dazzling them with blandishments and benefits. Socialists became "former Socialists," in part through the incessant propaganda directed at them, especially by such prominent people as Bürckel and by the new regime's Mayor Neubacher, who was himself a "former Socialist."[66] The appeal to them was based on the claim that National Socialism was the kind of Socialism along national lines that the Austro-Socialists had supposedly been fighting to realize all along. This was reinforced with special privileges, such as well publicized trips to the Altreich by tens of thousands of people from the workers' districts. A plan was put into effect of placing an even greater number of workers' children into private homes in the Altreich for vacations. But, the main ploys were of an economic nature. In the expectation of an economic upswing, there was hiring even prior to the creation of specific jobs, and many of those who had been dismissed as a result of the suppression of the Socialists by the defunct regime, were now rehired.[67]

A significant factor in the economic battle for the realignment of the Viennese in preparation for the plebiscite was the start of the removal of the Jews from economic life. Shopkeepers, businesses, and professionals benefited by this elimination of Jewish competitors; persons affected by the depressed employment market benefited by being assigned jobs left vacant by dismissed Jews. For whatever problems could not be solved quickly, the Jews served as ready scapegoats. And whoever was prone to balk at the new turn of events had the example of the persecution of the Jews as a visible and, hence, self-imposed instrument of his own terror-induced compliance.

The wooing of the Austrians was part of a massive campaign to realign them in time for the plebiscite. Nothing was left to chance. The pomp and melodrama was choreographed by the experienced master Albert Speer.[68] As the campaign approached its climax, the bigwigs of the regime were brought in for a well-orchestrated crescendo of appearances. The venue chosen for these spectacles was the Northwest Railway Terminal. Since the demise of the Habsburg Empire, it had been defunct, having been the main access to industrialized Bohemia and, not coincidentally, to the mines of its builder, the head of the Austrian branch of the Rothschild family. The relief depicting the builder was now removed, and the interior of the hall refitted for the stupendous rallies peculiar to the political process of totalitarian power. All of Vienna was decorated, every house with Nazi flags, every window with festive swastikas, as was every lamppost, every placard space, every lapel. But the main effort was reserved for the avenue approaching the Northwest Terminal. Here huge pylons were erected, more than two stories high, each of its four sides covered with a Nazi flag of equally heroic proportion, the whole structure crowned with a swastika enclosed in a wreath.

The Jews took in this spectacle of a world—which long ago, a few days ago, they had regarded as their world—swept up in a whirlwind of an incomprehensible enthusiasm. The youngsters among them saw it, too. Youngsters are impressionable and open to new experiences. But what the Jewish youngsters in Vienna had to apperceive was a world that to them had also become incomprehensible. Some of these youngsters were sitting in Viktor Löwenfeld's art class at the Chajes-Realgymnasium, the Jewish Gymnasium of Vienna.[69] They had missed school at the time of Purim because it had coincided with the Anschluss. To make up for it, Löwenfeld gave them the assignment to paint a Purim scene in watercolor. As usual, he structured the assignment by firing their imagination. He described the biblical scene of Mordechai sitting triumphant on a horse led by Haman, who had fallen from the king's favor when he was exposed as the persecutor of the people of Esther, the king's consort. As usual, the children worked diligently and, drawing from their perceptions of their new surroundings, many a pupil out of a naive, elemental defiance produced a Haman, bearded, albeit with a cowlick on his forehead, leading the horse through a throng of people cheering Mordechai, reviling Haman, along an avenue lined with pylons painted blue, gold, and white, and crowned with Stars of David.

Hitler gave the last of the speeches held at the Northwest Terminal the day before the plebiscite. Unlike the orators preceding him, he refrained from anti-Semitic cant. And, while Göring's coverage of the Jewish question may be regarded as restrained in comparison to that of others, it is of particular interest. He opined that Vienna had ceased to be—and admonished that it had to become again—a German city. Only when the Jews were removed from the economy and from the cultural sphere could Vienna again take on its special tasks as a German city. To make this happen, the Jews would have to leave. He said, "One cannot speak of a German city where there are 300,000 Jews." However, mindful of the unauthorized "Aryanisation" of Jewish businesses, he also warned that the liquidation of the Jewish presence had to proceed "systematically and with full deliberation."[70] He, in short, outlined the two main features of the ensuing program for carrying out the Jewish policy that the Nazis had in mind for Vienna: Get rid of the Jews, and do it by the use of available organs and in accordance with procedures provided by them. By grotesquely exaggerating the number of Viennese Jews, Göring also injected a sense of outrage and urgency into the liquidation of the Jewish presence in Vienna. This sense of outrage and urgency was unprecedented in the prior five years of the regime's dealing with the Jewish problem in the Altreich. It would provide a propitious incentive for bringing to fruition the hitherto rudimentary instrument of carrying out the regime's purpose and fuel its progress. It would also haunt the Jewish leadership, which the Nazis would install as an indispensable means of carrying out that purpose.

We will now turn to the rise of that instrument and the new kind of Jewish leadership.

Momentum and Instrument

"*Die Juden können gehen, aber das Geld lassen sie gefälligst da, das haben sie doch nur gestohlen.*" ("The Jews can go, but let them kindly leave their money behind: after all, they stole it.")[71] Göring spoke these words during one of the telephone calls by means of which he engineered the Anschluss. They were spoken in almost casual response to an insignificant point. Yet they reflect concisely the Nazi regime's policy as regards the Jews:

"The Jews can go": Jewish existence will be abolished.

"Let them leave … their money behind": In the process, the Jews must relinquish the means and trappings of their existence.

"They stole [the money]": In dismantling Jewish existence, ways will be found to justify that the Jews' right to exist is forfeit. The reason for this forfeiture is that they are Jews and, hence, that theirs is a stolen existence. Henceforth, the justification pronounced by Göring will be promulgated in as politic a circumlocution as may be available and superficially plausible.

Göring spoke as the plenipotentiary of the Four-Year Plan, that is, as the czar of the regime's economic development. Others might have summarized these three policy elements differently, according to their own attitudinal shade within the spectrum of Nazi ideology and their position in the regime; in any case, they were put into effect.

Politics of Anti-Semitic Ideology

Get rid of the Jews, strip them of their claim to existence, do so within the available frame of justification. The policy was simple; its implementation was not. The task was nothing less than formidable. Jews constituted 10 percent of the population of Vienna; their removal would take years, their expropriation countless maneuvers. After all, within the Altreich Jewish emigration had—in spite of the pressures—been cumbersome and desultory, and had been slowing down.[72] Hence, the pattern the Nazis brought with them when they took over Austria did not promise a speedy solution to the Jewish problem. As for the Jews of Vienna, they had enjoyed the status of equal citizenship until just a few days ago; though times may have become hard, it would have been foolhardy on their part simply to depart and leave everything behind. Also, in spite of the resistance by interests whose political preference was authoritarian, in spite of detractors on the right and on the left, modern liberalism had left more than a minimal effect on Vienna. The prevailing tendency had been to grant everyone the equal right of honest productivity and of protection in one's peaceful pursuits. Thus, even under the condition of an endemic anti-Semitism, a massive policy of squeezing the Jews dry and kicking them out would have had little of the support necessary for success. It would seem, therefore, that everything spoke against the practicability of such a policy. Yet, the new regime marshaled the motivation and the forces to put this policy into effect, recognized the obstacles as challenges to be met, transformed given factualities into instruments of execution, and above all committed to the task an executive machinery with an effective potential.

The motivational forces that provided the momentum for a successful and speedy execution of the policy can be located in three spheres. The first is the fundamental anxiety that spread among the Jews in the initial period of the Anschluss. We have spoken of this earlier, and we will have many occasions of recounting how this anxiety was renewed and intensified. Their world, the world with respect to which they defined and unfolded their very being, was disappearing, no matter to which aspect of it they turned, as if this world had been a mere specter. And worse, their new world—the world they were more and more finding themselves in, though they lacked the experience and the distance to define it—was a world that proved not to be "theirs," which was not a world for them. If this new "world" of Vienna's Jews was at all an arena for the realization of hopes and aspirations, if it was hiding any possibility at all for living a concrete life, then it was only that of escaping this world that was no world to another venue, no matter how uncertain the prospect of another world arising there that would be "their" new world. This anxiety, engendered by the terror of the first few weeks and reinforced in uncounted small and large ways in the ensuing period, would prove to be a *conditio sine qua non* for carrying out the Nazi policy against the Jews.

Furthermore, the enactment of the policy against the Jews could not have proceeded without the support and participation of the non-Jewish population of Vienna. In part, this was a matter of the groundswell of anti-Semitism being given free flow by the Nazi takeover. In large part, however, this motivational force was enhanced or engendered by the terror of the first few weeks. The actions against the Jews, perpetrated with impunity mainly by the hoi polloi of the new potentates, were a sufficient demonstration of the regime's way of dealing with whomever it deemed to be an opponent. The fact that the definition of "opponent" was not drawn merely along racial lines was amply shown by the arrest, vilification, murder, or suicide of respected fellow citizens who had been prominent in the government or in the political life of the pre-Nazi republic. Hence, what was happening to the Jews could readily be recognized as possibly happening to oneself. Anxiety leads to caution, and caution at the very least to acquiescence, which may be a mere minimum of support, but the minimum without which the maximum of perpetration could not succeed.

The decisive force propelling the vehement forward movement of the policy against the Jews, beginning with the Jews of Vienna, was the momentum of the regime itself. In its first few years, the Nazi Party carried out a remarkable consolidation of power. Within the framework of the constitution of the state, it succeeded in exercising governmental power beyond the limits of constitutional constraints. It subordinated the command structure of the military to its will and policy and, vitiating the Treaty of Versailles, asserted Germany's right to military equality among the nations. A vigorous economic policy not only led to practically full employment and recovery from the misery of the depression but increased Germany's productive performance, particularly in heavy industry, to threatening proportions. The legal and judiciary structures, as well as the administrative organizations of the state, the provinces, and the local jurisdictions were centralized and placed at the disposal of the executors of the party's policies. Finally, it installed an unprecedented organ for the execution of its policies, the SS, which incorporated one of the newly centralized administrative organizations, namely, the police. Except for the various ministries, the SS, in effect, superseded in authority all other administrative jurisdictions and had access to their capacities, regardless of whether or not they were structurally incorporated into the SS. The SS was responsible only to the party's command structure in accordance with the *Führerprinzip*, the "leadership principle."[73] The consolidation of power provided the Nazi regime with the wherewithal for implementing the larger segments of its policy of national advancement, a policy the party believed itself to be mandated to execute even as it believed itself to be the repository of the national will. The takeover of Austria and its consequences were not the onset of this implementation, but a dramatic manifestation of the momentum of its early progress. We may distinguish three areas of major concern in the period when consolidation gave way to the enactment of the Nazi regime's grand policies, which was the period into which the Anschluss falls.

1. One policy concern was to make Germany the undisputed *predominant power on the continent of Europe*. It was to provide the German nation with territories in eastern Europe and, thus, to secure for her ample reserves of agricultural land, raw materials for her industry, and elbow room for her enterprising and growing population. This policy goal was to be attained quickly and efficiently, that is, before

effective resistance to it could arise, and at the least cost to Germany. Since the implementation of this policy would inevitably lead to war, Hitler, when he was ready to implement it, informed the war minister and the commanders-in-chief of the armed forces to prepare the military for such an eventuality and for all the intermediate steps that would ensue. In order to decrease Germany's vulnerability, the first intermediate step was to be the takeover of Austria, the next the smashing of the Czechoslovakian state and the incorporation of its Czech part. How effectively this policy was enacted, how relentless the momentum of its implementation, can be measured by the fact that no more than four months elapsed between Hitler's secret meeting with his military chiefs and the Anschluss, only twelve months more until the several maneuvers leading to the demise of Czechoslovakia were completed, six months more until German troops stood before Warsaw, then two more years until they were advancing toward Moscow. The meeting at which Hitler convinced his military of the geopolitical necessity of the project—in an apparently brilliant four-hour-long dissertation—was secret.[74] Yet, the policy project was not. Hitler and his fellow ideologists were never reticent about formulating, developing, and promulgating it. It was, in effect, stated in *Mein Kampf*. No one took it seriously—except Hitler and his associates.[75]

2. Another major policy project of the Nazi regime was the *elimination of all opposition* to what it regarded as the German national will, whose trusteeship it had assumed. Who was an "opponent," which individuals, which groups, which nations? In part this was clear from the very beginning of the Nazi movement: political competitors, such as ideological socialists, and "Bolsheviks"; the traitors who lost the (First World) War; the practitioners of parliamentary democracy, who dissipate the national will; the supra-national churches, which destroy the genius and the instinct of the nation; the proponents of modern culture, who corrupt the nation's lofty spirit; unworthy races, such as Poles, Ukrainians, and Russians, who held sway over territories destined for the benefit of the German nation; but above all it was *the Jew*, who was to the Nazis *the epitome of the enemy*. What was "German," whose supremacy must be upheld and whose ascendancy over the peoples of the earth must be assured, this was as vague as such ideas inevitably are. However, although the Nazis could never succeed in their ongoing elaborate search for a scientific version as to what constituted Jewishness, their premise of what was "Jewish" was always clear to the Nazi ideologists, so clear that it served them as a foil for those occasions when what is "German" had to be defined:

The Jewish people are degenerate human stock and spread their degeneracy to the peoples among whom they are permitted to live freely. They are morally corrupt and they corrupt others. Themselves uncreative, they debase the creation and creativity of others; themselves unproductive, they arrogate the wealth of others unto themselves. Worst of all, by means of this accumulation, and by means of corruptive maneuvers—such as international finance and communism—the Jews, by nature weak and cowardly, increase in power as they seek world dominance, which they are well on the way to achieving. In short, the Jew is the antipode of the

German, and "world Jewry" is the pernicious victimizer of Germany and, in some insidious way, the cause of all its troubles.

The policy implied by an ideology that defined itself over against those whom it deemed to be its opponents followed as a logical step, especially as regards the Jews. From the time they came to power, the Nazis were vigorously inventive, even if not original, in ways to deal with opponents—from concentration camps and disfranchisement by decree to "protective custody" and forced suicide. The process of combating enemies was an indispensable component of the earlier policy of consolidation and proved to be of the essence in the larger policy enactments prepared for by the consolidation of power. The Anschluss as such marked and paved the way for the regime's stepped-up momentum in the pursuit of its opponents. As for the Jews, they were of course unique in the ideological roster of opponents, and were—especially in Vienna—the most accessible and visible of those opponents who could be neither neutralized nor absorbed into the Nazi movement and for these reasons alone subject to repression with renewed vigor. But, the upsurge in the enactment of the policy regarding the Jewish question, of which the Jews of Vienna were the first victims, did not merely ensue from these factors. The accelerated momentum was fuelled to no small degree by the mandate the regime received in the form of the unruly but welcome anti-Semitic outbursts with which the plain folk of Vienna legitimated themselves as new *Volksgenossen*.

3. Besides preparing for the drive to the East and smashing opponents, a third area of the regime's major policy concern during the time when consolidation gave way to implementation was to establish and maintain *German initiative in international affairs*. This may be seen as merely a corollary to the other two policy concerns, and in retrospect cannot be considered except in relation to them, but in the practice of the time its implementation seemed to proceed with only casual reference to the others. In this policy concern, Nazi Germany played on the fears of the various governments with which it conducted diplomatic relations. Foremost among these fears was the resurgence of Germany as a military power. Nazi Germany maneuvered this fear to its advantage by seemingly restricting itself to a legitimate sphere of influence of her own while granting others theirs, especially colonialist Great Britain. It justified the aggressive expansion of its sphere of influence by a pious reference to the commitment of the Versailles Treaty to national self-determination, and even to President Woodrow Wilson's "Fourteen Points."[76] This argument worked, especially on Great Britain, with respect to the Rhineland, the Saar Territory, Austria, and the Sudetenland. Its deceptive nature was revealed in March 1939, when Nazi Germany took the Czech part of Czechoslovakia; the attempt to revive the argument over the Danzig issue failed. At the same time, Nazi Germany received approbation for its relentless opposition to communism, a movement deeply feared by the nations of Europe, and for pursuing a policy of isolating Soviet Russia, on whose territory it had as yet secret designs. Thus, while seemingly exerting its growing influence mainly in this direction, it appeased or neutralized the fear which its increasing power provoked. If we recall that in the months

preceding the Anschluss, Nazi Germany formed its alliances with other authoritarian regimes of national resurgence that were bent on augmenting their spheres of influence, bringing about especially the Berlin-Rome Axis and the inclusion of Italy in the Anti-Comintern Pact, we can see that the policy of diplomatic initiative was in full force in the period under consideration. The fact that the leading powers of Europe, aside from facing internal problems, needed time to gain their bearings in the rapidly changing situation and to find new parameters for diplomacy provided additional force to Nazi Germany's initiative.

The less puissant nations, who had the most to fear from a resurgent German neighbor, were thus easy prey to Germany's temporizing diplomacy, which it practiced in order to enact its policy objectives at the least cost to itself. The means of diplomacy used with these governments are now familiar: either an appeal to the likeness of their objectives to Germany's, or failing that, the threat of terror. Nazi Germany's use of terror in dealing with representatives of small neighbors is well documented; see the way in which Hitler dealt with Schuschnigg at Berchtesgaden in February 1938, or with President Emil Hácha of Czechoslovakia in March 1939.[77] The appeal to national aspirations as objectives that others had in common with Germany was made to work in various ways. It worked in the final destruction of the Czechoslovak state, especially in plotting with the subversive elements that sought independence for Slovakia. It was also at play in the negotiations with Poland, when these were still at the stage of seemingly friendly temporizing.

In both of these cases, the ubiquitous element of the appeal to national aspiration as a common policy objective was the sort of political anti-Semitism that the Nazis had introduced into Central European statecraft and whose potential she was, in the period following the Anschluss, in the process of demonstrating: the removal of Jewish existence from the national state. A protocol of the negotiations between Göring and the Slovak plotters of October 1938 contains the following item: "The Jewish problem will be solved as in Germany."[78] And the protocol on the Polish side of German foreign minister Joachim von Ribbentrop's luncheon meeting with Józef Lipski, Poland's Ambassador to Berlin, in October 1938, mentions that "as a possible sphere for future cooperation between the two countries the German Foreign Minister specified joint action in … the emigration of Jews from Poland."[79] Since the emigration of its Jews had been a desideratum in leading circles of the modern Polish state, the result of such "joint action" was not unattractive to the representative of Polish interests; but the question whether such a stupendous undertaking could be carried out jointly without loss of Poland's freedom of action must have given him pause. Poland had over three million Jews, 10 percent of the entire population.

The anti-Semitic initiative in the dealings with the Slovaks and the Poles in October 1938 belonged to a more aggressive foreign policy, which the Anschluss portended and for which it provided the necessary momentum. However, it would be a mistake to think that with this initiative Nazi Germany was exporting a commodity that was entirely new. To be sure, it was Hitler himself who claimed, late in

1938, that he was merely exporting anti-Semitism, not National-Socialism.[80] But this claim was deceptive in two respects. What he euphemistically referred to as the "export" of anti-Semitism was in fact a matter of mining for resources already present within the regions of the negotiating partner's own mind. And, through the receptivity of the partner to the "import" of anti-Semitism, the partner was to be caught in the net of National-Socialism, not his own but Germany's National-Socialism, with all the grim consequences that were yet to come. If there was an original "export" article at play here, then it was not anti-Semitism, nor even its modern political form, but a *consequential execution of it as official state policy regardless of the guaranteed rights* that were the legacy of modern liberalism. It would also be a mistake to think of anti-Semitism as merely an occasional factor in the progress of the regime's diplomatic initiative, or even restricted to the period of its upturn. How intent Hitler was—and not only he but the tens of thousands and in time hundreds of thousands of executors of the Nazi ideology in all segments and at all levels—on insisting on radical anti-Semitism as a *sine qua non* of any politics he was prepared to countenance can be demonstrated by a minor incident reported by Churchill. In 1932, the year before the Nazis came to power, Churchill visited Munich. Ernst "Putzi" Hanfstaengl, an associate of Hitler's, came to speak with Churchill and to arrange a meeting between him and Hitler for the next day. During the conversation, Churchill held forth that one thing he did not understand about Hitler was his "violence about the Jews." The next day Hanfstaengl informed Churchill that the meeting with Hitler "could not take place."[81]

The accelerated momentum of the regime's policy implementation provided—together with the terror engendered among the Jews of Vienna and the subtle effect that the manifestation of this terror had on the general population—all the force needed for overcoming any obstacle and for using even the most recalcitrant means to increase the ensuing intensification of its anti-Semitic policy. The main vector of this momentum was the machinery of implementation that, at the time of the Anschluss, was essentially untried and, in fact, a mere potential whose very mode of operation needed as yet to be devised. In the following chapters there will be ample occasion to detail the development of the machinery that the ordinary Jews as well as their representatives had to face and to mention the persons with whom they had to deal. Before taking up the specifics of the story, the machinery that descended on Vienna has to be characterized in general terms.

SS: Executive Organ

Two determinants, mentioned earlier, of the intensified actions against the Jews when the Nazis took over Vienna were the policy of eliminating opposition and the presence of an elite organization for the execution of the regime's ideological policies. These two factors combined to designate one of the main *raisons d'être* of the SS. The mission of the SS, which led to its founding and determined its career and its elaborate development, was to safeguard the ideology that provided the focus of the Nazi movement and to safeguard the effective authority of the movement's executors (the leaders, the party, the nation itself) and thus to ensure the radical execution of the movement's policies. The internal means of its operation consisted basically of unrestrained initiative and freedom of action within the framework of a hierarchical command structure that was not to be challenged, in which each member was personally responsible to the leaders proximately, remotely, and ultimately above him. Externally, the SS operated with any amenable and available means; what was not amenable was circumvented or superseded. Where no means were available, they were devised and imposed. Internally, the method of its operation was a matter of the assignment of tasks, usually in general terms, which had the status of a peremptory order. This was matched by blind loyalty and obedience. The methods by which the SS operated externally comprised mainly directives and the posture of absolute authority, matched by the fear and terror that assured compliance.

It is no wonder, then, that one of the main functions of the SS was to deal with security, even as the momentum of the regime's policy implementation consisted to no small degree of destroying what its ideology defined as opposition. The development of the SS may well be characterized as the fulfillment of this function. The story of this development is noteworthy and has received due scholarly attention.[82] For our purposes, the following will suffice.

The SS was unique and must not be confused with certain precursors. Like other movements, especially after the First World War, the Nazi movement had a paramilitary political cadre. Before the Nazis gained power, the SS fulfilled this function; and, in fact, it was at first an offshoot of another such paramilitary cadre, namely, the SA, i.e., the *Sturmabteilung* (storm troop). One must bear in mind that the establishment of secret police and political police services was not unknown in Europe. What distinguished the SS was that (1) it had the capacity of functioning outside the law and of any constitutionally established jurisdiction; (2) it functioned at and through a seat of governmental sovereignty that had been centralized and reduced to a function of ideological policy aims; (3) it functioned through its monopoly over the power of enforcement; and as a corollary we should mention that (4) in the execution of its tasks it was accountable solely to the leader of the SS (Heinrich Himmler) and ultimately to the leader of the ideologically politicized state (Adolf Hitler).

It took many measures to establish this functional status; the process was protracted over many years and, in fact, never completed. At the time of the downfall of the Third Reich it was still going on. What were the decisive preconditions for its establishment? One was the usurpation and misuse of emergency powers provided by the constitution, a process confirmed by the "Enabling Act" of March 1933.[83] Consequent upon this act, the German legislature relinquished its power of legislation to the government, which exercised this power for an indefinite period of time and did so by issuing decrees. In time, this led to the method of *Führerbefehl*,[84] "order from the Leader," which superseded all other forms of "legislation" and, in effect, constituted the core of a phenomenon peculiar to the Nazi regime: It was the phenomenon of the sovereignty and the power of the state being taken over by the proponents of an ideology, hierarchically subordinate to the supreme leader, in order to carry out policy that, in the main, was not that intended by and, in fact, conflicted with the basic liberal provisions of the constitution.

Another precondition for the unique functional status of the SS was the process whereby *all the police* in Germany were incorporated in a central organization and thereupon, in effect, *subordinated* to the SS, that is, *to a nongovernmental, political agency*.[85] Wherever this subordination did not occur outright, it was effected through the personal union of two offices: the *Reichsführer SS* (National Leader of the SS) and the Chief of German Police, which together formed Himmler's official title.

A third precondition is of particular interest here. The SS was, in effect, a complex political police, whose task was to carry out the party's policies as they were received through orders from the highest leadership. It was of decisive importance that within this apparatus there developed political police organs with power not only to carry out the extra-legal policies of the ideological regime but also to decide the very mode of executing these policies—from overall planning, to mustering the means, to the minutiae of realization. These organs proved to be predominant within the SS and, hence, wherever Nazi Germany held sway. The main segments of this core of the regime's political police carried in their designation a reference to "security"—not insignificantly, since its main task was to make the world secure for the success of the Nazi ideology. Throughout the brief span of the regime's existence, the SS created an extraordinary number of offices and branches and undertook frequent reorganizations in accordance with the development of its tasks.[86]

As we turn our attention to the beginnings of the organized execution of the regime's Jewish policy in Vienna, we find two salient branches in charge of carrying out this policy. One was the *Sicherheitspolizei* (Security Police, acronym: Sipo), which included (1) the criminal police, which the regime had centralized, and (2) the *Geheime Staatspolizei*, which was known under the acronym Gestapo, the "Secret State Police."[87] The other was the "Security Service" (*Sicherheitsdienst*, or SD).[88] After the war started, the additional tasks resulting from the conquests in the east required a diversification of "security services," though still under central direction. This led to the establishment of the RSHA (*Reichssicherheitshauptamt*, Reich-headquarters of the [SS] Security Service), which combined the SD and the Security Police under one command.[90] However, the establishment of the RSHA was merely the official acknowledgment of what had been in effect all along, namely, the control of both services by the same person. He was none other than Heydrich, whose power and influence within the SS was second only to that of Himmler. Thus, even though the multiplication of offices resulted in their occasionally working at cross purposes and causing those who had to deal with them, such as the regime's victims, to experience considerable further confusion and harassment, the identity of the ultimate authority remained central and intact. A look at another, later development will serve as additional confirmation that this was the case.

The war brought not only a diversification of "security services" that the SS had to perform but also a wider geographical distribution of its operations. Thereupon, a new command structure was added at a right angle to the existing one, whereby all the SS operations in any one region under the sway of the regime was under the command of a regional "Higher SS and Police Leader" (*Höherer SS- und Polizeiführer*, or HSSPF).[90] In this way, the central leadership was able to maintain direct command access to the regional task forces without being encumbered by the channels of the various command structures. Thus, the mode of operation of the SS and of its "security services" was set up to give its task forces specific assignments in the execution of Nazi policy, to do so under strict central direction, to grant them initiative in the realization of these tasks, and yet to keep tight control over the process. Whatever was ordered from the center was done; nothing was done unless so ordered.[91]

From a historical perspective, it was both the Gestapo and the SD who were the executors of the regime's policy against the Jews in the period following the Anschluss. However, from the perspective of that time, it was not so simple. The Jewish functionaries of Vienna, and *a fortiori* the masses of Jews, who had to deal directly or indirectly with the Nazi officials, were left bewildered as to the connection, coherence, and precedence of the several authorities that required deference. The Gestapo was a well-publicized and feared presence. The SD remained in the background and was unknown to most of the Jews but turned out to be more dangerous for them. Both the Gestapo and the various relevant offices of the SD regarded themselves as the executors of the regime's Jewish policy. This is not to say that any of the jurisdictional disputes that took place between the two services was in any way decisive of the final outcome. These disputes were over which agency was to carry out which part or item of the Jewish policy that was understood the same way by both parties. For the most part, these disputes took place behind the scenes, although they involved the Jewish functionaries as if they were grain between millstones. The functional dispositions of the two services differed, and the SD was freer to do what needed to be done to rid the world under Nazi control of Jews. The Gestapo gained its authority by usurping the trappings and the functions of a normal police force, for example, to arrest offenders—especially for offenses of a political nature, interrogate them, keep them in custody, collect evidence, prevent wrongdoing, and so on. The offense of the Jew was that he or she was a Jew, was present where being a Jew was an offense, and owned property in a situation in which proprietary claims to any means of existence whatever was a right a Jew did not possess. The Gestapo, as an organization whose operation by its nature proceeded case by case and which maintained the semblance of legal procedure, would have little success in accomplishing a political task requiring large-scale, extra-legal maneuvering. Getting rid of the Jews was such a political task, and the Gestapo was an organization not well suited for being in charge of it.

It was a small handful of minor functionaries of a relatively obscure office of the SD, which heretofore had not had any task to speak of, that emerged as the executors of the regime's ultimate Jewish policy, *beginning in Vienna*. The Gestapo and the other agencies of the SS were in the foreground of the official actions against the Jews in the first few weeks and even months after the Anschluss. However, this handful of SD men worked to organize the execution of their task, no doubt authorized by orders they had brought with them from Berlin, and in a manner that, as far as possible, solicited the cooperation of the Gestapo, a cooperation expressed mainly by not interfering.

Who were these men? What were their qualifications? What power did they possess? What authority? How did they operate? With what means? In order to answer these questions, we have to take a closer look at the development of the relevant organizations, their operation, and their staff.

The Administrative Structures of Anti-Jewish Policy

The proponents of National Socialism made no secret of the fact that political anti-Semitism was an inherent and pronounced feature of their program. They consequently regarded it as their mandate to carry out this aspect of their program once they attained and consolidated their power. How to do it presented a problem; how far to go was an open question.

This question of how far to go was open because the program and the very nature of Nazi anti-Semitism were vague. It was a program in an ongoing process of articulation, a program that was carried out in steps, where the logic of each grim step followed from the realization of the previous step and in accordance with the opportunities of such realization as they unfolded within the larger career of the Nazi regime. The question of whether the ultimate "final solution"—the extermination of the Jews and the extirpation of Judaism as a living presence—undertaken from 1941 to 1945 had been projected by the ruling cadre of the Nazi regime perhaps as early as the mid-1930s has exercised many minds. Those who assert that such a plan had existed have to explain why no documentary evidence has been found so far in the tons of residue of a regime that was obsessed with recording the minutiae of its dismal performance. Those who deny the early existence of the project have to explain certain remarks in Hitler's opus *Mein Kampf*, or certain vituperations in Julius Streicher's vulgar and insipid but effective anti-Semitic sheet *Der Stürmer*, or certain passages in the SS periodical *Das schwarze Korps*. Clearly the ideological anti-Semitism sketched above was an idea to which the regime and its supporters were committed. Human beings live by ideas and when they act jointly, they rally around ideas. Ideas do not need to make *prima facie* sense. It is adherence to them that invests them with sense, the sense of doctrine and the resulting way of life, or the sense of political ideology and the resulting policy.

Unless an idea with pernicious potential is rendered harmless by one's own good sense or by effective political counteraction, or its realization is stopped along the way, the increasingly horrendous steps of its inherent dialectic are liable to be enacted unless—and until—the juggernaut of its adherents is crushed in a cataclysm of force. The idea of Nazi anti-Semitism was revealed as the idea of the German people having the right to decide whether and in what way the Jews have the right to exist. Once the right of arrogating such a decision was conceded—positively or by default—with respect to the Jews, there was no way of knowing where the resulting action would stop or whether it would stop at one's own people. Very few people gave any thought to the dialectic of ideas. Be that as it may, the logic of Nazi anti-Semitism was pursued with due energy.

But how to translate anti-Semitism into whatever may be designated as "policy"? One form of policy consisted of specific acts of persecution, such as the boycott of Jewish businesses on April 1, 1933. Another form consisted of the kind of defamation best exemplified by *Der Stürmer*, a Nazi newspaper, which had the effect of maneuvering and arousing latent prejudices against the Jews in favor of the regime's anti-Semitism. These forms of "policy," though useful to the implementation of the regime's overall Jewish policy, raised questions in the minds of its leading circles: On the one hand, if these policies were helpful at all, then it was not in ridding Germany of Jews—if that was the main policy—but at best in an auxiliary way. On the other hand, since these actions could be regarded as outbursts by party zealots rather than as expressions of articulate policies, what *was* the policy and how was it to be enacted? Another form of policy consisted of a series of decrees that dismantled the Jews' status as citizens and as members of a productive society. This process was effective within the limits defined by the individual laws. It also had the virtue of the kind of clarity that belongs to the established system of public law. However, while this process may have been indispensable, it did not define policy and intensified the question of underlying policy. In fact, among the predominant leaders of the regime there were diverse, if not downright contradictory, policies regarding the Jews. For example, in the mid-1930s, while Josef Göbbels agitated to get rid of the Jews, Göring thought that to do so would be harmful to the German economy.

It was in this ideological chaos—not uncharacteristic of National Socialism in general—that the development began of articulating the regime's Jewish policy and channeling it toward an orderly and relentless enactment. This development took place within the SS, which was emerging as the predominant instrument of the regime's power. As was said before, in its posture of a police force, the Gestapo's function was that of executing the regime's policy. Its function was not to determine the reasons for its actions but to proceed in accordance with set policy and on orders. It was the function of the SD to produce the reasons for the actions of the Gestapo. As a "security service," the SD was supposed to do so by gathering intelligence. However, what constitutes intelligence? For a normal governmental intelligence agency, this question is answered by pointing to the duly constituted branch of government that it serves and by the tasks given to it by its relevant superiors. The SD was not such an agency. It was a part of a political task force (*Politische Bereitschaft*) that operated in secret, outside of any governmentally determined parameters, and whose task was as open and vague as the ideology of which it was a key instrument. It developed methods of ideological control over both the ones whom the ideology designated as the elect as well as those designated as opponents. Basically, control was exercised by means of information gathered. However, what counts as "information" and how what has been gathered is to be understood as significant intelligence are determined by ideology. Yet, there is a conflict inherent in the juxtaposition of ideology on the one hand and information on the other, its meaning, its consequent reasons for actions, and the exercise of control. The latter are specific, while ideology is vague, and one cannot operate with them without articulating ideology. And this is what the SD proceeded to do, in particular with respect to the Jews as those who were, by ideological determination, the opponents *par excellence*. It should also be said that even as it was impossible to gather information without reaching back to formulate what constitutes intelligence, so it was unlikely that as powerful a tool as secret intelligence could be forged without reaching ahead and putting it to use. The use of information for purposes of police actions was the task of the Gestapo, at least within the jurisdiction of Nazi Germany proper. In the occupied territories, it was the SD that would have the function of political security police services. However, starting with Austria, the SD's function did—in at least one respect—extend to the area of enforcement of policy even within the boundaries of Nazi Germany proper, namely, as regards the Jews. In this way, the function of the SD collided with that of the Gestapo. Here, however, we see the rationale for the two services being united by having the same directorate, Heydrich, and by being two branches of the same organization, the SS, with Himmler as chief. Here we also see why key functionaries, such as Eichmann, could be switched from the SD to the Gestapo or, while belonging to the one, be assigned to the other. Similarly, agencies within these services were switched from the one to the other and back again.

At first, in 1933, the office in which the only Jewish desk within the SS was located was part of the Gestapo, in the headquarters of the Secret State Police (*Geheimes Staatspolizeiamt*). Characteristically, the office was the "Legal Section," and the desk concerned Jews and Freemasons. It was run by one Dr. Karl Haselbacher. Like many of the later cadre of SD protagonists, Haselbacher was young and had joined the Nazi Party *after* Hitler had come to power, for career reasons and not out of prior conviction. Similarly, there is no indication that he harbored any anti-Semitic convictions. However, his was a promising legal mind, and earlier that year he had been involved in formulating the first decree concerning the Jews, the "Law to Restore the Civil Service," which not only removed Jews from official positions but provided what served until the Nuremberg Laws of 1935 as an interim definition of "Jew."

A year later the SD established a Jewish Section. It was located within Department II of the SD, which dealt with *all segments of life* internal to Germany proper (*SD-Inland: Lebensgebiete*, Internal SD: Aspects of Life). Department II would be the most concentrated cell of Nazi power during the course of the regime's life. Several main sections of this department dealt with ideological "opponents," Main Section 1 with the Church, the Jews, and others. The Jewish Section carried the specific designation II/112.

What was the situation which defined the task and the performance of SD II/112 from its inception to the Anschluss of Austria, a period of less than four years?

The Jewish Section II/112

At the time Section II/112 was established, the regime did not pursue a Jewish policy that the leaders of the SS could recognize as worthy of the lofty ideology whose sentinel it was, or as precise as the paramilitary discipline of its executive organs required. The SD itself developed as the protector of the state's security against the kind of opposition that eludes definition by legislation and neutralization by judicial process. This kind of opponent was thought to be in conflict with the very soul and will of the nation whose proponent the Nazi movement was and whose protagonist was its leadership, with the SS as its spearhead. One of the memoranda issued from Heydrich's office and circulated within the SD in the months during which the reorganization developed that led to the establishment of the RSHA, spelled out these features as follows: In distinction from the Gestapo, the SD's "provenance is the political movement" and was designed to be "the exponent of the political will of the national-socialist movement for the purpose of [guarding] the state's security." Since the SD was concerned with the state's security through its concern with what harmed the nation, it proceeded "through political means, as the case may be even when no legal means are available as yet. Hence, it is the nature of the SD's task to take note and register (*Erfassung*) the phenomena that cannot as yet be apprehended through criminal law . . . [and] to prepare political means [to do so]."[92] In accordance with this prevailing sense of mission, the SD's approach to the solution of the Jewish problem consisted in gathering information aimed at the ideological clarification of the Jew as the enemy and at identifying the Jews in light of this clarification, devising the policy of neutralizing this enemy and marshaling the means of carrying out this policy. In gathering the information and in interpreting its meaning, the SD required nothing less than the dispassionate clarity of the scientific observer. However, the hermeneutic circle wherein this intelligence was developed remained closely circumscribed by what the SD leadership brought with them when they established Section II/112, that is, the ideological predisposition and the organizational mentality of the SD: what they wanted to see determined, what was being looked for, and what was seen. This is demonstrated by one of the two accomplishments of the initial director of Section II/112, Leopold von Mildenstein.

Von Mildenstein claimed to have had a benign attitude toward the Jews. Apparently he thought that the national resurgence to which the Nazi movement gave political expression and which excluded the Jews should be matched by a parallel resurgence among the Jews, a resurgence propelled by the exclusion of the Jews by the Nazi movement, and issuing in the Zionist movement. This, in effect, constituted the ideological clarification contributed by von Mildenstein; it had the virtue of directing the Nazi solution of the Jewish problem toward a palpable and feasible solution, namely, the emigration of the Jews of Germany to Palestine. (Presently and in the following chapters, we will have more to say about the policy of Jewish emigration to Palestine and elsewhere. At this point, we have to note that placing the stress on a policy of emigration did not address the ideological clarification of Nazi anti-Semitism in any fundamental way.) The fundamental identification of Socialists, Communists, and Democrats as opponents of Nazism was easy because it followed from obvious differences in conviction. According to Nazi anti-Semitism, Jews were opponents on racial grounds. To define this kind of opponent required the translation of differences of race into those of conviction. Von Mildenstein can be said to have contributed to that end by having the small staff he was assembling undertake research into the Jewish presence both in Germany and worldwide. What resulted was sadly out of keeping with reality. The data they received showed diversity among the Jews and a motley of groupings, which must have been bewildering to the Mildenstein team. With their ideological and organizational predispositions, they went to work to make sense of the data and to chart the results. The individual communities through which Judaism survived from generation to generation, the ad hoc groupings through which Jews sought to meet the threats posed by their perennially exposed situation, the tenuous contacts which they maintained in their pitiful dispersion: in the minds of these methodical investigators all that coalesced into a sinister, tightly woven web of "international Judaism." The opponent now had a persona. No matter that it existed only on their charts; the opponent being now palpable, the ways could be found for confronting the enemy.

For the time being, the prevailing policy was emigration, especially to Palestine. Hence, the ongoing research concentrated on the vicissitudes of Zionism. Von Mildenstein needed someone to assist him in this task. He found someone who had joined the SS three years earlier—not out of any Nazi convictions but who, when his attempts at a career in business had ground to a halt, had joined at the suggestion of a casual acquaintance of his. His name was Adolf Eichmann; and his casual acquaintance was Dr. Ernst Kaltenbrunner, who would succeed Heydrich as head of the RSHA. Kaltenbrunner was Austrian. Eichmann was born in Germany but raised in Austria. Eichmann's claim at his interrogation in Jerusalem that he was not anti-Semitic is credible. He was intelligent, and he was capable of doing a good job and eager to do so if given a challenging assignment that promised to advance his career. At the time when von Mildenstein was looking for an assistant, Eichmann was utterly bored with his assignment as a custodian of the SD's Masonic museum. The "Zionism" desk (SD II/1123), to which Eichmann was assigned and which he staffed until the Anschluss, was one of three within Section II/112. The other two were "Assimilationists" (II/1121) and "Orthodox and Charity Organizations" (II/1122). Thus overnight Eichmann became, in effect, the regime's expert in an area about which he had hitherto known as good as nothing, and under a predisposition of anti-Semitism which he had previously not harbored. It was a time in the development of the SD when Heydrich began to replace thinkers of ideological clarification with doers of detail work. However, Eichmann conscientiously set to work to acquire some measure of expertise in the intelligence and policy area in which he was—officially—expert. He read some books about Zionism, and not only those possessing the Nazi ideological tendency which his immediate superior Herbert Hagen had ferreted out. Apparently, his literature also included Böhm's *History of the Zionist Movement*.[93] Eichmann claimed to have taught himself some Hebrew, using a text by Samuel Kaleko. Reports to the effect that Leo Baeck gave him Hebrew lessons are not credible; and the rumor that Murmelstein taught him is, as our research indicates, certainly false.

Of the three desks within Section II/112, Eichmann's was the one that dealt most directly with a practical policy of meeting the Jewish opponent, that is, with the policy of emigration. Eichmann's and Hagen's junket to Palestine in 1937 to see the Zionist reality firsthand has been given ample publicity by Hannah Arendt in her book about the Eichmann trial. Von Mildenstein, the section leader who appointed Eichmann, soon relinquished his post to Kuno Schroeder. It was under Schroeder that work started in earnest of identifying Jewry as the foremost ideological opponent, of gathering and distributing intelligence about the ubiquitous tentacles of the hydra of world Jewry, and of steeling a cadre to oppose the foe by any appropriate means. By the time Eichmann had been at his new post one year, Section II/112 had a third leader, Hagen, who would remain in this position until the section was replaced in 1939 by Section IVB4 of the newly organized RSHA. Since IVB4 would be a section within the amalgam of the Gestapo and the SD, it would then be able to operate in an executive function in regard to the "final solution."

During his approximately three years as incumbent of the Zionism desk within SD II/112, Eichmann would participate in clarifying prevailing Nazi policy regarding the Jews and finding ways of putting it into practice. First, while Zionism counted as the preeminent means of ridding Germany of Jews through emigration, the kind of power base that would result from the establishment of a Jewish state would run counter to Nazi interests. Hence, that aspiration of the Jews would have to be counteracted. Second, for this reason and for others, emigration to Palestine could not possibly be an expeditious means of ridding Germany of Jews. Therefore, parallel efforts of emigration to other destinations would have to be added. However, emigration required money, including foreign currency. In the Altreich, a scheme of foreign exchange was provided in the mid-thirties for emigration to Palestine and in a limited way to other destinations. But the use of the scheme was limited; and the SD observers of all sectors of German life, including the economy, had doubts about whether such schemes were in the interest of Germany. The Jews would simply have to finance their emigration without taking capital or means of production with them and without tapping the Reich's access to foreign exchange. Third, voluntary emigration proved to be an extremely uncertain and slow policy. Hence, if emigration was to be pursued as a solution of the Jewish problem, then a more effective policy of emigration would have to be devised and instituted, a policy that a cadre of SD functionaries, having the means of peremptory authority at its disposal, could direct. It would, in short, have to be a policy of forced emigration. But how could the Jews be forced? To be sure, Section II/112 now possessed a map of the political structure of "world Jewry," which extended its insidious reach into the vital areas of German life itself. And the Zionism section diligently collected information on the progress of Jewish life inside and outside of Germany, cutting snippets from the press, subscribing to Jewish periodicals, keeping all kinds of Jewish groupings under surveillance, receiving reports from informants, and so on. And, in keeping with enforced internal SD procedures, the staff of Section II/112 steeled itself through indoctrination (under the tutelage of Professor Franz Six), training (competitive sports required), and policy conferences. However, none of this afforded them a hold on the Jews, a hold which would motivate the Jews of Germany to leave and the Jews outside of Germany to help them leave.

What was needed to that end followed from the logic of radical anti-Semitic ideology, whether this logic was articulated prior to the Anschluss or not. What was needed was a situation in which the Jews had no validity whatever: no status as citizens, no incumbency of civil rights, no material or spiritual validity, and thus no means of existing and no reason to continue, at least in Germany. Their existence would have to be at the sufferance and the disposal of the executors of the regime's policy, and thus they would be hostages vis-à-vis themselves and their friends outside. Within the headquarters of the SD the instrument for the execution of a radical ideological solution of the Jewish problem was being readied for the eventuality that the regime's momentum provided the opportunity. The opportunity came with the Anschluss.

The SD Command Structure

At the time of the Anschluss the command structure of the SD as the instrument of the regime's Jewish policy, was as follows:

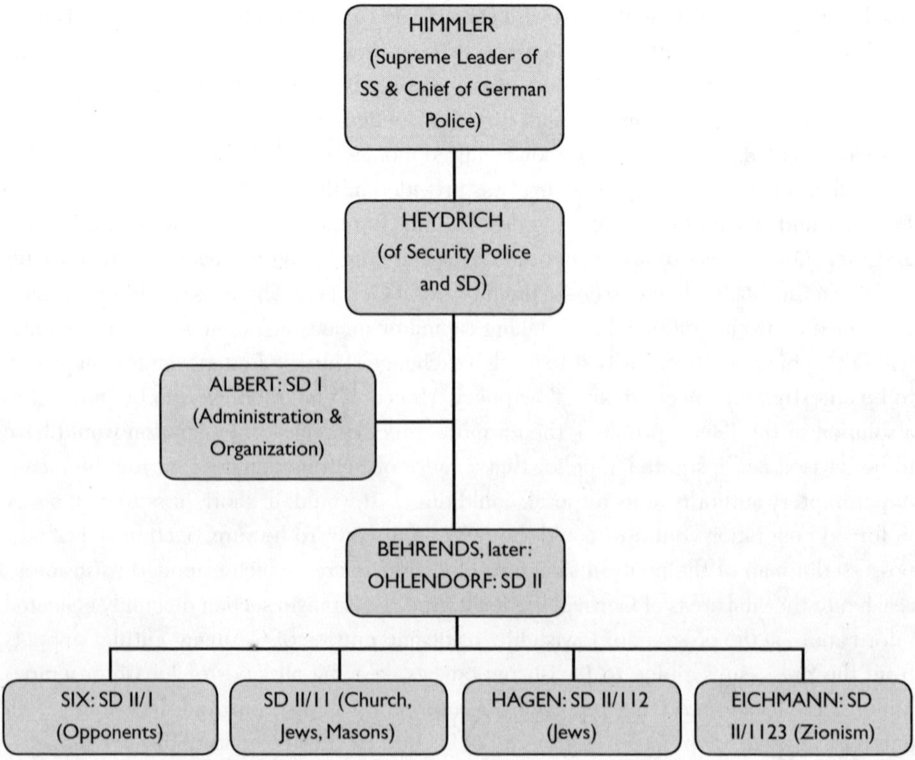

Some comments will clarify the significance of the chart.

1. SD headquarters was structured on an authoritarian, military-hierarchical pattern. The activity on any one level took place upon orders or authorization from above. What was produced at the lower level was reviewed by the higher level; no correspondence left a desk without clearance from above. Periodic conferences at all levels were required, as were briefing sessions of section chiefs by their superiors. Some matters, even those of a routine nature, had to be submitted to Heydrich. He also screened the intelligence produced by all sections before it became part of the periodic confidential intelligence reports distributed by the SD to the Sipo and the highest leaders, most of whom occupied posts in governmental ministries. All ranks within the SS, except for the three lowest, were "Leader" ranks and carried the word *Führer* in their rank-title. This meant they had to function as leaders within their assigned areas of competence and in subordination to supernal leaders. When Eichmann went to Vienna to "solve the Jewish problem" there, (a) he went under orders that issued from the uppermost ranks of Nazi leadership; (b) he continued to report to his superiors in SD headquarters in Berlin; (c) Hagen, who continued for a while as his immediate superior, functioned as his "inspector";[94] (d) he carried the additional title of *SD-Führer* within the newly established SS-*Oberabschnitt*

Österreich (SS Superior Regional Sector Austria), which, in effect, made him the plenipotentiary of the SD in matters of his competence.

2. The chart begins with Himmler as the ultimate chief of the organization to which Eichmann belonged. As chief of the SS and the police, the power wielded by Himmler was so immense that the SS has been regarded as a state within the Nazi state. However, it must not be overlooked that at the time of the Anschluss Himmler, and with him the SS in all its segments, was only one of the engines that provided the thrust for the momentum of the Nazi juggernaut. As chief of the German Police, Himmler was nominally subordinate to the Interior Ministry; as supreme leader of the SS, he was subordinate to the party leadership; and, most significant, as chief of the Gestapo, he was functioning as deputy to Göring, who had created the Gestapo and retained nominal control over it. In all these capacities, Himmler reported ultimately to Hitler; the fundamental purpose of the SS was, after all, to be at the disposal of the supreme leadership of the Nazi Party as the German nation's trustee of its destiny and executor of its will. Thus, policy devised and carried out by the SS was determined by the regime's supreme potentates, of which Himmler was but one. Nevertheless, the presence of Himmler and Heydrich at the uppermost reaches of the command line in which Eichmann was a subordinate meant that the struggle against the foe—a struggle in which Eichmann was the point man—would be carried out with deliberation, relentlessly, thoroughly, precisely, and discretely.

   The presence of Eichmann and Hagen at the bottom of the command line indicates that Heydrich was packing the infrastructure of the SD with technocrats whose importance in the operation of the SD would replace that of the professional men who in the earlier years helped to formulate the ideological foundations for the task of combating opponents, as well as the appropriate policy and structure of the SD. Two of these, Otto Ohlendorf and Franz Six, were in the command line at the time of the Anschluss. Six held a doctorate in political science from University of Heidelberg and was a professor at the University of Berlin. He was the main contributor to the effort of translating the ideological conception of the Jew from a racial concept to one of a cardinal political enemy. Possessing a sharp mind and being an effective lecturer, he provided the requisite ideological indoctrination during the years when the small staff of SD II/112 was preparing for its grim work. When Eichmann began his work in Vienna, he proved to be an able executor of policy. Hagen, as a home office supervisor of a project that turned out to be exceedingly complex for an average bureaucrat, was less effective. It was Six who really directed Eichmann's operations after the Anschluss. Like Six, Ohlendorf had an academic background. His contribution lay in the area of ideological theory and in devising precise ways of gathering detailed information that would gauge the mood in various "segments of life." As the SD's concern with opponents moved from ideological theory and intelligence toward action, the positions of professionals like Six and Ohlendorf became more managerial and eventually they were phased out of their jobs at headquarters. In time, Ohlendorf would become commander of *Einsatzgruppe* D, the task force that killed Jews in the southern sector of the Russian front; for a short time, Six would be a member of an *Einsatzgruppe* in the east as well, but not in a killing unit, and later a theoretician at the RSHA and in the Foreign Office.

3. At the time of the Anschluss, the unit to which Eichmann belonged was remarkably small. In fact, the main persons who would be associated with him more or less continuously fill only a small list: Besides the above-mentioned Hagen, some others from SD headquarters would join his expanding operation, including Theodor Danecker and Dieter Wisliceny. New personnel would be added over the years as the need arose at the various locations all over Nazi-occupied Europe. Most important among those who would assist Eichmann in Vienna and in Theresienstadt (the locales constituting the foci of this book) are Alois Brunner (to be known as Brunner 1), Anton Brunner (to be known as Brunner 2; not a member of the SS), Hans Günther, Rolf Günther, Karl Rahm, and Siegfried Seidl, among others. The Brunners were not brothers, as Aronson claims;[95] the Günthers were. At the time of the Anschluss, the ages of the main protagonists of the SD Jewish policy were as follows: Ohlendorf was 31; Six, 28; Hagen and Danecker were 25; and Eichmann, 32. Some, like Six and Ohlendorf, were methodical ideologists; some, like Danecker, were outright fanatics; all of them were young careerists, some, like Eichmann and Hagen, merely that. Their salary was good for young men at the beginning of their careers. If the staff of the SD, not only at headquarters, was small, then it was to a significant extent for budgetary reasons. The SD, unlike the Gestapo, was at the time of the Anschluss still strictly a party organization with no official access to any of the means or amenities of the governmental establishment. As director of both the Security Police (including the Gestapo) and the Security Services (SD), Heydrich provided a union of the two; but it was a personal union, not a real union, and it would not be one until he succeeded in combining the two in September 1939 as the RSHA. Until then, his official budget allocation was provided from party contributions, and his SD men would not have the benefits of civil servants. However, the SS had developed its own sources of income through the exploitation of the inmates in its network of concentration camps.[96] It would make sense that one reason that the SD sent its own emissary to Vienna to dispute the Gestapo's official executive jurisdiction over solving the Jewish problem was the promise of lucre. It is known, for example, that a justification for one of Eichmann's subsequent promotions was that he succeeded in enriching the coffers of the Reich and the organization. In any case, by that time, the handful of men who had gone so far from being gatherers of information and had trained so hard for the struggle against the foe had nothing to show for years of service and were ready for action. A memorandum written by Hagen to Eichmann—unbeknownst to him, and in fact to anyone, *one week before the Anschluss*—expresses the extent to which the contribution of SD II/112 to the solution of the Jewish problem had until then been as good as nil, and that whatever action there was had been undertaken by the Gestapo, whose relevant main office was IIB4:

> I request that in the near future material be assembled for a memorandum to C [i.e., Chief Heydrich] which should be prepared jointly with IIB4. It should demonstrate clearly that the Jewish problem cannot be solved on the present basis (financial difficulties, etc.) and that one will have to approach a solution in the area of foreign policy, as it had already been negotiated between Poland and France.[97]

Poor, simple-minded Hagen! No such thing had been "negotiated," although such a project had been broached by the representative of Poland in France. The Madagascar Plan to relocate Europe's Jews to the island of Madagascar fascinated the SD, and later it would be pursued up to a point by Nazi Germany. In any case, ready or not and unbeknownst to them, the time for action on the part of the men of SD II/112 was at hand. The memorandum was never sent; it remained within the office with a cryptic note at the bottom: "*überholt!*" that is, "outdated" by events.

The instrument of the solution of the Jewish problem was taken up by the momentum of the Anschluss and, riding on the momentum, would catapult the regime's policy regarding the Jews on a trajectory toward the final solution.

Chapter 3

"The Jews May Go!"

Jewish Organizations Past and New

On Wednesday, May 11, 1938, nine days after the IKG reopened, Josef Löwenherz presided over a meeting of sixty representatives of both the large and small Jewish organizations of Vienna.[1] There were no other meetings of this size and kind during the Nazi years. The list of those present included some of the leaders of Vienna's Jewish service and charitable organizations. One of them was Hermine Krüger, director of the *Krügerheim*, an institution for the care and training of neglected young women. Another was Dr. Berthold Löwenfeld, associate director of the *Waisenhaus Bisamberg* (Bisamberg Orphanage) and, as a specialist in the education of the blind, also associated with the *Israelitisches Blindeninstitut Hohe Warte* (Hohe Warte Jewish Institute for the Blind). The director of this prestigious institution, Siegfried Altmann, was also there.

The purpose of the meeting was, in effect, to inform those present that the organizations that they represented were to be liquidated. The terse record indicates that the meeting also revealed the new order under which Jewish existence was to continue, whatever its fate. Hans Kasztan, about whom we shall hear occasionally, acted as the recorder. Löwenherz was the sole speaker. He began by announcing that the assembled guests had been invited on orders from the Gestapo and were to be informed that their organizations were forbidden to engage in any organized collections of dues or contributions, that they—"insofar as they have not as yet been dissolved"—were to be subordinated to the IKG and were not to engage in any activity "*ohne Einvernehmen der Gemeinde*" ("without consultation with and the consent of the IKG"). Each one of these points was driven home several times: The authorities might release moneys for some welfare enterprises; the other organizations would have to wither away, and all of them would have to report their assets. All intercessions on their behalf would have to be made through the IKG. Finally, "the authorities wish that the IKG be and remain the center of Jewish life and tend to support the IKG in this activity." At the end of the meeting, Löwenherz announced that he was obliged to report the meeting to the authorities and that discussion was not permitted. Thanking the participants for their attendance, he requested strict fulfillment of these charges.

The meeting ended thirty minutes after it was called to order. Sixty people shuffled out, all of them in silence, most of them toward oblivion. Frau Krüger would be presiding for the next few months over the dissolution of the renowned home and training school, which she and her family had built; it had been a pioneer in its field since its founding in 1897.[2] Dr. Löwenfeld (later: Lowenfeld) would in time be superintendent of the California School for the Blind. Director Altmann would live out his last years in New York, whither he would take the guest book of the *Israelitisches Blindeninstitut Hohe Warte*—world-famous as a leading institution of its kind for over half a century, as the entries from visitors such as Pedro II, Emperor of Brazil, Elisabeth, Empress of Austria, Dr. Sigmund Freud, and hundreds more attest.[3] The meeting marked the end of an exceedingly vigorous organized life on the part of Vienna's Jews. All told, there were over four hundred and thirty Jewish organizations.[4] Some were large, such as religious communities with large synagogues, schools such as the Chajes-Realgymnasium, Zionist groups, veterans associations, and major charities. Some were small, like neighborhood ladies' aid societies, burial societies, fraternal groups, and *Landsmannschaften*. The liquidation of these groups proceeded steadily in the months following that meeting.

The liquidation of the Jewish organizations was not administered by either the SD or the Gestapo. The procedure for this liquidation evolved from a series of decrees, promulgated in the earliest period of the regime, whereby independent associations in all segments of organized society were disbanded or incorporated into the totalitarian embrace of the Nazi Party. This was effected, easily or brutally, in the case of political parties, the press, labor unions, and professional organizations—including in particular those serving the interests of art, culture, literature, research, and education. But, there were exceptions. Not all organized life could be absorbed by the party-state right away, for example, the churches could not. And by virtue of the special status of Jews and Judaism as the racial antithesis of the German folk, the instrument of whose promotion the party-state professed to be, neither could Jewish organizations be transformed for absorption by that entity in any positive sense.

The transformation of the Jewish organizations under the new regime thus proceeded from the same office as that of non-Jewish organizations. However, whereas the function of the latter was likely to be in some way accommodated or provided for in the elaborate structure of the party-state, the Jewish organizations were slated for extinction with temporary reprieve only if they could be made to serve the projected abolition of Jewish existence.

Most Jewish organizations were simply disbanded. Some, which the Nazis functionally modified or newly established, were permitted to exist, at least for a time, either for the purpose of ridding Germany of its Jews or for a purpose deemed ancillary thereto. Since the disbanding of independent organizations was provided for by decrees that in Nazi Germany had the force of law, it had proceeded in pre-Anschluss Germany on a case-by-case basis and was handled by the Gestapo as a police matter. For example, in a letter from the local Gestapo, dated April 17, 1937, the Hamburg Lodge of B'nai Brith was informed that it was "prohibited and dissolved effective immediately," as were its affiliated sister organizations and, either for good measure or out of sudden administrative efficiency, so too "all Jewish organizations of a similar type."[5] As its legal basis, the notification cited Clause 1 of none other than the "Decree for the Protection of the People and the State," which the new Nazi regime had Reich President Paul von Hindenburg promulgate the morning after the Reichstag fire, February 28, 1933. Clause 1 suspended certain provisions of the Constitution and instituted "restrictions on personal freedom, on the right to the free expression of opinion," including, among others there specified, "the freedom . . . of association."[6] The same letter also informs the Hamburg chapter of B'nai Brith that, pursuant to the law of July 14, 1933, providing for the seizure of "assets inimical to the People and the State," all the named organizations are declared to be thusly "inimical," their assets seized and credited to the city of Hamburg.

When the Nazis took over in Austria, they installed a *Stillhaltekommission für Vereine, Organisationen und Verbände* (Receivership Commission for Clubs, Organizations and Associations) as part of *Reichskommissar* Bürckel's staff. This centralized office provided for more effective abolition of politically undesirable organized life, better control over the seizure or use of available assets, and greater efficiency in dealing with the many organizations. Thus it happened that in matters pertaining to the dissolution of the Jewish organizations Löwenherz would be told by Eichmann (of the SD) to report to the commission in an arrangement imposed on Löwenherz by the Gestapo. As it happens, the official in the *Stillhaltekommission* with whom Löwenherz dealt would later be assigned to Eichmann's office and would participate in directing the last, major phase of the liquidation of Vienna's Jewry, the deportation of more than 48,000 Jews. His name was Anton Brunner, later known as "Brunner 2."

The procedure required each Jewish organization to fill out a questionnaire listing its assets and liabilities.[7] In time it was informed that it had been either dissolved or incorporated into a designated successor organization. The assets were kept in escrow for meeting remaining liabilities or for the use of the successor organizations. One of the major jobs that Löwenherz took upon himself in the ensuing months was to try to secure the remaining funds of the various dissolved charities for the use of the IKG's mounting welfare tasks. Each organization was assessed a hefty *Aufbauumlage* ("reconstruction charge"), which was really a euphemism for a contribution to *Reichskomissar* Bürckel's operating fund, and of course a respectable administrative fee.[8] In the case of the larger organizations, there were many problems of legal liability for debts and loans that the successor organizations were expected to assume together with the forced transfer of the properties to them. The IKG was not prepared to assume such burdens, and Löwenherz made frequent representations to this effect.[9] However, most of the organizations died quietly. One example of what was involved must suffice. It is a letter written by a Frieda Twersky, a *Rabbinerswitwe* (Rabbi's widow), addressed to Bürckel himself and presumably presented by Löwenherz to the Commissioner for Receiverships:[10]

> The *shul* "Jacob Joseph" has existed in my flat for many, many years. . . . The room facing the inner court serves as the prayer room. My husband was the last rabbi of this prayer house, where he suddenly died eight years ago in the fervor of the service. He left me and a boy, who

> was then five, without means. The society of like name was recently dissolved and the prayer house closed. The society is unimportant, poor, has few members, and its dissolution was no hardship on anyone. However, the prayer house is dear to a few very pious Jews. Its closing is very hard on them, and it is hardest for me who has been given modest support by the worshippers. . . .
>
> Only 10 to 12 worshippers come here . . . a quarter-hour in the morning, the same period in the evening, on holidays about 2 hours. . . . The room is neat; because of the lack of means, there is no organ, no leader, no servant. There are no complaints. Because of the high holidays, we would like to keep the prayer house for another five months at most; then the worshippers and I will leave Vienna. . . .

The bottom of the letter shows Commissioner Brunner's handwritten decision: "Private prayer houses have been strictly forbidden by the Gestapo and SD."

Of the hundreds of Jewish organizations, four were permitted to continue their existence until further notice, each with a function specified by the Nazi authorities.[11] One of these was the IKG. We have scant indications of how the new IKG came to be. We recall that IKG President Friedmann and Director Löwenherz were arrested on March 18, 1938, and the IKG closed. Emil Engel and some associates conducted some IKG business in the interim, especially welfare; he also had to produce money for the Nazis as a punitive measure for Jewish support of the late regime of Austria. While Friedmann, because of his association with the Dollfuss-Schuschnigg regime, counted as an "opponent" and was sent to Dachau, Löwenherz was kept at the Rossauer Kaserne, which now served as a political prison. Eichmann was charged with organizing the solution of the Jewish problem in Vienna in any way he was able. In the years prior to the Anschluss, he had been in charge of the "Zionists," a subsection of the SD dealing with "Opponents/Jews." Being the regime's "expert" on Zionism, he naturally assumed that the Jewish problem could be solved by sending the Jews of Vienna to Palestine. Since Böhm's *History of the Zionist Movement* had been published during Eichmann's tenure as resident expert on Zionism, he thought it best to summon Böhm to organize the Zionist exodus of the Viennese Jews to Palestine. This simplistic scheme was frustrated when Böhm refused the dubious honor thrust upon him and, in the face of Eichmann's anger, suffered a nervous breakdown from which he never recovered.

Eichmann must have been desperate for a feasible scheme that would bring quick results. Dr. William R. "Willy" Perl, who organized the illegal Perl transports to Palestine, reports that at that early stage Eichmann thought nothing of personally visiting holding rooms full of Jewish detainees, threatening and yelling at them to motivate them to emigrate. It was not long before Eichmann singled out Löwenherz as the one best suited for leading the Jews from Vienna across the borders of the Reich and to the Promised Land. There is no doubt that the imprisoned Löwenherz had the temerity to tell Eichmann that emigration required complicated preparation and had to proceed case by case, that many things had to be arranged in each case, that to the extent that emigration could succeed, it could not be restricted to Palestine, and that emigration to Palestine could be left to the organization that existed in Vienna for that purpose. It is doubtful that Eichmann was pleased to hear what Löwenherz had to say, and there are indications that Eichmann became violent against Löwenherz. In any case, Löwenherz stood his ground. The consequences are indicated in a two-page report that Eichmann directed to Hagen as his superior at headquarters in Berlin, dated April 23, 1938.[12]

Eichmann addressed Hagen as "*Lieber Herbert!*" ("Dear Herbert"), and started by saying that he was writing the report "with pencil for want of ink and pen"—not to speak of want of an office, typewriter, staff, and secretary. All that would come later, financed with Jewish money, apropos which he added at the end of the letter that "today's issue of *Völkischer Beobachter* (April 23, 1938) reports in big print on the front page that [the] 'Rothschilds are being expropriated'." For the time being, he had a leather satchel for an office, and the regime's authority over the Jews in his pocket. He reported to Hagen that Löwenherz had been released and that "preparations for the initiation of Jewish political activity are complete, particularly as concerns Jewish emigration." Eichmann was sure that "next week or so the IKG and soon after the Zionist shop will be opened." Most important, with a view toward the "political activity as concerns emigration," he charged Löwenherz and Dr. Alois Rothenberg of the Palestine Office (*Palästina-Amt*, or *Palamt*) "to prepare a precise action plan for the IKG and the Zionist organization, as well as a precise plan for the staffing of positions and personnel." The "action plan" would have to be submitted by April 27.

As soon as he was released, Löwenherz had to confer with Rothenberg of the Palestine Office and, consolidating what he considered in prison during Eichmann's visitations, to draft the assigned and unprecedented scheme of organizing the exodus of Vienna's almost 170,000 Jews and of some 10,000 more in the Austrian provinces. Eichmann's handwritten letter to Hagen is his first document in the fateful story we are telling; and the draft Löwenherz worked out with Rothenberg is his first document. Let us look at the features of the plan.

The title of the three-and-a-half–page document is "Draft of the Action Plan for the Establishment of a 'Center [*Zentralstelle*] for the Emigration of the Jews of Austria'."[13] The title indicates the need for the central coordination of all emigration efforts.[14] The plan came into being because the only emigration effort established in Austria since before the Anschluss was directed toward Palestine. Since Palestine could not absorb all those who would have to emigrate, there was need for emigration to move in other destinations as well. Inasmuch as emigration to Palestine proceeded under "its own laws and apparatus," emigration to other destinations would require an elaborate organization with many and diverse tasks that would have to be established from the ground up.

The three major new tasks projected for the Viennese Zionist organization were (1) to urge the British mandatory administration to increase the quota of permits for the Jews of Austria; (2) to develop the Youth Aliyah movement; and (3) to arrange for the foreign exchange necessary for permits available to "capitalists." The first of these tasks would prove to be well-nigh impossible, the third a task for Löwenherz rather than for Rothenberg.

The major point of the proposed action plan dealt with the tasks that a "Center for the Emigration of the Jews of Austria" to destinations other than Palestine would have to undertake. Presupposed for any and all emigration efforts was to secure all necessary and possibly useful information. This meant, first of all, gathering all domestic regulations pertaining to emigration, such as passport and property laws and, Löwenherz added more wisely than he could then have guessed, "their continuous amendment." Second, it meant

> tapping all conceivable sources of information concerning countries of destination . . . laws, regulations pertaining to immigration, settlement, and the practice of one's vocation. In order to obtain authentic information [the center] has to contact pertinent consular and central offices [of foreign countries], as well as agencies of public and private law, local administrations, scientific institutes, boards of trade, professional organizations . . .

Evidently this refers to the "Jewish political activity as concerns Jewish emigration" that Eichmann mentioned in his letter to Hagen and that Löwenherz was expected to "initiate." However, Löwenherz would learn very quickly that this sort of universal information gathering was impracticable and that contacting official agencies abroad was inappropriate, hence inadvisable and counterproductive, both for the proposed "center" as well as for individual would-be emigrants. According to the draft, additional information would be forthcoming from reports of fellow Viennese who had emigrated, about climate, ways of life, and prospects of earning a living. That Löwenherz considered such information gathering a feasible first stage of the proposed center's operation shows that he envisaged the emigration effort to proceed in an orderly, step-by-step fashion. He also thought the center would be in a position to negotiate with foreign jurisdictions (1) to gain immigration quotas or, where quotas were available, to increase them; (2) to secure opportunities for retraining abroad; and, with respect to individuals, (3) to secure workplaces for qualified workers.

To match the opportunities for immigration-plus-employment with the right would-be emigrant, Löwenherz included in the action plan of the center on the one hand, the registration of all *Wanderwillige* (those willing to emigrate), listing their qualifications, means, family members, physical condition, experience, and so on; and on the other, a "rational" informational campaign coupled with an advisory machinery. We will see that the registration of tens of thousands carried out by the new IKG would turn out to be futile and would only confuse the desperate Jews as to what the IKG could do for them, especially since Löwenherz would very quickly find out that the IKG was hardly in a position to secure these opportunities, much less to match them up with would-be emigrants.

However, the action plan turned out to be fully realistic in two respects: it projected making contact and negotiating with aid societies abroad and it assisted indigent Jews at every step of the emigration process.

And so the IKG was reestablished in order to function as the center for the emigration of the Jews of Austria, and Löwenherz was put in charge of carrying out the plan of action proposed by himself for the center. The apparatus of the new IKG would be as elaborate and complex as projected in the "action plan," and its services on behalf of the emigration effort and to individual emigrants would prove to be vital and indispensable, as would be its representation of the interests of the Jews. In the action plan, Löwenherz clearly foresaw that problems would be connected with carrying through the emigration of the Jews and with effectively representing their interests under the given circumstances. But, he did not—and could not—fully anticipate just how difficult and close to impossible the task would be. For example, on the very day (April 26) that he and Rothenberg completed the draft for submission by the deadline on the following day, a law was promulgated requiring Jews to report their capital, if above RM (Reichsmark) 5,000; in short, the "means" which, along with "qualifications," and so on, would facilitate their emigration would no longer be at the disposal of their Jewish owners. Thus, his performance at the various stages of the ensuing liquidation of the Jewish Community of Vienna and Austria will have to be measured against the fact that the precise difficulty of his task could not be anticipated, and by whether he could find ways of serving the interests of Jewish survival in the face of ever new challenges imposed by his Nazi overlords. One thing we, who have the benefit of hindsight, can say: The new IKG, as the projected "Center for the Emigration of the Jews of Austria," would be instrumental in what would prove to be the most successful, though laborious, Jewish effort of saving Jews through emigration under the Nazi regime, in spite of the fact that its capacities fell far short of what Löwenherz envisaged and what Eichmann expected.

The center that Löwenherz established and directed would again be known by its old designation of IKG for the following reasons: The title he had proposed for the center would later that year be adopted by Eichmann for the enterprise he would establish as the central place for the Jews to satisfy the official preconditions for emigration. It is especially ironic that the "Center (*Zentralstelle*) for Jewish Emigration" would also serve Eichmann as the SD headquarters for the final liquidation of Jewish existence in Austria through expropriation, deprivation, and deportation.

The IKG would have tasks aside from its officially assigned function of arranging for the emigration of the Jews of Austria to places other than Palestine. Subsidiary to this was the retraining of potential emigrants and the providing for the sick, the helpless, and the needy among those who had not yet emigrated. In addition, the IKG administered religious affairs insofar as these were permitted, as well as the assets the community had owned from the time before the Nazi takeover and the assets of the dissolved organizations whose successor the IKG would become. The IKG of Vienna would soon also supervise the activities and functions of the Austrian Jewish organizations outside of Vienna, as they were abolished, and would liquidate their assets.

The second permitted organization was the *Palästina-Amt Wien* (*Palamt*), the "Palestine Office of Vienna," which originally had been established by the Jewish Agency. It was now charged by the Nazi authorities with organizing Jewish emigration to Palestine. Of the over sixty regional and ideological Zionist organizations that existed in Austria prior to the Nazi takeover, five were now subordinated to the Palamt, the rest dissolved. In the period before the outbreak of the war, the Nazis regarded emigration to Palestine as offering the best chance of getting rid of the Jews. Therefore, since, at the time of the Anschluss, their main reason for organizing and dealing with the Jews was to foster emigration, they tended to treat the chief functionary of the Palamt as equal in importance to Dr. Löwenherz of the IKG. Originally Eichmann wanted Dr. Adolf Böhm, the highly regarded historian of Zionism, to be in charge. However, Böhm refused, and Eichmann's anger doubtless was a contributing factor in Böhm's collapse. Since Dr. Böhm was out of the picture, Dr. Alois Rothenberg was installed as director of the Palamt. For the first few months, he usually accompanied Löwenherz when he had to report to the authorities.

In his handwritten letter to Hagen, Eichmann mentions that soon after the reopening of the IKG and the Palamt, the *Agudas Jisroel* (Union of Israel) would also be reopened and a new organization established "similar to the *Hilfsverein [der Deutschen Juden]* (Aid

Association of German Jews)," the organization in Berlin administered by the *Reichsvertretung der Juden in Deutschland* to help indigent Jews to survive and to emigrate.

Thus, the Vienna Agudas Jisroel was permitted, for the time being, to function as a separate organization, its charge being to foster the emigration of orthodox Jews.

The new IKG was in a position to incorporate and build on the welfare department of the old IKG to meet its new needs. For this reason, it was not necessary to create a Viennese version of the *Hilfsverein*, which is what Eichmann had projected. Instead, of the almost one hundred and twenty welfare organizations that had existed until then—some of which were absorbed by the IKG, while most were dissolved—one was permitted to exist as a separate organization longer than any other during the Nazi regime, namely, the *Jüdischer Hilfsverband für jüdische Kriegsopfer, Invaliden, Witwen und Waisen* (Jewish Association for the Aid of Jewish War Victims, Invalids, Widows and Orphans). This was the only organization akin to a Jewish veterans' group that the Nazis permitted to exist. All four of the other regular Jewish veterans' organizations were dissolved. The IKG was required to subsidize this association. (We will hear about this group again in chapter 15 in the second volume of this work.)

In addition to these four organizations, a fifth one was permitted to retain, at least for a while and nominally, the autonomous status vis-à-vis the IKG that it had enjoyed heretofore, namely, the Viennese community of "Turkish" (i.e., Sephardi) Jews. Thereby hangs a tale; by pursuing it, we can have a preliminary glimpse of the function and the predicament of the new kind of Jewish leadership that was now emerging at the "reopened" IKG.

The Sephardi or "Turkish" Community of Vienna

We recall that at the meeting of May 11, 1938, Löwenherz had to announce the liquidation of Jewish organizations or their absorption by the IKG and that any negotiations to that end would have to be conducted through the IKG. Accordingly, in the days that followed, Engel met with representatives of a number of organizations, including the president of the *Verband der türkischen Israeliten [Sephardim] zu Wien* (Association of Sephardic Jews in Vienna). A few days later, the president of the Sephardim sent a request to the IKG that they inform the authorities that his association was not a *Verein* (club) but had the status of a legally recognized *Religionsgenossenschaft* (religious body).[15] Since the beginning of the century, the Sephardi community had enjoyed autonomous status, albeit within the framework of the law of 1890,[16] which established the IKG for the Jews of Vienna as the vehicle, sanctioned by public law, whereby they could practice their rites.

For the Nazis as well as the IKG, the point made by the president of the Sephardim was worthy of consideration: Austria, having been politically absorbed by Germany, was in the process of having its legal system aligned with that of Germany. Under German law, religious communities had the status of public entities and were tax exempt. Organizations such as "clubs" were private entities and as such liable to taxation. According to a law promulgated for all of Germany—including Austria—soon after the Anschluss, all Jewish communities lost their status as public entities and were supposed to be treated as private. In Vienna this became a matter of great concern to the Nazi authorities as well as the IKG, since Jewish organizations that were in the process of being liquidated or absorbed by the IKG had no further income; and the use of their remaining assets for the payment of taxes would not contribute to the alleviation of the snowballing impoverishment of the Jews but would exacerbate it. It is no wonder that, as we will see, much of Löwenherz's efforts in the ensuing period would be taken up with safeguarding the assets of the IKG and of the organizations that were being liquidated. Similarly, the authorities—from those who dealt with the Jews directly to the agencies dealing with various aspects of the economy and finance, to the newly installed government of the city of Vienna, and even to *Reichskommissar* Bürckel—recognized that it was in their interest to prevent the enforcement of decrees that would carry the impoverishment of the Jews beyond the point where it could be alleviated solely by means of Jewish assets.

The president of the Sephardi community no doubt made his point in order to maintain his old community's independence from the predominantly Ashkenazi IKG, whose modern, antecedent community was not officially established until the early nineteenth century. Even though autonomy was the motive of the Sephardim, we can see why their point was taken seriously by the Nazis. However, when it was evident that the Turkish community and its assets were small and could with greater efficiency be administered by the IKG, Löwenherz was instructed by Brunner, the Commissioner for Receiverships, and by the Gestapo to incorporate the Sephardi community. But, in response to Löwenherz's summons of the representatives of the Sephardim, the latter had Löwenherz arrange a direct meeting with the Commissioner for Receiverships, to whom they submitted, at his request, a statement of their position concerning the matter of the proposed incorporation of their community within the IKG.[17] Eichmann finally ruled on the matter during one of the times that Löwenherz had to report to him. It was the middle of August and the height of a mad whirl of activity, when all the major cogs of the laboriously devised emigration machinery were gaining momentum. The minutes of this meeting state Eichmann's "wish" that the Association of Turkish Israelites "while keeping their autonomy (*bei Wahrung seiner Autonomie*) be placed under the IKG and supervised" by Löwenherz.[18] In short, Eichmann would hold Löwenherz responsible for the incorporation of the Sephardi community regarded as a public legal entity. But, Löwenherz would have to find ways of letting the Sephardi community continue its relation of autonomy vis-à-vis the IKG as if nothing had changed in the status of the Jews. Further events will show that the resolution was untenable in this form.

Eight months later—after the major waves of expropriation, expulsion, forced emigration, and persecutions, including Kristallnacht—the Sephardi community, small to begin with, had dwindled and included only about one hundred destitute members, who were, like so many others, dependent on the IKG's meager resources, which were secured mainly through contributions from abroad. Early in April 1939, two leaders of the remnant of the Sephardi community, Dr. I. Haim and Albert Baruch, presented Löwenherz with a letter addressed to him but mailed to them. It was written by the president, Grand Rabbin Dr. Nissim J. Ovadia, of the World Sephardi Foundation—of which the almost defunct Viennese community of Turkish Jews was still a member—from its headquarters in Paris. Grand Rabbin Ovadia nominated a committee of seven to represent the interests of the

Viennese Sephardim, reminded Löwenherz that his budget was maintained by contributions by Sephardi as well as Ashkenazi Jews worldwide, requested that he transfer to the newly formed committee a fixed monthly sum, and suggested that he give the Viennese Sephardim equal treatment in matters of emigration.[19] Löwenherz met the two Sephardi delegates in the presence of Engel. In response to the content of the letter, he informed them that their organization had, in fact, been dissolved and that their movable assets were to be handed over to the IKG. (Their unmovable asset, the "Turkish" Synagogue [*Türkischer Tempel*], celebrated for its interior and exterior grace, had by then been destroyed during Kristallnacht.) Appropriate reports had to be made to the Gestapo as well as to Eichmann. Löwenherz told them that the IKG did not make any distinctions in the treatment of those who were dependent on it and, hence, was in no position to hand over to them a fixed monthly amount. However, he would see to it that the IKG's welfare department would give equal treatment to a list of about one hundred needy Sephardim that his visitors would prepare. As regards the two mass emigration programs for which the IKG was at that time responsible, the Sephardim would receive appropriate consideration.[20]

But the doughty Sephardim were not yet ready to give up. A few days later, Löwenherz received another letter, this time from Paul Goodman of the Spanish and Portuguese Jews Congregation in London. Goodman made inquiry regarding complaints about the

*The forecourt of the Turkish (i.e., Sephardi) Synagogue (*Türkischer Tempel*) in Vienna's Second District (Leopoldstadt) following Kristallnacht. (DÖW Foto 8392, 5/32 or DÖW Foto 8392 - 4/10)*

unequal treatment of the needs of the Sephardi Jews of Vienna. Trouble with the London community, the origin of a major portion of the contributions that sustained the Jews of Vienna, was what Löwenherz needed least. He answered Goodman that the complaint was unjustified, since all the Jews of Vienna received support regardless of whether they were Sephardi or not. He informed Goodman that the Sephardi community had been dissolved, that it was small to start with, that their former leaders estimated that there were only about one hundred needy people left, and that at present the IKG had sixty thousand needy people in its care. The whole matter was irresponsible and nothing less than *Brunnenvergiftung* (well poisoning).[21]

By return mail Mr. Goodman responded with an apology, and this ended the matter of the Sephardi Jews of Vienna.[22] For the pitiful remnant of the venerable community of Vienna's Sephardim, it was a last cry of defiance—albeit directed at Löwenherz and the IKG, as they were overwhelmed by the progress of incomprehensible events. Within the wider context of the liquidation of Viennese Jewry it was a small matter. The denouement of this affair shows not only that Eichmann's resolution of the problem of Sephardi autonomy was untenable but that the leadership function that Löwenherz was the first to exercise was just as untenable, for it meant that Löwenherz had to execute the policy that was handed down to him and was neither willed nor in accordance with the interests of those affected by it, that he had to be at the receiving end of the ire, frustration, and accusations of those who were the victims of the policy, and that he had to be the willing lightning rod of such outbursts in order to maintain the balance for the victims of services and benefits of which he was the provider and dispenser. The case of the dissolution of Vienna's Sephardi community serves to illustrate the problematic nature of the kind of Jewish leadership that was emerging in Vienna: in what way it had to be different and in what manner someone like Löwenherz was able to exercise such leadership. Indeed, we must ask why anyone would be willing to do so.

The way in which the liquidation of the Jewish organizations of Vienna was undertaken demonstrates how decisively the Nazis meant to proceed against Jewish existence in Vienna. It also reveals—in bare outline but unmistakably—that an unprecedented type of Jewish leadership was suddenly taking shape in Vienna. On the surface, it may seem that the structure of the leadership and the patterns of its operation followed lines familiar from the past, in particular those that had evolved for dealing with the Jewish question in the Altreich prior to the Anschluss. But, as we look more closely, we will see that this is not the case. Even though some of the features of this new way of exercising Jewish leadership did not emerge right away and required the trials of experience to assume their distinctive shape, in the main they were in place at or near the beginning. Let us take up some questions in order to elucidate this development.

The Organization of Vienna's Jewish Community under Nazi Rule

First: Whence its mandate, whither its responsibility? Vienna's Jewish leadership during the Nazi years did not derive its mandate from the Jews or from representatives of Jewish interests, nor was it based on duly enacted provisions governing such representations, as had been the case heretofore. The forced incorporation of the Sephardi community is a case in point. The IKG had, in effect, been abolished along with all other Jewish organizations. Henceforth, its existence as a functioning entity to which one turned or with which one dealt was no longer intrinsic to the will, needs, and interests of those for whose sake it supposedly existed. Henceforth, its presence as a legal entity, with assets and liabilities, with properties and obligations, was a matter of pragmatic temporary sufferance on the part of the Nazis pending its liquidation. Henceforth, the function of the IKG was external to its interests and to those of its constituency. All its efforts were now directed toward getting rid of this constituency. This was the very opposite of its original function of promoting the Jewish presence in Vienna and of serving its interests. From now on, the original functions of the IKG, to the extent that they were grudgingly permitted at all, were ancillary to that main function. To be sure, the "IKG" now presented itself, as before, under this designation, and the chief executive not only also operated under the original title of *Amtsdirektor* (Director of the Board), but was the same Dr. Josef Löwenherz. In this way, the operation and function of the IKG and its leadership bore the semblance of continuing what had existed up to then. Evidently this semblance served the interests of those whose fiat established the new IKG and installed its new—or reinstalled its old—leadership. Any thought Eichmann or his superiors in Berlin may have had at this time of making the abolition of self-organized Jewish life in Vienna complete by replacing the factually defunct designation of *Israelitische Kultusgemeinde* (Community of the Israelite Rite) with something like "Council of Jews" (*Judenrat*) ran afoul of practical considerations. One of these was that the Jewish World Congress and Jewish organizations in England and in the United States would balk at supporting any but an established Jewish organization. There is some evidence that the Nazis retained a semblance of the old IKG under precisely such pressures exerted by these organizations. Another was that the IKG would be a more effective and efficient instrument of dealing with the Jews if they felt that they were turning to their own familiar community organization. In effect the "reopening" of the IKG marked the emergence of a territorially restricted organization of Jews with an externally imposed *function* that was that *of ridding Vienna of Jews*, for the time being through emigration. The same pattern was to be repeated in other cities seized or conquered by the Nazis, in the same disguised form one year later in Prague and other Czech communities, and in explicit form one-and-a-half years later in Warsaw and other Polish communities. By then this explicit purpose would be formalized in Heydrich's directive of September 21, 1939. In the meantime,, the Viennese pattern was applied in the Altreich after Kristallnacht. The nominal abolition of the IKG—following what in effect had been its factual abolition on March 18, 1938, and its merely apparent "reopening" on May 2, 1938—occurred in November 1942, a year after emigration had been halted at Himmler's order, after the deportation to the east and to their death of most of the remaining Jews of Vienna had been completed, and when, for these reasons as well as that of the overt hostilities between the United States and Nazi Germany, support from the American Joint Distribution Committee (also known as the Joint or AJDC) had become useless and indeed impossible. It was only at that time that the designation IKG was supplanted by *Judenrat Wien* (Jewish Council of Vienna).

No organization like the new IKG, no such leadership had existed in Nazi Germany prior to the Anschluss. The *Reichsvertretung der Deutschen Juden* (National Representation of German Jews) was established and functioned to meet the needs of the various politically divided factions of Jews and of the scattered autonomous communities in order to represent and promote common actions and interests. The *Reichsvertretung*[23] was a body of representatives whose personal stature and authority enabled them to rise above the orientation of the faction or community they represented. It was a relatively small consortium of associates that formulated policy in the interest of German Jewry in response to the difficulties of the times and tried to find ways of acting vis-à-vis German authorities in accordance with such policy through representation, negotiation, or old, non-Jewish contacts. Even though the Nazi authorities desired the emigration of Jews, the *Reichsvertretung* did not feel constrained to consider it its primary task to facilitate emigration or to urge their Jews to pack up and go.[24] In fact, in the period prior to the Anschluss, they left matters pertaining to emigration largely to the various communities and to three national organizations, only one of which was fully incorporated into the *Reichsvertretung* at an early date, namely, the *Zentralausschuss für Hilfe und Aufbau* (Central Committee for Aid and Reconstruction). Sometime after the Anschluss, the organization of the Jews in Berlin and the Altreich was made to follow the functional paradigm instituted by the Nazis in Vienna as regards both the accountability and the provenance of mandates. Accountability to the Nazis was hardly a factor in Berlin, as can be seen from these passages in a report by Benno Cohn, one of the founders, in 1934, and main functionaries of the *Reichsverband Jüdischer Kulturbünde* (National Association of Jewish Cultural Organizations), whose establishment was sponsored by the *Reichsvertretung*. About the founding of the latter in 1933, Cohn reports that it

> . . . occurred without any official interference whatever. The Gestapo took no interest in it at all. Its founding was simply reported to the Ministry of the Interior, but the State took no interest in it either.[25]

In 1935, the relevant Nazi official attempted to install a new leadership of the Reichsverband, a move strongly resisted by both the Reichsverband and the *Reichsvertretung*. In Cohn's words:

> The whole thing is a chapter in the battle for Jewish autonomy. We regarded it as a battle for principles because, if we had given in, the Gestapo would soon have imposed on us a president of the *Reichsvertretung*. We were convinced, as were Baeck and Hirsch, that we had to fight this battle to the end in any case.[26]

Clearly the "battle for Jewish autonomy," which was fought in Berlin, was first lost in Vienna—and then in Berlin and points east. It could be fought in Berlin as long as the Nazi regime was in a state of consolidation that was also a period of learning how to deal with what they programmatically regarded as the Jewish problem. There is no better way of illustrating this than with a remark in Cohn's report: "After April 1, 1933 [i.e., after the boycott of Jewish businesses] there was at first no activity on the part of the Nazis in regard to Jewish affairs. [Otto] Kuchmann, the official commissioner, who was then a minor functionary"—and would in Vienna again be in a subordinate position—had to *ante-chambrieren*,[27] that is, cool his heels in the waiting room when he came to the headquarters of the main Jewish organizations, where he "was given a number like everyone else and had to wait his turn. At first the representatives [of the Nazis] were diffident, and broke that habit only gradually." By the time consolidation gave way to enactment of their policy, that is, by the time of the Anschluss and after, when they were confronted with the task of solving the "Jewish problem" in Vienna, the Nazis had not only learned how to behave in a manner befitting their authority—especially vis-à-vis a Jew, no matter who he was—but also that this enactment could hardly be entrusted to "Jewish autonomy."

How little the *Reichsvertretung* perceived the Nazi policy regarding the Jews as a threat implying a decisive liquidation policy, and how little they regarded the facilitation of emigration as their internally mandated Jewish responsibility, can be seen from the minutes of a discussion held by former members in January 1945 who were immigrants to Palestine, at a time when the fact—though not the horrendous details—of the catastrophe had become known. Reviewing the accomplishments of the *Reichsvertretung* in the first few years subsequent to its foundation, a certain Dr. Lubinski adds the following:

> At that time, we were able to realize an important positive fact: a solidarity that grew out of our need. . . . On the other hand . . . we were all guilty of a lack of foresight, of imagination. Indeed, I would venture to say that the successful organizational structure of the *Reichsvertretung*, which had its high points—intellectual high points such as the conference on adult education in Herrlingen—too often misled us and caused us to protract the process of liquidating German Jewry. We still believed at that time that it was possible, in this Hitler Germany, to work for a renaissance of Jewish culture and to arrive at a normalized organization of Jewish life. The historic guilt borne in common by all those who were responsible for the form of our communal life in Germany lies in that we believed we had much more time than was the case. I am reminded of the discussion in which we favored the preservation of the various [Jewish] communities. Thus, we delayed the emigration plans of individuals as well as the liquidation of the total [Jewish presence] and bear various degrees of responsibility.[28]

We have no interest in quoting these self-recriminations for choices under the duress of the period before the Anschluss for any reason other than to characterize, by juxtaposition, the determinants of the novel situation in Vienna. The policy of ranking emigration behind Jewish renewal under the condition of a fatherland straying into persecution of loyal patriots—a policy followed with discrete deliberation by the *Reichsvertretung* as the leading organization of German Jews—was surely not lost on the Nazis. The instrumentality of a body such as the *Reichsvertretung*, to whom the Jews deferred and through whom the Nazis could effect their policy regarding the Jews, was no doubt attractive to the Nazis. Less attractive, in fact subversive of Nazi policy, was the circumstance that the *Reichsvertretung* derived its mandate from the Jewish interests which it represented, and that its very establishment grew out of Jewish initiative. It is understandable, then, that the Nazis would not miss the unique opportunity afforded by the Anschluss of establishing in Vienna a Jewish instrumentality for solving the "Jewish question" that would suit their purpose without the hindrances of the earlier experience. Thus it happened that in Vienna:

- The Nazis installed a Jewish leadership on their own authority and answerable only to them;

- The Nazis installed a Jewish leadership with a mandate, designated solely by them, to rid Vienna of its Jews, for the time being through emigration;
- The Nazis installed a Jewish leadership at the head of an organization (the IKG) that, while continuing to exist as a real and legal entity, had in fact been abolished and reestablished under Nazi auspices;
- And the Nazis installed a Jewish leadership of an organization that retained a sufficient semblance of its former character to elicit the respect of the Jews of Vienna and the support of the Jews outside Germany.

From the Nazi perspective, there were other undesirable features to the status and the operation of the *Reichsvertretung*. Again we turn to a report that a former associate of the organization, Dr. Kurt Jakob Ball, wrote in May 1944 in Palestine.[29] Dr. Ball was a recognized authority on tax law. In the 1920s he had occupied a position in the German governmental tax administration and had briefly been assigned to the Ministry of Finance. He knew his way around his field, and he had contacts. Legislation promulgated in 1934 abolished the tax-free status of Jewish organizations whereby voluntary contributions were not subject to taxation. At first the established bureaucracies did not enforce this law because, on the one hand, discriminatory tax practices conflicted with the tax structure of the Weimar Republic under which they operated and, on the other, enforcement would have been beyond the capacity of their staff. However, inasmuch as Nazis were gradually installed in the different segments of the bureaucracies, the danger arose in 1936 that nonenforcement would cease. It does not take much imagination to see what this would do to the viability of these organizations, especially to their efforts of promoting emigration, or to the willingness of donors, especially overseas, to support them. Acting on Dr. Ball's advice and in part through his contacts, ways were found to prepare briefs that could be decided favorably by reasonable authorities, who saw that ruining the organizations through discriminatory taxation would not be conducive to a successful emigration policy. What is of interest here is not so much the fact that it was a Nazi official within the ministry who interposed himself and blocked a decision unfavorable to the Jewish organizations—at least until Kristallnacht—and thus changed the thrust of dealing with the Jewish question for all of Germany. Rather, what is of greater interest to us here is that it surely must have been entirely at odds with Nazi policy for Jews to prepare briefs for the relief of disabilities imposed by Nazi legislation, to do so on their own initiative and through official contacts which they sought out and activated as they saw fit.

Let us consider the case reported by Dr. Ball: No doubt the impetus of the Nazi law that gave rise to the case was the expropriation of Jewish assets. But in this case, one Nazi cause conflicted with another, namely, with Jewish emigration. Unless the Nazis took matters into their own hands through control and coordination, Jews could play off one cause against the other. Moreover, the Jews could do so with the collusion of a collegial network of the very civil service that the Nazis had been trying to take hold of intact and make it serve the policies issuing from their own ideology. In fact, the assumption of governmental power through the semblance of legality had been the paramount feature of the Nazi revolution and the main factor of the speed with which its aims could be executed. The process, although a matter of the swift succession of decrees and moves, had been gradual enough for the various establishments to continue their old practices and not to notice that the civil service had changed into an ideological service. It is an important part of this picture that one or the other official could be approached by reputable and respected former colleagues or associates who happened to be Jewish. To stay with the example of Dr. Ball's case, the Nazis surely had an interest in bending the cause of expropriation to clear the path for that of emigration. But unless this were to be effected by the Nazis themselves, they had no alternative but to perceive the existing situation as a corruption of their system of obedience to the supreme authority of the Nazi party and the agencies that made up the regime. Moreover, any possible interest the Nazis might have had in deciding, in a specific case, that emigration had precedence over expropriation would be predicated on the guarantee of Jewish performance. However, prior to 1939, there was no way for the Nazis to force the *Reichsvertretung* to execute a program fostering speedy Jewish emigration; for, while the *Reichsvertretung* would not have existed without accountability to the SD, such accountability did not include the responsibility to carry out mandates directed at a leadership installed for just that purpose.

The Nazis had an interest in having knowledgeable Jews articulate the problems encountered in the process of effecting Nazi policy regarding the Jews and in working out solutions to them, and perhaps even in presenting such matters before the relevant authorities; all these were tasks of the leadership that took shape in Vienna. For the Nazis, the aims in any such activity on the part of Jewish functionaries would have to be solely those derived from their policy regarding the Jews. Hence, such activity would have to be engaged in at the option of the Nazi authority, and the Jew engaging in it would have to be answerable to such authority, regardless of his acting at the same time in the interests of his fellow Jews. For all these considerations, the Nazis found a solution by installing a Jewish leadership answerable solely to them with a mandate designated solely by them. Vienna offered a unique opportunity to institute such a leadership.

Nazi Motives

Unlike in Berlin, in Vienna the Jews and their leadership could be isolated—without changing or restricting their location. They were isolated from the rest of the population by the severity of their stigmatization. The non-Jewish population in turn kept its distance because of its newfound convictions or the subtle terror of its own uncertainty. The law, that is, the governmental and administrative agencies, were all in the process of being abrogated and incorporated into instruments of a foreign ideological regime intolerant of any lingering indigenous authority. Any sort of recourse to the intercession of a potentially willing official who might still, or again, or only now be in office came into conflict with the uncertainty of his status. Characteristic of this situation are the instances of Jewish contacts with Dr. Hermann Neubacher, the Austrian Nazi who was installed as mayor of Vienna. Neubacher always received the Jews cordially and seemed to have been solicitous of their concerns. Yet, it became clear to all who sought him out that his office was, in effect, a dead end. He could claim not to have any information about the most outrageous actions against the Jews in the city of which he was the highest official. In short, the Nazi authorities from the Altreich had settled on Austria like a blight, running things as they saw fit, bypassing men like Neubacher who had helped the Nazis to power, and rewarding them for their efforts by installing them as window dressing.

One other highly significant factor of the novel situation of Vienna's Jewry was their isolation from the Jews of the Altreich. Upon the Anschluss, the *Reichsvertretung*, as the purported representative organ of all Jewish groups in what was now Greater Germany, volunteered to send an emissary to Vienna to advise and assist the Jews of Vienna in becoming the newest and largest community among its clients. This the Nazis forbade.[30] They would, in other words, deal with Vienna's Jews in a manner suited to their policy unencumbered by outside interference. This policy was in force from the beginning when, within two weeks of the reopening of the IKG, Dr. Heinrich Stahl, the President of the Jewish Community of Berlin, came to Vienna, apparently at the request of Löwenherz, who sorely needed advice on how to deal with the Nazi authorities and proceed with getting the Jews out of the trap that had closed upon them. Löwenherz had apparently requested leave to visit the *Reichsvertretung* in Berlin, which had been denied. However, at that time Stahl still felt free to travel to Vienna and came directly to Löwenherz's office. Kapralik reports what, according to Löwenherz, happened next:

> [Stahl's] visit . . . was a short one. After about half an hour Eichmann [SD] and Kuchmann [Gestapo] turned up in Dr. Löwenherz's office. Eichmann, raising his voice, ordered Dr. Stahl to depart immediately and forbade Dr. Löwenherz to have any contact other than in writing (limited to what was absolutely necessary) with the German communities. If Dr. Löwenherz needed advice about furthering emigration, he would be able to get this advice from Herr Eichmann. And he, Löwenherz, should not forget that emigration was the most important thing for the Jews of Vienna.[31]

It would, therefore, be untenable to maintain that the treatment of the Jewish question in Vienna was nothing less than a repetition of what had happened in Berlin, as the most thorough chronicler of the destruction of Austrian Jewry seems to maintain. To be sure, Rosenkranz adds that in Vienna in 1938 there did not only occur a catching up within a few months with what took years in Berlin, but novelties were established as well.[32] However, as we have indicated in this chapter, and as we will develop in the ensuing ones, the treatment of the Jews of Vienna was a new departure from the very start, and even the "catching up" with conditions in Berlin occurred within the context of this novelty. This novelty stands out glaringly if we compare the function of the IKG and its leadership with that of the *Reichsvertretung*. Moreover, in this sense the catching up will prove to have been reverse, that is, the novel function of the Jewish leadership was devised in Vienna and only then imposed on Berlin, and then Prague, and then Warsaw, and so on. Rosenkranz also attributes the "novelties" that he concedes with respect to Vienna to "the inclination on the part of the Austrians, especially the Viennese, to improvise rather than be bound by the scruples of printed provisions." This, too, seems to us to be misleading, since it implies that the enactment of Nazi policy concerning the Jewish question in Austria, especially in Vienna, took place under the aegis of Austrians. On this point, too, we have already indicated that with respect to the Jewish question no less than with respect to other sectors of governmental and ideological policy, the Nazis of the Altreich established themselves in Austria as decided rulers. We have absolutely no interest in protecting Austrians from the indisputable charge of having been diligent participants in perpetrating the outrages against the Jews. In addition, we have shown that Austrian anti-Semitism provided the impetus for the momentum of Nazi policy against the Jews. However, it must be stated that this policy, whose decisive enactment began in Vienna, was brought to Vienna by the Nazis of the Altreich and was administered by them in Vienna. No doubt most of their staff was recruited locally, from among the Austrians; but this does not explain the "improvisations" through which the novel aspects of the policy against the Jews were devised. Rather, improvisation was of the essence for a policy that was articulated in the very process of its unfolding enactment and which made use of existing resources in its pursuit, not the least of which were Jewish know-how, Jewish organization, Jewish service leadership, and the waxing and waning bonds of Jewish solidarity.

In short, in Vienna the Nazis could bring about the isolation of the Jews from any recourse, in effect delivering them to anyone who might offer them even the most tenuous relief from their exigency. The Nazis used that isolation in order to institute the framework for enacting their Jewish policy—a Jewish instrument, indispensable to the Nazis. Through the terror of persecution and the abrogation of rights, the Nazis educated the Jews as to the nature of their exigency, which was nothing less than that they had no right to exist. And the Nazis left it to the Jews to flesh out that framework in response to this knowledge. The ensuing sections and chapters will show how, in doing this, the new kind of Jewish leadership emerged.

Financing the Liquidation

On June 25, 1938, an urbane gentleman, Dr. Carl Kapralik, was at the French consulate to pick up visas for his wife and himself. He was a leading member of the Freemasons in Austria, and his visa was arranged for by Grand Master Camille Chautemps of the Grand Lodge of France, who had been premier of the last Popular Front cabinet, and whose resignation on March 10 no doubt added to the international power vacuum in which Hitler was able to effect the Anschluss of Austria. Before leaving the building, Kapralik was met by an emissary of a colleague in the field of international banking and finance, who was well known to him, with the request that he attend a meeting at the IKG concerning the transfer of funds. There Kapralik was informed that the IKG had been authorized to establish an office for international finance and he was importuned to be its director.[33]

Kapralik was indeed an eminently qualified expert in the legal aspects of banking procedures affecting the international transfer of funds. Because he was Jewish, his career had experienced serious setbacks during the Dollfuss regime. It is indicative of his standing in his field that in spite of religious and racial prejudice, he was put in charge of a central agency established by Austrian banks, whose task it was to arrange for the clearing of funds, which, counter to the treaties between Austria and its neighbors, had been blocked. When the Nazis came, Kapralik was of course dismissed. Because of this fact and the events since the Anschluss, his wife was close to nervous collapse, yet, when confronted with the request of the IKG, she said, "If the community needs you, you cannot refuse." So it happened that on June 27, instead of boarding a train to freedom, Kapralik entered and established a new office. He had no illusions about the risks: "Since allegations of lapses in the area of foreign exchange were, in Nazi Germany, a favored way of conducting persons to prison, any connection with foreign exchange was tantamount to putting one's head between the jaws of a lion."[34] The risk of the matter was the very reason why the services of a legal expert like Kapralik had to be secured; and this was the topic of the initial meeting and the terms of the contract by which Löwenherz appointed Kapralik. The contract specified that Kapralik would gather "legal and procedural regulations concerning foreign exchange"; organize an office that would advise prospective emigrants on such matters; "prepare proposals for transfers and for effecting transfers *in strict compliance with legal and exchange regulations*," and in consultation with the legal office of the IKG; he would also maintain "contact with the 'official' authorities, especially the *Devisenstelle Wien*," the Vienna branch of the German Exchange Office.[35]

Successful accommodation of the official interests represented by that office would solve a congeries of problems besetting the Jews of Vienna and their leadership, all related to finances. One problem was the increasing pauperization of Vienna's Jews, as more and more of them lost their jobs and livelihood. The assets of those who still possessed some were subject to arbitrary confiscation or blockage. Some businesses were plundered in the first few days of the Anschluss, some were closed. Within a few months, most of them were taken over in either a clandestine or an openly regulated process of "Aryanization," or else they were managed by an "Aryan" commissar. Many of them had to be sold at a fraction of their value, and even then the Jewish sellers saw little of their proceeds. Most of the Jews either had no liquid reserves to fall back on or these were soon exhausted. The need to work, earn, and eat would have been enough reason to arouse the Jews' motivation to emigrate, but of course there were others, such as the arrests or the constant threat thereof, chicaneries, beatings, rising restrictions, and disabilities. Yet, even if there were chances for emigrating, most of the Jews did not have the means to do so. No wonder that within two weeks of his taking office within two months of the Anschluss, Löwenherz considered it a basic factor of any solution to the Jewish question in Vienna that "half of them are completely without means," and he requested that the Ministry for Economic Affairs in Berlin be notified.[36] The pauperization of the Jews of Vienna not only frustrated emigration, it put an unbearable strain on the IKG. More and more people became dependent on the IKG for a meager meal, for subsidies to pay rent even for a most modest room, for the care of the aged parents of persons whose opportunities for emigration had to remain unused as long as they had to care for them.[37] Yet, even as the unprecedented demand for their services increased manifold, the sources of intake dwindled. Kapralik reports that by mid-1938 the monthly budgetary burden had risen to ten times what it had been in February, the month before the Anschluss. For all practical purposes, the Jews of Vienna had no more means of paying dues to the IKG; the contribution of the few who could and who retained some measure of access to their assets was a drop in the bucket.[38]

Access to foreign exchange was a problem distinct from that of having the means or the opportunities of emigrating. Some of the few countries that permitted immigration restricted it to persons who brought some capital with them. In this connection, the major problem concerned the recipients of so-called capitalist entry certificates to Palestine.[39] The Nazis permitted a monthly quota of ten Viennese Jewish families to obtain such certificates. Inasmuch as they had to present, upon entry, £1,000, which at that time amounted to US $5,000 or about RM 18,000, the question was how they might be provided with access to the requisite foreign currency.

The Reichsbank permitted the export of only RM 30 in foreign exchange (later changed to RM 10), and Jews had to apply for and receive permission for even this "free" amount. The only way to obtain such funds would be through a transfer scheme such as existed in the Altreich under the *ha'avara* (transfer) system or, since this possibility was not extended to Austria, under a scheme still to be devised, negotiated, and enacted. Aside from the capitalist certificates for Palestine, certain other countries required that immigrants possess various, usually smaller amounts of foreign exchange, and some restricted Jewish immigration exclusively to capitalists. Access to foreign exchange on the part of prospective emigrants was not the only financial problem the IKG faced, but it was the key to the solution of the other problems.

As we read the international press of those times, we realize that the fate of Vienna's Jews at the hands of the Nazis was well publicized. The concern of Jews and of Jewish organizations worldwide over the Jews of Vienna overshadowed their previous primary concern over the oppression of the Jews in Poland. One effective result of this concern was the readiness of the major Jewish aid organizations, mainly in England and the United States, to help the Jews of Vienna through the IKG. However, their contribution was neither unlimited nor unconditional.

If they were to be useful to the IKG in meeting its many and costly needs, ways had to be found of getting the most use out of the limited funds that were to be made available, and of making the restrictions and demands of the Nazi authorities amenable to the conditions of the contributing organizations. The Germans, aside from their strict enforcement of laws and regulations, had no intention of releasing more of the Jewish assets than were absolutely necessary for effecting emigration. Conversely, the aid organizations had no interest in making contributions that would end up in the coffers of the Nazis without being of substantial help to the Jews.

Thus the Nazis would have to refrain from enforcing the law whereby contributions to Jewish organizations such as the IKG would be subject to taxation or levy. In fact, the Jewish organizations in Britain and the United States did not wish their contribution to turn into reserves of foreign exchange that the Reichsbank would be very eager to secure. While the Nazis, in turn, would not wish to bring about the flow of foreign currency out of Germany, they could release blocked Jewish assets for use by the IKG, especially for the purpose of facilitating emigration.

Access to foreign exchange required a solution that was nothing less than formidable. Soon after he was installed as director of the "reopened" IKG, Löwenherz was involved in a complicated process of eliciting the various aspects of the problem while exploring remote possibilities, moving conflicting interests toward a workable solution, and facilitating an agreement by parties who were in a position to contribute the essential elements of such a solution.

One such party consisted of the Vienna branch of the *Devisenzentrale*, the German agency that governed foreign exchange, behind which stood the Reichsbank and the Ministry for Economic Affairs (*Wirtschaftsministerium*). The Devisenzentrale was represented by Carlheinz Raffegerst who, as an official in the main office in Berlin, had been in charge of foreign exchange matters connected with Jewish emigration from the beginning of the Nazi regime. He was ordered to Vienna three days after the Anschluss to fulfill the same function there.[40] In Berlin a major procedure had been the *ha'avara* system, whereby the export of industrial goods produced in Germany was substituted for the transfer of foreign currency.

In the *ha'avara* scheme, emigrating Jews with means could take some of their assets with them without dipping into German reserves of foreign currency; the British requirement that immigrants to Mandatory Palestine with "capitalist certificates" show assets in the amount of £1,000 was satisfied, and Germany's economic recovery was enhanced through export. In time, variants of this system were extended to emigration to other destinations. Behind the scheme was Dr. Hjalmar Schacht, the financial wizard who was the kingpin of the economic upswing in the early Hitler years and in 1933, when the scheme was negotiated, president of the Reichsbank. By the time of the Anschluss, Schacht was falling into disfavor, and certain considerations on the part of the ideological practitioners in the SD had gained the upper hand. Not only was it against their interest to make it possible for Jews to take any portion of their assets with them and in this manner strengthen the Jewish presence in Palestine but, in one of many instances where ideology made for perverse economic thinking, they considered the transfer scheme a threat to the inflow of foreign currency reserves. Thus, while *ha'avara* and related schemes continued in the Altreich until the outbreak of the war, the Nazis saw to it that it was not made available to Austrian Jews.

This is what Raffegerst communicated to Löwenherz, when he invited him for a first meeting on May 16. He asked how, in light of the Reichsbank's prohibition of the outflow of foreign currency, Löwenherz imagined the acquisition of exchange, which surely would become necessary in connection with the major effort at emigration the IKG was promoting. With the key factor of the—inaccessible—*ha'avar*a scheme no doubt in mind, Löwenherz assured Raffegerst

> . . . that well-to-do Jews would—after payment of all dues and taxes—be prepared to make a contribution of part of their assets, to be available for the emigration of Jews without means, if they were permitted to take the remainder in foreign exchange.[41]

Raffegerst in turn assured Löwenherz that while the release of foreign currency was not possible at that time, he considered the solution of the problem to be a pressing matter—especially in light of the pauperization of Vienna's Jews—that he would take up with the Ministry for Economic Affairs.

Löwenherz may also have had another matter on his mind. To judge from a passage in the weekly publication of the Jewish Press Agency of Switzerland (*Jüdische Pressezentrale Zürich*), Jews throughout the world were concerned about the matter, and it had bearing on the major efforts being mounted to assist the Jews of Austria. At the time when Löwenherz was released from custody to "reopen" the IKG, the Jewish Press Agency included the following in the news from Austria: Referring to the bad situation of the Jews of Vienna—unprecedented especially in comparison with the Jews of the Altreich—the editorialist opined that the misery was deepened by the fact that "the majority of wealthy Jews [had] already left Austria."[42]

Some of the wealthiest Jews were indeed among the first to leave. Some of the businesses of those who had succeeded in modern mass marketing, a success that earned them the ire of non-Jewish competitors given to less enterprising merchandising, had been forcibly taken over and in part plundered, and some of their owners had been arrested and mistreated. Older businesses were also taken over, their owners in effect dispossessed through confiscation of residences and other possessions and through blockage of accounts. Under extreme pressure to abandon their firms through precipitous emigration, these Jews availed themselves of the services of a small cohort of highly influential Nazi lawyers[43] to whom they assigned powers-of-attorney over their domestic holdings, from which the lawyers extracted exorbitant fees in exchange for passports and permits to leave the confines of the Reich within a specified period.[44] These services were not available to Jews who were less wealthy. Thus by the end of April the Swiss-Jewish editor could write with reference to this "majority of wealthy Jews" of Austria that "it is morally unbearable that someone who can afford to live in international luxury hotels *nichts übrig hat* for his indigent brothers."[45] The phrase *nichts übrig haben* has two meanings: "to have no concern" and "not to have anything left over." It was too early to tell on April 29, 1938 (the dateline of the issue of the *Jüdische Pressezentrale*), whether the new hotel guests from Austria would have *no concern* for the unfortunate brothers who were left behind in Vienna. Whether they *had nothing left over* for their brothers was a matter of fact, which could not be inferred from where they took lodging once they reached Switzerland, since the Nazi lawyers really did not leave them any access to domestic assets to which, through their lawyers, they retained legal title pending liquidation or transfer of title to an "Aryan." That these privileged refugees apparently stopped off—at least at first—at hotels they were probably wont to frequent in better times had no doubt something to do with the fact that the Nazis, in tacit exchange for *domestic* dispossession of the very rich by means of sudden expulsion, did not bother about their *foreign* holdings. And whether these richest Jews of Austria would "have anything left" of their *foreign* holdings for their brothers, it was also too early to tell at that time. In retrospect, the editor's rebuke and his tone seem puzzling and are not explained by the fact that it occurred on the same page as two indications that those who were not directly affected were doing their part—a report that £101,000 had already been collected in London for the Jews of Austria and a call to contribute to the "Zurich Relief Action for Austrian Jews." But perhaps it was not the behavior of the new refugees who came from Austria that was meant but that of their predecessors from the Altreich, since the writer also says, "*certain experiences* show, regrettably, that the richest Jews, even though they hold sufficient resources, do not take their moral obligation very seriously to participate, within the confines of their ability, in aiding those with fewer means."[46]

It is interesting to note the implication the writer draws from this "experience." He suggests a choice, a choice to be made on the neutral ground of jurisdictions that are not constrained to follow anti-Semitic policy, a choice under no other duress than that of an earnest motive to help:

> States or cities that grant them asylum would undertake a meritorious task if they were to involve these groups in a relief effort for the indigent, possibly by way of relevant Jewish communities or their aid organizations, and if they would make this a precondition for permitting even temporary residence.[47]

In short: First, the fight against totalitarian, ideological inhumanity was primarily of concern to those who had already become its victims. Second, the kind of choice that Löwenherz and others were about to make was a controversial choice because in effect it was robbery of the rich for the relief of those impoverished by an inhuman ideology, a choice which others "on the outside" were ready to make for these supposed rich.[48]

One other thing needs to be said before we go on recounting the solution of the financial problem of Vienna's Jews. The Zurich reporter's animosity toward the real or anticipated ostentation of the rich as they reached freedom, no doubt with a sense of relief though stunned by what they had to relinquish so quickly under pressure, casts a noteworthy sidelight. In spite of his relatively early realization that the way things were done with the Jews of Austria was dismally different, he shows that escape with body and soul seemingly intact tends to indicate that things were not as bad as claimed. At first this unfortunate attitude threw a discordant note into the reception of refugees, which a vast number of them—rich or poor—were to hear. Beyond that, the reverberations of such discord formed a distinct phenomenon of the Holocaust; they manifested themselves even this early in the perception of the role that Jews played in their victimization and, with respect to it, in a perception that often was determined by appearances rather than by an earnest and just regard for facts.

The liquefiable assets of the wealthier Jews were evidently very much on Löwenherz's mind as well. However, unlike some of his colleagues on the free side of the border, Löwenherz did not worry about how to deprive them of their assets. The Nazis were already doing this. His worry was whether ways could be found to draw off some of this ill-gotten Nazi loot for the benefit of the Jews, and to do so under the conditions under which he had to exercise his leadership. While waiting for word from Raffegerst, Löwenherz sought advice from what must have seemed the best source, the *Reichsvertretung*. This was no simple matter. The AJDC wanted their aid to Vienna to come through the *Reichsvertretung* in Berlin, and the availability of foreign exchange to be tied to the schemes already established in Berlin, mainly the *ha'avara* scheme. And of course, the leaders of the *Reichsvertretung* would have welcomed centralization in their hands because it would have meant greater access to foreign exchange for the orderly and leisurely process of emigration that they had established. In their earliest contacts with the Nazi authorities after the new IKG was opened, representatives of the AJDC and CGJ made representations to that effect. In his account of his and Alexander A. Landesco's trip to Vienna on behalf of the AJDC in early May, David Schweitzer reports that

> . . . we asked the authorities whether it would be possible for the *Reichsvertretung* und Hilfsverein to give the [IKG] the benefit of their five years' experience. . . . To this they gave a categorical "No" in reply.[49]

However, Mr. Rosen, writing on May 8, apparently a day or so after Schweitzer's visit, reported that Löwenherz was trying to obtain funds from abroad through the *Reichsvertretung*. Whether he would

> . . . succeed it is difficult to say. Up until this date the Gestapo has permitted neither the *Reichsvertretung* nor the Hilfsverein to communicate with the [IKG] or establish working arrangements with them. . . . Last week the Gestapo permitted Dr. Loewenherz to write a personal letter to Mr. Epstein [*sic*] of the *Reichsvertretung* asking for technical advice only.[50]

It was evidently in response to this letter that Dr. Heinrich Stahl, president of the Jewish Community of Berlin, came to Vienna to confer with Löwenherz at the IKG. We have seen how Eichmann in no uncertain terms ordered Stahl back to Berlin and forbade Löwenherz any other than written contact with his counterparts in the Altreich.[51] Henceforth whatever consultation concerning the primary task of emigration was to take place, it was to be with him, Eichmann, and with others only at his behest or with his approval.

However, Eichmann was out of town when a more promising opportunity arose for exploring solutions. On the morning of May 20 in the presence of Kuchmann of the Gestapo, Eichmann's rival for jurisdiction over the Jews, Löwenherz received in his office Dr. James Bernstein, who was director of HICEM in Paris, an immigration organization founded in 1927 whose name is an acronym of its sponsors: HIAS (Hebrew Immigrant Aid Society), JCA (Jewish Colonization Association), and Emigdirect (United Jewish Emigration Committee). In the afternoon a meeting took place with Dr. David Schweitzer, the vice-chairman and financial administrator of the Paris office of AJDC, this time in Kuchmann's office. HICEM was concerned with technical aspects of emigration, AJDC with relief work. Löwenherz took the opportunity to mention to both parties, that is, to the visitors from Paris as well as to Kuchmann, that none of the problems connected with emigration could be solved without the support of both the internal (German and Nazi) authorities and the external organizations. This pertained in particular to the financial aspects of the problems, the heart of which was represented by Löwenherz—as if in answer to the Zurich report—as being the fact that under present restrictions "formerly wealthy circles are not in a position to make available contributions for travel expenses of the indigent." To make such contributions possible, it would also be necessary not to expel them on such short notice. Very likely with reference to Eichmann's aborting the contact with Berlin and taking advantage of his absence, Bernstein suggested to Kuchmann that Löwenherz be permitted not only to visit Berlin but, like his counterparts in Berlin, to make monthly visits to Paris and London.

While these contacts were being initiated, a proposal was worked out whereby capitalists could save their capital and transfer it out of the country.[52] It is dated May 21, one day after the meetings with Bernstein and Schweitzer, five days after the meeting with Raffegerst. It is not clear who worked out the proposal or what was to be done with it, since Löwenherz and the relevant co-worker must have guessed by then that even if the proposal was practicable in the form in which it was drawn up, such an initiative would encounter a stone wall. The proposal may have been used in further discussions and negotiations as a scenario of the best possible case under existing laws and regulations. The details of the proposal seem to have consisted of reverberations of the advice Löwenherz had most likely received from Schweitzer and from Stahl before their meeting was aborted by Eichmann's intrusion. It was in fact an improved and generalized version of the *ha'avara* scheme. It provided for the use of Jewish capital for export purposes, resulting for five years (!) in an increase in industrial production and export, which would lead to a corresponding inflow of foreign currency, while at the same time drawing on the Reichsbank's foreign currency reserve only temporarily. Furthermore, the details of the scheme were to be different from case to case according to the size of the capital. The scheme would involve the incentive and enterprise of the individual Jewish capitalist. It is important to note here that the principle operative in devising this scheme was to benefit Jews by having this benefit serve at the same time the interests of Germany (export, foreign exchange) and its regime (Jewish emigration), insofar as these interests could be educed by exercising reason even under these unprecedentedly trying conditions. Now we know that a scheme with such a timetable was tragically out of line with the Nazi schedule for the elimination of the Jews. If the scheme did reflect Stahl's advice, then it is not surprising to see the five years the *Reichsvertretung* had until then been taking reappear in a scheme for the Jews of Vienna; Löwenherz must even at that early date have known that his Jews did not have this sort of time. But neither he nor Stahl could have guessed that five years hence most of those Jews of Vienna who were lucky enough to escape would have left stripped of all of their assets and some of them stripped of most of their assets, while the rest would have been murdered.

It is almost redundant to say that reasonable schemes were of no interest to the executors of Nazi policy concerning the Jews of Vienna. *They wanted to be rid of the Jews, and quickly,* and they wanted this at no cost to Germany and at the least cost to the Jewish assets of which they meant to take possession, and hence they wanted no outflow but rather the greatest possible inflow. Hence, they deployed tested means of arrest and assassination in order to fan the flames of urgency among the Jews of Vienna, in Löwenherz, and in whomever he might be able to enlist abroad in ridding Vienna of its Jews.

It is, therefore, no coincidence that at the time when the difficult process of fashioning the mechanics of emigration, of which the conferences on May 20 with the emissaries from Paris were an essential part, was being worked out, there began a concerted major wave of arrests of Jews, many of whom were brutally beaten and otherwise mistreated, and sent to Dachau. Spouses, parents, offspring crowded the IKG offices desperately appealing for intercession to secure the release of their relatives. Dr. Karl Ebner, a Viennese Nazi who used his experience as a police detective to make a career in the Gestapo, testified after the war at his pretrial interrogation that the May action against the Jews of Vienna was ordered by SD Headquarters in Berlin.[53] No doubt this explains Eichmann's brief absence from Vienna. However, the SD and the Gestapo were two segments of one organization,

Dachau concentration camp: Prisoners standing for roll call (June 28, 1938). (Bundesarchiv Bild 152-23-35A)

and it is not surprising that it was the Gestapo in Vienna that was directed to "arrest undesirable (*unliebsame*) Jews, especially those with previous criminal records, and to transfer them to the concentration camp Dachau."[54] Those who may wonder what kind of "criminal record" might have merited Jews such treatment should be assured that this designation was a canard; Ebner reports as an insider that "the Jews were seized indiscriminately." Only sturdy males were to be arrested by district police (!) and after a brief, prescribed interrogation, the prisoners were to be taken to a central collection facility and a dossier sent by special daily courier to the appropriate office of Gestapo Headquarters. Any searches or confiscations deemed necessary were reserved for the Gestapo.

Löwenherz did not succeed in any of his attempts at intercession. Mayor Neubacher informed him that the matter was outside his field of competence, and Hitler's plenipotentiary in Austria, Bürckel, refused to receive him and directed him to the Gestapo and thence to Eichmann.

Another tactic favored by the Nazis was applied by them to urge Löwenherz on, one which could not help but affect him personally. Jakob Ehrlich was taken by the SS from the concentration camp Dachau to a prison, where he was summarily executed. The ashes were sent to Löwenherz to give to Ehrlich's widow and teen-aged son with the message that Ehrlich was beaten to death by his fellow prisoners. Löwenherz needed no stronger indication of his position in the Nazis' scheme of things, or of what they wanted of him.

It is under the pressure of this desperate situation that the negotiations for a scheme were carried out that required the concurrence of the Nazis, that is, the SD (Eichmann), the Devisenstelle (Raffegerst), the Reichsbank, the Ministry for Economic Affairs, and, beyond the borders, that of the contributing relief organizations, namely, the American Joint Jewish Distribution Committee (AJDC, or the Joint) and the Central British Fund (CBF). Eichmann was in a terrible hurry to get emigration moving at a fever pitch and must have been annoyed that the terror effect of the arrests that he expected to result in a stampede was blunted by the sober reality of negotiable interests and regulations, which it was Löwenherz's task to represent.

It is most likely in this situation, charged as it was with tension and frustration, that the incident occurred for which Eichmann's pretrial testimony has so far been the only documented source. Eichmann reported that he struck Löwenherz but realized that this was no way to secure Löwenherz's cooperation and claimed to have expressed his regret to him. Not only Löwenherz, Eichmann, too, had to learn a *modus operandi* for this strange and novel working relationship. He also had to learn that simple terror[55] was not an effective alternative to the measured pace of emigration that had until that time prevailed in the Altreich. Decades later Kapralik was astonished to learn of this incident from Eichmann's testimony, since Löwenherz, even though he was wont to discuss his contacts with Eichmann with him, had not mentioned the incident.[56] Löwenherz's widow confirmed that her husband did not speak to others about the incident; to her he spoke of it not as Eichmann's striking but "insulting" him. It says something about the man's capacity of developing choices under his unprecedented duress that, in his wife's recollection, he countered Eichmann's brutality with the cool response, "You may be authorized to give me directives, but you have no right to insult me."[57] Kapralik reports that he had "repeatedly observed that Eichmann treated Dr. Löwenherz with a certain diffident regard."[58]

When Löwenherz saw him about the arrests, Eichmann hinted that he would be in a position to stop the arrests, if the outside organizations were to send lucre instead of legates. For this purpose, he permitted Löwenherz and the director of the Palestine Office, Dr. Rothenberg, to travel to London. Eichmann's instructions were simple: "See to it that you get some money." Upon his return, Löwenherz reported that the AJDC was prepared to make a monthly contribution of US $50,000 to be matched by an equivalent amount in British currency contributed by the CBF, albeit with the proviso that the imported foreign currency be available solely to the IKG for purposes of emigration, and not to the Reichsbank.[59] To Löwenherz's astonishment and relief, Eichmann was satisfied and undertook to gain the agreement of the Reichsbank and the Devisenstelle. The resistance of these two offices and no doubt others, especially the Ministry of Foreign Affairs, was motivated by Germany's tight foreign exchange situation. Yet, it would seem that not only Eichmann but also Raffegerst had done his homework.

On June 17 the time had arrived for Raffegerst and Eichmann as well as a representative of the Reichsbank in Berlin, Dr. Wolf, to inform Löwenherz and Rothenberg of the terms of the sort of scheme Löwenherz had been working for.[60] Wolf, incidentally, was a Nazi and, possibly without the knowledge of Raffegerst, a confidence man of the SD within the Reichsbank. The record of the meeting mentions a one-time scheme; however, it is indicative of the pattern followed henceforth. The record does not mention some of the factors at play, such as the source of the foreign currency. The AJDC and CBF were not identified as the sources, neither in the memorandum dated June 17 nor in that of June 24.[61] Basically, the scheme provided for emigrant families of no fewer than three members who, after payment of all taxes and levies, retained liquid assets of RM 30,000 to RM 40,000, to deposit this amount in a special account of the IKG. In return they would receive—in each case with the approval of the Devisenstelle—foreign currency at a rate considerably less favorable to them than the official rate of exchange. At this time, the rate was set at less than ten to one (e.g., for each deposit of RM 30,000 to RM 40,000, the official equivalent of RM 3,000 in foreign currency was released). Since the scheme was approved for seventeen families—against a deposit of about RM 600,000, foreign currency equivalent at the official exchange rate to RM 51,000 was released. At the same time, the equivalent of RM 200,000 in foreign currency would be released to emigrants who were indigent (the report speaks of 585 persons at RM 340 each).[62]

Nothing is said in the report about the balance of the deposit in this special account of the IKG. It was made available for the IKG's overwhelming task of feeding and housing and providing health and nursing care for the ever increasing number of destitute Jews. However, this part of the arrangement was subject to internal and external negotiation. Even though it was instituted as soon as funding by the AJDC and the CBF was assured, the apparently earliest record of its approval by Eichmann is dated August 17.[63] This and all other aspects of the scheme were to be subject to modification, setbacks, renegotiation, harsh measures, and wrangling as time went on. But basically, the delicate balance of risks and concessions whereby an unequal partnership robbed the rich to help the poor remained intact.

It would seem that this unique arrangement was hammered out between the participants who met in Vienna without the involvement of the *Reichsvertretung*. Four days after the Vienna meeting, Dr. Otto Hirsch of the *Reichsvertretung* reported to the AJDC that he had been informed by the Ministry of Economic Affairs that the funds that were to be made available for the emigration of the Austrian Jews would not be administered by the agencies that had been handling the *ha'avara* scheme but directly by the IKG in Vienna. Hirsch, therefore, requested that the AJDC contact the IKG Vienna for further negotiations.

The balance of risks and concessions was indeed intricate. The guardians of Germany's finances conceded to the Jews sole accessibility to the foreign currency contributed by the AJDC and the CBF, and together with this accessibility a rate of exchange far below the official one. The consequent risk of weakening the Reichsmark in the currency market was far outweighed by the guardians' considerable gain. They gained by making Jewish access to foreign currency possible without drawing on the Reich's reserves. They gained in preventing the threat of the sort of trade boycott that they broke by negotiating the *ha'avara* scheme, and they did so by means of a scheme that they thought was less favorable to the Jews. They gained by establishing a machinery of getting rid of what to them was a loathsome burden, namely, the indigent Jews. And they gained by ensuring that Jewish capital would not leave Germany.[64]

As to the AJDC and the CBF, not only did they knowingly become party to a scheme of exploitation and expropriation but, in conceding to the IKG the use of a sizeable portion of the proceeds for the relief of the poor rather than for emigration, they risked being expected and most likely also being pressed to do the same in Berlin and other communities of the Altreich.[65]

Löwenherz, in effect, conceded to the expropriation of Vienna's Jews, but in return gained a deflection of some of what was to be expropriated from the Nazi robbers to the IKG. He also risked the disapproval of all those on whose behalf he had worked out the scheme, without their knowledge, without their mandate, without their assent, and without their understanding.

In the scheme that was instituted at his behest, Eichmann, and through him the SD, may be said to have risked failure in several ways. First, it was a scheme that was as yet largely untried. Furthermore, its execution involved personnel and procedures that were not under the control of the SD. Also, it conceded to the Jews a certain latitude of choice, which in the Altreich—together with the relative absence there of the kinds of pressure of persecution that could be instigated in Vienna—made for a measured pace of emigration at best. However, Eichmann's gain, and that of the SD, was truly remarkable. The scheme provided that the motivation to emigrate that had been incited by means of terror among Vienna's Jews would be supplemented by the kind of management without which that motivation would remain ineffective. The scheme also showed that the means necessary for achieving the purposes of the Nazi policy regarding Jewish emigration could be brought about by activating and tapping Jewish know-how, Jewish initiative, and Jewish solidarity, provided it was handled in a manner that did not simply force but actually enlisted cooperation. Furthermore, the scheme provided experience in coordinating the various bureaucracies that make up a modern state with the administration of the purely political policies regarding the Jews.

All of these were procedural gains. Eichmann also achieved substantive gains. In the main he secured for the SD, as the organ responsible for enacting Nazi policy regarding the Jews, a functioning, well-financed executive agency at no cost to the SD. This is not to say that the organization, structure, procedure, staffing, and dynamic of the new IKG had advanced beyond its rudiments at the time when the transfer scheme was first confirmed. Most of this was yet to develop, and in response to needs arising from the tasks which the IKG was assigned or had assumed. Rather, the establishment of the scheme confirmed the IKG as having the capacity of, in effect, functioning as the executor of Nazi policy and of coming up with the ways and means of exercising this function. The IKG did Eichmann's job of enacting the policy of getting rid of Vienna's Jews, and with his permission the IKG used Jewish talent and Jewish assets to do the job. And more: Through the financial administration provided by the IKG, of which the transfer scheme was an essential part, there accrued to his office an "emigration fund" that safeguarded for his growing operation not only his independence from the purse strings of the SD, but a power base for as long as he would manage to keep his job secure, that is, for as long as there was a Jewish problem to solve and he contrived to have an essential service to offer in its solution. In time this fund, drawn from the assets of Vienna's Jews, would bear the major part of the costs for the Theresienstadt ghetto.

At the meeting of June 17 at which the transfer scheme was instituted, Löwenherz was instructed to announce that potential emigrants who were in need of arranging for foreign currency had to turn for advice to the IKG and the Palestine Office and not to the Devisenstelle.[66] Clearly, the prospect of having an untold number of persons applying, inquiring, and negotiating in ignorance and under pressure was unthinkable for Raffegerst who, Löwenherz was told, would be available only for a weekly meeting with him or with an expert to be designated by him. Thus it happened that a week later, on June 24, the IKG was empowered to establish an office for counseling and assisting potential emigrants in all questions that fell under the competence of the Devisenstelle, not only foreign exchange but also the export of assets—whether papers such as stock certificates, or professional equipment such as medical instruments, or valuables such as pianos, jewelry, and rugs.[67] In this way, it came about that Kapralik was appointed to establish such an office with, as mentioned above, a carefully defined area of competence to negotiate with Raffegerst on general questions as well as with respect to individual cases. Kapralik, as was expected and as it turned out, was a highly knowledgeable and resourceful expert, who founded and supervised a well-staffed office that gave valued service to its clients. His counterpart Raffegerst, whose approval was needed for all export of goods or moneys, restricted himself to enforcing the laws and regulations of the Ministry of Economic Affairs, the Reichsbank, and the Devisenstelle and was sympathetic to the Jews in areas where he was permitted some latitude. The working relationship between the two men would soon flourish into a friendship that was to be renewed after the war. Their cooperation lasted barely eight months, the period of the greatest emigration of Vienna's Jews.

A routine for handling most cases was soon established. The emigrants filled out two questionnaires, one concerning their liquid and negotiable assets, the other in case they were planning to take goods with them when they emigrated. Then, in consultation with the IKG Foreign Exchange Section (*Devisenabteilung*), the relevant papers were prepared together with required supporting documentation, the assignments of permitted foreign currency were made, requests for the clearance of goods were prepared and—in difficult cases—negotiated with the Devisenstelle. All that was needed was the approval of Eichmann and the signature of Raffegerst, where the former was more problematic than the latter. In its heyday, Kapralik's office, like Eichmann's later to be established Center for Jewish Emigration (*Zentralstelle*), processed more than two hundred and fifty cases daily. For the most part, Eichmann was content to let Kapralik and Raffegerst handle this most sensitive part of the financial aspect of emigration. However, so successfully did Kapralik negotiate and process the many problems and cases right under the nose of Eichmann that he found out through Raffegerst early in 1939 that he was no longer safe. It was then that Kapralik quickly immigrated to England. About a month afterward, Raffegerst was removed from his post because he was deemed to be too friendly to Jews, and transferred to a minor position in a branch office of a bank, where he survived the regime.[68]

Kapralik reports that the establishment of the IKG *Devisenabteilung* with the authority to negotiate and prepare the official processing of matters pertaining to foreign exchange was so far removed from what was thought possible that it had not been requested by

Löwenherz and came as a complete surprise.[69] In light of the endless waiting in line on the street outside of the Devisenstelle, exposed to the contempt of passersby and the chicaneries of storm troopers, it is understandable that Kapralik characterized the authorization of the IKG *Devisenabteilung* as a "concession" and even as a "favor" to the Jews. No doubt it was that, but no less a favor of the German authorities to themselves, since by means of this authorization they saved themselves the major expense and effort that processing the financial side of emigration would have required. And, as we have noted, Eichmann himself said that without the transfer agreement "emigration would in effect have been rendered impossible."[70]

A Shifting of Responsibility

However, the executors of the Nazi Jewish policy gained an advantage that can be recognized by the careful observer as a distinct phenomenon of the machinery of destruction and that seems to have manifested itself for the first time in connection with the IKG *Devisenabteilung*. It is the phenomenon of having the execution of harsh Nazi policy concerning the Jews appear to be a Jewish enterprise. That is to say that to the observer, and especially to the most immediately affected Jews, it was a Jewish official and a Jewish agency that enacted Nazi Jewish policy and apparently devised the ways and marshaled the means of doing so.

In the case of the operation of the IKG *Devisenabteilung*, as in so many later cases, the phenomenon first manifested itself in the form of complaints. The processing of most of the thousands of cases earned Kapralik's office the gratitude of its clients. But some of them objected to precisely those elements of its function that, seen by themselves, offended standards of fairness, yet made possible those conditions without which emigration and related enterprises would have been stymied. Some people resisted paying for the foreign currency assigned to them at more than the official bank rate—even though this rate was, aside from being the only one legally available to them, more favorable than any of the highly risky and illegal ways of obtaining foreign currency. Others objected to the fact that a sum of £1,000 was assigned only to emigrants to Palestine and not to others—even though this was a matter of external (British) regulation designed to attract the inflow of capital to Palestine. Still others imputed favoritism to the IKG for selecting a particular group of ten for the monthly quota of "capitalists' certificates" (*Kapitalistenzertifikate*) rather than one or the other of the dozens of other applicants who had been set aside or had to wait longer—even though the selection was made by the Palestine Office in conjunction with the main office of the Jewish Agency. Löwenherz worked out and negotiated the framework of the transfer scheme. The determination of the specific terms of the scheme was left to others and resulted from changing conditions beyond the control of IKG agents; and, of course, the execution of the scheme was largely out of his hands. Yet, Löwenherz was in charge and—already at this early stage—had to bear the brunt of the grievances. Toward the end of the year he would say to Kapralik what he said to others over the years as well: "*Der einzige Dank den wir je haben werden, wird der Undank sein*" ("Ingratitude will be the only gratitude that we shall ever receive").[71]

The work that Löwenherz and Kapralik performed in Vienna was ambiguous in a way in which the work of the Berlin *Reichsvertretung* prior to the Anschluss had not been. Indications are that the *Reichsvertretung* saw its task as one of temporizing and of Jewish renewal under progressively worsening conditions. The ambiguity of the leadership in Vienna was that under the condition of the sudden dismantling of Jewish existence, they saw it as their task to save Jewish existence. There is an indication that the IKG leadership was aware of the ambiguity of their work from the beginning. In the justification with which Kapralik introduced his report of the complaints mentioned earlier he wrote:

> It cannot be stressed enough that without this use of the foreign moneys which were contributed from abroad neither the work of the welfare office nor that of the emigration section would have proceeded. But under the circumstances [not proceeding with this work] was unthinkable, hence the IKG put up with the many complaints.[72]

Decades later, in our interview with him, Kapralik said of the scheme that he administered for the IKG, "No regrets."[73] What was not considered by those who complained against the IKG *Devisenabteilung* was that the harsh conditions imposed on its clients were in fact possibilities realized by the IKG leadership within the margin of choice discovered or devised by them under the duress of given facts. However, the Jews' gain of a meager measure of choice under duress was an immeasurable gain to the Nazis. What the Nazis gained in the IKG was more than a buffer. The very idea of a buffer was at odds with their stance and mode of operation because "buffer" implies the recognition of the validity of a potential counterforce from which one needs to be separated by means of a third entity. In this particular case, such a counterforce would have to be in opposition to the Nazi policy of dismantling Jewish existence, a counterforce which the logic of Nazi ideology certainly did not recognize as valid.

Although the Nazi regime was sensitive to public opinion abroad, it was so only for the purpose of advancing the enactment of its own policy, a policy which its ideology decreed to be the right one. The assumption was that the level of acceptance of this policy as right could be evoked or discerned in the policy of others. The role played by anti-Semitism in the diplomatic efforts of Nazi foreign policy has been mentioned earlier. What better confirmation of the validity of the policy of dismantling Jewish existence than its ostensible acceptance by the Jews themselves, and in particular its leadership, an acceptance convincingly demonstrated in actual practice? Practice, after all, bespeaks choice, and choice entails responsibility. The Jews of Vienna—who, in enacting their grim destiny, had to deal with the IKG—were permitted to encounter none other than the IKG functionary, whom they meant to hold accountable. The functionary, for his part, knew that the choice he made under the whip of the Nazi authorities brought accountability with it: on the one hand to his masters and on the other hand to his fellow Jews, to whom he was responsible in a unique and totally different way.

This squeeze play, within which the IKG leadership had knowingly to operate, had two noteworthy sidelights: First, Löwenherz, from the beginning, took great pains to record the fact that the harsh measures imposed on the Jews through him came down to him in the form of directives (*Weisungen*) from the Nazi authorities. He did this in two ways:

1. In Löwenherz's written account of each meeting with any of the Nazi authorities, he recorded each *Weisung* (directive) he received as such and each *Auftrag* (assignment, commission) as such. Most of these minutes had to be submitted to the respective authorities as *the official records* of the proceedings, sometimes with copies to certain other authorities. In this manner, Eichmann was kept abreast of Löwenherz's dealings with Raffegerst and with officials in Bürckel's and in the mayor's office. In this way also the two rivals for jurisdiction over the solution of the "Jewish problem" within the SS kept tabs on each other's dealings with the IKG, that is, the SD (Eichmann or his substitutes) and the Gestapo (Dr. Rudolf Lange, Otto Kuchmann, and others). Except for directives and other correspondence within the SD and the Gestapo, Löwenherz's minutes are the main records of the official minutiae of the execution of Nazi policy regarding the Jews of Vienna. Since the Viennese records of the Gestapo seem to have been destroyed in an air raid on their Viennese headquarters late in the war, since the whereabouts of the papers from Eichmann's office are unknown, and since no relevant records have so far surfaced in any of the papers of the Berlin headquarters of the SD, Löwenherz's own file of these minutes are the only fairly complete Vienna-related record of this kind. Löwenherz kept this record in a special personal file.
2. *Weisungen* (directives) from the authorities that the IKG had to transmit to the Jews via the Jewish newspaper—the publication of which was required by the authorities as an essential instrument of the execution of Jewish policy—were regularly identified as such.

The other sidelight of the squeeze play in which the IKG leadership had to operate concerns Eichmann's attitude toward the IKG. Since carrying out the Nazis' Jewish policy on behalf of the SD was his assignment in Vienna, the IKG had to perform exceptionably. It meant furthermore that Eichmann could not countenance any complaints from any quarter. For the executor of totalitarian ideology to entertain a complaint would be tantamount to conceding that the rightness of the ideology and its enactment were less than total. Eichmann also needed to forestall criticism from his superiors. This explains why Eichmann was constantly dissatisfied with the pace of emigration and baited the IKG leadership to perform better. It also explains his approval of the IKG as the device that he had created, and he was determined to exploit it to the fullest. As early as July 20, 1938, Löwenherz recorded the following item in the minutes of his meeting with Eichmann on that day:

> U'Stuf. [*Untersturmführer*] Eichmann further informed me that he requires the independence of Vienna to continue as before but will cause Dr. Eppstein and Dr. Rosenberg of the *Reichsvertretung* . . . to come to Vienna to inspect our enterprise.[74]

It further explains why Jews were required to deal—aside from specified and directed contacts with specific authorities—exclusively with the IKG. And it explains the fact that Löwenherz and his coworkers found ways of representing complaints and grievances to Eichmann not as such but by claiming instead that certain actions or regulations represented direct or indirect hindrances to their primary task of facilitating emigration. So convincing was this ploy that Eichmann used it himself to stop or rectify some of the unofficial and clandestine persecutions on the part of zealous storm troopers.

This is not to say that Eichmann opposed the persecution of Jews when it served his official purposes, including overt persecutions that were officially carried out. It will be recalled that he initiated a machinery that was considerably more radical and effective in terrorizing Jews than what had prevailed in the Altreich, and he was able to do so by means of the momentum provided by the outbreak of anti-Semitic manifestations in Vienna in the wake of the Anschluss. Also, the arrangement between the outside Jewish aid agencies, the IKG, the custodians of the Reich's finances, and himself gained its momentum under the pressure of the wave of arrests and "protective custody" in concentration camps that broke out late in May. This, too, was an action unprecedented in the Altreich. The end of the May action came one month after it began, that is, once the transfer scheme was in place. So successful was the action in the eyes of the SD that a similar action was tried, for the first time, in the Altreich as the Austrian action came to an end. As we will see in our discussion of Kristallnacht, Eichmann knew how to make use of official persecutions in order to speed up the execution of Nazi Jewish policy.

With the transfer scheme in place, he had a workable machinery for the removal of Jews and for controlling their assets. He now turned his attention to putting the machine to its work of chasing and looting.

Chase and Loot

With the initial transfer arrangement decided and the IKG *Devisenabteilung* installed, the pending enterprises could go forward. First, Löwenherz was sent abroad to obtain the contributions promised by the AJDC and the CBF and to negotiate for subsequent ones. How urgently the arrangement was needed was revealed during Löwenherz's absence, when the chief cashier of the IKG brought a problem to Kapralik, then in his second week in office: the imminent exhaustion of the IKG's cash reserves and bank balance. Kapralik took the written pledges of contributions from the AJDC and CBF to Raffegerst, who obtained a short-term credit of a quarter million Reichsmark for the IKG without further collateral,[75] surely a rare, perhaps even unique event in Nazi Germany. Once the transfer scheme was in effect, the IKG had to devise two financial programs, both of them with the approval of the contributors (AJDC and CBF), of the Jewish Agency (as agents for the British Palestine Mandatory Government for granting the capitalist's certificates), and of the German authorities, that is, the SD (Eichmann) and the Devisenstelle (Raffegerst). One program concerned the use of the foreign currency credited to the IKG (US $50,000 and £10,000 per month), the other the use of the proceeds from that portion of the assigned foreign currency for which recipients deposited Reichsmark in exchange either at the official rate or at a multiple thereof.

The use of the foreign currency credit changed according to the available immigration possibilities to countries that required proof of money assets. Australia, for example, required £200 per person, some Latin American countries £50. However, the main portion was assigned to capitalist's certificates at £1,000 each per family. Not only did these certificates require the lion's share of the available credits in foreign currency, they also provided the major share of proceeds in Reichsmark, which the IKG needed for its use. The normative version of the vital credit/use equation was the arrangement worked out between Löwenherz, Raffegerst, and Eichmann early in November 1938, immediately before Löwenherz left for negotiations abroad: half of the monthly contributions, £10,000, was to be used for the ten recipients of capitalist's certificates. These amounts of £1,000 each were to be assigned at a basic rate of RM 62.50 per £1.00, which was almost four times the official exchange rate. However, only half of the ten recipients of capitalist's certificates were to be assigned outright at this rate. The other five had to pay an additional surcharge (*Auflage*). The surcharge for these five certificates would be waived if, due to a lack of clients able or willing to bear this additional cost, the certificates would go unused and lapse.[76] The schedule of surcharges for a family of three persons was RM 2,000; of two persons RM 7,500; and for a single person RM 17,500. The surcharge would add at least RM 12,500 and at most RM 87,500 to the basic monthly proceeds of RM 625,000.

If only a single strand in the flimsy fabric of this credit/use arrangement were to break, the whole would become inoperative. Hence, it was important that there be no delays in clearing the recipients of capitalist's certificates either in Eichmann's own office or in offices issuing passports, handling tax and other financial clearances, and so on. It was also important that the full quota of ten certificates be made available by the British authorities. A desperate situation occurred as early as September 1938 when the British consulate stopped issuing capitalist's visas. Seven assignees of certificates were affected, who had already deposited in the IKG account the funds for the transfer of foreign currency.[77] The IKG, in turn, had already used up the deposits for its operations and would not be able to refund the deposits. One month earlier, Löwenherz had warned Eichmann of the potential for a crisis if there were to be a further delay in the processing of the seven cases.[78] Their clearance had been held up in the office of the *Reichsfluchtsteuer* (Reich flight tax), which was an especially stubborn bottleneck.[79] What to do now that a crisis far greater than envisaged had occurred? Löwenherz was out of the country, and Engel, who had been left in temporary charge, was beside himself. He proposed that Löwenherz and Rothenberg ask the Jewish Agency to intervene with the British government. If this did not work in time or at all, new means would have to be found for ensuring the continuance of the contributions and for realizing the urgently needed proceeds from them. This, in turn, would mean negotiating new transfer schemes with respect to countries other than Palestine. But, there were no such countries. Yet, without such transfer schemes, the seven depositors could be compensated neither in cash nor in the form of emigration possibilities. And of course, the IKG's obligations resulting from its aid to hundreds of indigent emigrants and thousands of needy could not be met and its efforts would collapse.[80]

And so would Eichmann's. He was intent not only on exacting performance from the IKG leadership, especially as regards finding solutions to problems, but on maintaining a functioning working relationship that bore some semblance of mutuality. When the initial transfer scheme was arranged, and even before the IKG *Devisenabteilung* was established and Löwenherz went abroad in early July to secure the first contributions, there were signs that the fury of the wave of arrests was abating.[81] Official and unofficial persecution had a function that was independent of—and hence interfered with—Eichmann's enrichment and emigration strategy. And even though Bürckel's urgent directive at the end of June to restrict arrests to cogent cases and to stop proceeding with undue severity[82] did not pertain specifically to Jews, one directive issued by Bürckel's office in mid-August to all Nazi service organizations—including the SS, the SA, and even the Hitler Youth—did: "No party member or member of a party organization is to engage anywhere in any action whatsoever against Jews without assignment from a supernal service office. Supervisors as well as leaders of subgroups are urgently requested to see to it that actions of this kind cease."[83]

Yet, the persecutions continued, and there are indications that they were directed from above. Especially in the weeks preceding Kristallnacht, the Jews of Vienna were increasingly subject to outrages which, added to the imposition of more and more restrictions, caused them to be even more desperate and confused than they had been before. Perhaps the most notorious incident, though not a major one, occurred on the eve of Yom Kippur.[84] It was a flagrant attempt at precipitously taking over Jewish homes in certain districts of Vienna as well as in several suburbs of the city. It was a time, writes Gerhard Botz, "when the terror of the Anschluss-days came to life again."[85] Many Jews were literally pulled out of their beds by uniformed SA men and other functionaries of the NSDAP, the *Nationalisozialistische Deutsche Arbeiterpartei* (National Socialist German Workers' Party), as the Nazi Party was known in German. They were told to pack their suitcases, to hand over the keys to their apartments on the spot, and to go immediately to the Danube Canal, where "there were ships standing by to take them to Palestine."[86] These ships, however, were nonexistent. Others were told to proceed to the Western Railway Terminal the next morning, where there were trains ready to take them for free beyond the German borders. They would only need their identity papers; no passports would be necessary, nor would tax clearances or any of the papers usually needed to leave Nazi Germany. Others, again, those from the suburbs, were loaded onto trucks and brought to Vienna,[87] again under the pretext of being shipped out. And still others were forced to sign away their homes without the "benefit" of such explanations. The misery, confusion, and helplessness of the people thus affected needs no description.

The burden of remedial or relief action placed on the IKG was very sudden and very great. Frantic phone inquiries reached Löwenherz, Kapralik, and Engel at home, who decided amongst themselves to tell everyone that nothing was known to the IKG of any such plans. On the following day, several thousand Jews appeared at the terminal at the appointed hour and were beaten and chased away. Having had to abandon their homes and keys, they had nowhere to turn but to the IKG. The named principals were called from Yom Kippur services and tried to initiate an intercession. However, they found that the action had been undertaken on a day when neither Bürckel nor Eichmann was in Vienna. Eichmann returned late in the afternoon, went straight to the IKG, chided their directors for letting the thing happen, and then—left alone in Löwenherz's office—was heard to yell into the telephone that this sort of thing sabotaged the emigration effort. Before the day was done, the people had cleared the IKG premises, obtained their keys from where they had left them and returned to their homes.[88]

Eichmann, then, could be said to have acted in response to Löwenherz's concern for the Jews in Vienna. But this must not be understood as a service rendered in recognition of rendered service; and of course, an Eichmann does not incur obligation vis-à-vis a Löwenherz. This was not, after all, an ordinary working relation, even though it may have had the semblance of such. Rather, the businesslike correctness with which Eichmann permitted—usually, not always—the transactions between them to proceed, his receptiveness to Löwenherz's intercessions—in some cases, not all—was a *modus operandi* that facilitated the progress and success of what was his task in regard to Nazi Jewish policy.

Within this mechanism of a harsh regimen oiled by motivated correctness and accommodation, Löwenherz and his associates in turn had to find ways of being proponents of Jewish interests that, at an early date, had shrunk to saving mere Jewish existence. There were several aspects to this complex task, each multifaceted and all of them connected: aid to the needy, representation vis-à-vis the domestic authorities and the agencies abroad, salvaging Jewish assets, administration, and emigration.

Emigration was of course the most important aspect of saving Jewish existence. For the IKG, it was also the most complex and frustratingly elusive task, elusive because its realization was largely beyond the control of the IKG. It depended first of all on the individual emigrant's will and capacity. Not every Jew felt in the same way and to an equal degree the anxiety over his very existence, an anxiety that we might have assumed terror had triggered within every Jew. Yet, there were some who decided that they could not possibly be the target of anti-Jewish measures, since they had not done anything wrong—as if the issue had been crime rather than racially defined Jewish identity. There were some who hedged their moment of decision with caution and temporizing, usually those who had assets to preserve and had succeeded so far in being left alone by the authorities. Then there were others who were paralyzed with fear or who, for lack of means or contacts or initiative, simply surrendered themselves to their dismal fates. Those who responded with defiance knew that only abroad was resistance not useless and not wasted.

Most of the Jews did not need to be directed in their anxiety. They were motivated to leave even before their reserves were exhausted, were prepared to abandon what little they might still have, ready even to leave loved ones behind if only to escape the land that no longer offered ground into which to sink the rootlets of existence. They needed no urging, and they went, especially the young who could fend for themselves and who did not feel tied to as yet unliquidated assets or to family obligations. But those who were not so young went, too, if they felt the vigor requisite for facing the uncertain future in preference to the dismal prospects of the more familiar present. They went if they had a place to go to, or if some border was open, or if they could cross it illegally. All went gladly. None went with a light heart. Austria had been their home, they had never considered it otherwise. They, or their fathers, had fought for the Emperor of Austria in the Great War. They were enchanted by the glowing verdure of alpine valleys, fragrant woods, and brisk rivers, by homely hamlets, charming villages, and the splendors of Vienna. Their minds and their very ways of life were shaped no less by the literary and cultural *genius loci* than by the distinctive tradition of Judaism that had developed there. This and little else they carried with them, this and a lasting bitterness.

Viennese Jews waiting in line for visas outside the Polish consulate on March 22, 1939. (AP Photo)

As this kind of precipitous, hence uncomplicated, escape reached its peak and then declined during the course of 1938, it became clear that the realization of the IKG's policy of emigration depended on another, more recalcitrant factor beyond its control, namely, on opportunities for immigration. Borders of European countries, which had been open to tourists and other temporary visitors, were closed or became subject to visa requirements when these countries felt threatened by a flood of "undesirable" refugees whose intended sojourns were indefinite and whose means were limited. We must not forget that it was in response to a request from Swiss authorities for the identification of Jews as Jews that German passports carried by Jews had a big red "J" stamped on the first page. The unexpected severity of Nazi Germany's actions against the Jews was well publicized by the press and alerted public opinion and governments worldwide to a rising refugee problem. Yet, the weeks and months would show more doors closing than opening and of the latter few more than grudgingly.

At the behest of the president of the United States, Franklin D. Roosevelt, an international conference on the refugee problem was convened in July at Evian les Bains on the French side of Lake Geneva. Löwenherz was permitted to attend the conference and to negotiate for more financial support and for emigration opportunities. So, for the second time in two weeks Löwenherz went abroad.[89] What he observed at Evian must have added to his realization of how terribly difficult the situation of Vienna's Jews was, how overwhelming his task. After nine days, the conference adopted a resolution. The preamble thereto reveals the context into which the convention placed the refugee question: Because of its sensitive nature, the problem addressed (the Jews) is not named. Instead, the conference speaks of "*l'émigration involontaire*" (of course the German translation in Vienna could speak only of "*Auswanderung*," that is, "emigration" not of its being "*involontaire*").[90] The convention takes particular note of the fact that emigration on a large scale could have adverse effects on the general economic situation ("*trouble l'économie générale*"), especially if it were to flow to countries with a depressed employment market, and would lead to consequences affecting the public order. Hence, responsible officials could be expected to consider the admission of refugees very carefully and then only within the bounds of existing laws and regulations—which, of course, were extremely restrictive. The problem could, in any case, only be addressed through intergovernmental cooperation, the key to which was held by the "countries of origin" (read: Nazi Germany), that had to permit the refugees to take their possessions and assets with them and to leave in an orderly manner.[91] The recommendations, for which these suppositions were a preamble, are less interesting: The participating governments should exchange information as to the kind and number of immigrants they can admit, according to their regulations. These countries, however, cannot be expected to bear the cost of emigration. The potential immigrants are expected to adjust to the economic conditions of their host countries; they must present documentation adequate for proving their refugee status. For the purposes of coordination, of exchanging information, of negotiating new possibilities of emigration, and so on, the participating governments formed an international committee with headquarters in London.

Löwenherz had no way of knowing at that time that the international committee would be ineffective in improving the chances for immigration. But he did realize even at this relatively early date that the situation was too exigent to wait for an intergovernmental organization to act quickly enough, especially since each of the participating governments most likely was waiting for the others to take the first step. Negotiations with individual governments for immigration within existing regulations, even if these were restrictive, were a different matter. They could proceed without the publicity of an intergovernmental committee. The Evian Conference, as it came to be known, offered ample opportunity for initiating such contacts and led to occasional results. In the open conference deliberations, the representatives of Britain, for example, were very strict in upholding existing regulations but more receptive outside the conference sessions. In the ensuing period until the outbreak of the war, Britain was—in comparison with other countries—quite forthcoming in admitting Jews, individually and in groups, albeit at the same time making the legal settlement of Jews in Palestine exceedingly difficult. Löwenherz knew that in any case Nazi Germany was not interested in the sort of "orderly" emigration that had, prior to the Anschluss, produced much temporizing and relatively meager results in the Altreich. Above all, he knew that the Nazi regime, to the extent that, bending to ineluctable necessity, it permitted some measure of orderliness to the emigration process, had no interest whatever in permitting the refugees to take their possessions and assets with them. Löwenherz knew that the pressure to find places of refuge was all on the Jews and on himself as their representative-spokesman-agent. The pressure issued from and was applied by the Nazi regime, and the Jews had nothing with which to apply counterpressure or to transmit the pressure to the governments represented at Evian. The Jews lacked status, validity, indeed any kind of power base that could have been brought to bear in representing their interests at a level at which sovereign powers interact. Their dire plight stirred the conscience of the nations—enough to arrange a conference but not enough not to state obliquely yet unmistakably that requisite action would hardly be politically feasible. Since the reason given was a matter of economics, Löwenherz knew that to be a selling item the refugees had to have more to offer than their dire need or their being Jews. Hence, he became even more convinced than before that he would have to make his Jews attractive to the potential host countries by ensuring that they would not be a burden but enhance their respective economies. To do so, they would have to bring with them some capital as well as a productive capacity that would not interfere with a precarious labor market.

Consequently, the rest of the year showed frantic action on the part of the IKG to offer, and of the Viennese Jews to attend, retraining courses (*Umschulungskurse*) and to provide youngsters, who were now excluded from the educational system, with some sort of schooling. Professionals and business people were now training to be butlers, manufacturers of toiletries, carpenters, and tinsmiths. Previously stay-at-home mothers were now preparing for jobs as domestics and seamstresses. Teenagers, dismissed from the Gymnasium where they had been preparing for university study, were learning to weave, smelt iron, and make brushes. Young Zionists, whose former activities consisted of studying the history of Zionism, the singing of songs, debating the politics of *Histadrut* (Labor Zionist) vs. *Mizrachi* (Religious Zionist) vs. *Betar* (Revisionist Zionist), and participating in the annual pilgrimage to Herzl's grave, were now undertaking *hakhshara* (training) by preparing to be pioneers in order to build *Eretz Yisrael* (Land of Israel). It is not known how many, if any, were able to build new lives based on these suddenly acquired skills, and it is doubtful that the retraining effort changed any immigration policies. Kapralik, one of those who made this extensive enterprise of *Umschulungskurse* possible, writes several decades later, somewhat bemused, that he is "unable to form a judgment about [their] practical value. . . . But [they] gave the participants something to do; no doubt [they] provided moral support."[92] Kapralik's judgment is based on the earliest experience with *Umschulungskurse*; as time went by, they became more and more important for the participants, especially the would-be emigrants.

Aside from this earnest effort on the part of the Jews of Vienna to prepare themselves for productive new lives as refugees in as yet undetermined host countries, some Jews, in their frantic desire to go to any place under any conditions, could not grasp the mainly economic reasons why immigration should be so difficult. Many devised reasonable-sounding schemes for the absorption of immigrants and were convinced that the reason why such were not instituted was that the potential host countries were not aware of the plight of the Jews or because the Jews had incompetent spokesmen. One such proposed scheme was to transfer the now unemployed Jewish insurance agents to positions to be provided by their colleagues in the field in the United States. By the time Löwenherz heard about it, the preparation of contacts was, to his dismay, making some headway, and he put a quick stop to this attempt of preempting positions and circumventing the competition for jobs in a potential host country's labor market. Such an attempt could have resulted in nothing but harm to the political atmosphere that determined immigration policy.

Among the concerns that Evian brought into focus, the one that was much more serious than the productive potential of the Jews was the necessity of avoiding their becoming dependents of the host country; it was, in short, the matter of securing Jewish assets for emigrating Jews. Before he left for Evian, Löwenherz submitted a preconference report to the Gestapo on the problems of emigration, which he concluded with what we already know to have been his prime concern:

> As long as there is no chance of exporting at least a part of their assets, wealthier Jews naturally cannot fulfill their intention of emigration, particularly since the relevant regulations governing immigration . . . call for proof that the required capital will be imported. In addition, only if a transfer scheme is granted would it be feasible to obtain those sums from wealthy emigrants, sums that are needed to finance in part the emigration of indigent Jews.[93]

This anticipation of the key position of the conference may seem puzzling, unless we conclude that Löwenherz was alerted to what would be the key issue of the conference when he went for his first trip abroad early in July. No doubt he also thought that it would be useful to bring the economic barriers to immigration into the open, so that ways could be found of breaking them down and of using them as pressure against Nazi policy. Additionally, the conference seemed to have held out the possibility of applying such pressure through diplomatic channels. Upon his return, Löwenherz immediately renewed his representations to Eichmann and to Raffegerst regarding the need to enhance the chances of immigration "on a large scale" to host countries through the only demonstrable way that was also of economic benefit to Germany, that is, through a scheme combining the export of liquid assets with the export of goods produced in Germany. Only this time, Löwenherz was able to back his request with the news that negotiations to this effect would be initiated with the German government. It was not recorded who would initiate them; however, it may be indicative that in this connection Löwenherz reported—possibly at the urging of representatives of the American Jewish organizations—that "especially [the United States of] America deserves much credit for the success of the conference."[94]

With or without collusion of the Ministry for Economic Affairs or the Reichsbank, the Nazis were content with their special transfer scheme for Austrian Jews. Eichmann thought that Löwenherz's main job in the economic sector of the emigration policy consisted of obtaining contributions of foreign currency from the aid organizations abroad, contributions that should be facilitated through what Eichmann regarded as a major concession on his part. What was the concession? Nothing other than his permission to release the foreign currency deposits distributed by the AJDC and the CBF for emigration purposes—which was the condition for the contributions to be made at all, as Löwenherz was quick to point out to Eichmann at the time when he reported the results of the Evian Conference.[95] The other aspect of Eichmann's "concession" consisted of releasing foreign currency against a multiple of their exchange value in German currency; but this meant nothing other than his permitting Jewish funds to be used to meet Jewish needs. Potentially, he was holding any and all Jewish assets hostage, according to the policy he had worked out with his home office, namely, that Jewish assets in Germany must remain in Germany. If Jewish assets were used to provide sustenance, care, and emigration expenses, this could not be helped. But, the *ha'avara* scheme of providing Jews with the products of German industry was, to the Nazi potentates, not the preferred way of keeping Jewish assets in Germany. Much preferable was expropriation on the grounds that Jewish holdings were amassed by ravishing the German national substance, that the Jews had accumulated wealth without giving anything in return. Hence, appropriation schemes attached to an emigration process that was quick and hasty were, at this period, the best way of retaining Jewish assets.

Of course, in this way loot was acquired not only by the new proprietors of Jewish businesses, the new owners of Jewish possessions, various tax revenue departments, the Reichsbank, agencies of the party (including Eichmann's home office in Berlin), but by Eichmann's own office in Vienna as well. This loot consisted not only of real estate—in March, Eichmann arrived in Vienna equipped only with a brief case, by the end of August his staff occupied the Rothschild palace—and of German currency, but also of foreign currency formerly held by Jews. It will be recalled that at the very beginning some of the richest Jews were permitted to keep their foreign holdings in exchange for being forced to abandon their domestic assets.

However, this changed when, according to a law promulgated on April 26, 1938, Jews had to report all their domestic and foreign assets.[96] The purpose of this law was not curiosity but expropriation. How to do this legally presented a problem. In August a draft for a second law concerning Jewish assets was circulated among the authorities in Vienna.[97] It had been prepared in June in Berlin and contained three far-reaching provisions. First, it was supposed to oblige every Jew to "offer" to the Reich his reported domestic and foreign holdings for possible use within the German economy. If the offer was accepted, compensation would be given according to the common value of the property, albeit in the form of a nontransferable government bond. The proposed law did not address what benefit or use the Jewish seller was to derive from the possession of the bond in case he emigrated or was in custody or was killed. The purpose of this provision was the orderly divestment of Jewish capital holdings and their assignment to the regime for its disposition as it saw fit. Second, the proposed law provided for the elimination of Jews from industrial management and from unions and denied them the right to acquire property. This provision was meant to accomplish the exclusion of the Jews from the German economy. A third major provision made Jews and their heirs liable—without application of any statutes of limitation—for any claims of damage in business transactions with non-Jews, if "the damage was caused through any behavior on the part of the Jew that ran counter to sound national sentiment" ("*entgegen das gesunde Volksempfinden verstossende Verhalten des Juden*").[98]

It sounds familiar: "The Jews can go, but they must be so good as to leave their money, since they stole it in the first place."

Sections 3 and 4 of the draft give away what lay behind this clumsy attempt to legalize appropriation: They provide for an administrator of the divestment who is to be assigned to the Minister of Economic Affairs but *appointed by the Plenipotentiary for the Four-Year Plan*, namely, Göring. Also, the "justification" (*Begründung*) that accompanies the draft law mentions that the content of Article V—providing the instrument of expropriation and its pretext—"corresponds to the personal wishes of Field Marshal Göring." If this law had been enacted, it would not have achieved its purpose. Dispossession by court decision, case by case, to the effect that Jews "committed fraud and deliberately inflicted economic disadvantages to or took advantage of non-Jews" would not—if at all practicable and reliable—have led to the quick and massive solution that was evidently sought. The events surrounding Kristallnacht would, as we will see, provide Field Marshall Göring with the pretext and the occasion to effect the economic side of the solution of the Jewish problem for all of the Reich, a solution on a scale more vast than the drafted law envisaged.

Clearly, there was an official eagerness to participate in the lucrative plundering of the Jews—using as its pretext the ideological image of the Jew as a parasite on the national substance—and to proceed in this concomitantly with their expulsion, which was gathering momentum in Vienna. This eagerness was becoming manifest in various quarters, so, for example, in the office of the Führer's Deputy Rudolf Hess, which secretly circulated a draft law for the "Settlement of Damages Inflicted on the German Reich by Jews."[99] The law would provide for a special fund to be collected by means of a surcharge levied on the Jews' income tax. The use of this fund would, of course, be dependent on the consent of the deputy of the Führer. The fund would also be used for "promoting the emigration of indigent Jews." However, we know that such provisions had by then already been made in Vienna through the special transfer scheme, and that concomitant control over Jewish assets and their appropriation had been preempted by the SD. No mention of this is made in the letter under cover of which the proposed draft was being forwarded by the office of the deputy to the Führer to Bürckel. It does, however, mention the reason why plans for its enactment were being suspended—"because it has not as yet been determined in what way the [proposed] Settlement Fund would be formed after the measures Göring is planning against the Jews are carried out." What is astonishing is not that the Führer's deputy and his staff wanted to secure a cut of the loot but that they seemed not to know that four months after the Anschluss there were hardly any Jewish earners of income left in Vienna to be taxed, much less to be levied with a surcharge, nor that according to the ideologically determined "measures" being "planned" by Göring there would soon be no such income at all in the rest of the Reich. However, the draft confirms (1) that the speed with which expropriation cum expulsion was proceeding in Vienna made the official regularization of the expropriation of Jewish assets a matter of high priority; (2) that Göring, as plenipotentiary of the Four-Year Plan, claimed a preeminent role in this matter; and (3) that the SD, as instigators and executors of the new momentum in matters of solving the Jewish problem, had preempted the initiative in receiving and disposing of the loot.

However, the proposed laws were not enacted and were to become redundant by decisions taken for the whole of the German Reich under Göring's more active direction in the wake of Kristallnacht. However, the confidential circulation of the drafts to the highest Nazi authorities in Vienna can be seen as programmatic for what was already being carried out there through Eichmann. He was able to do so with Bürckel's blessing, and due to the absence of continuity in law and usage resulting from the takeover and extinction of Austria, by means of an opportunistic initiative on his part that succeeded when representatives of other authorities who considered dealing with the Jewish question to be within their competency had failed, and under the constant control and direction of his superiors in Berlin.

So successful did the scheme of expropriation appear to be in spite of the "concessions" Eichmann claimed to have made, that what he mainly had to do in order to keep it functioning was to maintain the *conditio sine qua non* for its success, namely, a brisk pace of hasty emigration. This he did by applying pressure on the IKG, by making use of official and unofficial persecutions to pressure the Jews, most likely also by instigating such persecutions behind the scenes and by facilitating the emigration process, though selectively and within limits. Thus, we see expropriation as the emerging primary motif on the part of Eichmann's policy at this time. No wonder Löwenherz was unsuccessful in his persistent attempts to ensure what he, with Eichmann's encouragement, thought was the primary concern—the emigration effort—through securing Jewish assets for the purpose of emigration.

From the perspective of the *ex post facto* appraisal of the whole event of the destruction of the European Jews, we now know that what Nazi policy ultimately aimed at was neither emigration nor expropriation. The ultimate aim was to abolish the Jewish presence by any means possible, so also by uprooting the Jews and depriving them of the means of existence. Are there indications that at the time of the first period of Nazi rule in Vienna—which was the onset of the momentum that led to the community's actual destruction—the ultimate aim already was this destruction rather than merely ridding the Greater Reich of the Jewish presence?

In June 1938, at the stage at which the organized emigration effort was being established through the special transfer scheme for Vienna, some urgent messages passed between Eichmann and his home office. These reveal a "policy regarding the Jews" (*Judenpolitik*) within the SD and the Gestapo—a policy of the highest provenance, namely, from Himmler—to the effect of "preventing the emigration of Jews from the Reich to other European countries." For Eichmann the existence of such a policy was a command, a task for him as the executor of SD's Jewish policy in Vienna. However, it was not possible for him both to pressure the Jews to leave—as fast as and wherever they could—and to tell them that they could not flee to the most readily attainable refuges. To put this restrictive emigration policy into effect, he would need official backing and help. One such means would be a directive from Himmler. Hence, he asked for a confirmation that the policy in question existed in the form of an edict by Himmler, and that the Gestapo enforcement agencies officially be informed of it. He was told by his home office that this could not be because while Himmler "approved" of the policy in question, he did not formally enact it by means of an edict.[100] In order to rectify what to him was an impossible situation, Eichmann asked that the appropriate branch of the Stapo receive the "directive" (*Weisung*) to issue passports to Jews, whose validity would be restricted "if possible" to "North and South America, Australia, Overseas Island Groups, Africa, Palestine."[101] It is evident that Eichmann's request proved to be less than "possible"; while many of the "European states, especially central European states" would have been delighted to learn from the passports of unfortunate transients that Germany did not want to burden them with its Jews, such exclusions would surely have given them pause and made them wonder what was in the offing for a country on which Germany preemptively imposed its Jewish policy. Eichmann's request was, of course, not granted, and he proceeded to impel the emigration process whatever its destination.

But what does this exchange of messages tell us? It does not portend the destruction of European Jewry through extermination. It does indicate, however, that the policy then gathering momentum in Vienna was deliberately structured in such a way that its wider European context became apparent—that in all of Europe there was to be no place for the Jews. Precisely because the Nazi authorities were discrete about revealing their ultimate plans (e.g., by not making public schemes such as the proposed selective passport restrictions), none of these dismal plans were known or even guessed at by those who, whether inside or outside of Germany, whether Jewish or not, whether private or official, were concerned over rescuing the persecuted Jews of Germany.

What the leadership of the IKG surely knew by now was that its central task was to facilitate emigration. Its other formidable tasks, such as welfare and the preservation of Jewish assets, were moved away from the center. New departments were set up and large staffs were assembled to handle all of these tasks. The persons in places of primary responsibility had to be carefully selected. In time the staff that Löwenherz assembled amounted to about five hundred people. The organization and the assignment of responsibilities had to be such that the tasks of the traditional departments (religion, welfare, and care of the sick, old, and infirm) continued to be carried out under the new conditions of vast augmentation and paucity of available means. The execution of the IKG's unprecedented new tasks created special problems of staffing, organization, and performance. These tasks were in the main connected with emigration, secondarily with the management of Jewish assets (i.e., their retention and their liquidation). The new departments had to articulate the substance of their charge and acquire competence at the same time as the onslaught of clients began to make demands on such competence. Everything depended on finding the right people to be in charge of the most sensitive of the new departments and on persuading them to serve. We have recounted how this was done successfully in the case of the IKG *Devisenabteilung* and the appointment of Dr. Kapralik. Before the year was over, the IKG was organized into almost fifty departments and offices.[102] A few of these were directly carried over from the organization that existed prior to the Anschluss, such as the central executive offices (the directorate, office management, bookkeeping cashier, custody of properties, etc.) and the central administrative departments governing the specific tasks that are incumbent on a large Jewish community organization (welfare; cemetery; registry of births, deaths, and marriages; rabbinate; schools; personnel; hospital; nursing homes for the aged; etc.). Other departments grew out of the incorporation into the IKG of previously independent organizations as a result of their dissolution and centralization. All the old-age homes, schools, synagogues, soup kitchens, and their properties were now part of the IKG.

Emigration had, in normal times, been a minor concern of the welfare department. It had provided help to transients who were on their way from Eastern Europe to other countries. Now, however, the IKG had to provide counsel to the masses who were desperately eager to emigrate but did not know where to go or how to go about doing it. They needed help with the many formalities required by the various authorities within Germany as well as by representatives of foreign jurisdictions: with the legal, financial, and practical aspects of liquefying, transferring, relinquishing, and liquidating assets; with filling out forms required by finance departments, revenue services, passport offices, offices offering possibilities for emigration, and so on. Consultations about the legal and financial aspects were sensitive, and the departments dealing with such matters had to be in charge of carefully chosen experts, such as Dr. Kapralik. The constantly shifting labyrinth of the how and where of emigration, however, exceeded the competence of any available experts, if travel agents can be called such. The how and where of emigration required negotiation with and mediation among foreign jurisdictions, German authorities, private and public persons, organizations, and businesses. Many of the services offered by departments of the IKG that dealt with specific aspects of emigration depended on the negotiations conducted as well as information developed and obtained behind the scenes by Dr. Löwenherz and his closest lieutenants.

In the wealth of memoirs dealing with the initial period of the new IKG, one can find conflicting claims as to who actually organized the emigration effort. In consideration of the many levels and echelons at which the emigration effort had to be organized, and considering the discretion with which the most essential aspects of it had to be established, it can safely be granted that all these claims are true within limits, limits of which those making the claims were most likely not aware.[103] Those who organized a specific office dealing with emigration, those who carried out the procedures of a specific emigration effort, such as the children's transports or the illegal transports to Palestine, usually were far removed from where the negotiations for the very possibility of such projects and the determination of the means of carrying them out took place.

In effect, Eichmann stood aloof from both the mechanics and the execution of the emigration policies, as well as from involvement in the concrete situation of what was possible and what was not. It was the IKG that managed the emigration process, and within the IKG its central leaders Löwenherz, Murmelstein, and Engel, and with respect to specific tasks a loose team of additional experts and organizers. Some of their members, such as Kapralik for international money questions, were integral to the IKG structure, which Löwenherz had to build; others were affiliated with the IKG, such as, as of 1939, Storfer as organizer of overseas group transports.[104] Some who administered or organized specific emigration efforts worked outside of any affiliation with the IKG. The Palestine Office had its own specific task but worked in cooperation with the IKG, especially with regard to official emigration formalities and finances. The illegal transports organized by Dr. Perl proceeded only occasionally in cooperation with the IKG; since the Perl transports proceeded outside of legal channels, it was understandable that the IKG would try its best not to be compromised by any visible association with them.[105] However, for the same reasons the organizers of the Perl transports regarded the IKG as a last resort in case of failure. Entirely independent of any Jewish organization in Vienna was the Gildemeester action, which was established by Frank van Gheel-Gildemeester, a Dutch Quaker volunteer for the benefit of the emigration of persons who were—in Nazi racial terms—Jews, although they were Christian by religion. The separation of their respective spheres of activity was officially established very early.

From his elevated position of impetus and control, Eichmann displayed an ambivalent attitude toward IKG involvement with the nitty-gritty of the emigration process. On the one hand, he was dependent on the IKG eliciting, developing, and executing the complex and detailed mechanics of emigration. On the other hand, he was impatient with it, since he saw it as the obstacle to the speedy, regimented exodus he envisaged as his contribution to solving the Jewish question in Vienna. Undoubtedly, he thought that even when playing by the rules and attending to details, there must be an efficient way of moving groups rather than individuals. He soon thought he had found a way to show the plodding functionaries of the IKG how emigration ought to proceed. It was the fiasco of the Colombia transport.

The Colombia Transport and Its Aftermath

The recorded facts are few, but telling. On August 1 Löwenherz was directed by Eichmann to receive one Heinrich Schlie, who had come from Berlin where he ran a travel bureau affiliated with the Hanseatic Line.[106] The scheme was to arrange for a party of three hundred families to immigrate to Colombia in a group, apparently much in the manner of the tourist groups that experienced travel agents organize routinely. Herr Schlie would charter a ship from his Hanseatic parent concern and arrange for visas for the transportation of persons and baggage from Vienna to the port of embarkation and for the orderly discharge of the emigrants and their goods in part at Porto Colombo, in part at Cartagena. Eichmann would see about the passports and the expeditious handling of a minimum of other official formalities, while the lucky recipients of this fortuitous chance to escape would in quick order sell their possessions, quit their homes, pack their boxes and bags, and be ready in a matter of days.

All this was under way when the inevitable questions of foreign currency surfaced. On August 17 Eichmann directed Löwenherz to take up this question with Raffegerst and to be in touch with Schlie about the transfer arrangements. An *Aktennotiz* (memorandum) by Engel, dated August 21,[107] tells us that arrangements had been made whereby the group would be accompanied by Engel's brother who, by means of a letter of credit, would deposit at each of the two ports of destination as many multiples of US $140 as there would be discharged passengers over the age of seventeen; this was the landing fee required by Colombia. It was an exorbitant sum, considering that there were four hundred such prospective passengers, and that the total of US $56,000 would have amounted to more than half of the monthly contribution of foreign exchange from the AJDC. In addition the IKG would provide each person above the age of seventeen with US $20 and those under seventeen with US $10, so they would be able to reach an inland destination and establish themselves. Having discharged his duty, Herr Engel would return to Vienna. In other words, the competence of the IKG on tedious matters of detail was needed after all.

The next item in the records of the IKG is another report by Engel, dated August 31, the scheduled day of departure from Vienna to the port of Hamburg. It is a tale of the travails of the families who had gotten rid of everything—including domiciles and furnishings, who, if they still had jobs or businesses, had given these up as well, had hardly any money and only a few boxes at the shipping agency, and had no place to go.[108] What had happened?

Very simple: The kind of Colombian visas Herr Schlie was able to obtain were not valid for purposes of immigration.

What were the consequences and the repercussions of this fiasco? A memorandum drafted by Engel gives a hint of the desperate situation and of his own anguish. Engel suggested to Löwenherz that the authorities ought to return the fees that had to be paid for the preparation of the papers and that they should help in returning the homes and furnishings, which, under the pressure of time, were sold at a fraction of their value. The Aryan buyers, in turn, should be compensated for the ensuing loss. Shipping agencies should be enjoined to store the boxes for a while. The city welfare department should help in caring for the destitute would-be emigrants. Needless to say, nothing like this was attempted by Löwenherz. It was the IKG that had to help these unfortunates, though it could ill afford to take on this additional burden in the constantly burgeoning task of helping the indigent. Engel spoke of taking a loan of RM 100,000 "for a start."[109]

Of course, as for Eichmann, nothing was said by Löwenherz or his lieutenants. But his attempt at showing how things were done properly was a dismal failure, and the IKG's frustratingly plodding but energetic attention to fine points and details of what was possible and what was not, and of what were the ineluctable constraints, was confirmed as the only way of proceeding. Nothing was said, because Eichmann could not admit failure, and Löwenherz could not permit himself to discern it as such, much less to expose it; otherwise, whatever chance he had of serving the Jews by serving Eichmann would be jeopardized. For Eichmann the episode and the presence of the unfortunates of the aborted Colombia transport were a thorn in his side. When the first attempt at deportation took place fourteen months later, Eichmann made sure that the remnants from the Colombia transport were included. That Löwenherz and others at the IKG knew about his failure, and that his failure confirmed that they were indispensable for the job for which he meant to take credit—namely, getting rid of the Jews of Vienna—was a cause of Eichmann's resentment toward them. The relation of Löwenherz and of others at the IKG to Eichmann became even more delicate. It was now clear that Eichmann had to defer to the IKG when it came to carrying through the emigration process. Yet the form of absolute deference to him as the point man of the regime, for which the IKG represented the race of cardinal enemies, had to be observed. Eichmann's failure could be exploited by the IKG only by using the old ploy with renewed vigor, namely, the pursuit of a common goal: emigration. It was, therefore, in Eichmann's interest to speed up and alleviate the hardships of the emigration process.

A case in point was the major reform of the emigration process, which took place at the time when plans for the Colombia transport were breaking down. Many have taken credit for it: functionaries of the IKG, subordinates in the Gestapo and the SD, such as Wilhelm Höttl,[110] and Eichmann himself. It probably occurred to all of them because it was an idea whose time had come. Yet, as we related earlier in this chapter, it was Löwenherz who worked out a prototype of an organization dealing centrally with the complex emigration process and even proposed the name that Eichmann now adopted for the new organization facilitating the official emigration formalities, *Zentralstelle für jüdische Auswanderung* (Center for Jewish Emigration).[111] What led to its establishment?

The luggage of Jews being deported is loaded on carts for transportation. (WStLA, Volksgericht, A1: 871/1955)

Bureaucratic Hell

The daily life of being a Jew in Vienna in 1938 was like traversing several circles of hell. A special circle of hell was in store for those in the fortunate position of getting ready to emigrate. Various kinds of tax payments had to be brought up to date, and a series of tax clearances had to be obtained, even if the categories did not apply. A special tax, which Germany had imposed when it took over Austria, was the defection levy (*Reichsfluchtsteuer*), mentioned earlier. The relevant office was by no means the only bottleneck in the tortuously complex process, but it was a particularly stubborn one. Each clearance required waiting for the proper form at a certain time of day, sometimes day after day, then filling out the form, filing it, making payments, getting the clearance, paying fees, then filing the collected clearances at the office for the general tax clearance, and finally obtaining the overall tax clearance (*Steuerunbedenklichkeitserklärung*). Passports had to be obtained or brought up to date, requests for permission to emigrate had to be filed, permission then had to be obtained. Each of the offices—many more than can be mentioned here—was located in a different part of Vienna, each with its own office hours and procedures, each with its own ways of treating and mistreating the Jewish segment of its clientele. Each trip to an official agency was a terrifying experience. At most places, one had to wait in line, on the street and in all kinds of weather, for many hours and often the whole night. Frequently, this vigil turned out to be in vain if the Jew was not one of the 150 or so "lucky" ones who were processed that day, in which case he had to return and face the same perils once more. For, when the line was formed outside of the building, one had to run the gauntlet of the chicaneries of teams of storm troopers who had organized for this purpose, or the abuse of Hitler Youths and even solid Austrian burghers who were just passing by. Once inside the building, whether old or young, child or adult, one was exposed to the harassment of officious order-keepers, some of them Jews with a criminal record who had been hired by the Germans for this purpose, only in the end to be treated no better and even worse than "ordinary" Jews by the officials. All this took an endless amount of time and endurance and money.

With the establishment of the *Zentralstelle*, the many offices involved in the tedious emigration process were represented under one roof, and the Jewish clients could go from desk to desk in order to attend step-by-step to the carefully orchestrated sequence whereby they became expropriated and expelled, yet fortunate emigrants. The officials were still uncooperative, intimidating, and insulting, but the hard-pressed Jews avoided harassment on the street as well as the days and weeks of waiting all over Vienna, and the order-keepers were now employees of the IKG.

The importance of the establishment of the *Zentralstelle* for the development of the SD into an instrument for the kind of totalitarian activity that would turn out to be the "final solution" cannot be overestimated. It is commensurate with the establishment of the new IKG as a Jewish instrumentality for carrying out the Nazis' Jewish policy. The *Zentralstelle* effected the coordinated operation of disparate bureaucracies for the purpose of a policy motivated and administered by the SD. The IKG was a functioning agency of internal as well as external Jewry, whose mandate issued from the SD. Both developments became possible through the absolute sovereignty of the Nazi regime imposed on a country whose law and governance were rendered invalid. In this sense, it was a matter of course for both kinds of agencies to be reconstituted in a similar situation a few months later in Prague, when the Protectorate of Bohemia and Moravia was established upon the destruction of Czechoslovakia. In the meantime, a centralized *Zentralstelle* was established in Berlin, a city where law and government were now subordinate to the governance of the ideological regime.

Chapter 4

The Persona of the IKG Takes Shape

The *Beirat*

What was the organizational and command structure of the new IKG (*Israelitische Kultusgemeinde Wien*) which Löwenherz built, and what was its persona as it began to emerge in the first half year of its establishment?

It is instructive to look at the composition of the executive council (*Beirat*), which was appointed by the Nazi authorities to advise and assist Löwenherz. The tireless (unidentified) Swiss observer of the Jewish scene wrote as follows when he reported the announcement of what he took to be the new leadership:

> The selection of those whom the Gestapo appointed to the Directorate of the KG is puzzling. They are, aside from some assimilationists, mainly Zionists. On the other hand the official who made the appointments declared that Revisionists and advocates of a Jewish state did not come into consideration.[1]

While the Zurich editorialist had good reason to be puzzled by who was excluded from the list, he was somewhat hasty in dismissing some of those who were included as "assimilationists." The fact that most of the members of the council were Zionists indicates that, for the Nazis, Palestine was at that time the preferred destination for the Jews. Four of the eight members of the council were, in fact, more or less secular Zionists (Dr. Isidor Klaber, Dr. Ignaz H. Körner, Dr. Viktor Ornstein, and Dr. Leopold Plaschkes). The other four were anything but "assimilationists" in any sense of the word: Dr. Leo Landau was politically an independent, personally an orthodox Jew (and president of the Polish Synagogue), who favored Zionism. Dr. Mendel Rosenberg was also orthodox and represented *Misrachi* (*Mizrachi*), the religious-Zionist movement. Finally, Siegmund Bondi and Julius Steinfeld represented *Agudas Jisroel* (*Agudat Yisrael*), the orthodox organization that favored Jewish settlement of Palestine. There were several reasons for including these two: Löwenherz recognized that the *Agudas* had contributed greatly to the alleviation of suffering during the weeks when the IKG was officially nonexistent. Also, Dr. Neumann, who was the would-be *shtadlan* (intercessor/representative) in the period following the Anschluss, made strong representations for their inclusion. The reason the Nazis appointed them is precisely because they were not "assimilationists" in the Nazi sense of the word.

The Swiss observer's appraisal of the appointees as assimilationists was obviously inaccurate and might have been avoided by simple homework; it was also unfortunate. Ironically, two weeks earlier the same observer had commended the new leadership for another feature essentially not of its own doing but which had been imposed by the Nazi potentates, namely, its centralization. Apparently, contrasting the *modus operandi* that had prevailed in the Altreich, especially in Berlin, the observer reports:

> It is remarkable that they had evidently learned from the mistakes elsewhere—how far pressure from the authorities is at play is yet to be examined—by avoiding organizational fragmentation. The IKG . . . announced the establishment of a department for information and consultation in questions of emigration as a first stage toward a . . . central institution for emigration. The strict centralization, whose lack elsewhere caused important Jewish interests to suffer, is to be welcomed.[2]

On the one hand, the Zurich observer approved of the Nazi-imposed organizational framework within which the members of the new Vienna leadership took up their as-yet unknown task; on the other hand, he assigns the pejorative "assimilationists" to them, a pejorative intensified by its juxtaposition with "Zionists." At this time, however, there was, as yet, no discernible performance by which they might be appraised; hence, we must conclude that he faulted them on the basis of negative expectations that he supported by means of a factually misplaced pejorative. This was ominous, for it portended the onset of the later-to-be-familiar practice of faulting men and women in these and similar positions, and faulting them without regard for any pertinent facts other than that they were in that unfortunate position of leadership under the duress of the destruction process.

If anything needs explaining, it is not the presence but the absence of assimilationists in the council set up by the Nazis, as well as the absence of the Revisionists that is so puzzling to the Zurich observer. Assimilationists and Revisionists were anything but the same, yet both groups shared the disfavor of the SD and would not be considered for a position of forced leadership.

The Revisionists were programmatically dedicated to achieving the Zionist goal of reclaiming the ancestral land of the Jews and establishing a state in it through energetic collective action, action that could be vouchsafed solely by means of a decisive, paramilitary command structure. They adopted such an organization in the years of desperate struggle between the end of the First World War and the establishment of the State of Israel. Comparisons—which we regard as invidious—might suggest a superficial resemblance between these means adopted by the Revisionists and totalitarian nationalistic authoritarianism. It may also be thought that the Nazis, recognizing such a putative resemblance, would favor the Revisionists as their authoritarian kin. As a matter of fact, at the beginning, from 1933 to 1936, the Nazis did favor the ascendancy of Revisionist circles in the Jewish leadership, especially that of Dr. Georg Kareski. But, is the fact that Kareski was a Revisionist the reason that he was appointed by the Nazis as president of the Reich Association of Cultural Societies? The indications are that this was not the case.[3]

The Nazi officials, on whom the solution of the Jewish problem had devolved, were at that time in the earliest stages of on-the-job training. They had to learn how to define the ideologically postulated Jewish problem, they had to do so with respect to the givens of the Jewish actuality both in Germany and worldwide, they had to invent and project the ideologically mandated solution to the problem, and they had to learn how to use and shape the Jewish realities with which they had to deal in order to carry out their solution. Thus it happened that they placed great value on Vladimir Jabotinsky's moral influence, which derived from his role in the settlement of Palestine in the face of British opposition. But they were also sensitive to the boycott of German goods on the part of American Jewry, whose enforcement Jabotinksy continued to urge even after the *ha'avara* (transfer) scheme went into effect, by which it became possible to settle tens of thousands of German Jews in Palestine, and thus vitiated the boycott. As long as Kareski was thought to be in Jabotinsky's favor, and Jabotinsky was thought to be in a central leading position in world Jewry regarding the question of Jewish emigration from Germany, Kareski was favored by the Nazis, and then only by agencies that in time would prove to be ineffective in dealing with the solution of the Jewish problem, namely, Goebbels's Propaganda Ministry and, within the SS, the Gestapo. Kareski's credit with the Nazis began to slip when Jabotinsky dropped him, and Jabotinsky dropped him after Kareski mouthed Nazi cant that was as odious to Jabotinsky as it was uncomfortable to the Nazis: Kareski said, in an interview, that "except for relations determined by international law—the Nuremberg [racist exclusionary] laws correspond to old Zionist demands."[4] The Nazis dropped Kareski entirely when it became clear that he did not enjoy the confidence of the various groups of German Jews or that of the representative Jewish organizations beyond the borders of Germany.

Through their experience with the Kareski affair, perhaps more than any other, the Nazis learned that they could deal with what, to them, was the "Jewish problem" only (1) if they succeeded in finding a leadership that functioned centrally and unitarily by combining the various groupings and (2) if they secured the cooperation of international Jewish bodies through their dealings with the leadership of the German Jews. They also learned that the Revisionist connection would yield them neither.

Why did the representatives of German Jewry repudiate Kareski? There are two reasons that in fact represent two sides of the same coin. In order to understand the first reason, we recall that the different, highly politicized, groups of the German Jewish establishment accomplished—in confrontation with the unfolding realities of the Nazi regime—the not inconsiderable feat of creating nonpartisan, central associations devoted to specific concerns, which were responsive to the exigencies of the times: welfare, help to indigent emigrants, representation vis-à-vis the authorities, and Jewish renewal. These associations, though increasingly requiring the sanction of the Nazi authorities, arose from the will and initiative of the Jewish leadership. In the appointment of Kareski as president of the Reich-Association of Jewish Cultural Societies, the established Jewish leadership perceived the unprecedented installation of a Jewish leader who was not selected by Jewish choice but one who was foisted on the Jews. The Jewish leadership resisted in order to uphold the principle of Jewish autonomy, and for this reason repudiated Kareski.[5]

There was another reason. The policy of which Kareski was a forceful proponent and which he wished to effect in the Jewish cultural associations was a program exclusively oriented toward a radical Jewish nationalism. The representatives of the Jewish establishment wanted to carry forward a program of Jewish renewal, one which they had been favoring since the early part of the century, and which did not have such a pronounced nationalist orientation. Thus, there was a policy difference between Kareski and the establishment. Yet, this alone was not decisive. What was unacceptable to the representatives of the Jewish establishment was Kareski's attempt to have his policy prevail by using the authority of the hostile powers that installed him. They saw this as involving the Nazis in matters that should remain between Jews, and thereby as determining Jewish actuality by interests that were not only not Jewish but hostile to the Jews.[6] Thus, we see that the issue was once again that of Jewish autonomy.

Whether or not Kareski was wrong in attempting to impose himself through the authority of the Nazis as the leader of a radical solution to the Jewish problem, in this attempt he proved to be of no use to the Nazis. We do not need to decide whether, in winning this skirmish in the battle for Jewish autonomy, the German-Jewish establishment did the right thing for the preservation of Jewish existence, autonomous or not. The fact is that this self-consciousness, which in this case understood itself as autonomy, revealed to be the very instrument the Nazis needed for effecting their solution to the Jewish problem, one which they would henceforth seek to bring under their control. Vienna after the Anschluss would prove to be the ideal venue, if they would be able to find a way to do it. And they did.

After the Kareski affair, the Nazis resisted the ascendancy of the Revisionists, for the reasons we indicated. But another reason was also at play, namely, the Revisionist agenda of establishing a Jewish state in Palestine. This the Nazis opposed on grounds of ideology and foreign policy. On the one hand, Palestine seemed in their eyes to be the right destination for the Jews whom they wanted to get rid of. Linked to this goal was the fact that by shipping the Jews to Palestine they caused the British trouble in their relations with the Arabs. On the other hand, because of their opposition to the Jews, the Arabs were increasingly recognized by the Nazis as potential allies, particularly vis-à-vis the British; hence, they became more and more sensitive to Arab opinion regarding the settlement of Jewish refugees from Nazi Germany and looked for ways to promote these opinions. In the meantime, however, the emigration of Jews away from Europe, primarily to Palestine, was the Nazi aim in the 1930s. Insofar as the Revisionists were useful in realizing this particular goal, the Nazis supported them and gave them considerable latitude in carrying it out.

At the beginning of the Vienna phase, Eichmann still had to learn to make the distinction between two divergent ways of dealing with the Revisionists—denying them ascendancy and yet supporting their organized emigration efforts. The first of these is reflected in the deliberately announced exclusion of the Revisionists from the IKG council, which the Zurich observer noted. However, the other was taking shape at the same time when some enterprising Revisionists, through some deft maneuvering, managed to arrange a

A flyer printed in Vienna urging the boycott of shopping in Jewish stores: "Every decent fellow countryman, who voted for the Führer on April 10, 1938, supports us and doesn't buy from the Jew." (WStLA Historsche Kommission, A5: 24)

transport of almost four hundred young Jews—of all persuasions—that left at the beginning of June 1938. The transport was illegal in that its participants would enter Palestine without permits and would thus circumvent the quota by means of which the British meant severely to limit Jewish immigration to Palestine. Some of the maneuverings went against the official policy of Germany, such as making foreign currency available and, moreover, at the official rate of exchange.[7] This effort was primarily supported by the Gestapo but not by Eichmann. However, what was arranged through the determination, acumen, and *chutzpah* of a handful of Jews turned out to be precisely the sort of quick, orderly group emigration that Eichmann envisaged for Vienna and which he himself would never accomplish on a grand scale until the deportations to the concentration camps and death sites. Hence, he had good reason to do his part in making possible the subsequent transports organized by the Revisionists. Eichmann as well as other officials of the SD and the Gestapo came to witness the departure of the first transport on June 9, 1938, which was led by one of the main initiators of this action, Dr. Willy Perl. Perl had the participants line up in paramilitary fashion, and before they sang the *Hatikvah* (the Zionist and later Israeli national anthem) and boarded the train, he gave a brief speech:

> You are returning to your homeland from which Roman bands had chased your fathers. You are leaving Austria voluntarily, not as refugees. You will look back with favor to the time when this beautiful Austria was your home, but now you are looking forward to being pioneers of a proud Jewish future.[8]

Things were different in regard to the exclusion of assimilationists from the executive council of the new IKG. Long before 1938—when, starting in Vienna, they took the initiative in the solution of the Jewish problem—SD section II/112, the "Jewish" section of the SD department that dealt with "opponents," had progressed sufficiently in their definition of the Jewish problem for the concept of Jewish "assimilation" to have become an ideological red flag. This is summarized, for example, in a pamphlet entitled *The Jewish Organizations in Germany*, which was issued in April 1938 for intraparty information, as follows:

> The assimilationists, whose views were, until 1933, unconditionally dominant, are committed to the assimilation of Jews to their respective host nations, and, if need be, to their complete absorption therein. They represent the "German-Jewish" idea, and, especially the extremists among them, have known how to exert a certain influence that led astray those segments of the [non-Jewish] population who have not considered questions of race at all or have not wanted to.[9]

What the Nazis meant to exorcise in opposing Jewish assimilation was the conviction, springing from whatever motive, and the testimony thereto in whatever practical form, that one could be both a good German and a Jew. Such a conviction, if unopposed, would be tantamount to validation, and such practice, if not proscribed, tantamount to success. According to Nazi ideology, however, being German and being Jewish were diametrical opposites, and any compromise would continue to result in the sort of corruption of the German substance that the Nazis felt themselves mandated to stamp out radically and by any means. For this reason, the SD and the Gestapo checked the activity of any Jewish group which, in its policy of equal civil rights for Jews, would be expected to seek association with non-Jewish groups pursuing like interests, such as former (and now outlawed) political parties from the right wing to the left, as well as military and veterans' circles.[10]

It should be noted that the Nazi concept did not conform to the Jewish understanding of "assimilationist," so also not to the pejorative sense in which the Zurich observer peremptorily and wrongly dismissed some of the leadership of the new IKG. In the former sense a Jew, to paraphrase the cited Nazi pamphlet, becomes "absorbed" in the "host nation" so "completely" that he successfully hid his Jewish substance. No doubt many Viennese Jews had assimilated in this way and were completely unprepared for the advent of the Nazi reality in which their being Jewish suddenly became relevant to their very existence. However, no prominent Viennese Jew who might have been a candidate for inclusion in the executive council of the IKG was an assimilationist of this stripe. For Jewish consciousness, "assimilation" designated the problem of being Jewish in the modern world, a problem of increasing complexity; hence, it was a term in search of a definition that has proved to be perennially elusive. The problem grew, consequent upon the acculturation of the Jews with respect to secular ways and styles of life and the value modes that belong to it. It grew with respect to the professionalization and rationalization of the basic aspects of life, such as production, commerce, service, consumption, and general education. And it grew with respect to the exercise of the rights, privileges, and duties of citizenship in the modern state, liberal or not. All this raised questions as to the relevance, the centrality, and, in the end, the very nature of one's Jewish substance in relation to the task of securing and maintaining one's existence. "Assimilation" is a general notion, more an ideal type than a concept that has an explanatory, theoretical function; being related to the question of the substance of being Jewish in the modern world, it also has a value component. In this way, to some, assimilation meant the ineluctable condition and vital means of ensuring the future of Judaism, to still others it posed the unavoidable challenge that must be faced in saving Judaism, to others it remained the ever-present temptation whereby Jewish substance is dissipated, if such dissipation is not resisted. Each side had reasons to claim that the opponent's way was the way leading to the extinction of Judaism in the modern world.

The side not represented in the executive council was that of the Union of Austrian Jews (the "Unionists"), who pursued a policy of personal religious commitment to Judaism while securing and exercising their civil rights as Austrian citizens. This was precisely the sort of assimilation that the Nazis regarded as pernicious, and this is the reason why the Union was excluded from the new council. However, it must not be thought that the Unionists were assimilationists in any sense that cuts across the broad spectrum of Jewish opinion on this issue, and in particular not in the pejorative sense of the Zurich observer. There can be no doubt about the Unionists' commitment to preserving the substance of a life as Jews in the modern state; only, unlike the Zionists, they believed that it must be possible at the same time to carry out this commitment as Austrians in Austria. For most Zionists this constituted assimilation. There can also be no doubt that the Unionists vigorously represented Jewish interests within the parameters of Austria's political and social fabric. After World War I, they predominated in the IKG and in the Jewish elections of the IKG directorate. In 1932 a coalition of their Zionist opponents gained the majority. As of 1934 the Zionists Friedmann and Löwenherz functioned, respectively, as president and first secretary of the IKG, while the Unionist Dr. Josef Ticho, formerly president, was relegated to serving as second secretary.

Kapralik tells of an incident involving Löwenherz and Eichmann that concerned Dr. Ticho.[11] Despite his previous opposition to the Zionist solution, Ticho wanted to emigrate to Palestine. Approval for the release of the requisite foreign currency went through the usual channels and landed on Eichmann's desk. Eichmann was no doubt aware of the great rivalry for executive leadership at the IKG in 1934 between Ticho and Löwenherz. Insisting that the likes of Ticho—whom he called "a dog, an assimilationist"—"must never enter Palestine," Eichmann berated Löwenherz for supporting Ticho's emigration plans. We are no doubt grimly amused by Eichmann's show of Zionist zealotry, which he feigned as late as his pretrial interrogation in Jerusalem. The incident shows how the SD tried to use Jewish leadership as the instrument of solving the Jewish problem by activating what they believed to be Jewish motivation, by appearing to promote what they took to be Jewish interests. It also shows to what extent they considered the threat of Judaism to lie in assimilation.

According to its title, the Beirat was to function as a council advising the director, Löwenherz. However, in this function the Beirat was useless and ineffective, and for the following reasons: A council advises on matters of policy reflecting the interests that the councilors represent. The supposition operative here is that both the organization in which they function as councilors and its director exist for the purpose of carrying out such interest-determined policy. The Nazis wanted to retain the semblance of such a business-as-usual Jewish organization, since they evidently wanted to have ready access to an organized Jewish population and to ensure the cooperation of Jewish organizations outside of the Reich. Beyond that, the function of the IKG, as far as the Nazis were concerned, was strictly that of an organ executing Nazi policy and not policy for the benefit of the Jews. The sole function of the Beirat, therefore, was to advise the director on how to carry out what they were charged to do by those for whose convenience the organization existed. Hence, in its policy function the Beirat was useless.

The various services that the director had to provide and the negotiations and representations that he had to undertake were complex and specialized. Hence, the Beirat was also superfluous. Löwenherz did not need a body of advisors. And he did not and could not defer to a body of proponents of interests that they supposedly represented, for two reasons: First, Löwenherz was not in a position to be answerable to such a body. Second, the members of the Beirat, while they had the reputation of having been prominent members of the Viennese Jewish community, had no—and could not have any—constituency that chose them as its representative. As to the individual members of the Beirat, their expertise was either of no use at all or insufficient for what the operation needed. As independent professionals and experienced representatives of Jewish interests, they might have been good organizers of specific task forces. Yet, hardly any of them fulfilled a decisive function during the brief period of the Beirat's existence; the most notable exception was Dr. Leo Landau, who was very active in matters of welfare administration.[12]

There is evidence that the Beirat was consulted or acted as a body a mere handful of times. One time they had to respond to Eichmann's—again unprecedented—"suggestion," given to Löwenherz as soon as he returned from Evian, that the IKG relinquish its library and archive to the state "for the purpose of preservation and to keep it unified."[13] All of the members of the Beirat signed the declaration of relinquishment; one of them, Isidor Klaber, remembers that they had to do so under threat of arrest.[14] In any case the matter was really between Eichmann and Löwenherz who, in his minutes of the meeting with Eichmann, reports that Eichmann "declared—as he says, for my assurance—that both the Library and the Archive are to be brought in their entirety to Berlin, where they will be safe-kept and made available for scientific research."[15] Eichmann added that the matter must be kept quiet so that the transfer, which was to take place "in a few weeks," not cause "incorrect rumors on the outside"—which is understandable especially now that, through the efforts of Löwenherz, he had succeeded in gaining the cooperation of the Jewish organizations "outside" with his new kind of Jewish organization inside.

This need for secrecy may have suggested to Eichmann that a Beirat, consisting of makers of Jewish policy who were well-known and had connections abroad, may not be the best way to ensure such secrecy. No doubt the main function envisaged by the Nazis for a Jewish council was to spread the responsibility for the liquidation of Jewish existence to the whole spectrum of the Jewish Community. That the Beirat in Vienna did not usefully or effectively fulfill this function is underscored by the fact that within a year most of its members had managed to emigrate, five of them to Palestine, and were not replaced. Its only discernible function had been to lend the IKG an image that was attractive to the world outside and congenial to the Jews of Vienna. Once this was accomplished there was no further need for it. The kind of Jewish policy that the Nazis carried out in Vienna could and did proceed without a Jewish council. However, the idea of a Jewish council did not die. Looking ahead at the unfolding process of the Nazi liquidation of Jewry and Judaism in Europe, we recall that the idea of a Jewish council reappeared in Heydrich's *Schnellbrief* of September 21, 1939, when the SD began to organize the first stages of the final solution in Poland. In light of this reminder, we can better understand what the Nazi idea of a Jewish council really was, and that the indifferent experience with the Beirat in Vienna was an essential step in the Nazis' refining the idea into an instrument suitable to their grim task. The reported incident of the council being forced to sign the document whereby the Jewish Community of Vienna relinquished its precious library and archive portends its ultimate function, which was, in effect, to act as representative hostages to signify and ensure Jewish cooperation in the dismantling of Jewish existence. This is even more strikingly brought home by the report that the members of the council had personally to vouch for Löwenherz's return when he was sent to Evian.[16] After the dispersal of the Beirat into emigration, it became clear that Löwenherz, as well as his deputy Murmelstein, were in fact being held hostage; each had to vouch for the other's return from trips abroad.

The Lieutenants

Löwenherz found himself in an extremely demanding position that was primarily executive in nature. The policy decisions he should have been able to make had to be subordinated to his function as executor of Nazi policy. Whatever he might do to preserve Jewish existence had to be done within the framework of this forced function, case by case and wherever he perceived an opening for such action. His policies could not be based on principle or arrived at by deliberation. It is for this reason that an advisory council was of no use to him and was, in fact, an encumbrance. He needed trusted lieutenants to carry out specific tasks, such as Dr. Kapralik as chief of the Devisenabteilung. And he needed a personal staff, and in particular subordinate associates to function at his right hand. Löwenherz was fortunate to have found two right-hand men: Emil Engel and Benjamin Murmelstein.

At the time of the Anschluss, Engel was well over sixty years of age and close to retirement. He had been an employee of the IKG for decades and had worked his way up to become manager of its central operations. In this capacity, he worked immediately under the executive director—who, since 1934, had been Löwenherz—and had a residence assigned to him in the main building of the IKG. In the six weeks when the IKG was officially closed, he managed to maintain some essential services—such as welfare, hospital, and cemetery—from the venue of a nearby coffeehouse, to find funds for these services, and to help restore other services, such as some Jewish schools and synagogues. He was an able, energetic, and resourceful bureaucrat, and Löwenherz could rely on this dependable and effective lieutenant until he emigrated to the United States late in 1940.

At the time of the Anschluss, Murmelstein was only thirty-two years of age. Young as he was, he was recognized as a rising Jewish star both in Vienna and internationally. Like Löwenherz, he came from Lvóv (modern Lviv), the Jewish metropolis of Eastern Galicia. As a youngster, he had engaged in rabbinical studies and attended Gymnasium. After graduation in 1923, he settled in Vienna to study at the university and at the *Israelitisch-theologische Lehranstalt* (Jewish Theological Institute). The latter was Vienna's rabbinical seminary, established in 1893 and abolished with the Anschluss. In the forty-five years of its existence it was, before as well as after the fall of the Habsburg Empire, the main rabbinical seminary of the provinces comprising the Austrian portion of the Austro-Hungarian monarchy, which included Galicia. In the relatively brief life of the seminary, Murmelstein was its second-best graduate. The best was Zwi Perez Chajes, one of its earliest students, who would, in the period when Vienna changed from the capital of an empire to that of a small country, be Vienna's illustrious and revered Chief Rabbi. Until his untimely death in 1927, Chajes was one of Murmelstein's teachers at the seminary. In 1941, when Murmelstein was a candidate to succeed Marcus Ehrenpreis as chief rabbi of Stockholm, both Desider Friedmann and Löwenherz attested to Chajes' highest regard for Murmelstein's achievements as a rabbinical student.[17]

At the university, Murmelstein earned his Ph.D. (1928) in biblical literature and cognate studies at the Institute for Oriental Studies (*Institut für Orientalistik*). His main professor was Dr. Viktor Christian, a renowned scholar in his field. Murmelstein was also Christian's outstanding student, and as such held the promise of a successful academic career. For a Jew this was unlikely in Vienna. Christian tried to develop Murmelstein's chances for an appointment at Hebrew Union College in Cincinnati. Murmelstein, however, not only thought he owed it to Vienna, which had fostered his scholarship, to remain there, but most likely believed Vienna to be the most suitable venue for his career. If an opportunity for an academic appointment should develop, he would be ready with a record of publications. His dissertation was a hermeneutic treatment of the biblical figure of Adam in relation to the development of the doctrine of the Messiah.[18] It established his credentials as an interpreter of the Hebrew Bible with reference to the context of the ancient Near East on the one hand and to post-biblical literature, especially New Testament and other Christian literature, on the other. In this vein, he produced a number of studies in German and Hebrew that were published in major journals around the world.

In the absence of an academic post, his major effort was devoted to his rabbinic career, which commenced early and made rapid strides. At the age of twenty-four, Murmelstein was appointed rabbi of the community synagogue in Vienna's twentieth district (*Brigittenau*), one of the largest in Vienna. Its Jewish population represented all the major shades of Jewish opinion, from Unionist to Zionist, from *Histadrut* to Revisionist, from *Agudas* to assimilationist. Since this community was self-administered, Murmelstein's position as rabbi served him as an apprenticeship in the diplomatic art of making disparate elements work together. In those days, a rabbi was called upon to render decisions based on scripture and Talmud more frequently than is the case today. Murmelstein was also a gifted preacher. In Austria, schoolchildren were required to receive religious instruction and to participate in religious activities, hence synagogues offered religious services for children on Saturday afternoons. Murmelstein's revitalization of these services at his synagogue was emulated in the other synagogues of Vienna. He also shared in a more general way the

The faculty and students of the Israelitisch-theologische Lehranstallt *(Jewish Theological Institute) in Vienna 1936. Seated in the middle of the first row is the rector, Prof. Samuel Krauss. Rabbi David Israel Taglicht is fourth from the left. Benjamin Murmelstein is seated second from the right.*

concern of many other leaders of the Jewish Community over the Jewish education of the youngest generation. One expression of his concern was his frequent contributions to Jewish publications directed at the young.

Because of his oratorical gifts and erudition, Murmelstein was soon sought out as a speaker at occasions when the Jewish Community of Vienna had to be represented. At one such occasion in 1937, he spoke—in Esperanto—at the World Esperanto Congress, which was meeting in Vienna. Another occasion arose in July 1934, when Chancellor Dollfuss of Austria was murdered by a small group of Austrian Nazis who tried to take over the country, and memorial services were mandated at churches and synagogues. The official memorial of the Jewish Community was to take place at the central synagogue in the presence of representatives of the government. The chief rabbi was on vacation. Among those who were in residence, only Murmelstein was prepared to find the right words for the occasion and to muster the courage to speak them in this tense situation that was so dangerous for the Jews.

Murmelstein's teacher, Professor Christian—not an ideological Nazi, in spite of his party membership, but a German nationalist—was peripherally implicated in that *putsch* and arrested when the regime had reestablished order under the new, young Chancellor von Schuschnigg. Under Murmelstein's initiative, a group of his former students secured Christian's release.

Murmelstein's rabbinic and general Jewish studies intersected with his academic scholarship in a number of publications. Four of these are worthy of particular note: In 1937 there appeared a supplement to Alexander Kohut's famous *Arukh ha-Shalem*, an eight-volume dictionary of Talmudic terminology, under the title *Tosefet Arukh ha-Shalem*. Murmelstein was the junior participant of the team that prepared these comments; the others were older, distinguished scholars (Samuel Krauss, Bernhard Geiger, Louis Ginzberg, and Immanuel Loew).

In 1936 a certain P. Severin Grill was a candidate for an academic post at the Catholic Theological Faculty of the University of Vienna, apparently in post-biblical Hebrew literature. In support of his candidacy, he published a small work on the Talmud and the *Shulhan Arukh* (the "Set Table" of Joseph Caro), whose tendency was clearly misleading and damaging to Judaism.[19] The Union was willing to underwrite a Jewish response, and Rabbi David Taglicht (one of the senior professors at the Theological Seminary and soon to be appointed chief rabbi) designated Murmelstein as the one who possessed the knowledge to write such a polemical work on short notice, which he did. It was published with a foreword by Taglicht, under the title *Some questions for Prof. Dr. P. Severin Grill, O. Cist., the author of the theological tract "The Talmud and Shulchan Arukh."*[20]

At the time of the Anschluss, the Jewish publisher Josef Belf was ready to release to the market two weighty tomes by Murmelstein that were of general Jewish interest and were bound in the large format then fashionable in the cultivated mass market. One was *History of the Jews*,[21] the other an edition of the writings of Josephus.[22] The major topics of the *History of the Jews* are treated in four divisions corresponding to the four millennia of Jewish history. The connecting thread is that of wandering, and it follows the spiritual and geographical peregrinations of the Jews.[23] The two last sections of the book deal with anti-Semitism and Zionism. The section on anti-Semitism ends with the flight of Russian Jews to the United States and the establishment of the American Conservative and Reform centers of learning. Murmelstein observes there that:

> Once again the law of Jewish history is repeated, where Jews, forced to emigrate because of persecution, settle in a free place and become a decisive factor in its spiritual life.
>
> As on former occasions, it is the Jewish refugee from Eastern Europe, this time from Russia who—coming to America as the third wave, after the Portuguese and the Germans—takes his place in the [general] economy, while [internally] resisting any movement of reform.[24]

The book ends with the Balfour Declaration, which Murmelstein likens to the last words of the Hebrew Bible:

> Thus said Cyrus king of Persia: All the kingdoms of the earth hath the Lord, the God of Heaven, given me; and He hath charged me to build Him a house in Jerusalem, which is in Judah. Whosoever is among you of all His people—the Lord his God be with him—let him go up.[25]

Murmelstein offered this as an admonition to the Jewish people as they entered their fifth millennium under the political circumstances of those times, which, according to him, entered "a new stage" with the peace that followed World War I:

> In the newly established states the struggle for emancipation had to begin anew, and the downfall of liberalism has led to a changed situation in other countries as well.[26]

Among the political situations meriting Murmelstein's particular attention in his *History*, under which the Jews had to undertake their peregrinations, is the late period of the

Second Jewish Commonwealth (i.e., the late Second Temple Period). This period was marked by the problematic nature of maintaining Jewish existence under the threat posed by Imperial Rome. In this connection Murmelstein subjected the politics of Herod the Great to a reexamination using an original approach that was not taken up by scholars again until after the Second World War. His preoccupation with the problematic nature of Jewish existence brought him also to the study of Flavius Josephus and resulted in the edition referred to above. No doubt there was an aspect of timeliness to this topic. We will see that some who condemn Murmelstein's performance in Vienna and Theresienstadt see him as having deliberately regarded himself as playing a role like the one Josephus had played in his relationships to Romans and Jews.

Soon after Murmelstein was ordained as rabbi, he was appointed to the faculty of the *Lehranstalt*, where he taught Midrash and religious philosophy.[27] In order to supplement his income, Murmelstein also taught Religious Studies, which was a required subject in all Austrian schools, at a Gymnasium. In this connection, Murmelstein reported an incident to us (which could not be verified as yet from another source): With his older students he was wont to discuss pressing matters of Jewish concern. During one of these sessions, he was supposed to have ended an appraisal of the political situation of the Jews with the admonition that they leave Central Europe. Distressed parents caused the school administration to subject him to a disciplinary action on the grounds that he was needlessly scaring the youths, an action that resulted in a warning to him by the Gymnasium's administration.

In 1934 Murmelstein married Margit (Margarete) Geyer, who was related to him and stemmed from a prominent Hungarian rabbinical family. As coincidence would have it, the apartment into which the young couple moved was in the same building as that of Dr. Löwenherz, the first secretary and executive director of the IKG. One of the children of Dr. Löwenherz[28] was then a student of musicology at the University of Vienna and a former Gymnasium student of Murmelstein. In his capacity of gymnasium teacher, Murmelstein was known to Frau Löwenherz, who had taken a great interest in her children's education. She now took a friendly interest in the progress of the young couple, whose only child, a son named Wolf, was born in 1936. The relation between the two men, Löwenherz and Murmelstein, was different. There was a difference in age and in position between them, hence the relation between the two remained one of reserve, as befitted the rules of decorum prevalent at that time and place.

With the Anschluss, Murmelstein lost his teaching positions at the *Lehranstalt* and at the Gymnasium. His synagogue was closed for a while; when it was reopened, it came under the direct jurisdiction of the IKG, from which Murmelstein now drew his salary. But since his activities were curtailed and, as he phrased it, he wanted to give the community full value for their money, he was prepared to serve the community in any way he could. In preparation for hasty emigration, many persons needed to settle pending divorce matters, others wanted to get married to face the uncertain future together. We have seen that Murmelstein had already served as a junior member of the rabbinical court (on March 18, 1938). Murmelstein continued to attend to such rabbinical matters, but Löwenherz recognized that he was capable of more challenging assignments.

Löwenherz's son had finished his dissertation and needed only to present himself for the oral defense in order to complete the requirements for his doctorate. However, the Anschluss excluded all Jews from the university. A new administration had been installed by the Nazis. The new Dean of the Faculty of Philosophy was none other than Murmelstein's old mentor, Professor Christian. Murmelstein had to obtain permission to enter the premises of the university in order to see Christian who, owing Murmelstein a favor since 1934, arranged for young Löwenherz and the other Jews, who needed only a final examination to complete their studies, to obtain their doctorates or certificates.[29]

The third week of the new IKG saw the first issue of the weekly *Zionistische Rundschau* (*Zionist Review*), the only Jewish publication permitted in Vienna by the Nazis, and in fact mandated by them as the instrument of conveying their directives and facilitating the speedy liquidation of the Jewish Community. In conjunction with Chief Rabbi Taglicht, Löwenherz was preparing a brief and effective proclamation to the Jews of Vienna for the first edition. They had to find the right tone and the right words for calling on the Jews to reconcile themselves to the sudden end of Jewish existence in Austria, to muster the will to leave and make a new start in unknown venues, to rekindle the flame of their ancient faith, to renew their solidarity with their people, and to gather from their tradition the courage to survive their days of unprecedented trial. Taglicht and Löwenherz tried but saw that their draft was wanting. Löwenherz thought of giving it to Murmelstein, and Taglicht gladly concurred, remembering that he had chosen him for a similarly sensitive assignment two years earlier in the case of the Grill book. The proclamation, published over the names of Taglicht and Löwenherz, bears the stamp of Murmelstein's thought and prose. The very first sentences gather all the elements of the problematic nature of the situation, all the needs that would have to be met, and all the resources that would have to be activated:[30]

> We find ourselves at a serious and momentous moment; the imperative is "unity and trust in God." What divided us in the past is trivial and insignificant; what unites us today is great and imperishable. This sense of solidarity and of common destiny shall be the source of our renewed confidence. In the face of overwhelming new tasks, all that is petty and troublesome must recede and vanish. The changes in Jewish life are weighty and incisive, and many more upheavals are to come. Hence: Have faith in God, and be prepared.

Solidarity grounded on the foundations of a renewed Judaism must prove itself in practice; nothing else would enhance the chances of survival:

> Not one among us must be left alone in need and abandoned. Jewish compassion and charity must be in readiness to alleviate suffering, to assuage despair, and to rouse the will to live. . . .

But the purpose of survival is to find a place to make a fresh start:

> Soon many of us will be engaged in creating a new basis for life at some far place. Our Community has to provide this wandering with preparation and order, so that we do not fragment and dissipate our capacities. Those who leave should be assured that in their wandering they will be accompanied by the Community's love and solidarity.

We see here a clear reverberation of Murmelstein's conception of Jewish history as configured by "the people's global wandering." And the Land of Israel as the goal of this wandering is also not absent:

> The eternal yearning of earlier generations for Zion, the present hope of rebuilding Palestine will guide him and determine his direction.

Yet, realistically, the way to the ancestral homeland would be open only to a few:

> Not all will have the good fortune to head that way. Many have to take up their labor under new skies, in unfamiliar environs.

But once there and especially while still here, the Jews of Vienna are called upon to brace themselves and muster their strength for the staggering task ahead:

> We want to adjust to the new conditions with dignity and stringent discipline and, through extensive self-help and readiness for sacrifice, offer our Community the chance of further fruitful work.

The first target of such work was the younger generation of Jews. This had been the prime concern of the mentors of Vienna's community in response to the encroachments of assimilation, and the rescue of the youth was the first thought of its spokesmen after the Anschluss. Murmelstein, ever the educator of the young, formulated for the leaders of the community their present task with respect to the youth as follows:

> Our youth should not go out into the world without an identity, without something to hold onto, without self-assurance—but as the bearers of a great idea, endowed with inner assurance and with nobility of soul. A Jewish way of life and well-planned education will enable us to reach this goal.

As for the adults:

> We, too, have to reorient ourselves to new tasks and new conditions of life. Traditional writings as well as contemporary works, Jewish art and poetry should mold our lives and become the source of our motivation and our joy. In turning to the Jewish past, we seek the strength to endure.

This proclamation succeeded in dispelling any illusions that one or the other Jew may still have harbored, yet roused them to take courage. At the time, no one could have guessed the sad and bitter irony of the consoling words with which it concluded:

> Here [in turning to the past] we will find hope for the future, the hope expressed in the words, "God, who has always shielded Israel, will again be with us, and will not forget us, and will not leave us."

Murmelstein's way with words—always finding the right phrase, in direct exchange no less than in writing, always saying no more and no less than what needed to be said, always mindful of the effect to be achieved, always backed by a ready wealth of knowledge, information and ideas—would prove to be an asset that would stand him in good stead in the checkered career on which he was now embarked, and would be used with appreciation by Löwenherz. Even Eichmann and his lieutenants would rely on his reputation for proper phrasing (*stylisieren*), leaving it up to Murmelstein to determine the way their directives were to be officially phrased in the magazine *Zionistische Rundschau*, later the *Jüdisches Nachrichtenblatt* (Jewish Newspaper).

As for Löwenherz, it did not take long for him to realize that he needed an able and resourceful right-hand man, one who was loyal and unencumbered by habits of normal bureaucratic procedure or by commitments based on established prestige, and that he had found just such a person in Murmelstein. In later years, it would be said that Murmelstein had obtained his position of leadership within the IKG by usurpation. But in the files of the IKG for all to see is Löwenherz's appointment of Murmelstein, dated June 8, 1938, and effective June 15. Aside from keeping his position at his synagogue, Murmelstein was appointed as rabbi of the Great Synagogue of Leopoldstadt, whose pulpit had been vacant since the elevation of Dr. Taglicht to the chief rabbinate. Murmelstein was also assigned a number of other rabbinic functions, as well as that of consultant to the school department. One of the contract clauses outlining the many duties to which Murmelstein was appointed seems vague and unimportant but is most significant for the career on which Murmelstein was embarking for the next seven years—and whose ramifications were not known to him or to anyone at this time: It charges him with "carrying out all administrative tasks assigned to him permanently or temporarily by the Directorate."[31] The salary was set at a level second only to that of the director. Murmelstein would soon have his own offices and a personal staff larger than the director's.

The Persona

The new services that the IKG provided soon proved to be indispensable. The onslaught of clients waiting in line to make use of these services was overwhelming. This entailed various problems of internal discipline. More staff was needed to keep the traffic of clients moving in good order than the meager resources of the IKG could provide. Some of these keepers of order (*Ordner*) were youngsters or else impoverished men who were willing to do the job for a pittance. Others took the job on an honorary basis. There were various motivations for doing honorary service. Some wanted to help the community in time of need; some wanted to be near what was perceived to be the vital connections or sources of influence or privileged information; and some wanted to qualify for a paying job. The crowds of clients who were there for consultation or for filling out still another form about a matter dealing with emigration or finances or welfare or retraining waited for the most part in tense but patient desperation. The stairways were packed with several lines moving at different speeds to different offices. Inevitably, someone tried to get ahead or objected when someone let an old person get ahead. It was also inevitable that a head of family, whose lives depended on the speedy completion of his business, would balk at having an *Ordner*—whose suit had fit the year before and whose tie was evidently borrowed from his father—tell him that he could not proceed beyond a certain point until he was allowed to; many a cheek that had only recently experienced its first shave was graced with a rude and ruddy memento of client frustration. Some adult *Ordner* found no other way of mastering their fear of the crowd and fear for their pitiful livelihood than by treating the people with contempt or abuse. Some honorary helpers used their positions for their own advantage or that of their friends; in this way, many clients had to return day after day until they had their turn, while seeing others called to the front of the line.

While the leadership was not the cause of such internal corruption and infraction of disciplined performance, it was responsible, and hence the ultimate recipient of complaints. Hard pressed as the community leaders were to provide for unprecedented services and to meet the many external challenges to Jewish existence, they also had to face the equally unprecedented problem of internal discipline. Löwenherz and Engel, and in time Murmelstein, issued many a circular admonishing the section chiefs, the *Ordner*, the employees, and the honorary helpers to guard against discourtesy, brusqueness, unauthorized interventions, preferential treatment, loss of self-control, and the taking of bribes.[32] Appeals to Jewish solidarity in times of need and stress changed to admonitions to departmental chiefs to control their staff and in time to demands for impeccable performance at every level and eventually to strict disciplinary control by the uppermost echelon. No one would prove to be as effective in this administrative task as Murmelstein.

In this manner, the leaders of the new IKG were the first ones to be confronted with another unprecedented phenomenon associated with the unfolding destruction event, a phenomenon that would grow to be determinative of the perceived persona of the men and women who would find themselves placed in the position of forced leadership.

In Vienna in 1938, one aspect of the phenomenon was the severance of the Jews from the status of citizenship whereby they had possessed the civil rights and the protection of the modern liberal state. According to Nazi policy, the full import of which began to be revealed in Vienna in 1938, ***the** function* of the appointed representatives of the Jews, and, by extension, *of each of the Jews, was to dismantle Jewish existence*. This meant that in the effort of safeguarding their existence (through emigrating and—until then—surviving) the Jews were left to their own devices as individuals and family groups. The conditions of a more general context under which they were thus engaged were beyond morality and beyond legality: Externally, it was the good will and charity of the Jewish communities beyond the borders and of others who lived in relative safety; internally, it was the solidarity among all those who, aside from what divided them (e.g., social or economic status; commitment to their Judaism; merit and capacities; opportunities and connections), were confronted with the same threat of sinking into the abyss.

The Jewish leadership had no legal authority or safeguards, and no concomitant legal obligation to offer their services in support of survival and escape fairly and equitably, or to ensure that these services were used in a spirit of solidarity. The only available methods of enforcement were either Nazi authority or the appeal to and enforcement of Jewish solidarity. Naturally, the leaders eschewed the former, since it would not only lead to unthinkable consequences for their fellow Jews but to the loss of the leaders' own limited authority with the Nazis as well as with their fellow Jews; the leaders were also well aware how prone the Jews were to liken a Jewish leader to the Nazis.

They were left with the appeal to Jewish solidarity and its self-enforcement. This appeal gradually developed into a policy consisting of two major features: First, strict impartiality in rendering the various services and in exercising the various official functions of the IKG, and second, strict insistence on Jewish self-discipline. We will have occasion to see that, as the situation became ever more tense, Jewish self-discipline would prove not to be possible without some show of authority on the part of the leaders, coupled with an increasingly

A woman sitting on a park bench in Vienna marked "Only for Jews!" (USHMM 11195)

blind trust on the part of those who were being led. We will also have to look at the other side of the coin and see that as the Jews became more and more dependent on the IKG as their unavoidable and often only recourse, the IKG proved to be more and more useful to the Nazis.

One of the tasks assumed by the IKG was to make representations on behalf of specific cases. This pertained to pleading for the release of detained individuals or of those sent to concentration camps, as well as for gaining permission to develop special emigration opportunities. The line between such special pleadings and maintaining impartiality was thin, but definite. In any case, the leaders were left to their own devices in determining the location of this line and in adhering in their performance to what they considered to be right. Because the line was thin, there were complaints and accusations of favoritism. But because the line could be definitely drawn, the rectitude of the leaders was stringent, and their rejection of the accusations was as sharp as their refusal to give preferential treatment. This policy became particularly controversial in time.

The performance of the Jewish leaders in providing indispensable services to their fellow Jews was subjected to various kinds of scrutiny and expectations according to who was doing the scrutinizing. The Nazis preempted not just primary but exclusive claim to the services of the Jewish leadership. Under this duress, the leaders tried to find, develop, and exploit opportunities for ensuring what was surely not the Nazis' intention, that is, the survival of Jewish existence. In the ideal case, this opportunity consisted in *a convincing claim for the coincidence of Jewish interest with Nazi interest.* When no such claim could be made, these opportunities had to be pursued clandestinely. Even as the Nazis were sensitive about the inevitable negative publicity, especially abroad, that resulted from their anti-Semitic policies, they did not want it to be known that they could be tricked into being less than uncompromising in carrying them out.

The Jewish leaders, therefore, were monitored by the Nazis and had to be extremely guarded in the way in which they maintained the contacts with the representatives of Jewish organizations abroad. There were occasions when Löwenherz had to issue denials when papers of the free press abroad presented stories which the Nazis thought tended to put them in a bad light.[33] We also know that one of the most stringent conditions under which inmates were released from concentration camps was their pledge of silence within and outside of Germany about what they had seen and endured inside the camps. Gaining the cooperation of persons and agencies abroad despite this self-censorship was therefore integral to the task of saving Jewish existence.

The dependence on such discretion brought its own problems. One problem was that whereas Nazi sensitivity to the bad publicity was often a useful weapon against Nazi policy, some escapees and other Jews on the outside who publicized the truth in a show of defiance were committing acts that were potentially harmful to those left behind. There was another problem: The need for discretion was no doubt respected by the narrow circle of representatives of Jewish agencies that tried to help the Jewish leaders of Vienna. However, since there was no way of determining when it was imperative to be discreet, there was no way of making sure that discretion was exercised by the right person at the right time. The ramifications of the atmosphere of totalitarian threat and control were not always understood by those who breathed it, whether inside or outside of Nazi Germany; and yet, such understanding was vital for the exercise of Vienna's Jewish leadership. For these reasons, it was a good thing when Jews who felt slighted or ill-served or discriminated against came to the Jewish leaders in person. Such complaints could then be handled without upsetting the subtle balance of performance and secrecy. However, since some things could simply not be told or explained beyond a narrow circle, and since the leaders in Vienna had, from the very beginning, to render their service on behalf of Jewish existence without destroying their own ostensible usefulness to the Nazis, their competence or loyalty was always under suspicion. Their only show of strength that was both visible and permissible was their enforcement of Jewish self-discipline.

Part of the fault lay in the unreal expectations on the part of the Jews of Vienna as to what the new IKG could deliver. Soon after it reopened in May of 1938, it issued questionnaires to persons interested in emigrating, in order to help the IKG in assessing the situation. Tens of thousands of these were handed in. The information obtained in this manner merely showed how overwhelming was the task of getting one hundred and eighty thousand Jews of all walks of life, all ages, trained and untrained, with no experience in pulling up roots and wandering, for the most part with no connections, to emigrate quickly to—for the most part—nonexistent destinations. This information could not directly help anyone emigrate. However, the questionnaires were one of the factors that engendered the expectation on the part of the hard-pressed Jews of Vienna that the IKG had the competence and the means of relocating them. Also, since the Nazis quickly effected the centralization of all the remaining organized Jewish life in the IKG, and also deflected as much of the necessary official contact with Jews, channeling it instead in the direction of the IKG, the demand for performance on the part of its clients rose beyond reasonable expectations. When they were not met, the IKG was accused of nonfeasance and malfeasance.

For example: One person, who had lost his job and had very few reserves, spent the better part of six months registering in one consulate after another and writing to aid societies in various countries that were occasionally mentioned in the information provided to the *Zionistische Rundschau* by the emigration section of the IKG. This required obtaining forms, having letters of recommendation and previous employment documents notarized, and sending letters by registered mail, all of which takes money. By the time he realized that dutifully following what had seemed to be straightforward procedures leading to emigration was of no avail, he was at the end of his reserves and at the end of his rope. When he realized that for the first time in his life he would be dependent on handouts, he blamed the IKG for misleading him. Another man complained that while Polish Jews were emigrating at a brisk pace, he, as an old-time Viennese Jew, was being discriminated against. Evidently his family had settled in Vienna a few generations back and had lost contact with the more extended family abroad. Jews who had come from Poland more recently were more likely still to be in loose but sufficient contact with relatives to arrange for immigration sponsorship, especially to the United States.

And yet, the IKG provided services without which the majority of Viennese Jews would not have been able to emigrate. However, especially in the first year of the Anschluss, when most of the emigration took place, the IKG was not in a position to offer emigration opportunities but merely to help expedite those who already had places to go. Some of the services provided in good faith by the IKG did tend to foster an erroneous impression. One such service was advisory, offered by experts in various fields, and dealt with the qualifications for engaging in trades and professions in different countries, and the demand for immigrants in such fields. But this service, like others that also proved to be both useless and misleading, was discontinued; this justified change in policy gave rise to wrong interpretations and tended to arouse suspicion about the IKG and its leaders.

The very nature of forced leadership made it impossible for the hard-pressed Jews of Vienna to know what it took to exercise such responsibility. For example, the IKG made a point of identifying the sources of the information they published in their newspaper, whether it was information they were *required* to publish (such as *Weisungen* [directives] from the SD or the Gestapo) or information they were *permitted* to publish (restrictive immigration policies of various countries). Nevertheless, the ordinary, hard-pressed Jew tended to disregard the actual sources and tended to pin responsibility for restrictive measures on the messenger, squarely on the IKG leadership. Yet, the very ignorance of the ordinary Jew was the *conditio sine qua non* for Löwenherz and his associates to perform whatever leadership they were resourceful enough to provide.

Nothing points up this tragic misunderstanding more than what we heard expressed by a number of former Viennese Jews who had managed to escape or survive, an opinion which over the decades occasionally found its way into the writings of researchers who ought to have known better. It is an often-expressed opinion that Desider Friedmann's position as leader of Vienna's Jews was usurped by others, in particular by Löwenherz and Murmelstein, and that if he had been permitted to continue to lead, the fate of Vienna's Jews might have been different. Dr. Friedmann's work in representing Jewish interests in the difficult period after the First World War had earned him—justly—the highest regard of Viennese Jewry.[34] But this provides no justification for accusing Löwenherz and Murmelstein of usurpation, for the following reasons.

The Nazis were loath enough to deal with Jews, a fortiori with such as Dr. Friedmann, whom they had reason to regard as an enemy because, as we have seen, he had been the ranking Jew during the last regime of independent Austria and had collected a sizable Jewish contribution to the plebiscite campaign fund. When it came to Jews, the Nazis dealt with their appointees, not with freely chosen representatives. Since all Jews were offensive to them by their very nature, they tended to appoint Jews who were not objectionable to them on any other basis as well. The appointments they made were not meant to be honorific but functional, and for this reason they also tended toward younger and more vigorous persons than Dr. Friedmann, who was almost sixty, had a heart ailment, and was diabetic.

Supposing, however, that Dr. Friedmann had had the chance to continue as leader, would the fate of the Jews have been any different? The basic situation of the Jews would have been the same: Riding on a groundswell of Christian and social anti-Semitism, Nazi policy, as we have seen, was to exploit the Jews in every way, to destroy whatever validity they had as human beings and, ultimately, to eliminate them. It was a situation without precedent. Questions arise of what one has the power to do in a position of forced leadership, and of the attendant political and moral right and wrong. But these questions do not depend on who is the leader, or whose place he supposedly took, or who should have been the leader. They are questions, agonizing questions, of ethical principle. They do not pertain to Dr. Friedmann, simply because he was never forced into that position.

There is the further question of the choices such a leader may have had in this situation of deepening persecution and terror, and of how he exercised such choices while under duress. This question may be answered from the vantage point of historical perspective, given the advantage of historical distance. But again, Friedmann is not involved. For the issue would be the substance and manner of Dr. Friedmann's possible choices under such duress, and that could only be a matter of idle speculation.

The fact of the matter is that the duress under which these leaders had to make their choices was defined by their being Jews, which was sufficient reason for the Nazis' hostility. However, Friedmann, as we have seen, had incurred additional hostility, and this would have constituted one more obstacle to the exercise of what little but potentially decisive choices he might have had.

There is an ironic twist to this mindless talk about usurpation. Nothing would have been more gratifying to Löwenherz than to succeed in his repeated efforts to have the Nazis free Friedmann, either to emigrate or to help manage the IKG. Conversely, the Nazis knew that by holding Friedmann they were able to hold hostage Löwenherz's loyalty to him.

Needed: A New Thrust

With the IKG a functioning instrument of their will and with the *Zentralstelle* organized to speed the official looting and chasing of the Jews, the Nazi regime could be well satisfied. By building on the momentum provided by the Anschluss, it was carrying out its Jewish policy.

Yet as summer turned into fall, the frantic and chaotic tidal wave of emigration seemed to abate. Of course, this must not be construed as an indication that Nazi policy was being enacted less stringently. The opposite was the case, and Nazi Jewish policy would again be caught up in the regime's continuously accelerating momentum. This was the time of "Munich," when Hitler inveigled Britain into believing it could buy peace at the cost of Czechoslovakia's Sudetenland, that is, at the cost of abandoning to Hitler the last natural barrier between Germany and the East; when France was reluctantly prepared to fight if Czechoslovakia would; and when Czechoslovakia, abandoned by its friends, decided not to fight the invading German army.

It was also the time when the pressure of the Nazi regime against the other, more formidable "opponent," the Catholic Church in Vienna, led to an open polarization of the two sides, whereby faithfulness to the Church began to be the major focus of internal Austrian resistance, an effort that was as belated as it would prove to be ineffective, though in the end it turned out to be the one redeeming feature over against the Austrians' acceptance of Hitler.

On October 7 Cardinal Archbishop Innitzer officiated at the annual observance of the victory, in 1571, over the infidel Turks in the sea battle of Lepanto at the hands of the Christian League under the command of Don Juan of Austria. An unexpectedly large number of young worshippers crowded Saint Stephen's Cathedral.[35] There is some evidence of an organized effort to use the occasion to show the resistance of the Catholic youth to the regime's pressures against the Church. After the service, they conducted the cardinal to his residence, and while waiting—in vain—for him to show himself, they shouted slogans that were clearly provocative of the regime. News about the incident was spread by the rumor mill, since it was not reported in the press. What the Nazi paper *Völkischer Beobachter* did contain the next day was an attack obliquely but unmistakably directed against the Church and its leadership. At the same time, certain party units were placed on alert. In the evening, about fifty men, most of them members of the Hitler Youth, invaded and vandalized the archbishop's palace, demolished and removed valuables, and threw the rector of the cathedral out of an upper story window. They were looking for the cardinal but could not find him, as he had been conducted to safety. Police were called from within the palace and by others. However, it seems that the police knew beforehand about the action and did not arrive until an hour had passed, at which time the invaders retreated and no arrests were made. The day after, the Gauleiter of Vienna, Odilo Globocnik, and the Führer's plenipotentiary for Austria, Bürckel, were speaking at a rally and used the occasion to rail against Czechs, Jews, and "blacks" (i.e., clerics), thereby initiating a series of demonstrations against the Church, in the course of which the Jews were anything but forgotten.

The harassment and the sporadic, localized, and limited persecutions of Jews, the plundering of Jewish businesses, and the vandalizing of synagogues did not abate. There were even some major actions, such as renewed waves of arrests and cruel mock expulsions (all of which we recount in chapter 5). But, since one can become inured to what comes with tireless regularity even if it is a bitter fact of life, this period was perceived as one of relative stability rather than exacerbation. Nonetheless, there was tension, and people with connections were told that something was in the offing. It did not take long to happen, and what happened at the archbishop's palace in a small way would prove to have been a rehearsal for what would happen to the Jews in a dramatically big way.

Eichmann was committed to a successful (i.e., rapid) emigration program. Hence, he and his superiors were no doubt frustrated that the process did not develop into a brisk flow but was jelling into a laborious and bureaucratically plodding ooze. Instead of an effective but brutal expulsion, the executors of the Nazi Jewish policy had to let considerations of statutes and reason result in a regulated and steady but desultory emigration process. Eichmann's task needed fuel to speed up the program, the fuel of dread and anxiety. As before, he was not in a position to provide it, but he would have it soon from sources beyond his control and outside of the ladder of command, on which he still occupied a relatively low rung, namely, from foreign policy. The first step of the dismantling of Czechoslovakia having succeeded beyond expectation, the regime was ready to turn its attention again to internal opponents, that is, the Jews and the Church, and to initiate actions against the next external opponent, which was Poland. In the next chapter, we will see that it found a way of doing both at the same time.

Chapter 5

Kristallnacht

The Gathering Momentum

In order to understand the event of Kristallnacht and its ramifications, we have to see it within context. To this end we will first set the stage by revisiting some antecedents already discussed. Various motivations have been suggested for the vehement outburst of violence in November 1938 against the Jews and whatever Jewish institutions still remained. They can be reduced to two types that are, basically, related: (1) economic ones and (2) the perceived need, on the part of segments of the German population, to take out their frustrations in a violent manner on those whom they had been persuaded to consider responsible for their woes, for the ills of their society and, indeed, of the whole world. The government under Göring, assisted first by Hjalmar Schacht and then by Walther Funk, wanted to eliminate the Jews while retaining their assets. This did not seem to be succeeding well enough in the Altreich. Only about 20 percent of the Jews had left in five years,[1] many of the wealthier ones, especially at first, without leaving any substantial assets in Germany. The remainder was bloodied but not sufficiently bowed; much of what they had managed to retain was still beyond the "legal" reach of the regime. And Germany needed money: money for armaments, money to carry out plans for reconstructing the economy, and foreign currencies for trade with other nations. Yet, for a while the German Jews felt that their situation had deteriorated as far as it would. They had become second-class citizens, to be sure, but had remained citizens at some level.[2] They had been eliminated from public life, and the Nuremberg Laws had cut deep. There was a lull of sorts in the promulgation of anti-Jewish propaganda and measures until after the Berlin Olympics in 1936, which the rulers did not want to jeopardize.[3] Yet the contempt and hostility on the part of the media as well as the masses and their leaders became ever more palpable. The gradual resumption of the enactment and application of statutes and regulations claiming legal authority, in addition to their gradual elimination from social and economic life, drove the Jews ever deeper into a ghettoization that was as yet not physical but a state of mind. Nonetheless, many still felt that some sort of basic accommodation was possible and that emigration seemed the less desirable alternative, both for those who still had some means of support as well as for those who had nothing left and would go destitute into emigration, bereft of the support of their fellow German Jews. This was especially true of older people, who could not expect to make any life for themselves abroad, even if they had been welcomed into another country. German Jews were aware, to some extent, of what had occurred and was continuing to occur in Austria. And before long, there was reason for their faith in "it can't happen here" to waver. In spite of all that, they did not live in constant daily terror as did the Jews in Austria.

This "fool's paradise,"[4] as one may, in retrospect, call the situation of the German Jews until 1938, began to exhibit its darker side within months of the Anschluss. There was the enactment of more restrictive laws regarding the participation of Jews in the economic life of the country, and the registration of their property with the authorities,[5] which made Jewish assets accessible to the German state and facilitated Göring's plan to eliminate them totally from the German economy as quickly as possible. Jewish communities were no longer legal entities, which meant that membership was now voluntary and so were the contributions made to them by their members. In October 1938 all Jewish passports were recalled and were subsequently reissued to Jews only for purposes of emigration, albeit with a big red "J" stamped on the first page. This, apparently the brainstorm of a Swiss women's organization that wanted to make sure that Jews could be kept out of the country, turned out to be counterproductive, inasmuch as it negatively affected emigration and thus the handing-over of German Jewish assets to the German state. And the state very badly wanted these assets.

Sporadic attacks on Jewish persons and properties became more frequent and more vicious during 1938. Toward the end of May, the American chargé d'affaires in Vienna cabled the secretary of state that there had occurred "wholesale arrests of Jews. Many reported were sent to Dachau. Action reliably attributed to direct orders of Himmler and presumably intended to further demoralize Jews, facilitate spoliation and expedite exodus."[6] This action was followed, on June 15, by the arrest of 1,500 Jews all over Germany[7] who fell into a very broad category of "asocials," that is, anyone who had ever been convicted of anything at all, including traffic violations. These, too, were shipped to concentration camps, the condition of their release being speedy emigration.

Shops were looted and smashed that summer, for example in Berlin, and for the first time synagogues were demolished. When the museum *Haus der Kunst* (House of Art) in Munich was opened by Hitler, he ordered the beautiful neogothic synagogue across the street to be razed within twenty-four hours so German sensibilities would not be offended by it. Other desecrations and razings followed, as in Nuremberg and Dortmund. There was increasingly much anti-Jewish propaganda in the Nazi press. For example, in August an article in *Der Stürmer* referred to synagogues as "robber dens," and *Das Schwarze Korps* of November 2 wrote in an editorial, called "This Is Still Needed": ". . . arrests, seizure of property, prohibition of all business activity and possession of real estate," and went into detail about how this was to be accomplished. This campaign was to be a reply to the "declaration of war made by world Jewry against Germany."[8] Also, concentration camps were expanded, and "stars of David" were sewn by the inmates on prison uniforms.[9] This increase in the amount and intensity of anti-Jewish language, measures, and actions could not be a random occurrence; something was "in the air."

Indeed, what was beginning to be carried out at this time had been projected at least a year earlier. In 1937 the Jewish section of the SD head office had contended that "the most effective means for a more rapid 'solution of the Jewish question' was 'the wrath of the people (*Volkszorn*) turned into action . . . since the Jew has learned a lot through pogroms and fears nothing as much as a hostile mood that can turn spontaneously against him'."[10] What could point more directly toward the events of November 1938 than this?

As usual, the situation was much more acute in Austria. There had been hardly any letup in the sporadic, unofficial persecution between the immediate onset of brutality at the time of the Anschluss and the fall of 1938, no real breather, no pretext for the Jews to think that any kind of accommodation with Nazi Germany would be possible and life would be livable on any level. Beyond the new legal restrictions and pseudolegal regulations, the brutal acts of an organized or spontaneous nature made life terrifying and precarious.

When the initial period of official ferment of March and April came to an end, the organized brutality lost its momentum as its leaders became aware of its being inherently counterproductive. "Wild" aryanization, it was realized, was more of a liability than an asset, and the streets had been scrubbed clean. This was followed, until November, by the next phase: a time of administrative consolidation and the legalization of the basis for removing the Jews from the social and economic fabric of Austria. Now all measures against the Jews were to be put "on a legally flawless basis."[11] After all, "let everyone take note—Germany is a country ruled by law [*Rechtsstaat*]. . . . Nothing happens in our Reich without a legal basis . . . no pogroms are organized [here]."[12] Thus, the official methods were to be refined, while the aims remained the same. Yet most of the time, the means, at least in Austria, proved in their own way to be cruel and inhumane, too.

With the establishment of the *Zentralstelle*, some of the terrifying chicaneries and the wearying treadmill attending the emigration process was reduced, although there was still plenty of leeway for making things as difficult as possible for the Jews. Even during this period preceding Kristallnacht, the ranks of the Viennese Jews, and especially of those who were destitute yet had to leave the country within weeks, were swelled by those ejected forcibly and brutally from their homes in the provinces and forced to flee to Vienna and, if possible, abroad. These actions, whose purpose once again was to rid the rest of Austria—and especially the province of Burgenland, where the second largest number of the provincial Jews were at home—of its Jews, while retaining their assets, however meager, were usually ordered by the local governments in cooperation with the Gestapo. Often these Jews had to leave their homes within twenty-four hours. Compensation for the possessions left behind was ridiculously small or nonexistent, as were their chances of emigration. "Yugoslavia, CSR and various other countries have stopped the transit of Jews. . . . A number of Jews has decided to let themselves be baptized according to the Anglican rite in order to get permission to travel through Yugoslavia and enter Greece," thus according to the head of the State Police in Eisenstadt, the capital of Burgenland, in August 1938.[13] And from Wiener Neustadt, a city in Lower Austria, the regional Nazi party chief writes at about the same time: "The Jewish problem is being vigorously attacked, and we can ascertain with pleasure that a considerable emigration is taking place. The County Commissioner has ordered all Aryan landlords to give notice to the Jewish families to vacate their premises. Where they go—is of no interest."[14]

The expropriation of Jewish apartments and the forcible ejection of their tenants, as well as the appropriation of these apartments by Aryans, and especially by party members, was endorsed and encouraged by Gauleiter Odilo Globocnik and carried out with vigor, enthusiasm, and imagination by the rank and file. Sometimes a pretext was used to get the Jews out, for example, that an Aryan could not be expected to remain in the same house as a Jew. Ergo, the Jews must go.[15] Since most physicians in private practice had their offices and examining rooms right in their homes, they lost their homes together with their licenses to practice (July 1938).[16] The comrades' "desire for living space" seemed insatiable.

One of the most flagrant attempts at precipitously taking over Jewish homes occurred at the beginning of October 1938, during the Jewish High Holidays, in certain districts of Vienna as well as in several suburbs of the city. It was a time, writes Botz, "when the terror of the Anschluss-days came to life again."[17] Many Jews were literally pulled out of their beds by functionaries and members of the NSDAP (Nazi Party). They were forced then and there to hand over the keys to their apartments and were told to go immediately to the Danube Canal, where "there were ships standing to take them to Palestine."[18] These ships, however, were a cruel fiction. Others were sent to the railway terminal, where they were informed there were trains ready to take them, for free and without passports, beyond the German borders. Others, those from the suburbs, were loaded onto trucks and brought to Vienna,[19] again under the pretext of being shipped out. And still others were forced to sign away their homes without benefit of such explanations. The misery, confusion, and helplessness of the people thus affected needs no description. The burden of remedial or relief action placed on the IKG was very sudden and very great, as was its effort to have at least some of the apartments restored to their rightful owners, albeit with a lot or all of their contents missing. Much of the effort to reverse the effect of that clandestine terrorizing was performed by Löwenherz. His representations at the district Nazi offices are not documented in any records of the time but are attested to by a letter he received fifteen years after the events:

> Even though many years have gone by since 1938, neither I nor many other Jews will ever forget what you were able heroically to accomplish—at the risk of your life—on that Yom Kippur day for your fellow Jews in the 18th and 19th Districts [of Vienna], by helping them to return to their apartments after they were driven from them by a gang of Nazis. . . . You earned eternal gratitude for what you accomplished on that memorable Yom Kippur as well as by your deeds during the whole disastrous and cruel Hitler years.[20]

Generally, it was next to impossible to find any kind of replacement housing for those who had been thrown out.[21] Instead, the Jews were told that those who still had apartments had to share them with those who did not. Even this emergency solution usually did not work because the Aryan landlords refused to let their Jewish tenants sublet any part of their apartments. "The housing offices," writes Rosenkranz about a number of families who had been thrown into the streets out of their subsidized housing,[22] "refused to assign substitute apartments to those who had been evicted so that they were forced, during an [especially] cold October, to subsist in dilapidated military barracks that lacked windows, doors, and sanitary installations." It was not until October 29 that Eichmann officially permitted subleasing, and in effect ordered the owners and managers of apartment buildings as well as party officials to comply.[23]

The IKG also had to suffer the loss of many of its buildings and facilities during this period, since they were requisitioned at short notice by government and party agencies and officials. In July Löwenherz had been forced to send a letter surrendering the IKG's library and archive to the Gestapo.

There were other "legal" or officially sanctioned persecutions, for example, the elimination of Jewish students from the university mentioned above, and the reduction of Jewish Gymnasium students to fewer than 1/10 of their previous number. The five hundred who remained were concentrated in one Jewish school. Jews were eliminated from the media, the arts, as well as professional and trade organizations. Any Jew who could, by the widest stretch of the imagination, be replaced by an Aryan or whose position was not essential, lost this position overnight. "Aryan nurses could hardly be saddled with the care of Jews." The Jewish patients therefore had to be segregated in the public hospitals, and the IKG had to arrange for their nursing care.[24] Jews were forbidden by law to enter places of public amusement, were excluded from public baths (most apartments in Vienna did not have private baths or showers), were forbidden to enter most parks and recreation areas or even to sit down on public benches on the tree-lined streets. There was no place for them any longer.

During the same period, there were waves of arrests (this apart from the fact that individual Jews were always in danger of being arrested on the slightest infraction or for no reason). Of the approximately two thousand Jews who were arrested on or about May 24, most were sent first to Dachau, then, in August and September, on to Buchenwald[25] in order to make room for further mass arrests.[26] The brutality vented on these people was so great that soon boxes with their ashes were returned to Vienna, which their families could claim upon payment of a fee. They all had died of "natural causes," one of the favorites being pneumonia.

The "actions" against the Jews of Vienna during this period were often ordered and carried out by opposing factions within and outside of Austria. For example, while Göring wanted to preserve Jewish assets for the state enterprises under his control, the local Austrian party members may have wanted to seize the Jewish property for themselves. Thus, in Vienna, writes Kapralik, Mayor Hermann Neubacher, who was appointed by the Nazis, had the authority to sign documents relating to the Jews, but "in actuality did not presume to give any orders that were positive, negative or even neutral. Everything originated with the SS authorities and had to be submitted to the duo Eichmann (Jewish section SD) and Kuchmann (Jewish section Gestapo), who were, in fact, in a continuous jurisdictional dispute with each other, with the IKG in the middle."[27] Still, when it came to the Jews, the warring factions shared, at bottom, the three interlocking goals mentioned previously: (1) to get rid of the Jews by putting pressure on them to emigrate, using any means at their disposal; (2) to strip them of their possessions before and after their disappearance; and (3), at the same time, to allow the party faithful and anyone else who cared to join in to "blow off steam," as Hitler called it, that is, to safely to get rid of their frustrations through violence and brutality against people who could be counted on not to hit back. The extent to which each of these goals seemed to be the primary one depended on the particular situation, on where the directive for the operation originated and who carried it out, and on which interested party or historian interpreted it. And since the ostensible purpose of such an operation was not necessarily the real one, the triple skein of motivations and goals could not then—and cannot now—be unraveled in a manner that does justice to all the factors involved. Perhaps, part of the solution lies in looking at the somewhat divergent versions of the event which Karl Ebner, in his 1947 defense, calls the *Maiaktion* (May action) and seeing whether, cumulatively, we can come closer to what actually occurred.

The Maiaktion *and Its Aftermath*

On May 24 an express letter was sent by the Gestapo headquarters in Vienna to all local police stations: "An order has been issued [no indication as to its point of origin] to arrest immediately disagreeable Jews, especially those with police records, and to convey them to the Concentration Camp Dachau." Only German (Austrian) and stateless Jews were to be arrested, those over fifty only if highly incriminated. If any search for assets were to be conducted or assets to be confiscated, the Gestapo would handle it.[28]

From Ebner's perspective in 1947, the situation was somewhat different:

> In May 1938 the RSHA [*sic!*] ordered an operation against Jews in Vienna. We were instructed to arrest 4,000 relatively young able-bodied Jews and to get them moving in a westerly direction toward a place to be announced before their departure. A later order informed us that these people were to be deployed as a group in the western border regions (building of fortifications). Dr. Lange, for whom, according to his own statement, this operation constituted the first major assignment directed to him personally, put it into action enthusiastically. . . . The Jews were rounded up indiscriminately. . . . After about 2,000 people had already left, a telegram arrived from Göring prohibiting the operation. A few days later the RSHA [*sic*] also withdrew this order.[29]

According to Moser, the directive of the Gestapo of May 24 served to bring about the arrest of all the Jews who appeared on the "black list" kept by the Austrian Nazis.[30] From Gold we learn that the black list had been assembled by the Austrian Nazis during their period of "illegality." The aim and purpose of the operation, according to Gold, was, "on the one hand, the total elimination of the Jews from the political, economic and social life of Austria, on the other the effortless dispossession of the Jews at no cost [to the Nazis]."[31]

In his *Reichskristallnacht* Rosenkranz adds that the two thousand Jews arrested were of "superior social or professional stature,"[32] and in his later *Verfolgung* he states that the arrests "were not only of indiscriminately rounded-up Jews, but took place primarily according to proscription lists of young Jewish intellectuals, physicians, engineers, lawyers. Early in the morning, criminal police in civilian dress knocked at the victim's door and invited him to come along. . . . Thus, most were arrested with nothing but what they were wearing."[33]

But whether blacklisted or simply young and able-bodied, whether taken off the streets or out of their beds, these Jews were all subjected to brutality, and mental and physical torture, often of a very imaginative kind, which leads one to believe that some thought had been given to the methods to be employed. And the result, apart from trauma and death, was the desire, on the part of those thus abused, to leave immediately for anywhere at all, with just the clothes on their backs, happy to exchange all their possessions for their very lives. Thus, all three Nazi goals were achieved.

In the second half of October, another two thousand or so Jews were stopped on the street, searched, and arrested. It is claimed that Eichmann's purpose in these arrests, too, was to motivate Jews to emigrate. But they no longer needed this extra push.

There was also a steady increase, toward the end of summer, in instances of gratuitous violence and brutality against Jews. "A practice blackout was used to attack Jews and to rob them. The Jewish Rothschild-Hospital was so crowded with severely injured people that they had to be placed on the floors of wards and corridors and even in the garden."[34] In the 2nd District, which held the largest concentration of Jews, violence against Jews now occurred on a daily basis. Hitler Youth and SA vied with each other in vandalizing synagogues and houses of prayer, destroying and burning, smashing windows and furnishings, and robbing or desecrating sacred objects.[35] In vain did the IKG appeal to the state police. It then turned to the municipal police to ask for protection, since rumors were rife that further excesses were planned. According to the police reports sent to Bürckel between October 22 and November 7, there was not a day without Jews being subject to extortion, robbery, or violence in their homes and stores.[36] Rosenzkranz no doubt is correct when he states that "The pogrom of November 9/10, which represents a dramatic turning point for German Jewry, is differentiated, in Vienna, from the previous acts of violence only by two aspects: the larger scale and the mass arrests."[37]

It seems that the Austrian *Maiaktion* worked so well that about the middle of June the so-called *Juniaktion* (June action) was launched in the Altreich. Approximately 1,500 Jews were arrested on the pretext that they were "antisocial elements." Apparently, they were selected on the basis of four lists of Jews that had only recently been compiled in four different offices: the tax office, the criminal section of the police department, in the different Gestapo offices, and in the local police stations. These Jews, too, were sent to concentration camps.[38]

Was Austria being used as an experimental laboratory for the rest of Germany? And were these actions planned in order to try out the methods to be used come Kristallnacht? Or were they consciously put in operation as a prelude to what was to come? Historians differ in their assessments, and those who deny such a link shout "hindsight!" at those who claim to see one. Yet the Jews, especially those in Austria, experienced at that time a decided heightening of tension; they felt even more endangered and isolated. The failure of the Evian Conference added to their sense of isolation and their sense of abandonment to terror, while it gave confidence to the Nazi planners that their actions would remain unpunished by the international community.

But the Nazis could not afford as yet to thumb their noses at the other Western countries. In a speech before party officials in April of 1937, Hitler had made his approach to international politics very plain: "After all, we are quite clear about the ultimate goal of our policies. As far as I am concerned, it is always a matter of not taking a step forward that I might have to reverse again, and not taking any step that may be detrimental. You know that I always go to the outer limits of risk-taking, but I do not go beyond. . . . I want to destroy you [the adversary]! . . . to maneuver you into a corner such that you cannot fight back, and then you will get the thrust [of my weapon] right into your heart."[39] But, as it turned out, the Nazi potentates did not have to worry too much about risk-taking at this time. By following the events at Evian, as well as through private consultations with representatives of the Western countries, who wanted to preserve "peace in our time" at any price—especially if it was only at the cost of the Jews of Germany—the Nazi government was emboldened to proceed to the next big step in their anti-Jewish measures. Even Churchill, when he was asked by the Gauleiter of Danzig in July 1938 whether the German laws against the Jews would be an impediment to British-German relations, replied in the negative.[40]

On October 26 Himmler gave the order, "in agreement with the Office of Foreign Affairs," to arrest all Jews with valid Polish passports, cancel their residence permits, and ship them to the Polish border. This action was to be completed by October 29. "As many Polish Jews as possible, especially males, are to be shoved across the border by that date."[41] The idea behind the emphasis on men was the assumption that the rest of the families would then voluntarily follow their men into exile. Many of the Polish Jews managed to escape this action, but between 17,000 and 18,000 Jews, legal residents of the Reich but of Polish nationality, were summarily arrested directly off the street and from their homes. They were allowed to take only some hand luggage and 10 Reichsmark per person, and were taken first to prison and then to the railway station to be shipped to the Polish border. In some cases, whole families were taken; in others only the men. The background of this action is briefly this: In the spring of 1938, the Polish government enacted a decree of denaturalization, requiring all Poles living abroad for five years or more to get a stamp from a Polish consular official in order to retain their Polish citizenship. Whether they received this stamp or not rested on the discretion of the Polish official. Anyone failing to receive this stamp would be declared stateless. The main purpose of the decree seems to have been the desire on the part of the Polish authorities to prevent the tens of thousands of Polish Jews resident in Germany from returning or being returned to Poland by the Germans. Undeterred—or emboldened—by this ruling, the Germans sent the Jews to the Polish border. Poland, predictably, refused them entry, and thus, most of the 17,000 or so Jews were crammed without shelter in the freezing late autumn weather and with hardly any food into the no-man's land between Germany and Poland; and there they remained for a considerable time, if they did not first succumb to the conditions in which they found themselves.

This action took place in the Altreich. In Austria, matters took a somewhat different turn, one that, contrary to the by-now usual course of events, was for once less drastic and brutal than in the rest of Germany. Although there had been, parallel to the other actions, expulsions of some Russian, stateless, or Polish Jews since the Anschluss, there was no wholesale deportation of the Polish or formerly Polish and now stateless Jews on October 28 and 29 from Vienna. What made the difference? After all, the Polish and stateless Jews in Vienna were also detained at this time. But, whereas in the Altreich the Stapo and local police took care of the details of the expulsion as well as of the roundup, in Vienna

Eichmann wanted the IKG to do the dirty work for him of getting rid of the approximately 20,000 Polish Jews. They were given twenty-four hours to leave the country, a condition that could not possibly be met. Löwenherz obviously made this clear to Eichmann; for when he and Rothenberg met with Eichmann on October 29, Eichmann informed them that the time limit for the Polish and stateless emigration had been extended from twenty-four hours to four weeks. But Löwenherz and Rothenberg continued to press their point, arguing that even four weeks were hardly enough time to effect emigration; and Eichmann yielded once more, but on condition that "these people must exert themselves vigorously for permissions to immigrate; should emigration be impossible nonetheless [within four weeks] they should petition for an extension of their time limit."[42] And so, Löwenherz and Rothenberg, very cleverly and with great presence of mind, turned the deportation order into an emigration matter. And persuaded to treat it as such, Eichmann was forced to admit that the time limit placed on its execution was unrealistic and unrealizable. The immediate wholesale expulsion of Polish Jews was averted in Vienna.

One can only speculate about the reasons why this affair was handled so differently in Austria. But it seems clear that what was at play here was a different kind of what—for want of a better expression—one may call a "working relationship" between Eichmann's office and the IKG than that between the parallel institutions in Germany. This relationship could and did, at times, lead to some degree of amelioration for some of the Jews, as happened in this instance. At the same time, Eichmann's own ambitious plans were furthered in that, by seeming to give in to Löwenherz and Rothenberg, he was able to show that he was furthering emigration without causing the kind of expensive mess the 17,000 hapless Jews from the Altreich found themselves in. Gerhard Botz calls this relationship, based on mutually exclusive interests, a "division of labor between the persecutors and the persecuted,"[43] a designation that gets much closer to the truth than Arendt does when she speaks of Eichmann's "beloved Löwenherz"[44] and calls the latter "the first Jewish functionary actually to organize a whole Jewish community into an institution at the service of the Nazi authorities."[45] In any case, until Kristallnacht the situation of the Jews in Vienna was different from that of the Jews in the Altreich, and this fact was closely tied to the distinct way in which the IKG's and its leadership's status vis-à-vis Eichmann evolved. Previously, we reported that one of Eichmann's tasks was to see to it that the Jewish communities of Vienna and Berlin not only be treated differently from each other but be unable to compare notes or cooperate.

The deportation of the Polish Jews led to a situation that could not be predicted by the Germans but which could not have been more welcome to them, especially at this particular time.

On November 3, in Paris, Herschel Grynszpan, the 17-year-old son of Polish Jews, long-time residents of Hanover, received a postcard from his parents and sisters in which they informed him that they all had been deported to the Polish border and described the conditions under which they were forced to exist. On the following day, he read in the French Yiddish press about the deportations and the inhumane conditions in the no-man's land between Germany and Poland. Three days later, in his desperation and grief at his inability to do anything to help his family—he himself was at the point of being ejected from

France—he went to the German embassy and shot and severely wounded a minor consular official, Ernst vom Rath. Public attention was immediately focused on the shooting—but not on the situation that precipitated it.

This incident came at a most opportune moment for Germany, where the intensity of anti-Jewish propaganda and consequent feeling had risen to a fever pitch, and where the thunderclouds gathering around the Jews were in search of the spark that would ignite swift and brutal popular action against them. Herschel Grynszpan supplied this spark, and did so at just the right time. For the day on which vom Rath succumbed to his injury was—it is assumed—by coincidence a most important anniversary in the National Socialist movement. Murmelstein draws a straight line from November 9, 1918, through November 9, 1923, to November 9, 1938:

> A suggestive statement by Hitler of January 21, 1939, has been transmitted, which clarifies the connections. In a conversation [between Hitler and] the Czech foreign minister the following threat was heard: "The Jews did not stage the 9th of November 1918 in vain, this day will be avenged." What he was referring to is the proclamation of the [German] Republic by Philipp Schneidemann on November 9, 1918. However, the Kristallnacht as the twentieth anniversary celebration of the "Jew-Republic" goes to prove that the initiative originated from the same source as the one that attempted, on November 9, 1923, in Munich, to celebrate the fifth anniversary of the Republic in a special way.[46]

The former attempt, however, misfired; November 9, 1938, was right on target.

When, in 1936, David Frankfurter shot and killed Wilhelm Gustloff, the Nazi Gauleiter for Switzerland, the event did not pass unnoticed in the German press and in Nazi consciousness, but the waves created by this event were relatively minor: a special income tax for Jews, promulgated as a punitive measure,[47] and a bridge was named after Gustloff in Nuremberg in September 1937. At the dedication of the bridge, Julius Streicher gave an address in which he sketched the path which, according to him, the Jewish people had traveled through the millennia: "Everywhere murder; everywhere mass murder."[48] Streicher here made good use of the time-honored tradition of blaming Jewry as a whole for the dereliction, real or imagined, of a single Jew. Yet this event was not exploited any further at that time. Now things were different: the party hegemony was firmly established, the West did not want to rock the boat, and the escalation of actions against the Jews could proceed safely. Of course, both press and propaganda drew parallels between the Gustloff and the vom Rath affairs. The *Völkischer Beobachter* of November 8, 1938, warns in its lead editorial that "it is clear that the German people will draw its own conclusions from this new deed." It is an impossible situation, the article argues, that the Jews in Germany still lead the good life. . .

> . . . while the Jews abroad call upon the fellow members of their race to make war on Germany and to shoot down German officials. There is a straight line from David Frankfurter to Herschel Grynszpan. . . . The Jewish world press is again attempting to exonerate and exalt the perpetrator and to throw suspicion on the victim. . . . The shots fired in the German embassy in Paris will signify not only the beginning of a new German attitude in the Jewish question but, it is hoped, also give a signal to those foreigners who failed to realize up to now that it is, in the last analysis, the international Jew who stands in the way of an understanding between nations.[49]

Herschel Grynszpan following his arrest. (DÖW 2016 Grynszpan 001)

This emphasis on the fiction of the "international Jew" and his malevolent influence on world events was an important element in the directives issued by the German Press Service (*Deutsches Nachrichtenbüro*, or DNB[50]). The *Völkischer Beobachter*, the "flagship of the national socialist press" was, however, only one, although very likely the most influential, promulgator of what Benz calls the "scenario [scripted to express] the people's anger in November of 1938." As early as November 7, the DNB issued a communiqué informing the various German newspapers that they

> . . . must report on the attack . . . in the greatest format. . . . The news must totally dominate the front page. . . . In their own commentaries it must be pointed out that the attempted assassination on the part of the Jew must have the severest consequences for the Jews in Germany including the foreign Jews there. Using expressions consonant with the storm of indignation [that has broken out] among the German people it could be stated that the Jewish clique of emigrants that had put the gun into Frankfurter's hand was also responsible for this outrage.[51]

Prominent Jewish writers and intellectuals who had fled to France were to be mentioned in this connection, and a particular point was to be made of mentioning Emil Ludwig, who was a special object of hatred on the part of the regime.[52] The shooting was so important to the Propaganda Ministry's immediate aims that a directive later that day ordered a major address by von Ribbentrop before foreign journalists to be pulled from the front page in order to make room for the attack on vom Rath.[53]

On November 8 the instructions to the German press were to focus on the Jewish aspect of the shooting, especially on parallels with the Gustloff affair, and on the responsibility of international Jewry for the crime. And on November 9 the *Völkischer Beobachter* wrote: "The shots fired in Paris will not go unpunished. Of that Jewry can be certain." Another paper, *Der Angriff* (i.e., "The Attack"), called it a crime against the German people and spoke of "the imperative demand to proceed at once against the Jews with the most severe consequences. . . ."[54]

The ball was rolling, and it was not meant to stop. Vom Rath was expected to die. After all, what would have been the purpose of all the momentum built up by the Propaganda Ministry had he made a full recovery? And die he did. Even Hitler's personal physician, whom he had sent, together with a professor of medicine from Münster, to assist the French attending physicians,[55] could not—(or would not?)—save the junior consular official who, by all accounts, was not even a convinced Nazi. He did, however, oblige the Party by dying on the right day.

From the moment the news of the shooting reached the public, the Jews of Germany knew that the storm that they could feel brewing had found its spark and was about to engulf them. They did not yet know what precise form the catastrophe would take, and so uncertainty and dread were added to the chronic state of fear in which they lived. No one has made the claim that they expected their synagogues and houses of prayer to be torched, looted, and destroyed. Yet armed with our hindsight, we read the following in the *Völkischer Beobachter*, again in the November 8 issue, and draw our conclusions about what it portends.

The article is called "A Ramble through Vienna to View the Jewish Houses of Worship."[56] Four photos, two of rabbis and two of synagogues whose exact addresses are given, accompany the text, which emphasizes the fact that compared with the houses of worship of other religious communities, the Jewish ones "lack the appropriate decor." By the very inconspicuousness of their facades, they tell us that their function is not to call the believers to worship. Rather, they serve as the "lair" where the Jews spread the message to "despise, deprave, and destroy" all non-Jews.[57]

We must assume that this message was not brought by sheer coincidence at this particular time but was planned to coincide with the onset of the pogrom. Events bear us out.

Fanned by this media campaign, there occurred in various parts of Germany as early as November 7 and 8 individual acts of violence and vandalism against Jewish persons and property, so also against Jewish community buildings and places of worship. Thus, we read, for example, in the *Kurhessische Landeszeitung* of November 8:

> The bloody deed in Paris has aroused in Kassel and numerous towns in [the province of] Kurhessen spontaneous demonstrations . . . against Jewish stores and institutions. The populace gave expression in this manner to its anger and indignation, an indignation coming from its innermost heart. The smashed windowpanes and the damaged interiors of synagogues and other Jewish institutions are a spontaneous repayment to world Jewry, a repayment which the nation of agitators and swindlers has to blame on itself . . . [first of all, the synagogues were attacked, as the] most visible expressions of the Jewish striving for power . . . the will of the crowd could no longer be restrained.[58]

These acts, which at this stage still bore local character and were often initiated by the regional leaders of the NSDAP, many of whom also happened to be the mayors of the particular towns, were soon taken over and carried out enthusiastically by the ordinary citizenry, which found in them an opportunity to express their envy, settle real or imagined scores, enrich themselves, express the virulent anti-Semitism that had been drilled into them for so long, or simply let off steam through what had become a socially acceptable outlet. The favorable and approving manner in which these events were reported in the press caused the violence and hatred to feed on itself and to raise the momentum of the persecutions to an even higher level.

German Jewry frantically cast about for help from abroad. Wilfrid Israel, a British-born member of the *Reichsvertretung*, called on the British chargé d'affaires in Berlin "to express grave apprehensions that reprisals will be taken on Jews in Germany" and to ask for help. But neither he nor Chaim Weitzmann, who asked the foreign office to send a British non-Jew to Germany in order to help avert the pogrom he expected to start at any time, was able to secure any cooperation from the British: Lord Halifax had given instructions, it seems, "to do nothing that might offend Hitler and his minions."[59] And so German Jewry again stood alone.

The Event

The storm broke a few hours after the death of vom Rath, which took place on November 9 at 5:30 in the afternoon. We alluded earlier to the significance of this date in Nazi Germany's ideology: There were celebrations and commemorations, and there were the midnight swearing-in ceremonies for new SS recruits that were held at various locations throughout the country. But the main events took place in Munich, the city at the heart of the Nazi movement and the site of the abortive Beer Hall Putsch of 1923. Hitler, Himmler, Göring, Goebbels, Heydrich, the different Gauleiter, and other Nazi Party dignitaries came here to celebrate, to honor the Old Guard, and to give the speeches traditional for this occasion. Hitler had given a major address the previous evening in the *Bürgerbräukeller*[60] but had failed to make use of this opportunity to speak about the shooting of vom Rath. Neither did he speak about it at this evening's festivities: the dinner he attended together with prominent members of Party and SA.[61] Informed at approximately 9:00 p.m. that vom Rath had died, he held a long whispered conversation with Goebbels, too soft to be overheard, although some claim that he said, at the end, that the SA must have a chance to blow off steam.[62] Hitler then abruptly got up from the table and went back to his hotel without giving an explanation to his assembled comrades and indeed without giving his scheduled traditional address. The significance of his behavior could not have been lost on his old fellow fighters: Something very serious was up.

What was Hitler's strategy? Another fact is significant here: the time lag of two and one half hours[63] between vom Rath's death and Hitler's being informed thereof, a time lag that would seem excessive and therefore puzzling, considering that he had his own people in Paris, indeed at the bedside of vom Rath. Any one of them could—and perhaps did—pick up the telephone, or at the least have sent a cable immediately. Surely Hitler could—or would—have been informed within the hour. It seems, therefore, safe to conjecture that Hitler was, indeed, informed of vom Rath's demise but chose to make a public display of being told the news during the dinner, followed by an inaudible conversation with Goebbels and an exit observed and wondered at by all. This was a most effective ploy: It heightened the dramatic impact and made Hitler a key player without his having said a word. It also removed from his shoulders the onus for any actions that were to follow.

Hitler without a doubt thus preferred to remain in the shadows in regard to the propagandistic exploitation of the shooting as well as the consequent pogrom. His impatience with and anger at the relatively slow and cumbersome "legal" means of dispossessing the Jews were well known, and it was no secret that he was eager for a more radical, direct, even violent path to Jewish property. And so Goebbels, whether designated as such by Hitler or by his own choice, became the "front man."

Goebbels was singularly fitted to play this role. He was viciously anti-Semitic, ruthless, power hungry, and a seductive and convincing orator. The first and the last qualifications stood him in good stead now, for almost immediately after Hitler left—the meal was over by now—he stood up and gave the speech that signaled the comrades: let the pogrom begin! He announced the death of the young diplomat and then launched into a wild anti-Semitic tirade intended to rouse the most primitive passions and to focus them on the Jew, in his collective identity, as the archenemy. He informed his attentive audience that pogroms had already begun here and there in Germany (but failed to mention that it was his propaganda in the media which had incited them), and now used these early pogroms, these so-called spontaneous expressions of the righteous anger of the German people, to justify a general call to arms against the Jews, their possessions, and their institutions. He couched this call, however, in language that would sound ambiguous to the ordinary listener but held a clear and direct message for the initiates, for the old comrades and fellow fighters at the banquet: Further retaliatory actions were to be expected, he told them. And although the party was not to initiate or organize such actions, it was not to interfere should they arise spontaneously. This was understood by the party leaders present to mean that even though they were to initiate and organize, and also to execute, they were to make it appear as if the actions did not originate with them but with the people, and that they were brought about by the "seething soul of the people."

As soon as Goebbels stopped speaking, the party leaders rushed to the telephones to give instructions to the local bosses of their respective regions. The substance of Goebbels's speech was later—apparently, some time after midnight—distributed by teleprinter to all regional government offices with the instructions that they be passed on to the *Gau* propaganda chiefs. These missives were marked "secret—not for the press." After stating that there have occurred, in several regions, "considerable anti-Semitic demonstrations, in the course of which Jewish stores were smashed and synagogues torched" (thus telling the recipients what they were to do), Goebbels's message continues:

1. Such demonstrations are neither to be set in motion nor organized by the party.
2. If they arise spontaneously, they are to be allowed to run their course for the time being, but care is to be taken that no considerable economic values be destroyed.

3. If there is danger of fire, it is imperative that the assets of the German people be protected. . . .
7. This order is the final one for this evening; it invalidates all orders given previously regarding this matter insofar as they conflict with it.[64]

This directive was followed by a short addendum marked 2:45 a.m.: "Tomorrow [*sic*] there will take place in the whole Reich large-scale arrests of Jews. These arrests are to be carried out exclusively by the police."[65] By then, there was no longer any attempt made on the part of Goebbels to pretend that this action was confined to the expressions of anger on the part of "seething souls" or that this action was not an official one.[66]

After the meeting broke up there ensued a veritable chaos of authority (*Kompetenzenchaos*).[67] While the chain of command among the party officials and headquarters and the ranks of the SA had already begun to function, the SS, meeting at the Hotel Vier Jahreszeiten in Munich prior to attending the swearing-in ceremony for new SS members on the Odeonsplatz at midnight, knew nothing about what was going on until after 11:00 p.m. At that time, Heydrich received a telephone call from the *Staatspolizei* informing him that the regional propaganda office had issued an order for the initiation of an action against the Jews in which the police was not to interfere. Heydrich sent SS Group Leader (*Gruppenführer*) Karl Wolff to Himmler to ask for clarification and orders. Wolff found Himmler in Hitler's chambers and briefed him about the order. Apparently, Hitler and Himmler then agreed that the SS was to "keep out of it" except to "protect" the Jews and collect their property. Matters had to rest there until after the swearing-in ceremony. In the meantime, in Berlin, Heydrich's subordinate Heinrich Müller issued a directive before midnight that anticipated Heydrich's message. The directive did not refer to the death of vom Rath at all or to the consequent "seething soul of the people" as the triggers of the operation. This has led a number of scholars to conclude that the pogrom had been planned for approximately this time frame in any case, assassination or not. Müller also ordered preparations to be made for the arrest of up to 30,000 Jews, "primarily affluent" ones. If Jews were found in possession of weapons, the "most stringent measures" were to be applied (this at a time when Jews were still permitted to own them). Archival material in the synagogues was to be secured (this also has the flavor of preplanning). Plundering and theft were to be prevented in all instances.[68]

At 1:20 in the morning, Heydrich, following Himmler's instructions, was finally able to get off his express missive: The Propaganda Directorate was in charge; the state police had to obey its orders. Only such measures were to be taken that would not imperil German lives; the stores and homes of Jews may be destroyed but not plundered. Foreign nationals must not be molested, even if they were Jews. The police were not to prevent the demonstrations but had to make sure that the guidelines were adhered to. Archival material of historical value found in the synagogues and Jewish community houses was to be impounded. As many Jews, especially affluent ones, as could be fitted into the available jail space were to be arrested, and priority was to be given to healthy males who were not too old. The concentration camps were to be contacted immediately so that they could prepare to receive the shipments of Jews.

Messages crisscrossed Germany the rest of the night, with instructions going in one direction, reports of actions carried out in the other.

This, then, was the situation when all hell broke loose all over the German lands during the early morning hours of November 10 and continuing in some places, especially in Austria, until well after the operation had been called off. What made this night and the following day so different from the other persecutions of this time? After all, taken individually, each of the outrages against human decency perpetrated during this night and the following day had already occurred at various times and with varying severity in all parts of Germany, and especially in Austria. But Goebbels and his helpers had succeeded in orchestrating something unprecedented: The whole country was blanketed by their violence; no Jewish community was too small or insignificant to escape the terror. There was no fleeing through the back door to another street, another town, or another part of the country, for the same terror raged there too. This, then, was the truly novel aspect of the events of November 10: their simultaneity throughout the country, the immediacy of their execution following the order given, and the state of preparedness of the cadres designated to carry them out. There was no dearth, at two, three, or four o'clock in the morning, of hand grenades to be thrown into synagogues, of gasoline with which to douse their contents to let them burn at their brightest, of men and boys willing and trained to make use of these violent objects at such short notice. There can be little doubt that this campaign had been prepared well beforehand and that the "seething soul of the people," which was to have set these events in motion upon hearing of the death of vom Rath, was a fiction that fooled no one. Indeed, in Austria hardly any effort was made to keep up the pretense by having the SS and SA appear in mufti. Even uniformed groups of Hitler Youth were brought in to participate in the destruction of property. They stayed to perpetrate particularly cruel acts against the Jews they managed to catch.

The Jews of Vienna were not fooled, either. For the last few days they had already existed, according to Murmelstein, in a state of "almost unbearable tension."[69] The leadership of the IKG took a desperate measure to try and avert or at least reduce the extent of the coming catastrophe. It distanced itself publicly from the event in Paris and condemned it. The following declaration, dated November 8, was sent by the IKG to the Reich Commissioner for the Reunification of Austria with the German Reich:

> The IKG Vienna considers it its sacred duty to convey to the highest authorities of this country, in the name of all the Jews living in the *Ostmark*, the following declaration:
>
> The news of the bloody deed committed on the 7th of this month in Paris has deeply shocked all Jews living in Vienna as well as the other provinces [*Gaue*] of the *Ostmark*.
>
> According to Jewish teaching each human life is God's handiwork. It is the supreme duty of each of us to preserve and save it. Every attack against the life of our neighbor constitutes rebellion against the Creator. Each and every transgression of the laws of God and State must be damned [*muß verdammt sein*].
>
> The Jews living in Vienna and the other provinces herewith express their conviction that no one who remains connected to Judaism could be capable of such a deed. Whoever intentionally endangers human life has eliminated himself from our ranks.
>
> It has become incumbent on the Jews residing in this country to leave the homes they have occupied until now and to seek ways of living under different stars. All our efforts are directed toward doing justice to this task completely and comprehensively. If we seek to make contact

> with our brothers in faith in other countries, if we look for help from them, we do this only in order to be able to solve the question of emigration in a satisfactory manner. Everything beyond these parameters, everything directed against existing regulations is foreign to us and we reject it.
>
> For this reason what took place on the 7th of this month in the German Embassy in Paris constitutes a danger for Jewry. The lunatic author of this deed must be counted among those who, having come from Judaism, have lost the inner connectedness with it and constitute a serious peril for it.
>
> The Jews living in Vienna and the other provinces of the *Ostmark* urgently wish that the love of the heavenly judge preserve the life of the victim of this attack and return him to good health. May the villain, however, receive that punishment from the earthly judges which his evil deed deserves.[70]

We do not know who drafted the document, but we know who signed it. We also know that it was received in the office of the *Reichskommissar* Bürckel. Whether it was ever seen by him or read by anyone in the office cannot be established. The declaration is signed by Emil Engel, as acting head of the IKG, by Chief Rabbi Taglicht, by Rabbi Josef Babad, chair of the rabbinical council, and two members of the advisory board of the IKG. According to Rosenkranz,[71] Löwenherz's representative voted against the declaration. We have in our possession, however, a copy of the declaration signed by Engel, who was the de jure if not de facto representative of Löwenherz while the latter was abroad. It seems evident, therefore, that Landau was referring to the man who, in actuality, took over most of Löwenherz's functions at this time, namely, Murmelstein. This confirms Murmelstein's emphatic statement, made to us in 1977, that he refused to sign the document.

What does this declaration tell us about the situation of the Jews at this time, as their leadership saw it? Reading the effusive letter today one feels uncomfortable, almost embarrassed, and in light of our knowledge of what was to come, very sad. Writing it at all was clearly an act of desperation, in a situation of utter helplessness, a last hope to avert what was to come. The two main signatories, Dr. Engel and Rabbi Taglicht, were elderly men, dignitaries of the once thriving community, and personally courageous. Unfortunately, the language in which the letter is couched and the points it made must have been read by the addressee—if, indeed, he read it at all—as a confirmation of Jewish weakness. The moral stance expressed here, the reverence for life inherent in Judaism, must have seemed comical to those for whom individual life, and especially that of the Jews, had become devalued, and for whom the human being was expendable. But the moral lesson of the declaration would also have been a reminder to the Nazis of the morality they had rejected and might well have turned their amusement into anger, exacerbating rather than calming the situation—a tactical error on the part of the IKG. Further, there is the abject way in which the writers, in the name of all Austrian Jews, take upon themselves the yoke of emigration and give assurances of their total compliance with Nazi decrees. And finally, in writing the declaration at all, which at bottom constitutes an assumption of responsibility (read: guilt) for the act of one of its members, Dr. Engel and the other signatories support, in a sense, what the Nazis, and before them the churches, were wont to do: to hold the entire Jewish Community hostage to the act, real or imagined, of a single Jew. From this assumption of responsibility for the act of a fellow Jew, it is only a small step to the policy of visiting the punishment on the whole community. It did not matter that he placed himself beyond the pale of this community through his deed, since for the Nazi, as we know, the Jew remains the Jew under all circumstances. Ultimately, what was intended by the Jews to be an answer to the accusations against them and an appeal to the Nazis' better nature was bound to fail: the accusations were not based on reality and, hence, could not be refuted, and the Nazis' better nature was sorely lacking. The declaration turned out to be an exercise in futility.

From today's perspective we notice another flaw in what the IKG tried to do: it held no bargaining chip; there was nothing the Jews could offer the Nazis beyond unquestioning compliance, which the latter could exact at any time through increased pressure of a physical or psychological nature. Whether Murmelstein even vaguely understood at this early stage that the only hope of ever gaining the slightest advantage over the Nazi authorities lay in offering them—or seeming to offer—something big in return (and this worked only rarely), or whether his decision not to sign was based on his feisty nature and relative youth, we do not know. Subsequent events, however, seem to bear out the rightness of his negative decision.

As it turned out, nothing seems to have been gained by the leadership of the IKG by writing the declaration, whether on their own initiative or through pressure. If, as Rosenkranz believes,[72] the Gestapo had ordered the IKG via the *Reichsvertretung* to present such a document, noncompliance could have entailed, or could have been thought to entail, some form of punishment, perhaps of the Jewish leadership. In any event, the pogrom proceeded as planned, undeterred by the humiliation of the IKG.[73]

The aims of the operation were generally fourfold: (1) the destruction of the synagogues, (2) the smashing and confiscation of Jewish property, (3) the arrest and deportation of Jews, and (4) their eviction from homes, places of business, and jobs. In the provinces, there was the additional goal of getting rid of the Jews completely, by arresting them, by evicting them and forcing them to move to Vienna immediately, and in some instances, by killing them, as was done in Innsbruck, for example.[74]

There are detailed accounts of the accomplishments of November 10 from many of the units participating. Some of these reports are terse and businesslike, frighteningly so, such as the following one from a unit identifying itself as Sturm 4/11:

> . . . began at 6:00 a.m. and carried on until 22:00 hours. The following synagogues were destroyed:
> 13th district, Eitelberg Street (by fire)
> 15th district, Storchen Street (furnishings smashed)
> 15th district, Turner Street (by fire)
> 11th district, Braunhuber Street (by fire)
>
> House searches and confiscations were carried out in the homes of approximately 100 Jews. Several Jews were injured and some home furnishings smashed.[75]

SS-*Obersturmführer* H. Riegler, however, was much more voluble in his official report and presented the facts with editorial comment:

> . . . about the expiatory measures against Jews, which were carried out by the units of the 89th SS-troop on November 10, 1938, from 4:00 in the morning until 18:00 in the evening. Upon receiving the orders for the operation, the assault unit I/89 and the SS units 1/89, 2/89, 3/89

> were alerted to assemble immediately at their headquarters and to await further orders. Some of the men turned up as early as 1:25 a.m. at the troop headquarters and received further orders there. OStuf. Riegler, Schf. Sischka and USchf. Osel informed their units and went immediately to the 5th, 6th, 8th, and 14th districts. The Jewish synagogues [five synagogues are listed here] had already been almost completely destroyed, and now the remainder was destroyed also. The houses of prayer [two are listed] had not been touched as yet and were now destroyed by the members of the three SS units listed above. The battle readiness of the three Viennese units, which by 8:00 a.m. had reached a strength of 300 men divided into smaller groups, was put to the test in the course of midmorning. The units of the 89th SS-troop participated in the destruction of the following Jewish synagogues or carried the destruction out themselves: [there follows a list of fourteen synagogues in numerical order according to district and with their addresses].
>
> Further the Jewish synagogue in the Central Cemetery . . . the exploding and demolishing of individual Jewish properties was done mainly by the SS-VT with the help of our men and executed in such a manner that the neighboring houses and fellow Germans [*Volksgenossen*] were not endangered . . . the measures, approved after such a long period of restraint against Jewdom that is corroding our national character, were not only applauded by the whole population and especially by the SS, but were received with enthusiasm; and one may state that the SS, considering the time at its disposal, has done a thorough job.[76]

What reason could possibly be given for the destruction of these places of prayer and worship? The *Völkischer Beobachter* of November 11 (Viennese edition) had its answer ready: It was no wonder that popular fury was directed against the Jews and their communal institutions:

> They are, after all, the places where the Talmud, that doctrine so inimical to state and people, and especially the *Shulchan Arukh*, are taught and from where they are disseminated. . . . Never again will forces alien and inimical to the people be able to discuss and plan, under the guise and protection of "religious assembly," those measures which are then encountered at various places abroad and called "boycott movements" and "anti-fascist demonstrations," and which are directed against the Reich and the German people.[77]

A most persuasive argument, especially in light of the fact that hardly any "real" Viennese had ever been inside a synagogue and that the Talmud had long been assigned a sinister role by the Church. Introducing the outlandish-sounding *Shulchan Arukh*, a mid-sixteenth-century code of Jewish law, about which no one knew anything, was just icing on the cake. The good Viennese could sleep soundly at last; with their help, the seat of Jewish conspiracy had been destroyed.

> In the districts and streets in which, despite the aryanization of many stores, there are still more than enough places where Jewish "business acumen" is in evidence, the stores, against which the fury of the people was directed, had to be closed for protection. . . . In many a Viennese street, the windows of the Jew-stores were smashed, and thus a new identity card [*Visitenkarte*, lit. "calling card"] was created for Jewish stores. Looking at the shuttered stores and smashed shop windows, one can tell very clearly how many Jewish stores are still left in Vienna.[78]

This is how the *Völkischer Beobachter*, in the same article and in the same inimitable style—a mix of contempt, sarcasm, incitement, and verbal brutality—continues to deal with the smashing and vandalizing of stores and the looting of their contents. The "protection" offered above refers not to protection of Jews and their means of livelihood but to the attempt to salvage something of the stores' contents for the state or those worthy party members who, trained or not, were to be handed these places of business. Whatever merchandise could be salvaged was brought to collection points to be distributed later to aryanized stores or made available to the NSV, the Nazi Party's welfare organization. "Unfortunately," writes SS-Hauptsturmführer Josef Trittner in one of his oft-quoted reports, "in a few instances senseless destruction of the inventory and even plundering could not be avoided."[79] Truly an understatement.

Jewish homes suffered a similar fate. Wanton destruction and looting were the order of the day, and whatever the roving Nazi bands could not, or would not, take with them, was smashed, slashed, trampled, thrown out of windows, or otherwise made useless. It seems that quite a lot of the goods found in Jewish homes did not make its way into official depositories and storage places. For, whereas the stores were public places and their vandalization and robbing could be observed from the street and reported, apartments were less open to public scrutiny, and what went on there the perpetrators would not, and the Jews as a rule dared not, talk about. When the party members had had their fill of looting and smashing, the Jews were often told to pack up what was left and move out within twenty-four hours or even sooner. The official plan was to requisition the desirable, that is, smaller Jewish apartments. The Jews thus deprived of their homes had to move into large apartments and share them with as many Jewish families as could be squeezed in. These small apartments were considered instrumental in alleviating the housing shortage in Vienna without new houses having to be built. The apartments were then assigned to worthy party members, especially to the "illegals" who had joined in the 1920s. Through this action, Globocnik summarizes, approximately two thousand party members received suitable small apartments.[80]

Whereas the destruction of the synagogues was effected in a relatively organized and, if one may use the term, almost orderly manner, the situation was chaotic during the attacks on homes and businesses. "The operations against apartments and stores should have been carried out in a more disciplined manner," writes SS-HStuf. Trittner. And as regards the loot itself, he suggests searching the cellars of the SA and the NSKK, the organization of party chauffeurs. Amazing things would be brought to light, he continues.[81] Various and repeated attempts were indeed made by the Nazi authorities to recover some of the looted objects. On November 23, for example, the following telegram was sent from the SD Munich to the Gauleiter and Gestapo headquarters in Vienna: "During the operations, initiated by the population against the Jews, several departmental offices of the Party … had to take custody of valuables for the protection of German national assets. I command that such objects be handed over immediately to the nearest Gestapo office, in exchange for a receipt." Instances of theft, "which, unfortunately, may have occurred," are to be reported at once, as is the "reappearance of suspicious objects."[82] Apparently, some of the more conspicuous items were recovered, but most disappeared into the possession of bystanders as well as the party faithful, and no wonder. The people, that is, those who gave the matter any thought, felt they were entitled to all the goodies. Had they not been exposed for years, and especially during the past year, to Nazi and proto-Nazi propaganda, which told them that what the Jew owned was rightfully theirs, since he had stolen or otherwise wrested it from them in the first place? Had they not been told just the day before to take vengeance on him for the brutal murder in Paris of one of theirs by one Jew, a murder for which all Jews were to be held accountable? And what better way to make certain that the right people would receive this windfall than to have these right people help themselves to it directly?

And it was high time to do this. For had not the Jews continued to enrich themselves even after the Anschluss? Globocnik concludes his report dealing with the events of November 10 as follows:

> It should be noted that the Jews continued to do business of an unknown nature, as can be seen from the confiscated savings books, which show increased deposits for the months of June, July, and August. In September, considerable amounts were withdrawn from these deposits, which were used for the purchase of jewelry etc. with the intent to cart these assets off to foreign countries. Through the actions of police and party, tremendous losses of valuables [*Wertverschleppungen*] were prevented. . . .[83]

It would be years before the Nazi authorities gave up trying to get back some of the items lost to them through the self-help actions of individual party members. In April 1941, for example, the main Viennese party office sent a letter to the police president, head of the Viennese Gestapo, complaining that the office was still receiving inquiries regarding the "whereabouts of objects confiscated from Jewish ownership in connection with the operations of November '38. These questions cannot be answered most of the time because, in the course of the last 2½ years . . . the political leaders familiar with this matter had to be replaced by others who were not informed about these things." However, according to the writer's recollection, everything had been turned in and, in time, duly delivered to the Gestapo.[84]

There were other items of value that needed to be taken and secured for party and state, namely, Jewish and especially synagogue libraries and archives, as well as the contents of Jewish museums. A memorandum of November 16 from the Gestapo makes it quite clear that there were various government and party departments eager to have these materials. For example, the head archivist of the city of Vienna demanded the IKG's library as well as many books taken from private sources and synagogues, on the basis that these constituted an item of very great value for the city archive. He was told, however, that the Gestapo would have the final say in this matter. The head of the office for genealogy wanted to have the captured official records (births, marriages, deaths) of the Jewish Community for his *Sippenforschung*,[85] the search into bloodlines that could result in devastating consequences for many who thought of themselves as "good," that is, "pure" Aryan Austrians.

The terror of dispossession and destruction of property was augmented by the terror of arrests and the unimaginable brutality associated with them. As we have seen, the arrests were ordered by the highest echelons of the SS, by Müller, Heydrich, et al. The brutality accompanying the arrests was gratuitous. Whereas the High Command had wanted able-bodied males of substance to be taken into custody, no such niceties of choice were observed in Vienna or, by extension, in Austria. Jews of all ages were snatched away from wherever they could be found, at home, at their places of business, on the street, and whoever was not wearing the usual swastika pin, which only Aryans were permitted to wear, was fair game, as was anyone who "looked Jewish." Even women and children were not safe from arrest. SS, SA, police: they all participated in the game of "catch the Jew." For once, there was no friction between these groups, writes Rosenkranz.[86] Often a pretext was used for the arrest, such as the need for the Jew to come to the police station "to give information." Other pretexts were invented to lend a semblance of legality to the arrests. In the report from SD branch 8, we read that "all the known male Jews are to be visited, their homes are to be searched briefly for weapons and political reading matter," and then they are to be arrested. "[T]he orders . . . were given in such a way that every district group leader could understand that something incriminating must, in every instance, be found at the Jew's, if not legally then by a little imputation [*Unterschiebung*]. . . ."[87]

That this truly was the manner of proceeding is confirmed by the previously quoted article in the *Völkischer Beobachter* of November 11:

> During the visits and house searches in the Jew-apartments, which were carried out everywhere on Gauleiter Bürckel's orders, there was found incontrovertible evidence of [the Jews'] corrupting activity; this consisted of flyers with a content that was clearly inimical to the State, communist brochures, furthermore, foreign currency sewn into the seams of jackets and coats, and the most up-to-date weapons. These were represented by those questioned in their initial shock as harmless old models, of value only to collectors. Under the circumstances, it was very difficult for the police and political leadership to rescue the Jews from the fury of the people. Those who were thus taken under protection became acquainted with the benevolent institution of protective custody in the true meaning of the word.[88]

They obviously knew at the *Völkischer Beobachter* what was being done to those who had the misfortune to fall into the hands of their "rescuers." Trittner wrote in his report that "the treatment of the Jews was in the main very severe and degenerated most of the time into brutal beatings."[89] Rosenkranz presents a detailed account of some of what was done to the arrested Jews even before, and especially after, they were placed into the holding facilities prior to being shipped to the concentration camps; some were eventually released from the holding facilities, such as all women and children and those men whom even the SS doctors considered unfit. The sadistic inventiveness of the catchers and keepers knew no bounds; it was an orgy of torture, deprivations, harassment both physical and psychological. No one who survived it—and there were many who did not—was ever the same again. There were twenty-seven documented deaths in the worst of these holding facilities alone, and a figure of eighty-eight seriously injured at the same place is usually given. Botz speaks of 6,547 Jews arrested in Vienna, about 1,250 in the provinces; 3,700 were sent to Dachau immediately, 1,865 were not considered strong or healthy enough to be shipped there and were kept in police jails, sometimes for months. In the whole Reich, about 20,000 Jews were arrested.[90] This was the first time that large numbers of women were also arrested. Although they were not sent to concentration camps, "the inventiveness of their torturers reached unimaginable heights," writes Rosenkranz. While there were very few rapes, miscegenation being a serious crime in Nazi Germany, the women were forced to participate in sexually demeaning, even orgiastic, encounters.[91]

On November 11, the *Völkischer Beobachter* carried Goebbels's proclamation ending the persecutions, in which he writes: "In spite of the so very justified fury of all the

Germans, not a single hair on a Jew's head was touched; the world may credit this to the discipline of the German people."[92]

There is a dearth of information dealing with the reactions of the party members who were ordered to participate in the excesses of this day. The fact that these events could occur at all makes it quite clear, however, that the vast majority were willing and even enthusiastic participants. Yet there were some who seemed to have pity on the victims and tried, at risk to themselves, to alleviate their lot, especially in the victims' holding facilities. Most of those who had pity, however, were not personally friendly toward the Jews but were ideological anti-Semites who would have liked nothing better than to see Vienna and Austria *judenfrei*. For them it was a question of means and not of ends.

One anonymous Viennese SS-man left behind a brief report of his own involvement in the events of November 10, which led to his "conversion" away from the Nazism of his youth, a conversion he experienced on this day. He had received his orders at three in the morning, and together with

> . . . the order came the command: "The Jews you meet up with, are to be bumped off [*sind umzulegen*]. You'll be covered." The troop leader who gave this order was not any old criminal but a historian, a student at the University of Vienna, an eager beaver, to be sure, and irritating, but I never suspected him to be a murderer. Weeks later I found out that he himself did not "bump off" anyone. . . . We were then divided into groups and each of them was given a special task—mainly to destroy stores, to break into apartments, to destroy household goods, to mistreat the tenants, and to bring those who resisted to the police, where they would be arrested. One group was sent to the synagogue with cans of gasoline and other fuel . . . a part of my group had the intention of participating only "as if." . . . But at least half of the troop consisted of types who intended to commit "acts of heroism." They noticed the intention of others to try to get out of it. This immediately became the occasion for them to speak about obedience and to threaten. Because of this, many weakened. I saw them later, pale and with shaking hands, throwing paintings out of windows and smashing storefronts. . . . At first, disregarding an order seemed to me as bad as another act [i.e., to warn Jews]. I faced the choice of declaring war against a world that I had wished for since my youth. . . . I telephoned, I asked that Jews be warned. . . . The kingdom of my youth collapsed before the burning synagogues and the abused human beings.[93]

The above is an exceptional document and quite at odds with the usual information regarding popular reaction to be found in the reports tendered by the leaders of various groups in charge of the action on November 10. These reports often include an evaluation of the reactions to the goings-on, an evaluation that probably says as much about the evaluator as about the events and the reactions of the people to them. As we will see below, the "approval ratings" vary from high to negative. As we draw our conclusions from these evaluations of the popular reactions, we must also keep in mind that the Viennese, both bystanders as well as participants at some level, were reacting to different phases of the operation, such as the burning and desecration of the synagogues, the abuse, the plundering, and the sudden availability of apartments, in different ways. For example, the "decent" anti-Semites might have been glad to see the Jews forced to leave Austria but appalled at the attendant violence. Others were less concerned about the ultimate purpose of the exercise and more intent on grabbing what they could when they could. And any Jew who had the misfortune to be in Vienna at this time remembers the crowds that had formed around each burning synagogue, gawking and jeering, Jew-baiting, shouting approval at the actual perpetrators, and participating, at times actively but at least vicariously, in the mayhem enacted to cool down the seething soul of the people.

Wiesenthal and Gold quote from several reports in which the populace as a whole is said to be "satisfied" with the action; there is "undivided agreement," even "enthusiasm." The slight dissatisfaction is confined to the "obstinate Reds," who still hold on to their motto "Jews are human beings, too." Otherwise, there is "great satisfaction that at last decisive steps are being taken against the Jews."[94]

Rosenkranz also quotes another revealing passage from the same report:

> Shortly after the operation became known [among the people], a great crowd collected outside the district headquarters, which showed its approval of the action through joyous shouts. When [Jews] were brought [into the police stations], one could hardly keep the population from acts of violence and brutality against the Jews. Several times many, most of them workers, broke through [police] lines and beat up the Jews. In many instances, shouts were heard such as: "Beat them to death, the dogs. Teach them in Dachau how to work," and so on. . . . [P]eople, who up to this point had distanced themselves from the national socialist movement, were now motivated by this drastic action to join their voices to those of the national socialist populace.[95]

If this is a truthful report, then the brutality, rather than turning people away from the Nazi Party, motivated many of them to join it. In their eyes, it had now become the "party of action."

SS-HStuf. Trittner who, according to Rosenkranz,[96] collected incoming reports from the different units and then collated and summarized them for his superiors, presents us with conflicting pictures of the popular mood and, by extension, of his own attitude toward the events. Since we do not know the sequence in which he wrote the reports available to us, or to what extent what is contained in them is copied verbatim from incoming memos, we will not speculate on whether he had a change of heart but will let his words speak for themselves.

In one of Trittner's reports, dated November 11 and addressed to the SS main office in charge of the Danube region, he, too, mentions the tremendous masses of people watching the synagogues burn and "following the course of events with interest and expressions of approval; and, as far as they were not prevented from doing so, they began to participate actively in the actions. Likewise the arrest of Jews and the closing of Jewish stores and places of business were observed with ever increasing interest." One of the main reasons for the participation, vicarious or otherwise, and generally positive reaction on the part of the bystanders, is given by Trittner, who states that the people had "expected retaliatory measures against the Jews"; the press had also prepared them by hinting at such retaliation. But apparently, some anti-Jewish propaganda was spread right at the scene, either by the bystanders themselves or by agents provocateurs who had infiltrated their ranks. The source of the anti-Semitic propaganda does not become clear, since Trittner prefers to use impersonal and passive forms in his report:

> Reference was made to the exploitation of the Aryan population by the Jews during the Dollfuss-Schuschnigg era, to the many instances of Jewish fraud, and to the overweening

A synagogue, variously identified as one in Vienna or in one of its suburbs, aflame during the Kristallnacht pogrom. (DÖW 310[1])

arrogance with which the Jews had already attached themselves to the body of the people of Vienna. The Jews are now receiving their just reward and it is hoped that . . . they would now be driven out of Vienna once and for all. . . . Naturally, in the course of all of these actions, the Jews were not treated gently. . . . [When the action was called off around five that afternoon,] the order was obeyed in a disciplined manner, but many voices were raised regretting that the actions could not be continued, for today was the most opportune time to take care of the Viennese Jew-problem in a radical way.[97]

In an undated report, also signed by Trittner and also directed to the office in charge of the whole Danube region, he sings a slightly different tune: The popular participation is played down and "the unprejudiced observer immediately had the impression that the actions were ordered and organized." He stresses the senseless destruction, plundering and theft, and claims that these "naturally caused the strongest objections among the people." The brutality of the Hitler Youth, who participated at some locations, as well as the general brutality of the proceedings was "received most unfavorably. . . . Once these particulars became generally known, they had an oppressive effect on the general mood and served to do damage to the initial favorable reception of the operation in its entirety."[98] A slightly different report, also by Trittner, dated November 18, differs from the previous undated one in some other respects but retains all the passages regarding the negative evaluation of the general mood in Vienna.[99] Globocnik, too, evaluated the popular mood negatively but tried to rationalize away both the cause and its consequences. He blamed the negative reaction of the people to the way things were handled on the fact that the directives from the Altreich were vague and allowed too much latitude to the different groups carrying them out. For this reason, "a number of things occurred that shocked the people." Furthermore, he claimed that "one naturally sees only the negative aspects of such an event," and continued by stating that "the Party denies any responsibility for the actual negative consequences."[100]

There exist minutes of a meeting called to deal with the consequences of the recent events in the *Gauwirtschaftsamt*, the party's regional economic agency, on November 12. The participants included government officials ("middle-level politicians," as Botz calls them), financial experts, magistrates, and a high Gestapo official. These, according to Botz, were "typical representatives of 'legal,' economically motivated anti-Semitism," who had no use for "popular" anti-Semitism (i.e., the kind that expressed itself through violence and brutality), the reason being that the latter kind of anti-Semitism might not be amenable to control and threatened law and order.[101]

According to these minutes, the people present were unanimous in their opinion regarding the operation: ". . . disapproval and shock about the fact that . . . scandalous scenes took place that severely damage the reputation of the Party and the Reich. . . ." (The damage to the Jews was not mentioned.) "Pogroms and vandalism," they declared, "are not the means to solve the Jewish question. . . . [The] abuse, robbery, and plundering only caused disquiet among the people and many Party members." Lest we mistake this statement for an expression of humanitarian concern, we read "that recently the political leadership has generally interfered in the crassest way in the economic life, that the regional [party] leaders are bunglers and not able to grasp what trouble they make." In other words, what is being criticized here is the method and not the goal, and it is criticized not because this method is inhumane but because it produces undesirable results. And once again the communists are implicated: "The unleashing of the lowest instincts, the incitement to riot, in which a communist mob participated most prominently, undermines the authority of the State." Gauleiters Globocnik and Bürckel, however, were, at least according to this document, completely satisfied with the success of the action.[102]

The accusations recorded in the above minutes did not remain unanswered. They were contested by the SD, which, in its own report of November 21, countered that "even these circles can see the events only from the standpoint of an economic-capitalistic interpretation;" they do not see the "greater goals." This "intellectual upper class" has not yet grasped the meaning of National Socialism, the report goes on to say, and blames the press and radio for not having "treated the problems of National Socialist interpretation in a sufficiently incisive manner."[103] Obviously, even at this early stage, the program of the SD promises to go way beyond the mere dispossession of the Jews.

This difference of opinion regarding the methods to be used—"mere" dispossession vs. dispossession plus brutalization—reflected a divergence of views at the highest levels, with Göring on the side of the method bringing the highest gain to the German economy, that is, "mere" dispossession, preferably by legal means, and Goebbels representing the other side.[104] Gauleiter Bürckel, despite his professed satisfaction with the events, found it necessary to send a letter and report to Göring on November 18 explaining and, in a way, apologizing for the turn taken by the events in Austria. It is interesting to see how Bürckel, himself a "foreigner" in Austria, having come from the Altreich, subtly plays on the anti-Austrian prejudice that was rife in Germany and that he surely shared with Göring. Having been sent to Austria as the Commissar for the Reunification of Austria with the Reich, he saw his mission as "educating" the Austrian Nazis to share the exalted values of the German National Socialists. This proved to be difficult since, as he explains, "our comrades have had to suffer and put up with so much more under the Austrian system [of government] than those in the Reich. The supporters and upholders of this system with its sadistic chicaneries and persecution, with its pauperization of the masses, were—apart from political clericalism—the Jews. It was, therefore, a matter of course that, following the seizure of power, all the hatred turned against the Jews . . . based on this status of illegality the Austrian comrades developed an attitude towards many things that did not completely correspond to our ideas about property, personal decency in money matters, etc." Therefore, Bürckel goes on, he was faced with the tremendous task of reeducating the Austrian Party members. He managed to convince them of his way of doing things, he goes on, and he was faced only now and then with rejection based on the fact that he came from the Altreich. And just when he was making such good progress, the events of November 9 and 10 had to come and make a mess of his educational efforts. All this time, he claims, albeit without much justification, he had taken action against all instances of brutality. And now, "the police in Vienna gave the order to raze completely [*dem Erdboden gleichzumachen*] all Jewish property." All his political leaders have "thrown themselves against this frenzy of destruction," and some of their people were beaten up for their efforts. Whoever is familiar with the Austrian mentality, he goes on, will understand that such an action cannot be stopped from one second to the next. "What is permitted in this hour cannot be a crime in the next." The political leadership, "apart from a few swine," prevented general chaos in Vienna and did everything possible to rescue Jewish merchandise, "which we need so badly." The goods cannot be returned to the Jews because the original owners are unknown and also because "the Jews . . . are making the most unheard-of, mendacious claims." Christmas shopping,

Bürckel concludes, will greatly profit from all the captured merchandise.[105] We find in this interpretation by Bürckel of the pogrom as it took shape in Vienna an exemplary illustration of what Weinzierl refers to as the tension between the anti-Semitic mass movement in Vienna, which she describes as "local pogrom–anti-Semitism manifesting itself in unbridled excesses, plundering, robberies and extortion," and what she calls "the technocratic anti-Semitism operating with governmental pseudo-legal measures" that was favored by the Nazi leadership (such as Göring) in the Altreich and their satraps (such as Bürckel) in the former Austria.[106]

So far we have looked at the events of Kristallnacht through the eyes of the Nazi regime and its adherents. Before we turn to the victims, to the Jews as individuals and as a community, let us refer to Trittner one more time and to his quite astute though sardonic evaluation of the Jewish reaction. "The operation," he writes, "hit the Jews—although they really should have expected it following the death of vom Rath—with paralyzing force. Their mood was one of panic. . . . They were so paralyzed that even the usual hysterical outbursts did not take place . . . The eagerness of the Jews to emigrate will surely have experienced a great boost through the actions. We can be certain that, following today's events, the Jews will have given up the last vestige of their will to stay and defend themselves."[107] This initial paralysis is described also in the memoir of a Jewish witness to these events: "When the flames had died down and we saw the smoking rubble of our houses of worship . . . we were gripped by a paralyzing horror. Only now did we Jews grasp our real situation: that we were prisoners and threatened with death. Now the time before Kristallnacht seemed to us—in spite of suicides, harassment and torment—almost as a time of naive, busily carefree preparation for emigration. . . . Now all that remained to us was fear—the fear of death!"[108] The fear, panic, helplessness, and general demoralization of the Jews of Vienna had reached its peak. There were so many whose husbands, fathers, brothers, and sons had disappeared; and nearly all had lost homes, possessions, and livelihood. They were pursued without mercy, and there was no escape from the pursuers. All illusions about the basic humanity of the Viennese, about an outside world that would care enough to grant at least temporary asylum, lay shattered and burnt about them. They were desperately casting about for ways to alleviate their situation, yet at the same time, were leery of making any move at all for fear of enraging the Nazis even more. A report found in the files of the New York office of the Joint (American Jewish Joint Distribution Center, or AJDC), although referring specifically to something that occurred in Nuremberg, illustrates also the mood of the Jews of Vienna, that is, their panic and attendant paralysis at this time. The report is contained in a letter, dated December 2, 1938, from the Paris office of the AJDC to the main office in New York. Understandably, it is marked "most confidential . . . no publicity" because Jews could not be identified as the sources of the bad publicity worldwide without exacerbating the danger they were in.

There are other examples of both the terror of the Jews and of their fear of showing themselves as complainants over their fate at the hands of their persecutors:

George Roob, a non-Jewish American living in Paris, was in Berlin as of November 14 at the request of AJDC European chairman Morris C. Troper and also traveled to other German cities. He writes:

> While in Nuremberg I intended to intervene with the authorities in the case of Rabbi Dr. Heilbronner, who is in a concentration camp. Before doing so I sought the advice of the Jewish leaders there. They are so terrorized that they thought I was out of my mind. They pleaded with me not to approach the Gestapo, because it might do them harm, if a foreigner, be it Jew or non-Jew, would dare to aid Jews. I personally do not think any harm would result either for me or for them from my visit to the Gestapo, but seeing the frightened faces of my Jewish friends, I desisted from my intentions and Dr. Heilbronner is still in the concentration camp. I was told he is a sick man and will not stand the rigid regime there.[109]

In a report to the Joint, dated December 24, 1938, C. M. Levy recounts his trip to Vienna following Kristallnacht and describes the desperation of the Jews there. He tells of a meeting with Löwenherz, in which "Dr. Löwenherz stated confidentially that he had reason to fear that as many as 60,000 Jews will be arrested in January. He has not made this information public for fear of creating an even worse panic than exists at present."[110] Mr. Levy's report contains incongruities that need to be cleared away so we may get at the truth it conveys. The arrests (of mostly able-bodied men) during Kristallnacht amounted to a disturbing 6 percent of the Jews who were left in Austria at that time. But this fact does not justify the alleged projection of the arrest of 60,000 Jews, which would correspond to over 50 percent of the remainder and include men of all ages, women, and children. By no stretch of his imagination could Löwenherz envisage the Nazis' capacity of arresting in short order and holding 60,000 Jews—even if he had wished to exaggerate for effect, and in no way could he expect the officials of the AJDC to give credence to it. What Löwenherz did know and no doubt meant to impart to Levy was that Eichmann intended to use the momentum of Kristallnacht to put pressure on Löwenherz to the effect that he wanted all Jews out in the next few months—if not by the first anniversary of the Anschluss in mid-March, then by the Führer's fiftieth birthday on April 20—and that he threatened renewed mass arrests as early as the beginning of the next year if he did not see any progress in this direction. The figure of 60,000, which Löwenherz no doubt mentioned, corresponded to the number of Viennese Jews who had emigrated in the nine months since the Anschluss.

In addition, Levy's claim that Löwenherz withheld this information from the public for fear of increasing the prevailing panic is not credible.

First, let us consider the formal question: What access to the Jewish public did Löwenherz have? The newly established *Jüdische Nachrichten* (*Jewish News*) was primarily the Nazi instrument for promulgating the *Weisungen* (directives) handed down through Löwenherz; secondarily, it was the IKG channel for providing the Jews with information concerning emigration, available services, and bodily and spiritual survival, and was censored by Eichmann and his staff. Löwenherz was not the chief of a ghetto, such as, in a later phase, Rumkowsky in Łódź, where he could assemble and speak to multitudes of fellow captives about the evil decrees. Löwenherz did confide in a few intimates among his staff, but under conditions of the strictest confidence and trust. He would not have lasted long as the chief of whatever service the IKG was able to provide the Jews if he had been the source of rumors among the Jews that could have been traced only to him. What Löwenherz no doubt did mean to impart to Levy—as we will see in chapter 6—is the urgency of forestalling the imminent danger to the Jews by coming up quickly with workable immigration schemes.

Second, we need not doubt that Levy did indeed ask Löwenherz why he did not impart to the public his fears that another even greater wave of mass arrests may be in the offing, and that Löwenherz indicated that the public was sufficiently terrified, and that any intensification of their fears would be counterproductive to what the Jews needed most: a destination to emigrate to, and survival until it was their turn to leave. What Löwenherz most likely did not tell anyone but his most discreet and trustworthy counterparts in his dealings with the AJDC and CBF (Central British Fund)—and Levy was too casual a contact for that—was that causing even greater panic among the Jews would, at this stage of the liquidation, play into Eichmann's hands. Eichmann would welcome the chaos of a frantic Jewish populace, for he would thereby gain the justification for controlling them directly without the meddlesome mediation of the IKG. More important, the confusion that such terror would cause among the Jews, especially in consequence of Kristallnacht, was precisely what the IKG was even then representing to Eichmann as the major obstacle to what both Eichmann and the IKG wanted, namely, maintaining the emigration process at a high level. And this could be done only in an orderly manner, or it would fail.

Levy's report reflected the mood among the Jews six weeks after the events of Kristallnacht. They obviously feared that more of the same—and even worse—was to come, and that the regime of terror, far from abating, would only bring about the complete liquidation of Jewish existence in Vienna. The report also reflected the special pressures on the Jewish leadership; it did so, however, without Mr. Levy understanding with what urgency help was needed from the outside, without perception of the need to grasp the facts of their situation with accuracy, and without sensitivity for what the leadership under such duress can and cannot do, can and cannot say.

How prepared was the IKG for the pogrom itself, as well as for the onslaught of Jewish misery to follow? We remember Trittner saying that the Jews should have expected what was to come; and it is true that following the shooting of vom Rath and even preceding his death, a pall of dread and apprehension hung over the Jews in all German lands. But how does one prepare for a unique event and its unprecedented savagery? We must remember that the Jews were not privy to much that was going on in Germany; for example, the *Völkischer Beobachter*, which was Goebbels's mouthpiece and published his own rantings and ravings as well as those inspired and commanded by him, was not accessible to them; and they tried to ignore as best they could or explain away the propagandistic excesses in the daily papers and on the radio. The most reliable sources of information were those gentiles who were "insiders," that is, party members, but who had "their" Jews who, in their minds, were "different" from "the Jews" and therefore deserved to be warned of impending trouble. But this time they, too, did not anticipate the extent and severity of what was planned. No wonder, then, that the IKG, too, was unprepared for the event as well as for its ramifications for the organization itself. Dr. Kapralik calls the preparations for Kristallnacht "a well-guarded secret of the Nazi authorities."[111] Surely neither Löwenherz nor Rothenberg had any inkling of what was to come when they left for London to talk with the CBF and the AJDC. As was customary, they had the express permission to do so from both Eichmann and the Gestapo.[112] In any case, when the blow fell, it was the elderly Emil Engel who was in charge during the absence of Löwenherz and, according to Murmelstein, he simply was not up to the challenge of this day. "He folded up like an umbrella," said Murmelstein; enlarging on his metaphor, he compared him to an umbrella turned inside out in a gale.[113] Thus, until Löwenherz could again take over the helm following his return (the first documented meeting of Löwenherz and Rothenberg with Eichmann following their return was on November 29), the IKG was virtually without strong official leadership, and this at a time when the Jews, desperate for help as well as for information about their missing men, streamed to the IKG from all directions, including the provinces, from which they had been expelled. For them, it remained the only place where Jews might still find a sympathetic hearing. But what they found, at first, was destruction, disarray, and the Nazis.

The synagogue at Seitenstettengasse was the core of the administrative offices of the IKG. If it had been destroyed by fire, the rest of the building would have gone up in flames too, and with it all the documents, such as the files on the Jews and the financial records; indeed the whole apparatus would have been eliminated. Emigration would have come to a full stop. Bürckel therefore gave the order not to set this one synagogue on fire. But that did not save its splendid interior from destruction. "You must admit," Eichmann supposedly told Landau, "that we had to do at least this much."[114] Kapralik, in his memoirs, describes his experiences at the IKG on the morning of November 10:

> I was awakened on November 10 by a phone call from an acquaintance who advised me not to go to the IKG. This was followed by other telephone calls. I considered it my duty to go to the office of the Community and took a taxi. The streets were strangely empty, only police

The interior of the Stadttempel *(City Synagogue) in Seitenstettengasse trashed but not destroyed during the Kristallnacht pogrom. Restored after the war, it now serves as Vienna's main synagogue. (DÖW 12/32)*

> stood around everywhere. It became clear to me that Jews were being caught off the streets. [Arriving in front of the IKG building, he saw that the street was empty there also.] Only a man in SS boots and black pants but otherwise in mufti stood there and said to me, "Just go right into the Kultusgemeinde, but not by the main gate but the first door." . . . [B]ehind the door it was absolute hell. About fifty people, men and women [were there], who had come to the IKG, and about twenty Waffen-SS who were bellowing. The head of the emigration department, Friedmann, stood on a table. It was his task, it seemed to me, to say who belonged to the staff of the IKG. Two Waffen-SS took hold of me. I heard Friedmann call out: "This is Dr. Kapralik, the head of the Foreign Exchange department [*Devisenabteilung*]." It was about 8:00 a.m.
>
> I know nothing about the next two hours. I do not know how I came to sit in my office at about 10:00 o'clock, in an easy chair and not at my desk. Just then I heard terrible screams coming from a woman who was being beaten up in the hall. I heard her screams through the double doors of my room, even though the inside door was padded.
>
> There was no business being conducted. The SS let no one in, and men who had come to Seitenstettengasse were arrested immediately and carted away in waiting trucks. None of us were permitted to leave the building.

In the afternoon all male employees were confined to one room and had to wait there, not knowing what would happen to them. Eventually they were let go and told to come back to work the next morning. Kapralik and the other men who had come to work were the lucky ones, many of those who had stayed at home were caught and brought to the two police stations where the greatest horrors were perpetrated against the Jewish prisoners.[115]

Murmelstein, too, believed it to be his duty to come to the IKG. He describes his experiences in his manuscript:

> At three a.m. on November 10 the janitor of the community house at Tempelgasse [where Murmelstein had been the rabbi] informed me that the synagogue located there had "visitors." . . . I tried to get to the main office of the IKG in order to discuss with . . . Engel, who had his official residence there, what could be done. At the corner of the street I was snatched by SS troops in field gray . . . and brought into the main synagogue. . . . A group of SS men under the personal leadership of Eichmann were just then occupied with smashing the interior. There was a busy knocking and hammering like in a big workshop. When Eichmann saw me, he waved a crowbar in front of my face, screamed at me and had me taken away. Together with Engel I spent an hour under guard. Afterwards we were rudely ordered to go to our usual places of work. I had hardly begun to make sense of my impressions [of the situation] when the door was torn open in a brutal manner. Eichmann charged into the room, for a change waving a service pistol, and roared: "The emigration must continue, it must proceed at full speed."[116]

In Murmelstein's evaluation of his own behavior on that night, his pride in his courage and sense of duty—he called it craziness—was apparent: he did not bolt or hide himself, as many others did, but went to the IKG immediately and did not retreat even when he saw the building surrounded by SS.[117]

Unfortunately there is no testimony available, other than Murmelstein's, documenting Eichmann's actual participation in the destruction in the early morning of November 10, and Murmelstein regrets that he never had a chance to testify to Eichmann's actions at the IKG at his trial.[118] However, Kapralik, too, remembers Eichmann's presence there: "Toward two a.m. a SS-detachment under Eichmann's command approached [the IKG]. The doors were forced open, the building was occupied, the inside of the synagogue including the Holy Ark was destroyed, the Torah scrolls were torn and trampled. Eichmann occupied the Community offices in order to get there ahead of the SA, whose 'action' was scheduled for 4 a.m., and to prevent that the building, which Eichmann needed for administering the emigration, be burnt."[119] One can only marvel at the precise scheduling of the spontaneous show of popular ire.

Shortly after Löwenherz returned from abroad (November 24), he had to appear before Eichmann to report to him about the negotiations he had carried on in London and Paris. Murmelstein remembers Löwenherz telling him that "in the course of this meeting Eichmann tried, by means of leading questions, to find out what I [Löwenherz] had told about his [Eichmann's] heroic exploits of November 10," but his fishing expedition led nowhere. However, Eichmann apparently felt the need to give some explanation of his behavior: He simply had to be there during that night, he claimed; and even though he was unable to prevent the operation, he at least wanted to try to limit the damage. In this he claimed to have been successful, since he managed to prevent the destruction of the adjoining offices and especially of the emigration files, which he had to preserve at all costs.[120]

Beating both the men and the women employed at the IKG and at the Palamt who had come to work and arresting the men seems to have been a favored activity of the SS on that morning. Leo Landau reports: "The building of the IKG was surrounded by SS, which had beaten the Jewish order keepers bloody. In front of the building stood Gestapo vehicles. Whoever wanted to enter the building was beaten and loaded onto the vehicles. The eight to ten officials who were present [in the IKG building] were cut off from the outside world since the telephone exchange was occupied by the SS. They were kept [in the building] under constant threat of arrest until Eichmann arrived."[121] Apparently Eichmann came back at about 10 a.m. and demanded lists of the arrested officials in order to procure their release, his reason being that he wanted emigration to continue and these people were needed for the smooth functioning of the emigration apparatus.[122] Kapralik's and Murmelstein's recollections agree and complement each other on this point. However, Eichmann apparently was not as successful as all that in preserving the emigration files. In the *Aktennotiz* (memo) of November 14, documenting the first meeting of Engel with Eichmann after Kristallnacht, Engel brought up the fact that "part of the emigration files had been destroyed or ruined on the occasion of the occupation of the [main] synagogue and that it will be very difficult to reconstruct the material."[123] Nonetheless, emigration, with or without papers, with or without files, with or without money, had to continue, and do so at an accelerated pace, no matter what the difficulties were for the individuals involved as well as for the IKG. It was incumbent on the IKG to comply with the commands of Eichmann, no matter what, even though the problems seemed almost insurmountable.

Eichmann, in short, regarded the event of Kristallnacht as the fuel that would give the momentum of emigration the new thrust that he had been looking for.

The New Thrust

But was Kristallnacht truly the impetus, the tinder needed to light a fire under the recalcitrant Jews who still had not realized exactly how unwelcome they were in the country they called home, as the Nazis maintained? The answer to this question is many-faceted.

Immediately after November 10 the Jews had other priorities. In the interview of November 14 with Eichmann quoted above, Engel "regretfully has to report that, in view of the situation, an ordered emigration process is out of the question." The Jews, he goes on, are in such great despair because of the many men arrested and of the requisitioning of homes and property that they simply cannot think or act coherently. Their overriding concern at this time is not emigration but information about their missing men and their lost homes. Moreover, many of the men arrested were in the middle of arranging for their and their families' emigration, some were just about ready to leave when they were snatched off the streets or from their homes. This, too, is a setback for the emigration process. There were other immediate concerns, such as food for the soup kitchens, which had been stripped of all edibles by the Nazis, who also smashed the furnishings and equipment. Housing had to be found for those Viennese Jews who had lost theirs, as well as for the Jews who were driven out of the provinces and were now destitute. As many as four thousand desperate people came to the IKG daily at this time,[124] a figure that would increase to over six thousand by February.[125]

One important problem directly related to emigration, which had to be handled immediately by the IKG, concerned those families who had members too old or infirm to emigrate. (In the following chapter we will see how the IKG was involved in a major effort to find a place for these people to be taken care of for the time remaining to them, an effort that required protracted negotiations with Eichmann regarding securing financial means and the retrieval of properties.)

We have alluded to difficulties caused by the loss and destruction of emigration papers, including passports and boat tickets, of people ready to leave, due to the excesses of Kristallnacht and of the confiscation of money needed for emigration and immigration. This, too, led to delays and the interminable duplication of onerous chores already completed once. The situation was often coupled with the arrest of the head of the family and the expulsion of the rest from their home. The IKG had to work simultaneously to help replace lost documents and money, find temporary shelter, and get the men released in time to take advantage of the opportunity to leave, an opportunity which might be their only one. There also occurred catch-22 complications caused by conflicting regulations. For example, in his 34th Weekly Report, Löwenherz writes: "At present, in accordance with instructions, the documents needed to receive a passport are handed out only to those people who possess an immigration permit. However, in many instances the possession of a passport, of a certificate of good conduct or of proof of residence [from the police] is the precondition for receiving the permission to immigrate. Even the boat tickets for immigration to those countries which do not require a visa but landing money and money to show on arrival [*Vorzeigegeld*] can be obtained only upon the presentation of a passport." Löwenherz asks that special regulations be put in place for these kinds of situations.[126] It is no wonder, then, that when Eichmann ordered the IKG to work through the lunch hour Löwenherz informed him that not only was this already being done but that the offices in question were working twenty hours a day without a break[127]—an unheard-of situation in prewar Vienna where the two-hour lunch break as well as the break for *Gabelfrühstück* (second breakfast) and for *Jause* (afternoon coffee and cake) were de rigueur. And Kapralik in his memoirs confirms[128] that the IKG was open and working seven days a week. Closing to observe the Sabbath was no longer an option when lives needed to be saved.

A number of problems also arose out of the situation that were not related to emigration, such as the need for medical care for Jews, who were by now mainly dependent on Jewish doctors and the one Jewish hospital, the relatively small *Rothschildspital*. Aryan doctors and nurses could no longer be expected to treat Jewish patients, either by their own choice or because of pressure from the Nazi authorities, and Aryan hospital patients could no longer be expected to, or refused to, lie next to Jewish patients on the wards. A great number of the Jewish doctors had been arrested, even some who were attached to the hospital and were essential for its functioning; others had already emigrated. The hospital itself was bursting at the seams. At the same time the non-Jewish staff at the Rothschildspital, reports Kapralik, made special difficulties by performing their duties very poorly and with great reluctance, yet had to be kept on. The IKG breathed easier, he says, when, at the end of November, the local authorities made the non-Jewish staff leave "'since it was below the dignity of the Aryan nurses, and they could not be expected to take care of Jews.'"[129] There exists a letter from the director of the hospital to the administration of the IKG dated November 11 and received at the IKG on November 17, reporting on the situation at the hospital and the events of the previous day: fourteen wounded were brought in, four of them very seriously hurt. From the appended list, stating their names and injuries, it is quite clear how these people received their wounds. There were broken limbs, hematomas, stab wounds, concussions, teeth knocked out, noses smashed. All but one were males, ages 19 to 59. There were also three attempted suicides brought in, of which one, an 80-year-old woman, had already died. Further, two of the leading staff physicians, the head of the x-ray institute and a senior professor and *Hofrat* (court councilor, an honorific dating back to the monarchy) had been arrested at their homes, as was an orderly. The local party office sent guards to the hospital on the afternoon of November 10, who remained overnight, apparently to make sure that the hospital itself was not attacked. The emergency staff had to be augmented. There was so little space available at this hospital, which was never designed to take care of all the Jews in Vienna and was not equipped to handle the kind of emergency situations faced at this time, that even by pushing beds together and putting patients to bed in a waiting room, only fourteen more spaces could be created, for a total of 263 beds.[130]

Desperate Measures

And there were other pressing problems. Since most of the Jews no longer had a job to keep them occupied, and since it was believed that people who had a specific trade or specialization would have a greater chance at being accepted in a host country, the IKG had instituted a great number of courses in practical subjects. These courses were very popular. Attending them not only gave people something to do and to meet others in circumstances similar to theirs, but they felt that they were doing something toward their emigration. According to IKG figures, almost 11,000 people had taken these courses up to the end of December. However, Kristallnacht adversely affected this effort also. Sixty-four courses with over 800 students had to be canceled because the premises had been sealed, ten teachers and over 300 students had been arrested and were still in concentration camps at the end of December.[131] The number of course participants had shrunk to 2,500. Many Jews who would have been glad to attend were afraid to leave their homes, afraid to be part of a group that could be snatched at will. This situation was very detrimental to Jewish morale and had to be addressed by the IKG. Furthermore, now that the Jewish children were no longer allowed in the public schools, some alternative schooling had to be found for them, teachers had to be hired, localities requested from the authorities. Seeing to it that some semblance of meaningful life, of a life that looked toward some kind of a future, was preserved, was a great concern of the IKG at this time in order to counter the great despair.

And finally, there was a miscellany of problems and inquiries to be dealt with. For example, a Jakob Rothman, probably a functionary of the Döbling synagogue, informed the IKG on December 1 that his wife had been called to the police and handed a number of ritual objects from the Döbling synagogue, all of them badly damaged. He asked that the IKG take them over. Mr. Rothman was referred to the cemetery office, most likely to arrange for their burial.[132] There is also a letter from a real estate management company, asking the IKG to replace the smashed windows of a room rented by a Jewish organization and used for prayer. Engel replied that this organization was not the responsibility of the IKG and referred the agency to the Receivership Commissioner for Jewish Organizations (*Stillhaltekommissar*). There were inquiries about the liquidation of destroyed properties such as private synagogues and houses of prayer, the possible future uses of the real estate, and so on. In a memorandum to Eichmann, dated January 6, 1939, Löwenherz lists the bills paid by the IKG for the SS-guards who had been stationed at the IKG from November 12 on, whose main function, rather than to protect the building and the people in it, seems to have been to harass the already harassed clientele even further. The IKG had to pay them their wages (RM 1950.00), their bills at taverns (RM 1712.94) and coffeehouses (RM 514.78), as well as extra heat, electricity, and cleaning (RM 294.00), for a total additional financial burden of RM 4471.72.[133] We did not find any record of reimbursement.

When the first wave of panic and terror had passed and the Jews were able to think more clearly about the situation in which they found themselves, they realized that they were now placed irrevocably beyond the law. Those laws governing civil relations between people no longer applied to them. Even the most basic rights and protections accorded to human beings had been or were being withdrawn, either arbitrarily or by the imposition of new laws and regulations meant specifically for them. They had to get out if they wanted to have at least a chance at survival. Whereas before November 10 they might have weighed one destination against another, have hesitated and waited for better opportunities, they now realized that better opportunities were not forthcoming. They were not really wanted anyplace. The Nazis saw to that. For—as we have seen—at the same time as they were chasing out the Jews they made certain that the potential host countries did not want them, by sending them out with hardly more than the clothes on their backs. Norman Bentwich, who visited Vienna in August of 1939, less than two weeks before the outbreak of the Second World War, speaks about the fact that in Vienna the Nazis "prefer a disorderly to an orderly emigration."[134] When Bentwich went with Löwenherz to see Eichmann, he asked Eichmann outright why emigration could not proceed in an orderly manner in Austria; he also informed him that the Council for German Jewry could only support an orderly emigration. Eichmann gave him the cryptic answer ". . . that there were special circumstances in the *Ostmark* (Austria). Orders had been given in the highest quarters that the complete evacuation of the Jews must be carried out in the shortest time, and the statement about ordered emigration (made by Dr. Wohltat to the Inter-Governmental Committee assuring ordered emigration based on the help of other governments) did not apply there." It now becomes clear why Eichmann did not seem fazed at all, back in November, by Engel's statement that orderly emigration was impossible at that time: disorganized exodus, a mad dash for the borders, a lemming-like trek to nowhere fit right into Eichmann's scheme and into that of his superiors.

Herrmann Graml finds this seemingly contradictory behavior—intense and brutal pressure on the Jews to get out, coupled with the pressure on potential host countries to close off the escape routes—to have prevailed in all of Germany and ascribes it to the Nazis' determination not to let the Jews survive anywhere. His interpretation, crediting the Nazis with the desire "to make the earth uninhabitable for the Jews" even at this relatively early date, makes sense, especially in light of the events to come. To support his thesis, Graml quotes from a speech given by Himmler before SS squad leaders on November 8, 1938: "The Jew can no longer hold out in Germany. . . . We shall drive them out more and more with unparalleled ruthlessness. . . . Of course the other countries . . . are not anti-Semitic at present, but they will become so in time . . . so that someday the world will no longer have any room for the Jews."[135]

In the meantime, however, the Jews had to find room somewhere, and find it very quickly. An example of their attempts to engage the outside world in their struggle, an attempt that was as desperate as it was to a large extent hopeless, can be found in the files of the Gestapo, and is dated November 24–25, 1938:

> In a bundle of newspapers addressed to Julius Steger, New York, Hotel Vanderbilt, there was a 2-page typewritten "cry for help" of the "Jews of Vienna," in which we read the following:
>
> "America, England, France; Help us!
>
> "You, the leading and most powerful countries in the world, can do it. Several hundred million civilized people can protect 300,000 unhappy, tormented, despised, and beaten beings, if they seriously want to do so. We are not helped by radio reports and surely well-meant articles in the press, they often worsen our fate in this country. Open the doors of your consulates and palaces that belong to you in this country, counsel us there and give us real help; do not any longer watch from behind closed doors how an unfortunate crowd, which has stood in line on the street before your closed gates the whole night through, is mistreated by brutal bloodhounds, only to find out in the morning from your underlings that the exit permissions granted by you, all the affidavits and permits just lie there many months in your consulates and have not been attended to. Let your representatives in your senates and lower houses speak at last officially about the inhumanity we have to endure, powerless and unable to defend ourselves as we are. Let them discuss in these bodies possible ways to eliminate these horrible tortures!"[136]

We have no information regarding the identity of Steger, whether he informed the Gestapo, whether they intercepted the newspaper shipment, what action if any they took in regard to this desperate plea. We merely know that it did not influence the countries it addressed.

When we try to determine the exact emigration figures month by month starting with the Anschluss, we find that they are almost impossible to come by. Various factors account for this: Even though the IKG kept an accounting for each month and submitted those figures to the AJDC as a basis for calculating necessary contributions, they could be certain only of the number of Jews who had received financial help from them in order to be able to leave the country. The IKG files also yield the number of people who passed through the emigration process, who de-registered and thus made their presence—or absence—known. Many others—and we do not know how many—went illegally across the borders while this was still possible; these were mostly younger people who could pick up and go, who were adventurous or desperate enough to take chances, for example, to cross the Alps on foot by night, who could gamble on an uncertain reception abroad. It is known that the Nazis on occasion forced Jews illegally across borders, especially those holding Polish passports or those who were stateless. Still other Jews may have failed to register for emigration in the first place or may have somehow fallen through the statistical cracks. Furthermore, the emigration figures of the IKG during this time concern what the Nazis called *Glaubensjuden*, Jews by faith, whereas the figures the Nazis came up with often included also those who were considered Jews by descent, so-called *Rassejuden*, Jews by race but not necessarily by faith. Thus, the exaggerated figure of 300,000 Jews residing in Austria, which the Nazis liked to cite, was meant to refer to *Rassejuden*, whereas the IKG operated with the original figure of 180,000 Jews, all of them Jews by faith.

Another difficulty that arises where we try to check one set of figures against another is that the figures do not cover a comparable time span. For example, we do not know if totals were compiled at the beginning or the end of the month. Some lists give the number of Jews who have left, others the number remaining.

In spite of these reservations we can learn a few facts from the official IKG figures regarding emigration before and after Kristallnacht. Between the Anschluss and the end of October 1938, the IKG de-registered 47,165 Jews. Twenty-two percent of these emigrated with the financial assistance of the IKG. At first emigration was slow, but it more than doubled in June of 1938 to over 8,000, reached a peak in August (9,700), then dropped by about one third in September and by another 1,000 in October to not quite 5,600. There is a slight increase, into the 6,000s, in the next three months, then a rise to 7,200 and almost 8,500 in February and March 1939, respectively, followed by a sharp drop by over 2,500 in April 1939, after which the downturn continues. By June of 1939 the IKG was giving financial aid to 62.5 percent of all emigrants.[137]

When we interpret these figures we must keep in mind that it usually took an individual—and especially a family—months to ferret out a possible destination, make the necessary contacts, get the papers together, go through the emigration procedures, try to salvage some remaining assets to take along, find a berth on a ship, and so on. Most of the time spent on these procedures was beyond the control of the potential emigrants, and they could have done very little to shorten it. Further, and more important, we see no dramatic increase in the monthly numbers of emigrants after Kristallnacht, which was supposedly instigated to speed up emigration drastically. What did increase tremendously, however, were the efforts on the part of the IKG leadership to find destinations for people and to get them there as quickly as possible. (We discuss the heroic efforts of the IKG in the next chapter.) Gradually, more and more work and ingenuity were required, as well as increasing amounts of money, to find destinations for people who, as a group, by now were not as young as the earlier emigrants, had to consider their families, often with dependent children, or had fewer if any assets left, and were greatly limited by new laws as to what they could take along to start a new life God knows where. At the same time more and more borders were closing against the Jews—we recall that, as of October 1938, Jews were identified as such in their passports and were thus made all the more unwelcome abroad.

The most immediate emigration problem, however, was the conditional release of the men in the concentration camps. These were let go with the proviso that they leave the country within days or, at the most, two weeks. Otherwise, they were told, they would be sent back to Dachau or Buchenwald. The IKG leadership eventually persuaded Eichmann to extend this impracticable time limit to four to six weeks, during which time frantic efforts were made to find places for these men to go to. Apparently, these efforts were successful; we are not aware of any case where Eichmann had the opportunity to make good on his threat—truly a remarkable achievement by the IKG leadership. (The schemes devised to rescue the concentration camp releasees are discussed in chapter 6.)

Isolation and Abandonment

During the desperation and turmoil of these November days, the Jews of Vienna felt more isolated than ever from the world outside. The newspapers to which they had access did not report on the reaction abroad to the events of Kristallnacht, and most of their radios had been smashed, robbed, or requisitioned. The Jews could not know if the news of this latest outrage had reached the outside world at all. There was no sudden dramatic opening of borders, no noticeable effort by any power outside of Germany to interfere or to alleviate. But the news had gotten out, and for a few days the media abroad focused on what had occurred. They spoke of the pogrom "in terms of the utmost revulsion and horror." The foreign press was there when it happened, saw and heard firsthand and was able to take a few pictures. People in other countries realized for the first time what it meant to be a Jew in the Germany of that time.[138] On November 21, Paul Baerwald, chairman of the AJDC, sent a letter to "selected leaders or executive directors in larger cities" in the United States with an attached copy of an advertisement asking for contributions. The letter reads in part: ". . . the attached advertisement . . . appeared Friday morning and afternoon in every New York newspaper. So much publicity has been given in the American press to recent and current events in Germany, and so much sympathy has been aroused among the American public—both Christians and Jews—that it was our thought not to dramatize the situation. . . . What will interest you particularly in this advertisement is that we are demonstrating to the country that we are in close touch and cooperation with the organizations for the Catholic and the Protestant refugees." The advertisement speaks of the tragedy "which has overwhelmed not only Jews, but also Catholics and Protestants in Germany" and asks for contributions. The checks are to be sent to one of the four organizations listed—the AJDC, the United Palestine Appeal, the American Committee for Christian German Refugees, and the Committee for Catholic Refugees from Germany, and the moneys collected are "to be expended by them, respectively."[139] In other words, there would be no pooling of funds, to be brought into action wherever the greatest need arose.

Edith Ehrlich nee Schwarz's German Reich passport with the red "J" stamp identifying her as a Jew. An additional sign of her Jewishness is her middle name. All Jews had to assume as their middle names Sara, in the case of females, or Israel, in the case of males. (© CSE)

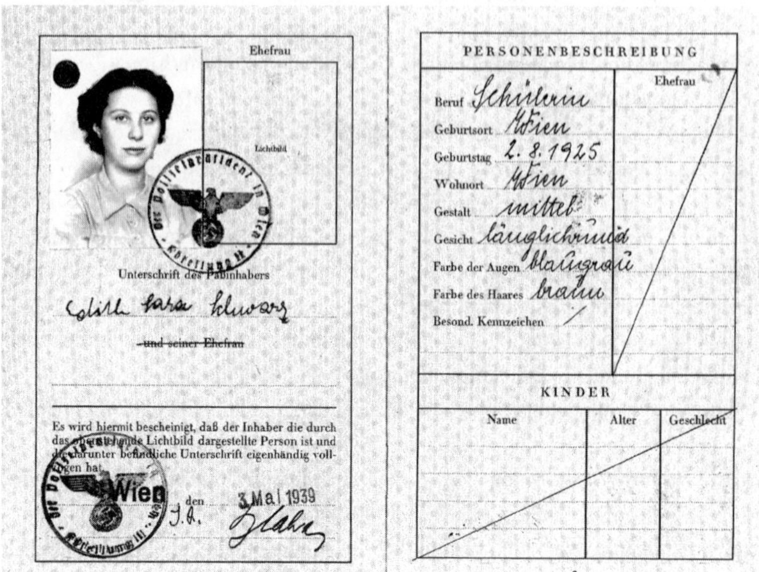

This is a very telling document. Even at this crucial time when shock and indignation were expressed by the media as well as by politicians and statesmen, not even as powerful an organization as the AJDC would have dared to speak out boldly on behalf of the Jews or to issue a call to arms against the outrages committed against them. Indeed, the letter and accompanying flyer almost make Kristallnacht sound like a natural cataclysm, a flood or a famine. And at a time when it was primarily the Jews by faith and their houses of worship that were the targets, the advertisement sounds as if Christians were equally victimized. Jews must not make waves, not even in America. Baerwald did not want to "dramatize the situation"—but what could have been more dramatic than the truth itself?

The media cannot interfere directly; only governments can do that and, for reasons of state or ideology, governments can refuse to do so. For example, in France, foreign policy considerations (Ribbentrop was expected on a state visit) dictated the course of events, and the press was asked—and to a great extent complied—to tone down their reporting of the events of Kristallnacht.[140] President Roosevelt, on the other hand, rebuked Germany in strong terms on November 15 and recalled the American ambassador, Hugh Wilson, "for consultations." The German ambassador to the United States, Hans-Heinrich Dieckhoff, was withdrawn in turn. In his dispatches, while still in the United States, he reported on the mood of the American public in light of the recent events in Germany. He found public opinion across the board "to be incensed against Germany and hostile towards her!" Even "respectable patriotic circles, which are thoroughly anti-Communist and, for the greater part, anti-Semitic" had changed their attitude toward Germany.[141]

Yet, America's shock and dismay did not change the deliberate pace of immigration to the United States; indeed, the emigration figures from Vienna to the United States for December 1938 were sharply lower than during the preceding months (only 31 people during the last week of December) because, as the IKG pointedly reported to the Joint, the U.S. consulate had closed for the Christmas holidays![142] When President Roosevelt was asked whether he would consider an alteration in the immigration laws to allow a greater influx of refugees at this critical time, he replied: "That is not in contemplation, we have the quota system."[143] Nor would he allow the unused portion of the 1937 immigration quota for Germany and Austria to be transferred to 1938.[144] The one immediate concession made by the United States in light of the situation was first to extend visitors' visas for another six months, and later to grant "long-term asylum to 15,000 fugitives then in the country on temporary visas."[145] It is doubtful that many Viennese Jews were among those 15,000.

In Great Britain moral indignation ran up against government policy. The country had staked much on "peace in our time" and the events in Germany threatened to undo the precarious relationship which British leaders had tried to establish. News of the pogrom was received with horror, a horror that was expressed in the media, in the House of Commons, and by some members of the clergy. Public opinion overwhelmingly considered the German treatment of the Jews to be "an obstacle to the good understanding between Britain and Germany."[146] Yet at about the same time Sir Samuel Hoare, Home Secretary, gave evidence of the "complete lack of relationship between the pogrom and the Government's foreign policy"[147] in his speech on November 24 to the Cambridge University Conservative Association, in which he "warned his audience that 'on no account must we fall from the height of exultation to which the world was lifted by the Munich peace to the slough of despondency in which there is no hope. . . . [T]the people in England and Germany wish to live at peace with each other and to see carried out in the spirit and letter the resolution against war signed by the German Chancellor and Mr. Chamberlain.'"[148]

Yet Great Britain was the one country that chose—or dared—to respond with a public gesture to the outrages perpetrated in Germany; yet, this response was not from one government to another, but a humanitarian one. Sir Samuel Hoare announced in the House of Commons the immediate admission of "as many Jewish children from Germany . . . as could be sponsored by responsible bodies and individuals." But "this concession was combined with a warning against the danger of mass immigration" because of the latent anti-Semitism in the country.[149] Britain's provision for the children's transports as well as the creation of a transit camp for able-bodied men at Richborough are discussed in the next chapter.

Finally, there was one reaction from various sectors of the free world that had apparently not been anticipated by Germany: the boycott of German companies and export goods, not only on the part of Jewish businesses and not only on a retail level. Many contracts were canceled, and the German armament industry as well as manufacturers of goods such as toys and leather goods lost a large percentage of their export business.[150] This was a devastating blow to Germany's foreign exchange and constituted a loss that had to be recouped—from the German Jews.

The November action against the Jews in Germany with its overt brutality visible to all, which had caused such negative reactions abroad, had run its course. No further action of this nature was perpetrated against the Jews within Greater Germany, partly because of this negative reaction, but largely because it was found not to be in the ideological or economic interest of the Reich. Germany, therefore, now chose to follow a different path to the total expropriation and humiliation of its Jews; it reverted to the path of legality. A veritable deluge of anti-Jewish legislation now engulfed the Jewish population. As usual, Vienna led the Altreich in anti-Jewish measures, for quite a bit of what was enacted at this time had already been put into practice there. But much of the legislation was new, even for Vienna, and devastating in its effect. The decisions to impose these harshest of measures were reached on November 12, 1938. Göring convened a meeting at the Reich Ministry of Aviation, which was attended, among others, by Goebbels, the Ministers of the Interior, of Economics, Finance, and Justice, by a spokesman for the German insurance industry, as well as by Heydrich; in short, all those senior officials attended who were involved in one way or another in what was euphemistically called the "solution of the Jewish question." Göring was furious about the loss to the Reich of the Jewish assets destroyed or robbed in the course of the pogrom, and he declared that he would have preferred the killing of two hundred Jews to the loss of such valuables.[151] A close reading of the minutes of the meeting provides the faint image of Göring glowering at Goebbels and Heydrich, both squirming in their seats.

This meeting had two main objectives: one was damage control, the other the creation of the means for the further dehumanization of the Jews. As we have seen, a tremendous amount of material damage was caused by the pogrom all over Germany, specifically through arson, vandalism, robbery. The destroyed and looted Jewish property—which the Nazis, in any case, considered to be potentially theirs—could no longer be distributed to worthy Aryans. The fact that stores and factories were demolished and their contents stolen or made unusable meant that no Aryan could become the new owner of a flourishing business. International trade suffered; the cities looked a mess, there were burnt-out ruins and smashed store fronts, often in the best parts of town, there was broken glass and other debris all over the usually so clean and tidy German cityscape. What was to be done? The conference participants came up with an inspired idea: make the Jews clean up the mess! After all, they were responsible for its creation in the first place, for if the Jew Grynszpan had not fired the fatal shot and killed vom Rath, the seething soul of the people would not have felt compelled to vent its anger in the manner described. And so the Jews were ordered to pay for the restoration of the *Strassenbild*, the streetscape, including the replacement of the shattered windows. The synagogues, which had been turned into blackened eyesores, were to be replaced, at Goebbels's suggestion, by parking lots. The Jews were also required to repair, at their own expense, the damage done to their homes and places of business.

Eduard Hilgard, the representative of the German insurance companies, wanted to know what was to be done about the insurance carried by the Jewish owners of businesses and homes. Was German money to be used to reimburse Jews? German insurance companies were known, after all, for the prompt payment of claims. Heydrich came up with the following idea, which was accepted: All such claims were to be paid; but as soon as the Jews received their reimbursement, the German government would confiscate it. Of course such confiscation did not apply to Aryan claims—and there were many such claims from Aryan landlords, especially for the replacement costs of expensive Belgian glass plate windows—and this money was lost not only to the German insurers but, more important, to the coffers of the Reich itself.

And so Göring and his guests thought up another scheme that would help to shore up German finances: A fine was imposed on the German Jews as a collective "atonement" (*Sühneleistung*) for the murder of vom Rath. This fine, to be collected by August 15, 1939, was set at one billion Reichsmark. The actual sum collected exceeded this amount; in the end, one billion, one hundred twenty-seven million Reichsmark were taken in.[152]

There was a good reason why the Germans chose this one-time levy over imposing a continuous taxation on the Jews, a reason that is explained by another edict issued on November 12, namely, a "decree which eliminated the Jews from German economic life."[153] This edict was a much greater blow to the Jews of the Altreich than to those of Vienna, since the latter had, in effect, already been eliminated almost completely from the Austrian economy. The decree did, however, supply the legal underpinning of the Austrian fait accompli. Among the provisions agreed upon on this day were those which stated that Jews could no longer own or manage retail or mail order businesses, practice trades or crafts, occupy managerial positions in business and industry; they also provided for the forced "sale" of real estate owned by Jews, in return for worthless receipts. But this was just the beginning. And once all their remaining sources of income had dried up, following the execution of this decree, there would soon have been nothing left to collect. Other regulations—following, in Göring's words, "blow upon blow"[154] logically upon those promulgated on this day—led in time to the complete dispossession and the total pauperization of the Jews. For example, in order to assess the individual Jew's share of the aforementioned levy, the Nazis needed to know exactly what assets he still possessed. Then, based on this information, these assets (bank accounts, stocks, bonds, etc.) could be blocked.[155] And to make sure that he could not, at the last minute, turn such assets into jewelry or, conversely, sell such jewelry, perhaps to have money to live on or to emigrate, all precious metals and stones had to be delivered up to the authorities. In return the Jews got a worthless receipt. Nothing could be retained by them, not even ritual objects such as Sabbath candlesticks, with the exception of wedding bands.[156]

Parallel with those decrees promulgated at the conference of November 12 that led to the total material dispossession of the Jews, there were others that robbed them of most of the status as human beings still remaining to them. Two aims seem to have been served by the discriminatory measures decided on at that time: one to "'buttress' the economic measures" enacted on that day (Göring's contribution), the other, to remove the Jews "from the public eye where they have a provocative effect"[157] (Goebbels's contribution). The Jew was to become invisible and, hence, nonexistent in the mind of the "real" German. Toward that end, streets in Vienna named after Jews were to be renamed, statues and busts of Jews were removed, as were monuments and busts made by Jews.[158]

Again, many of these measures were already in effect in Vienna, but they now received their official sanction. The Jews were now forbidden to attend public events or to take advantage of public facilities; to own weapons of any kind; to wear the national costume (such as a Dirndl dress or Lederhosen); even to own carrier pigeons.[159] A few days later they were denied access to public schools, including the university (from which Jews, at least in Vienna, had been excluded for months already), and their driver's licenses were withdrawn. On November 28, a police ordinance empowered government officials to limit the access of German and stateless Jews to certain parts of a town during certain periods. This made possible the imposition of curfews, "a first decisive step," Rosenkranz calls it, "toward the limitation of their freedom of movement."[160]

There was no outcry against these legal and quasi-legal measures and those to follow, neither on the part of the German public nor from abroad. This message was not lost on the Nazis, who, from then on, abstained from organized, overt violence against the Jews in Germany. They learned that they could achieve their ends much better through silent pogroms embodied in laws and ordinances. The Jews were now reduced to paupers, denied basic civil and human rights, and made invisible. Was their descent to the level of nonpersons, begun in earnest on November 10, the necessary precondition to the virtually unopposed—at least within Germany—physical elimination to come? In any case, as Göring stated at one point during the meeting of November 12, he would not want to be a Jew in Germany.

How right he was! For Kristallnacht was not only the occasion for Göring to withdraw from the Jews the last economic basis of their existence. It was not only the high point, so far, of venting on the Jews the meanness of the likes of Streicher's and Goebbels's contemptuous hatred. Indeed, it provided the upsurge of the momentum for solving the Jewish problem and also promoted the machinery that Eichmann devised for this purpose in Vienna as the only instrument capable of serving this purpose and worthy of being a model. Let us explain.

Reorganization of the SD

The Jewish Section (112) of SD Bureau II (Opponents) proved to be more than what it was intended to be. Its evolution in Vienna from gathering information about opponents into an instrument for liquidating them served as the impetus for redefining the function of SD Bureau II and constituted one of the many internal reorganizations of the SD that Heydrich undertook during the eventful year 1939. Redefinition of SD Bureau II began soon after Kristallnacht. The problem with the previous definition was that there was no continuity between the gathering of intelligence about "opponents" and any execution of policy indicated by the ideological interpretation of the information gathered. This is one reason for the jurisdictional conflict in which Eichmann found himself involved with the Gestapo, which, as the police organ, thought of itself as the proper executor of policy. In the weeks following Kristallnacht, we find Heydrich addressing these difficulties in several of his reorganizational directives. On February 24, 1939, after consultations with Himmler, he ordered the "organizational as well as personal coordination" (*organisatorische und personelle Angleichung*) of the Security Service (SD) with the Security Police:[161]

> The SS, as the supporting framework of the [Nazi] movement, directed by its special laws of military discipline and by its *weltanschauliche* [as determined by worldview] position, incorporates the state apparatus' sector "police." . . . [T]he police has been organically absorbed into the SS—not the other way around. . . . [I]t follows that—as a department of the SS—the SD is the bearer of a political aim. Aside from achieving this political aim through a prudently organized procedure, section by section, there is also the development of the concrete task of the total political information service, which is primarily the bearer and the very essence [*Inbegriff*] of the organization "SD," and which has its own proper dynamics to be derived in a law-like manner from its work.[162]

In light of the dynamics derived from its actual work:

> The main task of Bureau II will consist in the broad planning of the fight against opponents through research into their ideologies, *Weltanschauungen*, tactics of combat and strategies.[163]

In the case of Eichmann's extension offices of Bureau II, "broad planning of the fight against opponents," in this case the Jews, involved more than research into the nature and means of the "opposition." Heydrich's task of reorganization in light of the "dynamic derived from its work" did not so much pertain to Eichmann's extension of SD II/112 but to the function of Eichmann's main office in Berlin, i.e., SD II/1. What possible function did Heydrich envisage for SD II/1?

> From [a central] vantage point, II/1 could be assigned the education and training of a troop of "*active*" SS-men who, in a variety of professions, could be committed in a variety of ways in all areas of life and of opposition; [such a troop] would inevitably make the SD independent

> of future networks of observers, so as to enable it to engage in an action with "professionally trained" men in important cases and under disguise.[164]

It would be hard to dismiss the connection between these reorganizational projects and the experiences of Kristallnacht, and Eichmann's accomplishments. Kristallnacht showed that the ideologically directed SS was capable of tough action but that such action needed disciplined training, a discrete venue, a well-defined task, and central control. The example of Eichmann showed a number of relevant facts. It showed that the liquidation of an opponent who cannot be assimilated may require supplementary means more subtle than the hard-hitting action any SS-man is expected to be prepared for; that the nature of such means can be devised on the spot and that he can be trained for it while actually engaged in the action; that—while the extension agency is subject to "strict central direction"—in order for it to be effective, "the hands of the men at the front must be left free [to do their] work."[165]

Freedom of action on the part of the task forces charged with fighting opponents required that the umbrella of central direction provide coordination with other agencies, both as regards strategic policy and the nitty-gritty of tactical execution. This too can be seen to be the result of the experience of Eichmann's performance in Vienna as well as of the "chaos of authority" that prevailed at the time of Kristallnacht. We have seen how incensed Göring was over the economically destructive nature of Kristallnacht. In consequence thereof, as the plenipotentiary of the Four-Year Plan—and nominally in charge of the police forces, that is, the superior of Himmler and Heydrich—on January 24, 1939, he directed Heydrich, as the SS Chief of Security Police, to establish a central instrument for the liquidation of Jewish existence in Germany, to be called *Reichszentrale für die jüdische Auswanderung* (Reich-Center for Jewish Emigration). The center was to be established within the Ministry of the Interior, albeit under the leadership of Heydrich; it was to consist of a directorate and an executive office.[166]

The directorate would be a committee headed by Heydrich and consisting of delegates from all concerned ministries—the Foreign Ministry, the Ministries of the Interior, Economics, and Finance, and Undersecretary Dr. Wilhelm Stuckart. The staffing of the directorate tells us that the execution of the Jewish policy of the Nazi regime would henceforth be planned and conducted in a purposeful, coordinated, and orderly manner. Of course, policy would not be determined by the directorate; it would remain the prerogative of the highest echelons of the ideological regime and of the SD. However, the interests of foreign, domestic, and economic policy would have to be considered insofar as they were pertinent to and would further the execution of the Jewish policy. Notably absent from this committee were representatives from Goebbels's Ministry of Propaganda and Public Enlightenment; the enactment of Jewish policy needed the occasional services of the expert rabble-rouser, but when it came to the determination of strategies and tactics Göring wanted Goebbels to be kept at a distance. The presence on the directorate of Stuckart, who was high in the ranks of the SS as well as the undersecretary of the Interior, shows to what extent the Nazi Party had succeeded in staffing key positions of the various ministries and other governmental agencies (as well as business, finance, and industrial organizations) with party members. We clearly recognize in this memo the official involvement in Jewish policy of various governmental agencies, apparently for the first time. This would set a pattern determining later stages of the developing anti-Jewish policy, evidence of which is to be found in the protocol of the Wannsee conference of January 1942. Heinrich Müller, along with Stuckart and the named ministries represented on the directorate committee would, in fact, reappear later as members of the Wannsee conference.

The executive agency of the center was assigned to Gestapo Section II under the leadership of the Chief of the Gestapo Müller. It is true that the Gestapo and SD were not only both within the SS but were the two branches of the Security Police under Heydrich; it is equally true that any member of one could easily be transferred to the other. And yet, Eichmann was within the SD, and as such was answerable to a hierarchy of superiors different from the one whose leader was Müller. Moreover, the fight against enemies of public order was not the same as that against political enemies. Hence, as the reorganization directives cited above show, Eichmann's task falls more or less clearly under the SD's ideological policy enactment rather than under the Gestapo's police activity. To assign the central agency for the execution of Jewish policy to the chief of the Gestapo was therefore nothing short of an invitation to a massive jurisdictional dispute between the two branches of security service. Such rivalry may have been intended by Heydrich as the way to keep control over the performance of his subordinates. However, as we will see over and over again, to the Jewish functionaries who had to defer to both of these SS agencies, their rivalry in matters of Jewish policy was tantamount to millstones between which the hapless Jews were caught and ground.

Under central direction but with a free hand, Eichmann had indeed shown how to proceed. As we pointed out previously, what was needed was the instrumentality of a Jewish agency (1) that received its mandate from and was answerable exclusively to the protagonists of Nazi ideological policy; (2) whose interests coincided with those of the Nazi regime from which it received its mandate, interests motivated by the ambiance of duress; and (3) that the Jews of Vienna were made to depend on and that the Jews abroad supported.

Such an instrumentality would soon be needed in the Protectorate of Bohemia and Moravia, where Eichmann would install *Zentralstellen* and members of his—now trained and experienced—Vienna staff to direct them. Later it would be needed in the conquered territories of Poland. There the mode of liquidating Jewish existence would be grimmer, and so would the function of the *Judenräte*, for in Poland the Nazis would have a welcome and more discrete venue for their work.

In the meantime, such an instrumentality was missing in the Altreich, and the regime lost no time in using the momentum of Kristallnacht and Eichmann's experience finally to install it there. While he would continue to spend much of his time in Vienna, Eichmann was now given a headquarters office in Berlin. Vienna would become more and more a branch office of his agency, and the Vienna office would be left in the hands of his deputies. Still, Vienna was the model in accordance with which he meant to organize the liquidation of Jewish existence in Berlin, and through Berlin in all of the Altreich.

As in Vienna, this involved two coordinate agencies, one equivalent to the IKG, the other a *Zentralstelle*. But the preconditions differed. With the Anschluss the Nazis were able to operate in Austria in a situation in which the authority of established law and institutions had, in effect, ceased to exist. This vacuum of established authority was the precondition for the establishment of the new IKG as an agency mandated by the new potentates. At the same time, the IKG retained whatever legal status the Nazis found it useful to maintain and whatever semblance of continuity they thought it politic to uphold. This precondition was absent in Berlin. The *Reichsvertretung* was, after all, a body voluntarily established by the various Jewish communities of Germany in order to represent Jewish interests and to coordinate their activities aimed at ensuring the survival of Jewish existence under the trying conditions of the Nazi regime, and, if need be, to foster emigration. We saw earlier that the leading circles had fought hard to maintain the autonomy of the Jewish organizations vis-à-vis the Nazi authorities.

In January 1939 representatives of the *Reichsvertretung* and the Jewish Community of Berlin were told by Eichmann that the representation of all Jewish communities (*Kultusgemeinden*) and other recognized Jewish organizations in the Altreich would be combined under the title *Reichsvereinigung* (Reich Association of Jewish Communities); it would be the task of this umbrella organization to prepare a clientele of emigrants for a "central emigration agency according to the Vienna model."[167] Soon thereafter Eichmann informed Löwenherz of this plan, namely, that the jurisdiction of the *Reichsvereinigung* would be restricted to the Altreich and would not extend to the Jews of former Austria. Further, representatives from Berlin—Eichmann mentioned only Dr. Paul Eppstein—would visit Vienna "in order to familiarize themselves with the technical arrangements of the [IKG] emigration department."[168] Evidently Eichmann expected that the gentlemen would be quick to learn what was required of them in order to keep the mill of the *Zentralstelle* that he was establishing in Berlin fed with a sizable daily quota of would-be emigrants. Evidently this did not happen. For, while the waves of arrests of the June action and Kristallnacht intensified the motivation of the Jews in the Altreich to emigrate, the ideas of the representatives from Berlin on how emigration was to proceed were sorely at odds with what they saw in Vienna. And they said so. Thus it happened that at Löwenherz's *Vorsprache* (audience) of March 9 Eichmann handed him a letter addressed to the IKG by Heinrich Stahl, President of the Jewish Community of Berlin, which reads:

> [O]n the occasion of my visit to Vienna I was able to convince myself that the *Zentralstelle*, which is arranged for promoting and accelerating Jewish emigration in Vienna, is a very practical arrangement and that it shortens the emigration formalities considerably.
>
> At the same time I had criticized *your* [IKG] agencies, and expressed the opinion that this kind [of agency] complicated the preconditions for new chances of emigration and for maintaining the old ones.
>
> I wish to emphasize that I had no justification for this criticism.[169]

What had happened?

The letter was dated March 1, 1939, two days after the opening of the Berlin *Zentralstelle*[170] and of what Eichmann expected to be a fully functioning emigration enterprise on the part of the *Reichsvereinigung*. When he failed to discern the slightest hint of activity that would produce the expected throng of would-be emigrants, Eichmann summoned Stahl, Eppstein, and other leading representatives of the Jewish organizations in Berlin. The reason for the meeting was evidently Eichmann's impatience with the haughty gentlemen, who had not as yet deigned to be "completely in his power" and to warn them not to "dare take a single step without checking with him first," and "to shake a leg" and do his bidding.[171] As far as Eichmann was concerned, their autonomy was over and he let them know it.

Nineteen years later Benno Cohn, who attended this meeting shortly before his emigration, reported what he remembered about it. Eichmann began by taking the offensive, accusing those present of being the source for the stories in a folder full of foreign press clippings, in which he was referred to as a "bloodhound" who "wanted to kill the Jews." Then he chided them for something for which he had better evidence, namely, their past unauthorized trips to Vienna. Stahl, as the one who was implicated, is reported to have said: "It is a grotesque situation: Our brothers there are persecuted by you. It would be beyond our human powers not to speak to them." Someone who understands the situation of the Vienna Jews and their leadership reads this with astonishment: One could still speak this way to Eichmann at this stage and think that one could safeguard Jewish interests? Eichmann responded that contact with Vienna was strictly prohibited and threatened Stahl with incarceration in a concentration camp if it were to be repeated. Stahl was not finished and, referring to the massive expulsion of Jews that precipitated the events of Kristallnacht, he pointed out that deportations across borders were counterproductive. As we know, the IKG was able to forestall this expulsion in Vienna by virtue of its working relationship vis-à-vis Eichmann. And, at the time of the Berlin encounter under discussion, the people at the IKG were finding ways of telling Eichmann that forced emigration did not work. However, the Jews of the Altreich were about to be—but had not as yet been—placed under the conditions of leadership prevailing in Vienna, and they had not as yet found ways of dealing with Eichmann. Cohn's report continues:

> After this criticism Eichmann roared: "You old bag of shit. It's been a long time since you have been in the concentration camp. What do you think you are doing?" Stahl blanched, and said no more.

At this point Eppstein got up to speak. What he expressed was the heart of the matter, and this was precisely the obstacle that Eichmann had to remove. According to Cohn, he said:

> The gentlemen who are sitting here are representatives of German Jewry, not of the Gestapo, and they see themselves as elected by German Jewry and not as the recipients of orders from the German Reich. . . . We are accountable to our people for our conduct. If you talk to us like that, then we are not able to work with you. You can bring us to the camp at any time, and you can dispose of us there as you see fit. But if you approach us in this manner, then you cannot work with us.

Again we marvel at the way these men still felt free to speak with Eichmann, as if they were equals at a bargaining table, each exacting quid pro quo. And we cannot help but admire Eppstein for the courage to speak the truth and to find the right words. Eppstein is remembered for being a rousing speaker both in Berlin and in Theresienstadt. And yet, we have to step back and gain perspective. Like Murmelstein, Eppstein was educated and gifted with brilliance; unlike Eppstein, Murmelstein was circumspect. Like Löwenherz, Eppstein stood on his dignity, but unlike Eppstein's, Löwenherz's was a personal dignity that could not but affect Eichmann. Neither Löwenherz nor Murmelstein flaunted their superiority; Eppstein did and, perhaps more than anything else, that was his undoing.

At the meeting on February 28 Eichmann roared, in response to Eppstein, that he and his companion "will decide what has to be done after this impudence. You are dismissed. Wait outside." After a while the representatives of the Jews were told that the newly established scheme was to take effect as of Monday next. Every week the *Reichsvereinigung* had to send a certain number of Jews to the new Berlin *Zentralstelle* for the completion of emigration formalities; Eichmann's office would inform them every Wednesday of the required number. If the quota was not filled, sharp measures would follow. At 8:00 a.m. the next morning the representatives would have to confirm their compliance. Cohn reports:

> Among us a stunned silence. We had not thought that all that was so close at hand.
>
> I said: "I am responsible for emigration to Palestine, but the British Mandate makes difficulties, hence we cannot assume any guarantees for a certain number."
>
> [Eichmann]: "You will assume the guarantees!!"
>
> I: "We expect that the Jews will be treated with human dignity [at the *Zentralstelle*]."
>
> Eichmann roared: "That is *Greuelpropaganda* [horror propaganda]! Most likely it is you who is spreading [this] abroad! Everything will be taken care of [according to my directions] tomorrow morning!"

In effect the fight for Jewish autonomy—already lost in Vienna—was now over in Berlin also. "It was clear to us," Cohn writes, "we had to cooperate." How to concede the fight with dignity? They met and consulted until late at night:

> The need to emigrate was great. Until now the chasing around [for the necessary papers] to the different offices had been terrible. Concentrating the emigration offices in one place was practical. . . . We decided: Eppstein should go there tomorrow and deliver the declaration to the effect that we are interested and regard it as a normalization of the emigration process, but with the understanding that the deportations across the [Polish] borders would now cease, that we cannot assume any guarantees as regards numbers, and that—we repeat—we derive our mandate solely from the Jewish side.

Was Eichmann impressed? Not at all. Eppstein would appear the next morning because appear he must, and regardless of what he would say, his very appearance would testify to the fact that the leaders representing the Jews in the Altreich had, for all practical purposes, finally understood that they were the instrument by which the Nazi regime through him, Eichmann, dealt with all of the Jews. And if they were to persist in the conceit that they derived their mandate solely from the Jewish side, so much the better, for this would make them eminently suited to be the instrument that it was their function to be. The fact that, for Eichmann, the matter was already closed is confirmed by Cohn's report of what happened next morning:

> The following day Eppstein was received not by Eichmann but someone else, read the declaration to [that person], who received it without any comment.[172]

What Cohn does not report is that at the same time Stahl was forced to deliver the letter, which Eichmann then carried to Löwenherz in Vienna, perhaps to forestall Löwenherz losing confidence in the benefits of cooperation and attempting to assume autonomy.

The establishment of the Vienna model in the Altreich, the recognition—at the nerve center of the regime's Jewish policy—of what Eichmann had accomplished in Vienna, and the changes which this helped engender at that center, these spearheaded the new thrust consequent upon Kristallnacht. With this in mind, we can proceed to a consideration of what was to follow in the period prior to the war.

Chapter 6

Before the War

IT WAS ALMOST TEN MONTHS from Kristallnacht to the outbreak of the Second World War. The mode of carrying out the Nazis' Jewish policy in Vienna seemed no different in those months from what had been laboriously developed until that time. In the larger context the only difference was that the pattern of Vienna had been formalized by Nazi legislation and projected for all of Greater Germany. In Vienna Eichmann had a functioning machinery for meeting the bewilderingly many and disparate problems of isolating, expropriating, and expelling the Jews. All he had to do was to keep the machine moving at maximum efficiency, gain recognition for it, and hold it up as a model for the rest of the Reich. His influence in devising and effecting Nazi Germany's solution of the Jewish question was now extending beyond Vienna. And even though his responsibility in this regard would soon follow suit, he would spend much of his time in Vienna in order to supervise the machine he had devised and, more important, to motivate its functioning at full speed. And yet with regard to the pursuit of that solution and the role of the Jewish leadership, the period before the war shows some distinctive features that are significant for what was to follow. In a way the performance of both the SD with Eichmann as the point man and of the Jewish leadership at the IKG become routinized; what is significant is not the routine, but what becomes routine. This we will try to bring to light.

In the chronicle of these ten months following Kristallnacht we look in vain for the kind of dramatic and frightful major persecutions that filled the eight months before: the incessant brutalization, the unchecked looting, the legislation of one impediment after another, the waves of arrests, the official harassment, expropriation and other forms of impoverishment, and, as a consequence of all that, the deliberate destruction of the validity of the Jew as citizen. However, the palpable results of these persecutions provided an ambiance of duress in which the solution of the Jewish problem was effected. This ambiance was the context in which Eichmann could successfully apply the pressures to maintain a steady stream of emigration. If, in the ensuing ten months (November 1938 to September 1939), the number of emigrés was less than in the preceding eight, then only because the immigration opportunities decreased and because more and more Jews outside of Austria would compete for those opportunities. The additional Jews who would feel the motivation first experienced by the Viennese Jews were those of the Altreich, soon to be followed by the Jews of the Protectorate of truncated Bohemia and Moravia.

Forced Emigration

If the ambiance of duress fueled the motivation to leave, it also provided the condition for the fact and mode of choice exercised by those in the position of forced leadership. The duress was not simply a matter of the prevalence of terror; it was more fundamental. Terror is a matter of fears that are directed toward something definite, no matter how vague, no matter how unlikely yet possible. In the period before Kristallnacht the situation which unfolded for the Jews of Vienna was one of elemental terror: They lived in constant fear of the manifestations of their change from fellow human beings to outcasts, of the accompanying impediments mentioned earlier, and they were faced with bewildering obstacles to finding an escape and endless difficulties on the way to getting there.

This atmosphere of terror continued in the period from Kristallnacht to the outbreak of war, yet it does not characterize fully the duress that marked Jewish existence at that time. The aspects of terror now became functional components of an ambiance of duress that defined Jewish existence during this period. One might say that a degree of duress is an ineluctable factor of human life. The very humanity of a human being comes to light only in the way he or she responds to challenges, obstacles, frustrations, and dangers. In this sense duress cannot be and ought not to be eschewed, for it is by facing challenges that we invoke the resources of possibility, that we grasp at and realize the possibilities out of which we fashion our being and our humanity. The ambiance of duress that now defined the existence of the Jews of Vienna can best be described as the devastating realization that all possibility for fashioning life had been denied, that the very resources of possibility had been choked off. The Jews of Vienna found themselves at the brink of existence, or rather, confined in a space of duress, a space whose walls were pressing in on them. This is the basic meaning of the concept of "anxiety," that is, a perceived, experienced narrowness from which no agent would help one to break out. This distinction of the ambiance of duress from terror may be reminiscent of Martin Heidegger's differentiation of anxiety as *Grundbefindlichkeit* (i.e., as the fundamental state of being in which we find ourselves) from fear of something. But there is a difference: Heidegger thought he had identified a phenomenon of man's openness to Being, beyond the constructive activity of reflective thought. However, the ambiance of duress definitive of Jewish existence before the war was instigated, was deliberately caused, and was a manipulative instrument of policy, and in this sense was precisely a construction of thought, in particular of the totalitarian mind that was Nazism, its political movement, and its ideological policy.

Under these conditions the search for possibility on the part of the oppressed Jews was primarily a matter of finding a way of escaping the exigency of duress, and secondarily, but no less important, surviving until then. This, in effect, was the substance of the life of Vienna's Jews before the war. In this sense it was the task of the forced leadership at the IKG to be responsive to this exigency and to enhance such possibility.

This ambiance of duress prevailing among the Jews was also of fundamental importance to the Nazi authorities. It was, in effect, the main lever for exacting from the individual Jew and from the Jewish leadership the compliance with what, in accordance with official Jewish policy, was the Jew's raison d'être: The Jew's function was to get rid of the Jew. The duress of the Jews was thus the means whereby the Jewish functionaries became hostage to the Nazi authorities and were forced to carry out their assigned task of ridding Vienna of Jews.

But *mutatis mutandi*—and this is so easy to overlook—the Jewish leaders of Vienna had to and did find ways of holding the purpose that the Nazis pursued (by means of the Jews' duress) hostage to the leaders' attempt to alleviate the Jews' duress and enhance their chances of survival. How far such ways would lead into the thicket of impotence and abandonment will be traced when we recount the choices under the duress still to come but, at the time before the war, as yet not imagined.

As we have seen, there is no evidence that the Kristallnacht action was initiated by Eichmann or his home office or the SD or even by the SS, although they took charge of it once it was initiated. But from the beginning Eichmann knew how to use the events and effects of Kristallnacht to his advantage in carrying out his task.

The extent to which the emigration of Vienna's Jews had succeeded up to this point had been truly beyond any reasonable expectation, and Eichmann had done his part to facilitate the process by establishing the *Zentralstelle*. Yet the process whereby each person or family finds a place to go individually, and then goes through a laborious procedure of securing documentation, authorization, clearance, and passage was still tedious, and it threatened to mar his reputation as the one who was able to establish and motivate an effective process that the Altreich lacked. What he wanted, from the beginning, was for Jews to pick up their bags, board the trains, and leave en masse.

One can force masses to move only if one has jurisdiction over territory that is to be their destination. This was the case, for example, in 1915 when Turkey proceeded against the Armenians. However, Nazi Germany had no control over any territory beyond the borders across which they meant the Jews to move. In the first few months of the newly established IKG, it was one of the main tasks of the Jewish leadership to teach Eichmann that this emigration en masse was not to be and, after learning and devising the feasible emigration process themselves, to teach Eichmann what was involved and what he and the regime had to provide in order to make it possible. Now, with the ambiance effected by Kristallnacht, Eichmann meant to press the next best thing to mass migration, namely, the urgency of forced migration, including, if possible, the emigration of groups. Group emigration had been tried before, as we recall: The occasional Perl transports to Palestine were particularly successful. Eichmann's try at matching that Jewish enterprise (i.e., by his Colombia transport) had proved to be a dismal and embarrassing failure, a fact that the Jewish leadership could not allow itself to mention, which they kept, however, constantly in mind as Eichmann pressed for group migrations, and as the IKG and the Palamt tried to develop schemes of that kind which were not only feasible but legitimate.

One thing working in favor of realizing an intensified emigration was the arousal of public indignation outside of Germany over the reported brutal persecutions of Kristallnacht.

In no country would this prove to be more effective than in Great Britain. Professor Norman Bentwich, in one of his postwar memoirs dealing with his leading efforts to build on this public response and to organize schemes of rescue, says:

> Nazi "pogroms" were unleashed against Jews throughout Germany and Austria; synagogues and Jewish property were systematically burnt, and thousands thrown into concentration camps. . . . The British people were deeply moved, and renewed the tradition of asylum for the persecuted. Now the doors of England were more widely opened to the victims of racial hatred. . . . [A] wave of sentiment was stirred in all classes to find for them permanent homes or temporary refuge.[1]

It was up to the leaders of the IKG, especially Löwenherz, to impart to his contacts in London and the United States the urgency of the Jews' situation and of Eichmann's pressure and to direct their interest into channels of action. No doubt the coincidence of Löwenherz's being in England at the time of Kristallnacht proved to be fortuitous. After his return to Vienna and his contacts with Eichmann consequent upon a survey of the new deterioration of an already dismal situation, Löwenherz reported in English to the Council for German Jews in London, and in German to the American JDC office in Paris. What he had urged during his personal meetings had evidently become pressing reality:

> In the course of our repeated negotiations in Paris and London I have laid special stress upon the fact that an evacuation of the Austrian Jews will be very necessary within the next few months. Having returned from my journey I am convinced that the plan, phantastically as it may sound, must be realized immediately, in view of the fact that the Jews cannot stay here any longer.
>
> According to the most recent regulations the Jews are compelled to leave the German territory within the shortest time.[2]

As a result of Löwenherz's negotiations several group emigration schemes were already being arranged in Great Britain through the efforts of Jewish agencies and some prominent individuals. According to one scheme, women between the ages of 18 and 55 were admitted as domestics and found employment in private homes all over Britain. These women were from all walks of life, and they found positions mainly in middle-class families, where they kept house, cooked, served, and took care of children. They occupied servants' quarters, received modest wages, and were free to settle, to establish a new life, and, if possible, to arrange for the rescue of one or the other member of their families, a frustrating process even where it was successful but infinitely less oppressive than the corresponding process within Nazi Germany.

Another scheme negotiated by Löwenherz was devoted to the rescue of children. This was truly a charitable scheme because children were not employable and were completely dependent. For a similar reason this scheme was favored by the Nazi authorities: The Jewish children consumed assets without having produced any, they could be shipped off without the usual formalities having to do with the liquidation and expropriation of assets, and they could leave without taking anything of value with them. Löwenherz discussed the scheme with Eichmann, who issued his directives governing these transports at their meeting on December 2.[3] On that day the first transport of children, from Berlin, arrived in Harwich on the English Channel. The directives received by Löwenherz pertain to the composition of the first transport from Vienna—four hundred *Glaubensjuden* (practicing Jews) and one hundred *Nichtglaubensjuden* (nonpracticing Jews)—the time of departure, the procedure for preparing the transport (involving in particular the identity of the parents left behind), the provision of a collective passport for all the children, and so on. Two sets of directives are of particular interest. One pertains to assets:[4]

> (4) The parents must file a sworn statement that the children do not possess any assets and that the parents did not give them any assets along, either as a gift or through transfer. . . .
>
> (12) The children should take with them only the bare necessities; extra clothing, etc., is to be avoided. Every child is to be given a list of all items in his luggage . . . to be signed by the parents. The list is to be checked against the items actually taken. All lists are to be handed in [to the IKG], which will then submit it to the Foreign Exchange Office and Customs Headquarters.

Another directive concerns citizenship:

> (11) The only participants permitted in this transport are children who are German citizens or those whose stateless status has definitely been established through stateless passports. . . .

The point is clear: The assets of the IKG, considered to be part of the wealth of the German nation, should be used only to get rid of the German Jews. Foreign nationals should leave, too, but at the cost of the country whose citizens they are. The status of stateless Jews was a sore point with the Nazis, particularly since Poland had decided to revoke the citizenship of a large number of Jews who had left Poland many years before, thus rendering them, in effect, stateless. The problematic nature of this revocation was, as we have seen, the cause of the sequence of events of which Kristallnacht was the dramatic highpoint. And as we will see, these stateless Jews were under particular pressure to leave; yet the IKG was under constant harassment by Eichmann's *Zentralstelle* as it tried to protect them or to assist them in their emigration.

Another directive provided for chaperones to accompany the children. These adults must themselves be emigrants, preferably women going to England as domestics, a highly cost-effective measure. If IKG personnel had to be used, they may travel only to the border of Holland and then had to return; at the border the London Committee had to take over and arrange for escorts to the Hoek of Holland and the transfer of the children at Harwich.[5] In time the IKG requested that experienced personnel (i.e., the same two members of the IKG staff) accompany the transports, with permission to return; however, only Rosa Rachel Schwarz, the director of the children's section of the IKG welfare department, would be granted this permission.[6] Normally, with the exception of the chief officials of the IKG and the Palamt and of the corresponding personnel in the Altreich, no Jew who left Nazi Germany was permitted to return.

The trip took two days and one night by train, and one night by channel-boat. The parents were told that Dutch agencies would provide the children with food and drink once they crossed the border. In fact, however, they were only sometimes given an orange; usually all the children had to eat for the entire train trip were the bread-and-butter sandwiches that they took along for the German portion of the train trip. Usually they had nothing to drink until they boarded the ship. It must be noted that this was a matter of negligence on the part of the Dutch agencies.[7]

In England most children were taken in by families who provided them with home, shelter, and schooling, and others went to children's homes or to boarding schools, until they could fend for themselves, or in some cases rejoin their families wherever they had in the meantime, emigrated. Some orphans were adopted, some children came into situations where, in effect, they were unpaid servants; but that was the exception. All of them were fortunate to have escaped, their parents happy that they were saved even if they were never to see them again. As it happens, this was true in 80 percent of the cases: the parents of eighty out of one hundred children perished in the Holocaust.[8]

In his letter of November 28, 1938, to the Council for German Jews Löwenherz asks, in English:

> . . . most urgently to commence immediately with the mass-emigration of the children and juveniles already projected and to consider the Austrian juveniles to a respective extent upon this scheme.[9]

What he is requesting in this curious phrase, obviously constructed by his staff by consulting a German-English dictionary, are clearance for the first transport and general preference for Austrian children. There were good reasons for this request. First, aside from the particularly dire situation prevailing among the Jews of Vienna—still worse than anything experienced in the Altreich—was that the impoverishment of the Jews and of the Viennese community (again, more severe by far than that in the Altreich) left the children at a risk greater than the IKG could alleviate.[10] To back up his request Löwenherz provided statistics:[11]

Age groups	**(1)** **Number in Altreich** *Mar. 15, 1938*	**(2)** **Number in Austria** *Mar. 15, 1938*	**(3)** **Number in Austria** *Sep. 15, 1938*
0–6	7,200	9,200	6,900
6–14	20,200	10,400	7,800
14–16	8,300	6,400	4,500
16–20	18,600	9,000	6,800
20–25	12,900	11,700	8,500

A comparison of the first and second columns shows that at the time of the Anschluss the proportion of young people to the whole Jewish population was, in most age categories, much higher in Austria (total Jewish population ca. 180,000) than in the Altreich (total Jewish population ca. 375,000). The second and third columns show that in Austria the emigration of minor children was proceeding at a dramatically slower rate than that of youths ages 20 to 25.[12]

The first (and largest) children's transport of five hundred did leave soon, on December 8.[13] It cost the IKG RM 40,000 (i.e., RM 80 per child), for which Löwenherz received clearance from Eichmann on December 2. The IKG had to make all the arrangements for the list of participants, for the documentation, and for arranging railway passage at least to the border. In quick order other transports left, a process that continued until shortly before the outbreak of war, by which time more than 2,200 Austrian children who were *Glaubensjuden* had left for Britain.[14] Special time was set aside at the *Zentralstelle* for the IKG to complete the minimal clearance necessary to provide the children with travel documents and to permit them to leave Germany. In time the committee in charge of arrangements in London required that only those children be included in the transports who had a guaranteed destination in Britain; however, Murmelstein, during his first trip to London, negotiated a distribution of guaranteed and nonguaranteed participants.[15] At least one of the early transports was specifically for children who were destined for Orthodox homes.[16] Within a month of the beginning of the children's transports the process of dispatching them had become routinized and a matter of course, mainly through the efforts of lower echelons of the IKG. There was only minimal involvement by the leading officials, and no special clearance or further directives from Eichmann were required. Children's transports were also dispatched from the Altreich. Eichmann kept the operations of the IKG and of the *Reichsvereinigung* (Reich Association of Jewish Communities) strictly separate and reserved for his office the coordination of the respective transports. This caused occasional complications for the London committee receiving the arrivals.[17]

Even though the organization of the children's transports became routinized, even though the IKG's outlay for these transports made them per capita the most cost-effective emigration effort in which the IKG was in some way involved, the IKG still had to expend considerable effort to bring them about, even though no more than 2,700 children left in this way: almost 2,300 to Britain, the rest to Holland, Belgium, France, and Sweden.[18] The IKG's efforts comprised initial and subsequent negotiations, administration, and execution. But in comparison to other mass emigration schemes, the children's transports proved to be the easiest.

Early in the process these transports were expanded to include young persons 17 to 25 years of age, for men a most vulnerable age in light of the most recent wave of arrests. Murmelstein was sent to England early in January, ostensibly to negotiate this matter.[19] He was received by Professor Norman Bentwich,[20] who, after the Anschluss and especially in response to Kristallnacht, became the main Jewish activist in England for the rescue of the Jews of Germany. His wife headed the London committee (the "Children's Movement") to get Jewish children out of central Europe. Murmelstein's reputation as a scholar as well as Löwenherz's vigorous right hand had preceded him, but Bentwich, while pleased to make his acquaintance, wondered why another representation by the Vienna community was made so soon after Löwenherz's visit at the time of Kristallnacht. Murmelstein hastened to explain the plight of the men taken into "protective custody" during the Kristallnacht-pogrom and now languishing in concentration camps, most of them in Buchenwald, some in Dachau, with no chance of release unless they could leave Nazi Germany within four weeks. There were also those who had already been released under the proviso that they leave the Reich territory within that time. Murmelstein's plea for these most dire cases went hand in hand with a plan being developed under Bentwich's initiative, apparently in response to a proposal urged by Löwenherz. Whether some preliminary version of Löwen-

Jewish refugee children, members of the first Kindertransport *(children's transport) from Germany, arrive in Harwich, England. (United States Holocaust Memorial Museum, courtesy of Instytut Pamieci Narodowej. USHMM 02725)*

herz's proposal and Bentwich's project was discussed during Löwenherz's November visit is not known, but we have reason to believe that it may have been and that the letter of November 28 may in part have been a ruse vis-à-vis the Nazi authorities.

In Löwenherz's letter of November 28 the proposal is added to the information cited above[21] to the effect that according to the latest "regulations the Jews are compelled to leave the German territory within the shortest time." In the case of Austria, "the shortest time" was to be spring 1940, the second anniversary of the Anschluss, as Eichmann would continuously stress vis-à-vis Löwenherz during this period. Löwenherz proposed the following:

> [The Jews] could be placed and catered for at small expense[22] in camps and therefrom sent to the countries of immigration. They would be ready to do all work necessary which is not done by inhabitants in the devasteted [*sic*] areas, in order to do useful work up to the time of their emigration.[23]

What Löwenherz was proposing was the desperate scheme of settling a mass of people awaiting the realization of immigration possibilities on unused ("devasteted") land in Britain, where they would, at little cost to charitable organizations, fend for themselves, without taking jobs or developed areas away from the local population. Pressing home the urgency of the scheme, Löwenherz continues:

> Please pay your full attention to this question which cannot be postponed any longer with the Governments competent and with members of the Intergovernmental Committee. I am sure you will find a solution of this problem. No other solution does exist. Many thousands of Jews will be able to procure possibilities of immigration to various countries by friends and relatives without assistance of Jewish Organizations within the next weeks and months. The others, about 100,000, must be placed in camps to start from there their further migration.[24]

Löwenherz is realistic in not placing any hope in the efficacy of the Intergovernmental Committee established at the Evian Conference. He is, however, unrealistic in projecting the figure of 100,000 for the scheme he is proposing, even if it were to include not only Jews from Austria but also from the Altreich. As to Austria, Löwenherz must have realized that barely 100,000 Jews were left there by the end of November, and he also knew that the old and infirm could not be moved; in fact, much of his effort in the period under consideration would be taken up with anticipating the need to provide for this inevitable remnant of the Jewish population once the required emigration of its movable portion was successfully completed.

The scheme developed under the leadership of Bentwich called for reopening a military camp on private property that had been built in the First World War as a staging area for the British Expeditionary Force but had since been in disuse, namely, Kitchener Camp in Richborough, Kent.[25] Men whose ultimate destination lay outside the United Kingdom, in particular the United States or one of the Commonwealth countries, would be placed in this camp and would be granted temporary residence in Britain until they were cleared to move on. In the meantime, they would receive retraining in the camp. The first contingent would refurbish the camp and make it usable. It was projected that in time wives and children would follow.

So far the scheme seems to be innocuous. However, there seems to have been another feature to this scheme, as evidenced in its criteria of selection. In April 1939, long after the project had been under way, the Bulletin of the Coordinating Committee for Refugees published the description of a

> project for a Refugee Transit Camp similar to those in operation in Holland and Belgium but on a larger scale. . . . The Council for German Jewry, whose application to the Home Office has been considered with great promptitude and sympathy, has received approval for the establishment of such a camp on condition that it is responsible for the maintenance. . . .
>
> The persons for whom the camp is intended are men between the ages of 18 and 45 who have definite prospects of emigration to another country as far as possible within a year. . . . The selection of refugees is left entirely in the hands of the organisations on the continent; **no application to the British Agencies will be considered**. It is expected that there will be, roughly, 2,000 Jews from Germany and 1,000 from Austria, and that the remaining 500 will be selected by the Society of Friends, the Czech organizations and some of the Continental Committees. . . .[26]

The key phrases here are "men," "between the ages of 18 and 45," and "camp." After all, not only men but women too were awaiting immigration opportunities to materialize and were in urgent need to leave Nazi Germany in the meantime. Not only men between but also beyond those ages were in that position and in such need. And even if inmates of Buchenwald were to receive first consideration, men over 45 were also in custody or released with the proviso that they leave within four weeks.

And consider the political situation as it was developing in Britain at that time: At the end of September, Britain's Czechoslovak ally was sold out at Munich by giving the Nazi regime freedom to annex the Sudetenland, Germany's "last territorial demand." When Prime Minister Chamberlain stepped from the airplane upon his return from Munich, he held up the agreement and hailed it as the guarantee of "peace in our time." The "time" in question came to an end less than six months later, when Nazi Germany swallowed the rest of the Czech part of that hapless country and established it as a "Protectorate" of the Reich. It was the end of illusions, if there were any. From then on, the British knew there would be war. Others knew beforehand; some, like Churchill, were certain of it as early as 1935, when the German army marched into the demilitarized Rhineland. And they knew that time was short and had to be used for preparation. It may be said that the first jolt to illusion after "Munich" for those who still needed to be jolted came with Kristallnacht, with the reports of open brutality, massive arrests, and the filling of concentration camps.

What was in the minds of the Englishmen when they devised the scheme of a "Refugee Transit Camp" to which only men, moreover between the ages of 18 and 45, would be sent, and, as it soon turned out, with preference to those hardened by their victimization in concentration camps? We have already seen that the Home Office of the British government was involved in facilitating the scheme. These facts alone strongly suggest that the basis was being laid for a motivated cadre of fighting men. Thus we wonder also about Löwenherz's letter—written after his London meetings—in which he proposes the scheme. His proposal, which is on a scale much broader than the one with the implied paramilitary import, was no doubt written out of the sincere urgency of a desperate situation; but this may well have been merely the ostensible reason for the letter, the other being to function as decoy vis-à-vis the Nazi authorities for what may have been explicitly proposed to him or worked out with him under the impact of the reports of mass arrests that were coming in while he was in London.

The decoy, if it was such, had other features. First, the camp was projected and usually referred to as a "transit camp." This is the designation in the Bulletin of the Co-ordinating Committee, and more importantly in Vienna. Whereas Löwenherz, when writing to Eichmann, usually refers to it as "Camp," Murmelstein, for reasons which will presently become clear, never fails to say *Zwischenaufenthaltslager*, "transit camp."[27] But there are inconsistencies on the side of the British about treating the camp as an interim station for men headed to some other overseas destination. Inasmuch as those selected for the camp had to obtain British entry permits, we find Löwenherz—as part of the multilateral transactions that were necessary to make the scheme come true and to keep it going—at the British consulate in Vienna, negotiating with Passport Officer Berry and Vice-Consul Hardt. They were looking for certification from the U.S. authorities that the candidates for participation in the camp action did indeed have prospects of moving on to an American destination. However, Consul General of the United States in Vienna, Leland Morris, who was present at the meeting, was not in a position to divulge the registration numbers of those who were registered at the consulate under the quota system; he could not give an estimate as to when the persons in question would be due for processing, nor, we may safely assume, what their prospects were for qualifying for immigration once it was their turn. In his memorandum of this meeting Löwenherz recorded that while the British government was prepared to grant temporary residency even up to two years to persons who had affidavits from a guarantor in the United States, the "execution of this action on a large scale is frustrated by the American Consulate's refusal to verify the quota numbers, and [they] would honor the wishes of the English Consulate only in individual, pressing cases." Löwenherz also recorded Berry's suggestion that "appropriate representations" might be made at the State Department in Washington by the American Jewish Joint Distribution Committee (the Joint).[28] There is, of course, no indication that such representation was made, much less that it succeeded. And there would not have been time enough to wait for it; the camp scheme had to be instituted right away if it were to save those who were hard pressed to leave. Instead, there are indications that, from the beginning, enforcement of the requirement of a "definite prospect" of proceeding to another destination was anything but strict. Much less was the limitation of the sojourn in England to "as far as possible a year" enforced.

The selection of the candidates was, in fact, placed in the hands of the IKG, who thus acted as agent of the British government, though subject to British control and approval. The IKG selected persons whose prospects of continuing their emigration beyond the British "transient camp" were, in effect, nebulous; as regards prospects of continuing on to the United States, all they needed to show was proof of their quota registration at the U.S. consulate; not even an affidavit, much less one that would be acceptable for the granting of an immigration visa, was required.

Starting in February 1939, the section on emigration—a major feature of the new *Jüdisches Nachrichtenblatt* (Jewish Newspaper), Vienna edition—carried frequent notices concerning the transit camp in England. The name Richborough is mentioned for the first time on February 14. It is clearly stated that the applicant is supposed to have a definite opportunity for continuing his emigration within three to nine months. However, in apparent contradiction thereto, the reader is told that at the end of the training, which would be offered in a variety of fields, as well as and for a special group of young people in agriculture, there would be help for emigration to America or to the British colonies and dominions. In short, the idea of a transit camp was being upheld, but the requirement of previously secured further emigration opportunities was, at best, only nominal.

This is not to deny that many of the participants did, in fact, use the camp for transit purposes. Nor can it be said that applicants to or residents of the camp had the impression that the camp had paramilitary character.[29] Nevertheless, there was the danger—what with the choice of a former military encampment for the camp's locale, the restriction of participants by sex and age, and other features of which any intelligence service would quickly become aware—that the German authorities would soon become suspicious, rightly or not. As to those other features: not only did the British government give the project its approval, but the men who were put in charge of the camp were three officers of the Jewish Lads Brigade, namely, Jonas May, Phineas May, and R. Banks, who was "an instructor in physical training."[30] There were, then, good reasons for deflecting German suspicions that, with their cooperation, the IKG was recruiting an enemy force, and good reason for the use of decoys and the ruse that this was to be a camp for transients. The manner in which the scheme was formulated in Löwenherz's letter of November 28 may have played a part in this ruse.

We know how sensitive the Nazi authorities were to precisely this kind of possibility,[31] in fact to any show of hostility against Nazi Germany on the part of Jews and even on the part of non-Jews on behalf of Jews. The SD maintained an intelligence section that gathered information about the situation and the mood both within the various areas of Germany as well as in all the major countries worldwide. And, of course, the Gestapo and the SD, hence also Eichmann's offices, received the frequent periodic in-house intelligence briefings. Since all stations of the SD were supervised by the respective home offices in Berlin through the "inspector" system, a functionary like Eichmann was no doubt also alerted to potentially suspicious activities in his area of competence with the more or less implied order to bring it under control.

All this was known to the chief functionaries of the IKG and had to be kept in mind by them. For example, on January 5, 1939, Löwenherz was cited to Senior Secretary Kuchmann, the man in charge of Jewish affairs at Gestapo headquarters in Vienna. He had before him a clipping from the December 16 edition of the *London Daily Mail*, depicting a group of children from the first transport from Vienna as they arrived in Harwich after crossing the English Channel. According to the caption, the children were very tired and would find homes in England. Kuchmann made it clear that, acting upon instructions, presumably from Berlin headquarters, "if news reports directed against Germany were to appear with regard to the children's transports, further transports will have to cease." In response Löwenherz assured Kuchmann that "we have no interest in any reports whatever in connection with the children's transports" and that "in writing as well as directly" he would "ask the organizations which receive the children's transports to refrain from reports of this kind."[32] Murmelstein left a few days later on his first trip to London, and no doubt it was one of his tasks to urge this point. Löwenherz's reaction in this instance shows, first, how these functionaries of the IKG had to be alert at all times and ready to deflect the threat of a further intensification of the duress, a threat under which they themselves had to operate on behalf of the Jews. It indicates, secondly, the extent to which those independent agencies outside of Nazi Germany that endeavored to aid the Jews in the grip of persecution had to be persuaded by these functionaries to follow their lead in their dealings with the Nazi authorities. This was an almost hopeless task because there was no way for persons and agencies outside of the grip of Nazi Germany to comprehend what was involved in acting under the constraints of forced leadership, especially since the agencies had reason to regard these functionaries as their agents.

The incident with Kuchmann is fraught with ironies. If any reports can be said to have been "directed against Germany," then it was those about Kristallnacht, which precipitated rescue efforts such as the children's transports. Yet these reports were precisely the ones that proved useful to the Nazi effort of speeding up Jewish emigration. There was as such nothing harmful to Germany's image abroad in a report of Jewish children arriving tired after the stress and excitement of their first long journey ever, separated from their parents and coming to a strange country after crossing the North Sea in winter. Not only was the arrival of the first transport newsworthy but a report would be good publicity for a rescue effort which depended on finding homes for the children and on gifts from the public for its financing. Such favorable publicity for the enterprise would also aid Eichmann in his efforts to rid Vienna at least of the Jewish children. The contravention on the part of the Gestapo was, therefore, at cross purposes with what the SD and Eichmann were about and presents us with one minor example of the kind of jurisdictional rivalry between the two branches of the SS—with the functionaries of the IKG caught in the middle.

We have not found any evidence of any suspicion by the Nazi authorities about the nature of the Kitchener Camp scheme, or of such suspicion having been a factor in Eichmann's dealings with the IKG. In spite of the fact that Eichmann apparently had no objection to the emigration of men of military age to potential enemy countries, the IKG had to be concerned that a possible objection might prove to be an obstacle to the emigration effort. That this was no idle worry on the part of the IKG was in time borne out, albeit not until the outbreak of the war. It was not until two weeks into the war that, in connection with the question of continuing the emigration to Palestine, a mandate of Great Britain, now at war with Germany, that Eichmann confronted Löwenherz with the information that "Jews in Palestine declared themselves prepared for war service on the side of England." Löwenherz's response, at least in its recorded version, is a classic of subtlety and hidden meaning. He "stressed . . . that the Jews in Austria have always behaved loyally and that, by dispatching further transports to Palestine, we do not wish to arouse the semblance of disloyalty." Löwenherz's report of this confrontation ends with Eichmann's declaration that if the IKG could secure outside means for such transports, for example, from the United States, then such transports could continue.[33] In short, Eichmann, having carried out his obligation of confronting Löwenherz with received intelligence, resumed his task, made even more complicated by war, of driving out the Jews, even if they were to wind up in the army of what was now the enemy. This too would tend to suggest that any suspicions imparted to Eichmann about Kitchener Camp were ignored by him so as not to interfere with his succeeding at last in motivating mass emigration.

If any suspicion regarding the camp scheme should surface in the dealings with Eichmann, the IKG leadership would have to be able to claim to have done no more than in all innocence carry out the mandate handed down by Eichmann. Hence it was decided to relegate the execution of the scheme to the lower, less exposed echelons of the IKG staff. This proved to be simple in the case of the children's transport, but not now: The person in charge of the camp scheme would, by its very nature, find himself in an exposed position, would therefore have to act deliberately and with caution, and hardly anyone met this difficult qualification. The choice fell on Murmelstein. To be sure, Löwenherz continued to be the one who negotiated for financing, for disbursements, for clearance of individual transports, for special problem cases, for the release of concentration camp inmates, for the extension of deadlines by when those released had to leave the borders of the Reich. But, the minutiae of screening and selecting applicants, of dealing with the public, of recommending acceptances, of secondary negotiations with British authorities, especially of obtaining approval from them, of impelling forward the extremely laborious, complex, and sensitive process of documentation quickly enough to satisfy the time limitation hanging over those released from custody, all this was placed in the hands of Murmelstein. He himself maintained that at first he did not realize the possible military implications of the scheme, though he soon suspected them. Of course, no one ever mentioned anything of the sort, neither Bentwich nor the other contacts in England, nor Löwenherz, nor the British Vice-Consul in Vienna, with whom Murmelstein had to be in constant touch for the purpose of obtaining the British entry visas once the Commission in London approved the list of selectees.

The confirmation of Murmelstein's suspicions came, so he claimed, in two ways: On the one hand, when he was given a few hundred extra places to fill that had been left unused by Berlin, in spite of the fact that Berlin needed to dispatch released inmates across the borders as badly as did Vienna. Murmelstein figured that there could be only one reason why these places were being left unused by Berlin: There must be something about the scheme that made Eppstein hesitate out of fear. In Berlin Eppstein headed the welfare section of the *Reichsvertretung*, which, after Kristallnacht, had become the *Reichsvereinigung*; in this capacity he was in charge of the emigration effort in the Altreich and, to the Nazi authorities, not just nominally but executively, the man they had placed in overall charge. Having negotiated the camp scheme in London together with Löwenherz, Eppstein was in charge of it in Berlin. Murmelstein did not hesitate to make quick use of this windfall.[34] A second confirmation, in Murmelstein's mind, of the unspoken nature of the scheme was his inspection of the by then fully functioning camp, to which he was taken by Bentwich during his second trip to London in April 1939.[35]

The procedure for joining the camp was as follows: Notices of the plan appeared in *Jüdische Nachrichten*. It was a ray of hope for the desperate men who applied, for many more than could be accommodated, and for many more than qualified. The applications had to be screened, and Murmelstein was constrained to make selections in accordance with the stated criteria of eligibility. Furthermore, preference was tacitly given to those released from "protective custody" in the concentration camps or to inmates who would gain their release by being selected for the camp.[36] Murmelstein was, in effect, the authorized agent of the British Commission. He did not make the final decision but the preliminary selection, which was then subject to the commission's final decision. Once he was informed of the commission's decision, Murmelstein was authorized to sign the British entry permit. But before that could take place, the prospective participant had to be cleared by the many German authorities, especially as regards taxes and the relinquishment of property; then Murmelstein had to assign him to an available place on a transport; permit in hand, he would be issued the visa by the British consul; and finally, over Löwenherz's signature, the transport had to be cleared with Eichmann, with a copy to Gestapo headquarters.

The pressure by applicants on the IKG functionaries for inclusion in the project was great. Murmelstein and his staff could not receive the petitioners personally or they would have been besieged by people urging the priority of their case or that of their son or husband, and would not have been able to complete the outlined procedures. However, this meant that to the desperate confusion among the Jews was added a sense of betrayal.

Those who were perceived to have the means and the power seemed to refuse to help, and the suspicion soon arose that they were reserving places for those whom they favored.

It is in this situation that Murmelstein was able to muster an unusual combination of talents and abilities and, for better or worse, put them to use in carrying out a task which few, if any, besides him could have carried out. He was able to glean and remember relevant facts precisely and in detail, was circumspect yet quick in making justifiable decisions, gave his staff precise instructions, and saw to it that they were carried out strictly and on time. Murmelstein knew the abilities of the people he gathered around him and knew how to put them to use. Disloyalty, corruption, and indiscretion were not tolerated. Being himself utterly loyal to Löwenherz, he displayed an extraordinary degree of courage and presence of mind in dealing with the Nazi authorities. At the same time, his often intentionally and intimidatingly gruff manner helped him keep petitioners and seekers of special consideration at a distance, which did not serve to endear him or to enhance his reputation with the general public or with most of the enormous staff that crowded the IKG. Only those who worked in the uppermost echelons of the IKG knew and were able to appreciate the nature and the quality of his performance. Kapralik, who was still in Vienna and at the IKG in the first few weeks of the camp project, remembers Murmelstein as "a tower of strength."[37]

It was in connection with Murmelstein's administration of the camp project that the record shows the first complaints against him. People did not understand why some were selected while they were not. How could one explain to a person of 46 in most desperate straits but with impeccable proof of immigration possibilities to the United States that he was not eligible when he saw that his neighbor of 44 had been accepted, whose chances of moving on to an ultimate destination were highly questionable? How did one explain to a member of the IKG staff that his position would not enhance his eligibility? During our interviews, we showed Murmelstein a copy of an application by a man of 56 who had been released from a concentration camp. Murmelstein's decision was indicated by means of underlining the age, the word "impossible," and his initials. In response he said, "Pardon me, but what else could I have done?"[38] The British Commission would not have approved his proposed selection. Murmelstein also claimed that the severe strictures under which he had to make selections, coupled with the prevailing atmosphere of desperation, necessitated his moving with a bodyguard within and in the environs of the IKG. According to his report, he was, one time, assailed by a desperate releasee brandishing a knife, someone who was overage and thus not accepted into the camp program. The attack occurred in the stairwell of the IKG. Murmelstein and someone who was with him were able to subdue the attacker and disarm him. Murmelstein did not file a complaint with the police, since he understood the man's desperation and realized that the police were not there for the protection of Jews.[39]

In a passage we have quoted from the *Bulletin of the London Co-ordinating Committee* (April 1939) we find the sentence, "The selection of refugees is left entirely in the hands of the organizations on the continent; **no application to the British Agencies will be considered**." There is good reason for this statement and for the emphasis that appears in the original. As soon as the scheme was put in operation and Murmelstein's office was perceived as a bottleneck and as partial in its choices, refugees already in London began receiving complaints from friends and relatives in Vienna, which they in turn submitted to the commission. Murmelstein recalled that according to one complainant his, Murmelstein's, son was collecting bribes from those who, in return, were placed on the list of selectees; and yet, at the time Murmelstein's son was all of 3 years old![40] In consequence, the commission came to Vienna to see the situation for themselves. As usual, Löwenherz had to obtain clearance for the visitors and then submit a report of the visit to the Gestapo. On March 2, 1939, he reported the following:

> I report that Messrs. Julian David Layton, Adolfo Ernesto Gentilli, and Maurice Bernhard Baron have left. During their several days' stay in Vienna they selected ca. 1,080 men who may be considered for temporary sojourn in Kitchener Camp in Richborough in England and who will continue their travel from there to ultimate destinations, especially to Palestine and the United States of North America.
>
> The list of names of emigrants approved by the Commission will be sent from the IKG to the Council for German Jewry, to be submitted [by them] to the Home Office for the entry permits. The selectees will be dispatched by the IKG presumably in transports of 125 persons each.[41]

The commission's "several days'" work consisted of the detailed inspection of the files of all the applicants in Murmelstein's office and of confirming his selections and rejections. As a result, Murmelstein, in the official account of his second trip to London, was able to report that "both in London [i.e., at the Commission and at the Council] as well as in Richborough [i.e., among the transients from Vienna as well as the camp directors] it was declared that the organization of the transports from Vienna is exemplary, which facilitated the negotiations for additional places considerably."[42]

Löwenherz's mention of Julian Layton, a military man who was a member of the supervisory committee that developed the camp,[43] calls to mind the question of the possible military aspect of the camp project. In later years, Murmelstein claimed that Bentwich confirmed in his memoirs the correctness of this assumption. However, the confirmation is indirect.

The memoir in question carries the title *I Understand the Risks*. The subtitle is: "The Story of the Refugees from Nazi Oppression Who Fought in the British Forces in the World War." The main title is a phrase in the declaration which the political—including Jewish—refugees had to sign when, after joining the Pioneer Corps, they volunteered for overseas wartime duties. Nowhere in his account does Bentwich suggest that the camp had a paramilitary purpose. What he does say is that the way the activities and the communal life of the camp were organized and the experiences gained by the men "was also a valuable transition for the Army discipline to come."[44] While the inference which Murmelstein drew is not a necessary one, it surely is a plausible one. Under the circumstances, he believed that he had no discernible alternative but to proceed under the tacit assumption of its correctness. If he was to continue his dangerous work, he had to be prepared for the possibility of being confronted, directly or indirectly, with the compromising truth. He took this risk upon himself in order to get at least some men out of Austria. When war with Germany broke out, there was talk in England of interning all persons who, by virtue of their German citizenship, counted as "enemy aliens." The British government set up tribunals in order to

Jewish refugees gather around a table outdoors to listen to a record player at the Kitchener Camp. (United States Holocaust Memorial Museum, courtesy of Hilary Dalton. USHMM 45194)

separate bona fide refugees from others who may be suspect. Tribunals also visited Kitchener Camp. Only two of the men in the camp, which by then had surpassed its full capacity of over 3,500, were taken for internment. The rest were invited to join the army, not the fighting force, but the Pioneer Corps, albeit on an auxiliary basis. As it happened, this kind of service is precisely what the camp experience had prepared them for. Bentwich reports that "in the end 1,500 . . . were enrolled." Others, unless they continued their emigration to an ultimate destination, joined the war effort in some other capacity, which is to say that relatively few fulfilled—and none were forced to fulfill—the requirement of joining the camp as transients only.

Bentwich presents statistics about the number of Jewish refugees in Britain at large (including the camp) who joined the British armed forces and served in the war.[45] He also briefly accounts for the fact that once Nazi Germany invaded Holland and France, there was fear of invasion at precisely the coastal area where the camp was located. Wasserstein, in his more thorough report,[46] tells of the rumors that were rife, according to which the reason Holland fell so quickly to the onslaught of the German army was that Jewish refugees, fearful of the safety of loved ones still in Germany, were under pressure to spy for Germany. This, mixed with anti-Semitic sentiment that was not absent in Britain, caused refugees who were not in the army or engaged in other war work to be treated like any other "enemy aliens."[47] Hence the camp's remaining 700 inmates, together with many other refugees, including those male participants in children's transports who, in the meantime, had reached the age of 16, became enemy aliens and were interned. Bentwich reports that for these inmates of the camp "the conditions of removal were more considerate than for the mass of refugees in the country." He adds that it was none other than Julian Layton, by then a lieutenant (later colonel) in the Pioneer Corps, "who had been seconded for special service to take charge of the camp," and that the corps' rabbi was from Germany, Dr. Werner van der Zyl, who accompanied them to their internment on the Isle of Man.[48]

This, then, was for Murmelstein the postwar confirmation of the soundness of his inference about the nature of Kitchener Camp and of his *modus operandi* based on this inference vis-à-vis his British contacts, the Jewish public in Vienna, his staff, his colleagues at the IKG, and above all the Nazi authorities. He was convinced that Löwenherz and Engel (and, in Berlin, Eppstein) had known about the nature of the camp and that they had pushed on him the sensitive job of executing the scheme in Vienna. According to his own account, he used his subordinate and therefore less visible position to take initiatives beyond his competence, and pulled strings wherever it was possible and necessary: On his own he prepared a file of concentration camp internees. He had the usually cautious Löwenherz circumvent the Gestapo (who had authority over arrests, concentration camps, and inmates) and submit these lists to Eichmann asking for their release—a ploy that would work only if the internees were expedited within the stipulated time limit. As we have already seen, Murmelstein turned the camp scheme into a venue for the rescue of the internees. In cases where further emigration possibilities were lacking, he invented some so that the requirement of apparent transience could be fulfilled vis-à-vis the British Commission. He badgered the British vice-consul to work overtime to speed up the visa process. In the last week before the outbreak of war, when the consulate had shut down, he signed the two hundred remaining permits and sent the men across the border without visas.[49]

In Search of Feasible Schemes

The chaotic interplay of the vectors of pressure bearing down on the IKG leadership in the cases of the camp scheme and the children's transports illustrates the prevailing condition of forced emigration. But much more than these successes was needed, and the search for feasible schemes of mass emigration was on.

Shanghai was another possible destination for large-scale emigration, and it too was useful for quickly expediting men released from concentration camps. However, its usefulness was limited since Shanghai demanded an amount of money from immigrants which few Jews in Vienna were able to raise. A number of travel agencies in combination with minor shipping lines were prepared to arrange mass transports to Shanghai and other unspecified ports in China; but, aside from the doubtful nature of the offers, they required exorbitant deposits in U.S. dollars or British pounds. Neither the IKG nor Eichmann was willing to risk the sparse resources of the IKG in support of such uncertain schemes. And IKG participation in schemes that seemed feasible at first was denied when the shipping lines jacked up the prices. The IKG had good reason to have great reservations about the Shanghai transports. For example, a letter was received at the IKG on May 9, 1939, from a

Mr. B. S. Barbash, dated April 12. Mr. Barbash had an import-export business in Shanghai and appears to have been a leading member of the Shanghai Jewish Community as well as the chairman of a local aid committee. Hence, refugees who landed there wound up in his office inquiring about assistance. At this time, refugees from Austria were beginning to join those from Germany in greater numbers; but, whereas most of the German Jews had still been able to bring some money with them, these newest arrivals came, for the most part, without means. Mr. Barbash's letter, written in English, follows in full:

> Your favours, dated 20th. & 21st. ult. [i.e., March].
>
> It is absolutely useless for me to call these people, because the local Committee has not one cent at its disposal.
>
> It is a great mistake from "HICEM" [a Jewish immigration organization], Paris that they did not give any assistance to the emigrants from former Austria, because they gave only assistance to emigrants from Germany, and so the people arrived here without a cent.
>
> I recommend you send a copy of this letter to the "HICEM," Paris, and to draw their attention to the fact that most of the Jewish refugees here are in a very precarious situation: there have been here already cases of suicide for this reason. Please send also a copy of this letter to the "Joint," Paris and to the United States. They must find a way that the United States shall allow all these immigrants to go from Shanghai to America, and find money for their passage. This is the only one solution, as otherwise all these people are bound to starve here. I wrote many times to Berlin and Paris and gave them a picture of the situation, but they did not want to listen to my information. The local Jewish Community consists of 3,000 souls only, most of whom are poor, being Russian refugees. How can they support 8,000 people, and I would not be surprised that 50,000 people will come here little by little. . . .
>
> There are here no accommodations, no rooms, no shops, and NO JOBS. Business is dead and the interior is closed: only war conditions.[50]

The specter of the five-digit figure that Mr. Barbash hardly dared to envisage at the beginning of the trek to Shanghai became realized before long,[51] when well over 20,000, possibly as many of 30,000, refugees made Shanghai their interim station, albeit for a sojourn that lasted until after the war and the occupation by Japan, in most cases also after the civil war and the establishment of the Communist regime. How those people managed to survive is unfortunately not part of our story.[52]

However, the IKG did not need to wait for the arrival of Mr. Barbash's letter to have reason to be almost as deeply concerned over the question of what the emigrés would do at their destination, as it was intent on expediting the process of dispatching the distressed Jews of Vienna. The former concern was, in fact, a function of the latter. That concern was a reverberation of the reluctant responsiveness on the part of prospective host nations, a reluctance that had been evident to Löwenherz since he had attended the Evian Conference, and which in succeeding months he was consistently to encounter. Hence, while the leading functionaries at the IKG welcomed the prospect of having in Shanghai a destination that did not require visas and entry permits and were even prepared to assist the indigent with at least part of the considerable cost of the trip, they realized that sending their people where they would be a burden would be counterproductive to the overall emigration effort. In the apparently first major memorandum to Eichmann on the difficulties of financing mass transports (in this case to China) and of finding dependable transportation arrangements, Löwenherz adds:

> As we emphasized earlier, every collective transport can serve to influence public opinion in the country of destination in a manner adverse to further immigration, so that regulated immigration will inevitably meet insurmountable obstacles. Hence, from the standpoint of the technique of emigration, the immigrants' fate at their destination is significant, since it must under all circumstances be avoided that they become burdens to the Jewish aid societies; this would tie up large amounts of foreign exchange that might be withheld from the emigration effort in [Austria].[53]

Löwenherz concludes with the need for clearing such mass transports with the Jewish aid societies outside of Germany and asks permission to make appropriate representations. We will see that in this period the leading functionaries of the IKG were sent on a number of missions beyond the borders for precisely this purpose.

As regards Shanghai, on April 7, a month after the quoted memorandum, Löwenherz reported to Eichmann the dilemma in which the IKG found itself. On the one hand, the aid societies on whom the IKG depended "decidedly opposed, for cogent reasons, any subvention of emigration to the Far East." The ostensible "cogent reasons" consisted, no doubt, of the fact that by then Japan had control over Shanghai and its hinterland, as well as the rest of the coast of China, and that, because of the consequent unstable conditions, aid to the refugees would meet insuperable difficulties. Yet, the real reason may well have been that the Shanghai scheme confronted the aid societies with an upsurge of demands on their limited resources, especially now that, in the aftermath of Kristallnacht, the pressure on the Jews of the Altreich to emigrate posthaste was catching up with the pressure that the Austrian Jews had been feeling since the Anschluss.[54] On March 30, Engel, substituting for Löwenherz, was chided by Eichmann that the number of applicants for emigration documents in Berlin was beginning to exceed that in Vienna. Engel saw this as an "occasion" to "speak out against the forced pace of the transports to China" for the reason that the aid organizations took an "equivalent position" to that of Eichmann, which evidently means that the IKG was being "chided" by them. Their intent, however, ran counter to Eichmann's: Eichmann said "not enough," the aid organizations said "too much."[55]

At the same time, the IKG was besieged by desperate clients in need of passage to China for inmates in or ones already released from concentration camps; these people, "whose remaining [time] within the territory of the Reich is limited, often see the acquisition of such a passage as their only possibility of emigration." But the "difficult decision" regarding the IKG's participation, a decision which had been "due for some time," was now urged upon them by the fact that the Italian steamship line Lloyd Triestino required full payment for the complement of booked tickets by April 10. Hence "the IKG requests release of RM 200,000 from the funds set aside for emigration, and will examine each case as to eligibility and urgency."[56] Ten days later Löwenherz reports that of the 3,000 applicants for IKG subsidies for passage to Shanghai, 456 were deemed to be "especially urgent," for whom an "average amount of DM 350 each is required," and for which purpose Löwenherz requested release of appropriate funds. Once again, he assured Eichmann that the screening of the individual cases was strict to ensure that each could contribute according to his available means, and that the steamship lines would not extort additional charges.[57]

Löwenherz's memoranda to Eichmann concerning Shanghai, cited above, were typed on the typewriter in Murmelstein's office. This tells us two things. First, it confirms that the organization and execution of major emigration matters fell to Murmelstein—rather than to Engel who was and remained nominally in charge of the IKG emigration section—and consequently Löwenherz's relevant representations vis-à-vis Eichmann were heavily influenced by Murmelstein. Second, it tends to confirm Murmelstein's claim that in matters of emigration and the IKG's related competencies, there was considerable tension and even a tug-of-war between him and Löwenherz. It would seem that while Murmelstein was willing to have the IKG's resources in Reichsmark as well as foreign exchange disbursed wherever they were needed to facilitate emigration, Löwenherz was concerned to maintain substantial reserves for future needs and to preserve accountability.

The IKG, with Löwenherz as the man in its most exposed position, was accountable, first, to Eichmann, who had placed him and was maintaining him in his position of forced leadership, and who held the IKG's purse strings. Second, he was also accountable, under a gentlemen's agreement, to the aid organizations who were not only supplying the IKG with all the foreign exchange available to it but also provided a large amount of the funds that made up the monetary resources of the IKG's budget and reserves; moreover, one of those organizations, the Joint, regarded Löwenherz as its agent. Third, through his ethical commitment and responsibility, Löwenherz was accountable to the Viennese Jewish Community over whose eventual liquidation he was presiding. This community had, after all, chosen him as the executive director of its communal organization prior to the present situation, and it was the lives of its members, their assets, and their future that were in no small way now in his hands.

From Löwenherz's perspective then, since he was concerned to treat dwindling and sparse resources with a view toward all segments that were dependent on them as well as toward all those to whom he had to give an accounting, Murmelstein was the fiscally reckless executor of only one segment of the IKG's concern. From Murmelstein's perspective, things looked different: Because he thought that straining the IKG's resources, such as they were, in support of the forced emigration effort to be justifiable if it resulted in the rescue of Jews and if one could get away with it vis-à-vis those to whom the IKG was accountable, he saw Löwenherz's economy as a waste of precious resources. Decades later, in one of our interviews, Murmelstein had the following to say about this aspect of Löwenherz's *modus operandi* and of the working relation between them:

> **M**: Löwenherz says one should not overdo emigration, one also has to think about finances . . . with the result that so-and-so-many million marks were confiscated by Eichmann. [What] if they had not been, if they had been of benefit to the Jews? That was always the struggle between me and him. That he said he had to sell people dollars because he needed *Reichsmark*. Always was afraid of famine. And I told him, with the dollars we send the people away. . . . Therefore the *Zentralstelle* confiscated. But I predicted for him, I have always predicted. I told him, you will see, you are saving for Eichmann. When he called me he said, "For heaven's sake!"—I had approved the ship's tickets—"One cannot do this! I have no more

dollars for the old-age homes!" The old-age homes do not need any dollars, they have enough marks. . . .

LHE: [But] in general, when people were not able to get hold of dollars for ship's tickets either through relatives or contacts overseas, they could [obtain] dollars for the tickets by depositing marks. . . .

M: But what if one did not have the marks, if he was a welfare case? Should he have croaked? . . . [W]hat does one do in such a case? . . . I gave them the dollars. Löwenherz raged, I gave them the dollars. . . . What would one have done with the dollars? Some dollars remained frozen at the Joint in any case. Which had been at our disposal. If I had been lucky enough to speak with Löwenherz afterward [after the war], I would have said to him, "What happened to the *Reichsmark*? Eichmann stole them. What happened to the dollars? The Joint devoured them. Couldn't one have sent more people out?"

This is how it was: I approved the tickets. The [IKG] foreign exchange section had to obtain [from the authorities] clearance for the transfer of the foreign money for the tickets. You understand? And [Löwenherz] got the thing for his signature. Then he saw. And he always made a note requesting an additional explanation informing him how much the people had paid. And when he saw . . . that he had approved so-and-so-many dollars where people had not paid anything [in marks], he called me. Look: With me things were not so simple. When someone is blunt with me, rude, then I become even more rude. One fine day I told him, "See here, Herr Doktor, let me tell you something. We are, after all, not here to collect dollars, but to send people abroad. The Joint sends dollars for the purpose—and Eichmann wants the same—that we send the Jews away, not that we should have a bank account. In this one regard the Joint and Eichmann, as our supervisors, so to say, agree. And it is in this regard that you have to be contra." He understood, the direction the wind was blowing was fairly clear. . . . This means that he knew that I would not turn to Eichmann, but to the Joint. That he understood. After this discussion—we always went home together because we lived in the same building—he went home alone for a few days. It did not bother me.

MM [Margit Murmelstein]: There were many disputes. But, in general, he was a very fine gentleman. . . .

M: Löwenherz was a very fine gentleman. Only with regard to—I did not agree with many things that he did. And, in my opinion, many things happened that would not have happened if he had acted differently.[58]

Within the context of the matter immediately at issue, Murmelstein's somewhat sharp ex post facto appraisal of Löwenherz's seemingly excessive caution, two things stand out. First, as can be seen from the example of the tickets to Shanghai, in the end Löwenherz did plead with Eichmann for the allocation of available funds, yet not without presenting his reasons for caution and scruples, especially vis-à-vis the aid societies that would have had to be approached for continued funding—and all this apparently in form of a draft prepared in Murmelstein's office. The implication is that Löwenherz was decidedly appreciative of Murmelstein's thorough grasp of the needs and problems of emigration and of his unhesitating, forceful, and effective representation of required courses of action and their—at times—risky feasibilities. Second, Löwenherz may have seemed mainly—but was certainly not exclusively—concerned over money matters, leaving other matters to his lieutenants. Surely it was he who, for example, undertook the initial negotiations for the mass transports to England. But it was Murmelstein who gave shape and direction to the camp project and made it a going concern after it was set up by Löwenherz.

Time and again Eichmann pressed Löwenherz to go abroad to maintain and increase the flow of *Devisen* (foreign exchange or foreign currency). Constantly Löwenherz reported to him the British and the American aid societies' counterpressure to the effect that the Reichsmark raised through the availability of this foreign exchange were to be used for feasible emigration purposes only and not for any emigration "experiments" or for the IKG's social service and welfare budgets.[59] The IKG had to prepare a periodic accounting for the American Joint and the British Council for German Jewry,[60] even as it had to prepare frequent verbal and written presentations on money matters to Eichmann and other Nazi authorities. It is understandable that in spite of and in addition to all the ongoing matters of immediate concern under his purview, Löwenherz had to take the long view and wonder where the money for next month's emigration and service activities would come from, what the fiscal needs might be one year hence, how to manage since the local sources of revenue were drying up and being swallowed up by the insatiable extortionist regime represented by the various tentacles of authority implacably lording it over the Jews and the IKG.

"Get more *Devisen*" was Eichmann's constant refrain. And this, as well as negotiations for further possibilities of emigration, was the reason he supported Löwenherz's many travels to London, Paris, and Amsterdam during the period in question. It was in order to continue these negotiations that his lieutenants occasionally traveled abroad. Murmelstein went to London in January and in April. Engel, accompanied by Kapralik, went to London and Paris in February.[61] August finds Engel in Milan to clarify the status of the great number of Jews who were still arriving in Italy in spite of the anti-Jewish restrictions that Mussolini was beginning to impose in deference to the German partner of the Rome-Berlin Axis. The result was that only Jews possessing some foreign exchange and the prospect of moving to a further destination would be admitted to Italy. Eichmann approved the IKG's release of foreign exchange to Jews with German citizenship, but not to the stateless, from whom the Italians required 60 pounds.[62] While Engel was in Milan, Löwenherz received a call from Secretary Kuchmann at Gestapo headquarters, wanting to know where Herr Engel might be, and informing him that no permission for that trip had been issued to Engel, but only to one Herr Steinfeld. Löwenherz assured Kuchmann that Engel was travelling upon prior approval by Eichmann. Kuchmann objected that Engel did not understand anything about these matters. Löwenherz had to remind Kuchmann that Engel was the director of the IKG emigration section, and that he was engaged in efforts on behalf of emigration.[63]

We have seen that some of the most feasible emigration schemes required negotiation abroad, especially in England. Another small group, whose emigration presented special problems, consisted of the rabbis, cantors, and professional teachers of religion. The IKG had been primarily a religious organization, having grown out of the need to represent and to provide for the distinct requirements of Jewish life in the ambiance of modern society and the modern state. Times being what they were, the IKG's concerns soon grew beyond worship, ritual, rites of passage, charity, traditional teaching, and the training of rabbis and *melameds* (teachers) and comprised all kinds of concerns of Jews swept up in the life of modernity. But the religious concerns remained its core. With the closing of the synagogues and the expulsion of Jewish teachers (and students) from the schools, most of the rabbis, religious teachers, and cantors became charges of the IKG. The IKG provided these people with financial support insofar as it was not able to employ them in its new function of liquidating the Jewish Community. Some were employed in the rabbinical court, which continued to function, some were teachers in the schools that the authorities permitted the IKG to maintain, a few were employed at the IKG in administrative capacities.

Murmelstein is a case in point. Another example is Elimelech Rimalt. Like Murmelstein, Rimalt had come to Vienna from Galicia to study for the rabbinate and for a doctorate in biblical and cognate studies. With Murmelstein's help, he was able to secure a rabbinical position in the small Jewish community in Innsbruck in the alpine province of Tyrol. Soon after the Anschluss, he was chased out of Innsbruck. In Vienna he took over Murmelstein's pulpit when the latter moved to the Great Synagogue. When the synagogues were demolished at the time of Kristallnacht, Murmelstein took Rimalt into his staff at the IKG.

Employable or not, special arrangements were needed to provide this group of people with emigration destinations and, as was the case with other Jews, the urgency of the matter increased after Kristallnacht. By then the chief rabbi of the British Empire, Dr. Joseph H. Hertz, had established the "Chief Rabbi's Religious Emergency Fund for German and Austrian Jewry." On December 22, 1938, Löwenherz addressed a letter to Hertz, requesting that he arrange for an immigration permit for Rabbi Dr. Egon Lewin, who had been a teacher of religion, but who was now in protective custody and would not be released until his emigration could be assured. Löwenherz also mentioned, first, that the young man was the son of the 73-year-old Rabbi Professor Dr. Moriz Lewin, a scholar presumably known to the chief rabbi, *second*, that the elder Lewin had been the rabbi of the synagogue of Vienna's 13th District, presumably as a reminder that it was now defunct.[64] In response, the office of the Religious Emergency Fund sent a form letter informing the IKG of the usual preconditions that had to be met before application for a permit could be made, etc. etc.[65] Clearly, the matter of getting these people safely out of Vienna had to be urged in face-to-face negotiations. These had been started by Löwenherz in November 1938 and been brought to some measure of fruition by Murmelstein during his trip to England in January 1939. The latter reported having had "thorough discussions with the Chief Rabbi of the British Empire about the creation of immigration possibilities for religious functionaries." A list of applicants on behalf of rabbis from the Altreich had already been submitted to the Home Office for approval, and Murmelstein was able to gain Hertz's agreement to the submission of a second list, in which applicants from Austria would receive special consideration. In a report about this matter that Murmelstein had to submit to the Gestapo, he included a passage that may seem puzzling: "even in this case [of rabbis, etc.] it was determined that suitable consideration of [Austrian applicants] required information and advertisement."[66] This was meant to convey to the Nazi authorities that their objection to newspaper reports such as in the recent case of the overtired children arriving in Harwich were counterproductive to creating interest in helping Jews to immigrate and, thus, to the Nazi program of getting rid of the Jews.

After Löwenherz's renewed negotiations with Chief Rabbi Hertz during his trip to Lon-

Edith Ehrlich escaped Vienna on a Kindertransport *(children's transport) that arrived at Harwich, England, on May 15, 1939. Exactly seventeen years later to the day, she would give birth to her first child in the appropriately named city of New Haven, Connecticut (© CSE)*

don late in January 1939, he was able to report that he had received "the promise that in addition to the permits for rabbis, cantors, and religious teachers which were, thanks to our efforts, previously secured, the greatest efforts would be made to obtain further entry permits."[67]

Yet there was another hitch before the rabbis and others could be expedited. On February 13, 1939, Löwenherz wrote to Hertz, referring to their recent meeting and reiterating his and the IKG's appreciation for Hertz's efforts in obtaining entry permits for this special group and in helping them find ultimate destinations. Reminding Hertz of his declaration that his actions were undertaken on behalf of Jewry as a whole and not on behalf of a particular group, Löwenherz pointed out that clearly this is not the case "when notifications of the granting of permits are not directed to the IKG but to the Vienna branch of Agudas Jisroel," which in turn would notify the recipients. Löwenherz tried, as best as his problematic situation permitted, to explain to Hertz what difficulties obtained when the IKG was circumvented. On the one hand, the IKG, having always been the "sole religious organization for all Jews residing in Vienna," was the authority capable of giving references for "cultic functionaries" (rabbis, cantors, and religious teachers). However, since in this case the IKG was circumvented, persons appeared on the list of recipients of permits, a small list in any case, who were not known as religious functionaries either to the IKG or to other religious organizations. Moreover, the IKG was involved in the documentation procedure of all emigrants. This was why it was found that three of the persons included in the list were also recommended by the IKG for a Rabbi-Certificate to Palestine. Not only was it embarrassing to have the same persons appear on two lists of visa applications submitted to the Passport Office of the same British consulate, but "three Rabbis had the choice of two immigration chances [each], while others had none." At the end Löwenherz asked Hertz to put others on the list to fill the places left vacant by the ones who opted for Palestine.[68]

And so the exodus of Vienna's rabbis could proceed. Whether orthodox or traditional—in the manner that had developed in Austria in the nineteenth century and was taught at Vienna's *Jüdische Theologische Lehranstalt*, the rabbinical seminary that continued to attract students from the former Austrian crown lands even after the fall of the Habsburg Empire—they were careerists and eager to take up their vocation at new, friendlier venues. Within a few months the rabbis of the major congregations, now in effect disbanded, and the faculty of the seminary, now defunct, left with a generous severance stipend from the IKG in exchange for their renouncing all claims connected with tenure. Rabbis Dr. Moses Rosenmann, Dr. Artur Schwarz, and Prof. Dr. Kalman Kupfer left for Palestine.[69] Rabbi Josef Babad would wind up in the United States, as would Rabbi Prof. Dr. Julius Bach, a great orator, who would occupy a pulpit on Long Island.[70] Rabbi Dr. Hersch Zimmels left for England,[71] as would a number of other less well-known colleagues.

One of the last to leave, in April 1939, was the aged chief rabbi, Prof. Dr. Israel Taglicht.[72] It was the time of Murmelstein's second trip to England for negotiations with the London agencies, hence he was assigned to be the chief rabbi's escort on his journey of escape. Murmelstein told us the following incident from this trip to London: Chief Rabbi Hertz insisted on keeping his appointment with Murmelstein even though he was indisposed. When Murmelstein informed Hertz of the arrival of Vienna's chief rabbi, Hertz refused to receive him on the grounds that he could not honor a fellow rabbi who left his congregation at a time of persecution.[73]

And so it happened that Murmelstein was the only rabbi of a large congregation who remained among the Jews of Vienna. Not that he did not have any opportunities to emigrate. He was not a chief functionary like Löwenherz, nor a hostage like Friedmann or Stricker; Eichmann would have let him go. In fact, while in London in April 1939 he was asked whether he would not join the Camp Kitchener group.[74] Earlier in the year he had a chance to go to Palestine on a certificate as a rabbi. The certificate had, in fact, been issued to him, his wife, and his young son, Wolf. Yet, feeling that his work for the Vienna Jews was not done and that he owed it to them to continue, he passed it on to his friend Rabbi Dr. Elimelech Rimalt, who, together with his wife and little son thus entered Palestine under the name of Murmelstein.[75]

Other Jewish leaders who occasionally traveled abroad for negotiations were Rothenberg of the Palamt and Storfer. Rothenberg was involved with the mass transports to Palestine, even as the IKG was with other destinations. However, some mass transports to Palestine as well as to other destinations were of a nature that required organization not appropriate for either the IKG or the Palamt. This was to be Storfer's task. A specific transport project occasioned his appointment.

Seeking Safe Harbor

Since the beginning of the year, persons unaffiliated with either the IKG or the Palamt were planning a transport of young people to go to Palestine illegally as part of Aliyah Bet. It was being arranged by Maccabi (Ger. *Makkabi*), an international Jewish sports organization with Zionist leanings. At that time the Perl transports were still going to Palestine, but they were giving way to a wider enterprise that included prospective settlers who were not primarily from Vienna and neither included nor were arranged by as a rule the Revisionists. The planned Maccabi transport was clearly of the kind in which neither the IKG nor the Palamt could be officially involved, as Eichmann acknowledged at the *Vorsprache* with Löwenherz and Rothenberg on February 10. The relevant item of the *Aktennotiz* summarizes the administrative difficulty of this noninvolvement and Eichmann's initial refusal to solve it: "In the future such transports should not be arranged in Vienna, individual persons' preliminary steps can be taken care of and their emigration made possible by fulfilling the usual preconditions, but the putting together of the transports must take place outside of Germany [*die Zusammenstellung der Transporte hat im Ausland zu erfolgen*]."[76] However, more needed to be done in Vienna about ensuring the success of these transports in order to justify the IKG's inevitable involvement by providing travel funds and "fulfilling the usual preconditions" for emigration. Even if the arrangements for a transport were made outside of Germany, someone in Vienna had to take care of matters in which the IKG could not become involved. Yet the item in question ends with Eichmann's pronouncement that "No umbrella organization should be established for this sort of transport."

No "organization"—instead it was Storfer, who is first mentioned two weeks later when Löwenherz and Rothenberg appeared on February 23, 1939, for one of the frequent reporting sessions at Eichmann's office:

> It was suggested [by Löwenherz] that the overseas transports with which [according to Eichmann] the IKG ought not to concern itself be assigned to Herr Berthold Storfer, who will have to deal with the individual groups that will make the selection of [participating] persons. No separate organization is to be formed.[77]

One week later Eichmann's instructions are significantly more precise:

> SS Hauptsturmführer Eichmann wishes that mass transports to overseas destinations be placed under the supervision of Herr Berthold Storfer, who is to select his co-workers. He is to watch over the individual transports to be dispatched, inspect their financial dealings, ascertain the possibilities of transportation, and prevent [undesirable] persons from participating in this work who are unauthorized and who act in ways that conflict with each other. He is also to conduct the negotiations with shipping companies, and for this purpose is to maintain working relations [*Einvernehmen pflegen*] with the Travel Agency Schlie.[78]

The "Travel Agency Schlie"? The same Heinrich Schlie who organized the Colombia transport in August 1938? This transport was to have been Eichmann's demonstration to the Jews of how emigration should proceed, namely, en masse, but it turned out to be a debacle for the Jews and, worse, an embarrassment for Eichmann. This event, so painful for Eichmann, could not be mentioned by Löwenherz when he heard "Schlie"; but by fortuitous coincidence he could take up with Eichmann a matter of ongoing concern, precisely the kind of matter that prompted the need for the task that Storfer was charged to undertake.

Löwenherz had with him a letter from the Paris office of the Joint. The Joint referred to the fate of two groups of emigrants, one on the SS *Königstein*, the other on the SS *Carybia*; neither group had been permitted to disembark at its intended destination in Central America. According to Löwenherz's report to Eichmann, the aid societies abroad were "holding the IKG responsible for the failure" of these ventures, "even though the IKG had nothing to do with them." Hence, Löwenherz was constrained to direct Eichmann's attention to the "difficulties" which the same aid societies made for the IKG, societies "on which the IKG depends for support." These difficulties "arise from the sort of transports that are not properly prepared and are not dispatched to an assured destination." Eichmann conceded the cogency of the objections and requirements and, in the presence of Löwenherz, picked up the telephone to demand from the travel agency Zentrum that it "effect the expeditious landing of the passengers and refrain in the future from this kind of transport unless properly prepared."[79]

There were two sides to Eichmann's energetic admonition to Zentrum. In one sense it was a red herring, inasmuch as the kind of transport in question was precisely what he wanted. What had been embarrassing to him in the case of the abortive Colombia transport was, in the end, neither the fact that the affected Jews had had precipitously to abandon their possessions and to pay all the extorted taxes and charges, then were left destitute and dependent on the scarce resources of the IKG, nor the fact that for all their troubles the Jews did not arrive at their promised destination, but that the venture did not succeed in getting the Jews out of Germany. On the other hand, the call to Zentrum showed that the IKG's constant, vigorous representations kept Eichmann aware of the fact that success in getting rid of the Jews was conditional upon his taking into account considerations he could not care less about. Getting rid of the Jews required substantive performance on his part beyond issuing directives and applying pressures, and on his exacting such performance also from German agencies beyond the IKG's control. Four days after that telephone call Eichmann was able to report to Löwenherz that the Red Star Line had directed the SS *Königstein* to make one more attempt to find a port in Colombia(!), which would accept the emigrés, before directing it to return to Hamburg, its home port.[80]

How helpless the IKG was in dealing with German agencies can be seen from a record of a telephone conversation in Löwenherz's files from the time when the problematic nature of this transport—for whose arrangement, as we have seen, the IKG bore no responsibility—became clear. The date was January 24, 1939, a time when Löwenherz was out of the country and Engel took his place. Engel called Herr Wagner, the director of the Red Star Line in Hamburg, to inquire about the chances of finding a port of entry for the emigrés. Wagner denied any responsibility in this matter on the part of the Red Star Line; the responsibility, he claimed, rested solely with Zentrum, to whom they had leased the ship, and with the individual passengers.[81] In short, it was the situation of the Colombia transport all over again, with the commercial agencies pocketing the profits, and the authorities, including—and especially—Eichmann, the loot they had extorted, and the Jews paying the bill first with their assets, such as they might have been, and paying ultimately with their hope of escape—and all to no avail. The IKG had to assume responsibility for something they were not involved with in the first place.

It is, therefore, more than likely that it must have given Löwenherz pause to hear Eichmann say that the travel bureau with which Storfer, the designated agent for "overseas transports which the IKG ought not to concern itself with," would have to deal, would be none other than Schlie. To be sure, the "purpose" for maintaining "working relations" with Travel Agency Schlie was to "conduct negotiations with shipping companies." Yet, even though Schlie and its parent company would have had much time since the Colombia transport debacle to learn about the almost Sisyphean task of managing the forced emigration of the Jews, there was little reason to believe that they had learned more than how better to maneuver the interested parties, and especially Eichmann, into involving them in the lucrative transport aspect of emigration. But, inasmuch as there were many other travel agencies that were keenly interested in this business, one wonders: How else could Eichmann be maneuvered in this way other than—let us phrase it charitably—through the travel agents, and through them the steamship lines, joining the hard-pressed Jews in contributing to the "Emigration Fund" that he was accumulating? Eichmann was indeed beset by various agencies, all of whom requested a piece of the business. The major German steamship lines thought that overseas travel ought to proceed on their ships and even got the Interior Ministry on their side, especially at the time when the major phase of mass transports was getting under way.

On March 6, 1939, Eichmann had Löwenherz attend a meeting in his office with representatives of the North German Lloyd, headquartered in Bremen. The gentlemen declared their interest in "emigrants who receive travel moneys from the IKG taking Reich-German ships," and that "for the months of March and April many places are still vacant on German steamers." No doubt Eichmann was delighted to pass the pressure on to Löwenherz, who could not divulge the complexities and conditions of the foreign exchange arrangements on which the contributions of external aid societies depended; and Löwenherz had to inform the gentlemen that in cases where persons were constrained to leave Germany ahead of scheduled sailings, they could obtain a transit visa to Holland or to England only if they had bookings on Dutch or British ships. The gentlemen from Bremen assured Löwenherz that they could also arrange for such transit visas, and an appointment was set up at the IKG for further discussions that evening.[82]

It was after the gentlemen had left his office that Eichmann informed Löwenherz about Travel Agency Zentrum's attempt to have the SS *Königstein* discharge its hapless passengers in Colombia.[83] As a diversion from the dim prospect of success, Eichmann lectured Löwenherz, saying that the IKG should cease dealing with Zentrum and "altogether with small travel agencies." One can sense Löwenherz's attempt at restraint in the face of this comical instance of the schoolboy lecturing the teacher by his adding the following to the official record: "I informed [Eichmann] that the IKG has, for a long time, been in contact only with the large travel agencies."[84] But, of course, Schlie was precisely the kind of small travel agency against which Eichmann's advice was directed—and yet it was with Schlie that Storfer was to deal in cases where the IKG was not to be directly involved. To understand what was at play, let us look at another item of the same *Vorsprache* of March 6 where Schlie is mentioned:

> SS Captain Eichmann acknowledged and agreed that the proposal concerning the Shanghai transports submitted by the Hanseatic Travel Agency (Schlie) is not acceptable because they require a deposit of 10 pounds disembarkation fee and 50 for the possible return journey.[85]

Here Eichmann's interest becomes clear: It was not Schlie, because Schlie was one of the "small" agencies. What was of interest to Eichmann was the "large" travel agency, Hanseatic, for whom Schlie happened to have been the agent. But evidently there is something else, namely, the matter of economical and expeditious emigration, which was no less in Eichmann's interest than in Löwenherz's. For the sake of emigration Eichmann had to concede, as the case in point shows, that prepayment—in sparse foreign exchange!—of costs for a scheme that had no guarantee of success, moreover costs that were mutually contradictory: £10 for disembarkation, £50 in case disembarkation could take place, was unacceptable. The juxtaposition of the quoted items—contained in an official *Aktennotiz*—also shows that Löwenherz knew of Eichmann's interest in Hanseatic and that Eichmann was fully aware that he knew. Yet Eichmann expected Löwenherz to operate in accordance with his interest, at least to the extent of not interfering with Storfer's negotiations with Hanseatic, and to give support to viable mass transports arranged by Storfer with the allocation of funds for the indigent, as well as, when needed, with foreign exchange. Part of this game of dissembling was Eichmann's attempt, at the *Vorsprache* of March 6, to distract from his primary interest in dealing with Hanseatic by using Löwenherz to engage in futile negotiation with North German Lloyd.

We have discussed in unusual detail the matters surrounding Löwenherz's *Vorsprache* at Eichmann's office on March 6. What is of interest here is not only that the very documents that were submitted for the files of the authorities point unmistakably to Eichmann's enterprising ways of tapping both ends of the Jewish cash flow for the purpose of building his "emigration fund."[86] Of even greater interest is the fact that while Löwenherz could not flaunt what he knew, he had the courage to make use of the knowledge in order to obtain some of the moneys from Eichmann's "emigration fund" for the IKG budget, and to cause Eichmann to help recoup for the IKG some of the assets and proceeds taken by other Nazi authorities. But before we trace this frustrating chess game, let us conclude the matter of Storfer's appointment.

Storfer, as we have seen, was appointed in order to facilitate the group transports about which the IKG and the Palamt "ought not to concern themselves (*um die sie sich nicht kümmern sollen*)."[87] We need to clarify what Storfer's role was and what the reason for his position was.

A constantly increasing number of emigrants were becoming dependent on the IKG for the partial or entire expense of emigration. Hence, the IKG could not hold itself aloof from those enterprises of mass emigration that did not readily conform to all the mentioned strictures defining the IKG's parameters of action. Yet the IKG could not undertake to make arrangements for such enterprises, as it had done for "legitimate" mass transports mentioned earlier. But the IKG could do the next best thing: It could make sure that even these questionable schemes served the interests of the Jews—getting them to their destination, not wasting scarce resources, not enriching profiteers and extortionists more than was unavoidable, and not disappointing the rightful expectations of the ever watchful aid organizations. This is the reason that Löwenherz asked that Storfer be appointed. Storfer's job was to be that of a broker. He would negotiate mainly with carriers, or else he would monitor such negotiations by those who were arranging a transport on behalf of a group. He saw to it that no undue charges were levied, that the transport was technically viable (e.g., that the ship was relatively seaworthy), legally feasible, and economically sound. Only when this was the case would the IKG approve a transport scheme, approve the allocation of needed funds or foreign exchange, and make appropriate requests to Eichmann for approval and disbursements. Storfer had a lot of latitude in his dealings with German and other agencies, such as carriers and their representatives, but he was not an independent agent inasmuch as these dealings were also monitored by Löwenherz and his lieutenants, and in fact he had to proceed in constant consultation with them. Eichmann, in particular, insisted that no one, including private parties, were to start proceedings leading to group transports without prior consultation with the IKG.[88]

And, besides handling the transports with which the IKG and the Palamt "ought not to concern themselves," Storfer soon also acted as the agent of the IKG and the Palamt in negotiating for carriers of transports with which they were directly concerned. A case in point is the Maccabi transport, the arranging of which was, as we have seen, the immediate occasion for lending urgency to the appointment of Storfer. The Maccabi transport to Palestine, which was part of Aliyah Bet (i.e., illegal and hence "of concern" neither to the Palamt nor the IKG) was facilitated by Storfer; however, once it was arranged for, the IKG negotiated with Eichmann for the release of moneys to support it.[89] On the other hand, the IKG and the Palamt were directly involved in transports to Palestine that were "legal" (i.e., that fell within the "schedule" approved by the British government) and, while Storfer helped to arrange the logistics of transportation, the IKG wrangled with Eichmann over the release of the requisite moneys.[90]

Eichmann looked with favor on Storfer because, given the strictures imposed by the external sources of foreign exchange, by the travel and shipping agencies eager for profit, by the many cautions that the IKG had to observe, Storfer was the only one who could be fully devoted to realizing Eichmann's dream of mass emigration, and within limits he was succeeding.

Some of the transports to Palestine arranged by the Palamt were of a questionable nature, that is, they were "illegal." This was true especially after May 17, 1939, when the British, bowing to Arab pressure, issued their "White Paper" severely restricting Jewish immigration to Palestine. Arranging these illegal transports to Palestine now also involved Storfer's brokering. And all modes of emigration to Palestine—legitimate and illegal, individual as well as group—brought the IKG into play, since only the IKG was authorized to handle the financial aspects of emigration. Inasmuch as the £10,000 contributed every month by the British Council for German Jewry was used to provide "Capitalist's Certificates" to Palestine, requiring £1,000 per family, emigration to Palestine was one of the main producers of the IKG's revenue in Reichsmark.

The British scheme of issuing capitalist's certificates stood in ironic contrast to the White Paper, which, in deference to perceived Arab pressure, proposed drastically to limit Jewish immigration to Palestine for a period of five years, at the end of which immigration was to cease entirely. The certificates indicate the extent to which the British had reason to look with favor on the economic development of Palestine under Jewish initiative, a development that benefited not only Jews but Arabs as well. The White Paper, on the other hand, presents us with evidence once again that when it came to Jews—even at a time of their evident and increasing endangerment—political considerations outweighed sound economic ones.

The message was not lost on the Jews of Vienna or the IKG or Eichmann or the various echelons of Eichmann's superiors in Berlin. Information on British mandatory as well as foreign policy gathered by the German Ministry of Foreign Affairs was made available to and monitored by the branches of the Nazi organization. Summaries were passed down the various echelons and were certainly taken into account in policy determination and execution of the department in which Eichmann officiated. This is indicated by a remark Eichmann made to Löwenherz and Rothenberg on March 2, 1939. In connection with planning for their negotiations with aid organizations abroad, Eichmann said that he first wanted to await the outcome of the "Jewish-Arab conference."[91]

Eichmann was referring to what was euphemistically referred to as the London (or St. James) Round Table Conference, which took place between February 7 and March 17. Convened by the British government, it was anything but a Jewish-Arab conference. The delegates from some Arab states refused to sit with the Jewish delegation consisting of leading Zionists such as Chaim Weizmann and David Ben-Gurion. In effect, the British had to conduct two parallel, separate conferences. The British reason for convening the conference was that the Arabs' revolt against the Jewish settlement of Palestine was becoming intolerable, especially when war with Germany was becoming unavoidable, and Arab sympathies lay with a Germany that was anti-British and anti-Semitic. In effect, the British proposed what they would later issue as their "White Paper." The Arabs rejected the proposal because they wanted Jewish emigration to stop immediately, they wanted the British to end their mandate sooner, and they wanted to establish a purely Arab state. The disappointment of the Jews was abysmal, first, because emigration to Palestine was being throttled at the very time of European Jewry's most dire need; second, because the British opted in favor of the Arabs, who would not side with them in case of war, instead of the Jews, whose military support in a war against Germany was certain; and third, because the British proposal was tantamount to the abrogation of their mandate, which incorporated the promise of the 1917 Balfour Declaration, that is, a Jewish homeland in Palestine.

We can see that in addition to the other difficulties encountered by Vienna's Jewish leaders in their effort of finding ways of saving the Jews, they also found themselves caught in the wheels of world politics.

In matters of emigration, and especially in the frustrating search for feasible schemes, the men at the IKG had to monitor their master Eichmann, and they had to do so on the basis of a ready command of relevant knowledge and pitfalls. *Mutatis mutandi* Eichmann grudgingly deferred to the IKG in such matters. This can be exemplified by the "Bolivia project." On April 21, Eichmann informed Löwenherz that a counselor at the Bolivian embassy in Berlin had arrived in Vienna in order to propose to him a scheme of settling "a few thousand Jews" in Bolivia as farmers, and told him about some features of the scheme. Right away Löwenherz pointed to the questionable nature of the scheme: First, the amount of cash each immigrant had to show upon landing, stipulated at £50, conflicted with the officially required amount of £36; moreover, children did not have to show ownership of any money, much less the £30 required for this scheme. Second, according to the regulations known to the IKG, the only visas that were valid for immigration to Bolivia were those issued by the central government in La Paz and not the stipulated consular visas.[92]

Nevertheless, Eichmann ordered Löwenherz to discuss the matter with the counselor at the Grand Hotel, where he had taken temporary residence, not to agree to anything, and to report back to him three days hence. Löwenherz duly kept his appointment, which was not only with the counselor but also with his superior, the Bolivian consul. After explaining his concerns about the unusual financial requirements to the gentlemen, the consul explained to Löwenherz that more was at play than demonstrating the availability of funds to the immigrant, namely, a plan to divide a large estate into settlement parcels to be sold to the immigrants for pounds sterling. So that was it! We do not know what went on in Löwenherz's mind when he heard this, but we can imagine: The IKG would have to commit several months' worth of foreign exchange—most likely to persons who do not have the means to make the counter-deposit of Reichsmark that was so badly needed by the IKG—only for the would-be immigrants to be stuck with the commitment to pay for and take possession of a parcel of land that they have not seen, nor evaluated as to its condition or worth, and which, even if it should turn out to be arable and they would know how to till it, would be useless to them unless they also had the starting capital for machinery, seed, irrigation, and labor, not to speak of buildings, and to support themselves until the first successful harvest. Löwenherz's response is recorded—without comment by him or by Eichmann—in the *Aktennotiz* of his report to the latter: "The undersigned director emphasized to the two gentlemen that a project of this kind is not settled upon by granting the entry visas, and that the settlement of a large number of Jews requires extremely huge sums, and that this project cannot be considered without prior exploration with the large Jewish organizations abroad."[93] Concerned not to leave a stone unturned to find emigration opportunities, no matter how farfetched, Löwenherz did contact the organizations abroad, as we will see below.

This was not the end of the story. Hitting what must have seemed like the wall of a cumbersome bureaucracy in their direct negotiations with both Eichmann and Löwenherz in Vienna, the Bolivian gentlemen sought to win them for their project through those whom they must have thought to be their superiors in Berlin. Thus, on July 9 Löwenherz reported to Eichmann the receipt of a letter from Dr. Heinrich Stahl, President of the *Reichsvereinigung*, proposing the familiar Bolivia project. Löwenherz reminded Eichmann that the Bolivians had submitted some proposals that Löwenherz had forwarded to HICEM, since this organization would have to take up the financial burden of having the settlers make a start at their place of refuge. Eichmann must have been surprised that Dr. Stahl, in spite of past reprimands, again made unauthorized contact with Vienna, and advised Löwenherz to

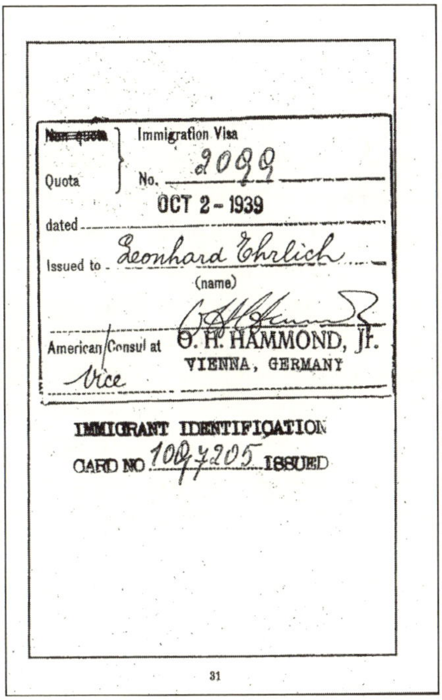

~~Non-quota~~ Immigration Visa
Quota No. 2099
OCT 2 - 1939
dated
Issued to Leonhard Ehrlich
(name)
American Vice Consul at O. H. HAMMOND, Jr.
VIENNA, GERMANY

IMMIGRANT IDENTIFICATION
CARD NO 1007205 ISSUED

31

Leonhard (later: Leonard H.) Ehrlich's coveted and life-saving visa to enter the United States. It was signed by U.S. Vice Consul Ogden H. Hammond, Jr., in Vienna, Germany [sic!]. (© CSE)

send a pro forma response, but he "does not wish for the IKG to remain in touch with Mr. Stahl."[94] To the best of our knowledge, this was the end of this particular Bolivia project in Vienna.[95] Whether the Bolivian landowner ever converted his useless holdings into pounds sterling, and his government's consular staff ever earned their kickback, we do not know.

Saving the Jews by supporting emigration, including the search and provision of feasible emigration schemes, was by no means the only concern of the IKG, as we have often indicated. In fact, these other concerns—the effectiveness of the IKG vis-à-vis the Nazi overlords, the provision of financial means, the survival of Jews still in Vienna—were ancillary to the success of the emigration effort. Let us take a closer look at them.

Present Worries, Worrisome Future

Eichmann kept the IKG under strict control as it exercised its mandated functions. The key was control over the performance of the leadership, mainly, Löwenherz, Murmelstein, and Engel.

The operative basis of control was the authoritarian leadership principle, which prevailed with deliberate stringency in the SS. For the individual SS-man, being at some level of authority and subordination defined his validity as a member of the elite that executed the will of the German nation as articulated by the Nazi Party's program and the supreme leadership; in turn, the supernal authority provided and validated the SS-man's freedom. On the other hand, control over the IKG leaders was total in the sense that they had no level of validity in the hierarchy of leadership-followership; whatever leeway of initiative they held was under the control of the SD. There were several means and manifestations of this control.

One of these concerned the way in which the IKG leaders received the substance of their executive function. By and large this occurred in the form of verbal *Weisungen* (i.e., directives) given either by Eichmann or his deputies or by authorities to whom they were directed by Eichmann for specific purposes, such as the *Devisenstelle* (German exchange office). Most *Weisungen* were given at meetings with Eichmann or his deputies for which Löwenherz and the other IKG leaders had to report either at the *Zentralstelle* or at Gestapo headquarters. The *Zentralstelle* was housed in the confiscated Rothschild Palace on Prinz-Eugen-Strasse off Schwarzenbergplatz, at the opposite end of the Inner City, about 15 to 20 minutes' walk from Seitenstättengasse, where the IKG was located. Gestapo headquarters were at the former Hotel Metropol at Morzinplatz, about 3 minutes' walk from the IKG. Upon occasion, *Weisungen* were spoken over the telephone, at times they were given when Eichmann or his deputies visited the IKG. We have not run across any written directives from Eichmann or the other Nazi authorities to the IKG, and we assume there were none.

Löwenherz or the others had to produce a written record of the verbal *Weisungen* in the form of *Aktennotizen* (i.e., memoranda for the files), which had to be sent both to Eichmann's office and to the Gestapo, with enough copies to be forwarded to headquarters in Berlin. Of course, copies were kept at the IKG, as the official record of their orders, and as such they preserve for history the documentation of the IKG's forced performance. The copy for Eichmann was delivered to him the same day and was provided with a cover sheet showing the date, the number of the yearly series of *Aktennotizen*, the month, a note saying "Enclosed is the *Aktennotiz* of the undersigned's *Vorsprache* of whatever date, duly submitted." In addition, over his title was Löwenherz's signature as *Amtsdirektor* (which was his title prior to March 1938) followed by *Leiter* (which is the title under which he was appointed by the Nazis). In his signature he never failed to style himself "Dr. Löwenherz"—at a time when the regime decreed the abrogation of professional degrees held by Jews.[96]

Weisungen *and* Aktennotizen

A few words have to be said about the principle underlying the procedure of *Weisungen* and *Aktennotizen*. According to the hierarchical military structure adopted by the executive organs of the Nazi organization[97] and modified by the discipline of the leadership principle, supernal orders must be obeyed, even if issued verbally, and especially in situations permitting no delay in their execution. Yet, even in situations that called for expedition, those who passed down orders knew that action groups needed to cover themselves by means of written orders. This is not surprising, considering the highly unusual actions the organs of this particular empowered party organization were called upon to carry out. As an example we saw how some units committed to the Kristallnacht action demanded written confirmation of orders frantically barked by telephone, only to receive conflicting and confusing orders. The situation of the IKG was such that they were in no position to request, much less require, a written and signed confirmation of a verbal *Weisung*. Can anyone imagine Löwenherz saying to Eichmann, "Herr *Obersturmbannführer*, I await your written instruction"? No, the truly diabolical nature of the procedure consisted in the recipient of the order being the one who wrote and signed it, while being bound to formulate it in the way in which the order was meant by the one who issued it, no matter how well or badly, no matter how clearly or vaguely it was uttered.

There were two noteworthy sidelights to this procedure. The first concerns the wording in which the *Weisungen* were recorded. When Löwenherz received *Weisungen* at a *Vorsprache* or by telephone, he took careful and detailed notes. This was not easy, because at *Vorsprachen* he, as well as the other Jewish functionaries, had to stand, while Eichmann sat. Returning to the IKG office, Löwenherz usually would discuss with his close associates what had transpired,[98] and, no doubt, the wording of the *Weisungen* resulted from these discussions, no less than the responses and courses of action. And yet, from a study of the style we can often tell who drafted a specific *Aktennotiz*, and whether the wording was that of Löwenherz, Murmelstein, or someone else. From the typeface we can usually also tell in whose office a memorandum was typed, but type and style do not usually coincide. Löwenherz's was a lawyer's style, dry, to the point, inclusive of the facts, considerations, reminders, and objections that he had voiced during the *Vorsprachen*. Engel, while sticking to bureaucratic definition, occasionally hints at the outrage he must have felt at having to function in the dismantling of the existence of those to whose service he had devoted his whole life. Murmelstein's style was conceptually economical, clear, and careful in recording only the minimum of what was directed, yet leaving open loopholes where he discerned them. This may suggest that the writers had some leeway in the formulation of the directives they received. In fact, Murmelstein reported to us that the Nazi authorities depended on his *Stylisieren* (i.e., his editorial skills), especially in the case of *Weisungen* that needed to be published in the Jewish newspaper. At least one time, so he told, there was some trouble between the Jewish leadership in Berlin and Vienna because of Murmelstein's more lenient formulation of a *Weisung* for the Vienna publication.

Second, we have to be very careful in evaluating this leeway in formulating the written record of the *Weisungen* that were given verbally by the Nazis. The reason is that the Nazis carefully and tirelessly censored everything the IKG leaders wrote in their *Aktennotizen*,[99] everything that went into the *Jüdische Nachrichten*, and every letter and report that was sent to foreign addresses, especially the aid organizations.[100] If the Jewish leaders exercised their leeway for the purpose of ameliorating a decree, then they had to do it in a way that would pass censorship and would have the minimum of repercussions in case the Nazis realized their lapse or the Jews' ruse. Murmelstein reports a case in point from the time when the emigration procedure was rationalized by establishing the *Zentralstelle*, and we stress that we have not been able to verify this. The IKG had to submit a design for a form which contained all the fees, taxes, and levies due that had to be recorded and processed on the way to receiving official permission to leave the Reich. After receiving Eichmann's approval but before the IKG sent the draft to the printer, Murmelstein claimed to have added an entry after the "total" of moneys due, headed "reduced to:."

In connection with the *Weisungen*, it must be emphasized that the IKG from the beginning took pains to inform the Jewish public, in particular in the Jewish newspaper mandated by the Nazis, that whatever was required of the Jews was a matter of *Weisungen* from the authorities and did not originate in the IKG.

The authorities required the IKG to produce a steady stream of reports in addition to the *Aktennotizen*. Many were ad hoc reports on problems and proposed solutions, minutes of consultations with authorities and aid societies, petitions, requests, reminders, position statements, and so on. A certain kind of required report was modeled on what was produced within the various organs of the Nazi Party machinery, especially the SD and the Gestapo, which was in turn modeled on traditional German police surveillance procedure. These were the *Tätigkeits- und Lageberichte* (activity and situation reports), which the IKG had to prepare and submit weekly, monthly, quarterly, and yearly.[101] The *Tätigkeitsbericht* (activity report) was, in effect, a report on the efficacy of the IKG's activity. It listed the number of Jews in need of meals, how many meals were served, how many presented themselves for emigration, how many were processed by the *Zentralstelle*, how many received emigration aid from the IKG, how many emigrated to which country, the IKG's outlays and receipts, the experience with *Devisen*, the enrollments in the various *Umschulungskurse* (retraining courses), the activities—especially as regards the traffic of clients—of the various departments and institutions of the IKG, including the Palamt (even though it operated semi-independently), and so on. In the parallel *Lagebericht* (situation report), the IKG dwelt on the main problems it had to deal with. Although the periodic reports were signed and submitted by Löwenherz, the writing was soon assigned to Murmelstein, who devised a standard form and style, which was repeated week after week. Reading these reports, it becomes clear how busy the various departments were, how much the IKG was under pressure to keep up the brisk pace of liquidation, and how much was added to their workload by having to maintain an up-to-date accounting of their productivity. The production reports compiled for the *Tätigkeits- und Lageberichte* were also used for the periodic reports that were submitted to the Joint and CBF mainly to account for the use of the moneys produced by their contribution of *Devisen*.

The IKG had to count on being visited by the Nazi authorities at any time, and any of its departmental files could be requisitioned or searched. Eichmann evidently considered the mountain of paperwork produced and accumulating in the files of the IKG to be an extension of his operation.

The travel of the persons going abroad on behalf of the IKG and the Palamt was of course strictly controlled. The main functionaries, Löwenherz, Murmelstein, and Engel, had to relinquish their passports while in Vienna and reapply for them whenever they needed them. Innumerable items in the *Aktennotizen* show how their travel had to be pre-authorized by Eichmann, for specified dates, destinations, and time frames, with the Gestapo frequently trying to control the movement of the functionaries for reasons of jurisdictional jealousy. Families stayed behind. The return of each of the three had to be personally guaranteed by the other two.[102] Gruen had to substitute for Rothenberg and Engel for Löwenherz during their respective absences.[103] We have a copy of the list of things that Löwenherz planned to carry with him on his travel to London in March 1939, which had to be approved by the Vienna *Devisenstelle*: a suit, five shirts, a half dozen starched collars, cuff links, sets of underwear, toiletries, medicines, papers, a brief case, a dictionary, and so on. At the bottom is Raffegerst's approval of the list, with only the gold watch and chain crossed out; how Löwenherz managed to keep appointments and meet trains we do not know.[104]

This tight control over the IKG functionaries also meant that these men had to exercise extraordinary caution in their dealings with their contacts while abroad. Whatever information about the problematic situation of the Jews in Vienna they were able to impart to their contacts when they met them abroad had to be given in a way that would impress on their listeners the need for special discretion in making use of it lest their continuing usefulness—on their part as well on the part of men in like positions—as representatives of Jewish interest vis-à-vis the Nazis go by the board. A leak of confidential information given, for example, by Löwenherz to his contacts at the Joint in Paris or at the London aid societies would have been disastrous.

The functionaries of the Jewish aid organizations who had direct contact with Löwenherz and Murmelstein—men at the Joint such as Mr. Tropper of the Paris office, Mr. Schwartz of the Lisbon office, and Mr. Bentwich at the CGJ—had due appreciation of the precarious situation under which they had to serve Jewish interests. Lower-echelon functionaries at the aid organizations, who were indirectly involved in aiding the IKG and similar organizations elsewhere, tended to have less insight into the nature of the position of persons like Löwenherz and Murmelstein and tended to regard them as willing tools of the Nazis. In short, without the insight and information received in direct, trustful contact, the tendency—which we first encountered in the case of the Zurich observer at the very beginning of the new form of Jewish leadership—was that anyone in this kind of position was automatically suspect.

The strict monitoring of the contacts with the aid organizations abroad extended to control over their visiting the IKG in Vienna. Each prospective visit had to be cleared with Eichmann. For example, shortly after Kristallnacht, Löwenherz requested approval for the visit of a certain Dennis M. Cohen from London. Eichmann not only approved but, in Löwenherz's wording in the official *Aktennotiz*, "even wished that a whole slew of commissions come from abroad to inspect our work." Clearly Eichmann was not merely interested in *Devisen* but took pride in and, for his own advancement, needed approbation for the "benign" machinery of expropriation and expulsion, which he had running in Vienna and which he was even then in the process of installing in Berlin. On the other hand, when a Frau Cahn of the "Aid Committee" in Geneva wanted to inspect the Viennese emigration organization, Eichmann ordered the IKG to consult with the "Society of Friends . . . whether such a visit is desirable," and to report to him.[105] There was less hesitancy on the part of Eichmann when a visit was in the offing by a person who represented proven aid efforts and thus someone whose cooperation and acquiescence in the execution of the Nazis' Jewish policy he had to secure and maintain. None other than Professor Norman Bentwich, Director of the British Council for German Jewry, was expected in August 1939; we will have something to say about Bentwich's visit below. Immediately before Bentwich's arrival Löwenherz had to submit a justification for the visit to the Gestapo.[106] And we recall that in the case of Engel's trip to Milan, Gestapo headquarters called

Löwenherz and questioned his qualifications for going abroad to negotiate about emigration matters. In effect such interference, on the part of the Gestapo, with the operations of the IKG to the point of harassment bespoke the perennial jurisdictional dispute with the SD, which caught the IKG in the middle and was to hound Löwenherz and Murmelstein throughout their dismal careers of forced leadership.

A relatively minor case in point in the period following Kristallnacht concerned the SS-men assigned to guard the IKG building and to protect the operations taking place within from marauding members of the "seething soul of the people." Being a police force, they were members of the Gestapo. After a few weeks, they presented Löwenherz with an outrageous bill for their recent food outlays during duty hours (i.e., luncheons with wine at restaurants, and coffee, pastry, and Schnapps at nearby coffeehouses). After ordering from Löwenherz a corrected accounting,[107] Eichmann, knowing full well that Jewish money was paying more than adequately for this "protection," assured Löwenherz the IKG would not have to pay this in the future, and apparently fixed things with his colleagues at Gestapo headquarters. However, the guards were either put out by the rude stoppage of their freeloading or else must have been bored and frustrated by their inactivity in the face of hundreds of powerless people in the building begging to be harassed. On March 2 Löwenherz records in his memorandum of that day's *Vorsprache* that "Eichmann again declared that the members of the . . . guard had no right to walk through the different offices and interfere with the functionaries' conduct of business, and he again held out the prospect of relevant *Weisungen* to the guard." The repeated use of "again" means that the subject had been broached a number of times, but the time was ripe for Löwenherz to commit the matter to the official record. Yet things must have gotten worse because in the record of the *Vorsprache* of only four days later we read, "Eichmann again stressed that the guard is not to enter the offices and is not to interfere in the business of the functionaries, and promised to issue relevant *Weisungen* once again."[108]

These occurrences underscore not only Löwenherz's and Eichmann's shared concern that nothing must interfere with the smooth functioning of the emigration process but also the limitations built into the Nazi machinery and the resulting limits of Eichmann's authority. These limits, of course, did not accrue to the IKG's benefit; rather they indicate how the IKG was caught between the mutually limiting authorities. We will illustrate this point by tracing how Löwenherz was made to shuttle between Eichmann, the Commissioner of Receiverships, Vienna's municipal administration, and others in the matter of restoring expropriated Jewish assets in order to provide for the sick, the aged, and the poor.

The IKG and the Zentralstelle

The official authority to which the IKG had to regard itself as subordinate was the *Zentralstelle* under Eichmann, which was an agency within the *Sicherheitsdienst* (SD), regardless of the indicated tug-of-war between the SD and the Gestapo. In some memoranda to various authorities, Löwenherz occasionally referred to Eichmann and the *Zentralstelle* as the *Aufsichtsbehörde* (supervisory authority). In his dealings with the Commissioner for Receiverships Brunner in the summer of 1939, Löwenherz was told by Brunner that before undertaking a certain action authorized by him Löwenherz had to submit a report to the *Zentralstelle*, to which Löwenherz replied "that without consent of the *Zentralstelle*, we, as a matter of course, do not undertake anything."[109]

The IKG was under a special kind of surveillance in the form of intense pressure to force the emigration process; hence, it was in the interest of the IKG as well as of the remaining Jews to keep the pace of emigration as brisk as possible. Eichmann constantly pressed for an increase of applications for emigration, for an increase in the number of emigrants to report for final processing at the *Zentralstelle*, and for a better performance by the IKG. And Löwenherz had to tell Eichmann that the pace was at the highest possible level and that disturbing the process could only be counterproductive.[110]

Thus, every Jew was held hostage to the Nazis' policy of getting rid of the Jews. This meant that every Jew was under pressure to find ways of getting rid of himself by emigrating. In various ways, the IKG and especially Löwenherz were the targets of even more intense pressure: first, by their function as executors of that policy; second, by their anguish over the duress suffered by the Jews for whose sake they served; and third, and this must not be overlooked, by virtue of their very function as executors because of which they tended to be falsely perceived by so many of their fellow Viennese Jews as willing tools of Nazi policy. The men of the IKG were well aware of this perception but, for the sake of those they served, they would not counteract it, even if they could.

One example: At the end of May 1939, nine months after the ill-fated Colombia transport, three would-be participants wrote to "*Comité voor bijzondere joodsche belangen*" ("Committee for special Jewish concerns") in the Hague, detailing the chain of events whereby they were left stranded and destitute when the transport was aborted, and complaining about the IKG's failure to make good on what they took to be their promise to arrange for alternative emigration at the first opportunity. The Comité forwarded the letter to the IKG with the request that they—inasmuch as it was written in "great desperation"—not "judge" these people but help them. In his reply to the Hague, Engel assures the Comité that the IKG does whatever it can to alleviate the misery of these people; however, it is not in any position to provide emigration possibilities.[111] We know the reason: For the most part, emigration had to be arranged by the individuals themselves. Although the IKG was involved in emigration schemes, participation was subject to defined eligibilities, which did not necessarily include the participant's ability to provide the requisite travel funds. And yet, the complainants state that, even though there have been transports to Shanghai and Palestine, they have not been included because they have "been stripped of all funds and are unable to contribute to travel costs."

Engel continues: "We must state that the [Colombia] transport was not initiated by us, and that against our express warning we were constrained to undertake the preparatory steps." There is no explicit mention—nor could there be—of who "initiated" the transport, nor who was "warned," nor the provenance of the "constraint"; but it was tacitly hoped that the Comité would understand. It was not possible to make those understand whose false impression Engel's statement was refuting. The complainants claimed that "On August 17, 1938, the IKG assembled, in great haste, a transport to Colombia, consisting mainly of craftsmen." They also related what the IKG did on behalf of the transport: "The participants were given a medical examination, vaccinated, photographed, their emigration papers were obtained, and regrettably they were made to quit businesses and apartments as of September 1, and to sell all movables, merchandise and household goods." In effect, the IKG was giving service to their people beyond the formalities of obtaining clearance with the authorities and within the constraints of having to carry out a scheme that they neither approved nor initiated. Yet, far from crediting the IKG with acting in this way under pressure from above on behalf of the prospective emigrants, the complainants took this as evidence that it was the IKG's hasty, incompetent, and injurious scheme that was at play; moreover, that having failed, it took little or no responsibility for this failure.

The other matter concerns the IKG's realization of the problematic nature of the persona that they presented to their sorely tried people, and that it was the inevitable and ineluctable condition of serving them. In response to the Dutch committee's plea not to judge but to help them, Engel says: "The abuse which these persons direct against the IKG and its functionaries is completely unfounded, yet we are neither offended nor resentful of them; we understand the desperation of these people and also understand that their rancor turns against the IKG as the only place against which they are able to complain."

We see that in addition to the censure—in the form of pressure by the Nazi officials and the monitoring by the external aid organizations—that the chief functionaries of the IKG had to bear silently, they were under the uninformed scrutiny of their Jewish charges and other Jewish observers abroad.

Of all the pressures applied to the IKG by the Nazis at this time, perhaps the most harrowing was the threat of randomly taking men into "protective custody" and placing them in concentration camps. There is no question that this was one of the main means used by the Nazis of "inspiring" the leading functionaries at the IKG to find emigration schemes, to find ways of financing the liquidation of the Jewish community, and to keep the gears of the emigration machinery running at full speed and at maximum efficiency. There is no question that these men were constantly reminded of the ready and inexhaustible supply of the fuel for persecution. We are astonished to find Löwenherz actually recording Eichmann's threat to this effect. In the record of the *Vorsprache* of March 16 we read:

> SS *Hauptsturmführer* Eichmann informed me that the number of applications [for processing at the *Zentralstelle* of the many formalities prior to emigration] has dropped and that, if it should happen that applications do not rise within the next two days, he will recommend measures which might have consequences like those in November.[112]

The threat was well understood by Löwenherz, for at the same *Vorsprache* he received Eichmann's approval of his leaving for Paris on Sunday March 19, namely, three days hence, for the sake of "obtaining *Devisen* and in regard to the IKG's budgetary concerns."[113] However, Löwenherz—mindful of what had happened while he was abroad "in November" (i.e., Kristallnacht), and knowing as well as Eichmann knew that the number of applications could not be jacked up in the two remaining days of that week—together with Rothenberg

> asked—considering past performance, and that immigration possibilities cannot be obtained mechanically—that [Eichmann] desist from any such measures. We pointed to the fact that,

> now as before, the will to emigrate is prevalent to the highest degree, but entry permits cannot be obtained so easily, and we are intent on obtaining new immigration possibilities.[114]

Another case in point is the incarceration at Buchenwald of two people treated by the Nazis as special cases: Desider Friedmann and Robert Stricker. In the past, Löwenherz had asked for their release, pleading their age (both were about 60), their frail health, and their chance of emigrating to Palestine as soon as they were released.[115] By now, the two could hardly count as enemies, but precisely because they were important enough to rate a special plea for release, elevated their value as hostages. On February 10, Eichmann informed Löwenherz that the two would "now" be released, though they were not permitted to emigrate. While Friedmann could be employed at the IKG in various and changing positions in the emigration effort, though not in any leading position, Stricker could not be employed in any capacity whatsoever. As a condition for their release, both Löwenherz and Rothenberg had to submit a signed statement declaring themselves responsible for seeing that Friedmann and Stricker would not leave Germany without the consent of the authorities.[116] Two weeks later, Löwenherz requested that Eichmann order Friedmann's release.[117] A similar reminder was given two months after Löwenherz was apprised that Friedmann's release had been approved.[118] We do not know exactly when the two were released. But, upon their release, Löwenherz was evidently in Eichmann's debt. And the usefulness of the two as hostages could just as well be maintained released as unreleased.

As it happens, Eichmann permitted the matter to progress to the point of letting Löwenherz suggest that he allow the two to emigrate. Eichmann gave his approval, albeit under one condition: They had to declare that once abroad they would not engage in any "publicistic activity directed against the Reich," and Löwenherz had to submit a signed declaration of liability to that effect. These statements had to be submitted in three days.[119] The declarations were duly delivered to Eichmann on June 26, with a request by Friedmann that his permission to remain in Vienna be extended to August 15; this request suggests that the two were released from the concentration camp with the usual condition that they leave Germany within a short time, usually four weeks. Eichmann approved of the declarations and requested that Friedmann report to him in person about the extension.[120] In light of the evident result of the interview, our imagination suggests a number of scenarios for its course, but we have no way of knowing how it actually went. A week later Eichmann informed Löwenherz that the passports of the two were ready and had to be picked up in person at the *Zentralstelle*; Löwenherz asked that Friedmann, being indigent, be charged a reduced passport fee.[121] Did the two receive their passports? It seems likely that they did not. In the record of the *Vorsprache* of August 12, there is this cryptic note: "There is no objection to the release of the passports of the wife and daughter of Dr. Desider Friedmann. The two women can pick up their passports and leave."[122] Needless to say, Frau Friedmann stayed with her husband in Vienna, in Theresienstadt, and in Auschwitz. The daughter found her way to Palestine, where she settled on a kibbutz, married, and raised a family.

What had happened? Again, we do not know. Friedmann and Stricker were hardly a threat to Nazi Germany, in or out of the Reich. However, if Löwenherz went so far as to

Dr. Desider Friedmann, president of the IKG, sitting behind his desk in 1934. It is unknown why there is white paint on this photograph. (ÖNB / Gersdorff Collection, Pf 40.063: D [1])

put his head into the noose for them, they were evidently too valuable to let them go. Was this Eichmann's idea? Or was he carrying out orders from above?

Not only the quick, but also the dead had to serve as hostages in one or the other chess game between the Nazi overlords and the leading Jewish functionaries. For some time, Rothenberg of the Palamt, with the concurrence of Löwenherz, had been requesting permission to transfer to Palestine the remains of Theodor Herzl, the founder of modern political Zionism, who had lived and died in Vienna and was buried there. To sweeten the pot, and in anticipation of the next round of negotiations in Paris and London, Rothenberg "hinted" at the *Vorsprache* of March 2 that the transfer might produce a special disbursement of *Devisen*.[123] But all that Eichmann agreed to was for Löwenherz and Rothenberg to hold out the possibility of such a transfer at their next sojourn abroad. Eichmann knew how "bringing home" the remains of the hero of Zionism to Palestine would lift the spirits of the hard-pressed Jews and, more important, what a slap in the face it would be to the Arabs whom the German Foreign Office was at that time intent on wooing into their anti-British and anti-Semitic camp. Hence, the reason he gave for not agreeing to the transfer right away was that he "first wanted to await the conclusion of the Jewish-Arab conference." Eichmann was referring to the St. James Conference that was in session at that time (discussed earlier in this chapter). From information routinely received through the channels of the SS, he must have known how the conference was going. And, no doubt with encouragement from above, he took up the matter of Herzl's remains a week later as follows:

> SS *Hauptsturmführer* Eichmann declared that he is prepared to release Herzl's remains, albeit providing that on this occasion the relevant Jewish organizations provide new emigration possi-

> bilities for 8,000 persons from Austria, and in this regard he charges the undersigned [Löwenherz and Rothenberg] to conduct the requisite negotiations during their sojourn abroad.[124]

Eight thousand new places for Jewish emigrants? Perhaps even to Palestine, or—to keep them from going to Palestine—to Britain? Perhaps the Grand Mufti of Jerusalem should be required to receive them with open arms? What an infernal joke!

The search for feasible emigration schemes was not the only preoccupation of the IKG leadership during the months before the war. It was a period when they were also beset by a bewildering array of worries, each of them demanding level-headed attention, all in some way interconnected.

Increasing Pressures

Some of the most pressing worries arose from the fact that the number of persons who, in one way or another, became dependent on the IKG, increased from month to month and from week to week. This dependence resulted, in the main, from the progressive impoverishment of the Jewish population, exacerbated by the final removal of Jews from all productive activity following Kristallnacht; from the fact that more and more ill and infirm as well as old people had to be left behind, as those who had cared for them took hold of their chances of emigrating; and from the continuing expropriation and expulsion of Jews from their homes. Thus, the Jewish population and its number of dependents changed in inverse proportion: The greater the success of forced emigration and the more the Jewish population decreased, the greater the number of persons in all categories of dependency.

A case in point is the provision of free meals by the increasing number of soup kitchens that the IKG maintained. In May 1938, when the new IKG began its operation, 10,000 people were eligible for a daily hot meal. By October, the month before Kristallnacht, the number had risen to over 14,000, in December to over 18,000.[125] Since the IKG had to report statistics to Eichmann and to the Joint not only about the number of meal recipients but also about the number of meals served, we can tell that except for two months, the number of meals actually obtained by each person was never fewer than twenty-six meals per month.[126] The two exceptions were June and November 1938: June because the wave of arrests tended to keep the Jews off the streets, November because for a number of days some of the soup kitchens had to suspend operation due to the plundering and spoiling of foodstuffs and the demolition of equipment, which were part of the Kristallnacht "festivities."[127] By the end of January 1939 the IKG reported to the Joint as well as to Eichmann that the number of daily meal recipients was approaching 21,000, and that they expected 30,000 before long.[128] In fact, in March 1939 the number of recipients had risen to 32,000, and the total number of meals served to 847,334 (December 1938: 533,176), and the number of soup kitchens to 16 (January: 14).[129] In his report of the inspection tour he undertook on behalf of the Joint, which took him to Vienna early in February 1939, Samuel Gurwitz wrote:

> [The kitchens] serve one meal daily, the people come with their pots and pans—pick up their slip informing the food distributors of the number of people in the family and the portions they

> are to get. Soup, potatoes, bread and vegetable salad is the meal that is provided. The kitchens are well managed, food deliciously prepared and everything moves very smoothly.[130]

The fare was vegetarian because the Nazis had outlawed the ritual slaughter of animals on the grounds that it was inhumane, and the importation of kosher meat was prohibitively expensive and subject to a persecutory application of import regulations. Merely the provision of *matzot* (unleavened bread) and related foods required for the period of Passover in March 1939 made a sufficiently noticeable dent in the IKG budget to be specially noted in their periodic report to Eichmann.[131] Aside from the soup kitchens, the IKG also had to provide meals at the hospital and nursing homes maintained by it.

Another example is financial relief. In the IKG's report for March 1939, we read the following:

> The elimination of the Jews from economic life [*Erwerbsleben*] has seen a noticeable increase in the number of applicants for support. Even segments of the middle class, whose modest savings have been used up through months without earnings, now have to turn to the IKG Relief Department for aid. The cancellation [by the public authorities] of support for [Jewish] persons, whose small pensions were devalued by the postwar [i.e., First World War] inflation, causes new segments to be dependent on the aid of the IKG.
>
> This month RM 274,852.14 were spent on cash payments, i.e., for help to pay for rent and other unavoidable expenses on the part of a great number of Jewish families living in Vienna, for the care of those families whose breadwinner has emigrated or for some other reason is not able to care for his dependents, for the support of religious functionaries, for the care and education of minors living with parents, in foster homes and institutions.[132]

Cash payments in March—with about 100,000 Jews remaining in Vienna—amounting to almost RM 275,000[133] must be compared with the total expenditure of RM 1,638,500 for all of 1938,[134] when the number of Jews in Austria was about 180,000 in March and about 117,000 by the end of the year.[135] Even if the two pre-Anschluss months are left out in calculating the monthly average for 1938, by March 1939, with a greatly reduced population, the amount budgeted for cash relief is two-thirds above the monthly average for 1938.

A significant number of the recipients of cash payments were the Jews from the communities in the provinces, whose Jewish population was concentrated in Vienna by 1939. This was the result of having the policy of making Austria "*judenrein*" begin with the smaller and more isolated communities outside of Vienna. The expulsion of some of the provincial Jewish communities began within days of the Anschluss and was carried out in a most brutal fashion in Burgenland, the easternmost province of Austria. Not only the Burgenland Jews but also those from other communities, who were expelled in a more orderly and official fashion, arrived in Vienna destitute, having had to leave their homes and possessions precipitously. It is for this reason that the proportion of Jews who needed cash support was greater for the Jews who had come from the provinces than those who had lived in Vienna all along. In June 1938 there were 2,053, mostly from Burgenland, who needed support; in December, the number had swelled to about 6,000.[136] In total there had been between 10,000 and 12,000 Jews living in provincial communities prior to the Anschluss; a goodly number of them had emigrated by the end of the year. Among those who were left, most were now destitute.

The IKG had to provide for the survival of the provincial Jews in many ways in addition to cash payments to individuals. Inasmuch as they were uprooted, they had to be provided with housing and with a modicum of furnishings. The financial support for their emigration had to be provided from the general emigration funds, in their case for the most part without their being able to contribute Reichsmark in exchange for the IKG's provision of *Devisen*. As we will see, the IKG was in time involved in trying to retrieve the assets of provincial individuals as well as of provincial communities.

The worries that preoccupied the IKG leadership were exacerbated by the debilities imposed on the Jews after Kristallnacht. Those concerns were distinct yet interconnected: How to take care of the sick, old, and disabled; how to secure the funds necessary for survival and emigration; and how to retrieve the Community's assets appropriated by different authorities.

Within a month of Göring's presiding over the meeting that decreed the final elimination of Jews from economic life, a number of directives spelled out the details. For the Jews in Vienna these were particularly harsh, vastly more so than in the Altreich. Whatever businesses were still in Jewish hands had to be sold, enterprises had to be liquidated, and proceeds, if any, had to be deposited in escrow accounts for meeting possible tax balances, liquidation costs, fees, asset levies and other exploitive assessments, and so on; they were available to the owners in a limited way only. For all practical purposes, the moneys were appropriated by the authorities, and the owners left destitute.

Added to this, the restrictions on living quarters were increased; more and more Jews were left homeless and had to be taken in by Jews who still retained their apartments. This was, in fact, the first hint of what, in retrospect, we can recognize as the concentration of Jews and, beyond that, their ghettoization.

Because of the emigration of the more vigorous, potentially productive, and self-reliant Jews, the ever increasing strictures affected the old, the sick, and the disabled segment of the Jewish population with particular urgency. Addressing their needs impelled the ensuing tug of war between Löwenherz, Eichmann, and other authorities over the release of funds from available accounts and over the retrieval of assets.

A major factor increasing the urgency of the problems facing the IKG at this time was the worry about what would have to be done for the Jews who would be left over after the great wave of forced emigration, whose completion Eichmann had ordered for the spring of 1940. In connection with the project of bringing emigration to completion by then, Eichmann projected the dissolution of the IKG. Without Jews, the IKG would have outlived its usefulness, and its remaining assets would be up for grabs. Löwenherz estimated that there would be at least 20,000 Jews too old or too sick or too infirm to emigrate.[137] Since the aid societies contributed *Devisen* only for emigration, there would be no further flow of *Devisen* with which to produce Reichsmark once emigration came to an end and, in turn, no money with which to finance, in part at least, the services required by those who would remain. Hence, the struggle for the wherewithal to take care of those who had to be left behind was coupled with that over the continued existence of an established representation of Jewish interests and concerns.

The old and the infirm were evidently a vexatious actuality for Eichmann. Like the children, most of them did not have any assets to speak of that could be milked upon emigration. Unlike the children, they could not be expedited across the borders of the Reich and would thus be consuming resources that would accrue neither to the insatiable agencies nor to the reserve of funds, which Eichmann was zealously building and hoarding. It was a problem that he could not ignore, and that Löwenherz did not let him ignore. It was a problem that provided Eichmann with additional pressure to apply to Löwenherz to find funds. It was a problem that Löwenherz had to consider as a source of additional leverage with Eichmann in his battle to help preserve and restore to the IKG officially purloined Jewish assets.

The problem of the Jews who, because of age or infirmity or for other reasons, could not emigrate or be expelled would have repercussions in the later stages of the unfolding Nazi policy and would affect the function and performance of men such as Löwenherz and Murmelstein.

For the time being, Löwenherz had to find ways of making Eichmann understand that his two intertwined projects would run up against unavoidable obstacles: The project of completing the emigration of all the Jews by an early date would be stalled because of the remaining old, sick, and infirm. And consequently, the plan of dissolving the IKG once emigration was completed would be frustrated by the need for a continuously functioning IKG to provide care for those who would be left behind. Furthermore, Löwenherz had to show that even if the moneys produced by providing *Devisen* were available for welfare, their use for this purpose would impinge on the emigration effort. In short, in this struggle Löwenherz's only possible strategy was to represent his own agenda as executing Eichmann's policy.

Under the increased stringency following Kristallnacht, the problem of the old, sick, and infirm insinuated itself in specific ways. There was a steadily increasing need for places in homes for the aged, for hospital beds for the sick in a situation in which hospitals and similar institutions excluded Jews, and for the means to help the increasing number of indigent stay alive. There was also the worry over the means to finance such care when, in the foreseeable future, emigration would have been reduced to a trickle and consequently the flow of *Devisen* would dry up. The upsurge in the expropriations of Jewish assets following Kristallnacht required Löwenherz to negotiate with various authorities and to persist in addressing the problem of the old, sick, and infirm.

Long-standing social legislation in the Altreich and in former Austria provided for the care of such persons through local and regional governmental agencies. Jews, no less than others, had paid taxes to be eligible for such services, and although now disenfranchised, they were entitled to them by law. Because of the elimination of Jews from the Reich's economic life and their consequent impoverishment and dependence, an increase in their demand for such social services was to be expected. It became necessary, therefore, to reduce, and if possible to eliminate, Jewish claims to public service funds. Hence, it was ordered that Jewish charitable organizations continue to exist and, taking the place of public services, provide for the welfare of Jews and thus reduce their claim to their public entitlements.

In Vienna, it will be recalled, the IKG was, in effect, the only relevant Jewish organization permitted to exist. Officers of all of Vienna's many Jewish service organizations, including some great foundations that had some assets left to speak of, were forced to transfer title to the IKG. This was not done to enrich the IKG but in order to have a material entity that could, on the one hand, be made to relinquish title to assets in a legal and orderly way and, on the other hand, be held responsible for any pending or future, legal claims against the no longer extant organizations. By the time of Kristallnacht, most of those assets, especially real estate, had been taken in receivership by Herr Brunner, the Commissioner for Receiverships, subordinate of Bürckel, the Führer's plenipotentiary for the incorporation of Austria into the Reich.

Clearly the matter of the old and infirm would now involve Löwenherz in trying to retrieve those assets and, therefore, in the maddening merry-go-round among, among others, the commissioner, Vienna's mayor's office, the Gestapo, and Eichmann as the regime's official authority over him. When, five weeks after Kristallnacht, in the wake of the newly increased stringency of the impediments, Löwenherz urged Eichmann to consider the matter, he was ordered to produce statistics: How many Jews were residents in institutions for the aged and the infirm? How many Jews were applicants for admission?[138] Next, early in January, Löwenherz raised the question of making available to the IKG the moneys that had been collected from the Jewish organizations when they were placed in receivership. There were two kinds of funds: First, the organizations' cash balances on deposit or in kind at the time of their dissolution. In regard to this money, Eichmann assured Löwenherz of his support in any inquiry to the Commission for Receiverships. Second, there was the assessed Reconstruction Charge,[139] most of which the IKG had to be liable for as the legal successor of these organizations. In regard to the latter, Eichmann hedged, claiming that he wanted to keep that money in reserve for the old and infirm "at the time when most of the emigrants will have left the Reich."[140]

Eichmann thus admitted that the money was available to him and that, if he wished, he could place it at the disposal of the IKG. On the other hand, he fended Löwenherz off by claiming to be keeping the money in reserve in order to take care of precisely that major need which Löwenherz was increasingly concerned about. Clearly, Eichmann was learning to play the game that Löwenherz had devised to play with him: the game of acting on the other's motivation. Only there was a difference: By virtue of their position relative to each other, Löwenherz's motive had to be revealed, while Eichmann could keep his concealed, as he did in this and every other case.

But the battle for the retrieval of assets was only now joined and would continue on many fronts. At first, the expropriations got abysmally worse. On February 23, Eichmann, in connection with Löwenherz's report of how many Jews had emigrated so far, estimated that between 20,000 and 25,000 would remain in Vienna at the completion of emigration one year hence, a figure evidently based on Löwenherz's estimate. Löwenherz then reported that additional homes for the elderly and the infirm had to be established and would have to be maintained, at a cost which the IKG was not able to meet. Furthermore, and this was the shattering news, the Commissioner for Receiverships assessed the IKG over RM 740,000 in fees for the foundations taken into receivership.[141]

What had happened? Apparently in reaction to Löwenherz's attempting to retrieve the assets of dissolved organizations taken in receivership, Commissioner Brunner decided to consolidate his hold on these assets and to solidify his position in dealing with the IKG. He did this by establishing, on February 6, 1939, an umbrella for these assets, with the Orwellian name "General Foundation for Jewish Welfare in Vienna" (*Allgemeine Stiftung für jüdische Fürsorge in Wien*), which seemed to imply that these assets would be placed at the disposal of the IKG. Thus, he was able to claim that the IKG had been given values for which he was required to assess it a combined reconstruction levy (*Aufbauumlage*) and administrative fee of RM 743,020.89 against their putative value. Until the IKG would pay up, Commissioner Brunner felt free not to release to the IKG any of the buildings or other assets and, in fact, to dispose of them as he saw fit.[142]

Evidently the IKG had no way of raising such moneys. Eichmann then ordered Löwenherz to submit another report, listing the foundations in question and showing their appraised value for the purpose of assessing the reconstruction levy as well as the other levies imposed by the commissioner.

At the same time, Löwenherz was summoned to Dr. Lange, chief of Vienna's Gestapo and State Police, in regard to the assets of the Burgenland Jews. In the Dual Austro-Hungarian Monarchy, Burgenland had been part of Hungary and the fiefdom of the old Hungarian house of Eszterhazy. In 1919 the predominantly German-speaking Western portion was split off and given to the newly formed Republic of Austria under the new name "Burgenland." It harbored many ancient Jewish communities. As soon as the plebiscite of April 10 was over, the Jews were summarily chased from their homes, most of them with nothing more than what they were wearing. It was a major instance of the barbarity let loose in the "gap of authority" that we characterized earlier. The State Police had not as yet been given specific orders and attempted on their own to secure the stolen assets for whatever official agency would, in the future, lay claim to them. They forced some Jews to sign papers relinquishing their assets and dragged them to the local registry to abandon their real property. Other Jews were set adrift on the Danube and eventually managed to land on the Slovak side.[143]

So wild was this rout and so cruel the chase that soon representations were made abroad. For example, in late April 1938, at the time when the IKG was officially closed, Engel received a letter from the consul of the United States in Vienna asking the IKG for clarification as to what was being done for these unfortunates. The refugees made their way to Vienna, where they became charges of the IKG, as we mentioned earlier.

Now Löwenherz had to report to Dr. Lange—it was Saturday, February 25, the Jewish Sabbath—and among other things had to listen to the following account:[144]

At the beginning of the Burgenland evacuation action most of the Jews who lived there declared—without any pressure being applied to them—that they relinquished their assets for the benefit of the emigration of indigent Jews.

The degree to which this relinquishment was voluntary is inadvertently and slightly, though sufficiently, indicated in the next statement: "In many cases the confiscation[145] (*sic*) of Jewish property was recorded by the courts by means of entries at relevant registries." Inasmuch as the separate Burgenland command of the State Police had in the meantime been dissolved and its duties had devolved on the *Leitstelle* (headquarters) in Vienna, the moneys would be at the disposal of Jews formerly from Burgenland, mainly to aid their emigration. The use of the moneys would be monitored by the governmental agency for the control of asset transfers (*Vermögensverkehrsstelle*), albeit in accordance with procedures set down and regulated by the *Staatspolizei*. The procedures required that the former Burgenland owners personally submit their claims to the Vienna Gestapo, certify their permission to sell their former assets, and sign over an assessed portion of the proceeds to the IKG for the purpose of aiding the emigration of indigent Burgenland Jews. The determination of the assessment would be left to the IKG, a typical instance of the Nazis putting the Jewish leadership in a position where they would appear to their fellow Jews as the executors of Nazi policy. The IKG would have to issue to the contributor a certification that the payment of the assessed portion had been made, to deposit the collected moneys in a separate account to be tapped only for the emigration of Burgenland Jews, and to submit to Gestapo headquarters a monthly accounting of credits and debits.

Did Eichmann pull some strings in order to retrieve some Jewish money from the clutches of the Gestapo, his perennial rival within the SS? According to the minutes that Löwenherz had to submit to Lange (at the Gestapo), it seems that Eichmann was not mentioned in the *Vorsprache*. Instead, we find Lange issuing a schedule of the kind of requirements that had hitherto been the exclusive prerogative of Eichmann. However, just how unqualified Lange was to hold his newfound sway over the Jews can be gleaned from Löwenherz's cover letter, with which he submitted the minutes of the meeting to Lange. In effect, Löwenherz pointed out that Lange's requirements could not be met for the following reasons: Of the approximately 3,500 Jews who lived in Burgenland at the time of the Anschluss, about 1,500 were now living in Vienna. Of these, 1,481 were dependent on the IKG (presumably Lange should have had no difficulty inferring why this was so). For the support of the unfortunate Burgenland refugees the IKG had so far spent RM 228,706.94; the unstated implication was that the IKG should be reimbursed for this expenditure out of the moneys in question. How much the IKG spent for the emigration of those who had left could not be determined because these moneys came from the general and not a special emigration account. In any case, about 2,000 had already emigrated and therefore—since that number included those who had properties and assets—they could not appear personally to make their claims. The inference was that Lange's generous scheme was not practicable and hence vacuous.

Parallel to the negotiations with Eichmann and with Lange, Löwenherz, with Eichmann's consent, resumed earlier contacts with Mayor Neubacher and magistrates in his office. After discussing the matter with Dr. Otto Schaufler, the chief magistrate (*Obersenatsrat*) in charge of welfare matters, Löwenherz brought the mayor a brief of almost seven pages. In it he outlined some pressing welfare needs of the remaining Jewish population and, referring to ordinances consequent on the special decrees following Kristallnacht, he submitted to the mayor his requests for relief.

He asked that the remaining Jews not be evicted from their homes, inasmuch as the emigration of over 70,000 Jews had made an adequate number of homes available to "other circles." Furthermore, after explaining the impoverishment of the Jews and how limited the available means were to meet these needs, Löwenherz requested "the intervention of public welfare insofar as Jewish welfare services are unable to help," as provided by the "ordinance concerning the public care of Jews" of November 19, 1938. Paragraph 35 of the ordinance provided for shelter, clothing, and care for the sick, and so on, as well as any other help that would aid the emigration effort. Referring to the need to provide new places for the old and the infirm, for which there were at that time 2,500 applicants, Löwenherz reminded Mayor Neubacher of repeated requests for the assignment to the IKG of facilities that could in time be furnished for the care of up to 4,000 people. Partial reimbursement to the city would be made with the proceeds from the sale of some of the assets of dissolved Jewish foundations once the Commission for Receiverships released them, as well as by transferring to the city title to the real properties of defunct and demolished synagogues. Löwenherz added that this provision would aid emigration because it would eliminate delaying emigration of persons who were caring for elderly or infirm parents. As regards the care of indigent and sick Jews in the Jewish hospital, Löwenherz requested that Vienna adopt the policy enacted in Berlin, where the city assumed the cost of such cases, a policy based on recent special legislation respecting the Jews. Finally Löwenherz requested the alleviation of a certain problem some would-be emigrants encountered in the process of obtaining permission to leave the Reich. A number of them were refused tax clearance because certain city departments made claims for past due taxes supposedly owed by persons with similar names or by relatives. To withhold certification of an indigent person would be counterproductive. Not only would such a person not produce any revenue, but he would lose the chance to emigrate, and hence continue to be a financial burden.

The brief also contained a request for the establishment of a health department within the IKG with authority over all health matters pertinent to the Jews of Vienna as well as to the emigration of Jewish physicians; this too was requested in accordance with special legislation pertaining to Jews. However, immediately prior to the meeting with the mayor, Schaufler told Löwenherz that the need for such a department was not as great as before and counseled that the IKG withdraw the request, which Löwenherz did.

After reading the brief, Mayor Neubacher made the following declarations: Jews were not to be evicted from their homes, and keys were to be returned to those who were evicted. Acknowledging the importance of expanding facilities for hospital care and for the care of the old and the infirm, the mayor expected that one of the private hospitals, which were then being transferred to the city, could be placed at the disposal of the IKG. The matter of the old and infirm, which Löwenherz represented as even more urgent, was to be taken up with Chief Magistrate Schaufler. The mayor would direct the relevant departments not to delay the emigration of indigent Jews for reasons of tax arrears in cases where there were no well-heeled relatives able to make payment. No decision could as yet be made about the requested contribution to the IKG's welfare obligations. However, the mayor directed that the IKG receive the city's contribution for the care of residents of the home for the aged.

A collateral matter was discussed when Löwenherz met with Neubacher and Schaufler on February 27—the matter of the employees in the Jewish hospital and facilities for the aged and infirm. One reason that Jewish patients had to be removed from public hospitals was that nurses and other personnel objected to taking care of Jews. Mayor Neubacher thought that, in turn, members of the nursing staff should have to leave the Jewish facilities. The mayor asked whether, when the nursing staff left, there would be enough Jewish nurses available. Löwenherz did not show how touched he was by the mayor's charming display of solicitousness because, truth to tell, he would have liked nothing better than to be rid of the bothersome staff. In the weeks before Kristallnacht, their ringleaders had squeezed concessions of outrageous salary demands out of him and were greater nuisances than they were worth. So he told the mayor, "difficult as it may prove to be, we shall provide a Jewish nursing staff." However, the personnel, including nurses, were quite content to remain employed at the Jewish hospital. Löwenherz records the reason for this paradoxical situation:

> Chief Magistrate Dr. Schaufler emphasized in my presence that, while he had been prepared to take over the nurses from our [Jewish] hospital, in accordance with the Mayor's previous orders, none of them had volunteered. His explanation for this was that the personnel at the hospital of the IKG were faring very well and their demands were met there to a greater degree than at municipal hospitals.
>
> He also stressed that, since the nurses in other private hospitals refuse to care for Jewish patients, the same standard has to be applied to the Jewish hospital as well.

No word about the extent to which the reassigned nurses would appreciate not having to take care of Jews—at a cut in pay.

In order to effect the regularization of this untenable situation of giving hands-on care to Jews, the mayor asked Plenipotentiary Bürckel for appropriate directives. A few weeks later, Schaufler informed Löwenherz of Bürckel's decisions. Now what? A Jew cannot fire an Aryan, especially from a cushy job. So, in June Eichmann got into the act and confessed for the record that he too thought that no Aryan ought to be employed in the Jewish hospital and, as usual, ordered Löwenherz to prepare and in short order submit basically unimportant statistics, this time an alphabetical list showing names of Aryan hospital personnel, their ages, positions, citizenship, professions, and former professions, as well as a similar list for the Jewish hospital employees.[146] Two weeks later, Löwenherz was able to report to Eichmann that the "recall of personnel from the hospital and the home for the aged is under way," and that its completion "should not take much longer."[147] After another fortnight, Löwenherz had to report that the personnel would be placed in other hospitals "in stages" and that this would take another eight to fourteen days.[148] Now the Gestapo entered the scene and, sniffing a police matter under its jurisdiction, issued the following directive by telephone to Engel: "70 employees of the hospital of the IKG are to be given notice or, as the case may be, dismissed no later than August 15, 1939, the younger persons first. Exempt are the doorkeeper, the switchboard operator, office workers, if any."[149] When that date rolled around, Eichmann directed Löwenherz to the effect that "personnel will surely be removed": nursing staff by August 15 and subordinate household staff "in stages" by September 30. Lists of remaining staff were to be reported so their transfer could be effected as well.[150]

However, the elimination of staff from the Jewish hospital was accompanied by an interesting footnote. It will be recalled that Löwenherz had asked for and was dissuaded from establishing a separate health department within the IKG with authority over all health matters pertaining to Jews. But now Löwenherz got a surprise: Coincident with the projected final removal of all Aryan personnel from the IKG hospital—including switchboard operators and office workers, if any—Eichmann told Löwenherz that at the behest of the Gestapo[151] the Jewish hospital would be under the surveillance of a Dr. Eduard Sponer, a police physician. The director Dr. Arnold Raschke and the IKG's administration of the hospital would continue as before, but Dr. Sponer was to begin his "control duties" (*Kontrolldienst*) the next day, August 15, and receive a hefty monthly salary of RM 750.00 from the IKG.[152] His one concrete duty that was spelled out was to issue medical certifications, which Jewish physicians were forbidden to do ever since their licenses to practice on the general public were withdrawn by special decree, although they were permitted to treat Jews.

A modicum of help did come from the municipality. Schaufler agreed to the municipality's support for an increased number of residents in the IKG old-age home, from 93 to 160. A pittance, but every little bit helped. He also permitted some disabled Jews, who needed constant care, to remain in the public institution for such cases in the suburb of Lainz; others, who did not need constant care, were to be placed in the public shelter for the homeless, including those who were now in the old-age home. We may wonder why the association of Jews and Aryans was acceptable in the case of persons who were derelicts or mentally disabled or tubercular though ambulatory. The reason can be gleaned from other items of Löwenherz's minutes of his discussion with the magistrates: The scheme would free some places for cases on the IKG's waiting list, thus reducing the necessity for granting the IKG additional facilities. In fact, the IKG also had to transfer cases from the hospital to nursing homes in order to free up beds for the sick. Most telling, however, is the fact that Löwenherz was informed that, with regard to the mayor's promise to assign a formerly private hospital to the IKG for an additional Jewish hospital and/or facility for the aged, "no decision has as yet been made."[153]

In short, the municipality was doing enough to claim that it had discharged its mandate, but not enough by far to make a real difference in meeting the needs of care and survival. But how did Löwenherz fare in his search to retrieve properties, assets, and funds appropriated by the authorities through the assessment of special levies?

Seeking Funds

When it came to Löwenherz's request for additional funds for various other pressing needs, Eichmann was very generous with moneys and funds that were not at his disposal, over whose disposition, however, he—by virtue of his position—exercised control. He eagerly grasped at Löwenherz's ideas to this effect, even as he found ways of temporizing about Löwenherz's attempts to tap his own resources.

A case in point was the question of the IKG sharing the emigration funds of the *Gildemeester-Aktion*. This *Aktion*—started as an informal initiative by Frank van Gheel-Gildemeester, a Dutch Quaker, to aid Jews—began in Vienna soon after the Anschluss;

before long, however, the aid was restricted primarily to Christian Jews, and its aim was restricted to furthering their emigration. Inasmuch as the IKG was basically an organization servicing those who were born Jewish and belonged to the Jewish Community, it was inappropriate for the IKG to be responsible for the support of Jews who had converted or who, because they were married to non-Jews or for some other reason, had dissociated themselves from the Jewish Community. Thus, with the approval of Eichmann, the work of support was divided along these lines between the IKG and the *Gildemeester-Aktion*. Yet, the matter turned out not to be so simple. Very often Jews who should have been served by Gildemeester came to the IKG and could not be turned away. Understandably, Löwenherz claimed that the IKG should share in the funds of Gildemeester, and Eichmann, always generous with someone else's money, agreed, especially since he operated more with the racial than the confessional conception of who is a Jew.

But the matter, apparently settled in principle, presented confusing specific cases, such as that of Wilhelmine Fischer, a Jewish woman from Graz. Since she was married to an Aryan, she should have been assigned to the *Gildemeester-Aktion*. Frau Fischer had six racially half-Jewish children and was six months pregnant. According to Eichmann's order, the *Gildemeester-Aktion* had to take care of the emigration of the Fischer children, but the IKG of that of Frau Fischer.[154] Of course, this solution did not sit well with the IKG, especially since their moneys were designated for persons who were Jews in every respect. But all Eichmann seems to have done to clarify such policy questions was to order, time and again, that Gildemeester hand over the cases of emigrating Jews by faith (*Glaubensjuden*) to the IKG.[155]

Were any of the Gildemeester funds assigned to the IKG? Not only did the IKG handle cases that would be appropriate for Gildemeester, but a "great part" of the donations to the Gildemeester fund were, in fact, made by contributors who were Jews by religion. Consequently, in December 1938 Eichmann promised Löwenherz that the IKG was to receive lump sums from that fund.[156] In January 1939 he promised that a decision would be taken within a month as to what portion of the fund would be allocated to the IKG.[157] A month later, Löwenherz was informed that the matter would take a while because the Gildemeester Fund would first have to be legalized as a public organization.[158] This was true, and for once one could say that the delay was beyond Eichmann's control. However, in other cases Eichmann blatantly reneged on promises of allocations or temporized endlessly.

Another case in point concerns the three transports that Storfer had arranged and that had been cleared by Löwenherz and Eichmann. Two of them were scheduled to go by Danube steamer to the Black Sea; there the passengers were to be transferred to an ocean-going vessel that would bring them to the coast of Palestine. One was scheduled to leave on April 29 with 720 passengers, the other the following week with 228 passengers. One day before the departure of the first transport, Eichmann authorized RM 70,000 for it—at RM 100 a head, a bargain for getting rid of 720 Jews—but required that a separate request be submitted for the RM 40,000 needed for the second transport at the time when it was scheduled to depart. At the same time, Löwenherz reminded Eichmann of the RM 27,000 authorized for a past transport of Jews from Graz. Eichmann thereupon told Löwenherz that he would issue a transfer authorization for the combined total of RM 97,000, and the

IKG official Richard Friedmann should come to pick it up at 3:00 p.m. In case the amount for the transport was needed before the transfer could be effected, Löwenherz was authorized to advance that amount from the account to which the IKG had direct access.[159]

Of course Friedmann was not given the transfer; of course the IKG had to advance the money from its own account; of course the transport departed as scheduled. A month later, during Löwenherz's absence, Eichmann told Engel that the outstanding RM 97,000 would be released in just a few days.[160] When Löwenherz reported to him one week after that, Eichmann requested a brief memorandum about the matter and promised to prepare the transfer that very day; and, of course, one week later Löwenherz had to renew the request for the transfer.[161] When Löwenherz raised the question again almost two weeks later, Eichmann informed him that the RM 97,000 had been transferred to the IKG account.[162] Löwenherz's report of Eichmann's response the next time he brought the matter up must be recorded verbatim: "Herr SS *Hauptsturmführer* Eichmann expressed his surprise that the RM 97,000 had not been transferred as yet, and issued a relevant order."[163]

Intent on getting rid of the Jews by an early deadline, Eichmann had no alternative but to dole out transfer authorizations and grudgingly even moneys from his "emigration fund." Yet, he meant to tap into the flow of officially expropriated assets for his own coffers and, perhaps more important, to keep what he had accumulated and have it grow. The IKG's efforts to retrieve expropriated assets received his blessings, at times even his active support, providing they were directed toward other authorities, such as the commission for receiverships. The main objects of Eichmann's squeeze play were the suppliers of foreign exchange with which the IKG obtained the Reichsmark for its budget. Hence, we are not surprised that two moves accompanied this squeeze play: On the one hand, Eichmann continued to direct Löwenherz to get more *Devisen*; this explains why Löwenherz maintained such an extraordinary travel schedule in this period. On the other hand, the aid societies increasingly used their purse strings to bring pressure to bear on Eichmann—of course through Löwenherz, and of course at Löwenherz's behest.

The IKG's main source of revenue was the capitalist's certificates to Palestine, of which ten per month were available for Vienna. The £1,000 per family which were required for this purpose were sold to wealthy Jews who had their assets frozen in blocked accounts. The few accounts left in the spring of 1939 had experienced considerable depletion through the atonement tax, which Göring had levied against the Jews for Grynszpan's assassination of vom Rath, and through the assets levy. Hence, the high multiple of the official exchange rate could not be borne by those who wished to avail themselves of such certificates. When the scheme was first set up, Eichmann insisted that the rate for the pounds sterling be set as high as RM 47.50 each, about three times the current exchange rate. In April 1939 the IKG and the Palamt agreed that this rate would have to be reduced to RM 30 per £1, and they asked Eichmann for his approval. The best deal they could get from him was that half of the certificates would be obtained at the lower rate, the other half at the higher, and that they were to inform the *Devisenstelle* accordingly.[164]

Eichmann knew that, by design, the Jews of Vienna had hardly any funds available. Hence, true to his generosity with moneys that were not his, he opined that *Keren Hayesod* (the United Jewish Appeal) and *Keren Kayemeth LeIsrael* (the Jewish National Fund), the funds to build up Eretz Yisrael (the Land of Israel) and to purchase its land, should be used to bolster the capitalists' ability to produce the money with which to obtain the certificates. His justification was that in Nazi Vienna these organizations were given permission to collect voluntary contributions on the grounds that they promote emigration.[165] But, by and large, the two funds collected money in the form of tiny contributions from a population that, even in their unprecedented penury, followed the *mitzvah* of charity by throwing coins into the *tzedakah* (charity) boxes held out by volunteers at the entrances of the IKG and the Palamt, as well as at the Jewish cemetery. In short, Eichmann wanted the IKG to be Robin Hood in reverse: In a scheme where some of the assets of the wealthy were saved from expropriation in order to help the indigent survive and emigrate, the indigent were to be enlisted to help the wealthy.

Tactics in the Battle for Assets

The battle for the retrieval of expropriated assets was joined at a time when Löwenherz's and his lieutenants' varied efforts to effect the forced emigration were at their peak. We have seen samplings of the tactics the Nazis used in this battle: In Eichmann's case, it was temporizing about approving funding, about authorizing funding, about releasing authorized funding, and even about reimbursing authorized funding advanced by the IKG. In the case of the municipality, it was a matter of a token dole while withholding the full measure of entitlements, and of giving grandiloquent assurances while content to leave actuality in the hands of the regime's policy executors. In the case of these executors, primarily the Receivership Commission, it was a matter of temporizing from the secure position of being in possession of the expropriated assets, a temporizing aimed at additional expropriation. The chief effect of these tactics was to pressure Löwenherz to produce funding for the IKG's welfare concerns, especially the care for the old and infirm, from sources other than expropriated assets. Ultimately, this meant that Löwenherz was to obtain foreign exchange from the aid organizations abroad for this additional purpose. This in turn meant that the only support he had in holding his ground in this frustrating chess game consisted of the aid societies' insistence on proceeding within the established parameters, refusing to open the floodgates of concession and compliance by going even one step beyond those parameters, and expecting that promises of funding and restitution of assets would be kept.

When Löwenherz went to Paris in May of 1939, it was time to confirm this support. Right after his meeting with him, Mr. Troper, the director of the Paris office of AJDC, wrote a letter to Löwenherz. In it he confirmed the report Löwenherz had made, particularly concerning the staggering financial burdens of the IKG under the increasing impoverishment and dependence of the remaining Jews. Reiterating that the budget for welfare and care must come from local sources, Troper pointedly says:

> We are pleased to learn that the *Zentralstelle* is prepared a) to make large sums available to you for emigration, and b) to assist you in gaining release of the assets of Jewish foundations and dissolved organizations. We acknowledge that based on this support you will, with the proceeds from the sale of securities and other assets, be in a position to ensure the continuance of the IKG's necessary welfare work, including the upkeep of the hospital and the homes for the old and infirm.[166]

Troper then informed Löwenherz that the promised May contribution from the AJDC of $75,000 (up from the usual $50,000) as well as £10,000 from the CGJ would be issued, albeit with the understanding that the mentioned restitution of assets was proceeding. Also, any allotments for June would be made with the understanding that none of the dollars or pounds allotted for May would have been spent for any purpose other than emigration. Finally, Troper reminded Löwenherz of the need to submit to the AJDC frequent reports detailing expenditures of dollars, pounds, and Reichsmark.

The point about the use of foreign exchange for external emigration in Troper's letter may have referred to a case in point, which Löwenherz also took up with Eichmann upon his return from Paris. It was the matter of $5,907.78 owed to HICEM, whose Paris office Löwenherz had also visited. Earlier in the year, HICEM had arranged for the settlement of some Jews from Vienna in Venezuela, at a time when Latin America was shut tightly against Jewish immigration. The condition for their permission to immigrate was that they bring with them a modest start-up capital in dollars. HICEM was to have parceled out to the arrivals a certain portion of the sum mentioned above. The dollars were to have come from the *Devisen* contributed by the AJDC and were paid for in Reichsmark, in the usual way, by the emigrants. In short, the dollars actually belonged to the emigrants, and the IKG held their Reichsmark in its account. The transport for this group was arranged by the travel bureau Zentral, which specialized in passage to South America, and which we have encountered before. When the people arrived in Venezuela, Zentral did not have the dollars to give to HICEM for their distribution. In Paris, Löwenherz was told in no uncertain terms that the matter must be settled. When Löwenherz confronted Eichmann with this matter upon his return, Eichmann declared that while "he is not saying 'no', he reserves the decision for himself, which he will announce in a week or two. At the same time he empowered me [i.e., Löwenherz] to apprise HICEM accordingly."[167] Almost three weeks later, upon his return from another trip abroad, this time to London, Löwenherz informed Eichmann that he had received another urgent reminder from HICEM and argued that it is "in the interest of smooth relations with the external organizations, whose support makes the conduct of the IKG's business possible" that this money be transferred forthwith. How fazed was Eichmann by this? His reply: Write a memo reiterating all the arguments.

While Löwenherz was successfully getting the backing of the aid organizations in his attempt to regain expropriated assets for the IKG's welfare and care budget, Eichmann seems to have been under the impression that American Jewry could be tapped for more *Devisen* than what the stubborn Löwenherz was able to obtain. What he needed was a better contact. He found him in Professor Dr. von Neumann (Heinrich Neumann von Héthárs), a highly revered, orthodox member of the Jewish Community of Vienna, a world-renowned physician, and, though a Jew, one of the stars of the famous but traditionally anti-Semitic Medical Faculty of the University of Vienna. In the weeks after the Anschluss, when the IKG was closed, he had independently tried to represent the interests of the Jews vis-à-vis the new potentates. Together with Löwenherz and Storfer, he had represented the Viennese Jews at the Evian Conference in July 1938. The most prestigious universities and research hospitals would have been honored to add him to their staffs, but he decided to remain with his people. He visited classes that the (religious Zionist) Mizrachi organizations maintained under the guise of training youngsters for pioneer work, he visited their agricultural retraining camps for would-be immigrants to Palestine, and he visited homes for the aged. Everywhere he went, this proud, bearded, and dignified man would, in exquisitely literate German, declaim and discuss intricate questions of Talmudic law and wisdom; and everyone would be fascinated, even if they did not understand, by the manifest epitome of unabashed Jewishness shining forth against the backdrop of its abject denigration. Rumor among the Jews had it that Neumann had been brought to Berlin to perform surgery on an anonymous patient—who everyone knew was Hitler.

For a long time Eichmann would not let Neumann go on his freelance mission unless he guaranteed that he would return within six months. Naturally, Neumann refused to go until Eichmann was convinced that his word was sufficient guarantee. And now that he was to leave, Eichmann found a way of maneuvering even this brilliant man. Evidently with a view toward the eagerness with which the nations opened their gates to the persecuted Jews, Eichmann's message to the world was "that Jews should not beg for the opportunity to enter other countries, since they were an asset rather than a liability." How did Neumann reply? Did he say, "Then what sense does it make to disenfranchise us and to chase us out?" No, more to the point, he said that "the reason the Jews had to act in the capacity of beggars in this connection was because of the forced emigration policies . . . the concentration camps and other coercive methods."[168]

Neumann's first stop was Paris, where he saw Troper soon after Löwenherz's trip in May. Troper sent a report of his meeting to Joseph Hyman, the executive director of AJDC headquarters in New York, where Neumann was heading among other places in the United States. Neumann indicated that he would like to raise money independently of the IKG and for activities other than those carried out by the IKG, some of them apparently under his, Neumann's, direction. Troper was quick to inform Neumann of some pertinent facts of life. First, that in each country the projects of the AJDC were carried out through only one central agency; in Austria it was the IKG. Second, the major fundraising that those times demanded was at that very time being carried out jointly by the AJDC, a National Coordinating Committee, and the United Palestine Appeal. Finally, no fund could be earmarked for special, independent projects. Troper warned Hyman: "We would hesitate to do anything which would decentralize the work in Austria."[169] Neumann arrived in New York on June 13, the same day as the letter; however, he apparently did not meet a group of representatives from the AJDC until July 28. After informing those present of the situation in Vienna and of his contacts with Nazi officials in Vienna and Berlin, Neumann placed himself at the disposal of the AJDC "for any constructive purposes." When Rabbi Jonah Wise closed the meeting, he assured Neumann that "the matter would be discussed and receive careful consideration, and that he would be communicated with in the not too distant future."[170]

In the meantime, in response to Troper's reminder of May 22 of the need to report expenditures and activities, the IKG submitted to the AJDC and the CGJ as well as HICEM and the Jewish Agency for Palestine, an elaborate, special, 25-page brochure in English, "Report of the Vienna Jewish Community: May–June 1939." The report was written not only to inform and reassure the aid organizations but to motivate Eichmann, who censored the report before it was dispatched to its destinations. On the question of the use of *Devisen*, the report states that "the foreign currencies put at the disposal of the Vienna Jewish community are *entirely and without any restriction* used for emigration purposes." (By "without any restriction" he evidently meant without exception.) On the question of the retrieval of expropriated assets, the report states:

> To the four Homes for Aged people already in existence wherein altogether 785 persons are placed, there are now coming two further homes with places for 300 people, as the reconstruction of the buildings put at the disposal for this purpose on the side of the authorities will be completed in the near future. In spite of the fact that essential parts of the reconstruction have been carried by participators of the retraining courses, the expenditures involved will be considerable.
>
> The IKG are of the opinion, it is true, that the funds for Homes for Aged people and other issues of social care would have to be raised in Vienna and have therefore submitted an extensive list of the Jewish foundations and other fortunes of Jewish charity to the *Zentralstelle* being the authority supervising the IKG, requesting them to use those amounts for the establishment and the maintenance of Homes for Aged people. The IKG hope to meet the understanding and consent of the authorities also in this respect. In view of the special urgency of the problem to provide places for more than 3,000 old and sickly people the work should necessarily be carried through without any delay.[171]

With the position of the aid societies reconfirmed in their letter of May 22, and again on record in the IKG report, Löwenherz could resume the unequal battle for retrieval of assets and, concomitantly, against impossible levies, with renewed backing. On June 5 Löwenherz gave a new presentation of the case at the *Vorsprache* at Eichmann's office. Eichmann directed him to prepare a report of the case with a list of the assets, their value, and the respective assessment of levies. "The report has to be so clearly arranged that someone who is not familiar with the matter would gain an impression of the true state of affairs."[172] On July 4 Löwenherz submitted his report.[173] He approached the matter contextually, that is, with a reminder of how the issue had arisen and of the restrictions on the use of *Devisen*: The IKG had requested the retrieval of the assets of the Jewish foundations, the defunct private synagogues and charities, as well as the proceeds from the sale of the properties of the former provincial communities "because, due to the progressive impoverishment of the Jewish population, the normal income of the IKG can cover only a fraction of the outlays for welfare." Furthermore, the moneys necessary in the period ahead to keep up the pace of forced emigration could be secured only if negotiations with external aid organizations were not disturbed by questions of the proper use of foreign exchange [currency]; such use would have to be restricted to the emigration effort. Löwenherz followed this by a summary compilation of the types of real properties. While this was not the itemization ordered by Eichmann, it made the situation clear enough.

Pointing to the difficulty of assigning specific valuation to many of the different properties and to the fact that the majority of properties was not included by the commissioner in the "General Foundation," Löwenherz arrived at summary valuations according to which the assessed fees amounted to an exorbitant 42 percent of an "extremely careful valuation." The estimated value of properties not included in the "General Foundation" amounted to RM 2,500,000. Löwenherz made a special point of mentioning that these assets were "in part confiscated, in part assigned to other organizations"; that is, they were outrightly expropriated, primarily for the benefit of a special corporation established by the plenipotentiary's commission for receiverships called "Reconstruction Fund—Assets Realization, Inc."[174] Moreover, these were assets that had "originally been available to the IKG for welfare purposes." The implication: If levies and fees were to be assessed against the assets to be placed at the disposal of the IKG, then a multiple of these fees would have been more than adequately covered by the value of the properties expropriated outright.

The estimated value of the real properties that were included in the "General Foundation," however, came only to RM 1,118,908. If one adds the value of the "other assets"[175] included in the "General Foundation," one arrives at the figure of 42 percent. This implied that without the "other assets," the assessed percentage of RM 743,020.89 would constitute 66.4 percent!

This was followed by a salient point. What was the commissioner's ostensible justification for assessing the reconstruction levy? It was his claim that the projected assignment of the assets combined under the General Foundation would constitute an actual enlargement of the IKG's holdings. And this is what Löwenherz emphatically denied. The reason for this was that all the properties in question and, as mentioned above, also the more valuable properties not included in the General Foundation had been at the disposal of the IKG's welfare concerns prior to the Anschluss. It was, after all, mainly through the private foundations, charities, schools, hospitals, and synagogues that the Jewish Community's concrete work was done. From this one may infer that there was to be no enlargement of holdings and only a partial restitution, hence no justification for the imposition of levies and fees.

On the basis of all these considerations, Löwenherz then asked that the commissioner for receiverships (1) cancel the levy and (2) transfer the administration of the Jewish properties included in General Foundation from the sub-commissioner to the IKG. Löwenherz added another request, one pertaining to 163 real properties of former Jewish provincial communities—including, in particular, 98 located in Burgenland. Shortly before Löwenherz finished the report, he was told by Brunner, in the presence of Eichmann, that the provincial communities no longer had the right to sell their properties. From now on, Commissioner Brunner reserved this right exclusively for himself.[176] In light of this, Löwenherz requested that this right be assigned to the IKG, with the proceeds to be used for the emigration of Jews formerly from the provinces and for the IKG's welfare budget.

We can guess what Eichmann thought of Löwenherz's presentation: Any assets that could be gotten from the commissioner reduced the likelihood that he, Eichmann, would have to tap his "emigration fund" and, far from enriching the IKG, would be under his control. However, any assets that Löwenherz did get would reduce the chances of ultimately succeeding in pressuring the external aid societies to increase the flow of *Devisen* for purposes other than emigration. If Löwenherz succeeded, then Eichmann would get the credit, and Löwenherz would be in his debt. If Löwenherz failed, the commissioner would be to blame, and Eichmann blameless. And when all was said and done, Löwenherz would be even less in a position to realize that all was a matter of bookkeeping among the various Nazi accounts, and that the various opponents in the game Löwenherz was forced to play were, in the end, one and the same.

The Tightening Financial Noose

But Löwenherz and the other leaders at the IKG did know, and this knowledge added another worry to those already plaguing the leading men at the IKG. As far as Eichmann and other Nazi authorities who were constantly monitoring the activities of the IKG were concerned, they might come to realize that Löwenherz and his lieutenants were beginning to know too much. We recall that early in 1939 Kapralik was forewarned, presumably by Raffegerst, his German contact, about his increasingly dangerous position, whereupon he obtained permission to make a quick exit. This was a far cry from what happened at the later, lethal stages of the unfolding Holocaust to all but a handful of Jews in positions of forced leadership. But Kapralik's case was a portent that could not go unnoticed by Löwenherz and especially Murmelstein: To be in that position meant having one's head in a noose, being constantly at risk. One was bound to know more than the Nazis could risk permitting the Jews to realize and to remember. For the Jewish functionary, to be under such risk diminished the effectiveness of his actions on behalf of the Jews. Not that Löwenherz or his lieutenants thought themselves indispensable. But clearly by then there was no one who could, for all practical purposes, take their place. To risk making a false step and, as a result, be removed, would be tantamount to defection. The Jewish functionary had to find a *modus operandi* that would obviate the risk of knowing too much, if he would continue to function for the benefit of the Jews as long as he survived. For Löwenherz, this meant reminding Eichmann only of previously decided or agreed-upon specifics, never broaching topics beyond matters of received directives, and never mentioning failures such as the Colombia transport. For Murmelstein, it meant pretending ignorance, which created room to operate within the framework of received directives so he could act to the greatest benefit of the Jews while giving the impression that he observed the letter of the directive.

In the meantime, the matter of the foundation assets was reaching a crisis situation. On July 7, three days after Löwenherz submitted his report to Eichmann, the office of the commissioner informed him that Brunner had decided to sell two of the properties included in the General Foundation—the proceeds to cover part of the assessed levy and fee, and that he was ordering Löwenherz to submit "all the documents required for an orderly execution of the sale at the real estate registry."[177] Löwenherz, upon presenting the matter to Eichmann, was ordered by him to prepare a report, the second one about this matter in one week. Here Löwenherz reiterated that the expropriation of assets worth RM 2,500,000 should adequately cover any assessed fees, that the external aid organizations insisted that welfare and care budget needs extending what could be realized from the sale of *Devisen* for emigration be covered from domestic sources, and that the present and increasingly difficult negotiations with these organizations were undertaken on the basis of official assurances (i.e., Eichmann's) that the levy would be canceled. Hence,

Löwenherz asked Eichmann to cause the commissioner to release the properties in question to the IKG, thereby ensuring that sales would be under the control of the IKG, that "formally and factually" the demand for the levy be withdrawn, and that proceeds from the sale of any of these properties be reserved for "welfare concerns, especially for the maintenance of homes for the old and infirm."[178]

One week later, this matter was a major topic during the *Vorsprache* at Eichmann's office prior to Löwenherz's leaving for what, in the summer of 1939, was a monthly trip abroad to negotiate with the external aid societies. Löwenherz reminded Eichmann that the recent notification by the CGJ of the allotment for July was coupled with the understanding that the matter of the release of funds for "welfare, especially the maintenance of homes for the old and infirm, independently of [external] support" was proceeding. In order not to disturb the next round of negotiations, Eichmann informed Löwenherz that a third party was being brought into the proceedings, presumably to mediate the matter between the commissioner and Eichmann-plus-Löwenherz. A special office at the *Zentralstelle*, which would include a delegate from the *Vermögensverkehrsstelle* (government agency for control of asset transfers),[179] would process the requests that had been submitted by the IKG for the restitution of assets, the cancellation of levies, and the sale of realties. To take the wind out of the sails of the recalcitrant and suspicious aid societies, Eichmann "empowered" Löwenherz to inform them that "the required levy will be revoked and requisite directions will be issued for releasing the foundations and other assets for the IKG's use." For good measure, to impress the external organizations with the high priority given to emigration from Vienna, Eichmann wanted Löwenherz to inform them that in light of their "support of the IKG's emigration effort . . . emigration of Jews from the Protectorate will be kept to a moderate level in order to utilize available immigration opportunities for Jews from the *Ostmark* [Austria]."[180] At the same time, since part of the Sudetenland portion of the former Czechoslovakia was now incorporated into former Austria, Löwenherz was instructed that the IKG serve the Jewish population in these parts in the same way as other provincial communities.[181]

After Löwenherz's return from Paris and London, Eichmann informed him that Commissioner Brunner was working on the remission of the levy and the release of the properties.[182] Löwenherz reported to Brunner two days later. He asked Brunner what would be left for the establishment of new homes for the aged and the infirm if the designated properties were sold to cover the assessed levies, especially in light of the fact that the most valuable properties and assets had been confiscated. Brunner responded that the matter of the remission was under consideration, and that the question of transferring the confiscated properties "either to the IKG or to the *Zentralstelle* for welfare use" would be decided in eight to ten days, apparently by Bürckel himself. As to the provincial properties, Brunner's superior, the General Commissioner for Receiverships, required that they be sold. Furthermore, the sale of the two properties that were to have covered the assessed levy had, in fact, been effected. However, Brunner assured Löwenherz that no sale was made below assessed value, except for properties needed for public purposes. In any case, the IKG was required to join the commission in endorsing the sales documents. To Löwenherz's objection that he was not at liberty to make sales endorsements without orders from Eichmann, Brunner told him to inform Eichmann of what he had been told and to ask Eichmann for the appropriate order. The proceeds of the sale of properties would be available for Jewish welfare purposes, after determination and settlement of debts owed by the respective foundations. In this connection, Löwenherz reminded Brunner of the IKG's advance of a considerable sum against one of the two foundations in question and that reimbursement of that sum would have to be considered in the respective settlement.[183]

Brunner approved the conversion already under way of some former foundation properties to homes for the aged and infirm. Upon being informed of the great delays in the progress of these projects (evidently due to the stipulated use of laborers), Brunner approved the use of Jewish labor.[184]

In addition, Brunner did not approve the transfer of the administration of Jewish provincial cemeteries to local parishes or foundations of the Roman Catholic Church. Instead, the cemeteries would be transferred to local jurisdiction in return for "the commitment to take the Jewish cemeteries under its care for the legally mandated time; thereby these cemeteries will best be protected."[185]

In this atmosphere of temporizing on the part of the authorities, marked by assurances immeasurably greater than the accompanying token-like tangible results, Löwenherz was invited by the nervous aid organizations abroad to attend a meeting at which all of them would consult about questions of emigration, and at which his presence was "absolutely necessary (*unbedingt erforderlich*)."[186] The meeting would be held in Paris immediately after the 21st World Zionist Congress in Geneva, which Löwenherz and Rothenberg (of the Palamt) were also scheduled to attend.

Another attendee of that congress was Norman Bentwich. Before the congress began, he came to Vienna to represent the CGJ's position to Eichmann on matters concerning Löwenherz's most sensitive dealings with the authorities. Eichmann was ready for him. After he expressed his appreciation of Bentwich's support of the IKG and its Director Löwenherz, Bentwich proceeded to raise questions that concerned him.

His main point was the matter of disorderly, forced emigration. His major points were that the pace of emigration had to slow down; that the aid organizations could not keep up the present rate of support; that the demands on their resources in various countries due to forced emigration were too great; that the German representative to the Intergovernmental Committee, Ministerial Director Helmuth Wohlthat, had pledged the German government's cooperation in a process of orderly, measured emigration; that since such a measured pace was being maintained in the Altreich, it ought to be instituted in Vienna; and that the orderly emigration of the projected additional 45,000 Viennese Jews could be effected within eighteen months, but the deadline of spring 1940 was unrealistic.

In his response Eichmann again said that he appreciated the difficulties of the aid organizations and asked Bentwich to take his constraints into consideration. Agreements respecting the more measured pace of emigration in the Altreich could not be applied to Austria, where, according to orders from on high, emigration had to be completed by spring 1940. In order to facilitate this special project for Austria, Eichmann told Bentwich, as he had recently told Löwenherz, he was limiting emigration from the Protectorate of Bohemia and Moravia.

Bentwich next raised the question of the IKG's welfare budget, especially the care of the sick, aged, and infirm. The aid organizations, generous in their support of emigration, should not be burdened with and could not bear the costs of welfare. Hence, he requested the release of foundation assets to the IKG for their welfare services and the revocation of the levies assessed against them. Eichmann declared that the release of the properties would take place and expressed hope that the assessment would be revoked.

The worry about closing the IKG after the completion of forced emigration came up as well, a worry that was intimately connected with the care of the Jews who would be left behind. Here, too, Eichmann was firm in declaring that the IKG would continue under its present legal status and independently of the *Reichsvereinigung*. In addition, "The organization of its activity would then be effected in accordance with proposals of its present director [i.e., Löwenherz]."

In response to Bentwich's question about continuing the schooling of very young children in schools maintained by the IKG, Eichmann was less certain.

The information for our summary of the meeting between Bentwich and Eichmann is drawn from Löwenherz's official record submitted by him to Eichmann and written that same day, August 14.[187] Three days later, on August 17, as soon as he was out of the country, Bentwich wrote his own summary of the meeting as well as of the impression he gained during the two or three days he had spent in Vienna.[188] The date is important because it shows that Bentwich wrote the account before he had a chance to meet Löwenherz again at the Zionist Congress. The two accounts of the meeting are essentially the same. This—for the researcher of this sensitive and controversial topic most welcome—corroboration of Löwenherz's account by an independent outsider is unique and, for this reason, noteworthy.

One item is mentioned by Bentwich that was not and could not be mentioned by Löwenherz. Before Bentwich left Vienna, Löwenherz said to him, with reference to Eichmann's assurances concerning the release of properties and the revocation of the levy, "that he doubted that there would be any change. There will not be any modification of the present ruthless policy in Vienna, unless some strong influence is brought to bear in Berlin, and definite instructions are issued from Berlin."[189]

In his "Report" to the aid societies, Bentwich gives us a unique glimpse by an important outsider into the IKG's operation:

> The work of emigration is organized, with remarkable thoroughness and devotion, by the IKG. . . . The Jewish Communal offices in the Seitenstettengasse [name of street] are a curious rabbit warren; but the elaborate procedure which requires reference to a score of government offices and the filling in of scores of forms is carried through methodically and expeditiously. It is a tribute to the Vienna spirit that punctuality and politeness are maintained.[190]

Another interesting sidelight in Bentwich's report concerns his meeting with U.S. Consul-General Morris, the highest official representative of the United States after the ambassador was withdrawn when Austria lost its independence. Discussing the situation of the Jews of Vienna under the duress of forced emigration, Morris told Bentwich

> that he had not realized altogether the extreme pressure that was being used to force out the Jewish population, nor the quantity of the emigration. He was prepared to send a report on the matter to the Department of State as soon as he received the necessary material.[191]

We do not know whether Morris obtained the material he deemed necessary for ascertaining what had been going on all around him and his organization for well over a year or whether he submitted the report he was prepared to send.

Löwenherz's reported appraisal of the dismal nature of the situation was uncannily correct. (We wonder where he, as well as Engel and Murmelstein, drew the strength to continue to go through the motions of endless negotiations in spite of their knowledge that by and large it was futile and to no avail.) Indeed, there is corroboration of Löwenherz's appraisal from none other than Eichmann. He waited until Bentwich, with his assurances fresh in his mind, had left the country, and Löwenherz had left as well, before making his next move. While Löwenherz was attending the Zionist Congress, Engel, as acting director, was given the directive to file an unprecedented "correction" of two passages in Löwenherz's *Aktennotiz* of the August 14 meeting between Eichmann and Bentwich. The first concerns Eichmann's response to the question of the restitution of the assets of the foundations; the second concerns the integral continuance of the IKG after the projected end of emigration. To show the difference in the two formulations, and thereby to show how Bentwich was being maneuvered, we are juxtaposing the two texts, Löwenherz's account on the left, and Eichmann's "correction" on the right:[192]

Aktennotiz, Aug. 14	*Weisung*, Aug. 21
The funds, foundations, and assets of organizations will be released and placed at the disposal of the IKG for welfare purposes.	The attempt will be made to have funds, foundations, and assets of organizations be released and placed at the disposal of the IKG for welfare purposes.
Upon completion of the emigration process the IKG, whose legal public status will be preserved and will neither be subordinated nor made equal to that of the *Reichsvereinigung* . . .	Upon completion of the emigration process the IKG, about which it will be decided at that time whether its legal public status will retained, will . . .

Löwenherz's correct appraisal of the maneuvers on the part of the various Nazi authorities indicates that he and his lieutenants had gained insight into the way they were being dealt with by their overlords, which not only added to their worries about the future but would be the one constant worry underlying all the others that might arise. In the case under consideration—the release of means to cover costs of care, to prepare for anticipated future needs, and to pay for emigration transports—the question was, why the manipulative temporizing, why the assurances and promises followed by reconsideration, modification, and reneging? In this case, the answer is clear: What had been expropriated would not be returned; what had been extorted would be retained; if the Jews did not have the means to take care of their own, let them do without; squeeze the Jews abroad for whatever they were worth. And the IKG's response is clear as well: To stay at your post, futile as it may

Delegates attend a session of the International Conference on Refugees at Évian-les-Bains (July 6–15, 1938). Among those pictured are Myron C. Taylor (right), James McDonald (second from the right), and Norman Bentwich (left) in conversation with Henri Bérenger. (USHMM 67488) (S. Adler-Rudel, Before 1933 and After: The Evian Conference on the Refugee Question, *Leo Baeck Institute Yearbook (1968) 13 (1): 235–73, doi:10.1093/leobaeck/13.1.235.)*

seem, and with the stubbornness learned in two millennia of exile; to stay your course, to find ways of pressing and of renewing your case, and of presenting your case as being ultimately in the interest of the Nazis.

But the insight that would from now on inform the underlying worry was that the Nazis did not do anything without a purpose. And, of course, they kept their purpose well hidden from the Jews. And, of course, the Jewish functionaries could not ask why they received a *Weisung*, or, if they were to ask, they would have to wonder in what way the Nazi's response was manipulative, as surely it was. The reason that insight would be such a pervasive undercurrent of worry was that the Jewish functionaries would, in their enforced ignorance, have to second-guess the possible purpose of a move on the part of their masters. Few of the men, placed in their position, would have had the acuity of perception, honed by the experience of almost day-to-day contact during a protracted period of most intense activity, that Löwenherz and Murmelstein had acquired. Yet even for them it was an almost hopeless task to guess the purpose of the Nazis' moves and, as the case may be, to figure out how, in their own impotence, they would have to make choices that would, under the given circumstances, best save their Jews and best ensure their survival.

The Nazis never did anything without an ulterior aim. This was now the operative principle. Murmelstein, too, had plenty of reason to wonder what this aim was. Among other things, his scholarship was being tapped more and more frequently to write the briefs that would bolster Eichmann's expertise in Jewish matters, and he would wonder why Eichmann was interested in these particular topics.

Löwenherz, Murmelstein, and Engel must have often wondered what the Nazis intended by Eichmann's and the Gestapo's conflicting claims of jurisdiction over the Jews and the IKG. Arendt thinks that the chaos of authority was part of the maneuver of playing off one party against the other and, therefore, a means of totalitarian control. However, this did not pertain to the situation of the IKG and its functionaries. The Jews were to be eliminated and, hence, had no normal validity as subjects of control. In such absence of validity and in such a state of substantive impotence, for Jewish functionaries to attempt to use the conflict of Nazi jurisdictions for the putative benefit of the Jews by means of nothing but one's wit would be a dangerous game, which some seem to have played at a later stage, especially in Theresienstadt. The situation in Vienna during the stage of emigration required clarity. During the highly intense and multifaceted activity of the IKG leadership in the weeks before the outbreak of the war, it was time for such clarification.

Navigating Bureaucracies

At the beginning of August 1939, Löwenherz had to report to Kuchmann (in charge of Jewish affairs at the Gestapo), who wanted to know by what right the IKG submitted reports and requests to other authorities—Kuchmann no doubt had the most recent dealings with the Commission for Receiverships in mind—only by way of the *Zentralstelle*. Löwenherz's response was that Eichmann repeatedly prohibited direct submissions. On orders of Dr. Karl Ebner, a superior at the Gestapo criminal department,[193] Kuchmann then ordered Löwenherz to submit a signed declaration acknowledging that "in future such questions are to be treated only in direct communications to the Gestapo headquarters." Löwenherz acceded to this order, noting that he would submit the matter to Eichmann.[194] A few days later, Kuchmann called Löwenherz, challenging him on the matter—mentioned earlier—of Engel's trip to Milan in connection with the mounting problem of Italy's closing of its borders to Jewish refugees.[195] Eichmann then informed Löwenherz of the clarification he had worked out with his colleagues at the Gestapo. All the IKG's submissions regarding emigration matters were to go to the *Zentralstelle*, similarly all requests for official travel on the part of personnel of the IKG and the Palamt. Direct submissions to the Gestapo were those concerning "matters of organization," such as the employment of personnel, requests to hold religious services, and permission for the arrival of foreign visitors. Questions of overlapping authority were to be submitted to the *Zentralstelle* which, if appropriate, would take them up with the Gestapo.[196] The Gestapo was to receive one copy of the periodic reports as well as listings of the IKG's retraining and other courses.[197]

Löwenherz's prediction, expressed to Bentwich, that the "ruthless policy" against the Jews would not change, "unless some strong influence is brought to bear in Berlin," that is, without radical political pressure on the powers at the very center of the regime, manifested its truth in a frightful way. Saving the Jews was evidently not on the agenda of world politics. Yet only world politics could bring the requisite pressure to bear on Berlin. This would be possible only if the world, and not merely the Jews, not only felt but actually were threatened by Berlin. It was only a few months earlier that Hitler strode to the lectern of the Nazi Reichstag to read a letter he had received from U.S. President Roosevelt appealing for peace, in light of the many countries that had reason to feel threatened by Germany's evident aggressive designs. As Hitler began to read the long list of threatened countries Roosevelt mentioned, there was a ripple of laughter from the assembled delegates of the Reichstag—a ceremonial one-party body "elected" as part of the plebiscite that endorsed the Anschluss. The laughter swelled as the list went on and reached a telling high point at "Palestine." Now the time was at hand for the world to feel threatened.

When Eichmann directed Engel to emend the record of his conversation with Bentwich, the 21st Zionist Congress was under way in Geneva. The main controversy of that congress was the policy to be followed vis-à-vis Great Britain in light of their issuance of the White Paper projecting a cut-off date for Jewish immigration to Palestine and limiting immigration until then. One day after Eichmann's call to Engel, the news of the Hitler-Stalin pact had a particularly devastating effect on the mood of the congress. It adjourned soon after that, having been the shortest Zionist congress ever, and the last for the six years of the war, whose imminent outbreak the news of the pact portended. Weizmann had advised that instead of protesting Great Britain's White Paper one should quietly keep up the illegal immigration. Ben-Gurion had counseled defiance against Britain on both counts. Löwenherz listened with a heavy heart, knowing full well that for the last eight months Britain had been the major source of immigration chances for the Jews of Vienna, and that Palestine—by way of illegal transports more than by legal ones—was at that very time a major destination for them. In fact, in order to safeguard these transports, Löwenherz had disguised the emigration figures for Palestine shown to Bentwich by throwing them together with the figures to Shanghai under the destination rubric "Asia," but Bentwich was not fooled by this.[198] It was with a sense of doom that the congress came to a close on August 24, the day the meeting of aid organizations convened on the premises of the Joint in Paris, where Löwenherz headed from Geneva. It would be his last trip there. He could have eluded the Nazis by staying there but returned to his post in Vienna shortly before war broke out on September 1, 1939.

Everything was disrupted by the war: the IKG's frantic emigration effort, Eichmann's various schemes attendant on ridding Vienna of its Jews by spring 1940. To normalize his enterprise under the new, as yet undefined, conditions, Eichmann now traveled between his Berlin headquarters and his branch office in Prague, and a new name appears in Vienna, that of his deputy, SS *Hauptsturmführer* Rolf Günther. One of the interrupted schemes was the campaign to have Löwenherz get more *Devisen*. Because of Britain's entry into the war against Germany, there would be no more pounds sterling from the CGJ, and only the Joint was left to be tapped. Early in September, Günther told Löwenherz that emigration must be completed by spring of 1940 as planned. How this was to be accomplished he left to the IKG, though he did allow that, since group transports would be difficult to arrange, individual emigration was the order of the day. Löwenherz spelled out the difficulties connected with this and stated that a slow emigration to the United States was now the most promising possibility.

When Löwenherz brought up the matter of financing the IKG's welfare budget but before he had a chance to elaborate, Günther told him that he was free to contact the Joint "and find new ways of getting *Devisen*." Günther had not mastered Eichmann's knack of temporizing, and with this blunt challenge he revealed what the chess game really had been about throughout the previous months. To drive the point home, Löwenherz was also told that restitution of moneys advanced by the IKG to provincial communities could not as yet be made; and that RM 200,000 from Eichmann's emigration fund for the youth *aliyah* transport, which he had grudgingly promised after weeks of vacillation, would not be forthcoming.[199] The explicit linkage of financing the IKG and "get more *Devisen*!" was the theme of several items of Löwenherz's next meeting with Eichmann. It was also revealed at this meeting that through Rothenberg's contacts in neutral Geneva, arrangements could proceed for continued emigration to Palestine. On the other hand, Eichmann confronted Löwenherz with the report mentioned earlier, that Jews in Palestine had volunteered for war service in the British military.[200]

It was becoming clear that Eichmann was on tenterhooks over the disruption caused by the new conditions and in search of possibilities that would save his enterprise, attainments, and performance. For the IKG leadership, the task was to fathom Eichmann's moves that were sure to come, in the meantime, to stay the course with regard to emigration and to press the search for means of survival, especially of the old, sick, and infirm. Many Viennese Jews had relatives in Poland, so also Löwenherz and Murmelstein; and anxiety over what was happening in Poland and what would happen to the Jews there once the campaign against it was over, added to their burden of care.

PART II

Captivity

Chapter 7

Prospects of a Kingdom to Come

The Nisko Project

We come to a chapter that deals with a short period of time—a few weeks in the fall of 1939—and with relatively few people—a few thousand Jews, a handful of Germans. It is a pivotal episode in the inexorable progress of the liquidation of Jewish existence in Europe. This episode has often been overlooked[1] or considered a failure.[2] Its limited action bears many of the earmarks of later events, containing such disparate elements as the deportation of Jews and the final expropriation of their property, pretexts and elaborate lies, intrigue and cover-up, harassment, poor planning, death, unquenchable Jewish optimism and gullibility, and international indifference. It is, in fact, a grand rehearsal of what was to come.

In late 1939 the Jews still remaining in Austria and those in the Moravian portion of the Protectorate of Bohemia and Moravia, who, besides those of Polish Silesia, were the primary targets of this action, had their hope for orderly emigration shattered by the German invasion of Poland and the consequent extension of the war to France and Great Britain. They knew they had to get out fast, but where could they go and how would they get there? With the outbreak of the war, the emigration machinery of the IKG, together with the Palamt and other Jewish organizations, began trying to find alternative routes and alternative destinations, but they had limited success. However, two groups were being readied for emigration, one to Palestine and one to Bolivia, the latter being organized by the Maccabi sports club. Emigration to the United States was proceeding at its usual halting rate, but alternative travel routes had to be devised for those lucky enough to receive the coveted U.S. visa, routes that avoided French, British, and German ports. On September 11, *Hauptsturmführer* (SS Captain) Rolf Günther, at that time Eichmann's second-in-command in Vienna, informed Löwenherz "that the emigration program is to continue and that special attention is to be given to individual emigration since there are difficulties connected with group emigration." All the difficulties notwithstanding, Günther continued to make demands as if nothing had changed. He spoke of the previously planned "big emigration project to be carried out by spring of 1940," and, of course, more money had to be found. Löwenherz was permitted to resume contact with the American organizations "and to explore new ways to get foreign currency to be used for emigration."[3]

But there were also other ways in which the people at the IKG were kept busy. On September 25, Günther informed Löwenherz that a history of the Jews was to be written, dealing specifically with the Jews in Vienna, the former Austrian provinces, and Southern Moravia, which was now incorporated into the *Ostmark*. Günther was very specific about what he wanted:

> The papers have to contain the historical development of the Jewish community organizations [*Kultusgemeinden*] in the individual provinces and Vienna and must consist of original thoughts. This should not be a compilation from existing books.
>
> The use of sources should be indicated by marginal notes. The books are to have 30 pages each, and two of them, treating the same subject in a [more] exhaustive manner, have to contain 200 typewritten pages each.
>
> If possible the work has to be delivered by October 9.[4]

There is a certain Mad Hatter quality in all this, both in what is demanded as well as in the readiness, on the part of the IKG, to comply. No questions were asked—or answered—as to the possible use of this exercise. Even today we can only speculate as to why this history was important, and at this particular time. The demand for it came two days after Heydrich's meeting with the chiefs of the *Einsatzgruppen* (mobile killing task forces) and four days after his famous circular[5] (September 21, 1939) dealing with "total measures" of an unexplained nature concerning the Jews, more immediate measures including the concentration of the Jews of the occupied areas of the East in cities and the establishment of *Ältestenräte* (councils of elders) to head these concentrations. Heydrich asked for "the most thorough preparation" for these actions and those to follow. Perhaps Eichmann, working hand in glove with Heydrich and always wishing to appear the expert, considered such a historical project, which he could then claim as his own, as a part of this "thorough preparation"; there would be plenty of "facts" to impress his colleagues with when they went about making plans for deporting the Jews across the Vistula River[6] and setting up the *Ältestenräte*. Whether the choice of the target date for the report was arbitrary or not, it seems to mesh very neatly with the events of the first few days in October.

In any case, orders are orders, whether they make sense or not; and Dr. Löwenherz delegated Dr. Leopold Moses and Dr. Murmelstein to write the required history in its long and short versions. The kind of pressure these men must have been under to finish on time is reflected in Löwenherz's later request to Günther to leave Murmelstein in Vienna, in which he mentions "that within the last 16 days [Dr. Murmelstein] worked through 11 nights at the IKG."[7]

Another bit of busywork makes more immediate sense in light of the ensuing developments. On September 8 and 15, 1939, the *Jüdisches Nachrichtenblatt* (Jewish Newspaper) carried the announcement that "for important reasons" the IKG finds it necessary "to make a register of all Jews living in Vienna." Without having registered in the manner required, the Jews would not be able to make use of the IKG "in matters relating to emigration, welfare and all other questions" (which covers just about everything), "since help will be extended only on the basis of the personal data furnished at this time."[8]

It seems to be the accepted opinion that such a registration could have taken place only or primarily at the behest of the Nazi authorities. To cite two examples: Rosenkranz emphasizes what he calls the added sanction, that is, the statement regarding the consequences of not registering, and adds: "in the case of such announcements one must however keep in mind they all were censored and edited by Eichmann so that the paragraph in question, or its formulation, could be Eichmann's work."[9] Adler is not as cautious as is Rosenkranz in his phrasing and places his emphasis on what he calls the "totally subjugated Jewish corporate body" (i.e., the IKG Vienna) and the "indispensable precondition" for such total subjugation, namely, that all those important data of the Jews within the "area of competence" of this corporate body be known. Calling particular attention to the fact that the *Jüdisches Nachrichtenblatt* was published at the command of and controlled by the *Zentralstelle* (central office), Adler concludes that Eichmann and Company meant to gather information that would later on be especially useful for purposes of deportation.[10]

The implication of the collaborative nature of this Jewish census and, by further implication, the complicity of the Jewish leadership, is clear. Yet, there are certain aspects of this situation that must be considered lest we, too, remain mired in this somewhat simplistic interpretation. First of all, the wording of the notification itself: It is the IKG itself that claims to be the initiator of the action. Usually, if a Nazi directive was to be publicized, the source of the directive would be given in the form of a reference to the "authorities." There is no reason to believe that, in this instance, the Gestapo or the SD would be finicky enough to hide behind the IKG or have any reason to believe that the Jewish population would obey more readily if there were no mention of Nazi pressure. Second, the language is rather mild, the so-called sanctions may occur if this directive were disobeyed; the IKG expects with certainty that this call would be heeded and adds that a complete listing would be necessary so that it can better serve the community. And finally, it makes available alternative dates if someone cannot (for important reasons, of course) appear on the appointed day.[11]

Leaving aside for now the ultimate purpose to which such a list could be—and was, eventually—used, let us consider whether the IKG might have had reasons of its own for such a census. What was the situation of the Viennese Jews in September 1939? Suddenly, the major avenues of escape to east and west, meager and difficult as they had been, were blocked. Nonetheless, the pressure by the Nazis for the Jews to get out did not let up; Eichmann's *Zentralstelle* needed a steady flow of clients in order to have a reason to continue existing in the relative ease and security of Vienna; the moneys derived from the highly inflated fees related to the granting of exit permits must continue to enrich their coffers; and Eichmann's prestige as emigration expert—and his hoped-for promotions—were at stake. Moreover, during the past year or so, the IKG, the sole protector of Vienna's Jews, had gradually lost reliable count of its membership, through legal emigration that somehow bypassed it; through individual illegal emigration it never knew about; through arrests, deportations, expropriation of housing, and other population shifts; as well as through death and impoverishment. Since an indefinite number of these changes in population had been brought to its attention, it makes sense that the IKG needed to know as precisely as possible the number and status of those who remained under its care. This was also the opinion of Murmelstein[12] who added that the Nazi authorities had an entirely wrong (i.e., much too high) estimate of the number of Jews living in Austria at the time of the Anschluss as well as of the number remaining at the outbreak of the war. Hence, proof had to be presented of the correct number of Jews who still were there and could reasonably be expected to emigrate and how soon; how many were no longer in a condition to do so, such as the old and infirm, and would need care in Vienna, perhaps for years to come; how many children needed some schooling; how many impoverished persons needed soup kitchens; and, depending on the numbers in these different categories, a projection of moneys and facilities needed; and, last, of the minimum Jewish personnel required to carry out and administer these various services. And overriding all these considerations were Eichmann and Company's constant pressure and threats and arrests designed to speed up the emigration of the Jews, a number of whom were no longer there.

How important was this list for the Nazis? It was a convenience, to be sure, for all kinds of purposes up to and including deportation. Could they have done without it? No doubt. They knew from other sources how to find their Jews and had used, and would continue to use, other means to round up the Jews whenever they wanted. For example, when, at about the same time, the Gestapo wanted to arrest the stateless Jews in Vienna and to expel or incarcerate them, they managed to find them even without this list: On September 10, in the course of his visit to the Gestapo, Löwenherz asked what the circumstances surrounding the arrests were. He was told that the old prisoners would be released soon, but about the others no directive had been received.[13] The next day he was told by Günther that the emigration possibilities of the expelled stateless Jews need not be reported to him anymore,[14] possibly because they all had been arrested.

Assuming that the census was undertaken at the initiative of the IKG, possibly with an indifferent SS concurring, the registration did come in handy for SS purposes when, two weeks later, SS Captain Rolf Günther ordered a list, one original and four copies, to be drawn up of all Jews still in Vienna. Some of the items demanded in this list are interesting in the light of subsequent events, and the memorandum as a whole is a good example of the interest, on the part of the Gestapo, in the details of the life of each individual listed, an interest whose sinister implications become clear very soon:

> The list of the names has to be made separately for Vienna and for the provinces. The provinces are to be arranged by counties [*Gaue*], Vienna by districts and within the districts according to streets.
>
> All lists are to be typewritten. The district lists are to be numbered consecutively, starting with number 1. The district lists are to contain: family name, first name, year of birth, occupation; in the case of married women who do not work at a particular occupation, "wife" is to be written in; apartment; in the case of roomers, the name of the landlord or the room number. Citizenship. In a separate column is to be stated whether the person is with or without means. A person with means is someone who has assets of over RM 5,000; in these cases it is to be stated under Remarks whether the assets consist of cash, securities, real estate, etc. It should also be stated under Remarks whether the person is under arrest, in the hospital or nursing home, if he is crippled, draws disability benefits, and so on.
>
> All males between 15 and 55 years of age are to be registered as able to work unless they are complete cripples. Separate lists are to be made for people in the hospital or nursing home.
>
> Furthermore, one list of physicians and one of engineers is to be drawn up. The list of

physicians is to be divided into those who are allowed to practice and those who are not; also, in all cases the field of specialization is to be entered.

Of course all other columns contained in the apartment lists are to be completed.

All lists, arranged by districts, and bound, are to be handed in by Wednesday, September 27, at 10 a.m.[15]

Now that all the Jews remaining in Vienna were neatly listed, numbered, and categorized in one original and four carbons, the time had come for the Nazis to make use of the information that had been gathered and intended for the benefit of the Jews.

Mission to Moravia

Löwenherz was summoned to Rolf Günther on October 10[16] and was given the order to send to Mährisch-Ostrau [Ostrava, a larger city in Moravia] three days hence the four most important men in charge of organizing emigration, where they were to report to Eichmann. They could expect to stay away for three to four weeks. Besides Murmelstein, the men in question were Julius Boschan, the IKG liaison at the *Zentralstelle*, Dr. Mauricy Moses Grün of the Palamt, and Berthold Storfer, the liaison with the shipping companies and arranger of all kinds of legal and illegal group emigration transports. There was no direct mention of the purpose of this trip. However, it could be assumed that it stood in some connection with the next order, also given on October 10, namely, that the IKG choose 1,000 to 1,200 men who were in a condition to emigrate and able to work, and put them in a list, again in alphabetical order, again in five copies. Again the same kind of information was required as had been a little over two weeks previously. Place of birth and number of dependents were the new features this time. Somehow it became clear right away that this was not merely another list but that these men were going somewhere to do something, although neither the one nor the other is specified. The orders were restricted to giving information as to what kind of people were to be ready to go: artisans of all kinds, carpenters and technicians were preferred; they were to be chosen from among German nationals and stateless persons of Polish birth. Former inmates of Dachau and Buchenwald who were supposed to leave the country immediately were to be included. Members of the Palestine and Bolivia transports would also be added to the list if they met the requirements. Murmelstein[17] mentioned that the members of the Colombia transport, which Eichmann had tried to organize and which had turned into such a personal failure for him, were also to be sent along. There was no official confirmation for this in any of the *Aktennotizen* of the time, but it would make sense that this was an oral command by Eichmann not meant to show up in writing, an expedient to help Eichmann rid himself of those who were living proof of his bungling. One interesting specification was that only poor Jews may go. However, they would have to hand over whatever gold or jewelry they might still possess.[18] What to take along: tools, building materials and supplies, provisions for three to four weeks, heavy and work clothes, and up to RM 300 per person. Furniture and other belongings would have to be sold, presumably to get the 300 marks together. Other participants: ten physicians, who were to bring along all their pharmaceuticals and instruments; a group of transport leaders to be appointed by the IKG; people to be in charge of individual railway carriages;

and people to keep order (*Ordner*). Ten Jews on the list were to be singled out as having special organizational ability. All participants would have to be ready to leave within three days from date of notification.

These were the main points of what was disclosed to Löwenherz, according to his minutes. If he was told anything else that would make the situation any clearer, there is no record of it. In any case, he found himself in a very difficult spot. In keeping with the intention of Heydrich's circular of September 21—which was, of course, unknown to Löwenherz—the responsibility for the execution of this order lay on his shoulders and those of his co-workers,[19] the most important of whom he was going to lose right at this time, at least for this crucial period. He had, moreover, been given the order to select those who were to go. The situation was novel, unique in his experience, an unprecedented action containing the features of emigration, deportation, and arrest, without a revealed destination, purpose, or length of stay. It meant the giving up of homes (the sale of furniture indicated permanent removal) and the rendering asunder of families for an indefinite period of time. Yet, such was the desperation of the Jews of Vienna that even this sorry substitute for emigration looked good to a great number of them. If nothing else, it seemed preferable to the cul-de-sac into which they had been driven. It seemed a glimmer, no matter how faint, at the end of the tunnel.

This glimmer was soon to be extinguished.

Of course, the interest of the Nazi authorities did not lie in the direction of creating a viable Jewish settlement in the east but rather in expelling the Jews from the area that now comprised greater Germany. On October 10 the head of the SD and security police for Bohemia and Moravia wrote to Josef Bürckel, the Gauleiter of Austria, from Prague:

> Over Sat./Sun. I was in Vienna for a short time, to discuss, among other matters, Jewish problems. . . . Eichmann . . . informed me of the visits of a representative of yours who was working toward a speedy solution of the Jewish question in Austria. There is hope that a large number can be deported. As soon as this project can actually be carried out, Vienna will inform you immediately. In any event I am hopeful that this problem will be solved with finality in short order.[20]

And again on October 17, in a memorandum regarding a discussion held on the previous day by Eichmann, Dr. Ebner of the Vienna Gestapo, and Dr. Becker from Bürckel's staff, we read that Eichmann had received "personally" from Bürckel "full authority [*sämtliche Vollmachten*] over the resettlement project." Indeed, the resettlement from Vienna was to be carried out at an increasing tempo. No obstacles were to stand in the way of speedy deportation, this at the beginning of the war, when the whole rhythm of German life, both civilian and military, was still in the process of change and readjustment. Special trains and food for the trip and the first few weeks would be arranged, a troop of police guards to accompany the trains would be furnished, employees of the housing office would be assigned to secure the apartments vacated by the Jews, and last but not least, the Jews themselves would be apprehended, all this by courtesy of Bürckel.[21]

The immediate gain, on the part of the Viennese, would be material: Everything beyond the 50 kg of personal effects or tools of the trade had to be left behind by the Jews, the RM 300 that they could get together by the sale of their belongings were amassed by their being paid ridiculously little for a great many items. Even more important, apartments became available to the Viennese, or rather to those segments of the population that had some kind of priority or connections. The National Socialists were never able to live up to their promise of alleviating the perennial housing shortage in Vienna; and of course the outbreak of the war drastically curtailed the creation of new apartment buildings. In fact, the government had begun seriously to consider throwing all Jews out of their homes and housing them in barracks. Having them deported would enable the government to fulfill their obligation to the Viennese at very little cost. Thus, we also read in the same memorandum that "the Gauleiter [Bürckel] is overjoyed that [in light of this project] the planned removal of the Jews into barracks does not need to take place, since the costs of the construction of such barracks would have come to RM 500 per head."[22]

Much has been said about the identity of the originator(s) of this deportation plan, who were its main proponents and opponents, and what were their real intentions. For example, Goshen, focusing on Eichmann on the one hand and the Czech Jewish community on the other, has presented a careful and convincing genesis of the action from this perspective.[23] Since the Vienna Jewish community and especially its leadership stand at the center of our investigation, our approach is somewhat different. Based on the material at our disposal, we place this action within the wider context of the general Nazi scheme of making the European Jews disappear from sight of the "Aryan" population. We have to ask ourselves to what extent Nisko (hardly more than a railway stop in western Poland, near the River San) represented the decisive first step in this process, to what extent it was planned as such, or whether it turned into that primarily through accident or fortuitous circumstance or other factors.

In any case, things happened rather quickly, especially between the end of September and October 18. Indeed, as early as September 14, we find the protocol of a conference of administrative heads, held in the newly established RSHA (the headquarters of the SS), which includes a statement by Heydrich to the effect that Himmler (the head of the SS) was making suggestions to Hitler regarding the Jewish problem in Poland, about which only he, Hitler, could make a decision, since events of considerable impact on foreign affairs were involved.[24] Only one week later, Heydrich was able to report about a further conference at which the Führer had approved the deportation of Jews into the Government General (Eichmann was present at this second meeting).[25] And yet another week later, Alfred Rosenberg could write in his diary for September 28/29 (i.e., during and immediately after the signing of the German/Soviet agreement regarding the division of Poland) that in a series of talks among Hitler, Himmler, Rosenberg, and the group of Gauleiter in the east, Hitler provided the first guidelines for the reorganization, by nationalities, of the conquered territories.

On October 6 Hitler gave his "peace" address, which was meant to reassure Britain and France, who had declared war on Germany when it invaded Poland, and to persuade them to desist from waging that war, an overture that found little resonance in the west.[26] In this speech, Hitler found opportunity to refer to the attempt, on the part of his government, to "regulate and bring order" into the Jewish problem.[27] It is not clear in what way he meant to win over the West by this projected solution, whether it was to reassure those who feared

ES STELLTE SICH HER/
AUS/DASS DER BOL/
SCHEWISMUS NICHT EIN
KAMPF FÜR EINE SOZIALE
IDEE WAR UND IST/SONDERN
EIN POLITISCHER KAMPF
DES JUDENTUMS ALLER
LÄNDER GEGEN DIE NATIO/
NALE INTELLIGENZ ALLER
VÖLKER

ROSENBERG

An anti-Semitic saying by Alfred Rosenberg that was distributed as an "inspirational" flyer: "It has turned out that bolshevism neither was nor is a struggle for a social idea, but rather a political struggle waged by the Jewry of all lands against the national intelligence of all peoples." (WStLA, Hauptarchiv-Akten - Kleine Bestände: Zeiträume und Ereignisse, A81 Nationalsozialismus 1)

brutal repressive measures against the Jews or to please the anti-Semites of Europe with the prospect of removing the Jews from their midst. What is certain and worthy of note is twofold: First, it represents a confirmation of Hitler's involvement in the planning of some action regarding the Jews under Nazi control. Second, the lack of reaction to his speech includes also a lack of reaction to his remarks regarding the Jews. This was a good portent for the planners of the final solution of the Jewish question. They understood that they did not need to shape this policy with one eye on public opinion abroad. It was an ominous portent for the Jews who—though they were not aware of it at the time—could count on very little beyond indifference from the very nations whose political ethos was formed by the ideas of freedom, justice, and equality.

The deportation of Viennese, Moravian, and Silesian Jews to Nisko, Poland, did not take place in isolation. They were not the only groups of people who were being moved around like pieces on a chess board during this time. The conquest of Poland had opened up new possibilities as well as new territories for the Germans, possibilities for putting into practice their up-to-now fairly vague plans regarding the enslavement, displacement, and/or elimination of what they considered inferior races. It had also opened up the possibility of bringing together and enriching those of German extraction who had been living in pockets distributed among other nationalities, primarily in eastern and southeastern Europe. In a sense, one can speak of a master plan according to which all of these population shifts were to take place. But when it came to the actual carrying out of this plan, there occurred a diffusion of responsibilities and actions. There were sub-plans and counterplans, immediate plans, and top-secret overall plans to be realized in the future. The documents reveal a frantic scurrying around, a jockeying for position among those who wanted the new *Völkerwanderung* (migration of peoples) to be considered their very own scheme and their very own bailiwick. Orders were given and withdrawn (often by others), preparations went awry or were lacking altogether, the aims and needs of one agency conflicted with those of another. The Jews affected were to a great extent unaware of the wider implications of the agitation in the world around them and of the role all this could and would play in their immediate future. We, however, can at least attempt to sketch out the broader context of their situation.

Deporting Jews

The Nisko deportation was not the first one attempted or carried out from Central Europe. As we know, the precedent for this was the summary expulsion of thousands of Jews who were Polish nationals that gave rise to the events of Kristallnacht (discussed in chapter 5). On September 8, 1939, only a week after the beginning of the war, there was a secret directive distributed by the Gestapo in Frankfurt-on-the-Oder over Heydrich's signature to all major Gestapo offices, to wit: First, male Jews of Polish nationality were to be arrested, the members of their families to be registered; of course their assets were to be confiscated, but enough was to be left to the family members as seemed necessary to support them. Second, those Jews were to be registered ("as inconspicuously as possible") who had once held Polish citizenship or had originally come from Poland. The purpose of this action was the deportation of all of these "at a given point in time" into that area in Poland that was not to be incorporated into Greater Germany. In the meantime, members of the first group could individually be sent to concentration camps. Exempt from this deportation were those Jews needed for the furtherance of emigration, such as Löwenherz and Murmelstein, both of whom had been born in what was then Poland. Gestapo Vienna was to make contact with Eichmann regarding this matter.[28] Eyewitness reports confirm that Jews meeting these criteria were shipped out of Vienna shortly after the beginning of the war.

We do not know where in Poland these Jews landed. There exists, however, a transcript of a teleprint sent to Eichmann in Prague from Stapo Brünn (Brno) dated October 3, 1939, in which a functionary of IIB4 reports that Jews who had been deported to Poland were trying to come back to the Protectorate; some were incarcerated in Mährisch-Ostrau (Ostrava in Moravia), the majority were again shipped into Polish territory. Besides these deportees, there were also Jews who had apparently left the Protectorate after the German takeover and had tried to save themselves by crossing into Poland. The fact that at least a number or possibly all of them were stateless or had been born in Poland is mentioned, as is the supposition that it was the German military in Poland which induced them to return. The German civil government in Poland did its part by stating that it had no objection to the westward migration of the Jews. Our Gestapo man plaintively asks for instructions on what to do if all the Jews were to come back.[29] Unfortunately no answer could be found in the files, but one can see from later developments how the Nazis responded in practice.

From the middle of September there is a telegram, from one army unit to another, signed by a chief of staff, ordering that the Jews of that portion of newly conquered Upper

Silesia, which was being incorporated into Greater Germany, were to be shipped eastward across the River San immediately.[30] And on the 18th of that month, a conference took place between Gauleiter Josef Wagner (Breslau aka Wroclaw), Dr. Franz Stahlecker (Vienna), and Councilor (*Regierungsrat*) Hermann. The secret minutes of this meeting speak of a planned deportation of eight thousand Jews to Galicia. There follows an enumeration of the administrative work involved—"the dwellings of the Jews must be subjected to an inventory, their property, no matter how insignificant, must be secured. . . ." To avoid terrible consequences, their work could not be left to untrained personnel, and Wagner insisted that he get the proper help, especially since a great number of apartments had already been secured.[31]

On the same day, back in Nisko, one of the few German inhabitants had been elected mayor. He lost no time in advising the Jewish residents "to remove themselves across the San."[32] But deportation or mere advice to leave the territory did not account by any means for all the exodus of Jews toward the east or for the flight of other nationalities. And having once been "encouraged by various means" to go east, these people were meant to stay there and not return. On September 21, a directive went out from the Army High Command in Łódź: "Polish and Jewish refugees from Western Poland who had fled east across the San, the Vistula, and the Narew [rivers] are to be prevented from returning to Western Poland."[33] And on the 26th: "Refugees of Ukrainian, Polish and Jewish ethnic identity are to be prevented from going west across the Vistula, even between the bridges, by all means available including the use of weapons."[34]

That such a population policy brought all kinds of outrages with it cannot surprise us, since it gave all groups not directly or officially victimized ample opportunity and ideological justification to plunder and kill. A few examples from diaries and reports from the German side will give us an inkling of the situation. The German district president of Jarosław, Poland, reported on October 1 to his superior in Krakow that the "lower strata of the local population have managed, during the past few weeks, to get hold of considerable amounts of valuables mainly through plundering. The concepts 'property' and 'order' have disappeared." He requested a German expert to keep an eye on the abandoned Jewish landed property.[35] And on October 19, he wrote to the same address: "At least 90% of the Jewish population of the county fled across the San to Russian territory when the demarcation line was redrawn (approximately 12,000 people). All their assets were left behind. In this process 80% of all the businesses of the district . . . have become *herrenlos* [ownerless] and just as many residential houses, apartments, farming real estate. The local population began to plunder. . . . Securing these assets . . . has been my main task." And again he asked for someone who would take care of abandoned Jewish property—apparently his first appeal had remained unheeded. In the meantime, he had placed ethnic Germans and refugee Lithuanians into the Jewish businesses, but he was completely at a loss whether he had done the right thing since he did not know if ethnic Germans were to be settled in his territory or shipped back to Poznan and Western Prussia to form closed colonies.[36]

We see that securing Jewish property had become a main concern of the newly created German administration in Poland. The newly appointed territorial commissioner (*Land-*

kommissar) of Nisko, in his "War Diary" begun on October 1, breathed a sigh of relief, as it were, in describing his various administrative duties: "[My] work was made much easier by the fact that the actions against the Jews [*Judenaktionen*] had already been finished. [I] merely had to order an inventory of secured [*sichergestellte*] Jewish possessions. . . . We still have to place trustees into those Jewish businesses that are still closed."[37]

Of all the German agencies involved, it seems to have been the army which, at least at first and in the higher echelons, tried to some extent to preserve a modicum of humanity and to stem the tide of violence accompanying the conquest. So, for example, General Walter von Brauchitsch on September 24: "excesses against the local population, in which even officers had participated and which endanger the prestige of the army, must be fought with the strongest measures including court-martial and punishments severe enough to serve as deterrent. Neither must the army participate in police executions."[38] Other army reports, from the same general area and time, deal with SS activities, such as the burning of synagogues and the incarceration and shooting of Jews in territories controlled by the army. Such actions were generally carried out under the noses of the army and within its jurisdiction, "without reporting to me first" as one lieutenant general plaintively phrased it. Attempts were reported of trying to limit shooting and arrests, from a planned 10,000 to a mere 800 in one instance. "The Führer would hardly approve of the shooting of all the Jews," wrote the general. He had gained the impression, however, that the SS had come to undertake some action against the local Jewry "as a whole." Of course the Jews doubtless deserved strong measures if they misbehaved, he went on, but the SS actions seemed inappropriate and brought unrest and excitement into the populace.[39]

One example of such unrest and excitement said to have been caused by the Jews of the region is found in a situation report by the district president of Pińczów who, after quoting statistics regarding the number of Jews in the larger towns in his district, wrote on October 19 to Krakow: "One cannot even say that these numbers are approximately correct since a lively migration seems to have begun among the Jews which, however, could possibly be due to housing burnt-out Jews in other domiciles."[40] In spite of all the measures taken against them (forced labor, punishment, confiscation, etc.), "the Jews still constitute an element of unrest." He claimed that they have been convicted of inflating prices, of swindling as well as of violent acts; moreover (though there is no proof), it had been reported to him that they were arming themselves in order to stage a revolt with the aid of the Soviet Russians; in the expectation of their liberation by the Russians, the Jews were said to have supplied themselves with red armbands.[41]

Yet, the army, too, was just as glad to get rid of the Jews. In a directive of October 10 from the General Staff dealing with the safeguarding of the demarcation line, we read: "Jews and Poles who want to cross for good the demarcation line into the Russian interest sphere are to be granted transit. In cases where the Russians refuse to accept them, it is to be left to the people to pass through the line on their own responsibility, with the agreement of the office dealing with deportation." However, this applied only to Jews (and Poles) who were fugitives and already near the border; further evacuations of Jews and Poles still living in border towns were to be stopped for the time being.[42] Thus we find two actions alluded to in this directive: first, the "encouragement" of undesirables to leave German territory, and second, a confirmation of the fact that deportations had actually been carried out by this time.

The "humanity" of the soldiers had its limits, however. There are two sworn depositions by Jewish survivors who had lived in Tarnobrzeg, a town on the German side of the San River. Both tell in detail how in early October 1939 all the Jews were rounded up by German soldiers, were forced to leave everything behind and brutally driven by these soldiers down to, as well as into, the San River and made to cross to the Russian side. This was done with absolutely no regard for age or infirmity and caused great loss of life, mostly through exhaustion and drowning, as well as unimaginable hardships for those who managed to survive.[43]

During this time the ethnic Germans were also being uprooted, faced hardships, and basically were caught up in a population policy which, though meant to result in their eventual benefit—at least that was the claim—could not but exacerbate the general confusion. Thus, in a secret situation report sent out by Himmler's office on October 18, we read of the ongoing migration of ethnic Germans from Estonia and Latvia, about 70,000 to 80,000 in all, back to the Reich. These re-settlers were expected to take all they owned with them[44] and hence made great demands on transportation facilities. This westward migration seems to have been less problematic even though it often met with resistance from the "native" Germans back in the old Reich. In Hungary, the resident Germans had to be assured that they could remain and would not be forced into resettlement, at least not for the time being. In the South Tyrol, which had been given to Italy after World War I, on the other hand, the great majority (90 percent, it is claimed) was "giving thought" to going east but did not like the area suggested, since, for these vintners, the climate in Poland was too harsh.[45]

So far the material available has allowed us to open a few small windows into the chaotic landscape of the occupied Polish territories immediately following the German conquest. A few situation reports dated just a few weeks later give us a somewhat better insight into what was going on, what was planned, and what was projected as the result of the resettlement policy. Even though these reports take us into November, that is, beyond the time when the Nisko transports took place, basically the overall situation did not change nor would it do so in the intervening weeks.

The first situation report, dated October 28, was written by an agency of the *Wehrwirtschaftsdienst* in Łódź, an office concerned with military economy. Here the claim is made that the projected and in part started resettlement of 6.75 million Jews and Poles in the Government General (German-occupied Poland) would bring about a disorganization and paralysis of the economy, especially since "it apparently is to be executed without consideration for military, civil and economic concerns. . . . Serious internal political dangers are to be feared." Since the military was the biggest customer of the region, it would have to have the right to demand "that the resettlement action take into consideration the war economy needs of the conquered territories."[46] When this report was issued, the first Nisko transport was ready to leave Vienna, on October 20.

On November 5, the date of the second report from the same office, there still seemed to be no clarification regarding the resettlement. According to one account, for example, 250,000 Jews from Łódź were to be deported quickly into the Government General. Baltic Germans were expected to take their place, notwithstanding the fact that all the Germans from Łódź who had gone—or had been forced to go—east, had not yet returned. There were still refugee camps at the demarcation line, a situation that had surprised Himmler greatly during a visit to the area, especially since the camps did not make "a very beautiful impression." The report continues: "Where in particular instances the great streams of people within the Government [General] are to be deported to and resettled seems to be still unclear. Directives are discussed that begin with the words: To be deported into the area around Kielce, . . . one will have to avoid the error of generously determining regions [for settlement] without knowing their possibilities for housing under the present conditions," and so on in the same vein.[47] Attached to this document is a report by Dr. Peter-Heinz Seraphim dealing in detail with the consequences of the resettlement policies on the German defense industries, policies the execution of which, according to Seraphim, "rests with the *Reichsführer* SS as the autonomously deciding authority." The plan under discussion comprised the resettlement of over 6 million Poles and over 630,000 Jews roughly from Western to Eastern Poland and the bringing in of 274,000 Germans. Of course this was not sufficient to keep up the economic life of the area, which contained necessary war-related industries; moreover, agriculture would be devastated. Seraphim suggested that Germans be brought in from Russia as well as from Germany proper to make up the losses, at least in part.[48] But this, too, would have been insufficient, even if it had been practicable. Seraphim's conclusions: immediate resettlement without immediate replacement means total economic standstill, since "indiscriminate deportation of Jews is economically disadvantageous." The main consideration was the demands of the economy, especially war production. Resettlement undertaken by independently acting local initiative was counterproductive. And (how little it takes to seem humane in this environment!) even though Seraphim's stated interest, too, was primarily the achievement of a higher level of productivity, "But it is also not a matter of indifference what happens to the deported people. . . . The Jews are kept occupied doing different kinds of forced labor; but we do not necessarily make economically purposive use of their energies."[49]

At about the same time as these situation reports were written, reports that are so critical of the scheme of deporting many to make room for a few, plans were worked out in greater and lesser detail—and some even carried out—to do just that. One such plan was the one discussed in the minutes of a meeting held November 8 in Krakow between the highest SS officials in Poland. SS Brigadier General Bruno Streckenbach, who had been assigned the central planning of the resettlement, revealed a master plan he had submitted to Himmler, to take the place of Himmler's original, apparently less stringent plan. It is possible that Streckenbach referred here to a directive from Himmler, dated October 30, in which Himmler ordered the deportation of all Jews from the formerly Polish provinces that had been incorporated into the Reich, to take place between November 1939 and February 1940, as well as the removal of certain groups of Poles from approximately the same areas.[50] Streckenbach's first recommendation was for closing off the eastern borders more effectively, since the Poles and Jews who had been shipped into the Government General, that is, the area between the Bug and the Vistula rivers, were again migrating westward. Streckenbach went beyond Himmler's declared intention to suggest, among other things, the removal of Jews and Poles from the Altreich as well, and gave an approximate figure of one million Jews and Poles to be evacuated by the end of February 1940; of these, 400,000 were to come from West Prussia. These were to be replaced by ethnic Germans, approximately 150,000, of whom 7,000 to 8,000 had already returned. Streckenbach would make arrangements for transport with the German railway to have trains ready by the middle of November, first of all for the deportation of Jews and Poles. Only after these West Prussian regions had been "cleared" to some extent, would the trains bring the ethnic Germans back to the homeland. He ruled out the use of highways because of the difficulties of guarding and otherwise taking care of the "undesirables." Finally, he went into detail regarding the bolting shut (*Abriegelung*) of the way back for the deportees.[51]

There exists also a telegram, dated November 10 and signed by Heydrich, this time from the Gestapo in Danzig, one of the important places from which Jews and Poles were to be deported. This telegram speaks of the plans as divided into a *Nahplan* (immediate plan) and a *Fernplan* (long-range plan, stated at that time to be the ultimate—secret—aim). The *Nahplan* (i.e., the immediate deportation of Jews and Poles) was to be administered locally and carried out by the Security Police who were to deal also with the tasks connected with the evacuation. The *Fernplan*, however, was to be planned "here" in Heydrich's office; it would be determined, with finality, from there, and would be binding for all the eastern provinces.[52] It is interesting that both Heydrich and Streckenbach refer to Himmler, the former apparently to Himmler's directive of October 30, Streckenbach to his own suggestions submitted to Himmler. The chronology is unclear, that is, whether Himmler received Streckenbach's suggestions before or after he sent his directive, whether Heydrich was aware of Streckenbach's plan, and whether his telegram was an indirect response to it. In any case, there seems to exist an underlying tension between Krakow and Danzig as to who was in charge, who had Himmler's ear, and so on. The only clue to how this tension was resolved lies in the absence of further communication from Streckenbach but many more from Heydrich. There is, in fact, a further order from Heydrich, dated November 28, this time from Berlin, addressed among others to Streckenbach, giving instructions on how to effect the *Nahplan*: 80,000 Jews and Poles were to be deported in the next two weeks from the Warthegau (one of the formerly Polish regions, newly incorporated into Germany) to make room for 40,000 Baltic Germans; 5,000 were to be sent away per day. Their selection was up to the local SD administration. The deportees would have to secure their own supplies.[53]

We can see from this sampling of plans, alternative plans, and even counterplans, none of which referred to the Nisko deportations nor seemed to be learning from them, how small a part in the overall resettlement action of 1939 the Nisko plan actually played. Yet the Nisko resettlement is paradigmatic of the general confusion regarding the treatment of "undesirables," is relatively well-documented, deals with the group of people who concern us most, and can teach us something about the role of the Jewish leadership at a time when

SS Brigadier General Bruno Streckenbach in ca. 1944. (Bundesarchiv Bild 183-R63691)

the rules of the next phase of the game played by the Nazis were not yet rigidly established, when there was no precedent for the Jewish leaders to go by and no one knew what to expect. Yet, before we can return to Vienna and the situation there, we must make one more excursion into the background of the action. This time we will look at its antecedents in Germany and what was foreshadowed by them.

Displacing Jews and Other "Undesirables"

We have already mentioned the plans, devised around the middle of September, to deport the Jews into the Government General. Heydrich's memorandum of September 21, 1939,[54] sent on the day on which the last meeting of the chiefs of the *Einsatzgruppen* of the SD took place and directed to them, is already quite detailed. It deals solely with the Jews although, as we have seen and will see again, Poles and other "undesirable" nationalities were also slated for deportation and were in fact deported. However, it contains a few items of special importance for us: first of all, the mention of an "ultimate goal" (*Endziel*) regarding the Jews, to be kept "strictly secret." This ultimate goal (not yet the same as the "final solution" (*Endlösung*), although the two terms are often conflated) is not stated explicitly here but can be assumed to be the goal of making Western and Central Europe *judenrein* (free of Jews) by shipping those Jews who survived all other brutalities to the Government General to live—and die—in their own colonies in a fashion presumably like what we know about the later ghettos. In order to carry out these "planned all-inclusive measures," an immediate goal had to be reached first. Here Heydrich specified the different regions he wanted totally cleared of Jews right away: Danzig (Gdansk), West Prussia, Poznan, and Eastern Upper Silesia. If total evacuation were impossible, then concentration in a few cities would be the alternative. In the remaining occupied territories, with the exception of the area to the east of Krakow and lying along the demarcation line where Jews were merely to be counted, a small number of places of Jewish concentration were to be established near railway junctions—an indication, perhaps, that this was to be no more than a temporary way station for the Jews of this region. The exclusion of the above-mentioned region from both "purification" as well as concentration may well indicate that this area had already been at least considered for the eventual settlement of the Jews.

An important feature that distinguishes the treatment accorded the Jews from others on the "unwanted" list was the establishment of *Jüdische Ältestenräte*, the Councils of Jewish Elders, which played such a pivotal as well as a frequently misunderstood role in Nazi policy and its execution. The main points pertinent to our present discussion are (1) the composition of the councils, consisting of rabbis and other leading personages; (2) their being constrained to assume full responsibility for carrying out Nazi orders; and (3) the counting and classifying of Jews. Also of interest is the reason to be given[55] for concentrating the Jews in the cities, which was, as we have seen, the ostensible reason for the circulation of Heydrich's memorandum, namely, that some Jews had allegedly participated in sniper attacks and plundering. It is difficult to see why Heydrich included this transparently mendacious reason, unless he was following the established pattern of making Jews responsible in this way, too, for what was to befall them, a pattern, as we have seen, so successful the previous year in the devastation of Kristallnacht. It also served to complement, in its own fashion, the responsibility placed on the bent shoulders of the Jewish Elders.

Another milestone in the displacement of the many to make room for the few is recorded by Rosenberg in his diary entry of September 29, 1939, mentioned earlier, in which he sets down his conversation with Hitler of that day. The latter preceded the outline of his plans with his characterization of Poles and Jews: "The Poles: a thin Germanic layer, below this, dreadful stuff. The Jews, the most horrible one could possibly imagine. . . . Only the hand of a lord and master, certain of its goal, could reign here." It was Hitler's plan, possibly suggested by Himmler, to concentrate "the whole of Jewry," including those of the Reich, as well as all elements considered unreliable in any way at all, between the Vistula and the Bug rivers. At the former border Hitler meant to create "a broad belt of Germanization and colonization," a German "bread basket," and a strong German peasantry, and to settle here "good Germans from the whole world." Between the Jews in the east and the "good Germans" in the west Hitler envisaged some approximation of a Polish state.[56] Truly a grandiose scheme!

Rosenberg received the bulk of this information later than some others in leading positions, for example, later than Walter von Brauchitsch, the head of the German military in Poland, who found out from Heydrich on the 22nd that there existed a plan to create a Jewish state under German administration near Krakow, in which other "undesirables" were also to be settled.[57]

At this early point in the war, Germany still held out for a peaceful settlement with the West, for an accommodation with England and France with the possibility of some kind of rudimentary Polish state remaining after Germany and Russia had helped themselves to the territories they wanted. Hence, settlement and resettlement plans for Jews and the other "undesirables" as well as for ethnic Germans remained relatively vague and tentative. But when the Allies did not swallow the bait dangled before them by Hitler in his "appeal for peace" on October 6, mentioned earlier, there was no more reason to hold back.

The first important act was to establish a chain of command. Heydrich had announced to the meeting of administrative chiefs of the RHSA (headquarters of the SS) and the heads of the *Einsatzgruppen* as early as September 21 that Himmler would be named "Settlement Commissar."[58] On the day following Hitler's speech, Himmler was officially installed as head of all matters pertaining to "the strengthening (*Festigung*) of German folkdom," with the charge to return the ethnic Germans to the Greater Reich, to eliminate (*ausschalten*) harmful influences (by now we know who is meant), and to create new areas for settlement. Himmler was given all powers necessary to carry out these interrelated programs and assumed the appropriate title of Reich-Commissar. He had thus become "the prime executive of Nazi Germany's [living-]space policy (*Raumpolitik*),"[59] especially since he already was in charge of the SS and was now able to draw on any other administrative units and individuals concerned with the east in order to carry out these policies. Within our present area and time frame, Heydrich worked closely with him or in his spirit, and Eichmann with Heydrich, his function in this matter being that of general director of planning and execution. And Eichmann, as Heydrich's subordinate, played one of the leading roles in planning as well as execution, having, by virtue of the structure of the SS organization considerable freedom of initiative in both. Yet, even now the chain of command must not be understood as monolithic; there was duplication and duplicity, contravention of orders, and individual initiative both to be exercised and to be squelched.

In any case, things were beginning to happen. Two memoranda from Berlin, dated October 6 and most likely authored by Eichmann,[60] are simultaneously prelude and first step in the wholesale elimination of the Jews in Germany and former Austria as well as in the Protectorate. The first memorandum deals with preparatory steps in Berlin, that is, making further lists from the lists of Jews from these areas, lists already in Nazi hands. Now these were to be organized geographically and according to the Jewish organizations to which these individuals were assigned. Maps had apparently been supplied by the Jewish communities, and these were to be brought up-to-date. The Jews possessing Polish citizenship who had already been arrested were to be entered on another list, which was to be put together by Gestapo offices, most likely those in whose prisons they were confined. A further step was the removal of Jews of foreign citizenship other than Polish and, perhaps most interesting, "extracting (*ausziehen*) the assets of the indigent Jews to be deported."[61] Apart from the now all-too-familiar expropriation of property even from those who hardly had any, we have here the first indication that poor Jews in particular were to be deported at this time. The lack of further explanations in this memo leads us to suspect that more explicit information must have been communicated in an undocumented way.

The second memorandum is more specific. It is based on an order given by Gestapo-Chief Heinrich Müller to plan for the deportation of 70,000 to 80,000 Jews from the district of Kattowitz (Katowice, Poland). For the time being they were to be deported eastward across the Vistula River. At the same time Jews from the Mährisch-Ostrau (Ostrava in Moravia) region could also be deported, as well as all Jews from Poland to be found there, who had tried to hide in this area because of the events of recent times. And now comes a paragraph whose ominous language seems to adumbrate what is to come and gives us a clue as to what the reason might be for this particular expulsion at this particular time: "This activity is to serve mainly to gain experience in order to be able, on the basis of the experiences gained in this way, to carry out the evacuation of larger masses."[62]

From our vantage point, knowing the fate that befell millions, an essential component of which was the deportation of large masses, we might be tempted to assume that these planned deportations were meant to be the prelude to the later mass deportations to the death camps. There is no evidence for this, especially since we have no indications from this early period that the so-called final solution had reached the actual planning stage. Rather, the scenario seems to be the following.

We have seen above the orders given and the first attempts made at a grand overall resettlement plan for the whole of Nazi-occupied Eastern Europe, in which all ethnic Germans were to be brought "home," to be resettled either in the Altreich, where there was little available space, or, in the main, in the eastern border regions of the now-expanded Greater Germany, populating those sections of what used to be Poland that (1) were the most fertile and thus most capable of supplying a livelihood for the new settlers, as well as (2) constituting a living bulwark against the Soviet east. In order to accomplish this, the desirable areas not decimated sufficiently in the course and bloody aftermath of the war had to be cleared of their undesirable populations, of all the Jews, most of the Poles, and other non-Germanic ethnic groups such as Gypsies or noncooperating Ukrainians, criminals including the intelligentsia (if these had somehow missed being shot), and so on. These, again, had to be shipped somewhere else, at least for the time being, either into cities or into malaria- and dysentery-infested swampy and unproductive regions where, the pious hope was, they would be decimated "naturally"; perhaps the Russians could be persuaded to look the other way when these people were driven into Russian territory, or the Russians could somehow be persuaded to take them.

And so the Jews were chosen over all other peoples once again, this time to be guinea pigs. Whether the idea of the Nisko project originated with Eichmann, as he claimed in Jerusalem, he was, as so often in his career, in the right place at the right time and knew how to take hold of a chance when he saw one. The war had made his lordship over the emigration process practically redundant once emigration had virtually dried up because of the war, and with it the work of his outfit, which at this time had its headquarters in Berlin and branches in Vienna, Prague, and at times in Mährisch-Ostrau. It thus appeared that Eichmann was in great danger of losing his extra incomes and extra perquisites. Now an entirely new field of endeavor opened up to him, and he saw its inherent possibilities: if not emigration, then relocation. The figures on his chess board were once more his to move. His expertise in emigration acquired mainly from Jewish functionaries, especially in Vienna, could be applied here. Having made himself an expert on the Jews in the eyes of his superiors, he also realized that of all the groups of "undesirables," the Jews were the ones least in a position to resist, yet they were the best organized. In short, they were the most vulnerable and hence best suited to be the first pawns to be moved in the grand scheme of reshaping the face of Europe. The experiences garnered during this first great exodus of Jews could then be applied to all the Jews, but by no means exclusively to them.

Why the figure of 70,000 to 80,000 was chosen is unclear. It certainly does not seem a workable figure, especially under the condition of an unsettled and totally unready country and population. Since neither of the memoranda of October 6 gives any projected dates for the completion of the action and the concurrent or subsequent collection of experiential data, we need not assume that the numbers mentioned constituted anything other than a figure high enough to impress local functionaries. Within three days, the projected figure became much higher, but the instructions were not any less vague.

Having sketched some telling features of the general context, the focus of our attention can return the Nisko interlude itself.

Preparations for Deportations and Cancellations Thereof

On October 18, the following item appeared in the *Mährisch-Schlesische Landeszeitung*, the new German newspaper of this region newly incorporated into Greater Germany:

> **Exodus of the Jews from the Ostrau Region**
>
> On Tuesday the male Jews of the Ostrau region were ordered by their IKG to report at two locations in Mährisch-Ostrau in order to be registered. They brought all their materials needed for emigration and thus they were deported from our region. In this way, a beginning has been made in Ostrau, which had once been so defamed as a "Jew-town," for a "general Jew-exodus," and Greater Ostrau is regaining the honest reputation of a city of work and honest commercial life. Surely no decent person will cry a single tear for the former rulers over the Ostrau economy of which they were, in actuality, only its parasites.[63]

The response to this article from German official quarters was immediate. The SD's daily report of October 19 from Mährisch-Ostrau, signed by Alois Brunner, includes the above newspaper item and reports that "exception was taken to it today by us and that, in the absence of the editor-in-chief, his deputy was ordered to come to this office this afternoon." He did not show up, but the editorial representatives of the Czech newspaper, who had also been "invited" but could not afford to ignore the invitation, did come and were instructed as follows: First of all, if they wanted to print articles about Jews, they had to check with Brunner's office. Further, what was reported in the *Landeszeitung* did not constitute an "exodus of the Jews from the Ostrau region," nor were the Jews being "deported."

> It was pointed out that the Jews who left today on the transport have merely been sent for *Umschichtung*[64] and are not constrained in their actions, nor do they stand under any kind of supervision by the authorities.
>
> This voluntary action on the part of the Jews, carried out by the IKG Mährisch-Ostrau, has, as has been mentioned, the purpose of *Umschichtung* and preparation for emigration. The settlement area is located within Reich-German territory and the Jews are not prevented from emigrating from there.[65]

This was the line handed to the editors by Brunner, presumably with a straight face, a line which they would do well to follow, no matter where the truth lay. For, as Murmelstein claimed, "at that stage . . . the Nisko action was passed off as a project of the Jewish organizations, as an attempt to further the occupational *Umschichtung* and the emigration of the Jews."[66]

What were the facts behind this fiction?

We have discussed the *Aktennotiz* of October 10, on which day the IKG was first informed of the planned deportation and the preparations to be made for it. It is only in the next-to-the-last sentence that a hint is given as to the general destination, that is, to Poland ("*nach Polen*"). However, there is no mention of what the deportees could expect once they got there. At this time Eichmann had not yet chosen the exact location of the camp, and on the basis of the Vienna documents of this time, there is no indication that a plan had been worked out regarding what the people were to do after they arrived. However, the Mährisch-Ostrau records tell us what, apparently, the Jewish leadership did not yet know or was not allowed to reveal. Three memoranda dated October 11 refer to meetings held on the 9th and deal with the deportation of Jews from Kattowitz (Katowice) and Mährisch-Ostrau (Ostrava). Even though Vienna is not mentioned, it is quite clear from the contents that they were also applicable to the Jews of Vienna (whom Eichmann quite possibly included in this action on his own initiative, since no records have been found thus far authorizing him to do so). It was a busy day for Eichmann and Rolf Günther, meeting with the Nazi civilian top administration of Kattowitz, with the military commander of that region, and also with the head of the Gestapo in Mährisch-Ostrau, a meeting in which Alois Brunner and Theodor Dannecker also participated. The two first-mentioned memoranda are signed by Günther, the third is signed by Dannecker. The first two, in which the respective authority is asked for cooperation (which is granted), tell of—for the time being—two planned transports each from Kattowitz and Mährisch-Ostrau. The experiences garnered from them are to be reported, the reports to be submitted to Himmler, who would most likely send them on to Hitler. For the time being, the memorandum states, "the Führer has ordered the *Umschichtung* of 300,000 indigent Jews from the *Altreich* and *Ostmark*." After these first transports there would be a waiting period until the general deportation of Jews is ordered. Eichmann also asks that Gauleiter Wagner be informed.[67]

At the conference in Mährisch-Ostrau, Eichmann divulged more details about the purpose of the transports and claimed that he was acting in accordance with SS Senior Colonel Müller of the Gestapo, Berlin. Here he spoke of only one "Jew-transport" each from Kattowitz and Mährisch-Ostrau, to be put together "soonest," in such a manner that these transports could be placed as advance troops, so to speak, in the area earmarked for the reception of the first transports, an area comprising the region Rozwadów-Annopol-Kraśnik-Southwest Lublin. This Jewish advance troop would have the task of erecting a barracks village, designed to serve as a transitory camp for all transports to follow.

That the accommodations would not be luxurious can be gleaned from another item in the memorandum, namely, that the IKG Ostrau had been ordered to submit building plans plus a list of necessary materials. This list was considered too generous, especially since Eichmann and associates "intend, on principle, to house the Jews in the barracks *zweischichtig*"—which can mean in two layers (upper and lower bunks) or in two shifts, one group to sleep by day, the other by night. Either or both might have been planned. "In any case," Dannecker concludes, "we can start off by cutting the estimate in half."

And how did Eichmann and Co. plan to finance the remaining 50 percent? With Jewish money, contributed voluntarily, of course: "The Jews in Mährisch-Ostrau contributed to the IKG in Mährisch-Ostrau—after prior appropriate instruction to the IKG by party member Brunner—RM 300,000 as a gift, out of their frozen accounts, the purpose being the construction of retraining (*Umschulung*) camps for the facilitation of emigration."[68] The process of deception coupled with pressure was in full swing.

The memorandum further states: "In distinction from the later transports, in which no consideration will be given to the age or sex of the Jews to be resettled, the Jewish advance troops will consist exclusively of less-well-off male Jews fully able to work." Then follow details about matters of a bureaucratic and practical nature, similar to what was demanded in Vienna, emphasizing, however, the role of the Jewish *Ordner*, that is, those Jews who would be responsible for the smooth functioning of the transports, right down to the kinds of check lists each *Ordner* would have to carry. The distribution of Jews in the trains is interesting in that the skilled workers were to travel as one group and the unskilled ones as another so that, at the destination point, the latter group could unload the building materials and the former could start putting up the barracks. Reading these instructions, one cannot but be impressed by the meticulous care with which all these details had been worked out, details that included the sources for building materials, cooperation between the transport command and the railway, the question of food and heating materials for the camp; and the exchange of the RM 300 to be brought along by each Jew into Złoty. This meticulousness merges into the ridiculous when we read that

> . . . prior to the departure of the transports a wooden board, measuring two meters, is to be put up on which are put small number tags—attached by means of thumb tacks—corresponding to the number of Jews to be shipped out, numbered backwards starting at the locomotive. . . . [T]he Jews intended for a particular car must line up in three rows . . . each *Ordner* has a list (one original, three copies) in a binder . . . in addition to lists (also in quadruplicate) regarding the content of each individual car transporting materials.[69]

According to Eichmann, Stahlecker had told him on October 10 (*sic*) that the *Reichsprotektor*, Konstantin von Neurath, had given his approval for the resettlement of the Jews in the Protectorate. His only condition was that their reception and/or distribution in Poland function perfectly—an interesting comment in light of later developments. There is a reference to Vienna hidden in this memorandum, namely, the *Zentralstellen* of Prague and Vienna are immediately to put together guard units for these transports. There seems to be no reason for the inclusion of Vienna if transports from there had not been planned, at least by Eichmann. This first transport is referred to as a *Mustertransport*, one that would function as model or pattern for the ones to follow. The end of this long memorandum deserves to be quoted verbatim:

> At the same time the Jews are to be handed an exact plan dealing with arrival for entrainment (by exact schedule) and for the entrainment itself. This plan serves to make their arrival as inconspicuous as possible and is meant to make the Jews themselves mainly responsible for

> its orderly execution. This is in the interest of preserving a certain "voluntary character" and is also necessary for achieving as inconspicuous a departure of the transport as possible. The Jews are to be told to appear "without dependents," i.e., no one is allowed to accompany them to the entrainment. All good-byes will have to be said inconspicuously.

Dannecker concludes the memorandum by stating:

> The IKG has to pay 50K for each Jew included in the transport. How they get this money is their business.[70]

The four men of Vienna who were ordered by Eichmann's office to report to Mährisch-Ostrau—Murmelstein, Storfer, Grün, and Boschan—all had some knowledge of organized emigration matters. The same can be said of Jakob Edelstein and Richard Friedmann, the two functionaries from Prague who received similar orders.

It was less than six months between the establishment of the Protectorate (in what was left of Bohemia and Moravia) and the outbreak of the war on September 1. During these months, the emigration of Jews from there had been desultory. The Nazis had fully expected the Vienna/Austria pattern to work in Prague/Protectorate as well, that the indigenous anti-Semitism, given free reign, would motivate the Jews to make a dash for the borders, and that all the Germans would have to do then would be to step in with a bit of a push and organization. This was, after all, the period when one of the instruments of the regime's foreign policy was to "export" political anti-Semitism by playing on ubiquitous traditional Jew-hatred. This sentiment was, of course, anything but absent in the Czech provinces. Yet, the liberal democracy that was the handiwork and legacy of Thomas Masaryk,[71] the founder and first president (1918–1935) of the Czechoslovak Republic, had left its imprint on the Czech mentality, and this was one reason for the failure of this particular Nazi policy.

There were also other reasons: The Czechs were themselves victims of the rapacity of Nazi Germany and of their abandonment by their allies, France and Great Britain. In effect, Nazi Germany found itself in the—up to this time—unprecedented situation of imposing its rule on an unfriendly population. In addition, Eichmann was so intent on the priority of making Austria *judenrein*, that he deliberately held back the emigration effort in Prague (as we have mentioned in the previous chapter). Furthermore, compared with Vienna and Austria, the Germans took their time in imposing their organization on Prague and the Protectorate. And finally, the persons who were put in the position of forced leadership in Prague were in their own way prepared for a leisurely, measured pace of emigration.

These leaders from Prague were, in the main, functionaries of Zionist organizations. As such, their conception of emigration was oriented almost exclusively toward fostering the Jewish settlement of Palestine, and especially toward preparing young pioneers for the agricultural development of that country. Even though the Czech Zionists were at odds with the community of those who regarded themselves as Czech national Jews (in German *Tschecho-Juden*), the offices of both groups in Prague were, in fact, in the Jewish community building. In Vienna, it will be recalled, the IKG and the Palamt were separate. In time, the two Prague groups would, in effect, function in unison, especially at the insistence of the Nazi authorities. Among the group of Zionist leaders Edelstein was the youngest; but he was very energetic, and he soon was the group's main contact vis-à-vis the Nazi authorities. At first he and his companions had reservations about dealing with the Germans. They soon found out, however, that the choice was not theirs. They were functioning not at the sufferance of the German authorities but under their mandate. Within six weeks of the occupation of Prague—and of Britain's issuance of the White Paper of 1939 limiting Jewish immigration to Mandatory Palestine—Edelstein was sent to Palestine to obtain immigration possibilities for Czech Jews, with negative results. In the summer of 1939, it was time for the Germans to proceed more vigorously with the execution of their Jewish policy in the Protectorate. The expected pogroms against the Jews on the part of the indigenous population failed to materialize; hence, the Nazis did not have this excuse by which to impel the Jews to emigrate. The Nazis, and specifically Eichmann, had to revert to the other weapons in their arsenal. There were the discriminatory laws, the registration of property, Aryanization, and so on. Plans were afoot to concentrate the Jewish population of the Protectorate, which was more widely scattered than that of Austria; to bring them all to Prague proved to be impracticable, but they were confined to a few urban localities. Therefore, Eichmann set up a Prague *Zentralstelle für jüdische Auswanderung* (Center for Jewish Emigration), accompanied by the requirement of a daily quota of would-be emigrants, a figure twice as high as what could possibly be achieved. Other *Zentralstellen* were established in Mährisch-Ostrau (Ostrava), where the Zionist Otto Zucker was the leading Jewish functionary, and in Brünn (Brno). Since Edelstein seemed to be ineffective in organizing the emigration of the Jews, Eichmann did two things. First, he summoned Storfer to Prague for a brief visit to facilitate and coordinate Edelstein's arrangements for whatever group transports to Palestine he was able to organize. Second, Eichmann ordered one of Murmelstein's most able assistants in the IKG Vienna's emigration effort to Prague to organize the indispensable Jewish side of the emigration procedures. He was Richard Friedmann, who was still in his twenties. Friedmann arrived in Prague at the end of August, a few days before the war brought emigration to a halt.

In short: The intense and relentless pressure on the Jews to leave, which we know from Vienna, was not applied in Prague during the brief time preceding the outbreak of the war. The leading functionaries of the IKG Vienna responded to this pressure by saving their Jews through a brisk emigration process and by reducing their persecution through developing and maintaining appropriate working relations with the Nazi authorities. The pressure as well as the response to it were also lacking in Prague.

In fact, Edelstein soon harbored the illusion that the reason for the low level of persecution in Prague and the deliberate way in which emigration from the Protectorate was proceeding was due to his taking a strong stand vis-à-vis the Nazis, in evident distinction from the unfortunate conjunction in Vienna of a submissive leadership and the resulting harshness of persecution and precipitous emigration.[72] At least, he told as much to Moshe Shertok when he met him in Geneva in February 1940, a few weeks after the end of the Nisko episode. At that time, he was desperate to find, somewhat late in the game, immigration opportunities for his Jews and to secure funding from organizations such as the Joint (the American Jewish Joint Distribution Committee). We find it hard to believe that in evaluating both situations, those in Vienna and in Prague, he was simply succumbing to the logical fallacy of *post hoc ergo propter hoc*. It seems more plausible that by discrediting the performance of the Viennese functionaries, Edelstein wished to make his own creditable.

By virtue of his reassignment to Prague, Friedmann constituted, together with Edelstein, the Czech contingent of the panel of six experts in emigration matters who were meant to form, at least at the beginning, the cadre of Jewish leaders in charge of the resettlement whose location had at that point—October 10—not been determined.

Once they arrived in Mährisch-Ostrau (in Czechoslovakia), the four functionaries from Vienna and the two from Prague were to report to the *Zentralstelle*. However, even though we know that SS Captain Rolf Günther gave the order, we have two versions about to whom they were to report. According to the *Aktennotiz* by Löwenherz of October 10, they were to report to Eichmann;[73] according to a memorandum from Mährisch-Ostrau regarding these functionaries,[74] as well as according to the letter of summons each of them received individually,[75] they were to meet with Günther, which they did as a group on October 16.[76] In this *Aktennotiz*, dated October 13, the purpose of their trip is spelled out, namely, to participate in the first transport, the one from Mährisch-Ostrau.[77] The purpose of the transport is mentioned neither in the Löwenherz *Aktennotiz* nor in the summonses.

Löwenherz was extremely loath to lose, even if only temporarily, his right-hand man, Murmelstein. He knew enough by then to consider that one could not be sure that any of the four would return at the promised time, and immediately mentioned his reservations regarding Murmelstein's absence to Günther, asking that he be allowed to remain in Vienna. He was told that Murmelstein should go along with the others for a few days, but to submit a petition that Murmelstein be allowed to return to Vienna.[78] This Löwenherz did, saying that "Dr. Murmelstein is directly attached [to the office of] the Director [i.e., Löwenherz] and participates in an outstanding manner in all the jobs involving great responsibility." Löwenherz went on to detail some of the recent projects Murmelstein had been involved in and then threw in a phrase that has given offense to some historians, such as Adler, namely, that Murmelstein could perform "very valuable services in the resettlement of the Jews from Vienna to Poland." Adler criticizes this sentence, as well as the whole tenor of the petition, by saying that Löwenherz's "servility seems to go a bit far, especially the reference to the 'very valuable services' of [his] protégé on the occasion of a 'resettlement' to Poland would have been better left unsaid."[79] Adler seems to read some sinister implications especially into this latter phrase and thus to throw a shadow on Löwenherz's stewardship. But if we discount our hindsight regarding "settlement in Poland," the remark, within its context, is more likely a desperate casting around, on the part of Löwenherz, for an especially good reason—at least in the eyes of Günther—for leaving Murmelstein where he was, rather than the example of eager Jewish collaboration that Adler sees in it.

Finally, Löwenherz summarizes his arguments by stating that "Dr. Murmelstein belongs to the few persons who are indispensable for the administration of the IKG in Vienna." Since there was no pressure on Löwenherz to plead for Murmelstein in this manner, we must assume that he described the latter's role correctly or, at the very least, that he saw his role in this light. Murmelstein, in our interviews with him, stated categorically and repeatedly that, unhappy and worried as he was about this new assignment, he never asked

Löwenherz to intercede on his behalf. To give extra weight to his request, Löwenherz mentioned that he would be prepared to suggest a replacement for Murmelstein. On the following day Löwenherz submitted a petition to this effect, nominating Robert Prochnik, Murmelstein's young and able assistant, to go instead of Murmelstein.[80] Murmelstein told us that Prochnik actually volunteered to take his place,[81] but Löwenherz kept this fact from Günther because Günther definitely wanted Murmelstein to go and because Murmelstein refused Prochnik's offer.

Günther forwarded the petition to Eichmann in Mährisch-Ostrau, repeating Löwenherz's contention that without the "Jew Murmelstein" the apparatus of the IKG is endangered and that he "supposedly cannot be replaced by anyone."[82] However, after Günther discussed the matter with Eichmann, the order stood, and the original four designees from Vienna left for Mährisch-Ostrau on October 16. We will soon see how they fared.

In the meantime, Eichmann finally set out to find a site for the camp. He took with him *Oberführer* Stahlecker, and both flew to Warsaw on October 12 to continue their search in style—in two requisitioned cars, one Mercedes and one Lancia. As Günther outlined the purpose of their trip, they were going to find a suitable territory, investigate the availability of food and possibilities for housing, and determine the route and final destination of the train transport.[83] Somehow, the problems of food and housing were swept under the rug; and it is open to question what the term "suitable" means as applied to the territory they finally settled on. However, on October 15 Eichmann was able to wire from Krakow to Günther in Mährisch-Ostrau: "Train station for transports is Niesko (*sic*) on the San."[84] This piece of information was all that was necessary to get the trains rolling.

But Vienna, Mährisch-Ostrau (Ostrava), and Kattowitz (Katowice) were not the only places anxious to get rid of their "undesirables." There is an interesting exchange between Oberführer Arthur Nebe, head of the Security Police in Berlin, trying to get hold of the peripatetic Eichmann in order to find out how quickly he could get rid of "his" gypsies. His first call for help came by telephone to Mährisch-Ostrau on October 12; in a plaint strongly reminiscent of the situation in Vienna, he said: "If the deportation of the Berlin Gypsies in particular were to be delayed for a longer period of time, the city of Berlin would be forced to build special camps for the Gypsies, which could be done only at great expense and with even greater difficulties." Nebe wanted to be called back.[85] The reply sent to him by telegram on the 16th and signed by Eichmann gives us an idea of Eichmann's plans as well as of the impression he wanted to convey to Berlin:

> Regarding the Gypsies . . . on Oct. 20, 1939, the first transport of Jews will leave Vienna. 3–4 wagonloads of Gypsies can be attached to this transport.
>
> Continuous transports are now leaving regularly for the time being from Vienna . . . Mährisch-Ostrau . . . Kattowitz. . . . The simplest method is . . . to attach a few cars of Gypsies to each transport. Since these transports take place, as it were, according to a train schedule, we can expect a smooth execution of this matter.
>
> Regarding tackling the Altreich I can report that this will not take place until 3 or 4 weeks from now.[86]

What is of particular interest in this telegram is the choice of language by Eichmann. He makes it sound as if transports were already being sent even though not a single one had left as yet. But Eichmann did not intend to be questioned closely on this matter by Nebe and became unavailable, in part due to his trip east, from which, however, he returned on October 15. On the 18th Hstf. Braune, apparently an aide of Nebe's, called again to complain that nothing had been heard from Eichmann, not even that the telegram had arrived. He spoke to Günther, who assured him that Eichmann had tried in vain to reach Nebe or his assistant on the 17th by telephone from Mährisch-Ostrau. After reading the telegram to Braune, Günther suggested the next transport from Mährisch-Ostrau on the 25th for the Gypsies, since the first one had left "today," consisting of 901 Jews. Apparently, it never came to that, since there are no further communications from Nebe's office nor any evidence that Gypsies were ever sent to Nisko or even as far as Vienna from Berlin. There was some talk in Vienna of sending Gypsies along with the Jews, but Viennese Gypsies were meant, and even they never joined the Nisko exodus. None of the Nisko returnees questioned remembered seeing any evacuated Gypsies in or near the camp.

Even before Eichmann set off to find a site for the camp, Günther was already arranging with the transport command for a train, consisting of thirty-three freight cars and seventeen coaches, to transport the first group of deportees plus building materials from Mährisch-Ostrau, scheduled to leave on the 18th. At the same time, he gave notice that another transport, this one from Kattowitz, was scheduled for the 20th. Günther invoked the name of Hitler and called the transport "an attempt at the resettling of Jews ordered by the Führer." He also mentioned all the other high administrators who had promised full cooperation. It would have been hard to refuse him, and the railway carriages were promised. Nonetheless, one can sense a certain lack of enthusiasm if not actual reluctance on the part of the railway authorities, especially in light of the fact that the exact route could not yet be planned. However, Günther wanted at least the freight cars in place so that the loading of the building materials could begin as quickly as possible.[87]

The IKG in Mährisch-Ostrau was also active during this preparatory stage; even the head of the youth department, Hanna Steiner, was employed in an activity that was becoming so dear to the Nazis, the making of lists of Jews. Parts of a report sent by Steiner to the *Zentralstelle* may be enlightening:[88] "I am just now finishing the desired register of citizens of the Protectorate arranged alphabetically and according to sex. I take the liberty of mentioning that the lists were made with carbons." He goes on to explain that because of "untrained help mistakes have crept in," which he is trying frantically to correct and promises to hand in the corrected sheets as they are finished. "I ask you to exchange [the corrected copies] for the originals so that I can correct these also."

"I am working at this time on lists of men between 17 and 35 and 36 to 60 years of age and am as far as the letter 'K'. Even before I finish these two lists, work will begin on the male artisans. I shall take the liberty of asking you personally what other lists you would like. . . ." How pleased they must have been at the *Zentralstelle* that their strategy towards the Jews was paying off in such naive attempts at cooperation, coupled with the hope of thereby ameliorating the harsh treatment!

In his report, Wilhelm Bienenfeld makes a point of stating that Löwenherz, "*contrary to his orders to make short shrift of assigning* [Jews to the transports to Poland], *called for voluntary participation*."[89] While it is difficult to reconstruct precisely how the men were finally chosen for the two transports from Vienna, and hence to establish to what extent this action can be called "voluntary," there is no reason to doubt Löwenherz's desire to keep the action voluntary, and we have seen previously that the Nazis had a stake in preserving this appearance vis-à-vis the outside world.

We do not know how many people responded to Löwenherz's urging nor how many of those were actually eligible under the guidelines laid down by the *Zentralstelle* as well as in light of the concern on the part of the IKG not to send men who would not be up to a labor transport going east. We also must not lose sight of the fact that the term "voluntary" is to be understood here as a mere relative term in distinction from other methods that could have been—and later were—applied, including rounding up people off the street, as well as from their homes, and shipping them off directly.

A summons, undated but sent out prior to October 17 by the IKG Vienna and apparently addressed to men eligible for Nisko, states:

> By order of the authorities a large transport of Jews 18–50 years old and able to work will leave for Poland for the purpose of initiating colonization work.
>
> You have been proposed by the authorities [for this transport] and therefore have to appear on October 17 at 2:00 p.m . . . at the IKG. . . .
>
> If, contrary to expectation, you were not to obey this summons ordered by the governmental authorities, you will have to ascribe to yourself all ensuing consequences.
>
> Attention! Attention! Even persons who have already reported must *unconditionally* obey this summons.[90]

Obviously, there was an earlier invitation issued by the IKG to apply for participation in this transport, and a number of people must have responded and made voluntary application. It seems that the quota demanded by the *Zentralstelle* for these transports had not been filled; and it is for this reason that the summonses containing the cited passage were sent out by the IKG to men who would fit the requirements, and most likely had to be sent on orders from the *Zentralstelle*. The people to whom the summons was sent have only been "proposed" (*in Aussicht genommen*), not selected. There were, as we have seen, reasons to be exempt from this transport, such as age, infirmity, the possibility of immediate emigration, and having a job or a pension.

There is no indication as to whether this summons pertains to the first or the second transport. Adler assumes that the first transport is meant,[91] but certain considerations seem to point to the second: The first indication of the official date of the first transport is the *Aktennotiz* dated October 16 that, according to Günther, the transport was to leave on Wednesday, October 18.[92] Even if the IKG had immediately informed the candidates for the transport, they could not possibly have gotten all their papers together, including passport photos, and made all necessary preparations (i.e., giving up their homes, selling their furniture and other nonportable goods) to be ready to leave by the 18th. And even though the Nazis had no compunctions about making life difficult for the Jews, they would have been practical enough not to set such an unreasonable deadline. Not until the *Aktennotiz* of October 17 do we read that Günther announced that the first transport would not leave until the 20th.[93]

We recall that in the matter of the Gypsies, Eichmann's wire to Nebe of October 16 states that the first transport from Vienna would leave on the 20th. It is quite possible that

Günther already knew of this date when he spoke to the author of the *Aktennotiz* of October 16 but still gave the date as the 18th, perhaps to increase the pressure on the Jews. In any case, the timeframe involved makes the summons more likely to refer to the second transport than to the first.

Rosenkranz quotes two paragraphs from what he states is an information sheet sent to the individual participants on the first transport.[94] This sheet gives no clues as to the voluntary nature of the project; indeed, Rosenkranz uses it to emphasize the pressures applied to the participants on this transport. We can imagine the immediately sobering effect the following passages must have had, especially on the eager volunteers who had, rightly or wrongly, invested so much of their hopes in this venture:

> We are obliged to bring to your attention most emphatically that your absenting yourself from the transport would be connected with the gravest difficulties for you. If you were to fail to appear at the collection point at the correct time, you would be fetched from your apartment by the police authorities.
>
> We beg you to be convinced that everything possible is being done, on the part of the IKG, that can be done in order to ameliorate the hardships that are unavoidable in the case of such a transport. It is in the interest of all participants for each and every one of them to avoid anything that could cause difficulties for himself or his companions.

Even within the context of the general situation in Vienna this seems rather strong language at the very beginning of the venture, even before anyone had lived through or observed the send-off of the first group, and before any reports of hardship on the road or on arrival had trickled back from the east. And yet, it is said that people volunteered for the second transport. How can we reconcile this with the demand, on the part of Günther—related in the above-mentioned *Aktennotiz* of October 16—that the list, which had been submitted and from which a number of people had to be eliminated due to physical disability or other reasons, had to be brought up to a thousand again? "This number," said Günther, "must leave on Wednesday." How did Löwenherz get replacements at such short notice? All we do know is that the number of deportees from Vienna on October 20 was 912, almost one hundred less than Günther had insisted on. Still, somehow, there were many who took part in this as well as in transports to Nisko other than from Vienna, who should not have been allowed to go for reasons of age, ill health, or infirmity.

We do have an apparent confirmation, from Brunner of the *Zentralstelle*, of the voluntary nature of the first transport. In a memorandum dated October 23 and addressed to two officers of the SS, he states, among other things, "The participants of the first transport consisted of volunteers."[95] However, this statement must be taken with a grain of salt, not only for the reasons given above but also because the Nazis were, at this stage, concerned about creating and preserving the myth of the voluntary nature of the settlement. Stretching the truth had never posed much of a problem for the Nazis at any level of the hierarchy and was as common—though not as deadly in its effect—in interactions between party members as between them and the Jews.

We must mention the crowning piece of misinformation to accompany the first transport to Nisko: "[Rolf] Günther stated to Dr. Löwenherz at the railway station: The people who are leaving would be grateful to him, they are going into ordered working conditions, will be sufficiently and well fed and housed, and Dr. Löwenherz can completely set his mind at rest about the fate of the people."[96] However, two days earlier Brunner, in a memorandum addressed to Eichmann and others—that is, not for the consumption of the Jews—was closer to the truth:

> After completion of the barracks village in Nisko, the Jews who arrived with the first transport will be distributed on a continuous basis [*fortlaufend*] into the former Jewish villages in the area or into the interior of the country. . . . Besides, each transport is accompanied by 25 police officers under the leadership of a police chief, who must prevent by force of arms any danger of flight.[97]

The discrepancy is obvious. For the Nazis the scheme was a manipulative fiction. And yet, the reality of what awaited the people once they arrived in Nisko was even worse that what the Nazis projected.

In this memorandum, Brunner does not speak about the "voluntary" nature of the transport (since the memo was meant for Eichmann's eyes, he surely could dispense with fancy) but mentions that "the transports are put together by the IKG Vienna . . . and [that] Jewish transport leadership is responsible for the transport." There is, however, an insertion in parentheses after "Vienna" that is puzzling and even ominous in tone, that is, "as long as this is still possible." Does this mean that the IKG would run out of eligible people and that the *Zentralstelle* would take over the deportations? Or that Brunner foresees the IKG itself being dissolved and sent to Nisko? Or is this remark of little importance? What we do know is that the municipal government of Vienna expected to be rid of all of its Jews in the near future and was willing to do anything to bring this about.

It is possible that Brunner was taking his cue from a conference on October 16 between Eichmann, Ebner of the Gestapo Vienna, and Becker from Bürckel's office, at which Eichmann was told that he had been given "all full authorizations" by Bürckel "personally" for the Polish resettlement action. Bürckel, as Becker explained, "had even asked to accelerate the resettlement from Vienna." And Becker promised to remove any and all obstacles to the resettlement by going directly through Bürckel. The obstacles he mentions are those of a bureaucratic nature as well as delays caused by putting together the trains, obtaining the police escort, procuring food, *Erfassung* of Jews, which means, laying hold of them either physically or through registration, and getting extra help from the housing office. The latter was an important consideration since the Jewish apartments, and whatever was left in them, had to be secured for the right people and "wild Aryanization" had to be prevented. Indeed, according to Becker, all of the Jewish real estate in Vienna was to be handed to a trust company that would give the proper payments to the *Zentralstelle*. This, too, would prevent a "precipitous Aryanization" of the abandoned real estate. If these measures were not taken, said Ebner, reiterating Becker's argument and emphasizing it most strongly, then "November [1938] conditions" could arise, that is, the unauthorized masses could enter the Jewish premises and help themselves to all the goodies left behind rather than have them go to the privileged few.

Ebner further promised "to reroute the whole apparatus at his disposal for the resettlement and to take proper measures in the *Erfassung* of the Jews." Even the Jews in Viennese jails would go; he would arrange for all the imprisoned Jews to be sent in the second transport. He even wanted to include the stateless Jews, who were also in custody but were not under criminal jurisdiction, to be put into the second transport and to send the ones from the concentration camps directly.[98]

The prospect of sending along these unfortunates and thus filling the quota for the second transport was held out to Löwenherz during his meeting with Brunner on October 23.[99] However, we do not know to what extent, if at all, this ever came about, or whether they were the ones to bring the final number of deportees up to the 672 who, according to Rosenkranz, left on the second transport.[100]

There had been a lot of discussion between Brunner and Rolf Günther on the one side and the IKG on the other regarding the number of deportees, the *Zentralstelle* holding out for 1,000—indeed, as we have seen, they wanted five transports of 1,000 people each during the next two weeks. Even before the first transport left, there were already plans being made and carried out for the further transports. On October 17 two meetings took place, one between Brunner and Löwenherz, the other between Günther and "the undersigned"[101] who might have been Engel. At this time the second transport was still scheduled to leave on October 24, and a third was projected for the 27th—in all 3,000 able-bodied men were meant to be deported within eight days.

Günther wanted a projection of how many people could still be procured for Poland, and the IKG came up with the approximate number of 500. This was not good enough for him, and he ordered that the exact number be submitted to him by 9 o'clock the following morning, a number that then would have to be adhered to under all circumstances. To Günther's question why the original number given to him of 830 people was not being adhered to, he was told that the list had originally been drawn up on the basis of voluntary enrollments. In the subsequent medical examinations of the candidates, it turned out that about 300 among them were in such poor physical—and some even mental—condition that they were totally unfit for a labor transport; in short, the IKG functionary argued that the inclusion of the unfit would constitute a grave liability for this transport and the work it was to do.

The argument that these people would suffer grievous bodily and, in some cases, psychological harm was not advanced. No doubt questioning their potential contribution to the efficiency of the camp was a better bargaining chip. But that, too, did not work. Günther could not be budged, having apparently lowered his expectation to 830 from 1,000, and gave the order to replace the dropouts with other people. Should this prove impossible, the people who had applied in the first place would have to be put back on the transport list without consideration for their condition.[102]

This is a very important order in the light of later developments because it puts the aims of the Nazis into proper perspective. At least from where we stand now, it is evident that the first concern of Günther et al. was not the creation of a viable living space but a dumping ground for the Jews, and that the idea of the work camp was merely a front, window dressing to fool the gullible Jews and anyone else who might care about what happened to them. Did the "undersigned" at that point catch a glimpse of what was really in store for the men going east? Did he—and others, with whom he shared this information—feel that they had been cheated and had, in turn, albeit unknowingly, cheated those who relied on them and would have to continue to do so to meet the demands of the Nazi authorities? Again, we do not know.

On the same day, October 17, Löwenherz had a meeting with Brunner, who demanded an exact list of all Jews still in Vienna up to age 55 who met the qualifications for a work transport, and he reiterated that at least five transports had to leave within two weeks. Löwenherz asked permission to reduce the number of participants since it was impossible to assemble this great number unless wives and children could go along and be counted among the 1,000. But Brunner was not amenable to this, and for each of the next two transports he insisted on a thousand males only. He did promise to boost the numbers of those eligible by adding inmates of Dachau and Buchenwald. As we have seen, Brunner knew that Ebner and the Gestapo were prepared to send inmates directly from the concentration camp to Poland. Löwenherz now asked permission for these to return home to be outfitted by their families.[103] Brunner's positive reply to this request came at Löwenherz's meeting with him on October 23, as mentioned above, when Engel was also present. They brought statistical tables with them to show that they had signed up 600 men for the next transport and asked once more for a reduction in the number. The reason, given in greater detail than before, was no longer a dearth of volunteers but of healthy men in this age group, who did not live in mixed marriages or did not have a chance at emigration in the very near future either to the United States or to Palestine. Things would change when wives and children could come along. "In spite of the greatest exertions and most rigorous examination of those who were summoned [to the IKG and who claimed exemption], 2,000 men per week cannot be assembled, older men could only be considered if their wives could accompany them, since these men are, for the most part, ill and need nursing care." The deep impression made on Brunner by these arguments can be gauged by his response, namely, to fill up the second transport to 1,000 "tomorrow" and to prepare for the third transport.[104]

Löwenherz and Engel also told Brunner that the IKG had made itself highly unpopular among the Jewish population by organizing these transports. But it was willing to suffer this "odium" in order to help people in their preparations for the journey and to make it possible for them to take along the luggage and money allowed.[105] Of course Brunner did not respond to this at all; it was none of his concern. But for us, this circumstance is significant, for it shows that the original enthusiasm among the people for this project had faded; even without reports from the front lines, as it were, people saw how quickly volunteering brought about coercion and hardship. And the IKG had no message of hope or optimism to counter suspicion and accusation. All it could do—and did—was to try to ameliorate the hardships of deportation, a role that would be forced on it so many times in the ensuing years.

There is another *Aktennotiz* from the time immediately prior to the second transport of a meeting on October 25 between Brunner and Prochnik, Murmelstein's assistant, an unusual circumstance in itself. This *Aktennotiz* differs from the others by its brevity and also by the subtle difference in the tone in which it was written. We hear no attempt to please the "Master," and its terseness and bluntness, typical for Prochnik himself, sounds refreshing. Apparently, Prochnik brought another 145 passport applications for the second transport, whereupon "Herr Brunner demanded the supplementation [of applications] up to 1,000. . . . I said to this that this figure cannot be reached, rather only about another 60 applications can be prepared. Herr Brunner repeated the demand for 1,000 . . . or else the *Zentralstelle* would take other measures. . . for Tuesday, Oct. 31, a transport of 1,000 men has to be put together. To this I said that such a number cannot be found."[106]

As it turned out, Brunner had merely been bluffing about making up the number of deportees to 1,000, nor did the other threatened transports come off. The third one, due to leave on the 28th, was first postponed to the 31st and then canceled, as were all subsequent ones to Nisko, albeit not without causing great hardship to those who had been selected for it. For in the meantime, people, including pregnant women and women with children, slated for this nonexistent transport, were housed in a shelter for the homeless after having been forced to give up everything except their luggage and the money permitted to them, which by now had been raised to RM 400. They were still there on November 8, when Löwenherz was told that the transports to Poland had been stopped until February. The men had to continue staying at the shelter, ostensibly for a transport being prepared, but Löwenherz managed to get at least the pregnant women and those with children eliminated from this transport and secured permission for them to leave the shelter and return to their previous accommodations.[107]

Why were these men still kept in the shelter? Did Eichmann want to assert his power, save face, or did he not know what to do with them? The last seems least likely, since he would have had no compunction about simply putting them out into the street, which is more or less what he did a month later. Rather, it seems that he was trying to push through at least one more transport, as he had managed to do from Mährisch-Ostrau (Ostrava). There is some evidence that Eichmann was still trying to clear Vienna of its Jews at this time, as he had promised to do, counting on the promised help of Bürckel and the Vienna Gestapo. Apparently he also relied on information received from Brunner to the effect that individual transports from Vienna could still be attached to prisoner transports. Hence, he continued to prepare for this third transport, which, however, failed to materialize despite his and Bürckel's efforts.[108] This hope on Eichmann's part would also help to explain the elaborate fairy tale he foisted on Löwenherz on October 27 about Nisko, which he made Löwenherz pass on to the Jews of Vienna[109] (we discuss this matter at the end of this section).

In any case, these men were still in the shelter on December 12, since an *Aktennotiz* of this date states that Engel, as the representative of Dr. Löwenherz, who was in Holland at the time, was informed that the shelter where the last people chosen for the transport to Poland were still living had to be cleared by January 15. By this date, all the men remaining there would have had to have immediate emigration possibilities. Were the IKG unable to secure these for the men by this date, they would be shipped to Buchenwald.[110]

Finding the "Right" People to Deport

As we leave the Viennese Jews on their ill-fated journey to Nisko—or rather Zarzecze, as the actual site of the camp was called, Nisko being the nearest railway station—and before we take another look at the situation as it developed at the camp, we ought to clarify an aspect of the situation that was peculiar to Vienna and did not apply to Kattowitz (Katowice) and Mährisch-Ostrau (Ostrava), the other two collection points for Nisko. It is the question of the actual availability in Vienna of men eligible for these transports and how this compared with the situation at the other two locations. Vienna had been in the midst of an extremely vigorous emigration effort when the war brought all this activity to a virtual standstill. And of course, the first to leave, after the Anschluss and until the outbreak of the war, belonged to the age cohort that would have been needed for the Nisko enterprise, which included the ones who were still young and adventurous enough not to hesitate pulling up roots, those poor or at least poor enough not to have to worry about liquidating assets, and those still unencumbered by families and not burdened with parents too old to emigrate yet too young to be left forever. In addition, there were those who had just the skills that made them at least somewhat attractive to potential host countries, which were the skills most in demand for Nisko. Many of the younger men had wasted no time after the Anschluss and especially after Kristallnacht to find a border to be crossed illegally, a mountain pass to be scaled in the dark of night, or a berth in the Aliyah Bet to be preferred to a plank-bed in Dachau or Buchenwald.

On the whole, Mährisch-Ostrau and especially Kattowitz still had considerable pools of younger men, poor or impoverished by recent events. The IKG of Mährisch-Ostrau and other Czech communities had just begun to gear up for emigration, while the men of Kattowitz (in Polish Silesia) never had the chance to do so. There the age spread among the Jewish population had not altered substantially, and there was no preponderance of the old and infirm or of women and children.

Events surrounding the dispatching of the Nisko transports took a rather chaotic turn during these last few days of October. Attempts have been made to sort them out, for example, by Goshen and Murmelstein, but since these tend to present us with a more orderly picture than is warranted, a more or less chronological survey of some salient documents may serve to illuminate the nature of these events with all their confusing and contradictory turns.

There is an—unfortunately undated—transcript of a conversation between Rolf Günther (Mährisch-Ostrau [Ostrava]) and Zimmermann (Brünn [Brno]) regarding a transport of about 300 Jews from Brünn to be added to a Mährisch-Ostrau transport. Most likely this was the first transport from there since, according to information dated October 24, the second one from Brünn was attached, in turn, to the second Kattowitz transport. The cars with these Brünn Jews were attached to a regularly scheduled train, the transcript tells us, and the trip would take about seven hours.[111] We have no further information as to why Jews from so far away should also have been sent at this time, but it would indicate that Mährisch-Ostrau and Kattowitz were collection points for their regions, for the Moravian portion of the Protectorate in the one case and for the formerly Polish portion of Silesia in the other. This highlights another difference between these regions and the situation in Austria, where practically all of the Jews were concentrated in Vienna.

Günther asked some interesting questions of Zimmermann that point to another concern of the Nazis, namely, that only the right kind of people be sent. He wanted to make sure that no Jews who had foreign citizenship were included from Brünn and had Zimmermann go over the lists once more to make sure. Of course, Czech and Polish Jews were no longer foreigners. Furthermore, "Berlin does not wish that Jews who are married to an Aryan woman and have children with her be deported." Here Zimmermann had to admit that there were about 50 men included who fell into this category, and Günther told him in no uncertain terms to take them off the list. Günther also asked whether war invalids and other invalids with 60 percent disability or seriously ill persons were slated to go. This Zimmermann denied. But now he revealed that he had included 25 percent women in the transport as well as about 20 to 30 children over six years of age; however, as he reassured Günther, "all of them healthy and fit to work." Günther quashed this, too, since for the time being only males would be allowed to be sent, even if the women and children, as Zimmermann had to admit, had Polish citizenship. Günther admonished Zimmermann once more to check the nationality as well as the mixed marriage status of the deportees.[112]

A teleprinter conversation of October 18 and a *Tagesbericht* (daily report) dated the 19th, from the SD in Mährisch-Ostrau, deal with some difficulties connected with the deportation.[113] Of special note in the cited *Tagesbericht* of October 19 are certain reports by the IKG Mährisch-Ostrau. According to them, a number of well-to-do Jewish women left Mährisch-Ostrau with their children "in the direction of the Protectorate." It is unclear where these people went, since there is no further record of them. Also, "wild rumors" were being spread regarding the transport that had just left, namely, that it was still standing on a railway spur 7–8 km outside of Mährisch-Ostrau and that the deportees were being used for forced labor (i.e., road building). They were supposed to be extremely badly housed and fed. The IKG was told to find out the names and addresses of the people spreading these rumors and to report them.

Another item in this *Tagesbericht* deals with the registration of Jewish women and children by the IKG Mährisch-Ostrau. For the next transport, unmarried women and those living alone, in addition to married women without children, married women with children up to age 6, and married women with children of school age (i.e., up to age 14) were to be registered. The IKG Mährisch-Ostrau would on its own get hold first of all of those Jewish women who were unmarried or alone, aged 14 and up, further of those women who were married but childless and whose husbands had already gone with the first transport. The IKG Mährisch-Ostrau, the report continues, asked that the women who were to be deported and whose husbands were already in Nisko be allowed to take their children.[114] One would assume that there would be some uniformity of plan, as regards the sending of women and children, between Vienna and Mährisch-Ostrau (we lack such information about Kattowitz), especially since the same team of Nazi functionaries was involved (Eichmann, Günther, and Brunner). Viennese women and children were not to leave until the third transport; they were, however, scheduled for the second transport from Mährisch-Ostrau.

Simultaneously with all these plans and preparations, there were intimations of the approaching end of the enterprise. SS-*Oberführer* Müller informs Eichmann's office in Mährisch-Ostrau "that the resettlement as well as the deportation of Poles and Jews into the region of the future Polish constitutional state must be centrally directed. Therefore, permission to do so must be obtained from this office on principle." According to Günther, who forwarded this message to Eichmann, the latter was given a copy of this notice at the railway station in Kattowitz, while the entrainment of the transport was taking place, the original having been sent to Mährisch-Ostrau and forwarded by Brunner. The latter, Günther claimed, could not be reached any more that evening because of a break in the telephone connections. He asked Eichmann urgently to let him know whether the second transport from Mährisch-Ostrau and Kattowitz, scheduled for the following week, would be allowed to leave. It was Günther's guess that the notice from Müller must have been connected with Eichmann's latest conference in Berlin.[115]

On October 20 Günther informed the authorities in Kattowitz that a transport of almost 875 Jews from there, Königshütte (Chorzów), and Bielitz (Bielsko-Biała) had left for Nisko. Most likely there would be a further transport of Jews that would also contain women leaving Kattowitz and Mährisch-Ostrau.[116] This is the first indication of the combined transport mentioned above. However, on the very next day Günther was informed by the main office of the Gestapo in Brünn through Councilor (*Regierungsrat*) Hermann that, on the basis of an order from the RSHA (SS headquarters), all deportations of Jews had to cease. Hermann could not say whether this order applied to the whole area of the Reich. When asked by Günther whether the second transport from Mährisch-Ostrau, which according to his knowledge had already been discussed between Eichmann and Müller, could leave, Hermann announced that this transport could not be dispatched either.[117]

Back in Vienna, Brunner at the *Zentralstelle* sent a report to two SS functionaries, dated October 23, regarding the first transport from Vienna, which had left on the 20th. In it he speaks, for the first time, of difficulties with the German railway regarding the deportations. Apparently, the German railway officials claimed that the whole stretch to Nisko was overloaded with military transports and refused to schedule the transport of Viennese Jews until eight days later. However, Bürckel's office intervened with the heads of the railway in Berlin and the transport was able to leave on the 20th. For military reasons, however, the next one would not be able to leave until the 27th.[118]

In the meantime, Eichmann had made a quick trip from Krakow to Mährisch-Ostrau on the 22nd to meet with Günther. The result of this meeting was a memorandum dated the 23rd, signed by Günther and sent to the SD main office for distribution to the various main Gestapo offices. It is a long memorandum dealing with the resettlement of the Jews and the manner in which the transports were to be carried out.

Much of this memorandum merely reiterates what had been required, on a bureaucratic level, from the very beginning of the Nisko action regarding the registration of Jews, what they were to take along, the role of the IKG, and so on. A few points bring new information;

others, however, are worth noting not because they are new but because of the emphasis placed on them. Under "preparations," the first item is that "the exact registration by name of the impecunious Jews of German, Polish, and Czech citizenship as well as of stateless Jews, is to be carried out promptly." Also, "immediately after receiving the official order, the Jewish community has to see to it that the transports are put together in the prescribed number (1,000 persons) and prepared in accordance with orders."

The Jewish community had to collect an assessed amount from each Jew to be deported (except from those who were under 17 or totally destitute) according to the following schedule: RM 10 from those whose assets amounted to up to RM 1,000 and RM 50 from those who had assets of up to RM 5,000. This money was to be handed over to the Nazi officials in charge of the transport.

Furthermore, "Jews assigned by the Jewish communities for a particular transport are, for the sake of expediency, to be concentrated in suitable halls near the railway station. The Jews have to appear with their luggage, since after the elimination [of unqualified persons] the entrainment will begin immediately." Only those would be disqualified who were "war- and work-disabled persons (over 50% disability) as well as those seriously ill." Obviously to avoid any possible leniency on the part of Jewish doctors, "Aryan doctors are to be consulted in special cases."

There are detailed instructions about letting the railways know well ahead of time the size and composition of the trains needed (e.g., third-class cars for the Jews, second-class cars for the accompanying police, freight cars for baggage and materials, the freight cars being the hardest to obtain since they were needed for military purposes). The Gestapo was to be informed punctually of the departure times of the trains so that the Gestapo, in turn, could notify the Army High Command.

For each passenger car for the Jews, the Jewish community was to supply one container with water for washing and one with tea or coffee. The cars were to be searched for weapons, foreign currency, and jewelry. The accompanying police troops were to be equipped with pistols and rifles with sufficient ammunition. After entrainment, no Jews, other than the Jewish transport subleaders and the physicians, were allowed to leave their railway cars.[119]

Many of the above details are self-explanatory and need no further comment. Especially noteworthy, however, is the timing of this memorandum. It was issued at a point when the transports were being discontinued—only temporarily, it was claimed—and yet it is worded as if this were the very beginning of the action, as if these were instructions on what to do in the future rather than a belated information sheet on what had been the procedure. Not only does the memorandum order a registration of impecunious Jews, which had already taken place in Vienna, Mährisch-Ostrau, and Kattowitz, but a great number of these people had been, or were in the process of being, shipped out on the basis of this very registration. We can only speculate about the purpose of this exercise. Was it to defy the rival Gestapo by presenting them with a fait accompli, an ongoing venture they could not stop at this time? Or was it meant to pacify them by acting as if they were being kept informed of ongoing activities? Was the memorandum meant to impress certain superiors with the administrative know-how and organizational prowess in standardizing procedures

Jewish deportees building barracks in Oppeln (Opole) in the General Government (May 1941). (DÖW Foto 5553 - 6/35)

evident from its content? Or is it no more than empty posturing in the face of inevitable defeat?

No matter what, the tug-of-war continued. For October 24 we have three memoranda from Mährisch-Ostrau initialed by Günther, two dealing with assigning trains for transports, the third a record of a telephone conversation with Eichmann in Berlin. In what is obviously the earlier of the two memoranda, Günther asked the German railway administration in Oppeln (Opole) for two special trains, each to hold up to 1,000 people, to leave from Mährisch-Ostrau and Kattowitz, respectively. He managed to have them promised to him, albeit for later than he originally requested; the delay, he was told, was necessitated by the "major troop movements" and "laborer transports." Also, before the railway administration would agree to do its best, Günther had to call to the attention of the railway administration the "importance for the Reich" of the trains he was requesting.[120]

In the telephone conversation with Eichmann in Berlin, Günther was informed

> that the deportations from the Protectorate for purposes of resettlement are, for the time being, to be discontinued until further notice, and that the women who are registered for the next transport are not to be deported for the time being; the reason for this [Eichmann] could not give over the telephone.
>
> Since in Mährisch-Ostrau the preliminary work for the next transport is already relatively far advanced and a large number of Jews who wanted to flee Mährisch-Ostrau have in the meantime, been arrested, the request was made that—in order to preserve the prestige of the local state police—at least one transport of the available men be allowed to leave.
>
> Eichmann was agreeable to having . . . up to 400 male Jews deported. It was intended that this partial transport be attached to the transport leaving Kattowitz on October 27.

Günther also found out that Müller wanted to know all the details about each transport, whether from Vienna, Kattowitz, or Mährisch-Ostrau, and ordered that Nisko be informed of its imminent arrival.

And finally, Eichmann asked that this call be paid for by the Stapo. He assumed that the local Mährisch-Ostrau police had made the telephone connection and was thus responsible for its costs.[121]

The discrepancies in this memo are obvious. Are the transports to be stopped or not? If yes, then why give instructions for further transports, and if not, why say that they are? And why is Eichmann making it sound as if he were the one making the decisions (for example, agreeing to having the 400 "available" men shipped out)? Why be so mysterious about not being able to talk freely on the telephone? One possible explanation would be that he was speaking from a public phone or someone else's office, which is perhaps the reason for his unusual request to have the Stapo pay the bill, and that he believed a third party was listening in. This would account for his attempted secrecy as well as for the pretense that he was the one wanting the transports stopped. Tantalizing glimpses of behind-the-scenes machinations is all we get.

Apparently on the basis of the above conversation with Eichmann, Günther telephoned once more with Oppeln, asking for two transport trains as before, but this time for passenger cars for up to 400 people from Mährisch-Ostrau plus two cars for the police escort, plus a train for 1,000 Jews from Kattowitz. The Mährisch-Ostrau cars were to be attached to the larger train in Kattowitz, and they would travel together to Nisko from there.[122] And this seems to be what eventually did indeed take place.

In spite of all the many memoranda and telephone conversations, communication among the different agencies did not always function smoothly. In a situation report from Berlin, dated October 25, 1939 (the day following the last three communications), at a time when Eichmann either was still in Berlin or had just left, we read the following, put out by Himmler's office: "In the *Ostmark* [Austria] the resettlement of the Jews has begun. Approximately 3,000 Jews were sent with the first three transports to Poland. They received tools for the erection of a barracks village from the IKG Vienna."[123] It is clear that Himmler's office was misinformed, although we do not know who had provided the misinformation. It is, after all, unlikely that the first transports from Vienna, Mährisch-Ostrau, and Kattowitz were lumped together, as is implied by the claim that the IKG Vienna supplied all 3,000 with tools, which would not make sense under these circumstances. There is, however, a stamp on this secret document stating that "this report is intended solely for the addressee personally and contains information which is being sent without having been checked, for the sake of its timeliness."[124] In spite of this disclaimer, it would be interesting to know who fed Himmler's office with this piece of misinformation, its most outstanding characteristic, apart from the grossly inflated figure, being again the implication that the resettlement of Jews was in full swing and would continue.

As we have seen, the last attempt to push through a transport from Vienna did not succeed, ostensibly because the rail facilities were needed for the transport of laborers for the harvest of root vegetables and for troop transports to the western front.[125] There was, however, one more shipment of Jews from Mährisch-Ostrau on November 1, which was different from the others in that at times some or all of the 322 men of this transport are referred to as "prisoners." According to the *Tagesbericht* from Mährisch-Ostrau to the *Zentralstelle* Vienna, a group of Jews from Prague was brought in (*eingeliefert*, which usually refers to prisoners) and entrained on November 1, together with six Jews who had already fled from Nisko (and perhaps tried to return home), plus one Aryan prisoner who chose voluntarily to go to Nisko. These men did not rate passenger cars but were shipped in ten freight cars and sent toward Kattowitz. They only got as far as Sosnowitz (Sosnowiec), however, supposedly because the transports had been discontinued due to the flooding of the San River and the consequent washing away of its bridges. On Eichmann's order, the Jews immediately built a temporary camp in Sosnowitz and were to continue on to Nisko, on the first transport permitted to go there. Until then, the IKG Sosnowitz would see to their needs.[126] A corroboration of the fact that this transport took place—though not of the reason given for its not reaching Nisko—is contained in a letter from Gestapo section IIb/IIe Mährisch-Ostrau to Eichmann in Vienna, dated December 12, reporting a communication from Kattowitz:

> In accordance with a letter from the IKG Mährisch-Ostrau of November 22, 1939, there should be on deposit for the people belonging to the last Jew transport destined for Nisko from Mährisch-Ostrau in the blocked account of the IKG . . . Kc [Kčs] 24,325. Due to the discontinuance of the transports to Nisko, the participants of the above-mentioned transport were housed in an assembly camp in Sosnowitz. . . . [T]he upkeep of the camp entails great expense and a forwarding of the Jews is out of the question for the time being.[127]

No further information is available about the fate of these people but, since no further transports to Nisko were permitted, it is highly unlikely that they ever got there.

So much for the actual mechanics involved in starting, carrying out, and eventually ending the Nisko transports. But we must go back a few days and report on one last masterpiece of deception—or at least attempted deception—perpetrated by Eichmann on the Viennese Jewish community.

Eichmann's Jewish Homeland

We have an unusually long *Aktennotiz* dated October 27, 1939, the day after the second and last transport left Vienna, regarding a meeting between Eichmann and Löwenherz that summarizes the Eichmann version of the new Jewish homeland.[128] We can evaluate the following excerpts even before discussing the actual conditions in and near Nisko or the fate of those who were sent there. We will keep them in mind as we look at the documentation to follow, based on reports by those who had actually "been there."

First, it was made clear that the whole resettlement project was taking place under Eichmann's direction. Löwenherz continues:

> In the spirit of the regulation of the Jewish question planned by the government of the Reich, a majority of the Jews living in the Altreich, the *Ostmark*, and the Protectorate is to be resettled in the area between the San, Bug, and Vistula [rivers] in Poland. The whole action is to be carried out in the most humane manner and is meant to make it possible for the Jews to move around there freely, to settle and to build up their livelihood. To a great extent the rural areas are depopulated and must be rebuilt. The arriving Jews are brought into a newly erected barracks camp where they may spend one day and one night. In this barracks camp, in which up to now there are only primitive accommodations for 1,000 people, food and medical attention is taken care of. The physicians accompanying further transports, other than those staying in the camp, can settle freely in the areas assigned to the Jews, take up their practice, just as all other Jews are permitted to carry out activities corresponding to their occupational preparation, because in this region the Nuremberg laws and other limiting decrees are not valid. The representatives of the IKG Vienna and of the Protectorate, who already are present in this area, are to create branch offices (*Exposituren*) that take the arriving Jews under their wing, advise them and make it possible for them to settle in the individual villages. They are allowed to travel freely in the area and have been furnished, for this purpose, with the proper letters of recommendation by the district presidents of the areas and the commissioners of the army. Within the next two weeks they have to present their suggestions to SS-Hstf. Eichmann.

Eichmann further stated that transports had already left Austria and the Protectorate and that the first transports from the Altreich would commence within three weeks. And then follows a statement by Eichmann which, in the light of later events right up to the end of the war, is really more significant than appears at first glance.

> The humane way in which this action is carried out is to be expressed also by the fact that . . . Eichmann is ready to give his permission to journalists and representatives of large Jewish organizations abroad to go there in order to convince themselves right on the spot of the way in which [this action] is executed.

Consequent upon these communications, Löwenherz

> took the liberty of raising the following objections: The IKG, which of course carries out the task assigned to it, meets with great difficulties within the Jewish population because it is accused of having promoted this action and is sending the people into an uncertain fate. Many fear that the men are again being sent to a concentration camp. There are also grave questions about the possibility of rebuilding [the area] economically and there are fears that the Jews, by taking over the locales abandoned by the fleeing [indigenous] population, will again be exposed to anti-Semitic attack. Also, only a part of the [Viennese] population can be brought there because older people, the sick, and invalids cannot be resettled under any circumstances.

Further, Eichmann agreed that the IKG was to invite voluntary participation and insisted, at the same time, on 1,000 people per transport from Vienna, at least until the Jews from the Altreich could be used to make up the number demanded. A representative from the *Reichsvertretung der Deutschen Juden* (National Representation of the German Jews) in Berlin was to come to Vienna to see how things were done there as regards these transports. Also included among them would be those in "protective custody" in Viennese jails as well as in Dachau and Buchenwald (it seems we have heard this before), in addition to about 400 of the 1,000 young people preparing themselves for Palestine by working in *Hakhshara* (training) camps since, as Eichmann said, the resettlement in Poland also needed these experienced young people.

Of the many other related topics touched upon here, the following are of special interest to us: Löwenherz used the opportunity to inform Eichmann that normal emigration to the United States and Palestine had resumed and that during the last few days between 80 and 100 people per day were being processed; and in this connection, he again asked that Murmelstein be released because he was urgently needed in Vienna. To this Eichmann responded that "Dr. Murmelstein was competent to render very valuable services in integrating the immigrating Jews and that he must remain in Poland for the time being. In about two months those [functionaries] who are now there will return and others will be sent in their stead." Eichmann did approve of the regular emigration from Austria and stated that those in Poland would also be allowed to emigrate, but not until the war was over. Löwenherz also mentioned that Morris Troper of the Joint would like to meet with him in Geneva to discuss the financing of the regular emigration. In this connection Eichmann repeated his invitation to outside organizations to visit Poland to inspect the resettlement project, and this time he invited specifically the representative of the Joint to visit there with Löwenherz and Rothenberg. This seems to be the first documented instance of Eichmann extending invitations, invitations that were either not kept or were fake in one way or another, that came too late to make much difference, or that indirectly did more harm than good.

One last noteworthy feature of this memorandum is one that demonstrates the interaction at this time between Eichmann and the IKG. Löwenherz writes: "In order to facilitate the execution of the action, I suggested publishing a proclamation in the *Jüdisches Nachrichtenblatt*. . . . Eichmann agreed to this and demanded that the draft be submitted to him still in the course of this morning," the meeting with him having begun at 9:00 a.m. It was a bold move on the part of Löwenherz, suggesting, as it does, that the whole matter be out in the open. Yet Eichmann was not to be outdone. In spite of the unreasonable demand that the draft be submitted forthwith, it apparently was completed at the stipulated time. But a postscript was then added to the *Aktennotiz* to the effect that Brunner called that afternoon to inform Löwenherz that the proclamation was not to appear at this time in the *Nachrichtenblatt* but in the form of posters in the IKG and the Palamt. Furthermore, the second paragraph was to be deleted and in paragraph 6 the adjective *schweren* (arduous/difficult/grave) was to be deleted.

Rosenkranz quotes a few passages from a "Draft for a Proclamation,"[129] which he includes in his section on the Nisko transports. He gives no indication of the date, but it is evident that it is the proclamation under consideration here. Rosenkranz prefaces these excerpts by writing: "The illusion of a free settlement which different groups—organized since the Anschluss for purposes of emigration and settlement—were striving for, is also reflected in [the following] proclamation" by the IKG. Among the excerpts given by Rosenkranz the following are pertinent:

> According to communications to [the IKG] Vienna received from the most competent sources, the Jews immigrating into the region determined upon may settle and act freely and build up their livelihood.
>
> Temporary shelter and food will be supplied. Representatives of Jewish organizations are at the disposal of arriving Jews right on the spot.

This is almost verbatim what we read in the *Aktennotiz* quoted at length above; and it seems quite clear that we have before us parts of the proclamation issued by Löwenherz following his meeting with Eichmann on October 27, the "most competent source" obviously being Eichmann himself. Since the whole proclamation starts out by stating that the IKG has been given the task of carrying out the resettlement project by the *Zentralstelle*, Löwenherz seems to have done all he could under the strict censorship alluded to above to let people know that the information and evaluation of the project did not originate with him. Unfortunately, the necessary subtlety of his message was lost on many readers of the proclamation, then as it is today, for the following reasons.

The Jews in Vienna were isolated without being segregated; their lives were spent under the public scrutiny of hostile surroundings. They were never closed off in a ghetto. Yet, within the confines of a ghetto such as Łódź, the Jews were able to speak among themselves about their dismal condition and about what their captors were inflicting on them. There are records of Chaim Rumkowski addressing his fellow inmates of the Łódź ghetto in public assembly about their captors' latest demands. Such an open and uncensored address was impossible, as well as forbidden, in Vienna; the informational isolation of the Jews, coupled with Nazi censorship, served to protect the Aryan public from information that would cause disturbance among them. Such disturbance was to be prevented at all costs. Therefore, the security service (SD) as well as the police branch (Gestapo) of the SS kept constant watch over what was on the mind of the public; and a *Stimmungsbericht* (mood report) was a rubric in their weekly *Lagebericht* (situation report), recording public reactions to the latest action against the Jews.

The Nazis' efforts to have the Nisko transports proceed smoothly may have been fumbling improvisations, but whatever reason the Jewish leadership may have had for its suspicion, such suspicion could not be imparted to their Jews in a manner recognizable to the authorities, and its effect on the Jewish leaders' conduct had to be restricted mainly to caution and vigilance in their desperate dealings with their overlords.

The Promised Kingdom

After all the preparations, frustrating on all sides, and after all the confusion leading to the cancellation of the project practically at its very inception, a few hundred Jews did have a chance to glimpse the kingdom that the Nazis had promised them.

What was it like?

When Eichmann traveled to Poland to find a proper locale for the camp, the little town of Nisko on the San River[130] and the surrounding countryside must have made a good impression on him. Nisko itself seems to have been a town of about 5,000, more German than Polish in character, manifesting everywhere the German influence of the Franke family, the local lords of the manor that stood in the center of town. The town itself was described as clean and friendly in appearance, all the amenities and necessities of a county seat were there, including good preparatory schools. Of course, the Jews were not to be settled in Nisko; it merely contained the railway station from which they would have to walk a few miles to reach the less hospitable region of their campsite. Nisko County in general, we are told, consisted mainly of forests, but there was some grazing land and some agriculture. Whatever industry there was, was concentrated in a small northerly section.

However, before October 1, Nisko itself was totally overrun by the German military, which had requisitioned all usable space and which provisioned itself up to 50 percent from what it could take from the farmers of the county, thereby causing general food shortages as well as the danger of famine. On September 29 the new German county commissioner arrived at last. His work was made much easier by the fact that the actions against the Jews had already been completed by the Gestapo. They almost totally cleaned out the Jews in more ways than one, including taking all their money and jewelry. All that was left for the commissioner to do was to register the real property left behind by the Jews, install his own people in Jewish stores (on October 5), and consider Nisko's "Jewish problem" solved.[131]

This "pleasant" interlude, however, did not last long. The information section of the 44th Division issued a report on October 25 dealing with recent events in the jurisdiction of the district president of Janów-Lubełski, a town approximately 35 km northeast of Nisko. The language in which these events are told is itself noteworthy, although not unexpected; and the events themselves furnish a corroboration, apart from some minor discrepancies, of what Murmelstein and other Jewish sources relate of their experiences during this time.

> For the last three days many Jewish fugitives have been arriving in the area east of the San and the Vistula [rivers], coming from the west . . . and the Reich. The vice president of the Jewish Emigration Committee in Vienna came to see me on October 23 and informed me that by this time 3,000 male Jewish immigrants (mostly from Vienna) had been shipped to Nisko, of whom a majority has already been deported across the San. During the last two days 5,000 Jews have passed through Janów-Lubełski itself. On the eastern bank of the San, opposite Nisko, a camp for fugitives, i.e., immigrants, is being built and one train of emigrants also carried lumber, etc.
>
> These immigrant Jews have practically no cash and only the most rudimentary clothing. During the conference of the district presidents, which took place . . . in Lublin yesterday, other district presidents reported similar things; however, up to now the . . . civil government has not been informed of any [such] planned action on the part of the Reich. On the contrary! The civil government has been charged with . . . liberating the economic life of the region as far as possible from Jewish influence. This has been initiated by the use of all [possible] measures up to now.
>
> This haphazardly initiated influx of [Jews] would . . . bring about . . . through these undesirable individuals—who do no real work but are merely parasites and profiteers—even more disorder in the economy.[132]

The consequences for the local population, the report continues, could be catastrophic since in this most heavily war-ravaged area there was a lack of food and shelter. What the troops did not get, the Jews hid. The door was now open for black-marketeering and usury on the part of the Jews. "The native population, consisting of small farmers, [is] unintelligent, totally at the mercy of the Jewish traders, and will be their first victims." (In the war against the Jews, even the pretense of compassion for the Poles was a valuable weapon.)

The report then brings up questions to be faced by the administrators of the district: Who was to prevent murder and mayhem, theft and plunder, and who was to be protected? If it was to be the non-Jews, then why let the Jews willy-nilly into the territory? Or was the civil or military government supposed to protect the Jews from the "justified" defensive measures of the non-Jews? This dilemma "could tarnish the unblemished shield of the military" by the government, either by protecting the Jews against the "justified anger" of the non-Jews or by allowing or even promoting pogroms.

The report closes with a dire warning about the consequences of allowing this "source of trouble" to remain unchecked.

We have quoted at length from this memorandum in order to document the total opposition, on the part of the local German government agencies, to the settlement of the Jews in this region. They pulled out all the stops, as it were, and threw in all the anti-Semitic clichés in order to press home their main point. This point, however, is a valid one: They were not informed of nor prepared for that influx into this war-ravaged region. Eichmann and Co. had refrained from making any arrangements for the reception of the Jews and even from ascertaining whether this region was in any way suitable for the professed purpose of the venture. Could he really have thought that such preparations and considerations were unnecessary? Or was it an integral part of his plan, even then, for a "natural" decimation of the Jews, which was abetted even by the physical nature of the territory he had chosen? Or was it merely monumental indifference to the fate of these people, once he had removed them, as promised, from the major populated areas in the new eastern parts of the Reich? And did he count on this efficient removal of the Jews as a stepping stone in his career, as just another ploy to impress his superiors?

An indication of what was really happening to the Jews—other than their supposedly enriching themselves at the expense of the poor Polish peasants—is contained in the entry of October 28 of a war diary kept by the High Command South in that region. Here we get a foretaste of what we will find again in the firsthand reports of the Jews who had been in Nisko. The diary refers to events at the Przemyśl pocket, formed where the San River bends from an easterly to a northwesterly flow. Jews from German-held Galicia, and also from the direction of Nisko, who wanted to flee to Soviet-held Lwów (German Lemberg, Ukrainian Lviv) would have to enter this pocket and cross the demarcation line at that point, which is about 10 km east of Przemyśl.

At the San crossing point, this diary states, there were great crowds of refugees and Jews who wanted to cross over into Russia, while others, on the Russian side, wanted to come over to the German side. But this was not so easy; the Russians wanted this border traffic stopped. The people on the German side were desperate; no food or shelter was available. It was the end of October, the beginning of a long, cold, and rainy season (there is no so-called Indian summer in this part of Poland). Many tried to swim across the San River, which, as we already know, is flood-swollen at this time. Many fugitives drowned, others were shot by the Russians as they were crossing. Those managing to get across to the German side from the Russian shore (among whom most likely there were Jews who had been forcibly separated from their families and were trying to find them again) were caught and handed over to the Gestapo. Moreover, the Russians were constantly complaining that the SS was regularly forcing Jews to cross the San at night to the Russian side.[133]

While the war diary does not specifically refer to Nisko Jews, it indicates the kind of fate they suffered when, according to Eichmann's scenario, they were to have been distributed and received, in an orderly manner, into the villages and towns and Jewish communities around Nisko.

On October 31 Julius Boschan, the liaison the IKG had to assign to the *Zentralstelle* Vienna, sent his "first" (and only available) report to Löwenherz from Nisko.[134] It is a strictly factual account of events plus a repetition, down to the very terminology, of some of the plans Eichmann outlined to Löwenherz, as well as instructions which, to those who have learned to read between the lines, contain hidden information about conditions. We will concentrate on what is new to us here as well as pertinent to our investigation.

The six Jewish representatives met with Rolf Günther as ordered on October 16 and were instructed to aid the IKG Mährisch-Ostrau in its preparation for the first transport. After its arrival in Nisko on the 19th, the participants were "transported" to the other side of the San River to a site about 7 km from Nisko, where the building of the barracks was immediately begun. About 500 Jews (mainly skilled workers and artisans) were employed in the erection of the buildings, "while the remainder, in accordance with the basic idea of the resettlement action, were scattered into the surrounding villages."[135]

The Jewish representatives reported to Eichmann, as they had been instructed to do, both in Nisko and at the campsite, and were informed of the dimensions of the territory allotted to the Jews for resettlement, its eastern border extending to about 10 km to the west of the Russian line. A special *Zentralstelle* would be created to take care of the arriving Jews. In the different "temporary stopover camps" (*Etappenlager*), branch offices (*Exposituren*)[136] would be set up that were at least 7 km from the "transit camp" (i.e., Zarzecze) in order to take care of the Jews coming from the latter and to move them on.

Eichmann further informed Boschan that "the legal position of the settlers rests, for the time being, on the decree that the Jews become settlers here. When a 'truncated' Poland (*Rumpfpolen*) is created, this legal position is to be confirmed when negotiations take place."[137]

All the Jewish representatives, with the exception of Boschan himself, were sent out to make contact with Jewish communities and to set up, in conjunction with them, a *Zentralstelle* to prepare for the resettlement action and left on the 23rd for Lublin by way of Janów. Boschan remained in the camp as representative of the IKG Vienna and had the task of preparing the distribution, by stages, of the arriving Jews into the villages lying in the direction of Lublin. His first project was the establishment of an emergency hospital and a transit camp 8 km away in Pysznica, both of which were already functioning very well by the time he wrote his report. Three more transit camps were to be established in the next few days.

The morale in the camp was good, he wrote, there were no infectious diseases, there was enough food, and Boschan hoped to keep the men healthy and able to work.

Then Boschan discussed the arrival of the first transport from Vienna. Of the 912 men, only 34 artisans were kept in the camp. The others went on into the surrounding villages. The building materials, as well as the food, that were brought along by this transport remained in the main camp, however. Of the 672 participants in the second transport from Vienna, which arrived on October 29, 92 were left in the camp, again all artisans. After a short rest and refreshment, the rest of the men went to the next transitory camp in Pysznica, where they were received by "our" functionaries and kept overnight. The next day, they were transported by wagon to the surrounding villages chosen for this purpose, under surveillance by an escort.

Boschan and his assistants were trying to register all the Jews passing through the temporary camp so that contact with them could be maintained.

And finally, Boschan tried to give some advice to participants of future transports. First of all, he urged them to take along a lot of potable liquids—water, tea, and coffee—since the water in the region was "not unobjectionable," also water for washing in the trains as well as brooms to clean them. Solid boots were important—no regular shoes—two pairs if possible, warm underwear, and work clothes (he even uses the English "over-alls"). The most important things are to be packed in the rucksack in such a way that the rucksack could be carried for at least two or three hours. Any food packed would have to be taken along in the rucksack.[138]

It is quite obvious that the six functionaries in Nisko knew the details of Eichmann's plan to scatter the Jews before Löwenherz was informed of them on October 27, and of course Boschan had no way of knowing if and to what extent Löwenherz was aware of it at all. We know that by the time Löwenherz received Boschan's report, sometime after October 31, he already had been told that the Jews would gradually be distributed in the area to settle and begin a new life. What new facts was he able to gather from Boschan's letter? First of all, he learned the number of Jews who stayed in the camp, at least for the time being, compared to the number who had to go on immediately after having disembarked 4 km or 5 km up the road. Quite clearly the transit camps to receive them had not been built at the time of the first transport, which meant that these men really had no place to go. There was no indication in Boschan's letter that the outlying villages were prepared or willing or even able to receive them.

The other five Jewish representatives were, at least temporarily, removed from the picture, their whereabouts unknown. Obviously Boschan had not heard from them during the eight days they were gone, otherwise he would have mentioned something; nor had any information filtered back about possible support from other Jewish communities such as Lublin. He was clearly working in a vacuum, trying to take care of the men arriving and remaining in Zarzecze, keeping track somehow of the others, building waystations and outposts to who knows where. That the first emergency hospital was operating so well was good news, to be sure, but why was it already in full swing? The physicians accompanying each transport should have been able to take care of minor problems right out of their black bags; there were no epidemic or infectious diseases, as Boschan emphasizes. What, then, was keeping the hospital occupied? A disturbing question. Another puzzle: Why, if the Jews were allowed to settle freely, did they need to be taken out of the transit camp under escort? From Boschan's advice to further deportees, Löwenherz was able to gain various facts: The water supply at the destination was inadequate at best and possibly polluted. How much drink could people take from Vienna to eastern Poland? The mention of washing water for the trains hinted at poor hygienic conditions. The emphasis on sturdy shoes told something about the terrain. The urgency that came through in Boschan's advice to put the most important items, including food, into rucksacks and to be prepared to carry them for long stretches raised questions regarding the fate of the supplies taken along in suitcases, and brought home the certainty of long marches to unknown destinations. It was quite a lot of information that Boschan was able to smuggle out of the camp right under the noses of the Nazi censors and in perfectly innocuous terms!

Rosenkranz is highly critical of this report by Boschan: "Boschan, a close co-worker of Murmelstein, veils idyllically the situation in the Nisko camp in the spirit of Eichmann's maneuver of deception."[139] From later incidents, we know that Eichmann often wanted leading Jews to write reports home from their place of deportation, and Boschan's letter seems to be the first instance of this kind. It was not difficult to persuade Boschan to do so, inasmuch as he was one of two or three men the IKG had to assign to the *Zentralstelle*. In this position, Boschan took his orders directly from Eichmann and associates and not from the IKG. His performance at the *Zentralstelle* on behalf of the Jews was and has been regarded as suspect, also by the leading men at the IKG. Thus, Rosenkranz's attribution of his being "a close co-worker of Murmelstein" serves to throw suspicion on Murmelstein. To be sure, Murmelstein was sitting in Lublin at the time when Boschan wrote his letter, and thus not in a position to be requested to write "idyllically veiled reports in the spirit of Eichmann's deceptive maneuvers." But later incidents will show that, unlike others, Murmelstein was the one who was always suspicious enough to evade such requests on the part of Eichmann and associates. In this instance, as in others, Rosenkranz's interpretation seems to be colored by his general evaluation of Murmelstein. There is no doubt that the very writing of the letter was a maneuver on Eichmann's part. This can be inferred from two facts: First, the letter indicates that one of Eichmann's men left in the camp censored the letter. Second, the only way the letter could have reached Löwenherz at the IKG was—in the absence of a postal service or of the Jews' access to such—if Eichmann wanted him to get it and if Eichmann's staff forwarded it through their own channels. And yet, as we have shown, Boschan was very clever in the way he hid his crucial information behind a supposedly idyllic veil.

It is difficult to imagine how much more explicit Boschan could have been in his report under his strictly monitored conditions and most likely under pressure to write a positive evaluation of the Nisko project for home consumption. Perhaps the best way to illustrate the strictures under which the IKG and its outposts had to operate as well as the lack of understanding of this situation (both at that time and from our retrospect when, in the light of subsequent events, we surely should know better) is an exchange of letters deposited, like the Boschan report, in the Central Archives in Jerusalem.

Leo Fuchsgelb, the brother of a deceased higher functionary of the IKG, wrote on November 7, 1939, to the editors of the *Jüdisches Nachrichtenblatt*:

> For the last few weeks a resettlement of the local Jews has been going on about which the most fantastic and disquieting rumors are being spread. Your paper, which is the only agency capable of informing the local Jews about measures concerning them, has not reported about this action with a single word. I believe that a precise authentic publication of all the details concerning this action would be of more interest to your readers at this time than. . . [Here Fuchsgelb mentions recipes for available foods and other items either well-known or of no particular interest.]
>
> So why has the editorial board not found it necessary to report about this action and put an end to all the rumors being spread around?[140]

Two weeks later the editor of the paper replied as follows:

> We are responding to your letter of the 7th only today because—and we admit this openly—we needed a long time until we could decide to take a position at all, in the face of so much naiveté as you expressed in your letter. In the meantime, you may have realized that limits have been placed on our publication activity beyond which we may not go, especially in the action mentioned by you. No matter how important [details] about the use of ration cards . . . are, surely many other things would deserve to be treated sooner and in greater detail. But this is impossible for certain reasons. We believe that you will now understand our "reticence." Yours truly[141]

Needless to say, none of this appeared in print.

The Fate of the Transports

But back to Nisko. We now have three distinct groups of Jews involved in this venture, the six representatives of the IKG, those Jews who stayed at the camp in Zarzecze, and those who were driven beyond the camp into the surrounding countryside with no place to go. This third group was the biggest. Goshen writes:[142]

> Immediately upon arrival [in Nisko] the train was unloaded, the deportees, the building material and food brought across the San. On a bare meadow near the village of Zarzecze we stopped and began to work immediately. A group of Jewish skilled laborers (among them contractors) erected a guard room and sleeping facility for the [police] escort, another group the roof and walls of a barracks which, after a few hours, protected us somewhat from the rains that lasted through the night. Eichmann . . . had received the unwilling guests sitting on a horse and told them that first of all they would have to find water, since the existing wells are polluted: "Otherwise you will all croak."
>
> [The next morning] 300 to 400 deportees were led out of the camp, escorted for a few kilometers and then left to their own devices; the only instruction was that returnees would be shot on the spot.[143]

Of the first Vienna transport, only a small number of deportees was smuggled into the camp by the Jewish camp administration, some were tolerated quietly by the SS commandant; but most of them were forced to keep going. Most of these Viennese deportees as well as the ones from the later Kattowitz and Mährisch-Ostrau transports only saw the camp "from a distance," says Goshen. Altogether about one tenth of deportees from all three centers (i.e., about 500) stayed at the camp in Zarzecze until its dissolution in April of 1940.[144] Of these, 198 were from Vienna, and all of these returned to Vienna at that time.

According to Goshen, conditions at the camp, once it was established and the transports were stopped, were fairly tolerable. The inmates were all younger men, in relatively good physical shape and able to work, even in the harsh Polish winter. The food was adequate to keep body and soul together; the guards were in part almost human in their treatment of the Jews. It seems they did not exactly enjoy being there, either. The work was hard and constant from sunup to sundown, mainly in logging and similar operations. Of course, no attempt was made to create any kind of settlement other than a slave labor camp, which, in effect, this turned out to be, nor to get the Jews started in any kind of an occupational venture, which Eichmann had claimed to be the purpose of the enterprise.[145]

But these inmates of the camp were vastly better off than those who had been chased away and those who were still held in the concentration camps. Three documents illustrate the fate of the Jews who were not lucky enough to be left in the camp at Zarzecze. The first is a letter dated January 10, 1940, to the AJDC in Warsaw, written by one of the men who had gone as far as Ulanów and stayed there, at least up to that time. The second is a draft for a petition to search for the Jews lost in Russia, apparently addressed to a governmental agency of the restored Republic of Austria and written in 1946 by the Jewish transport leader of the first Nisko transport. And last, we cite the copy of an unsigned letter, written by the leader of a small group of men who went as far as Bełzec, dated February 8, 1940; it is no longer a cry for help but a goodbye to his friends, his situation and that of the men in his charge being totally hopeless.

We will begin with the letter to the AJDC and use the others to fill the details:

> The hopes of most of those removed from Vienna against their will unfortunately were not fulfilled in any manner whatsoever. After three days of train travel that was fraught with deprivations and psychic tortures of the worst kind—we were not allowed to leave the car or compartment, no possibility for washing, many hours without anything to drink, hermetically sealed windows, under strictest guard, removal of all identity documents, etc.—we arrived in Nisko. . . . After a 2½ to 3 hour march, in pouring rain, we arrived in Zarzecze, where, on a meadow, a barracks camp was just being built. . . . While the majority of the Viennese was standing there looking at the situation not knowing what to do, they were suddenly assaulted by the locals, during which time they lost almost all of the luggage they had taken with them out of the passenger cars. With the exception of artisans, who were kept in the camp, the others had to march on, most of them toward Lublin, thereby forced to give up most of their big luggage that had been brought along for them in the freight cars. But since they did not find any place in the assigned region where they could have stayed, many turned toward the Russian border, hoping to encounter better conditions on the other side. But only a part of this group was able to reach its goal. Many, unable to bear the hardships any longer, stayed with compassionate people in the villages, where they are now living far from any contact with the rest of the world.[146]

Of the second transport from Vienna, about 600 men were forced to continue to Pysznica, a transit camp about 5 km distant, which we mentioned above, where they spent the night. The next morning, still exhausted from the trip, they were forced to continue on foot to the village of Kwidzów, 14 km away. This march turned out to be one of the worst experiences of the whole trip:

> Apart from the fact that the way led . . . through territory threatened by bandits and highwaymen, there were obstacles that made the greatest demands on the physical constitution of the participants. Sick, old, and physically frail people [so much for the fiction of age limits and rigid physical examinations!] had to go through water up to their necks as well as through swamps; the porters exploited their plight through extortion of the worst kind, refused to go further and demanded more and more wages.[147]

In the meantime, it had gotten dark and a number of participants, unable to orient themselves, lost their lives in the swamps. The rest, cold and wet as they were, camped out that night. The porters made common cause with the bandits and appropriated baggage including rucksacks right off peoples' backs and threatening their lives. It is not clear how many did not make it to Kwidzów, since there was no list of participants in this forced march. Many of those who did make it by now owned no more than the clothes on their backs. Since they could not remain in Kwidzów, about half decided to keep on going to Ulanów, 28 km away, while the others headed toward Lublin. Of those who finally got to Ulanów, in all about 170 men, the majority decided to go on to the Russian border. Of these, many were once more held up by bandits, who took what had been overlooked before. At that point the police put a stop to the robberies. Forty people remained in Ulanów; their situation, writes our correspondent, became more critical from day to day, even though eventually a few of the suitcases that had to be abandoned at the beginning of the trip could be recovered and their contents used for barter. Also, the Jewish leadership in Zarzecze tried, to the extent of its ability, to send help to the people in Ulanów, but its means were limited. No help was to be expected from the local population—the Poles were hostile, the Jewish population poor and unable to help. The situation was tenuous especially since the local authorities could make their stay in Ulanów impossible and they, too, would have to head for the Russian border. They tried, albeit without success, to get in touch with the IKG Vienna. They did hear, apparently by way of Zarzecze, that the IKG had tried to help, but until then without success. The mood among the Jews from Vienna was extremely depressed, especially since they also worried about the fate of their families. The letter ends with a plea for help "before it is too late."

The second document mentioned above, the petition by the transport leader of the first Viennese transport, Ernst Kohn, fills us in on certain aspects of the situation in Vienna before the transport left as well as on some details regarding money matters. Taking up the narrative at the point when people received letters telling them they were picked for resettlement, we read that when the people arrived at the IKG for further instructions, they were told (unfortunately we do not know by whom) that, once in Poland, they would be sent to a region abandoned by the Polish civilian population, where they would be assigned a farm to which they could later on bring their families. They were then examined, apparently by Jewish doctors, and almost all of them were found to be suitable for the transport. No exceptions were made, neither on the basis of possibilities for emigration, such as affidavits to the United States, nor on the basis of mixed marriages. The transport leaders were also told that at the point of arrival the men would be met by functionaries of the IKG who were already there, and that they would take them to their quarters. However, in place of the IGK functionaries, the SS under the command of *Oberscharführer* Dannegger (*sic*) was there to welcome them. During the trip, the Jewish transport leaders were ordered to take all their money from the deportees. Each man was then handed 150 Złoty, regardless of how much money he had brought with him; and since the exchange rate agreed upon was 1:2, a very unfavorable rate to begin with, most men should have been given 600 Złoty. The rest remained in the hands of Dannecker, who claimed this money in the name of the SS, ostensibly to cover the costs of the transport.[148] During the second Viennese transport, the exchange was supposed to have been properly executed, Kohn says. Also, all personal documents had to be collected so that the deportees were left without any kind of identification.

Kohn's description of the arrival in Nisko and the march to Zarzecze is in agreement with that of our first correspondent, except for the addition of details such as the escort from the railway to the camp being composed of Viennese police and SS men, and that the porters, who were to help with transporting the suitcases, had to be paid between 10 and 20 Złoty each by the deportees. These were not let into the camp but were told to keep going; within two hours none of them would be allowed to be seen in the area. This latter order was given emphasis by the salvos of shots both from the SS escort and the police troop. Even though no one seems to have been hit, people panicked and fled north toward Lublin, leaving their luggage behind. Kohn also speaks of being attacked and robbed by the local population. The abandoned luggage of both transports from Vienna remained with the SS command in Nisko. Close to 1,400 people from Vienna, says Kohn, chose to try their luck on the Russian side, in the former province of Galicia where some of them found work and were left in peace for six months. During the summer of 1940, however, the Russians carried out a registration of these people, at which time they were given a choice of three options: (1) they could opt to become Russian citizens, (2) they could return to the German side, or (3) they could go abroad. Only a small percentage opted for Russian citizenship; most wanted to go back to find their families, and a few, who had had emigration possibilities before being shipped to Nisko, wanted to go abroad. Those who opted for citizenship were gradually put to work for the Russians. The other two categories, which constituted the great majority, were rounded up during the night, put together into transports, and shipped to the east, most of them to Siberian labor camps under the control of the NKVD (the Soviet secret police). The work in these camps was extremely hard, and most of the men were not up to it. The motive expressed by the Russians for treating the men who had opted for options (2) and (3) in this manner was that these people were "socially dangerous individuals" and had to be treated as such; they were given terms of from three to eight years in the labor camps. Of these, twenty-two had returned to Vienna by 1946; the fate of the others is unknown.[149]

The third document, dated February 8, 1940, and sent from Bełzec (Poland), makes no reference to the Nisko project. All we know is that this is a group of fourteen men from Vienna and that the man who writes this letter is the leader of this small band. Since many of the deportees from Nisko who had to keep going east no matter what formed small groups, choosing one of their own to be the leader, it is very likely that we are dealing with such a splinter group of Viennese Jews from one of the Nisko transports, but we cannot document this. In any case, their situation is paradigmatic of the kind of misery encountered by Jews who found themselves destitute and stranded in Poland at this time. He writes:

> My very dear friends! . . . Nothing matters to me any more. . . . I have given up all hope of ever leaving this filthy mess. . . . We live in the midst of a population that is absolutely hostile toward us. We live on an island of hate and contempt. Among the German military we are considered as Jews, the Poles think of us as Germans, the local Jews see us as intruders. If we cannot pay for our shelter today, we shall be out on the street tomorrow. With a temperature of –26°C [–15°F] it is impossible to heat the shack in which we 'live'. The straw on which we sleep is damp and rotting, and we all suffer from rheumatism. The snow outside reaches up to our hips, and our clothing is wholly inadequate. Some of us have no shirts. We are 14 comrades and have only 12 pairs of trousers between us, so that two people always have to stay inside. . . . We do not get paid for the work we do, so we cannot look around for a more lucrative source of income. . . . We eat . . . only one meal per day, either potatoes, spuds, or *pommes de terre*. . . . Added to this are the vermin. . . . [S]ometimes I nauseate myself. There is no opportunity to wash halfway properly. . . . [T]he sanitary conditions are gruesome. There are no toilets, metabolism is taken care of, totally without embarrassment, publicly on the highways. The polar temperatures . . . cause bladder and kidney ailments. . . . Of course we have no money to buy medicine. There is no chance of getting well. I, too, suffer dreadfully. Together with us, in a small room à la ice cream parlor, in which 14 people live, by the way, with running water—running down the walls, of course—there is also a young woman with her husband. She is not Viennese . . . and is even poorer than we are, if this is possible. Her lungs are severely affected, and yet we cannot put her out into the street because she would be completely lost. We are glad that, although we have nothing at all, we are still able to help, at least a little bit, someone still worse off.[150]

He goes on to say that he has lost all hope and, under the circumstances, it no longer pays to fight for one's life. He regrets only one thing, namely, that he will never be able to thank his friends for their love and care.

There is no comment adequate to embellish what is expressed in this letter.

Murmelstein's Journey

From the fate of the ordinary Jew caught up in the struggle for survival in the Poland of 1939–40, we must now turn to the adventures of the Jewish functionary who, together with four of his colleagues, was sent out to prepare the way for these ordinary Jews to come after them and to arrange for their proper reception in the designated part of Poland. The only available firsthand account of this fruitless endeavor is that of Murmelstein. We will follow his trail both in what he wrote and in what he related to us.

Even though all six of the functionaries had orders to call on Günther in Mährisch-Ostrau, Murmelstein was ordered to visit him separately in order to receive special instructions. Günther laid before him Eichmann's grandiose plan of a special settlement area for the Jews and ended by saying that Murmelstein must get great satisfaction from participating in the realization of those plans. Murmelstein did not show the expected enthusiasm and countered by speaking of his activity in the emigration section in Vienna and how he had just been in the process of revamping the emigration process, which had been temporarily halted by the outbreak of the war. He described the plight of those who had practically completed all of their extensive preparations for an immediate emigration: Not only were they suddenly shipped to Poland and torn from their families, but these families were now sitting in Vienna rather than emigrating with their husbands and fathers.

Günther replied to this in a manner that made a deep and lasting impression on Murmelstein; he referred to it frequently in our interviews with him, and it seems to represent a symbolic watershed for him, precisely because of his familiarity with Christian theology and its implications for the history of the Jews over the previous nineteen hundred years: "The prospect of becoming king of the Jews does not seem to entice you particularly." Murmelstein, in whom this whole conversation had brought about a state of turmoil and confusion, merely managed to stammer "There is no kingdom of the Jews—king of the Jews is an inscription on the cross," aware of the implications of such an "honor."[151] Murmelstein never told any of his colleagues about Günther's offer, nor was it ever again referred to by the Nazis. But Murmelstein believed that the enmity with which he was regarded later on by Edelstein, especially in Theresienstadt (Terezin), had its origin in the fact that Günther preferred to see him, Murmelstein, alone, rather than Edelstein.[152]

After assisting the Mährisch-Ostrau IKG in completing preparations for the first transport, as they had been instructed to do by Günther—and, according to Murmelstein, after the deportees had to sign statements to the effect that they applied voluntarily "for retraining"—the six functionaries joined the train of deportees. For some reason, the train stopped at Krakow. There they saw Jews being forced to work on the railroad tracks. Somehow these forced laborers discovered that this train, disguised as it was as a military transport, contained Jews being shipped to the east. They attempted to come close to the cars but were brutally chased back by the train escort. They had been so close that they could have looked into each other's eyes, but the eyes of the Jews outside seemed dead. They stared at the Jews on the train without really seeing them, nor did they seem to notice their surroundings but seemed to retreat into themselves. This interlude, too, and the image of these obviously traumatized Jews, impressed itself deeply on Murmelstein.[153]

There has been considerable controversy about a seemingly minor point, namely, Eichmann's appearance and/or speech either at the train station in Nisko or on arrival in Zarzecze. Arendt claims it was not Eichmann at all but Erich Rajakovic (Rajakowitsch). Goshen opts for Eichmann at the railway station, as we have seen. Murmelstein insists that it was Eichmann, who was known in person to only a very few of the deportees at that time, and that he received the men not at the railway station but at the future campsite. The relative importance of pinpointing this event lies in the fact that the one witness at the Eichmann trial in Jerusalem who reported on this incident correctly transmitted the gist of what Eichmann said but testified that it was said at the Nisko station. Thereupon Eichmann, the defendant, could solemnly declare that he had held no speech at the station. Murmelstein, who stood in the very front row of the crew, within a few steps of the speaker, and who knew Eichmann from Vienna, of course, was absolutely positive of the place and the identity of the speaker. Aside from this, Murmelstein and Goshen corroborate each other's memory of Eichmann's speech. According to Murmelstein, Eichmann said that there were supposed to be cases of typhoid, cholera, and dysentery in the area, and that the danger of

The train station at Nisko today. (By (GRAD) - Own work, CC BY-SA 3.0, https://commons.wikimedia.org/w/index.php?curid=11075699)

infection must be addressed first of all. "At this point Eichmann paused for effect, looked around smiling and added with sinister calm: 'Otherwise you'll have to die.'"[154]

The people Murmelstein describes as being driven away from the camp to the accompaniment of warning shots were mostly older men. "After a few days the roads were paved with pieces of luggage, which the old people were no longer able to carry. What they still tried to drag along, summoning their last bit of strength, was taken from them by . . . robbers and . . . marauders." Soon Jews with gunshot wounds were lying in the surrounding villages and had to be taken care of by doctors coming on foot long distances from the base camp. "In the forests, however, remained the corpses of the murder victims and of those so badly injured that they lacked the strength to drag themselves to the nearest settlement and bled to death." In the face of this development, the functionaries felt completely powerless, and the burden of their inability to change things for the better became all the heavier in light of the expected arrival of women and children. What would happen then?[155]

Repeatedly questioned as to the manner in which the settlement was to take shape, Eichmann finally came up with his solution: The Jews were to chase the Polish peasants from their farms and occupy them in their stead; or, as he is quoted by Murmelstein, to whom he said it, "kick the peasants in the arse." This advice is uncannily reminiscent of the way in which the population of Vienna appropriated Jewish homes, businesses, jobs, and property. Did Eichmann really think the Jews would do the same? "The veil . . . was lifted," continues Murmelstein, "there was nothing behind it. A little band of Jews was doomed to perish in a pestilent and war-devastated, bandit-ridden region."[156]

The last hope of the Jewish functionaries lay in making contact with the established Jewish communities in the area and asking them to take in the deportees. Over the centuries it had become as traditional and commonplace as it was necessary for Jewish communities to help one another when disaster struck. After several requests to Eichmann, he finally agreed to let five of the six functionaries travel to Lublin to make contact with the Jewish community there. On the way they were to explore possible sites for Jewish settlement. They were each given a pass and letter of protection to allow them to travel without being apprehended and shot by the Germans. These documents were essential, since the area swarmed with military police and SS *Einsatzgruppen*; the Jews knew nothing of the latter, but Eichmann was well acquainted with them and their function. There was also the ever-present danger of marauding bands of the local population against which the passes were of course powerless. However, Eichmann had a vested interest in the safe and sound return of the functionaries since, at this time, the Nisko action was still being promoted as a voluntary program on the part of the Jews, aimed at expediting their retraining and emigration. The "IKG Group," as they were known, was needed for purposes of camouflage. And this group, writes Murmelstein, was still naive enough at this point to assume they might bring about an improvement of the situation in Nisko.

The first town that seemed to offer the possibility of housing the Jews was Janów-Lubełski, some 30 km from Nisko, 25 km from the camp at Zarzecze. Janów was completely reduced to rubble except for three houses, with most of the population dead or gone. Still, living among the rubble would be preferable to camping out in the forests. This is where the functionaries spent the night. The next morning Murmelstein and Friedmann went to see the German district president, who, upon realizing who they were and what they wanted, was speechless with shock and finally managed to tell them that he had just sent away the last Jews from his county.[157] Apparently, he and his colleagues in the other counties had interpreted the Nazi policies to mean that they were to chase "their" (i.e., Polish) Jews to the east, whereas Eichmann, Günther, and their crowd wanted to chase the Jews from the Altreich, the former Austria, and the Protectorate into this very region. We saw earlier in this chapter the shock waves created by this new situation among the district presidents. The IKG group, on the other hand, hoped that this unwillingness to accept these displaced Jews might bring about a cessation of deportations. Yet the ones who were already there and had no place to go still had to be taken care of, and so, in part on foot, in part on peasant carts, the five continued their journey to Lublin.

The Lublin Jewish community promised to help all those who managed to make their way there but could not make any promises beyond that since it was under the strictest control and surveillance by the SD. In fact, the arrival of the Nisko emissaries had to be reported to the leader of the local SD, who ordered them to stay put and refrain from any activity until told otherwise. In the meantime, he would obtain instructions from higher up.

The functionaries had to wait in Lublin for ten days, during which time two pogroms took place in the Jewish section; they were then ordered to return to Nisko for fresh instructions from Eichmann. In Zarzecze, a real functioning barracks camp had been erected in the meantime, with surprisingly tolerable living conditions, making use of the skill and initiative of the Jews who had remained in the camp. But not all the news was good: One group of Jews, chased out under an SS escort unfamiliar with the terrain, had been driven into a swamp. Under orders not to allow returnees, the SS refused to let the Jews turn around, formed a chain behind them and drove them further into the swamp and into destruction. It could not be determined whether any of them managed to escape or if all of them drowned.

The day after their return from Lublin, Eichmann told the functionaries that there would be no more transports for the time being but that emigration from Vienna and Prague, by other, more devious routes, was again a possibility. There were certificates for Palestine waiting in Trieste. They had their work cut out for them. From Eichmann's very choice of words Murmelstein could pick out verbatim several phrases that he, Murmelstein, had used on Günther during their meeting in Mährisch-Ostrau. Shortly thereafter, the five left for their respective home bases. Boschan seems to have stayed on longer, possibly until the dissolution of the camp in April 1940.[158]

We do not know the exact date on which the other three returned to Vienna, but an *Aktennotiz* dated November 9 reports a meeting at the *Zentralstelle*, at which Murmelstein and Grün are listed as participants.[159] Thus, their whole venture, including the ten days of sitting and waiting in Lublin, had lasted little longer than three weeks.

Only three weeks, but a far journey into another dimension of the abyss, the contours of which had yet to be discerned.

Future Prospects

What were the conclusions drawn and lessons learned from the Nisko venture by the main participants?

In answering this question we cannot restrict ourselves to those on whom we concentrated in our account of this episode, that is, the Viennese Jews and their leaders who had been assigned to Nisko. The event occurred within a wider context of participating parties. The highest echelon of Nazi authority was involved, the echelon at which Nazi policy was determined and which ordered its execution, usually leaving the mode of execution to the trial-and-error methods of its underlings. This is the level at which we find Hitler, Himmler, and Heydrich.

The next echelon involved was that of Eichmann and his associates. This was the echelon charged with directly carrying out the policy regarding the Jews, a policy that was handed down to Eichmann one stage at a time. He executed this policy as he understood it, fluctuating between seeing his job as carrying out orders on the one hand and as an opportunity for exercising his own initiative on the other.

And there were the Jews themselves, and in particular the Jewish leadership. What difference did Nisko make as regards their representation of the interests of the oppressed Jews; the relationship of the Jewish leadership to their Nazi overlords; and the relationship of this leadership to the only contact Jews had with the outside world, the representatives of the AJDC? And, of course, the response of the outside world to Nisko is not only of interest but has wider implications.

The quick resettlement of 70,000 to 80,000 Jews from the regions of Kattowitz and Mährisch-Ostrau was to have been an opportunity of gathering experience in moving large masses of people. Eichmann considered this scheme his opportunity to be in charge not only of that resettlement but, as he claimed in his meeting with Löwenherz on October 27, of the decreed resettlement to Poland of all Jews from the Altreich, Austria, and the Protectorate. Whether there had actually been such a decree and whether he was actually put in charge is a moot question. The facts are as follows.

First, there was talk, at the highest level of the regime (i.e., Hitler and Himmler), of a grand shifting of populations. This talk was strictly a matter of Nazi ideological policy, for which Himmler's appointment as Commissar for the Consolidation of German Ethnicity may serve as an illustration. The talk was not a matter of the politics of the possible; indeed, when the attempt was made to implement the substance of the talk, it ran afoul of realities. In any case, the populations that were to be shifted around were those of the conquered territories, whether incorporated into Germany or not. Getting rid of the Jews in the incorporated territories was part of the grand shift of populations. However, by the ideologically determined special status of the Jews, the scheme of moving the Jews out functioned independently of the grander scheme, and it included the previously established and—as yet incompletely executed—policy of clearing Germany of Jews.

Second, with the conquest of the western part of Poland, the opportunity seemed at hand to implement the grand scheme of expanding the living space for Germans by restricting that of Poles, and to implement the sub-scheme of ridding that space of Jews. The appropriate instrument existed, that is, the SS and its subsidiaries, such as the SD and the *Einsatzgruppen*. Its authority was established, and its units were in place in Poland, to the occasional chagrin of the army. Since Poland as a newly conquered territory was still a military zone, matters of order and consolidation of the new authority were the concern of the army. In spite of the fact that Germany rapidly installed civilian agencies at all levels of governmental authority and in all major segments of organized social life, the SS had freedom of movement and of maneuvering independently of these authorities, especially during the initial, confusing period of consolidation. However, the recalcitrant ways of reality would not bend to the totalitarian will no matter how grandiose, no matter how decisive. The military knew that disturbing elements cannot be controlled when there is a chaotic stream of homeless refugees. Economists knew that crops are not raised when peasants are uprooted. Local administrators knew that order is not established when the orders of one authority are countermanded by another. And the railway officials knew that priorities had to be set when orders exceeded the means available to carry them out.

Thus, policy came into conflict with the apparent opportunity of implementing it. The policy was upheld, only the mode of its implementation had to be changed. This was the conclusion that the Nazis had to derive from the experience of the Nisko episode. The specific nature of the conclusion depended on the echelon at which it was derived, and even then it had to be inferred in large part from the context of later events.

Eichmann saw that the resettlement could not start up, much less succeed, unless prior and complex arrangements were made, and that it could not simply be left to the cleverness of the functionaries of the desperate Jews. The arrangements involved territorial jurisdictions; local policies, especially as regards the Jewish question; questions of the German economy; problems of supply and provisioning; logistics of transportation, of policing and guarding; and the availability of housing, means of productivity, and of exchange; etc. No doubt Eichmann understood that such arrangements had to be negotiated and secured at echelons outside of and considerably above the level of his competence and operation. Henceforth, he would have to restrict himself to making immediate arrangements, ensuring appropriate authorizations from above, to the extent that his limited authority made this possible, consolidating his sphere of authority and thereby enhancing it, and above all, continuing to succeed in contriving to obtain Jewish cooperation.

Further events show that in fact Eichmann would never again attempt on his own to establish a place that would receive Jews. His activity would be restricted to getting rid of Jews by forced emigration and deportation. The Nisko episode ended for him with the disbanding of the camp that the Jews had built. This happened in April 1940. By then, much larger labor camps had been established by agencies of the SS that had been charged specifically with this task. One such camp was in the vicinity of Nisko, in Bełzec; another was in Auschwitz (Oświęcim). While the Nisko camp was a labor camp and anything but a picnic, the atmosphere was sufficiently relaxed for some of the inmates to have been able to escape. At the point when the camp was disbanded, Eichmann used a ploy that he no doubt thought would confirm his position vis-à-vis the Jews as a benign executor of the Nazi policy concerning the Jews. He ordered the 198 Jews who had joined the camp from Vienna and who were still all there at the end, to return to Vienna. They constituted barely 12 percent of those who had left Vienna less than half a year before, and they must have known at least some of the terrible things that had happened to some of the others who had been driven away. Nonetheless, in light of his apparent magnanimity, Eichmann may have been hoping for favorable reports by way of mouth of the kind of life that could be expected when he planned the arrangements and executed them.

However, by the time the returnees arrived in Vienna, the Jewish leaders had drawn their own conclusions from the Nisko experiment. We have a fairly clear and informed idea of what they inferred, an idea which, however, differs from what had been believed in the past. Perhaps most telling in this regard is the judgment of Rosenkranz:

> After his return to Vienna, Murmelstein, probably at Eichmann's bidding, declines to prepare an official report, even for Löwenherz. But they [Murmelstein and Boschan] cannot prevent the leaking of rumors that are more frightening than the reality. As the people were disembarking from the trains they had been fired upon with machine guns already in place, and only a few of them, fleeing in all directions, had remained alive. These rumors caused the relatives remaining in Vienna to storm the IKG in panic.[160]

Rosenkranz is basing himself on the following passage of a memoir by one Mulisch Mautner:

> After the occupation of Poland all Polish citizens [in Vienna] were collected and Rabbi Murmelstein, who was well known as the liaison of the Gestapo, was placed at the head of this transport. So as to organize further transports, Murmelstein, after his return, declined to submit an official report to the IKG. However, it filtered through that at their arrival, the Jews were fired on from mounted machine guns as they disembarked from the train, and only a few of them scattered in all directions insofar as they succeeded to flee.[161]

The credibility and reliability of Mautner's report can be inferred from our account so far. Rosenkranz himself discerns that what Mautner reports as fact is merely rumor. Yet, he gives credence to Mautner's claim that Murmelstein declined to submit a report about Nisko to Löwenherz. The above passage from Rosenkranz was published after our interviews with Murmelstein. However, Rosenkranz had indicated in an earlier publication how seriously he took the quoted passage in Mautner.[162] Hence, we confronted Murmelstein with this quotation, and he was appalled. There were good reasons for the lack of an official report, and the validation of those reasons does not depend on Murmelstein.

In the first place, we have already seen from the *Aktennotiz* of October 27 that Löwenherz spoke to Eichmann at that time about the anxiety among the Jewish population regarding the settlement project and that rumors were being spread about it. Hence, Murmelstein's return (as well as that of Grün and Storfer) during the first week of November came at a time when rumors were already rife among the Jews. We know this also from the exchange of letters between Fuchsgelb and the *Jüdisches Nachrichtenblatt* cited earlier. Second, Murmelstein was outraged that Rosenkranz, as an expert on this period in history, should fail to see the extreme danger as well as futility of even attempting an official "honest" report of events in and around Nisko—not that the minimum of facts (e.g., only 12 percent of the Jewish contingent from Vienna had been allowed to remain in the camp and that the rest had been hounded to God knows where, with heavy casualties and no information on survivors) would have been particularly reassuring. And third, Murmelstein insisted most strongly and repeatedly that he briefed Löwenherz in complete detail on what went on in the Nisko area—but, of course, under the strictest secrecy.[163] We can trace the effect of this briefing on Löwenherz—who, as we have seen, had already become very suspicious of the scheme—in the result of Löwenherz's meeting with the representatives of the AJDC, especially Mr. Troper, in December of 1939 in Amsterdam. At that time, the Joint decided that there would be no more moneys forthcoming for Vienna, unless the deportations to Poland were halted.[164] For the Joint to issue such a strong ultimatum, there must have existed a very compelling reason, namely, a full briefing on the Nisko facts and their implications for the survival of the Jewish community. And nothing that Eichmann had said or done could have led the Jewish leadership to believe that Jewish survival played any role in his plans.

It must have taken a considerable amount of insistence on the part of Löwenherz to make Troper understand the portents of the Nisko experience and to move the AJDC to issue their ultimatum. We infer this from what, according to Murmelstein, Löwenherz reported to him after returning from Amsterdam. When the topic of the late resettlement to Nisko was broached, Troper's initial comment was, "That is the solution!" If Nisko had revealed any bona fide intention by the Nazis to resettle the Jews in Polish territory, it would indeed have been a solution of sorts to the "Jewish problem." Löwenherz had to disabuse Troper of the notion that Nisko was even remotely a "solution."

Instead, Löwenherz and Murmelstein were convinced that when it came to resettlement, the Nazis had absolutely no intention of benefiting the Jews and only meant to give the appearance that such benefit was intended in order to ensure Jewish cooperation. Based on the Nisko experience, Löwenherz and Murmelstein now saw clearly that assurances were not to be trusted, that blandishments must arouse suspicion, and that promises had ulterior motives. They were more convinced than ever that directives were to be passed on explicitly as directives of the authorities, and that only directives and nothing beyond directives were to be carried out. There would be no volunteering to engage in an enterprise that the Nazis wanted done, no calls for volunteers.

Not all the functionaries who were in Nisko drew the same inferences. In time Edelstein readily welcomed the chance to be the one to build the Theresienstadt ghetto from scratch. To him it would represent the opportunity to show how deportation followed by resettlement in a Jewish enclave ought to proceed, moreover under a Jewish leadership that was clearly superior, and it seemed to him an ideal way of preparing a great number of young and of more experienced people for the Jewish return to Palestine, the land of their fathers. Convinced that he and his hand-picked cadre of volunteers would build a productive Jewish society better than the Nazi bunglers who improvised Nisko, he apparently did not realize that, no matter what came of his efforts, his success would play into the hands of the Nazis. Some say that Edelstein's enthusiasm for building and ruling Theresienstadt was a result of certain inferences he drew from the Nisko experience, that resettlement to the east (i.e., Poland) meant death.[165] But, this is a wild guess; there is no evidence that Edelstein drew such an inference, neither does his effort on behalf of Theresienstadt imply such.

After Nisko, Edelstein was, in effect if not in title, the chief representative of the Czech Jews vis-à-vis the Nazi authorities. And evidently, he thought that dealing with them required a posture of dignity and guileless openness.

As regards the former, Bondy reports an incident that occurred at the time when Storfer first came to Prague to be introduced to Edelstein in Eichmann's presence. When Storfer walked up to Eichmann, the latter shouted, as was his wont "*drei Schritte vom Leib*," which means "three paces from my body." Jews had to keep their distance from their Aryan overlords, and the then current way of enforcing this was by means of the cited command. Persons like Storfer and Murmelstein, who occasionally had to explain documents or reports on emigration to Eichmann, were often permitted to come closer to his presence and even to sit nearby. However, it is doubtful that Storfer, when he entered the room in Prague, had any reason to break the rule of "three paces." Hence, it is safe to assume that the command was shouted for the benefit of Edelstein. What was Edelstein's reaction? "Describing this incident to the staff of the [Prague] Palestine office, Edelstein remarked, 'If Eichmann had treated me like that, he would not have extracted another word from me.' The most important quality in dealing with Germans, he said, was to preserve one's dignity."[166] A few pages later, Bondy reports that Edelstein "spoke . . . of the burden it was to be in daily contact with the Germans, stressing that he did it out of a sense of obligation. Somewhat ironically, he spoke of those 'delicate souls' who knew that the job had to be done for the general good but were not prepared to contaminate themselves through contact with the Germans," a sentiment for which we have considerable understanding, showing as it does Edelstein's awareness of the degree to which men in his position were held suspect by his fellow Jews. Yet, this apparently did not prevent him from making uninformed judgments concerning the chief functionaries in Vienna, nor did it make his own performance, especially in his relation to the Nazis, transparent to himself. Bondy continues: "For him, the constant contact with the SS was an incessant battle with fear. Edelstein was no undaunted heroic figure; it was enough to look at him: a bespectacled Jewish clerk, who shrank from violence and had never in his life raised his hand against anyone. Sometimes, when he was unexpectedly called to the Gestapo, he would feel a weakness overcome him, turn pale, and have to go to the toilet—yet he went, his stomach in turmoil, but never betraying his fears."[167]

The posture of dignity and the effort to overcome fear seemingly left Edelstein with few reserves for being circumspect and suspicious in his direct dealings with the Nazi Germans. Bondy reports an episode, which to our minds illustrates Edelstein's naiveté in trying to deal man-to-man with his overlords, apparently unaware of possible dire consequences. At their meeting in Geneva in February 1940:

> Edelstein told Nahum Goldmann . . . that he had once asked a senior official in the German administration why the Germans were so bent on Jewish emigration, now, during the war, when the younger emigrants might very well join the British army. To which the man had replied that thousands of young Jews were apt to constitute a danger to the Protectorate in times of internal unrest, whereas a few thousand more or less British soldiers would not change the course of the war.[168]

We recall how discreet Murmelstein knew he had to be when, even prior to the outbreak of the war, he maintained an attitude of guarded ignorance as to what he believed to be the nature and purpose of the Richborough camp, which he supplied with able-bodied men. And now we hear of Edelstein guilelessly broaching the topic of potential Jewish militancy with the Nazi authorities. How they must have welcomed his enthusiasm for helping them concentrate those potential troublemakers in Theresienstadt! And we cannot help surmising that by revealing his awareness of this potential, Edelstein may, in effect, have helped, unwittingly to be sure, to strengthen German resolve to transfer thousands of able-bodied Jews from Theresienstadt to Auschwitz—as well as eventually Edelstein himself. In the film *The Bridge over the River Kwai*, the British officer (played by Alec Guinness) who, guilelessly, made it possible for his fellow prisoners of war to build the railway bridge for their Japanese captors, is heard to say, as he sees British commandos destroying the bridge, "What have I done?" We have no report of a similar belated epiphany from Edelstein.

The eventual establishment of the Theresienstadt ghetto, at least in its function as an *Altersghetto* (ghetto for the old), was also related to some of the inferences Löwenherz and Murmelstein drew from the Nisko episode. Even though the resettlement action was suspended, Eichmann had indicated that it would resume in the not-too-distant future, and Löwenherz and Murmelstein had no reason to doubt that. The only problem was how to prepare for it. In particular, Murmelstein urged on Löwenherz a policy of doing what could be done not to let the old, the sick, and the infirm go on any further resettlement transports, as well as to find other pretexts for keeping Jews from being deported. When the Nazis became serious about purging Vienna of Jews and it became clear that even the old, the infirm, and the sick would have to leave, Murmelstein carefully began hinting to Eichmann about the benefits of establishing a settlement specifically for their care, and he was certain that his carefully phrased suggestion ultimately resulted in the establishment of

Theresienstadt.[169] In fact, in German documents of that time, Theresienstadt was, in fact, referred to as an *Altersghetto*.[170]

Murmelstein's firsthand experience of Nisko revealed overwhelming hardships, and he concluded that only those with a strong constitution and well-supplied with the proper necessities had any chance of surviving them. Hence, care had to be taken that future deportees be outfitted for the harshest weather and be prepared for the worst sanitary conditions, for unreliable and meager means of sustenance, and for the most dire threats to their lives.

Löwenherz and Murmelstein knew of no outcry abroad against the resettlement deportations. They heard no voices raised because the Jews were once again abandoned to this new dimension of persecution. They knew that the only recourse was their contact with the free Jewish organizations through the AJDC, which was permitted only under the condition that it be useful to the Nazis as a source of money to aid emigration. And, as we have seen, Löwenherz and Murmelstein were able to persuade the AJDC to make such contributions conditional upon the end of deportations. But this was not enough.

What was needed in a war in which the Jews were held hostage by a victorious Nazi regime, with no relief in sight, was a radical program of opening the doors of immigration. Another inference the Jewish functionaries in Vienna drew was that against the odds of acutely restrictive wartime conditions the emigration effort had to be renewed, and in fact reinvented, with even greater vigor. (In chapter 9 we recount how 12,000 more of Vienna's Jews were saved in this way.)

There is one inference the Jewish leaders of Vienna did not and could not draw from the Nisko experience. No doubt Nisko showed that the perils of deportation were such that many of even the hardiest would perish. But there was nothing that would prepare the leaders for the horrendous enterprise of planned extermination. Their assumption that they now knew the worst that the Nazis could do to them was the Achilles heel of their informed mistrust of their Nazi overlords.

No doubt Eichmann and the others who dealt with the Jews through the Jewish functionaries of Vienna expected them now to be increasingly wary and to try to restrict their cooperativeness to those directives that they did not recognize as harmful to the Jews. Hence, in order to keep the Jews and their functionaries in even greater ignorance and isolation under even tighter control, surveillance and censorship became more than ever a primary instrument of dealing with them as the solution of the Jewish problem inexorably moved from stage to stage. This too was a consequence of Nisko.

Those concerned with the Jewish question at the highest echelon of the Nazi regime were also involved in the Nisko experience, and not only at the theoretical level of sketching out a grand resettlement scheme. We saw, for example, that Himmler's office was keenly interested in the progress of what they thought was the beginning of the removal of the Jews from Greater Germany to the east. What were the inferences drawn from the Nisko experience at this level?

The Nisko experience taught that to rid the Greater Reich of its Jews by means of mass resettlement gave rise to conflicts with other policy priorities. Resettlement of the Jews needed prior planning, but planning involved the manpower and the cooperation of agencies that were carrying out other tasks related to policy. One could not tell a regional authority—installed in the conquered territory that was home to more Jews than Nazi Germany had ever had under its jurisdiction before—to rid his bailiwick of his Jews only to settle other Jews there. One could not make room for the resettlement of Germans by deporting Poles from some regions, only to have the Poles of other regions replaced by Jews. One could not provide even the minimal means necessary for the most primitive Jewish settlement without depriving other policy priorities of food, housing, materials, real estate, supervisory personnel, administrative services, transport, and so on. One may rid Greater Germany of Jews in this way, but Nazi Germany's "Jewish problem" would not be solved by transposing the Jews and the "problem" from one place to another within the areas under German control.

The Nisko enterprise was not only planned in a haphazard manner, it also showed that this sort of plan had to be undertaken within a larger context. Even if we consider only those other contextual priorities we have mentioned, we must conclude that the Nisko solution to the "Jewish problem" proved to be neither the most practicable nor the only feasible one. It does not take much imagination, at least in retrospect, to see the direction in which those officials were heading, who were bound by the logic of their overriding goal of getting rid of the Jews. The inferences drawn from the Nisko experience by those who determined Nazi policy at the highest echelon had to influence their plan for the next time.

The next time began on June 22, 1941, with the German invasion of Russia and the prospect of incorporating another unprecedentedly large Jewish population. The Nazis were ready. *Einsatzgruppen* of the SD would act as killing squads, decimating the newly conquered Jewish communities as the front advanced. In the former Polish territories, which would then be in a more settled situation in the rear of the military front, Jews could be brought to carefully installed killing centers. The deportation of the Jews could proceed without squandering territory and other means of resettlement, and it would take place according to the pattern first established for the Nisko transports: registration, 1,000 per transport, selections and exceptions, forms filled out, taxes paid, goods sold or left behind, financial assets "voluntarily" relinquished, Jews outfitted with warm clothing, good shoes, some money, extra food, other assistance from the IKG, guards, and so on.

Chapter 8

The Tightening Grip

Context: September 1939–October 1941

When he returned from Nisko, Murmelstein took up his accustomed place alongside Löwenherz, Engel, and the others in the well-oiled machinery of the IKG (*Israelitische Kultusgemeinde,* the Jewish Community of Vienna). This was by no means a return to some kind of normalcy, where Nisko was merely an interruption. Abnormality had become the norm, and the normal *modus operandi* of the IKG was to be alert and responsive to the modifications of the duress resulting from changes in the situation. There was no way for the IKG to expect or anticipate or in any way control them. This is what fundamentally defined the duress in all of the seven years under consideration. And yet, in their desperate attempts to save their Jews, the leadership had to muster their practiced intuition and skills to respond to the ever new modifications in the pressures brought to bear on them.

As fall merged into winter 1939, the main officials of the IKG were still—or again—at their posts. However, the situation had changed, and the duress modified. In this phase of the liquidation of Vienna's Jewish community the situation was fluid and would continue to change, as did the concomitant pressures, making a characterization of the distinctness of this phase difficult. To complicate matters, the time parameters of this phase overlap those of the next and final one, the central feature of which are the deportations, the threat of which was, however, an additional factor in determining the character of the present phase. This phase extends over the two years from the outbreak of the war to the fall of 1941, when Himmler issued the order to stop any further emigration of Jews. We were able to characterize the phase lasting from Kristallnacht until the outbreak of war as one in which the IKG had to operate within an ambiance of terror designed to motivate speedy emigration with the least expenditures of resources. Now, however, we are faced with a phase whose characterization requires clarity about what actually happened to the Jews during this time, as well as about the broader contexts, including world politics.

During this time, the Jews experienced an intensification of their abandonment and isolation concomitant with the tightening grip over them. In consequence, the leadership of the IKG was increasingly and as never before subject to their pressure, coercion, and control. The leadership's fundamental impotence in dealing with their overlords became more and more glaring, so that oftentimes their only—and usually futile—resource was their wit. Yet, in spite of decreasing means and increasing obstacles, they marshaled their staff for a massive effort to save as many of the Jews as possible.

In earlier chapters we alluded to the bearing of world politics on the extent to which Nazi Germany felt free to unfold its Jewish policy. Now, however, the broader context of the world political scene played a decisive role in defining the duress under which the Jews would find themselves in the ensuing phase. This context was now dominated by the changing fortunes of the war, the salient events of which we must keep in mind since they have bearing on the fate of the Jews.

It began in late summer 1939 with the German-Soviet Pact and the ensuing campaign that swiftly obliterated Poland, its territory divided between Nazi Germany and the Soviet Union. When, true to their treaty commitments, France and Great Britain declared war on Germany, Germany's western border became a frontline, albeit without any discernible consequence. The Germans referred to their Polish campaign as a *Blitzkrieg* (lightning war) and to the war in the West as a *Sitzkrieg* (haunch-sitters' war). It lasted until April 1940, when Germany secured its northern flank by taking Denmark and Norway with hardly a shot being fired. One month later, they began to repeat the maneuver devised at the turn of the century by then Chief of General Staff Alfred von Schlieffen for the eventuality that the German Imperial Army had to invade France. The plan called for marching into neutral Belgium, then making a flanking maneuver to the left into France; "let the cuff of the last man on the right touch the Channel," von Schlieffen admonished. In the First World War, the maneuver turned into the disastrous trench war, a bloody stalemate broken only when the Western Allies invented and deployed tanks, and also by the German Navy's reckless submarine warfare that caused the entry of the United States into the war. This time, however, the Germans had tanks. Nonetheless, France was ready, lining its direct border with Germany with the stationary fortifications and tank obstacles of the Maginot Line and, secure in their knowledge of the impenetrability of the Belgian forests, neglecting to complete them at their border with Belgium. Germany took the neutral Netherlands in four days, neutral Belgium in two weeks, and from there, driving through the impenetrable forests, easily breached the Maginot Line, the rightmost tank getting its treads wet on the beaches. In a trice Germany had occupied the Atlantic Coast from Norway in the north to the borders of Spain, which was sympathetic to Nazi Germany's fascism but, recovering from its brutal civil war, would remain neutral throughout the war. In June 1940 Germany accepted the humiliating surrender of France in the same railway carriage in which Imperial Germany had signed the humiliating armistice in November 1918.

Having gained predominance in the west and center of the continent, Nazi Germany turned to carry out its designs on the Balkans, where Mussolini's Italy had already gained a foothold in Albania. Italy joined the war on the side of its Axis partner when it was clear that France was about to fall before the onslaught of the German juggernaut. As 1940 was drawing to a close, giant Italy invaded tiny Greece, only to be bogged down because of the fierce resistance of the Greek fighters. In spite of Croat leanings toward Germany and Yugoslav Prince Paul's[1] readiness to accommodate Germany, the predominant Serbs among the peoples and the army of Yugoslavia rejected these moves, earning the country a furious military reaction by Germany in the spring of 1941. This made it possible for Germany to relieve its hard-pressed Axis partner in Greece, with the result that Germany now also predominated in the southern Balkans.

The incursion into Yugoslavia and Greece had not been on the Reich's military schedule. Hence, this additional success fatefully delayed what had been planned for spring 1941, namely, the treacherous invasion of Nazi Germany's ostensible ally, the Soviet Union. Instead, it began on the first day of summer. By the end of 1941, the time of the conclusion of the phase under consideration, Germany had conquered vast reaches of the Soviet Union, with no sign yet of the dismal fate that its massive armies would meet; this lay at least a year ahead. Until December 7, 1941, Great Britain was still the only Western nation in defiance of Nazi Germany, battling Field Marshall Rommel in North Africa.

None of these breathtaking successes, or the ones to come, were lost on the German population, on the captive nations, or on the Jews. And as we will see, none of these successes was without effect on the development and execution of Nazi policy regarding the Jews.

After the fall of Poland, in October 1939, a joke circulated among the Jews of Vienna. A radio program is interrupted for a special announcement: "Amid the jubilation of the population the Führer is entering the Old City of Tokyo at the head of his victorious troops." A Viennese is heard to comment: "Åber jetz *wird* er sich's Gnack brechn (but this time he *will* break his neck)." A Viennese joke, but it might as well have been the expression of the old grim Jewish humor, suited to the situation. It was a knowing humor, knowing that Hitler's breaking his neck in our lifetime was even less likely than his marching into Tokyo. It was the beginning of the realization that nothing less than the defeat of Nazi Germany could save the Jews. But, given Nazi Germany's unrestrained success, there was no glimmer of such a possibility on the horizon. Later, much later, when the appearance of this glimmer should have given rise to hope, it would not be certain that there would be any Jews left even to entertain such hope. And yet, the leadership at the IKG had to work toward both ends: getting Jews out of Nazi Europe and saving Jews for the distant day of deliverance.

More immediately, the joke indicated the dawning of a new dimension of the sense of the abandonment and isolation of the Jews. Near the end of chapter 6, we mentioned Löwenherz's telling Professor Norman Bentwich, the leading British advocate for the Jews under Nazi rule, that nothing less than diplomatic pressure on Berlin would help the Jews. But now, with Nazi Germany triumphant and evidently ready to take on all comers, there was no one left who might, by any stretch of the imagination, be in a position to pressure Germany about its Jewish policy. Great Britain, which, in spite of the White Paper of 1939 that had cut off Jewish immigration to British Mandatory Palestine, had been the country most ready to receive Jewish refugees, even if only on a temporary basis, was, in any case, now out of the picture. The United States was not of a mind to pressure Germany, and how seriously the United States was taken in Berlin was amply demonstrated by Hitler's public ridicule of Roosevelt's appeal for peace.

Given Germany's successes, the plight of the Jews was last on the agenda of the nations of the world, something that the Jews as well as the Nazis realized. The regime, it will be recalled, was secure in its conviction that anti-Semitism was its most successful export. And the extent to which the world's heart was bleeding for the plight of the Jews was, in spite of the bad press engendered by the outrages against the Jews, amply demonstrated by the glaring lack of welcome mats for the Jews anywhere in the world. With Germany at war, threatening one and all, the Jews were now completely abandoned and delivered to the Nazi regime to do with as it would see fit.

In addition to public ostracism, control, restriction of contacts, and the atmosphere of terror that had hitherto marked the machinery of the Jews' isolation, the conditions of war greatly increased their isolation. Much of the non-Jewish population of Vienna would continue to support the regime, especially its Jewish policy. Even though as the war wore on many Austrians became disillusioned with and even opponents of the regime, they would continue to knuckle under to it. But for almost all of them, the Jews in their midst were the enemy; or else they were the handy scapegoat for all the suffering, deprivations, and casualties that came with being at war. In any case, the Jew was the parasite who had food and shelter but who, unlike the *Volksgenossen* (countrymen), was exempt from risking his life for the fatherland.

Things looked quite different from where the Jews stood. Their meager prewar contacts and support from abroad were now eliminated, sharply curtailed, or manipulated according to the whim—or plan—of their oppressors. The more the IKG felt the tightening of the vise of their impotence, the more the Jews became dependent on the IKG, whether for their means of escape or their means of survival.

In this chapter and the following ones we will see the specific factors of the situation that marked this phase as it affected the remaining Jews caught in wartime Vienna and determined the activity and the function of the IKG and its leadership. This chapter will deal with the tightening of the Nazis' chokehold on the Jews of Vienna and, in particular, on the IKG. In the next chapter we will deal with the effort to save more Jews through emigration, which was a desperate effort to open doors of escape and pave ways thereto. And finally, in chapter 10, we will report on an activity the leading men of the IKG were engaged in in the midst of the turmoil of trying to save the Jews: They were telling about the tragic—yet proud—past of the Jews and about their dismal present. Their audiences included "their" Jews so as to encourage them in an increasingly hopeless situation, the Nazis so they may know whom they were destroying, their outside contacts as a cry for help, and posterity as a testimony of unconquerable spirit.

The New Regime

Until the outbreak of the war on September 1, 1939, the task of getting rid of the Jews was left in the hands of Eichmann and his *Zentralstelle*. The process they supervised was that of emigration, a laborious process as we have seen, which in any case seemed to have ground to an irremediable standstill under wartime conditions of indeterminate duration. All the political, administrative, and service authorities that governed in Vienna—Mayor Neubacher, Plenipotentiary Bürckel, the Gestapo, the municipal Housing Bureau, and the Labor Bureau—were now faced with the urgent question of how to get rid of the remaining Jews. It seemed as if the matter had, in effect, slipped out of the hands of SD-112 and in particular of Eichmann. No wonder that he eagerly took the opportunity of directing the Nisko project and worked hard to regain a handle on the solution of the Jewish problem through his network of *Zentralstellen* after the demise of Nisko.

Meanwhile, as soon as the war broke out, other Nazi Party as well as governmental authorities in Vienna got together for a concerted effort to give priority to the stubborn Jewish problem in Vienna, in part by enlisting the highest authorities in Berlin. This urgency marks the defining context of the situation of the Jews and of related events between the outbreak of war and the onset of deportations. A look at some of the written record of this effort will bring this context to light.

Four days after the outbreak of hostilities, Walter Rafelsberger began a letter to Erich Gritzbach, the Ministry Director assigned to Göring as Plenipotentiary for the Four Years' Plan, as follows:

> Recent events call for new and speedy steps to remove the Jews of Vienna. It is known to me that in the next few days relevant Reich departments will be apprised of this situation, and the NS-Party *Gau*-leadership as well as the Burgomaster of Vienna, and, in any case, *Statthalter* [Bürckel] will ask for help to remedy it. Together with these officials I consider it necessary to inform you and the General Field Marshal [Göring] of the new situation and what it requires.[2]

These other officials did indeed contact the relevant Reich departments about the situation. In fact, Mayor Neubacher wrote to Economics Minister Walther Funk the same day Rafelsberger wrote to Göring's office. Like Rafelsberger, Neubacher claimed that even after the emigration of 110,000 Jews, there were still more than 150,000 in Vienna. He advanced two reasons that "we in Vienna are preoccupied with the Jewish problem" and he asked Funk "to concern himself with this problem."[3]

First, "such a mass of evident enemies of the state influences public opinion under all circumstances." It is incredible how even a "mass" of cowed, disenfranchised, politically, socially, and spiritually isolated and controlled people can be claimed to have the power to influence public opinion. But such was the nature of the ideological view of the Jews. Rafelsberger was also constrained to justify the "new situation and requirements." While his argument was convoluted and not without inconsistency, it was more clever and plausible than Neubacher's and inadvertently revealed his concern over the loyalty of the Viennese proletariat to the Nazi cause, especially now that Nazi Germany was at war: "We cannot prevent the great number of Jews, who have no discernible occupation, from constantly developing flash-points of resistance in workers' quarters. Moreover, in recent days Jews have been observed to disport themselves in an increasingly impudent manner. Thus the danger could arise that the populace would proceed to remedial actions on their own, which, under the present circumstances, must be seen as especially undesirable." Rafelsberger too—incredibly—feared the possibility of the Jews' influence on the populace, but the conclusion he drew is the opposite of Neubacher's, namely, that the people would proceed against the Jews vigilante-style.

Neubacher went on to give vent to his concern that a mass of Jews "could be the cause for excesses, which must be prevented." Curiously, this expression of fear stands in marked contrast to his concluding remark in his letter to Funk, assuring him that "in Vienna things are working well [*alles klappt*] and, according to the observations of all authorities and party officials, the populace is maintaining a completely calm attitude and the best possible discipline." The remedy suggested by Neubacher would remove the Jews to camps, away from population centers, where they would be put to useful work. And in connection with this suggestion, Neubacher revealed what, in his position as mayor, was the real reason for getting rid of the Jews of Vienna: "Such an action would also relieve the housing market that is so tight, especially in Vienna."

Rafelsberger proceeded more knowledgeably and circumspectly. He reported that the "dejudaization of private enterprises has practically been completed." He should know, since, as a member of the SS and in his function as Director of the Nazi Party's Economics Bureau and of the Office of Asset Transfer, he had been in charge of the organized Aryanization of Jewish businesses in Vienna from the beginning. His success in that regard carried weight with Göring, who was the one who, from the time of the Anschluss, demanded and motivated the elimination of Jews from the economic life of Vienna. Continuing his report, Rafelsberger pointed out that

> because of the methods followed so far, more than two-thirds of Jewish non-agricultural real estate in Vienna is still owned by Jews. For this sector measures repeatedly proposed by us will . . . be necessary, i.e., the appointment of non-Jewish building managers, and the takeover of these building properties by a financial consortium.[4]

While it is true that the expropriation of some buildings had not been carried out as yet and they were still under nominal Jewish ownership, it is also true that Jews were no longer in control of their management or in a position to derive any rental profit from them. What this passage indicates is that the vigorous ongoing expropriation would be intensified.

Rafelsberger proceeded to discuss the expulsion of the Jews by providing the following background:

> Clearly more urgent is the immediate removal of the 150,000 to 180,000—the remnant of originally about 300,000 residents, who are still in the country—who are pensioners or proletarians. In these times this great number of Jews poses a political danger of considerable significance.[5]

He spelled out the proposed solution in greater detail than Neubacher did in his letter to Funk:

> We regard the removal of the majority of the Jews to forced labor camps, which must be scattered over the whole Reich, as the only effective chance of immediately meeting those dangers. We are thinking mainly of road construction, brickyards, and different kinds of large factories, where Jews can be employed in segregated sections. Personally I am convinced that it is absolutely indispensable that the Jews be barracked in camps and appropriately guarded. Uncontrolled distribution of the Jews over the whole Reich would diminish the extent of this political danger in Vienna but would spread it over the whole Reich.[6]

Rafelsberger concludes: "Appropriate proposals are being worked out at present with the Labor Bureau and economic organizations and will be submitted shortly to relevant offices."

In the weeks to follow there was indeed a lot of activity. Statistics were gathered, proposals formulated, problems confronted, solutions grasped at, courses of action redirected, and appeals to higher authorities submitted. Most telling is a letter from Bürckel to Neubacher, telling him that he had appointed Dr. Becker, a member of his staff, to examine the "question of a large-scale internment [of Jews] in mass camps, and how such a measure would affect the housing market."[7] Becker's survey produced a memorandum with many appendices. One of these discusses the logistics of creating the sort of barracks camp with simple amenities for Jewish families of 6,000 persons in Gändersdorf, especially the different inexpensive options for the removal of fecal matter and liquid waste.[8] We know from the Nisko project (see chapter 7) that Bürckel favored this kind of camp. However, inasmuch as Becker's completion of the study coincided with the onset of the Nisko action, the memorandum reports, somewhat prematurely, that "Berlin agrees that in this first action [of evacuating all the Jews from the territory of the Reich] all the Viennese Jews will be included."[9] By way of a contingency plan, the memorandum states: "In case the total solution of the Jewish problem is not effected through the relocation to Poland, the rest of the Jews . . . will have to be located in barracks."[10] In any case, the conclusion is that "the most dire need for housing in Vienna will be met to the extent that Jewish housing is vacated."[11]

For the Housing Bureau all this studying and planning did not do enough to evict Jews from their housing. On October 3, 1939, they tried to enlist the Gestapo's "decisive" help in having evicted Jews actually leave their rooms: "Through their impudent demeanor the Jews make the work at the Bureau burdensome . . . they declare themselves ready to vacate their apartment at a certain date, let themselves be issued assignments for other housing, and on the date they do not vacate because of illness or financial difficulties. . . . This [tactic] has spread among the Jews so that no Jew would think of meeting the deadline." And Dr. Leopold Tavs, the Deputy Director of the Housing Bureau, was, unbeknown to him, grasping at straws but anticipating future actions when he asked Bürckel "to persuade SS Reichsführer Himmler, first of all, that of the entire Reich, the Viennese Jews be transported [to Poland] first; and, second, that whole families be transported. This is the only solution that would alleviate the Viennese housing situation at least for the first half of 1940."[12] The letter was not received in Bürckel's office until October 27, a day after the last transport to Nisko had left Vienna. And when Eichmann was preparing for additional transports in spite of resistance from all manner of offices superior to him, Himmler personally had to issue his curt directive on November 8: "Because of technical problems I forbid the deportation of Jews to Poland until further notice. Deportation can take place only upon my directive."[13]

We do not need to give further details of all the different deliberations and machinations, nor of conflicting plans and expectations on the part of the many authorities who had one or the other interest in the solution of the Jewish problem in Vienna at the beginning of the war. What we have learned is sufficient to indicate the atmosphere prevailing among the authorities right from the beginning of the phase under consideration. As far as the Jews were concerned, all this took place behind the scenes, but it forms the predominant context of pressure on the Jews and on the IKG. How this would affect them we saw in part in chapter 7, with more details to follow in this chapter, when we discuss the evictions from dwellings, the IKG's struggle to retain assets and the proceeds from their sale, the entry of Jews into the forced labor market, as well as the control, the extortion, the exploitation, and so on.

Beyond that, we have to note that the offices represented by these documents formed a powerful lobby to have Vienna be first in Nazi Germany's program to eliminate the Jews, pressure to which Berlin was receptive. In time they would be a source of pressure to resume the deportations interrupted by the end of the Nisko project. While there is no hard evidence at that point in time to the effect that getting rid of the Jews would have to involve extermination, there are hints that those who determined Jewish policy in Berlin would be led to the conclusion that extermination would prove to be the only feasible means toward that end.

Before leaving the documents connected with Becker's survey of the Jews of Vienna at the beginning of the war and the new initiatives detailing what to do with the Jews, it behooves us to take a look at what the documents reveal about Jewish demography. In chapter 7 we reported that the IKG undertook a registration of Jews as of September 15, 1939. Since we did not find any trace or indication of a Nazi directive ordering this survey, we asked Murmelstein why it was undertaken. According to him, the Nazis labored under the impression that at the time of the Anschluss there were 300,000 Jews in Vienna; this exaggerated figure presented the IKG with even more difficulties in their dealings with the Nazi authorities as to budgeting for welfare needs as well as with more pressure because the IKG was incapable of speeding up the emigration of so many Jews, and it presented obstacles in their effort to protect those who had not yet left nor ever would. Since this proved to be a particularly vexing obstacle in the IKG's already difficult position vis-à-vis the Nazis, Löwenherz and Murmelstein had to find a way of dispelling it, and registration was the answer. The documents in question (e.g., Rafelsberger's letter of September 5, four days after the beginning of the war to Göring's office) confirm Murmelstein's explanation. And Löwenherz, when he reported to Eichmann at the beginning of December that there were only 58,000 Jews remaining in Vienna, referred to the September survey as the one "conducted by the IKG Vienna."[14]

According to the Nazis' assumption, there should still have been about 190,000 Jews in Vienna when the war broke out, close to 110,000 having emigrated by then. The number of Jews who registered at the IKG came to 65,612, to which 768 youths had to be added who were away on agricultural retraining in preparation for emigration to Palestine.[15] This figure was evidently not available when Rafelsberger wrote his letter, but it found its way into the surveys submitted to Becker five weeks later. With 66,000 Jews remaining plus 110,000 emigrated plus a certain number of deaths there were the approximately 180,000 Jews residing in Austria at the time of the Anschluss. This figure was provided by the official Austrian census, where one had to indicate religious affiliation, if any; it is the figure with which the IKG had been operating.

But according to the Nazi theory, there were 300,000 Jews. Enter the Nazi distinction between *Glaubensjude* (Jew by faith) and *Rassejude* (Jew by race), the latter including Jews who had left the Jewish community, had converted to Christianity, had mixed parentage, or were living in a mixed marriage. According to Nazi ideology, the Jews they wanted to be rid of were all of them (i.e., the *Rassejuden*). Hence, if the IKG was able to account for 180,000 Jews, the remaining 120,000 of the stipulated 300,000 Jews must be *Rassejuden*, who were not *Glaubensjuden*. And if the IKG was able to account for a remnant of 66,000 Jews, then a goodly portion of the 120,000 *Rassejuden* whom the IKG could account for must still be in Vienna, that is, those who had not died or emigrated. This was the reasoning reflected in Rafelsberger's statement that "150,000 to 180,000—the remnant of originally about 300,000 residents who are still in the country" and in Neubacher's claim that after the emigration of 110,000 Jews, there were still more than 150,000 left in Vienna.

However, the authorities who were required to obtain and submit reliable background information to Dr. Becker availed themselves of sources which revealed that the stipulation of 300,000 had been a myth. The Vienna branch of the Interior Ministry, in its report to Becker, accepted the IKG figure of 66,000 *Glaubensjuden* remaining in Vienna, which they obtained from the *Zentralstelle*.[16] In August 1939 all those considered Jews had to apply for new identity cards identifying them as *Rassejuden*, which comprised Jews by faith. A survey of the number of applications at the various district police offices resulted in a total of 105,354, from which fewer than 1,000 had to be subtracted to account for those who were able to emigrate in September. Inasmuch as everyone had to be registered at the district police station, the survey also included 5,899 Jews who were foreign nationals and 7,128 stateless Jews, who for the most part were former Polish citizens. The report rounded off the total of racial Jews actually still in Vienna to "between 100,000 and 110,000," which is quite a different sum from the one based on the original erroneous stipulation. Another report submitted to Becker at the same time originated in the Organizational Office of the Nazi Party. From a similar survey of identity card applications and of foreign residents' registrations as of October 1 at the district police stations, the numbers are: 99,353 Jews who were German nationals and 13,000 who were foreign nationals or stateless. The total: 112,353 Jews,[17] which in essence corroborates the other survey. An interesting sidelight: A statistical report submitted to Becker at the same time by the Asset Transfer Office, which was Rafelsberger's bailiwick, reflects knowledge of the updated statistics but continues the claim that in 1938 there were 300,000 *Rassejuden* in Vienna.[18]

But no matter how many Jews were left in Vienna, a number of authorities began to take an interest in getting rid of them. The fact that the nation was at war stimulated them to action. The war also seemed to have brought the emigration efforts administered by Eichmann and the *Zentralstelle* to an effective stop and made their further usefulness in getting rid of the Jews questionable. No doubt Eichmann felt that his indispensability and that of the agency he had organized were at stake. The eagerness with which he had arranged the Nisko project and the ill-disguised disappointment when it was stopped by higher powers speak to that. However, in the weeks of uncertainty about who had the handle on the execution of the constantly evolving Jewish policy, it was Eichmann, with the blessing of his superiors, who was consolidating and centralizing his position and that of his agency. As various authorities began to look for ways of getting rid of the remaining Jews, the ruling echelons in Berlin, recognizing the need to maintain central control over policy and the means of executing it, confirmed Eichmann and his system of *Zentralstellen* as their ready instrument. The agitation by the various authorities, especially those in Vienna, to remove the Jews no doubt needed to be kept in check by the central authorities but also constituted a significant and welcome impetus to advance Jewish policy to the next level.

In effect, Eichmann, his agency (the *Zentralstelle*), his staff, and all those who often only tangentially acted as his agents would soon present themselves as a new regime under which the IKG would have to function and by which the Jews would experience ever greater duress. Let us look at the outlines of that regime, whose formal structure kept changing in the phase under consideration.

While Eichmann was engaged in organizing the abortive Nisko resettlement and had to travel from Mährisch-Ostrau (Ostrava) to Nisko and from Berlin to Kattowitz (Katowice), Löwenherz and his deputies were confronted with new men when they had to report at the *Zentralstelle*. They soon found that this was not a temporary change but indicated a reorganization of the SD machinery executing Jewish policy. We recall that as early as the period following Kristallnacht, Eichmann was in charge of directing the leaders of the *Reichsvereinigung* (Reich Association of Jewish Communities) and specifically of the Jewish community of Berlin to institute the machinery necessary for a processing center for expediting the emigration of the Jews of the Altreich, much like the one he had established in Vienna. Eichmann also set up a similar machinery in Prague, when Nazi Germany marched in in the spring of 1939. Now Eichmann had his main office in Berlin at the newly established RSHA, the *Reichssicherheitshauptamt* (Reich-headquarters of the Security Service [SS]) presided over by Himmler and Heydrich, into which all the regime's security services had been consolidated following the conquest of Poland and the consequent expansion of security operations. This indicates that Eichmann's operation designed for the liquidation of Jewish existence in Greater Germany was from then on under direct control and supervision of the chief decision makers, administrators, and executors of Nazi Jewish policy.

Eichmann would occasionally make his rounds, stopping in Vienna and Prague at his branch offices. Löwenherz or his deputies would report to him on these occasions. Normally, Löwenherz was summoned to Berlin for a day or two, where he would report to Eichmann directly. There Eichmann would deal with him, usually along with Eppstein representing the *Reichsvereinigung*, Dr. Hirsch representing the Berlin community, and Edelstein, sometimes accompanied by František Weidmann, representing Prague. For day-to-day business in Vienna, Eichmann's lieutenants would be the contacts to whom Löwenherz and his main associates would have to report. In Berlin Eichmann would usually deal with Löwenherz directly on main points and leave it to his lieutenants to settle details with Löwenherz before he returned to Vienna. This way of dealing with Löwenherz served to restrict his maneuverability vis-à-vis Eichmann even more than before and to restrict his ability to secure the means to save the Jews and to sustain the ones who needed care. Frequently Eichmann would listen to Löwenherz state his case and request that he submit an *Eingabe* (statement/application/report), or he would say he would consider it, only to have one of his lieutenants tell Löwenherz that what he requested could not be done, that it was out of his hands, that it was too late, that it would be done at a later date, that it was about to be done, that it would be done in stages, or that Eichmann was still considering it. In this way Eichmann interposed between himself and Löwenherz someone whose power consisted of issuing decisions that he did not have the power to make or to reverse. It would be futile for Löwenherz to present arguments to Eichmann's lieutenant, who most likely would listen to them and then find reasons to reject them; only on occasion would the lieutenant actually intercede on behalf of the IKG with local authorities or with Eichmann. Eichmann was the only one who could intercede on behalf of the IKG with the central governmental authorities in Berlin but only if it served his interests. In effect, the governmental authorities, whether on the ministerial level in Berlin or on the local level in Vienna, were in collusion with the Nazi authorities in liquidating Jewish assets and Jewish existence altogether, although not without conflicts of interest, which the IKG found itself caught in the middle of.

Within the SS the rivalry continued between the Gestapo and the SD (*Zentralstelle*) as to the jurisdictional parameters of dealing with the Jews. A somewhat amusing example is the following: A few days after the outbreak of hostilities, it occurred to someone at Gestapo headquarters that while the nation was engaged in fighting a battle of annihilation with an external enemy, one could not have an internal enemy running around freely. So one morning Löwenherz received a telephone call to report "immediately" to Room 316 of Gestapo headquarters, a few hundred feet downhill from the IKG. There an unnamed SS man handed him a four-point declaration to sign. The first point decreed that "The IKG is to build its own air-raid shelters." Löwenherz understood this to mean that the IKG was to build air-raid shelters for all the Jews in Vienna. We quote Löwenherz's record of the ensuing exchange:

> Whereupon I declared that we are most certainly not in a position to build air-raid shelters for all the Jews, whereupon I received the answer, that most certainly all Jews who live in private [apartment] buildings will make use of the air-raid shelters that are there. The IKG needs to provide air-raid shelters only in buildings that it owns.—To this I remarked that we have already provided for air-raid shelters in the official building of the IKG, in the hospital and the old-age homes.[19]

The other points concerned a special curfew for Jews as of 8:00 p.m. to take effect on that very day. "Whoever breaks this prohibition, will be punished." This order must not be published in the *Jüdische Nachrichten* (Jewish Newspaper) but announced by means of notices in the soup kitchens and buildings of the IKG. How the Jews were to be informed before the order went into effect that evening is not recorded.

As the days were getting shorter, the men at the Gestapo decided they did not want to have Jews wandering about in blacked-out Vienna and moved the curfew forward to 4:00 p.m. This proved to be an excessive hardship, and Löwenherz asked for a revocation.[20] When the promised decision on the matter was not forthcoming, he pointed out that the emigration and other work of the IKG, the Palamt, and Storfer's office had to suffer when the employees had to be home by 4:00 p.m.[21] Two days later Kuchmann from the Gestapo called Löwenherz to tell him to post announcements in the soup kitchens of the new curfew of 6:30 p.m.[22] However, when this was also not suitable for especially long working days at the offices dealing with emigration, Kuchmann instructed the IKG and the Palamt to list officials who had to work beyond the time of the official curfew and to submit the lists to Gestapo headquarters on the respective days.[23] This provision would be extremely important in the middle of 1940 when, owing to the forced reduction of the IKG staff, the persons working at the IKG had to work into the night.

Who were Eichmann's lieutenants? They came from the cadre of young SS officers who had been assigned to him after he took up his post in Vienna and who were trained by him to deal with the Jews in matters of liquidating the Jewish community. We met the brothers Rolf and Hans Günther at the time of the Nisko episode (see chapter 7). In the phase under present consideration, Rolf Günther was Eichmann's deputy at his headquarters in Berlin and his right-hand man wherever he needed to be represented in matters dealing with the liquidation of the Jews. Occasionally he would stand in as Eichmann's representative, especially whenever Eichmann preferred not to be challenged by Löwenherz's deferential probing. Hans Günther was assigned to be Eichmann's lieutenant in Prague and the Protectorate of Bohemia and Moravia, and in time would deal with matters connected with the Theresienstadt ghetto. In Vienna Eichmann's lieutenant, who would, for the present phase, be the main official for Löwenherz and his associates to report to, was Alois Brunner. The Nazis as well as the IKG personnel referred to him as Brunner 1 to distinguish him from Anton Brunner. Eichmann's lieutenant for Berlin (i.e., for the Jews in the Altreich) was Theodor Dannecker, who would occasionally also deal with Löwenherz in Eichmann's stead.

Thus, the prevalence of a new regime presented itself to Löwenherz only indirectly, at least for a while. Occasionally, indications of the changeover came from Eichmann, the earliest of these at a *Vorsprache* (meeting) in mid-November 1939. On the previous day, Eichmann had given his version of why the Poland action had been suspended, supposedly until early the following year. Now he told Löwenherz that a commission from Berlin had inspected the *Zentralstelle* that morning in order to determine whether it should continue to operate. Eichmann said that its continuance would depend on the emigration effort and pressured Löwenherz to produce estimates of how many emigrants could be processed in the next few months.[24] In other words, when the Nisko project fizzled out as soon as it began, Eichmann had reason to be worried about his future usefulness despite his new status at the RHSA in Berlin. He therefore did not even hint at it until he felt secure enough in his new position to use it for putting pressure on Löwenherz.

The new regime was in place when Löwenherz had to report to Eichmann at the *Zentralstelle* Berlin on December 19, after he had finally been able to meet with Morris C. Troper of the Joint (American Jewish Joint Distribution Committee). Eichmann explained that there was now a general *Reichsstelle für jüdische Auswanderung* (Reich-center for Jewish Emigration), whose directorship he "had taken over." The *Zentralstellen* in Vienna, Berlin, and Prague "would operate separately, and none will be superior or subordinate to any other."[25] Eichmann also announced that he would spend half a month in Berlin, the other half traveling between "Vienna, Prague, and the General Government in Poland." Löwenherz was expected to report to him once a month in Berlin, where those matters would be settled "whose decisions depend on the *Zentralstelle* Berlin."[26] It should be noted that Eichmann, in his function as director of the *Reichsstelle*, was not only, as heretofore, responsible for the *Zentralstellen* in Vienna, Berlin, and Prague but also for an unnamed

Eichmann's right-hand man in Vienna, Alois Brunner, who is often referred to as Brunner 1 in order to distinguish him from Anton Brunner, aka Brunner 2, who was also active in Vienna during the Nazi era. (DÖW 1642[2] Alois Brunner)

function with respect to the Jews in Nazi-conquered Poland. This fact was duly noted by Löwenherz in his *Aktennotiz* (memorandum), and kept in mind.

The full scope of Eichmann's new parameters of responsibility became clear to Löwenherz early in 1940, when he had to report to Eichmann in Berlin, and later in Vienna. While in Berlin, Eichmann ordered Löwenherz and Rothenberg to inspect the institutions and operations of the Reich Association of Jews in Germany (*Reichsvereinigung*), the Jewish Community of Berlin, and the Berlin Palestine Office (the Palamt). It will be recalled that when Eichmann established the Berlin *Zentralstelle* about a year earlier, he had tried to motivate the Jewish leaders of Berlin to expedite their emigration process by having them visit the IKG in Vienna so they could learn what the process should be like. The men from Berlin were appalled by the forced emigration process that prevailed in Vienna. And they said so, only to be whipped back into shape by Eichmann. Now, at the beginning of 1940, the Jewish leadership in Berlin had long forgotten their insistence that the emigration procedures be followed in a proper and measured way, as well as their questions as to whether the application of Eichmann's pressure was conducive to the kind of working relations they found acceptable. These three Jewish agencies in Berlin were now duly toeing their mark, though it was a bit late in the game.[27] So, while in Berlin, it was now Löwenherz's turn to inspect the Berlin establishment.

Löwenherz's (and Rothenberg's) report ran to over five pages. As an afterthought Löwenherz gave the Berlin setup a better report card than the colleagues from Berlin had given Vienna a year earlier, and he hinted at what Berlin had failed to observe in Vienna, namely, that the conditions under which they had to do this unpleasant job were extremely harsh:

> The persons responsible for the *Reichsvereinigung* as well as those responsible for the Jewish Community of Berlin earnestly wish to solve the tasks assigned to them, to accommodate prevailing conditions, and, within the confines of available possibilities, to meet all obligations, especially in the area of emigration.[28]

Directly or indirectly Löwenherz took notice of the difference between the way things were done in Vienna and in the Altreich, and in particular in Berlin. In Austria Jews in the provincial communities were expelled or ordered to move to Vienna (this process would be completed in the phase under consideration). Such concentration of the Jewish population was not feasible in the Altreich because, as Löwenherz's inspection report mentions, only 90,000 of Germany's remaining 200,000 Jews lived in Berlin; the rest were distributed over 2,600 localities and 800 Jewish communities.[29] According to a decree of the Interior Minister, the *Reichsvereinigung* had overall responsibility for all Jewish organizations in Greater Germany (with the exception of former Austria); these organizations included all the Jewish communities, the aid organizations, and the Palamt Berlin. Yet there was a division of function among them, especially regarding the complex emigration process. The *Reichsvereinigung* was in charge of the whole process, but it left obtaining emigration documents to the various communities since such documents, especially tax clearances, had to be obtained locally. The *Reichsvereinigung* took care of helping to find immigration possibilities, booking and paying for passage, and routing the emigrés. Until its dissolution later that year, the Palamt Berlin operated largely autonomously "because of its special character and its rights and duties regarding emigration to Palestine."[30] Löwenherz was astonished to find that the *Reichsvereinigung* maintained a regular school system at both primary and upper levels, some measure of religious services, a cinema, and occasional theater presentations and concerts. It also issued the Berlin version of the *Nachrichtenblatt* (newspaper) with a circulation of 36,000.[31]

But what struck him most were the differences in the financial situation. In comparison with the struggle Löwenherz had in Vienna, the situation in Berlin must have seemed paradisiacal to him, a fact that would have considerable impact on the painful liquidation process to which Vienna was subjected in 1940. What were some of these differences?

Berlin vs. Vienna

The first item we mention here may seem trivial, but in light of what we will relate below it is anything but. The Palamt Berlin maintained a retraining program for 1,300 children and youngsters in preparation for their emigration to Palestine (*hakhshara*). The program consisted of young participants working in groups, presumably at farms and factories, moreover "for appropriate recompense, which alleviates the cost of the *hakhshara* program."[32]

According to the decree of the Interior Ministry mentioned above, the *Reichsvereinigung* was the legal successor of all Jewish "associations, foundations, and organizations" that were dissolved by the Nazi regime, and as such all their assets, "especially real estate and securities," devolved on the *Reichsvereinigung*. Unlike the IKG Vienna, the *Reichsvereinigung* in Berlin was able to make use of these assets to support its emigration effort and to meet its obligations such as welfare, medical services, old-age homes, and schools. In his report Löwenherz pointed out that the welfare budget of the Berlin *Reichsvereinigung* was proportionately considerably smaller than that of Vienna. For example, while during the summer months of 1939 Vienna fed up to 37,000 persons a day in their soup kitchens, Berlin fed between 5,000 and 6,000. The reason he gave was that "the [economic and social] stratification of the population in the Altreich was and is much more favorable than in the *Ostmark*."[33] What Löwenherz was obliquely referring to was that the Jewish communities in Germany were, by and large, much older than the one in Vienna, some dating back to Roman times. Therefore, the Jews were better established, and even though the emancipation of the Jews in Germany did not antedate that in the Austrian lands, over the centuries the Jews of Germany had suffered less by comparison from persecution and prejudice.

As the dismal financial bind of the IKG steadily worsened in the months to come, Löwenherz would remind Eichmann of certain facts about the financial situation of the *Reichsvereinigung* vis-à-vis the Berlin *Zentralstelle*, which must have flabbergasted him. The Jewish Community of Berlin was still collecting dues (*Kultussteuer*) from its members whereas the collection of dues to the IKG had ceased with the Anschluss. More important, in Berlin it was not the *Zentralstelle* that assessed and collected the *Auswanderungsabgabe* (i.e., the amount that emigrants had to pay from their remaining assets to receive their passports) but the *Reichsvereinigung*! Löwenherz reports:

> So far this emigration tax has brought in RM 18,000,000, and has enabled the RV [*Reichsvereinigung*] . . . to fulfill . . . its obligations in the areas of emigration, welfare, schooling, and religious observance, duties incumbent on it according to the decree cited above. The RV's right of immediate collection of the emigration tax enables it to determine a long-term budget for its internal expenses and to accrue reserves needed for unexpected outlays.[34]

That these financial arrangements of the *Reichsvereinigung* pertained only to the Jews of the Altreich points once again to the fact that the Nazis meant to keep the solution of the Jewish problem in former Austria separate, even though it was now an integral part of Greater Germany. Eichmann, as we know, had greater latitude in manipulating the Jews and their leaders under the condition prevailing in Austria as the result of the Anschluss (i.e., where rights and laws were largely suspended together with sovereignty). German law could not be established simply by supplanting the validity of Austrian law, which, for many reasons and in many instances, it was useful to retain. But retention of the old side by side with the new was bound to cause conflicts among various Nazi authorities who had an interest in the liquidation of Jewish assets while maintaining the semblance of legality, thereby multiplying ways in which pressure was applied to the Jewish leaders. For the Altreich the fact that all the "associations, foundations, and organizations" were incorporated into the *Reichsvereinigung* (and both the *Reichsvereinigung* and the communities, including the large one in Berlin, counted as such organizations) meant that, according to the Nazi decree, they now were private enterprises much like corporations, and any income they had was taxable. Thus, they were liable to pay and did indeed pay taxes, as did the Jewish Community of Berlin, against the dues collected from their members. The *Reichsvereinigung* and the Berlin community did this as a matter of course, among other reasons because they had ample income for meeting their operational expenses. Among other worries about the IKG budget, Löwenherz was concerned that the IKG not be declared a corporation under German law and thus be taxable but retain its status under Austrian law as a public institution. Evidently the Interior Ministry as well as sectors of the Nazi party machinery, particularly as represented by those who, under Bürckel, were charged with completing the alignment of former Austria with the Altreich, saw no reason for the IKG to be treated differently from the *Reichsvereinigung*. It appears, therefore, that the continuation of the IKG's status as a public institution was under threat at that time. While in Berlin, Löwenherz again pressed for a favorable resolution of this matter, and Eichmann assured Löwenherz that the IKG would retain its character as a public institution for the year 1940 "in principle."[35] It will become clear that Eichmann's accommodation of Löwenherz on this matter was not only a necessity for Löwenherz but also Eichmann's means of profiting in Vienna.

On another matter Eichmann would not budge, no matter how often Löwenherz would spell out its reasonableness, namely, permitting the IKG to be the direct recipient of what in Vienna was most often called the "passport fee," which was the most important source of Eichmann's growing "emigration fund." Eichmann would only occasionally, and then extremely grudgingly, release some of these funds so that the IKG could meet its obligations.

We do not know why Eichmann permitted the *Reichsvereinigung* in Berlin to collect the "emigration tax" directly and to build up a sizable reserve. We can only guess. Now that most aspects of the emigration process were centered in Berlin as the place where the travel agencies as well as other pertinent offices and especially the foreign consulates were located, it may have been politic not to put so much overt pressure on the Jews and their agencies, in the same way and for the same reasons as the anti-Semitic outbursts ceased during the Olympic Games of 1936. And, of course, Eichmann knew that the *Reichsvereinigung* was doing a splendid job of accumulating a fund that they had no way of using up as long as he was in charge. He could, therefore, bide his time until the money would devolve on his *Zentralstelle* enterprise. In the meantime, he had Vienna to enrich his fund for purposes he himself did not as yet know.

The separation of the operations of the IKG from those of the *Reichsvereinigung* and its subsidiaries had important advantages for the IKG, especially regarding the access to *Devisen* (foreign currency) from the Joint. Nonetheless, Löwenherz could not but be struck by the greater duress under which he had to operate, especially in regard to money matters. Why then did Eichmann have Löwenherz inspect the *Reichsvereinigung* and the Berlin community? Most likely it was not so much to receive recognition for having instituted in Berlin what the Berlin community inspectors had been so dismissive about in Vienna, only to be humbled into submission themselves, but to let Löwenherz realize that the regime he was under was, in fact, harsher and would increasingly be so, as Löwenherz would begin to find out only a few days after returning to Vienna from Berlin. Another reason may have been to put the leadership in Berlin on notice that what they established in emulation of Vienna was at Eichmann's sufferance and merely temporary, and that the next stages of duress were in the offing.

The centralization in Eichmann's hands of all direct dealings with the Jewish leadership consisted, in the main, of coordinating the lower executive authority of the regime's "security" policy by consolidating the central command structure. This was in keeping with the restructuring that established the RSHA shortly after the outbreak of the war, as we discussed in chapter 2.

Accordingly, when Eichmann visited Vienna soon after the meetings in Berlin, we find him telling Löwenherz that he would henceforth "supervise all Jewish institutions, and will have to be informed about all details, especially about the organizations abroad with which the IKG is in contact." In this capacity Eichmann ordered the "inspection of the IKG's entire correspondence," the files of which would have to be submitted, to be returned to the IKG "in a few days." Eichmann assured Löwenherz that he was "convinced that the IKG conducted and conducts the entire correspondence within the parameters of its authority [*im Rahmen der Befugnisse*]." In case one or the other IKG official should prove to have exceeded these limits, Eichmann would "instruct [Löwenherz] to correct that official in an appropriate manner." And he added: "No other consequences will follow from this inspection."[36]

Control over and censorship of the IKG's contacts with the foreign aid organizations, especially correspondence, was nothing new. What was new was not so much that Eichmann required the submission of back files; in principle the authorities had considered the IKG to be their agent all along, and hence IKG files to be their property and subject to their inspection. What was new was that Löwenherz had been put on notice that control over the IKG—and through it over the Jews—would be tightened. However, this tightening would proceed in such a manner that, in accordance with Eichmann's wish, the working relation between his office and the IKG would not be disturbed. Absent in Eichmann's notice is any reference to the condition of war necessitating extreme caution in foreign contacts. However, we can guess that this situation was very much on Löwenherz's mind, especially since Eichmann would continue to support, and in fact push, illegal transports to British Palestine and the various risky and delicate contacts these transports would entail. In what follows we will see signs and instances of the tightening of the control, the censorship, the pressure, and the extortion that marked this phase of the unfolding liquidation of the Jewish Community of Vienna.

Liquidating Jewish Assets

Another aspect of the consolidation and centralization of Eichmann's operation concerned the management and liquidation of the assets not only of the IKG but of the Jewish communities in the provinces and of the Jewish foundations. According to Nazi legislation, as we know, all private organizations of a social, fraternal, or charitable nature or special interest groups (such as automobile clubs) had to be incorporated into the corresponding Nazi organizations or else dissolved, unless permitted to exist nominally independently (such as the German Red Cross). When, with the Anschluss, Bürckel was appointed commissioner for the so-called re-association of the *Ostmark* with the German Reich, a department of his organization dealt with the liquidation of such organizations in former Austria. Anton Brunner (see chapter 2) was the member of that department who had been appointed as Commissioner for Receivership of Assets of disbanded Jewish organizations. However, the SD, with Eichmann as point man, was in charge of the solution of the Jewish problem in the *Ostmark* and thus also of the liquidation of the Jewish assets, both communal and private. We have also seen that immediately after Brunner 2 (to distinguish him from Alois Brunner aka Brunner 1) had begun his work, Eichmann's office had received the sanction of the Ministry of Finance and of the Reich Economics Office (*Reichswirtschaftsamt*) to guide the economic aspect of the liquidation. This setup meant not only that Eichmann and Brunner 2 pursued conflicting interests and exercised conflicting authority vis-à-vis the Jews, the IKG, and Löwenherz, but also that whenever Brunner proceeded peremptorily with the liquidation of Jewish assets, Löwenherz was able to seek recourse from Eichmann on the grounds that it was in his interest to retain the use of these assets for the IKG. Now, however, it was time for the regime to tighten control over the use of these assets and to concentrate on liquidating them.

Hence we find that when Eichmann visited Vienna in February 1940, he spelled out for Löwenherz what was involved in his being the "supervisor of all Jewish institutions," which he had first mentioned to Löwenherz in January. Eichmann had been appointed by Reich Commissar Bürckel as Special Trustee for the Assets (*Sonderbevollmächtigter für das Vermögen*) of the IKG Vienna, of the provincial Jewish communities, as well as of the "General Foundation for Jewish Welfare in Vienna,"[37] into which all the Jewish foundations of Vienna had been incorporated. Since the assets of these foundations had formerly been under the control of Anton Brunner in his capacity as Commissioner for Receiverships within Bürckel's office, under the new arrangement Brunner would now be subordinate to Eichmann.

Eichmann also informed Löwenherz of the relation of the IKG to him and to the *Zentralstelle* in light of the new regime's additional parameters of authority. While he reconfirmed the administrative status of the IKG with respect to the subjects of his trusteeship, Eichmann made two things clear: First, the disposition of each of the three segments of the Jewish assets—IKG Vienna, provincial communities, and the General Foundation—would be treated separately. Second, the administrative status of the IKG would be under Eichmann's "control," where "he reserves for himself final decision."[38] The legal difficulty inherent in this arrangement became clear to Löwenherz when Eichmann added that the liquidation of the assets of the provincial communities was to proceed as expeditiously as possible but that the IKG Vienna was not to have the status of the legal successor of the provincial communities. Evidently this was in conflict with the proposal for a legally sound procedure that Löwenherz had been directed to prepare and that he submitted on December 31, 1939. On the basis of his proposal, he said, "the liquidation could proceed without difficulty (*anstandslos*)." Eichmann's procedure, however, would leave Löwenherz vulnerable as the executive of the IKG; hence he told Eichmann that to carry it out he would need "a formal confirmation." We doubt that such was issued by Eichmann. Instead, the topic would come up time and again and, as now, Löwenherz never failed to record the matter in his *Aktennotizen*. In the meantime, he told Eichmann that the liquidation procedure would be handled by the legal and technical departments of the IKG, albeit under his careful supervision.[39]

In spite of Eichmann now being formally in control, with Anton Brunner as his subordinate, Löwenherz would still have to deal with the latter regarding the use and liquidation of assets, since he now functioned as Eichmann's agent. Nonetheless, Brunner would still tend to proceed peremptorily with the liquidation of assets, would still present Löwenherz with *fait accompli* sales of properties, and would still demand that Löwenherz sign the legal transfer papers. Brunner was not a member of the SS, hence could not show up clad in the authority of the black uniform, but would make up for that lack by sporting the huge party badge reserved for those who had joined the Nazi Party when it was still illegal in Austria and by throwing his weight around in a sharp and unpleasant way. He would continue to play an increasingly important role in carrying out the liquidation of the Jewish Community of Vienna.

The intensification of control over the IKG—over its internal business and external contacts, over the Jews generally, as well as over the corollary censorship of what they wrote and said—manifested itself in various ways and in various venues.

Some control/censorship was engendered by wartime conditions. For example, when Löwenherz was in Berlin in January 1940, he reported to Eichmann that telegrams from Jews with visas, who were requesting their sponsors in the United States to pay for their passage in U.S. dollars, were not accepted by the Post Office. Löwenherz explained to Eichmann that this was detrimental to emigration to the United States, inasmuch as the few remaining neutral passenger lines plying the U-boat-infested waters did not accept Reichsmark, and the IKG's access to *Devisen* was limited. Eichmann told Löwenherz to let the telegrams be collected and precensored by the IKG, and then submitted twice a week to the *Zentralstelle* for its censorship and dispatch, and that he, Eichmann, would make appropriate arrangements when he came back to Vienna the following week.[40] In Vienna in the meantime, later the same day, Murmelstein had to report to the *Zentralstelle*, where he was told by Brunner 2 that "in principle telephone calls and telegrams are forbidden" for private persons; in "especially urgent cases" permission could be obtained if it was applied for early enough.[41] With these confusing directives in mind, Löwenherz submitted a memorandum before leaving Berlin, on the basis of which Eichmann agreed to permit the IKG to submit to the *Zentralstelle* up to one hundred precensored telegram texts pertaining to emigration each week. The IKG as well as the Palamt were also authorized to submit telegrams to organizations abroad.[42] The censorship of their correspondence with these organizations, both incoming and outgoing, would later need further regulation when the staff of the *Zentralstelle* realized how voluminous it was. First Brunner 2 informed the IKG that henceforth only one copy of their letters needed to be submitted, later that all copies of outgoing letters needed to be submitted in one batch once a week.[43] Finally, a few months later, copies of letters received from abroad did not need to be submitted anymore; instead, a bimonthly list of senders accompanied by an indication of the subject matter.[44]

Censorship of correspondence with foreign organizations is indicative of the tightening control over the IKG's contact with these organizations. Löwenherz's and Murmelstein's trips abroad had to be prepared in great detail on the basis of Eichmann's directives, strictures, and consent. Inasmuch as the operations of the IKG continued to be largely financed by the Joint, reports to them had to be prepared and translated into English. These reports had to be submitted for censorship to the *Zentralstelle* with a version in German that was certified as being in complete accord with the English.[45] Since such reports were also subject to wartime censorship, the *Zentralstelle* provided Löwenherz with permission to export forty copies of the IKG report in English to what, unbeknownst to him, would be his last direct contact with representatives of the Joint.[46] Bentwich's visit to Vienna and Eichmann shortly before the outbreak of hostilities between Nazi Germany and Great Britain would be the last time Eichmann received an official of one of the aid organizations. Even then he merely granted Bentwich an interview; there were no negotiations. Negotiations were left to the Jewish intermediaries under his control. When Löwenherz informed Eichmann early in 1940 that Troper (of the Joint) wished to come to Vienna, Eichmann told him that Troper could not come.[47]

Occasionally a Jew would approach one of the leading German authorities with his or her concern by mail. Such letters were then redirected through channels to the appropriate Nazi official, normally Eichmann or his staff at one of their outposts. Since he was in charge of controlling and dealing with the Jews, surely nothing rankled Eichmann and his staff more than when this happened. There were several such incidents in the first year of war, and whenever they occurred, Löwenherz was told to have it stopped. For example, in mid-1940, when the Nazis tried to complete concentrating the Jews of Austria in Vienna, the few isolated Jews who were still living in the provinces were told through their local authorities to move to Vienna. Two sisters, Therese and Franciska Ruzička, had been lifelong residents of Stein, in the midst of the romantic vineyard region on the banks of the Danube called the Wachau. When they were told to move to Vienna, they did what their parents would have done when the Emperor was still reigning at his residence in Vienna: They appealed to the Führer Adolf Hitler at the Reich-Chancellery in Berlin. So, when Löwenherz was in Berlin for the June meeting, Eichmann told him that such appeals "constitute an unnecessary burden on the authorities." The IKG had to tell all Jews in Austria through the *Jüdisches Nachrichtenblatt* that "individuals are not entitled to direct themselves to officials with wishes and appeals." Instead, such communications had to be submitted to and screened by the IKG and, if appropriate, directed to the relevant office by way of the *Zentralstelle*. As to the Misses Ruzička, the IKG would have to see to it that they move to Vienna and be given a warning.[48] Despite the notice in the *Jüdisches Nachrichtenblatt*, six weeks later Brunner 1 told Löwenherz that an appeal similar to that of the Misses Ruzička was submitted to Hitler at the Chancellery. Löwenherz was "again" directed to publish in the *Jüdisches Nachrichtenblatt* "that direct applications by Jews to higher authorities are inadmissible, and that Jews . . . are to direct themselves solely to the IKG."[49]

Very often authorities other than the *Zentralstelle* were involved in matters that concerned the Jews and the IKG, such as the postal and telegraphic services, the various labor departments, various local governments that wanted real estate belonging to or controlled by the IKG, tax offices, housing, and other municipal bureaus, and last but not least other Nazi authorities. Inasmuch as such authorities sometimes conflicted with the aims, interests, and jurisdiction of the *Zentralstelle*, the *Zentralstelle* tried as much as possible to control the IKG's contact and transactions with those authorities. Brunner 1 and Eichmann often let Löwenherz deal with these authorities directly. There were obvious reasons for that. One was that it was politic for the ruling Nazi Party (as represented by the *Zentralstelle*) not to assert their overruling authority too frequently, especially in dubious cases, even when the governmental authority could claim to be within its rights. Also, in this way Löwenherz could be informed by authorities other than the *Zentralstelle* that nothing could be done about whatever problem the IKG or the Jews were facing. And, of course, the Nazis would interfere on behalf of the IKG when their own interests were directly or indirectly involved, but only when there was promise of success, thereby enhancing their sorry prestige with the IKG. Inevitably this resulted in the IKG being in the middle of another frustrating squeeze play. When the Viennese Housing Bureau, ever in need of dwellings occupied by Jews, wanted the IKG to submit charts showing the progress of Jewish emigration, Brunner 1 told Robert Prochnik, Murmelstein's assistant, not to honor the demand because only the *Zentralstelle* issued orders to the IKG.[50] However, when the same bureau evicted Jews and expected the IKG to move their effects, Brunner 1 told Löwenherz that the Housing Bureau, not the IKG, should provide the trucks.[51] On the other hand, when Brunner 2, in charge of the liquidation of Jewish assets but as such now nominally under the jurisdiction of Eichmann, failed to act on pending matters, Löwenherz submitted a list of these matters to Brunner 1, requesting his intercession with relevant authorities.[52]

The tightening grip on the operations, performances, assets, and leadership of the IKG went hand in hand with the increased isolation of Löwenherz and Murmelstein from the Jews outside. Few had Troper's insight into the necessity of giving the IKG leadership trusting support in their task of saving Jews under unimaginably difficult circumstances. The greater their isolation, the more telling were the rare incidents that served to show them that they were being watched by their fellow Jews outside. They IKG leaders were isolated, even from most of the staff at the IKG, for they could not reveal to them the special pressures they were under in having to deal with the Nazis on their behalf. The following incident may serve to demonstrate this.

In February 1940 Professor Cyrus Adler of Dropsie College received a letter from Agudas Jisroel (Agudat Yisrael or Agudah) in the Hague, appealing to him "in a matter that undoubtedly will have your wholehearted attention and interest such as it has ours." In it the request was made that Adler arrange for a monthly contribution of $1,000 to help provide Jews under Nazi rule with kosher food. While the letter mentioned both Vienna and Krakow, the former was singled out for special attention:

> Apart from the general lack of ordinary food . . . there is also the provision with kosher food that causes difficulty. For instance in Vienna where there are still some 60,000 Jews living under the worst conditions, about 25,000 of them are publicly fed every day! If we cannot send sufficient oil and other [foods] from here at regular intervals, it will not be possible to keep up this Jewish kitchen. . . . Especially at this time of the year, towards Pesach, the want of aliments and the distress is doubled.[53]

A secretary at Dropsie College forwarded the letter to Henriette Buchmann in New York, who gave it to Rabbi Leo Jung, who submitted it to the Joint; a penciled note reads: "Rabbi Jung was informed of JDC provision for Passover supplies."[54]

The matter was not new to the officials of the Joint. A few days earlier they had received a letter from an Agudah office in Brooklyn, reporting that they had

> just received verbal information and written requests from our organization in Vienna pertaining to kosher fat and oil. . . . The situation is a really desperate one because this kosher fat is the main base for household cooking, and the only fat that can be procured is margarine and the religious element will not avail themselves of this *trefe* [non-kosher] impediment. . . . [Having been] informed that the [requisite] fat can be procured through Romania or Hungary . . . this situation could be easily remedied by the allotment of $3,000 [to be sent here] . . . and the actual disposition of the kosher fat should, in our opinion, be given to the Agudath Israel of Vienna. . . . [I]f you prefer . . . the IKG, then we suggest you ask that the matter be handled by the only orthodox representative of the IKG, Mr. Julius Steinfeld.[55]

We are not surprised to read in the Joint's response that they "have received similar requests from organizations in this country on behalf of various orthodox groups." They assured the Agudah that they had cabled their Paris office to inquire whether kosher Passover foods and shipments from Hungary and Romania could be obtained without incurring additional expenses. Any such shipments, however, would have to be distributed by the IKG, where Agudah was represented by Mr. Steinfeld.[56] Representations were also made by the chief rabbi of Belgium, Dr. Joseph Wiener, through the Brussels office of the Joint, to which both Löwenherz and Murmelstein responded during their meeting with Troper in Budapest in March. Löwenherz's verbal response was circulated for confidential staff information at Joint headquarters in New York. He explained that due to wartime rationing the IKG was no longer "in a position to carry out its soup kitchen activities strictly in accordance with the ritual prescriptions owing to the fat shortage." However,

> the existing stock of vegetable fats was therefore put aside for a kitchen preparing meals for orthodox persons. There are of course only small quantities available and it is feared that kosher meals will have to be suspended in the near future.

We know that even if the Dutch and Swiss Agudah had succeeded in sending all the required foodstuffs, if the IKG had been able to secure an import license from the authorities, and if food inspectors had refrained from condemning the food out of sheer meanness, there was another factor to consider. It was the factor of duress, which those outside of Nazi Germany were never in a position fully to appreciate, especially those who pursued simple agendas without consideration of context, such as "providing our Brothers in Central Europe," as it says in the letter from Agudah in The Hague. But such caution was precisely what Löwenherz had to impart, adding the following to his response, as Troper reported it:

> The Jewish Community [i.e., the IKG], aware of the importance of this problem, is trying its best to comply with the religious prescriptions. Supplies from abroad would be most desirable. However, it should be previously ascertained that such deliveries from abroad will not be the signal for eliminating Jews from obtaining food altogether. A special treatment of the Jews may indeed provoke anger and have legal consequences. In any case the [IKG] will examine the

> situation carefully and appeal for help in due time after having made sure that no prejudice will result from those activities regarding other Jewish interests.[57]

The men at the IKG were truly alarmed, for it was evident that there was a concerted campaign going on, provoked by someone in Vienna, that was disturbing the delicate balance they tried to maintain in standing up to the increasing pressures by the Nazis, serving their people with ever dwindling means, and securing the continued support of the overextended Joint. Löwenherz and Murmelstein came to the conclusion that they had to respond to the verbal inquiry from Dr. Wiener, the chief rabbi of Belgium, which had been transmitted to them by Troper. Deferentially, but in no uncertain terms, and under letterhead of "The Rabbinate of the IKG Vienna," Murmelstein sent the official response to Chief Rabbi Wiener via the Brussels office of the Joint, "[i]n order to state precisely the true state of affairs vis-à-vis the rumors that are circulating." He explained how many people were dependent for food on the IKG, in soup kitchens, in the hospital, and in homes for the aged and the young. Before the war, when food was not rationed, "no sacrifices or pains" were spared by the IKG to supply these people strictly in accordance with ritual regulations. This changed with the outbreak of the war. The resulting restrictions made it impossible to obtain strictly kosher supplies for provisioning a greater number of dependents than those who needed to eat "only according to ritual." For this reason, of the sixteen kitchens maintained by the IKG:

> [A] big kitchen, located where half of the Jews of Vienna [have been concentrated], was chosen as the one where conformance with religious rite is being continued. The preparation of food in that kitchen is done under the supervision of strictly religious persons, appointed by the rabbinate of the IKG, who have the responsibility of seeing that all religious laws are observed rigorously. At the same time the kosher kitchen makes certain that the offered food is in no way worse than that of the other kitchens. . . . [N]ot only the distributed food, but the bread is also made ritually in the same kitchen. . . . The IKG endeavors to supply that kitchen with sufficient quantities . . . also in the future, barring unforeseen changes.

There follows a strong statement of appreciation for the Joint's supply of matzoth for the forthcoming Passover and an account of the extent and success of Vienna's emigration effort that could not have taken place without the Joint's massive support. Murmelstein concludes:

> [W]e consider it gratuitous and harmful to have to turn to this magnificent Committee about a matter that we can and should completely take care of within what is our proper sphere of activity.
>
> The rumors circulating abroad concerning our kosher kitchen are, therefore, incorrect and constitute a humiliation of the IKG, which nonetheless does all in its power to satisfy the religious needs of its members.
>
> For the sake of truth I implore you, dear Chief Rabbi, to convey the contents of this letter to Rabbi Dr. M. Friedinger in Copenhagen, the rabbis in Saarlouis and Amsterdam, to Mr. Rottenberg in Anvers, and also to the sender of the circular, Rabbi Jacobsen, with a note stating that the IKG Vienna abundantly fulfills its duty in the domain of religion even today.[58]

We note with sadness beyond irony that within a few weeks those who in Belgium, Holland, and France questioned the performance of the IKG would be faced with choices under duress in their own persons, those in Denmark within a matter of days.

Löwenherz's written response confined itself to a covering letter to the Joint in Brussels, enclosing "a letter by our rabbinate to the Grand Rabbi, Dr. Wiener, at Brussels." He adds, "I trust that the incorrect rumours will now be finally eliminated."[59] Was Löwenherz's trust misplaced? Joint Brussels forwarded a copy of his and Murmelstein's letters to Joint New York, whose receipt was acknowledged by Moses A. Leavitt, saying that:

> We are very glad to have this information, part of which we are using for publicity in the Yiddish press. . . . Mr. Troper did not see this letter while he was here, and you may . . . wish to call his attention to it when he is next in Brussels.[60]

Troper did not get to Brussels, and most likely neither did Leavitt's letter, for it was written three days before Nazi Germany invaded Belgium and the Netherlands. As to the use of Murmelstein's letter for the Joint's publicity in the Yiddish press, it is not difficult to guess that it helped to discredit Murmelstein in a venue that was fortunately and happily far removed from having to make choices under duress. Thus, we have reason to believe that Löwenherz's trust was misplaced.

Given the increased censorship under the new regime, we can understand that no correspondence from the IKG to its contacts abroad left Vienna without prior censorship by the *Zentralstelle*. In other words, this troublesome complaint by the Agudah must have been known to and have had the attention of the Nazis, and therefore turned out to be counterproductive. When Löwenherz reported to Eichmann in Berlin in June 1940, a few days after the fall of Belgium and the Netherlands, he was informed that the Agudah in Germany had "voluntarily" dissolved, and directed Löwenherz to have the Vienna Agudah cease its activity as well and to dismiss their representative Steinfeld from the *Beirat* (executive council). Löwenherz passed on Eichmann's directive to Steinfeld in the presence of Murmelstein. In order to prepare for the liquidation, Jakob Ornstein, the other remaining leader of the Agudah, requested from Löwenherz an accounting of the financial activity of the IKG, to which he acceded. A month later Brunner issued the directive dissolving the Agudah as of that time and ordered that it submit a liquidation report regarding finances and personnel.[61] Thus ended, in a manner similar to the dissolution of the Sephardic community a year earlier, the seemingly independent representation of orthodox Jews in Vienna, which it had seemed politic to the Nazis to permit to function up to that time.

Within a year the Palamt, the office in charge of emigration to Palestine and of selecting young Zionists for training camps that would prepare them for pioneer work, would also be dissolved. The only remaining Jewish organization, besides the IKG, would then be the Veterans Aid Organization.

Financial Stranglehold

For those in charge at the IKG nothing was more determinative of the tightening grip than the growing deterioration of the IKG's financial position from dangerously precarious to desperate, a deterioration caused, bit by bit, in various ways and by various means, mainly by Nazi authorities, especially Eichmann and his lieutenants. Central to the financial deterioration was

- the manipulation of the *Devisen* the Joint made available for emigration purposes,
- the control over the IKG budget and expenditures,
- the temporizing by the *Zentralstelle* over the release to the IKG of direly needed funds,
- the arbitrariness in the sale of assets and properties and in making proceeds from the sales available to the IKG,
- ordering the IKG to advance funds from its meager reserves to other Jewish communities, promising and then failing to refund the money either outright or when needed, and so on.

No other Jewish leadership under the yoke of the Nazis had to steer through such destructive maneuvers while undertaking moreover a similarly frustrating emigration effort, caring for those who were left behind, and worrying about those who would never emigrate. No account could even come close to being complete, and we doubt that such an account can be given. We can only trace some of the madly intertwined strands.

Manipulation of Devisen

Until the end of 1941—at which time emigration came to a halt and the United States entered the war—the basis for the source of moneys funding the IKG budget was the allotment of *Devisen* in U.S. dollars from the Joint. For this reason we begin our account with the regime's maneuvers with respect to the IKG's access to these precious *Devisen*.

With the beginning of the war and Great Britain now an enemy, Eichmann was confronted not only with a curtailment of emigration but also with the sudden cutoff of half the supply of *Devisen*. In the records of the early contacts of the *Zentralstelle* with Löwenherz under these new conditions, we can sense this concern when Löwenherz is urged to get *Devisen* and to get the remaining Jews to emigrate to the United States.[62] The increased supply of *Devisen* needed in case emigration were to pick up again would now have to be supplied solely by the Joint. However, the contact with the Joint was also disrupted, since the European main office had been in Paris, with branches in other cities. Coinciding with the onset of the Nisko venture, Troper informed Löwenherz by telephone that more *Devisen* would be available to Vienna through Amsterdam, which, however, would not be allowed to be used for illegal immigration to Palestine.[63] In spite of the Nisko interruption, the IKG was able to initiate a new, though small wave of emigration, making use of available *Devisen*. However, to negotiate for a future supply, Löwenherz would have had to see Troper personally, which Eichmann would not permit.[64] Troper was willing to come to Vienna, but Eichmann would not hear of it.[65] When the matter assumed new urgency after the Nisko venture had fizzled out, Löwenherz told Eichmann that direct contact with Troper was indispensable.[66]

Hence, Löwenherz would be permitted to see Troper soon, after all. However, the meetings would now require more extensive preparation than they would have before the war. Permission for Löwenherz to leave for the meetings would be granted at Eichmann's convenience, without regard for the urgent needs of the IKG. This too served to put Löwenherz under increased pressure.

Morris C. Troper, the head of the American Joint Distribution Committee in Europe during 1938–42, and his wife (center) pose with Jewish refugees on the deck of the ill-fated MS St. Louis *in the port of Antwerp, Belgium, on June 17, 1939. (United States Holocaust Memorial Museum, courtesy of Betty Troper Yaeger. http://collections.ushmm.org/search/catalog/ USHMM 01175A)*

In preparing for the first wartime meeting with Troper, both Löwenherz and Eichmann sought to stake out positions regarding the conditions under which negotiation for *Devisen* would succeed. Wartime restrictions on emigration and the threat of renewed resettlement to Poland were the new and salient factors under which Löwenherz's negotiations with Troper and his preparatory maneuvering with Eichmann had to proceed. When, upon the return of Murmelstein from Nisko, Eichmann explained to him and to Löwenherz about the supposedly temporary stop of the resettlement to Poland, he made it clear that it would be resumed in three months' time and would involve all Jews who had not yet emigrated. Löwenherz pointed out, as he would over and over again during the next year, that between 22,000 and 25,000 Jews would not be able to emigrate because of age and disability. Eichmann shot back: that's too many, Vienna had to be cleared (*geräumt*) of Jews by the end of 1940, details to follow.[67]

Eichmann knew that the Joint was now the only source of outside support for the Jews of Vienna and that it wanted to facilitate matters as best it could. He surmised that the Joint would help no matter what but thought it politic not to put Löwenherz into an impossible negotiating position. Hence, he agreed when Löwenherz tied the contribution of *Devisen* by the Joint to a continued emigration effort without mentioning the threat of transports to Poland. Löwenherz explained that, in any case, only a limited number of Jews who could not emigrate would be eligible for resettlement to Poland; as mentioned previously, 22,000 to 25,000 would have to remain. He stressed that according to "the census conducted by the IKG," there were 66,500 Jews in Vienna at the time of the outbreak of the war. Now, three months later, 58,000 remained. Emigration in November, originally projected at 2,500, actually amounted to 4,420. On this basis, Löwenherz held out the possibility of ridding Vienna of all Jews who were able to emigrate by the stipulated end of 1940. Wisely or naively, Löwenherz did not add "all other things being equal." He had no way of anticipating the obstacles to the emigration effort that would be posed by the next phase of the war or the disastrous stoppage of visas by the U.S. consulate as of mid-1940. In any case, Eichmann agreed to Löwenherz's projection as a basis for the meeting with Troper, reiterating that he wanted emigration to be completed by the end of 1940. And grandly, as if it were up to him, Eichmann declared that he was prepared to refrain from Poland transports on condition that the Joint provide *Devisen* until the end of 1940 and the IKG were committed to emigration. Löwenherz could not promise the former. Instead, he referred to the record of the IKG's past performance. Also, he wanted to be able to say to Troper that Eichmann would provide the IKG with subsidies out of the "emigration fund" amassed by the *Zentralstelle*.[68] It was not difficult for Eichmann to agree to this, but we will see to what extent he was forthcoming with such subsidies. If the Joint could make the provision of *Devisen* conditional on the release of subsidies, Eichmann could make the release of subsidies conditional upon the *Devisen*. A perfect squeeze-play, with Löwenherz, the IKG, and the Jews of Vienna caught in the middle.

Löwenherz finally met Troper in Amsterdam during the first half of December 1939. It is at that time that Löwenherz told Troper in confidence the truth about the "resettlement" action at Nisko. This revelation formed a significant background to what, a week later, Löwenherz reported about the meeting to Eichmann in Berlin. He told him that Troper had agreed to make *Devisen* available for emigration under three conditions: first, that there be no further Poland transports; second, that the status of the IKG as a tax-exempt public organization be retained through 1940; and third, that the *Zentralstelle* grant greater subsidies to the IKG,[69] now that emigration required greater amounts of *Devisen* for each emigrant, since most of them lacked access to a corresponding amount in Reichsmark. Troper pledged the Joint's support of the IKG; however, he required regular accounting of IKG budget outlays and regular meetings with Löwenherz. Even though Eichmann agreed to these three conditions, Löwenherz thought it necessary to urge again that there be no Poland transports in 1940; not only were such transport not feasible, but they disturbed the Jews. The fact that the Joint pledged support is a testimonial to the performance of the IKG, he said, and that performance justified carrying emigration to its successful conclusion in a calm atmosphere, without special measures against the Jews. If emigration continued at a steady pace, Eichmann pledged, there would be no Poland transports.[70] In retrospect we can understand that he refrained from extending the pledge to "quiet atmosphere" and to "no special measures against the Jews," about which we will learn later in this chapter.

We do not know at which point Löwenherz was informed that the use of *Devisen* would henceforth be subject to a new rate of exchange, namely, RM 5.00 per $1.00, instead of the multiples thereof that had prevailed before the war. This was not the idea of Eichmann or of his superiors in the SD. Instead, the *Reichswirtschaftsamt* (Reich Economics Office), ever strapped for foreign exchange and mindful of the need not to cheapen the value of the Reichsmark on the international money market, saw this as the proper time to stop the exchange of dollars for multiples of the official fixed exchange rate in Reichsmark, which at about RM 3.65 per $1.00 was, in fact, even now below the reduced rate permitted to the IKG and the *Reichsvereinigung*.

This new monetary regime no doubt suited Eichmann well. After all, the amount of *Devisen* that would be provided would easily accommodate the flow of emigration, which could be expected to remain at its slower rate. The *Reichsvereinigung* would, at all events, not be affected by the reduced income that the new exchange rate would provide. As to the IKG, the resulting forced reduction of income would be a welcome means of applying pressure to economize further, to agree to the sale of their assets, to motivate them to ever greater emigration efforts, and to obtain more and more *Devisen* from the Joint; all the while the Reichsmark of individual Jews, which might have been given to the IKG for more costly *Devisen* exchanges, would remain dormant until the time when they could be expropriated. The Joint objected to the low rate and through Löwenherz conveyed requests for change. To no avail; there was nothing they could do short of abandoning their support of the IKG and their relief work at other places, which they would not do, as the Nazis knew.

For the IKG the new exchange rate caused a dramatic worsening of its financial status. It generally meant that the IKG would take in a considerably lesser amount than heretofore in corresponding Reichsmark to meet its budgetary needs. Also, the emigration picture had changed. There were now fewer emigrants than during the earlier period of forced emigration, and even fewer opportunities for emigration. And yet, emigration had become more costly, since routing people in wartime was becoming more and more complicated, and most available passages had to be paid in *Devisen*, especially U.S. dollars. Even though the corresponding amount in Reichsmark for the dollars had become less than before the war, the ability of the remaining Jews to reimburse the IKG in Reichsmark had in its turn decreased considerably. As a result, the IKG was developing a dependence on new sources of income, a dependence that would increase as 1940 progressed to nothing less than crisis proportions, something that Löwenherz had not been able to foresee, least of all when he met Troper early in February.

Thus many aspects of the tightening grip on the IKG and on the Jews of Vienna, especially in regard to their means of emigration and survival, were intimately connected with the *Devisen* provided to the IKG in this phase by the Joint. Let us look at how this story unfolded.

When Löwenherz reported to Eichmann in Berlin on January 15, 1940, he had to submit statistics about foreign nationals who were recipients of welfare from the IKG. When Eichmann looked at the tables and saw that they included citizens of the United States, he informed Löwenherz that the consulate had registered objections to the *Zentralstelle* charging U.S. nationals passport fees, which all other Jews who were cleared for emigration by the *Zentralstelle* had to pay. Eichmann's standpoint was that, in principle, the

IKG was not to grant benefits nor make *Devisen* available to anyone who was freed from paying the passport fee. This was a confirmation of the prevailing state of affairs, according to which the IKG was nothing other than an agency of the *Zentralstelle*, and the tasks and enterprises of the IKG as well as the means available were under the strict control of Eichmann and his lieutenants. However, since the *Devisen* necessary for emigration now came solely from the United States, Eichmann, "in consideration of the small number of persons involved . . . and since [the IKG] depends on the goodwill of the consulate in regard to emigration, [did] not wish to cause the IKG any difficulties, and recommended that the IKG conduct negotiations with the U.S. consulate in a careful manner."[71] The sacrifice of the passport fees from the handful of Americans who would be processed by the *Zentralstelle* would surely not make a dent in its "emigration fund" and would be well worth keeping both *Devisen* from the Joint and the emigration visas from the U.S. consulate flowing steadily; he could leave the difficult negotiations in the hands of Löwenherz. But that did not mean that Eichmann was forthcoming with the subsidies to the IKG, whose resources were dwindling to an alarming degree. A week after Berlin, Löwenherz reported to Eichmann in Vienna and informed him that from the beginning of October 1939 to the second half of January 1940, the IKG had made $225,000 available for ship passages. However, since the IKG was able to collect from emigrants only a small portion of the corresponding value in Reichsmark, Löwenherz asked Eichmann for RM 500,000, which Eichmann granted, albeit in two monthly installments.[72]

Early in February Löwenherz met Troper in Budapest, mainly to negotiate for *Devisen*. One of the factors determining the negotiations with Troper was the new exchange rate. But, another factor needs to be mentioned here. Soon after the conquest of Poland, when somehow some news reached the West of how the Jews were faring under the political overlordship of the SS, the Joint prepared to give aid to the persecuted communities. But how could that be done without handing the Germans *Devisen* in exchange for Reichsmark and Złoty? Thus it happened that Löwenherz suggested to Troper

> the possibility of obtaining new *Devisen* in connection with the projected welfare action by the Joint in Warsaw and in other regions of the General Government of Poland. I [Löwenherz] proposed a preliminary transfer of $100,000 to the IKG Vienna, and was prepared to apply for approval [of the scheme] to the *Zentralstelle* and to the *Devisenstelle*, so as to transfer RM 500,000, which equals 1,000,000 Złoty, to the institutions in Warsaw that will be designated by the Joint and approved by the German authorities, and to use the *Devisen* for emigration purposes.[73]

Löwenherz then argued that by means of that scheme "the IKG would be in a position to finance the emigration to America and thus prevent its coming to a halt." (Little could he foresee that the reason for the virtual standstill of emigration to the United States later that year would not be a lack of *Devisen*.) In his report to Eichmann, Löwenherz continued:

> With the completion of the initial transfer the basis will be established whereby it will be possible to bring in larger amounts in *Devisen*, and to make them available for purposes of emigration not only to the IKG Vienna, but also to the RV Berlin.[74]

Eichmann enthusiastically endorsed Löwenherz's scheme and said that he would submit it to the RWM (*Reichswirtschaftsministerium*, Reich Ministry for Economics) for approval.

He thought that "emigration from Poland is surely out of the question, hence the use of *Devisen* released for welfare efforts in Poland for the purpose emigration from the *Ostmark* and Altreich is to be welcomed."[75] Apparently Troper wanted to come to either Vienna or Berlin to negotiate the scheme, possibly also to inspect conditions at the IKG, as Bentwich had done shortly before the outbreak of the war; but Eichmann told Löwenherz that this was not possible "at present." However, he wanted Löwenherz to continue his efforts of obtaining more *Devisen*. Löwenherz, anticipating that the scheme would be put in operation, asked Eichmann, apparently at Troper's request, for an advance from the *Zentralstelle* of the RM 500,000 to be transferred to Warsaw. Instead, as we know from later developments, Eichmann asked Löwenherz that the IKG advance that amount and promised reimbursement by the *Zentralstelle*. We also know that Eichmann temporized about returning the money, and we don't know that he ever did.

What we do know is, first of all, that as long as Nazi Germany and the United States were not at war, the effort of the Joint to provide aid to the hard-pressed Jews of former Poland was financed by Jewish money largely from IKG Vienna, and to some extent also by the *Reichsvereinigung* Berlin. Second, far from helping the IKG in this effort by means of appropriate releases from the "emigration fund," Eichmann and his agents used this effort by the IKG as an additional lever to choke off its financial basis.

A few days after Löwenherz had first presented the scheme to Eichmann, Troper, who had in the meantime, returned to the new European Joint headquarters in Brussels, telegraphed Löwenherz that he had informed Joint headquarters in New York of the scheme Löwenherz had presented. New York needed to be assured that the Złoty transfer could be effected and that the Warsaw bureau would be able to make use of it "properly." Furthermore, New York felt that the exchange rate should be at least double the proposed US $1.00 to RM 5.00. Troper needed Löwenherz's response right away because he was about to take a ship for New York. When Löwenherz informed Brunner 1 by means of a translation of the telegram, he was told that the transaction was feasible and that Joint Warsaw would be able to use the money "properly." He told Löwenherz to draft a telegram to that effect addressed to Troper and to submit it to him "today for censorship." No mention was made of relaxing the tight exchange rate.[76] When, a few days later, Löwenherz reported to Eichmann that the Joint had approved the transfer of $100,000, Eichmann, in turn, told Löwenherz that the RWM approved the corresponding transfer of "RM 500,000 = Złoty 1,000,000," and that he expected them to give their official confirmation in a few days, when Löwenherz would be in Berlin. At the same time Eichmann informed Löwenherz that the *Reichsvereinigung* Berlin, which had "somehow" gotten wind of Löwenherz's scheme, had asked for approval of a similar transfer scheme and was prepared to transfer twice Vienna's amount to Warsaw. However, such an amount was out of the question; the participation of the *Reichsvereinigung* Berlin would come into consideration only to the extent that Vienna had no use for a transfer offered by the Joint.[77] And that was it, at least for now. Five days later, in Berlin, Eichmann told Löwenherz that the *Reichsvereinigung* Berlin had received approval for a similar transfer of $100,000, but, as in the case of Vienna, for RM 500,000 only. All future transfers of this kind would have to be approved by the RWM on a case-by-case basis.[78] Now we are puzzled: How did the *Reichsvereinigung*

Berlin "somehow" find this out? The fact that in the intervening five days he had obtained clearance for the *Reichsvereinigung* to participate in the special transfer scheme tells us that Eichmann's rejection of Berlin's participation was a ploy to deflect Löwenherz's contact with the *Reichsvereinigung* on this matter.

In Berlin, Löwenherz handed Eichmann an application addressed to the RWM for the transfer under the conditions earlier stipulated by Eichmann, namely, that most of the *Devisen* were to be used for emigration costs for indigent emigrants, without recompense in Reichsmark to the IKG, the rest to be negotiated against recompense, according to the emigrant's available Reichsmark, case by case. It turned out that the application was a formality for the record because the RWM had preemptively approved the scheme. Eichmann now told Löwenherz that approval for the specific steps would be forthcoming from the *Devisenstelle* in Vienna. In anticipation of the Reichsmark to be realized in this way, Löwenherz asked permission to effect, for the time being from its own account, the transfer of RM 500,000 = Złoty 1,000,000 to Warsaw. Löwenherz then reminded Eichmann of his previous application for a contribution from the *Zentralstelle* to cover part of this outlay, inasmuch as the amount in Reichsmark to be realized from those who could afford it would fall short of the RM 500,000 that the IKG was advancing to help the Jews in Poland. Whereupon Eichmann suggested to Löwenherz to get as many Reichsmark as possible for the *Devisen* left over after the indigent emigrants had been processed; after that Löwenherz was to submit an accounting together with a new application for a contribution from the *Zentralstelle*, on the basis of which Eichmann would decide whether or not such a contribution would be made.[79]

The Joint found itself in a new and extremely tight situation. It needed to increase its expenditures in support of the Polish Jews under the heel of Nazi occupation, deprivation, and persecution, and the only way it could do so was by supplying Vienna and Berlin with large amounts of additional *Devisen* for their emigration efforts. It also needed to continue supporting Vienna, again by means of monthly contributions of *Devisen*, though at a reduced rate; for April 1940 Vienna received $40,000.[80] Because of the war, the Joint had to carry this burden alone. And it had to supply *Devisen* at exchange rates that were much reduced from before the war. In this desperate situation, the little control the Joint could exert over the use of the *Devisen* consisted in requiring more frequent reports and budgets from the IKG. They were, of course, aware of the fact that these reports and budgets were closely censored by the *Zentralstelle*, and the only way in which they could have any inkling of what really went on was when Löwenherz met with Troper or his representatives. However, they could not apply strictures to the IKG or even set conditions on their release of additional *Devisen* on the basis of what Löwenherz revealed in strictest confidence because the reason Eichmann and his agents permitted Löwenherz to meet with representatives of the Joint was to negotiate for more *Devisen*. The prewar refrain "get more *Devisen*" was still voiced by Eichmann and Brunner 1,[81] but any control that the Joint had over the terms and conditions of their release to the IKG was lost to the new restrictive measures and censorship exercised over the IKG and its finances.

Eichmann blithely expected the IKG to advance the Reichsmark needed for the transfers to Warsaw out of its nonexistent reserves. When Eichmann was in Vienna in mid-

April, he gave Murmelstein the go-ahead to continue negotiating with the Joint for another $100,000 transfer on behalf of Warsaw and promised to obtain the support of the RWM. Murmelstein told Eichmann that advancing the respective exchange value in Reichsmark for the first transfer had placed the IKG in financial difficulty and reminded him that Löwenherz had asked for a contribution from the *Zentralstelle* to offset that outlay. But Eichmann, as so often before and after, responded that he would make the decision at a later date.[82]

We recall that the reason Löwenherz needed to see Troper in Brussels was to get more *Devisen*, a trip that had long been planned. On May 4, Brunner 1 informed him that the report to the Joint, drafted in English by Margarete Feiler, which he was to take to Troper, was approved, but Löwenherz still had to submit a statement to the effect that the German translation, on the basis of which approval was granted, truthfully represented the English original. When on May 10, 1940, Germany invaded Belgium and the Netherlands in preparation of its campaign against France, Troper and his staff cleared out of Brussels. Löwenherz's meeting with Troper could not take place, and it was not clear where and when another meeting could be scheduled.[83] However, when Löwenherz saw Eichmann on May 14, he was able to report that, according to a cable received that day, the Joint offered another $50,000 for the Polish transfer scheme but demanded RM 7.50 per $1.00 instead of the previous rate of RM 5.00. Eichmann explained that the RWM would not approve any amount other than RM 5.00 for the Polish transfer, whether it was effected by the *Reichsvereinigung* Berlin or the IKG Vienna. Löwenherz had already been informed by Brunner 1 that the asked-for rate was denied and had in turn to inform the Joint of that by cable.[84]

Since the outbreak of the war in September 1939 until this time, May 1940, the IKG had received over a million dollars for emigration purposes and, so Löwenherz reported to Eichmann, despite the difficult and frequently changing conditions under which emigration could be arranged, they were able to expedite the emigration of 15,000 Jews by religion (*Glaubensjuden*) during this period. This averaged out to about $65 per emigrant. Since the *Devisen* necessary for the emigration of just one person exceeded that amount by multiples, the figure meant that many of the emigrants had been able to obtain the necessary *Devisen* from their benefactors overseas. Nonetheless, Eichmann reiterated his demand that emigration be speeded up and, in connection with it, that Löwenherz negotiate for more *Devisen*. However, Löwenherz had to remind Eichmann that by this time, the IKG had advanced RM 750,000 for the Polish transfer without being able to recoup that amount from emigrants in exchange for *Devisen* made available for their emigration, since most of them were indigent. Hence, in order to offset this debit, he asked for release of the funds from the *Zentralstelle* that he had repeatedly requested and which had repeatedly been promised by Eichmann. Eichmann thought he might make that release later that month of May.[85]

The extent to which Troper and the Joint trusted Löwenherz to make the right use of the funds made available to him can be seen from their release of a large amount of pounds sterling in connection with a problematic group transport to Palestine (that we will discuss in chapter 9). Apropos that release, Löwenherz reminded Brunner 1 that the handling of the moneys derived from *Devisen* released to him, Löwenherz, affected all parties concerned over the continued flow of *Devisen*: "Mr. Troper honored me by his decision, but thereby placed me under a specific obligation. . . . The Joint has so far made large amounts available for emigration, and naturally places great value on the *Devisen* being used for that purpose with as little restriction as possible."[86]

While in Berlin in mid-June, Löwenherz was ordered by Eichmann to join the directors from Berlin and Prague in proposing a suitable way of apportioning among them the available places on transports to the United States via the Far East. Löwenherz told Eichmann that he did not wish to appear to be in competition with the others but insisted that Vienna deserved a larger proportion of available places since, unlike the other two, the greater part of its budget in Reichsmark came from the sale of *Devisen* for emigration purposes. Löwenherz left unsaid what Eichmann knew well, namely, that the income in Reichsmark from the expenditure of *Devisen* was relatively low, and his repeated pleas to make up the deficit with contributions from the *Zentralstelle* had so far been largely futile; the resulting shortfall was approaching crisis proportions.[87]

At that time the Joint had assigned $40,000 for the Poland transfer. In order to speed up the corresponding transfer to Warsaw, Löwenherz asked that the application for clearance be submitted to the RWM right away, while he was still in Berlin, instead of awaiting his return to Vienna. Dannecker was prepared to make the submission to the RWM as soon as telegraphic advice from Joint Warsaw was received as to the distribution of the proceeds among Warsaw, Łódź, Sosnowitz, and Pressburg (Bratislava).[88] Löwenherz prepared and submitted the application that very day, June 13, but it was not approved by the RWM until July 16. In August Brunner 1 told Murmelstein that the *Zentralstelle* received from the RWM the approval to transfer to Warsaw the amount corresponding to $40,000 contributed by the Joint for that purpose and wanted to know whether this was the same approval received by the IKG. Murmelstein explained that the approval that had been received by the IKG from the RWM stipulated that the rate at which the *Devisen* may be assigned on behalf of emigrants would be RM 5.00 per U.S. dollar. Thereupon, the IKG had sent a request to the RWM for permission to negotiate the corresponding exchange rate in Reichsmark with each emigrant case by case. Murmelstein also told Brunner that the approval now received by the *Zentralstelle* no doubt contained the approval of that request, and he asked Brunner to issue this amended approval to the IKG.[89]

In the meantime, the IKG had received another $25,000 from the Joint for the Warsaw transfer of RM 125,000. On August 9 Löwenherz had asked Eichmann to intercede at the RWM for permission to effect the transfer. By the time Löwenherz reported to Eichmann in Berlin almost four weeks later, he still had not been told to go ahead and, concerned about the need for the money in Warsaw, asked Eichmann about the status of his request. Eichmann "held out the prospect" of an intervention at the RWM. The phrase in Löwenherz's *Aktennotiz* is "*in Aussicht stellen*," literally, "to hold out the prospect," which implies that Eichmann did not promise to intervene but that he was temporizing. Why? At the same meeting Eichmann gave Löwenherz the task of making a very large assignment of *Devisen* to a specific individual in Berlin. Since this was against all the rules under which the Joint made *Devisen* available to the IKG, we believe that Eichmann was holding the transfer to Warsaw hostage in order to apply pressure on Löwenherz to comply with this unusual demand in spite of the obstacles.[90]

There is another reason to suspect a connection between temporizing about effecting the Warsaw transfer and manipulating Löwenherz to engage in an improper use of *Devisen*. Before Löwenherz reported to Eichmann, Brunner 1 prepared him for his going to Berlin. First, Brunner 1 gave Löwenherz a list of which IKG assets he had to tabulate and told him to bring the tables with him to Berlin, among them an account of the *Devisen* available to the IKG, with details as to what part was committed to emigrants in the process of leaving and what the available balance of Reichsmark was that had been realized from this assignment of *Devisen*.[91] It was Eichmann's curiosity as to what *Devisen* were available to the IKG that points to the special scheme of which Brunner 1 first informed Löwenherz. He said that a Jewish enterprise was being liquidated in Berlin, in connection with which it would be possible for the IKG to realize RM 500,000 for $20,000 (a ratio of 25:1!), which amount was to be transferred to the Jewish party upon his emigration. Löwenherz should be prepared to speak to Eichmann about this matter in Berlin five days hence.[92]

In Berlin the "enterprise" (*Unternehmen*) turned out to be "assets" (*Vermögen*), and the amount in Reichsmark corresponding to the $20,000 turned out to be one million, at an astronomical and unprecedented ratio of 50:1![93] Evidently some Germans thought that acquisition of that property was well worth a considerable portion of it, namely, one million Reichsmark; equally evidently, the as-yet-unnamed Jew was refusing to sign over his property without the guarantee of a sizable capital outside of Nazi Germany with which to start over. It was also evident that Löwenherz's need for *Devisen* and his contact with the Joint were the only means of effecting this scheme and that Eichmann's hold over the purse strings of the IKG was the only usable instrument.

Löwenherz told Eichmann that "in principle the IKG does not effect such a sizable transfer for an individual; however, this being a special case, he would have to get the agreement of the Joint, which [he] will attempt to do in consideration of the large rate of exchange, so as to obtain for the IKG RM 1,000,000 for emigration and welfare purposes."[94] Eichmann replied that once the matter had progressed to a certain point, he would have the person in question contact Löwenherz to begin direct negotiations. We can see how anxious the German side was to realize this windfall, when three weeks had passed and Eichmann had not heard from Löwenherz. Brunner 1 then told Murmelstein that the matter must be initiated with the Joint so as to accelerate this transaction. Murmelstein responded that immediately after he had received the instructions from Löwenherz in Berlin, the request was sent to the Joint in New York and that the IKG would immediately transfer the amount upon receipt of the agreement from the Joint.[95]

Meanwhile Löwenherz had found out from Dr. Hirsch of the *Reichsvereinigung* Berlin that the person in question—who now had a name: Carl Kutschera—did not have any emigration prospects and that he had asked the emigration section of the *Reichsvereinigung* to help him emigrate. Therefore, Löwenherz now told Brunner 1, "since there are only a few emigration countries that come into consideration, it will, under the best of circumstances, be several months" before a place could be found for Mr. Kutschera; receipt of the stipulated exchange value in Reichsmark for the projected $20,000 would have to wait until then.[96] Soon thereafter, Brunner 1 informed Löwenherz that, according to information from Berlin, chances for Mr. Kutschera's emigration were good, so that the transfer of the $20,000 should be realizable in the foreseeable future. But, in response to his question as to whether the Joint New York had agreed to the transfer, Löwenherz reported that he had not as yet heard but hoped that when the time came they would agree to it.[97]

It was then that the problematic nature of the matter began to emerge. At the end of October Brunner 1, in the presence of an unidentified gentleman, informed Löwenherz that Kutschera would arrive in Vienna "today or tomorrow." Assuming that Joint Chairman Troper would issue to Löwenherz the release for the transfer when they would next meet in Lisbon, Brunner 1 suggested that Löwenherz not protract the negotiations with Kutschera. Instead, he should issue a declaration that the IKG would transfer $20,000 to Kutschera from its own reserve of *Devisen* in case he sold his real estate in Berlin and Kladow. Brunner 1 assured Löwenherz that he could count on the approval of this transfer by both the *Zentralstelle* and the *Devisenstelle*. While Brunner 1 doubted that the full amount of the projected RM 1,000,000 could be realized, he wanted Löwenherz to get the highest possible amount without unduly protracting his negotiations with Kutschera. Löwenherz declared that he expected that whatever corresponding amount in Reichsmark for the sale of $20,000 would result from his negotiation with Kutschera would be placed at the ready disposal of the IKG. At this point the unnamed gentleman, evidently a representative of the RWM, said that the proceeds from the sale would be at Kutschera's disposal only upon approval of a number of authorities and agencies; furthermore, it would take up to two months for the settlement of capital gains taxes and the Reich defection levy. A final addendum to this litany of obstacles came from Brunner 1, who instructed Löwenherz to use his time in Lisbon to find emigration possibilities for Kutschera. Löwenherz, in his frustration, agreed to make inquiries but insisted, in accordance with his earlier declaration, that the question of Kutschera's emigration chances was unrelated to the right of the IKG to have the amount of Reichsmark corresponding to the $20,000 at its ready disposal.[98]

When Löwenherz saw Eichmann in Berlin in early December, there was talk about an agreement that had in the meantime been reached with Kutschera regarding the corresponding amount of Reichsmark for the $20,000, and of Löwenherz planning to see him while there about arranging the exchange. In the *Aktennotiz* there is no indication what amount in Reichsmark was agreed upon, only a handwritten marginal note that the report is in a separate file.[99] We found no indication that the deal materialized, much less any information about what happened to Kutschera.

In connection with the order for an updated report about past cash flow as well as the assignment of *Devisen* by the Joint, and about the IKG's corresponding receipts of Reichsmark, Brunner 1 ordered Löwenherz to present a similar report with respect to the Aid Organization for Non-Mosaic Jews, which actually operated independently of the IKG. Brunner added that since this organization did "not have direct access to *Devisen*," Löwenherz should simply say that for purposes of the emigration of Jews under its care, "*Devisen* are made available by the Society of Friends, the [Protestant] Mission, and the [Roman Catholic] Caritas Association." This is interesting because it indicates that, unlike the Joint, which supplied *Devisen* directly for the emigration of Jews by faith, the Christian organizations contributed the needed *Devisen* to the authorities, which makes sense, given that the Aid Organization for Non-Mosaic Jews was headed by a member of the Nazi Party.[100]

On September 16 Löwenherz submitted to the *Zentralstelle* an application addressed to the RWM, asking permission to transfer RM 100,000 to the Joint office in Krakow in exchange for an additional $20,000 contributed by the Joint for that purpose. Ten days later Brunner 1 informed Murmelstein that permission would be granted, but added—out of the clear blue sky—only upon his obtaining information as to the way in which a portion of that amount would be used for the care of the Jews of Łódz.[101] Löwenherz telephoned the Joint representative in Krakow, who informed him that unless instructed by Joint New York, he could not forward to Łódz any portion of RM 20,000 from the RM 100,000. He promised to get in touch with New York but doubted that they would change their instructions.[102] This is understandable, because Krakow was in that part of conquered Poland called the "General Government" by Nazi Germany, whereas Łódz, called Litzmannstadt by the Germans, was in the area newly incorporated into Germany ("Wartheland"), and as far as the Joint was concerned, had the same status as Vienna or Berlin. Löwenherz, therefore, expressed his reservations about the scheme proposed by Brunner 1 "because I would be in danger of the Joint ceasing to effect the Poland transfer via Vienna," and he added that if that were to happen, "it would have very unfavorable financial consequences for Vienna."[103] And both Löwenherz and Brunner 1 understood that the financial interest of both the IKG and the *Zentralstelle* were at stake. How then could Brunner 1 carry out the instructions he had received, that is, to supply Łódz with means derived from those slated by the Joint for Poland? First, he permitted Löwenherz to transfer the whole amount of RM 100,000 = Złoty 200,000 to Krakow. Then he told Löwenherz to prepare a new application to the RWM, requesting permission to fix the exchange rate for the $20,000 slated for Krakow at RM 6.00 instead of RM 5.00 per dollar. In this way Löwenherz could realize the additional RM 20,000 that were needed for Łódz; and that amount would be paid from the account of the IKG directly to Łódz, instead of via Krakow.

Löwenherz had no alternative but to comply, and in November, the next time $20,000 were received in exchange for funds slated for Krakow, the matter was handled the same way without further discussion, and the Łódz ghetto received its portion.[104] By the time Löwenherz saw Eichmann in Berlin a few days later, Löwenherz had received notification from the Joint that another $30,000 was available for the Polish transfer, if Vienna was in a position to make use of this amount. Since he needed Eichmann's consent, Löwenherz had waited before answering. In discussing the matter with Eichmann, Löwenherz pointed out that the IKG could use the additional *Devisen*, since the normal contribution of *Devisen* was insufficient for present emigration needs. Since the IKG was permitted to take in Reichsmark at an exchange rate greater than what was permitted to be sent to Krakow, not having the *Devisen* for the Poland transfer would also be detrimental to the IKG. Eichmann approved Löwenherz's request to accept the *Devisen* and instructed him not to transfer the full amount to Krakow as yet and, since Łódz would be getting the recently cleared RM 20,000, to await further instructions about the new amount. Löwenherz used this opportunity to reveal to Eichmann that he had heard from Rumkowski that Łódz had received a sizable subsidy, in light of which the money the IKG had been forced to send to

Łódz was really a "supplement" (*Zuschlag*), and also to ask that in the future Vienna not be required to transfer any more money to Łódz.[105]

The episode with Kutschera and the scheme of grafting subsidies of Jewish money from Vienna onto transfers to Poland show the extent to which the Nazi authorities used the increasingly dire financial straits of the IKG, brought about largely by their design, to pressure the IKG into dubious financial schemes. One time Brunner 1 went so far as to suggest that Löwenherz use moneys in escrow in "*Konto* (account) D" for IKG purposes. At that time, according to the *Aktennotiz*, Löwenherz had again asked for the release of proceeds from the sale of assets, which Eichmann had promised for October, and also for a subsidy from the emigration fund, which was "often promised" and without which the IKG "cannot meet its financial obligations despite the most stringent savings measures." Brunner 1 assured Löwenherz that "the plight of the IKG was well known to him, and he had reported it to Berlin; in the meantime, he counseled" the use of account "D." This account held moneys in escrow that were collected by the IKG in exchange for *Devisen*. Löwenherz rejected Brunner's suggestion, reminding him that he could not use these moneys until corresponding amounts in *Devisen* had actually been transferred.[106] If Löwenherz had taken Brunner's suggestion, it would have been he who would have had to answer for it, not Brunner 1, if some inspector from the *Devisenstelle* or the Finance Office had found the irregularity.

The constant risk involved in dealing with *Devisen* and the duress consequent upon these dealings can be seen from a specific question the IKG had to deal with in December 1940. The spokesman of the IKG Legal Department had to report to Chief Inspector Löffler of the Vienna *Devisenstelle* about payments to consulates in connection with emigration to Shanghai. He explained that Shanghai was one of the few places where emigrants could still go, however only as transients to an ultimate destination that was recorded by a visa in their passport. Since the U.S. consulate had stopped issuing visas, the only visas obtainable for ultimate destinations were those from South American countries, which the Travel Bureau Postelt in Hamburg was able to arrange with the respective local consulates for a hefty fee of about RM 1,200 per person, albeit with the proviso that recipients not make use of the entry visa. Since these payments were made with moneys derived from *Devisen*, the chief inspector was concerned; however, since the payments were made to recipients within Germany, Löffler was able to reassure the IKG official that the transaction was "completely legal." However, Löffler reminded him that, according to a circular issued a year earlier, the RWM was against the payment of bribes (*Schmiergelder*) to consulates, and that it would not release funds for that purpose from collateral accounts.[107]

A telling example of how Eichmann and the *Zentralstelle* used the withholding of Reichsmark corresponding to assigned *Devisen* as a means of incremental pressure pertains to the Palestine transport mentioned earlier. In January 1940, when Löwenherz and Storfer reported to him in Vienna, Eichmann informed them that the amount of RM 300,000, which he had approved for the next Palestine transport organized by Storfer, would be released when arrangements for the transport were complete and it was ready to leave.[108] However, Storfer had many difficult and protracted arrangements to make before the transport would become actuality. The main reasons were (1) that the prospective participants' immigration to Palestine was illegal and (2) that Palestine, being under the British Mandate, was technically at war with Nazi Germany. Shipping the contingent down the Danube to the Black Sea, and thence through the Mediterranean, which was patrolled by the British, and landing them undetected in Palestine was a formidable challenge even for an expert like Storfer. While the process of making arrangements was going on, Löwenherz earmarked the requisite *Devisen*, for which he would need corresponding Reichsmark to meet the budget of the IKG. When the time was near for the actual release of the *Devisen*, Eichmann made the conditions for releasing the corresponding contribution of RM 300,000 more stringent, saying it would have to wait for his approval of the report about the preparation of the transport, once Storfer submitted it.[109] Storfer was in a position to do so fairly soon, after he transferred £13,800 that Löwenherz made available from the pounds left over from the prewar contribution of *Devisen* by the London aid society. Consequently, Löwenherz requested that the approved RM 300,000 in exchange for the pounds advanced by the IKG be released. But Brunner 1 now issued an additional condition for the release, namely, that he be informed that the transport was actually ready to leave.[110]

To make the situation even worse, the Lowlands were invaded by Germany and fell; the victorious armies were forging ahead in France; the British force, exposed by the surrender of Belgium, was being rescued at Dunkirk; and France was about to fall. Löwenherz, who was to meet Troper in Brussels, met him in Budapest instead. When he reported in Berlin upon his return, Eichmann opined that under the changed political situation, there was no chance the transport would still be dispatched. Löwenherz countered that he would be able to advance arrangements for the transport in Budapest and asked that Eichmann not make any decision until he heard from Storfer, who was expected in Berlin the next day.[111] As for the previously approved RM 300,000, Eichmann merely reiterated what he had Brunner 1 say five weeks earlier, notwithstanding Löwenherz's plea that the IKG was strapped for money,[112] and he did so again three weeks later.[113] Sometime later Brunner 1 explained to Löwenherz that "release of this amount can hardly be expected before the embarkation of the emigrés in Pressburg [Bratislava]."[114] When the number of participants from Vienna in the projected transport increased from 800 to 900, Löwenherz asked Brunner 1 to persuade Eichmann of the need for money in addition to the RM 300,000 already approved.[115]

The matter had been seething for well over seven months when it reached a boiling point in mid-August—for both sides. First Brunner 1 reminded Löwenherz that the amount in question "will be paid the moment the passengers embark in Pressburg" and not sooner. But then he increased the pressure: Eichmann would not consider any of the other requests for subsidies for August until the transport was dispatched, including the request for the additional contribution for the transport as well as restitution for moneys advanced by the IKG for retraining camps. Löwenherz took this opportunity to go on record about the discrepancy between the performance of the IKG and the failure by the *Zentralstelle* of making good on the promised support:

> [T]he IKG has made great sacrifices on behalf of this transport, has transferred the [requisite] *Devisen*, and has constantly supported Mr. Storfer in his efforts without being in a position to

> influence the actual dispatch of the transport. The financial situation of the IKG is such that it will not be able to maintain its many-branched facilities without the approval of the subsidy for August.

These included the various welfare programs, hospitals, and homes for the old, orphans, and other dependents. Additionally, the IKG was incurring new expenses for another old-age home that the authorities ordered the IKG to establish. Löwenherz continued:

> Thanks to careful fiscal management it has, until now, been possible to fulfill all financial obligations, even though emigration has been greatly reduced; however, the reserves of the IKG, being depleted, are no longer sufficient for us to continue [our efforts] without worry, and this despite extensive saving measures and curtailment of all expenditures. The monthly IKG budget is RM 800,000, and has to be regularly met, hence I am asking SS Lieut. Brunner to make representations to SS Capt. Eichmann to approve the subsidy for August, before the departure of the transport.

Based on such strong arguments, one would expect Brunner 1 to again take up the matter of the release of the funds with Eichmann or at least promise Löwenherz that he would do so. Not so. Brunner 1 had been waiting for this opportunity to use a situation over which the IKG had no control to apply pressure, and his response was curt: He "suggested" to Löwenherz that he "indicate to Storfer the consequences that would arise if dispatching the transport were to be delayed or not to take place at all"[116]—as if Storfer really needed this expression of encouragement.

When the transport left at last at the beginning of September, Eichmann finally permitted the release of RM 300,000 plus an extra RM 75,000 to reimburse the IKG for the additional expenses incurred for it. At the same time Eichmann released a subsidy of RM 300,000. These amounts were to be disbursed immediately by the Vienna *Zentralstelle*.[117]

The Struggle for Control over Budget, Expenditures, and Assets

The vexing problem of the legal status of the IKG persisted throughout 1940. It was of great importance that it maintain its status under Austrian law as a not-for-profit organization. One benefit—for both the IKG and the *Zentralstelle*—was the avoidance of tax assessments due from corporations. However, the various German governmental agencies dealing with economic matters were agitating for their share of revenue. In preparation for his first meeting with Troper after the onset of war, Löwenherz broached the question with Eichmann, who informed him that, for his part, Bürckel agreed to continue this status but that the matter would have to be considered in Berlin.[118] In May 1940 Löwenherz informed Brunner 1 that the Chief Presidium of the Vienna branch of the Finance Office was conducting an audit of the IKG in connection with an assessment of corporate tax as well as trade tax. Eichmann had told Löwenherz a number of times that the legal status of the IKG as a public institution would be maintained. Especially in light of the fact that the IKG had to take on the administration of the defunct foundations incorporated into the General Foundation for Jewish Welfare, it was important that the IKG retain its tax-exempt status as a public organization. Because of the audit, it was urgent that Löwenherz's recent request for intervention with the Chief Presidium be acted upon.[119] Soon thereafter

Brunner 2 informed Löwenherz that Herr Thieme, corporate tax officer at the Finance Office, had ruled that the assessment of the corporate tax for 1938 would be canceled and that no assessment would be made for 1939 and 1940. On the other hand, Thieme said that the IKG would have to pay sales taxes. He also thought that the General Foundation for Jewish Welfare had to pay property taxes for their real estate; but Löwenherz denied that the IKG was liable for such a tax. Thieme even thought that some sort of tax should be paid for the moneys collected at soup kitchens, since this was paid as recompense for that service by the IKG. Löwenherz pointed out that this was not so, since the food was given for free, and whatever contributions were made by those who frequented the soup kitchens were given without a corresponding performance by the IKG.[120]

When Löwenherz reported to Eichmann in Berlin in June, he was again assured that the IKG would continue to retain the legal status of a public organization, as well the tax exemption connected with that status, including exemption from corporate tax.[121] Nonetheless, a few weeks later Brunner 2 informed Löwenherz that, contrary to the previously reported ruling of the Finance Office, the exemption of the IKG from property tax and trade tax for the year 1938 might not be possible. Inasmuch as the Chief Presidium had, in fact, decided against the exemption, the only recourse left was to appeal directly to the RWM. As regards the corporate tax, Brunner 2 would intervene with local authorities, and he wanted Löwenherz to prepare the necessary documentation. In desperation Löwenherz referred to declarations concerning this matter on the part of Eichmann and Brunner 2 himself and reiterated that the exemption from corporate tax was based on the fact that the budget of the IKG was financed by contributions and was kept in balance through the support of the Joint and the *Zentralstelle*.[122] Within days of this meeting Löwenherz reported to Brunner 1 that, contrary to his and Eichmann's assurances that a corporate tax would not be levied against the IKG and the General Foundation, the head of the Finance Office had decided that this tax was due in the case of one of the defunct organizations incorporated into the Foundation. Löwenherz also reported that he had asked Brunner 2, in his capacity as special trustee for the assets of the IKG and the General Foundation, to intervene in order to confirm the tax exemption.[123]

Somewhat later Brunner 1 informed Murmelstein that the corporate tax would not be levied against the IKG, although it could not be avoided in the case of the General Foundation. In response Murmelstein mentioned that not only would the IKG not be able to pay such a levy but imposing it on the IKG would make it impossible for the Joint to make further contributions in support of the emigration effort.[124] In this way Murmelstein reminded Brunner 1 of what was at stake in this matter not only for the IKG but also for the *Zentralstelle*. In Berlin Löwenherz broached the matter again. All Eichmann was able to tell him was that the IKG would "most likely" be exempt from the corporate tax, but he should be in constant touch with the Vienna *Zentralstelle* in their pursuit of that matter and inform them in a timely manner of the due dates of all tax bills. The IKG should also undertake steps to ensure exemption from property tax.[125]

Eichmann well knew that the only steps the IKG was empowered to undertake was to submit requests to the *Zentralstelle* and to remind the people there of their own interest in granting them. The end of the year was approaching and with it the deadline when Eichmann's guarantee of the IKG's tax-exempt status would run out. Whatever little chance there was of extending that status into the next year would depend on deflecting the assault on that status in the year of its constantly contested guarantee. Hence, in order to effect the needed regulation of these problems, Löwenherz submitted to the *Zentralstelle* a statement on all aspects of the matter of tax exemption, together with a request for intervention on behalf of the IKG. Löwenherz requested the opportunity to make a personal representation to the president of the Finance Office, but Brunner 1 denied his request, saying that he would represent the IKG.[126] Löwenherz also mentioned that the IKG Graz was similarly tax exempt, since it had the same legal status as the IKG Vienna, and asked that appropriate representations be made vis-à-vis the officials in Graz by the local subsegment of the SS, who were informed about the matter.[127]

However, the struggle continued without resolution and was renewed time and again, especially since Herr Thieme of the Vienna office of the Finance Department was not convinced of the status of the IKG as a public institution. He in particular thought that realizing Reichsmark in exchange for *Devisen* contributed from abroad by aid organizations constituted taxable profit. Löwenherz again impressed on Brunner 1 that the loss of its tax-exempt status would ruin the IKG financially and "would, of course, contradict the assurances [with respect to this matter] which, at the behest of Eichmann, I [Löwenherz] had repeatedly given [to the contacts] abroad," that is, the Joint. Brunner said that he would again intervene in regard to the matter, and regardless of the outcome, "taxation of RM receipts from *Devisen* was in any case out of question."[128]

When late in November Löwenherz saw Eichmann's deputy Rolf Günther in Vienna, preliminary to his reporting to Eichmann in Berlin a week later, Günther told him that, according to Eichmann, the *Reichsvereinigung* Berlin was liable to taxation. It was clear to Löwenherz that he would have to explain the legal basis for the tax-exempt status of the IKG to Günther from scratch, which he did. Thereupon Günther opined that these receipts were not taxable and directed Löwenherz to submit a statement summarizing all "the legal and practical reasons that justify tax exemption." Apparently the statements that Löwenherz had submitted repeatedly in the past had either not been shared with or were not read by Eichmann's right-hand man.[129]

In Berlin Löwenherz continued negotiating with Eichmann, reminding him that rulings pertaining to legal status in the Altreich explicitly excluded the *Ostmark* and asking for an extension of the tax exempt status through 1941. Eichmann stated that whatever happened, a tax levied for Reichsmark receipts derived from the use of *Devisen* contributed from abroad was "in any case out of question."[130]

Back in Vienna Löwenherz submitted yet another statement and asked Brunner 1 to intervene on behalf of the IKG's exemption from corporate tax.[131] On December 20 Brunner 1 again saw Thieme, who decided that the General Foundation was definitely liable for taxation and, since the IKG had already paid a tax levied against the General Foundation, it would have to pay further taxes levied against it. Brunner 1 relayed the news but told Löwenherz that these taxes were not high. The Finance Office for Corporations also deemed the institutions of the IKG to be liable for taxation and would issue a tax bill to that effect in January 1941. Furthermore, the IKG itself would also receive a tax bill, which also would not be high. In any case, receipts of Reichsmark in exchange for *Devisen* would not be taxed. Löwenherz, of course, objected that the IKG was not a corporation and that its institutions were not run for profit. All Brunner 1 could advise was that they wait and see what would develop.[132]

Finally, the end of 1940 being only days or even hours away, Löwenherz, to be on the safe side and in anticipation of the legal wrangling that would no doubt ensue, asked Brunner 1 to confirm to the Finance Office the decision of "pertinent higher authorities" to recognize the legal status of the IKG as a public institution up to December 31, 1940.[133]

We have mentioned that when by mid-year 1940 the funds available for meeting the IKG budget were restricted to an alarming degree, Löwenherz had to turn to the *Zentralstelle* for help. We already know the reasons: The amount of Reichsmark the IKG was permitted to obtain in return for *Devisen* spent for emigration purposes was a fraction of the special rate of exchange that had prevailed in 1938 and 1939. Furthermore, most of the people who were fortunate enough to emigrate and who were assigned to the respective group transports did not have the Reichsmark to recompense the IKG for the *Devisen* spent to arrange for these transports. Similarly, for example, recompense to the IKG in Reichsmark for the *Devisen* spent in preparation of the special Palestine transport would not be released until the transport was actually dispatched much later that year. The *Zentralstelle* dawdled with the reimbursement of the considerable amounts in Reichsmark that the IKG was required to advance for Joint relief operations in Warsaw, Łódz, Krakow, and Sosnowitz. Proceeds from the forced sale of assets, whether those of the IKG Vienna or of the dissolved provincial communities or Jewish organizations, were in funds and accounts over which the IKG did not have free control nor to which it had access. Neither were the moneys in the *Sperrkonti* (frozen accounts) of people who had emigrated readily available.

Thus Löwenherz had no alternative but to press Eichmann with respect to his previous requests, dated April 18 and May 31, 1940, for subsidies from the "emigration fund." Eichmann finally approved the release of RM 300,000 on June 12,[134] and on Löwenherz's insistence, of another measly RM 200,000 on July 15.[135] In August Löwenherz reported to Brunner 1 that the experience of the first seven months of the year showed a deficit despite the reduced budget and that a balanced budget would not be possible without a steady subsidy from the *Zentralstelle*, and requested that Brunner 1 intercede with Eichmann accordingly.[136] However, the urgent need for subsidies handed an additional stranglehold to the Nazis, as demonstrated by the events recounted or still to be told. The last subsidy from the "emigration fund" was released in September 1940, and despite the dire straits the IKG found itself in, despite the reports Löwenherz had to submit, despite his requests to supplement the bits and pieces he was able to scrape together from different sources, in spite of his persistence in calling the bluff of the orchestrated temporizing and maneuvering on the part of Eichmann and his team, no more subsidies would be forthcoming from Eichmann and the *Zentralstelle*.

We have seen that Eichmann also delayed or even withheld the release of funds from accounts nominally belonging to the IKG. Not only did he tighten his grip over the moneys as the year turned into fall, but other authorities followed his lead. In November Löwenherz reported to Brunner 1 that the Vienna municipality had stopped paying unemployment compensation to Jews, sending them instead to the IKG for help. For Brunner 1 this was an additional occasion to pressure Löwenherz to continue the negotiation with the municipality for a monthly contribution to the welfare budget, a negotiation that had proved to be futile in the past. Löwenherz reported: "SS-OStuf. Brunner declared that I should consider this kind of decision [of cutting off unemployment compensation] as an opportunity to intervene at the respective section of the municipality and of submitting for consideration the subsidy of the IKG, urged months ago." And he added this bit of practical wisdom, which Löwenherz no doubt had failed to think of himself: "With a lump sum contributed by the Vienna municipality the IKG would be in a position to meet its welfare commitments."[137]

From what we have related so far we can recognize certain factors of the financial squeeze-play that was being enacted, factors beyond the manipulation of *Devisen* contributed by the Joint. Let us examine some of the prominent developments of this tightening grip.

Financial Finagling

On his trip to Vienna in mid-May 1940, Eichmann had promised a subsidy for May from the *Zentralstelle* reserve designated for "America migration." On May 31 Löwenherz confronted Brunner 1 with a graph showing that during the four months from February to May the IKG had released or spent RM 2,921,768, which represented the equivalent in Reichsmark of *Devisen* released without recompense to finance the emigration transports. Now, however, he was asking for a contribution of RM 600,000, which was urgently needed to cover the financial obligations of the IKG. To clinch the point, Löwenherz said:

> Incidentally, in accordance with SS-Hstf. Eichmann's understanding, I assured the President of the Joint Distribution Committee, Mr. Troper, that the IKG could count on respective contributions from the *Zentralstelle*, and I am convinced that he will raise this question at the imminent negotiations in Budapest.[138]

Brunner 1 promised to refer the matter to Berlin, which did not alleviate Löwenherz's urgent need to meet the immediate financial obligations of the IKG.

Löwenherz received Eichmann's reassurance that the IKG would, for the time being, retain its legal status as a public institution and thus avoid corporate taxes. But when he justifiably asked Eichmann to support his attempt to gain welfare contributions from the municipality, Eichmann thought that "all steps in that direction were futile" and that contributions from the *Zentralstelle* were a substitute for support by the municipality. Löwenherz countered "that in the past [Eichmann] had promised me the amounts that were paid by emigrating Jews for passport fees, and the IKG would have been able to meet its budgetary obligation more easily if it had had the right to collect the passport fees directly." In other words, Löwenherz was telling Eichmann that the fees were collected for the IKG, not for the *Zentralstelle*. Eichmann understood this, of course, and, understanding it, had no difficulty in finding a way of weaseling out: "SS Hstf. Eichmann declared that these contributions are, naturally, at the disposal of the IKG, and they will come in very handy at a later time, when it will have no further income under the title 'emigration.'"[139]

By mid-1940, the amount of money amassed by Eichmann for the passport fee levied by the *Zentralstelle* on the 120,000 Jews who had left by then was considerable, inasmuch as it was assessed in proportion to the amount of property the emigrants had to report as of January 1, 1938, before the Anschluss and before they lost their sources of income and their assets. And now that previous sources of revenue had been curtailed or eliminated, the time had come for Löwenherz to tap supposedly available sources, in particular Eichmann's emigration fund, which had been built with the passport fees. Instead, Eichmann temporized and reserved for himself—though actually in keeping with the Nazi plans for the Jews of Vienna, plans which were even then being formulated in Berlin, of course unknown to Löwenherz or to any Jew—the decision when and how to tap the fund, thereby increasing the financial stranglehold on Löwenherz and the IKG.

In addition to the many regular periodic financial reports that the IKG had to submit to the *Zentralstelle*, the IKG was often ordered to prepare summary reports for certain periods or certain activities or status reports as of given dates. In August 1940, when the IKG had to find or liquefy assets of any amount that could be used to finance the IKG operations, Brunner 1 referred to a graph the IKG had had to prepare at the beginning of this period of tightening finances. The graph showed the assets of the IKG as of October 31, 1939, among other things an outstanding balance of RM 291,000 in accounts receivable. Brunner 1 ordered Murmelstein to report the present balance of that account and how much would be retrievable. Murmelstein reported three amounts: a loan of RM 86,735 by the IKG Vienna to the IKG Graz, a loan of RM 7,000 to the home for the disabled and the blind *Hohe Warte*, and a debt of RM 20,000 owed for *Devisen* released by the IKG to the Committee for Jewish Overseas Transports (i.e., Storfer's Palestine transports). All three of these moneys were under control of the *Zentralstelle*, and their retrieval would be a matter of their releasing these funds to the IKG. Murmelstein did not mention this, since he did not need to. Especially the debt owed by Graz had been claimed by Löwenherz a number of times, as we know. Other amounts, totaling RM 86,170, were loans granted by the IKG to Jewish organizations before the Anschluss (in Murmelstein's words: "before the new order"), organizations that no longer existed. However, "a part of these amounts is secured by real estate, insofar as these organizations have been incorporated into the IKG, together with their immovable assets," which is to say that these assets, too, were retrievable upon their release to the IKG. Murmelstein took the opportunity to cite the example of the assets of the defunct Julius Fränkel Foundation for stipends in the amount of RM 58,300, which had been transferred to the IKG with the condition that they be used to aid the emigration of Jewish students. However, these assets were being held in escrow at the Vienna *Länderbank* (Provincial Bank), and they "have not as yet been released to the IKG."[140] In other words, Brunner's attempt to goad the IKG into retrieving dormant accounts receivable instead of constantly asking for subsidies from the "emigration fund" and other Jewish assets held by the *Zentralstelle* backfired, albeit without benefit to the IKG.

The extent to which control over funding was increasing can be seen from Löwenherz's extensive review of the financial situation of the IKG when he reported to Eichmann at the RSHA in Berlin on September 4, 1940. After receiving a report about the movable and immobile assets of the IKG from Löwenherz and reassuring himself of their extent,

Eichmann granted the aforementioned release of RM 375,000 to reimburse the IKG for expenses incurred for the Palestine transport, which had finally, after all these months, been dispatched, as well as a "subsidy" of RM 300,000. He was also prepared to release up to RM 500,000 from the proceeds of assets to be sold in September and October. However, the IKG would have to make do with these amounts through October, in addition to any income that the IKG might realize.[141]

If the need should arise, Eichmann would authorize his emigration fund to acquire the securities owned by the General Foundation for Jewish Welfare at prevailing rates. These, we recall, were the remaining assets of the dissolved Jewish welfare organizations, whose functions had now devolved upon the IKG. These assets were now under the control of Eichmann, though Brunner 2 continued as the executor of their liquidation. Eichmann would spend funds from the emigration fund he had been accumulating to acquire securities that would appreciate in value, thereby transferring money to the Jewish welfare reserve account, the release of which he, of course, controlled as well.

Löwenherz again inquired about the debt of RM 86,000 owed by IKG Graz to IKG Vienna, which Murmelstein had mentioned only two weeks earlier when he reported to Brunner 1. Eichmann told Löwenherz that this "will be refunded under any circumstance," but he did not say when or under what circumstances. Instead, he told Löwenherz he had to report to him personally again when it came time to consider funds needed to meet expenses in November and December, at which time he would also consider the proposed funding for 1941. Löwenherz suggested that the Vienna municipality contribute a monthly welfare allotment of RM 300,000, and Eichmann ordered him to undertake steps to secure such contribution from the municipality.[142] We recall that when Löwenherz raised this matter three months earlier, Eichmann had told him that "all steps in that direction are futile." Now however, in December, we find that Löwenherz had to report to Eichmann about the progress of his negotiation with the municipality concerning this contribution.[143] Löwenherz also requested a monthly subsidy of another RM 300,000 from the *Zentralstelle*, pointing out that the request was justified in that it was tied to *Devisen* approved for emigration and that the rate of subsidy granted to the IKG by the *Zentralstelle* for *Devisen* received from abroad and released for the purpose of emigration could be expected to continue to decline. Eichmann, as was his wont, responded by saying he would consider this at a later time but, in the meantime, the IKG would have to realize additional savings.

Löwenherz answered that the IKG had been operating in the most frugal way, in accordance with the changing demands on its budget. In fact, as Löwenherz reminded Eichmann, the present monthly budget of the IKG in the amount of RM 850,000 was approximately half of what is had been one year earlier, in August 1939, when expenditures connected with the last few months of the prewar emigration effort were at a high point. However, the considerable savings in this area were now counterbalanced by the increased demand for the care of the sick and the aged, for new facilities that had to be established, and for additional personnel who had to be employed, if the IKG was to continue providing its many necessary services. This presentation touched on two sensitive issues: the forced dismissal of personnel and the pressure to reduce the expenditures on behalf of people who were in one way or another dependent on the IKG for basic care and services.

Both of these issues ran parallel to the increasing control over the accessibility to the IKG of its sources of funding. It is significant, yet not surprising, that Eichmann responded to Löwenherz's warning about the precarious state of the IKG's capacity of operating under the draconian rule over its funding by ordering him to see whether additional personnel could be dismissed from the home for the aged and the hospital and to report how many former employees were receiving pensions or other allowances from the IKG. Löwenherz pointed out that not only were pensioners by law entitled to their pensions but also that he, Eichmann, had already "drastically reduced" (*empfindlich gekürzt*) these pensions.[144]

Eichmann had promised to release RM 500,000 from the proceeds of assets sold during September and October, admonishing Löwenherz that with this sum, together with the other funds to be released, Löwenherz would have to make do through October. Based on this promise, Löwenherz proceeded to honor the financial commitments of the IKG. In November 1940 he reported to Brunner 1 that since RM 200,000 of the money Eichmann had promised by the end of October had still not been released and since Löwenherz had included that amount in preparing his budget, the continued operation of the IKG had become impossible. Moreover, despite the strictest savings measures, the IKG could not meet its obligations without the funds accumulated by the *Zentralstelle*. Brunner 1 responded that he had reported the financial emergency situation of the IKG to Berlin, evidently without an alleviating response. He therefore offered Löwenherz a nifty interim solution: Why not use the moneys held in escrow for the IKG in the deposit account D at the *Länderbank*? It would have been very nice if Löwenherz had proceeded to do that, because it was illegal and, since Brunner's suggestion was not in writing, Löwenherz would have had to suffer the consequences. Hence Löwenherz pointed out what Brunner 1 knew—after all, that was the point of his joke—that moneys deposited in that account could not be withdrawn until the *Devisen* had actually been transferred. As it happens, Löwenherz continued, because of the forced emigration to Shanghai, as well as to Central and South America, he was able to withdraw some of that money, and this was the only reason why the IKG did not have to shut down any of its offices as yet. However, the IKG also had to meet payments for deliveries from Aryan businesses, to the Vienna municipality, to various tax bureaus, and so on. In sum, because the RM 200,000 were not released, the IKG would be in dire straits within the next few weeks until certain schemes that were in the works, as Löwenherz hoped, would come to fruition. Finally, Brunner 1 promised to intercede once again in Berlin about release of the RM 200,000.[145]

A consequence of Brunner's intercession was that Eichmann sent his deputy, Rolf Günther, to Vienna to prepare the next step in Eichmann's maneuver, which would require Brunner 1 to play his role. Thus, one week after his meeting with Brunner 1,[146] Löwenherz had to report to Günther, who wondered what the IKG would need for December 1, when bills would come due. Löwenherz informed Günther that the IKG needed RM 300,000 "unconditionally." He would be able to obtain RM 100,000 of this amount from the deposit account in exchange for *Devisen* to be released in the next few days for emigrants who would be leaving. But the remainder would have to be covered through the immediate release of the RM 200,000 promised for the end of October. Günther, a master of straight-faced temporizing prevarication, stated that the authorization for their release might arrive as early as later that day. We know that it did not, for the following reasons: For many weeks there had been talk about arranging a meeting between Löwenherz and Troper of the Joint. Troper was now planning a winter crossing of the Atlantic to Lisbon in order to meet Löwenherz and the principals from Berlin sometime in December. However, ships plying the Atlantic in wartime did not run according to any schedule. According to when the Lisbon meeting could be arranged, Löwenherz was supposed to have a preparatory meeting with Eichmann in Berlin and leave for Lisbon from there. Now, however, Günther told Löwenherz that if the meeting with Troper were again postponed, he would have to report to Eichmann in Berlin on December 5. And there, ten days after Günther held out the imminent release of the RM 200,000, Löwenherz had to bring up the matter again.[147]

As for the December budget, Löwenherz told Günther that thanks to "extreme savings measures," only RM 700,000 would be needed, RM 400,000 of which would, if all went well, derive from income and moneys in exchange for *Devisen*. The remaining RM 300,000, however, would have to be covered by a subsidy from the *Zentralstelle*, which Löwenherz now requested.[148] It was very important for Löwenherz to secure the money for December because he was scheduled to be absent a good part of the month to report, as he had just then found out, twice to Eichmann in Berlin and then to leave for Lisbon to meet with Troper. Not only did Löwenherz not want to leave the IKG without secure financing during his absence, but it was of vital interest to the IKG to represent a sound financial picture to Troper, which, he presumed, was of interest to the Nazis as well.

Therefore, when Löwenherz presented the same report and request for December that he had given to Eichmann's emissary Günther, Eichmann seemed ready and assured Löwenherz, in the presence of Brunner 1 who had come to Berlin as well, that he would order the release of RM 300,000 by the Vienna *Zentralstelle*.[149] Yet the matter was not over, for the dance of extortion continued. A few days before he went to see Eichmann in Berlin, when Löwenherz was busy with an appeal to the Vienna municipality and other matters in preparation of his meeting with Eichmann, Murmelstein reported to Brunner 1 in his stead and was advised that Löwenherz should be prepared to report to Eichmann about his efforts to obtain a monthly welfare allowance of RM 300,000 from the Vienna municipality.[150] This Löwenherz would in any case have been ready to report on. But now, in Berlin, Eichmann informed Löwenherz that the release of RM 300,000 was only by way of an advancement against the grant by the Vienna municipality of a monthly lump sum of RM 300,000 for the IKG welfare budget, as if the welfare deal were a done deal. Löwenherz must have been reassured to no end by Eichmann's declaration that for the sake of the "settlement" (*Verrechnung*; read: extortion) the Vienna *Zentralstelle* would now be supportive of the IKG's "appeal" (*Ansuchen*) to the Vienna municipality and would try to have the "contribution for welfare that is to be approved by the Vienna municipality be in force already for December."[151] Of course.

To explain: We recall that Löwenherz thought the Vienna Municipality ought to make this grant and that Eichmann said that it was not he, Eichmann, but Löwenherz who should apply for it. Löwenherz's reasoning, no doubt, was that the taxes Jews had paid for social security, including especially those who had emigrated, would in any case exceed what Vienna would disburse to the IKG. However, the municipality had no interest in making payments other than to qualified individuals, if it had to, and under present conditions would get away with refusing even individual payments to Jews. The Nazis at the *Zentralstelle* would welcome having the municipality take over a hefty part of the IKG claim on the "emigration fund," which they so diligently amassed from the Jews. But they would not want to appear to be interfering with the governmental authorities (that were actually also under the thumb of the Nazis, though via a different hierarchy of authority), that is, as long as they could send a hapless Jew to do it for them. What better way to pressure Löwenherz to succeed than to withhold the RM 200,000 that were part of the money promised for October, and in December finally to release RM 300,000, albeit as an advance for the not-at-all assured generosity of the municipality in granting what the Jews were entitled to in any case?

It came, then, as no surprise to anyone that by the time Löwenherz saw Brunner 1 again on December 10 and 11, the Vienna municipality had rejected Löwenherz's appeal for a monthly welfare contribution of RM 300,000, much less one beginning as of December. Consequently, Brunner 1 was in a position to tell Löwenherz that since all other funds were frozen at present, the release of RM 300,000 would be possible only upon Löwenherz's transfer of the securities that the IKG Vienna had deposited for safekeeping at the *Länderbank* and the *Credit-Institut* to the liquidation account of the assets of the former provincial Jewish communities of Austria. He assured Löwenherz that the value in excess of that amount would be made available to the IKG, "probably" (*voraussichtlich*) next month. He also assured Löwenherz that the remaining assets in real estate would remain in the possession of the IKG, since "no more houses will be sold," a ploy Löwenherz had heard on a number of occasions in the past. He further assured Löwenherz that, in case the Vienna municipality did come through with a monthly contribution of RM 300,000, he would try to prevent them from laying claim to the "General Foundation for Jewish Welfare in Vienna," a foundation that Eichmann controlled and whose money came from liquidated Jewish organizations.[152]

On both days of that *Vorsprache* (meeting) Löwenherz insisted that "retention of this asset [the securities] is absolutely necessary (*unumgänglich erforderlich*) for the IKG because it would otherwise lose credit both domestically and abroad." Furthermore, "in light of its diverse tasks and the increasing number of duties, the IKG cannot be left without assets." Löwenherz reiterated for the umpteenth time that the monthly subsidy that the IKG was supposed to receive from the "emigration fund" had not been forthcoming since September. Instead, the IKG had been forced to meet its expenses from the fund of the welfare foundation and from the liquidation account from sold properties. And now, the amount whose release was promised for December was to be drawn from the assets of the IKG. Brunner 1 did not need to say that he had been maneuvering bit by bit to effect precisely the depletion of these funds and assets, nor did he divulge what Eichmann and the powers-that-be in Berlin were saving the "emigration fund" for. Löwenherz would find out soon enough.

By the time Löwenherz was ready to leave for Lisbon via Berlin and the RSHA, a trip that had again been postponed, this time to the beginning of January 1941, he reported to

Brunner 1 that in spite of the proceeds of RM 300,000 from the sale of the securities that had been deposited at the *Länderbank* and in spite of his having tapped all remaining available reserves, the IKG could not meet its bills due on January 1. Brunner 1, who had just returned from again reporting to Eichmann in Berlin, informed Löwenherz that Eichmann had approved the release of RM 300,000, which would take place the following week.[153] In other words, Löwenherz would have to leave before the moneys came through and would not be in a position to report to the Joint that the IKG budget was covered.

Liquidation of Provincial Community Assets

The role that the IKG Vienna was forced to play in the liquidation of what was left of the provincial communities forms a particularly painful episode in the tightening grip on the IKG and its finances. When in December 1939 Eichmann announced the impending liquidation of the Jewish communities in the provinces, Löwenherz of course laid claim to the proceeds from the sale of their assets for the emigration and welfare efforts of the IKG and requested that no *Aufbauumlage* (reconstruction levy) be assessed against these sales. Eichmann, however, pointed out that while the IKG Vienna was the administrator of their emigration and welfare needs, it was not the legal successor of the provincial communities, thus leaving the question of tax exemption up in the air.[154] In connection with the topic of the provincial communities, Löwenherz raised the question of reimbursement for the sizable sum that, at Eichmann's order, the IKG Vienna had to advance to the IKG Graz for purposes that are not clear. It was a matter that would drag on for all of 1940, until it reached an utterly unsatisfactory resolution. Because the financial situation was beginning to worsen and because Löwenherz had little or no control or oversight over the assets of the provincial communities, he was anxious to have the matter of their liquidation proceed expeditiously. Since the status and mechanics of Eichmann's trusteeship were still not settled in January 1940, he told Löwenherz that regulating the liquidation of the communities in the provinces was still under consideration.[155] The trusteeship matter was still not regulated in February when Eichmann told Löwenherz that, once his appointment as special trustee of the properties of the IKG and the provincial communities was in place, he would leave the administration of relevant matters to the IKG, "reserving for himself the final decision" on any and all matters. The provincial properties were to be sold by the IKG Vienna, which, Eichmann reiterated, was not to be construed as being their legal successor. Since the legal discrepancy in the status of the IKG that was inherent in this scheme was evident to Löwenherz, he told Eichmann that the IKG could proceed only upon formal confirmation and that any such actual procedure would be handled, under Löwenherz's supervision, by the IKG legal department. In this connection Löwenherz referred to an earlier statement (dated December 31, 1939), proposing a relevant legal ruling to govern the form of the liquidation.[156] Unfolding events will reveal that his advice was not followed.

Löwenherz was told that the question of the sale of realties belonging to the IKG Baden to the city of Baden would have to wait until that regulation was in place. In the meantime, Heinrich Fleischmann, who was taking care of the business of that community, was to be informed that he was not entitled to make any official commitments to the town regarding any sales.[157] However, all along a number of provincial matters had to be dealt with that would not wait until Eichmann's trusteeship was regularized. For example, Löwenherz again asked for the reimbursement of DM 86,735 advanced by the IKG Vienna to the IKG Graz—to no avail—and for release of proceeds from the sale of realties in Graz, Linz, and Wiener Neustadt.[158] When an insurance company in Znaim owed RM 24.10 to the Jewish Community (*Kultusgemeinde* or KG) of Misslitz (Miroslav), the IKG was ordered to effect the transfer of that amount to the account of the KG Misslitz, without implying that the IKG had any legal interest in this matter.[159]

Early in March 1940 Eichmann informed Löwenherz that Bürckel had appointed him special trustee for the liquidation of the assets of the provincial Jewish communities (*Kultusgemeinden* or KGs), and in this capacity he would "direct and empower the IKG Vienna to effect" that liquidation.[160] The mechanics of the involvement of the IKG in the liquidation of the assets of the provincial Jewish communities raised some questions. Thus, when Löwenherz and Murmelstein reported to Eichmann in Vienna at the end of March, they expressed their concern whether the IKG would incur any fees in connection with the projected reassignment of the provincial properties to the IKG Vienna. In response Erich Rajakovic, the legal expert of the Gestapo, spelled out a twisted way of effecting the reassignment, evidently in the expectation that the statutory obligation for the IKG to spend its increasingly limited and increasingly controlled funds could thus be avoided, not out of consideration for the IKG but out of the knowledge that what was the IKG's was ultimately the Nazis'. Rajakovic explained that because the directors of the provincial KGs had emigrated, the Ministry of Religious Affairs and Education would appoint Löwenherz as their new director. "In this capacity [Löwenherz] will actively participate in the liquidation of the assets of these KGs and will effect the liquidation under the supervision of the Special Trustee for the Assets of the IKGs in the *Ostmark*." Thus it was Löwenherz, and not the agents of the Nazi Party, who would transfer the provincial assets to the tax-exempt IKG Vienna. Since IKG Vienna would not be the legal successor of the provincial Jewish communities, it would not be liable for any of their outstanding debts.[161] There was only one such debt, the major debt owed by IKG Graz to IKG Vienna with which we are familiar. Löwenherz of course wanted this money returned to the IKG Vienna, "even if it had, in the meantime, been submitted to the *Aufbaufonds*" (the fund for reconstruction).[162]

Not all matters pertained to the selling of assets. The liquidation of the provincial Jewish communities also involved relocating the Jews remaining in the provinces to Vienna. This action began in spring 1940 and was directed by Brunner 2. When he gave notice that the Jews of St. Pölten must move to Vienna by April 1, that is, within ten days, Murmelstein requested and was granted an extension to April 15.[163] Soon afterward, he was told that the Jews of Misslitz would have to come to Vienna and that the IKG would have to make the arrangements.[164] The new arrivals were relatively few, but because of the increasingly tight housing situation, the IKG was overwhelmed with this sudden broadening of its responsibility. Brunner 2 directed the IKG to provide housing for the Jews of Misslitz and for those who would soon be arriving in Vienna from other places in the provinces. In response to Murmelstein's prediction of the resulting turmoil, Brunner 2 offered to inform the municipal housing bureau accordingly,[165] which, coming from Brunner 2, was anything but a reassuring promise. When the deadline for these expulsions arrived on April 15, Murmelstein took advantage of Eichmann's presence in Vienna and informed him that several of the persons in Misslitz were between 80 and over 90 years old. Eichmann permitted an extension of the deadline to May 1 and, in the absence of someone who could organize their move to Vienna, for someone from the IKG to take charge.[166] Brunner 1 was also monitoring the removal of provincial Jews to Vienna. Acknowledging that the move of the Jews of Misslitz to Vienna had been completed, he informed Murmelstein that the Jews from St. Pölten had to be in Vienna by May 10, those from Amstetten, Krems, Tulln, and Wiener Neustadt by May 27. Those who had official permission to stay longer were to be reported individually. Those in institutions were exempted.[167] However, since only Jews from the Austrian provinces were required and indeed permitted to move to Vienna, a certain Johanna Sara Schwarz, age 73, had to be told, for example, to return immediately to Berlin.[168]

At this time Brunner 2 continued doing the work he had formerly done as the Commissioner of Receivership for Jewish Properties, but now he was working out of the *Zentralstelle* as the agent of Eichmann in his capacity of special trustee for the liquidation of not only big but also small Jewish assets, so also of those in the provinces. How small can be seen when Prochnik had to report to him early in April 1940 on behalf of the IKG to receive a string of orders. Brunner 2 wanted a report about the RM 800 belonging to the Jewish Community (KG) of Lackenbach, which had been given to the former rabbi of Lackenbach for safekeeping. He wanted particulars about a parcel of land in Döbling (a district of Vienna) belonging to the IKG Vienna. He wanted the application for the transfer

The entrance to the village of Brunn am Gebirge in the Mödling district, just a few kilometers south of Vienna. The sign at the entrance reads: "Jews not wanted." (WStLA Fotoarchiv Gerlach, FC1: 6634M)

of parcels belonging to the *Chevra Kadisha* (Jewish burial society) of Mödling (district) to be submitted to the respective office of the provincial government rather than to his former office as Commissioner of Receivership. Similarly, he wanted the IKG to apply for the official cancellation of the lost savings account book of the KG Tulln, showing a balance of RM 549.01. As regards the report filed in May 1939, according to which the balance of RM 5,500 owned by the KG Hollabrunn was confiscated by the local party office, Brunner 2 claimed the president of the KG Hollabrunn, Oskar Skutetzky, used the money to pay debts incurred by the local *Chevra Kadisha*, and Brunner 2 wanted the IKG Vienna to investigate and report. Finally, Brunner 2 informed Prochnik that the balance of RM 127.60 of the Jewish savings and credit club of Hollabrunn has been transferred to the liquidation account of the IKG Vienna.[169] The KG Hohenems was said to have a balance of about 3,000 lire in Merano (Italy), and Brunner 2 wanted Löwenherz to obtain a report about it.[170] Another time Löwenherz was assured that the liquidation of the KG Lackenbach would not be delayed, inasmuch as their debts exceeded their accounts receivable by only a few hundred Reichsmark.[171] When someone in the village of Zlabings (Slavonice) bei Waidhofen, historically and currently in Moravia but at that time incorporated into the Reich, wanted to rent the Jewish cemetery there, the IKG had to submit an application to that effect to the *Zentralstelle*. Brunner 1 directed instead that steps be initiated leading to the sale of the cemetery to the village, so that they as owners would be renting the cemetery, and not the IKG.[172]

The major concern during the liquidation of the provincial Jewish communities was the sale of their properties. Sales were arranged mainly by local officials in collusion with Nazi officials, often from agencies other than the *Zentralstelle* or from the office of Brunner 2. These sales could not be completed until Löwenherz signed the sales contract on behalf of the IKG Vienna. Löwenherz was concerned about the amount and disposition of the proceeds from the sales, and with good cause. He was not consulted about the sales price, and he had to fight a constant battle to save the proceeds from taxation and to secure them for the use of the IKG. Once the sales contracts were approved by the IKG, they had to be submitted to the trustee's office for signing before they could take effect, such as in the case of the contract for the sale of real estate to the Linz Postal Service.[173] One time Löwenherz reported to Brunner 1 that Notary Dr. Adolf Reiter submitted contracts for his signature for sales of real estate owned by the Jewish communities of Neunkirchen, Wiener Neustadt, and St. Pölten. Löwenherz had not signed them because the sales prices were too low. On the one hand, he was pressured by Eichmann to get the highest possible prices because proceeds from these sales had to defray the costs of emigration and pay for the welfare of Jews from the provinces. On the other hand, Brunner 1 opined that higher prices could hardly be expected when the buyers were towns or villages.[174] When Löwenherz submitted the *Aktennotiz* containing his objection and Brunner's opinion, Brunner 1 ordered Löwenherz to sign.[175] When he saw Eichmann in Berlin a few days later, Löwenherz reported his objection to the low prices at which he had to sell the properties in the provinces; Eichmann consoled him by saying that the sale of two properties were in the offing, at prices above the value estimated by the IKG, although he could not as yet tell Löwenherz which they were, only that they were not in Vienna.[176] Eichmann also assured Löwenherz that he

*A memorial plaque affixed to the house in which the synagogue of the Jewish Community of Hollabrunn in Lower Austria (*Niederösterreich*) was located until the Community was eradicated in September 1938. (By Herwig Reidlinger (Own work) [CC BY-SA 3.0 (http://creativecommons.org/licenses/by-sa/3.0)], via Wikimedia Commons)*

would order that the proceeds from the sale of provincial properties, which were deposited in a special account, would be released to the IKG after deduction of the *Aufbauumlage*, which had to be paid in its entirety. Löwenherz asked that the release actually be effected, not only because the IKG had to advance RM 86,000 to Graz but also because it had to advance RM 100,000 for the emigration and welfare of Jews in the provinces.[177]

The pressure on Löwenherz to sign sales agreements over which he had no control continued unabated. When he objected to the low sales prices for still other properties, this time of former communities in Burgenland, Brunner 1 again said this could not be helped in cases where properties were sold to local administrations, and Löwenherz "should sign in the name of the communities."[178] One evening at 7:00 p.m., as he was leaving for the day, Löwenherz was confronted by Notary Dr. Reiter, who wanted him to sign sales agreements for a number of provincial properties. Although he was being placed under intense time pressure because of the approaching curfew, Löwenherz was able to ascertain that one property in Krems and several in Eisenstadt were being sold at far below their actual value. Instead of signing under pressure, Löwenherz submitted a report to the *Zentralstelle*, asking for its intervention with the local administrations with the aim of increasing the sales prices. However, Brunner 1 told him that this was no longer possible and that if anyone criticized Löwenherz about this matter, he should say that the sale had been made at the order of the *Zentralstelle*.[179]

Löwenherz had warned Eichmann that the legal status which the *Zentralstelle* assigned to the IKG with respect to the liquidation of the assets of the provincial communities, was highly questionable. Hence, it came as no surprise to the men at the IKG when Bürckel's office passed on a ruling it had received from the Ministry of Internal and Cultural Affairs, according to which "the liquidation of the provincial communities through the IKG Vienna, without its being their legal successors, is impossible." Moreover, considerable transfer fees would have to be assessed on the sale of these properties. The matter did not come as a surprise to Brunner 1 either, but all he would say was that Eichmann would take up the matter when he was in Vienna two days hence.[180] Two days later, Löwenherz had to report to the *Zentralstelle* at the unusual time of 4:00 p.m. He was not received by Eichmann but by Brunner 1. Considering the number of directives Brunner 1 handed down concerning various liquidation matters, it was clear that Eichmann had been in town that day. As to the matter at hand, it was also clear that Eichmann had done his work: Brunner 1 informed Löwenherz—in the presence of Dr. Rajakovic—that "the ruling by the Ministry for Internal and Cultural Affairs, Dept. IV, dated June 28, 1940, promulgated on July 10, 1940, to the IKG by the Governor [Bürckel] in Vienna, State Administration, Section Ia, VB, is incorrect." The presence of Rajakovic, who was the legal expert of the Gestapo and thus the party's main legal authority in Vienna, was meant to prevent any confusion on Löwenherz's part as to which authority he was to follow in this matter. However, it also had the effect of the governmental authority eating crow and confirming that when it came to directing Nazi policy vis-à-vis the Jews, the SD was in charge by way of Eichmann and his *Zentralstelle*.[181]

The procedural and legal problems of liquidating Jewish assets, especially those of the provincial communities, must have seemed like the Mad Hatter's Tea Party. Just how bewildering it was, from a standpoint of proper bureaucratic procedure, can be gleaned from a record of an exchange between Löwenherz and Dr. Mayer. Mayer was an official of the Nazi government (*Statthalterei*) of Lower Danube (*Niederdonau*), which at that time included the former province of Lower Austria (*Niederösterreich*), the northern part of former Burgenland, and areas of the Moravian part of the Sudetenland. Mayer was in charge of the liquidation and purchase of Jewish assets in his province.

Mayer asked two questions. He wanted to know whether Löwenherz was empowered to make statements concerning the KGs in Lower Danube that were legally valid and whether he was legally empowered to dispose of their assets. All that Mayer could find was a vacuum, and he had no inkling as to who had the right to dispose of the assets.

Löwenherz responded that according to a ruling of the Federal (*sic*! Did he mean Reich?) Ministry of Religious Affairs and Education, he was appointed director of the KGs in the *Ostmark* in his capacity as director of the IKG Vienna. According to a second ruling by the ministry, all provincial KGs were dissolved as of August 1, 1940, with the exception of those in Graz and Lackenbach. The assets of the provincial KGs had already been sold, most of them to local municipalities.

And now Löwenherz explained the byways of legality over which the sales were effected: Eichmann was appointed, according to a ruling of said ministry, as special trustee for the assets of the KGs in the *Ostmark* and of the General Foundation for Jewish Welfare in Vienna. Recently, when Eichmann resigned from that post, Löwenherz was informed by the chief magistrate of Vienna that the *Zentralstelle* (i.e., the Center for Jewish Emigration in Vienna) "has to take care of the supervision of the assets administered by the IKG."

The actual sale of the provincial assets was implemented by Herr Brunner of the office of the special trustee, and Löwenherz's involvement consisted merely in receiving the sales contracts for signature from Dr. Reiter.[182] Löwenherz also informed Mayer that according to Brunner 2, he had nothing to do with the assets of the formerly Moravian KGs that had been incorporated into Lower Danube because those had already been sold by the Commissioner for Receivership in Reichenbach.

Mayer was astounded. Wasn't the Commission for Receiverships originally established in Vienna for the purposes under consideration? Löwenherz explained that the commission had jurisdiction only over the assets of organizations that, unlike the KGs, did not have the legal status of public institutions; therefore, the commission had nothing to do with the assets of the KGs.

Mayer explained to Löwenherz that, in his opinion, even though the Commissioner of Receiverships was not empowered to conduct the sale of Jewish community assets, he was entitled to determine what assets there were and to supervise the orderly conduct of sales. In connection with an inspection trip Mayer had found that a synagogue building in Misslitz was still unsold, and the reason he needed to consult Löwenherz was to determine who had the legal right to conduct the sale. However, since Löwenherz's empowerment was reduced to signing the sales contracts that were negotiated by others, he suggested, in response to Mayer's quandary, that he get in touch with the *Zentralstelle*.

Nonplussed, Mayer opined that the *Zentralstelle* could not possibly have anything to do with the matter at hand, since it had no official concern other than the emigration of Jews. Löwenherz must have been delighted to inform Mayer that the Center for Jewish Emigration was under the direction of Eichmann, who at one time had been appointed special trustee for assets of KGs in the *Ostmark*.

The interview ended with Mayer asking Löwenherz to prepare a summary of what he had told Mayer and to submit it together with copies of the pertinent ministerial documents.[183]

When Löwenherz submitted the report of his meeting with Mayer to Brunner 1, Brunner 1 told him that the proceeds from the sale of the assets of the formerly Moravian KGs had been used for meeting the reconstruction levy due from the IKG Vienna.[184]

In June Eichmann informed Löwenherz that the liquidation of the provincial assets would have to be completed forthwith. The office of the trustee would soon be abolished. The IKG would retain its status as administrator of assets under the supervision of the *Zentralstelle*.[185] A few months after that, in order to wrap up the liquidations, the *Zentralstelle* ordered the IKG to report which assets ("realties, accounts, securities, etc.") of the Jewish communities of Innsbruck, Hohenems, and Kobersdorf had been sold or redeemed, and to prepare a list of those which as yet had not. On the basis of this list, the *Zentralstelle* would arrange for their liquidation.[186] As it happened, the Ministry of Religious Affairs and Education had ruled that the provincial KGs be dissolved by August 1, 1940, and that their assets be transferred to the IKG Vienna. Since this ruling would provide the IKG with a small measure of influence over the determination of sales prices, Löwenherz requested that the sales contracts executed before that date be changed accordingly. Brunner 1 agreed and empowered Löwenherz to negotiate the matter with Dr. Reiter.[187]

When the liquidation of all the other provincial KGs was effectively completed, there remained what had been the major problem for the IKG Vienna all along, the liquidation of the assets of the IKG Graz. The Jewish Community of Graz, the capital of the province of Styria, had been the largest of the provincial communities and had long been dissolved in all but legal status. Unlike the other provincial KGs, the liquidation of Graz dragged on. The reason was that its assets were encumbered by debts, the greatest of which, as we know, was the money owed to the IKG Vienna, which, as we also know, Löwenherz was very eager to recoup.

When the deadline for completing the liquidation of all provincial KGs was at hand, Brunner 2 informed Löwenherz that he had succeeded in settling the outstanding matters concerning Graz. First, the IKG Vienna would retrieve, if not all, at least a major portion of the RM 86,735 advanced at the behest of the *Zentralstelle* to KG Graz. Also, the municipality of Graz would take over certain obligations, except for the claims of some moving companies that had been storing the goods of emigrants, which, for whatever reason, had not been shipped and had hence been incurring storage charges. The municipality decided that the moving companies could keep the goods as compensation.[188] The news that only a portion of the Graz debt would be retrieved was worrisome, and Löwenherz broached the subject again when he next reported to Eichmann in Berlin. Eichmann assured Löwenherz that the RM 86,000 (*sic*) that the IKG Vienna advanced to Graz would in all events be refunded.[189] In Vienna Löwenherz told Brunner 1 that he would prepare a summary report about the liquidation of the Graz KG and asked the support of the *Zentralstelle* in conducting the remaining liquidation.[190] Löwenherz saw Brunner 1 a few days after he handed him the report and asked that he consider the suggestions he had made. Brunner 1 said that he would study the report and that the liquidation of KG Graz was very complicated.[191] A week later Löwenherz found it necessary to ask Brunner 1 to intervene immediately with the finance bureau of Graz concerning the tax exemption of the KG Graz. Brunner promised to do so and wanted the legal department of the IKG to prepare an appropriate brief, with specific reference to the indebtedness.[192] In the brief he submitted to the Finance Bureau of the Municipality Graz, with a copy to the *Zentralstelle*, Löwenherz declined any tax liability by the KG Graz on the grounds of its being a public organization, a point he had to insist on, if for no other reason than that he needed this status to prevail in the case of the IKG Vienna. With the brief on record, he now asked Brunner 1 again for intervention, possibly through the Graz section of the SS, "who are well informed about the local KG."[193] When another month had passed, Brunner 1 told Löwenherz that he was in contact with the Graz municipality and would continue to pursue the matter of the liquidation of the KG Graz. For his part, Löwenherz said that he was anxious for a prompt resolution because he was counting on the restitution of the advanced RM 86,000, which would result from the liquidation of the KG Graz.[194]

On December 19, after still another month, when Löwenherz was about to leave for Lisbon for his meeting with Troper, Brunner 1 told Murmelstein that he had finally been to Graz the day before concerning the liquidation of the assets of the KG Graz. First he reported that the legal counsel, Dr. Julius Israel Spieler, who had represented the interests of the KG Graz, had not undertaken his task "with requisite care, and thereby had harmed the interests [of KG Graz] to an essential degree." Specifically, he supposedly had failed to dismiss the Aryan school janitor [*Schuldiener*] Franz Schäfer of the defunct Jewish school. In the meantime, however, the municipal pension fund of Graz had accepted Schäfer as pensioner, but the health insurance costs that had in the meantime been paid would have to come out of the proceeds from the sale of the assets. However, back at the IKG, Murmelstein found a copy of a letter to Franz Schäfer, dated December 12, 1938, informing him that "IKG Graz had ceased its activity, and therefore it can no longer use his services." He also found that the legal validity of that letter was confirmed by the provincial court of Graz.[195]

Brunner also informed Murmelstein of the disposition of the sale of the assets of the IKG Graz. The cemetery together with the adjacent acreage, the synagogue building, the community administrative building, the school building with its garden, and another building would all be taken over by the municipality of Graz for RM 55,000. Out of this amount, aside from the expenses connected with Herr Schäfer, there would be costs for the demolition of the synagogue building, all of which would amount to the stipulated proceeds. Or, as Brunner cheerfully said, once all these expenses were covered, "the whole amount seems more or less spent." Murmelstein remarked that the IKG Graz owed IKG Vienna RM 86,000, an amount that hardly seemed covered by the projected liquidation of its assets.[196] Up in arms, Löwenherz called Brunner 1 the next day and objected to the municipality of Graz offering RM 55,000 for the whole lot, whereas heretofore they had offered this amount for the administrative building alone. Brunner 1 declared that the matter was finished; nothing else could be done, except what he had ordered.[197] And so the sales contract prepared by the municipality of Graz was forwarded to Löwenherz for his signature. After examining the contract, Löwenherz submitted to Brunner 1 a report about his reservations regarding the contract: The claims of a number of creditors were not considered in the projected distribution of the proceeds from the sale; it was illegal to give preference to one creditor to the detriment of another. Referring to the contract and his report, Löwenherz broached the matter at the last *Vorsprache* prior to his leaving for Lisbon via Berlin. In what was surely the longest *Aktennotiz*—800 words—of the thousands he wrote and saved for posterity in his special file, Löwenherz carefully recorded that Brunner 1 claimed that he had carefully read both papers, that according to Brunner 1 each of the claims was being satisfied, mainly by the municipality, that no further claims against IKG Graz existed, that the claim on the part of the municipality of Graz to RM 33,700 had been granted by Brunner 2 and nothing could be done about that; that he, Brunner 1, did not see any reason for any reservations about the contract; and that he ordered Löwenherz to sign it and to tell Dr. Reiter to send him a copy. Brunner 1 also wanted all the matters and explanations about the case that transpired between them to be summarized in a separate statement and would see to it that it was signed by the municipality together with the contract.[198]

This saga of the liquidation of the IKG Graz and of Löwenherz's attempt to recover the debt of RM 86,000 was the final chapter in the history of the provincial communities, some of which dated back to medieval and some possibly to Roman times.

Struggle over Assets in Vienna

The matter of the assets of the IKG Vienna, including those of the defunct foundations, was even more complicated than those of the defunct provincial communities, which were liquidated outright. There were many contravening interests at work, and Löwenherz was caught in the middle. Löwenherz desperately needed those assets. Brunner 2, having the job of liquidating the assets of defunct Jewish organizations, was ever ready to arrange the sale of one or the other object to anyone who was interested, especially municipal departments. Since officially he was doing the job on behalf of Eichmann and the *Zentralstelle*, he felt free to proceed on his own to arrange for sales, that is, apparently without prior clearance with Eichmann, who was, sadly, Löwenherz's last resort. Eichmann, however, had an interest in using these assets to tighten his control over the IKG by manipulating its precarious financial condition. We have already seen the means available to him: interceding with other authorities, supposedly on behalf of the IKG, promising Löwenherz that there would be no further sales, temporizing about the release to the IKG of proceeds from such sales, letting his henchmen tell Löwenherz bad news, and so on. There were many more objects at risk, more protracted transactions than we can trace here. Typical of what transpired are the cases of the building on Bauernfeldgasse, which the IKG was using in 1940 as its only orphanage, and of the former famous Home for the Blind at Hohe Warte, which the IKG was now using as a home for the disabled.

When Eichmann was appointed special trustee for the assets of the IKG, he told Löwenherz that unlike the assets of the provincial KGs, all of which were to be liquidated, only individual objects that were not needed for the operations of the IKG Vienna were to be sold. For such objects Eichmann wanted the IKG to obtain "appropriate offers," subject to his approval.[199] Some of the buildings needed by the IKG were properties that had belonged to private charitable foundations. Since these defunct foundations did not have the public tax-exempt status that still applied to the IKG, sales of these properties were always in danger of being taxed by one or the other authority. One of these was the office of Plenipotentiary Bürckel, whose Commission for Receivership administered the liquidation of Jewish foundations; the liquidation of their assets was a source of revenue for the *Aufbauumlage*, the reconstruction levy. And while he now functioned as the agent of Eichmann, Brunner 2 continued his work as commissioner for receiverships. This means that, since he was the executor of the regime's plan to liquidate Jewish properties, he was ready to facilitate their acquisition by any interested party, especially municipalities. While Eichmann was also engaged in the liquidation of the Jewish presence, he had an interest in maintaining the IKG's operations while reducing it as much as was practicable. Brunner 2 was not part of this aspect of Eichmann's task.

The result was a highly confusing situation for the IKG in its increasingly hopeless battle to retain ownership and use of properties, to maintain control over sales, to avoid undue taxation, and to obtain the release of proceeds from sales to cover its budget. This difficulty made itself felt very soon after the authority of Eichmann (and his *Zentralstelle*) and Brunner 2 (in charge of receivership of assets and properties of Jewish organizations declared defunct) supposedly merged. Let us focus on the two properties, mentioned above, whose retention was of utmost importance to the IKG.

Essential Properties

One day Herr Back, the director of the IKG orphanage at Bauernfeldgasse, came to see Murmelstein to report that State Commissioner Beran had visited the orphanage in the company of several gentlemen, who were evidently interested in acquiring the building. Murmelstein right away telephoned Brunner 1, explaining that it was the only remaining orphanage of the three that had originally been made available to the IKG. Brunner agreed that under the circumstances, the sale of the building was out of the question and would see to it that a statement to that effect be issued by the Office of the Special Trustee,[200] Brunner 2. As usual, a request had to be filed by the IKG, which meant that the matter was left dangling.[201] When Brunner 2 ordered Löwenherz to submit floor plans of the building, he was hardly reassured when, upon his "protesting against the sale of the building," Brunner 2 assured him that it would continue to shelter the orphans.[202] Hence, when Löwenherz next reported to Eichmann in Berlin, he again pleaded for the retention of what was the only remaining orphanage.[203]

Another building needed by the IKG, which others had their eyes on and which Löwenherz had to struggle to keep, was that of the aforementioned former Home for the Blind at Hohe Warte, which now was used to house also the deaf and disabled. The transfer of the building had been arranged without the prior knowledge of the IKG; but, as the official administrator of the assets of the General Foundation, the IKG was now told to clear the building by June 1, 1940. Not only was the buyer eager to take possession, but the *Aufbaufonds* was eager for its share of the prospective proceeds. When Eichmann was in Vienna in mid-April 1940, Murmelstein obtained his promise to consider the matter of leaving the building "for its present use."[204] The next day Engel was called to Brunner 2, who had been charged to inform him that "after consultation with Eichmann and with the *Aufbaufonds* the sale will, for the time being, not take place" and that the IKG could disregard the order to clear it.[205]

The conflict of authorities regarding the sale of properties, during which Löwenherz had to plead with Eichmann and his agents against Brunner 2, who was supposed to be working under Eichmann, was a terrible burden on Löwenherz. We do not know whether this is the reason that the position of the special trustee was discontinued.[206] But, did the situation for Löwenherz and the IKG improve with the apparent reversion to the separation of those authorities? Hardly, as we will see. Eichmann and his agent Brunner 1 could pose as the ones in charge of and as guardians of IKG interests against the aggressive designs of Brunner 2. Yet, by supporting and effecting the liquidation process, they could claim that if things went wrong for the IKG, then it was against their best efforts. They could also use the liquidation process as an additional way of tightening their financial stranglehold on the IKG.

At mid-year, Eichmann told Löwenherz at the RSHA Berlin, in the presence of his counterparts from Prague (Edelstein and Weidmann) and Berlin (Eppstein), that he would not order any "further sales of properties owned by the IKG and the General Foundation," which could have meant that such sales would still take place at the order of Brunner 2, though with Eichmann's tacit consent. Continuing, Eichmann reiterated the IKG's legal but practically nonexistent responsibility, this time assigning to it the status of trusteeship: "The administration of these properties and of the securities will have to rest on the IKG as trustee [*Treuhänder*], under the control of the *Zentralstelle*." Eichmann then declared that proceeds from the sales of properties after payment of the reconstruction levy would be put at the disposal of the IKG to cover its welfare needs, but only with his permission. That the sale of properties in Vienna would continue and that the proceeds would be grudgingly meted out was old news to Löwenherz; evidently Eichmann was not only directing himself at Löwenherz but also meant to make a point to his Prague and Berlin counterparts. He concluded by telling Löwenherz that the specifics of Vienna's finances would be discussed one-on-one the next day.[207]

When the orphanage building on Bauernfeldgasse was again inspected—this time by the *Volksdeutsche Mittelstelle*, an aid organization for ethnic Germans—and Löwenherz submitted another strong statement concerning its indispensability to the IKG, Brunner 1 gave him a convoluted assurance that was anything but reassuring: "[T]he inspection of the object . . . in no way implies that it will be used for other purposes. If this were to happen, then another suitable object will be assigned to the IKG."[208] But things were being done behind Löwenherz's back. Three weeks later a gentleman from the *Volksdeutsche Mittelstelle* with a name that was surely not ethnically German, Herr Szucsits, came to the building, presented himself as the new superintendent, and announced that the building had been sold and that renovation work to adapt it to the needs of the *Mittelstelle* would commence in five weeks. Löwenherz, judging this to be a matter for the Gestapo, rushed a request for intervention to Gestapo headquarters, explaining that the building was used to house 156 orphans, that the IKG had no other facility for them, and asked that it be permitted to retain it. Soon after, Kuchmann telephoned to tell Löwenherz that, on orders of Counsel Ebner, Löwenherz was not to sign the sales contract. Kuchmann also "promised to get in touch with Brunner 1 and inform him that the Gestapo does not wish that this house be taken from the 'General Foundation' and be used for other purposes."[209] But the matter was not subject to the Gestapo's wishes and did not end there.

Only one week later it was discussed again when Löwenherz asked Brunner 1 that the orphanage at Bauernfeldgasse as well as the old-age home at Wasnergasse be retained. Brunner 1 "did not know whether this would succeed in the case of the orphanage." But remembering his recent promise that "another suitable object would be assigned," Brunner suggested that the orphans be distributed among other homes maintained by the IKG. Löwenherz said that was impossible because the other homes were already overcrowded. Brunner had another idea: He would inspect the homes, and if he found that there really was no room for the orphans, then each one of them would be placed with a Jewish pensioner. Löwenherz explained that the children received schooling at the orphanage, for which the IKG had no other facility. Aside from that, placement of the 156 orphans with pensioners would be insuperably difficult, "because most pensioners, like all other Jews, no longer have their own apartments," and once again he pleaded to be allowed to keep the last remaining orphanage.[210] A few days later Brunner 1 informed Löwenherz that the orphanage building would have to be vacated in ten days and that the children would have to be placed partially in the home for apprentices and partially in the Lele Bondi Home (*Heim*). When Löwenherz mentioned that in addition to those in the orphanage there were 190 children for whom there were no places available, Brunner decided "to place about 100 of them with Jewish families who were still in possession of their own apartments" and to save space he ordered the IKG to provide tiered bunk beds for that purpose. He also promised to support the IKG's application for the necessary rationed raw materials. It was a lost cause. This was the time when, in addition to the tightened financial constraints and the forced sales of properties, the Jews were being concentrated in increasingly crowded housing. All Löwenherz could do was to say that it would be impossible to evacuate the building in ten days.[211]

The facility at Hohe Warte was not out of danger, and the IKG had to find ever new ways of pleading to be allowed to retain it for its use. At the end of November Brunner 1 ordered Murmelstein to have the IKG, in its capacity as administrator of the defunct Jewish foundations, submit a request to him for the municipality officially to dissolve the defunct foundation Home for the Blind, for which the building had been established in the late nineteenth century. He cautioned Murmelstein to make fullest possible use of the available space and to employ resident patients for needed services regardless of their advanced age.[212] In 1941, between the first and second sets of deportations, the home was used increasingly for the aged. Being a valuable property, it was inspected by the Cultural Department of the Municipality, and Löwenherz requested Brunner's intercession.[213] When a similar inspection by a medical army officer occurred a few weeks later, Murmelstein told Brunner that if the building were to be requisitioned, "the IKG would be confronted with the insoluble task of providing other shelter for the present residents." He said that the problem of this building was a case in point of the impossible situation of buildings that had belonged to now defunct foundations and were assigned to the IKG for temporary use. Since Eichmann had announced the eventual liquidation of the IKG, Murmelstein suggested that title to this building be transferred to it, which would then be liquidated together with the rest of the IKG. Brunner was interested and ordered a report, including the legal aspect of such transfer.[214]

Curtailed Operations

We have seen in some detail how Löwenherz and his lieutenants fought an incrementally losing battle to forestall the liquidation of the IKG, which the Nazis pursued by tightening the financial stranglehold while yet insisting that the IKG continue its effectiveness in performing its various essential functions. As we have seen, these functions were differed according to the views from the respective perspectives of the Nazis and the IKG.

Löwenherz continued his struggle to fend off the manipulation of *Devisen*, to control the sale of assets, to obtain the proceeds from these sales, to secure subsidies from the "emigration fund," to badger one or the other of the powers that be for the release and reimbursement and contribution of funds, to retain exemption from taxes and levies, and more. Löwenherz also sought, successfully, to practice frugality in budgeting and in expenditures. However, Eichmann and the *Zentralstelle* used all those financial strangleholds to apply pressure on the IKG radically to reduce expenditures on operations by forcing them to dismiss staff, to reduce remunerations, and to reduce or eliminate pensions and related obligations.

One case in point was the old problem of separating Aryans from Jews, which was taken up in earnest toward the middle of 1940, when the war had begun to heat up. Aside from the ideological mandate, there were other, more pressing reasons. One was connected with the plan of liquidating the Jewish presence in Vienna, another with curtailing the expenditures of the IKG. There were collateral benefits for the Nazis: By separating the Aryans, they increased the isolation of the Jews through segregation. By withdrawing Aryans from employment at the IKG and at other institutions the IKG was permitted to maintain, they freed them for potential employment in the incipient wartime economy. By withdrawing them from Jewish properties, they removed an additional obstacle to the eventual appropriation of these assets. There would prove to be difficulties with carrying out this plan. Indeed, it would never entirely succeed. However, there were occasions when it meshed well with other Nazi aims.

The removal of Aryan personnel began about the time when pressure on the IKG tightened in two ways: in the forced reduction of expenditures and in the forced reduction of staff through dismissals (discussed below). It was at this time that the IKG shifted into overdrive to get as many Jews as possible out under the increasingly impossible wartime conditions. On May 20, 1940, Brunner 2 came unannounced to Löwenherz's office to issue a number of orders pertaining to the use of IKG assets, which was meant to include the use of funds for operations and remuneration. In item six the order reads as follows:

> Aryan personnel will be removed from all operations of the IKG pursuant to official orders. Jewish substitute personnel must be remunerated at considerably lower rates, in order to realize savings. The fact that the [replacement] personnel to be used will be not be certified, but will be untrained people hired as needed, is one of the reasons justifying the lower rates.[215]
>
> Mechanics and skilled workers are to be taken from the pool of technicians. I [Löwenherz] declared that we are in a position to provide Jewish personnel in place of the departing Aryan personnel.[216]

Löwenherz was no doubt relieved to have an official order to be rid of the Aryan employees, many of whom were increasingly troublesome and, for whatever work they deigned to perform, commanded excessive wages. He must also have been glad to find some remunerative employment for a few Jews, and he knew that the Jewish substitutes would not be people whom Brunner 2 contemptuously dismissed as "untrained . . . hired as needed." Less pleasant was the fact that it was Löwenherz, the Jewish employer, who had to give the Aryan employees notice of their dismissal. The effect of this pernicious practice of forcing the Jew to be the bearer of bad news ordered by the Nazi authorities was no more benign when the recipient was an Aryan than when he or she was a Jew. The only difference was that the Aryan had recourse; the Jew did not.

Three days after he received the order to dismiss the Aryan employees, Löwenherz reported the inevitable problems to Brunner 1.[217] By law, dismissed workers had to receive severance pay at a specified rate. In earlier days the IKG had given those who left their employ additional emoluments; this practice continued after the Anschluss, when Aryan employees left. Now these dismissed from their jobs demanded similar benefits with the support of the party organizations protecting workers' interests. The party of this one-party state was, after all, the National Socialist German *Worker's* Party (NSDAP, *Nationalsozialistische Deutsche Arbeiterpartei*). Löwenherz, who was under orders to deal with all authorities through the *Zentralstelle*, now told Brunner 1 that the IKG was financially in no position to pay more than the legally mandated severance pay. Brunner 1 told him that no additional demands would be made by any party organ, such as the German Labor Front (DAF) or the district party office (*Kreisleitung*). But that was not the end of it, for Brunner 1 was mistaken in thinking that he could speak for party organs other than his own without prior agreement. No wonder, then, that the official consideration of this matter moved to the high echelons of the RSHA in Berlin.

On June 6 Dannecker at the RSHA telephoned to inform Murmelstein that Löwenherz's suggestion of reducing the pensions of retirees who were also beneficiaries of annuities was not to be extended to Aryan pensioners of the IKG.[218] The peremptory decision on the part of the *Zentralstelle* that Aryan employees be dismissed ruffled a lot of feathers, resulting in a conference at the *Zentralstelle* on June 19 with both party and governmental agencies involved in this controversy. Since Löwenherz had not yet returned from Berlin, Brunner 1 informed Murmelstein the next day that the *Zentralstelle* had "inadvertently refrained from notifying the Reich trustee for labor in the *Ostmark*" of the plan to dismiss the Aryans from the IKG, even though notification was required if more than nine persons were involved. Since this was the case, Brunner 1 was now constrained to direct the IKG "for the time being to continue the employment of those dismissed [Aryans] insofar as their number exceeds nine; among the nine whose dismissal will remain valid are to be mainly those who have, in the meantime, found employment elsewhere."[219] While Brunner now knew the official regulation to which he was constrained to conform—at no cost to him but to the Jews—he now also knew how to get around it. Murmelstein's *Aktennotiz* continues as follows: "At the same time the directive is issued [by Brunner 1] to carry out the dismissal of all Aryan employees at the IKG by July 31, 1940, in such a manner that by August 1 no Aryan would have to remain in the service of the IKG." In other words: Dismiss them a few at a time but never more than nine at once. Murmelstein had been assured that the IKG would not have to submit special requests to the Reich trustee for permission to carry out these dismissals, since Brunner 1 claimed to have pre-arranged it.[220] However, it was not until July 5 that Brunner 1 was able to report the Reich trustee's actual approval of all dismissals as of July 31, a deadline which, Brunner admonished, would have to be met.[221]

There were exceptions to the dismissals. Dr. Sponer, the officially appointed Aryan supervisor of the Jewish hospital, required the retention of the Aryan doorman, telephone operator, and furnace stoker. The authorities wanted the Aryan water-kettle tender of the old-age home to remain at his post. All Aryan janitors of buildings used by the IKG for their various purposes were to remain. On the other hand, only those Aryan employees of the Jewish cemetery were to remain who were married to Jews.[222] This rule was subsequently extended to Aryan employees in all IKG enterprises, yet with the restriction that "Aryans married to Jewesses must be dismissed, while Jews married to Aryan women may remain."[223] The employment by Jews of Aryans was subject to the Nuremberg laws of 1935, which among other strictures restricted the ability of Jews to employ Germans; for example, the continuing employment at the Jewish cemetery of Ernestine Bica, who was not married to a Jew, required the approval of the Gestapo, of which Löwenherz was informed in due time.[224]

Aryan nurses who lived in the Jewish hospital and the old-age home had to move. The IKG had to help find them suitable living quarters.[225] Late in 1940 there were still Aryan residents in Jewish buildings, and the IKG was told to submit a list of them. Löwenherz was referred to the Municipal Housing Office to facilitate a swap of Jewish and Aryan apartments.[226]

The German Labor Front was also represented at the meeting with the *Zentralstelle* on June 19. They demanded that dismissed employees receive the same extra emoluments that were in the past granted by the IKG to departing hospital employees. Löwenherz pointed out that while the IKG did and would continue to meet legally mandated obligations to dismissed Aryan personnel, the additional demand would contravene the savings measures that the IKG had to undertake, measures such as the "dismissal of 140 employees, and the cancellation of compensation for overtime." For the time being, Brunner 1 promised to make representations to this effect before the German Labor Front.[227] However, when Brunner 1 telephoned Murmelstein two weeks later, he informed him that the Labor Front demanded hefty severance benefits for the dismissed Aryans; in fact, they issued a schedule: RM 50 for unskilled laborers, for others "much higher contributions, including RM 200 and RM 600 for nurses of the old-age home at Seegasse 9." Murmelstein demurred that such voluntary contributions on the part of the Rothschild Hospital over and above legal mandates had been possible in earlier times but now the IKG lacked the requisite funds.[228] A few days later Löwenherz was directed to submit a list of dismissed and not yet dismissed Aryan employees, including the nature of their employment and salary level.[229] The reason for this demand would soon become clear. After a few more days we find Löwenherz again arguing against severance contributions above legal mandates, and Brunner 1 again agreeing.[230] Finally, at the time of the deadline, Brunner 1 informed Löwenherz of the settlement that he had been able to negotiate on behalf of the IKG: The IKG had to transfer to the German Labor Front the lump sum of RM 6,000, which they would distribute, according to seniority, age, and number of dependents, to those dismissed Aryans who had been in the employ of the IKG for a long time. To add insult to injury, while assuring Löwenherz that the *Zentralstelle* had tried to keep the settlement as low as possible, Brunner 1 stated that it might have been lower "by RM 1,000 to RM 2,000" had there not been the precedent of the generous severance benefits granted by the Home for the Blind Hohe Warte, a foundation which at that time was not as yet incorporated into the IKG.[231] And there is more: By August 1 this institution, like all other enterprises under the supervision of the IKG, had substituted a reduced staff of Jews for the dismissed Aryans. But by August 20 Brunner had complained about the excessive number of employees at the Hohe Warte; Murmelstein explained that because of the ordered dismissal of Aryans and of stateless Jews, the staff had already been reduced.[232]

It must have rankled Eichmann and his men at the *Zentralstelle* that another agency of the party referred the matter of extra severance benefits to the upper echelons of the SS, and thereby had gotten their hands into the IKG till, supposedly the sole privilege of SD Section 112. And so they waited a few months and, when everyone was busy with wartime Yuletide cheer, Brunner 1 issued the following directive to Löwenherz:

> All former Aryan employees and their dependents, as well as dependents of employees now in war service, are to be informed by the IKG in writing that the financial condition entailed by the process of liquidating the IKG does not permit any further contributions [by the IKG] of any kind, including voluntary ones. The contributions have to cease as of January 1, 1941. Should they need further support, the persons affected by this are to be directed to turn to the Welfare Office of the Municipality of Vienna.
>
> Upon prior notification of Dr. Sponer [the Aryan supervisor of the Jewish hospital] the Aryan telephone operator is to be given notice.[233]

Brunner 1 also agreed that recent salary reductions, which he had ordered for all Jewish employees of the IKG, be extended to the Aryans still in the employ of the IKG; "in case of objections on the part of any of them, they should be directed to the *Zentralstelle*."[234]

The removal of Aryan personnel from Jewish employment was a special concern of the Nazi regime but, as we indicated, was carried out in connection with the pressure on the IKG to reduce expenditures by dismissing part of its personnel, all part of the plan of the eventual liquidation of the IKG and of the presence of Jews in Vienna altogether.

It all started very quickly. On June 12, when Löwenherz was in Berlin, he was given the following directive:

> SS Captain Eichmann indicated that in light of reduced emigration possibilities the IKG would have to effect savings and demanded that by June 20, 1940, a list be submitted of current [Jewish] employees who can be dismissed. Reduction of staff should be done in such a way that the most capable ones remain in office in any case, and that the effectiveness of the organizational apparatus remain intact.[235]

We do not know the number of persons slated for dismissal, nor the pace at which the dismissals were proceeding, but a few days after Löwenherz returned to Vienna with Eichmann's directive, Brunner 1 directed Murmelstein by telephone to submit a list of persons to be dismissed, including addresses and dates of birth, and to instruct them to report to the *Zentralstelle* immediately upon leaving the employ of the IKG.[236] To press the point, the demand for this list was repeated when Löwenherz reported to Brunner 1 two days later, this time with the addition of the dates of dismissal.[237] At the same time Löwenherz was directed to prepare a list of all persons remaining in the employ of the IKG, arranged by IKG departments and by institutions maintained by the IKG. Presumably Löwenherz took this list with him when he was summoned to Berlin for the second time in three weeks. It is doubtful that Eichmann took time to study the list before telling Löwenherz that he was being "charged with terminating 100 additional employees of the IKG within four weeks."[238] Directly upon leaving the RSHA, Löwenherz telephoned Vienna to inform Engel of this development and conveying the message that preliminary work would have to begin immediately.[239] The list of employees slated for dismissal was then submitted to the *Zentralstelle*, which had to clear the matter with the Viennese office of the Reich Trustee for Labor as well as the Labor Bureau. Upon their approval Brunner 1 told Löwenherz to proceed with the dismissals.[240]

Eichmann's directive to reduce staff while retaining the IKG's effectiveness left it largely to the IKG's discretion to determine when staff reductions would lead to ineffectiveness. Evidently the purpose of the list of persons employed at the IKG and its various institutions, which the IKG was required to submit, allowed the *Zentralstelle* to retain control over the IKG's staffing. Thus we find that in August 1940, when Brunner 1 voiced concern over the high number of persons employed at the home for the blind and disabled, Murmelstein reported to Brunner that there were 160 residents in the home and that preparations had been completed to receive 30 more. Since most of the residents were disabled, the size of the staff could not be reduced any further. While some payroll savings had been realized by exchanging well-trained for lower-paid and untrained staff, savings could not be extended to the size of staff.[241]

The exchange between Brunner 1 and Murmelstein was to be a rehearsal of the question of "staff reduction vs. effectiveness" for when Löwenherz reported to Eichmann in Berlin at the beginning of September 1940. The main agenda item of the meeting was the IKG's budget. Löwenherz reminded Eichmann that the monthly budget had been reduced to RM 850,000, about half of one year earlier, the period immediately preceding the outbreak of war, and that the various saving measures, of which staff reduction was a part, had yielded RM 76,000. What Löwenherz did not say out loud was that this amount constituted barely 9 percent of the lowered budget, but Eichmann no doubt understood. Löwenherz then opined, with barely suppressed sarcasm, that "saving measures alone do not suffice to keep the IKG effective," and added that with the imminent opening of a new old-age home and a children's hospital the institutional staff would, in fact, have to be increased. Eichmann, however, ordered a study of the staffing at the hospital and the old-age homes; the study was to be undertaken in consultation with Dr. Sponer, the Aryan supervisor of the Jewish hospital, and with a view toward an additional reduction of 30 of the hospital staff. He also ordered a report on the activity of the employees in every department of the IKG.[242]

At the IKG the ten weeks following this meeting were taken up with pursuing the laborious emigration effort that was fraught with such difficulties. While the pressure to realize savings through additional staff reductions lessened during this time, Löwenherz was beset by all kinds of other pressures exerted by the Nazi authorities regarding finances. But on November 25, 1940, Dr. Ebner of the Gestapo and SS Captain Guenther representing Eichmann showed up unannounced at the IKG. They were accompanied by Brunner 1 of the *Zentralstelle*, recently promoted to SS First Lieutenant, and SS First Lieutenant Grevenik. The wording of Löwenherz's official account of the "inspection" tells the story:

> The gentlemen had each of the [IKG] officers and department chiefs step up and report about the activity of his respective department. Then they made the rounds of all the offices in the buildings [of the IKG], inquired from individual officials about their activity, and issued to the undersigned Director [Löwenherz] the following directives:
>
> (1) The number of officials and orderers employed in the different offices and departments is again to be reduced by 100. This cutback is to be carried out with care to maintain the effec-

> tiveness of the IKG. Receiving the directive, I [Löwenherz] informed [them] that together with experts I would examine the status of the staffing, but that I doubt that a cutback of 100 officials and orderers would be possible.

The list of employees proposed for cutback and of those who were to remain was to be submitted to the *Zentralstelle* and to the Gestapo by December 1.

> Notices [of dismissal] have to be issued for the end of December. If appropriate, the places of the dismissed employees are to be filled with pensioners who may still be useful for service.[243]

This was followed by a directive to cut the salaries of employees with monthly net earnings above RM 100, with the exception of Löwenherz and Murmelstein.[244]

The next morning Löwenherz had to report to Günther, who admonished him on behalf of Eichmann that "the effectiveness of the IKG must be preserved" and that Löwenherz ought to "retain the service of the most capable and reliable employees." For his part Löwenherz pointed out

> that the reduction of 100 employees would be impossible, the more so in consideration of the fact that the [remaining] employees in the central offices of the IKG number 215, and not 270, and [I] asked that in the interest of the services [rendered by the IKG] the number of [required] dismissals be reduced.[245]

Günther demanded an organizational plan of the IKG and detailed proposals for cutbacks in staff and salaries and told Löwenherz that he would be informed about the decision regarding cutbacks. The following day the matter of cutbacks was the subject of extensive deliberation when Murmelstein reported to Brunner 1. Ebner's and Günther's directive concerning the list of all IKG employees by department was now amended to include the personnel serving at the soup kitchens.[246] Murmelstein took the opportunity "to beg leave to mention" a number of the IKG's concerns connected with the Nazi's latest move to force a cutback in staff. The cutbacks of the previous months had left the IKG so sorely decimated that if this latest move were to be carried out as directed, it would leave the IKG operating with merely a skeleton staff. In Murmelstein's words, "the required number of 100 . . . cannot be met without endangering the operation of the several offices and institutions." Hence Murmelstein had to use the well-practiced stratagem of making it appear that the IKG's proposal of a minimal additional cutback actually accorded with the demands of the authorities for continued efficient operations. The previous day Löwenherz had pointed out to Günther that the number of remaining employees was 215 and not 270, a number that Günther had brought with him from Berlin on the basis of one of the many lists the IKG had had to prepare that year but which was now outdated. Murmelstein now explained that the "result" of the cutback to be proposed by the IKG

> can be expected not to lag far behind the 100 [dismissals stipulated by the authorities] and would amount to about 90; it must be stressed that, insofar as the issued directive projected the reduction of personnel in the offices located in the [IKG] office buildings at Seitenstettengasse 2-4, [that reduction] will be achieved, since the status as of the 25th was not 270 but 215.[247]

Brunner 1 had no rejoinder to offer and told Murmelstein that Löwenherz could present the matter to Eichmann for his decision when he reported to him in Berlin in the near future.[248] He reiterated this point when, on the day before Löwenherz's departure for Berlin, Murmelstein submitted to him the reports concerning the employment of staff in various departments, saying that "on the occasion of his reporting to SS Major Eichmann, [Löwenherz] will, in an appropriate presentation, have to justify the manner and extent of the cutback."[249] When—thus forewarned and as well prepared as one can be under those circumstances—Löwenherz, in the presence of Brunner 1, reported to Eichmann in Berlin, he pressed the point that a reduction below the now projected 168 employees would jeopardize the effectiveness of the IKG that he was ordered to maintain. He also pointed out the prospective need for additional staff upon the imminent opening of the children's hospital and the eighth old-age home. Eichmann replied that upon careful examination of all the reports submitted to him by Löwenherz, and presumably also by Nazi officials, he would make a "final decision."[250]

Murmelstein presented to Brunner 1 a second concern at the *Vorsprache* of November 27, pertaining to the feasibility of reducing his personal staff. When the gentlemen from the Gestapo and the SD arrived for their inspection tour, Murmelstein's office was the first to be viewed. At that time the appropriate form of reporting to the inspectors had not been settled on either side, hence, as Murmelstein told Brunner 1, "the presentation of the actual extent of the tasks on the part of the individual employees (*die Darstellung des eigentlichen Wirkungskreises der einzelnen Angestellten*) was not made thoroughly [enough]. . . . Permission is requested to present the actual and prevailing tasks of these sections."[251]

There followed the most definitive description of the role that had devolved on Murmelstein in the third year of his position as Löwenherz's personal assistant. Now that Engel, who had long served as the IKG office manager, had emigrated, Murmelstein fully functioned as the chief executive officer, internally responsible only to Director Löwenherz, and, in fact, acted as Löwenherz's deputy. The operative procedure was for Löwenherz to inform Murmelstein of whatever needed to be done and for Murmelstein to see to it that the appropriate machinery of the IKG got it done. Murmelstein's immediate tasks were divided into two areas.

One comprised the different matters that, in light of the control by the Nazi authorities and of Germany being at war, were extremely sensitive:

- "Putting the entire incoming mail in order" (*"Ordnung des gesamten Posteinlaufs"*). This means not only that Murmelstein's office distributed incoming mail to the respective departments but implies that he was the one person at the IKG who monitored the entire operation and kept a watchful eye on the situation of the Jews insofar as it was reflected in mail received at the IKG.
- "Precise registry of foreign correspondence." A registry of correspondence to and from persons and agencies abroad was required by the Nazis, and Murmelstein had to bear this responsibility; in fact, the IKG's letters abroad had to be submitted to Brunner 1 for censorship and approval.

The other area, comprising a number of different matters, amply demonstrates the duress under which the IKG was laboring, where choice was limited or nonexistent, the *Zentralstelle* being the IKG's absolute taskmaster:

- "Carrying out all orders concerning the two retraining camps." The retraining camps (*Umschulungslager*) were by then regarded by the authorities as nothing other than labor camps, except that the IKG had to pay for the upkeep of the workers.
- "Drafting and registering all submissions directed to the *Zentralstelle* and the Gestapo, as well as to several authorities . . . drafting of reports to authorities." Murmelstein's skill in finding the best formulation in submitting requests and in interpreting directives, his role as the author of periodic reports to the authorities, and as monitor of routine and other reports have been mentioned before.
- "General foreign language correspondence." In this regard Dr. Margaret Feiler of the IKG Correspondence Department was, until her emigration early in November 1940, Murmelstein's valued amanuensis.
- "Drafting reports . . . for the aid organizations abroad." Here too Murmelstein was adept at finding the right wording and format.
- "Preparation of the statistical tables and graphs produced by the IKG." The importance of statistical reports in dealing with the authorities cannot be overestimated. Not only did such reports provide the necessary proof of the productivity of the IKG and thus assure permission for its continuance, but they also functioned as a basis for the continued support of *Devisen* from the Joint. Furthermore, they served to correct the authorities' mistaken impression of the size of the Jewish population in 1939; and they were also useful as proof of the IKG's reliability vis-à-vis the ever suspicious authorities.
- "Registry of all incoming and outgoing telegrams, as well as preliminary examination of [outgoing] telegrams to be submitted to the *Zentralstelle*." The registry was required by the *Zentralstelle*, and the drafts of outgoing telegrams had to be submitted for censorship and approval.
- "Submission of character references for *Ausgereiste*." This item seems puzzling; Murmelstein speaks of *Ausgereiste* (people who had departed from the country presumably on their own volition), not of *Ausgewanderte* (emigrants), which would imply duress. Most likely it was a matter of emigrants at an interim location who needed such a certificate to move to a country that required it, the IKG being the only place in Nazi Vienna prepared to issue such a document for a Jew.

The employment at the IKG of stateless Jews, for the most part persons who had been citizens of the now defunct Poland, posed a special problem for the authorities. We recall that the sudden attempt to get rid of Jewish residents of the Altreich who had immigrated to Germany from regions that reverted to newly established Poland after the First World War and who had not bothered to take out German citizenship, precipitated the crisis that culminated in Kristallnacht. In Vienna, within a week of the outbreak of the war, Jews from the Polish parts of the former Austrian Empire, who had also neglected to become citizens of the Republic of Austria, were arrested and kept for weeks under open skies in Vienna's great sports stadium under the worst conditions, in the expectation that, upon the completion of the conquest, they would be sent to Poland. Hence, in light of the control exercised

The synagogue of Klosterneuburg, on the Danube River just north of Vienna, in flames during the Kristallnacht pogrom. (DÖW 3030[10])

by the labor bureau over the employment of citizens, especially in wartime, the *Zentralstelle* took up the dismissal of "stateless" Jews as an additional opportunity of proceeding against them, as well as of realizing savings in the expenditures of the IKG. Löwenherz's request for the retention of "stateless persons whose service is indispensable" had to be cleared by Brunner 1 with various authorities. We do not know whether he obtained their approval. At one point, he told Löwenherz that he expected it "in 1 to 2 days." This was not good enough, for it left Löwenherz with a choice of two equally risky courses of action: either retain people whose employment might prove to be illegal or dismiss needed staff, thus preempting the decision of the authorities. Hence, he obtained Brunner's permission to continue their employment until the official decision had been handed down. Three weeks after the "1 to 2 days," Brunner 1 told Murmelstein that a ruling had not yet come down but that he would continue to support the IKG in its effort to retain these persons.[252]

The dismissal of so many staff members threw the IKG operations into turmoil. It was the time when the frantic effort to save the Jews under the outrageously frustrating conditions was getting under way, an effort that we will outline in chapter 9. Even though the opportunities for emigration were much fewer than before the war, the effort required by the various IKG departments to get each individual out had become incomparably great and complex. And now this effort had to be undertaken with an increasingly reduced staff. This was possible only by greatly extending the working hours per day. The extended work hours required additional compensation that, however, in most cases amounted to a measly RM 20 a month.[253] Even before the dismissals started, the core staff in charge of emigration had had to put in late hours; this invariably included Murmelstein and other people such as Feiler. As the hectic emigration effort reached high pitch and was accompanied by waves of dismissals, the number of staff having to work many more hours often numbered forty. This was not a simple matter. Since the Jews were under curfew, each day the list of persons who had to work beyond the curfew time (which in the summer of 1940 was 9:00 p.m.) had to be prepared hours before and taken downhill to Room 314 of Gestapo headquarters on Morzinplatz. The list was signed by Murmelstein and provided with the following note: "The above employees of the IKG Vienna are engaged today [date] in urgent business beyond the normal office hours, hence cannot start their way home prior to 9 p.m. It is requested that this be taken note of with approval."[254]

The Jews of Vienna never knew who the Nazis were who decided their fate. But they did know who Murmelstein was, whom in their misfortune and frustration they were prepared to blame. Murmelstein was constantly in danger of attack. At the IKG, he kept to his office suite most of the time, occasionally shuttling to Löwenherz's office; at times he had to report at the other end of Vienna's Inner City at the *Zentralstelle*. He supervised the various departments under his responsibility through a small staff of associates, only a few of whom really knew what transpired behind the padded double doors of IKG Room 7. Because of the sensitive nature of his position and his responsibilities, especially vis-à-vis the Nazis, discretion required that he keep contacts with the many persons employed at the IKG to a minimum, determined by need. He had reason to know that every word that was overheard could be grist for the rumor mill, every person he would receive, each call for a secretary could be blown up into a scandal. As he would tell us in one of the interviews, "whenever a sneeze was heard in Room 7, they would say *Gesundheit*! at the *Zentralstelle*." Murmelstein had reason to mistrust even his secretary. This situation had many effects. For one thing, whether he left for home before or after the curfew hour for the brisk walk of about 20 to 25 minutes, he was invariably accompanied by three of his associates who acted as bodyguards, among them Feiler and Prochnik.

The IKG made it clear that the dismissals were carried out on orders issued by the Nazi authorities. But this left the many employees who were affected frustrated over having lost their meager income and angry when they saw that others were retained at the IKG. They thought they knew where the blame lay and where to complain in their desperation. Thus it happened that a few weeks after the dismissals began, Margaret Feiler was summoned to Kuchmann at Gestapo headquarters. We recall that it was the SD, not the Gestapo, that supervised the IKG; this meant that the dismissals were under the direction of the SD and not of its rival Gestapo. We have also mentioned that the SD was known only to a few at the IKG; most Jews knew only of the Gestapo. Kuchmann, incidentally, was held in low esteem by those of the IKG staff who had contact with him. Why did Kuchmann want to see Feiler, who was not one of the leading Jews at the IKG? It seems that Kuchmann had received complaints that the reason some people were dismissed and Feiler was not was that she was having an affair with Murmelstein. By way of a response, Feiler angrily hit her outstretched palm on Kuchmann's desktop. This was a provocative gesture coming from a

Jew, and Feiler knew that the time had come to leave her post at the IKG and Nazi Germany, which she did. Feiler was one of several women about whom this rumor was spread, and authors whose research did not advance beyond the collection of gossip have felt no compunction about citing it as a significant truth. Feiler told us that, as a matter of fact, she had no such liaison with Murmelstein. To be sure, Murmelstein could be charming toward women and had an eye for attractive females, but he had no illusions about his own appearance. Also he was constantly on guard against corruption among the IKG staff and could not afford to make a wrong step himself. In Feiler's decided and informed judgment, there was, in any case, no chance of any such goings-on in Murmelstein's office. The times were too busy, the work too intense, and Frau Murmelstein was there every day to bring him his meals. Occasionally his associates would gather for a short while in his office to relax, and one of the young men would play the guitar and sing some Yiddish songs, which Murmelstein favored. But then it was quickly back to work!

■ ■ ■

The financial stranglehold, including the curtailment of the IKG operations, turned out to be merely a preliminary maneuver on the part of Eichmann's new regime in tightening its grip on the IKG and the Jews of Vienna. There were other maneuvers, some of which affected the general population of Vienna's Jews. By means of all of these stratagems the Nazis were aiming at the eventual liquidation of the IKG and of the Jews it served.

Marks of Captivity

The tightening grip over the IKG was reflected in the increased deprivations suffered by the Jews of Vienna and the increasingly desperate conditions under which they tried to survive. They were captives of a regime aiming to liquidate their very being. We will describe just two salient aspects of their captivity in greater detail: the evictions and the labor camps. However, we must stress that this is not the whole story. The Jews of Vienna also had to contend with a number of other deprivations. Like all people in wartime Germany, the Jews' access to food and goods was restricted by rationing. However, the amount and variety of food available to Jews was more meager and of lesser quality, and it was available only at certain stores and during two afternoon hours on two days of the week. Clothing was practically unobtainable by Jews. Furthermore, used wool items had to be relinquished without recompense for fabric recycling; all sorts of other goods, such as tools, had to be similarly given up. Besides having to abide by the curfew, travel on certain routes of the public tramway system was restricted; and where it was permitted, Jews had to stand on the rear platform, and even from there any irate patriotic Aryan could feel free to chase or throw them off the streetcar even while it was in motion. And so on and so forth.

The mark of captivity that brought about the greatest isolation of the Jews in the midst of a teeming city was their having to wear the yellow star with the legend "Jew," a regulation instituted toward the end of 1941. We will discuss it in the chapter on the deportations in the second volume.

Evictions

Making housing available for Aryans by evicting Jews from theirs had been an ongoing project since the Nazis took over Vienna. For the authorities this posed many problems similar to the wild Aryanization of businesses right after the Anschluss. One of the vexing questions was: On what legal basis could the evictions be implemented, especially since in both Austria and Germany renters were protected by law? Another question was: Who had the rights to the apartments vacated by eviction? In the period following the Anschluss, someone who wanted a Jewish apartment could go to the local party office and institute eviction proceedings against the Jewish inhabitants. Often these proceedings consisted of nothing other than threats, but sometimes there were summary evictions, even arrests. There was a need for these evictions to proceed case by case according to what under the Nazi regime constituted legal norms. For example, we have before us the decision of the Municipal Court of the Eighth District of Vienna, dated February 9, 1939, authorizing the owners of the building at Tendlergasse 3 to give notice to Professor Bernhard (Bernard) Floch to vacate his apartment by May. The reason given: "The Aryan tenants of the building . . . refuse having to live any longer [in the same building] with non-Aryan tenants."[255]

What was needed, however, was appropriate legislation. The case of the Floch eviction demonstrates how Berlin took up the initiative of the people and of the rule of the Nazi Party of Vienna in order to produce such legislation, namely, the law of April 30, 1939, concerning "Rental Relations with Jews." On July 8, 1939, Martin Bormann, the Führer's deputy and chief of staff, sent the following circular (marked "CONFIDENTIAL!") to all regional party leaders (Gauleiter):[256]

> The law is meant to provide the possibility of dissolving housing communities comprising Germans and Jews which may still exist on the basis of the rent protection law, and to carry out a more just distribution of housing space . . .

And here follows the mendacious justification which we have come to expect to find in connection with Nazi policy respecting the Jews:

> . . . inasmuch as, in proportion to the size of their population, Jews possess an excessive amount of housing space.

Bormann continued:

> Consequently, by means of the law, care will be taken that housing space available in Jewish houses, in part especially abundant, will be put to better use by taking in additional Jewish families.

This was the basis for the concentration of Jews within the great population centers, beginning in Vienna, especially during the period under consideration. In his interpretation of the usefulness of the law, Bormann also provided the basis for the requests two months later that under wartime conditions Vienna be the first in ridding itself of the danger posed by the Jews and for channeling these requests through the various authorities, as discussed above:

> In order to prevent disturbances of public safety and order, the elimination of Jews from Ger-

> man housing and placing them elsewhere must be undertaken according to a plan. For this reason the law provides for municipalities to be involved to an essential degree.
>
> In cooperation with relevant higher officials [*Hoheitsträger*] of the Party, mayors . . . are directed to issue certificates for the suitable placement of Jews. Higher Party officials will have to examine whether Jews can be placed in Jewish buildings. Where this is indicated, he must see to it that the appropriate certificates are issued by the mayor.

In principle, then, this put the party in charge of the eviction and concentration process, and the municipal authorities in a subordinate position as executors. By giving it legal sanction, the law and its official interpretation were to provide for the orderly execution of the process, now that it was to move into high gear. But, it was not at all clear in what way the process was to be regulated or how to undertake it, and how it affected the roles of various Nazi authorities who had an executive function in the solution of the Jewish problem. At the same time the need for the housing inhabited by Jews was perceived by municipal as well as other authorities as all the more urgent; the fewer Jews who were left who occupied separate housing, the better. Emigration provided a solution of sorts, but the outbreak of war appeared to put a stop to it. Bürckel, we recall, motivated by the urgency of vacating Jewish housing for Aryans, had welcomed the chance of shipping the Jews to the newly conquered Polish territories and even contemplated transferring those left in Vienna in the meantime, to barracks. The Nisko project halted before it had really begun and thus failed to provide the desired solution. The perceived need for housing persisted and became greater even as the solution faded away. While Eichmann still had the assignment of ridding Vienna of its Jews, carrying it out involved more than vacating Jewish housing for the use of Aryans. For example, the process of providing the documentation required for would-be emigrants and the routing of their passage to their destination was tedious and time-consuming. Also, the official persecution of Jews had to be kept within bounds by the consideration that the Joint, the only remaining aid organization to provide *Devisen*, would use them as leverage to prevent the worst excesses. Also, if the Jews were driven from one place, where would they live until they emigrated, died, or were deported?

By the time the war broke out, the Nazi Party was firmly in control of every little corner of Vienna. It was an unmistakable display of totalitarian power down to the smallest detail and to each individual, an ideological governance duplicating in an overarching way the established governmental authorities. Each block of every street was effectively ruled by a *Blockwart* (block superintendent) who, while not necessarily a member of the Nazi Party, was appointed by and answerable to the party. It was his job to mobilize the *Volksgenossen* under his guardianship for whatever the war effort required of the populace, to monitor their attitude and behavior, and to make sure everyone's needs were fairly met in keeping with the available rationed means. (In the later war years the power of the *Blockwart* would literally be one over life and death.) If Jews resided in his bailiwick, it was his responsibility to see that what they did and what they got was in keeping with their being Jews. Among other duties, he had to report to the local party office how many Jewish apartments there were at the addresses for which he was responsible, how many rooms there were, and how many Jews resided in each apartment. The need to take over housing occupied by

Jews could thus be met by evictions ordered by the local party office and carried out by the *Blockwart*. Jews who had a room designated as "extra" were required to take in persons evicted from their own place. The process of eviction and concentration of the Jews seemed to be well under way and under the control of the party and their agents.

It was not long before the inevitable difficulties arising from this situation became a major concern of the IKG. It was one of the matters Löwenherz presented to Eichmann as early as the *Vorsprache* in Berlin in January 1940, some four months after the outbreak of war. Eichmann temporized and demanded that Löwenherz submit "a relevant list" by way of the *Zentralstelle*. Evidently there was nothing that Eichmann and his staff could do about this matter. And the bad situation only got worse. By the time of Löwenherz's next *Vorsprache* at Eichmann in Berlin at the beginning of March 1940, the situation of forced evictions had become critical:

> I [Löwenherz] reported about the crowding of several Jewish families in single inappropriate flats or in shops, and indicated that this practice leads to disease, even to epidemics, and asked for intervention with the Housing Bureau.

Eichmann's response? He

> informed me that in many parts of the Reich German *Volksgenossen* also have to suffer under similar conditions. That practice is caused by [present] circumstances and can hardly be changed. I [Löwenherz] am free to intervene in this matter with Deputy [Commissioner] Tavs [of the Vienna Housing Bureau]. However, SS Captain Eichmann does not believe that much can be done in this matter.[257]

Captain Eichmann was right about the futility of dealing with the Housing Bureau. By staffing the directorates of vital municipal agencies with proven Nazis, the Plenipotentiary Bürckel, the highest Nazi official in former Austria, wanted to make sure that the party was in control of all governmental and civil agencies that had bearing on the success of his regime. Surely Vienna's Housing Bureau was such an agency. Bürckel had ambitious plans for solving Vienna's housing shortage by means of building projects . . . and by the eviction of Jews. The plans for building projects were frustrated because the bureau overestimated the available means and materials as well as the available workforce. They were too late in any case, since the war effort soon had priority. Also, Bürckel was unsuccessful in staffing the bureau with qualified party men. Hence, when the war broke out, the only feasible solution left was the eviction of Jews. However, according to the survey made for Becker's report, all that could be expected from that scheme, even when the "total de-Judaization of Vienna" (*Totalentjudung Wiens*) was accomplished, would be to provide housing only for those most urgently in need of it. In fact, as stated in the conclusion of the report, "until the [postwar] resumption of construction, there will be constant pressure on the Viennese housing market, resulting from the fact that [of 60,000 apartment houses] 10,000 Viennese houses are ready for demolition."[258] At about the same time as the completion of Becker's report, Bürckel placed Dr. Leopold Tavs in charge of the Housing Section at his headquarters; the Housing Section included the party's building program for Vienna.[259] Tavs was one of the leading Nazis in Vienna in the period leading up to the Anschluss. Even though he was more competent and better suited to the job than the Nazi Party's man in the Housing

Bureau, he could do little under the conditions of war to alleviate the housing shortage other than to work hand in glove with the party, to which he owed exclusive allegiance, by ruthlessly forcing the eviction of Jews and their concentration in ever more crowded dwellings regardless of whether they were suitable for habitation.

It was a process that ran independently of the jurisdiction and authority of Eichmann. Was Eichmann wrong about sending Löwenherz to the Housing Bureau, thereby sanctioning the Housing Bureau's right to deal with the Jews directly? No, because he evidently knew that, unlike matters of control over Jewish assets, the Nazi Party's control over municipal matters lay outside his parameters of authority. Only rarely could Eichmann and the *Zentralstelle* assert their jurisdictional prerogative vis-à-vis the consortium of the Housing Bureau and the party's governance. One such instance occurred when, soon after Eichmann assured Löwenherz of the futility of dealing with the Housing Bureau, this bureau demanded emigration statistics from the IKG, and Brunner asserted the *Zentralstelle*'s sole jurisdiction over the Jews.[260]

Not to be upstaged, Kuchmann at the Gestapo informed Löwenherz in May 1940 "that the evictions will cease entirely."[261] The reason Löwenherz had to report to the Gestapo at that time was as follows: The evictions were continuing, and the Housing Bureau had moving firms transport the belongings of the Jews who were being evicted to their new quarters. Since the Jews were unable to pay the movers, the movers turned to the Gestapo, and the Jews turned to the IKG. Even earlier, at the time when the authorities were engaged in the campaign of "Vienna first," the Housing Bureau, frustrated at the apparent recalcitrance of some evicted Jews, had sought to enlist the Gestapo to enforce the evictions,[262] even though this was neither a police matter nor in the interest of the solution of the Jewish problem over which the SS had jurisdiction, and even though there were frequent jurisdictional disputes within the SS between the SD (Eichmann and the *Zentralstelle*) and the Gestapo (Kuchmann). Kuchmann now told Löwenherz that the Jews did not have to pay for the moving charges nor was the IKG to contribute toward them.

Matters were, of course, neither as simple nor as settled as Kuchmann said they were. But his declaration clearly indicated that something would have to be done to put some order into the process of freeing up Jewish housing, not for the sake of the Jews but for the sake of not having overlapping jurisdictions at loggerheads. In particular the willful eviction activity by the consortium consisting of the Housing Bureau and local party leaders needed to be brought under control. Only one authority could set the matter straight, not the SD, not the Gestapo, not the Vienna municipality, and not the local party officials, but the officials of the party's overall governance in Vienna that had set that activity in motion in the first place. Accordingly, Karl Scharitzer (Scharizer), as Deputy Gauleiter of Vienna, issued the following directive concerning *Judenumsiedlungen* (here: "relocation" of Jews) and circulated it to the Gestapo, to Tavs of the Housing Office, and to the regional party leaders (*Kreisleiter*):

> Upon consultation with the Gestapo, I order the immediate cessation of all relocation of Jews by the Party. Such relocation actions may not be undertaken by regional Party offices [*Kreisleitungen*] even with the agreement of the police and the Housing Office.
>
> The implementation of relocation is exclusively incumbent on the Housing Office or other

> governmental authorities. Regional Party functionaries may submit suggestions for desired relocation of Jews to the Housing Office.

Did this mean that the party functionaries would have to defer to the ostensibly governmental Housing Bureau? The very opposite was the case, as is unmistakably indicated in the concluding sentence of the directive, which we will render in its convolutedness:

> It is especially necessary that, with regard to the cases which, because of the herewith ordered cessation of the action, remained outstanding, [and] in particular where Aryans had been issued certificates of assignment, to report to the Housing Bureau that I have ordered speedy implementation.[263]

We do not know whether the officials of party and municipality were satisfied with the orderly process that had been established. We do know that for the Jews matters did not improve, neither with regard to evictions nor to any other duress of that period. For all practical purposes, the process mandated by Scharitzer was nothing other than a confirmation of the way things were being done anyway.

In August 1940 Bürckel was replaced by Baldur von Schirach, who, eager to give the impression of benefiting Austria, was quickly enlisted for the campaign to evict Jews from dwellings desired by Aryans. Therefore, as expected, Scharitzer soon produced another "C o n f i d e n t i a l !" circular dealing with the "relocation of Jews" and prefaced it as follows:[264]

> In light of the dire housing emergency, the Reich Director [von Schirach] wishes for the immediate resumption of a planned and thorough *Umsiedlung* of Jews.

Umsiedlung has two meaning: "relocation" and "resettlement." As "relocation" it means moving from one dwelling to another. "Resettlement" implies moving to a different geographical location. In light of the subject matter of the rest of the circular, *Umsiedlung* seemed to have the sense of "relocation," moving Jews to ever more crowded Jewish apartments. However, a more ominous meaning is adumbrated, for later that fall von Schirach would put pressure on the highest authorities in Berlin to get rid of the Jews of Vienna altogether and immediately. In the meantime, Scharitzer outlined in greater detail than in the earlier circular the process of evicting and concentrating the Jews through the collusion of the party and the Housing Bureau. In summary, the circular provides for the following division of labor:

> It is incumbent on the Party to ascertain which Jewish apartments are to be vacated, and to work out suggestions where the persons who have been removed from vacated apartments are to be assigned. Only the Housing Bureau is to assign vacated dwellings or move Jewish households.

Regional party leaders (*Kreisleiter*) were to list all Jewish homes through their local party managers (*Ortsgruppenleiter*). Jewish dwellings were easily identified since the ration card of the head of household bore a "J" (for "Jew"). The local party manager would decide which Jewish apartments could hold more Jews and how many. They were to exercise caution "that no epidemic or other danger result from overcrowding." (Evidently Löwenherz's concern expressed to Eichmann half a year earlier did make an impact.) And on this basis the local leaders were to "suggest" how many apartments could be vacated. The regional party leader would then determine the resulting movement of Jews and the assignment of vacated dwellings and would submit appropriate "suggestions" with the surveys to the Housing Bureau, which was thus reduced to coordinating and executing the action. Thus the party gained the advantage of concentrating the Jews in a limited area and in a manner befitting their new status. Apartments of Jews who were foreign nationals and of war veterans wounded in action were exempt, at least for the time being. In accordance with a directive from Himmler, regional party leaders were instructed to speed the eviction of Jews from buildings situated on main thoroughfares; the reason for this and similar restrictions was to prevent Jews from observing the movement of troops and war machinery. Finally, the local party managers were "most earnestly directed not to mention to Jews the purpose of the surveys, and generally keep [the surveys] as confidential as possible." Since the surveys were to be completed by November 1, it was to be expected that a major effort at eviction would be in the offing after that date.

One week after this "confidential" circular, Löwenherz reported to Brunner 1 the difficulties caused by the evictions and subsequent overcrowding, and pointed out that the housing shortage in Vienna was not being eased in any significant way, but that the IKG was saddled with additional financial burdens. When Brunner 1 told him that the IKG ought not to pay for moving expenses, Löwenherz explained that this was unavoidable, especially in cases of persons "who repeatedly had to change their dwelling in the past half year, some even six times." This may have been unwelcome news to Brunner 1, especially since it involved an unnecessary strain on the IKG budget, which he was mandated to keep tight. Yet, all he could do was to tell Löwenherz to submit a list naming those "who had to move repeatedly in the last six months."[265]

When Löwenherz submitted the required list one week later, he again stressed the dire straits in which Jews found themselves:

> This survey shows that for Jews, who had already been living in extremely crowded and most wretched conditions, additional unnecessary expenses arise from repeated evictions, and that consequently the IKG is adversely affected, since those totally impoverished people must be able to place their furnishings [somewhere].[266]

Löwenherz recorded that "Brunner declared that in the next few days a discussion of this matter would take place among the relevant offices."

The provisions of Scharitzer's circular evidently went into effect after November 1, the deadline for the completion by the local party leaders of the surveys of available Jewish dwellings. What was the effect of Brunner's discussion with the relevant authorities? In an unusually lengthy item in his *Vorsprache* at Brunner 1 on November 19, Löwenherz recorded the emerging crisis:[267]

> I described the extremely dismal housing condition of the Jews, and the prevailing mood of desperation intensified through the new relocation action. Yesterday two suicides were reported that were connected with that action. It is feared not only that the number of suicides will increase, but that epidemics will arise. Jews, who had been assigned to living quarters by the Housing Bureau, now have to leave them and move to other, overcrowded rooms. Many of the assigned rooms lack the means for heating and cooking. Cramming (*Zusammenpferchen*)

> married and unmarried, young and old people together in one and the same room leads naturally and inevitably to quarrels and the danger of the outbreak of epidemics.

In his response Brunner 1 reflected the results of the discussions that he had had in the meantime, with the relevant authorities. He "explained that this relocation action is being undertaken on higher orders not only in Vienna but in the entire Reich and the Protectorate." This was a canard because, as we know, and as Brunner 1 must have known but Löwenherz could not, the prevailing policy was "Vienna first." In any case, the next statement did not offer the reassurance it was perhaps meant to convey: "Jews may stay in the rooms assigned to them until their emigration." Emigration? What about the old and infirm, who could never emigrate, not to speak of those who would have to wait for a long time in crammed quarters for the chance to emigrate? And, as if he were answering these unspoken questions in Löwenherz's mind, Brunner 1 said, "Amelioration of these conditions could not be effected even upon appeal to *Herrn Reichsstatthalter* [von Schirach]." This is not surprising, since von Schirach, even more than his predecessor Bürckel had been, was the driving force behind the expulsion of the Jews of Vienna. Also, did Brunner's phrase "until their emigration" suggest that the crowding of Jews was merely temporary and thereby constituted an unintended first hint of the plans for the impending resumption of the deportations? And if so, did Löwenherz's antennas pick up the signal?

In light of that year's history of evictions and crowding, culminating in the exacerbated action of November 1940, Brunner's next declaration could hardly have been reassuring to Löwenherz: "Jews may be evicted from their housing only if they are assigned to rooms with sanitary facilities. With respect to cases where such reassignment does not conform to these requirements, the IKG's agent should intervene on their behalf at the Housing Bureau and direct its attention to the discrepancies in the assigned housing." Then what? By then the Jews would have had to quit their previous housing and be stuck at the new. Surely, no one would expect the Housing Bureau to provide a staff of inspectors to condemn all the faulty assignments "suggested" by agents of the party.

On the matter of the IKG straining its tight budget by subsidizing the moving costs of indigent Jews, Brunner 1 had a suggestion: Send an official of the IKG to SS Lieutenant Buchleitner, the official party manager of transport in Vienna, with the names of twenty Jews who could help indigent Jews to save money by moving their belongings instead of using Aryan labor. Löwenherz responded by saying that "the IKG had been strongly attacked [by the Jews] at the time of the earlier housing action and must not expose itself to the accusation that it throws Jews out of their apartments or that it collaborates in it." Two comments on this exchange: First, Löwenherz was telling Brunner 1 in an indirect but blunt way that what was happening to the Jews in the eviction action was that they were literally being "thrown out." Second, Löwenherz did not wish to exacerbate the situation to which he and the other leaders at the IKG learned to be sensitive early on, namely, the fact that the Jews, in spite of their always being told that what was being done to them was by directive and decision of the Nazi authorities, were prone to blame their proximate fellow Jew rather than the anonymous Nazi oppressor. While this perception fitted into the grand scheme of the Nazis, it had to be kept within limits, so as not to undermine Löwenherz's usefulness. Hence, Brunner 1 agreed that "the IKG must not present itself in an official capacity"; nonetheless, he instructed Löwenherz to send the list of twenty men in order to save poor Jews the cost of employing Aryan laborers.

Since Brunner and the *Zentralstelle* could be of as little help in this crisis as Eichmann was earlier in the year when the eviction situation was less dire, Löwenherz made representations at the Housing Bureau a few days later with Brunner's permission.[268] He reiterated the dismal details of hardship resulting from the evictions and from "the cramming together of Jews in inadequate rooms . . . devoid of appropriate facilities for sanitation, heating, and cooking." He spoke of the "assignment of Jewish tenants to rooms already fully occupied," and that the "Jewish tenants thus crammed together are unable to keep the rooms in good order and to maintain the most primitive rules of cleanliness and sanitation." Löwenherz, therefore, "asks for a change in the present practice of assignment and pointed out that the relocation that is being carried out will hardly relieve the housing market but will likely lead to the spread of epidemics."

What was the response of Dr. Wedel, who worked in the Housing Bureau under Dr. Tavs? Löwenherz recorded that Wedel

> sees the difficulties of the relocated Jews. At the same time he informed me that Deputy Dr. Tavs carefully worked out the plan and will not deviate from it. Individual cases of hardship can be ameliorated upon the objection of tenants. Dr. Wedel promised to convey all my complaints to Deputy Dr. Tavs upon his expected return a few days hence, and to inform me of the result. . . . An immediate meeting with Dr. Tavs is not possible.

It is clear that nothing came of this penultimate attempt at intervention. When Löwenherz was in Berlin two weeks later in preparation for his trip to Lisbon to meet with the representatives of the Joint, he brought up the matter one more time with Eichmann, who was as powerless over the Housing Bureau as ever. When Löwenherz mentioned the danger of epidemics, Eichmann perked up and "thought that because of the possible danger of epidemics the Gestapo headquarters Vienna would be competent to intercede, and directed SS 1st Lt. Brunner to gather reliable information concerning the apartments vacated in connection with the action, and to report results to him."[269] But, when Brunner ordered Murmelstein to provide such statistics a few days later, Murmelstein had to tell him that they were not available and that all he could provide was guesswork.

Thus ended, for all practical purposes, the IKG's effort to provide some relief to the Jews of Vienna in this desperate situation. Some relief would come with the deaths of some Jews by suicide or old age or disease or deprivation. Most relief would come only with the emigration of a few and the deportation of many.

Labor Camps

Not all the Jews remained in Vienna. Some went to retraining camps and other places of employment. But, were they more fortunate than the loved ones they left behind in Vienna?

In the winter of 1939–40 the war was well under way, though temporarily at a standstill. As the regime was gearing up for campaigns yet to come, able-bodied men were called to arms as soon as they were old enough, and additional labor forces were recruited for the war industries and the growing demands of the peripheral segments of the economy. The Jews, slated for removal from the areas under the control of the Nazis, had been excluded from the economy, from duty to country, and from any contribution to their "host nation" whatsoever. Instead, they were supposed to leave and relinquish their remaining assets to the coffers of the Nazis. But now, the war made the emigration effort even more laborious and sluggish; and the Jews, waiting for their turn, consumed food, occupied housing, used up assets and resources, and neither produced anything nor risked their lives facing the enemy.

Since the remaining Jews would not disappear and could not be put away, the next best thing would be to put at least those who were capable to maximal use at the least cost. As early as the first week of the war Rafelsberger wrote to Göring's office that "the only effective possibility of immediately meeting this danger" of Vienna's "tremendous number of Jews (*Unzahl von Juden*)" forming "flashpoints of resistance" was

> the deportation of the majority of Jews into forced labor camps. . . . We are thinking mainly of labor at road works, brick works, as well as greater factories of all kinds that can employ Jews in closed sections. It is my personal conviction that it would be indispensable to quarter such Jews in barrack camps under appropriate guard. . . . Appropriate proposals are being worked out in consultation with the Labor Office and economic organizations.[270]

At the same time Mayor Neubacher wrote in the same vein to Economics Minister Funk:

> A national emergency situation of longer duration requires that decisive measures be taken in regard to cities where large masses of Jews are still residing. I am assuming that in the near future the Reich will declare that the Jews would have to be put to work; this seems absolutely necessary, and we would welcome quickly instituting such a measure. However, in this case it would not be possible to commit such a mass of Jews. We are therefore of the opinion that the Jews of Vienna and in [other] German cities be distributed in a number of labor camps all through the Reich.[271]

The concerted effort of doing just that began early in the spring of 1940, in the weeks before the war in the west began in earnest with the invasion of Norway and Denmark on April 9. The instrumentality of putting Jews to work was the *Arbeitsdienst* (labor service) or *Arbeitseinsatz* (labor force), the mobilization of a labor force organized by the official Labor Bureau (*Arbeitskammer*), which operated at local levels throughout the Reich under the auspices of the *Deutsche Arbeitsfront* (DAF), the German Labor Front directed by Robert Ley, one of the chief Nazis. However, the use that was made of Jews for labor service was, in effect, the logical next step in the enactment of the regime's Jewish policy.

The precedents and preconditions for what Jewish labor service turned out to be were already in place. According to Nazi ideology, Jews were parasites and should be made to engage in labor to justify their existence. In addition, gathering opponents of the regime in concentration camps and forcing them to do hard labor seems to have been one of the innovations of the Nazis, who thereby combined the precedent of Soviet labor camps with that of the detention camps of Dollfuss's Austrian fascist regime. But there were also more specific precedents. When the Jews lost their livelihoods, many prepared for emigration at *Umschulungskurse*, the retraining courses mentioned earlier. This program, while offered by the IKG, was monitored by the Nazi authorities. An important segment of the program consisted of preparing young Zionists for emigration to what was then called Palestine. This program, called *hakhshara*,[272] was to enable them to be pioneers in reclaiming the land and making it as arable as it was in ancient times, a land that had been neglected and despoiled in the intervening centuries. The *hakhshara* program grew out of the rise of modern Zionism and had been well established by the time of the Anschluss. Löwenherz was able to continue the program within the parameters of the *Umschulungskurse*. However, under the Nazis *hakhshara* became severely structured. No longer would a handful of students spend their summers helping at a farm in exchange for a straw mattress and good country food, nor would they spend their evenings sitting around a campfire singing Zionist songs. Now the venue consisted of a few large Jewish farms or small industrial enterprises from which the owners were expelled, but which the Nazis permitted to be worked by the free labor of young Jews eager to qualify for emigration.

The participants were carefully selected by the leaders of their respective Zionist organizations, mainly the secularist *Hechalutz* ("The Pioneer") and the religious *Misrachi* ("Eastern"). The leaders were also supervisors of the youngsters in their work schedules and in their daily living routines. The leaders as well as their charges were under the constant surveillance of a resident member of the SS, who was usually in his black uniform. The work schedule was hard and unchanging. Rising between four and five, after prayer and breakfast the participants assembled in military formation to receive the order of the day and their assignments. A kitchen crew brought a noontime meal to the fields. Evenings, after supper and the prayer of thanks, everyone threw their aching backs and limbs gratefully on his or her sack of straw. Once a week, there was a day of rest with a gathering of the whole contingent, of course under the watchful eye of the SS man. One of the authors (i.e., LHE), who participated in *hakhshara* shortly *before* the outbreak of the war, remembers *Tisha b'Av*, the fast day commemorating the destruction of the ancient temples in Jerusalem. The camp leaders naïvely thought that the youngsters would be able to stay in their quarters for the duration of the fast and to sit on the floor for the reading of *Eikha*, the Book of Lamentations. In no uncertain terms, the SS man put a stop to this and, on a cloudy and windy day, had us out on the field, working as usual but without food. Occasionally, when the coast was clear, our leader had us rest on the ground to survive the day.

With the outbreak of the war, the *hakhshara* camps had become work camps, where Jewish labor engaged in production that was useful to and required by the Nazis. Moreover, they served as models for similar *Umschulungskurse*, which were now usually called *Umschulungslager* (retraining camps) but were in effect labor camps, to which Jews were assigned who were eager to have room and board as well as some occupation, even though they received hardly any earnings. Even before the concerted action of impressing Jews for labor service got under way, the Nazis designated Jews for labor at these retraining camps. There were, for example, some men left over from the Nisko project. At the time the Nisko action was terminated, a number of participants had already been gathered for a third transport. Many of them had given up their living quarters and relinquished their belongings. Being destitute, the IKG was ordered to settle them at a homeless shelter that the IKG owned at Gänsbacher Street in the tenth district of Vienna. The home was now called a camp (*Lager*), and in effect its inhabitants were detainees.

They, as well as the IKG emigration machinery, were placed under pressure to make their early emigration a matter of the highest priority. Part of the pressure consisted of Eichmann's order to liquidate the "camp." Late in January 1940 Löwenherz was able to report to Eichmann that some of the residents had the chance of emigrating overseas, and while arrangements were being made for some to emigrate to Russia, others were being considered for illegal transports to Palestine.[273] However, several small contingents from the camp in Gänsbacher Street were sent, on orders from Brunner 1, to the retraining camp at Altenfelden.[274] All this served as precedents for making use of Jews for the *Arbeitseinsatz*.

At first glance, it would seem that the venture was a happy confluence of various interests: The Labor Front was able to deploy a badly needed labor force; the SS provided idle Jewish consumers for labor service; the enterprises to which they were assigned made good use of them; the hard-pressed Jews had something to do and earned something with which to help keep their families alive; and the welfare budget of the IKG would experience some relief, especially now that the budget had been placed under even tighter constraints and control. Yet, for the Jewish factors of this equation things were anything but rosy; rather, they were full of trouble and hardship. A look at Löwenherz's dealings with the authorities concerning some of these camps is instructive.

When Austria became part of Nazi Germany, its name was changed to its ancient designation *Ostmark*.[275] The borders of Austria's provinces were redrawn, some of the Sudetenland was incorporated into provincial territory, and provinces, too, were renamed. Upper Austria (*Oberösterreich*) became Upper Danube (*Oberdonau*). While Hitler, for reasons of personal spite, was content to let Vienna atrophy into a provincial backwater, he had big plans for Linz, the capital of the region he regarded as his home. The province now found itself in a privileged position. Other interests also had their eyes on Upper Danube. In the nineteenth century, when Emperor Francis (Franz) Joseph I ordered the glorious rebuilding of his residence city of Vienna, the city's engineers pioneered the smooth-surfaced, hard-rock pavement that has lasted well into the automobile age. To this end, the city acquired granite quarries of the highest quality in Mauthausen, a small town near Linz. So great was the reputation of the stone from there that as soon as the Anschluss was completed, moves were under way to make it available for the grand building projects in the main cities of Germany proper, as planned by Albert Speer. The SS had already founded a corporation for the production of building materials such as stone and brick carried out by captive labor. Thus it happened that less than two months after the Anschluss the SS had succeeded in leaning on Vienna's new city fathers sufficiently to lease them the quarries for a low price, and a year later to sell them to the SS.[276] Thus the newest part of Nazi Germany had the distinction of having a concentration camp of its own, one which would become notorious for its brutal stone quarry. There is evidence that from the beginning the potential for the punishing brutality of the quarry was the Nazis' motive for its acquisition. Less than two weeks after the Anschluss Bürckel said in a speech preparatory to the plebiscite discussed in chapter 2:

> We might be about to discover a factory or a quarry with a sign reading "This plant employs only Jewish laborers"! (Uproarious laughter.) We would designate it as a model plant. So, don't worry, your *Leit* [bowdlerized Yiddish for "people"[277]] are in business again.[278]

At about the same time, the new Party Governor (Gauleiter) August Eigruber was reported as bragging that because of its special merit Upper Danube would have the distinction of harboring the concentration camp of traitors from all of Austria.[279] He was no doubt referring to the reason for the urgency of establishing that new concentration camp at Mauthausen, that is, the concentration camps Dachau and Buchenwald could not fully accommodate the waves of arrests following the Anschluss.

By early 1940 Mauthausen concentration camp had a number of satellite camps. And with the availability of SS guards trained for extension service, the precinct around Mauthausen was well suited for having *hakhshara* and retraining courses turn into captive labor camps. Originally there were several *hakhshara* camps at formerly Jewish agricultural properties: in Altenfelden near the former German border, in Waidhofen over the border of Lower Danube, and in Traunkirchen in the Alpine foothill region known as Salzkammergut, none more than 40 miles from Linz and Mauthausen. At a distance of about 60 miles, in Styria, lay a camp at Eisenerz, which had been Austria's source of high-grade iron ore that could be mined on the surface since the Middle Ages.

The reason the IKG was interested in involving their Jews in the labor force was, as we have said, financial: It would give Jews a chance to earn some money and thereby provide the IKG's welfare budget with some relief. Some Jews were still receiving weekly payments from their unemployment insurance, which was an official governmental social service. Thus, this service too had an interest in the employment of Jews. The candidates for assignment to the workforce were screened for physical fitness. The screening was done by the Nazis, inasmuch as they regarded Jewish doctors to be too lenient. However, right away a problem arose. Those deemed unfit lost unemployment benefits, meager as they were, on the grounds that theirs were not cases of unemployment but of disability. When, in consequence, the Jews thus dispossessed of their paltry benefits turned to the IKG for support, Löwenherz reported to Brunner 1 that the workforce failed to have a positive effect on the IKG budget. This new drain on the IKG welfare budget was not in the interest of the Nazi authorities either. But when Löwenherz asked Brunner 1 to see to it that those unfit for labor service continue to receive unemployment benefits, all that Brunner 1 did was promise to investigate whether the cancellation of benefits was ordered by some higher authority.[280] We do not know the outcome of Brunner's investigation, but the incident indicates that all manner of authorities, bureaus, and personages were very quick to grasp at pretexts for combining exploitation with the further expropriation of Jews.

Aryans who were recruited into the wartime workforce away from home were properly housed, paid, fed, and outfitted. Not so the Jews. Everyone involved—Bürckel's office as the Nazi Party's central office in Austria, the *Zentralstelle*, SS monitors, employers, local labor bureaus, and regional Nazi officials—looked on the commandeered Jews as labor material to be exploited with the least expenditure of resources, even if these were Jewish resources that were being held captive. In their exploiting, the different agencies worked hand-in-glove and engaged in a tug-of-war; and the Jews, including the IKG, were caught in the middle. A case in point: Early in June 1940 the *Zentralstelle* had selected a contingent of workers to be sent to Traunkirchen, presumably to work alongside young *hakhshara* participants in local wood products industries, mainly in the production of cardboard. Prochnik received the order for the IKG to dispatch the men to Traunkirchen and to submit the bill for incurred expenses to the *Zentralstelle* for reimbursement by the Linz branch of the *Statthalterei*, the Party Governor Bürckel's office.[281] The bill came to RM 3,548.40. A few days later, the bill was returned to the IKG on the grounds that the governor's office was to be approached only for the train fare of the 248 men sent to Traunkirchen, which at RM 10.80 per person amounted to RM 2,678.40. The additional amount of RM 870.00 in the original bill reflected RM 10.00 spending money contributed by the IKG to eighty-seven of the most indigent members of the group. Technically it was wrong for the IKG to include this amount in the bill for train fare, and if on the side of the IKG the matter had been handled directly by Löwenherz rather than by lieutenants such as Prochnik, it would have been billed correctly, and the allowances would have been quietly absorbed in the IKG budget. But, under the given circumstances the IKG was now told that the contributions totaling RM 870.00 were to be returned to the IKG by the respective beneficiaries through payroll deductions. Engel's request that the contributions be gratuities from the account of the IKG was denied on the grounds that the laborers in question received "legally prescribed full pay, from which a deduction of RM 10.00 would not be a substantial burden." Engel was also instructed that the IKG apply to a Herr Zeitlinger, the camp director of the enterprise to which the men were assigned, for the required payroll deductions. As to the train fare advanced by the IKG, reimbursement was made by the treasurer's office at Linz, inasmuch as the enterprise in question turned out to be the Traunkirchen branch of the Reich road construction project,[282] a governmental enterprise.[283]

Other groups of Viennese Jews were also employed in road building, presumably with granite blocks quarried by the less fortunate inmates at Mauthausen. The men so employed by the firm ASDAG at Eisenerz soon found out to what extent Jews could count on receiving "legally prescribed full pay." At the beginning of July, right after his return from Berlin, Löwenherz reported to Brunner 1 about the increasing number of complaints about the insufficient food given to the Eisenerz contingent. He was told to take the matter up with the Labor Bureau, which had mediated the employment of the Jews.[284] To what effect he did so, we find out when two weeks later he faced Brunner 1 with the report on how ASDAG responded to the complaint that was forwarded to them by the Labor Bureau. Löwenherz had, in the meantime, received a letter written by one of the "174 Jewish workers." The letter was handwritten and mailed to the IKG in spite of the prevailing censorship. We will reproduce it here in full. In reading it, let us consider that this was mid-1940 and concerned a work contingent recruited by the Labor Bureau for employment by a private firm. It was not 1942 in the Warsaw ghetto. It was not 1943 in a concentration camp that also served as an extermination camp. In fact, it was not even a concentration camp, such as nearby Mauthausen. The supervisors were not SS camp guards but managers of a road-building firm. The meanness of these do-it-yourself persecutors and exploiters speaks for itself:[285]

Eisenerz, July 14, 1940

To the Jewish Community—Vienna

The Vienna municipal employment office has up to now referred 174 Jewish workers to the ASDAG Company, which is in charge of constructing the new national highway in Eisenerz.

The workers were promised 57 *Reichspfennig* [Reich cents] per hour, and this was raised to 60 *Pfennig* in accordance with the law of May 9, 1940. For a short time, the company paid this amount. On June 23, 1940, this amount was lowered to an average of 40 *Pfennig* per hour, supposedly because wages must reflect productivity.—But when the wages were handed out on July 12, 1940, a further radical change had gone into effect and, with few exceptions, the contingent was allotted an hourly wage of only 11 *Pfennig*.—Since the usual workday consists of 9 hours, the people thus affected received RM 0.99, while the [per diem] charge for room and board is RM 1.30. Thus it happens that more than half of the contingent is unable to scrape together the cost for their upkeep.

If these workers are entitled to a marriage increment, that difference is deducted from this increment by the employer. If a worker has no such increment, then, as was announced today, he will be deprived of the usual food and will receive merely bread and soup.—If the debt, which totals about RM 350, is not paid in the next few days, the construction management threatens to have the workers arrested, i.e., to turn them over to the Gestapo.

In this extreme situation we therefore plead most urgently that the IKG transfer this amount to the administration of the camp and to intervene immediately with the proper authorities in order to prevent such measures.

The reason given for this reduction in wages is an alleged inadequate performance and, it is claimed, a refusal to work. In this regard it must be said that, according to the skilled [non-Jewish] workers, the amount of work produced by the great majority of the [Jewish] group is completely satisfactory and on the same level as that of the Aryan workers. The only ones not measuring up are old, sick, or weak persons who are not able to keep up. Even the threat of the severest measures and possible transfer to forced labor cannot get these people to do more.

Characteristic for the spirit with which the Jewish workers are treated is the order issued today that from now on our group is not permitted to receive money or food packages from home to supplement our insufficient food supply. Any packages arriving nonetheless would be confiscated and sent to the NSV [the Nazi welfare organization].—I would also like to point out that for the last few weeks we did not receive the extra allowance that had been allotted for the hardest labor; at the same time there is constant pressure on the workforce for ever greater productivity. As additional punishment for our supposed low productivity all leaves are canceled as of today, and we are not allowed to go home even in dire emergencies (such as the death of close relatives).

This description of conditions represents only a small part of the actual picture.

For this reason we urgently ask that you intervene energetically with the proper authorities and to do everything possible to rescue the 174 Jewish workers employed here, who are under constant pressure and unending threats, from physical, emotional, and financial ruin.

We ask once more that you take the seriousness of our situation fully into consideration and not leave any stone unturned to bring about an improvement in the conditions here in accordance with the regulations dealing with the utilization of Jews for work.

[signed] *The non-Aryan workers of the ASDAG Company*

P.S. Because of the recently instituted severe measures and the newly introduced strict censorship of all correspondence, please exercise the greatest caution in making use of this letter.

The reduction of hourly pay from RM 0.57 to RM 0.11 was hardly a scheme whereby the men could sustain their families and save the IKG welfare expenditures. (In those days 11 *Pfennig* translated to about 4 U.S. cents, the cost of two copies of a daily newspaper.) The absurdity of the company charging the men for their upkeep, such as it was, which it was supposed to provide, and deducting the charge from their pay, with the result that on payday all the men received was a pay-slip showing an amount *they owed the company* and had to pay lest they faced dire consequences, is mind-boggling. All the IKG could do was to submit the matter to the Labor Bureau in Vienna and, at their suggestion, to the branch in Eisenerz, with copies to the *Zentralstelle* and the Gestapo.[286]

Whether or not the matter was rectified, the episode also indicates the attitude of some people who were not directly charged with carrying out Nazi policy regarding the Jewish problem, and the opportunities grasped by them to make their unofficial contribution to that cause, at least in the form of further exploitation. It was the same contempt for the Jews and the denial of their humanity that prevailed in Austria and provided the Nazi regime at the time of the Anschluss with the momentum for stepping up its anti-Jewish policy and thereby, at least initially, gaining the acquiescence of the Austrians. But, like the wave of zealous and unauthorized Aryanizations at the time of the Anschluss, it indicated that the welcome and needed momentum would have to be controlled, especially now that the war provided more and more opportunities for the regime's solution of the Jewish question to move into higher gear. In particular, it was the SD section 112, being the coordinating and main executive organ for the solution of the Jewish question, that encountered problems of control as it involved other agencies in the handling of the Jews, including those within the party structure and even internal to the SS itself. Until such problems merited the attention of levels of the apparatus that could solve them, Brunner 1, operating at his relatively low level, would have his delicate work cut out for him: Locally, he would have to do ad hoc coordination, while keeping his ears cocked to what, unbeknownst to him, may have been—to use his words—"ordered by some higher authority" other than the chain of command directly above him. Above all, he would continue to exercise sharply his absolute authority over the Jews, while taking care to restore the ever disappointed semblance of confidence in him on the part of the men at the IKG. Without this semblance of confidence, Brunner's work would not be impossible, but it would be much more laborious. Without his encouraging such confidence through a modicum of performance on his part in support of the IKG's interests, the IKG would be left with no recourse to accomplish its task of saving Jews.

A sequel to Löwenherz's effort at alleviating the hardships at Eisenerz, about which the IKG had received so many complaints, was an order that Brunner issued to Murmelstein: "Messages addressed to the work camp Eisenerz are to be directed by way of the *Zentralstelle*, while those addressed to other work camps can be sent directly." Murmelstein had to report to Brunner 1 that the IKG "departments concerned were notified in accordance with the received directive."[287]

Löwenherz, to whom the participation of the Jews in the *Arbeitsdienst* (labor service) was of vital importance, spared no opportunity of promoting it while trying to gain control over the problems which arose. Inasmuch as the *Zentralstelle* summoned the candidates for labor service from their lists of Jews, it happened that men over the age of 50 were called up. Upon Löwenherz's worried inquiry, he was assured that they would not have to serve. If there were any that were summoned, then only because "one cannot tell in advance how old the summoned Jews are. Upon submission of proof of having reached the age of 50 they will not be taken into labor service."[288] But a few weeks later Löwenherz was directed to have fifty able-bodied men report to the *Zentralstelle* for labor assignment. The men were to be selected from among Jews fed at the soup kitchen; as for their ages, their years of birth were to range from 1880 to 1923.[289] In short, the IKG's concern to experience savings in their welfare budget, in this case the soup kitchens, was used to have the IKG make the primary selection of candidates and, with the recruitment of men between 17 (1923) and 60 (1880), the assurance that no one over 50 would be drafted fell by the wayside. Later on, the quoted letter from the Eisenerz contingent would confirm for Löwenherz not only the indiscriminate recruitment of old and unfit men on the part of the SS, but the impossibility of their useful employment.

The IKG had good reason to be concerned over actually getting hold of the projected savings. Except in the rare instances when the IKG had to dispatch the recruits or had to submit a list of candidates, they had no way of knowing whom the SD had actually drafted and whom the Labor Bureau had accepted into labor service. Hence, with the permission of Brunner 1, Löwenherz requested from the Labor Bureau a list of men already drafted and any future lists, apparently without response. When he presented the matter to Brunner 1, he was assured that the IKG would be given the lists.[290] When the draftees continued to receive welfare payments from the IKG because the lists had still not been obtained, Brunner 1 told Löwenherz that some of the lists that he had received had been forwarded to the IKG. As to other and future lists, they could be compiled only bit by bit and one at a time, "due to the small number of personnel available to the Labor Bureau."[291] But the enlistment of Jews into the workforce resulted in savings to the IKG only slowly, if at all, and in fact increased outlays, such as train fares, whose reimbursement was similarly delayed. Consequently, when Löwenherz met with Eichmann in Berlin early in August 1940, he asked, besides other outstanding financial matters, that "due to the financial condition of the IKG" this too "be settled speedily."[292]

Löwenherz's many concerns about hardship conditions at the work camps prompted Brunner 1 to make an inspection tour in August 1940.[293] In the "retraining camps" (*Umschulungslager*) of Windhag and Doppl, both in Altenfelden, he "issued orders to ensure sufficient and good food." He found that the families of some of the workers had sent them food packages out of their own meager rations. Brunner 1 now told Löwenherz that this would not be necessary and instructed him to inform the families not to do so any more. We see that, aside from addressing Löwenherz's concerns, the purpose of Brunner's trip was to inspect the work performance of the Jews employed there. He found "that the young laborers worked with zeal, while with few exceptions the older persons are not performing satisfactorily." The young laborers were mainly teen-aged *hakhshara* participants, whom their leader Aron Menczer instructed to work hard in order to impress the Nazis and to qualify for emigration as pioneers to Palestine. In comparison with the young, the efforts of older recruits must have seemed to be flagging.

Brunner 1 had promised that on his inspection trip he would make a decision about releasing Aron Menczer from labor service at Altenfelden. Menczer had been selected—deliberately, as Löwenherz would find out more than a year later—from among the first candidates summoned to the *Zentralstelle*. Being the able leader of the Youth Aliyah activities, such as Zionist schooling and preparation for emigration to Palestine, including *hakhshara*, he was in a vital position where he could not be spared. Hence, as soon as he was drafted, Löwenherz asked for his return. He was told that Menczer would be released after he worked at Altenfelden for two weeks, presumably side by side with his young charges.[294] It was more than two weeks later when Löwenherz again asked for Menczer's release and another month until Brunner 1 made his inspection tour after which he would decide on his release.

The relief of the IKG welfare budget through the recruitment of Jews for remunerative labor service was as much in the interest of the *Zentralstelle* as of the IKG. A demonstrable coincidence of interests of some kind had been a meager but the sole means of leverage available, which, as we know, Löwenherz had developed and of which he availed himself from the beginning. This factor was also operative from the early stages of labor service. For example, at the June 1940 *Vorsprache* in Berlin, Löwenherz asked Eichmann about extending labor service to the employment of women. He added that "relief of the IKG's welfare budget [would] to a high degree depend on [the women's] proper remuneration." At that time Eichmann informed Löwenherz that, unlike in the Altreich, the employment of Jewish women in Austria would have to wait.[295] In time women were employed in Viennese factories, often as the only wage earners in their families. Nonetheless, that did not save them from deportation.

With the exception of Eisenerz, the conditions in the labor camps within the larger radius of the concentration camp at Mauthausen were not as hard and brutal as in the concentration camp itself; and the men and boys were not imprisoned within the confines of the camps. However, the Jewish workers were strictly monitored by the Nazi authorities. This control pertained both to "labor" camps (*Arbeitslager*) and to "retraining" camps (*Umschulungslager*), which included *hakhshara* camps. The difference between the two kinds of camps seems to have been that the recruits in labor camps received some kind of monetary remuneration from the firms to which they were assigned, while those in the retraining camps received in the main only pocket money. We mentioned earlier that it was different in *hakhshara* camps in the Altreich. In his inspection of the Jewish organizations in Berlin, Löwenherz saw that there were several *hakhshara* projects, with some of the youths receiving "appropriate remuneration, which considerably eases the financing of the *hakhshara* program."[296] Evidently the supposition operative for Austria was that participation in *hakhshara* camps was purely for voluntary retraining.

Because the retraining program was an enterprise of the IKG sanctioned by the *Zentralstelle*, the latter also kept these camps under minute and direct supervision. This pertained not only to requests and complaints but in particular to the performance of the participants, their care, and their subsidies by the IKG and by their families. As regards the subsidies the participants received from the IKG, Brunner 1 directed that for those under 20 it was not to exceed RM 0.20 per diem, for the older ones RM 0.30. At the then current international rate of exchange this translated to about 6 U.S. cents and 9 U.S. cents, respectively. Furthermore, family members were forbidden to send them money.[297] Not long after Brunner 1 stopped even this restricted subsidy: "Shelter and ample food is being provided, the workers are also getting appropriate pocket money, hence their support by the IKG is in no way required and is to cease."[298] The prohibition against sending the labor camp participants supplementary foodstuffs would be reiterated over time.

When Löwenherz asked that workers engaged at labor service be released from work for the High Holidays, he was told that the Labor Bureau could not arrange this and that he should refrain from submitting such requests to them.[299] Löwenherz then asked that the participants at the two retraining camps at least be freed from work on Saturday, October 12, "the highest Jewish Holiday," Yom Kippur. Brunner 1 told him that he would issue directives to that effect with respect to the Doppl camp; in Windhag, however, part of the crew had to do the scheduled work. This shows the extent to which these retraining camps were, in fact, labor camps, with the difference being that the respective employer most likely did not have to pay proper wages for the Jews' labor. Since the retraining courses were meant to run for a limited time, participants were to vacate their places and make room for others. However, the *Zentralstelle* was interested only in there being enough of a workforce. We have seen that, when the labor service started, the *Zentralstelle* screened Jews for their fitness to do labor. At the same time, they began screening for substitutes at the retraining camps, only to turn the job over again to the IKG a short time later, evidently because the retrainees had proven to be good workers. These facts explain the following: In September 1940 Löwenherz asked for the release of fifty members of Youth Aliyah who had been at the Altenfelden/Doppl work camp—Löwenherz refers to it thus in the *Aktennotiz*—for over three months, so they could be given theoretical and language instruction in preparation for emigration to Palestine. According to Brunner 1, "these youths will be released as soon as appropriate replacements are made available,"[300] that is, by the IKG. A few days later Murmelstein was ordered by Brunner 1 to have the IKG produce another twenty men each for the Doppl and Windhag labor camps—Murmelstein's *Aktennotiz* refers to them as retraining camps. Murmelstein responded that, while "all that is necessary" would be done to fulfill this demand, the "success of this effort is uncertain." Whereupon Brunner issued a threat:

> In case the IKG should not be in a position of nominating the appropriate number of persons, the *Zentralstelle*, in its official capacity, will make the selection.[301]

We can imagine that the process at the *Zentralstelle* of selecting an able-bodied workforce was not as benign as that at the IKG. In any case, Brunner's concern was to use the resource of Jewish laborers to fill the respective labor/retraining camps with the required number of workers, and the IKG had to see to it that their numbers were maintained. When, for example, the number of workers at the labor camp Traunkirchen fell below the requirements because of emigration, Murmelstein—Löwenherz was in Berlin at the time—was given the following directive:

> To replenish the number, the *Zentralstelle* will, in the next few days, mail out summonses and examine each individual for his physical fitness. To this end, alphabetical lists [of candidates],

> including year of birth and address, are to be submitted by the IKG, based on available information.[302]

What was the reason for this demand? After all, a constantly updated list of all the Jews remaining in Vienna was available at the *Zentralstelle*. Apparently, Brunner 1 saw fit to accommodate the IKG's perennial concerns about the elderly. It was only a month earlier that Löwenherz had asked Brunner 1, prior to his October inspection of the labor camps, "for the release of the older Jews who were not able to do the work."[303]

Brunner 1 kept control over who was to be impressed for labor service. Aside from one's age and physical condition, there were other factors. We have seen that some detainees who had been slated for the aborted third Nisko transport were dispatched to labor camps. But released detainees from concentration camps had to emigrate within the mandated time, lest they be returned there; they were not permitted to join the labor force.[304] Former IKG and Palamt personnel, whom the *Zentralstelle* had forced the IKG to dismiss, were for Brunner 1 preferred candidates for labor service. On December 4 a man named Hausknecht was suddenly slated by the *Zentralstelle* to join a labor transport to Traunkirchen. He was the bookkeeper of the Palestine office, which was being dissolved on Eichmann's orders, and its affairs were in the process of being transferred to the IKG. On that day, Murmelstein asked Brunner 1 to delay Hausknecht's departure until the transfer of the books and accounts of his office had been completed.[305] We have already seen that Jews who depended on the IKG for support, even if only to the extent of being beneficiaries of the soup kitchens, were preferred targets for labor service. When "35 to 40 able-bodied Jews" were needed from one day to the next for some outdoor labor in Vienna, they had to be recruited from the soup kitchens and welfare rolls.[306] Another source of recruits for labor service was a sizable group of "remigrants" (*Rückwanderer*) from Italy. These were Jews who had emigrated to Italy, where, because of Mussolini's accommodation to Nazi Germany's anti-Jewish policy, they were to have been interned. However, the southern Axis partner found it more convenient to deport these Jews back to the northern one. One contingent arrived in Arnoldstein, Carinthia, from where they were sent to Vienna and right away impressed into labor service. The ones who arrived in Innsbruck, Tyrol, were not so lucky. Some were arrested, and some were sent to the concentration camp at Dachau. Dr. Hirsch of the Berlin community was able to negotiate for their release and for them to be sent to Vienna, where they would also be drafted into the labor force. This was done with the cooperation of Löwenherz, who arrived in Berlin soon thereafter.[307]

A special recruit for labor service was a certain Theodor Spitzer, who was found in the vestibule of a coffeehouse, which Jews were forbidden to enter. The IKG was ordered to send him to the retraining camp Windhag at his own cost and without any support from the IKG.[308] While this incident illustrates one Nazi mode of staffing the camps with Jewish labor, we must note that Spitzer could consider himself fortunate not to have been dealt with more severely.

All along, the IKG had to recruit replacements for or additions to the workforce at the camps. Thus, for example, at the time of the first set of deportations Brunner 1 ordered Murmelstein to provide, from one day to the next, two groups of ten young Jews for the Doppl retraining camp. They were to be single and without dependents; however, if married men were to be included to bring up the total, then only if they had evidence of a chance for emigration.

The fact that the labor camps at Doppl and Windhag were technically retraining camps meant that the IKG had to provide for the upkeep of the participants. Eichmann promised that the IKG would be reimbursed for the outlay. However, the matter was not so simple. For example, in February 1941 the section "Administration" of the *Zentralstelle* in Vienna required that the IKG pay for expenses incurred for the retraining camps in the amount of RM 51,639.22. Later, the IKG was informed that for the time being that amount did not need to be paid, which was confirmed by Brunner 1 during a telephone conversation with Murmelstein. When Murmelstein appeared at Brunner 1 for a *Vorsprache* later that day, he was told "for reasons of bookkeeping (*aus verrechungstechnischen Gründen*) it is necessary that the IKG submit [payment]. The amount advanced for this purpose should be reimbursed to the IKG, in accordance with Eichmann's promise."[309] One week later Brunner 1 said that the amount had to be paid by the IKG by April 10. In light of the increase in the IKG's outlay in proportion to the absence of any of the promised reimbursements, Löwenherz said that the IKG would compile an account of all such advances together with a request for reimbursement, which Brunner acknowledged (*hat es zur Kenntnis genommen*).[310] However, it turned out that the IKG had to continue paying for these camps without reimbursement. This is indicated by Löwenherz's informing Brunner 1 in May that to avoid large outlays, the IKG would henceforth request monthly billing.[311]

What the smaller monthly bills were like can be seen from the cost incurred by the IKG for the participants in the camps as reported by Murmelstein to Brunner 1 on June 6, 1941. For the camp at Doppl the expenses were as follows (all amounts in Reichsmark):[312]

Board	2,822.00
Pocket money	493.00
Clothing	36.40
Travel	339.70
Tools	13.60
Medical	32.16
Misc. expenses	204.22

The expenses on board for the 31 days of May means that there were on average fifty-five men at the camp, since their food cost on average RM 1.65 per diem, less than half a U.S. dollar at the then prevailing exchange rate. They received on average 87 *Pfennig* a day pocket money to buy additional food and whatever else they needed. Even at these low rates of reimbursement, these people were fortunate compared to the deportees.

At year's end, between the second set of deportations and the onset of the final major deportation of 1942, Löwenherz was informed that the camp at Doppl was being dissolved. The contingent of workers would remain in the service of the Manner Company, which would make provision for their upkeep. In the meantime, the IKG would have to advance the money, for which the firm was expected to reimburse the IKG. The contingent would remain under the supervision of the *Zentralstelle*, albeit through the IKG. The leader of the group, Gustav Engelmann, would have to report "noteworthy events" to the IKG, which then had to be included in the monthly reports from the IKG to the *Zentralstelle* with the costs incurred and the condition of the workers. Engelmann was further required to sell the group's remaining tools and other materials (that had been furnished by the IKG) to the company and to send the proceeds to the IKG.[313]

There is a revealing aspect to this changeover from a work camp posing as a training camp to a work camp assigned to the Manner Company. It will be recalled that the Zionist youth leader Aron Menczer was sent to the work camp near Linz as part of the Youth Aliyah contingent in mid-1940 and that Löwenherz kept requesting his release, only to be given promises that were never kept. Most recently, Murmelstein had asked Brunner 1 for his release since Menczer had been at the camp for fifteen months. Brunner 1 assured him that Menczer would be part of the group soon to be released.[314] When this did not materialize, Löwenherz renewed the request. Brunner 1 then told him that he had nothing against the release of Menczer but since Menczer had been committed to the camp by the Gestapo, he would get in touch with them about the matter.[315] Now almost three months later, as the camp was being transferred to a private firm, with Menczer still there, the question came up again. Brunner 1 handed Löwenherz two requests for furloughs, from the contingent leader Engelmann and from Eduard Israel Herz. He told Löwenherz he was to process the requests. How? The two "should remain in the camp and not come to Vienna," and as an afterthought he added, "the same goes for Aron Menczer, who also works there."[316]

Thus, when the work camps were dissolved, Löwenherz's hunch was confirmed: It had seemed evident to him almost from the beginning of the retraining camps that the work camps represented a form of captivity for the participants; and though they were not concentration camps, in the case of someone like Menczer, they came close to functioning as such.

From the beginning, Löwenherz and Murmelstein worked hard to free the inmates of the concentration camps. This had been possible only if, upon the release from these camps, the detainees had had the opportunity of emigrating within a short time, usually within four weeks. By mid-1941 the situation was exacerbated by the severe reduction of emigration opportunities, by the recent stoppage of visas to the United States, and by the threat of the resumption of deportations. Löwenherz thought that the chance of employment for Jews might be a way out for concentration camp inmates. When he requested the return of young inmates of Buchenwald and their absorption into the labor force, Brunner said "at the present time, out of the question!"[317]

In April 1940, at the beginning of the program to draft Jews for labor service, Murmelstein, as the one in charge of the IKG's emigration effort, was told that persons joining the labor service or their families must continue their preparations for their emigration. As the end of 1940 approached, there was a marked increase in the number of Jews who were taken into the labor force. While Löwenherz was in Berlin, Murmelstein was informed that this increase would continue but that no opportunity must be missed for the emigration of those doing labor service. To this end, a special section was to be established in the IKG emigration department, which would provide documentation and guidance services for these special cases and arrange for a timely return to Vienna of those for whom emigration arrangements have been completed.[318] During the forced decimation of the IKG staff throughout the year 1940, the IKG emigration department had not been spared. Nonetheless, this additional task was taken on by Murmelstein and his remaining associates, since the many factors of the tightening grip made the frantic effort to save as many as possible through emigration the main order of business in the phase under consideration.

It was not the drafting of the Jews of Vienna into labor service but the way in which they were impressed into it by the Nazis that made it an instance of increased pressure. This leads logically to our next chapter, in which we will adumbrate the frantic efforts of the IKG to save as many Jews as possible under the extreme and multifaceted pressure that was imposed upon them by the Nazi regime. The outbreak of the Second World War provided the Nazis with an excuse to hasten and deepen their anti-Jewish policies. The Jews had no right to exist in the Nazi universe. However, until the Jews could be eliminated in some form or other, they were to be subject to exploitation, expropriation, and enslavement.

Chapter 9

Frantic Effort to Save 12,000 More

WARTIME HAD BROUGHT WITH IT a deepening of the desperate situation of the Jews of Vienna. Not only did hope for the eventual emigration of all the Jews who still remained diminish for some and vanish for many, but after Nisko the threat of deportation hung over them like the sword of Damocles. The central task of the IKG during this phase was, therefore, to save as many as could be helped through emigration and to find ways of saving those who would have to stay behind. This task had to be undertaken in spite of the financial stranglehold that the new regime applied to the IKG, including the pressure to reduce the staffing and curtail its various activities. The complex task of emigration turned into a frantic effort—that of saving the remnant was quixotic and hopeless; yet both were in some ways nothing less than heroic. They were carried out on behalf of a captive population of cowed but desperately hopeful Jews.

As we move to sketch that frantic effort that ran parallel to all aspects of the Nazis' tightening grip on the Jews, let us keep in mind that the condition of war provided the Nazis with the opportunity to carry the logic of their Jewish policy a significant step further. The Jews' right to exist in domains under Nazi control was, as before, forfeit. Until such time as this forfeiture could be realized in the case of each Jew and in every concrete aspect of Jewish actuality, Jews and things Jewish were chattel, to be exploited, expropriated, and enslaved.

In the sixteen months between the reopening of the IKG under the control of the Nazis and the beginning of hostilities, 106,000 of the 180,000 Jews of Austria had emigrated, most of them at least in part due to the efforts or services provided by the IKG. The persecutions of the first few weeks, culminating in the wave of arrests and brutality in May and June 1938, no doubt provided the impetus, as did the events of Kristallnacht. Although the outbreak of the war put a brake on the emigration effort, in the weeks following it was still possible to make arrangements for those Jews to leave whose emigration process had been in the works before September 1. In this way, by the end of 1939 an additional 11,000 Jews were able to emigrate. And the Nisko affair removed another 1,000 Jews, albeit not to emigration. This means that by the end of 1939 there were still about 58,000 Jews in Vienna, of which about 23,000 were considered incapable of emigrating. This left almost 35,000 Jews as possible candidates for emigration. Of these the IKG managed to send forth 6,500 in 1940, and in 1941—until Himmler ordered the end of emigration in October 1941—about 6,000 more. Saving these 12,500 by emigration took a tremendous effort on the part of the staff of the IKG, beset as they were by the other pressures (as discussed in preceding chapters). An exhaustive account is not possible, but we will look at this effort and highlight some pertinent aspects.

The outbreak of war only heightened the need as well as the desperate urge to emigrate. It also provided the Nazis a golden opportunity to tighten their grip on the Jews, who found themselves more and more in the situation of captives with no other future than deprivation, impoverishment, increasingly crowded housing, enslavement, and the threat of deportation. The policy of deprivation was only secondarily designed to provide the thrust of increased emigration. The financial stranglehold, coupled with tight control over contacts with people and agencies abroad, also had the effect of thwarting rather than promoting the thrust. Thus the Nazi policy of deprivation and control was, to a significant degree, at cross-purposes with the Nazi policy to have the Jews emigrate.

Not only Nazi policy but world events seemed to conspire against the beleaguered Jews in 1940 and 1941. As if the conquest of Poland and the subsequent entry of the Allies into the war were not enough, the year brought further hostile actions and with them further restrictions. The parts of the world to which the Jews could emigrate or through which they were at least allowed to travel to their final destination, if they were lucky enough to find such, were getting fewer and smaller. The invasion and violation of Belgium and The Netherlands in May, Germany's conquest of a part of France in June and its hegemony over the rest, all served to choke off one escape route after another. Italy's declaration of war on the Allies the same month restricted the southern escape route. An alternative passage to the south, mainly down the Danube River, soon meant running the gantlet through the territories of German sympathizers and allies and, if it could be attempted at all, was beset by foreseeable and unforeseen dangers and calamities. And all this happened on top of the unexpected and unexplainable choking off of visas to the United States which we discuss below.

The only official source of information the Jews of Vienna had was, as we have seen, the *Jüdisches Nachrichtenblatt* (Jewish Newspaper). Since the paper was censored word for word by the Nazis, its editor-in-chief, Dr. Emil Reich, had the unenviable task of making the usual bad news somehow inoffensive to the authorities and palatable to the readers, without straying too far from the truth as he knew it. Reich and his contributors had to choose their words very carefully, so much so that, if we did not know the sorry situation of the time, we would consider some of the formulations used to circumscribe events to be ridiculous. To cite just two examples: The Anschluss was a "realignment of the state of affairs";[1] the Second World War that had recently begun was "the change in the relations between the nations that had occurred the previous year."[2] Badly needed information about emigration was either nonexistent or not helpful, especially when published under orders issued for their own reasons by the Nazi authorities. In the spring of 1940, when Germany began to heat up the war by invading Denmark and Norway, Murmelstein received instructions from Brunner 1 that reflected Eichmann's anxiety about the negative effect of the renewed hostilities on the emigration effort. He is reported as

> wish[ing] . . . that in one of the next issues an article appear about the results of emigration up to this point, the present situation and the outlook for the future. In connection with this article [the Jews] are to be instructed to get in touch with their relatives abroad for the purpose of procuring immigration possibilities and providing ship passage.[3]

But how to impart to those relatives the increasingly desperate situation without having the censored letter result in accusations of spreading *Greuelgeschichten* (horror stories) and earning a free trip to a concentration camp?

As it happened, it was not as if the Jews abroad were not aware of the increasingly dismal plight of their captive brethren. As early as February 1940—that is, five months into the war and before the full extent of deprivations and the stranglehold on the Jews of Vienna were enacted—a report on "the general situation of the Jews of Vienna" was sent to Joint (American Jewish Joint Distribution Committee) headquarters in New York from Geneva, outlining all aspects of the incipient crisis: the evictions, the crowding of old and young together in unhygienic conditions, the restricted food supply, the dependence of 85 percent (about 45,000) of the remaining Jews on IKG soup kitchens, the lack of heating, the employment of Jews for menial labor without pay, the dismal prospects of the old and the sick, and so on. What was the source of this information? Perhaps not entirely, but surely to a large extent, the source must have been both Löwenherz during his meeting with Troper in Amsterdam and Murmelstein during his trip to Budapest. What conclusion did the report draw as to the proper response to the ominous conditions in Vienna? "Emigration is the only solution of the Jewish problem and the only way to save Jewish lives. . . . 120,000 Jews have already emigrated from Vienna. The emigration of a further 25,000 people has to be carried out without delay."[4] But the main source of emigration possibilities that remained at that time was the United States. What happened to it will be recounted in the last section of this chapter.

The Jews of Vienna, now more than ever dependent on the IKG, looked to it for relief even in matters of emigration possibilities, over which the IKG had no control. The situation was as impossible for the Jews to understand as it was for the IKG to explain. Some examples from the correspondence of Dr. Reich of the *Jüdisches Nachrichtenblatt* will illustrate this.

A Herr Kohn sent a letter and submitted an article dealing with emigration questions generally and with his hopeless situation in particular. Reich replied with care and compassion, and, reading between the lines, we can guess what could not be said even in private correspondence. Mr. Kohn is told that the article he submitted "contains much that is correct. However, neither the topic nor the content allows its publication." Reich then replied to the letter accompanying the article, agreeing with the writer's observation that "there is a paucity of information regarding emigration emanating from the IKG." Yet, the correspondent was wrong, Reich continued, in assuming that the leadership of the IKG was not pursuing the Jewish interests regarding emigration with sufficient vigor. He did hint, however, that the IKG functionaries were not always the most patient of men: "Whatever can be said about emigration possibilities will be told to the petitioner by the IKG in a more or less humane manner and with more or less patience."[5]

The very fine line that the newspaper as well as the IKG had to tread between what they knew and what they were allowed to say publicly on the one hand and the pressure exerted by the ever more desperate people approaching the only Jews they considered to be in the know and to possess any power over people and events and expecting these people to "do something!" on the other, no doubt led to irascibility on the part of the IKG functionaries and the creation of myths and the belief in all kinds of rumors on the part of the Jews. Seeing others lucky enough to emigrate, and wondering why they themselves failed to find a safe haven, brought out rivalries and prejudices that had lain dormant. Early in 1940 Reich answered a long epistle by a Herr Stössel, in which he claims that Jews born in Poland were "constantly" (*ohne Unterbrechung*) receiving visas to the United States whereas the "native-born" Viennese Jews received none. Here Reich got a bit impatient and called this prejudicial differentiation "especially ridiculous given today's circumstance," but then proceeded to explain patiently that the Jews who had immigrated to Vienna from Poland (the so-called *Zugereisten*, who had often been looked down upon by the "genuine" Viennese Jews) were more likely to have relatives who had emigrated to the United States decades earlier and were now well established enough to supply the coveted affidavits.[6]

While the individual Jews trying to emigrate faced their own kind of nightmare and felt moreover that too little was being done by the Jewish officials in charge of helping them leave, they were not aware of the fact that these officials had entered a different kind of nightmarish realm in which just about every promising avenue of escape was hedged with pitfalls of the most unexpected kind, where every effort seemed to be stymied, a world in which bureaucracy reigned supreme and individual needs seemed to be way down on the scale of priority.

Thus the emigration officials of the IKG and others, especially those charged with making arrangements for Jews who were forced to leave immediately and whose only recourse were illegal transports, had to do their work under pressure from every direction. There was the pressure from the Jewish population desperate to leave. There was the overwhelming problem of finding destinations, transit routes, money, tickets, visas, reliable travel agencies, and shipping companies, and having it all come together in spite of conflicting information, demands, and schedules. By no means least was the pressure exerted by the Nazi authorities and their organs with their unmistakably threatening undertones, employing their unrestricted power of control.

In 1940 we find repeated expressions of displeasure on the part of the *Zentralstelle*, especially Alois Brunner (aka Brunner 1), with the pace of emigration. For instance, in January Brunner 1 demanded a list of people housed in a home on Gänsbacherstrasse. These were persons who had been collected for the aborted third transport to Nisko, Poland. He decreed that the emigration possibilities of each individual were to be listed "in red ink," together with their final destinations and dates of departure. Murmelstein pointed out that because of "the present situation regarding the technicalities of emigration it is almost impossible to abide by the individual deadlines for departure from the Reich," and asked that this circumstance be taken into consideration.[7] In May Löwenherz was told that "the figures of emigration from the *Ostmark* are not satisfactory, an increase is absolutely necessary. . . . [Löwenherz] pointed to the fact that the IKG is making every possible effort to promote emigration, but one must consider the constantly increasing difficulties."[8] Until this time the directives from the *Zentralstelle* had specified that the questionnaires to be filled out in order to receive a passport must not be handed to the applicant until he could prove that his emigration was imminent. However, Brunner 1 now insisted that the number of passport applications be increased and for this reason even those who were not ready to leave "but intended to do so in the foreseeable future" would now have to be given the questionnaires and the strict instructions from the *Zentralstelle* would have to be eased henceforth.[9] It seems as if Brunner 1 himself was under pressure from above and wanted to make use of this ruse in order to pad the emigration figures.

In his interviews with us, Murmelstein threw a significant light on the background and reasons why Eichmann and, therefore, Brunner 1 were so eager to have more people apply for emigration papers at the *Zentralstelle* and why the Jews were so reluctant to commit themselves to the emigration process in this manner. We get a glimpse here of the inner workings of the SD (security service) and its affiliated network, things that could not appear in any *Aktennotizen* (memorandums) and were only whispered about among insiders. Beginning with the war, when the busiest escape routes to or through France and England were cut off, the Jews were reluctant to apply for passports because they did not know if and when they would be able to use them. And getting a passport, Murmelstein told us, meant being given a deadline for leaving, a deadline that most applicants were not able to adhere to under the uncertain wartime conditions. And we know what the penalty for noncompliance with the order to leave by a certain date was. "Eichmann ranted and raved," since the purpose of the *Zentralstelle* was to issue travel documents, and "no passports, no *Zentralstelle*." The people employed there were nervous, as was Eichmann. They feared that if they were seen as not fulfilling their primary function, they would be called up into the military and even sent to the front. They enjoyed their sinecure and would do anything to hold on to it. Hence, the amount of "business" had to get out of its slump and increase drastically, and the Germans working at the *Zentralstelle* would have to seem indispensable (*unentbehrlich*) on the home front.[10]

Furthermore—and Murmelstein considered this the *nervus rerum*, the heart of the matter—there was the question of money. Each Jew who passed through the *Zentralstelle* had to pay out a whole lot of different fees under different names, such as the *Auswandererabgabe* (emigration levy) and the *Reichsfluchtsteuer* (levy on leaving the Reich). The emigration levy was Eichmann's discretionary fund, and a lot of it may have gone into his own pocket. Officially this money was the emigration fund, that is, it was intended as a reserve to finance some of the emigration expenses of the IKG and some of the illegal transports to Palestine. In the previous chapter we saw how Löwenherz had urged the release of this reserve and how Eichmann withheld release as part of his financial stranglehold, only to make belated contributions in the end. But the bulk of the money that he did not keep for himself went to subsidize other ventures. For example, when one of the two biggest Viennese department stores, Gerngross, was Aryanized and a party functionary was brought in as commissar to run it, he ran it right into the ground. Eichmann used a great deal of the

Auswandererabgabe to help the store avoid bankruptcy. And so it turned out, we were told, that the IKG had to go to the commissar to beg for the money that should rightfully have been theirs. The most diverse projects, Murmelstein said, lived off this emigration levy. Eichmann was clever, he was one of the most influential among his comrades, and he gave a helping hand to them and others. He was known to have "a limitless supply of money" to use as he saw fit. And this supply threatened to dry up, all because the Jews refused to stand in line at the *Zentralstelle*. His secure and profitable niche was threatened, and the specter of taking an active—though unwilling—part in the war loomed before him and his minions. No wonder he went "berserk."[11]

At times the officials at the *Zentralstelle* came up with their own ideas. In November 1940, for instance, Brunner 1 found an item in a Frankfurt newspaper dealing with the possibility of the Virgin Islands being used as a stopover for emigrants. Even though Murmelstein was convinced that there was nothing to this report, he had to obey and follow it up.[12] It turned out, of course, that the IKG had to do a lot of extra work to be able to report that, as was expected, this scheme "hardly comes into consideration in the near future." Nonetheless, Löwenherz had to humor Brunner 1 by promising that the IKG would follow up on this and would alert the Joint to be ready to assist possible emigrants to these islands with food and housing.[13]

Transporting Jews also seems to have been good business, and there was apparently stiff competition for their money. In November 1939 a large transport of emigrants from Prague, the Altreich, and Vienna heading for illegal entry into Palestine assembled in Vienna, left for Bratislava, and from there on a Yugoslav ship for their voyage down river to the Black Sea.[14] The Yugoslav ships usually anchored near the berths of the DDSG (*Donaudampfschiffahrtsgesellschaft*, Danube Steamship Company) ships, and in this way the DDSG found out about this particular transport. Obviously, the Yugoslavs were going to earn a pretty penny, money that Director Schöpf of the DDSG felt should go to his company; and all of a sudden he waxed patriotic: he "complained that foreign ships are being used to transport Jews from Germany" and threatened to file a complaint with the proper authorities. He also wanted to know whether he could expect that Viennese Jews would be shipped out in the near future. Rolf Günther was not very sympathetic since, as he writes, in recent times the DDSG had refused to supply ships for transporting Jews, evidently in a display of the sort of super-anti-Semitism the Austrians displayed after the Anschluss. Obviously, they themselves were to blame if they lost out on this lucrative deal.[15] Nonetheless, in time, given the failures experienced with Yugoslavian and Slovakian ships that were hired by persons other than Storfer, it would be ships of the DDSG that would successfully complete the river voyage leg of the Palestine transports.

The great difficulties connected with bringing the Palestine transports to fruition is the subject of the first section of this chapter ("Palestine Transports"). Two other sections ("Groups and Routes via the Far East" and "Groups via Spain and Portugal") will deal with the efforts of routing emigrants to other destinations. Finally, the United States of America, the most desirable destination, presented difficulties in addition to the problem of routing and will be discussed in a fourth section ("Destination: USA").

Palestine Transports

Emigration to Palestine required a special and major effort in the months from September 1939 to the end of 1940. This does not mean that a major number of Viennese Jews was involved, as can be seen from the following statistic:

Year	Month	Number of Persons to Palestine	Total Number of Emigrants (for comparison)
1939	September	151	1,157
	October	347	3,390
	November	1,300	4,601
	December	809	2,087
1940	January	22	1,030
	February	11	965
	March	61	1,135
	April	37	820
	May	20	631
	June	0	59
	July	0	165
	August	0	133
	September	897	1,036
	October	0	108
	November	15	198
	December	0	216

We see that the major number of emigrants for Palestine left in the last few weeks of 1939 and in September 1940. However, it is one thing to emigrate, another to immigrate. Thus, the lower numbers and lulls in no way reflect a lull in activity on the part of those who were involved in the arrangements for emigration to Palestine. It took a lot of work to organize a transport and after the participants had emigrated—that is, passed the borders of Nazi Germany—it took even more work to dispatch them to the coast and thence to the shores of Palestine. What were the various pressures, dangers, obstacles, and manipulations that made up the substance of this effort?

Difficulties of Emigrating to Palestine

With the beginning of the war and Great Britain's entry into it, legal immigration into Palestine, meager as it had been, became highly problematic, since Palestine was a British mandate and there was no contact between the warring parties. In the months between the outbreak of the war and Italy's entry, it became increasingly clear that Italy would not make its ships or ports available for Palestine transports. And so, beginning in the fall of 1939, there were sporadic attempts at chartering ships for larger groups, which were to carry motley bands of Jews down the Danube River to the Black Sea and from there, it was hoped, into the Mediterranean Sea for a landing—in the case of an illegal transport, a secret landing—on Palestinian shores. Some of these transports were illegal and were part of the wave of illegal immigration into Palestine at that time, known then and in history as *Aliyah Bet* (*Aliyah* = "ascent," as immigration to the Land of Israel is called; *Bet* = B); and some were not illegal. For the latter, certificates of immigration were obtained from the Jewish Agency for Israel (founded in 1929) according to the British schedule of allotments of ten thousand annually then still in effect in accordance with Great Britain's White Paper of 1939. But, of course, neither the British authorities nor the Jewish Agency could be represented when Britain and Germany were at war.

Vienna is strategically located on that part of the Danube that is deep enough for larger river ships and is, therefore, the homeport of the Danube Steamship Company (DDSG), that had been established when most of the navigable Danube was within the Habsburg Empire. Vienna was also the terminus of other shipping lines. It became, therefore, the place from which not only the Viennese Jews but also those from the Altreich and the Protectorate of Bohemia and Moravia would come to start their journeys downriver. However, at the beginning of the war it was thought that the journey from Vienna by the DDSG would take them only the 40 miles (about 65 km) downriver to Bratislava, the capital of Slovakia. This small province had recently become an independent state for the first time in history, as a result of the dismemberment of Czechoslovakia in March 1939. From there the voyage to the coast would have to be arranged with other carriers. We will see that a lot of problems resulted from this, and a great part of the solution hinged on the DDSG becoming the carrier for the journey downriver.

The question of emigration to Palestine was broached at the first *Vorsprache* (meeting) after the war started, when Rolf Günther warned Löwenherz that the emigration effort must continue under the new conditions and be completed by the spring of 1940. Löwenherz reported that he did not see any way to continue emigration to Palestine under the given circumstances.[16] However, one week later this was a major topic when Löwenherz and Rothenberg reported to Eichmann. This was the time when Eichmann expressed concern over reports that Jews from Germany were joining the British forces, and Löwenherz assured him of the loyalty of the Jews.[17] Regardless of why Eichmann raised the subject with Löwenherz, he told Löwenherz that the Palestine transports were to continue, but the means of financing them would have to come from abroad. Rothenberg, who had been exploring different possibilities, reported that he received promises from Geneva (whether from the World Jewish Congress or the Jewish Agency is not clear) that ships would be made available at the cost of $60.00 per person.[18] No doubt this refers to oceangoing ships that would take the emigrants from a Black Sea or an Aegean port to the shores of Palestine. The reference to the Geneva agency indicates the complicated international network of different agencies and of both positive and negative interests that came into play, often at cross purposes, in the bewildering effort to realize these transports: the aid organizations, the Zionist activists (whose agenda it was to bring the right kind of illegal immigrants to Palestine), the shipping companies, the tourist and travel agencies, the providers of moneys, the holders of purse strings, the profiteers, the governmental agencies, and the bureaucrats.

The planning of the Palestine transports began in the fall of 1939, shortly before the outbreak of war. In August 1939 Edelstein, possibly at the behest of the Jewish Agency, was trying to organize a transport to Palestine for his *halutzim* ("pioneers" from the left-wing Zionist movement). A Mr. Gruenberg, an agent of the Jewish Agency, came to Vienna to obtain Eichmann's permission to go to Prague "to participate in organizing the [Prague] transports." Eichmann permitted him to go to Prague with Storfer and also to travel there "repeatedly . . . provided it is not too often."[19] This was a few days before the Twenty-First Zionist Congress, scheduled to take place in Geneva, Switzerland, from August 16 to 26, 1939. From Vienna, Löwenherz and Rothenberg were permitted to attend the congress. Edelstein and nine other delegates came from Prague.[20] A meeting of the Jewish Agency was to take place after the congress, which Storfer was given permission to attend.[21] All this may have given the Jewish Agency as well as Edelstein the impression that Storfer was authorized to be at their service in their effort to arrange for transports of Zionist pioneers to Palestine. Nothing was further from Eichmann's mind; just the opposite: It was the Jewish Agency that was to facilitate the Nazi effort to rid Greater Germany of its Jews. And, of course, Storfer expected nothing other than that any outside agency would place itself at the disposal of those who, like himself, were engaged in helping their fellow captive Jews escape.

In Vienna three agencies were involved in making the transports possible. While there was a clear division of tasks, their efforts required close coordination. First, the men in charge of the Palamt, as sub rosa agents of the Jewish Agency, would negotiate for the provision of emigration certificates for legitimate entry into Palestine; they were also in charge of the *hakhshara* (training) programs, in this way providing a cadre of trained young participants in the transports. Second, it was Storfer's responsibility to make the arrangements for all aspects of moving the legal as well as the illegal transports from Vienna to their destination, including negotiations, on-site inspections, and drawing up contracts. Finally, the IKG had the responsibility for keeping the emigration effort alive and to make the necessary means available.

The stage was set for the first wartime Palestine transports of emigrants from Vienna, Prague, and the Altreich, which had been planned since shortly before the war. Storfer was in the process of making the arrangements, when Löwenherz was summoned to Rolf Günther and told to send Storfer, Murmelstein, and two others to Mährisch-Ostrau (Moravian Ostrava); it was the beginning of the Nisko venture. One of the two others was Dr. Grün, the second in charge at the Palamt. That meant that Dr. Rothenberg, the director of the Palamt, was to remain in Vienna. Puzzled, Löwenherz asked whether the Palestine transport that Storfer had arranged could proceed. It seems Günther was not prepared for this question and peremptorily said "that this is not the case at this time, but that I [Löwenherz] am authorized to include in the list [of Nisko participants] able-bodied men who have been accepted [in the Palestine transport]." For good measure Günther said that the Bolivia transport arranged by the Jewish sports club "Maccabi" was now also "out of the question" and that those slated for it could also be included in the Nisko list.[22]

It was for good reason that Löwenherz had requested that Murmelstein be left in Vienna; he was, after all, the essential organizer of the IKG emigration effort and indispensable at a time when under wartime conditions new ways had to be found of bringing the emigration effort to fruition. And yet, even in Murmelstein's and Storfer's absence, even though burdened with the ominous developments of the Poland transports, and even in the face of Günther's officious discouragement, it is evident that Löwenherz continued his effort on behalf of the projected Palestine transport. Two days after reporting to Günther, he received a telephone call from Troper at his new location in Amsterdam. After Troper informed him of the Joint's readiness to continue its contribution of *Devisen*, Löwenherz broached the question of the Palestine transports. Troper told him that Joint headquarters in New York refused to underwrite the Aliyah Bet. Löwenherz responded with the assurance that the Joint would have nothing to do with Aliyah Bet. Instead, the scheme would be for Vienna to "send individual [small] groups ahead, and then inform him [Troper] as to the respective disbursements of required funds." The meaning is clear: The transports would not appear to have been organized in Vienna. The participants would travel to nearby Slovakia in small groups and assemble there for the transport. While there, their upkeep would be subsidized by the Joint. The cost of the transport, though assembled and in part arranged by Storfer, who was headquartered in Vienna, would be met with funds made available outside of Nazi Germany. While the Joint would not be the provenance of these funds, they would help secure them. For this reason Löwenherz asked Troper to intercede with the British Council for German Jewry to disburse the £29,000 still owed to the IKG Vienna.[23]

The plan of sending the participants out of the country before arrangements were made regarding their transportation to the coast and from there to Palestine was very risky and not in keeping with Löwenherz's or Storfer's usually cautious ways of making sure all necessary prearrangements were in place. It indicates the pressure exerted by Eichmann's increasingly urgent demand to resume emigration and by the initiation of the resettlement to Poland. Sending the people ahead poorly prepared would contribute to the impending difficulties.

When the first Nisko transport had left and the second one was being readied, Löwenherz "asked" (*bat*) Brunner 1 to make it possible for the 800 young people at the *hakhshara* camps who were slated for the Palestine transports to leave. The cost of $35,000 would be met by means of *Devisen* made available by aid organizations abroad. Löwenherz also requested that the organization remain in the hands of Storfer's office without the interference of travel bureaus. Brunner 1 assured Löwenherz that travel bureaus were not authorized to arrange special transports to Palestine.[24] By the time he reported to Eichmann a few days later, Löwenherz had increased the number of *hakhshara* participants to bring the number of the upcoming transport to 1,000 participants. Eichmann said that only 500 to 600 were permitted to go; the rest would have to go to Poland where able-bodied and well-trained young people were needed.[25] The next day Brunner 1 reiterated this restriction and also informed Löwenherz that all except three *hakhshara* camps were to be dissolved.[26] Both Eichmann and Brunner 1 knew at that time—but did not disclose—that there would be no more Nisko transports. Thus, when, after their return from Nisko, Murmelstein and Grün reported to Rolf Günther together with Löwenherz and Rothenberg, they were told that the Palestine transport may go ahead and—we are not surprised—the number of participants was to be augmented.[27] Another foursome dealing with emigration, this time with Storfer instead of Grün, was told again, and not for the last time, that the participants would have to leave Vienna in small groups and take ship "in Pressburg" (Bratislava). The *Aktennotiz*, which was the official record to be sent to Berlin, had to be corrected to say take ship "outside the country." This shows the sensitive nature of Eichmann's dealings with transports to Palestine, which was enemy territory, while at the same time he was frantically trying to motivate whatever emigration would still be possible.[28]

Before long, Löwenherz had to report to Eichmann that the Joint had declined to broker the disbursement of the remaining allotment of pounds by the British Council for German Jewry. Since this spelled difficulties for the Palestine transport, Löwenherz would use his upcoming meeting with Troper in Amsterdam to ask the Dutch aid organization to make the arrangements.[29] However, Löwenherz managed to "overcome great difficulties" in getting the Joint to agree to providing the *Devisen* needed for the Palestine transports to be organized by Storfer's office.[30]

Löwenherz now found out that, in spite of Brunner's assurance that travel agencies were not authorized to arrange special transports to Palestine, the Viennese branch of the Hanseatic Travel Bureau—in other words, the notorious Herr Schlie—was doing precisely that, charging RM 1,200 per person. How did Löwenherz find out? He was told by the IKG officials who were assigned to the *Zentralstelle* that passports for persons who had signed up for the transport had been presented to the authorities for the *Sichtvermerk*, the entry that was the final authorization for leaving Germany. Among the persons slated for the transport were children ages two and older and very old persons (*Greise*) up to age 93. Reporting this matter to Eichmann, Löwenherz expressed his doubts that Hanseatic had access to the *Devisen* needed to carry the transport through. Moreover, Löwenherz felt "constrained to point out that a transport of persons not carefully selected, even if it succeeded in landing, would endanger future transports because Palestine clearly values the immigration of the kind of able-bodied people needed for developing the country." Löwenherz recorded that Eichmann "thought that this transport too was organized under Storfer's supervision," a clear admission that, contrary to Brunner's assurances, he had known about this. And Löwenherz was able to respond by saying that Storfer, with whom he had already spoken, had nothing to do with this particular transport.[31]

This situation does not come as a surprise, inasmuch as we have learned on several occasions that Eichmann had had contact with travel agencies, and especially with Schlie, who had ideas about emigration schemes that were more lucrative (to them and, therefore, to Eichmann) than practicable. Eichmann evidently needed to be reminded of this every so often, especially at a time when he was again anxiously trying to motivate an increase in emigration. Of course, the travel agencies had recourse to another venue: the Gestapo. While Löwenherz was in Amsterdam for his first wartime meeting with Troper, Murmelstein was summoned to the Gestapo and ordered to have the IKG release RM 30,000 to clear 330 Jews from Burgenland for the transport arranged by Herr Schlie of Hanseatic. Murmelstein replied that "the IKG is certainly prepared to support any transport that would help the emigration of Jews by faith (*Glaubensjuden*)." However, in this case, "since the question of *Devisen* is not clarified, the realization of this transport is, in the opinion of the IKG, not sufficiently assured." In any case, the matter had to go through the *Zentral-*

stelle, and Brunner informed the Gestapo that the IKG could not release the money without authorization.[32]

Some clarity was gained when Löwenherz reported to Eichmann in Berlin on his way back from meeting with Troper.[33] First, Löwenherz was able to report that the laborious gathering in Slovakia of 800 participants in the Palestine transport had been completed. Second, arrangements for another transport of 500 to 600 was "about to be completed."

Still another transport of 800 to 1,000 was being planned, for which *Devisen* in the amount of $55,000 were already reserved. Löwenherz indicated that there would be many difficulties to overcome in connection with the organization of the transport. For example, certain groups of people whom the authorities required to be included in this transport had to be held at readiness; both of these groups were composed of indigent people. One group consisted of the residents of Gänsbacher Street, a temporary shelter for those who had to give up all their assets when they reported to what was to have been the third Nisko transport, the other were those released from the concentration camps Dachau and Buchenwald. Löwenherz asked for the release of RM 300,000 to defray these and other costs that the IKG was about to incur for Storfer's organization of the transport. We know from the previous chapter the extent to which Eichmann used the delay in dispatching this transport to tighten the financial stranglehold by withholding reimbursement of the money spent. We also recall that the inclusion of concentration camp releasees and some of the Gänsbacher residents was not only required by the Nazis but, considering the special constraint these people were in, it accorded with the IKG's obligation to get these people out any way and as quickly as they could. However, these people were hardly the kind of young pioneers the Jewish Agency wanted; this too would contribute to the coming troubles.

With respect to the transport arranged by Hanseatic Travel Bureau, Eichmann assured Löwenherz that he had ordered the *Zentralstelle* not to issue *Sichtvermerke* to the participants "until there is proof of their visa for the final destination [*End-Visum*]" and that the go-ahead would not be issued until "the ship owner Nikolopoulos deposits in escrow 17,500 pounds outside of the country [Germany] and to the order of Hanseatic Travel Bureau as guarantee of the trouble-free completion of the transport and its landing in Palestine."[34] We do not know whether Mr. Nikolopoulos or anyone would take such a risk, much less whether Eichmann's statement to Löwenherz was meant merely for effect. Eichmann's assurance about the *Sichtvermerke* is very, very curious: He gave it on December 17, 1939, well over two weeks after the participants of the Hanseatic transport had left Vienna for Pressburg (Bratislava). The fact that the unreasonable demand made by Hanseatic could not be met, and that for this reason the people were given *Sichtvermerke* by the *Zentralstelle* and sent to Pressburg without an assured final destination, explains the sorry fate of that transport.

For Storfer, the work on the transports that he was organizing was just beginning, as was the odyssey for their participants—work and odyssey that would stretch over the next year.

At the end of 1939 there were two illegal transport groups headed for Palestine: Most members of the first group left Vienna for Pressburg in November. Most of the second group left Vienna at the beginning of December. Both groups were joined in Pressburg by relatively small contingents from the Altreich, from Danzig (now Polish: Gdansk) and from the Protectorate. The first group was arranged by Storfer on short notice after he returned from Nisko, in the expectation that he would be able eventually to arrange for maritime transportation to Palestine. In the meantime, the group was stuck in Pressburg.

The second group consisted of about 800 people from Vienna and smaller contingents from other areas. The transport of this group was arranged by the Hanseatic Travel Bureau, initiated by the action of the Jewish Agency with the consent of the Gestapo and, apparently, with Eichmann's encouragement. Having been initiated and carried out without the IKG's and Storfer's involvement, the arrangements for this transport lacked his attention to detail as well as his planning and foresight, and it was in trouble from beginning to end. Like the first group, it assembled in Pressburg, to the consternation of the Slovak authorities. Initially the transport was meant to consist of young Zionist pioneers, mainly the Youth Aliyah teenagers from the *hakhshara* camps of *Mizrachi* and *Hashomer Hatzair*, as well as older members of *Hechalutz*; but, as we have seen, the *Zentralstelle* insisted that children and older people were included.

One of the pioneers was Susanne (Susi) Melzer, at that time 19 years old, and a leader in the Vienna *Mizrachi* movement.

The Vienna contingent left about December 1, 1939. While they waited in Pressburg, they were joined by the Berlin, Danzig, and Prague contingents; altogether the group now consisted of about 1,100 people. When the Slovak authorities threatened to send them all back across the border, the backers of the transport were able to provide a ship of the DDSG. Right away the fatal flaw of the amateurish arrangements by the Hanseatic Travel Bureau made itself felt. The ship was an excursion ship, which for decades had plied the Danube through the Balkan lands with happy vacationers and honeymooners. But now the ship was overloaded with refugees. So, when after a few miles the ship arrived at the Hungarian border, the authorities soon saw that the passengers had no guaranteed destination and sent the ship back. Even if the passage down river could succeed, the DDSG now realized the risk of being stuck with the passengers. The captain discharged the group at Pressburg, and the ship returned to its homeport in Vienna. But now, the Central Association of the Jewish Communities of Yugoslavia was able to arrange for three small Yugoslav Danube steamers, *King Nicola*, *King Dushan*, and *Queen Maria*, to pick up the group. This got the group through Hungary and into Yugoslavia, where they were stuck.

Pressburg is an old city guarding, since Roman times, the approaches to the Carpathian Mountain Range where the Danube, flowing from the west, bends southward toward the Hungarian plain. The Danube bend of about 15 miles (25 km) is the extent of the river within Slovakia. Glad to have escaped Nazi Germany, the 800 participants in the first transport were waiting in Pressburg for the arrangements of their journey downriver and on to Palestine to be completed. But the affair ran into difficulties. The Slovak ship, on which they were to sail, proved not to be river-worthy, fortunately before they were to embark. While waiting, the participants soon finished whatever food they had brought along and also ran out of the small amount of money they had been permitted to take along. After New Year's Day 1940, Dr. Rothenberg, the director of the Palamt, went to Pressburg to see whether he could straighten out the various problems. When he reported to Eichmann in Berlin, he requested that another official of the Palamt, Dr. Alois Rottenstreich, be sent to Pressburg to supervise the group for two to three weeks, or until they could embark on their river journey. In the meantime, Rothenberg and Storfer would also go to Pressburg to finalize the arrangements with Čedok, the Czechoslovak travel agency. Rottenstreich was to be in charge of the Austrian participants only, and not of the Hungarians who had joined the transport.[35]

As it turned out, none of the arrangements could be finalized; the situation turned into a nightmarish muddle of competing agencies and carriers, and of organizations in various countries working at cross-purposes in their desire to help. And Storfer, instead of being in charge, found himself in the middle of that chaos, the recipient of pressures from all sides. By March 1940 it was Edelstein in particular who, on behalf of his particular interests in expediting his *halutzim* and deeming himself the one who represented the Jewish Agency, had begun to interfere with the arrangements being developed. This interference would reach crisis proportions in the weeks to follow. In light of the fate of the emigrants stuck in Pressburg and those in Yugoslavia, and anticipating the resumption of movement in the spring, it was time to bring some order into the Palestine emigration scheme. Evidently at the urging of Murmelstein and Storfer, Eichmann had the principals report to Berlin in March to bring order into the arrangements. Murmelstein, who drafted the *Aktennotiz*, significantly lists Edelstein first among those who reported to Eichmann in the presence of his deputy Rolf Günther and of Dannecker as the one in charge of the Berlin *Zentralstelle*. The other Jewish functionaries reporting were, besides Storfer, three from Berlin: Otto Hirsch, Eppstein, and Lyon.[36]

Eichmann declared that all proposals for Palestine transports from the Altreich, the Protectorate, or Austria, whether submitted by "organizations"—meaning the Jewish Agency as represented by their agents in neutral Switzerland—or by travel bureaus, whether received by German officials or by Jewish offices, would have to be transmitted to Storfer. Storfer would have to examine such proposals for feasibility and submit a preliminary report to Eichmann. Upon his approval, the "required negotiations and preparations must begin" and be reported to Eichmann. No transport would be allowed to be dispatched except upon approval by Eichmann, which would be contingent on proven arrangements for ships downriver from the seaport and from there to the destination, for all necessary transit visas, and for landing in Palestine. "What counts is that all technical difficulties that could arise in carrying out the transports be prevented, if possible, and that a uniform way of handling the matter be achieved for the Altreich, the Ostmark, and the Protectorate."[37]

Eichmann also wished "that an explicit declaration by a Jewish organization in a neutral country be submitted [to him], to the effect that it would guarantee its assistance with the landing [of the transports in Palestine]. Such declaration is not to be a general one, but is to be issued specifically for each transport."[38] Murmelstein pointed out the insuperable difficulty of Jewish organizations in Greater Germany making contact with Jewish agents in Palestine, even by way of neutral countries, a point reiterated by Löwenherz and Storfer when they reported to Eichmann in Vienna three days later.[39] This consideration was decisive in bringing the interference to an end a few weeks later.

Three days later, Eichmann again told Löwenherz, Murmelstein, and Storfer in Vienna that Storfer was the one responsible for the organization of all transports to Palestine. He would have to examine and, with Eichmann's approval, decide on all proposals submitted by travel agencies and negotiate with shipping companies, ship owners, and other relevant carriers. And Eichmann would not pass on any proposals submitted to him without their prior examination by Storfer.[40] At the same time Löwenherz was able to report that the remaining £13,800 from the British aid organization, the disbursement of which he had sought in Amsterdam three months earlier, were about to be transferred via the Service de Transmigration du Comité d'Assistance aux Réfugiés Juifs in Brussels—just in the nick of time, since a few weeks later Belgium and the Netherlands would be invaded and overrun by Nazi Germany.[41]

Was everything now in place for the emigrants stuck in Pressburg to be sent on their way? Not at all. Indeed, the matter reached crisis proportions, while Storfer traveled to and fro, telegraphed and telephoned here and there, all the while reporting to the IKG and enlisting their assistance and cooperation.

April 22 found Storfer in Pressburg. The next day he reported in person and in writing about the visit. Slovak officials "are furious and threaten to send our emigrants back to the German border unless we send them on by the end of the month." Storfer was taken to the police, who wanted him personally to see the plight and the despair of the emigrants at the camp where they were held. But first he was escorted to the Interior Ministry, where he was questioned for three hours and had to sign a statement, explaining the money transfers and contracts connected with the transport arrangements. The Interior Ministry then decided that either the emigrants would be dispatched by the end of the month or they would be subject to drastic measures. Because of the delay at the Interior Ministry, Storfer asked to be excused from the visit to the camp, and the police relented.

Before returning to Vienna, he met with the representatives of the Jewish organizations in Pressburg, who were aware of the full extent of the Interior Ministry's recalcitrance: They would not permit any funds, even of external provenance, to be used for any relief work other than for domestic Slovakian Jews. There was just enough money from local charitable contributions to feed the stranded emigrants for two more days at most. Even if one could get a permit for a transfer by means of a bribe (i.e., by allocating part of the possible proceeds for non-Jewish relief work), there would—after the Joint's loan of 200,000 Slovak koruna (crowns) for the upkeep of the emigrants was paid up—be just enough money left to feed the emigrants until the end of the month, that is, for one more week. The daily outlay was 12,000 crowns. If Storfer could come up with the money to continue provisioning the stranded travelers, then the authorities might permit them to remain until they were able to continue the journey. Storfer asked, "Where am I going to take the crowns from? Not to mention that a daily expense of 12,000 crowns would be a disaster for us." The Jewish representatives were desperate; they wanted to help but saw no way out. Storfer related one incident that illustrates this desperation: "Frau Fleischmann clung to me like a drowning person, and simply did not want to let me go."[42]

The other transport was also in trouble, not the one arranged by Storfer but by the Hanseatic Travel Bureau on behalf of the Jewish Agency with the approval of the Gestapo (and since Hanseatic was involved, no doubt also with the collusion of Eichmann). Shortly after New Year's Day 1940, the news reached Vienna that the transport of around 1,000 people, most of them the Vienna contingent that had left in December, was stuck in Yugoslavia near the Romanian border. In order for Storfer to go there to straighten things out, he needed a visa that the consulate refused to issue. The IKG sent a telegram to Savez Jevrejskin Veroispovednin Opština (the Association of Jewish Communities in the Kingdom of Yugoslavia) in Belgrade, asking them to arrange with the authorities for a consular transit visa for Storfer, valid for ten days. In their delayed response, the president and general secretary of the organization informed the IKG that the authorities would not permit transit travel by train for anyone as long as the transport was stuck in Yugoslavia. And, considering that the Danube was iced over, this state of affairs was expected to last for the rest of the winter.

What had happened? The transport had attempted to make the journey to the Black Sea coast before the severest winter freeze. As we know, when, for good reason, the DDSG refused to transport the group, they were sent on Yugoslavian river ships. The Yugoslavian ships had already passed safely through Slovakia, Hungary, and Yugoslavia. Starting about fifty miles downstream from Belgrade, the Danube formed the border between Yugoslavia and Romania, until it begins its easterly flow and constitutes the border between Romania and Bulgaria. This was the official point of entry into Romanian territory, and here the transport was stopped. Why? The arrangements for this voyage had not been made by Storfer and, lacking his thoroughness and expertise, they were flawed. Storfer would not have sent the group out prior to the assured availability of an ocean liner. For this group the Jewish Agency was supposed to arrange for such a ship, which they did not do. Thus, when the three Yugoslav ships arrived at the Romanian border, the same thing happened as when the DDSG ship tried to enter Hungary: The Romanian authorities refused to let the passengers transit Romania in the absence of prior arrangements for their transfer to an ocean vessel. The ships turned back to the nearest Yugoslav river port, namely, Kladovo. The Yugoslavia/Romania stretch of the river was very difficult to navigate. Most major obstacles were removed at the end of the nineteenth century, but many remained. Kladovo lies near the notorious narrows known as the Iron Gates. At the narrows, the river is deep and swift. At Kladovo the river is broad, its waters are shallow, and it gets iced over in winter. The ships could not proceed. The passengers of the Palestine transport had to live on the three small, unheated ships, and the ships were iced in for the winter in Kladovo.

The Association of Yugoslav Communities did not have the necessary means to take care of the stranded travelers. With the rental of the ships and the food and incidentals for over 1,000 persons, the daily expenses amounted to the equivalent of US $1,300. The president of the Association of Yugoslav Communities wrote, "In consideration of the given facts, all interested parties must combine their means to create the possibilities for moving the transport from here, and thereby clear the way for other transports," for until this transport would be sent on its way, the Yugoslav authorities would not permit the transit of any other. All the Association was able to do to alleviate the situation was to arrange for the thousand plus people to be taken from the "winter mooring" to the nearest railway station, which was 30 miles away, "as soon as the ice conditions permit" and then to send them on to an Adriatic port.

Jewish refugees from the Kladovo transport in a makeshift kitchen on board one of the vessels in Kladovo harbor. (United States Holocaust Memorial Museum, courtesy of Ehud Nahir. USHMM 32972)

Until then the emigrants would be stuck in suffocatingly close quarters, amidst the accumulating filth, on three small, unheated ships that were frozen at their winter mooring. After a few weeks the passengers were permitted to stretch their legs and walk on land for brief periods. As soon as the river thawed sufficiently for the ships to move, the shipping company discharged the refugees and retook possession of the ships. The emigrants were then distributed, some in town, some in barracks, and some in a tent camp. Being in the vicinity of malaria-infested bogs, undernourished and plagued by vermin and filth, many took sick, especially with skin diseases; there were even some cases of typhoid fever and polio.[43]

The offer to send the emigrants to an Adriatic port was useless, even if well meant. The destination that was needed was not an Adriatic port but a Black Sea or an Aegean one. This meant that Storfer would have to negotiate with Romanian and not with Yugoslavian authorities. In Yugoslavia he would have to be granted permission to have the transients stay until he could obtain permission for them to travel through Romania and remain there until they could actually set sail. In this baffling bureaucratic stalemate, the only way the Association of Yugoslav Communities could manage to have Storfer come to Belgrade "for one or two days" was for him to obtain a visa to Romania, and with it obtain a transfer visa through Yugoslavia.[44]

But it never came to that. By late April the ships were still iced in their winter harbor, and Storfer was faced with straightening this mess out at the same time as he had to handle the matter of the group stuck in Pressburg, as well as dispatching the next group transport that was to include the Gänsbacher Street inmates and those released from concentration camp.

The mess of those two stuck transports is madly complicated, and we can merely try to untangle some of the main factors and actors.

Transports in Limbo

Foremost was the constant Nazi pressure to get the Jews out quickly and cheaply. At the IKG Löwenherz was challenged to keep the emigration efforts going under the changing wartime conditions and to maintain and even increase the allocation of *Devisen* from the Joint. The Joint was not prepared to have the *Devisen* be used for any emigration schemes to Palestine, especially illegal ones. Löwenherz had to find ways of financing these transports that would not run counter to the Joint's strictures. Permits to enter Palestine legally, under the restricted schedule of the White Paper of March 1939, were seldom granted, and when Löwenherz in Amsterdam and Murmelstein in Budapest met with the Joint representatives, they also tried to obtain such permits through contacts with representatives of the Jewish Agency.

But now we have to come back to Edelstein. We related in chapter 7 that Murmelstein saved Edelstein from having to remain in the Nisko camp by telling Eichmann that in Edelstein's absence the assignment of immigration certificates to Palestine by the Jewish Agency would suffer.[45] In order to obtain such certificates, Eichmann called Edelstein to Vienna early in February 1940, and from there sent him to Geneva to meet with representatives of the Jewish Agency, the most prominent of whom was Moshe Shertok,[46] who had stopped in Geneva on his way from Palestine to London. It was the time after the transport of emigrants to Palestine got mired in Pressburg. The group included some 200 young *halutzim* whom Edelstein had sent from the Protectorate.

No doubt as frustrated over this unfortunate snag as were the men in Vienna who had arranged the transport, Edelstein tried to advance his own agenda for a trouble-free emigration to Palestine. There seemed to have been several elements to this.[47] First, most likely thinking to improve his position by discrediting the men in Vienna, he reported to the Jewish Agency that unlike them, those leaders in Prague who were Zionists had enough backbone to stand up to the Nazis, and for this reason the people there did not suffer the "ill treatment" that in Vienna had "reached insufferable proportions." According to Shertok, Edelstein said:

> The Zionists' rise in power and prestige has put [us] in a position to assume leadership of the [Protectorate] community, and the Zionist officials have become the focus of recovery, of mutual assistance efforts and self-help, of finding a way out and a shield against despair.[48]

Regrettably, this was patently inaccurate; and the persons whom Edelstein met in Geneva were surely aware of it, that is, not only Nahum Goldmann, who was President of the World Jewish Congress at the time, but even Shertok. For the men in Vienna—Löwenherz, Rothenberg, and even Murmelstein—were also Zionists, though their agenda was to save Jews by emigration no matter what the destination, and no matter what their age.

Edelstein also painted a dark picture of his experiences in Nisko, stressing the details of the torment to which the Germans subjected him and the other Jewish functionaries, "the humiliating wiles, the physical torture, the blows and injuries." Perhaps in light of this, Edelstein's interlocutors reached the conclusion that the situation of the Jews at large was hopeless, and out of loyalty to their fellow Zionist leaders they were motivated to save at least them and their families. Again we quote from Shertok's journal:

> Should all hope be lost, and there will be no way to save the Jews in enemy countries, we will demand that the government give us a limited number of permits for colleagues who have disregarded their own safety so that others could be rescued.[49]

In fact, while in Geneva, Edelstein secured certificates of entry into Palestine as well as entry visas to Switzerland for himself, Otto Zucker, and some of the other leading Zionists in the Protectorate, as well as for their families. Edelstein also asked for a certificate for František Weidmann—the young lawyer whom the Nazis installed as the director of the Jewish Community in Prague—for, in the words of Ruth Bondi, "though he was not a Zionist, his conduct was always irreproachable; if fate had forced them all together, it would be unfriendly and unfair to forget him."

This leads to another element of the agenda Edelstein was pursuing, namely, that the effort of emigration he meant to motivate was centered on a select group, young pioneers. Not only was Edelstein under pressure from the leadership of the *Hechalutz* movement in Prague to provide emigration for the *halutzim*, but it was in the interest of the Jewish Agency that no one who would add to the depressed labor market be sent to Palestine; only those who could be counted on to contribute to the development of the Jewish homeland would be welcome. This also accorded with the interest of the Mossad. The Mossad, working unofficially on behalf of the Jewish Agency, occasionally succeeded in organizing illegal transports to Palestine. Bondi describes the Mossad as "[not] really an institution [but] a handful of enterprising young men dedicated to their cause, operating without an orderly budget."[50]

In spite of this, and even though the performance of the Mossad had been disappointing, Edelstein, in desperate commitment to his agenda, entered into a gentlemen's agreement with the Mossad during his hectic two days in Geneva. The terms provided for the Mossad to arrange the safe transport to Palestine of 2,400 young Jews from the Protectorate, including some of those stranded in Slovakia, within the next few weeks; the arrangements were to include shipping down the river to the coast as well as by oceangoing vessels to Palestine, transit visas, and orderly debarkation. In return, Edelstein committed himself and his associates in Prague: First, to provide £23 per person (that is £55,200 for 2,400 persons!); second, not to enter into negotiations with alternative organizations and to let them know of all other projected transport schemes; third, not to agree to any other transport scheme without the Mossad's approval.[51]

Did Edelstein now have control over a going concern of transporting select *halutzim* to Palestine? Aside from the fact that he had no access to even a fraction of the exorbitant sum of £55,200, the Mossad was in no position to arrange for the emigration of captive Jews from Nazi territory, to hire river ships from Vienna to the Black Sea, or to obtain transit visas for the participants; but it would be a while before Edelstein would fully realize that. It was the men sitting in the Danube city of Vienna, who had the capacity and knowhow to be in charge of such schemes, and it was on them that Edelstein and those who were backing him would have to depend for the time being. Thanks to Edelstein's independent machinations, Eichmann confirmed, as we know, that transports schemes had to be arranged or at least reviewed by Storfer.

It would soon become clear that the Mossad could not deliver, and in that respect the substantive points of Edelstein's agreement with them were for naught. It was at this time that Edelstein called for a two-day consultation in Prague with Löwenherz to take place on April 14 and 15.[52] We do not know what the agenda was; but the conjecture is not far-fetched that he would propose to tie in with Storfer's efforts what, thanks to the Mossad, he had failed to achieve on his own. When Murmelstein reported to Brunner 1 in Löwenherz's stead, he was told that Löwenherz was not to travel to Prague, since the consultation could not take place.[53] It seems that Edelstein thereupon motivated the Mossad agents to take over the task of getting the Prague *halutzim* to Palestine. The Mossad people did so in short order and with a vengeance. Folk wisdom tells us that cuckoos lay their eggs in the nests of other birds. There the cuckoo offspring, growing larger than its host-siblings, soon push these from the nest, to wind up as the sole survivors. Something like this was about to be attempted.

One point of the agreement with the Mossad was still functional, and when it came into play it caused gratuitous trouble for Storfer, when the situation with the stuck transports reached crisis stage. The point at issue was that Edelstein was not to agree to any transport schemes without the approval of the Mossad. And, by implication, approval presupposed that the participants were properly selected Zionists, preferably young *halutzim*, and that the shipper would provide seaworthy ships and guarantee orderly landing in Palestine. The Mossad group did find a Turkish ship for the transport of a group of *Hechalutz* members; and, since the Nazi authorities insisted on Storfer's approval, the Mossad exerted considerable pressure on him. He finally gave in, even though he had no way of ascertaining the viability of the arrangement. In any case, he was told that the deal with the Turkish ship was assured.[54]

Believing the Prague *halutzim* to be taken care of, Storfer felt free to move the Pressburg people from their miserable internment and to prevent the Kladovo people from being summarily dispatched to the Adriatic. He did so by entering into a contract with the

Athens/Piraeus ship owner and leading member of the Greek national ship cartel, Socrates Avgherinos. No sooner was this done and it was time to arrange for payment from the pound account that was recently transferred from Brussels to Amsterdam, that Storfer again heard from the Mossad group, namely, from Mr. Kantor and Moshe Averbuch at their headquarters in neutral Geneva. Their deal with the Turkish ship had fallen through and, unable to make headway in providing for the emigration to Palestine of their people or of the hapless stranded emigrants, they found new ways of pressuring Storfer. They now insisted that the Prague *halutzim*, for whom they failed to arrange transportation, be given preference for places on the ship or ships contracted by Storfer; they also voiced great reservations about the qualification for immigration to Palestine on the part of the participants selected for the transports by Vienna.[55]

To make their demand stick, they first of all assigned Mr. Zameres (Shmarya Tsameret), the representative of the Mossad in Athens—residing at the Hotel Grand Bretagne—to inspect the arrangements made by Avgherinos under contract with Storfer. Second, without Storfer's knowledge, they had traveled to Amsterdam, where they were able to persuade the Joint not to authorize the Dutch Refugee Committee, who were holding the pounds on behalf of the Joint, to release the money until they received Zameres's signed approval of the transport project, that is of the arrangements made by Avgherinos.[56] In short, lacking the ability to arrange for transport, and based on the gentleman's agreement they had made with Edelstein, they pursued their own ends by using that agreement to hold Storfer's efforts at moving the stranded emigrants hostage. Interestingly enough, shortly before Kantor and Averbuch "surfaced" (*aufgetaucht*—Storfer's term) in Amsterdam, the Danzig community had transferred $30,000 and then another $10,000 in payment for the Danzig contingent in Storfer's transport; the sum was duly released for its purpose before it would also have been subject to the Kantor-Averbuch ambush. In Storfer's restrained words, these payments could be duly effected "when misleading persons do not interfere." Albeit, much earlier Danzig had transferred $6,000 "on account" to Averbuch, an amount which, as Storfer reported, Averbuch had not returned.[57]

Meeting Avgherinos in Piraeus, Zameres demanded to know the details of the arrangements he had made for Storfer and gave him to understand that he was not prepared to approve the scheme and recommend the release of the contracted funds until Avgherinos cooperated. Avgherinos now realized that he would not receive payment, which was then already past due, resulting in the loss of the availability of the ship in question. It was not certain that a substitute ship could be found; if it could, Avgherinos informed Storfer through his legal representative in Vienna, it would cost £5 more per person.[58]

Before leaving Pressburg, Storfer telegraphed Zameres that "in consideration of the consequences" he should recommend that Kantor release the payment to Avgherinos. He also called Rottenstreich in Vienna and told him to telephone Zameres and speak to him in a like vein. From his telephone conversation with Kantor, Storfer gained the impression that a telegram from Edelstein might put a brake on Kantor's "machinations." Evidently, he must have guessed that Edelstein and the Mossad group were in cahoots. Since Edelstein could not be reached while Storfer was in Pressburg, he planned to travel to Prague to speak with him personally.[59]

But there was another wrinkle to the plot.

Before leaving for Prague, Storfer received a telegram from Rottenstreich informing him that he had spoken with Zameres, who responded that Storfer should "urgently prevail upon Avgherinos" to give him the information he requested in accordance with his orders from the Mossad, "otherwise his signature is not attainable." Rottenstreich added that "if possible [Storfer should] telegraph Avgherinos because he threatened to break the contract." Storfer thought that Avgherinos could not be expected to share his business secrets with someone like Zameres; the reason being that Zameres was an agent of the Mossad, a group represented by Averbuch, who was known in Athens to be Avgherinos's "antagonist and competitor."[60] In other words, Zameres was hired to be the intermediary between Avgherinos and the Mossad in their attempt to gain control over the transport laboriously being organized by Storfer. Accordingly, Storfer right away wired Zameres that Avgherinos "refuses to release his business secrets. You can get all information from me. Telegraph at once what you want to know. I again point to the grave consequences of your interference."[61]

While this sad comedy of Jews obstructing Jews was going on, only slightly out of view of the Nazis, Storfer got a reminder he did not need, from the source of the paramount pressure: Brunner 1 told him "if we take our time, we shall soon experience the steps [that will be taken]." What steps would be taken did not need to be spelled out, inasmuch as Brunner 1 also informed Storfer that Eichmann was "in consternation last night" to learn that the transports were still stuck.[62]

A number of urgent problems hung in the balance: moving the Pressburg group downriver, moving the Kladovo people downriver, securing available ships that would pick them up at the Black Sea port, organizing other transports (including the Prague *halutzim*), and financing of all this. And the solution to all these problems depended on calling off the obstruction initiated by Kaplan-Averbuch-Zameres. There followed a flurry of activity to do just that. The first tactic was to meet the key players head-on—Edelstein, Kaplan, and Zameres. The second tactic was to maneuver around them and enlist the cooperation of Avgherinos and the Joint.

As for Zameres, Storfer had not received an answer from him to his telegram by the time he arrived in Prague. But there were several conversations with Kaplan. Rottenstreich, after a telephone call with Kaplan, received a telegram from him to the effect that Avgherinos should be told to give Zameres the information that he was charged to obtain for Kaplan. Kaplan then wired Rottenstreich Zameres's message that he was:

> INCAPABLE PERFORM JOINT-TASK PROJECT-INSPECTION BECAUSE OUR PARTNER [AVGHERINOS] REFUSES[63]

Well, the obstruction was now represented as the doing of the Joint! By return wire Rottenstreich told Kaplan that Avgherinos refused to divulge his business confidences to "third parties" and reiterated that the latter was ready to declare "us" (Storfer's office acting on behalf of the Vienna Palamt and IKG) in breach of contract. Rottenstreich did not mince his words. He told Kaplan that while he was prepared to give him information, the matter was of no concern to Zameres. The consequences would be catastrophic should Zameres continue to block payment to the ship owner with the *Devisen* Vienna acquired by means of the transfer to Warsaw. "This outrageous chicanery must cease!"[64]

But Kaplan was unmoved. In Prague, Storfer got Edelstein to speak earnestly with Kaplan for half an hour to no effect. Instead, Kaplan leveled two serious complaints against Storfer. First, he accused Storfer of having deserted him in the matter of the transport that got stuck in Kladovo. The Kladovo matter was not Storfer's fault; but by shifting the blame onto him, he was telling Storfer that the group behind Kaplan meant to save face and that the motive of rectifying the Kladovo situation was behind the maneuver of laying claim to the transport facilities that Storfer had arranged. Kaplan also claimed that Storfer's and his Vienna associates' selection of participants in the transports ignored the preferences by the people in Palestine. In other words, as far as they were concerned, the men in Vienna were there to fulfill the agenda of the Mossad, not that of saving as many Jews as they could, no matter who they were, no matter what their age. Kaplan also continued to insist on being informed of what ships were being hired and under what flag they were sailing. And, to drive his pressures home, he wished for a personal meeting with Storfer.[65]

Before we look at what came next, let us clarify what we have just recounted. Edelstein's independent initiative had proved to be vacuous. In fact, he was revealed as nothing but the instrument of forces he thought he had enlisted for his own agenda of settling Prague pioneers in Palestine. These forces did not have the means of enacting Edelstein's agenda. But, thanks to the information that Edelstein had given to them in fulfillment of their gentlemen's agreement, they used surprise tactics to try to avail themselves of the means organized by Storfer in order to use them for their own purposes. Edelstein's usefulness to them ended with his performance of his part of the bargain. To be sure, from their standpoint, the intentions of these feisty fighters for the future Zionist state were good, and we cannot but admire them for their sense of enterprise. But, sadly, engaged as these men were in their own agenda, they had no inkling of what was incumbent on them: The duress under which the Jews of Nazi Europe found themselves and under which the leaders and agents of these Jews had to make choices, required that those outside place themselves at their disposal, and not the other way around. Only a few of the persons in the forefront of assistance efforts had learned this, mainly Troper and Schwartz of the Joint, as well as Bentwich of London. Instead, unknowingly, the Mossad representatives used the Jews in their misfortune as a resource. Yehuda Slutsky, the Israeli historian, surely overstated things when he claimed that "[d]uring the war years, [the Mossad's effort] became an operation for rescuing Jews from extermination."[66] How well this was borne out with regard to the Kladovo group remains to be seen.

For Storfer and his associates it was time for the second tactic.

First Avgherinos had to be pacified and dissuaded from considering the contract breached. While still in Prague, Storfer called him. Avgherinos was angry. He did not want to have anything to do with Zameres, considered him an impudent person, and had no intention of sharing any information with him or with Averbuch. He complained that Storfer had left him in the lurch, while the Greek National Shipping Cartel, with whom he had contracted for a second ship, gave him one twenty-four-hour extension after another to meet his obligation. Storfer asked Avgherinos to be patient while he cleared up the "Zameres incident," which he promised to do forthwith.[67]

Back in Vienna, Storfer and Murmelstein reported to Brunner 1, who brought up a report he had received stating that the completion of the contract with Avgherinos was being held up by the unexpected requirement that the release of £13,800 be subject to the signature of a third party. Murmelstein was fully behind Storfer's efforts, his policy based on his firm conviction that it was better to send Jews on an uncertain voyage than to risk their being caught within Nazi territory. The two men explained to Brunner 1 that the "obstacle is based on the machinations of another group that wants to seize the ships for their own use." Brunner 1 ordered them to get rid of the obstacles and get the transport moving. He stressed that "the steps undertaken for self-serving purposes by the people headquartered in Geneva could lead to grave consequences," which the two men well knew but needed to have spelled out in the official record. They also reassured Brunner 1 that the arrangements made by them were "correct and sound" (*korrekt und reell*) and that the matter was getting their attention. Murmelstein right away drafted a telegram and received Brunner's permission to send it to Amsterdam, in which he explained that the *Devisenstelle* authorized payment of the £13,800, that payment to Avgherinos could not be delayed, that Storfer's examination of all aspects of the arrangement was thorough and adequate, that Zameres's intervention was gratuitous and pointless, that the Pressburg people as well as the transport of an additional 850 emigrants from Vienna had to be moved, that delay of only one day would lead to a catastrophe, and that he expected agreement by return wire.[68]

Later that same day Storfer, who understood that the main reason that the group tried to muscle in was to provide a ship for their group of emigrants stranded in Kladovo, decided, as a matter of accommodating the antagonists, to wire Athens to send a ship for them. Since any proposed telegram had to be submitted to the *Zentralstelle* for censorship, it was not long before he got a furious telephone call from Brunner 1, telling him that this matter was not Storfer's concern. He should stick to his own business, namely, to relieve the impasse of the Pressburg group and to make arrangements for the additional Palestine transport from Vienna. Brunner 1 planned to report this matter to Eichmann and warned Storfer again that he must not think that he could take his time in settling the matter.[69]

To Storfer, having Murmelstein's support was all-important for neutralizing the interference of the Kaplan-Averbuch-Zameres group, for unblocking the release to the payee of the Joint funds that were transferred to Piraeus, and for confirming the substantive support and confidence in his work on the part of the IKG, meaning primarily Löwenherz. Storfer, therefore, took this opportunity to spell things out. He knew that Löwenherz tended to be cautious and worried about emigration schemes such as Storfer's illegal immigration transports to Palestine. He reminded Löwenherz of the absolute necessity of getting the Pressburg group on its way. He reminded him of the necessity of organizing the next transport of Viennese Jews, consisting of "D[achau] and B[uchenwald] people and of persons who cannot remain" (that is, the Gänsbacher group) because of "other coercive measures of the central authorities they must finally and unconditionally go away." For this reason Storfer could not entertain the scruples recently voiced by Löwenherz, namely, whether there were any guarantees connected with the transports, especially in regard to their proceeding smoothly, and whether it might not be advisable to use the payment stoppage as a pause to allow for reconsideration of the scheme. Storfer's response was curt and unsparing:

> Our overseas journey jolts along rough roads, one has to expect that. All I was able to do was to take maximal precautions; no one could do more. It is possible that on the way to Palestine, the final destination, there will be a lot of unpleasant surprises. But we cannot allow ourselves to be overly pessimistic; otherwise, we could not embark on this difficult path.[70]

Storfer was equally blunt with the Joint. He insisted that they were "obliged" to validate the release of funds to the IKG that had been made available, without letting themselves be misled by spoilers. If the Joint, in the absence of Troper, would turn out to be the cause of damage to the transport project, they would bear the responsibility for the consequences. "We are beset from all sides, and in case misfortune should strike us which is the Joint's fault, then we will roll our misery over on the Joint." Storfer requested that the IKG also make the appropriate urgent representations to the Joint but warned that Avgherinos would not divulge the name of his ship, its flag, or any of his business secrets.[71]

Löwenherz was, indeed, in the center of the storm and, in fact, the one who had primary responsibility for the transport. He was responsible to the Joint for financing emigration schemes that promised to be successful. He was responsible to the *Zentralstelle* for a vigorous but low-budget emigration effort. During all the weeks of difficulties with the Storfer transports, he was constantly admonished by Brunner 1 and Eichmann himself to have more emigrants report to the *Zentralstelle* for processing and was reprimanded because not enough people did so. And, feeling responsible for the safe passage of his emigrants and their assured arrival at their destination, Löwenherz was cautious and circumspect, to the frustration of both Murmelstein and Storfer.

Early in May Löwenherz received an order from Brunner 1 to go to Brussels to arrange for the unblocking of the Piraeus payment, and Storfer was sent to Geneva to straighten things out with Kaplan and the Mossad.[72] Löwenherz never made it to Brussels because on May 10 Germany invaded Belgium. Somehow he managed to make a direct appeal to Troper, wherever he was at that time, and on May 23 he received the following wire from Saly Meyer, who represented the Joint in Switzerland:

> TROPER WIRED STOP EMPOWER ATHENS TO RELEASE PALESTINE EMIGRATION FUNDS AT DISPOSAL LÖWENHERZ STOP[73]

Reporting this to Brunner 1 in the presence of Storfer, Löwenherz said that while he felt honored by Troper's decision, it placed him under some specific obligations because in case the transport were to fail, the Joint's confidence in him would be shattered, and there would be no future allocations of *Devisen* for emigration. To make sure that the purpose for which the *Devisen* were to be spent would be met with the least amount of trouble, Löwenherz would withhold his go-ahead for disbursement until Storfer could get the following assurances from Avgherinos: First, whether immediately upon payment of £13,800, the ship could be made seaworthy and leave for Sulina, the Romanian river-ocean transfer port in the Danube delta. Second, whether Avgherinos had any additional demands, in light of the lateness of the payment and the possible resultant change in the exchange rate. Upon

Avgherinos's satisfactory response, problems with hiring a ship for the river portion of the voyage would have to be settled with the DDSG.[74] Löwenherz then went to Budapest to regulate all outstanding matters pertaining to the transports with the Jewish organizations, especially with Bertrand Jacobson representing the Joint.

The crisis of the Mossad interference was over, but the transport was far from getting on the way. The war had picked up pace. The Netherlands and Belgium were overrun, and France was next. This was the opportunity for Italy to enter the war on the side of Nazi Germany. The Nazi authorities now considered the Mediterranean Sea a war zone, thus effectively putting a stop to the special transports to Palestine. On June 12, 1940, Löwenherz reported to Eichmann in Berlin that his negotiations in Budapest provided all the preconditions for dispatching the transports. Eichmann thought that under the new circumstances the Palestine transports would not be able to take place. Löwenherz asked that he postpone his decision until he heard from Storfer, who was expected the next day, and until there was greater clarity about the changing conditions.[75]

The next day, which was the day Paris fell to the German army, Storfer joined Eppstein, Hirsch, and Löwenherz as they reported to Dannecker in Berlin. In a long presentation Storfer voiced his judgment that the transports could proceed even under the new conditions, and he detailed the arrangements that should be made pending the authorization by the authorities to proceed. Löwenherz detailed the complex financial aspects of the project, involving transfers and exchanges of *Devisen* from Vienna, the RV (*Reichsvereinigung der Juden in Deutschland*, Reich/National Association of Jewish Communities/Jews in Germany), Danzig, and Prague, as well as refundable and non-refundable security deposits, Storfer's concern over the return of deposits in case the transports did not materialize, and so on. Dannecker directed Storfer to contact Avgherinos about the feasibility of sailing the Mediterranean with Italy at war and ordered him to Athens to inspect the prospects firsthand as well as to negotiate amendments and renewals of contracts. Storfer thought that moving the Pressburg people had priority and should be taken care of before the sailings of the ships contracted with Avgherinos.[76]

In Athens Storfer was able to ascertain that there was no interruption of traffic between the ports of Constanta (Romania) and Piraeus and between Piraeus and Beirut in addition to Tel Aviv. The Greek passenger ship *Ileni* was being readied to take 300 passengers to Tel Aviv, and "the ship owner and all the seamen have not the slightest hesitation to sail." The captains and owners of four steamers, the availability of which had long ago been arranged by Storfer, "are determined to carry through the trip." The captains, "capable experts" and "reliable," had received the charts and knew the safest route, that is, by way of the Greek island of Rhodes. Storfer was able to find out that the ships were Spanish, though one of them sailed under the Panamanian flag. At his orders three of the ships left Piraeus for Sulina (a port in Romania) to await the arrival of the passengers; regrettably, inasmuch as these had not left for their Danubian journey, the waiting would incur extra charges.[77]

The stumbling block at this time was the Joint. The £13,800 that Troper had placed at Löwenherz's disposal was, with the clearance by the *Devisenstelle*, duly transferred to Athens for payment to Avgherinos. But because of the safety and feasibility questions raised by Italy's entry into the war, and in order to clear up the questions raised by all the different parties interested in the transports, Löwenherz was told by Mr. Jacobsen, the Budapest representative of the Joint, that Mr. Troper required the retro-transfer of the pounds. Löwenherz had repeatedly, and to no avail, warned Jacobsen that if the £13,800 were to be retro-transferred, then a cumulatively much greater amount of previous transfers by Vienna, Prague, and Danzig would be lost.[78]

For this reason, after reporting the information from Athens to the participating leaders of Vienna, Prague, Danzig, and the RV while in Berlin on July 4, Storfer was requested to write a report for the Joint, addressing all outstanding matters of concern and motivating them to give their go-ahead. He certified that the DDSG had provided good ships and had obtained the necessary Yugoslavian and Romanian transit authorizations, but unless they could proceed in short order, they would have to use the ships for other purposes. With reference to the Edelstein-Kaplan accusations, Storfer wrote that "[w]e are fully mindful of the wishes of the country of immigration, and the selection [of participating emigrants to Palestine] is carried out by the Jewish Selection Committee, the Palestine Offices, and ourselves." Although ready to deal regarding these matters with any "authoritative offices," he would not deal "with any person who just happens to present himself to us," a clear reference to Kaplan, Averbuch, and Zameres. In particular, he and his associates were "ready to comply, to the best of our ability, with the well-meant intentions of the Joint. . . . In the name of thousands we are indebted to the Joint for its kindly disposition."[79] And he issued an admonition:

> No need to tell you of the urgency and necessity of getting these people to their destination. We only have to mention 1,000 Pressburg people, etc., etc. Nevertheless we can tell you with good conscience that it was not the necessity for the transport that decided us [finally to go ahead with the transport at this time], but the assurance that there was no danger in carrying it through.[80]

Storfer also addressed the two matters of great concern to the Joint, matters that more than any other factor led to the present difficulties, namely, the stranded transports in Pressburg and Kladovo. Storfer laid the blame for the debacles squarely on the "carelessness of unauthorized persons" whose "preparations, to put it mildly, were superficial." The reason that the people got stuck in Pressburg was that the Danube steamer, hired by the Mossad, which was to take them downstream capsized before it could take on its passengers. "In order to remedy the situation," Storfer and his Vienna associates, as the "responsible and authorized" persons, "have taken the matter completely in hand." Storfer only hoped that when they arrived at their destination, Palestine "will not close its doors to our pilgrims."[81]

As to Kladovo, Storfer reported that when he was in Athens a week earlier, he was shown a ship that was listing and "evidently in need of repair," for which the Averbuch group had advanced $40,000. The Greek authorities were making trouble about the flag and the crew. Storfer suggested that someone be "authorized to look into the matter and get a picture of the present financial situation." While in Athens he also tried to get in touch with Zameres to get information about Kladovo. "But, strange to say, he hesitated speaking to me."[82] Referring to Zameres's claim to be the representative of the Joint, Storfer asked what precisely his role was.

On the basis of Storfer's report that all arrangements had been made for the transport to start on its way, Löwenherz and the corresponding leaders of the participating communities decided to go ahead, and he wired Troper to tell Jacobson to withdraw the retrotransfer order. By return wire Troper requested clarification. In response, Löwenherz wrote to Troper that he and his colleagues were satisfied that Storfer had made arrangements that were responsible and the best possible and that some of the oceangoing ships hired by Storfer had arrived at the Black Sea port ready to take the passengers to Palestine. Moreover, the DDSG had provided a few good ships for the river journey and is "surely interested in their safety." In fact, its director had "thoroughly examined the whole stretch to the [ocean] harbor, and, on the basis of his observations is prepared to proceed with the transport." Löwenherz pressed home the need for the Joint's final cooperation in this matter by summarizing the plight of the very people for whom all these efforts had been made:

> Out of humane considerations, we have to take care of the emigrants who are still in Vienna by making it possible for them to leave; months ago they were stripped of their assets and are still waiting. Dispatching the transport is even more important for the persons in Pressburg; their departure would dispense of the need to provide them with further support.[83]

Once the transports of the Vienna and Pressburg contingents were dispatched, Löwenherz and Storfer would see to the settling of the Kladovo matter, as agreed to in Budapest. Until then, it was also agreed, Vienna would contribute $10,000 for the upkeep of the Kladovo people. Nevertheless, a week after this letter was sent, Löwenherz found out, to his great consternation, that the Joint had docked Vienna $16,000 instead, which he strongly protested.[84]

In the meantime, internal pressures continued. The extent to which the long delay in sending the transport served Eichmann to tighten the financial stranglehold on the IKG was discussed in chapter 8. On the morning of July 15, 1940, Brunner 1, reiterating the authorization of the transport, admonished Murmelstein to include as many of those released from concentration camps as possible; otherwise, they would be sent back.[85] In the afternoon he ordered Löwenherz urgently to advise Storfer to dispatch the Viennese participants in Pressburg and those who were still in Vienna right away, regardless of the state of readiness of the Prague and Berlin contingents.[86] A few days later Murmelstein told Brunner that according to Storfer, of the six persons nominated for participation by the *Zentralstelle*, one woman was not Jewish by faith and the others, due to the state of their health, were incapable of participating in the transport.[87] Could it be that the *Zentralstelle* ordered specific individuals to be included in emigration transports? This was soon clarified, when Brunner 1 indicated to Löwenherz that these people were included by the Gestapo and would be removed from the list if they should prove not to be Jewish by faith or ill.[88]

But before arrangements for the new Vienna transport could be completed, there was another kind of internal pressure, a very curious one. We mentioned that one of the main concerns for the representatives of the Mossad was the selection of the right transport participants. In pursuit of this goal the Mossad also enlisted the Joint, as the Storfer documentation indicates, and they did so even after their interference was effectively neutralized.

But even when this seemed settled, it was not the end of the matter. There was another recourse, namely, Eichmann himself. Murmelstein, in his interviews with us, gave his version of what was at play. As far as he was concerned, it was Edelstein, and not so much those who were behind him (the Mossad) who had brought about the situation. Be that as it may, it was Edelstein who was now the only point man left for bringing the last possible internal pressure to bear on behalf of the Mossad's—and his—interests.

As we know, Vienna, Berlin, and Prague had an agreement concerning the apportionment of participants in the Palestine transports. At the time when it looked as if the Mossad would arrange for a transport of Edelstein's *halutzim*, Vienna was at the beginning stages of organizing the transport that would finally leave in September. In anticipation of his own transport, Edelstein, according to Murmelstein, declined to use his allotment in the Vienna transport and apparently got Eppstein to decline, too. Murmelstein then felt free to fill all the available openings with applicants from Vienna. There were not enough young *halutzim* left in Vienna; most eligible young people had emigrated before the war, and most of the remaining ones who had been in *hakhshara* camps had been sent to Pressburg and were now waiting there. Hence, Murmelstein was able to fill some, perhaps even the majority of the places, with people other than *halutzim*. As mentioned previously, the IKG was under pressure from the *Zentralstelle* to include participants from two additional groups: the ones quartered in Gänsbacher Street, who had been slated for the Nisko transport that did not leave, and the releasees from Dachau and Buchenwald. There is evidence that Edelstein was under similar pressure with respect to the Nisko returnees in Mährisch-Ostrau (Ostrava), some of whom were included in the Prague contingent. When the Mossad initiative failed, Edelstein had tried to arrange a meeting in Prague. By the time the ensuing interference was neutralized and France fell, it looked as if the Vienna transport would never be realized. But then when things began to look promising again in late July 1940, Edelstein became interested in securing these places for his *halutzim*, which he had spurned a few months earlier. For what happened next, we will present excerpts from the inimitable ramblings of Murmelstein's rhapsodic account:

> An illegal transport . . . was supposed to go to Palestine. And at that time there was one person who believed in the transport. One had to be *meshugge* [crazy] to believe in it. . . . I believed that if the people do not get to Israel [*sic*] . . . then they get to where the devil is, but it is better for them to be there than here, I mean Vienna. There had been the first transports to Poland . . . of Auschwitz or similar things I could not have had any inkling, but for me it was enough what I had seen in Nisko to say to myself, better not. So the transport was put together. . . . Of course, we did not have many youths; they had emigrated; but, what can I say, included were some whores. Excuse me, it is important to say what sort of human material there was, but they were human beings, and it was a matter of saving them from death. . . . It caused me pangs of conscience whether such human material belonged in . . . Palestine. But on the other hand, it also caused me no pangs of conscience to say these people do not belong in Poland. . . . What could a woman of 45 or 50 expect in Poland. . . . [S]ooner or later they chase her into a bog and she will perish. . . .
>
> I knew . . . the transport would leave. Where it arrives, I could not care less; let it get stuck in Romania, let it get stuck wherever, only away from here, because here it stinks. . . . I acted to save people and not for the sake of ideology. Ergo, when they said they don't need the places, I said, "thank you." All of a sudden things get serious. Now they want the places again. But

look . . . there are third parties involved. What should I tell these people, whom I called, who have paid for their journey, who might have started to liquidate [their assets] and for a long time had no apartment . . . and are sitting on their luggage . . . and now I should tell them, "No, Herr Eppstein and Herr Edelstein have changed their minds and you will stay here." . . . I did not come to them, "give me places," but they wanted to be the smart ones while I am the idiot, occupying myself with things that are not feasible while they, the smart ones, know that it cannot be done. . . .

One fine day . . . there was a call from Berlin: "Murmelstein!" "Sir!" "You are to report to *Obersturmführer* Eichmann tomorrow at so-and-so o'clock." "Yes sir!" Now I could muse all night about what happened—is it something good, is it something bad? . . . I got to Berlin, report at the guard and say, "My name is Murmelstein and I am supposed to report here." He looks it up and says, "Not only report, also wait." So I wait. As I am waiting, Eppstein comes marching in and Edelstein. . . . They keep their distance. My God, I thought, distance, distance. They probably know already what was decided about me. It's not healthy; it's infectious. Finally we get in. Eichmann sits there, performs the whole comedy, has his own head office—you know it reminded me of a character in the Yiddish theater: "*Groisser Melekh*" [sarcastic: "great king" or "big chief"]—So he says, yes, he heard people are making trouble. He plays the benefactor: there is a war, but nevertheless out of his infinite goodness he lets people out to Palestine, even though he knows they are enemies of Germany, and yet people make trouble, etc.—and then he scowls at me. It was all rehearsed—and therefore he decided the following: First, and once and for all, when the transport leaves, it may not return; there must not be any difficulties with the landing; the Zionist *Halutz* organization must assume the guarantee that the transport can land. All this was, of course, Edelstein's suggestion, namely, that we should send the lists to Switzerland, so that they can be examined from Israel [*sic*], and then the transport can leave, and he points out that whoever sabotages will get to know him, and now he is already up on the roof [looking down on everyone]: "You, Eppstein, did you understand me?" "*Jawohl*!" "And you, Edelstein, did you understand me?" "And you, Murmelstein?" "*Nein*!" "How come? What didn't you understand? You are becoming stupid?" "Maybe I am becoming stupid, but no, I do not understand; there is a law which says that one may not get in touch with enemy countries, also not by way of neutral countries." So, now one saw a balloon into which one sticks a needle and it bursts. You realize, I did not have the time to consider the matter because they wanted to confront me with a *fait accompli*. "It's forbidden by law." Silence. After a while, a *Donnerwetter* [thunderstorm] over all of us, for now he was furious, for now he understood that they had led him on the ice, that they wanted to misuse him, that he—so to say—hit a wall and I was it; it hit home, for he was not dumb—Arendt, she can write what she wants[89]—he was no genius, he was a good bureaucrat. . . . Alas, if he had been stupid, it would have been better for us. And suddenly there was a *Donnerwetter* and in a trice we are outside with the instruction: The [transport] lists that have been drawn up are valid, and the people have to leave, and if they don't leave, they will all go to the concentration camp, and we with them, etc., and he does not want to see us anymore, and out of here. The matter was finished. Eppstein and Edelstein left and did not look at me, as if I was air.[90]

The string of interferences, which delayed the dispatch of the transports at least two months, was finished.

On September 5 a cable from Löwenherz arrived at the Joint headquarters in New York:

DEVISENGENEHMIGUNG 6284 TRANSPORT STORFER GLUECKLICH ABGEGANGEN KONNTEN WEITERE NEUN PERSONEN ANSCHLIESSEN STOP DRAHTUEBERWEISET SCHWEIZERISCHE KREDITANSTALT ZUERICH DOLLARS SIEBENHUNDERT GUNSTEN SOCRATES AVGHERINOS ATHEN

(FOREIGN EXCHANGE APPROVAL 6284 STORFER TRANSPORT SUCCESSFULLY

> LEFT NINE ADDITIONAL PEOPLE COULD BE ADDED STOP WIRE TRANSFER SWISS CREDIT INSTITUTE ZURICH SEVEN HUNDRED DOLLARS FOR SOCRATES AVGHERINOS ATHENS)

What it means is that the transport was under way on its river ships without any problems and that with permission of the exchange office (*Devisenstelle*), $700 ought to be released to Avgherinos's—likely private—Swiss bank account.

After the transports were on the way downriver, Eichmann ordered Löwenherz to have Storfer's office monitor their progress and inform the Vienna *Zentralstelle* twenty-four hours before their expected arrival in Tulcea, the river harbor at the point at which the Danube divides into its delta. At that time, Eichmann would undertake the necessary steps for the transports to continue proceeding trouble-free, in particular through waters under "Italian sovereignty," which raises the question of what Eichmann might have been referring to by use of this latter phrase. Surely not the Black Sea; most likely he was referring to the entire Mediterranean Sea, even the eastern parts that the transports would have to traverse to reach the coast of Palestine.[91] Eichmann must have had some knowledge that Mussolini was about to claim sovereignty over the entire Mediterranean, where he meant to operate his wartime naval forces. Having assured safe passage through "Italian sovereignty," Eichmann continued, he would then also monitor the progress of the three maritime ships, and, upon Storfer's report of their safe landing, would give the go-ahead for the departure of the next transport, the one slated for the *Rosita*, the fourth maritime ship.[92]

Eager as he was for the realization of the next transport, Eichmann was concerned for the first three ships to arrive as planned. As the weeks of waiting dragged on, Brunner 1 took the opportunity of Löwenherz's raising the issue of the "catastrophic situation" of the eviction of Jews (discussed in the section on "Evictions" in chapter 8) to connect the possibility of its alleviation with the IKG's efforts "to place Jewish families on the next transport to Palestine." In particular he instructed Löwenherz that the *Rosita* was to be reserved solely for Jews from Prague and Vienna; in fact, Vienna must have the majority of places. Löwenherz reminded Brunner 1 that the actual arrangement would have to wait until the landing of the ships now at sea and mentioned that in selecting participants their capacity of helping in the development of Palestine would have to be a major factor.[93] Shortly before the three oceangoing vessels arrived at the coast of Palestine, he told Brunner 1 that an early start of the *Rosita* transport via the Danube was "unlikely, even impossible" because of the impending winter conditions. However, one could also consider an overland route to the Romanian seaport. Brunner 1 then told Löwenherz to order Storfer to cancel the contracts concerning the *Rosita* but to reserve the right to contract for its use at a later date.[94]

As for the fortunate participants, we have to imagine them crowded on small river ships, picking up their greatly relieved companions in Pressburg, consuming their provisions as they moved through Hungary and Yugoslavia, passing the unfortunates still stranded in Kladovo, passing through the Iron Gates and into Romania, and finally landing in Sulina. We do not know how long they stayed in Sulina or when they transferred to the oceangoing vessels. We do know that nearby Romanian Jewish communities helped to provide for them. Then they boarded the three ships waiting for them. They passed through the

Bosporus and the Dardanelles into the Aegean Sea, southward then eastward along the coast of Asia Minor, around Rhodes, then south again along the Levantine coast.

Could Löwenherz rest assured that the protracted effort had safely succeeded? Could the Joint be satisfied that its support has been well used? Could Edelstein and the Mossad breathe easier now that *Eretz Yisrael* has been settled with more *halutzim* and more fighters? Was Storfer's hope fulfilled that at their destination they "will not close its doors to our pilgrims"?

The effort of realizing the Palestine transports, resumed after neutralizing the Mossad interference, took place under the cloud of fast-moving wartime events. When these efforts finally came to fruition in September, the emigrants setting sail downriver to the Black Sea were not traversing a placid Balkan region far from the war and proceeding into a tranquil Romania. Things were heating up there as well. In June 1940, while the world was watching the drama of the fall of France, the Soviet Union demanded the return of and summarily occupied the portion of the Bukovina region ceded to Romania at the conclusion of the First World War.[95] At the end of August, at a conference convened in Vienna, Romania, under pressure from Germany and Italy, had to return to Hungary a large portion of the Transylvanian region Hungary had ceded to Romania under the terms of the Versailles Peace Treaty. As the Palestine transports were departing Vienna and Pressburg in early September, Ion Antonescu—Fascist, anti-Semitic in a country that had a Jewish population of 800,000, and sympathizer of Nazi Germany—became head of the Romanian government; King Carol fled Romania with Mme. Lupescu, his Jewish mistress and wife-to-be; his young son Michael V, thought to be pliable, was placed on the throne; and Romania had to cede another stretch of its territory, this one to Bulgaria. In October, as the three ships were loading at Sulina and then proceeding through the Black Sea, German troops landed in the Romanian Ploesti region to protect the oil fields. As the ships were proceeding past Greek waters, Greece, after rejecting Italian demands for the use of its naval bases so their navy could ply the waters of *mare nostrum*, was invaded by Italy from Albania, and British troops landed on Crete and other Greek islands. A little later, Hungary and Romania joined the Berlin-Rome-Tokyo Pact.

In time the three ships made it to the shores of Palestine. It was well into November. The Romanian Jewish newspaper *Renasterea Noastra* reported the messages received from Palestine. As previously arranged, the messages were forwarded to Storfer. Storfer reported the messages, without comment, to the organizations of the five places that had provided participants in the transports: Vienna, Berlin, Prague, Danzig, and Brünn (Brno). Löwenherz then had to relay them to Brunner 1. From Storfer's report, supplemented by some later accounts, we can reconstruct what happened.[96]

Two of the ships arrived first, the *Pacific* and the *Milos*, and were intercepted by the British coastal police. Their approximately 1,800 passengers were regarded as illegal immigrants. While the British Mandatory Government expressed sympathy for the emigrants, they felt constrained to follow wartime regulations issued that year prohibiting entry to Palestine and to deem it against the interest of the country to allow illegal entry. It was decided to send the passengers to some British colony for the duration of the war and then decide where they should go other than Palestine. It was also decided to apply the same treatment should other ships with illegal immigrants appear.

Soon another ship did appear, the *Atlantic*, the third ship of the Storfer transports with passengers from Vienna, the Protectorate, and Danzig. Altogether there were 1,645 people (some say 1,800), including not only "young Zionists and *halutzim*" but also hundreds of women, old people, and 150 children. Some had relatives in the country. In spite of the fact that there were plenty of unused entry certificates available under the schedule of the 1939 White Paper, in spite of the vigorous efforts of the Jewish Agency to have them stay, and in spite of reported uproars and even riots, the British Mandatory authorities insisted on their removal to a distant colony. The reason was once again that "Jewish illegal immigration poses a danger to the interests of Palestine." Pending their removal, they were interned in a camp.

In time the almost 1,800 passengers from the *Pacific* and the *Milos* were transferred to the *Patria* lying at anchor in Haifa harbor, a small French passenger ship that had been requisitioned by the British, to be taken to Mauritius, a tiny island in the Indian Ocean, about 500 miles east of Madagascar. Then the inmates from the *Atlantic* were brought to Haifa to join the others for the journey on the *Patria*. When about 130 of these had embarked, there was an explosion, causing the ship to list and in a short time it sank. The police, the military, the harbor personnel, and other civilians immediately undertook rescue operations, bringing most of the people to shore. There were some deaths. The uninjured were brought to a camp, the wounded to public and to Hadassah hospitals. According to the official communiqué, "clothing and food were contributed from all over the country. All newspapers praised the aid operation undertaken at the risk of life by the police and the military."

What had happened? The official communiqué speaks of "an explosion from an unknown cause." David Blasberg, one of the passengers of the *Milos*, was able to send a letter to a Rubin Schapira in Sulina, who forwarded it to Storfer, in which he reported that the explosion on the *Patria* had been "simulated," that the losses were "relatively few," and that the passengers who had been on the *Milos* and the *Pacific* were well. Simulated? Since there was no way for deaths to be simulated, how simulated could the explosion have been? Blasberg no doubt wanted to reassure the people back home. But deaths, any number of deaths, could not be ignored. Hence, again: What had happened?

In a desperate attempt to keep the *Patria* from sailing, some explosives had been brought aboard with which to disable the engines. This was not an easy job, and with the precious cargo of hundreds of people—refugees from hell—aboard, it called for a professional saboteur. We do not know whether the *Haganah* (the prestate Jewish paramilitary force), as is claimed, handled the job, only that the explosives ignited at the wrong place and at the wrong time, causing the disastrous loss of lives. The initial official communiqué stated that 22 dead were found. Later sources say that more than 250 died, of whom 209 were found and buried.

The Mandatory Government took pity on the survivors of the *Patria*, possibly at the orders of an embarrassed British government, granted them certificates of entry from the quota of the current schedule, and established a special commission of inquiry into the

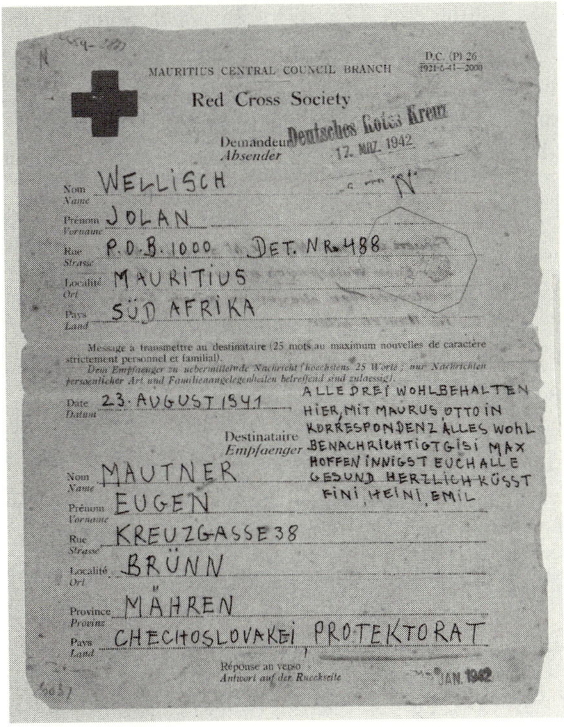
MAURITIUS CENTRAL COUNCIL BRANCH
D.C. (P) 26
1921-6-41—2000
Red Cross Society
Deutsches Rotes Kreuz
17. MÄRZ 1942
Demandeur
Absender
Nom / Name: WELLISCH
Prénom / Vorname: JOLAN
Rue / Strasse: P.O.B. 1000 DET. NR. 488
Localité / Ort: MAURITIUS
Pays / Land: SÜD AFRIKA

Message à transmettre au destinataire (25 mots au maximum nouvelles de caractère strictement personnel et familial).
Dem Empfaenger zu uebermittelnde Nachricht (hoechstens 25 Worte; nur Nachrichten persoenlicher Art und Familienangelegenheiten betreffend sind zulaessig).

Date / Datum: 23. AUGUST 1941

ALLE DREI WOHLBEHALTEN HIER, MIT MAURUS, OTTO IN KORRESPONDENZ ALLES WOHL BENACHRICHTIGT GISI MAX HOFFEN INNIGST EUCH ALLE GESUND HERZLICH KÜSST FINI, HEINI, EMIL

Destinataire
Empfaenger
Nom / Name: MAUTNER
Prénom / Vorname: EUGEN
Rue / Strasse: KREUZGASSE 38
Localité / Ort: BRÜNN
Province / Provinz: MÄHREN
Pays / Land: CHECHOSLOVAKEI PROTEKTORAT

Réponse au verso
Antwort auf der Rueckseite
JAN. 1942

Telegram sent from Mauritius by Jolan Wellisch of Vienna to her brother-in-law in Brünn (Brno), Czechoslovakian Protectorate, notifying him that she and her family are safe and well. Although her brother-in-law responded in a positive manner, eventually he and his family were murdered. (United States Holocaust Memorial Museum, courtesy of Henry Wellisch. USHMM 59942)

cause of the sinking of the *Patria*. The 1,645 passengers from the *Atlantic*, who were fortunate enough not to have embarked on the *Patria* before it sank, embarked on the *Atlith* on December 9, 1940. When they found out that, unlike those who had survived the *Patria*, they would have to leave for exile, they staged a hunger strike—to no avail. They arrived in Mauritius shortly before the New Year, as reported in *Renasterea Noastra* on January 1, 1941.

Because of the upheavals and impending wars in the Balkans it was becoming clear that trying to route illegal transports to Palestine via Danube River ships and especially via Romanian and Greek ships was not only dangerous but futile. But Storfer did not give up. While in Berlin around the New Year, he asked Prochnik, who represented the IKG in Berlin on matters relating to routing emigrants to their overseas destination, to investigate the possibility of routing emigrants to Palestine via the Soviet Union to Odessa, and to take ships from there to Palestine. Prochnik had found out that this kind of emigrant (i.e., Jews who were Zionists) would not be offensive to the Soviet authorities; they would treat the matter merely as a technical problem of transporting people. The only sticking point was the matter of the transit visas, which were issued only upon proof of having a destination beyond the Soviet Union. However, Prochnik was given to understand that the presentation of a paid ship's fare would do. He also found out the details of the available route by train from Berlin via Warsaw, Minsk, Moscow, and Kiev to Odessa. The cost for the stretch within the Soviet Union would be US $100 per person. Alternatively, the route could circumvent Moscow and go directly from Minsk via Kiev to Odessa, which would reduce the cost to $70.[97] Presumably, Prochnik spoke unofficially to his contacts at the Russian consulate and at the Intourist office. Acknowledging receipt of the information, Storfer thought both routes would be too expensive and that a possible route via Krakow and Lemberg (Lwow/Lviv) would cost considerably less. He added, "I shall get back to you about this matter."[98] He never did.

What was the fate of the Kladovo group? Now that these first three transports had finally been dispatched, Storfer was going to take up the task of dislodging the around 1,000 people, most of them from Vienna, and send them on their way. Unbeknownst to Storfer, when the ships carrying the Pressburg group and the third group transport passed Kladovo, the authorities were in the process of moving the people who had been stranded there. These included not only those among the 1,100 who had survived the harsh winter conditions but a number of others who had fled illegally to Yugoslavia from Austria, Germany, and Poland, and who had joined the original Kladovo group. Despondent and furious after nine months of having had good reason to feel betrayed and abandoned by the faraway Zionist leadership that had brought them there, the group may have been expecting finally to be transported downriver to embarkation in Sulina. But no, they were taken upriver instead, to Belgrade, where the tributary Sava River issues into the Danube, then a few miles up the Sava to the rural Serbian town of Šabac, where they arrived in late September 1940. While life at Šabac was better than in Kladovo, the refugees were still abandoned to an uncertain future. In any case, it is doubtful that the IKG and Storfer ever knew of their new location. No doubt the Joint, who supported them through its Yugoslav contacts, did know, as did the Mossad. In time more refugees joined the group, swelling their number to 1,400. The Mossad appeared to have made several attempts at securing a seagoing ship and of arranging river ships to take them to the Black Sea, but all of them failed. In spite of their frustration and renewed despondency, some of the refugees were able individually to motivate their contacts in Palestine to secure landing certificates.

Even if the group had stayed at Kladovo, it would have been too late for Storfer to make arrangements to keep them safe, since there was turmoil now in the Balkans, Romania, and Greece. There was no way for Storfer to arrange for a Greek ship to pick them up at Sulina, and therefore no way for him to arrange for their passage there from Kladovo. With Italy at war, there also would have been no way for the Yugoslav authorities to make good on their threat to ship them to an Adriatic port. It was this impasse that had moved the Yugoslav authorities to ship them to Šabac.

When Bulgaria followed Hungary and Romania in joining the Rome-Berlin Axis, Yugoslavia was completely surrounded and, under the leadership of Prince Regent Paul, also joined the Axis on March 25, 1941. The next day a coup group overthrew the Regent, declared Yugoslavia neutral, and placed Prince Paul's nephew, who was still a minor, on the throne as King Peter II. Furiously the Germans, poised for the imminent invasion of the Soviet Union, instead poured into Yugoslavia, which capitulated on April 17 after eleven days of fighting.

Before the German troops arrived, some 200 of the Kladovo group who had been able to secure certificates of entry to Palestine escaped Šabac, made their way to the coast, and reached their goal.[99] The remaining 1,100, of whom 800 were from the original group, soon found themselves under the occupation of the German Wehrmacht (army), which had placed Serbia under military rule. The military government brought the institution of the Nazi Jewish policy with it, as carried out by the SS. Soon the refugees were confined to a concentration camp on the outskirts of Šabac. Their confinement, at the beginning of summer 1941, coincided with two developments that sealed their fate. First, the war of attrition began, which the Yugoslav Partisans, led mainly by communists under the leadership of Josip Broz Tito, waged against the German occupiers. It was a struggle that would last until the Germans were driven from Yugoslavia in the last stages of World War II. Second, with the assault on the Soviet Union, the first stage of the systematic extermination of the Jews began.

The Fate of the Kladovo Group

The steps leading to the outbreak of World War I had begun with the assassination of the successor to the throne of the Austro-Hungarian Empire, Archduke Franz-Ferdinand, during a state visit in Sarajevo, the capital of Bosnia-Herzegovina. The assassin was Gavrilo Princip, a teenage member of a Serbian group of conspirators. That war led to the end of the Habsburg Empire as well as to the downfall of glorious imperial Germany. Now, twenty-seven years later, this was not forgotten. What better payback than to install General Franz Böhme, an Austrian, in Belgrade as the Supreme Commander of the Wehrmacht in Serbia, commanding occupation units consisting mainly of fellow Austrians? While the main force of the Wehrmacht was engaged in the war against the Soviet Union, units began to engage the roving bands of partisans in the mountains of Serbia. When one of the early skirmishes with the partisans resulted in the death of twenty-one soldiers of the Wehrmacht, the Austrians, having to prove that they were up to the task, decided to improve on the ancient Roman maneuver of decimation by ordering a "centimation." But, there was no way for them to seek out 2,100 partisans in the mountains, and it would not do to alienate the Serbian civilians at this early stage of occupation. Unfortunately, the lowlands surrounding Belgrade offered a solution. The Austrian General Dr. Walter Hinghofer, headquartered at Šabac, ordered a punitive massacre of 2,100 Jews and communists by his unit, which consisted mainly of Austrians. Included among the victims were all the adult male members of the Kladovo group. The men did not know of their impending fate, since they were taken from the camp on the pretext of being needed for labor assignment. These Jewish refugees, it must be noted, were slaughtered not by the SS but by the Wehrmacht, moreover by a unit that consisted mainly of fellow Austrians.

The women and children remaining in the camp also never knew of the fate of their men. In January 1942 they were moved to a concentration camp for Serbian Jewish women and children, established in former fairgrounds at a place near Belgrade called Sajmište, where many died of exposure and undernourishment. The commander of the camp was an Austrian, SS Corporal Herbert Andorfer. In March 1942 those who survived received the welcome news that they would be transferred to better quarters. Beginning in March there was a daily truck that would pick up four to five dozen inmates, followed by a truck with their remaining belongings. At the entrance to Belgrade the truck would halt. The operator would debark long enough to move a lever that redirected the exhaust fumes into the interior of the closed truck. By the time the truck had passed through Belgrade the passengers were dead; the truck continued to the north of the city to a place where a ditch dug by some prisoners the previous day awaited the mass burial of the corpses. Three months later all 7,000 of the women and children of the camp had been "resettled." One of these unfortunate women was Susi Melzer, who was mentioned briefly in connection with the "Palestine Transports" earlier in this chapter. She was 21 years old.

The Mossad group was, in the pursuit of its own agenda, surely well intentioned; yet we cannot avoid the truth that their ineptness led the emigrants to their unfortunate confinement in Kladovo and that the delay caused by their interference was, though unintended, the major factor in delivering them to their dismal fate.

Groups and Routes via the Far East

There were some Jews who were fortunate enough to have a destination to emigrate to, who had successfully completed all the daunting steps leading to the *Sichtvermerke* in their passports (i.e., to their clearance to leave the Reich), and whose passage was paid for, which meant for most of them by means of the *Devisen* provided by the IKG. Yet they still needed travel arrangements to be made for them under the restrictive conditions of wartime. The men at the IKG worked frantically at the seemingly endless task of devising travel schemes and carrying them to completion on a case-by-case basis and in the face of constant difficulties. These schemes consisted of sending emigrants in groups over complicated and often circuitous routes to their destinations and in this way managing to save as many as could be saved before the door to emigration was slammed shut. The machinations involved in this are described in what follows.

In addition to and complicating the usual problems related to emigration, the outbreak of war posed new problems for the staffs of the IKG and the RV in their task of finding avenues still open for getting emigrants out of Europe. This task became maddeningly more difficult when the war heated up in the spring of 1940. The usual transatlantic routes via Atlantic ports were no longer available, nor were the ships sailing under the flag of the United States. When the availability of the ports and ships of Germany, the Netherlands, France, and Great Britain fell prey to the war, there had been talk for a brief time of using Italian ports and liners to transport emigrants to America, but this too fell through. First, a difficulty developed concerning emigration by way of Italy, which had nothing to do with Italy itself but a lot with the attitude toward Jews even as they were leaving Germany. In April 1940 Brunner 1 related the following: The directorate of the German Reich Railway (*Deutsche Reichsbahn*) wrote to him at the *Zentralstelle* to point out that there had been "complaints" (*Anstände*) about Jewish emigrés traveling first class in the express trains to Italy. Brunner 1 therefore gave the order that the emigrés would have to travel as a group in third-class carriages only, and the directorate of the Reich Railway would have to be informed whenever such a group was traveling. Only those too old or ill to travel third class, which consisted of rows of hard benches, would be allowed to travel second class, but only on the overnight trains. However, Brunner 1 "emphasizes that these instructions must not result in any reduction of emigration whatsoever."[100] While there are no details furnished, we must keep in mind the fact that "good" Aryans did not want to share any space at all with Jews. Sometime before the war, to forestall related difficulties, the Nazis restricted Jewish travel on railway trains except for purposes of emigration or with special permission. Emigrating Jews were to travel in separate carriages, or at least in separate compartments, and to travel in groups so as to occupy fully the designated space. Subsequently, as early as May 4, before the invasion of the Low Countries, Brunner 1 authorized the inclusion in the *Jüdische Nachrichten* of a warning against travel to Italy, even by those in possession of a passage on an ocean liner.[101] A memorandum by Murmelstein from that time instructed those at the IKG who advised would-be emigrants on the process of obtaining refunds for cancelled passages on the Italian Line and the United States Line. The memorandum also advised that since "it is not expected that ships would be sailing from Italian ports [in the foreseeable future], all who already have their luggage in Genoa or Trieste should order it shipped back [to Vienna]" at their own expense with the assistance of the IKG.[102]

Aside from the need to segregate Jews from Aryans on trains, dispatching emigrants in groups became a necessity for other reasons as well. Emigration matters were becoming impossibly complicated. Even assuming that an individual or a family had managed somehow to find a destination that would accept them, and assuming that this family had overcome all hurdles, there still remained the problem of getting from point A to point B. Other countries had to be traversed that might be at war with Germany or occupied by Germany and hence off limits, or were afraid that the emigrants might decide to stay in them, or simply did not want to be bothered, or demanded unconscionable sums to allow transit. The immigration visa might be contingent on the transit visa at the same time that the transit visa was made dependent on the immigration visa. Each visa had a certain period of validity, and while one consulate sat on its hands, the other one rescinded the visa because the stipulated time was up and would not renew it. Travel agencies of greater and often much lesser honesty, and a number of individuals making spurious claims of being experts in arranging passage, took advantage of this desperate situation and offered their services, frequently for fees that the emigrant could not afford and the IKG could not countenance paying. This was the case especially whenever the emigrants were forced, as they were so often, to book passage early, even before the other visas were granted and formalities concluded. Situations arose in which an emigrant or a whole family had spent their or their overseas guarantors' money for passage, only literally to miss the boat at the last minute because of incomplete papers. This, of course, would be a devastating blow: to the individuals because the money was no longer available; to the IKG because its greatest efforts were directed toward getting as many as possible out; and even to the Nazis, who were still involved in the emigration effort.

Arranging group transports was, then, the solution to this impasse. There had been group transports earlier, as we have mentioned, mainly to Central and South America and of course to Palestine. Group transports had the advantage that the IKG could buy blocks of passages so that if one or more of the scheduled emigrants were unable to leave, others could take their place and no tickets would remain unused and no money would be lost.

Dealing with a number of visas at a time, the consulates were able to save time and effort and were more likely to cooperate. Furthermore, only a limited number of travel agencies and shipping lines, if possible those that had proven their reliability, needed to be dealt with; and gouging and outright cheating of emigrants were substantially reduced, even though not eliminated.

Of even greater concern now was to find routes over which to dispatch the groups to the remaining overseas destinations, such as North and Latin America, and the Far East, which meant mainly Shanghai and in a few cases the Philippines. There followed a flurry of activity, on the part of the staffs in Berlin and Vienna, to find ways of reaching the Far East by a land route, whence ships would have to take the emigrants across the Pacific to their destinations in the Americas. In June, at the time when the Allied front in France was collapsing before the German onslaught, Löwenherz, Storfer, Eppstein, and Hirsch had to report to Eichmann and Dannecker about the progress of that effort. Eichmann and Dannecker were extremely anxious for quick results, and from one day to the next required a full report about "Emigration to North and South America via the Far East."[103] The report proved to be the basic framework for a major scheme to route groups of Jews out of Europe.

Arrangements for this routing were complex and presented many difficulties, and Eichmann's and Dannecker's pressure for them to secure "a special ship for the purpose of regular voyages" and "to bring the efforts as quickly as possible to a favorable conclusion"[104] made Löwenherz's, Eppstein's, Hirsch's, and Storfer's job even harder.

What the four men stated in their report was the result of planning, exploration, and negotiations begun late in 1939 to put in place ways to reach the Far East. The idea of a land route through the Soviet Union apparently originated with Murmelstein and was explored by Storfer, when the war sealed the Atlantic ports but opened up the overland route with the friendship pact of August 1939 between the Soviet Union and Nazi Germany. Vienna's participation in the scheme had been interrupted when Murmelstein and Storfer were ordered to Nisko. At that time the RV temporarily took the lead, in agreement with the IKG Vienna and the Prague Jewish Community.[105] The subject of emigration from Nazi Germany to or by way of the communist Soviet Union was a touchy subject in spite of the friendship pact. Nonetheless, Löwenherz first broached the subject indirectly with Eichmann at the first Berlin *Vorsprache* in mid-January 1940. He used the pretext to gain Eichmann's permission to use his presence in Berlin to contact the Russian General Consulate, to explore with them the matter of the "dependents (wives and children) of persons who are there," by implication referring to the survivors of Nisko who may have succeeded in crossing over to Soviet territory.[106] As we know, Eichmann was very eager to get rid of the "dependents" who were stranded at Gänsbacher Street. However, Löwenherz had other matters in mind, namely, a way to the Far East via the Soviet Union. At the same time Eichmann "expressed his skepticism about all projects dealing with group transports" but authorized Löwenherz to explore the matter in consultation with the RV.[107] It is understandable that in January 1940 Eichmann was skeptical about group transports at a time when the Mossad's Palestine transports were getting stuck in Kladovo. However, he was soon persuaded to have all group transport schemes approved by Storfer as to feasibility. Thus, in June, by the time the turmoil of war frustrated the emigration business of his *Zentralstellen* as never before, his skepticism had given way to nervous insistence.

When Löwenherz went to the Russian Counsel General during his January sojourn in Berlin, he was told that transit visas would be issued to persons who had all requisite documentation, in particular valid visas to their ultimate destinations. Early in June 1940 the first list of a group of eleven from Vienna was ready for Russian transit visas, being in possession of transit visas through Manchuria and Japan, as well as the *Steuerunbedenklichkeitsbescheinigung* (certificate of overall tax clearance). According to a directive from the *Zentralstelle*, a recommendation was required "from proper authorities," that is from the Reich Foreign Office, to the Russian General Consulate in Berlin. Murmelstein then submitted the list of emigrants who were ready to be dispatched to the *Zentralstelle* with the request that they obtain the required clearance from the Foreign Office. Presumably Löwenherz took the request with him when he went to Berlin a week later and submitted it there. This case shows that until the IKG assigned a delegate to further their emigration efforts in Berlin, the RV Emigration Section had the advantage of being where all the consulates and relevant travel and shipping offices were located.

What was the scheme outlined by Löwenherz and his Berlin counterparts, which gained Eichmann's and Dannecker's immediate approval?

All the projected routes led to Moscow and from there, by Trans-Siberian Railroad, to the different destinations or embarkation points. To get to Moscow, the emigrants—from the Altreich, Vienna, and the Protectorate—had to assemble in Berlin at a given time. They then traveled in a group through Lithuania, Latvia, and Russia to Moscow. Each of these countries required a transit visa for each individual. No transit visa was issued unless a passport showed a visa to an ultimate destination. This presented difficulties for travel to Shanghai by the overland route: Since this route led through Chinese territory occupied by Japan, it required a Japanese transit visa. Only with such a transit visa would Manchuria issue a transit visa, and only with these in hand would the Soviet Union issue one, as would in turn Latvia and Lithuania.

There were two routes to Shanghai. One was the land-sea route, which traversed the full length of the Trans-Siberian Railway from Moscow to Omsk in Siberia, to Krasnoyarsk, and ended in Vladivostok. There a ship would take the travelers around Korea (which was under Japanese control), through the Sea of Japan and the East China Sea to Shanghai, with a stop at the tiny port of Tsuruga on the north shore of the Japanese island of Honshu. This route, though much longer and more laborious, had the advantage of not requiring a transit visa for Manchuria.

The other, more direct land route to Shanghai led from Moscow, Omsk, and Krasnoyarsk to Tayshet, where the carriages were separated from the Trans-Siberian Railroad train and sent south to Irkutsk and around Lake Baikal. At Manchouli (Manzhouli) the travelers crossed into Manchuria. Manchuria, under Japanese control, was an independent country named Manchukuo (Manzhouguo). Japan established the last Emperor of China—and the last of China's Manchu dynasty—as the Emperor of Manchukuo. Only Japan and the Axis partners Germany and Italy officially recognized the country. This was fortunate for the emigrants, since for this reason Manchukuo maintained a consulate in Berlin; and early in

1940, at the request of the Reich Foreign Ministry, it was prepared to issue transit visas. Applications for Vienna had to be channeled through Eichmann's Berlin office by way of the IKG and the Vienna *Zentralstelle*.[108]

There were additional complications connected with dispatching emigrants to the Far East. For a while the Russian transit visas were issued upon certification by the emigration section of the RV. But soon a recommendation by the Reich Foreign Office was needed. Also, Russia issued only a very small number of transit visas to travelers to Vladivostok because it was a fortified city, and the Soviet Union was painfully aware of tensions with Japan. One of the reasons for routing some of the emigrants to Shanghai by way of the Japanese port of Tsuruga was that Japan wished to have control over those who were not traveling with a prior permit to enter Shanghai. Since an office of HICEM (an immigration organization founded in 1927; the name is an acronym of its sponsors: HIAS, JCA, and Emigdirect) was established in Shanghai to aid Jewish emigrants in transit in the Far East, the Japanese made it relatively easy for Jewish migrants to go there. Shanghai continued as an international city even under Japanese occupation, and permission to enter Shanghai was given by concessionaires representing certain nations to anyone who was in possession of US $400. The RV and IKG attempted to gain Japanese transit visas for emigrants, who had the $400 but no permit, to Shanghai to be sent through the easier Manchuria route.

The access route to overseas destinations also went by way of Manchuria: to Harbin—which had a Jewish community, consisting mainly of refugees from the Russian revolution—and to Mukden, and from there to Pusan in the south of Korea. In Pusan, the Korean port facing Japan, they would take a ship to Shimonoseki on Honshu Island, where they would take the train to one of the major Japanese ports: Kobe or Yokohama. There were several lines operating from there to the west coast of America, small ocean liners of 14,000 to 17,000 tons sailing twice monthly. Two of them flew the flag of the United States, the President Line and the Barber Line. There was also the Japanese Nippon Yūsen Kaisha Line (NYK). All three lines sailed from Yokohama to San Francisco. Only the NYK could be used to reach the west coast of South America or the West Indies (for example, San Domingo). The ship would take its passengers to Balboa, the Pacific terminal port of the Panama Canal, where one could change ship to one's destination.

While the journey to the west coast of North as well as South America headed directly eastward, access to the east coast of South America doubled over westward from Yokohama, via the Osaka Nyosen Line, through the Indian Ocean, around South Africa and the Cape of Good Hope, and—traversing the Atlantic Ocean—to Argentina. This was a journey from Berlin (13.5°E x 52.5°N) via Siberia to Yokohama (139.5°E x 35.5°N) to the tip of South Africa (20°E x 35°S) to Buenos Aires (58°W x 34°S). To travel 71 degrees latitude, one had to traverse 316 degrees—in effect, more than three-fourths of the globe!

Smaller Japanese ships took some groups of emigrants for a short end-lap from Japan to the Philippines.

Normally the voyage from Berlin to Japan would last seventeen days. The actual voyage from there across the Pacific to America would take another seventeen days. For waiting in Japan for the ship one would have to allow another week.

What were the costs for such circuitous journeys over such great distances and over territories and on ships of so many flags? From the beginning of the war, passage on ocean liners had to be paid in U.S. dollars. But, until June 11, 1940, the time when the directors met with Eichmann and his deputies, the voyage both over land and by land-and-sea could be paid for in Reichsmark. Now, however, while the Soviet Union continued to accept Reichsmark, the voyages in Manchuria and China had to be paid for in U.S. dollars. This meant that the entire voyage to America by way of the Far East cost, on average, US $260. To that one had to add personal costs, such as for food, especially on the Trans-Siberian Railroad and in Japan.

This was the scheme, theoretically complex but feasible. In practice, however, dispatching the groups of travelers had to be arranged group by group and individual by individual, and it involved the tireless labor of Jewish officials at many locations and at various stations working as if they were a team. In its practical execution the full complexity of the scheme made itself felt, straining its feasibility to its limits, and at times to a breaking point.

While in Berlin, Eichmann directed Löwenherz to agree with Eppstein and Hirsch on a formula for dividing available passages among the three communities. Löwenherz pointed out that Vienna "did not wish to be in competition with the others and would proceed in cooperation with the Berlin and Prague organizations." However, Vienna was especially in need of an ample number of places since its income in Reichsmark depended essentially on the expenditure of *Devisen* for passages.[109] For the purpose of reserving ship passages, the three participating communities agreed to apportion available places among Berlin, Vienna, and Prague according to the ratio of 47:37:16. It was also agreed that any places not used by Prague would be divided equally between Berlin and Vienna.[110] One week after this agreement was officially set down in the report to Dannecker, Victor Löwenstein, the leading official in the RV emigration section, informed Löwenherz that he had been able to secure twelve passages on the run to the east coast of South America (Brazil and Argentina), scheduled to sail from Kobe on July 15. Since Prague required two places, Berlin and Vienna took five each, at a cost of US $204 per passage. At the same time, Löwenstein informed Löwenherz that Prague required only 10 percent of a block of passages reserved for a sailing to the United States, and they agreed that Vienna's portion would be upped to 40 percent.[111] This proportion of 50 (Berlin):40 (Vienna):10 (Prague), which was originally recommended by Dannecker,[112] would prevail more often than not in the succeeding period, at least as an operative guideline.

Three days later Murmelstein reported a telephone call he received from Löwenstein about Prague not being able to make use of the ten places on the SS *Rakuyo Maru*, which was scheduled to sail from Yokohama on July 27, 1940, but to reserve these places on later sailings. Hence, Löwenstein suggested a re-allotment of the next five sailings as follows:

Date	**Ship**	**Allotment of Places**
July 27	*Rakuyo Maru*	44 places for Vienna instead of 40
Aug. 8	*Heian Maru*	15 places for Vienna instead of 16
Sep. 4	*Hikawa Maru*	15 places for Vienna instead of 16
Sep. 18	*Hie Maru*	15 places for Vienna instead of 16
Sep. 22	*Heyo Maru*	39 places for Vienna instead of 40

In either case, Vienna would have a total of 128 places. Of course, Murmelstein agreed.[113]

The following day, Friday at 6:45 p.m., Löwenstein informed Löwenherz that four second-class places had become free on the July 22 sailing of the *Hikawa Maru*, at a cost of US $140 each, plus boarding fee, head tax, and funds for incidentals during the transit through Manchuria. After they agreed to share two places each, Löwenherz instructed the appropriate documentation department of the IKG to take charge of the two places, to prepare all necessary documents (passports, applications, and photographs), and to submit them to Murmelstein on Sunday, June 23.[114] In other words, they had all of a Saturday, the Sabbath, to finish the documentation within 35 hours for the two fortunate, as yet anonymous emigrants, and to submit the documentation for final in-house processing in Murmelstein's office, who would then direct it to the proper authorities and to Berlin. Considering that the sailing was scheduled half a world away exactly one month later, there was surely no time to lose.

At the time Eppstein, Löwenherz, and Hirsch were writing their report, most of the places on the ships from Japan to the United States were booked for months ahead, mainly because American citizens were heading home owing to the ominous developments in Europe. For this reason the IKG and the RV had begun negotiations with NYK to hire a ship exclusively for emigrants to America, and they requested Troper to do likewise with American lines. Before leaving Berlin at the time of the June 1940 meeting, Löwenherz joined a representative of the RV to consult with the Berlin agent of NYK about the progress of those negotiations. They were told that the traffic of the American returnees would soon be finished and that there would then be plenty of spaces. As to the matter of a special ship, the response of the latest telegraphic inquiry at the home office indicated that they were waiting for a directive from the Japanese authorities, without which they could not go ahead. In dire need of escape routes and mindful of the pressure by the Nazis, Löwenherz and his associate told the agent that "at this time it is mainly Jewish emigrants who are using the shipping line to North and South America, resulting for [the NYK Line] in an extraordinary business opportunity, which it is in their interest to exploit as quickly as possible, especially since, thanks to the Joint, the passages will be paid in U.S dollars."[115]

Nothing became of the scheme Löwenherz explored with the NYK Line while in Berlin. His place was in any case at his home base in Vienna, his job to provide the wherewithal for all the concerns arising on behalf of the remaining Jews in Vienna. He had a staff in place to carry out the new routing of groups of emigrants via the Far East. While cooperation with the RV was absolutely necessary, their mandate was to care for the Altreich Jews and—even within the context of cooperation in emigrations matters—the RV and IKG had been and would continue to be in competition. Clearly, the IKG needed someone in Berlin to represent the interests of Viennese Jews in emigration matters. Löwenherz requested and was granted permission to send such an agent.

The man selected for the task by Murmelstein would turn out to be a key player in the arena where the battles for visas, for routes, and for places on trains and ships were being fought. He was a young man by the name of Robert Prochnik. He had been a law student but, like all Jewish students, had to leave the university after the Anschluss. During his abbreviated university career, he had joined a *Studentenverbindung*, an academic fraternity, to which several influential Jews of Vienna belonged, a fact that worked to his advantage after his university studies came to an abrupt end. After he had tried—and failed—to escape to Belgium, an alumnus of the fraternity, Professor Bettelheim, introduced him to Löwenherz, and in 1939, at age 24, he found employment at the IKG. At first he worked as a volunteer doing menial jobs, but he was soon given more responsible assignments. His association with Murmelstein dates from this early period of service at the IKG. Prochnik was acknowledged to be highly intelligent and committed to whatever work he was assigned. Murmelstein could rely on Prochnik as a loyal, discreet, effective, and efficient assistant. Being very much aware of his intellectual acumen, he, like Murmelstein, seems not to have suffered fools gladly. More about that later.

One of the reasons why an agent had to represent the IKG in Berlin was that when Austria became part of the Reich, Vienna became a provincial capital. This meant, among other things, that foreign countries would no longer maintain embassies or, in some cases, even fully staffed consulates there. Furthermore, the main offices of the travel agencies and shipping lines were now to be found in places like Hamburg and in time almost exclusively in Berlin. It made sense, therefore, for the IKG to post a highly capable agent to Berlin in order to be on the spot when passages were available or visas given out. There was also the matter of cooperation with the other Jewish community organizations, the RV in Berlin and the IKG Prague. Berlin was now also predominant in the number of remaining Jews; and, unlike many other cities in Nazi Germany, especially unlike Vienna, the status of the Jews was almost residually privileged, and their public isolation and persecution was at a minimum. Tactically, not only documentation but negotiations concerning emigration matters would be greatly facilitated by face-to-face meetings rather than only through correspondence or occasional telephone conversation. Taking all these factors into consideration, the *Zentralstelle* authorized Löwenherz to send a representative of the IKG to Berlin for an indefinite period of time, one who was familiar with emigration problems and procedures. Being eminently qualified, Prochnik was chosen to be this representative. His task, as he explained in his deposition for the Austrian courts

> consisted primarily in procuring the necessary transit visas as well as ship passages and train tickets for those already in possession of visas to their final destination. We also procured fake visas for supposed final destinations (Cuba, San Domingo) that made it possible for some people to get at least as far as Shanghai or Lisbon.[116]

Prochnik also explained the difficulties connected with this work in light of the fact that there were very few berths available on the ships and very few seats on the Trans-Siberian Railroad; the consulates involved were anything but helpful. In light of all the roadblocks erected by the authorities, he was forced to resort to "totally illegitimate means" to further emigration, such as ignoring the directives issued by the *Zentralstelle*. This made his work, which was risky to begin with, even more dangerous.

Prochnik, according to his testimony, used all kinds of ruses to get results at the end of the Nisko fiasco when the remaining Viennese members of this sorry troupe were to return to Vienna to a home they no longer had. Prochnik, by all accounts, did not "look Jewish," and it seems that he capitalized on this lucky circumstance and profited by it, for others and surely also for himself. One way in which he emphasized his non-Jewish looks, and the one that is cited more often than any other, is the fact that he wore boots "like the SS."[117] This, in the minds of many, meant that he was a collaborator. But the facts tell us a different story.

Prochnik was sent to Berlin in June of 1940, and immediately plunged into a sea of interconnected problems, some of which will be exemplified in what follows. Any summary account fails to convey in full the incredible complexity and the frantic nature of this last-ditch effort, the tenacity, the attention to each case, the courage, and even chutzpah necessary to wring the least concession out of bored bureaucrats and avaricious dealers in human misery. Prochnik was in constant contact with the IKG, mainly by mail; long-distance phone calls were less frequent. Most of the immense correspondence between Prochnik and the administration of the IKG was between him and Murmelstein, who was at the command post and in whose hands all the different strands of the various emigration efforts came together and were coordinated. Fairly frequent letters were reports to the *Amtsdirektion*, the central office of the IKG; they reached Löwenherz first and then Murmelstein. Some correspondence dealing with travel arrangements passed between him and Storfer. Prochnik, of course, was not the only one involved in the practical aspects of this never-ending struggle.

Prochnik's letters convey the atmosphere of that time and place. Many are long, detailed, and hastily written missives typed at the end of long, exhausting, and frustrating days, letters that he tried to finish in time to run to the train station and send them on the overnight train that left Berlin for Vienna at 11:00 p.m. Even though most of the travel arrangements were made for groups of emigrés, each case presented its own problems and each individual or family had to be checked on and guided individually. Sometimes Prochnik injected a kind of grim humor into his letters; sometimes he got sarcastic in the face of human failings, especially when he felt people should have known better: "Perhaps [they] . . . should write down everything they need [to know] since, apparently, they can't keep anything in mind."[118]

Even though this evidence from the forefront of the ongoing battle for visas, reservations, passports, money, and so on is somewhat sketchy (since apart from missing letters we also lack information about phone calls and face-to-face meetings), enough material remains to allow us to understand the overwhelming difficulties of the unique situation into which this young man was thrown. There were a number of factors, all of which had to be considered at the same time; and if Prochnik failed to follow up on one, a project might come to naught in spite of all the planning that had gone into it; and the emigration possibilities of a whole group might be jeopardized, if not lost. The evidence in the letters of the stress brought on by the responsibility placed on Prochnik's shoulders is palpable, as is his constant concern that he might have overlooked something—a possible snag, a new route, a new more or less receptive consular official who would have to be approached differently. Regulations, many of them arbitrary, the personalities of the people he had to deal with, both Nazi and Jewish and neither/nor, the changing face of Europe, time constraints—all these had to be taken into account. Coordination of all that went into getting an individual or a group past all the obstacles and onto the train or plane or to a ship scheduled to depart literally half a world away, and that would get them beyond the reach of the German behemoth, was one of the keys to success as well as one of the most difficult things to achieve. A few glimpses of his activities in the very first weeks after his arrival give insight into this world of almost Kafkaesque twists and turns.

Prochnik's Kafkaesque Experiences in Berlin

When Prochnik arrived in Berlin in June of 1940, the major Mediterranean and Atlantic ports had been lost as available embarkation points, so that basically—apart from the illegal transports to Palestine, with which Prochnik was not involved—there were two directions left in which the emigrants could be sent, albeit with great difficulty. One way led to the southwest, through Spain and Portugal, for travel to the east coast of the Western Hemisphere. The other went by land and sea, and sometimes in part by air, across the Soviet Union and Manchuria to Shanghai—which would still take Jews with some capital—or through Japan across the Pacific to the West Coast of the United States. In his deposition Prochnik prided himself on having contributed "substantially" (*wesentlich*) to the opening of the route through German-occupied France, Spain, and Portugal in 1940.[119] But when he first got to Berlin, it was the emigration to and by way of the Far East that was of paramount importance as well as difficulty.

It was not only the transit countries or the final destination that could cause difficulties at the last moment. On June 26, 1940, shortly after he got to Berlin, Prochnik reported that he found out from Löwenstein of the RV that German customs had begun to delay the emigrating Jews at Eidtkunen (sic; should be Eydtkuhnen), the East Prussian border crossing into the Soviet Union via the Soviet Zone of occupied Poland and Latvia. They had to leave the train and could not continue on their journey until the next day. This meant that the Viennese Jews—who first had to travel to Berlin, where they were taken in hand by the Jewish Community, fed and housed, and then continued from there together with the Berlin contingent—had better leave a day earlier to make sure not to miss their connection in Moscow to the Trans-Siberian Railway, lest all their travel arrangements (i.e., bookings and reservations) would be invalidated. That this was no false alarm becomes quite clear from Prochnik's letter of July 1, in which he reported that because of the delay at "Eidtkunen" a group of Berlin Jews had missed the Trans-Siberian train and, hence, also the Japanese ship, the *Rakuyo Maru*, on which they were to continue their travels.[120]

A difficulty Prochnik alluded to in a letter to Murmelstein was the minimum of cooperation he was given by the RV. Indeed, there was a fierce competition between Berlin and Vienna for available places on ships, trains, and planes, and this in spite of the distribution ratio of 5:4:1 that Berlin, Vienna, and Prague had agreed upon. Two weeks later Prochnik reported that the Lithuanian and Latvian visas, which Moscow insisted on, were no longer available; in fact, the Lithuanian consulate had already packed up and was ready to leave. This meant that refugees could no longer go to Moscow by train to catch the Trans-Siberian Railroad. The only remaining possibility was to fly from Berlin to Moscow, and of course there were much fewer places available. Air travel in those days was still the exception rather than the rule; and single-propeller passenger planes seated twelve passengers at most. And seats, according to Lufthansa, could not be reserved without the Russian visas, which would take a few more days. Prochnik feared that the RV would try to reserve all of these for itself by using "straw men," as he phrased it, whose papers to Shanghai were all in order, to hoard (*hamstern*)[121] these few seats and then reassign them once the Russian visas came in. While he was negotiating with Lufthansa, Herr Sänger of the RV came in and "exploded" when he saw Prochnik there, probably in his turn afraid of "the other side"—Vienna—snatching the airplane reservations. Eventually they did come to an agreement, for this time at least.

But now another difficulty arose. Toward the end of July 1940 Prochnik wrote a two-and-a-half page, single-spaced letter to the IKG, detailing in breathless prose the last-minute foul-ups and his efforts to save at least some of the situation. A few excerpts should convey the atmosphere. To understand the problem, we must keep in mind that for the almost weeklong trip across Siberia one needed to purchase a train ticket as well as a seat reservation.

> [Y]esterday morning there was danger that I would have to send all people back to Vienna. . . . When I went to pick up the tickets [for the Trans-Siberian train] from HAPAG [the German travel bureau] I was told that the seats were not available. . . . Wladimirov [claimed] that he could not give out more seats than were at his disposal . . . and suggested that he send the people to Moscow with tickets and let them buy their reservations and provisions there. However, he could not issue the tickets because he was not allowed to sell them without bed reservations. . . . For three and a half hours I beseeched Wl. not to leave me up in the air and to help me, without success. All I accomplished was that he . . . threw me out twice [but without success] so that he finally left the office himself. But I didn't let go and followed him everywhere. Finally he tried to escape to the toilet, but I stood guard at the door and descended on him again when he emerged. . . . In the end he was ready to call Moscow and told me he could give me the places on Monday or Tuesday. . . . I told him that the people had to leave yesterday already. . . . You cannot imagine what methods I had to use . . . to prevent the break-off of negotiations. . . . I called him a criminal who causes people's misfortune, I begged him to save the lives of twelve people. . . . [A]nd finally the head clerk began to cry, and he, too, started sobbing . . . . [A]t one-thirty he offered me five reservations, he could not risk more, at a quarter of two I had talked him out of eight, and by two he was ready at last to give me all eleven.[122]

There was good reason for Prochnik to go directly to the Russian Travel Agency to secure places on the Trans-Siberian train: The group in question had to be in Japan for the sailing of the *Heian Maru*, scheduled to leave on August 14. In the next three weeks the tickets had to be sent to Vienna, the persons had to be brought to Berlin, to Moscow, via the Trans-Siberian to the Pacific coast, then to Japan. Since HAPAG, which was supposed to do the booking, did not pursue the matter with due vigor, Prochnik complained about their unreliability and about a number of other things. He reported that Lufthansa was understandably incensed over the practice on the part of the RV of booking a set of flights to Moscow via Königsberg [later, Kaliningrad], only to issue the tickets to passengers with names different from those for whom the flights were booked. These substitute passengers were then stuck in Königsberg because they had left Berlin without a Russian transit visa and could not proceed to Moscow. Prochnik begged the IKG most urgently (*aufs eindringlichste*) not to send people against his advice and contrary to his request that they not be

The MS Heian Maru *of the Nippon Yūsen Kabushiki Kaisha ("NYK Line") moored at the Great Northern Dock in Seattle in July 1941.Many of the passengers waiting to disembark were Jewish refugees from Austria and Germany. (Seattle Post-Intelligencer Collection, Museum of History & Industry, Seattle. All Rights Reserved. Property of MOHAI Seattle)*

sent, and further asked that certain routes of travel, such as a flight by way of Stockholm, which he had mentioned to the IKG as mere possibilities, not be communicated to would-be emigrants as fact. If the IKG could not refrain from doing this, then he would have to keep quiet about such matters to avoid making people crazy.[123]

The war situation being what it was at that time, travelers had to count on considerable delay for Russian transit visas, at a minimum three days. Not only Jewish emigrants from Vienna as well as from Berlin needed visas, but German and other businessmen, as well as Japanese travelers. Prochnik even mentioned Albanian diplomats. None of them could obtain visas right away. There was only one consular official to process the visas, and she could do only 80 to 100 a day. Since Prochnik's submissions of thirty applications would have taken a huge chunk of the daily workload, he agreed to pick up ten completed applications on each of the following days. He requested of Murmelstein that properly completed (in triplicate with photograph at the upper right-hand corner) and documented visa applications be forwarded to him for submission to the consulate well in advance of the applicants' travel deadline, accompanied by all the necessary proof papers, including the passports with Lithuanian transit visas, tickets, and so on. And to be sure that his home base in Vienna knew what his assignment was like, Prochnik added:

> I do not always have time to be busy at night [with the preparation of incomplete documents], as was the case today; from 9 a.m. to 8:30 [p.m.]. I was on the go, though mainly waiting, at noon briefly at home to see whether the passports have arrived and to call you, I did not eat all day, only smoked, in the evening I vomited, until 10:30 p.m. I still had to write—and yet one cannot accomplish all that one wants to because it is impossible for one person to manage all that running, talking, waiting, etc., which normally takes a whole staff.[124]

For reasons we do not know, the Russian consulate, or at least its visa office, moved a number of times, so also toward the end of August 1940, causing them to close for business. Prochnik reported that for this reason he would not be able to complete arrangements for dispatching a current group. He estimated that as many as fifteen people who had tickets for the Trans-Siberian would not be able to make the train for lack of a transit visa. Also, the consulate would no longer accept applications from individuals, except in rare cases, and they were advised to apply through agents (i.e., a travel bureau, the RV, or Prochnik). On the other hand, they "accept ridiculously few" applications even from these agents "so that there ensued a wholly impossible situation."[125]

There were also complications and problems with other links in the chain along which the emigrants would be dispatched to the Far East. In mid-September Prochnik reported that, "as expected," the Manchurian consulate "made difficulties" about granting transit visas for two of the six applications that Prochnik had submitted, requiring each of the two to show a permit to carry *Devisen* in the amount of at least $47.[126] The very next day he reported that as many as twenty-seven participants of the RV contingent booked to sail on the *Heyo Maru* on September 22 would not make the departure because they were not able to obtain their Manchurian visas on time. The loss of twenty-seven passages to America was, of course, a catastrophe for the RV. And it caused trouble for Vienna as well as for Berlin because the travel agency that had arranged for the addition of a special carriage for the Trans-Siberian group transports threatened to cancel the arrangement altogether if such a situation were to occur again.[127]

Half a year later, some passengers from Vienna were held up in Manchouli because, according to new, previously unannounced regulations that went into effect after they had departed from Berlin and Moscow, they did not have enough *Devisen* with them to exchange for the local currency, Japanese Yen, as was now required. *Vaad (Waad) Leumi*, a Jewish aid organization that had a temporary branch office in Harbin, sent a telegram to the IKG requesting the immediate transfer of an exorbitant amount in U.S. dollars. In answer to their inquiry to Prochnik, Murmelstein explained to the emigration section of the RV that he was expecting an explanation of the request from *Vaad Leumi*, which he would check against his records. He would then ask the Joint to transfer the appropriate dollar amount to Harbin.[128] It soon became clear that there was a new regulation regarding the transit of refugees by way of the troublesome Manchurian route to the effect that the passengers were given vouchers for their room and board while in Manchuria. Also a credit in the amount of US $20 had to be exchanged for Yen upon entry into Manchuria; this was not returnable and hence "lost." The vouchers were issued either by MER (*Mitteleuropäisches Reisebüro*, Central European Travel Bureau) or by Hanseatic; Prochnik reported that the people there had never seen a voucher and were confused about what to do with them.[129]

In light of these and other complications Prochnik suggested that the route via Vladivostok to the Japanese ports would be preferable. In November 1940 he had reported to Murmelstein that the Russian consul in Prague issued transit visas to emigrants from there for travel via Vladivostok to Shanghai. He planned to consult with Richard Friedmann, who had been transferred from Vienna, where he had worked for the IKG, to Prague to organize emigration, to see whether it might be possible to obtain such visas in Prague for emigrants from Vienna.[130] In time visas to Vladivostok were issued in Berlin, but this routing was problematic. In April 1941 a large contingent of emigrants from Vienna and Prague arrived too late in Vladivostok and missed the steamer that was scheduled to take them to Japan. While they waited for the next ship, due to leave on April 20, they were running up hotel bills that would have to be covered by Vienna and Prague.[131] At the same time Prochnik reported that transit through Russia had been suspended until the beginning of May, which meant that a number of emigrants who were being processed for early May sailings would have to be rescheduled for later in May, in the hope that transit through Russia would be resumed in time. However, because of the desirability of providing a route that would avoid Manchuria, Prochnik pursued the Vladivostok alternative and found that the difference in cost was negligible: Moscow to Kobe via Manchuria cost US $251.70 in soft-seat class and $221.30 for hard seats. Via Vladivostok the journey cost $259.30 and $224.00, respectively. The main drawback of the Vladivostok route was that the connection to it left every ten days, while the connection via Manchouli was available every three to four days. Also, reservations for the Vladivostok connection had to be made ten days in advance. "If it is possible [to make all these arrangements]," Prochnik wrote, "I consider [the routing via] Vladivostok more favorable."[132] Prochnik wrote this report on May 5, 1941; little did he know how futile these arrangements would be once they were firmed up.

We have mentioned certain difficulties connected with travel to Moscow to board the Trans-Siberian train. There was the fierce competition with the RV for places on Lufthansa flights to Königsberg and from there to Moscow. For those who took the train to Moscow there were difficulties obtaining transit visas to Lithuania and with the border crossings that would lead there. This indicates that the emigrants were routed to Moscow via the Baltic rather than by a more direct route. But, why? The reason seems obvious. On October 6, 1940, Prochnik reported that as of that day train traffic for emigrants could be routed to Moscow by way of Warsaw. Not only would this route be more direct, not requiring transit through the Baltic, but it would also provide a more efficient connection. Since the train was scheduled to arrive in Moscow before noon, the emigrants would not have to stay in a hotel overnight as heretofore but could board the Trans-Siberian, which was scheduled to leave at 5:00 p.m. on the same day. The date on which this route was made available to emigrants was not chosen arbitrarily. It took the Germans one year from the time they seized Warsaw to gather all the Jews from there and the surroundings, to concentrate them in one place, and to fence them in. The Warsaw ghetto was completed on October 2, 1940.

Now the Nazis could finally let Jews traverse the city and the region without seeing what Murmelstein and the others who were Nisko-bound saw as they passed through Krakow in October 1939, and without being in the position to carry their tales abroad.

Not all complications, changes of regulations, and difficulties in coordinating efforts pertained to countries that had to be traversed along the escape route. When the scheme of routing the emigrants via the Far East went into effect, an exit clearance in the form of a "recommendation" from the German Foreign Office was needed before the list of emigrants requiring transit visas could be submitted to the Russian consulate.[133] Soon Prochnik had to submit these applications in duplicate not directly but via the Berlin *Zentralstelle*.[134] Then, SS Sergeant Richard Hartmann of the Berlin *Zentralstelle* informed him that the Foreign Office required that for each transit visa applied for, country by country, every emigrant on a group list had to submit a separate application for Foreign Office clearance, and that the set of applications submitted via the *Zentralstelle* be accompanied by proof of payment (i.e., a receipt of money transfer) for a processing fee of RM 2 for each application, country by country.[135] This may seem like a minor annoyance and a minor outlay, but it indicates the literally dozens of papers that had to be filled out and the innumerable details that had to be attended to, in sequence and on time, by the harassed individuals—and all that under the supervision and coordination of the various sections of the IKG concerned with the emigration process.

Other problems concerned the procedures, the scheduling, the stages, and the execution of the emigration process. One time Prochnik advised the IKG that inasmuch as the transit visas were valid for a limited time only, they should not be applied for prematurely but when reservations for seats on the Trans-Siberian were in place. Hence, it would be preferable that individuals not apply themselves but let the IKG handle the matter. Also, because of the volume it would be best to apply for the transit visas in blocks, as was done in Berlin, though not more than twenty to twenty-five at a time, since the Russian officials tended to be "*schwerfällig*" (hard to budge).[136] Another time he advised the dispatching section of the IKG not to send two different groups to Berlin at the same time, if at all possible, the reason being that upon their arrival, travelers from Vienna were met by a guide delegated by the Berlin community. If it should happen that a contingent from Vienna, whose documentation was complete, was led to the Berlin contingent for joint embarkation on the train, then no one competent would be left to take over and guide another group arriving at the same time that still had to obtain its visa for transit through Manchuria.[137] There was no end of trouble with respect to transit visas for Manchuria. Because the regulations changed frequently, some of the people from Vienna had to apply during their brief stay in Berlin before boarding the train to Moscow. Once Prochnik had to take care of two ladies in charge of a group of eight emigrants. He described them as "surely the clumsiest one could find" and suggested that in the future the IKG send people who could write. Prochnik had to fill out all eight applications for the Manchurian visas for them, which he minded "less because of the work than the loss of the time [he] needed to eat lunch."[138]

The RV was generally helpful in receiving the Vienna contingents for their brief stays in Berlin pending the departure of their trains to Moscow or to Lisbon. The competition between Berlin and Vienna lessened in time; and an atmosphere of reliable cooperation prevailed. But there were exceptions, mainly with respect to money matters. On September 6, 1940, Dr. Braun of the RV emigration section wrote to the IKG emigration section (i.e., to Murmelstein) that the Joint had requested the immediate transfer of US $1,000 to the Kobe Jewish Community, supposedly to take care of transients who had arrived too late for the departure of their ship from Kobe and Yokohama. On the basis of the 5:4 ratio stipulated for places on ships, Braun demanded that Vienna transfer its share, namely, $400. In his response, Murmelstein assured Braun that the transfer of $400 had been arranged but told him in no uncertain terms that he knew of no tardy arrival of a contingent from Vienna, that in any case the Viennese emigrants were provided with required *Devisen* for their expenses *en route*, that the transfer has been arranged on the dubious chance that emigrants from Vienna had to be supported by the Jewish Community of Kobe, and that because such transfers had to be justified and cleared with the *Devisenstelle* "and for other reasons," the RV must in the future gain the agreement of the IKG before they committed themselves to a transfer that entailed committing Vienna to a portion.[139] The matter of a *Hilferuf*, a "cry for help," for supposedly stranded emigrants in Kobe may have seemed strange to Murmelstein. A few days after that exchange, a letter arrived at the RV with a copy for Vienna, which reached Murmelstein on September 14. It was from Max Birman of the affiliate of HICEM in Shanghai. He reported that some people who took the Lufthansa flight to Moscow were detained in Königsberg because their Russian transit visas were issued for a different route, namely, the route by train. They missed their connection with the Trans-Siberian Railway and, hence, the ship in Japan. Others missed the ship because they stayed in Manchouli to await the arrival of their luggage, which was delayed. This may explain that *Hilferuf*. But to the tune of $1,000? Could it be that the needs, beyond the money they carried with them, of the temporarily stranded emigrants served as a convenient pretext for the Kobe aid committee to help provide for the sudden influx of Mirer Hassidim from Lithuania?

However, there was another dispute about money between the RV and Murmelstein.

We have seen how the stranglehold on the financial position of the IKG reached a crisis point as 1940 came to an end. It was the time when Löwenherz was in Lisbon and, as his deputy, Murmelstein was temporarily in charge at the IKG. We do not know whether Löwenherz's absence was a pretext for Murmelstein to act on an idea he had of relieving the situation somewhat or a coincidence; perhaps he had Löwenherz's blessing. Murmelstein thought that Löwenherz was too cautious in spending available money for emigration, desiring to keep a reserve for someday taking care of those who would not be able to emigrate, especially the old and the infirm. But by then there would be no more income from the transfer of *Devisen* for emigration. Murmelstein was no less concerned for the old but thought that when the time came, the IKG would have to exploit the opportunities that would then offer themselves. One thing he was convinced of, and the experience of 1940 bore him out, that any reserve the IKG might accumulate would not be under the control of nor be freely available to the IKG and should therefore be used now as needed. Also, Löwenherz was impeccably correct in trying to avoid doing anything on behalf of the

Jews of Vienna that would appear to be in unfair competition with the RV. However, Murmelstein knew that this caution extended mainly to the distribution of places on trains and ships and that Löwenherz himself had gained the permission of the authorities to exchange U.S. dollars for Reichsmark at a ratio of 1:6, rather than the required 1:5 that continued to be the ratio for the RV. He also knew that the RV not only had a sizable reserve but that it had control over it, and that Vienna, because of its share of the Poland transfer, had access to a goodly amount of *Devisen* for emigration purposes. Moreover, for most of the period under consideration Vienna had more *Devisen* for emigration than it could use, whereas Berlin had fewer. The dollar-Reichsmark ratio of 1:5, which the *Reichswirtschaftsamt* (Reich Economic Office) had imposed, was a factor in the financial stranglehold on Vienna; but because of the different financial situation of the RV, it had no such effect in Berlin. The stranglehold on Vienna was only to a small degree relieved by raising the ratio to 1:6.

Thus on January 5, 1941, while Löwenherz was away, Murmelstein spoke with SS First Sergeant Adolf Girzik, representing Brunner 1, who was in Berlin, and asked that the IKG be permitted to provide emigrants from the Altreich with *Devisen*, moreover at the same higher rate of 1:6 as the IKG had been permitted for emigrants from Vienna; this would provide Löwenherz with a little additional relief for the hard-pressed IKG budget. Girzik relayed the request to Brunner 1, Brunner 1 to Eichmann, and when he returned to Vienna, Brunner 1 informed Murmelstein that Eichmann had granted the request. Upon the consent of the *Devisenstelle*, the scheme went immediately into effect.[140] When Löwenherz returned from Lisbon via Berlin, the matter was a *fait accompli*, and what with the ensuing turmoil caused by the first set of deportations, it did not come up for discussion.

In the ensuing months the IKG always had more *Devisen* than were needed in Vienna, and Berlin made use of them. Occasionally, when there were few emigrants, the IKG conceded to the RV its monthly allotment of *Devisen*, albeit always "without prejudice" to Vienna's future needs. Seven months after Murmelstein's initiative, when war had closed the route via the Soviet Union to the Far East, and the only remaining route via Lisbon was in highest gear, Murmelstein finally heard from the RV, requesting an explanation "on what basis the IKG approved *Devisen* for transfer to Jews living in the Altreich." Murmelstein then obtained Brunner's permission to inform the RV that in the matter in question "the IKG had been proceeding entirely in accordance with the consent and permission of the supervisory authority,"[141] that is, the *Zentralstelle*.

Over the months there were considerable problems with the necessary transit through Japan. On August 11, 1940, Grete Breuer, the secretary and one of the senior assistants in Murmelstein's office, went to the General Consulate of Japan to obtain information about current regulations governing transit visas and the extension of permits to Shanghai. The Japanese authorities required that an applicant for a transit visa be in possession of a destination visa that would be valid for at least two months. The reason was clear: It took a lot of time, starting from when the visa was issued, then making travel arrangements, reaching the Japanese port, and until the expected arrival at the destination. The Japanese authorities did not want to be saddled with people whose visas were about to or did run out and who therefore could not proceed. For stateless persons Japan required a minimal duration of validity of three months, as well as credit for US $60 and proof of paid passage. As for permits to Shanghai, without the approval of the Japanese authorities in Shanghai the Vienna consulate could no longer grant extensions to emigrants whose permits had run out because of delayed travel arrangements. However, in cases with a confirmed date of departure from Vienna, the General Consulate would be prepared to telegraph Shanghai, provided they were reimbursed for the expense.[142] To make sure that the then current list of names for the needed permits was accurate, Murmelstein, on the same day, telegraphed a list of forty-four names to the affiliate of HIAS and HICEM in Shanghai. He included the request that they obtain the approval of the authorities in Shanghai (without which the Vienna consulate could not extend the permits of the named persons) and to wire both the approval to the consulate and a confirmation to the IKG that the matter had been accomplished. Mr. Birman of the Shanghai Jewish Central Information Bureau answered by letter, dated August 15 and received at the IKG and on Murmelstein's desk on September 14:

> We doubt that the Japanese consul [in Shanghai] would inform the consul in Vienna by wire concerning the extensions. They have certain rules, and, in our opinion, they will not depart from them. We fear that they will carefully re-examine the position of the applicants before they might possibly grant extensions. And to obtain these, new applications have to be submitted. At least this has been the practice until now. We are informing you of this so that those under your care do not entertain excessive hopes. The matter will not be regulated as simply as you might think.[143]

Additionally, Birman reported "for your orientation" that during the previous week three ships had arrived from Darien with one hundred emigrants, who had applied for their permits in January, February, and March of that year. "As you can see, the granting of permits is very slow. It is no use to press for greater speed, it will only lead to unpleasantness. Please inform the persons concerned. In any case, they can rest assured that all will be done on behalf of a smooth completion. . . ."

Transit through Japan and the territories under its control did not run smoothly, though Japan did not exhibit the ideological anti-Semitism of Nazi Germany. The regulation that went into effect in August 1940—that all transients through Japan had to show ¥20 or US $5 for each day of their sojourn in Japan—referred to "all passengers" and not specifically to Jews.[144] And yet, we must take note of the following items that appear in related documents. On September 17, 1940, Murmelstein sent Prochnik a list of persons who had problems either with transit visas or with Shanghai permits. One of these persons was Rosche Kreuter, a child. Murmelstein added that Rosche's mother, Marie, would receive the Japanese transit visa as a matter of course because, though a *Glaubensjüdin* (Jew by faith), she was an Aryan by race,[145] and as such her passport did not identify her as a Jew. A few days later, on October 5, Prochnik reported that "according to as yet unverified reports, the Berlin Consulate of Japan will from now on make the issuance of transit visas for German passports with 'J' contingent on proof of a credit account."[146] The fact that between these two dates, on September 27, 1940, Japan joined the Rome-Berlin Axis in a tripartite pact designed to "promote the prosperity of their peoples" is coincidental. The reason the Japanese authorities found it convenient to make use of the Nazi policy of marking the Jews as such in their passports was the same as the ostensible reason why Switzerland originally requested that practice. They did not wish to be saddled with refugees stranded in their land with limited means and nowhere to go.

One "promotion of prosperity" was taken seriously, though it had less to do with the tripartite pact than with the commercial exploitation of refugees from the senior Axis partner. Because of the difficulties encountered in dispatching emigrants in time to make use of the block of ship passages that the RV and the IKG had reserved months ahead of the scheduled sailing, some of the tickets had to be cancelled. In October 1940 Ommeren, the travel bureau in Berlin through which the reservations had been made, announced that on behalf of the NYK Line it would charge an exorbitant fee of 15 percent for every cancellation of a named passenger, though this fee would be credited in case he or she were to be scheduled for a later passage.[147]

Another example: The Bassel family from Vienna had purchased tickets for a second-class cabin on the *Hikawa Maru*, due to sail from Kobe on September 9, 1940, and from Yokohama on the eleventh. On the morning of the day the ship was to sail from Yokohama, the Bassels had to pay ¥15 per person for service in the second class. Half an hour before sailing, they were given tickets by the "committee" in a third-class cabin, supposedly because second class was sold out. They also received a voucher in the amount of US $180.00 for a refund of the difference in price, plus the dollar credit that was required for embarking. The voucher was to be redeemed at the Joint in New York or Chicago. Once they had set sail they found out that there were vacancies in all classes, fifty berths altogether; and the ship's officers told them that the ship never sailed fully occupied. In Seattle, the Jewish Committee received them and the other refugees, took them to hotels, took care of them, and asked them whether they had enough money to take them to their destination. When in answer the Bassels showed them the voucher they had received in Yokohama, the good people of the Committee had a good laugh and assured the Bassels that they had seen many such "vouchers."[148] Was this another instance of the enterprising promotion of prosperity on the part of the NYK Line? It is doubtful; more likely the $180 plus the dollar credit was pocketed by the Kobe committee, possibly to care for the Mirer Hassidim and other escapees from Lithuania, whose case is discussed below. In any case, no harm was done: The Bassel family settled safely in their new country even with the loss of their capital, and we can hope that the Mirer were well cared for.

In March 1941 the Japanese consulates in Europe were directed not to issue any more transit visas except to those who had valid Japanese permits for Shanghai. The official reason given was that there were about 2,000 Jews, mainly from Lithuania, who were stranded in Japan without a final destination. Prochnik reported that he heard from Japanese contacts that the real reason for the visa cutoff was retaliation for the United States' refusal to grant transit visas to citizens of Japan. We do not know whether this reason was true or just a rumor. In any case, Prochnik reported that the Japanese steamship lines were making representations with the authorities in Tokyo to ease this restriction.[149] The fact that the visa cutoff was in force is documented in a letter Prochnik sent to a Hannover travel bureau together with vouchers for four tickets on the *Hikawa Maru*, due to sail on April 14, 1941. The reason for the cancellation was that the passengers "had been unable to

The MS Hikawa Maru *of the Nippon Yūsen Kabushiki Kaisha (NYK Line) serving today as a museum ship berthed at Yamashita Park, Naka-ku, Yokohama, Japan. (© CSE)*

obtain the Japanese transit visa" and, Prochnik added, "the measures taken by the Japanese authorities make reservations of places on Japanese ships impossible for the time being."[150] A few weeks after he first reported about the visa cutoff, Prochnik found out more about it from a Japanese man who had recently come from Japan and from the Ommeren travel bureau, and from a Japanese newspaper, which he forwarded to the IKG. There were indeed about 2,000 Jewish emigrants in Japan who had no place to go, and the Japanese authorities wished to prevent the "formation of a white proletariat," "in spite of their loyal attitude." Most of the emigrants came from Lithuania, where their emigration was aided by Moses Bockelmann in Kovno (Kaunas), acting as agent of the Joint.[151] Evidently this group included the members of the Hassidic Yeshiva at Mir and their relatives, who had left for Kovno and Vilna after Lithuania was incorporated into the Soviet Union. These emigrants did not need Russian transit visas. The Russians transported them to Vladivostok and put a few at a time as passengers on freighters that plied the coastal waters to Japan and Shanghai. Over 1,000 of the Lithuanian emigrants had Japanese visas, apparently issued by a consul, but the authorities were going to declare them invalid.

After the outbreak of war between Japan and the United States, the Japanese deported the Jews stranded in Japan to Shanghai. Sometime after the war the Mirer Hassidim were brought to the United States, where they established their yeshiva in Brooklyn. But in the spring of 1941 the route via Japan was closed for emigrants from Vienna, Berlin, and Prague.

In connection with his explanation of what was behind the Japanese visa cutoff and in the apparent expectation that emigration to Shanghai would continue, Prochnik again held out the possibility of circumventing Manchuria by routing groups via Vladivostok. In fact he reported that Shakhanov, his contact at the Soviet Intourist office in Berlin, was planning to travel to Moscow in July to arrange for this routing. Shakhanov also suggested that there might be employment possibilities for skilled emigrants in the war industry of Chungking (Chongqing), China. They even figured out what sort of visa would be required and what the costs might be.[152]

But all that was too late. On June 22 Nazi Germany entered the territory of its partner in the friendship pact signed twenty-two months earlier on a broad front. On June 25, 1941, Prochnik reported that Intourist now was the enterprise of an enemy state and would soon submit the final statement of the IKG account. And Herr Runes, the last fortunate emigrant from Vienna on the Far East route, who was according to the schedule on the Sverdlovsk-Omsk stretch of the Trans-Siberian Railway at the outbreak of hostilities, was now presumably in custody or interned in Omsk.[153]

All that was left in the frantic effort to get Jews out of Nazi Europe was the route via Spain and Portugal.

Groups via Spain and Portugal

Much preferable to the long route to America—through the breadth of the Eurasian continent and the vast Pacific Ocean—would be a voyage across the Atlantic. But the war closed all the Atlantic ports that had been available for passenger traffic. The search for a likely port now focused on Lisbon, Portugal. Two difficulties presented themselves for realizing this possibility. One concerned finding ships that were capable of making that run and owners ready to risk their ships. The other concerned finding routes to get the emigrants from Nazi Germany to Portugal. Both of these difficulties were reflected in a telephone conversation between Eppstein and Löwenherz one week after the June 1940 meeting in Berlin, where the arrangements for the Far East route were finalized.

In mid-June Eppstein reported that negotiations for the Greek ship *Nea Hellas* to undertake the transatlantic voyage had fallen through because it was unable to make it to Lisbon.[154] The reason became evident two weeks later, when Storfer was in Athens to finalize arrangements for the ships that would take the Palestine transports to their destination. One of the owners, the Goulandris brothers, explained that the ship was supposed to pick up 300 passengers at Jaffa; but since the Italians, who had entered the war on the Axis side, would consider them to be British subjects, they would not have let them pass through the Straits of Messina, which was the ship's prescribed course. In addition, the Greek government did not permit the SS *Corinthia*, which was to transfer a contingent of emigrants from Piraeus to the *Nea Hellas* in Lisbon, to traverse the Mediterranean under the present conditions. Thus the *Nea Hellas* was berthed in Lisbon without any passengers. Hence, Mr. Goulandris had no alternative but to decommission the ship in Lisbon in order to save the salary for its crew of 100 and the insurance premium for a transatlantic voyage, which he expected to run to £40,000.[155]

Eppstein also reported that the American Express Company might be prepared to institute a passenger service from Lisbon to the United States. For this eventuality, negotiations had been entered into with neutral Switzerland to bring the emigrants by direct flight from Zurich to Lisbon. The Swiss would grant a transit visa only to emigrants in possession of a steamship ticket out of Lisbon and would not permit them to stay in Switzerland for any length of time. Parallel negotiations had been initiated for transporting emigrants to Lisbon on Yugoslav carriers,[156] presumably out of Rijeka.

While in Athens, Storfer found that "a group of serious shippers under the leadership of Sokrates Avgherinos" was prepared to outfit the 4,000-ton SS *Attiki* for transporting emigrants to America via Greece. The ship, small as it was, would carry 800 tourist- or third-class passengers at US $200 each, and 200 first- and second-class passengers at $250, thereby grossing $210,000 per run. The emigrants would come to Greece, where their transit would be "guaranteed"; in this way their transit through Yugoslavia would be "automatic." The emigrants would embark at the ship's homeport of Piraeus. Other passengers could embark in Messina (Italy), Barcelona (Spain), and Lisbon (Portugal). The voyage from Piraeus to Lisbon would take ten days. It would take another ten days to reach New York. The Atlantic leg of the journey would lead past the Azores, the best route for navigability and the most tranquil. Storfer reported that he "has inspected the ship together with her captain and considers the project to be quite realizable."[157] One may wonder whether Avgherinos, in his leading position in the Greek shipping cartel, would have a better chance than Goulandris to gain Greek governmental permission to travel the hostile waters of the Mediterranean, or the cooperation of the Italians. In any case, the search for a Western route to America was on.

One way under consideration of getting emigrants from Germany to Lisbon was by airplane. Murmelstein found out, probably from Prochnik, that after the hostilities between Germany and France ceased and the Vichy Government was firmly in place, the German airline Lufthansa was about to schedule regular flights from Berlin via Stuttgart and Lyon to Madrid, where there would be a connection to Lisbon. Upon inquiry, Murmelstein learned that while this route would not normally be available for transporting emigrants, exceptions would be made in special cases. Hence, Murmelstein reported to Brunner 1 that the IKG would make use of this possibility, once it materialized.[158] When it did materialize, it provided the possibility for a rare and slow trickle of individual or very small groups of emigrants to fly to Lisbon to catch a ship to America. The arrangements had to be made person by person through the concerted efforts of the IKG in Vienna and by Prochnik in Berlin. In mid-September Prochnik informed Murmelstein that he was able to book passage on an available ship for three ladies from Vienna—Freda Hurd, Margarete Loria, and Guida Loewy—as well as flights from Stuttgart to Madrid, train fare from there via Barcelona to Lisbon, and meals and lodging. The moneys that had to be transferred amounted to US $20 per person for train and hotel, RM 200 for the flight, and US $200 for the ship ticket. The latter consisted of $175 for passage, the remainder for taxes and fees. The ship in question was none other than the *Nea Hellas*. We do not know under what flag she sailed, only that she was now under the control of American Express.[159]

The work that went into dispatching these three emigrants was enormous. The provision of documentation, travel arrangements, and financing had to be done for each individual. This was unavoidable. However, time constraints imposed by the dangers, the obstacles, the restrictions, the limited means, and the competent personnel made it that much more urgent to dispatch emigrants in groups. Instead of negotiating person by person, it was more efficient to purchase blocks of passages, fill an entire coach of emigrants, obtain transit visas for a whole list of persons, and so on. To this end, the experience of dispatching the three ladies yielded an important factor in the equation of the group transports by way of Lisbon. On September 5, 1940, the Portuguese consul in Vienna informed the IKG that transit visas to Portugal would be granted to Jewish emigrants, even stateless ones, provided that they had a paid passage on a ship.[160] With this in hand, the IKG applied for a similar guarantee of transit visas for Jewish emigrants to the United States through Spain, only to be refused "according to a telegram received from the Spanish Foreign Office in Madrid."[161] However, with the letter from the Portuguese consulate in hand, Murmelstein urged the Spanish consulate to relent, which they did, though apparently not in writing but only verbally. Murmelstein recorded the call he received: "The Spanish General Consulate in Vienna informs by telephone that as of today it will issue transit visas to those Reich-German passports that are marked with 'J'. Visas will *not* be issued to stateless or foreign passports."[162] We cannot stress enough the importance of this decision on the part of the Spanish government. While the Franco regime was sympathetic to the Nazi regime as regards fascist authoritarianism, it remained neutral in the war, and by that decision showed that it did not share the anti-Semitic nationalism of the Nazis. The guarantee of Spanish transit visas, which Löwenherz and Murmelstein helped to secure, was an essential element in saving about 1,000 Viennese Jews, in addition to another 5,000 from the Altreich and the Protectorate.

On September 14, 1940, immediately upon receiving the information from the Spanish consulate, Murmelstein called Prochnik to finalize the arrangements for these three ladies. But much more needed to be done to arrange for a feasible program of group transports to Lisbon.

Groups such as these would have to travel by train. The trains would leave from Berlin but in order to reach Madrid, would have to traverse Vichy France. In other words, they would have to travel through a France that was fully under the jurisdiction of the German military, as well as through Vichy France, which was also under German occupation and restricted by the Wehrmacht to persons having officially sanctioned business. Jewish emigrants did not fit the qualification of permitted business. Only organs of the Nazi Party could overrule the Wehrmacht. Prochnik had orders from Murmelstein to overcome this formidable obstacle, and he was the man to do so, even if, as he said, he had to resort to "totally illegitimate means." His task was to secure an agreement to permit the transit of Jews from Germany to Lisbon, which the RV had already unsuccessfully attempted to do. Both the *Deutsche Reichsbahn* (German national railway) and the Supreme Command of the Wehrmacht insisted that the Gestapo and *Zentralstelle* be direct parties to such an arrangement; however, they declined. Prochnik now resumed negotiations with the railway and the army, declaring that he was acting on the orders of the *Zentralstelle* on behalf of Jewish emigration from the *Ostmark*. What he did not mention was that he was a Jew himself. The authorities considered him to be a Gestapo official and granted him the necessary agreement. Only then did his identity as a Jew become clear to them. Luckily, the officials he had dealt with did not denounce him after all, and he got away with his hide intact,[163] and more important, with a vital element in the route to Lisbon in place.

Another element was the technical execution of the transports. This was placed in the hands of Herr Keppler, the director of MER, located on Potsdamerplatz in Berlin. As in the case of other group transports, the logistics had to be coordinated by Storfer, and the arrangements of MER had to pass his inspection. Thus, when the first Lisbon transport was finally being readied, Storfer was in Berlin. When he had completed his work, he was able to get a seat on a flight back to Vienna. Since he had to leave for the airport precipitously, he missed giving his final reports verbally to his contacts. Upon arrival in Vienna, he wrote a number of letters: to Keppler of MER; to Löwenstein, who, as head of the RV *Hilfsverein* (Aid Association), was in charge of emigration in Berlin, and thus not only the counterpart of Murmelstein in Vienna but also the emigration coordinator vis-à-vis the central authorities; to the Berlin *Zentralstelle* as the coordinating authorizing authority; and to Prochnik as the representative of the interests of Vienna's Jews.[164] From these letters we can reconstruct what he accomplished in Berlin. Storfer's inspection there of the first Lisbon transport was important. Unlike the transports to Palestine, which Storfer had to guide one by one and step by step to their final dispatch, the subsequent Lisbon transports could normally be dispatched according to the pattern set for the first transport.

With MER, Storfer made sure that adequate carriage space was booked for the expected participants from Vienna, Berlin, and Prague, that the departure and arrival was scheduled, and that the transit documentation and the necessary authorizations were in place or applied for in a timely fashion and at the appropriate offices.

Having consulted with and inspected all participating agencies connected with arranging the transport, Storfer presented himself at the *Zentralstelle* at the RSHA (Reich headquarters of the SS) on Kurfürstenstrasse 116 and verbally outlined the main features of the project; there was no opportunity to go into details. He was told that MER had to submit a written report on the details of the technical execution of the project, and to include photocopies of transit permits from France, Spain, and Portugal. Storfer pointed out that First Lieutenant Bresser assured MER that the OKW (*Oberkommando der Wehrmacht*/"Supreme Command of the Wehrmacht") would issue a permit for the emigrants to pass through France, albeit upon prior agreement by the *Zentralstelle* to the emigration of the Jews. As for the transit through Spain and Portugal, relevant visas issued to the passports of the individual passengers would suffice, and therefore no general transit permit was needed. Storfer asked that the *Zentralstelle* agree to the projected transport of approximately 140 emigrants to leave on November 27 in three carriages; and he received their agreement conditional upon submission of the stipulated documents.

Storfer informed MER accordingly, and they sent a letter to the *Zentralstelle* with the heading: "Group of Jewish emigrants No. 1 to Lisbon (and overseas)," describing the plan of having the group of Jewish emigrants assembled in Berlin leave on November 26, to be joined by another group in Frankfurt the next morning. There the carriages with the Jews would be sealed for their transit through occupied France via Paris to Hendaye on the Gulf of Biscayne, which lies on the border between France and Spain. MER then requested a statement addressed to the director of the *Deutsche Reichsbahn* in Frankfurt to the effect that transporting the Jewish emigrants as suggested was approved by the *Zentralstelle*. A second statement they requested was to be addressed to the OKW in Berlin to the effect that the *Zentralstelle* agreed to the transit through occupied France and that either a collective pass or individual passes be issued. MER also mentioned that the RV *Hilfsverein* would submit a statement certifying that all the participants in the transport were in possession of Spanish and Portuguese transit visas and overseas immigrant visas.[165] The letter was addressed to "*Reichsführer SS*," that is, Himmler, and duly signed "*Heil Hitler! Mitteleuropäisches Reisebüro.*"

It was barely three weeks until the scheduled departure from Berlin on November 26. The permit from the *Zentralstelle* to the *Deutsche Reichsbahn* and to the OKW would not be issued until the various Jewish agencies had assembled the list of participating emigrants with certified documentation, and Storfer had signed it. And until then, much needed to be done. A letter Prochnik wrote to Storfer on November 13, less than two weeks before departure, shows what a cliff-hanger this was. We remember that on November 6 Storfer received a conditional agreement from the *Zentralstelle* for a transport of 140. Prochnik now reported that according to Löwenstein, there were only 86 firmly booked ship passages available: 65 for Berlin and 21 for Vienna. Prochnik hoped that an additional seven places on the Portuguese steamer *Angola* and five places on the Spanish *Cabo de Hornos* would become available for Vienna, increasing this contingent to 33 emigrants; with 6 expected from Prague, this brought the entire group to 104, again far short of the stipulated 140. Since MER had proved ineffectual as regards ship passages, Prochnik asked Löwenstein to contact Norddeutscher Lloyd (shipping company) in Bremen to confirm the additional passages. Löwenstein would also have to contact various travel bureaus and agencies to find people who had booked ship passage on their own and who could fill the empty places on the train. To make matters worse, the *Zentralstelle* required the final passenger list two days hence, and Storfer present in Berlin to sign it.[166]

The Individual Transports

The first transport left on November 27, not with 86 passengers, not with 104, and not with the originally stipulated 140, but with 148: 106 from the Altreich and 42 from Vienna, but none from the Protectorate; and they left not in three but in two carriages sealed in Frankfurt for the duration of their transit through France.

One of the passengers was an elderly physician and former professor at the Medical Faculty of Vienna University, Dr. Weinberger. And, to paraphrase a Shakespearean phrase, thereby hangs a nasty tale, which we will tell mainly in Murmelstein's words. First, however, let us present the cast of characters: Dr. Weinberger was a friend of Dr. Emil Tuchmann, who was the physician in charge of the Jewish Hospital during the Nazi years and had been appointed as the Jewish *Vertrauensarzt* of the Gestapo, and in fact signed himself as *Vertrauensarzt der Geheimen Staatspolizei*, "Privy Physician of the Gestapo." As such Dr. Tuchmann not only had ready access to Kuchmann, who headed the Jewish desk at Gestapo headquarters in Vienna, but took the liberty of free access to the offices and officials of the IKG, a privilege he felt entitled to by his being Löwenherz's personal physician. Prior to the Anschluss, Dr. Weinberger had been a prominent member and generous supporter of the Jewish Community of Vienna. Laudable as this was, it should not have entitled him to special status in the dire situation in which all the Jews in Vienna equally found themselves and should most assuredly not have led to special consideration and privileges. In such a situation no one was in a more sensitive and a more exposed position at the IKG than Murmelstein. Being in charge of emigration, his policy was to be unbending in treating everyone the same way; he regarded anything that interfered with this as corruption, which he fought accordingly. Frau Grete Breuer was Murmelstein's secretary, and as such privy to the sensitive matters that were his responsibility and required utmost discreteness and loyalty on her part.

When the list of participants in the first Lisbon transport was finalized and ready to be submitted to Brunner 1 at the *Zentralstelle*, this is what happened in Murmelstein's (M) account between him and Löwenherz (L):[167]

> L called me and said, Professor Weinberger . . . must leave. . . . I knew that this was a case of favoritism, and had to be contained. In this connection [L] was like a woman who ought not to be saying "yes." Politicians are like that, they say "yes" to everyone. [L said] "He must leave." I answer, "All of us must leave. The list is now complete." . . .
>
> [L:] "No, take someone out, and put him in." [M:] "No, I won't do it." Thus it went back and forth.

This was at the height of the financial squeeze play into which Eichmann had forced the IKG, and the IKG was sorely strapped for money. In view of this Murmelstein continued:

> Look, [Weinberger] benefited the IKG financially by buying a lot of U.S. dollars. But for this reason I wanted him out, because the Joint does not contribute dollars for doing business. . . . For the dollars one sends Jews away. . . . [L:] "No, the man has given a lot of money to the IKG." [M:] "But you gave him dollars." . . . [L:] "No, you must do it." Then I said, "The list has gone [to Brunner 1]; there is nothing I can do." But the list was not gone. Next day L calls me and says, "Dr. Tuchmann told me that the list is not gone. Frau Breuer told him." She was [the secretary] in my office, and Frau Breuer was transferred forthwith. She flew out [of my office] so that the stairs shook! And Mr. Tuchmann, I banned him from my office [*Zimmerverbot*]. Yet I was constrained to accept Herr Weinberger, because L was boss. . . . I said, "Imagine how it is when, at this time, wartime, one says to someone who is on the list, you have to wait for another transport to Lisbon." But I had to do it.

But, as Murmelstein said, "the case of Weinberger is not finished; it goes on." In fact, it is only now beginning:

> Weinberger was merrily included; I had to do it. Brunner railed that I shifted the list, always, he says, this shifting! And he was right. It was a shifting. And on Saturday evening the train was to leave. Saturday afternoon I was in my office at the IKG; I, a rabbi, sit in the office [on Shabbat] and work. It was a matter of dispatching sixty Jews. Someone announces Professor Weinberger. What might he want? . . . He said, "I do not wish to leave this evening." [M:] "Why, first you move heaven and hell to force me to give you a place in today's transport, and you do not wish to leave? What happened in the meantime?". . . There was also his wife and the 90-year-old mother-in-law. I had told L, for the money I would have given [her] a place in the

> old-age home. Whether a 90-year-old woman dies after two weeks in America or here, it is all the same. . . . But he overruled me. I could not prevail against money.
>
> All three, he says, we have to stay. How come? [Weinberger:] "You know, I own a building which I have not sold as yet. I wanted to leave it behind, but I changed my mind. I would like to sell it and give the marks to the IKG, and buy dollars from the IKG. But for that I need time." Do you understand? For that I would lose three places. These places cannot be filled any more, impossible. Three ship passages are lost. This is swinish! Every place is a matter of life and death. Then there is the negotiation with the *Zentralstelle*. The railway carriage went through occupied France. They knew exactly how many persons are on the list. . . . There are ladies present here otherwise I would have told. . . . I told him what I thought of him. Right? I threw him out. I told him that the SS would pick him up because I would have to report that he is not leaving, I would have to report that not all places are taken. Because the carriage travels with an escort, travels through occupied French territory with an SS escort. One cannot hide that.—Forty-five minutes later L called: have I gone crazy?
>
> EE: Did [Weinberger] leave?
>
> M: He left.
>
> LHE: Had to leave?
>
> M: Had to leave.
>
> LHE: You insisted?
>
> M: Of course. What would you have done?

Another passenger on the first transport was Dr. Margarete (later Margaret) Feiler, one of Murmelstein's most able assistants during her brief tenure at the IKG. Referring to her, Murmelstein continued:

> She wrote to me Herr Weinberger stopped at the Joint in Lisbon, complained about me, that I screamed at him, that I threatened him with the SS. I did not threaten him. I merely told him, made it clear to him, the SS would pick him up because the carriage travels under escort, right? [sarcastic:] "I threatened with the SS, screamed at him, yelled!"—I made a mistake; with reference to Dr. Feiler, I should have written a letter [to the Joint] and explained the matter, right? But I thought, if they do not write, I will also not write to them. . . . Dr. Tuchmann got *Zimmerverbot* . . . because of the Weinberger case: He spied!! . . . Tuchmann had the stupidity to call himself "Privy Physician of the Secret State Police [Gestapo]." Privy Physician of the Gestapo!! . . . How can a Jew be Privy Physician of the Gestapo?! At the IKG he was . . . the liaison, the denouncer, the spy of the Gestapo..

After this episode Tuchmann respected the *Zimmerverbot* and stayed clear of Murmelstein. Frau Breuer, who was a very competent secretary, was reinstated in Murmelstein's office after a few months of punitive banishment.

The second Lisbon transport was being readied even before the first one had left. This one left from Berlin in four carriages, one each on successive days from December 9 to 12, with 157 emigrants from Berlin, 3 from Prague, and 36 from Vienna. Altogether there would be 25 Lisbon transports. Most of them followed the pattern of the second transport, where, on successive days, a single sealed Jewish carriage was attached to the regular train from Berlin via Frankfurt and Paris to Madrid. Even though the departure of most of the transports stretched over several days, each participant in a numbered transport had a personal number as well. It was important for the participants to display both numbers, for example, on their luggage. After the last transport was completed, the IKG was required to prepare and submit to the authorities a summary statistic.

The table below is based on the copy submitted to the Vienna Gestapo. It shows a slow and desultory start. The beginning of some regularity in the scheduling of transports in February and March 1941 coincided with both the resumption of the granting of U.S. visas and the first deportations from Vienna. The hiatus marked by the aborted transport no. 13 was the result of the crisis that led to the invasion of Yugoslavia. The transports resumed with ever larger contingents in May and became very large when the assault on the Soviet Union cut off the route to the Far East, and the route to Lisbon was now the only one left. The last two transports proceeded under the specter of the second wave of deportations from Vienna and coincided with Himmler's order to stop emigration altogether. The last transport left about a month before the United States entered the war.

The table also shows that the percentage distribution of places (50:40:10 agreed upon by Berlin, Vienna, and Prague) fell by the wayside, collectively and for all transports individually. For all twenty-five transports together, the distribution was Berlin 80.9 percent, Vienna 16.5 percent, and Prague 2.6 percent. There are several reasons for this discrepancy. In response to the special duress the Nazis applied to them, the exodus of the Jews of Austria was successfully carried out due to the efforts of the IKG, especially those of

Special Transports of Jewish Emigrants to Spain and Portugal

Transport Number	Number of carriages	Date	PARTICIPANTS FROM Altreich	Protectorate	Ostmark	Total
1	2	Nov. 27, 1940	106	—	42	148
2	4	Dec. 9–12	157	3	36	196
3	1	Jan. 8, 1941	35	—	—	35
4	3	Jan. 21–23	128	2	24	154
5	1	Feb. 4	33	7	—	40
6	1	Feb. 13	38	1	24	63
7	3	Feb. 25–27	184	1	33	218
8	3	Mar. 3–5	128	5	5	138
9	2	Mar. 11–12	77	4	5	86
10	2	Mar. 18, 20	98	—	17	115
11	4	Mar. 25–28	214	3	41	258*
12	3	Apr. 1–3	165	8	—	173
13	—	—	—	—	—	—
14	2	May 7–8	74	9	41	124
15	4	May 17–20	257	1	9	267
16/17	7	May 23–29	438	19	125	582
18	9	June 5–13	328	20	123	471
19	2	June 18, 23	105	2	18	125
20	11	Jul. 14, 15, 17–24, 31	615	37	125	777
21	11	Aug. 6–15, 19	677	12	66	755
22	7	Aug. 26–28, Sep. 4, 8–10	353	10	37	400
23	2	Sep. 25–26	32	5	44	81
24	8	Oct. 8, 15–-21	416	7	87	510
25	3	Oct. 29, 31, Nov. 3	150	—	79	229
TOTALS			**4,808**	**156**	**981**	**5,945**

* Including the rest of transport no. 10.

Source: *Sondertransporte jüdischer Auswanderer nach Spanien und Portugal*, Nov. 6, 1941. DÖW 2825.

Löwenherz and of Murmelstein. Thus, at the time of the group transports to Lisbon, most of the Austrian Jews who could find a destination had already left. The frantic efforts to expedite the remainder coincided with the schemes for group transports, the last of which turned out to be those to Lisbon. It was different with the Jews of the Altreich, who did not experience the sudden brutal pressure to leave until later. The massive exodus of German Jews coincided with and was frustrated by the outbreak of the war. The restrictions which wartime placed on emigration, necessitating the scheme of limited group transports, was the main reason for putting a brake on the excessive demand on available places by Berlin, by means of the agreement 50:40:10. The discrepancy in the actual distribution among participants in the Lisbon transports also showed that the Jews of the Altreich could make use of the German quota for emigration to the United States, whereas the Austrian Jews, and especially the Czech Jews, had to be placed on a waiting list for visas because the number of Austrian and Czech quotas were much more restricted and few visas were issued. And, as we know, the German Jews still had greater means available for qualifying for destinations requiring immigrants to bring some capital, such as Cuba.

While the Weinberger case was not typical, it shows that dispatching each transport required attention to unforeseen details, case by case and up to the last minute. After all the documentation had been assured, including visas, transit visas, and bookings, and all official authorizations for departure had been checked, including those from the tax offices and the police, and the assets and dwellings had been liquidated, the logistics of the journey had to be arranged. The group from Vienna had to arrive early enough to join the other groups on the train leaving from Berlin, but not so early that they would have to be put up by the RV *Hilfsverein* for any length of time. The Vienna contingent was put up in a home owned by the RV, where they received coffee in the morning and modest meals. As late as the time when the twenty-fourth transport was being readied, the RV reminded Vienna that the participants would be required to bring ration coupons for their stay in Berlin for each day for 25 grams of food in general, 20 grams of fat, and 50 grams of bread.[168] They also had to bring extra ration coupons for 50 grams of bread that they would receive in Frankfurt before the carriage was sealed. Prochnik responded that it was best that the participants surrender their ration coupons to the transport leader in Vienna, who would hand them to the responsible people in Berlin and Frankfurt.[169] Since wartime ration coupon booklets were issued once a month, the emigrants were permitted to keep only enough ration coupons for their needs during the journey and had to hand the rest to the authorities before they were permitted to leave the Reich's territory. In Lisbon the emigrants were provided with lodging and board by the Joint until they set sail; there were no provisions for them in transit through Spain; and one time the participants had to be instructed to take enough bread with them for the journey through Spain.[170]

Another recurring problem concerned luggage, which had to be treated in a prescribed fashion. Since the SS border guards closely inspected all luggage, there was often a delay until they finished checking before the carriage could be sealed in Frankfurt. Some people had their luggage pre-inspected and sealed in Vienna; while this was desirable, it was not a requirement.[171] For the trip from Vienna to Berlin, the large pieces of luggage were checked; while for the trip to Lisbon, the luggage accompanied its owners wherever they were sitting. People who had to stay in Berlin for one or more nights between their arrival from Vienna and their departure on the group transport had to leave their large luggage at the railway station. They were instructed to bring a small piece of luggage with their necessities for their stay in Berlin and to keep it light, since each passenger had to tote it by himself to the home where he was staying. As for the larger pieces, some people did not close and secure their pieces; so they arrived with their contents spilled. To make the division of stored luggage by group transports possible, they were also advised to mark each piece with the number of their transport, followed by their assigned personal number within the transport, and to fasten the tag with string or wire. One time a person stored his travel documents in his big luggage and, since it arrived late, he was left without documents and could not take his place on the train to Lisbon.

Berlin also asked to be informed of any participants who were ill or had some disability, so they could be picked up at the train. Inasmuch as the last transports occurred at the time when Jews were already required to wear the yellow star, and the arrivals from Vienna only had one for their overcoats, they were given a second star in Berlin.[172] The reason was that, even though the Jews were in a segregated carriage, while still in German-controlled territory they had to sit there showing the star on their jackets or dresses.

A major amount of detail work on a case-by-case basis concerned documentation. Let us look at a few examples connected with transit visas. The Portuguese authorities required that each applicant submit a signed application and a passport photo and the passport. To simplify procedures, in preparation of specific transports these three items were collected by the IKG and sent in batches to Prochnik in Berlin, who submitted them to the Portuguese consulate. This made sense because sometimes the applicants did not have the required proof of their ship passage but Prochnik did, since he was in constant touch with MER. For example, in connection with making arrangements for overland travel and for transit visas for transport 24, Prochnik informed MER that the Joint had booked a block of passages on the SS *Serpa Pinto* to San Domingo; and Prochnik and Dr. Braun of the RV had decided on how to divide them between Vienna and Berlin.[173] Problems arose when individual emigrants initiated their applications by making direct inquiries to the consulate in Berlin, while Prochnik did the same for the group of which such applicants were a part. Though annoyed by such duplication, the consul replied to all inquiries, sometimes in a manner that overly sensitive petitioners misunderstood. Cowed by the experience of their persecution, they took recourse by lodging complaints at the embassy, which only resulted in the consul becoming angry at Prochnik. In July 1941 Prochnik had to inform the dispatching department (*Abfertigung*) of the IKG that "in the future I cannot process these cases because the consulate justifiably objects to such double processing (read: annoyance)."[174] Only a few days after this incident, Murmelstein had to send to Prochnik the application for Rosina Stern, informing him that she had sent her passport directly to the consulate.[175] Another application sent to Prochnik at about the same time had no signature and was not accompanied by a passport photo because the petitioner, Isak Unterberg, was still away doing labor service.[176]

One other example: Early in April 1941, MER received a notification from their contact in Lisbon, the travel Bureau Marcus & Harting, Ltda. The Director of Policia de Vigilancia e Defensa do Estado had notified them that passengers who take a Spanish ship would have to embark at the appropriate Spanish harbor (i.e., at Bilboa rather than at Lisbon) and would not be issued Portuguese transit visas.[177] This case confirms the suspicion that transit visas could not be issued by the Berlin consulate without prior approval by the Portuguese authorities in Lisbon. It seems that earlier in the project, the lists of transit applicants were submitted by Prochnik to the Joint in Lisbon, and they "procured" (*erwirkt*) from the authorities approval of the list, whereupon the Berlin consulate issued the transit visas. Later the approval was processed through the travel bureaus.[178] We can imagine under what time constraints the different steps of documentation had to proceed and how inviolably final the lists had to be.

These few fleeting examples have to suffice to indicate the kind of minutiae that were involved in the unsung and thankless but frantic effort to get as many out into an inhospitable world before the gates closed for good. The main destination of the emigrants who went to the Americas via Lisbon (and Bilboa) was the United States. Emigration to the United States during wartime had a history all its own, to which we now turn.

Destination: USA

By the middle of 1940 the emigration process became trying as never before. The arrangements made in Vienna had to be coordinated with Berlin, some aspects also had to be finalized there, and the immigration section of the United States Consulate in Vienna had to work in coordination with its Berlin counterpart. The only legal destinations of note were South America, Shanghai, and the United States. The main route to South and North America at that time led through Lisbon, where the Joint and HIAS had located what in effect was their only remaining office on the European continent. The actual emigration of those who were duly documented was the end result of a time-consuming, costly, and complex process of multilateral negotiation, tight scheduling, and a maddening process of coordination. It is against this background that we have to view the impact of the crisis brought about by the stoppage in issuing of immigrant visas to the United States that unfolded in the middle of 1940.

In light of the complexity of this process, it was necessary for the IKG to know how many visas the U.S. consulate could issue in the ensuing months, in order to initiate the process well ahead of time for the qualified emigrants. Under the quota system U.S. visas were valid for a limited time only. If, once visas were issued, all the other arrangements were either not completed in time or encountered some unforeseen obstacle, the visas would lapse and were rarely reinstated without going through the whole process again. A lapsed visa would then not only be lost to the would-be immigrant but would most likely be lost altogether because it would still be counted as part of the limited number of the yearly quota.[179] The fall of the Netherlands in May and the subsequent campaign leading to the fall of France late in June 1940 disrupted the flow of emigrants who had visas, since their escape routes were now cut off. These concerns prompted Löwenherz to see U.S. Vice Consul Thomas Hohenthal at the consulate in Vienna on July 1.

On the question of what number of visas would be available in the quota year then starting, specifically in July and August, Löwenherz was told that

> [the U.S. consulate in] Vienna was being informed by [the consulate in] Berlin month by month as to the number of visas assigned to Vienna under the pertinent (i.e., German and Polish) quotas but that this time Vienna had not as yet been informed.

On the question of whether visas, which lapsed as a result of the "events" (the campaigns on the Western fronts), could be renewed or extended, Hohenthal said that relevant applicants would have to prove that the visas lapsed through no fault of their recipients. They, as well as new visa applicants, would henceforth also have to prove, and Löwenherz would have to certify, that they were in possession of paid passage on specific sailings. Löwenherz was given appropriate forms for this purpose.[180] Lest the reader miss the vicious circle of this new requirement, let us point out that would-be immigrants would have to book passage as part of the qualifying process, that is, before they knew whether they would be able to satisfy all the other requirements of the U.S. immigration authorities and before they knew that they would actually be issued their visas. This was a blueprint for a debacle in which emigrants denied their visas would have booked passage in vain, a passage that would in any case have to be purchased with U.S. dollars. Dollars were unavailable to Jewish emigrants and would have to be remitted by the Joint or contributed by generous sponsors in the United States through the Joint. The IKG quickly had to find the only way in which such a debacle could be prevented, namely, to buy blocks of passages on available steamers, using foreign exchange made available by the Joint, and make these places available to people assured of being issued visas. In cases where the visas were not issued, the passages could be reassigned. Löwenherz's record of the meeting with the Vice Consul stressed the stringency of this requirement:

> [T]he consulate will issue visas to, and process visa applications only of those who can prove that they are in a position to make the journey to the United States. . . . Issuance of visas to persons who cannot fulfill these requirements is out of the question.[181]

Hohenthal made one concession to Löwenherz, who asked whether "it might be possible to secure the issuance of individual visas, which for financial reasons are most important to the IKG." Hohenthal consented, if "all other conditions are met" and "if it is not a matter of too great a number of such visas."[182]

To meet the new requirement of securing prior passage, the Jewish leadership spared no effort to ferret out even the smallest blocks of available passenger space, which was shared by Vienna, Berlin, and Prague, as we have seen. And yet, emigration to the United States was reduced to a minimum when it became clear that the flow of visas, grudgingly issued in the best of times, was reduced to a trickle. At first it seemed that the reason for this reduction was the upheaval caused by the conquest of Western Europe and hence only temporary. However, it persisted month after month, and the Jewish leaders felt that they had run up against a wall that they had to penetrate, though they were at a loss as to how to go about doing so.

The Jewish leadership in Berlin felt the urgency to speed up emigration somewhat late in the game, and even then they were bent on doing things in an orderly and measured way. Dr. Julius Seligsohn, a leading member of the *Reichsvereinigung*, carefully researched immigration procedures to the United States and, in the spring of 1940, prepared a brochure about the United States immigration laws and the complex steps that would-be immigrants would have to follow. Three days after his meeting with Vice Consul Hohenthal in Vienna, Löwenherz was in Berlin, where he, with Edelstein, Weidmann, and Eppstein, were informed by Dannecker that the draft for Seligsohn's brochure had been approved by the Propaganda Ministry for publication by the *Jüdischer Kulturbund* (Cultural Federation of German Jews) and that it would be submitted for censorship to the Berlin *Zentralstelle*, whose director was Danneker. At that time it was beginning to be apparent to the Jewish leaders that the issuance of visas was being blocked by the consulates. Hence, when the brochure was cleared for publication, Seligsohn referred to the blockage by adding a foreword:

> After I had completed this manuscript, there occurred a serious tightening of the North American immigration procedures. There has been no change of the law, hence the validity of the regulations described herein remain in force. . . . At the beginning of July the government in Washington directed its consular representatives to apply a more stringent standard in evaluating the proof of qualification for immigration; if there is any reason for doubt, the issuance of visas is to be denied, even if the increased severity in applying such standards results in unfilled immigration quotas. Consequently . . . the consulates have resorted to the most severe requirements . . . [regarding] the financial guarantees [of affiants] as well as the character of the applicant . . . [such as] his biography, prior convictions, other questions of [his] trustworthiness. If the consuls have any doubts that the particular applicant would be a desirable and useful citizen of the United States, they would not issue the visa.[183]

Seligsohn's remarks present the bare facts of the blockage. They do not explain the reasons for it, as Reich, the editor of the Vienna *Jüdisches Nachrichtenblatt*, accurately observed in connection with quoting them:

> The sudden cutting-off of immigration to the USA resulted from the conduct of the American consular representatives, which is said to be based on a directive from the Washington government. Despite all efforts on the part of officials who are at work here [at the IKG] on behalf of emigration to gain insight into the relevant context, the underlying cause of that directive could up to now not be clarified.[184]

In the meantime, the pressure on Löwenherz originated not only from the desperate Jews of Vienna and the recalcitrant consular officials, but also from the Nazis. For example, in mid-July Brunner 1 gave Murmelstein "the order to pursue the emigration of the Weinbach [family], who are in possession of an American visa since May 1940"[185]—as if Murmelstein or Löwenherz had any control over the U.S. consulate. At the end of August Löwenherz reported to Brunner 1 that he had again been at the consulate and, as in the recent past and "despite urgent inquiry" on his part, had not been able to obtain information as to the number of quota places available in the coming month and thereafter; and he added, "The IKG sedulously continues its efforts to obtain passages to the USA by way of Lisbon."[186] Three weeks later he was at the consulate again, this time consulting with Consul Paul S. Guinn himself; he had his secretary along, Frau Breuer, who recorded the minutes of the meeting in some detail.[187] Vigorously pressing his case on behalf of his charges, Löwenherz

> described the general situation of the Jews living in Vienna and pointed to those who, having been waiting for two years, had coped with everything [*alles auf sich nahmen*] buoyed up by

> the hope of reuniting with family members who had emigrated, or of building a new life in the United States.

After giving some examples of cases where the withholding of visas was simply incomprehensible, Löwenherz

> declared that it seems to me as if the work of the American consulate is actually pointless if all persons who are summoned are refused visas.

Consul Guinn gave as close an admission of what was at play, as he was able:

> They are at the American Consulate in Vienna, as at all other consulates, [merely] paid officials who had to follow regulations and the law. All his sympathies rest with us and the Jews, and it would be his greatest joy if he could issue an unrestricted number of visas.

Guinn saw only one possible way out of this impasse, namely, "to let our friends in the USA intervene in Washington." While "no one would welcome a change in tendency more than he," he felt that he could give Löwenherz added ammunition in his appeal to the American friends of Vienna's Jews by divulging that

> at the end of this month [September 1940] the personnel of the consulate will be reduced by one-third and that the purely administrative work connected with the 60,000 people who at this time are still registered will proceed more slowly.

Löwenherz suggested that surely the majority of the mentioned 60,000 registrants had already emigrated and that if the consulate reduced its list accordingly, it would summon fewer applicants and hence issue more visas. Guinn replied that the decision concerning the issuance of a visa did not depend on any one person, such as the examining physician, but on a committee consisting of all the consuls. Yet, as Löwenherz reported, Guinn meant to sound a hopeful note:

> [Guinn] is not as yet in a position to say what the future chances are for people who had been refused [a visa in the past]. The fact is simply that there is a chance—if there is a change in tendency. He would counsel individuals that their relatives in the USA do all that is possible to change the decision of the consulate.

Taking up this point, Löwenherz said that he would submit a list of the different types of cases in a memorandum to the Joint, "in which he will describe the plight of those who wish to emigrate to the USA." In light of the frank exchange that had taken place, and to smooth the way for the future, Löwenherz added that he

> will take the liberty of sending to the American consulate a copy of that memorandum, in order to document that it is in no way a statement directed against the consulate, but a characterization of the situation.

The memorandum in question was in the form of a four-page, single-spaced letter to Troper in New York, dated October 3, 1940, and translated into English that for our purposes has to be paraphrased rather than quoted.[188] Löwenherz tells of the many kinds of senseless refusal of visas in cases of unquestionable qualification. Summarizing, he says, "we are, of course, not authorized to criticize the activity of the consulate and are glad of every case of a Jew of Vienna who receives the chance to emigrate, yet we have to note that in some cases consent is given where the qualification is less than in many other cases where immigration is refused." Not only did this hamper emigration per se, but with the requirement of proving paid passage before the visa application could be processed, many reserved passages were lost when it turned out that visas were refused. Löwenherz was, therefore, asking the Joint to exert influence with respect to three types of cases: The first concerned visa recipients who missed meeting the four months' deadline for entry into the United States as mandated by immigration law because of snags in making all the complex travel arrangements; for these Löwenherz requested renewal. The second concerned people who, after they had successfully passed all the steps of qualification, were not issued visas because their quota was filled; for these cases he pleaded issuance of visas from the pool of the quota year that had started in July. These people suffered the additional hardship of having liquidated their homes and assets in anticipation of their emigration. And the third concerned people who had never been summoned, even though they had been on the waiting list for a long time; for these cases Löwenherz asked that processing be resumed in accordance with existing U.S. emigration laws.

However, the "tendency" that Guinn had talked about persisted, and the need for action at the highest level on the part of "friends" in the United States to try to resolve the crisis was as dire as ever. Such action, he must have thought, was best urged in a personal meeting. At the time of his December *Vorsprache* at Eichmann's RSHA office in Berlin, Löwenherz discussed a number of common emigration questions with Dr. Otto Hirsch of the *Reichsvereinigung*, especially questions pertinent to Löwenherz's impending personal meeting in Lisbon with Joint President Troper.[189] The report of their meeting contains the following:

> Since the practices of the American consulate are the same in the Altreich and in Vienna, we shall enjoin the Joint to intervene at the State Department in Washington because the issuing of visas to the United States of North America is most important for the future course of emigration.

Two days before he left Vienna for his January 1941 meeting with Joint officials in Lisbon, Löwenherz

> was informed by the American consulate that a substantial relaxation in the issuing of immigrant visas was about to be instituted. Since May 1940 . . . there had been practically no issuance of immigrant visas. . . . According to the new procedure all applications for visas filed subsequent to May were to receive immediate consideration. Thereafter, all expired visas were to be reconsidered . . . and all applications for visas which were rejected were to be reviewed.[190]

Whether Troper or other Joint officers already had, directly or indirectly, made representations at the State Department as a result of Löwenherz's letter is not known. Whether—in case such representations were made—the "tendency" was changed as a result cannot be known. Whether the consulate's call to Löwenherz was deliberately timed to coincide with his imminent departure for Lisbon is also not known. Löwenherz had actually received an indication that a relaxation of the blockage was in the works a few days before the call from the consulate.[191] The effect was that, for the time being, Löwenherz deemed it politic not to risk disturbing the sensitive relations he maintained with the Vienna consulate, and thus he refrained from doing what he had set out to do, namely, causing his Joint "friends" to make representations at the State Department:

> [I]n view of the fact that the entire procedure has changed, Y [Löwenherz] feels that no intervention should be undertaken before one has the opportunity to learn in what way the consulate will act during the next period.[192]

Nevertheless, he told the representatives of the Joint (Troper had left Lisbon for New York before Löwenherz's arrival) about the manner in which the consulate had been proceeding and about the attitude of its staff, which they included in their report to the New York home office:

> [T]he physicians of the American consulate were particularly severe to a point which might be termed anti-Semitic in establishing the basis on which they rejected applicants for reasons of health. The consuls themselves questioned applicants along irrelevant lines or put questions concerning internal matters in the U.S. to which it is quite likely large numbers of American citizens residing in the country itself would not know the answers. The Vienna [consul] further stated that he would not accept affidavits from wealthy men, as he did not feel such people would assume the responsibility they undertook, such guarantee being given for reasons of sympathy, nor would he accept so-called friendship affidavits.[193]

This report shows that by interviewing the people who were refused visas, the IKG brought to light some disturbing facts about the goings-on at the U.S. consulate in Vienna. But the cause of the "tendency" that prevailed there, to the chagrin of the IKG concerned with facilitating emigration and relieving the misery of thousands of desperately frustrated would-be emigrants, was a mystery to them. Unbeknownst to them, a policy of choking off immigration to the United States had in 1940 become a concerted effort initiated mainly by two officials at the State Department, as documented and related by David Wyman. One was Assistant Secretary of State Breckinridge Long, "who was continually exercised about possible immigration of Nazi agents . . . [and feared] infiltration by German subversives," in fact believing "that Nazi agents trying to get to the United States disguised as refugees gravely threatened the nation's safety."[194] The other was Avra Warren, who headed the Department's Visa Division.

The speed with which the Netherlands were overrun gave rise to some panic in Great Britain. Giving credence to the rumor that this speed was the result of spying by refugees pressured by the Nazis, out of fear for the safety of relatives left behind,[195] the British proceeded to intern aliens, including Jewish refugees. Wyman reports that in May 1940, even a few days before the Germans "invaded the Low Countries, . . . Warren was at work on proposed legislation for stricter immigration controls to protect the country from subversive aliens."[196] The stated need for such legislation was based on the consideration that under laws then existing the issuance of visas could be refused to applicants who have "subversive connections or intentions" only in the case of visitors and not of immigrants. In the absence of such a law, and until such legislation was enacted a year later, Long devised a method of procrastination within the consulates that processed applicants:

> We can delay and effectively stop for a temporary period of indefinite length the number of immigrants into the United States. We could do this by simply advising our consuls to put every

> obstacle in the way and to require additional evidence and to resort to various administrative devices which would postpone and postpone and postpone the granting of visas.[197]

Instructions in accordance with this new policy went by circular cablegrams to consular officers worldwide and were reinforced by a four-month tour of the continental European consulates on the part of Avra Warren, chief of the visa section. To Margaret E. Jones, an American emigration worker active in the American Friends Service Committee, whom he met in Vienna, Warren said that the reasons why "immigration from Germany was being terminated" was that

> President [Roosevelt] wanted to stop the flow of aliens into the United States, particularly those coming from Germany . . . because some refugees had been connected with fifth column activities, because anti-Semitism was rising in the United States, and because of the need to use German [quota] visas to move refugees out of England and Shanghai.[198]

In connection with relating some examples of hardship the new policy caused among would-be emigrants in Vienna, Wyman says:

> Indications that the State Department did not want the severity of the new restrictions generally known soon appeared in Vienna. Following Warren's visit, the consulate continued to permit refugees to nurture hopes of obtaining visas and let them spend weeks and money assembling documents and affidavits, fulfilling all the other American and German requirements, and arranging ship passage, only to reject them after the final interview.[199]

The applicants in Vienna, who had been strung along in this way and, having run the course with apparent success only to be told that they would not receive their visas, were puzzled as to the nature of the obstacles. They had no way of knowing that the problem lay not with them, their qualifications, the financial strength of their guarantors, or their documentation, but was a matter of the State Department's policy. This policy required the consular officers to find any reason whatsoever for withholding the issuance of visas.

Dr. Feiler, one of the most valuable members of the IKG staff, decided to make use of her chance to immigrate to the United States in the period under consideration. In November 1940 she was one of the very few to whom a visa was issued in Vienna. Half a century later she told us what she had always believed to have been the reason for her success. In her official capacity at the IKG she had spoken to many would-be emigrants who, in their desperation over not obtaining a visa for the United States, had turned to the IKG emigration section. Feiler asked them detailed questions about their cases, and what they were asked at the final interviews with the consular officials. One of the questions that consistently recurred was whether the applicant had voted the last time there had been a free election in Austria (i.e., before 1934), and, if so, for what party they had voted. Among the parties the two main choices were the conservative Christian-Social Party and the anti-Bolshevik Social-Democratic Party. Most Austrian Jews, whether politically conservative or not, found it difficult to vote for the Christian-Social Party, since it harbored most of Austria's anti-Semitic tendencies. Hence, they voted Social-Democratic. And, naturally, when asked, the applicants answered truthfully. Feiler noted that none of these were given visas and concluded that it was a matter of the United States' fear of communism. When it was her turn, she said that she had voted for some obscure minor party and, when she received her visa without much ado, she concluded that this was the key. No doubt this was a necessary but not a sufficient condition for the positive decision. We surmise that Consul Hohenthal's concession may have been more decisive in her case, according to which even under the policy of visa stoppage, visas would be issued in individual cases that, for financial reasons, were very important to the IKG. We know that Dr. Feiler went as an emissary of the IKG to the Joint, where she was, in fact, employed from the time of her arrival in New York until her retirement in 1971.

In January 1941, soon after her arrival in New York, Dr. Feiler reported to the Joint and was presented with ten questions.[200] Inasmuch as she had belonged to the inner circle of professionally trained people working at the IKG on matters of emigration, she was in a position to answer most of them. The questions dealt with "emigration procedures" at the IKG, for the most part connected with the transfer of the foreign exchange necessary for emigration, that is, the funds made available by the Joint, and with regulations pertinent to emigration to various non-American destinations. Not one of the questions dealt with the puzzling visa stoppage about which Löwenherz had spoken in Lisbon at about the same time.

The officials at the Joint may have been under the impression that the crisis had been resolved. If so, they were soon disabused of the notion, especially when the deportations started. On March 11, 1941, the Lisbon office sent a cable to the Joint in New York:

> WE BELEAGUERED HERE DAILY EVER INCREASING NUMBERS HAVING RELATIVES LION HEART CITY [i.e. Vienna] AND RECEIVING FRANTIC LETTERS CABLES UNLESS BOOKINGS MADE IMMEDIATELY THEY WILL BE SENT NEUSTADT [i.e., Poland] STOP. . . .WE UNABLE COPE SITUATION. . . ONLY PROMISE IN ORDER QUIET APPLICANTS REFER MATTER ISKULT [i.e., IKG] THEIR ATTENTION STOP HAVE YOU ANY SUGGESTIONS[201]

A similar cable arrived on March 13 from the Joint in Budapest:

> AUTHENTIC REPORTS INDICATE LIONHEARTS DEPORTATIONS UNABATING OUR OFFICE HERE AVALANCHED BY FRANTIC REQUESTS FOR AFFIDAVITS EMIGRATION HELP SYMPTOMATIC PANIC REIGNING THERE[202]

Lest we think this is only the panic attending the beginning of the deportations, an earlier cable, from Löwenherz to Troper can set us straight:

> ALTHOUGH SINCE MIDDLE JANUARY VISA DISTRIBUTION AGAIN REGULATED THE US CONSULATE VIENNA STARTED MUCH LATER WITH NORMAL HANDLING OF CASES STOP SINCE THEN ONLY A LIMITED NUMBER OF VISAS BECAUSE THERE ARE VARIOUS DIFFICULTIES ON THE BASIS OF INSTRUCTIONS FROM WASHINGTON STOP WOMEN WHOSE HUSBANDS ARE ABROAD RECEIVE NO VISAS EVEN IF SPONSOR AGREES AND GUARANTEES STOP MANY MEDICAL REJECTIONS STOP NUMBER OF QUOTA NUMBERS EXCEEDINGLY SMALL IN PROPORTION TO TOTAL NUMBER STOP WE URGENTLY REQUEST INTERVENTION WITH STATE DEPARTMENT WASHINGTON FOR RELAXING THE INCREASED SEVERITY OF THE REGULATIONS IN ORDER TO OBTAIN SEVERAL HUNDRED QUOTA NUMBERS FOR VIENNA STOP. . . . ESPECIALLY URGENT THAT YOU TAKE CARE OF ABOVE SINCE END OF QUOTA YEAR IS APPROACHING[203]

The officers and staff of the Joint were beset with all kinds of inquiries, from individuals and other aid societies, all in one way or another concerned with what the Joint could do to save the Jews of Vienna. One such inquiry came from two members of the refugee artists' colony in Hollywood, the composer Erich Korngold and the writer Lion Feuchtwanger. In response Joint secretary Moses Leavitt assured them

> that the Jews of Vienna are not forsaken . . . but one of our chief problems is our lack of funds. We [could] spend $3,000,000, if we had the money, for transportation from German countries [i.e., Altreich and Austria] alone.[204]

Two weeks later, in a bulletin directed to "Welfare Fund and community executives," Joseph C. Hyman, one of the officers of Joint, gave a seemingly more realistic figure:

> In January of this year [1941], about 42,000 Jews were left in Vienna. Deducting the aged, the infirm . . . at least 20,000 desperately seek to emigrate. To do that would run . . . about $8,000,000. If we were to give up every other kind of work all over the world and just devote ourselves to emigration transportation, we would not begin to have enough to meet such a staggering demand.[205]

Whether $3,000,000 for "transportation [of emigrants] from German alone" or $8,000,000 for those from Vienna alone is the better projected estimate, we will never know. However, neither figure takes into account the money in the Joint's newly established account to hold transportation deposits made by panicky relatives, even though it is mentioned by both Hyman in his bulletin and Leavitt in his letter. Leavitt, in fact, states that the account had already reached "over $1,600,000, of which a large share is for the emigration of people from Vienna."[206] And evidently it continued growing. It would thus appear that available funds outpaced the flow of emigration from Vienna as well as from Berlin and Prague.

The labored pace of emigration caused by blockage and slowdown at the U.S. consulates, as well as by the immense difficulties of devising and arranging transportation routes, may have been in accord with the Joint's evaluation of its capacities. Yet, Löwenherz's warning during the January meeting in Lisbon, which arrived in New York a few days prior to news of the deportations, must have been ringing in their ears: "The Jews have an absolutely black future, and to move them before the 'final accounts are in' would be a saving of Jewish lives." The exacerbation of the situation caused by the February/March deportations must have worked like a confirmation of Löwenherz's warning and like a call for more decisive action. The documents do not tell us to what extent the Joint and the other Jewish leadership in the United States answered that call by making representations in Washington, particularly at the State Department, to speed up immigration procedures to the full extent provided by law. Under the prevailing political climate, which included anti-Semitism, there is reason to doubt that such pressure would have worked and reason to believe that it would have been counterproductive.

For the Joint the matter was thus reduced to a question of money. The funds that could be raised were limited, and whatever funds were available had to be used for a variety of purposes and at many locations in the world. The captive Jews of Poland were starving, refugees stuck at many interim stops had to be housed and fed from Lisbon to Shanghai, other refugees were stranded at ports from Romania to Japan, destitute and awaiting ships to their destinations, and neither last nor least, but also not first and foremost, the Jews of Vienna needed foreign exchange to pay for passage to their refuge. How to urge the Jews in the United States to greater sacrifice without unduly alarming them? How to rouse them to their sense of duty without seeming to play on their alarm and fear? How, in fact, could one inform them of the urgency? What evidence could be advanced in support of it, other than the frantic telegrams from some individuals to their relatives?

At the Lisbon meeting Löwenherz "was asked whether it would be possible for him to go to the United States to participate in the fund raising campaign . . . should the JDC feel it advisable to invite him."[207] Can we imagine the tall, dignified gentleman, sartorially impeccable (including starched collar), speaking in lawyerly cadences and accented English, convincingly telling of the plight of the Jews of Vienna and the urgency of the situation? The idea was preposterous. Löwenherz would have had to appear at fundraisers before select audiences consisting of people who could pledge leadership gifts and people who could spread whatever he had to report to communities which, in turn, might make smaller contributions. What he told would have made its way to the press and not only to the Jewish press. But, Löwenherz could not have related precisely the sort of jarring truths that would have effectively motivated a successful fundraising drive; and the message was bound to reach the well-organized Nazi information network. We know how the Nazis reacted to the spread of what they called *Greuelgeschichten*, "horror stories" or "malicious rumors of atrocities." And how could Löwenherz have then gone back to face the music, since he well knew what would await him?

But how could he not have gone back, inasmuch as his wife as well as his deputy Murmelstein would have functioned as hostages for his return? In fact, he and Murmelstein would have had to sign an agreement that Murmelstein would be hostage to Löwenherz's "proper conduct" while abroad. Another concern would have been the possibility of his taking ill and not being able to return.

Correctly evaluating his situation, Löwenherz said that "it would be impossible for him to obtain permission to leave the country merely for purposes of campaign."[208] On the other hand, Löwenherz thought "that if he [were] invited to participate in conferences and plans in connection with matters of emigration from Vienna, there is some likelihood that permission might be secured." This was not only a matter of his being more effective as a negotiator in the businesslike confines of an executive office. Both he and the Nazis were interested in his negotiating with the Jewish aid organizations for the sole purpose of getting the Jews out of Vienna and Europe. For this purpose he was permitted to leave for brief contacts with the closest representatives of these organizations in Europe. However, if his effectiveness in securing increased aid in response to the desperate need might be increased by a visit to the United States, he had to show a willingness to go. Keeping all this in mind, Löwenherz cautioned that if an invitation to the United States were to be issued, it should not be couched in general but personal terms: "Should the invitation be a general one, it is possible that the [Nazi] authorities might send some technician [like Storfer] from the committee [i.e., the IKG], which would not serve [the Joint's] purpose at all." Ever mindful of the unique nature of his position and of the vital need for his presence in Vienna, as well as both the importance and hostage function of Murmelstein, Löwenherz noted that a personal invitation to him "should contain some language to the effect that our committee is sure that from among his colleagues and collaborators, it will be possible to find someone who will be able to carry on the program of the KG during his absence."

We mentioned that at Joint headquarters there was awareness abroad that it had reached the limits of its capacity of responding to the ever deepening crisis. Löwenherz must have perceived this. No doubt he also saw that someone was needed to help break through these limits, someone who, like himself, knew firsthand about the relentlessness of the Nazi policy of ridding Europe of Jews. Besides himself there was no one who would be more qualified to do so and, even more than himself, there was no one he could trust to "behave properly" who would be more effective in speaking frankly with people than Murmelstein. It is, therefore, no coincidence that the "Personal Matters" appended to the minutes of the Lisbon meeting contains an item on "Dr. Benjamin Murmelstein" about whom, as is written there, "there has already been a special file of correspondence . . . with New York."[209] What is most interesting is Löwenherz's request "that the matter be pursued as energetically as possible." Murmelstein's position as an emissary of the Jews of Vienna—and not only theirs—would have been ideal, if his immigration under the non-quota provision had been "pursued energetically" and succeeded. In the innocuous position of a professor or rabbi in Cincinnati, Philadelphia, or New York, with his wife and son safely by his side, he would have been in a secure position to help rouse the Jewish community of the United States to greater effort. But, as we have seen, even Löwenherz's urging "the energetic pursuit of the matter" did not help, and a great opportunity to help the Jews of Vienna was lost.

Therefore, in March 1941 Mr. Leavitt of the Joint could do no more to allay Korngold's and Feuchtwanger's concern than "to point out that the Jews of Vienna are not forsaken, and that the JDC is exercising every effort to aid them—but one of the chief problems is our lack of funds."[210]

In March 1941 the abyss of Nazi Germany triumphant was inexorably deepening: It was one month before the invasion of Yugoslavia, three months before the attack on the Soviet Union, barely nine months before the United States would also be drawn into the war. And with it, for the Jews the last gates of escape were slamming shut.

■ ■ ■

While still in Lisbon, Löwenherz took the opportunity of writing a letter to his son Siegmund, who was at the beginning of an academic and musical career in Chicago, though soon to be drafted into the U.S. army.[211] He gave the letter to the gentlemen from the Joint to mail to Siegmund.[212] Löwenherz took this, the only and as it happened last, chance to testify, from his own unique perspective and unencumbered by the need to speak officially, to the conditions in Vienna not quite three years after the Anschluss. He asked Siegmund to share the letter with certain relatives, but otherwise to be circumspect about mentioning it: "one has to be very careful because any information that arouses the slightest suspicion will cause great unpleasantness."

About the impoverishment of the Jews, Löwenherz reported that

> the conditions are becoming unspeakably sad, and day by day they are becoming worse. About 42,000 of the 46,000 Jews who live here depend on support by the Community [i.e., the IKG].

> The Community struggles with great financial difficulties, since the outlays are increasing and the sources of income steadily decreasing. Without the support of the Joint I would not be able to lead the Community.

The housing problem that Löwenherz described in his letter was even worse than what he was able to state in the record of his *Vorsprachen* with the Nazi authorities:

> To all that we had to suffer so far, there now is added a housing catastrophe of unimaginable magnitude. People are herded together 6 to 8 in a room, where married and unmarried, healthy and sick, old ones and children have to live together. Often they are assigned to rooms that cannot be heated, without lights and [access to] water. With the greatest effort it is possible to get relief in individual cases, but by and large the prevailing tendency is to make it impossible [for the Jews] to remain in the city [Vienna].

Löwenherz himself was not spared:

> We also received an order to vacate. I am sharing, in all aspects, the fate of the Community members; however, after a day's hard work I need the assurance that the four walls are ours alone. The traffic of clients comes not only to the Community, but a lot also to our home. [Your mother] takes care of it excellently and in the evening she reports to me all that transpired.

The deprivations suffered by his people were Löwenherz's most urgent concern:

> Jews are forbidden to possess radios or telephones. Shopping for food is restricted to two hours; the rations are very meager, and milk, fruit, and other nutritious foods [*Naehrmittel*] may not be sold to Jews. One can subsist only with occasional gift packages from friends in neighboring countries. . . . Difficulties with clothing are added to concerns over nourishment. Jews do not receive rations for fabrics and shoes. Poverty forces most of them to sell their clothes in order to eat. The acquisition of new [clothing] is impossible.

However, the main concern in this desperate situation was the need to find immigration destinations. Löwenherz told Siegmund that two months previously they were able to dispatch about 1,500 people to Palestine, and they had safely landed. "You can imagine the great organizational and financial difficulties that were connected with such a transport;" but, "I do not think that another transport can be arranged in the near future."

Löwenherz had heard before leaving for Lisbon that after the stoppage of emigration to the United States, the consulate would again be issuing visas. He reported that about 10,000 were in possession of viable affidavits and, since they registered for the waiting list in 1938, they could be ready to emigrate if only their visas were issued. The first priority—for second visas—should go to those who had previously received their visas but, because of the military campaigns in the Low Countries and France, could not leave before the visas ran out. The second priority concerned parents whose children sent them affidavits; the difficulty there was that it was not certain whether they had established themselves well enough to satisfy the financial guarantee requirement. Generally, Löwenherz wrote, aside from the United States "there are no other larger emigration possibilities." As regards his own chances of emigration, Löwenherz had this to say:

> The stoppage of emigration [to the U.S.] has also delayed Mutti's ("Mother's") and my chances of emigration. I was able to obtain the emigration permit [from Eichmann] for Engel but not for myself. The members of the Community [i.e., Löwenherz's main associates at the IKG]

> were desperate when they heard that I was going to Lisbon because they thought that I was ready to emigrate. Of course, I shall return, because I cannot and I will not leave the Community in the lurch. In the next few months I shall try to take soundings as to my emigration and nominate a deputy. Whether I will succeed in getting the permit cannot, of course, be predicted.

As it turned out, Löwenherz would have no chance to take soundings about his possible emigration; his trip to Lisbon would be both his last trip abroad and his last consultation with the Joint, and he would have no access to Eichmann again until fairly late in 1941.

Chapter 10

Lessons in Judaism

DURING THE PHASE UNDER CONSIDERATION in this chapter, the leaders of the IKG had to dance to several conflicting tunes under a pressure that had become even more extreme. At stake was the survival of the Jews still in Vienna by means of facilitating their emigration as well as by devising ways for those left behind to stay alive. Nonetheless, the leadership harbored no illusions. In August 1939, even before the outbreak of the war, Löwenherz had told Norman Bentwich, who had become the main Jewish activist in England for the rescue of the Jews of Germany, that there would be no change in the ruthless treatment of the Jews of Vienna unless outside pressure were successfully brought to bear on Berlin. There was not a chance of that then, and not now with Nazi Germany as master of the continent. Hence, in January 1941, when Löwenherz was in Lisbon to meet with officials of the Joint (American Jewish Joint Distribution Committee, AJDC)—what would turn out to have been for the last time, he and Paul Meyerheim, who represented the *Reichsvertretung* (Reich association of Jewish communities), are recorded as

> repeatedly [stating] that under present circumstances and uncertainties everything [possible] must be done to [bring] as many Jews as possible out of Germany, Austria, and the Protectorate. . . . [They insisted] that it is actually a matter of life and death, that regardless of the outcome of the war the Jews have an absolutely black future, and to move them [out] before the "final accounts are in" would [constitute the] saving of Jewish lives.[1]

In effect, this warning was a lesson about the dire state of Judaism and what urgent action needed to be taken to counter it. Indeed, it was the final one of the many lessons in Judaism that the Jewish leaders under Nazi rule, and especially the Vienna leadership, had to teach prior to their final cutoff from the outside world. Along with working at fever pitch, they had to reflect on the present reality and the history of the Jews, on what the present demanded and what hope was held out by the lessons learned from the past, on the truth of their faith and the validity of their ethos, and on the perfidy of their enemies and the sources of their own strength. Such lessons had to be articulated according to the audience toward which they were directed, whether the Nazis or the Jews, the old or the young. No one was more driven in this work at the IKG than Murmelstein. And no one worked harder at finding the right tone in formulating such lessons in accordance with his audience. Perhaps the choice of approach and language would make a difference, even if the topics were determined by the situation or prescribed by Nazi fiat.

In 1940 the Nazi authorities ordered the leading Jews to prepare and submit studies on specific subjects. Submitting reports on activities, lists of people possessing certain attributes, and general lists of populations, addresses, assets, statistics, and so on had been part of the dealings between the Jewish functionaries and the Nazi authorities all along. But some of the studies now ordered were different, or at least they appear so from the privileged position of retrospect.

The Directors Plan a Final Solution

It all started innocently enough, when in January 1940 Eichmann ordered Löwenherz to submit a

> register of all Jewish institutions that are active worldwide in the area of Jewish political life and welfare. This also includes religious communities [*Kultusgemeinden*] and the larger organizations of orthodox, Zionist, and other orientations. In the case of the Zionist organizations, the various subgroupings are to be considered.[2]

This account of the complex organization of Jewish life was, no doubt, meant to supplement, corroborate, or correct the information gathered over the years by SD II/112, which, it will be recalled, had started off as a tiny research section dealing with that segment of the "enemies" and "opponents" of the Nazi movement that comprised the imagined Jewish world conspiracy. However, now that the section had grown into an executive agency dealing with the realization of the Jewish policy mandated by Nazi ideology, they had to know in greater detail than what their amateurish information provided with whom they would have to deal in their contacts with the likes of Löwenherz.

More intriguing was another study ordered at the same time.

> Dr. Murmelstein or Dr. Moses should write a brief paper about Gabriel Ri[e]sser, a few pages, purely factually, without any personal note, and submit it to the *Zentralstelle*.[3]

Unfortunately, we could locate neither the result of this directive nor the reason for it, and we might wonder what interest Nazi ideologues and policy executors might have taken in this brilliant German Jew of another era, who was in the area of constitutional law the greatest proponent and advocate of the emancipation of the Jews in German lands. And why the stipulation that the Jews carry out their assignment "without any personal note"?

Gabriel Riesser had stood up effectively for the equal status of Jews in German society and in the German body politic.[4] Hence, we need not wonder about the reason for the Nazis' interest in Riesser, the political Jew whose actions and ideology were diametrically opposed to their policy of racial-national necessity. As to the matter of their watchful concern over the Jew's "personal note," it is, in the case of Riesser, difficult to anticipate where the Nazis would draw the line between the "personal note" and the "strictly factual." As to Murmelstein, they might have consulted his *Geschichte der Juden* (*History of the Jews*), where Riesser is taken up in a chapter dealing with the period of emancipation and Jewish renewal in the nineteenth century. There Murmelstein does not mention Riesser's performance at the National Assembly in Frankfurt (1848–1849); instead he says

> violent actions were repeatedly instigated as a pretext for suppressing the rights of Jews. In Hamburg this method of brutal force brought forth the most significant fighter for the rights of German Jews. After his application for admission to the bar was rejected, Gabriel Riesser (1806–1863) placed himself fully at the service of Jewish emancipation. In several writings he advocated equal rights for Jews, at the same time decidedly rejecting baptism as a way thereto: "There is only one baptism for admission to one's nationality, the baptism of blood in the common battle for freedom and country."[5]

"Brutal force"? "Violent actions . . . instigated for suppressing the rights of Jews"? "Equal rights for Jews"? "Advocating" and even "fighting" for them by the power of the written and spoken word? Could one tell the Nazis the blunt truth? If they knew nothing about Riesser other than his name, they were simply in need of information to strengthen their ideological backbone in regard to their Jewish policy. If, on the other hand, they did have an inkling of Riesser's significance (and their specific injunction against "a personal note" would speak for this), then the order for the study may have had an element of testing its author's impudence. In either case, writing the report must have taken considerable skill

The title page of Benjamin Murmelstein's History of the Jews *(*Geschichte der Juden*). (© CSE)*

GESCHICHTE DER JUDEN

DES VOLKES WELTWANDERN

VON

DR. B. MURMELSTEIN

DOZENT AN DER ISRAEL. THEOL. LEHRANSTALT IN WIEN

VERLAG JOSEF BELF, WIEN

in presenting the full weight of the truth of the matter without seeming to interject a "personal note." None of the leading Jewish functionaries possessed this skill more than Murmelstein. It was a matter of bluntly expressing no more and no less than what needed to be said, yet being cautiously sensitive to the Nazi's readiness to detect a note of resistance to their battle against those they considered their "opponents." We will have occasion in the course of this chapter to see the degree of their suspiciousness, and that this caution did not always succeed.

■ ■ ■

In the first week of July 1940 the leading functionaries from Vienna, Berlin, and Prague were ordered to Berlin for a combined *Vorsprache* at the RSHA (Reich headquarters of the SS). The first meeting of Löwenherz, Eppstein, Edelstein, and Weidmann with Eichmann took place in the afternoon of July 3. After some routine matters, the emigration effort came up, and it was agreed that the arduous task of routing emigrés through the Far East had to continue, and their routing through Portugal had to get under way. In this connection Eichmann broached the need for a final solution to the Jewish problem. It was two weeks after June 22, when France had accepted the harsh terms of surrender; it was also the beginning of what would become known as the "Battle of Britain" and what Nazi Germany thought was the beginning of the end of the war; and no one present at that meeting would have imagined that one year hence, on another June 22, the war would expand with Germany's invasion of the Soviet Union.

In anticipation of the end of a war that Germany had, in effect, already won, the Nazi regime needed to plan for the event under the novel condition of a victorious and preeminent Germany. Most pressing was the Jewish problem, which had turned from the project of eliminating Jews from the German national body politic to ridding the entire portion of Europe under the predominance of Nazi Germany of Jews. How to accomplish this? Among the plans that prevailed among the Nazis at that point was the plan to ship them all to Madagascar. From a much later document, we learn that by August 1940 the Foreign Office Section D-III had

> [designed] a plan for the final solution of the Jewish question, for which the island of Madagascar would be demanded from France [as part of a] peace treaty, the execution of which, however, was to be assigned to the RSHA. In accordance with this plan *Gruppenführer* HEYDRICH was commissioned by the Führer to implement the solution of the Jewish question in Europe.[6]

This document shows that the war provided the opportunity for a final solution of the Jewish question, that the plan for it was being jelled in the first year of the war, and that the Führer authorized its implementation and entrusted Reinhard Heydrich, the director of the RSHA and Himmler's right-hand man, with it. Before the fall of France provided the possibility of focusing on the plan of shipping the Jews to Madagascar, the Foreign Office needed to gain clarity about questions of alternatives, feasibility, logistics, means, and costs. A consideration of alternatives, especially within wider contexts of foreign relations is testified to in an in-house memo of the Foreign Office Section D-III, which was written almost three weeks before the fall of France. Because of its great interest, we quote the memo in its entirety:

> Berlin, June 3, 1940
>
> Brief review of urgent tasks of Sec. D-III
>
> 1. Request from the Reich-Foreign Minister [von Ribbentrop] a fundamental determination of German war aims in regard to the Jewish question. The possibilities are:
>   a. all Jews out of Europe,
>   b. separation of East- and West-Jews; in order to paralyze the America-Jews, East-Jews, who are more potently procreative and competent in the Talmud, remain in German hands as security (Lublin?); West-Jews out of Europe (Madagascar?)
>   c. Jewish national home in Palestine (danger of a 2nd Rome?)
> 2. Begin closer discussions with interested internal German authorities of Party, governmental, scientific; determine their plans and coordinate with the wishes of Reich Foreign Minister.
> 3. Gather relevant information (number of Jews in each country, the financial means and the transportation necessary for the evacuation [of the Jews], and the likely time periods, etc.).[7]

Whatever decisions were to be made, whether in coordination with von Ribbentrop's wishes or not, would be executed by the SD (*Sicherheitsdienst*, "Security Service," the SS intel agency) under the executive command of Heydrich and would be based on the primary input of the SD; and whatever information would be needed to arrive at the decisions would be elicited by the same SD. Thus, it does not come as a surprise that Eichmann, as the regime's point man on Jewish affairs, was charged with gathering the information needed for planning a final solution of the Jewish question; and he did so in a manner befitting his expertise; that is, he asked the Jewish functionaries, whom he had gathered in Berlin, for a plan. Specifically he said, very delicately:

> It is likely that at the end of the war an overall solution of the European Jewish question will have to be put into effect. It will be a matter of dealing with about four million Jews in the European countries under consideration. Individual emigration will not be sufficient for their resettlement, although in special cases permission for individual emigration will continue to be granted.[8]

Eichmann, as we see, did not use *Endlösung* ("final solution"), the expression that came into currency later on; instead he spoke of *eine Gesamtlösung der europäischen Judenfrage* ("an overall solution of the European Jewish question"). By "Europe" he meant the part of the continent that was then under the control of victorious Germany and its allies,[9] control that Eichmann represented as a fait accompli. The shock of Germany's furious vanquishing of France, which had been, until then, the traditionally dominant power on the continent, was reverberating among the captive Jews no less than around the world. But, that the dismal turn of events portended a final disposition according to which Jews would have no place on this continent at all was no doubt something that was, even then, more than what the four men were able to absorb or deal with. And these four men had not merely their own survival to be concerned over but that of hundreds of thousands, the burden of whose care was thrust upon them.

At this time Eichmann asked them a question: Have the gentlemen given any consideration to or made any plans with regard to such an overall solution? The four must have looked at each other. Who would answer? All the record tells is: "This question was answered in the negative." Thereupon Eichmann ordered them to prepare "in brief outline the different angles from which such a plan would have to be considered." The four responded to the effect that "such a plan could be carried out only if an actual territory were set aside for the settlement, and if the financing—especially by means of public funds [*staatliche Mittel*]—of emigration as well as of the process and the organization of settlement were secured." Eichmann must have heard the oblique reference to the "emigration fund," which he had amassed and which Löwenherz had been trying to tap. He said "that at this time it is merely a matter of stating guidelines that would make it possible to carry out such a plan of emigration without friction or hardship for either party, and to do so within three to four years." Löwenherz, Eppstein, and Edelstein were leading Zionists in their respective venues and as one pointed to Palestine, which with its "half million Jews" constituted "the best point of departure for the absorption and settlement of great masses of Jews," and declared that such a settlement project could best count on the "participation of Jewish aid organizations." But Eichmann knew what he wanted and said that "specific plans regarding the territory and form of settlement" had not as yet been determined. He left the meeting expecting the report to be submitted the following afternoon.

The meeting was continued with one of Eichmann's men in Berlin, Theodor Dannecker, then at the rank of *Obersturmführer* (first lieutenant).[10] To the objection that the time frame stipulated for preparing the report presented difficulties, Dannecker reiterated that this should merely be a preliminary reaction to the whole problem and that, even though no specific territory had as yet been decided upon, an actual country could be mentioned by way of an example. The men took this as a cue to mention Palestine again, but Dannecker demurred to the effect that Palestine was not large enough, and—not having Eichmann's acumen—he revealed the real reason: "it is possible that the Arabs would make trouble." The men, who would not be deterred, offered the rejoinder "that in its [then] present size Palestine" should be able to hold three million Jews, and, if it were "to comprise Transjordan, [it] would solve the entire problem in question." The men were hinting at the fact that, according to the Balfour Declaration, the Palestine that was to be the homeland of the Jews would comprise not only the territory west of the Jordan River but also that which had been separated from the Palestine Mandate in 1920 as "Transjordan."

The reader will have noticed that Murmelstein was missing from this caucus of directors. This was curious for two reasons. First, in questions of the complicated logistics of the emigration effort Murmelstein was at least as experienced and involved as any of the ones whom Eichmann assembled to consider the matter. Second, whenever Eichmann—in his capacity of the regime's resident expert on Jewish matters—had to present to his superiors well-documented authoritative studies on any relevant topic at all, it was his wont to turn the task over to "*dem Jud*" (the Jew), as he referred to Murmelstein.

Was there a reason that Eichmann did not call on Murmelstein to join the others in drafting the assigned project? We believe there was.

Earlier in that spring of 1940, probably between the June 3 in-house Foreign Ministry memo and the fall of France, Murmelstein had been ordered to write a study on a related matter. In retrospect—since he was not privy to the plans and deliberations of the uppermost reaches of the Nazi regime, nor did he know of that memo—he interpreted (fairly accurately) the reason for this assignment to be that, with the German armies poised to complete the subjugation of Europe under Nazi control, the Nazis realized that the Jewish question could not be solved by means of the laborious emigration process and that they would have to consider a territorial solution. One such territorial solution was the rationale behind the study Murmelstein had to prepare. He told of this as follows:[11]

> Though accustomed to the strangest wishes and assignments from Eichmann, I was surprised when I was informed that I had to prepare for him, in the shortest time possible, a treatise, based on historical sources, on the development of the idea of a Jewish national state. I was to stress especially the historical implicatory background of the solution of the Jewish question. If this final solution was to be based on Jewish history and literature, then there was no alternative to the equation: final solution of the Jewish question equals settlement in Palestine. In a voluminous essay I steered toward this only possible solution. Apart from the historical ties, I believed I could point to the technical advantages in respect to transportation based on the geographic situation of that country. In conclusion I opined that the responsibility for the political and administrative implementation of this venture as a whole would have to be assumed by the power that would predominate in the Mediterranean after the war was over.
>
> In accordance with instructions, the IKG passed the finished voluminous manuscript on to the *Reich-Zentralstelle* in Berlin. We did not have to wait long for Eichmann's reaction. He was furious that I had dared to doubt the ultimate victory of Germany. According to him, I should not have spoken of a "predominant power" but explicitly of the German Reich, which had, after all, practically won the war and would have to be considered the predominant power when it was over. Apart from this political gaffe on my part, my paper seemed to have been acceptable, since apart from this reprimand there were no further repercussions. Nevertheless, the fact that I was ignored by Eichmann for quite some time seems to have constituted a stern reproof for my audacity. But whenever he needed a report, he knew he merely had to turn to the IKG and his order would reach me, albeit indirectly.

The incident shows, on the one hand, that by excluding Murmelstein Eichmann shifted the question to one of technical logistics and, on the other, that Löwenherz, well prepared by Murmelstein's experience, avoided provocative language, while he and his companions confirmed Murmelstein's promotion of Palestine as the preferred territorial solution.

Let us return to their caucus:

The directorate of the three Jewish communities (Löwenherz from Vienna, Edelstein and Weidmann from Prague, and Eppstein joined by Hirsch from Berlin) sat until late into the night and much of the next day to prepare their proposal for the "overall" solution, which they submitted at the stipulated time on July 4, 1940. They entitled it "Settlement of Jews from European Lands in Settlement Territories Placed at [Their] Disposal outside Europe." The parameters of the report were set by their immediate impromptu responses to Eichmann and Dannecker. A preamble stipulated three presuppositions for the projected settlement:[12]

1. Provision of a suitable territory, where a permanent settlement of the Jews can be ensured under healthful, legal, and economic conditions conducive to the unfolding of the productive powers of the Jews, as well as to the creation of a commonwealth.
2. Availability of the material and financial means for effecting both the emigration and the settlement.
3. The time span set aside for executing the plan of settlement should be great enough to ensure sufficient preparation of the logistics of emigration and placement.

These presuppositions are, in effect, a summary of the positions that Löwenherz and Eppstein, and to a minor degree Edelstein, had over a period of time struggled so hard and frustratingly to maintain vis-à-vis Eichmann and his deputies. To Eichmann, and generally to the Nazis, they were, in turn, the massive rocks of reality blocking the way to a solution to the Jewish problem "without any hardship" for them. As far as the Jews were concerned, these rocks had to be scaled no less by the Nazis than by the Jews, an effort which, as it turned out, the Nazis intended to avoid at any cost.

The three sections of the Jewish functionaries' proposal for an overall solution, which followed these presuppositions, could not but confirm the Nazis' worst expectations regarding the success of the methods they were applying at that time to rid their world of Jews. And overall the sections contained necessary steps and conditions they did not want to face.

The first section characterized the territory suitable for Jewish settlement. Not only would there have to be enough land for an initial population of four million as well as soil suitable for cultivation, but the "climate must not preclude the possibility of living and working on the part of people who hail from Europe, as it would, for example, on Madagascar." There had been talk, even before the war, about Madagascar as a possible destination for all of Europe's Jews; and now that France was conquered, the Nazis considered this project as the best territorial solution and wanted to revive and seek to realize it through the subservient Vichy government. The Jews did not know this but correctly anticipating it, they tried to forestall it. Moreover, if resettlement were to proceed as speedily and smoothly as the Nazis wished, the territory would have to be easily accessible, especially by ship. The directors then identified Palestine as the territory that best fitted all these stipulations, and they made a forceful case for it. However, they added, "[P]roviding several settlement territories would make simultaneous development efforts possible at various locations" and suggested "sparsely settled regions such as Alaska, Australia, Brazil, New Zealand, and Rhodesia."

The means and logistics were covered in the second section of the document. On the basis of their experience with individual settlements in Argentina, they estimated the cost "per family including real estate to be above $4,000." In comparison, the cost of similar settlement in Palestine fluctuated between $1,000 and $3,000. But in any case, the cost of settling four million Jews would amount to several billion dollars. Aside from this, there would be need for building materials, tools, machinery, livestock, seed, and other agricultural inventory. As regards the logistics of transporting four million settlers during the course of four years, the report advised that those capable of undertaking the initial development go first, to be followed in time by the old people. Efficiency would be enhanced by having the settlement not too distant from Europe—an allusion to the preference for Palestine—or by developing several settlements simultaneously. In any case, with one thousand emigrés per shipload, including their belongings and the various materials of the kind mentioned, the completion of the project in the allotted time would require four thousand sailings or three departures daily.

The estimates were arrived at on a moment's notice, but they were close to the mark. And they were staggering to both the Jews and the Nazis: to the Jews because the estimates showed that the chance of the project's realization was so beyond any possibility that only blind hope could sustain them in continuing their efforts to save as many Jews as possible in the tedious way that had proved to be the only possible one. To Eichmann it must have meant the end of the illusion that one could have the Jews pack up and leave en masse. To the Nazis generally, the impossibility of such a scheme must have now become clear, and this realization must have served not only as confirmation that emigration, the present course of action, was never-ending, tedious, inefficient, and expensive, but that the logistics of a territorial solution would hardly be less so. The impracticability of the scheme surely must also have served as an additional impetus to let the logic of their ideology regarding the Jewish problem direct them to a more radical solution, and preferably under the cover of the war they were certain of winning.

The need for step-by-step preparation, implementation, and execution of the scheme, appropriately protracted over time, was detailed in the final segment of the document.

We can only speculate, as we did above, what effect the directors' draft of the overall solution to the Jewish question may have had on the Nazis. And we may venture guesses as to its effect on some of the drafters. For Löwenherz it must have meant a confirmation to stay the course, to worry about finances and assets, about the old and those left behind, and to continue the massive effort directed at getting a few more Jews out. For Murmelstein it must have reinforced his determination to find a way of settling the old at a place where they could be taken care of. And for Edelstein it must have seemed that the Nazis were sincere in letting the Jews prepare for a massive Jewish settlement of Palestine.

About a month after the directors submitted their draft for a final settlement of the Jewish problem in Europe, Brunner 1 told Löwenherz to obtain a copy of Adolf Böhm's *History of Zionism*, and Löwenherz promised to do what he could.[13] Eichmann had entered the picture soon after the Anschluss; as the SD II/112 expert on Zionism—an expertise based on his supposed acquaintance with Böhm's book—he thought that the solution to the Jewish problem in Vienna lay in expeditiously shipping the Jews to Palestine. To that end he had Böhm appear before him in order to put him in charge of that scheme, which would soon reveal itself as being impracticable. Böhm was in consternation and had a nervous breakdown from which he never recovered. Early in 1940 Löwenherz was ordered to find out Böhm's whereabouts.[14] And now, in August 1940, apparently by way of a follow-up to the directors' urging Palestine as the preferred destination for the final solution, came the request for Böhm's book. Löwenherz knew that Eichmann viewed it as the fundamental statement on Zionism. We are left to wonder what sort of stratagem lay behind this request. Did the Nazis really need to study Böhm's book? Did they suspect that the book would show the directors' preference for Palestine to be part of a conspiracy? Or did they mean to reinforce Löwenherz's belief that the Nazis meant to act upon the directors' project, especially the preference for Palestine? In any case, Löwenherz assigned the task of finding a copy to Murmelstein; the item of the *Aktennotiz* in Löwenherz's file is annotated with the initial "Dr. M," with which Murmelstein normally indicated that he had received the respective directive assigned to him by Löwenherz, and sometimes that it had been carried out.

The Historian

A month later, in September 1940, Murmelstein was directed to write four studies on specified topics, which he finished in three weeks and submitted to Brunner 1 on September 30, 1940, all the while continuing to attend to his other duties. Again we may wonder why the Nazis needed this information, and we may begin to wonder whether, for them, there was any connection between the chosen topics of all the studies ordered that year. And if we wonder how Murmelstein acquitted himself in this additional lesson in Judaism without interjecting an offensive "personal note," we have, in this case, copies of the four studies for our perusal.

The *Aktennotiz* recording Murmelstein's submission of his studies—he refers to them as *Zusammenstellungen* ("compilations)"—to Brunner lists them as follows:

1. Polish regions as goal and origin of Jewish wandering (23 pp.)
2. Origin and development of the Jewish dialect (24 pp.)
3. Jewish rites and customs[15] (71 pp. plus draft 12 pp.)
4. Jewry in Poland[16] (35 pp.)

Item (3) is a set of essays of varying lengths on the following topics:

The Jewish [ritual] immersion bath (9 pp.)
Jewish [ritual] slaughter (22 pp.)
The Jewish funeral (18 pp.) and, in draft form, Jewish death customs (12 pp.)
Jewish circumcision (10 pp.)
The Jewish divine service [*Gottesdienst*] (12 pp.)

We will first consider items 1, 4, and 2, which are related by being historical in nature and substance; we will discuss them as a set and in that order.

Polish Regions as Goal and Origin of Jewish Wandering

In this essay Murmelstein showed that Jewish migration to the region occurred from west and east, the latter preceding the former by centuries. He recalls that what would become the "Polish regions" were, from prehistoric times on, part of the path of the "amber road" to the Baltic deposits of amber, and that in antiquity Greek and Jewish merchants had traveled this road. After the Greeks had passed from the scene, settlements of Jewish merchants remained west of the Caspian Sea and along the Black Sea, with outposts farther inland. The Turkic tribe of the Khazars established their rule in that region in the seventh century, remaining predominant there well into the tenth century. Through their commercial connections, Jewish settlers contributed significantly to the economic development of the Khazar kingdom, and their rulers as well as many of the people converted to Judaism. In the tenth century the kingdom began to be challenged from many quarters, primarily by the Byzantine Empire and the as-yet predominantly pagan Russian groups, but also by the rise of Italian mercantile city-states, which began to expand their commercial interests along the Black Sea. It was thus a mainly Jewish army that fought these wars and established garrisons that later developed into towns and cities in what is now the Ukraine and Poland. Place names such as Kiev attest to their Khazar and such as Żydów to their Jewish origin. When the Khazar kingdom declined, in spite of its conversion to Islam, the Jewish settlers profited the new overlords through their agricultural skills and as large-scale traders with wide-ranging connections. Murmelstein noted that the interconnection between the Jewish populations in the areas under consideration and those in other areas (such as Spain, the Germanic lands, and Italy) were maintained throughout the centuries and proved useful to the peoples among whom the Jews lived. This was, in particular, the case in the development of Poland as a nation and a state. While Jews from the east were the first Jewish settlers of Poland, the main Jewish influx later came from the west, impelled by the persecutions connected with the Crusades and the mercantile development in German lands that made the Jews dispensable. Murmelstein went so far as to suggest that even the motives of the Crusades, purportedly religious, were mainly economic.

In Murmelstein's essay, the main waves of Jewish settlement in Poland, and the waves that were of the greatest import, were those of German-speaking Jews who came from the German lands. He credits these Jews with importing the so-called Magdeburg Law to Poland. The laws pertaining to Jews legislated by Polish sovereigns were also based on German models. While, over several centuries, persecution and expulsion played a major role in this eastward migration, the motive of economic opportunities was hardly less important. Moreover, the emigration of Jews to Polish regions prepared the way for similar migrations of non-Jewish Germans. As Murmelstein wrote:

> The opportunities for employment offered in Poland were no less decisive for the mass settlement of Jews, who spoke German and who dressed like Germans, than the numerous actions directed against them. Simultaneous emigration to Poland on the part of Christian Germans, who had not been exposed to persecution at home, points to the economic motive. The fact that the Jews in Poland retained the German language and German dress also proves that they saw themselves not as exiles but as an advance party to the East.[17]

Murmelstein also saw the economic impact of the terrible decimation of the Jews of Poland perpetrated by the Ukrainians during their great revolt (1648) against the Polish landlords. On the one hand, the overland trading route between the Middle East and Europe that Jews had maintained for a thousand years was severed, never to recover again. On the other hand, the remigration of many of the remaining Jews to the German lands filled a need after the devastation caused by the Thirty Years' War (1618–1648): "Commerce had come to a standstill. [Hence,] the employment of Jewish enterprise and Jewish capital in rebuilding were not merely tolerated but eagerly enlisted."[18]

For the Jews remaining in Poland there followed a period of increasing misery and stagnation, which they could escape only by emigrating to Western Europe and beyond. But when Western Poland fell to Prussia as the result of the partitions of Poland in the late eighteenth century, the Jews residing there remained in place because they welcomed their connection with the German lands from which their ancestors originated. Murmelstein added that their remaining was

> also to be attributed to the national-politically based desire on the part of governmental circles not to diminish the German-speaking part of the population. . . . [However, when the authorities] attempted to secure the German character of the eastern provinces by bringing in settlers, . . . the political significance of the Jews was reduced, and, because of the distinction made between Germans and Poles, their economic situation became untenable. . . . As a result, there began an internal migration to the West.[19]

The background against which these words are to be read is, first of all, Article 8 of the Program of the National-Socialist Party, dated February 24, 1920:

> 8. Any additional immigration of non-Germans is to be prevented. We demand that all non-Germans who immigrated since August 2, 1914 [i.e., the outbreak of the First World War] be forced to leave the Reich.[20]

That this was directed especially against Jews is clarified in another article:

> 4. Only a member of the people [*Volksgenosse*] can be a citizen. Only those who are of German blood can be *Volksgenossen*. . . . Hence no Jew can be a *Volksgenosse*.[21]

Second, Murmelstein's words were written less than two years after the events surrounding Kristallnacht. It will be recalled that these events began with Nazi Germany's enactment of Article 8 of their program, that is, by expelling those Jews to Poland who had migrated from formerly German parts of Poland after August 2, 1914.

Summing up, we see Murmelstein showing that Polish regions had been throughout history more the goal than the origin of Jewish wandering, in particular from the West. To make this point, Murmelstein placed the topic within a wide context of history and geography. He made use of all the knowledge that he had acquired to write his *History of the Jews* (*Geschichte der Juden*), yet with a difference: He selected facts from various periods and brought them together in extremely concentrated form to serve an interpretation that was distinct from the one in his *History*. When he spoke of the "West" as the area from which the Jews drifted toward Poland, he usually meant the German regions. He also showed that the pertinent Jewish migrations, as well as the places where they settled, were determined by economic motives. And economic motives were the determining factor in the recurring expulsions of the Jews from one or the other region—or in their repression, their persecution, their displacement, their temporary usefulness and acceptance—rather than the prejudice and discrimination resulting from religious motives. The unstated implication—unstated because of its pertinence to the situation at that time—was clear: Stated reasons for persecution had been nothing more than pretexts for the exploitation of the Jews, who lacked political power to back up economic success, reasons that also served to obfuscate the real reason, namely, the chance of economic exploitation.

Jewish migration to or from Poland, wrote Murmelstein, benefited German no less than Polish lands. Moreover, in the centuries of the second millennium, it was as Germans that the Jews undertook, or had to undertake, the migration to and from Polish regions, to the economic benefit of both Poland and Germany. Especially the reference to the Jewish experience in the formerly Polish lands in the nineteenth century seems to be an allusion to the ill-fated Nisko settlement and suggests Murmelstein's apprehension that it portended a repetition of the history of sending Jews as a vanguard, only to replace them when they have served their purpose. To him it must have been an ominous possibility, for it meant that the renewed replacement of the pioneering Jews by German settlers would not proceed in as benign a fashion as before, when the replaced Jews were able to undertake an "internal remigration." In any case, in Murmelstein's essay, Jewish enterprise was stressed and, while German capability was not denigrated, Germans could be seen as simply taking advantage of the path that the "German" Jews had cleared.

Jewry in Poland

To a great extent this essay deals with the same historical material as Murmelstein's previous essay. But there is a difference. For example, in connection with the Jewish westward migration following the upheavals of the seventeenth century, Murmelstein's emphasis shifts from the benefit to the Germans to the impact on Jewry and Judaism at large:

> In the wake of the Thirty Years' War German commerce had become paralyzed and offered new opportunities for Jewish enterprise and Jewish capital. But internally, the immigration, or rather, remigration of Jews from Poland to Germany signified a renewal. The deliberately religious and national sentiment of the remigrants from the east was, however, of even greater import for the newly established communities in Holland, most of whose members had been Marranos [forcibly Christianized crypto-Jews] who had for a long time belonged to the Catholic Church. . . .
>
> Sabbatai Sevi's messianic movement, which had originated in Smyrna, threw all of Jewry into an ecstasy that was followed by painful disappointment. That this upheaval passed without grave consequences is largely due to the Polish Jews, who were by then dispersed over the entire Jewish world.[22]

In contrast to the renewal engendered among Jewry at large by Jewish emigrants from Poland, the Jews who remained in Poland sank into misery, largely because of oppression by local lords, a condition that prevailed when Saxon (i.e., German) kings ruled Poland. The minority among the Jews who had the wherewithal to buy the lords' favor formed

> a privileged Jewish caste, which was joined by the rabbis and the powerful members of the communities, while the broad masses were abandoned to misery. Far and wide there was no prominent person to be found who, by virtue of authority or acumen, would be qualified for leadership.[23]

Murmelstein followed this censure of failed Jewish leadership under duress with a tribute to the Polish Jew who effected Jewish renewal by showing the worth of the Jew even in abject misery:

> In this environment appeared arguably the most significant personality of Polish Jewry, namely, Israel, called Baal Shem [Tov]. . . . He recognized the malaise of the Jewish masses, sunk into ignorance because of their plight, plundered by the state, disdained by their leaders.[24]

Ever so delicately Murmelstein hinted that the message of the Baal Shem Tov (ca. 1700–1760) was also addressed to the masses, who in a tradition rooted in the Hebrew Bible attributed their misfortune to transgressions on their part rather than to prevailing forces of evil under which it was their lot to suffer:

> To those despairing over their sins he proclaimed that even in the depth of evil man can become one with God. It is not erudition that raises man up, but yearning for goodness.[25]

Murmelstein must have deeply regretted that this passage would only reach readers for whom it would be too subtle, and that there was no way of assuring his fellow Jews of Vienna that, contrary to Nazi ideology, they suffered duress not as punishment for their sins but because they found themselves "in the depth of evil."

While Murmelstein's account of the fate of Polish Jewry under Prussian and Russian rule after the partition of Poland is similar to that of the earlier essay, he now added an interpretation of the usually celebrated policy of "tolerance" in Galicia, the Austrian part of Poland:

> The treatment of the Jewish part of the population and its problems was directed from Vienna without precise knowledge of the situation and without regard for historical givens. The enlightened absolutism of the Habsburgs was determined to Germanize the Jews in order to maintain through them a counterbalance to the Polish population. The schools that were established for this purpose were to be paid for by surrendering articles meant for religious purposes. Legislation invaded the most personal matters and even went so far as to officially assign Jews to specified professions.[26]

With the emancipation vouchsafed by the Habsburg Empire's constitution of 1867, the stage was set for a freer pursuit of Jewish life and interests. However, Murmelstein was critical of the fact that the various leading circles of Galician Jews failed to develop their own means of representing Jewish interests in the political arena:

> Poles and Ruthenians now endeavored to expand their national domains at the cost of the third part of the population [the Jews]. . . . Polish big landowners finally succeeded in gaining the Jewish vote, thanks to the help of the assimilated [Jewish] intelligentsia. They were also supported by the Hassidic leadership, which saw in independent Jewish politics a danger to religious life.[27]

Thus Murmelstein saw danger in Jews' entrusting their fate either to assimilation or to involvement in secular political movements, or to retreating to the deceptive safety of an enclave of tradition without responding to the challenges of the political givens. Ruefully he noted that "the [Jews'] surrender of their own interests" did not prevent the formation of Polish nationalistic parties, boycotts against the Jews, and finally, explicitly anti-Semitic movements, especially among the Ruthenians in East Galicia:

> In the end, an openly Jewish politics would remain the only solution, and in Poland, as elsewhere, its proponent would [prove to be] be the Zionist organization.[28]

A major portion of the essay deals with the period starting when the Polish state was reconstituted after of the First World War until 1939, when it was destroyed by Nazi Germany and the Soviet Union. The majority of the population consisted of Poles, but one third consisted of sizable groups of minorities.[29] Each of these inhabited specific regions, except the Jews, who, although distributed throughout Poland, were concentrated in cities. Each of the minorities pursued their own nationalistic politics, which resulted in hostilities, especially between Poles and Ruthenian Ukrainians. While Jews studiously avoided taking sides, these conflicts turned into anti-Semitic outbreaks from both ethnic groups. Murmelstein, a native of Lemberg (Lwów), the meeting ground of Poles, Ruthenians, and Jews, spoke from direct experience in recounting these conflicts and pogroms. The newly established state was obliged to conform to the Minority Treaty that it signed at Versailles in June 1919. Hence the Jews were granted a constitutionally guaranteed status as an emancipated minority. However, as so often happens, such guarantees are one thing, the politics of discrimination another.

The new Poland was beset by insuperable problems. The first president of Poland elected under the new constitution was immediately assassinated by a nationalist who, like many others, was enraged by the fact that the election was decided by the votes cast by minorities, in particular the Jews. The government of a predominantly agrarian nation tried to force the development of industrialization so as to render Poland independent of more developed countries. However, owing its reestablishment to the United States, France, and other victorious nations, and being in need of their support—squeezed in as Poland was between two hostile neighbors—it had to pursue its domestic policies with an eye to foreign policy. In one instance the proposal by anti-Semitic legislators of an official restriction of Jewish enrollments at Polish universities was rejected for reasons of foreign policy. Yet such restrictions prevailed unofficially at several universities, especially in medicine. Discrimination took many circuitous routes, for example:

> There is no doubt that in many respects [the Poles] were dependent on the Jews. The business sector of the new state needed to find avenues for export, and nothing was more suitable to this end than to engage experienced Jewish merchants. However, once such relations were established, the business was always taken from the Jews and transferred to Polish firms or to cooperatives. Where this was impossible, the state stepped in, establishing its own enterprises against which no competition was possible.[30]

Governmental actions were initiated whereby discrimination against Jews was practiced without any apparent violation of the Minority Treaty. In Murmelstein's words:

> [F]orty-five percent of all Polish Jews lived in cities with a population of more than 20,000. . . . In formulating new tax legislation, it sufficed to give preference to the rural population, i.e., to localities of fewer than 20,000 people, in order to aim at the Jewish population without provoking talk about anti-Jewish measures. On the other hand, certain advantages that Jews may have enjoyed because of their dense settlement in cities were removed by attaching to certain cities some rural suburbs with great masses of non-Jewish inhabitants.[31]

The discrimination against the Jews not only ran counter to the Minority Treaty but was counterproductive to the well-being of the struggling new state. According to the inaugural statement of the reform government installed after the national revolutionary hero Marshal Józef Piłsudski's coup d'état in 1926, "the exclusion of the Jews is damaging to the effort of reconstruction, and can no longer be tolerated."[32] However, this reform was not to have the desired result, as Murmelstein reported in concluding this essay:

> Inasmuch as the general amelioration expected from reform did not materialize, and the entire population had to suffer under the economic crisis, the government felt forced to appropriate the weapons of the nationalistic opposition, among them Jew-baiting. . . .

> Those in authority—being unable to fulfill the duties thrust on them—contrived to drag the Jewish question to the foreground, the solution to which they thought to have found in emigration. Actually, however, they had no clear idea of the goal of such a movement or whether it could be carried out.
>
> The government resisted only halfheartedly the raids and actions against Jews instigated by the All-Polish camp, not only because [these events] offered the opportunity of speaking about Jews, but, more importantly, of remaining silent about other problems whose solution [it] dared not take up.[33]

The grave problems facing Germany following the First World War were different from the contemporaneous problems of the new Poland. Yet the role of anti-Semitism, born of a facile nationalism, in avoiding the frustrating labor of facing those problems was strangely similar. The cited passage is the closest that Murmelstein could dare to state this outright. He added these last words:

> Only the rising political tension in 1938 portending the coming war distracted attention from the Jewish question.[34]

In the midst of this account of the dismal experience of the Jews in the reconstituted Poland that they so loved, Murmelstein gave a report that seems spoken from the heart:

> It is indicative of the indomitable national strength of Polish Jewry that under these desperate conditions and despite dire need it would not forgo its cultural development and, in spite of its poverty, established a school system out of its own funds, a system that was capable of fulfilling all requirements.[35]

Origin and Development of the Jewish Dialect

Murmelstein did not address directly the old canard that Yiddish is a corruption of German, but neither did he sidestep the issue. Offering arguments, he was able to dismiss some of the theories that had been offered for the existence and persistence of Yiddish: that it is the result of the special legislation that has tended to isolate Jews; that it is a matter of racial inheritance; that it meets the need to communicate among members of the commercial class to which Jews essentially belong; or the sinister need for a means of secret communication. Instead, Murmelstein considered the origin, development, and persistence of Yiddish to be an instance of a phenomenon that is not unique to the Jews, namely, a common language as a function of the coherence of a religious community. He was able to point to the connection of Greek and Latin dialects to Christianity, of Southern German (*Oberdeutsch*) to German Catholicism, Luther's Central German to German Protestantism, and to the fact that the adoption of the language of Luther's bible translation as the standard "high German" did not occur until much later. Referring to historical linguistics, Murmelstein reminded his readers that Jews started speaking German when they came to German lands by the middle of the first millennium, and he demonstrated how Yiddish is suffused with Southern German usage in its vocabulary, grammar, and pronunciation. As the German-speaking Jews spread to the west and to the east, other elements entered the language, so that 60 percent of modern Yiddish is of Germanic origin, 15 percent Slavic, and 25 percent Semitic, the latter being mainly religious in nature. Furthermore, even as the other German language(s) developed, so did Yiddish, splitting into subdialects and developing various kinds of literature that were influenced by other literatures, and in turn influenced and had parallels in others:

> The new direction taken by Jewish literature in the seventeenth century is connected with the regression that also occurred in Germany as a result of the Thirty Years' War. Serious literature was dominated by mysticism and superstition, the coarse character of *commedia dell'arte* predominated in entertainment. Avid readers were fed lurid novels. No less heart-wrenching than these were literary accounts of the Cossack Rebellion and of the slaughter of whole Jewish communities in 1648, only they had the advantage of being true. These events aroused an interest in discovering similar occurrences in the past. There now appeared historical accounts of the persecution of Jews in the Middle Ages. Family chronicles and diaries transmit a vivid picture of that stormy time in which Jewry awaited a messiah and, in the full sense of the word, suffered bloody disappointment.[36]

This passage, written for the Nazis in 1940, reveals the literary tradition of testimony and remembrance of Jewish suffering and persecution, and it hints at the seeds of spiritual renewal in the depth of despair. If Nazi planners of their Jewish policy had paid attention to this passage, what implications might they have gathered from it as to the eventual turn that policy would have to take? In answer to this question, we turn to the following impromptu remarks made by Heinrich Himmler in 1943 to officers of the killing squads, and we are gripped by what it says about the Nazi design to suppress the Jewish spirit, to kill the Jews, to annihilate their remains, and to extirpate anything that might testify to what was done to them and that might evoke their memory and renewal:

> Every Party member says, "The Jewish people will be exterminated, quite clear, can be read in our Program, exclusion of the Jews, extermination, will do." And then they come, all the good eighty million Germans, and everyone has his decent Jew. Of course, the others are swine, but this one is a top-drawer Jew. No one who talks like that has observed, no one has gone through this, but most of you know what it means when 100 corpses are lying next to each other, or 500, or 1,000. To have stuck it out and—aside from exceptions of human weakness—to have remained decent, this has made us tough. This is a never recorded, never to be recorded page of honor in our history.[37]

And we juxtapose this with Hannah Arendt's words, written in 1963:

> It is true that totalitarian domination tried to establish these holes of oblivion into which all deeds, good and evil, would disappear, but just as the Nazis' feverish attempts, from June 1942 on, to erase all traces of the massacres . . . were doomed to failure, so all efforts to let their opponents "disappear in silent anonymity" were in vain. The holes of oblivion do not exist. Nothing human is that perfect, and there are simply too many people in the world to make oblivion possible.[38]

But back to Murmelstein:

He wrote that the "mystical ardor" [*Schwärmerei*] of those dismal times was followed by "sober times of enlightenment," which, in its "areligious" turn, sought to abolish "the Jewish dialect that was rooted in faith" and replace it with an artificial, "anemic" construct. It was the romanticism of the nineteenth century that effected "a decisive turn" in the mentality of "the West":

> The nations recognized that the customs and language of a people, far from being antiquated deadweight that had to be overcome, were the fountainhead of national renewal. For the eastern [i.e., Russian] Jews this kind of choice would not come easily; they hoped that by assuming the national [Russian] character they would experience an amelioration of their political and economic situation. It took the anti-Semitic movements of the 1880s, which unleashed the wave of pogroms, to show that the solution of the Jewish problem was not to be found in assimilation. Jewry should shoulder its destiny with conviction and draw the requisite strength from its ethnic character.[39]

Aside from the expressed interpretation of recent Jewish history, this passage is an allusion to certain contemporary parallels: In Russia, national renewal deteriorated into overt anti-Semitism, which, in turn, served as an impetus for Jewish national renewal. While the anti-Semitic movements of the 1880s in Germany did not deteriorate into overt action until the Nazis came to power, they did provoke a strong Jewish reaction, expressed as a deliberate religious-national renewal. However, unlike in Germany, in Eastern Europe renewal was intimately tied to Yiddish—in spite of the Zionist recovery of Hebrew as a modern language—and to cultural enterprises of various kinds, most notably the establishment in 1925 of the Jewish-Scientific Institute in Vilna.[40] As Murmelstein ended the essay, he combined the themes of the cohesive quality of Yiddish among the Jews scattered over many parts of the globe, of the Jews' fatedness to wander, and of the derivation of Yiddish from German:

> Beyond the ocean, millions of immigrants . . . speak the English of their surroundings and are, like all Jews, closely tied to the Hebrew that, together with them, was driven from its . . . homeland 2,000 years ago; yet among each other they cultivate the language . . . which at one time their forebears took with them from the Alps to the Rhine and thence to the Vistula, to the reaches of Russia, the Manchurian steppes, and the islands of Japan on the rim of the Pacific. The millennial bond of Jewish wandering, Jewish fate, stretches across lands and seas.[41]

Murmelstein gives no quarter here: Yiddish, far from being a corruption of German, is no less a vigorous and legitimate dialect thereof than the current standard of "High German." National renewal that is corrupted into intolerant exclusivism can only strengthen Jewish pride and its own renewal out of the resources of Jewish history, legacy, and faith. And the Jew has the courage and resiliency to respond to persecution by resuming his wandering and taking root again, carrying his precious heritage with him, as did countless generations before. This is the lesson in Judaism that Murmelstein transmits, taking the assigned topic of "The Jewish Dialect" as his point of departure.

The Talmudic Scholar

The sections on rites form a distinct set of Murmelstein's lessons in Judaism for those who ordered them. The assigned topics of the three historical writings discussed above seemed clearly keyed to the question of removing the Jews from a European continent that was to be the fiefdom of Nazi Germany. We saw how Murmelstein tackled these topics, obviously aware of the subtext of his assignment. We cannot assume a similarly clear understanding with respect to the topic of rites. Murmelstein became convinced early on that the Nazis

Rabbinic court as photographed by the Nazis during their raid on the IKG on March 18, 1938. Benjamin Murmelstein is standing on the right. (DÖW 2761[2])

did nothing without having a definite purpose in mind, and equally convinced that guesswork on his part was a better indicator of Nazi intentions than what the Nazis claimed, if they said anything at all. In the case of their curiosity about Jewish rites, their intentions were not as obvious. No discernible policy seemed to be connected with topics such as the ritual immersion bath (*mikveh*), circumcision, or kosher slaughter. Instead, questions—and, if possible, confirmation—of the Nazis' ideologically determined views of Judaism seemed to have been at play. And Murmelstein must have guessed that he was to supply this confirmation. Yet in his expositions Murmelstein made use of all opportunities of disputing and counteracting such views.

The Nazis were heirs to the modern secular anti-Semitism that came to full political bloom in the nineteenth century, an anti-Semitism that was, in turn, informed by the millennial tradition of theologically determined Christian hatred of Jews. The Nazi movement was of too short a duration to have added anything new or distinctive to the idea of anti-Semitism. Nazism, finding itself so quickly empowered politically, was in a rush to put the inferences drawn from the anti-Semitic focus of its ideology into practice, to the effect that the salvation and subsequent glorification of the German people required the extirpation of Jews and Judaism from its midst. They filled in the vast theoretical blanks of their ideological anti-Semitism by taking over what they had received from their antecedents, using it for justification and indoctrination, as needed.

Invidious views of Judaism were promulgated through mass propaganda, especially through *Der Stürmer*, the vulgar and graphic anti-Semitic weekly published in newspaper format in Nuremberg by Julius Streicher, the Gauleiter of Franconia. Each issue was prominently exhibited in display cases in every neighborhood in Nazi Germany for the enlightenment even of those who would not spend the 20 Pfennig for a copy of their own. Jews from Vienna well remember their consternation when, shortly after Kristallnacht and just in time for St. Nicholas' Day and Christmas, the Christian season for gift giving, the windows of even the most respected bookstores of newly Nazi Vienna featured what was to be that year's best-selling children's storybook: *Der Giftpilz* ("The Poison Mushroom"). It was Streicher's special contribution to the proper edification of the tender Aryan minds of the new Germany. The mushroom on the cover was a pale greenish-yellow—in German iconography the color of poison—and bore the features of the stereotypical *Stürmer* Jew. The stories were short enough for the waning bedtime attention of very sleepy youngsters. Each was accompanied by graphic *Stürmer* artwork, and all the stories were displayed in the bookstore windows. One story told of the lecherous Jew who would seduce young Aryan girls; another of the Jew trying to insinuate himself with sweets to children of both sexes; another of what "Solly" learns from the rabbi's Talmud lesson, namely, that the "goyim" are here to be exploited; another, that the Jews were shirkers in the war; another, that they torture animals; as well as other stories in the same vein.

Of course, the pretentious high-mindedness of the SS elite looked down on such graphic obscenity, clumsy ideas, and coarse rhetoric. Their newspaper, *Das Schwarze Korps* ("The Black Corps," a reference to the SS uniform), brought more "factual" and more "researched" articles about Jews, Jewry, and Judaism.[42] But what the paper published was still the same ideologically determined anti-Semitic nonsense. In any case, *Das Schwarze Korps* could not compete in popularity with *Der Stürmer* for the minds of the *Volksgenossen* hungry for enlightenment.

An entirely different approach was taken by Joseph Goebbels who, as Minister of Propaganda and Public Enlightenment, functioned as the general arbiter of the arts in Nazi Germany. His favored medium was film, and his rabid hatred of Jews was reflected in his sponsorship of anti-Semitic films, the most important of which began to be shown in the months after the war started, namely, *Der ewige Jude*[43] and *Jud Süß* (*Jew Suess*). Accompanied by a sickening scene of a swarm of rats released from a sewer, *Der ewige Jude* contains the memorable line:

> When rats appear, they carry epidemics and destruction abroad, the same as Jews do among people.

It is especially against the background of *Der ewige Jude* that we have to try to discern the possible motivation for the Nazis demanding these studies, especially the ones concerning rites. This film shows Jewish practices in a sinister light, including the vivid filming of the ritual slaughter of a cow, sparing no detail. Himmler himself ordered the film to be shown to all members of the police and the SD. Clearly Murmelstein did not see the film, since Jews were not permitted to attend the cinema. But the content of the film was no secret, and neither was its tendentious nature. They were the givens of modern European culture. The topics of ritual slaughter, of circumcision, and of the rites surrounding death reflect the traditional attitude about alleged Jewish barbarism, the topic of *mikveh* reinforced the canard about Jewish prurience, the topic of synagogue service that about Jewish conspiracy. The Jews of Vienna remembered their helpless torment at having obviously hostile people come in to observe their supposedly sinister high-holiday services shortly before the synagogues were destroyed during Kristallnacht.

In writing the segments of the study of rites, Murmelstein drew on his prodigious knowledge of rabbinic Judaism and of the history of religion. The individual essays maintain an objective tone. While the core of each essay is the treatment of the respective topic, Murmelstein placed it within a wider context, primarily that of the phenomenology of religious sentiment and the religious practice of peoples everywhere. Regarding the pernicious lies—old and stale but rife in the Nazi mind—connected with the assigned topics, we find that Murmelstein took the bull by the horns and, purely by setting the record straight, dismissed them for what they are. In relation to this corrective, we also find in the essays an underlying note of reproach, which takes many forms. Both the corrective and the "reproach" had to be inserted subtly and cautiously. Murmelstein usually provided a context for the particular rite at the beginning of each essay in order to create an atmosphere for the ensuing treatment.

The Ritual Bath

In the case of *mikveh*, the style of the introduction is an unusual one for Murmelstein:

> The image of a spring hovers before the wanderer in the African or Asian desert as the very essence of bliss; oftentimes it is an illusion, deceiving and leading him astray and to perdition. But when he is able to carry the refreshing liquid to his lips, to remove desert dust and sand from aching feet, he seems to see in the limpid depths the palace of a mighty divinity, to hear in a wave's murmur the chant of supernatural beings.[44]

Poetry was most decidedly not Murmelstein's style, and in a communication to the Nazis surely out of place. Was this a test Murmelstein devised to see whether the essays were actually read? Or was it to blunt the pointed reproach that suffuses this essay and is very explicit at one point? This is the more likely explanation, for after the quoted introduction, the essay continues as follows:

> Mediterranean man, plagued by heat and thirst, turns water into divinity and primal matter—even as Nordic man, ever beset by rain squalls and cold, stretches his hand to the warming sun and sees in it the primal source and power.

The latter term of this juxtaposition is a veiled reference to the ancient, worldwide symbol of the sun that the Nazi party appropriated as their emblem, known in English by the Indian word swastika. By means of this sentence, the thrust of the essay is aimed at contraposing the Jewish rites of purity and sanctification through water to the paganism of the latter-day "Nordic man."

Murmelstein shows that the association of water with the divine spirit is to be found at the very beginning of the Hebrew Bible and, citing the prophets, he presents the ancient Jewish view of seeing water as the symbol of life and of the power of God. He also shows the Jewish origin of the various Christian rites of baptismal purification. Among the many

Jewish rites tied to the use of water, Murmelstein points to the ablutions by the high priest on Yom Kippur, the Day of Atonement, when the Temple still stood in days of old, in order to wash away the sins incurred by the people of Israel. He mentions that the *sopher*, the Torah scribe, immerses himself in the ritual bath before entering especially sacred passages on the parchment. Observant Jews prepare for the sanctity of Shabbat, the Sabbath, by visiting the *mikveh*. Disarming prurient interest so often exhibited by non-Jews with regard to Jewish practices or attributed by them to Jews, Murmelstein delicately reports that "whenever nature has approached her with its admonition, a woman commits her body to living water, again to be ready for love and motherhood."[45]

Much space in this brief essay is taken up with the traditional precepts of how immersion is to proceed and with the structure of the *mikveh* that is based on them. For ritual immersion the water has to be, in any case, "living" and not still water, such as the water of the Jordan or some other river or the ocean. The idea of building *mikva'ot* ("ritual baths," plural of *mikveh*) and sluicing flowing water through them arose when, within the diaspora, Christian law forbade Jews to bathe with Christians.

Murmelstein gives a brief history of *mikva'ot* in Vienna, the earliest documented one dating to 1309. The last one, built by the recently established IKG shortly before the First World War, had of course separate sections for men and women. And here Murmelstein ends his account as follows: "After the rearrangement of circumstances in 1938" (i.e., after the Anschluss), the newest *mikveh*

> was turned into a bath whose doors were opened also to persons who, rejecting the deeper background of religious realization, scorned the ritual bath as a monstrosity of superstition.[46]

Murmelstein ends the essay by drawing a parallel to the recent transformation of the IKG from being "originally a corporation of purely religious concerns" to "assuming tasks comprising ever widening areas of daily Jewish life and to structure them according to given circumstances."[47]

Circumcision

Murmelstein's treatment of the rite of circumcision[48] as an apparent response to the allegations of Jewish barbarism is concise. He shows that even though circumcision was not universally practiced among Jews in biblical times, the rite is ancient; biblical references to the use of stone knives date the rite to Neolithic times. At the time of Murmelstein's writing the medical profession advocated circumcision for medical and hygienic reasons. Nonetheless, in Europe this advice did not make any headway. However, Murmelstein says, Jewish circumcision of boys eight days after they are born is not a matter of ensuring medical benefits but a biblically mandated ritual that is connected with the ancient idea of sacrifice and to the acceptance of the child into God's covenant with Abraham, the first to have been circumcised. Circumcision of the eight-day-old child as a symbol of entering the covenant is in any case more humane and less painful in his opinion than circumcision at age thirteen as entry into manhood, as it is practiced by Muslims (Murmelstein says

"Arabs"). This observation is meant as a corrective to invidious views. In passing, Murmelstein also mentions the cruel practice on the part of some non-European peoples of female circumcision (actually, excision), which is abhorred in Judaism. The questions of the procedure of and exceptions to circumcision are not of interest here. What is of note is Murmelstein's reference to the occasional adoption of circumcision by others in history, such as by members of the Roman nobility, and the reverberation of Jewish circumcision ritual in the Christian celebration on the eve and the day of the New Year, which used to be called *festum circumcisionis Christi* ("Feast of the Circumcision of Christ"). The reproach enters in Murmelstein's account of attempts by secular authorities to forbid the Jewish rite of circumcision, such as that of the King Antiochus Epiphanes of Hanukkah fame or that of the Directorate under Robespierre. He has no kind words for Jews who, like the Hellenizers of old, would refrain from and even try to reverse the mark of circumcision.

Burial Customs

Two versions of Murmelstein's treatment of Jewish burial customs were found in the IKG's files. One is a preliminary draft of twelve pages,[49] the other the carbon copy of the eighteen-page version that was submitted to the Nazi authorities.[50] Most of the informational material of the draft was taken verbatim into the final version but elaborated with references to related historical phenomena and to recent discussions of specific topics. A case in point is Murmelstein's treatment of what was most likely the reason for the Nazis' interest in Jewish burial customs, that is, the widely held anti-Semitic opinion that the Jewish practice of burying the dead on the day of death bespeaks Jewish barbarism. In the draft Murmelstein says:

> When a person dies, those present ascertain death by placing a down feather under the nostrils. If the feather remains motionless, it is taken as proof that breathing has ceased. Regardless of this proof, death is, of course, certified by a physician. The corpse is not touched for a quarter hour after death has occurred, so as to make certain.[51]

But in the final version the following is added:

> In principle, the departed is to be buried on the day he died. According to Talmudic interpretation, anyone who leaves a corpse in his house overnight violates a prohibition, for the soul may enter the abode of God only after the interment of the body. . . . Postponement of burial is possible only to await the arrival of far-off next of kin. Aside from these views one can find the justifiable precept, dating back to ancient times, to guard the departed for three days because of the danger that he might not be dead.[52]

At this point Murmelstein adds Mendelssohn's famous confirmation of this caution:

> In recent times Moses Mendelssohn endorsed a waiting period of three days, while the orthodox side held fast to the Talmudic prescription.[53]

Murmelstein compares this ancient custom with modern regulations:

> In Central Europe the period between the occurrence of death and interment is, at the present time, regulated by the sanitation police.[54]

The quoted reason for the Talmudic view on early burial—that the soul cannot enter the divine presence until after the body is returned to the earth—indicates what, for Murmelstein, is the main religious motive of the many details of Jewish burial customs. The details pertain to the rites of death, to the preparation of the body, its progress to the burial site and placement in the grave, and to mourning and remembrance. While the emphasis is on the burial customs that have evolved in the lands of the former Habsburg Empire, in particular in the culture of the shtetl (Jewish village), Murmelstein mentions variants in different Jewish cultures, ancient and later antecedents and derivatives, and he differentiates between matters of faith and superstition.

Two themes of Jewish piety inform Jewish burial customs: purity of the soul and charitable service. They are central in Murmelstein's discussion of the rites of dying, the symbolic significance of the ablution of the corpse and the death garments, which prepare the soul to stand before God's seat of judgment, and of practices such as the covering of mirrors. The essay stresses the theme of charity with respect to the loving service selflessly rendered the dying and the dead. This too is clearly an attempted corrective to anti-Semitic slander. Thus Jews have the duty to attend the dying, bringing them comfort and prayer, and helping their purification through their confession of sins and of faith in God's judgment. Murmelstein relates that following this confession, the final words spoken by the dying and by those attending the dying are those of the concluding service (*Neilah*) of the Day of Atonement (Yom Kippur): *YHWH hu ha'elohim.* These words, spoken when the prophet Elijah prevails over the worshipers of Baal (1 Kings 18:39), are usually translated as "The Lord, he [alone] is God." However, with his rabbinical insight into their meaning as the culmination of the Day of Atonement, Murmelstein translates them as *Gott ist der Weltenrichter*, "God is the Judge of the World" or "God is the Universal Judge."

Loving service is also the motive behind preparing the corpse for burial, conducting it to the grave and burying it, giving of alms along the way, and keeping the memory of the name and teaching of the departed alive in succeeding generations. The latter Murmelstein relates to the special role of the children of the deceased in the rites of death. They may not be present at the washing of the parent's body because of the biblical prohibition against uncovering one's parent's nakedness (Leviticus 18:7); this is one of the tasks of a community's burial society. The children observe the period of mourning by saying *Kaddish* and express their piety toward the departed by naming their own children after their forebears and raising them in the spirit of their piety. Murmelstein writes: "No matter how great the pain, no word of complaint is directed against the Judge, whose messenger is death." Returning to his favorite theme of Jewish wandering, Murmelstein continues:

> The place where the earthly vessel has found its rest is the destination to which children return when, in the course of Jewish wandering, lands and seas have separated them from the place of the joys of youth and of the mourning for their families.[55]

Murmelstein also explores the controversial question of whether bodily interment is biblically mandated and cremation prohibited; but even if cremated, the remains are to be interred in the sanctified earth of the community's cemetery. Cemeteries must remain intact. If secular authorities appropriate a Jewish cemetery, Jews are required to gather and reinter the bones of the departed.

This was said at a time when the IKG, mainly through Löwenherz, was in a continuous struggle with the Nazi authorities to keep Jewish cemeteries from being appropriated by municipalities for various profane purposes. When, a year later, the municipality requisitioned the Währinger Friedhof, which was Vienna's main Jewish cemetery in the nineteenth century, the exhumation and re-interment of the remains proceeded as much as possible in accordance with Jewish customs of piety. (We will discuss in the final section of this chapter, "Exhuming a Glorious Past," the exhumation of the Währinger Friedhof and how the IKG offered another lesson in Judaism by way of an account of the accomplishments of those whose remains had to be transferred.) It is possible that permission for the IKG to proceed with a proper exhumation was very likely determined in part by the reproach implied by Murmelstein's account of what Jewish piety required with regard to the safekeeping of cemeteries and the need for proper reburial.

A similar subtle reproach is inserted in connection with the loving service incumbent on the next of kin of saying *Kaddish*. Murmelstein reports:

> Heinrich Heine, who fled the ranks of the Jews and, alienated from his people, was unable to take root in any other soil, ruefully laments before he dies:
>
> *Keine Messe wird man lesen, kein Kaddosch wird man sagen;*
> *nichts gesagt und nichts gesungen wird an meinen Sterbetagen.*[56]

Murmelstein's censure of Heine's apostasy was written at a time when the Nazis foisted on the IKG the emigration and other concerns of persons who were Jews only by Nazi racial definition and who, as converts, had left the care and jurisdiction of the Jewish community.

This emphasis on the primacy of loving, selfless service in Jewish practice permeates both versions of Murmelstein's thoughts on the subject. The draft begins as follows:

> The highest degree of loving service to one's fellow man is rendered when this fellow man lacks the wherewithal to offer his gratitude for the service, and when the one who renders the service knows from the beginning that thanks for his service can never be offered. These preconditions are fully satisfied in service to the dead.[57]

A similar statement introduces the version that was submitted; however, unlike this later version, the draft version succeeds in bringing the theme of loving service full circle by reiterating it at the conclusion:

> The name of the departed should not only be inscribed on the tombstone, but should live on in the family. . . . The traditional perpetuation of the name should not be merely a gesture; rather, the descendant is to be brought up in the spirit of the forbear. The grandchild should continue the grandfather's tradition and transmit it to his descendant. Each generation should teach the next—unchanged, unadulterated, and ever the same—that the supreme principle of a Jewish family must be the realization of true love.[58]

The version that was submitted expresses the same thought, not in terms of a veiled admonition to the Jews but by testifying to the conviction that the people of Israel live and must and will continue to live:

> In the meantime, a new generation has arisen. The name of the deceased is not only recorded

> on the gravestone, but among his descendants he has found those who, as the living bearers of the Jewish tradition, form the links in its millenary chain.[59]

To act on this conviction that this chain must not be broken was the task Murmelstein set himself in his emigration effort. Little did he suspect at the time he wrote this essay how close the Nazis would come to frustrating that conviction and what role he would have to play to save a remnant of Jews.

This brings us to the question: What lesson in Judaism might the Nazis have learned from this essay? Consider that it was hardly more than nine months after what Murmelstein wrote about Jewish burial customs reached the desk of the Nazis that their *Einsatzgruppen* began in earnest to carry out their assigned task of ridding the world of Jews once and for all. To this end the Jewish way of death was surely counterproductive, tied as it was to pious remembrance and perpetual renewal. The Jewishness of the Jews had to disappear, together with the Jews. The community would assemble not to render service to the dying and dead but to die together, unprepared to face their Judge. The children would not conduct the remains of their parents to their resting places; instead, children would be conducted to their deaths by parents with their nakedness uncovered. The question of bodily interment or cremation would be resolved in favor of cremation, the intermingled ashes dumped into pits or washed downriver, without a tomb to await the coming of the Messiah, without a name memorialized in stone, without a child to say *Kaddish*, without descendants to perpetuate the name and the living tradition, without a place for families to which to return that was the venue of the joys of youth and of their mourning. There would be no more links in the millenary chain, no youth, no family, no mourner.

Ritual Slaughter

With respect to no other Jewish custom was the accusation of Jewish barbarism as common and as palpable as that against ritual slaughter. Nonetheless, Murmelstein succeeded in tackling no other topic as directly without seeming to be concerned about offending Nazi sensibilities. The points Murmelstein made and the reproach he clearly stated required a particularly detailed treatment and a complex argument, all of which he successfully projected in his opening passage:

> The fundamental mark of Jewish slaughter is that its practice is rooted in faith. At first glance it may seem curious that the manner of killing a living being is governed by religious writ down to the very details of its execution; from here it is but one step to the concomitant appreciation, or rather depreciation, of a way of looking at things [*Weltanschauung*] according to which such is possible. From a truly Jewish point of view such an accusation is to be rejected, and so is the defense customary in an age of liberalism, which, based on a materialistic orientation, took advantage of facile rationalistic claims in order to demonstrate how ancient commandments are in agreement with hygiene. . . . [Ritual] slaughter is the result of millennial development, rooted in paganism, refined in scriptural teaching [*Lehre*], and adapted through tradition to the circumstances of the times. . . . If, unlike other rites, it did not fall into oblivion, . . . it is because, according to the Jewish perception, it makes possible killing of domestic animals with the least pain, and . . . to keep their flesh in a state that is the most healthy for human nutrition.[60]

Murmelstein shows how the ancient Hebrews, no less than other ancient peoples, regarded animals as fellow living beings, and how animals, especially the mighty steer, were symbols of valued attributes.[61] The Hebrew Bible teaches that "animals, no less than man, owe their lives to God's grace," and enjoins Jews to provide for the needs of animals even if it means breaking the Sabbath. From the dawn of the Jewish people, the killing of animals was connected with offering the life that was taken to God, the source of life; partaking of man's portion of the sacrificed life was possible only as a ritual symbolizing communion with God. The blood of animals was spilled on the altar, since it "was and is forbidden to partake of blood, regarded as the source of life and hence as the divine part" of living beings. In this way Murmelstein indirectly counters the pernicious accusation of blood-libel, which had been resurrected—especially in Austria-Hungary—within memory of those whose lives stretched back to the nineteenth century, and which *Der Stürmer* spared no pains to publicize. Murmelstein also shows that while the Christian sacrament of Holy Communion is an offshoot of the ancient Jewish meaning of sacrifice, there is a significant difference:

> Within Judaism [the idea of] sacrifice did not develop into a unique miracle; instead, it developed into ritual slaughter as the presupposition for partaking of meat, i.e., an act of religious solemnity by which living beings are wrested from their natural state and sacrificed with special restraint and awe.[62]

By way of a Christian confirmation of the Jewish attitude toward animals and slaughter, Murmelstein cites the scholar Heinrich Cornill, pointedly referring to him as an "Aryan." Cornill wrote at a time when Christian clergy were adding fuel to the rising modern secular anti-Semitism:

> Israelites also ascribed a soul to animals, and recognized them too as creatures of God; while God subordinated animals to the dominion of man, He did not thereby deliver them defenselessly to man's willfulness.[63]

Almost half of the essay's twenty-two pages are taken up with the details of ritual slaughter: the piety, experience, and skill of the slaughterer; the preparation of the place and the implement; the design, care, and testing of the blade; the speedy and painless positioning and binding of the animal; the exact exposure of the neck; the position of the haft in the hand; the precise location and depth of the cut; the precise, single, instantaneous movement of cutting by sliding the knife, not by pressure; and the bloodletting, accompanied by the invocation of the Divine Name. The process of throwing the animal on its side, binding, positioning, and cutting is supposed to be done within one minute's time.

Murmelstein adds the results of modern anatomical and physiological research to show that the process of Jewish slaughter as it was developed over the millennia causes, in fact, the least pain and suffering among them than current alternative methods of slaughter. In all cases, death is the result of bleeding to death, whether internally or externally, and Jewish slaughter hastens this process more than any other. The deadening of the animal's sensibility to pain is similarly hastened more effectively by Jewish slaughter than any other because the location of the cut severs the supply of blood to the brain. Also, Murmelstein maintains, stunning by any of the various methods then in use for non-Jewish slaughter immobilizes the animal but neither eliminates nor hastens the loss of pain. However, scientific research into the phenomena attending death reaches its limits, beyond which all that remains are "mutually conflicting claims; what is important is the conviction that nothing was left undone to lower the dying creature's pain."[64]

All this is discussed by Murmelstein with reference to the frequent accusations leveled against Jewish slaughter on the grounds that it is cruel to animals. While such accusations have arisen in most countries of Western Europe, it was Nazi Germany that expressly forbade Jewish slaughter in one of its earliest legislative acts, on April 24, 1933. At the same time it legislated the stunning of animals prior to slaughter. Feeling relatively free, in the case of the topic of ritual slaughter, to voice the reproach directly, Murmelstein writes:

> Of course, a comprehensive account [of Jewish ritual slaughter] from the Jewish side, cannot—even under observance of the restraint that is called for in principle—avoid emphasizing what speaks in favor of Jewish slaughter, and to point out the shortcomings of other killing methods.[65]

Hygienic and economic reasons speak most clearly in favor of Jewish ritual slaughter:

> The greater durability of meat drained of blood is generally known and indisputable, as is the fact that the Jewish way of slaughter removes the greatest amount of blood from the animal in the shortest time. . . . [R]otting occurs later, and the meat is generally much less suffused with pathogenic organisms.[66]

This, writes Murmelstein, is documented through scientific research. Furthermore, meat that is drained of blood is more concentrated, and hence more economical. However, such hygienic and economic considerations are not decisive:

> An attempt to decide the matter in this way would be as appropriate as an appreciation of the pharaonic pyramids exclusively from the standpoint of the tourist trade.[67]

What is important for Jews is

> to avoid using raw force and to proceed, to the greatest possible extent, without inflicting pain. . . . [Judaism] is in principle opposed to all killing, as must be the case with a religion that lays claim to divine love and grace.[68]

These essays, which Murmelstein had to write at the bidding of his Nazi masters, most likely constitute the last known, perhaps the only attempt by a Jew to impress on the Nazis the basic decency, indeed nobility, of the Jewish tradition and way of life. He did this in an objective yet impassioned way, and he demonstrated one last time the unfounded nature of the lethal Jew hatred and the evil Nazis perpetrated as its consequence.

Travails of a Captive Press

The Nazis were not the only beneficiaries of Murmelstein's effectiveness in producing appropriate lessons in Judaism. To the Jews Murmelstein directed himself in the only periodical that they were allowed to publish and obtain. We saw that it was Murmelstein who had been chosen to write the first proclamation to the newly captive Jews of Vienna when, in May 1938, the *Zionistische Rundschau* ("Zionist Review") began to be published. After it had to be replaced by the *Jüdische Nachrichten*, Murmelstein and Löwenherz together were regarded as the publishers, with Dr. Emil Israel Reich as the editor. The paper was intended by the Nazis to be an instrument of informing the Jews of whatever they wanted them to know or do. However, they allowed additional material to be published in line with their permission for the *Jüdischer Kulturbund* to exist. Goebbels's Ministry for Propaganda and Popular Enlightenment considered the paper to be under its charge both as a publication and as a cultural organ. Additionally, the Gestapo and the *Zentralstelle* exercised strict censorship. There was tight and ever tightening control over whether and which Aryan businesses would be able to place advertisements in the paper, whether stateless Jews would be permitted to subscribe, over the list of those who received free copies, the size of the paper, the size and frequency of the issues, and so on.

Murmelstein, as the chief executor of the IKG emigration effort, was frequently involved in preparing copy about the matter of greatest interest to the Jews—the opportunities, regulations, difficulties, and procedures of emigration. However, he also contributed articles about topics in Jewish history and brief editorials; usually the signature "drm" identified Murmelstein as the author, but some were left unsigned but are easily identifiable by their distinctive style. The editorials were often of a religious nature, in the form of *drashot*, "sermonettes." Let us give some examples.

Two weeks after the outbreak of the war, on the same front page that called on the Jews to register for the census (discussed in chapter 7), we find Murmelstein's holiday sermon/editorial "*Rosch ha-schanah*." He reminds the readers that until the time of the Babylonian exile the holiday was referred to as *yom ha-zikkaron*, the day of remembrance, and only afterwards also as *Rosh Hashanah*, the day beginning a new year. His interpretation is as follows:

> A Judaism that only knew a day of remembrance was condemned to lose its country and its freedom. The miracle of its resurrection after the Babylonian captivity consisted mainly in that the people learned to grasp the concept of *Rosh Hashanah*, of eternal renewal.

The lesson for the Jews under the new condition of a war against Poland, from where the families of many of the Jews of Vienna had come, was to sustain hope and not to give in to despair as expressed in excessive supplicatory prayer.

Eleven months later, as the grip on the Jews was tightening and the Nazis were ordering various studies, Murmelstein's message of sustaining hope, even against all hope, was connected with the fast of Tisha b'Av (the ninth day of the Jewish month of Av (aka Ab) in July/August), and, appropriately, it was tied to the theme of wandering that had underlain the conception of his *History of the Jews*. The editorial, entitled "Tisha b'Av, the Day of Wandering,"[69] reminds the reader that—always on the ninth day of the month of Av—Solomon's temple as well as the second temple were destroyed in 586 BCE and 70 CE, respectively, Betar, the last fortress of the "freedom fighters" under the leadership of Simeon Bar Kokhba, fell to the Romans in 135 CE, and the expulsion of the Jews from Spain was completed in 1492; and he tells how each of these shattering events was followed by wandering and migration to another place. And the lesson:

> Verily, a dismal date, over which fateful and grave events in a time span of two thousand years cast their shadow. Yet, these millennia between the first expulsion from Jerusalem and the expulsion from Spain are clear proof of the people's strength and of its capacity for wandering without losing its roots in its native soil.

Murmelstein recounts the many peoples and places on earth—pointedly including the regimes of Europe ruled by the "Goths"—to which their wanderings took the Jews, wanderings that commenced on a ninth day of Av only to lead them back to their point of origin:

> [By way of] . . . the Euphrates, the Nile . . . splendid Alexandria, eternal Rome, the Gothic West, the Ukrainian steppe, the African desert, the American prairie, the path of the wandering Jew [leads] back to the Jordan. . . .
>
> No matter what was inflicted on the Jewish people on the ninth day of the month of Ab, it always was a day when not only their dispersal but also their wandering back to the Promised Land began. This consciousness is the source of the strength to endure, the strength to wander, the strength to build anew.
>
> Though the mourning of the ninth of Ab has lasted for thousands of years, it cannot last forever. It must come to an end with the completion of the coming restoration.
>
> Thus spoke the Eternal to the prophet Zachariah: For the house of Judah the fast of Ab will be turned into joyous gratification and festive remembrance. Hold fast to truth and peace.[70]

By the time of Hanukkah the mood had markedly worsened. Hanukkah, the Festival of Lights, is a post-biblical observance of liberation from the pagan (i.e., Hellenistic) assimilation that the Seleucid ruler Antiochus IV Epiphanes tried to enforce. To be sure, the editorial recalls the will and determination with which the Jews of the former Austria took up the task of emigration, and the tremendous difficulties that had to be faced to make emigration possible:[71]

> For 180,000 Jews the watchword was to conclude what has been, to renounce the present, and to direct their gaze toward the future.

But then

> [w]hen in spite of all the added difficulties and obstacles the flow of Jewish emigration from the *Ostmark* reached its high point and salvation seemed imminent, it became a trickle: The initial events of the war quashed innumerable hopes and reduced many months of preparation to futile labor.

The IKG's effort to make the rescue of Jews possible under these increasing, ever changing difficulties is also recalled, as if to remind the readers that they were not totally abandoned:

> The war draws ever smaller circles, and before long all paths seem blocked. Devotion and enthusiasm for the work of emigration still motivate us to bring groups of emigrés to harbors lying clear across the Asian continent. Not thousands, not hundreds, but every single departure represents a task accomplished only through the commitment of all our strength.

Hope must be held high, but without any illusion:

> The light of the future is flickering and waning. . . . The light of new life across the seas, now a mere glimmer, seems at times extinguished. After years of preparation and expectation, tens

> of thousands look to the flickering light with bated breath. Uneasy forebodings alternate with joyous hopes: Will the last tiny chance vanish or will [our] yearning find new gates opening?

It was Hanukkah, so now Murmelstein recalled the miracle of old, when the Temple was cleansed of the invasion of pagan rites and symbols, and when at its rededication, according to later legend, one day's supply of consecrated oil lasted eight days:

> The tiny lone flame rose and fell in the huge candelabrum, every moment it seemed to falter and die. A people's faith and confidence effected the miracle, they seemed to give new strength to the light . . . *the miracle of those days* . . .

And the lesson:

> In *our days* goal-directed effort, a sense of community, and readiness to make sacrifices must pave the way for every striving toward emigration and every yearning for a new future, until each of these hopes is fulfilled and the problem of the Jews living in the *Ostmark* is solved.

Many a Jew would remember the line from Friedrich Schiller that they had learned in school:

> *Noch am Grabe pflanzt er die Hoffnung auf!*[72]
> He plants hope even at the grave.

For who among the 55,000 remaining Jews would have guessed earlier that such desperate hope would have to be upheld? Who among them would guess, even at that time, that within two years most of them would be beyond hope, beyond life, without graves to remember them by, and without graves on which to plant hope?

Dr. Murmelstein's editorial appeared on December 23, 1940, as usual on the front page of the *Jüdische Nachrichten*. It was accompanied by a drawing of a Hanukkah menorah, with candles almost burned down, together with an appeal for contributions to Jewish winter relief. The lead article, authored by the paper's editor Dr. Reich and evidently based on information furnished by Murmelstein, dealt with an emigration problem that had developed, "The Problem of Immigration to the USA." Both themes—charity and emigration—were now paramount in the paper and in Murmelstein's articles. At the beginning of the winter season the paper carried prominent appeals for contributions to the IKG's effort to take care of those in need of care, and Murmelstein wrote the editorials on behalf of the IKG. In the first of these, on November 1, he asked the readership for contributions to help the IKG maintain the *Umschulungskurse*, the retraining programs that boosted morale while preparing potential emigrés for useful employment abroad: The idea was

> to enable emigrés . . . to attain skills for an independent vocation. . . . [T]he IKG was able to give many thousands the joy of work, to restore their self-confidence, and . . . impart knowledge and the capacity to earn. . . . Sexagenarians climbed ladders to escape the depths of hopelessness; a 15-year-old, engaged in laying electric cables, sees before him the light of a new vocation. All are motivated by the desire to emigrate and begin a useful life. . . . For thousands this dream has become reality, thousands are waiting. . . . Their effort must not have been in vain. Former Viennese Jews, now happily employed, confirm the success of the retraining project. The readiness on the part of Jews still in Vienna to make a contribution will ensure the continuance of the project.[73]

The 15-year-old electrician-in-training was one of Murmelstein's protégés, Kurt Mezei. Three months later, with the onset of the deportations, the Nazi authorities would close all *Umschulungskurse*, and Kurt, one of the few who would escape deportation, would serve as IKG electrician until almost the end.

As the campaign for charity continued, other aspects of the deep and deepening need were taken up, such as the cause of dependent children:

> [W]hether we are dealing with a lively baby boy who is to be raised into a young Jew, or with an incurably paralyzed girl who could not be taken abroad by her parents, they are individual lives for which the Community as such must take responsibility.
>
> The IKG is charged with bringing sunshine and joy into the lives of more than 150 orphans. . . . But even the eyes of those children whose parents are still there to protect them are filled with tears when hunger is not allayed and cold is not dispelled. Nurseries and day schools open their gates to hundreds every day to offer nourishment and shelter, warmth and care. . . . Purposeful direction is also indispensable at the onset of puberty so as to guide the adolescents' first steps into adulthood and supervise them with care. . . .
>
> Where there is no mother, where there is no father at a youngster's side, where parents are not able to care for their child, we all have to step in. Each one of these children has a claim on the Community. None of us may shirk his duty.[74]

The next editorial addressed a need that, if anything, was even closer to Murmelstein's heart, namely, the needs of the aged. Before the Anschluss, most of the old people were cared for in the time-honored way, at home with their family, usually with their children. Hence there was only one Jewish home for the aged in Vienna. Now, however, younger families had to leave their elderly parents behind as they emigrated to an uncertain new start in a new land. In addition, the old people were even more severely affected than the middle-aged by the impoverishment of the Jews. Hence the IKG had to add to the number of homes for the care of the aged. (We saw in chapter 6 in the section on "Present Worries, Worrisome Future" how the IKG had to do battle with the Nazi authorities to keep the properties needed for that purpose from being expropriated.) By the end of 1940 the IKG maintained seven such homes and was about to add another. And for this too they needed the charitable support of their remaining Jews. Murmelstein wrote:

> Love for parents caused pain and anguish over the uncertain fate of those who had to remain in Vienna. In distant lands the possibility beckons of starting a new life; here an infirm father, an aged mother had to be left to their fate. This burden weighing upon the emigrants should be lifted so they can turn their attention to their new labors free of worry.

After describing what had been accomplished in the care of the aged, Murmelstein continues:

> Parents of children who emigrated are now able to withdraw to a world where they live with memories and wistful hopes. Every letter from overseas lets hearts beat faster, sparks longing, and carries the seed of a tacit expectation that a reunion in the far-off distance will yet be possible. For many a little mother who, aided by a nurse, leaves the home to follow the call of a child, this dream has been realized. And the gates of the home are again open to save yet another Jewish mother from hunger and cold.

And the lesson:

> Our Community is small, our capacities have become limited, but the call to love the neighbor

> has remained the same. No Jew in Vienna in the last years of life must, lonely and abandoned, be delivered to need and misery. The goal can and must be attained, if every one of us, in remembrance of our own parents, makes an offering to help the parents of our neighbor.[75]

Next came the appeal for the poor:

> Care of the poor has always been among the most important duties of every Jewish community, and accordingly was laid down in the statutes of the IKG half a century ago.

Murmelstein had to keep in mind that Eichmann had come to Vienna determined that the many poor Jews be expedited quickly and en masse, as well as the fact that the IKG was engaged in an ongoing struggle to justify an increasing budget for the poor on the grounds that emigration was helped thereby. Hence he had to exercise care to phrase things in a manner acceptable to the Nazi censors no less than to the Jewish reader:

> Many recipients of financial support left Vienna in the wave of emigration; however, since many breadwinners preceded their dependents for destinations overseas, the number of those who needed such support was not only constantly replenished but was greatly enlarged. Yet a person's suitability for emigration must not be curtailed by his need and deprivation.

Major means of support for the needy were cash payments, free meals in soup kitchens, medical and nursing care, and gifts of clothing and household furnishings. Recipients of the latter were both those remaining as well as those leaving Vienna, for

> provisioning indigent emigrants was not only of great help to the specific recipient, but a matter of preventing their attracting attention at their destination because of their shabby appearance and thus furnishing an excuse for the closing of borders [to further Jewish immigration].

And the lesson that was drawn from this was:

> The IKG strives to protect its needy members from hunger, cold, and lack of shelter. The task is great, available means small. Every one of us in a position to help has a sacred duty, which must be fulfilled through offerings freely given before it is too late.[76]

Caution about what to print and how to phrase it was an art and science that could be mastered up to a certain point. One could never take the full measure of this antagonist, for whom every Jew was an "opponent," how much more so a Jew who was clever and who was in a position of leadership, even if this leadership had been forced on him, and thus one who had influence over his fellow Jews. A case in point is the uproar over a sentence printed in the Vienna edition of *Jüdisches Nachrichtenblatt*[77] about the time when the Jewish leaders were turning out studies on specified topics, and Murmelstein's career as an editorialist went into high gear.

Every week the *Nachrichtenblatt* provided a small space for sayings from Jewish religious writings, normally under the title *Spruch der Woche* ("Saying of the Week"). During the laying-out of issue 69, dated August 26, 1940, there developed a gap on page 3, which, on Dr. Reich's request, his co-worker Frieda Rosenthal filled with a *Spruch der Väter* ("Saying of the Fathers"), an allusion to *Pirkei Avot (Pirke Aboth)*, usually translated as "Sayings of the Fathers," an ancient compilation of ethical sayings in part from pre-Talmudic times. While the saying chosen by Rosenthal ("Do not do unto your fellow what is hateful to you") was by Hillel, who is amply represented in *Pirkei Avot*, this particular saying did not come from there. But, no matter. Every issue, after being censored by the *Zentralstelle*, was released for distribution to recipients according to three lists: Aside from the list of subscribers and that of the recipients of free copies (Jewish institutions mainly in Vienna), there was a list of required recipients. These were the various Nazi agencies concerned with Jewish affairs. Of the seventy-seven required copies, thirty-nine went to various offices of the Reich Ministry for Propaganda and the Enlightenment of the People, including two copies to the Ministry's offices in Vienna.[78] When these men saw the "Saying of the Fathers" in issue 69, they telephoned the *Zentralstelle*, probably berating them for their careless censorship of the Jewish publication. Brunner 1 telephoned Dr. Reich, the editor, to pass on the compliment, but apparently it was too late to recall distributed copies or to stop further distribution.

It was a marvelous opportunity for the Propaganda Ministry—which, despite Dr. Goebbels's rabid Jew hatred, was like a fifth wheel in the execution of Nazi Jewish policy—to make a difference. Right after Brunner's call, Löwenherz was off to Berlin for one of his *Vorsprachen* at the RSHA. While there, he was called before *Obersturmführer* Kochanowski, who was in charge of Jewish matters at the Propaganda Ministry. Kochanowski ordered Löwenherz to reduce the Vienna edition of *Jüdische Nachrichten* by 1,000 copies per issue and to submit a list of recipients of free issues, which would be examined by Kochanowski personally and reduced as he saw fit.[79] The main item of business concerned the editor, Dr. Reich. Kochanowski confided to Löwenherz that because of the offensive *Spruch der Väter*, "a higher authority"—this can only mean Kochanowski's superior, Hans Hinkel, or, more likely, Goebbels himself—demanded the cessation of the Vienna edition altogether, but "in the interest of the Jews of Vienna he succeeded in having the order rescinded."[80] However, Dr. Reich was to be dismissed; upon Löwenherz's "urgent plea," Kochanowski agreed, "after considerable hesitation," to leave Reich at his post but issued the following orders: Löwenherz must speak to Reich about the matter in "an earnest form and emphatically," and Reich had to submit a letter of justification designed "to prevent further cumbersome investigations in Vienna." Reich also had to submit a list of sources for the material published in the paper, a list of his staff and their function, and to identify the person who selected the offensive saying.[81]

Directly upon receiving Kochanowski's judgment and orders from Löwenherz, Reich prepared and mailed the required lists and in a covering letter gingerly stated his justification and apology:

> [I]n conformance with received directives [Löwenherz] reproached the undersigned for the first sentence published under the "Sayings of the Fathers," which could be interpreted in a manner that renders its publication impermissible. Coupled with this reproach was the admonition, given in earnest and emphatic form, that in future [I] am to fulfill the duties as responsible editor even more carefully than hitherto.

Reich then thanked the Propaganda Ministry for permitting him to continue. As for the "Sayings of the Fathers," he stated that both he and his co-worker Rosenthal, "who had made the selection"

State Councilor (Staatsrat) *Hans Hinkel in uniform as an SS Major General* (Brigadeführer) *(1939–1944). (By Bundesarchiv, Bild 183-S70002)*

> are guided only by the motivation to present its literal meaning to Jewish youth for educational purposes. In no way did we consider an interpretation that, in the sense of extant regulations, would disallow publication.
>
> The undersigned regrets the publication most profoundly and begs . . . that the above justification be acknowledged.[82]

Reich deftly managed to offer an apology Kochanowski could not but accept, without in any way conceding the Nazi interpretation under dispute of the lesson in Judaism to young Jews, nor even that he had any inkling of what that interpretation might be. In addition, Reich did not mention that Rosenthal regularly obtained from Murmelstein compilations of suitable, brief quotations for her to choose as needed.

What was it about Hillel's version of the old Jewish "golden rule," first mentioned in Leviticus, that put a whole hierarchy of the German Reich up to a minister's level into such consternation? After all, Hillel simply said: "Do not do unto your fellow what is hateful to you." How did this affect the Nazi mind? Pangs of conscience? Or did they detect a reproach no matter how subtly stated? Or even fear that the Jews might get ideas? The former are not likely. As to the fear of rebelliousness, let us recall that on May 1, 1943, near the end of the Warsaw Ghetto uprising, Goebbels wrote this in his diary:

> [There are] the exceedingly serious fights in Warsaw between the police and even a part of our Wehrmacht on the one hand and the rebellious Jews on the other. The Jews have actually succeeded in making a defensive position of the Ghetto. Heavy engagements are being fought there which has even led to the Jewish Supreme Command's issuing daily communiqués. Of

> course this fun won't last long. *But it shows what can be expected of Jews when they are in possession of arms.*[83]

What we see at work here is the sort of control that is the backbone of a totalitarian regime, where censorship of the press is an extremely serious means of control. This pertained a fortiori to the newspaper of the segment of the population that was, according to the prevailing ideology, the premier target of control. The paper was, in fact, mandated by the Nazi authorities for the purpose of exercising control specifically over the Jews. Its purpose was not to benefit them or to provide them with an organ for expressing or partaking of what they valued as their culture. To be sure, the masthead identified the paper's publisher as *Jüdischer Kulturbund in Deutschland*, the "Jewish Cultural Association in Germany." But this was a canard, for the *Kulturbund* was nothing other than an instrument of such control, being sanctioned for that purpose by Goebbels's Ministry of Propaganda.

In the first section of chapter 3 we recounted how, for its founders, the *Kulturbund* in Berlin was connected to what they perceived as their struggle for Jewish autonomy. The Nazis granted the Jews of the Altreich the illusion of Jewish cultural autonomy and the consequent conceit of Jewish self-assertion until well past the Anschluss of Austria.

There were two reasons for this: At that early stage the regime was politically and technically not yet ready to proceed with the solution of the Jewish problem; and temporarily and conditionally permitting a seemingly autonomous *Kulturbund* gave them a front for the pursuit of their agenda.

The Anschluss gave the Nazi regime the opportunity to put into practice their solution of the Jewish problem. The mechanics of dealing with the Jews and liquidating their presence, developed in Vienna as a paradigm for proceeding in the Altreich, was described in chapter 3. However, the presupposition for that process was the coordination of the various Nazi agencies and echelons dealing with Jewish matters and the consolidation of their various activities. Some decisive steps in this consolidation and coordination occurred at the time of the Anschluss. The most important of these was the designation of SD section II—hitherto restricted to ideological policy research concerning "opponents"—to be the executor of Nazi Jewish policy, in coordination with other agencies.

In this way we find that the Propaganda Ministry's responsibility was defined as "political and cultural-political leadership" in all matters that could be comprised under "culture." In this capacity it established its Section IIA, whose chief carried the title *Reichskulturwalter*, which means Reich Superintendent of Cultural Affairs. The incumbent of this office was Hinkel. His subordinate responsible for "the surveillance of the cultural activities of non-Aryans within the confines of the Reich" was Kochanowski.[84] Inasmuch as Hinkel had as early as the Anschluss achieved the high rank of SS *Oberführer* (equivalent to Senior Colonel), he had, in effect, one foot in each of the two powerful agencies dealing with Jewish matters. As a rule, within this complex machinery there was no cooperation between agencies without underlying rivalry, even conflict. Himmler, deeply steeped in the mystique of ancient Germanic culture, may have thought of Hinkel as his man at the Propaganda Ministry, while Goebbels may have thought of Hinkel as his man within the SS. Thus, especially at the lower echelon of concrete policy execution, the coordination of the activities of these agencies was not a foregone conclusion and needed to be worked out.

In Vienna, too, the work of the Jewish section of the *Reichskulturkammer* ("Reich Chamber of Culture") consisted in controlling the Jews in order to facilitate the liquidation of Jewish life. And here, too, this was accomplished by holding out the promise of the establishment of a Viennese branch of the *Kulturbund*, which would offer cultural activities. There are, for example, the minutes of the October 1938 meeting of department chiefs Franz Six, representing SD II, and Hans Hinkel, representing Propaganda Ministry IIA, each accompanied by relevant subordinate staff. On behalf of Colonel Six, Herbert Hagen, as headquarters leader of SD Section II/112 (Opponents/Jews), explained to Hinkel

> that it is not expedient to delay the process of liquidating Jewry in Austria by establishing a cultural organization. . . . [I]t would serve no purpose to initiate such an establishment at this stage. . . . Hinkel agreed completely but pointed out that it is necessary that the Jew Hellmer—whom he [Hinkel] had originally charged with the formation of the Jewish cultural organization in Vienna—not be informed of the true state of affairs but be kept in the dark about plans for the establishment of the organization and to string him along until early next year.

What was the reason for this official deception? Hellmer was the owner of a theater in Frankfurt/Main, and at Hinkel's insistence rented it to the city for a yearly fee that was still being paid to him. Hellmer wanted half a million Reichsmark to sell the theater. While Hinkel considered the price reasonable, he thought that when the sale would indeed go through,

> Hellmer must never receive payment. If Hellmer were to be pressured to emigrate there would be the danger that he would transfer his demand [for payment] to a foreign national, hence Hellmer is to be strongly urged to remain in the Reich by letting him wait.
>
> For this reason it was ultimately agreed to charge the *Kulturbund* in the Altreich to assemble the cast for a Jewish theater in Vienna, to maintain it with their own funds, and to do this without a separate organization.[85]

Colonel Six now understood, agreed, and gave orders to inform his people in Vienna accordingly. Of course, Eichmann and his associates were by then perfecting their own methods of expropriation by stringing Jews along in various ways. In our account so far, the most visible way of playing this game concerned the properties of the Vienna and provincial communities administered by Löwenherz.

To the Nazis the publication of the *Jüdische Nachrichten* was not a privilege they granted to the Jews for the free and autonomous expression of their essence but an instrument of control through the only medium they permitted. If the Jews perceived the publication as a privilege, so much the better, because the conceit of privilege could only serve as welcome means of control, in addition to control through censorship.

Löwenherz and his closest associates understood the parameters within which they could operate and, beyond informing the Jews of official directives as well as of matters of emigration and survival, they felt the need to find ways, within those parameters, of serving the spiritual needs of hope, pride, and faith. For these reasons extreme caution and watchfulness was called for in preparing and editing and, beyond that, in managing the paper. Hence Löwenherz's plea for the retention of Reich is not surprising, for he, too, was aware of those parameters. Understanding them, he knew that he was in an exposed position vis-à-vis the Nazi authorities. Yet in a special way, he was also the lightning rod neutralizing the flashes of frustration and incaution on the part of his readers. Many of them seemed unaware of the strictures under which he had to work.

When, after the Anschluss and the closing of the IKG, the Jews of Vienna had nowhere to turn in their confusion and panic, some wrote letters to the *Jüdische Rundschau* in Berlin, which was then the officially mandated Jewish paper in Germany. Before the IKG was reopened in Vienna and before the Viennese edition of that paper was established, Hagen, writing on behalf of SD headquarters, addressed the following request to Hinkel:

> *Die jüdische Rundschau* of April 5, 1938, writes in a lead article that they have received numerous letters from Austria after the changeover. Since there is great interest here in receiving these letters, it is requested that you approach the *Jüdische Rundschau* and the other Jewish papers and request their submission of the letters they received from Austria.[86]

It is interesting to note that at that time and place SD II/112 did not as yet claim controlling authority over the files of Jewish organizations and that Hinkel's office was asked to "approach" the *Rundschau* and "request" the letters. Hinkel's office took the letters, submitted them to SD II/112, but added: "Whether the publishing house withheld additional important letters, cannot, of course, be verified."[87] The tone of this exchange of letters in Berlin in 1938—"approach," "request," "cannot be verified"—tellingly shows what a difference Eichmann's handling of the IKG Vienna made in forging SD II/112 into a tool of executing the solution of the Jewish problem.

In spite of, or because of, the persecution experienced by the Jews of Vienna, they tended to look for straws to grasp at, straws of comfort and belonging. The *Jüdische Nachrichten* was such a straw, especially in the deepening despair of wartime, when, imprisoned within a seemingly invincible Nazi domain, their isolation from the world of freedom was almost complete. It fell to Dr. Reich to respond in writing to letters to the editor from readers who expressed concerns, whose airing was inappropriate to the situation in which all of them found themselves. Some did so through ignorance, and some of the letters were written by people who certainly should have known better. Reich, knowing that his files were no less subject to censorship by Nazi authorities than the published newspaper, responded with acumen by setting the correspondents straight, sometimes sharply, but more usually in a kindly manner. One correspondent bitterly complained in a long letter that the IKG provided Jews originally from Poland with opportunities to emigrate to the United States, neglecting the Jews who were natives of Vienna. Reich rejected the distinction native and newcomer, explaining that the provision of emigration opportunities was not in the hands of the IKG and that the reason why natives of Poland had better chances of being sponsored by relatives in the United States was that more Jews from formerly Russian Poland and from Galicia had emigrated to the United States than Jews whose families had settled in Vienna.[88] An old woman was disabused of the notion that the IKG could make representations to the authorities on behalf of Jewish children and the elderly to lift the prohibition against Jews using parks.[89] Murmelstein's assistant Prochnik, who, as the IKG representative on emigration matters in Berlin, was enjoying the freer atmosphere there, away from the oppressiveness of Vienna, wrote to Reich that his "journalistic pen had come alive again" and he would, aside from "a certain laziness to which I am sometimes prone," be prepared to write contributions on any suitable topics that Reich might suggest.[90] Reich responded by pointing out that only topics concerning emigration were of interest and that these must originate from the IKG, in particular from Dr. Murmelstein, adding:

> Aside from that, I was glad to note the cheerful tone that you sounded in your letter. I hope to note the same positive mood in you when you visit Vienna in the near future.[91]

Dr. Victor Frankl, a physician at the Jewish Hospital, and others submitted articles, all of which Reich had to reject for the same reason he could not accept Prochnik's offer. An author named Siegmund Ortony, who wanted to submit an article on the usefulness of learning foreign languages (as if the IKG did not arrange for many such courses already), was told that his contribution was not written in a "manner conforming to presently prevailing conditions. It would not do to make propaganda for English as the world language [Germany was then already at war with Great Britain]. Other remarks of yours also make one wonder."[92]

With the step-by-step liquidation of the Jewish organizations that the Nazis had at first allowed to continue, we find that the Vienna branch of the *Kulturbund* was reduced to offering the IKG's program of *Umschulungskurse*, which were supposed to prepare participants for emigration. When the emigration effort wound down, these courses were abolished by the authorities; and, finally, the activity of the *Kulturbund* in effect consisted solely of the publication of the *Nachrichtenblatt*. When the authorities abolished the *Kulturbund*, the publication of *Nachrichtenblatt* was assigned directly to the IKG. And in 1943 the *Nachrichtenblatt* was also abolished.

Dr. Emil Reich was deported with the 43rd transport (marked IV/12), which left Vienna on October 1, 1942, and arrived in Theresienstadt the next day. From there Reich was deported with transport Er to Auschwitz on October 16, 1944.[93]

■ ■ ■

In the meantime, however, since the primary official purpose of the *Nachrichtenblatt* was to aid emigration, appropriate articles appeared in the paper for as long as it made sense to address the subject. And, as Reich wrote to Prochnik, Murmelstein, in charge of the IKG's emigration effort, had to control the contents and was one of the main sources of information for Reich's articles about emigration. The other main source was Dr. Julius L. Seligsohn, who, as chief of the *Reichsvereinigung* section on migration aid, held a position in Berlin corresponding to Murmelstein's in Vienna. Perusing the issues of the *Nachrichtenblatt* of those years, we see indeed that matters connected with emigration tend to predominate. Some were articles about experiences of those who were fortunate enough to have emigrated. For example, issue 65 (August 12, 1940) has two such stories from unnamed contributors. One is from a physician who was in charge of establishing the military clinic of an army encampment in the jungles of Bolivia. The other is from a lawyer in Northampton, Massachusetts, who could not find employment, while his wife worked as a housekeeper. Rudolf Beck, a musician, reported in issue 86 (October 25, 1940) about an immigrant's impressions about American life in Chicago. He wrote about drug stores, the summer wardrobe (straw hat, white or yellow/white shoes, never without a jacket, sometimes without a necktie), and living-room furnishings. He denied that Americans put their feet on the table. He told about the summer concerts in Grant Park:

> I went because I coached one of the lady singers taking part. . . . The acoustics were quite poor, the audience was nonetheless satisfied with the performance, at times even enthusiastic. The orchestral part of the program did not lack the "William Tell Overture," a piece that, at this time, is *au courant* in Chicago.[94]

Evidently Mr. Beck had not as yet been exposed to "The Lone Ranger." He included details about his professional life as a coach, accompanist, arranger, and transcriber, and as a performer at formal parties. He advised future emigrants about employment opportunities:

> How else can one make money here? With good baked goods and pastries. Made in the Viennese manner, such things would be well received here (according to Viennese standards sweets-shops here are simply awful): things like *Pischinger Torte*, rum-puffs, Pressburg crescents, Viennese napoleons, possibly also Viennese apple strudel and Viennese *Milchrahmstrudel*.[95]

However, with wartime rationing, which was especially stringent for Jews, there was little chance for any *Umschulungskurse* to give instruction to those who may have been interested in preparing for such an upscale pastry business in emigration.

Most of the major articles dealing with emigration matters concerned the ever fewer immigration opportunities and the increasingly burdensome travel restrictions. As soon as Murmelstein returned from Nisko late in 1939, he began to provide Dr. Reich with information summarizing how many Jews by faith had emigrated, how many were left, what help the IKG had given to facilitate emigration, and what problems the emigration effort would have to face in the future. Hence many of the relevant articles of the subsequent eighteen months reflect the information Murmelstein submitted on behalf of the IKG. There were some glitches, at least at first, when Reich obtained emigration information from other sources, not always with fortunate results.

Soon after his return to Prague from Nisko, Edelstein also became concerned about emigration. Realizing how far behind Vienna and Berlin Prague was in the emigration effort compared, he had the Prague edition of the *Jüdische Nachrichten* publish a list of Jewish aid societies in the United States and their addresses, with the suggestion that readers write to them for affidavits. This was done in spite of the fact that Prague had Richard Friedmann, experienced as a former assistant of the IKG emigration team, who was reassigned by the authorities to show Prague how to proceed. Without consulting with the IKG, Reich reprinted the Prague article in the Vienna edition of January 2, 1940. All of a sudden, offices of American aid societies, including local ones, were besieged by hundreds of letters, appealing for help to emigrate. The reaction was not long in coming. On January 23 Löwenherz received the following telegram from Troper, of the Joint:

> advised by Newyork several hundreds letters requesting affidavits received Hias Nacomref Jointdisco lastdays from your committee stop appreciate explanation unquote.[96]

In his first response to Troper, Löwenherz expressed puzzlement as to how this could be attributed to the IKG (he also asked for the meaning of "appreciate explanation unquote"). After the source for these letters became clear, Löwenherz wrote an official letter of reprimand to Reich, informing him that according to that telegram, "organizations in America have been assailed with wholly useless requests for affidavits." What was worse, the IKG Vienna, which

> has repeatedly been asked not to divulge addresses of organizations, is made responsible for this and has been asked for clarification as to how this could have happened.

As a matter of fact, before the Prague article was reprinted in the Vienna edition, Reich had been informed by Löwenherz that the aid organizations did not wish this kind of publicity, and that

> articles in the Jewish paper in Prague can in no way be a model for [Vienna], since [the people in Prague] have as yet little experience in the area of emigration.[97]

Löwenherz, therefore, had no alternative but—"convinced that you wish to promote and not damage our effort"—to request that in questions of emigration the paper restrict itself to "information and publications from the IKG."[98] For Reich this was not the end of it. The *Reichsvereinigung* in Berlin sent him a translation of a letter they had received from Sanford M. Treguboff, Secretary of the San Francisco Committee for Service to Emigrées, explaining why appealing to anyone other than relatives for affidavits was useless. Aside from that, the process of responding in the negative to the hundreds of letters was more than their office could handle without disrupting their aid work.[99] In his response, Reich left no doubt where he thought the fault lay:

> Because of the apodictic and confident way the Prague article was written, we thought that an affidavit action had been initiated in the USA through committees and organizations.

Reich here reflected a sentiment that was surely not only his:

> We regret that with our article we caused an excess of work for the committees in the USA, but even the gentlemen overseas will well understand that we on this side cannot pass up any possible chance of promoting emigration. In the end the disappointment experienced here, when it became clear that it was all a false hope, is more to be deplored than the inconvenience of overtime in America.[100]

It is doubtful that this message was transmitted to the good people in the United States, but in those times and under the prevailing conditions it would have been a needed lesson about the dire state of European Jewry.

The issues of the *Nachrichtenblatt* straddling New Year 1941 presented a series of major articles concerning the problems of emigration that had developed in 1940 and the uncertain outlook for the year then beginning. By then the war had closed off all but a few immigration countries. Of the remaining ones the major one by far was the United States. However, the number of visas granted at the American consulates to qualified emigrants had been radically reduced in the second half of 1940 (as recounted in chapter 9). The people in Berlin were no less bewildered than those in Vienna. Dr. Seligsohn of the Berlin *Reichsvereinigung* tried to research the matter, and the first in Reich's series of articles presented whatever clarity Seligsohn was able to gain.[101] He held out hope for easement in certain cases, that is, those that fell outside the quota ("non-quota") and those who qualified for "first and second preference." The details of the article show how scant the hope for anyone to qualify was.[102] The non-quota categories were meant for spouses and minor children of citizens of the United States, persons born on the American continent, clergy, and university faculty. The preference categories were similarly narrow.

The Rabbi

Murmelstein had his own problem with immigration to the United States; hence, the non-quota category of clergy concerned him personally. Immersed as he was in the work he had been doing at the IKG since the Anschluss, he had neglected to register for a visa at the United States consulate. Under the quota system the waiting list was long and overloaded with people who, like him, fell under the Polish quota. However, inasmuch as his career interests were in academic research, in teaching in a rabbinical seminary, and in a major rabbinic pulpit, he thought he should not have any difficulty in securing an appointment that would circumvent the quota restriction.

A few years before the Anschluss, his mentor at the University of Vienna, Professor Christian, returned from an American conference on biblical studies with a promise of a position for Murmelstein at Hebrew Union College in Cincinnati, in no small part on the basis of Murmelstein's collaboration on Alexander Kohut's *Tosafot Arukh ha-Shalem* (published in 1937). Murmelstein decided not to apply, since he felt indebted to Vienna, where he had received his higher education and had been given recognition for his work. But after the Anschluss and before he became committed to the role as Löwenherz's right-hand man, Murmelstein sent out inquiries regarding suitable positions, mainly in England but also in Holland and the United States. The response of one of the correspondents, Chief Rabbi of the British Empire Joseph Hertz, sums up the situation for someone even as eminently qualified as Murmelstein:

> I find I have not answered your letter of the 10th of April. The delay is due solely to the fact of the extreme difficulty of finding academic positions such as you require. I am getting into touch with Drs. Stephen Wise and Cyrus Adler in regard to your application and the many others of a similar nature which reach me from Germany, Austria, and now also Hungary.

We have already mentioned in chapter 6 in the section on "In Search of Feasible Schemes" that at the height of Murmelstein's early activity on behalf of the IKG emigration efforts, he had donated his certificate of entry into Palestine to his friend Rabbi Dr. Rimalt and that a few weeks later, during his April 1939 trip to London, Professor Bentwich offered him a chance to emigrate to England. But by then Murmelstein was too involved in a job he felt he had to see through.

After Murmelstein returned from Nisko, he found a letter from Dr. Ernst Max in Stockholm, dated October 16, 1939. Max was a friend of his who had worked at the IKG after the Anschluss and who had been able to emigrate to Sweden. He told Murmelstein, "Today I bring important news to your attention, which, I hope, could be very significant for you and your future." The news: The Chief Rabbi of Sweden, Professor Dr. Markus Ehrenpreis, "is not well and has informed the [Board of Directors of the Jewish Community] of his wish to retire in the coming year. The board received this news with sincere regret, and in closed session set aside a considerable sum to be used for honoraria for trial sermons." Max spoke of Ehrenpreis's prestige and the power he wielded in his community as well as the emoluments that went with both. He added: "His successor must have his approval." Max urges Murmelstein to apply: "I believe that, if at all possible, you should not let this unique opportunity go by, and . . . among the other recommendations, it would be good to have one from Troper. . . . Officially, the matter is still secret." Max offered to pass along any necessary correspondence.[103]

By 1940, with the last desperate emigration effort well under way, though of necessity winding down, Murmelstein thought that he had paid his debt to the community for his education and early career, having been instrumental more than anyone else in helping the Jews of Vienna to emigrate. But Murmelstein still had his sight set on the United States. Early in 1940 he was sent to Budapest on IKG business, where he met Troper. We do not know whether he ever asked Troper for a recommendation to be sent to Stockholm. In July 1940 he asked Troper to help him get an appointment in the United States. He must have been puzzled when he received no response. Writing to Troper in September, Löwenherz referred to Murmelstein's letter and mentioned that since Murmelstein had not registered, he would have to immigrate into the United States under a non-quota category. For this reason, Löwenherz briefly sang Murmelstein's praises and asked Troper to help Murmelstein "secure a suitable position and the chance to emigrate." Evidently with regard to Murmelstein's ongoing emigration efforts at the IKG as well as the difficulty he foresaw of securing Eichmann's permission for Murmelstein to leave, Löwenherz added: "Most likely a considerable amount of time will have go by before he will be able to emigrate, but for understandable reasons Dr. Murmelstein wishes to make the necessary preparations."[104] A handwritten note on the draft of the letter indicates that it was to be given to Murmelstein for translation into English and for sending it off. In January 1941 Herbert Katzki, one of the officials at the Lisbon office of the Joint, mentioned in a situation report to Troper that a dossier had been established on behalf of Murmelstein and that Löwenherz "requests that the matter be pursued as energetically as possible."[105]

But it was no use. Before long, Murmelstein found out why through Dr. Margarete Feiler, one of his most able assistants, who most likely is the one who translated Löwenherz's letter into English. Feiler was a lawyer who, at the time of the Anschluss, had completed the lengthy internship required in Austria and was about to start her career. Instead, she told us, she had to take a position at the IKG, where she was in charge of the most sensitive correspondence. In November 1940 she had to emigrate in a hurry when her firm stand during an appearance at the Gestapo made her position dangerous. Since she had to travel by way of Portugal, Löwenherz gave her the assignment to report to the European representatives of the Joint, which had by then been transferred to Lisbon. It was there that she found out that in the United States Murmelstein had, in effect, been blacklisted. Murmelstein had asked her to look up his contacts in the United States on his behalf, among them Rabbi Dr. Leo Jung, originally from Uherský-Brod in Moravia, who, in effect, confirmed what Feiler had found out in Lisbon, all of which she reported to Murmelstein.

After all, Rabbi Jung was one of the persons through whom the complaint about the provision of kosher foods earlier in 1940 had circulated, and no doubt Jung was the recipient of other rumors about Murmelstein.

Murmelstein now officially applied for the Stockholm position, the opening for which had by then been publicized. Nothing but the strongest support would provide any chance of success. When Löwenherz was in Berlin in January 1941, he enlisted the support of Rabbi Dr. Leo Baeck for Murmelstein's candidacy and wrote to Ehrenpreis that "Dr. Baeck had the kindness to point to the special qualifications of Dr. Murmelstein and to recommend him highly as a scholar." Twice in this letter he referred to Murmelstein as his "closest associate" and mentioned Murmelstein's "extensive knowledge, deep sensibility, and impeccable character." Löwenherz was "convinced that he is rendering the community of Stockholm . . . a service in recommending Dr. Murmelstein as [Ehrenpreis's] successor."[106] Ehrenpreis answered immediately with certain questions, to which Löwenherz responded at length "in order to dispel certain reservations and unclarities,"[107] of which there were five. The first concerned Murmelstein's experience in the rabbinate. Löwenherz related that until he was 16, Murmelstein had almost exclusively devoted himself to rabbinical subjects. At the Jewish Theological Seminary his academic achievements were second only to those of the late Chief Rabbi Chajes. As a rabbi since 1929, he had officiated at the synagogues of the two districts of Vienna with the greatest populations of Jews and at hundreds of rabbinical functions on an annual basis. In what surely must have been a strong sequel to this point, Löwenherz reported that

> Dr. M. was the only Viennese rabbi who remained at his post even after the recent [political] reorganization, rejecting proffered chances of emigration out of a sheer sense of duty, and that, for the sake of the [remaining] Jews, he fills an extremely responsible and difficult position. He also carries out the rabbinic functions of the Temple at Seitenstettengasse.

On the question of Murmelstein's performance as preacher, Löwenherz reported that

> [h]is sermons are always substantive, never formulaic; his voice is pleasant and carries well. He is adept at captivating his audience with clear and generally understandable presentations, never speaks in an unctuous or pathetic manner; popular and demagogic mannerisms are foreign to him, neither does he assume the role of a *maggid*.[108] [Because of h]is talent of adjusting [his message to a particular] audience, the directorate of the IKG has selected him to speak at formal [official] religious observances.

A third question concerned Murmelstein's teaching. Löwenherz told of his teaching in schools attended by Jewish students hailing from "the better circles, though frequently alienated from Judaism." He managed to stimulate their interest in studying Jewish subjects "to a greater degree than they had been used to at home." In response to Ehrenpreis's concern about Murmelstein's religious position, Löwenherz tells of his coming from a

> strictly orthodox family and leading his life in a manner befitting a rabbi. Yet his views are moderate and he judges the members of the congregation with liberality and without intolerance. . . . His wife comes from a distinguished Budapest family, keeps an exemplary Jewish household.

The papers that Löwenherz had submitted with his earlier letter included a picture of Murmelstein, which led Ehrenpreis to voice concern about his "unspiritual looks." Löwenherz promised to send a more recent picture and assured Ehrenpreis that "Dr. M. presents himself well and also knows how to maintain dignity and tactfulness in dealing with the authorities."

Even though Ehrenpreis did not ask about Murmelstein's record as a scholar, Löwenherz recalled how in a conversation the late, "unforgettable Chief Rabbi Chajes characterized Dr. M. among the most brilliant students of the seminary. This circumstance caused Dr. M. to be appointed as lecturer at a very young age." He suggested that Ehrenpreis also request letters of recommendation from former IKG President Desider Friedmann and from Murmelstein's senior associate in preparing *Tosafot Arukh ha-Shalem*, Bernhard Geiger, then residing in New York. Whether Ehrenpreis ever wrote to Geiger is not known. He did write to Friedmann, who responded at length on March 11, 1941. While for the most part Friedmann's appraisal was in agreement with Löwenherz's, one of his points is worth reiterating: At the Theological Seminary Murmelstein

> counted among the best, one can say the most distinguished students, and Rector Dr. Schwarz as well as Professor Dr. Chajes had the highest hopes for him. . . . In 1931 [when Murmelstein was 26 years old], by way of carrying out a legacy of the late Chief Rabbi Dr. Chajes [who died 1927], Dr. M. was appointed as Lecturer at the Seminary, where he taught Midrash and Philosophy.

Friedmann mentioned one important new point: "I am convinced that, with his subtle Talmudic and rabbinic knowledge, Dr. M.'s ability to make rabbinic decisions and to preside over a board of rabbis is beyond any doubt."[109]

In anticipation of his possible appointment in Stockholm, Murmelstein and Löwenherz managed to obtain from Eichmann a letter of permission to emigrate, a document he would keep until the end of the war. Yet, in spite of the massive effort, nothing came of the matter. Ehrenpreis decided to stay at his post until after the war, while Murmelstein kept at his post and was the only Viennese rabbi who stayed with his dwindling, hapless community until he, too, was deported.

■ ■ ■

Among the studies ordered by the Nazis one more needs to be discussed, namely, Murmelstein's brief treatment of *The Jewish Divine Service.*[110] If those who ordered the study hoped to find here a basis for the oft-repeated claim that the Jewish religious service is in some way connected with a Jewish conspiracy against non-Jews, they were sorely disappointed. The service, he wrote, consists of "prayer, teaching, and symbolic acts."

As Murmelstein argued, at one-time prayer was no more than the confession of beliefs and the expression of hopes; supplications for the provision of basic needs and for the good of the community were added later, especially "the return to Palestine." There are "two main prayers, central to all services." One is the *Shema*.[111] Among the few passages to illustrate its contents, Murmelstein chose the following from Deuteronomy 11:14–15: "I will give the rain of your land in its season"; "I will give grass in thine field for thine cattle"; "You too shall eat."[112] The other main prayer is usually called the *'Amidah* (the "standing" prayer) in the United States, and in Europe the *Shemoneh 'esreh* (the "eighteen" benedictions); hence, Murmelstein referred to it as *das Achtzehngebet* ("the eighteen prayer").

Among the examples from it cited by Murmelstein we find "Thou sustainest all the living through Your loving-kindness" and "return in mercy to Jerusalem, Thy city."[113] Aside from the prayers in the synagogue offered at daily services and on the occasion of the five major holidays (Rosh Hashanah, Yom Kippur, Sukkot, Passover, and Shavuot), there are prayers at home for the perennial cycle of the Jewish calendar, as well as for rites of passage.

Teaching, Murmelstein wrote, has always been a matter of reading portions of the Torah and from the Prophets and interpreting them. The reference to symbolic acts reiterates the stress on the Jewish yearning for a return to the ancient homeland. These acts are

> historical reminders of the solemn service in the Temple in Jerusalem and of life in the Holy Land, and serve to keep alive the yearning for the reestablishment of the Jewish commonwealth.[114]

Murmelstein described the history of the structure, arrangement, and function of the synagogue, the laws of purity pertaining to participation in communal services, and the order of the service. The timing of the three daily services

> takes the occupations of the Jews into consideration; it was not the intention to keep an individual from his work because of his religious duties in the House of God, because work is also considered a religious duty.[115]

The topic of music merited Murmelstein's special attention because, according to him, "among Jews . . . cult and music appear to be so closely tied that, historically, their religious service knows only prayer that is sung." The readings from the Scriptures that constitute part of the teaching segment of synagogue services are chanted in the form of set phrases (tropes), "the musical notations for which rank among the oldest in the world."[116] The melodies of prayers, Murmelstein surmised, originally arose out of the mode of reciting the scriptural readings, and in the course of time melodies were adapted from the various musical traditions that the Jews encountered in their wanderings. While originally members of the community took turns chanting the readings and leading the prayers, in time fewer and fewer were able to do so, especially since the singing of the prayers became increasingly more demanding, requiring talent, training, and a pleasing voice. Murmelstein, drawing on his *History of the Jews*,[117] described the movements throughout the centuries aimed at reforming the synagogue service in accordance with the times and indicated the special place occupied by the modern Jewish community of Vienna:

> The decisive turning point in the area of synagogue music is connected with the history of the Jews in Vienna. The opening of the new synagogue . . . in 1826 was accompanied by the development of a form of religious service . . . aimed at solemnity while retaining its Jewish character. At the same time as Preacher[118] Isak Noa [Isaak Noah] Mannheimer [acted as rabbi], Salomon Sulzer served as cantor; in his four-volume work *Lied Zions* [Heb. *Schir Zion* or "Song of Zion"] the latter created the musical aesthetics of the new vocal music for the synagogue.[119]

Murmelstein emphasized that the first volume contains contributions from contemporary non-Jewish composers such as Sulzer's friend Franz Schubert; the later volumes show more and more a return to the Jewish idiom:

> Sulzer's work, while bearing the imprint of the musical culture of Vienna, rejects any radical reform and is suffused with noble sublimity and religious solemnity.[120]

Murmelstein was highly critical of the reforms introduced by certain modern movements, such as the substitution of songs sung in German for the Hebrew prayers or

> the insane attempt to delete all those passages from the prayers that mention the yearning to return to Palestine. Such bungling interference cannot alter the millennial tradition of Judaism.[121]

Instead, Murmelstein continued,

> [t]he historical development [of Judaism] from the time of Moses to the most recent times shows the Jew the way to the Hebrew language and to the land of his fathers. At the very core of the service, unchangeable, is the prayer: "To Yerushalayim [Jerusalem], Thy city, return in love, and take your dwelling therein as you have foretold. Build it soon in our days as an eternal edifice."[122]

Murmelstein concluded the essay with the words sung by the congregation as the scroll of the Torah is returned to the shrine after the scriptural reading:

> Lead us back to you, Eternal One, we wish to return. Renew our days as in ancient times.[123]

We may be puzzled by this essay. There is no discernible reproach or corrective aimed at invidious stereotypes. While there is the reaffirmation of tradition and of the centrality of Torah, Hebrew, the yearning for a return to the Holy Land, and the traditional Jewish idiom, there is no overt attempt at criticism other than against aberrant assimilative reforms within Judaism. The explanation may lie in the fact that Murmelstein and Löwenherz were working very hard—and would before long succeed –in having the Nazi authorities permit the reintroduction of regular weekly religious services at the Central Synagogue and refurbishing it for that purpose, after it had been partially demolished at the time of Kristallnacht. It had since functioned as an emigration office. Officially scheduled services had generally been forbidden; the exceptions were holiday services at the homes for the aged and the hospital. It is possible that private clandestine *minyanim* on a small scale had continued to assemble. Generally, however, after Kristallnacht, Jews had observed their devotions individually, including during the major holidays.

At the time Murmelstein's studies were submitted, Löwenherz tried to gain permission from the authorities to close the IKG offices temporarily to enable employees to observe the coming High Holidays, Rosh Hashanah on October 3–4, 1940, and Yom Kippur on October 12. On September 19 he was told by Brunner 1 that the Municipal Labor Bureau was not the proper authority for granting such permission.[124] On September 27 Murmelstein also spoke with Brunner 1 about this matter and was told that the IKG would be allowed to close down for the holidays provided a skeleton crew manned the telephone and kept the service log. Julius Boschan and Hans Kasztan, the two employees of the IKG who were assigned to external service at the *Zentralstelle*, had to take turns.[125] Three days later Murmelstein handed in the ordered studies.

Regular services at the Central Synagogue, the only one to survive Kristallnacht, began again in the spring of 1941 at the time of Passover. The authorization for the services was obtained by Löwenherz. The administration—such as the collection of contributions, the sale of tickets for the High Holidays, and the assignment of seats— was left to Inspector of Schools Dr. Isidor Oehler, who often functioned as cantor. The order of service and overall responsibility were in the hands of Murmelstein, who was the only officially appointed rabbi left in Vienna. While Murmelstein was concerned with providing the congregants meaningful and traditional services, the arrangements evidently had to conform to the strictures of the authorities. In fact, everything about the services was controlled by the Gestapo under the supervision of Inspector Otto Kuchmann, who worked for the Jewish section of the Gestapo in Vienna. Care had to be taken to submit prior reports, outlining the service itself and any arrangements other than the routine Sabbath services and the occasional weekday *minyan*. In addition, a Gestapo officer was often present, especially during the holiday services. Sermons had to be in German and, in principle, the text had to be submitted in advance for censorship. The IKG files containing copies of the studies ordered in September 1940 also contain copies of two of the first sermons given by Murmelstein after the resumption of services, namely, those given at Shavuot, the Feast of Weeks, in 1941.

Making use of his early experience as a pioneer in the conduct of services for young people, Murmelstein now arranged special services for the few remaining younger Jews. The typescript of Murmelstein's minutes of the planning session tells what was involved in arranging the first of those youth services, to be held on the afternoon of the first day of Passover 1941.[126] Altogether there would be 450 youngsters from 13 to 16 years of age: 150 from institutions of the IKG (orphanage, home for children, and the school that had to be referred to as an "activity institution") and 300 from the Youth Aliyah. Aaron Menczer, the leader of the latter group, had by then been at the labor camp for almost a year and could not himself be party to the administrative aspects of the planning and the seating of the groups by age and sex, nor of their supervision. The order of the service, which had to be brief, was devised by Murmelstein and consisted of a minimum of prayers selected for their relevance, readings from the Torah, and a brief sermon by Murmelstein. The three Torah readings were to be followed by hymns familiar to the youngsters, *Malchutcha*, *Adir hu*, and *Halleluyah*. The service would end with *Alenu*, the ancient acceptance of the Jewish mission, and *Adon Olam* ("Eternal Lord"), a medieval hymn extolling God. In Murmelstein's handwriting, *Hatikvah* (the Zionist anthem) was added at the end, evidently at the behest of the Youth Aliyah leader, who took Menczer's place in his absence. Other notables of the Jewish community and their spouses also attended the event and were seated in the loges reserved for them.

The youth service for Shavuot was held on the eve of the festival. In ancient times the feast coincided with the year's first harvest, and in rabbinic times it was associated with the revelation on Mount Sinai, seven weeks after the exodus from Egypt. In his sermon Murmelstein took up the question of the relation between celebrating the gathering of the first fruits and recalling the revelation. In his exegesis he quoted the key passage of the commandment: "Six days you shall labor and do all your work, but the seventh day is a sabbath dedicated to the Eternal One, your God" (Exodus 20:9–10). It would be wrong to see this simply as the commandment enjoining the Israelites to keep the Sabbath, for "in full and complete conformance with Jewish teaching" it is no less the commandment to observe the Sabbath rest as it is the commandment to work. In support of this point, Murmelstein referred to some passages in the Talmud, such as "Whoever devotes himself exclusively to study without also engaging in labor, has fallen into sin." Hence, "the feast of revelation . . . would be incomplete if this day were not also a feast of giving thanks for the harvest, for the fruits of one's labor." The lesson to be taken from this was that

> [t]oday, more than ever, we know how to appreciate the blessings of work. We pursue, as if it were a promise, the hoped-for chance to emigrate and to work for a home and to take root. . . . In our daily bread, gained by our labor, God's grace reveals itself clearly and distinctly. For thousands of years the human spirit has endeavored to grasp and explain the revelation at Sinai. The revelation of the golden sheaves upon the field needs no exegesis. . . . Hold fast to your Judaism and be ready to take your place: May these be your guiding stars on the way to the future.

Two of the teenagers at the service were the twins Ilse and Kurt Mezei. Kurt had become bar mitzvah, with Murmelstein officiating, at the synagogue on Kluckygasse in 1937, and was employed as a runner in Murmelstein's office. Ilse would also be employed as the IKG's telephone switchboard operator. Their mother, Margarete Mezei, had taken employment at the IKG in 1938 when her husband, Maurus (Moritz) Mezei (1886–1944), an author, translator, and journalist, had to leave the country because he was a Hungarian citizen. Frau Mezei worked in the correspondence section of the IKG and typed and corrected many of Murmelstein's reports, including the ones under consideration. We will have ample occasion to refer to these three people again in the second volume.

Murmelstein's Shavuot sermon to the adults was built around the reading: "They [the children of Israel] departed from Rephidim and came to the wilderness of Sinai." These

Author and journalist Maurus Mezei. (DÖW 9443[2])

words, taken from Exodus 19, occur at the beginning of the Torah reading on the first day of the festival and introduce the story of the revelation at Sinai. The thrust of the lesson Murmelstein preached was twofold: first, the importance for Jews of having a home of their own, namely, the land of their fathers, and to hold fast to it; and second, the significance of their receiving the revelation while wandering in the wilderness:

> For us this is not a report of ancient times, but the immediate present, and the palpable actuality of a community that has done with the past, makes do without the present, and directs its gaze toward an uncertain future. Words like these signify the daily reality of parents who have for years endeavored to follow their children. They focus on a facet of the lives of those who had thought repeatedly to stand on the threshold of fulfillment, only to have their hopes dashed again and again. Nonetheless we wanderers on the long and onerous path to distant goals are not permitted to despair or lose heart.[127]

At this point Murmelstein reiterated the reading in a wider context: "They journeyed, they were able to rest, and had to move on. *They departed from Rephidim and came to the wilderness of Sinai*. There the Almighty appeared to them." Only the emphasized passage is a true reiteration of the biblical text; the rest is a summary of what comes before and after. What comes after is indeed God's revelation. But, as for the respite at Rephidim, as the listening worshippers were no doubt painfully aware, it was anything but "restful": First the Israelites, desperate with thirst, rebelled against Moses, and then they waged a hard-fought battle for survival in their first encounter with the treacherous Amalekites, their perennial enemies. In the Bible the episode ends with the words: "[The Lord] will utterly blot out the memory of Amalek from under heaven. . . . The Lord will be at war with Amalek throughout the ages" (Exodus 17:14, 16). This, of course, could not be said within earshot of Nazi listeners—who, aside from objecting to the warlike tone of this passage, might possibly have been aware that, through the ages, "Amalek" has been the collective name given by Jews to their enemies—and had to be said by means of a textual ellipsis. Murmelstein concluded by saying

> we know that God sheds his grace on those who, in search of a new homeland, always have but a brief time to rest and then must move on. Strengthened and encouraged, we pray: "O Father, let us come to you, we wish to return."[128]

It was a desperate kind of encouragement that was being preached here. It came a few weeks after the Nazis suddenly staged the first five deportations, which stunned the Jews of Vienna and the leaders at the IKG. It was not known if and when the deportations would be resumed. In the meantime, the Jews were allowed to hold services. We will consider the possible connection between the deportations and the resumption of services in our second volume.

The number of people attending services at the Central Synagogue was strictly controlled by the authorities, hence seat assignments had to be obtained on a first-come, first-served basis in the six weeks prior to the holiday services. Ordinarily, holiday services could only be advertised within the building of the IKG,[129] not in the *Jüdisches Nachrichtenblatt*. Those who could afford it had to pay for seats for High Holiday services with a contribution to the IKG welfare fund. In 1941 RM 10,134.50 were collected. Some seats were reserved for leading members of the IKG staff, as well as for honored members of the community, such as the two main Jewish hostages Desider Friedmann and Robert Stricker, the philanthropist Frau Hermine Krüger, and Frau Erna Patak, a leader in Jewish women's organizations. Dr. Emil Tuchmann, who was the medical director of the Jewish Hospital, felt slighted because he was not granted a seat among the other leading members of the IKG staff. He was informed by Dr. Oehler that on order of Löwenherz he had the honor of offering him an honorary ticket: "It gives me pleasure to carry out this order, and at the same time I beg leave to express the most heartfelt good wishes for the coming holidays."[130] The Nazis permitted the Jewish veterans of the First World War to maintain their own organization and to enjoy special privileges; these, however, were to be provided by the IKG. The veterans requested that eight seats in front be reserved for war invalids; and with Murmelstein's approval, Oehler informed their director, Siegfried Kolisch, that such seats would be made available and held in reserve until thirty minutes before the beginning of services.[131]

Special permission was obtained from Kuchmann for services at two locations in addition to the newly established High Holiday services at the Central Synagogue and the services permitted in earlier years at homes for the aged and the hospital. The local Nazi Party office objected to one of these locations "in spite of the permission granted by the Gestapo"; therefore, Kuchmann ordered that "only a few persons take part. [And] bearded men are advised to go elsewhere."[132]

Elaborate regulations and personnel assignments were made to ensure that the High Holiday services were brief and concluded on time; that there would be no ostentation in the display of ritual objects, such as Torah decorations; that worshipers came and left individually and did not congregate in front of the synagogue; and that there would be a sufficient number of people to keep order placed in the different sections of the synagogue to ensure decorum, in particular during *Yizkor*, the service of pious commemoration of departed family members, traditionally a time for free expression of sorrow, a sorrow surely exacerbated by the dismal times.[133]

For Sukkot, the Festival of Tabernacles, there arrived, via the Italian port of Trieste, a shipment of *lulavim* (palm and other branches) and *etrogim* (citrons); these are the plants and fruit displayed in connection with the hymns of thanksgiving for the autumn harvest recited during this festival. These objects have been shipped by Jews living in the Holy Land to diaspora Jews since ancient times. But now it was wartime. Yugoslavia and Greece were occupied by Nazi Germany. This was also the time of the seesaw battle for North Africa between Rommel and Montgomery, and there was hardly a square mile of Mediterranean waters that was not being patrolled by one or the other navy. What neutral trader could have brought that shipment of ceremonial produce from British Palestine to an Axis port? Ninety-three sets of *lulavim* and *etrogim* arrived in Vienna in usable condition, of which nineteen were assigned to services held at various places, and seventy-four sold to duly listed individuals who were able to make a contribution, most of them RM 10, to the IKG welfare fund.[134]

Soon after the High Holidays and the Feast of Tabernacles in 1941, the deportations resumed in earnest, but the services at the Central Synagogue would continue almost to the end. Murmelstein's arrangements for the order of service would be retained even after his own deportation.

Exhuming a Glorious Past

In the process of liquidating the assets of the defunct provincial communities, the local municipalities had their eyes especially on Jewish cemeteries. And since the assets of the IKG Vienna were slated for liquidation, the question of acquiring the Jewish cemeteries of Vienna also came up. However, according to received law, cemetery grounds could not be used for other purposes, if they contained burials less than ten years old. Hence, only two Jewish cemeteries in Vienna came into consideration: The medieval one on Seegasse was surrounded by buildings and for that reason not available. Aside from that, it had historical value, for it contained a tombstone that commemorated a carp, which, it was said, cried out "*shema Yisrael* (Hear, o Israel") as it was about to be killed, which is the last prayer to be uttered on one's deathbed. Since the fish was thought to be a *dybbuk*, a creature that had been taken over by a tormented soul, the fish was buried as a pious person.

The other cemetery to meet the above-stated criterion was the Jewish section of the Währinger Friedhof, the cemetery in the District of Währing. And so it happened that one of the projects that kept the IKG busy in the lull between the first five deportation transports and the next five was the exhumation action. The central municipal building administration had requisitioned a major part of the Währinger Friedhof, ostensibly for the purpose of building a public air raid shelter on it. The Währing Cemetery was established at the turn of the nineteenth century, at the time when the Jewish community of Vienna was being re-established in the wake of Emperor Joseph II's quasi-liberal emancipation decrees and the liberalization that swept Europe after the turmoil of the French Revolution. The cemetery held thousands of Jewish graves, including most of the prominent members of the Jewish community from about 1810 to the 1870s, when the "First Gate" of the vast Central Cemetery (*Zentralfriedhof*) was dedicated as holy ground for Jewish burial, soon to be followed by the "Fourth Gate."

The decision as to how to proceed with the exhumation was made during an inspection of the cemetery on June 6, 1941. It was conducted by *Baurat* (building councilor) Dr. Kalina, in the presence of *Baurat* Adametz (an architect and presumably the one who would oversee the building on behalf of the municipality); Dr. Brachtl, representing the Health Department of the 18th District where the cemetery was located; Herr Schreiber, the Aryan superintendent of the cemetery; and three men representing the IKG: Dr. Löwenherz, Dr. Heinrich Dessauer, and Dr. Ernst Feldsberg, the latter the IKG official in charge of Jewish cemeteries and burials. The record of the meeting was prepared by Kalina and signed, by way of agreement, by all participants. It was accompanied by a set of photographs of the area on which the shelter was to be erected.[135]

Kalina brought along the plan of how to proceed with the exhumation, which had evidently been decided upon by the various municipal and Nazi authorities prior to the meeting. According to their scheme, any remains found in connection with preparing the ground for the building project would be gathered by a representative of the IKG and

The main Jewish ceremonial hall (Zeremonienhalle) *of the central cemetery* (Zentralfriedhof) *of Vienna following its devastation on Kristallnacht in November 1938. It has since been restored and serves once again in its original function.* (*DÖW Foto 9972 - 20/32*)

placed in provided containers, which would then be transported to the Jewish section of the Central Cemetery. The IKG would not be burdened with the cost of this phase of the exhumation but would take over responsibility for the remains once they were delivered to the Central Cemetery. No exhumation tax would be levied for the required exhumations. However, they would have to be approved by the Health Department of the 18th District (Währing), and the transfer of the remains to the Central Cemetery by that of the 11th District (Simmering), where the Central Cemetery was located.

The IKG was to announce the projected exhumation in the next issue of the *Jüdisches Nachrichtenblatt*, dated June 10, in order to give descendants ten days to request permission to undertake individual exhumations and to transfer gravestones at their own expense.

Aside from such privately claimed gravestones, the IKG would be able to request the transfer of honorary gravestones (*Widmungsgräber*). All other stones would be stored at a location in the cemetery not as yet needed for building. They would be at the disposal of the authorities, and the IKG would have no further claim to them. The IKG also "raises no objection to the utilization of the said part of the cemetery, and reserves the right to claim compensation for the said portion of the lot on the occasion of negotiations with Department I/6 of the municipal administration for the sale of the entire area of the cemetery."

Löwenherz had no choice but to agree. His concern was that the exhumation and reinterment proceed in accordance with the precepts of Jewish piety. The task of finding and gathering the remains was a formidable one, especially since Kalina seemed to suggest that the IKG proceed together with the building crew's preparation of the ground for the building project. Proper exhumation and reburial according to Jewish practice was different from what prevailed among Christians in Austria, where old churchyards in rural localities and small towns were periodically cleared of skeletal remains. These were then stored in a charnel house (in Austria called a *Karner*) adjoining the parish church. In larger communities, skulls were provided with the name of the deceased and the year of death, and were placed on shelves on top of the respective remaining bones. In other communities the bones were simply heaped in the *Karner*, there to await the resurrection at the end of days in helter-skelter fashion. It was this that Kalina may have had in mind when he imparted to Löwenherz the procedural directive according to which the IKG might gather any remains found during the preparatory phase of the building project. But, in the words of Murmelstein's report concerning Jewish burial customs,

> [c]emeteries must remain intact. If secular authorities appropriate a Jewish cemetery, Jews are required to gather and re-inter the bones of the departed.

This is what the crew from the IKG, under supervision of Dr. Feldsberg, now proceeded to undertake with great care.

In various ways, many of the remains were difficult and time consuming to remove. The exhumations began one week after the inspection with the most recent burials from the 1860s and 1870s. These graves were not only the most readily accessible but, being closest to Währinger Hauptstrasse, the main thoroughfare of the 18th District, they occupied the portion of the cemetery designated for the projected air raid shelter. Some of the graves were those of parents or grandparents of persons still living in Vienna but too old to emigrate and were claimed by them for reburial at the Central Cemetery. For the most part these graves either held the remains of prominent persons or were in keeping with the elaborate display of middle-class success that began in the Biedermeier era following the Napoleonic wars and increased during the course of the nineteenth century. Some of the remains were in burial vaults, and some in metal or stone sarcophagi, even if, as required by Jewish custom, the actual coffin was made of wood. Some sarcophagi were in brick chambers embedded in the earth. Some remains had to be extracted from roots that had grown into the coffin. Some graves had elaborate stone settings or heavy gravestones that had to be dismantled. Unlike granite markers, most sandstone markers had deteriorated and were of no further use. The exhumed remains were stored for the inspection by the municipal physician (*Stadtphysikus*), which normally took place once a week. Placed in wooden coffins, the remains were then transported to the Central Cemetery and there re-interred. Some family groups were placed in a common coffin.

Feldsberg's crew would proceed with the exhumations with proper care, bit by bit making room for the excavation machines working alongside them. Feldsberg prepared periodic *Tätigkeitsberichte* ("activity reports"), which was a standard Nazi requirement. In the *Tätigkeitsberichte* Feldsberg reported the location and the state of the graves that had been cleared, what kind of work was required, the condition of the remains found in them, the identities of the persons buried there, when they died, and their contribution, if any, to the life of the Jewish and the general community. It is doubtful that all of these particulars

An Austrian charnel house, or Karner, *in Hallstatt, Upper Austria* (Oberösterreich) *in 2012. (© CSE)*

were required by the Nazi authorities. However, we note that some of this information was not obtainable from the gravestones or the IKG's burial records but evidently was gathered through at least a modicum of research. In this way the IKG compiled a proud record of the presence of Jews in Vienna in recent history, during an age of industrial, economic, intellectual, and spiritual upswing. Vis-à-vis the Nazis it was, in effect, another lesson in Judaism; although, even more than in the case of the previous lessons discussed, it is unclear what conclusions the Nazis might have drawn from it. For the Jews, this record eventually formed a basis for the genre of memorial books that sprang up after the Holocaust to remember destroyed communities. Here, however, it was not the community that was in the final stages of its destruction that was memorialized, but some of the forebears that gave birth to it.

In the records of the IKG, the copies of the *Tätigkeitsberichte* are, for the most part, addressed to Dr. Moses, with the request that he submit the legends on the tombstones of those whose exhumations were reported. Dr. Moses was evidently at the cemetery recording the legends of the markers in Hebrew and German as they were being dismantled. Dr. Moses was a historian and collaborated with Murmelstein in writing some of the lessons in Judaism discussed earlier. Most likely the impetus to implant information about the contribution of Jews to the splendor of Vienna and hence to the culture of modern Europe came from Murmelstein.

The careful and necessarily deliberate pace of exhumation came to an end a few weeks after it began. One of the last graves exhumed in that phase yielded the remains of Wilhelmine Strauss, who died in 1851 at age 25, her daughter Hermine, who died in 1852 at age 4, her husband Albert, who died in 1886, and a certain Albert Strauss, who died in 1877.[136] The exhumation was requested by Paula Lippmann, who was one of their relatives. Feldsberg's report recounts that Wilhelmine and Albert were the parents and Hermine, the sister of Adele, the "wife of the waltz king Johann Strauss [Jr.]." An 11-foot (3.5 m) high stone in the shape of an obelisk crowned by a harp marked the Strauss grave, indicating that this Strauss family into which the waltz king married was musically gifted, as was his own Strauss family. Most likely the families were related in past generations, although the waltz king's immediate forbears had converted to Catholicism.

In the two months since the work had begun, fewer than seventy exhumations had taken place. Now the area needed for the building project had to be cleared. In the last three weeks of the slow exhumations, digging machinery had already been moved in to excavate the foundations. A mass exhumation took place that extended to areas of the cemetery with less elaborate tombs, including graves without markers. A list of the names of those buried in the affected sections was made based on the cemetery records; and the list was deposited at the Central Cemetery. However, since only those names were on record for which there were grave markers, the list had to remain incomplete. Nonetheless, 2,005 names were recorded.[137]

As the excavations progressed, the earth containing remains was loaded on trucks that dumped and spread the loads at several designated sites. The IKG, therefore, had to provide crews at each of these places, which gleaned the bones from the dumped loads and deposited them in large coffins. The filled coffins were brought back to the Währing Cemetery, where the remains were moved to crates. These were then taken by the municipal authorities to the Fourth Gate of the Central Cemetery. There the remains were placed in mass graves by an IKG crew, with the skulls facing east (i.e., toward Jerusalem), as required by tradition. Surprisingly, the municipal building authorities cooperated to the extent of digging only to a depth of two meters (6 to 7 feet), which was the maximal depth for burials. Only afterward did the excavation proceed to the required four meters. However, since the excavation also continued on Saturdays, the pious bone gatherers had to break the rule of observing the Sabbath. Some bones were fractured by the operation of the excavation machinery. "The Rabbinate" (i.e., Murmelstein) directed that these fragments also be gathered for proper reburial. Since the IKG crew could not interfere with the work of the building crew, the municipal workers were asked to pick up and deposit bone fragments in coffins provided for this purpose and to do so while under observation by the IKG crew.[138] But this was the only concession by municipal authorities to Jewish piety.

The construction project needed an area for site huts and for storing building supplies. To prepare an area of the cemetery that was adjacent to the building site for this purpose, the workers simply flattened the gravestones. While the burials were not disturbed, the IKG crew could neither undertake any exhumations nor record who was buried in that area.[139]

The continuous watch by men of the IKG laid bare an additional major grave, that of one Moses Karpeles, whose remains could only be recovered with extreme difficulty, since he was buried in a metal coffin within another metal coffin, which, in turn, was inextricably walled in. The corpse had to be removed by breaking the end walls of the metal coffins at the side of the head. The remains were found to be intact (i.e., not skeletonized), and the traditional burial clothing and tallit in which he was shrouded were still intact.[140]

Before the interruption of the orderly pace of the exhumations, Feldsberg had submitted a list of 116 "graves, in order of [cemetery] groups, which are recommended for special care in consideration of the stature of the persons buried therein."[141] Only about a third of these were exhumed and re-interred during a second phase, including the graves of some prominent Jews who lived and died in Vienna during the early phase of its modern Jewish community. Some examples of those on Feldsberg's list include:

- Jews who fell during the Revolution of 1848, among them Dr. Adolf Kolinski, age 27, a candidate for the rabbinate.
- Moritz Hartmann, connected with the political upheavals of 1848, who not only participated in the fight for liberty but was a delegate to the All-German National Assembly at Frankfurt. He died in 1872, age 51.
- There was Israel Hönig von Hönigsberg (1724–1808), an entrepreneur and the first Jew to be knighted, by Emperor Leopold II.
- Salomon Edler von Hertz, another businessman who received a patent of nobility, had the distinction of having been the last official representative of the Jews in Austria under the system of Toleration.
- Several scions of two other distinguished families were buried there, the Wertheim (sometimes, Wertheimer) and the Arnstein families, who, because of their financial positions, were able to exert some influence on behalf of Jewish interests, especially during the reign of the Empress Maria Theresia (Theresa).
- Among the notable Jewish scholars was Jehuda Löb Ben-Ze'eb (1764–1811) who, according to *The Jewish Encyclopedia*, was a member of the *Haskalah* (Jewish Enlightenment) and "the first Jewish grammarian and lexicographer of modern times."[142]
- The IKG crew searched in vain for the remains of Meir Obernik, which were said to be in the grave of his stepson. Obernik (1764–1805) was a translator and commentator of some books of the Bible, and he belonged to the first group of modern scholars to use Hebrew as a literary language. He also collaborated on the journal *Meassef*.[143]
- Jacob Goldenthal was Professor of Oriental Languages at the University of Vienna in the nineteenth century, a time when Jewish university professors were a rarity.
- Dr. David d'Allemane, who died in Vienna in 1869, age 39, was Professor of Philosophy in London.
- Josef Fischhof (1804–1857), pianist and noted interpreter of Bach and Beethoven, was Professor at the Vienna Conservatory.

Some who were buried at the Währing Cemetery were, by virtue of their far-flung connections, employed in international relations:

- Salomon Brandeis-Weikersheim (1813–1877) was the Consul General of Great Britain.
- Siegmund Edler von Wertheimstein (1797–1854), Director of the Austrian National Bank, was Royal Spanish Consul.
- A Dutch descendent of Jews driven from Spain and Portugal at the end of the fifteenth century, Count Joseph Henry Teixeira de Mattos, Consul General of the Netherlands, died at age 70 in 1898. His and his wife's were among the last burials at the cemetery; they were buried near their son, who died in 1858 at age 24.
- Karl Ritter (Knight) von Weil (1806–1878) was Privy Councilor at the Ministry for External Affairs.
- Adam Nathan Freiherr (Baron) von Arnstein (1748–1838) was Swedish Consul and holder of the Order of Wasa.

Here we must mention von Arnstein's wife, who was buried nearby, Franziska ("Fanny") was one of the daughters of Daniel Itzig, the Court Jew and Court Banker of the Prussian King Frederick II the Great. Bright, educated, and charming, Fanny established in the Vienna of Joseph II the kind of salon she knew from Berlin, which soon became Vienna's leading salon. During the Congress of Vienna (1815), which in the aftermath of the Napoleonic wars would establish forty years of peace based on the balance of powers, diplomats and councilors from the great powers of Europe would meet at her salon, among them luminaries such as Austria's Klemens von Metternich, France's Charles de Talleyrand, Great Britain's Sir Arthur Wellington, and Prussia's Karl von Hardenberg. Aside from also being a leading organizer of Jewish as well as general charities for the poor, she supported the arts (e.g., the founding of the *Gesellschaft der Musikfreunde*, "Society of the Friends of Music") and was the sometime sponsor of Mozart.[144]

Among the many other philanthropists buried at the Währing Cemetery were Leopold Ritter von Lämel (1790–1867), Prague City Councilor knighted by Emperor Franz (Francis), and Hirsch Kolisch (1788–1876), the founder of the Austrian Institute for the Deaf-Mute.

Some distinguished rabbis were also buried there:

- The exhumation of Meier Popper-Almas (1767–1841) was requested by former residents of Burgenland, who held the memory of this famous preacher in great reverence.
- Rabbi Chaim Baruch Maestro (died 1817) came to Vienna from Hebron.
- Rabbi Lazar Horowitz's remains were among the last ones exhumed. He had been called to Vienna by Isaac Löw von Hofmannsthal because he favored a more orthodox rabbi than the liberally inclined Rabbi Mannheimer. Though generally strict in his many rulings and responsa as President of the Rabbinical Council of Vienna, Horowitz was able, for the sake of peace within the communities that consulted him, to accept some latitude in interpretation where inconclusive rabbinic tradition permitted.[145]
- Josef Szanto (1816–1873) was the first Jewish chaplain of the Imperial Army.

Among other military men buried at the Währing Cemetery were:

- Simon Wertheim, Lieutenant of the Mounted Sharpshooters Corps, one of the first Jewish officers after Jews were admitted to military service in the Imperial Army, who died at age 34 in 1811 during the Napoleonic wars.
- Edmund Schwarz, M.D., Corvette Captain of the Imperial Navy, who circumnavigated the world on a scientific mission and authored its medical report.
- Benjamin Salomon Spitzer, who undertook two circumnavigations for the young United States, died in Vienna in 1820 at age 45.

The second phase of exhumations and re-interment proceeded desultorily. By September 5, 1941, Feldsberg reported forty-one exhumations. After that, there was a pause of three months for the following reasons: First, the Jewish High Holidays, and second, all available IKG personnel were employed in connection with the second set of deportation transports. On December 10, five more exhumations were reported; on December 15, six; on December 24, seven; and on January 3, 1942, two more.

A number of the people on Feldsberg's list achieved their prominence by being the financiers of rulers. Considering the Nazis' vituperation against what they perceived as the perniciously predominant *Weltfinanzjudentum* (international-finance-Jewry), it is understandable that Feldsberg did not mention that fact.

The last exhumations were those of Isak Löw Hofmann von Hofmannsthal and Isak Noe Mannheimer and their wives.[146] There is something ironic in this juxtaposition, for the two were antagonists at the time of the rise of the modern Jewish community of Vienna. In particular, they were at odds about the turn that Judaism would have to take to survive in the world of political and social equality, for which Jews had long yearned and to which they would have to adjust. Mannheimer, a Danish Jew, who was deeply influenced by the reforms engendered in Berlin by Moses Mendelssohn, was brought to Vienna as a teacher of Hebrew and Scriptures and appointed as "preacher" when the first modern synagogue was established. The Imperial authorities did not permit him to have the title of rabbi, but he was so regarded by his fellow Jews that in time he was considered chief rabbi of Vienna. Because of the strong adherence to tradition on the part of the Jews who were coming from the provinces to settle in Vienna, Mannheimer compromised his Reformism and retained Hebrew as the liturgical language, as well as all the rituals and their associated commandments, and he encouraged the collaboration of Cantor Solomon Sulzer in developing traditional chants for the modern ear. Mannheimer's prayer book, which included his translation of the liturgy into German to facilitate understanding by those worshippers not versed in Hebrew, became standard throughout the Austrian part of the Austro-Hungarian Empire.[147] Hofmannsthal viewed what he regarded as Mannheimer's Reformism with suspicion and, therefore, invited Rabbi Horowitz to Vienna to solidify a more traditional orthodoxy among the community's Jews. Mannheimer facilitated the survival of Judaism under the pressures of assimilation and anti-Semitism, challenges that Mendelssohn did not anticipate. It would take a goodly part of the nineteenth and twentieth centuries for the development of more traditional orthodoxies to face up to these challenges. In the meantime, as was the case with Moses Mendelssohn's descendants, the

Opportunistic composer Richard Strauss (on the right), who had a Jewish daughter-in-law, raising his arm in what appears to be a half-hearted "Heil Hitler" in 1938. (WStLA Fotosammlung allgemein FC - Positive: C 124/9.1)

son of Hofmannsthal, the proponent of strict traditionalism, converted to Christianity. In his report, Feldsberg remembered him, aside from his having been a businessman and philanthropist, as the "grandfather" (should be great-grandfather) of the poet and librettist Hugo von Hofmannsthal.

It was winter when the last two exhumations took place. Germany and Japan were at war against the United States. Himmler had put a stop to all emigration. And soon the deportation of the remaining Jews of Vienna would begin in earnest. There are reports of further exhumations, but there was no more major effort.

The beginning of the exhumations at Währing Cemetery coincided with the onset of the systematic murder of the Jews behind the advancing front in the war against the Soviet Union, which began at that time. We do not know why the Nazis permitted the pious exhumations and re-interments in Vienna. Were they meant as a distraction or as a reassurance for the Jews of Vienna, or even for the general population? The Nazis and others could not have been very happy to be reminded of the Jewish connections of the "Waltz King" or of Hofmannsthal, the librettist of the great Richard Strauss and author of the modern version of the medieval morality play *Jedermann* (*Everyman*), the mainstay of the yearly Salzburg Festival. Were the killing pits of the East meant as a grisly perversion of the way the Jews proceeded in their pious task in Vienna: Have the Jews dig their own graves, line them up tightly in their graves, and kill them where they would come to eternal rest, obliterate their identity and the record of their ever having existed? While the obliteration of the quick was proceeding, that of the dead would have to wait a bit longer.

■ ■ ■

[This concludes the first volume of *Choices under Duress of the Holocaust*. The second volume, scheduled to appear about two years after the first, deals with the subsequent fate of the Viennese Jewish Community during the remainder of World War II. A major focus of the second volume is on the actions of the Viennese leadership following their deportation to the ghetto of Theresienstadt/Terezin. — Ed.]

Notes

Foreword

1. Anna Hájková, "The Last of the Self-Righteous: Claude Lanzmann's Version of Benjamin Murmelstein," *Histoire@Politique: Politique, culture, société*, September 18, 2014, http://www.histoire-politique.fr/index.php?numero=32&rub=comptes-rendus&item=499.
2. Hannah Arendt, *Eichmann in Jerusalem: A Report on the Banality of Evil* (New York: Viking Press, 1963); Raul Hilberg, *The Destruction of the European Jews* (Chicago: Triangle Press, 1961); Isaiah Trunk, *Judenrat: The Jewish Councils in Eastern Europe under Nazi Occupation* (New York: Macmillan, 1972).
3. Doron Rabinovici, *Eichmann's Jews: The Jewish Administration of Holocaust Vienna, 1938–1945* (Cambridge, UK: Polity Press, 2011), 71, 73.
4. Dan Diner, *Beyond the Conceivable: Studies on Germany, Nazism, and the Holocaust* (Berkeley: University of California Press, 2000), 117–29; and Dan Michman, "Jewish Leadership *in Extremis*," in Dan Stone, ed., *The Historiography of the Holocaust* (London/New York: Palgrave Macmillan, 2005), 341–63.

Preface

1. Leonard H. Ehrlich, "Philosophical Faith and the Future of Mankind," in *Philosophical Faith and the Future of Humanity*, ed. Helmut Wautischer, Alan M. Olson, and Gregory J. Walters (Dordrecht/Heidelberg/London/New York: Springer, 2012), 35–44; idem, "Fragments of a Philosophical Autobiography," *Existenz* 5, no. 2 (2010): 7–59, http://www.existenz.us.
2. _____, "Geschätzt und gescholten: Benjamin Murmelstein in Wien 1938–1943" ("Treasured and Reproached: Benjamin Murmelstein in Vienna 1938–1943"), *S:I.M.O.N.*—**S**hoah: **I**ntervention. **M**ethods. Documentati**ON**. It is available online at http://www.vwi.ac.at/index.php/veranstaltungen/simon-wiesenthal-lectures/icalrepeat.detail/2008/05/13/6/-/leonard-h-ehrlich-geschaetzt-und-gescholten-benjamin-murmelstein-in-wien-1938–43.
3. _____, *Karl Jaspers: Philosophy as Faith* (Amherst: University of Massachusetts Press, 1975).
4. _____, *Fraglichkeit der jüdischen Existenz: Philosophische Untersuchungen zum modernen Schicksal der Juden* (Fermata philosophica; Freiburg [Breisgau]/München: Verlag Karl Alber, 1993).

Chapter 1

1. A German-language immigrant newspaper that was published in New York.
2. I collected the *Kalenderblätter*. When it was time to pack up and emigrate, my father permitted me to pack only one.
3. Herbert Rosenkranz, "The Anschluss and the Tragedy of Austrian Jewry 1938–1945," in Josef Fraenkl, ed., *The Jews of Austria: Essays on Their Life, History and Destruction* (London: Vallentine, Mitchell & Co., 1967).
4. Hugo Gold, *Geschichte der Juden in Wien: Ein Gedenkbuch* (Tel Aviv: Olamenu, 1966).
5. H. G. Adler, *Theresienstadt. 1941–1945: Das Antlitz einer Zwangsgemeinschaft, Geschichte Soziologie Psychologie* (Tübingen: Mohr, 1955); idem, *Die verheimlichte Wahrheit: Theresienstädter Dokumente* (Tübingen: Mohr Siebeck, 1958). [The former book has recently appeared in English translation as *Theresienstadt 1941–1945: The Face of a Coerced Community* (trans. Belinda Cooper; New York: Cambridge University Press, 2017) — Ed.]
6. [This book has recently appeared in a German translation: Benjamin Murmelstein, *Theresienstadt: Eichmanns Vorzeige-Ghetto* (trans. Karin Fleischanderl; Wien: Czernin, 2014) — Ed.]

7. Isaiah Trunk, *Judenrat: The Jewish Councils in Eastern Europe under Nazi Occupation* (New York: Macmillan, 1972).
8. Clipping from 1961, date and page not known.
9. [These tapes have been donated to the United States Holocaust Memorial Museum in Washington, D.C., where they have been digitized and are accessible to researchers. The typed transcription of the tapes is also to be found there. — Ed.]
10. Thirty years later, *The New York Times* reported that the restriction was still in place. At that time, the position of the United States—which had supplied of much of the archival material and is a signatory of the group of nations that established the Tracing Service—was that sixty years after the end of the war the material ought to be opened to researchers and copies be made available to other archives. See Roger Cohen, "U.S.-German Flare-Up over Vast Nazi Camp Archives," www.nytimes.com, Feb. 20, 2006. It was only in November 2007 that the archives were finally opened up.
11. [On Dr. Kapralik (1895–1993), see Anthony Grenville, "Charles Kapralik," *The Association of Jewish Refugees Journal* (Dec. 2013), www.ajr.org.uk/index.cfm/section.journal/issue.Dec13/article=14001. — Ed.]
12. [Following LHE's death, the materials, consisting of both papers and audio tapes, were donated to the United States Holocaust Memorial Museum in Washington, D.C. — Ed.]

Chapter 2

1. A detailed day-by-day account of the takeover of Austria, March 9–15, 1938, is given by Dieter Wagner and Gerhard Tomkowitz, *"Ein Volk, ein Reich, ein Führer!": Der Anschluss Österreichs, 1938* (München: Piper, 1968); in English: *Anschluss: The Week Hitler Seized Vienna* (New York/London: St. Martin's Press, 1971). For a documentation of the takeover, see Heinz Arnberger, Winfried R. Garscha, and Christa Meitterrutzner, *"Anschluss" 1938. Eine Dokumentation* (Wien: Österreichischer Bundesverlag, 1988), which was compiled for DÖW (Dokumentationsarchiv des österreichischen Widerstands [Documentation Archive of the Austrian Resistance]) with introductory essays by various contributors.
2. The authors' taped interview with Dr. Emil Lehmann, New York, on January 25, 1979.
3. Deuteronomy 25:17–19.
4. Lehmann interview.
5. Wagner and Tomkowitz, *Ein Volk*, 133; *Anschluss*, 88.
6. Ibid., 194; not in the English edition. Kurt von Schuschnigg, *Im Kampf gegen Hitler: Die Überwindung der Anschlussidee* (Wien: Amalthea, 1969) 33, 429.
7. About Hitler's entry into Linz, see Wagner and Tomkowitz, *Ein Volk*, 288ff. The episode of the first public expression of Nazi anti-Semitism is not mentioned by Wagner and Tomkowitz but is from the authors' memory.
8. "Bericht von Dr. Leo Landau," Yad Vashem Archives, Jerusalem (hereafter, YV) 01/244, 10f.
9. Siegfried Kolisch to *Jüdische Historische Dokumentation*, Feb. 1, 1948. DÖW 21582/4.
10. Wagner and Tomkowitz, *Ein Volk*, 331f; in English: 219f.
11. The man's name was Josef Ehrlich, the father of one of the present authors.
12. The emergency welfare efforts are reported by Schwarz and confirmed by Landau. See Rosa Rachel Schwarz, "Zwei Jahre Fürsorge der Gemeinde Wien unter Hitler," YV 01/73, 1f. Also Landau, "Bericht," 11.
13. See Schwarz, "Zwei Jahre."
14. Schwarz reports the photographing in "Zwei Jahre," 2. The archive of KZ-Gedenkstätte Dachau has the original filmstrip, from which the authors obtained copies of some of the frames; some of these are displayed in this book. Some of the photographs are also in DÖW. [The editor was unable to find these copies, perhaps since most of the files had by then been donated to the United States Holocaust Memorial Museum in Washington, D.C. — Ed.]
15. [This picture is reproduced in chapter 10. — Ed.]
16. Jonny Moser, *Die Judenverfolgung in Österreich 1938–1945* (Wien/Frankfurt/Main/Zürich: Europa-Verlag, 1966), 7.
17. Gold, *Geschichte der Juden in Wien*, 62.
18. Ibid., 64.
19. Schuschnigg, *Im Kampf*, 97.
20. Wagner and Tomkowitz, *Ein Volk*, 133; in English: 88.

21. See Jonny Moser, "Die Verfolgung der Juden," in Wolfgang Neugebauer ed., *Widerstand und Verfolgung in Wien 1934–1945: Eine Dokumentation Vol. 3* (Dokumentationsarchiv des Österreichischen Widerstandes; Wien: Österreichischer Bundesverlag für Unterricht, Wissenschaft und Kunst, 1975), 195.
22. See the "Friedmann" entry in Georg Weis, *Totenbuch Theresienstadt 1: Deportierte aus Österreich* (Wien: Jüdisches Komitee für Theresienstadt, 1971), 34. More will be related about Friedmann in later chapters of this book.
23. Gold, *Geschichte*, 48.
24. See the "Stricker" entry in Weis, *Totenbuch Theresienstadt*, 140.
25. About Ehrlich, see Gold, *Geschichte,* passim.
26. Ibid., 1. sequel, Feb. 14.
27. Ibid., 2. sequel, no date.
28. Ibid.
29. Ibid.
30. See Frederic Morton, *The Rothschilds: A Family Portrait* (New York: Atheneum, 1963), part IX, "Hitler versus Rothschild."
31. Great Britain, France and Italy counted as the protectors of the independence of Austria.
32. *Neues Wiener Abendblatt*, March 17, 1938, 7; cited in Botz, *Wien*, 93.
33. Wagner and Tomkowitz, *Ein Volk*, 309.
34. *Reichsgesetzblatt 1938*, Part 1, no. 28, issued Berlin, Mar. 18, 1938, 257.
35. Ibid., no. 37, Mar. 24, 1938, 303.
36. A copy of the four frames of the placard are in DÖW 1554.
37. Franz von Papen, *Der Wahrheit eine Gasse* (München: P. List, 1952) 491f; in English: *Memoir* (trans. Brian Connell; New York: Dutton 1953 [1952]), 432.
38. So reads the report of the meeting in the files of the archbishopric of Vienna that was written by Dr. (later Bishop) Jakob Weinbacher, who, as Innitzer's secretary, accompanied the cardinal together with Chaplain Johann Jauner von Schrotzenegg. However, only Jauner was present at the meeting between Innitzer and Hitler. Innitzer and Jauner are the only sources for Weinbacher's report, Innitzer the only source for von Papen's notes. See Viktor Reimann, *Innitzer: Kardinal zwischen Hitler und Rom* (Wien: Molden, 1967), 98.
39. See Weinbacher's report in the archive of the Vienna archdiocese as cited in Reimann, *Innitzer*, 101; also Erika Weinzierl, "Christen und Juden nach der NS-Machtergreifung in Österreich," in *Anschluß 1938: Protokoll des Symposiums in Wien am 14. und 15. März 1978–Wien 1981* (Veröffentlichungen der Wissenschaftlichen Kommission des Theodor-Körner-Stiftungsfonds und des Leopold-Kunschak-Preises zur Erforschung der österreichischen Geschichte der Jahre 1918 bis 1938, München: Oldenbourg, 1981), 179f.
40. Botz, *Wien*, 119; Botz cites *Reichspost*, Mar. 13, 1938, 5.
41. Weinzierl, "Christen und Juden," 179; also Botz, *Wien*, 120.
42. Botz, ibid.
43. The Dollfuss-Schuschnigg regime operated under an experimental interim constitution conceived along the lines of the encyclical *Quadragesimo anno*, issued in 1931 under the pontificate of Pius XI, as a successor to and on the fortieth anniversary of Pope Leo's XIII encyclical *Rerum novarum* (1891). The earlier encyclical sought to lay the basis for a Christian response to the polarization of modern class divisions between possessing capitalists and laboring masses. The later encyclical sought to supplant the class structure of society by suggesting a political structure of the state in accordance with vocational groupings (*Stände*, i.e., estates or corporate associations), which would cut across class lines and be members of an integral political unity, each contributing to the whole in accordance with its vocation, and guided by Christian charity. In light of the political as well as economic failure of the new democratic Republic of Austria, Dollfuss, less than fifteen years after its establishment, and less than two years after the promulgation of *Quadragesimo anno*, instituted the experiment of the *Ständestaat* (corporate state). There were no precedents for this experiment. For the democratic and liberal mentality, it was antidemocratically authoritarian ("Fascist"). For the Nazis, it was an obstacle to their gaining power. In this context, we have to understand the attempted Nazi coup of 1934, resulting in the murder of Dollfuss. Years later, Schuschnigg, who had succeeded Dollfuss, gave a sober assessment of the experiment but chafed under such designations as "clerico-fascist police-state—the unconstitutional constitution." (See Schuschnigg, *Im Kampf*, 98ff.) Be that as it may, it must be noted that von Papen sought to reconcile the German Catholics to the Nazi regime by pointing to the conformance of

its social program with the suggestions of *Quadragesimo anno*; similarly Pope Pius XI, the promulgator of the encyclical, approved of the social program of Mussolini's regime and did not break with it until 1938 when, upon Hitler's urging, Mussolini instituted an anti-Semitic policy in Italy.

44. See note 40.
45. Because of the predominantly Roman Catholic population of the Saar Territory, the Catholic Church's endorsement in the matter of the Saar plebiscite was of vital importance to the Nazi regime. The maneuverings of the regime to attain that endorsement have been the subject of many studies. Our references to this event are based mainly on Guenter Lewy, *The Catholic Church and Nazi Germany* (New York: McGraw-Hill, 1965), 182–201; Gerhard Paul, *"Deutsche Mutter, heim zu Dir!" Warum es misslang, Hitler an der Saar zu schlagen: Der Saarkampf 1933–1935* (Köln: Bund-Verlag, 1984), therein esp. 233–56.
46. Bornewasser was bishop of Trier. Church jurisdiction over the population of the Saar territory is divided between the bishops of Trier and Speyer.
47. Erika Weinzierl, *Zu wenig Gerechte: Österreicher und Judenverfolgung 1938–1945* (Graz: Styria, 1969), 98; Reimann, *Innitzer*, 236f.
48. The bishops of Salzburg carry the title of Prince-Bishop or Sovereign-Bishop (*Fürst Bischof*) from the time when the bishop of Salzburg was also the ruler of the duchy. Subsequently, the duchy was crown-land of the Habsburg Empire and a province (*Land*) of the Republic.
49. Solemn Declaration, see note 6 supra.
50. Ibid.
51. Walther Hofer, ed., *Der Nationalsozialismus: Dokumente 1933–1945* (Frankfurt/Main: Fischer Bücherei, 1957), 30.
52. Ibid., 31.
53. Raul Hilberg, *The Destruction of the European Jews* (Chicago: Quadrangle Books, 1961), 14ff., 666f.
54. Weinzierl, *Zu wenig Gerechte*, 98ff; Reimann, *Innitzer*, 231ff.
55. Weinzierl, ibid., 99.
56. That the Catholic Church of Austria suffered this setback within a few weeks of the endorsement is a matter of bitter irony. What, after all, motivated Cardinal Innitzer and the other bishops in working out the endorsement with Bürckel? It was precisely their concern that the traditionally predominant role of the Church in the education of the young—a role that was protected by the concordat between the Vatican and the Imperial government negotiated in 1855 to counteract the anticlerical tendencies of an age of liberalism, and which continued in force after the fall of the Habsburg Empire and the establishment of the Republic—not be declared null and void through the incorporation of Austria into Nazi Germany. As it happens, the concordat between Nazi Germany and the Vatican of 1933 had been declared—by Bürckel—to be invalid for the Saar Territory on the grounds that the latter did not belong to Germany at the time the concordat was negotiated. And, of course, even if the validity of the 1933 concordat were to be regarded as extensible to Austria, by 1938 the provisions guaranteeing to the Church its traditional role in educating the young had been violated by the Nazi regime. That this motivation was at play is reflected in Innitzer's promise to Hitler "that the Austrian Catholics will be the most loyal sons of the great realm . . . provided that schools and churches may continue to enjoy the freedom vouchsafed in the Concordat, and provided primarily that the Church will not be excluded from the education of the young, as happened in the Reich" (Weinzierl, "Christen und Juden," 179). It is curious that in spite of Innitzer's confronting Hitler with the latter fact, Hitler's response to Innitzer was to promise him "everything," a promise accepted by Innitzer at its face value.
57. Weinzierl, *Zu wenig Gerechte*, 98.
58. Gold, *Geschichte*, 55, 71.
59. Genesis 4:9.
60. See Botz, *Wien*, 139ff, for an account and a discussion of this episode.
61. Ibid., 143.
62. Ibid., 141.
63. See ibid., 141; Botz cites Oskar Helmer, *50 Jahre erlebte Geschichte* (Wien: Verlag der Wiener Volks-buchhandlung, 1957), 183. See also Jacques Hannak, *Karl Renner und seine Zeit: Versuch einer Biog-raphie* (Wien: Europa-Verlag, 1965), 648ff.
64. In an interview with the authors.
65. Botz, *Wien*, 147f.
66. Ibid., 129ff.

67. Ibid., 134ff.
68. Ibid., 169.
69. Personal recollection of the authors.
70. Botz, *Wien*, 163.
71. Wagner and Tomkowitz, *Ein Volk*, 294; in English, *Anschluss*, 198.
72. See, e.g., Herbert A. Strauss, "Jewish Emigration from Germany," *Leo Baeck Institute Year Book* 25 (1980), Table VII, 326.
73. About the "Leadership Principle," see Karl Dietrich Bracher, *Die deutsche Diktatur: Entstehung, Struktur, Folgen des Nationalsozialismus* (Köln: Kiepenheuer & Witsch 1969), 370ff.
74. The protocol of Hitler's meeting with the chiefs of the *Wehrmacht*, Werner von Blomberg and Werner von Fritsch (both army) and Erich Raeder (navy), is known as the "Hossbach minutes"; also present were Konstantin von Neurath as foreign minister and Göring in his many capacities as the second most powerful man in the regime. The protocol was used at the Nuremberg Tribunal and is published in *Akten zur Deutschen Auswärtigen Politik 1918–1945* (Baden-Baden / Göttingen 1950ff), series D, vol. I, 25ff. In English, *Documents on German Foreign Policy 1918–1945*, part D, vol. I, document no. 19 (London, 1948ff). Excerpts in Hofer, *Der Nationalsozialismus*, 193ff. Cf. Alan Bullock, *Hitler, A Study in Tyranny* (New York: Harper & Row, 1964), 367ff; Bracher, *Die deutsche Diktatur*, 334ff.
75. About Hitler's war plan see Bracher, *Diktatur*, 330ff; Karl Dietrich Bracher, Wolfgang Schulz, and Gerhard Sauer, eds., *Die nationalsozialistische Machtergreifung: Studien zur Errichtung des totalitären Herrschaftssystems in Deutschland 1933/34. Vol. III, Die Mobilmachung der Gewalt* (Frankfurt [Main]/Köln: Ullstein, 1974), 85f; also Hitler's *Mein Kampf*, book II, ch. 14.
76. No. 10 of the "Fourteen Points" states that "The Peoples of Austria-Hungary . . . should be accorded the freest opportunity of autonomous development"; no. 12 is a similar reference to "other nationalities which are now under Turkish rule." The difficulties of drawing political lines congruent with the distribution of nationalities is alluded to in no. 13 with respect to the reestablishment of the Polish state: "An independent Polish state should be erected which should include the territories inhabited by indisputably Polish populations." The stress on establishing and guaranteeing the sovereignty of national states is reiterated in no. 4 of the "Four Principles" in Wilson's speech to Congress on February 11, 1918: "[A]ll well-defined national aspirations shall be accorded the utmost satisfaction that can be accorded them without introducing new or perpetuating old elements of discord or antagonism." Binding settlements of questions of territory or sovereignty should be left to a League of Nations, according to Wilson's speech of July 4, 1918. Germany dissociated herself from the League of Nations within nine months of the appointment of Hitler as chancellor. For President Wilson's "Points" see *Encyclopaedia Britannica*, Vol. 9 (Chicago/London/Toronto, 1951), 566. On Germany's leaving the League, cf. Bullock, *Hitler*, 321ff.
77. The duress under which Schuschnigg and Hácha had to deal with Hitler has often been described. See, e.g., Bullock, *Hitler*, 422ff, 483ff.
78. Hofer, *Der Nationalsozialismus*, 221.
79. Cited in Bullock, *Hitler*, 493.
80. Hitler's telling remark was made and elaborated in his conversation on November 24, 1938, with Oswald Pirow, who at that time held both the Defense Ministry and the Ministry for Economic Affairs of South Africa. Pirow had urged Hitler to maintain the momentum of cooperation with the government of Great Britain, signaled by the latter acceding to Hitler in the recent Munich agreement ceding Czechoslovakia's Sudetenland to Germany. Among the ways Hitler could safeguard Britain's cooperation would be to offer an acceptable way of solving the Jewish question. Hitler's rejection was uncompromising: "The problem would be solved in the near future. This is his unshakable will . . . The Jews will one day disappear from Europe." The suggestion that the Jews be ceded some territory, say in a former colony of Germany's (which Germany lost together with the First World War), was vehemently rejected. It is in this connection that Hitler opined to Pirow that he was "merely exporting an idea. This [idea] is not National-Socialism . . . [but] anti-Semitism." Cf. Helmut Krausnick, "Judenverfolgung," in Hans Buchheim, Martin Broszat, Hans-Adolf Jacobsen, and Helmut Krausnick, eds., *Anatomie des SS-Staates*, Vol. 1 (3rd ed.; München, 1982) 280ff. Krausnick cites from *Akten zur Deutschen Auswärtigen Politik 1918–1945*, series D (1937–1945), Vol. IV, *Die Nachwirkungen von München* (Baden-Baden, 1951), 291ff.
81. Winston S. Churchill, *The Gathering Storm* (Boston: Houghton Mifflin, 1948), 83f.
82. The main works about the SS, on which our account is based, are Hans Buchheim, "Die SS—das

Herrschaftsinstrument" in Buchheim et al., *Anatomie des SS-Staates*, vol. 1, 15–214 (an early version of Buchheim's study is available in English translation as "The Position of the SS in the Third Reich" in Hajo Holborn, ed., *Republic to Third Reich*, New York, 1973); Heinz Hoehne, *The Order of the Death's Head: The Story of Hitler's S.S.* (trans. Richard H. Barry; New York, 1971); Shlomo Aronson, *Richard Heydrich und die Frühgeschichte von Gestapo und SD 1931–1935*, diss. Berlin 1967; as well as on various rolls of documents of the Nuremberg Tribunal.

83. See Bracher, *Die deutsche Diktatur*, especially 230ff.
84. See note 70.
85. For a precise account of this process, see Buchheim, "Die SS," 35–59.
86. See Bracher, *Die deutsche Diktatur*, 381ff; Buchheim, "Die SS."
87. See Buchheim, "Die SS," 35ff; Hoehne, *The Order*, passim.
88. See Buchheim, "Die SS," 59ff; Hoehne, *The Order*, ch. 9.
89. See Buchheim, "Die SS," 66ff; Hoehne, *The Order*, ch. 10.
90. See Buchheim, ibid., 113ff.
91. See Hans Buchheim, "Befehl und Gehorsam" in Hans Buchheim, Martin Broszat, Hans-Adolf Jacobsen, and Helmut Krausnick, eds., *Anatomie des SS-Staates*, Vol. 1 (3rd ed.; München, 1982).
92. "Die Eigenständigkeit des Sicherheitsdienstes," no signature, no date (ca. spring 1939), AHS/GSA, T 175, Roll 239; also IZG, MA 433, frames 680–683.
93. Adolf Böhm, *Die zionistische Bewegung* (2 vols., Berlin: Jüdischer Verlag, 1935–1937).
94. Within the SD, the role of "inspector" was modeled on the Prussian inspector of the civil service and the army. According to SS regulations, the function of the inspector was to "maintain contact, instruct and supervise. He has no power of command, and no leadership function, but in the main the right to suggest improvements." Heydrich kept control over men on far-flung extension assignments in their execution of their many tasks. In order to streamline his control system, Heydrich, in February 1939, gave all the *SD-Führer* within *SS-Oberabschnitte* the additional title of Inspector of Security Police and vice versa. This means that as of that date Eichmann carried both functions. See "*Dienstanweisung*" (service directive) issued by Stabskanzlei I 11, Feb. 22, 1939; AHS/GSA: T 175, roll 239 (also IZG: MA433). Hagen actually exercised the function of inspector (see his reports of inspection trips to Vienna, Oct. 31, 1938 and May 16, 1939). However, as explained above, Eichmann would carry the title of Inspector himself, and, by virtue of his accomplishments in Vienna, would in time outrank Hagen, and Hagen would be his subordinate in the liquidation of Jewish existence in Paris.
95. Aronson, *Heydrich*, 280. The two Brunners are often thought to have been one and the same; see, e.g., Hoehne, *The Order*, 445.
96. See Aronson, *Heydrich*, 267.
97. "II/112 Hagen" to "II/1123" (i.e., Eichmann), handwritten date: Mar. 5, 1938; USNA T175, Roll 413.

Chapter 3

1. "Protokoll über die am 11. Mai 1938, 5 Uhr nachmittags, im Sitzungssaale der Kultusgemeinde stattgefundene Besprechung" (Minutes of conference held at the IKG meeting room, May 11, 1938, at 5 p.m.), CA:A/W (Central Archives for the History of the Jewish People, Jerusalem), 300.
2. For correspondence and other documents pertaining to the dissolution of the Krügerheim and of other endowed welfare and service organizations, and of the liquidation of their properties and assets, see CA: A/W 301.1.
3. The guest book of the *Israelitisches Blindeninstitut Hohe Warte* is deposited at the Leo Baeck Institute, New York.
4. "Überblick über das jüdische Organisationswesen im Lande Österreich," CA: A/W 299. This is a report prepared for and submitted to the Gestapo. Pages 1–5 consist of a summary of the structure of Jewish organized life prior to and subsequent to the Anschluss. Page 6 is a list of *Kultusgemeinden* in Austria. Aside from Vienna, there were thirty-three Jewish communities organized as *Kultusgemeinden*, most of them in the provinces of Lower Austria and Burgenland. Pages 7–29 are lists of other Jewish organizations, which are summarized as follows:

Synagogues and prayer houses	79
Zionist	82
Scientific and cultural	24
Chapters of Agudas Jisroel	8

Veterans	4
Welfare and service	119
Schools	24
Student	22
Sports	11
Professional	24
Landsmannschaften	7
Social	6
Savings	6
Miscellaneous	20

5. Gestapo Hamburg/Staatspolizeistelle to Veranstalter des Logenheims der Hamburger Logen des U.O.B.B. Max Spier, Apr. 17, 1937. YV 02/1127, also WL 504a.
6. Hofer, *Der Nationalsozialismus*, 55.
7. See, e.g., "Fragebogen" dated May 25, 1938, concerning "Verein zur Unterstützung jüdischer Kleingewerbetreibender," CA: A/W 722.
8. See, e.g., "Einweisung" dated Oct. 18, 1938, concerning "Verein der Verwaltungsbeamten der israelitischen Kultusgemeinde," CA: A/W 722.
9. See, e.g., Groser to Engel, Feb. 1, 1939; Engel to Groser, Feb. 21, 1939; Engel to Krüger, May 7, 1939. CA: A/W 301.1.
10. Twersky to Bürckel, July 15, 1938. CA: A/W 301.1.
11. For the following, cf. "Überblick," above.
12. Eichmann to Hagen, Apr. 23, 1938, EICH (Eichmann Trial Papers) 1512.
13. "Entwurf des Aktionsprogramms einer zu gründenden 'Zentralstelle für die Auswanderung der Juden Oesterreichs,'" YV 30/94.
14. It should also be noted that Löwenherz had not as yet found out that Austria had in the interim become the *Ostmark*.
15. Vorstand des Verbandes der türk. Israeliten to IKG, dated May 25, 1938. CA: A/W 301.1.
16. See "Gesetz vom 21. März 1890 betreffend die Regelung der äusseren Verhältnisse der israelitischen Religionsgesellschaft" (Law concerning the Regulation of the External Relations of the Israelite Religious Body), in *Reichsgesetzblatt für die im Reichsrathe vertretenen Königreiche und Länder* (Law Gazette for the Austrian Part of the Austro-Hungarian Empire), fascicle 18, Apr. 15, 1890, 109, item 57. Among the activities regulated by the law are religious schools, ritual baths, ritual slaughter, hospitals, nursing homes, old age homes, poor houses, cemeteries, and synagogues.
17. Löwenherz to "Verband der Türkischen Israeliten," July 22, 1938; Vorstand des Verbandes der türk. Israeliten to Löwenherz, Aug. 1, 1938. CA: A/W 301.1.
18. AN *Vorsprache* Löwenherz at Eichmann, Aug. 17, 1938; Löwenherz papers at the Leo Baeck Institute, New York; hereafter L-papers.
19. N. J. Ovadia and O. Camhi to Loevenhertz [sic!], Mar. 14, 1939. CA: A/W 464.
20. Memorandum for the files concerning the discussion of April 6, 1939, with the representatives of the Sephardi Jews in Vienna, Messrs. Dr. I, Haim and Baruch. CA: A/W 464.
21. Goodman to Löwenherz, Apr. 14, 1939; Löwenherz to Goodman, Apr. 17, 1939. CA: A/W 271.1.
22. Goodman to Löwenherz, Apr. 20, 1939. CA: A/W 271.1.
23. Cf. Max Gruenwald, "The Beginning of the 'Reichsvertretung'," *Leo Baeck Institute Year Book* 1 (1956), 57ff.
24. About the mode and pattern of Jewish emigration in Germany prior to the Anschluss of Austria, see Werner Rosenstock, "Exodus 1933–1939: A Survey of Jewish Emigration from Germany," *Leo Baeck Institute Year Book*, vol. 1 (1956), 373ff; Herbert A. Strauss, "Jewish Emigration from Germany: Nazi Policies and Jewish Responses," Part 1, *Leo Baeck Institute Year Book* 25 (1980), 313ff; Part 2, *Leo Baeck Institute Year Book* 26 (1981), 343ff.
25. Benno Cohn, "Um die Legitimierung des jüdischen Kulturbundes in Deutschland—ein Kapitel des Kampfes um jüdische Autonomie nach 1933," typed transcript of a lecture, Tel-Aviv, June 3, 1945, 1. YV 01/6.
26. Ibid., 7.
27. Ibid., 1.
28. Notes by Dr. Kurt Jakob Ball (Ball-Kaduri) of the discussion following Dr. Herzfeld's lecture on the founding of the *Reichsvertretung*, Tel-Aviv, Jan. 1, 1945, 1f. YV 01/10.

29. For the following, see "Der Steuer-Abwehrkampf der Reichsvertretung," an 8-page typed report by Dr. Kurt Jakob Ball (later: Ball-Kaduri), May 1944. YV 01/1 see also *Yad Vashem Studies*, vol. II, 178.
30. See, e.g., internal memorandum by SD II/112, dated Mar. 15, 1938. EICH 1509. The memorandum reads in part: "What was not to be suspected has happened, the [RV] wants to effect the Anschluss also for the fellow members of their race [*Rassegenossen*] in Austria. [On April 14, 1939] the RV even had the impudence . . . of asking whether there are any reservations about their representative's entry into Austria. . . . Of course the request was denied."
31. Carl Kapralik, "Wien 1938/39." Original typescript deposited at LBI/NY, 10f.
32. See Herbert Rosenkranz, *Verfolgung und Selbstbehauptung: Die Juden in Osterreich 1938–1945* (Wien/München: Herold, 1978), especially chapters xi to xiii.
33. Kapralik, "Wien 1938/39," 15f.
34. Ibid., 16.
35. Appointment of Kapralik, dated June 27, 1938, in "Beschluss-Buch nr. 67" (from May 22, 1938, to July 24, 1938), CA: A/W 88/64.
36. AN Löwenherz's first meeting with Raffegerst, May 16, 1938; L-papers.
37. Cf. Kapralik, "Wien," 12. See also reports from that period in the files of AJDC Archives, file 28/ folder 445. For example, J. Rosen of the Poland Branch (Warsaw) of the European Executive Offices (Headquarters: Paris) writes from Warsaw (May 8, 1938) to the Main Office (New York) about his trip to Vienna: "The Gemeinde has been permitted to reopen a few days ago. Dr. Löwenstein [*sic*] and Mr. Engel are trying desperately to do everything in their power but their possibilities in every respect are very limited . . . thousands are besieging the soup kitchens where close to 9,000 people are being fed daily . . . all the Gemeinde can do for the desperate people is to give the neediest a few Marks. In cooperation with the Council for German Jewry we have been supporting the kitchens but this is growing to proportions where the amounts we have been able to give them are utterly insufficient." In the "Office memorandum on the visit to Vienna by Mr. Landesco and Mr. Schweitzer," no date, but the visit took place "shortly after the [IKG] was permitted to function again," i.e., about the same time as Mr. Rosen's. On p. 2 we read: "General kitchens were visited and it was agreed that this activity, done quietly and efficiently, thanks to the devotion of a number of volunteers, should be extended to cover this urgent need; within a short time it is planned to extend the number of kitchens to feed 12,000 persons."
38. Kapralik, "Wien," 12. According to the "Report by Messers. Schweitzer and Bein on their recent trip to Vienna and Berlin," dated Aug. 18, 1938, and filed at the AJDC Paris Office, the "income of the [IKG] . . . from Jewish Community taxes . . . [has] fallen from RM 355,000 in January to RM 92,000 in July." As regards budget for the period May 3 to July 31, they report: "Ordinary Budget . . . RM 340,200," which, however, includes for "General Relief" the extraordinary amount of RM 160,000; "Extraordinary Budget . . . RM 787,200," which includes Soup Kitchens RM 208,000, Food Packages RM 35,000, Relief RM 126,000, Relief to Intellectuals and Provincial Communities RM 93,600.
39. This was based on the 1933 *Ha'avara* (transfer) Agreement that allowed Jews possessing sufficient funds to emigrate from Germany to British Mandatory Palestine, thereby enabling Nazi Germany preemptively to get around anticipated trade restrictions.
40. AN Löwenherz's first meeting with Raffegerst, May 16, 1938; L-papers.
41. Ibid.
42. *Jüdische Pressezentrale Zürich*, vol. 21, no. 988, Apr. 29, 1938, p. 6; available at LBI/NY.
43. Especially the law office of one Dr. Gallop, one of whose former law clerks, according to Kapralik, was Dr. Erich Rajakovic, an illegal Nazi, who became the Gauleiter of Vienna. With this connection, Dr. Gallop was able to engage in an efficient fleecing operation. Kapralik, "Wien," 4f. On Rajakovic's role in this earliest phase of effecting the Nazi Jewish policy in Vienna, see also William R. Perl, *Operation Action: Rescue from the Holocaust* (New York, 1978), passim.
44. At the time the IKG was reopened, there were still a few cases pending of rich Jews having to leave within a short time but having no place to go. Soon after his release and installation in his new position, Löwenherz mentioned the urgency of such cases at the first meeting with David Schweitzer, the vice-chairman of the AJDC European Executive Council in Paris. "Office Memorandum on the Visit to Vienna by Mr. Landesco and Mr. Schweitzer," no date (early May 1938), AJDC SM Archives, file 28/ folder 445.
45. *Jüdische Pressezentrale*, vol. 21, no. 988, Apr. 29, 1938, p. 6.
46. Ibid. Our emphasis.

47. Ibid.
48. At least one person had the idea of raising funds for the relief of the Jews of Austria by means of the forced taxation of all Jews worldwide, not only of the victims. Among the recommendations made in "Digest of Report by Captain B. M. Woolf on his Visit to Austria Made to the Council for German Jewry [London] July 25, 1938," we find the following: "D. That in order to raise funds in every country in the world, an attempt be made to institute a levy on every Jew, in place of the method of voluntary contribution." How such a levy could be enforced in any of the pertinent jurisdictions is not stated, much less how such a levy could be raised in a nondiscriminatory way.
49. "Office Memorandum on the Visit to Vienna by Mr. Landesco and Mr. Schweitzer," no date (early May 1938), AJDC SM Archives, file 28/folder 445.
50. Rosen to AJDC New York, May 8, 1938.
51. Kapralik, "Wien," 10f.
52. "Vorschlag betreffend die Auswanderung des in jüdischem Besitz befindlichen Kapitals im Lande Oesterreich" (Proposal concerning the emigration of Jewish capital in Austria). CA: A/W 2540.2.
53. Interrogation dated July 22, 1947. Pretrial interrogations of Dr. Karl Ebner in the case against him at *Landesgericht für Strafsachen Wien*, case Vg 12 g Vr 1223/47; copy deposited at DÖW 8919/a. In his testimony Ebner says that the order came from "*Reichssicherheitshauptamt*" which, however, was not established until September 1939; he means SD headquarters Berlin.
54. "Schnellbrief Gestapoleitstelle Wien an alle Bezirkspolizeikommissariate" (Express Letter [from] Gestapo Headquarters Vienna to All District Police Commissions), May 24, 1938, "Betrifft: Festnahme von Juden" (Re: Arrest of Jews); YV 030/17, item 5.
55. Eichmann's readiness to use the brutal strong-arm methods typical of the SS in the early period of his service in Vienna is amply attested to by Perl, *Operation Action*.
56. Kapralik, "Wien," 39.
57. Authors' interview with Sophie Löwenherz, New York, Jan. 25, 1979.
58. Kapralik, "Wien," 39.
59. Ibid., 12f.
60. AN Meeting at *Devisenstelle Wien* of Raffegerst, Wolf, Eichmann, Löwenherz, Rothenberg, and two other unidentified Germans, June 17, 1938; L-papers.
61. Ibid. and AN Eichmann's and Raffegerst's visit at IKG office of Löwenherz. Also present: Rothenberg. June 24, 1938; L-papers.
62. AN June 17, 1938.
63. AN Conference between Löwenherz and Raffegerst at *Devisenstelle* Wien, Aug. 17, 1938; CA: A/W. 2540.2.
64. At the end-phase of the negotiations leading to the transfer scheme, Eichmann recorded a meeting between himself, Wolf of the Reichsbank, Raffegerst of the *Devisenstelle*, and Dr. Siegert representing the Ministry for Economics (*Reichswirtschaftsministerium*). The following excerpt is of special interest:

    The emigration through transfer of major capital (*Grosskapital*) from Austria is to be prevented.

    As regards the feature of the scheme, according to which the foreign currencies donated by AJDC and CBF are deposited outside of Germany (and out of reach of the Reichsbank) and made directly available to emigrants at exchange rates other than the official rate, Eichmann reports that if the foreign currencies had to be made available in the normal way, that is, through middlemen of the sort of transfer schemes that had been instituted in the Altreich, the result would have been that no foreign exchange would have been available for the region of Austria, and hence emigration would in effect have been rendered impossible.

    Eichmann also states that the *Devisenstelle Wien* would have to work in close cooperation with his office and that it would not be permitted to process any Jewish application for foreign exchange without paperwork being countersigned by his office. See Vermerk for II/112 (Eichmann's home office in Berlin), dated June 14, 1938; EICH 1511.
65. At the time negotiations of the preliminary transfer scheme neared completion, Bernhard Kahn, chairman of the (Paris-based) European Executive Council of the AJDC, wrote to Mr. Schiff in London, who would be representing the AJDC in forthcoming negotiations with CGJ. The matter of providing the IKG with funds for relief work was very much on his mind. It seems that Norman Bentwich, who had been taking an interest in Vienna from the beginning of the Anschluss, had proposed an immediate

monthly contribution of £10,000 for relief work, an extremely large sum. Kahn reports that in his discussion with Bentwich he thought that "it would be much better to begin on a smaller scale and increase, if absolutely necessary, than to reduce the amounts on account of lack of funds." Kahn was also worried that if in Vienna one would supplant the portion of the relief work that was to be done by municipal welfare agencies, then the agencies in the *Altreich* would follow suit. (Dr. B. Kahn, Paris, to Otto M. Schiff, London, June 10, 1938; AJDC SM Archives, file 28/folder 445). A few weeks later (July 28, 1938), we find Kahn writing to Paul Baerwald at AJDC's New York headquarters, in which he implies that it is not the AJDC but the London Council that is hesitant about using the funds for relief work:

> I am still much afraid that some day the Council will leave us all the relief and refugee work. Lord Samuel . . . tried to tell us to take over all relief work and the Council would give funds only for emigration and training.
>
> When convinced that this cannot be done, Lord Samuel then went on to say that they need . . . statements [to that effect] . . . namely that they give funds for constructive work. I could only reply that the JDC needs such statements as well . . . in connection with fundraising! It cannot be said of the JDC that it does only relief and soup kitchen work. (Kahn to Baerwald, July 28, 1938; AJDC Archives, ibid.)

66. AN June 17, 1938; also CA: A/W 2540.2.
67. AN June 24, 1938; also CA: A/W 2540.2. The memorandum makes it clear that neither domestic nor foreign stock certificates could be exported, nor could domestic or foreign insurance policies be transferred. Especially valuable medical equipment, including X-ray machinery, could not be exported.
68. Kapralik, "Wien," 36.
69. Ibid., 13.
70. See note 30.
71. Kapralik, "Wien," 39.
72. Ibid., 20.
73. Authors' interview with Kapralik, London, May 15, 1980.
74. AN *Vorsprache* Löwenherz at Eichmann, July 20, 1938; L-papers.
75. Kapralik, "Wien," 17f.
76. AN Nov. 5, 1938; L-papers. This unsigned memorandum was apparently written by Kapralik.
77. AN after Sep. 15, 1939; L-papers. It is apparent that Engel wrote this unsigned and undated memorandum during Löwenherz's absence in London.
78. AN *Vorsprache* Löwenherz and Rothenberg at Eichmann, Aug. 17, 1938; L-papers.
79. The *Reichsfluchtsteuer*, i.e., "defection levy," was enacted at the time following the First World War when Germany, in its tight economic situation, sought to stem the outflow of capital, assets, manpower, and expertise. Now it was a neat way of adding to the expropriation of the assets of the Jews, who were thus being penalized for fleeing while being chased out.
80. See AN after Sep. 15, 1938; L-papers. In spite of the terseness of the memorandum, Engel's almost frantic state can be discerned.
81. See Kapralik, "Wien," 22.
82. Bürckel to all Gauleiter, June 29, 1938, DÖW 9409.
83. Sobolak to "Sämtliche Dienststellen der Partei . . .," Aug. 18, 1938, YV 030/17, item 6.
84. This incident is documented in Löwenherz to Stapoleitstelle Wien, Oct. 9, 1938, and in Kapralik, "Wien," 24ff. It is discussed by Botz, *Vom "Anschluss" zum Krieg*, 397; Rosenkranz, *"Reichskristallnacht,"* 13f; Rosenkranz, *Verfolgung*, 157; and Weinzierl, *Zu wenig Gerechte*, 58.
85. Botz, *Wien*, 397.
86. Ibid.
87. Rosenkranz, *Verfolgung*, 157.
88. Kapralik, "Wien," 22.
89. The American journalist and author Vincent Sheean attended the Evian Conference as a reporter. In his book *Not Peace but a Sword* (New York, 1939), 91f, he reports the following in his account of the conference: ". . . I saw friends from Vienna. One was Dr. Neumann . . . another was Dr. Löwenherz, the head of the [IKG] . . . who had been thrust into the position of responsible chief for his people during the most terrible ordeal of their modern history. They were rather agitated, and rightly so: for they had come to Evian to represent the Jews of Austria, the people about whom this meeting had been summoned, and they were barred from attending it. . . . [T]he secretariat . . . had prepared for a limited number of delegations, for the press, and for nothing else. . . . I gave my ticket to Dr. Löwenherz . . . Dr. Neumann . . . [was] unable to enter."

90. Typescripts of both French and German versions were filed at the IKG; see CA: A/W 2491.
91. Two days after the opening of the Evian Conference, on July 6, 1938, Ernst von Weizsäcker, *Staatssekretär* (Undersecretary) of the German Foreign Office, wrote a circular to the German consulate nearest to Evian (Geneva) and to some German embassies (London, Paris, Rome, Washington, Warsaw) and legations in nearby countries that were especially vulnerable or would in time be solicited as allies of Germany (Belgrade, Bucharest, Budapest, Prague, Sofia). Some points in it are of interest to us. First, they take note that "No country is prepared to accept the emigrant German Jews, in particular if they are without means." Second, responding to the British Ambassador's query directed to the German Foreign Minister Joachim von Ribbentrop as to whether Germany would cooperate with other countries by allowing the transfer of Jewish capital, von Weizsäcker says that this has to be denied, since Germany could be expected to permit the transfer of the capital accumulated by Jews—especially after the [First World] War. It is noteworthy that a kind of transfer had by then been arranged in Austria. Weizsäcker to Embassies and Legations, July 8, 1938, EICH 462.
92. Kapralik, "Wien," 33.
93. Löwenherz to Geheime Staatspolizei Leitstelle Wien, CA: A/W 2491.
94. AN *Vorsprache* Löwenherz at Eichmann, July 20, 1938; L-papers.
95. Ibid.
96. *Reichsgesetzblatt* 1938, Part I, no. 63, Berlin, Apr. 26, 1938, 414ff.
97. See "Zweite Anordnung auf Grund der Verordnung über die Ankeldung [*sic*! should read Anmeldung] des Vermögens der Juden vom 26. Apr. 1938," article V, section 10,1. See also section 11,2; the reference therein to "section 8" is a mistake; what is meant is section 10. Draft forwarded under cover of Raffegerst (in his capacity as Staatskommissar in der Privatwirtschaft) to Barth (Bürckel's personal assistant), Aug. 8, 1938; NA: T84/Roll 13 and IZG: MA145/1, frames 10266ff.
98. Ibid., p. 10, frame 10275.
99. Draft sent under cover of von Hummel to Bürckel, July 18, 1938; NA: T84/Roll 13 and IZG: MA 145/1, frame 10279ff.
100. Leiter der Zentralabteilung II/112 (i.e., Eichmann's home office in Berlin) to SD-Führer des SS-Oberabschnitts Österreich II/112 (i.e., Eichmann in Vienna), June 21, 1938; NA: T175/Roll 413.
101. Eichmann to Sicherheitshauptamt II/112 Berlin, June 24, 1938; NA: T175/Roll 413.
102. CA: A/W 568.1. The offices and departments can be grouped as follows. The departments and offices under (3) and (4) were entirely new and were established to meet the tasks resulting from the new conditions. Some of the offices in other groups were similarly new, such as Murmelstein's office. Others assumed unprecedented expansion and importance, such as certain administrative offices and welfare departments. Even the school departments were essentially new because the Anschluss necessitated the provision of schooling for children who were no longer permitted to attend public school, and the employment of their teachers.

    1. Central administration: 3 offices (Directorate: Löwenherz; Special tasks: Murmelstein; General office manager: Engel).
    2. Administrative departments: Bookkeeping; Cashier; Correspondence; 2 Personnel offices; Technical; Registration; Accounting; Legal; Custody of properties.
    3. Special task departments: Tax; Housing; Provinces; Economics; Supervision and internal order; Blocked currency; General advice; Liaison with *Zentralstelle*; Retraining programs.
    4. Emigration departments and offices: Foreign currency; Emigration advice; Processing; Research and investigation; Passport and other documentation; Booking of passage.
    5. Welfare departments: Medical; Clothing; Free meals; 6 Old-age homes; Hospital; Relief.
    6. Religious departments: Rabbinate; Cemetery; Religious education; *Mikveh*.
    7. *Matrikelamt* (Registry of births, marriages, deaths).
    8. School department: Teachers; Schooling for children.

103. In his memoir obtained by Ball-Kaduri and deposited in his archive, Dr. Leo Landau reports about his activity from the Anschluss to his emigration in February 1939. Attached appointment letters from Löwenherz (dated May 10 and 31, 1938) show that he was one of the eight members of the *Beirat* (see chapter 4), and that he was asked to take over the honorary positions of Chief of the Relief Department and the "newly established Section for Emigration and Retraining." In the memoir, Landau shows that the letters, which he apparently carried with him, came in handy one time when he was interrogated by the Gestapo and in danger of being sent to Dachau. By means of the letter, he could claim to be in charge of the emigration effort, which the Gestapo did not wish to disrupt, and they let him go. (See

Landau, 17.) However, Landau's position in the emigration department was not very important, and in fact, dubious. It was different with his organization of the retraining effort, and especially with his relief work. In this area he had rich experience before the Anschluss, which he brought to bear on the difficult task of providing help, especially free meals, to thousands of Jews pauperized as the result of the Anschluss. Recognition for his vigorous work in this regard is not diminished by pointing to his exaggerated claims in other directions, e.g., "I led the Sections for Retraining, Relief and Foreign Currency" (*Ich hatte das Referat der Umschichtung, der Fürsorge und die Devisenstelle*. Landau, 12). The *Devisenstelle* was organized and staffed by Kapralik (see above), and Landau was not among the staff.

104. Regarding Storfer and group transports, see chapters 6 and 9.

105. The British government was, of course, opposed to illegal entry into Palestine; hence, Jewish organizations in Britain had to be very careful about supporting this kind of immigration. Aside from this, different Jewish organizations had reasons of their own to stay clear of such support. After the first illegal transport of 380 young men and women left Vienna on June 6, 1938, Perl wrote to the CGJ for a contribution of £7 per person for their maintenance in Athens, where they had become stranded (Perl in Vienna to Stephany in London, June 13, 1938). After they finally landed illegally in Palestine, the Council as well as the AJDC were approached for funding the settlement of these people. Normally, settlement was funded by the Jewish Agency, which, under President Chaim Weizman, worked in cooperation with the British Home and Mandatory governments. Since the Jewish Agency was the main force in gaining schedules of immigrant permits to Palestine, they dispensed the funds for the costs of settlement. But, for this reason they also hesitated supporting the settlement of illegal immigrants. The AJDC, on the other hand, as well as all other relief agencies, left all matters dealing with the settlement of Palestine to the Jewish Agency. When the telegram request to help in the case of the 380 illegal settlers reached the AJDC in New York, it was directed back to Dr. Kahn, Chairman of the Paris Office. On July 22 Kahn reported back to Mr. Hyman, Executive Director in New York. He explained that the telegram "signed by Mr. Jabotinsky is not from . . . the real 'General' Jabotinsky—the Jewish 'Fuehrer'—but from his little son." Furthermore, the 380 had been sent by the Revisionists with the help of the Gestapo, who "provided" some of the funding. (There is no evidence that the Gestapo had provided any funding, and if they had "provided" funds, these would have come out of the pockets of Vienna's Jews, whose purse strings were held, through the IKG, by Eichmann of the SD.) Kahn correctly recognized the transport as the beginning of a scheme of illegal immigration. (While it was the first such transport after the Anschluss, it was, in fact, the fourth in what would later be called the "Aliyah Bet [Immigration B]," the first three having left—also from Vienna—in 1937. See Perl, *Operation Action*, 405.) The AJDC, Kahn said, may "contribute toward the transportation expenses of legal immigrants," but they do not help immigrants to Palestine after their arrival, whether legal or illegal. And, regardless of whether or not the AJDC approved of illegal immigration, if they would contribute even merely to the transportation costs, "the Gestapo would . . . insist that we help in the transportation of another 1,000 people waiting to be smuggled in the same manner with the help of the Gestapo and the Revisionists." (Kahn to Hyman, July 22, 1938, in response to Hyman to Kahn, July 6, 1938, concerning the telegram from Jabotinsky in London to JTA [Jewish Telegraph Agency, New York], July 3, 1938; all AJDC SM Archives, file 28/folder 445.)

At the same time (July 26, 1938) a similar negative decision was formally made by the CGJ executive in response to a similar appeal to them. Their refusal stated very clearly what their concern was: The Council "deprecates all emigration which is not properly organized and which does not make proper provisions for the welfare of the emigrants. The [CGJ] cannot in any way encourage illegal immigration into Palestine." (Cited by Perl, *Operation Action*, 86f.) Inasmuch as the AJDC and CBF/CGJ were then embarking on a scheme of pooling their contributions in support of emigration in Vienna, it would not do for them to support what in the eyes of the government under whose jurisdiction the CBF operated would be illegal.

Löwenherz, in turn, was obliged to follow suit, because the IKG was now being financed by the two organizations and, in effect, he was the *sub rosa* agent of the AJDC in matters representing Jewish interests in the former Austria. However, as we will see, not even emigration targeted for illegal immigration could proceed without IKG involvement in matters of official documentation and foreign exchange.

The main complication that the Revisionists had to face in securing financial support for Aliyah Bet from Jewish organizations resulted from their break with the General Zionist movement, a break initiated by their leader, Vladimir Jabotinsky. The illegal transports, however, did not include only

Revisionists. For example, Perl, in his letter to the CGJ of June 13, 1938, says the 360 [*sic!*] "belong to various Jewish associations in Vienna—General Zionists, New Zionists [Revisionists], Aguda[s Jisroel] and Makkabi." In his telegram of July 3, 1938, to the AJDC New York, Jabotinsky reports that they "appealed [to the] Austrian Relief Council" (*sic*; he means the Council for German Jewry) and claims that "Zionist majority influenced refusal," referring in this way to the General Zionists in distinction to the Revisionist Zionists. In the end, the "illegal" Aliyah Bet initiated by the Revisionists was able to get an appreciable number of Jews out of Nazi Europe, also in the years between the end of the World War II and the end of the Mandate in 1948, and got them settled in Palestine, a feat hailed by all concerned.

106. AN Eichmann's telephone call to Löwenherz, Aug. 1, 1938; L-papers.
107. In-house memorandum by Engel, Aug. 21, 1938, CA: A/W 2505.
108. In-house report by Engel to Löwenherz (*Bericht an die Amtsdirektion*), Aug. 8, 1938; CA: A/W 2502.
109. Ibid.
110. For Höttl's testimony at the Eichmann trial, see: www.holocaustresearchproject.org/nazioccupation/hoetll.html.
111. Henceforth: *Zentralstelle*.

Chapter 4

1. *Jüdische Pressezentrale Zürich*, vol. 21, no. 994, June 10, 1938, p. 4; available at LBI/NY.
2. *Jüdische Pressezentrale Zürich*, vol. 21, no. 992, May 27, 1938, p. 5; available at LBI/NY.
3. Much valuable material on Kareski, especially by persons in leading Jewish positions in Berlin in the 1930s, is to be found in the archive compiled by Dr. Ball-Kaduri and deposited at Yad Vashem. See, e.g., (1) the German translation of the record of the rabbinical court trial (1937) of Kareski's accusation of libel against *Hitachdut Olei Germania* Organization of Immigrants/Zionists from Germany (the original Hebrew record is missing); YV 01/112. (2) Minutes of the Meeting of "Zionists from Germany," Topic: Kareski, date: Mar. 5, 1959; YV 01/245. (3) Ball-Kaduri's "Einige Bemerkungen zum Konflikt . . ." dated July 1944; YV 01/93. (4) Ball-Kaduri to Yad-Vashem, Feb. 20, 1958; YV 01/112a. (5) Benno Cohn, "Um die Leitung des jüdischen Kulturbundes in Deutschland—ein Kapitel des Kampfes um jüdische Autonomie nach 1933" (About the directorship of the Jewish cultural association in Germany—a chapter of the struggle for Jewish autonomy after 1933), dated June 3, 1945; YV 01/6.
4. See Benno Cohn, "Um die Leitung," 5.
5. Ibid.
6. There was a time when Nazi officials still met with representatives of the Jews about matters of Nazi Jewish policy. At a meeting in the Reich Ministry of Propaganda (in 1936) Kareski, as the Nazi-imposed president of the *Reichsverband jüdischer Kulturbünde*, tried, in the presence of Nazi officials, to force his "anti-assimilationist" plans for the *Reichsverband* against the recalcitrance of the Jewish leadership. Cohn had the temerity—unimaginable less than two years later!—of responding, still in the presence of the Nazi officials, that "with the Nurenberg [racial] laws a line was drawn. It is now up to the Jews to structure their own lives. The substance of the *Reichsverband* is a question internal to and would have to be discussed within the Jewish Community. In his presentation Kareski overlooked 150 years of assimilation; we [Jews] have to find our way back gradually." See Cohn, "Um die Leitung," 6.
7. The Jewish leaders in Berlin were also hesitant to make use of the illegal route to Palestine, a hesitancy they regretted in retrospect. See, for example, Ball-Kaduri's record of a discussion held on May 20, 1958, by him, Benno Cohen, and Jews who had been in leading positions in Berlin in the 1930s: "Verschiedene Informationen über die jüdische Situation in Berlin in den Jahren 1933 bis 1940" (various information about the Jewish situation in Berlin in the years 1933 to 1940), YV 01/226. One participant reports that in 1938 they were approached by a certain Herr Segall, who had arranged illegal transports in other parts of Europe. They met him with suspicion and rejected him: "according to my present opinion [1958] we were very stupid then [1938]" (p. 6). Others voiced similar opinions: "For us [in Germany] we rejected the system used by the Revisionists in Austria. They let the illegal *aliyah* [immigration to Palestine] be arranged by private agents who accepted participants according to the amount of money they were able to pay, and in part they transported them under terrible conditions. We tried to make the transports in a more humane manner and to arrange them ourselves, but in fact we lacked experience. . . . From the standpoint of the simple rescue of the greatest number of people we have to say, in retrospect, that the Revisionists' system was right" (p. 4).
8. As reported by Wolfgang von Weisl, "Illegale Transporte" in Josef Fraenkel, ed., *The Jews of Austria*:

Essays on Their Life, History and Destruction (London: Vallentine, Mitchell & Co.), 172. Von Weisl as well as Perl had been organizing illegal transports in Central Europe since the mid-1930s.

9. *Die jüdischen Organisationen in Deutschland*, a pamphlet issued by the *Informationsdienst/Rassenpolitisches Amt der NSDAP—Reichsleitung* (Information Service of the Reich-Directorate of the Nazi Party Office of Racial Policy), Apr. 10, 1938, no. 42, 1. NA: T175/roll 508, frame 374110; also IZG: MA 557.
10. In a note about "The present situation of Judaism in Germany" in the file of SD section II/112 (where Eichmann was subordinate to Hagen) dated Sep. 13, 1936, we read: "In their struggle against National-Socialism the Jews make use not only of their own institutions but cooperate closely with other groups of opponents. Thus, in recent times good Jewish relations to circles of Catholic clergy could be discerned. This danger was enhanced in the attempt to comprise all non-Aryan Christians in the newly founded Paulist Society. In like manner it was ascertained that even today there are still Jewish protagonists of the illegal struggle of the KPD [German Communist Party]." NA: T175/roll 508, frame 374092; also IZG: MA 557.
11. Kapralik, "Wien," 38. Kapralik does not refer to Ticho by name, only as "Dr. T."
12. See Landau's memoir, YV 01/244. Regrettably, Landau presents an exaggerated appraisal of his importance and performance as a member of the *Beirat*.
13. Copy of Löwenherz to *Geheime Staatspolizei*, July 19, 1938, attached to AN *Vorsprache* Löwenherz at Eichmann, July 20, 1938; L-papers.
14. Isidor Klaber, "Vom Einmarsch Hitlers in Österreich bis August [1939]," YV 030/9-8. On Nov. 7, 1938, the *Beirat* also met under duress in order to draft a required statement dissociating the Jewish Community from Herschel Grynszpan's attack on Ernst vom Rath. The statement is discussed in chapter 5.
15. AN *Vorsprache* Löwenherz at Eichmann, July 20, 1938; L-papers.
16. Klaber, "Vom Einmarsch Hitlers."
17. See Löwenherz to Prof. Dr. M. Ehrenpreis, Feb. 10, 1941; D. Friedmann to Ehrenpreis, Mar. 11, 1941. Both in CA: A/W 181,1.
18. *Adam, ein Beitrag zur Messiaslehre* (Adam, a contribution to messianic doctrine), diss. University of Vienna, 1927.
19. P. Severin Grill, *Der Talmud und Schulchan Aruch: Eine theologische Studie für weitere Kreise* (Graz/Leipzig: U. Moser, 1934).
20. Benjamin Murmelstein, *Einige Fragen an Prof. Dr. P. Severin Grill, O. Cist., Verfasser der theolog. Studie "Der Talmud und Schulchan Aruch"* (Wien: Union österreichischer Juden, 1935).
21. Murmelstein, *Geschichte der Juden: Des Volkes Weltwandern* (Wien: Verlag Josef Belf, 1938).
22. Murmelstein, *Flavius Josephus* (Wien: Verlag Josef Belf, 1938).
23. A few months after the Anschluss, Murmelstein would publish an article about Jewish wandering in the weekly newspaper authorized by the Nazis, *Zionistische Rundschau*.
24. Murmelstein, *Geschichte der Juden*, 390f.
25. Ibid. 406. 2 Chronicles 36:23 cited according to the Jewish Publication Society translation of 1917.
26. Ibid. 406.
27. See Wiener Magistrat/section 2 to Vorstand der israelitischen Kultusgemeinde, Feb. 3, 1938; CA: A/W 270.1.
28. Siegmund, later Levarie (Hebrew for Lionheart, a direct translation of the German Löwenherz).
29. This was told to us by Murmelstein and, in the case of Löwenherz's son, corroborated by the latter in our interview with him in 2000.
30. *Zionistische Rundschau*, no. 1, Vienna, May 20, 1938, 1.
31. Executive decision (*Beschluß*) no. 7130, dated June 8, 1938, in *Beschlußbuch* (Record book of executive acts); CA: A/W 88/64.
32. See the various in-house circulars in CA: A/W 2502.
33. This happened, for example, when the *Daily Mail* (London) showed tired Jewish refugee children arriving in England. This incident is discussed in chapter 6. AN Löwenherz telephone conversation with Kuchmann, Jan. 5, 1939; L-papers.
34. It was for this that the new Jewish Community, which slowly arose after the Nazi period, might have set him monuments, not for his martyrdom.
35. Documents pertinent to this event are excerpted in *Widerstand und Verfolgung in Wien 1934–1945*, vol. 3: *1939–1945* (2nd ed., Vienna, 1984), 36–42. For a historical account, see Botz, *Wien*, 383–88.

Chapter 5

1. Shaul Esh, "Between Discrimination and Extermination," *Yad Vashem Studies* 2 (1958): 85.
2. The Nuremberg Laws (Sep. 15, 1935) differentiate between *Reichsbürger* (citizens) and *Staatsangehörige* (nationals eligible for passport and liable for taxes); the Jews became the latter, having lost their political but not all of their civil rights through these laws. See Hofer, *Nationalsozialismus*, 284f.
3. Cf. Krausnick, "Judenverfolgung," 271f.
4. See Hannah Arendt, *Eichmann in Jerusalem* (New York: Viking Press, 1963), 40.
5. Esh, "Between Discrimination," 87.
6. *Foreign Relations of the United States of America, 1938*, vol. II, 374; quoted in Esh, "Between Discrimination," 81.
7. Ibid. Cf. also *Anatomie*, vol. 2, 76f; and Jonny Moser, "Die Entrechtung der Juden im Dritten Reich," in Walter H. Pehle, ed., *Der Judenpogrom 1938. Von der 'Reichskristallnacht' zum Völkermord* (Frankfurt [Main]: Fischer, 1988), 120.
8. AJDC Archive, File 632. A report by a former employee received in New York office, Mar. 9, 1939.
9. Cf. Lionel Kochan, *Pogrom: 10 November 1938* (London: A. Deutsch, 1957), 34.
10. Quoted in Avraham Barkai, "Schicksalsjahr 1938" in Walter H. Pehle, ed., *Der Judenpogrom 1938. Von der 'Reichskristallnacht' zum Völkermord* (Frankfurt [Main]: Fischer, 1988), 105n.
11. Botz, *Wien*, 243.
12. VB, Apr. 26, 1938, as cited in Botz, *Wien*, 248.
13. Rosenkranz, *Verfolgung*, 89.
14. Ibid, 94.
15. Ibid., 156.
16. Gold, *Geschichte*, 85.
17. Botz, *Wien*, 397.
18. Ibid.
19. Rosenkranz, *Verfolgung*, 157.
20. Letter Leopold Ferster (Vienna) to Löwenherz (New York), Sep. 24, 1953; L-papers.
21. AN *Vorsprache* Löwenherz and Prof. von Neumann at Senator Dr. Schaufler (newly appointed advisor for Jewish affairs for the municipality of Vienna), Aug. 5, 1938, items 1, 7; L-papers.
22. Rosenkranz, *Reichskristallnacht*, 14.
23. AN *Vorsprache* Löwenherz and Rothenberg at Eichmann, Oct. 29, 1938, item 12; L-papers.
24. AN *Vorsprache* Löwenherz at Dr. Lange (Gestapo), July 29, 1938; L-papers.
25. Moser, *Die Judenverfolgung*, 7f.
26. Rosenkranz, *Reichskristallnacht*, 12.
27. Kapralik, "Wien," 7. Kapralik mixes up the locations of the persons in this dispute; he erroneously has Kuchmann teamed up with Eichmann. In fact, Lange was Kuchmann's superior at the Gestapo.
28. Moser, *Judenverfolgung*, 6.
29. Ebner's testimony, DÖW 8919.
30. Moser, *Judenverfolgung*, 7.
31. Gold, *Geschichte*, 84.
32. Rosenkranz, *Reichskristallnacht*, 12.
33. Rosenkranz, *Verfolgung*, 87.
34. Rosenkranz, *Reichskristallnacht*, 14.
35. Gold, *Geschichte*, 86–87; Rosenkranz, *Reichskristallnacht*, 14f; Rosenkranz, *Verfolgung*, 157f.
36. Rosenkranz, *Verfolgung*, 158.
37. Ibid., 158.
38. Arthur Prinz, "The Role of the Gestapo in Obstructing and Promoting Jewish Emigration," *Yad Vashem Studies* 2 (1958): 211.
39. Krausnick, "Judenverfolgung," *Anatomie des SS-Staates*, vol. 2, München, 1982, 270.
40. Rosenkranz, *Reichskristallnacht*, 9n.; Hermann Graml, *Der 9. November 1938* (Bonn: Bundeszentrale für Heimatdienst, 1957), 17n.
41. Trude Maurer, "Abschiebung und Attentat," in Walter H. Pehle, ed., *Der Judenpogrom 1938. Von der 'Reichskristallnacht' zum Völkermord* (Frankfurt [Main]: Fischer, 1988), 60f. Maurer's article is an excellent and detailed discussion of this affair.
42. AN *Vorsprache* Löwenherz and Rothenberg at Eichmann, Oct. 29, 1938, item 1; L-papers.

43. Botz, *Wien*, 249.
44. Arendt, *Eichmann*, 47.
45. Ibid., 63.
46. M-Ms., 45.
47. Hilberg, *Destruction*, 53 and 100; Graml, *Reichskristallnacht*, 11. Frankfurter was a Yugoslav national studying in Switzerland, according to Graml, medicine, according to Hilberg, rabbinics. Gustloff was the leader of the Nazi organization of German nationals operating in Switzerland; his title was *Landesgruppenleiter*. The assassination occurred in February 1936, before the summer Olympic games held in Berlin. Hence official reaction to the assassination was relatively mild, and the punitive tax was not imposed until a year later, in February 1937.
48. Hilberg, *Destruction*, 656.
49. Graml, *Reichskristallnacht*, 17f.
50. The DNB was the semi-official organ of the Nazi regime, whose function it was to coordinate the German press and to bring it into line with what the Reich Ministry for the Enlightenment of the People and for Propaganda wanted the people to believe.
51. Wolfgang Benz, "Der Rückfall in die Barbarei," in Walter H. Pehle, ed., *Der Judenpogrom 1938. Von der 'Reichskristallnacht' zum Völkermord* (Frankfurt [Main]: Fischer, 1988), 15.
52. Ibid., 16.
53. Kochan, *Pogrom*, 42.
54. Ibid., 43f.
55. Uwe Dietrich Adam, "Wie spontan war der Pogrom?", in Pehle, ed., *Der Judenpogrom 1938*, 76.
56. The author here uses the unusual term *Glaubenshäuser*, which translates literally as "houses of faith" or of "belief," whereas he refers to *Gotteshäuser* ("houses of God"), the usual designation for houses of worship, when he refers to other religions. The implied difference must have been obvious to the reader.
57. Botz, *Wien*, 398f.
58. Benz, "Rückfall," 17f.
59. Kochan, *Pogrom*, 44f.
60. The site of the Beer Hall Putsch.
61. The SS met separately at a different location.
62. Kochan, *Pogrom*, 51.
63. In 1938 Germany was on central European time, France on west European time, a difference of one hour.
64. "An alle Gauleitungen. Vertraulich nicht für die Presse," DÖW, Bürckel files.
65. Ibid. DÖW.
66. DÖW 3051.
67. Adam, "Wie spontan," 83.
68. 7th Army Documentation Center, PS-374, National Archives, Washington, D.C.
69. M-Ms., 44.
70. Amtsdirektion der IKG Wien to Reichskommissar für die Wiedervereinigung Oesterreichs mit dem Deutschen Reich, Nov. 8, 1938, signed by Emil Engel (for the directorate of the IKG), Israel Taglicht (as chief rabbi), Josef Babad (as president of the Rabbinical Council [*Rabbinatskollegium*]), Viktor Prustein and Julius Steinfeld (for the *Beirat*); DÖW 9426.
71. Rosenkranz, *Reichskristallnacht*, 33. Rosenkranz bases himself on the memoir by Leo Landau, 11, YV 0-1/244, which page was not available to us at Yad Vashem.
72. Ibid.
73. Another plausible interpretation would be that this humiliation of the Jewish leadership constituted an important element of the pogrom as well as of the Nazi program in general. Cf. Peter Loewenberg, "The Kristallnacht as Degradation Ritual," *Simon Wiesenthal Center Annual* 2 (1985): 309ff.
74. See "Niederschrift. Geheime Reichssache," Report by SS UStf. Fast of SD Unterabschnitt Tirol to SD-Donau, Nov. 12, 1938; DÖW 1780.
75. Simon Wiesenthal, *Als die Tempel brannten. Vor 25 Jahren.* 1963, 4, DÖW 3097.
76. Ibid., 4f.
77. Document 148, "Bericht des Völkischen Beobachters über 'judenfeindliche Kundgebungen in Wien,' 11.11. 1938," in Wolfgang Neugebauer, ed., *Widerstand und Verfolgung in Wien 1934–1945: Eine*

Dokumentation Vol. 3 (2nd ed.; Dokumentationsarchiv des Österreichischen Widerstandes; Wien: Österreichischer Bundesverlag für Unterricht, Wissenschaft und Kunst, 1984), 278.

78. Ibid.
79. Trittner reports to DS-Oberabschnitt Donau, DÖW 1000.
80. Globocnik Report, undated, DÖW, Bürckel files.
81. Trittner reports, DÖW 1000.
82. Bürckel files, 26, DÖW.
83. Globocnik Report, DÖW, Bürckel files.
84. YV 030/17.
85. "Aktenvermerk der Gestapo Wien betreffend beschlagnahmte Bücher und Matriken, 16. 11. 1938," DÖW 1456, in *Widerstand*, item 152, 281.
86. Rosenkranz, *Reichskristallnacht*, 43.
87. Wiesenthal, *Tempel*, 5.
88. Botz, *Wien*, 403.
89. Ibid., 401.
90. Ibid., 402. Rosenkranz (*Reichskristallnacht*, 45), referring to Gestapo figures, corroborates the number of arrests in Vienna, i.e., 7,800.
91. Rosenkranz, *Verfolgung*, 159.
92. Botz, *Wien*, 403.
93. DÖW 3021, 6ff.
94. Wiesenthal, *Tempel*, 5; Gold, *Geschichte*, 90; Rosenkranz, *Reichskristallnacht*, 42.
95. Rosenkranz, ibid.
96. Rosenkranz, *Verfolgung*, 162.
97. DÖW 1000.
98. Ibid.
99. Botz, *Wien*, 401.
100. Globocnik report, 4; DÖW, Bürckel files.
101. Botz, *Wien*, 404.
102. "Aktennotiz des SS-Hauptscharführers Seliger über die Sitzung im Gauwirtschaftsamt wegen der Vorfälle am 10. 11. 1938," dated 12.11.1938, *Widerstand*, item 149, 279f.
103. Rosenkranz, *Reichskristallnacht*, 58.
104. We discuss Göring's evaluation of Kristallnacht and his subsequent actions in the final section of this chapter.
105. Reichskommissar für die Wiedervereinigung Österreichs mit dem Deutschen Reich. Schreiben und Bericht an Ministerpräsident Generalfeldmarschall Göring, geheim, 18.11.1938. Institut für Zeitgeschichte/München PS 2237, cited in Hans Safrian and Hans Witek, *Und keiner war dabei: Dokumente des alltäglichen Antisemitismus in Wien 1938* (Wien: Picus, 1988), 185ff.
106. Ibid. See Erika Weinzierl's "Introduction," 15.
107. DÖW 1000.
108. DÖW 3021.
109. AJDC Archive File 632 (Kristallnacht), 8.
110. AJDC Archive File 439, 2f.
111. Kapralik, "Wien," 28.
112. It is an intriguing question whether this permission was granted for this particular time in the foreknowledge of what was to take place on or about November 9, and whether Eichmann and the Gestapo expected their rapine of the IKG to run more smoothly with these two men out of the way.
113. M-Tapes II-16A, 291. (Tapes available at https://collections.ushmm.org/search/catalog/irn105866.)
114. Rosenkranz, *Reichskristallnacht*, 43. Rosenkranz quotes from a page of the Landau report, which was not available to us at Yad Vashem.
115. Kapralik, "Wien," 28ff.
116. M-Ms., 46. In our interviews with Murmelstein he added that Eichmann had also threatened to shoot him.
117. M-Tapes II-16A, 291.
118. Cf. M-Tapes and M-Ms, ibid.
119. Kapralik, "Wien," 28.
120. M-Ms., 46.

121. Rosenkranz, *Reichskristallnacht*, 44. From a page of Landau's report not accessible to us at Yad Vashem.
122. Ibid.
123. AN *Vorsprache* Engel at Eichmann, Nov. 14, 1938, 2; L-papers.
124. Ibid.
125. Report by Samuel Gurvitz to the Joint, undated, following his return from a European tour that included Vienna in February 1939, 5; AJDC Archive.
126. Ibid., 28.
127. Löwenherz Report: Löwenherz and Rothenberg at Eichmann, Nov. 29, 1938, 7. For a slightly different version of this exchange, cf. AN *Vorsprache* Löwenherz and Rothenberg at Eichmann, Nov. 29, 1938, item 10; L-papers.
128. Kapralik, "Wien," 30.
129. Ibid., 31.
130. Direktor, IKG Spital to Leitung der IKG, Nov. 11, 1938; CA: A/W 270.2.
131. "34. Wochenbericht der [IKG] Wien vom 3. Jänner 1939 zugleich Tätigkeits- und Lagebericht für die Zeit vom 2. Mai 1938 – 31. Dezember 1938" (34th Weekly Report of IKG, Jan. 3, 1939, also Activities and Situation Report for the period May 2, 1938, to Dec. 31, 1938); YV, 11.
132. Jakob Rothmann to IKG, dated Oct. 1, 1938 ([*sic*!] correctly: Dec. 1, 1938), CA: A/W 301.1.
133. CA: A/W 165.1.
134. Norman Bentwich, "Report on a Visit to Vienna" for the Council for German Jewry, Aug. 17, 1939, 3; AJDC Archive: file 440.
135. Graml, *Reichskristallnacht*, 189f.
136. "Tagesrapport Gestapo Wien, Nr. 11," Nov. 24–25. 1938; NA: T84 roll 13/frame 39790, quoted in *Widerstand und Verfolgung*, 270f.
137. Figures based on "Report of the Vienna Jewish Community May–June 1939," 1f, AJDC Archive.
138. Kochan, *Pogrom*, 125. Kochan's summary of reactions outside of Germany still seems to be the best one, and in this segment we rely frequently on his findings.
139. AJDC: file 632.
140. Kochan, *Pogrom*, 129.
141. Ibid., 131f; 131n.
142. "34. Wochenbericht," 1; YV.
143. David S. Wyman, *Paper Walls: America and the Refugee Crisis 1938–1941* (Amherst: University of Massachusetts Press, 1968), 73.
144. Kochan, *Pogrom*, 136. According to Wyman, *Paper Walls*, 221, only 42.1 percent of this quota had been used up in 1937.
145. Wyman, *Paper Walls*, 213.
146. *News Chronicle*, Nov. 28, 1938, quoted in Kochan, *Pogrom*, 141.
147. Kochan, *Pogrom*, 141.
148. Ibid., quoted from *The Times* (London), Nov. 25, 1938.
149. Ibid., 142.
150. Hilberg, *Destruction*, 25f.
151. Cf. for example, Hilberg, *Destruction*, 27. A number of books and articles report, in greater or lesser detail, on this meeting and the anti-Jewish measures to come out of and to follow it; e.g., Hilberg, 26ff; Graml, *Reichskristallnacht*, 177ff; Moser, *Judenpogrom*, 121ff; Rosenkranz, *Verfolgung*, 164; Kochan, *Pogrom*, 110ff.
152. Graml, *Reichskristallnacht*, 179.
153. Ibid.
154. Rosenkranz, *Verfolgung*, 165.
155. Decree of Dec. 3, 1938, ibid.
156. Ibid.
157. Kochan, *Pogrom*, 116.
158. Rosenkranz, *Verfolgung*, 165.
159. Cf., for example, Moser, *Judenpogrom*, 123.
160. Rosenkranz, *Verfolgung*, 164.
161. The "coordination" was no doubt merely a matter of internal convenience. The officially sanctioned

reorganization did not occur until the establishment of the RSHA in September of 1939. Hence, the "coordination" made the later official reorganization a *fait accompli*.

162. "Reorganisation" issued by Stabskanzlei II 11, Berlin, Feb. 24, 1939, pp. 1, 8f; NA: T175, roll 239; also IZG: MA 433.
163. Ibid., 22.
164. Ibid., 25; emphasis in original. In this "Reorganization" memorandum we take note of the plan for "a troop of active SS-men" who would be "professionally trained" (through "directedness by special military discipline and by ideological attitude") for whatever task to which they might be "employable" (*einsetzbar*); of the fact that they would involve men "in a variety of professions" (*vielgestaltig auch in beruflicher Hinsicht*); and that they would not only operate far from their original function of observing but far from any "network of observers," moreover "in disguise" (*in getarnter Form*). In retrospect we can recognize here the seeds of the project of the training and commitment of the killing task forces (*Einsatzgruppen*) of a later phase of the solution of the Jewish question.
165. Ibid., 21, 23.
166. Heydrich to Foreign Minister, Minister of Economics, Minister of Finances, Undersecretary Stuckart, dated January 30, 1939; for copy of the letter to the Foreign Minister, see EICH 1368.
167. Report by Benno Cohn, "Vorladung von Vertretern des deutschen Judentums vor die Gestapo (Eichmann) im März 1939"; part of the Ball-Kaduri collection of testimonies, YV 01/215. Also AN *Vorsprache* Löwenherz and Rothenberg at Eichmann, Feb. 10, 1939, item 4; L-papers. It should be noted that Benno Cohn, referring to the Gestapo, did not know that he had reported to the SD.
168. AN Feb. 10, 1939, ibid., item 3.
169. Vorstand der Jüdischen Gemeinde Berlin to IKG Wien, Mar. 1, 1939; attached to AN *Vorsprache* Rothenberg and Löwenherz at Eichmann, Mar. 9, 1939, item 1; L-papers.
170. AN *Vorsprache* Löwenherz at Eichmann, Feb. 23, 1939, item 1; L-papers.
171. See Eichmann's first extant letter from Vienna, handwritten in pencil, dated May 8, 1938, one week after the opening of the new IKG. This letter is quoted at the beginning of this chapter.
172. Cohn, "Vorladung."

Chapter 6

1. Norman Bentwich, *I Understand the Risks: The Story of the Refugees from Nazi Oppression Who Fought in the British Forces in the World War* (London: Gollancz, 1950), 25.
2. Löwenherz to Council for German Jewry, Nov. 28, 1938, CA: A/W 2545.1.
3. AN *Vorsprache* Löwenherz and Rothenberg with Eichmann, Dec. 2, 1938, items 1, 2, and attachment; L-papers.
4. See ibid., attachment.
5. Ibid., attachment item 10.
6. AN *Vorsprache* Löwenherz, Rothenberg, Storfer at Eichmann, Mar. 8, 1939, item 3; L-papers.
7. As a matter of fact the Netherlands also took in children's transports, and Löwenherz made trips to Amsterdam to negotiate for them (Engel to *Zentralstelle* and to Gestapo, Jan. 31, 1939, CA: A/W 165.1); altogether over one hundred children left Austria in this way (see Rosenkranz, 185). The Dutch also sheltered resident and transient refugee Jews as well as their own Jewish fellow citizens during the entire period of the ensuing Holocaust as well as they could, even under the brutal occupation by Nazi Germany. The fact that most Dutch Jews were shipped to extermination camps was less a matter of Dutch collaboration than of the oppressive nature of the German occupation. The record of the Dutch people with regard to the Jews is matched by none, with the possible exception of the Italians.
8. LHE's sister and EE belonged to the lucky 20 percent who were reunited with their parents.
9. Löwenherz to Council for German Jewry.
10. In time, once the transports got under way, there would even be requests for children's transports from Jewish communities not within the domain of Nazi Germany, i.e., from Hungary and Poland. We can only guess at the reason. Was it a premonition of things to come? Was it a matter of perceiving an opportunity to provide some children a chance of a better life or to escape the disabilities caused by the anti-Semitism prevailing in Poland and Hungary?
11. Löwenherz to Council for German Jewry, op. cit.
12. Taking the number of Jews remaining in the Altreich at the time of the Anschluss to have been ca. 375,000 (see Werner Rosenstock, "Exodus 1933–1939, A Survey of Jewish Emigration from Germany,"

LBI/YB, vol. 1, 1956, 377; and Herbert A. Strauss, "Jewish Emigration from Germany, Nazi Policies and Jewish Responses (I)," LBI/YB, vol. 25, 1980, 341), and the Jewish population of Austria at that time to have been ca. 180,000, the percentage of the population in the various age categories in the Altreich (column 1) and in Austria (column 2) yields the comparison implied by Löwenherz's statistics:

Percentage of Young People in the Jewish Populations of the Altreich and Austria

Age groups (yr.)	Altreich	Austria	Emigrés 3/12/38–9/15/38
0–6	1.2%	5.1%	25%
6–14	5.4%	5.8%	25%
14–16	2.2%	3.6%	29.7%
16–20	5.0%	5.0%	24.5%
20–25	3.4%	6.5%	38%

Column 3 indicates the percentage of children and youths who had emigrated from Austria between the Anschluss and Sep. 15, 1938.

13. See AN *Vorsprache* Löwenherz and Rothenberg at Eichmann, Dec. 2, 1938, and attachment; L-papers.
14. See Rosenkranz's tabulation, loc. cit.
15. Murmelstein's report, dated Jan. 19, 1939, was forwarded to the *Zentralstelle* and Gestapo over Engel's signature (CA: A/W 165.1). In it he says:

> The English organization . . . intends to accept in the near future mainly children who have found guarantors in England. . . . It was necessary to indicate most strongly that [such] a restriction of children's transports is not feasible and that a preference for guaranteed children would render the IKG unable to consider urgent cases. . . . In the end it was determined that . . . toward the end of January there would be a transport of nonguaranteed children.

However, among the Jews of Vienna the rumor made the rounds that according to the IKG there would be no more children's transports, which was reported to London. On January 30, Grete Exiner (later Exiner-Westman), who was the executive of the Children's Movement in London, telephoned Engel at the IKG for an explanation. She confirmed that at present the movement would accept guaranteed children and that nonguaranteed children would be accepted soon again (AN telephone call Exiner to Engel, Jan. 30, 1939; L-papers).

16. AN telephone call Eichmann to Löwenherz, Dec. 20, 1938, item 3; L-papers.
17. See telephone call Exiner to Engel, Jan. 30, 1939, op. cit.
18. According to Rosenkranz's tabulation gathered from various sources; op. cit., 185f. In his memoir, written in 1972, Kapralik reports that according to notes he made in 1940, 2,300 Jewish children from Vienna came to Great Britain in the children's transports. He adds: "I think this number is too low." However, it is borne out by Rosenzweig's tabulation. See Kapralik, "Wien," 32.
19. See AN *Vorsprache* Löwenherz and Grün (Palamt) at Eichmann, Dec. 16, 1938; item 5 is a notice that at the end of December Eichmann would issue permission for Murmelstein's trip, whose officially projected purpose was to "prepare the January transports, especially of youths ages 17 to 25." See also Murmelstein's report, dated Jan. 19, 1939, op. cit.
20. M-tapes II-16A, 293f. Norman de Mattos Bentwich (1883–1971) was the scion of an English part Ashkenazi, part Sephardi family that was active on behalf of Jewish causes, especially Zionism. His father Herbert, a lawyer and community activist, established the Zionist movement in Great Britain and settled part of his family in Palestine. Norman was a legal scholar and lawyer in the colonial service. Before the First World War, he became commissioner of courts in Cairo, where he also lectured at the law school. After frontline service in Palestine, he was appointed attorney general of the British Mandatory Government of Palestine, where he introduced British law and legal procedure. In 1930 an Arab attempt was made on his life, and in 1931 he resigned his post because of the increasingly anti-Zionist policy on the part of Great Britain. As of 1932 he was Professor of International Relations at Hebrew University in Jerusalem. From 1933 to 1936 he also served as director of the League of Nations' Commission for Jewish Refugees from Germany. With this background it was a matter of course that he took a leading and independent position within Great Britain as an activist on behalf of Jews persecuted by Nazi Germany. (Benjamin Jaffe and Cecil Roth, "Bentwich," *Encyclopaedia Judaica*, ed. Michael Berenbaum and Fred Skolnik, 2nd ed., vol. 3, Macmillan Reference USA, 2007, 381. *Gale Virtual Reference Library*, go.galegroup.com/ps/i.do?p=GVRL&sw=w&u=yorku_main&v=2.1&id=GALE%7CCX2587502551&it=r&asid=ac0cae993d878deba959752798acf7f6. Accessed Nov. 29, 2016).
21. Löwenherz to Council for German Jewry, op. cit., see note 2 above.

22. In *Wanderer in War 1939–45* (London: Gollancz, 1946), Bentwich reports that "The cost of feeding the men, and feeding them well, was less than 9*d*. a day; and the total cost of maintenance, including the allowance of pocket money, was less than 10*s*. a week" (10).
23. Ibid.
24. Ibid.
25. See Norman Bentwich, *I Understand the Risks*, 25ff; also Bentwich, *Wanderer in War 1939–45*, 9ff.
26. *Bulletin of the Co-ordinating Committee for Refugees* 3, London, Apr. 1939, 22f. Emphasis in original.
27. Some examples: Murmelstein's use of *Zwischenaufenthaltslager* (transit camp) in his handwritten drafts for Löwenherz's report to the Gestapo of May 2, 1939, concerning Murmelstein's second trip to London (L-papers); a similar draft for Löwenherz's report to the *Zentralstelle* of May 11, 1939, concerning the citizenship of men selected for the camp (L-papers). See also Murmelstein's typed drafts for Löwenherz's official requests of various dates for processing the documentation of projected groups destined for the camp; similar drafts for Löwenherz's requests for approval of Murmelstein's trip to London (all in CA: A/W 165.4). For Löwenherz's use of "camp," or "Richborough Camp," or "Camp Kitchener," or "camp in England" see, e.g., AN *Vorsprachen* Löwenherz at Eichmann, Feb. 16, 1939, item 1; Apr. 17, 1939, item 10; June 26, 1939, item 10; Aug. 11, 1939, item 2; all in L-papers.
28. AN of Löwenherz's consultation at the English consulate, Jan. 4, 1939; L-papers.
29. The authors have known a number of persons, including relatives, who were in the camp, and they denied knowing of any military plans for the residents.
30. Bentwich, *I Understand the Risks*, 28; see also *Bulletin of the Co-ordinating Committee for Refugees*, 23.
31. For example, in a memorandum (dated Apr. 28, 1939) to the German embassy at Sofia, Mr. Jakubowski, the German consul at the Bulgarian seaport of Burgas, reports the departure of the *Atios Nikola*, a Greek steamer, "small" and of "ancient construction," with Jews from central Europe bound for illegal immigration to the British Mandate of Palestine. There are two significant passages in the memorandum. The first deals with German sensitivity to the possible military value of Jewish refugees to the British:

    > In spite of the fact that immigration permits cannot be granted by the mandatory authorities, according to reliable sources the English have agreed to permit tacitly the illegal disembarkation at unpatrolled coastal stretches. Among the passengers there are about 350 men, all with past military service; according to credible statements to the British authorities, these men form a welcome addition to the Jewish police force.

    The second passage exemplifies the concern over the international image of Nazi Germany as regards the treatment of Jews:

    > In the mood of the Bulgarian population SS *Atios Nicola*'s prolonged 14 days' stay in Burgas worked to the detriment of Germany, because the many Jewish emigrants, idly frequenting the coffeehouses, liberally spread the worst horror propaganda (*Greuelpropaganda*).

    "Jakubowski, Deutsches Konsulat, Burgas to Deutsche Gesandtschaft, Sofia, Apr. 28, 1939," in John Mendelsohn, ed., *The Holocaust: Selected Documents in 18 Volumes, Vol. 6: Jewish Emigration 1938–1940* (New York/London: Garland, 1982), 215.
32. AN *Vorsprache* Löwenherz at Kuchmann, Jan. 5, 1939; L-papers.
33. AN *Vorsprache* Löwenherz and Rothenberg at Eichmann, Sep. 17, 1939; L-papers.
34. M-tapes, II-11a, 195; II-16a, 295.
35. Murmelstein mentions his inspection of the camp in his handwritten draft for Löwenherz to the Gestapo and the *Zentralstelle*, May 2, 1939; L-papers.
36. Murmelstein thought that the placement of former concentration camp inmates constituted 80 percent of the total. M-tape II-11A, 195.
37. Kapralik, 40.
38. M-tape II-16A, 295.
39. M-tape II-10A, 170.
40. M-tape II-16A, 294.
41. Löwenherz to Gestapo headquarters, Mar. 2, 1939; CA: A/W 165.3.
42. Murmelstein's handwritten draft, dated May 2, 1939, for Löwenherz to Gestapo headquarters and the *Zentralstelle*; L-papers.
43. Bentwich, *I Understand the Risks*, 27.
44. Ibid., 28.

45. Ibid., 176f.
46. Bernard Wasserstein, *Britain and the Jews of Europe 1939–1945* (London: Institute of Jewish Affairs / New York: Oxford University Press, 1979), ch. 3, 81ff.
47. Kapralik, in the prefatory remarks to his memoir, mentions that he too was interned in what he calls the "atmosphere of panic" prevailing in the summer of 1940; Kapralik, 1. The order to intern all German foreigners, and that would include the Jewish refugees, ultimately came from the new Prime Minister Churchill's effort to devise the defense of Britain against the expected German invasion. In his *History of the Second World War*, Churchill does not mention the internment order. However, in the chapter dealing with the plans for home defense he cites a letter he wrote to the Secretary for the Colonies, Lord Lloyd, dated June 28, 1940. Churchill, in need of the sizable British force held in Palestine, reproves Lord Lloyd for "the anti-Jewish policy which had persisted for some years. . . . If the Jews were properly armed, our forces would become available. . . . I think it is less than a scandal that at a time when we are fighting for our lives these very large forces should be immobilised in support of a policy which commends itself only to a section of the Conservative Party" (Winston S. Churchill, *History of the Second World War, Vol. 2: Their Finest Hour* [Boston: Houghton Mifflin, 1949], 175). This confirms that anti-Jewish sentiment tended to determine policy; yet, it also shows that anti-Jewish policy was not the primary determinant of the internment of Jewish refugees in Britain during the initial period of the Churchill government.
48. Bentwich, 33.
49. M-tape II-10A, 172; M-tape II-16A, 292f; M-tape II-11A, 195.
50. B. S. Barbash to IKG *Auswanderungsabteilung* (i.e., emigration section), Apr. 12, 1939; CA: A/W 165. By the time Barbash's letter reached Vienna, HICEM had responded to his pleas, and for a time he administered their aid effort in Shanghai. According to Kranzler, Barbash's "amateurish, though well-intentioned efforts to provide the necessary aid to thousands of refugees, forced HICEM to move its Harbin office to Shanghai by September of 1939, and put it under the direction of Meyer Birman." David Kranzler, *Japanese, Nazis & Jews: The Jewish Refugee Community of Shanghai, 1939–1945* (New York: Yeshiva University Press, 1976), 98. Kranzler reports that the Jewish refugee community of Shanghai included, besides those from Germany and Austria, and those from Russia mentioned by Barbash, some who had fled the rising persecution of Jews in Iraq.
51. The exact number of refugees from Germany and Austria who came to Shanghai may never be known. Kranzler reports that in 1943 there were 17,000; in 1944 the ghetto that the Japanese established held 14,245, of whom 3,942 were from Austria. In 1945 there were 13,496. These figures do not tell us about births and deaths or about the movement of Jews from Shanghai to other localities in China. See Kranzler, *Japanese, Nazis & Jews*, 115 and 606.
52. An example: A cousin of one of the authors, released from Dachau in spring 1939, bought passage for a considerable amount of money supplied by his father and spent the war years in the interior of China, where he joined a traveling circus in which he played a role unheard of in those parts, namely, a clown. Most refugees in Shanghai were not so fortunate, not because they were not as enterprising, but because they had families, including children, or were women or older people.
53. Löwenherz to Eichmann, memorandum "Betrifft Sammeltransporte nach China," Mar. 8, 1939; CA: A/W 165.3.
54. By the middle of 1939 a considerable effort was under way to help the ever larger number of refugees in Shanghai sustain themselves. Especially HICEM gave the needy refugees checks in U.S. dollars. While these checks, and those which relatives from the United States sent to the Jews of Shanghai, were not large, the favorable exchange rate made it possible for a person to feed himself for less than three dollars a month. See Kranzler, 98.
55. AN *Vorsprache* Engel at Eichmann, Mar. 30, 1939, item 3; L-papers. Engel's response to Eichmann does not differ from the one which Löwenherz would have given. This confirms what one of our informants, Dr. Margaret Feiler, reported to us at the office of the AJDC (the "Joint") in December 1974, namely, that Löwenherz had frequent informal meetings with his lieutenants to discuss his meetings with Eichmann and other authorities and to consult and determine policy; Engel and Murmelstein were his chief lieutenants.
56. Löwenherz to *Zentralstelle*, Apr. 7, 1939; CA: A/W 165.4.
57. Löwenherz to *Zentralstelle*, Apr. 17, 1939; CA: A/W 165.4.
58. M-tape II-15B, 280ff.
59. "Bericht der IKG über ihre Tätigkeit in den ersten drei Monaten 1939," 3.

60. See, e.g., from this period the following reports in Joint file "AJ": "Translation of Report of Jewish Community, Vienna for January 1939"; "Translation of Report of Jewish Community, Vienna, January 14, 1939"; "Report of the Vienna Jewish Community, May–June 1939."
61. Soon after his return Kapralik found out, presumably from Raffegerst, his German counterpart, that because of his function in the extremely sensitive area of foreign exchange, which put him in contact with German as well as foreign officials, he was under suspicion at the Gestapo and might be in danger of arrest, and so he emigrated.
62. AN *Vorsprache* Löwenherz, Rothenberg, and Storfer at Eichmann, Aug. 12, 1939, item 1; L-papers.
63. AN telephone calls Kuchmann and Löwenherz, Aug. 7, 1939; L-papers.
64. Löwenherz to Hertz, Dec. 22, 1938; CA: A/W.
65. Religious Emergency Fund to IKG, no date, received Jan. 16, 1939; CA: A/W.
66. Murmelstein's report to Gestapo, Jan. 19, 1939; CA: A/W 165.1.
67. Löwenherz to *Zentralstelle* and Gestapo, Feb. 1939; CA: A/W 165.2.
68. Löwenherz to Hertz, Feb. 13, 1939; CA: A/W. Löwenherz must have been sensitive to the problem from the time of his consultation with the British Passport Officer on January 4. In the official memorandum recording the substance of the consultation we read: "In regard to the issuance of 10 rabbi certificates the IKG together with the Palamt is to submit a ranking, also a brief memorandum in which [Löwenherz] and the chief rabbi [of Vienna, Taglicht] jointly indicate which of the rabbis are really rabbis and had functioned as such in Austria." AN consultation Löwenherz and Rothenberg at Passport Office, British Consulate, Jan. 4, 1939, item 2; L-papers.
69. *Beschlussbuch* (IKG ledger of administrative decisions) nr. 72/items 7920f, 7928f; nr. 74/item 8135. CA: A/W 88/69, 88/71.
70. *Beschlussbuch* nr. 73/items 8032f, CA: A/W 88/70; nr. 74/item 8137, op. cit.
71. *Beschlussbuch* nr. 74/items 8147f, op. cit.
72. Ibid., items 8193f.
73. M-tapes II-13A, 232f; II-15B, 278.
74. M-tapes I-5A, 66.
75. This was reluctantly and indirectly confirmed by Rimalt in our interview with him in Tel Aviv, May 1977. Cf. M-tapes I-5B, 72; II-13A, 235.
76. AN *Vorsprache* Löwenherz and Rothenberg at Eichmann, Feb. 10, 1939, item 5; L-papers.
77. AN *Vorsprache* Löwenherz and Rothenberg at Eichmann, Feb. 23, 1939, item 5; L-papers.
78. AN *Vorsprache* Löwenherz and Rothenberg at Eichmann, Mar. 2, 1939, item 1; L-papers.
79. Ibid., item 2. See also "Bericht der IKG über ihre Tätigkeit in den ersten drei Monaten 1939," op. cit., 3.
80. AN *Vorsprache* Löwenherz and Rothenberg, Mar. 6, 1939, item 2; L-papers.
81. AN Telephone consultation Engel and Wagner, Jan. 24, 1939; L-papers.
82. AN *Vorsprache* at Eichmann, Mar. 6, 1939, item 1; L-papers.
83. AN *Vorsprache* Löwenherz and Rothenberg at Eichmann, Mar. 2, 1939, item 1; L-papers. Before the end of March, "Jewish aid societies abroad succeeded, thanks to their efforts, in having the passengers [of the *SS Königstein*] land in Venezuela." See "Bericht der [IKG] über ihre Tätigkeit in den ersten drei Monaten des Jahres 1939," 3.
84. AN *Vorsprache*, Mar. 6, 1939, op. cit., item 2.
85. Ibid., item 5.
86. It is no wonder that Löwenherz regarded the IKG's carbon copies as the most important documents of that period, which he compiled and kept in his desk during those years, and reacquired when, in 1946, he was finally able to emigrate to the United States. It is strange that the Israeli police, to whom Löwenherz lent these papers in preparation for the Eichmann trial, made so little use of them and did not even do so in connection with Eichmann's interest in the Hanseatic Travel Agency.
87. See AN *Vorsprache*, Feb. 23, 1939, op. cit.
88. AN *Vorsprache* Löwenherz, Rothenberg, and Storfer at Eichmann, Mar. 8, 1939, item 1; L-papers.
89. It was difficult to get Eichmann to release the necessary moneys. In the case of the Maccabi transport, as in other cases, he released less than was requested by the IKG. (See AN *Vorsprache* Löwenherz and Rothenberg at Eichmann Feb. 10, 1939, item 5; AN *Vorsprache* the same with Grün and Storfer, Apr. 17, 1939, item 2; AN *Vorsprache* Löwenherz, Apr. 21, 1939, item 1; L-papers.) The Maccabi transport of 948 persons finally left in two parts on Danube steamers around May 1; 906 embarked on the SS *Liesel* at the Danube Delta port of Tulcea, Romania. The *Liesel* left on May 17 and was captured by the

British off the coast of Palestine on June 2. The captain of the *Liesel* was given a nine-month prison sentence, but the crew was acquitted. The participants were detained but released on June 4, an easier fate than that of many a transport of the more than sixty of Aliyah Bet. (See Perl, *Operation Action*, 406.)

90. AN *Vorsprache* Murmelstein and Storfer at Eichmann, June 19, 1939; AN *Vorsprache* Löwenherz at Eichmann, June 23, 1939, item 2; AN *Vorsprache* Löwenherz and Rothenberg at Eichmann, July 9, 1939, item 6; L-papers.
91. AN *Vorsprache* Löwenherz and Rothenberg at Eichmann, Mar. 2, 1939, item 4; L-papers. About the conference, see Walter Laqueur, *A History of Zionism* (New York: Holt, Rinehart and Winston, 1972), 522ff.
92. We can see here to what extent Murmelstein, Engel, and the emigration staff had to engage in research and had to keep Löwenherz abreast of such minutiae.
93. AN *Vorsprache* Löwenherz and [Mauricy Moses] Grün (Palamt) at Eichmann, Apr. 28, 1939, item 2; L-papers.
94. AN *Vorsprache* Löwenherz and Rothenberg at Eichmann, July 9, 1939, item 9; L-papers.
95. Later that year, other immigration schemes to Bolivia began to materialize, which HICEM was prepared to underwrite with start-up funds for the new immigrants.
96. See AN *Vorsprache* Löwenherz at Eichmann, Aug. 14, 1939; L-papers.
97. That is, the SS (SD and Gestapo) and even the SA.
98. This was reported to us by Dr. Margaret Feiler, who was often called in by Löwenherz to be a member of this circle of intimates. Prior to the Anschluss, Dr. Feiler had been a practicing lawyer. During her employment at the IKG, she drafted official correspondence and documents. When, in 1940, her firm stand during an appearance at the Gestapo made her position dangerous, she took the opportunity to immigrate to the United States.
99. See, for example, the corrections of Löwenherz's AN of Aug. 14, 1939, which Engel was ordered to submit on Aug. 21, 1939; L-papers.
100. With reference to the IKG's first annual report to the Joint and CBF, Löwenherz notes the following in the AN of his *Vorsprache* at Eichmann of December 28, 1938: "The report to the foreign organizations, drafted in English, is approved and can be forwarded" (item 10; L-papers).
101. Löwenherz records Eichmann's directive for the submission of the first yearly report: "The yearly report of the [I]KG is to be submitted no later than January 3 [1939] and must contain, strictly separate, the (a) Activity and (b) the Situation Report. The report is to be supplemented with relevant tables and illustrations. The report of the Palestine Office is to be modelled on the model of that of the [I]KG." AN Dec. 28, 1938, item 12.
102. Löwenherz, Rothenberg, and Engel had to sign the following statement submitted to Gestapo headquarters and drafted by Murmelstein: "The undersigned declare that they wish to assume responsibility that Dr. Benjamin Murmelstein of the IKGW Directorate, who will proceed to England in order to discuss the expansion of youth transports, will return to Vienna after 10–12 days to resume his duties." This was accompanied by a copy of Löwenherz's request for a temporary entry visa for Murmelstein, addressed to the British Passport Control Office, Vienna, which contains the following passage: "[Murmelstein's] trip was approved by the appropriate authorities under the proviso that the aforementioned will resume his duties in the Directorate. . . . The responsibility for [his] meeting this obligation has been assumed by the undersigned . . ., Rothenberg . . . and Engel." CA: A/W 165, 1.
103. See, e.g., AN *Vorsprache* Jan. 10, 1939, item 6; L-papers.
104. Löwenherz to *Devisenstelle* Wien, Referat 60, Mar. 17, 1939, with Raffegerst's approval; YV: 030/4, file "Dr. J. Loewenherz."
105. AN *Vorsprache* Löwenherz, Grün, and Storfer at Eichmann, Apr. 17, 1939, item 6; L-papers. The Society of Friends was the umbrella organization for the "Gildemeester action," which soon after the Anschluss took care of the interests of Jews who had converted to Christianity, later, under Eichmann's orders, only of persons who were racially only part Jewish. Racially 100 percent Jews had to be taken care of by the IKG, whether religiously Jewish or not.
106. Löwenherz to Gestapo Leitstelle Wien, Aug. 11, 1939; L-papers.
107. AN *Vorsprache* Löwenherz and Rothenberg at Eichmann, Jan. 4, 1939, item 2; L-papers. In a memorandum to Eichmann, dated Jan. 6, 1939, Löwenherz lists the bills paid by the IKG for the SS-men who had been stationed at the IKG since Nov. 12. (See CA: A/W 165.1.) The IKG had to pay them their wages (RM 1,950.00), pay their tavern bills (RM 1,712.94), bills at coffeehouses (RM 514.78), as well

as extra heat, electricity, and cleaning (RM 294.00), a total of RM 4,471.72. We did not find any record of reimbursement.

108. AN *Vorsprache* Löwenherz and Rothenberg at Eichmann, Mar. 2, 1939, item 5; AN *Vorsprache* Löwenherz and Rothenberg at Eichmann, Mar. 6, 1939, item 7; L-papers.
109. AN *Besprechung* (discussion) Löwenherz with Brunner, Aug. 2, 1939, item 3; L-papers.
110. See AN Nov. 14, 1938; Nov. 30, 1938, item 4; Dec. 2, 1938, item 6; Jan. 10, 1939, item 2; Feb. 16, 1939, item 1; Mar. 16, 1939, item 3; May 18, 1939; May 26, 1939, item 4; June 5, 1939, item 7; June 23, 1939, item 8 (also accompanying special report concerning a wave of harassment such as evictions, which tended to disturb the emigration process); June 27, 1939; July 16, 1939, item 5; July 31, 1939, item 2; Aug. 3, 1939; Aug. 14, 1939, item 3; L-papers.
111. Ehrmann, Laufer, Fürst to Comité foor Joodsche Vluchtlingen (*sic*), May 28, 1939; Comité voor bijzondere joodsche Belangen to IKG, May 31, 1939; IKG (Engel) to Comité . . . , June 11, 1939. CA: A/W.
112. AN *Vorsprache* Löwenherz and Rothenberg at Eichmann, Mar. 16, 1939, item 1; L-papers.
113. Ibid., item 2.
114. Ibid., item 1.
115. See Löwenherz's letters to Gestapo *Leitstelle* (headquarters) and to Eichmann on behalf of Friedmann and, separately, of Stricker, dated Jan. 5, 1939, CA: A/W 165.1.
116. AN *Vorsprache* Löwenherz and Rothenberg at Eichmann, Feb. 10, 1939, item 1; Löwenherz and Rothenberg to *Zentralstelle* c/o Eichmann, Feb. 10, 1939; L-papers.
117. AN *Vorsprache* Löwenherz and Rothenberg at Eichmann, Feb. 23, 1939, item 7; L-papers.
118. AN *Vorsprache* Löwenherz, Grün, and Storfer at Eichmann, Apr. 17, 1939, item 11; L-papers.
119. AN *Vorsprache* Löwenherz (only) at Eichmann, June 23, 1939; item 9; L-papers.
120. AN *Vorsprache* Löwenherz (only) at Eichmann, June 26, 1939, item 1; L-papers.
121. AN *Vorsprache* Löwenherz and Rothenberg at Eichmann, July 31, 1939, item 3; L-papers.
122. AN *Vorsprache* Löwenherz, Rothenberg, and Storfer at Eichmann, Aug. 12, 1939, item 7; L-papers.
123. "*. . . eine Andeutung, dass vielleicht anlässlich der Überführung ein Separat-Betrag in Devisen für Auswanderungszwecke erwirkt werden könnte*" [". . . his hint, that a separate amount of foreign funds could perhaps be procured on the occasion of the transfer"]. AN *Vorsprache* Löwenherz and Rothenberg at Eichmann, Mar. 2, 1939, item 4.
124. AN *Vorsprache* Löwenherz and Rothenberg at Eichmann, Mar. 9, 1939, item 4; L-papers.
125. "34. Wochenbericht der [IKG] Wien vom 3. Jänner 1939 zugleich Tätigkeits- und Lagebericht für die Zeit vom 2 Mai 1938–31 Dezember 1938" (34th Weekly Report of IKG, Jan. 3, 1939; also Activities and Situation Report for the period May 2, 1938, to Dec. 31, 1938), 14; YV.
126. Calculated on the basis of statistics in ibid., 14.
127. In the IKG report to Eichmann and the Gestapo, Murmelstein phrases it as follows: "The decrease in November is due to the circumstance that during the course of this month the soup kitchens were closed for a week." Ibid.
128. "Tätigkeitsbericht der [IKG] Wien im Monate Jänner 1939" (Activities Report for Jan. 1939), 2; YV. "Translation: Report of Jewish Community Vienna for Jan. 1939," 2; Joint Archive.
129. "Tätigkeitsbericht der [IKG] im Monate März 1939" (Activity Report of IKG to Eichmann and Gestapo for Mar. 1939), 6; YV. "34. Wochenbericht . . .," op. cit., 14.
130. Samuel Gurwitz's handwritten report, 11f; Joint Archive.
131. "Tätigkeitsbericht . . . ," Mar. 1939, op. cit., 6; YV.
132. Ibid., 5.
133. Ibid., 8.
134. "Einnahmen und Ausgaben im Jahre 1938" (Income and Outlay in 1938), Supplement to "34. Wochenbericht . . . ," op. cit.
135. Population statistics computed according to information in IKG reports to Eichmann and Gestapo.
136. "34. Wochenbericht . . . ," 15f.
137. The estimates of the number of Jews who would remain in Vienna after the forced emigration action was completed, fluctuated: According to AN Löwenherz at Eichmann, Feb. 23, 1939, item 2, Eichmann thought "one will have to reckon with 20,000 to 25,000 Jews remaining here." Four months later, in connection with Eichmann's plans to close down the IKG once the emigration was completed, Löwenherz advised that "about 25,000 to 30,000 Jews will have to remain in Vienna, hence the liquidation of the IKG is not advisable. The IKG will have to provide for those who are left behind by means of nursing homes for the aged and for the infirm, for food service, for burials, etc., and also to pursue

emigration efforts for them, though on a smaller scale. There is no doubt that in the course of the next few years the younger people will send for their parents or grandparents, insofar as they find an occupation" (AN June 23, 1939, item 8). During his meeting with Eichmann, Bentwich, accompanied by Löwenherz, speaks of "23,000 to 25,000 Jews who will have to remain" (AN Aug. 14, 1939). All references to L-papers.

138. AN *Vorsprache* Löwenherz at Eichmann, Dec. 16, 1938, item 3; L-papers.
139. *Aufbauumlage*; see ch. 3.
140. AN *Vorsprache* Löwenherz and Rothenberg at Eichmann, Jan. 10, 1939, items 2 and 3; L-papers.
141. AN *Vorsprache* Feb. 23, 1939, items 3 and 4; L-papers.
142. See Löwenherz's report to Eichmann concerning *Allgemeine Stiftung* . . . , dated July 4, 1939; also the accompanying request for cancellation of assessment, dated July 9, 1939. L-papers.
143. Ignàc Schulcz, a Social-Democratic, Slovak member of the Czechoslovak Parliament, reported to his government the case of fifty-one Jews from Kittsee, whom he saw in Bratislava. They included "old men, women, children, who lacked the most necessary clothing. . . . [They] were chased to the Danube, and in spite of entreaties of fellow citizens who were Christian to leave some of them in Kittsee, they were all put into a boat and launched. . . . At about 1:30 a.m. they made landfall at the Czechoslovak shore, not far from the border village Theben. . . ." "Information, aufgenommen vom Abg. Ignàc Schulcz am 20. IV. 1938 in Bratislava," YIVO Occ 6a-3.
144. AN *Vorsprache* Löwenherz at Lange (Gestapo headquarters), Feb. 25, 1939, accompanied by Löwenherz's covering letter to Lange, dated Feb. 27, 1939; L-papers.
145. Beschlagnahme (confiscation).
146. AN *Vorsprache* Löwenherz at Eichmann, June 12, 1939, item 4; L-papers.
147. AN *Vorsprache* Löwenherz at Eichmann June 26, 1939, item 5; L-papers.
148. AN *Vorsprache* Löwenherz at Eichmann July 9, 1939, item 4; L-papers.
149. AN Gestapo telephone directive, July 12, 1939; L-papers.
150. AN *Vorsprache* Löwenherz at Eichmann, Aug. 14, 1939, item 1; L-papers.
151. Eichmann actually said "*im Einvernehmen mit*." While this literally means "in agreement (or consultation) with," it can have the contextual connotation of following orders.
152. See AN *Vorsprache* Aug. 14, 1939, item 1; L-papers.
153. AN discussion (*Besprechung*) Löwenherz with Schaufler and municipal officials, Mar. 14, 1939; L-papers.
154. AN *Vorsprache* Löwenherz, accompanied by Grün and Storfer, at Eichmann, Apr. 17, 1939, item 7; L-papers.
155. See the following AN *Vorsprachen*: Löwenherz at Eichmann Dec. 19, 1938, item 2: "IKG and Palamt are entrusted exclusively with questions of emigration of Jews by religion, whereas *Gildemeester-Aktion* is to restrict its activity to nonconfessional Jews." June 12, 1939, item 1: "from now on Gildemeester is not to concern itself with Jews by religion, and is to relinquish all pending relevant cases to the IKG." L-papers.
156. AN *Vorsprache* Löwenherz at Eichmann, Dec. 20, 1938, item 2; L-papers.
157. AN *Vorsprache* Löwenherz and Rothenberg at Eichmann, Jan. 10, 1939, item 1; L-papers.
158. AN *Vorsprache* Löwenherz and Rothenberg at Eichmann, Feb. 16, 1939, item 3; L-papers.
159. AN *Vorsprache* Löwenherz and Grün at Eichmann, Apr. 28, 1939, item 1; L-papers.
160. AN *Vorsprache* Engel at Eichmann, May 28, 1939, item 3; L-papers.
161. AN *Vorsprache* Löwenherz at Eichmann, June 5, 1939, item 4; and June 12, 1939, item 2. L-papers.
162. AN *Vorsprache* Löwenherz at Eichmann, June 23, 1939, item 5; L-papers.
163. AN *Vorsprache* Löwenherz and Rothenberg at Eichmann, July 9, 1939, item 12; L-papers.
164. AN *Vorsprache* Löwenherz, Grün, and Storfer at Eichmann, Apr. 17, 1939, item 4; L-papers.
165. Ibid.
166. Troper to Löwenherz, May 22, 1939; German translation submitted to Eichmann; L-papers. Regrettably, the English original is not available.
167. AN *Vorsprache* Löwenherz at Eichmann, June 5, 1939, item 5; L-papers.
168. Joseph J. Schwartz AJDC in-house memorandum to Paul Beerwald, July 31, 1939; AJDC archive file AJ 440.
169. Troper, AJDC Paris, to Hyman, AJDC New York, June 6, 1939; AJDC archive file AJ 440.
170. Joseph J. Schwartz AJDC in-house memorandum.
171. "Report of the Vienna Jewish Community: May–June 1939," AJDC archive file AJ.

172. AN *Vorsprache* Löwenherz at Eichmann, June 5, 1939, item 2; L-papers.
173. Report "VII-5 Allgemeine Stiftung für jüdische Fürsorge in Wien. Weisung vom 5. Juni 1938," dated July 4, 1939; L-papers.
174. *Aufbaufonds-Vermögensverwertungs-G.m.b.H.*
175. "*Sonstige Vermögenswerte.*"
176. In-house information circular, Löwenherz to directors of provincial communities, June 26, 1939; L-papers.
177. Report "VII-5/2 *Erlassen der Aufbau-und Verwaltungsumlage für die allgemeine Stiftung für jüdische Fürsorge in Wien. Weisung vom 9. Juli 1939*" [In regard to release from the reconstruction and administrative fee for the "General Foundation . . ." according to directive of July 9, 1939], dated July 9, 1939; L-papers.
178. Ibid.
179. A governmental office regulating the transfer (literally, movement) of assets.
180. AN (dated July 16) *Vorsprache* Löwenherz and Rothenberg at Eichmann, July 15, 1939, item 1; L-papers.
181. AN *Vorsprache* Löwenherz at Guenther, Aug. 11, 1939, item 1; L-papers.
182. AN *Vorsprache* Löwenherz and Rothenberg at Eichmann, July 31, 1939, item 5; L-papers.
183. AN discussion (*Besprechung*) Löwenherz with Brunner at the *Zentralstelle*, Aug. 2, 1939, item 1; L-papers.
184. Ibid., item 3; L-papers.
185. Ibid., item 2; L-papers.
186. See draft of memorandum (Löwenherz to Eichmann) "VIII-25 *Auslandsreise*" dated Aug. 9, 1939; L-papers.
187. AN *Vorsprache* Löwenherz at Eichmann in sometime presence of Bentwich, Aug. 14, 1939. Items 3 to 7 deal with the matters discussed in the presence of Bentwich. L-papers.
188. Norman Bentwich, "Report on a Visit to Vienna," dated Aug. 17, 1939; AJDC file AJ 440. A copy of the "report" was evidently submitted to the AJDC, thus indicating that Bentwich was an emissary to Eichmann of the highest echelon of the Jewish establishment on the matters mentioned, as well as an inspector of the IKG as their agency in Vienna.
189. Ibid., p. 4.
190. Ibid., p. 2.
191. Ibid., p. 5.
192. AN nr. VIII-40/2 of *Weisung* (directive) received by Engel, dated Aug. 21, 1939, regarding *Weisung* as in Löwenherz's AN dated Aug. 14, 1939; L-papers.
193. After the deportations, when dealings with the remaining Jews were declared to be police matters and consequently the Gestapo was finally assigned sole jurisdiction over them, Ebner would be the last supervisor over the IKG.
194. Löwenherz's draft (handwritten by Engel) AN VIII-9 "Weisung der Gestapo Leitstelle Wien," dated Aug. 3, 1939; L-papers.
195. AN Kuchmann's telephone call to Löwenherz, Aug. 7, 1939; L-papers.
196. AN *Weisungen* by telephone Guenther to Löwenherz, Aug. 11, 1939; L-papers.
197. AN *Vorsprache* Löwenherz, Rothenberg, and Storfer at Eichmann, Aug. 12, 1939, item 2; L-papers.
198. Bentwich, "Report," 4.
199. AN *Vorsprache* Löwenherz at Günther, Sep. 11, 1939, items 1, 2, 4; L-papers.
200. AN *Vorsprache* Löwenherz and Rothenberg at Eichmann, Sep. 17, 1939; L-papers.

Chapter 7

1. The Nisko episode is not treated in Hilberg, *Destruction of the European Jews*.
2. Arendt considered it an "utter fiasco." See Arendt, *Eichmann in Jerusalem*, 75.
3. AN *Vorsprache* Löwenherz at Rolf Günther, Sep. 11, 1939, items 1, 2; L-papers.
4. AN Rolf Günther's visit at Löwenherz's IKG office, Sep. 25, 1939; L-papers.
5. *Chef der Sicherheitspolizei* [Chief of Security Police, i.e., Heydrich] to *Einsatzgruppen der Sicherheitspolizei* [Security Police Task Forces], Sep. 21, 1939; EICH 775. This document has been reproduced at various places, e.g., in *Faschismus-Getto-Massenmord* (edited by Jüdisches Historisches Institut Warschau, Frankfurt/Main, 1962), 37f; English in Trunk, *Judenrat*, 2f.

6. Memorandum from "Ech" (Eichmann?), dated Berlin, Oct. 6, 1939, to *Zentralstelle Mährisch-Ostrau* (Ostrava in Moravia) (received Oct. 8, 1939) regarding orders received from SS-*Oberführer* (Brigadier General) Heinrich Müller. The transmitted orders provide for "shoving" (*Abschieben*) 70,000 to 80,000 Jews from the area of Kattowitz (Katowice) as well as the Jews from Mährish-Ostrau "at first in an easterly direction across the Vistula." Significantly the memorandum ends as follows: "In the main this activity is meant to serve the gathering of experience, on the basis of which large-scale evacuations can be carried out." Wiesenthal Archive, Vienna, file M-O.
7. Löwenherz to *Zentralstelle Wien*, dated Oct. 11, 1939; subject: "Petition to refrain from sending Dr. Benjamin Israel Murmelstein to Mährisch-Ostrau." Untitled collection of documents published in Prague in the 1960s, 7.
8. *Jüdisches Nachrichtenblatt*, Vienna edition, Sep. 8, 1939.
9. See Rosenkranz, *Verfolgung*, 213.
10. Adler, *Die verheimlichte Wahrheit*, 126f.
11. *Jüdisches Nachrichtenblatt*, Vienna edition, Sep. 8, 1939. Neither Rosenkranz nor Adler takes note of the first two facts in their reference to this announcement.
12. M-tape II 10A, 176ff.
13. AN *Vorsprache* Löwenherz at Gestapo, Sep. 10, 1939; L-papers.
14. AN *Vorsprache* Löwenherz at Rolf Günther, Sep. 11, 1939, item 5; L-papers.
15. AN *Vorsparche* Löwenherz at Rolf Günther, Sep. 23, 1939; L-papers.
16. AN *Vorsprache* Löwenherz at Rolf Günther, Oct. 10, 1939, item 1; L-papers.
17. Murmelstein typescript, 56.
18. Addendum (dated Oct. 11) to AN Oct. 10, 1939; L-papers.
19. Clause 1 of the section of Heydrich's memorandum of Sep. 21, 1939, dealing with the establishment and function of the *Jüdische Ältestenräte*, specifies that the councils "are to be made literally *fully responsible* for the exact and timely execution of all directives issued or yet to be issued." (Emphasis in the original.) See note 5.
20. DÖW 9376.
21. Memorandum [*Vermerk*] by Brunner, dated Oct. 17, 1939, recording discussion held Oct. 16 by Eichmann, Ebner, and Becker; Wiesenthal Archive Vienna, file M-O; also DÖW 2527.
22. Ibid.
23. Cf. Ze'ev Goshen, "Eichmann und die Nisko-Aktion im Oktober 1939," *Vierteljahresheft für Zeitgeschichte*, Nr. 1/1981, 74–96.
24. Ibid., 79.
25. Ibid.
26. Churchill's comment about this "peace offer": "[Hitler] felt sure His Majesty's Government would be very glad to accept the decision reached by him in Poland, and that a peace offer would enable Mr. Chamberlain and his old colleagues, having vindicated their honour by a declaration of war, to get out of the scrape into which they had been forced by the warmongering elements in Parliament. It never occurred to him for a moment that Mr. Chamberlain and the rest of the British Empire and Commonwealth of Nations now meant to have his blood or perish in the attempt." Winston S. Churchill, *The Gathering Storm* (Boston: Houghton Mifflin, 1948), 484f.
27. Murmelstein typescript, 54.
28. Secret Directive No. 191 332 issued by Heydrich Sep. 7, 1939 to all *Stapoleitstellen* (regional State Police Headquarters) and Inspectors of the Security Police, and through Wolff at Himmler's Gestapo Headquarters to regional and municipal governing authorities and police directors. EICH 1633.
29. Telegram Zimmermann of *Stapoleitstelle* Brünn (Brno) to Eichmann at *Zentralstelle* Prague, Oct. 10, 1939. Wiesenthal Archive Vienna, file M-O.
30. General Quartermaster to Army Group South and others; after Sep. 11, 1939; actual date illegible. IZG: MA113/6.
31. Secret memorandum from Stapo Mährisch-Ostrau to Gestapo/*Stapoleitstelle* Brünn, Sep. 19, 1939. Wiesenthal Archive, file M-O.
32. Proceedings against Dreiser, archive of *Zentrale Stelle der Landesjustizverwaltungen*, Ludwigsburg, cited in Goshen, "Eichmann und die Nisko-Aktion," 83fn.
33. "Besondere Anordnung Nr. 28 für die Versorgung der 8. Armee," issued by *Armeeoberkommando* (Army Headquarters) 8, Łódz, Sep. 21, 1939. IZG: MA-113/6.
34. "Besondere Anordnung Nr. 25," issued by *Armee Oberkommando* 10, Sep. 26, 1939. IZG: MA-113/6.

35. "*Der Landkommissar, Jaroslau*, to *Chef der Zivilverwaltung*, Krakow," Oct. 19, 1939. IZG: MA-682.
36. Ibid.
37. Transcript of "*Kriegstagebuch* [War Diary]" of Landkommissar Nisko begun Oct. 1, 1939, 1. IZG: MA-682.
38. Transcript of "*Geheime Kommandosache* [secret orders]" issued to major army units and commanders by Army Commander-in-Chief von Brauchitsch at his headquarters, Sep. 24, 1939. IZG: Files of the 8th Army, IZG: MA-113/6.
39. Report of the Commander of the 8th Army in Łódz, written in Włocławek, Sep. 25, 1939, Files of the 8th Army, IZG: MA-113/6.
40. "Burnt-out" = *abgebrannt*; this word also is used as a colloquialism meaning "bankrupt." Both meanings might be operative here.
41. *Lagebericht* (situation report) by *Landrat* (regional council) of the Pińczów region to chief of the civil administration in Krakow, Kazimierza Wielka, Oct. 19, 1939. IZG: MA-682.
42. Supplemental directive "Concerning: Securing the Demarcation Line" by General Command (for the chief of the general staff) to relevant divisions, Oct. 8, 1939. IZG: MA-113/6.
43. Translation into German of deposition by Roman Kaniewski, Krakow, Sep. 2, 1945, War Crimes Unit Document EJ-10; and of deposition by Syma Weikselbaum, Tarnobrzeg, Aug. 31, 1949, War Crimes Unit Document EJ-12. IZG.
44. Secret report about the internal political situation, based on reports filed by local offices of the SD and Gestapo, issued by Heydrich's office, Oct. 18, 1939. IZG: MA-441/1.
45. Secret report on the internal political situation issued by Heydrich's office, Nov. 8, 1939. IZG: MA-441/1.
46. Secret report about armament logistics for the period Oct. 7 to 28, 1939, filed by *Wehrwirtschafts-Inspektion Ober-Ost*, Łódz, Oct. 28, 1939, p. 7. NA: AHS/GSA microfilm T77, roll 618, frame 806006; also IZG: M638.
47. Situation report of *Rüstungswirtschafts-Inspektion* XXIII, Łódz, Nov. 4, 1939. NA: AHS/GSA microfilm T77, roll 618, frame 805750-1; also IZG: M638.
48. Report by Dr. Seraphim, *Wehrwirtschaftliche Auswirkungen des Umsiedlungsvorhabens im deutschen Verwaltungsgebiet Polens* (Defense-logistical effects of the projected resettlement plan in the German-administered Polish territories). This report is appended to the situation report cited in the previous note, 1f. NA: AHS/GSA microfilm T77, roll 618, frame 805754ff; also IZG: M638.
49. Ibid., 6f, frame 805759f. We should not miss a noteworthy point in what Seraphim says here. In the face of deportations, the Jewish leadership of ghettos such as Łódz and Theresienstadt attempted to make the captive communities indispensable to the Germans, in some cases to the German war industry, as a means of having them survive. Seraphim's point makes these later, desperate attempts by *Judenräte* more realistic than they are usually judged to be.
50. *Anordnung* (Directive) 1/II, dated Oct. 30, 1939, by Himmler in his capacity as Reich-Commissar for the Establishment of German Folkdom. EICH 1397.
51. Record of a consultation held by the SS leaders of SS police and security operations in the Government General in the former territories now incorporated into Greater Germany, dated Nov. 11, 1939. Topic: Master plan of the evacuation of Jews and Poles from and resettlement of German nationals to the newly incorporated territories. Speaker: SS-*Brigadeführer* (Major General) Streckenbach, in charge of central planning of this two-way migration. EICH 1458.
52. Telegram by Heydrich to some regional higher SS and police leaders in the former Polish territories, now incorporated into Germany, dated Nov. 28, 1939. Topic: The SD is in charge of removal of Poles and Jews from the new German territories. EICH 1459.
53. Transcript of a directive from Heydrich to SS leaders in Krakow and Poznan concerning the evacuation of Jews and Poles from the Warthegau, dated Nov. 28, 1939. EICH 1460.
54. See note 5.
55. In the German phrase "*hat zu gelten*," *gelten* has the connotation of "to pass for [the truth]," i.e., of a tacit admission of an untruth.
56. Hans-Günther Seraphim, ed., *Das politische Tagebuch Alfred Rosenbergs 1934/5 und 1939/40* (München: Deutscher Taschenbuch Verlag, 1964), 99.
57. See Goshen, "Eichmann und die Nisko-Aktion," 79n.
58. Martin Broszat, *Polenpolitik*, 21, cited in Uwe Dietrich Adam, *Judenpolitik im dritten Reich* (Düsseldorf: Droste Verlag, 1972), 252.

59. Adam, *Judenpolitik*, 252; cf. also Krausnick, "Judenverfolgung," 290f.
60. Cf. Goshen, "Eichmann und die Nisko-Aktion," 84.
61. Memorandum from Eichmann in the files of *Zentralstelle* Mährisch-Ostrau concerning preparations in Berlin for the deportation of Jews, dated Berlin, Oct. 6, 1939; no addressee. Wiesenthal archive, file M-O.
62. Memorandum from Eichmann in the files of *Zentralstelle* Mährisch-Ostrau reporting his consultation with Müller, dated Berlin, Oct. 6, 1939; no addressee. Wiesenthal Archive, file M-O.
63. Copy of clipping in Wiesenthal: file M-O.
64. In communicating with each other about the Nisko action, the Nazis referred most of the time to *Abschiebung* or *Abschub*, i.e., "deportation." Only rarely did they apply the term *Umsiedlung* ("resettlement") to Jews; this term was usually reserved for what was being done with ethnic Germans and other less 'undesirable' groups. As for Jews, areas were *gesäubert* of them, i.e., "cleaned out/purified"; and Jews were *deportiert* ("deported"). How did Eichmann and his associates refer to this action vis-à-vis the Jews and, to some extent, the general public? Their favorite term was *Umschichtung*, especially in regard to Nisko, a term which was at that time linked with *Umschulung*. *Umschulung* ("reeducation/retraining") was a project carried out by the IKG with the approval of the Nazi authorities, for the ostensible purpose of teaching the Jews certain trades that might be useful to them in the country of their immigration. But its main purpose was to give the people something to do and, indirectly, to foster the hope that they would be allowed to practice their newly acquired skills in a new life somewhere else.

    Umschichtung means a "regrouping," a social reshuffling, and can thus be understood within the context of *Umschulung* as well as *Umsiedlung*. Thus, the professed purpose of the Nisko plan was to present the Jews with an area in Poland where they could acquire new skills to use in future emigration or, in the case of artisans, make use of their old skills to enable them to set up a new community, in which each member would contribute productively to the whole. No longer would the Jew be a "drone" or a "parasite" on the Aryan body, a stereotype so zealously promulgated by the Nazis that even some Jews were beginning to believe it about themselves and thus felt that, at least in part, they had coming to them what was being done to them. By clever manipulation, the two terms *Umschulung* and *Umschichtung* were becoming synonymous. The following may serve to illustrate this: On October 13, an order sent to the *Zentralstelle* Mährisch-Ostrau reads that a certain Jew, a resident of Mährisch-Ostrau, "is to be held in immediate readiness in order to be transported to a reeducation camp (*Umschulungslager*)." He was evidently intended for the first Nisko transport. See copy of order from Mährisch-Ostrau Gestapo Section II A; Wiesenthal: file M-O.
65. "Tagesbericht," dateline: "Mähr. Ostrau, Oct. 19, 1939", signed by Brunner; Wiesenthal: file M-O.
66. Murmelstein typescript, 72.
67. *Vermerk* (record) of *Vorsprache* Eichmann and Günther at Roden, Mähr. Ostrau, Oct. 11, 1939, initialed by Günther (and Roden?); see also *Vermerk* of conference in Kattowitz of Oct. 9, 1939, between Eichmann, Günther, Civil Administrator Fitzner, and Major General Otto von Knobelsdorf; Wiesenthal: file M-O.
68. *Vermerk* concerning "Arbeit in M. Ostrau" (work in M-O), i.e., a conference between Wagner, Eichmann, Rolf Günther, Brunner, and Dannecker, signed by the latter, dated Oct. 10, 1939; Wiesenthal: file M-O.
69. Ibid.
70. Ibid.
71. Thomas Garrigue Masaryk was of humble origin, with Czech, Slovak, and German family connections. He obtained his Ph.D. in philosophy in Vienna. At first he taught at the Universities of Vienna and Leipzig, where he met his wife, Charlotte Garrigue, the daughter of the president of a New York insurance company. When Prague's Charles University was divided into a German and a Czech part, Masaryk became professor of social philosophy in the latter. In time he became politically active in various ways. He took strong stands against anti-Semitic outbreaks such as blood libel accusations. Equally strongly, he criticized the Austro-Hungarian Empire's increasing subordination to the international policies of the German empire. As an elected member of the Austrian Parliament and as an indefatigable researcher and publicist, he was a leader in the fight against the Austro-Hungarian Empire's oppression of Slavic nations. In this way, Prague became the focus of liberation movements of South Slavs no less than Czechs and Slovaks. With the outbreak of the First World War, he escaped to the West, and was a moving spirit in the eventual dissolution of the Austro-Hungarian Empire and the

creation of Czechoslovakia and Yugoslavia. Masaryk died a few months before the Anschluss of Austria and a year before Czechoslovakia was sold out at Munich.

72. Ruth Bondy, *"Elder of the Jews"—Jakob Edelstein of Theresienstadt*, translated from the Hebrew by Evelyn Abel (New York: Grove Press, 1989), 182f. Bondy writes: "Edelstein told Shertok that there were people in the Berlin Jewish community who in specific instances knew how to stand up to the Germans. 'Whereas in Vienna [so Shertok quoted Edelstein in his diary] the people are spineless, and as a result ill treatment there has reached insufferable proportions.'"
73. AN *Vorsprache* Löwenherz at Günther (*Zentralstelle* Vienna), Oct. 10, 1939, item 1; L-papers; also EICH 1135.
74. *Vermerk* concerning *"Abstellung von jüdischen Funktionären"* (assignment of Jewish functionaries) according to an order from Eichmann, Mähr. Ostrau, Oct. 13, 1939, initialed by Rolf Günther; Wiesenthal: file M-O.
75. Murmelstein typescript, 56. See also copies of carbon copies (sent to *Zentralstelle* Mährisch-Ostrau) of the summonses issued by *Zentralstelle* Prague to Jakob Edelstein and Richard Friedmann, dated Oct. 14, 1939, signed by Burger; Wiesenthal: file M-O.
76. According to Murmelstein, the group met with Günther twice. Murmelstein, however, met with him separately, in accordance with special instructions that he was given while still in Vienna, "in order to receive an important communication." Cf. Murmelstein typescript, 56f.
77. AN *Vorsprache* Löwenherz at Rolf Günther, Oct. 10, 1939, item 1; L-papers.
78. Ibid., item 2.
79. Adler, *Der verwaltete Mensch*, 131.
80. Letter Löwenherz to *Zentralstelle*, Oct. 11, 1939; L-papers.
81. M-tape II/13A.
82. Rolf Günther (*Zentralstelle* Vienna) to Eichmann (*Zentralstelle* Mährisch-Ostrau), Oct. 11, 1939; Wiesenthal: file M-O.
83. *Vermerk* by Rolf Günther (Mähr. Ostrau), Oct. 16, 1939; Wiesenthal: file M-O.
84. Telegram Eichmann (Krakow) to Rolf Günther (Mähr. Ostrau), Oct. 15, 1939; Wiesenthal: file M-O.
85. SS HStuf. Braune (SD Hauptamt Brünn) to SS Ostuf. Wagner (Mähr. Ostrau), received by Rolf Günther, Oct. 13, 1939; Wiesenthal: file M-O.
86. Eichmann to R. Günther, Oct. 16, 1939; Wiesenthal: file M-O.
87. Rolf Günther to Ziegler of *Transportkommandatur* (transport command center) Oppeln, Oct. 13, 1993; *Vermerk* by Rolf Günther regarding second conference with *Transportkommandatur* Oppeln, Oct. 14, 1939; Wiesenthal: file M-O.
88. Steiner to *Zentralstelle*, Oct. 14, 1939; Wiesenthal: file M-O.
89. Bienenfeld "Report," 15, emphasis in the original, cited according to a transcript in EICH 783. The fact that Löwenherz tried to keep participation voluntary could, of course, not be stated in the official *Aktennotizen* on which the Bienenfeld report is mainly based. This fact was no doubt a matter of confidential decision within the leading echelon of the IKG.
90. Emphasis in original. YV 030/4, file "Dr. J. Loewenherz 39–46"; see also Adler, *Der verwaltete Mensch*, 132.
91. Adler, *Der verwaltete Mensch*, 131f.
92. AN *Vorsprache* Löwenherz (?) at Rolf Günther, Oct. 16, 1939; L-papers. This AN is unsigned, otherwise unidentified, and written on a typewriter with Pica script; Löwenherz's secretary usually used a typewriter with Elite script. However, there is at least one AN from this busy period (Oct. 28, 1939) signed by Löwenherz, written on the typewriter on which the AN Oct. 16 is written.
93. AN *Vorsprache* Löwenherz (?) at OStf. Hans Günther, Oct. 17, 1939. See previous note.
94. CA: A/W 2737, as cited in Rosenkranz, *Verfolgung*, 217.
95. *Vermerk* by Brunner (*Zentralstelle* Vienna) concerning *"Ersten nach Polen abgehenden Transport von Juden aus der Ostmark"* (first transport of Jews from Austria to Poland), Oct. 23, 1939; DÖW 8919/b.
96. Bienenfeld Report, 15, EICH 783. Günther's assurances to the anxious Löwenherz watching the entrainment procedures must have been reported to Bienenfeld verbally; needless to say, they do not appear in the *Aktennotizen* from which Bienenfeld drew most of the material for the *Bericht* (report).
97. *Vermerk* by Brunner (*Zentralstelle* Vienna) concerning *"Umsiedlungsaktion der Juden aus der Ostmark nach Polen"* (Relocation project of Jews from Austria to Poland), Oct. 18, 1939; DÖW 2527.
98. *Vermerk* by Brunner (Vienna) of a conference between Eichmann, Ebner (Gestapo), and Becker (Bürckel's staff), Oct. 17, 1939; Wiesenthal: file M-O.

99. AN *Vorsprache* Löwenherz and Engel at Brunner, Oct. 23, 1939, item 1; L-papers.
100. Rosenkranz, *Verfolgung*, 217.
101. AN *Vorsprache* at Günther, Oct. 17, 1939; L-papers. See note 92.
102. Ibid.
103. Bienenfeld "Report," 15.
104. AN *Vorsprache* Löwenherz and Engel at Brunner (*Zentralstelle*), Oct. 23, 1939, items 1, 2; L-papers.
105. Ibid., item 1.
106. AN *Vorsprache* Prochnik at Brunner, Oct. 25, 1939; L-papers.
107. AN *Vorsprache* Löwenherz, Rothenberg, Murmelstein, and Grün at Rolf Günther, Nov. 8, 1939, item 2; L-papers.
108. See telegram Brunner (Vienna) to Eichmann (Mähr. Ostrau), dated Oct. 28, 1939. Brunner reported on the notification received from Müller (Gestapo HQ Berlin), namely, that the army had to give precedence to transports of laborers harvesting root crops in the occupied territories and to those delivering the crops. Also, a subsequent request to the directorate of the *Reichsbahn* (Reich-railway) to squeeze the Jew transports into the prisoner transports (*die Einschiebung der Judentransporte in die Gefangenentransporte*) was rejected because the army's transfer of troops from the east to the western front precluded the shipment of Jews to the east. Finally, Brunner reported that he was asking Müller at Gestapo HQ Berlin (!) as well as Bürckel's office to find ways of letting this transport be pushed through nonetheless (*trotzdem durchdruecken lassen*); Wiesenthal: file M-O.
109. AN *Vorsprache* Löwenherz at Eichmann, Oct. 27, 1939; L-papers.
110. AN telephone Eichmann to Engel, Dec. 11, 1939; L-papers.
111. Transcript of teleprinter communication between Günther and Zimmermann, no date; Wiesenthal: file M-O.
112. Ibid.
113. Transcript of teleprinter conversation between Brunner (in Mähr. Ostrau) and Günther (in Brünn), Oct. 18? (*sic*!), 1939; *Tagesbericht* (daily report) by Brunner (M. Ostrau) regarding *Baumaterial* (building material), Oct. 19, 1939; Wiesenthal: file M-O. On a general level, the teleprinter exchange points significantly to the cumbersome collateral difficulties connected with the Nisko deportation. It shows that deportation for resettlement as it was conceived at this early stage must have seemed to the Nazis an unacceptably inefficient way of getting rid of Jews. The difficulty in question was that of procuring lumber for the barracks in Nisko. In the cited exchange, Günther and Brunner discussed problems encountered in bringing lumber from Slovakia across the border: Ten private cars had to be requisitioned. Slovakian and German border officials were making difficulties about bringing out the lumber. An SS officer reported that from now on he would need written permission from the Slovak authorities in order to bring out additional shipments. Brunner was taking the necessary steps to continue bringing the lumber across. The IKG Mährisch-Ostrau was instructed to supply the manpower for loading the lumber onto the freight cars. Hence, the Nazis must have yearned for a more efficient way of getting rid of the Jews!
114. Ibid.
115. Günther's postscript to the record of a telephone message from Blumenfeld concerning Müller's notice, no date, apparently addressed to Eichmann; Wiesenthal: file M-O.
116. *Vermerk* by Günther concerning "*Unterrichtung der Behörden vom Abgang des Judentransportes*" (Official Report of the Departure of the Jew-transport), Oct. 20, 1939; Wiesenthal: file M-O.
117. *Vermerk* by Günther concerning "*Abtransport von Juden nach Polen*" (Expediting of Jews to Poland), Oct. 21, 1939; Wiesenthal: file M-O.
118. *Vermerk* by Brunner (*Zentralstelle* Vienna) concerning "*Ersten nach Polen abgehenden Transport von Juden aus der Ostmark*" (First transport of Jews from Austria to leave for Poland), Oct. 23, 1939; Wiesenthal: file M-O.
119. *Merkblatt* (memorandum): instructions for Stapo stations concerning "*Umschichtung von Juden—Durchführung der Transporte*" (Shifting of Jews—transport procedures), no date; Wiesenthal: file M-O. Much of this memorandum is a summary of procedures whose development was reflected in documents that we have cited, including *Aktennotizen* of the IKG; hence, it seems clear that it was prepared in the latter part of October 1939 by *Zentralstelle* Vienna for the satellite *Zentralstellen* that actually were, or were to have been, involved in the Nisko transports.
120. Three memoranda by Rolf Günther (Mährish Ostrau), dated Oct. 24, 1939: "*Anforderung eines Trans-*

portzuges für die nächsten Transporte von Juden ab M-O und ab Kattowitz" (Request for a transport train for the next transports of Jews from M-O and from Kattowitz), "*Abtransport von Juden*" (dispatching of Jews), "*Abstellung von Sonderzügen zum Transport von Juden*" (assignment of special trains for transporting Jews); Wiesenthal: file M-O.

121. "*Abtransport* . . . ," ibid.
122. "*Abstellung* . . . ," ibid.
123. IZG: T-175, roll 258, MA 441/1.
124. Ibid.
125. Telegram Brunner to Eichmann, Oct. 28, 1939; see note 108.
126. *Tagesbericht* by Brunner (*Zentralstelle* Mährish Ostrau) to Rolf Günther (*Zentralstelle* Vienna), Nov. 3, 1939; Wiesenthal: file M-O.
127. Wiesenthal: file M-O.
128. AN *Vorsprache* Löwenherz at Eichmann, Oct. 27, 1939; L-papers.
129. "*Konzept zur Bekanntmachung*," CA: A/W 2736, as cited in Rosenkranz, *Verfolgung*, 216f.
130. The San River together with the Vistula, into which it issues about 50 km northeast of Nisko, formed the demarcation between the German and the Soviet "spheres of influence" according to the secret clause of the Nazi-Soviet Pact of August 23, 1939, agreed to between Foreign Ministers Joachim von Ribbentrop and Vyacheslav Molotov. This was the prelude to the outbreak of Germany's *Blitzkrieg* that annihilated the first Republic of Poland. Nisko lies in the southern part of the region whose main city is Lublin, one of the few places where the Polish army was able to organize a fierce resistance to the German onslaught, and the last to fall, on October 5. When Warsaw fell at the end of September, Stalin personally renegotiated the details of the spheres of influence with von Ribbentrop. In exchange for the inclusion of Lithuania in the Soviet sphere, Stalin offered the Germans the area between the earlier demarcation line and the Bug River. In the southern portion, where the upper reaches of the San flows eastward toward Przemysl, the new and the old demarcation lines coincided. To reach the city of Lwów (in Ukrainian: Lvov or Lviv) on the Soviet side from Nisko, one would have to go southeast along the San and cross the demarcation line at Przemysl. Stalin's largesse—a rural area, relatively sparsely populated, a region of villages and shtetls—was now chosen to be the area of Jewish settlement. The Bug River, the new demarcation line, could be reached from Nisko by going due east. However, the main road from Nisko to the bigger towns likely to have a significant Jewish presence and ultimately to Lublin, led northeast. There are many morasses in this region, and especially the terrain between Lublin and the Bug is swampy and treacherous and can be deadly for the unwary stranger.
131. Transcript of "*Kriegstagebuch des Landkomissars Nisko, begonnen am* 1. 10. 1939" (War diary of county commissioner of Nisko, begun Oct. 1, 1939). NA: T501, roll 211, frames 512ff; IZG: MA 508.
132. Report of *Aufklärungsabteilung* (information section) of 44th Division, Budzyn, Oct. 25, 1939; Bundesarchiv/Militärarchiv Freiburg: RH-53-23, H.K. XXXIV. Courtesy of Ze'ev Goshen.
133. *Kriegstagebuch Grenzabschnittkommando Süd* (War diary of boarder-section-command south), handwritten, entry Oct. 28, 1939; IZG: AKZ 2909/62, MA 113/6.
134. Julius Israel Boschan, *Erster Bericht* (first report) to Löwenherz, dateline Nisko-on-San, Oct. 31, 1939, 5 pages; addendum dated Nov. 3, 1939, 1 page; both parts are handwritten, signed by Boschan, and marked by a Nazi censor: "*gesehen*" (seen) followed by an illegible signature and dated November 2 and 4, respectively. CA: A/W 271.2.
135. Ibid., 2.
136. Ibid. Cf. also Eichmann's speech to Löwenherz in AN Oct. 27, 1939, cited above.
137. Boschan, *Erster Bericht*, 3.
138. Ibid., 4f.
139. Rosenkranz, *Verfolgung*, 344n1.
140. Leo Fuchsgelb to *Schriftleitung* (editor) *des Jüdischen Nachrichtenblattes*, Nov. 7, 1939; CA: A/W 495.1 (file: correspondence of *Jüdisches Nachrichtenblatt*).
141. Dr. Emil Reich (editor of *Jüdisches Nachrichtenblatt*) to Leo Fuchsgelb, Nov. 21, 1939, CA: A/W 495.1.
142. Ze'ev Goshen, who was himself one of the men in the first transport from Mährisch-Ostrau, is our source for the most reliable information regarding the camp itself, both in his articles and from his conversations with us in the summer of 1984.
143. Goshen, "Eichmann und die Nisko-Aktion," 91.

144. Ibid.
145. Conversation with Ze'ev Goshen, 1984.
146. Carbon copy (without name or signature) of letter to *Joint in Warschau* [Warsaw], Ulanów, Jan. 10, 1940; CA: A/W 2749. How this copy came to the IKG Vienna is not known. It is a letter of about 1,800 words typed single space on three pages.
147. Ibid.
148. Of course these had been and would be covered from other sources, i.e., IKG and other Jewish sources of funding.
149. DÖW 2528. Moser identifies the author of this "draft of a report to an [Austrian] government agency in 1946" as "Ernst Kohn, the leader of the first transport from Vienna." Cf. Moser, *Judenverfolgung*, 18.
150. CA: A/W 2749.
151. Murmelstein typescript, 55f.
152. M-tape II/10B.
153. Murmelstein typescript, 67.
154. Ibid., p. 67f. According to Goshen, Eichmann said, "otherwise you croak"; see above.
155. Ibid., 69f.
156. Ibid., 71.
157. An army captain of the *Aufklärungs-Abteilung* (information detachment) of the 44th Division relates this meeting between Murmelstein and the district president of Janów in a report "*Vorkommnisse im Sicherungsbezirk Krasnystow*" (events in the security zone Krasnystow), dateline Budzyn, Oct. 25, 1939. While he does not mention Murmelstein by name, he refers to the "vice president of the Jewish emigration committee in Vienna." The copy of this report, deposited at the archive of the University of Haifa, was made available to us by Ze'ev Goshen.
158. Murmelstein typescript, 71f.
159. AN *Vorsprache* Löwenherz, Rothenberg, Murmelstein, and Grün at Rolf Günther, Nov. 9, 1939; L-papers.
160. Rosenkranz, *Verfolgung*, 344n1.
161. Mulisch Menasche Mautner, "Bericht aus Wien 1938–1942," 5; YV 01/163.
162. Herbert Rosenkranz, "The Destruction of the Jewish Community in Austria 1938–45" in Joseph Fraenkel, ed., *The Jews of Austria* (London: Vallentine, Mitchell, 1965), 508.
163. Cf. M-tapes II2A.
164. AN *Vorsprache* Löwenherz at Eichmann, Dec. 19, 1939, items 1 and 1a; L-papers.
165. See Chaim Yahil, "Edelstein, Jacob," *Encyclopedia Judaica* 6, 365.
166. Bondy, *"Elder of the Jews,"* 143.
167. Ibid., 148.
168. Ibid., 180.
169. Murmelstein also believed that this purpose of Theresienstadt was frustrated by Edelstein to whom, in all fairness, the projected settlement was presented in a different light by the Germans. In the second volume, which deals in the main with Theresienstadt, we will see the uses to which the Ghetto was put, especially by the Nazis, the tensions among the motley grouping of inmates and their fate, and the performance of the Jewish leadership, in particular the chiefs of the Jewish Council, namely, Edelstein, Eppstein, and Murmelstein.
170. The German philosopher Karl Jaspers kept a diary during the time of extreme danger for himself and his Jewish wife, Gertrud. In his entry for August 28, 1942, we find the following: "There is some talk about Theresienstadt. It is supposed to be possible to live there. There is something seductive in such talk: to remain alive after all. And yet: Deportation is tantamount to execution. Life there is like in the prison of a concentration camp. But, first and foremost: What is capable of affording confidence in such an 'old-age home'? No message comes from there. Mail is 'temporarily' prohibited." Karl Jaspers, *Schicksal und Wille: Autobiographische Schriften*, edited by Hans Saner (München: Piper, 1967), 161.

Chapter 8

1. Prince Paul was Regent in Yugoslavia during the minority of his nephew, King Peter.
2. Rafelsberger to Gritzbach, Vienna, Sep. 5, 1939. DÖW 9403.
3. Mayor Neubacher of the City of Vienna to Funk, Vienna, Sep. 5, 1939. DÖW 9402.
4. Rafelsberger to Gritzbach, Vienna, Sep. 5, 1939. DÖW 9403.

5. Ibid.
6. Ibid.
7. Bürckel to Neubacher, Sep. 25, 1939. DÖW 9386.
8. "*Schaffung eines Barackenlagers für 6,000 Juden bei familienmässiger Unterbringung*" (establishment of a barracks camp for 6,000 Jews to be accommodated by families), report by Vienna Municipality Department of *Bauwesen* (construction), Oct. 9, 1939, 2. DÖW 9380.
9. "*Auszug aus der Denkschrift über Judenumsiedlung und Wohnungsbedarf in Wien*" (extract from the memorandum in regard to relocation of Jews and housing needs in Vienna), Oct. 12, 1939, 1. DÖW 9379.
10. Ibid., 2.
11. Ibid.,10.
12. Tavs to Bürckel, Oct. 18, 1939. DÖW 9386.
13. "Himmler to *Höhere SS- und Polizeiführer*" (superior SS and police leaders), Nov. 8, 1939. YV: IV-05/122/39.
14. AN *Vorsprache* Löwenherz at Eichmann, Dec. 2, 1939, item 1; L-papers.
15. Löwenherz used the round figure of "about 66,500 Jews" as a basis when he reported to Eichmann that by November 30, 1939, there were about 58,000 Jews left in Vienna. This figure was derived from the IKG survey. See ibid.
16. *Ministerium für innere und kulturelle Angelegenheiten* (*sic*. Evidently they used stationery left over from the old Austrian Interior Ministry) to Becker, Vienna, Oct. 5, 1939. DÖW 9386.
17. "Personenstatistik" by NSDAP Gau Wien Organisationsamt, Vienna, Oct. 5, 1939. DÖW 9380.
18. "Personenstatistik" by the Vermögensverkehrsstelle, no date, signature illegible. DÖW 9386.
19. AN *Vorsprache* Löwenherz at Gestapo, Sep. 10, 1939; L-papers.
20. AN *Vorsprache* Löwenherz at Brunner, Nov. 23, 1939, item 4; L-papers.
21. AN *Vorsprache* Löwenherz, Rothenberg, Storfer at Brunner, Nov. 27, 1939, item 5; L-papers.
22. AN telephone call Kuchmann to Murmelstein, Nov. 29, 1939; L-papers.
23. AN telephone call Kuchmann to Murmelstein, Dec. 4, 1939; L-papers.
24. AN *Vorsprache* Löwenherz and Rothenberg at Eichmann, Nov. 4, 1939, item 1; L-papers.
25. AN *Vorsprache* Löwenherz at Eichmann, *Zentralstelle* Berlin, Dec. 19, 1939, item 5; L-papers.
26. Ibid., item 13.
27. In fact, Löwenherz expected that in 1940 the quota numbers of immigrant visas to be assigned to the U.S. consulate in Vienna would exceed those in Berlin because registration at the Berlin consulate had occurred at a slower rate. See AN "Bericht ... über die am 16. und 17. Jänner 1940 im Auftrage . . . vorgenommene Besichtigung . . . ," 2, L-papers. In English: Report of the Undersigned Directors of IKG Vienna and Palamt Vienna about the inspection of the institution of the Reich Association of Jews in Germany, of the Jewish Community in Berlin, and of the Palamt Berlin, as well as the conference with the representatives of these organizations, undertaken on January 16 and 17, 1940, on orders of SS Captain Eichmann.
28. Ibid., p. 5.
29. Ibid., items 1, 2.
30. Ibid., items 2, 3.
31. Ibid., items 7, 8, and 9.
32. Ibid., item 4.
33. Ibid., items 5, 6.
34. Ibid., 1f.
35. AN *Vorsprache* Löwenherz at Eichmann in Berlin, Jan. 15, 1940, item 3; L-papers.
36. AN *Vorsprache* Löwenherz and Storfer at Eichmann, Jan. 26, 1940, item 1; L-papers.
37. AN *Vorsprache* Löwenherz at Eichmann in Vienna, Feb. 19, 1940, item 1; L-papers.
38. Ibid.
39. Ibid.
40. AN *Vorsprache* Löwenherz at Eichmann in Berlin, Jan. 17, 1940, item 2; L-papers.
41. AN *Vorsprache* Murmelstein at Brunner 2, Jan. 17, 1940, item 3; L-papers.
42. AN *Vorsprache* Löwenherz at Eichmann in Vienna, Jan. 26, 1940, item x; L-papers.
43. AN *Vorsprache* Prochnik at Brunner 2, Feb. 5, 1940. AN *Vorsprache* Löwenherz at Eichmann in Vienna, Feb. 19, 1940, item 5; L-papers.
44. AN *Vorsprache* Murmelstein at Brunner 2, Aug. 16, 1940; L-papers.

45. AN *Vorsprache* Löwenherz at Brunner 1, May 4, 1940, item 2; L-papers.
46. AN *Vorsprache* Löwenherz at Brunner 1, Oct. 31, 1940, item 6; L-papers.
47. AN *Vorsprache* Löwenherz at Eichmann in Vienna, Feb. 19, 1940, item 4; L-papers.
48. AN *Vorsprache* Löwenherz at Eichmann in Berlin, June 12, 1940, item 2; L-papers.
49. AN *Vorsprache* Löwenherz at Brunner 1, July 29, 1940, item 1; L-papers.
50. AN *Vorsprache* Prochnik at Brunner 1, Mar. 29, 1940; L-papers. The reason Prochnik was called to the *Zentralstelle* was that Löwenherz and Murmelstein were in Berlin on matters pertaining to illegal Palestine transports.
51. AN *Vorsprache* Löwenherz at Brunner 1, July 23, 1940, item 2e; L-papers.
52. AN *Vorsprache* Löwenherz at Brunner 1, July 15, 1940, item 2; L-papers.
53. Letter Dutch Migration Department of Agudas Israel (The Hague) to Cyrus Adler, Feb. 18, 1940. Joint Archive, AJ.
54. Covering letter Claire Goldman (Dropsie) to Henriette Buchmann (New York), Mar. 11, 1940. Ibid.
55. Letter Immigration Office of Agudath Israel Youth to Joint, Mar. 4, 1940. Joint Archive: file AJ.
56. Letter Irwin Rosen, Joint to Immigration Office of Agudath . . . , Mar. 6, 1940. Ibid.
57. "Notice no. 8" (undated). Joint Archive: file AJ.
58. Murmelstein's letter (in French) to M. le Grand Rabbin Dr. Wiener, Mar, 19, 1940. Joint Archive: file AJ 440.
59. Löwenherz to Miss Emanuel, Joint, Brussels, Mar. 19, 1940. Joint Archive: file AJ 440.
60. Memorandum Leavitt to AJDC Brussels, May 7, 1940. Ibid.
61. AN *Rücksprache* Löwenherz, Eppstein, and Hirsch with Dannecker at RSHA Berlin, June 12, 1940, item 3; L-papers. AN Steinfeld at Löwenherz and Murmelstein at IKG, June 18, 1940; L-papers. AN Ornstein and Steinfeld at Löwenherz and Bienenfeld at IKG, June 6, 1940; L-papers. AN *Vorsprache* Löwenherz at Brunner, July 15, 1940, item 1; L-papers.
62. See AN *Vorsprachen* Löwenherz at *Zentralstelle*, Sep. 9, 1939, item 2; Sep. 17, 1939, item 2; L-papers.
63. AN telephone call Löwenherz and Troper, Oct. 12, 1939; L-papers.
64. AN *Vorsprache* Löwenherz at Eichmann, Oct. 27, 1939, item 4; L-papers. We recall that at the time when Eichmann was triumphantly under the impression that the Nisko venture was the beginning of the "emigration" of the remaining Jews of Vienna—though only a few days before being disabused of that delusion by superior authorities—he told Löwenherz that he could not see Troper in Geneva but would soon be able to invite him to inspect the settlement of the Jews in Poland.
65. AN *Vorsprache* Löwenherz, Murmelstein, and Storfer at Eichmann, Nov. 13, 1939, item 1; L-papers.
66. AN *Vorsprache* Löwenherz at Eichmann, Nov. 27, 1939, item 1; L-papers.
67. AN *Vorsprache*, Nov. 13, 1939. Ibid.
68. AN *Vorsprache* Löwenherz at Eichmann, Dec. 2, 1939, item 1; L-papers.
69. AN *Vorsprache* Löwenherz at Eichmann in Berlin, Dec.19, 1939, item 1; L-papers.
70. Ibid., item 4.
71. AN *Vorsprache* Löwenherz at Eichmann in Berlin, Jan. 15, 1940, item 9; L-papers.
72. AN *Vorsprache* Löwenherz at Eichmann, Jan. 26, 1940, item ix; L-papers.
73. AN *Vorsprache* Löwenherz at Eichmann, Feb. 19, 1940, item 3; L-papers.
74. Ibid.
75. Ibid.
76. AN Löwenherz re: enclosed transcript and translation of telegram from Troper and telephone call with Brunner 1, Feb. 25, 1940; L-papers.
77. AN *Vorsprache* Löwenherz and Rothenberg at Eichmann, Mar. 2, 1940, item 4; L-papers.
78. AN *Vorsprache* Löwenherz, Storfer, and Grün (Palamt) at Eichmann in Berlin, Mar. 7, 1940, item 3; L-papers.
79. Ibid.
80. AN *Vorsprache* Löwenherz, Storfer, and Murmelstein at Eichmann, Mar. 30, 1940, item 6; L-papers.
81. See AN *Vorsprache* Murmelstein at Brunner 1, Apr. 24, 1940, item 1; L-papers.
82. AN *Vorsprache* Murmelstein at Eichmann, Apr. 15, 1940, item 5; L-papers.
83. As it turned out, the next meeting took place in Budapest a month later.
84. AN *Vorsprache* Löwenherz and Grün at Eichmann, May 14, 1940, item 1; L-papers.
85. Ibid., item 3.
86. AN *Vorsprache* Löwenherz and Storfer at Brunner 1, May 23, 1940, item 1; L-papers.
87. AN *Vorsprache* Löwenherz at Eichmann in Berlin, June 12, 1940, item 5; L-papers.

88. AN *Vorsprache* Löwenherz, Eppstein, Hirsch, and Storfer at Dannecker at RSHA Berlin, June 13, 1940, item 2; L-papers. The name "Pressburg" may seem strange. There is no locality in Poland whose German name is Pressburg; it is the German name of Bratislava, which at that time was the capital of independent Slovakia, an ally of Nazi Germany. What was at play was the Palestine transport that was stranded there. See chapter 9.
89. AN *Vorsprache* Murmelstein at Brunner 1, Aug. 20, 1940, items 4 and addendum 4; L-papers.
90. AN *Vorsprache* Löwenherz, Hirsch, and Weidmann at Eichmann at RSHA Berlin, Sep. 4, 1940, item 5; L-papers.
91. AN *Vorsprache* Löwenherz at Brunner 1, Aug. 30, 1940, items 1 and 2; L-papers.
92. Ibid., item 3.
93. AN *Vorsprache* Löwenherz at Eichmann in Berlin, Sep. 4, 1940 (not the same as Löwenherz, Hirsch…), item 1; L-papers.
94. Ibid.
95. AN *Vorsprache* Murmelstein at Brunner 1, Sep. 27, 1940, item 4; L-papers.
96. AN *Vorsprache* Löwenherz at Brunner 1, Oct. 8, 1940, item 1; L-papers.
97. AN *Vorsprache* Löwenherz at Brunner 1, Oct. 17, 1940, item 1; L-papers.
98. AN *Vorsprache* Löwenherz at Brunner 1, Oct. 31, 1940, item 1; L-papers
99. AN *Vorsprache* Löwenherz at Eichmann at RSHA Berlin (also present, Brunner 1), Dec. 8, 1940, item 8; L-papers.
100. AN *Vorsprache* Löwenherz at Brunner 1, Sep. 19, 1940, item 5; L-papers.
101. AN *Vorsprache* Murmelstein at Brunner 1, Sep. 27, 1940, item 1; L-papers.
102. AN *Vorsprache* Löwenherz at Brunner 1, Oct. 1, 1940, item 1; L-papers.
103. Ibid.
104. AN *Vorsprache* Murmelstein at Brunner 1, Nov. 27, 1940, item 1; L-papers
105. AN *Vorsprache* Löwenherz at Eichmann at RSHA Berlin (also present, Brunner 1), Dec. 8, 1940, item 2; L-papers.
106. AN Löwenherz at Brunner 1, Nov. 29, 1940, item 1; L-papers.
107. AN *Vorsprache* Murmelstein at Brunner 1, Dec. 16, 1940 (dated Dec. 17), item 1; AN *Vorsprache* (signature illegible) at Chief Inspector Löffler, Dec. 16, 1940; L-papers.
108. AN *Vorsprache* Löwenherz and Storfer at Eichmann, Jan. 26, 1940, item xi; L-papers.
109. AN *Vorsprache* Murmelstein at Eichmann, Apr. 15, 1940, item 4; L-papers.
110. AN *Vorsprache* Löwenherz and Storfer at Brunner 1, May 4, 1940, item 5; L-papers.
111. AN *Vorsprache* Löwenherz at Eichmann in Berlin, June 6, 1940, item 4; L-papers.
112. Ibid., item 6.
113. AN *Vorsprache* Löwenherz at Eichmann at RSHA Berlin, July 4, 1940, item 2; L-papers.
114. AN *Vorsprache* Löwenherz at Brunner 1, July 23, 1940, item 2c; L-papers.
115. AN *Vorsprache* Löwenherz and Murmelstein at Brunner 1, Aug. 4, 1940, item 2; L-papers.
116. AN *Vorsprache* Löwenherz at Brunner 1, Aug. 14, 1940, item 3; L-papers.
117. AN *Vorsprache* Löwenherz at Eichmann at RSHA Berlin, Sep. 4, 1940, item 2; L-papers.
118. AN *Vorsprache* Löwenherz at Eichmann, Dec. 2, 1939, item 2; L-papers.
119. AN *Vorsprache* Löwenherz and Storfer at Brunner 1, May 4, 1940, item 4; L-papers.
120. Memorandum to IKG Legal Dept. re: meeting Brunner 2 and SS Lieut. Grevenik at Löwenherz, May 20, 1940, item 11; L-papers.
121. AN *Vorsprache* Löwenherz at Eichmann in Berlin, June 12, 1940, item 11; L-papers.
122. AN *Vorsprache* Löwenherz at Brunner 1 (also present, Brunner 2), July 29, 1940, item 2c; L-papers.
123. AN *Vorsprache* Löwenherz and Murmelstein at Brunner 1, Aug. 4, 1940, item 4; L-papers.
124. AN *Vorsprache* Murmelstein at Brunner 1, Aug. 20, 1940, items 4 and addendum 4; L-papers.
125. AN *Vorsprache* Löwenherz at Eichmann in Berlin, Sep. 4, 1940, item 4; L-papers.
126. AN *Vorsprache* Löwenherz at Brunner 1, Oct. 17, 1940, item 2; L-papers.
127. Ibid., item 3.
128. AN *Vorsprache* Löwenherz at Brunner 1, Nov. 19, 1940, item 3; L-papers.
129. AN *Vorsprache* Löwenherz at Rolf Günther, Nov. 26, 1940, item 3; L-papers.
130. AN *Vorsprache* on Dec. 5, Löwenherz at Eichmann in Berlin (also present, Brunner 1), Dec. 8, 1940, item 5; L-papers. Thieme had recently declared to the legal consultants of the IKG that he would abstain from taxing the receipts of the IKG if its legal status as a public institution were confirmed. Eichmann, however, had to confess that the "central authorities" in Berlin made difficulties about the

matter, but he would instruct the *Zentralstelle* Vienna to use Löwenherz's recent memorandum and documents from higher authorities in the files of the *Zentralstelle* to secure the legal status and tax exemption of the IKG at least through the rest of 1940.

131. See AN *Vorsprache* Löwenherz at Brunner 1, Dec. 11, 1940, item 3; L-papers.
132. AN Löwenherz on telephone with Brunner 1, Dec. 20, 1940, item 1; L-papers.
133. AN *Vorsprache* Löwenherz at Brunner 1, Dec. 29, 1940, item 4; L-papers.
134. AN *Vorsprache* Löwenherz at Eichmann in Berlin, June 12, 1940, item 6; L-papers.
135. AN *Vorsprache* Löwenherz at Eichmann at RSHA Berlin, July 4, 1940, item 2; and letter Löwenherz (in Berlin) to *Zentralstelle* Vienna confirming Eichmann's release of funds, July 4, 1940; L-papers.
136. AN *Vorsprache* Löwenherz and Murmelstein at Brunner 1, Aug. 4, 1940, items 1 and 2; L-papers.
137. AN *Vorsprache* Löwenherz at Brunner 1, Nov. 19, 1940, item 6; L-papers.
138. AN *Vorsprache* Löwenherz at Brunner 1, May 31, 1940, item 2; L-papers.
139. AN *Vorsprache* Löwenherz at Eichmann in Berlin, June 12, 1940, item 11; L-papers.
140. AN *Vorsprache* Murmelstein at Brunner 1, Aug. 20, 1940, items 7 and addendum 7; L-papers.
141. AN *Vorsprache* Löwenherz at Eichmann at RSHA Berlin, Sep. 4, 1940, item 2; L-papers.
142. Ibid.
143. See AN *Vorsprache* Löwenherz at Brunner 1, Dec. 4, 1940, item 2; L-papers.
144. AN *Vorsprache* Löwenherz at Eichmann at RSHA Berlin, Sep. 4, 1940, item 2; L-papers.
145. AN *Vorsprache* Löwenherz at Brunner 1, Nov. 19, 1940, item 1; L-papers.
146. AN *Vorsprache* Löwenherz at Günther, Nov. 26, 1940, item 1; L-papers.
147. AN *Vorsprache* Löwenherz at Eichmann at RSHA Berlin, Dec. 8, 1940, item 1; L-papers.
148. AN *Vorsprache*, Löwenherz at Günther, Nov. 26, 1940, item 1; L-papers.
149. AN *Vorsprache* Löwenherz at Eichmann at RSHA Berlin, Dec. 8, 1940, item 1; L-papers.
150. AN *Vorsprache* Murmelstein at Brunner 1, Dec. 4, 1940, item 2; L-papers.
151. AN *Vorsprache* Eichmann at RSHA Berlin, Dec. 8, 1940, item 1; L-papers.
152. AN *Vorsprache* (continuing from the previous day) Löwenherz at Brunner 1, Dec. 11, 1940, item 1; L-papers.
153. AN *Vorsprache* Löwenherz at Brunner 1, Dec. 29, 1940, item 1; L-papers.
154. AN *Vorsprache* Löwenherz at Eichmann, Dec. 2, 1939, item 3; L-papers.
155. AN *Vorsprache* Löwenherz and Rothenberg at Eichmann in Berlin, Jan. 15, 1940, item 4; L-papers.
156. AN *Vorsprache* Löwenherz at Eichmann, Feb. 19, 1940, item 1; L-papers.
157. AN *Vorsprache* Jan. 15, 1940, item 2; L-papers.
158. AN *Vorsprache* Feb. 19, 1940, item 1; L-papers.
159. Ibid., item 2.
160. AN *Vorsprache* Löwenherz, Storfer, and Grün at Eichmann in Berlin, Mar. 7, 1940, item 8; L-papers.
161. AN *Vorsprache* Löwenherz, Storfer, and Murmelstein at Eichmann, Mar. 30, 1940, item 7; L-papers.
162. Ibid., item 8.
163. AN Brunner 2 telephone with Murmelstein, Mar. 21, 1940; L-papers.
164. AN *Vorsprache* Murmelstein at Brunner 2, Apr. 8, 1940, item 3; L-papers.
165. AN *Vorsprache* Murmelstein at Brunner 2, Apr. 12, 1940, item 5; L-papers.
166. AN *Vorsprache* Murmelstein at Eichmann, Apr. 15, 1940, item 8; L-papers.
167. AN *Vorsprache* Murmelstein at Brunner 1, Apr. 24, 1940, item 3; L-papers.
168. AN *Vorsprache* Murmelstein at Brunner 1, Apr. 26, 1940, item 3; L-papers.
169. AN *Vorsprache* Prochnik at Brunner 2, Apr. 9, 1940, items 1–6; L-papers.
170. AN (addressed to IKG Legal Dept.) Löwenherz, Brunner 2, and Grevenik at IKG, May 20, 1940, item 6; L-papers.
171. AN *Vorsprache* Löwenherz at Brunner 1, Aug. 13, 1940, item 3e; L-papers.
172. AN telephone call Murmelstein with Brunner 1, Oct. 18, 1940; L-papers.
173. AN (addressed to IKG Legal Dept.), May 20, 1940, item 8; L-papers.
174. AN *Vorsprache* Löwenherz at Brunner 1, May 31, 1940, item 6; L-papers.
175. AN telephone call Löwenherz with Brunner 1, June 3, 1940; L-papers.
176. AN *Vorsprache* Löwenherz at Eichmann in Berlin, June 12, 1940, item 8; L-papers.
177. Ibid.
178. AN *Vorsprache* Löwenherz at Brunner 1, July 15, 1940, item 4; L-papers.
179. AN *Vorsprache* Löwenherz and Murmelstein at Brunner 1, Aug. 4, 1940, item 5; L-papers.
180. AN *Vorsprache* Murmelstein at Brunner 1, July 13, 1940 (dated July 15, 1940), item 4; L-papers.

181. AN *Vorsprache* Löwenherz at Brunner 1 (also present, Dr. Rajakovic), July 15, 1940, item 3; L-papers.
182. Interestingly, Brunner 2 continued as executive of a special trusteeship whose special trustee had not only resigned but left the supervision of the IKG with respect to its assets to the *Zentralstelle*, his agency in Vienna, a function that consisted in telling Löwenherz to sign legal instruments over which the IKG had no legal control.
183. AN *Vorsprache* Löwenherz at Dr. Mayer, Sep. 10, 1940; L-papers.
184. AN *Vorsprache* Löwenherz at Brunner 1, Sep. 19, 1940, item 11; L-papers.
185. AN *Vorsprache* Löwenherz at Eichmann in Berlin, June 12, 1940, item 8; L-papers.
186. AN *Vorsprache* Löwenherz at Brunner 1, Sep. 19, 1940, item 2; L-papers.
187. AN *Vorsprache* Löwenherz at Brunner 1, Oct. 1, 1940, item 5; L-papers.
188. AN *Vorsprache* Löwenherz at Brunner 1 (also present, Brunner 2), July 30, 1940, item 3d; L-papers.
189. AN *Vorsprache* Löwenherz at Eichmann at RSHA Berlin, Sep. 4, 1940, item 2; L-papers.
190. AN *Vorsprache* Löwenherz at Brunner 1, Sep. 19, 1940, item 12; L-papers.
191. AN *Vorsprache* Löwenherz at Brunner 1, Oct.1, 1940, item 4; L-papers.
192. AN *Vorsprache* Löwenherz at Brunner 1, Oct. 8, 1940, item 3; L-papers.
193. AN *Vorsprache* Löwenherz at Brunner 1, Oct. 17, 1940, item 3; L-papers.
194. AN *Vorsprache* Löwenherz at Brunner 1, Nov. 19, 1940, item 4; L-papers.
195. AN *Vorsprache* Murmelstein at Brunner 1, Dec. 19, 1940, item 1; L-papers.
196. Ibid.
197. AN telephone call Löwenherz with Brunner 1, Dec. 20, 1940, item 2; L-papers.
198. AN *Vorsprache* Löwenherz at Brunner 1, Dec. 29, 1940, item 3; L-papers.
199. AN *Vorsprache* Löwenherz, Storfer, and Grün at Eichmann in Berlin, Mar.7, 1940, item 8; L-papers.
200. AN by Murmelstein, Mar. 13, 1940; L-papers.
201. See AN *Vorsprache* Löwenherz and Grün at Eichmann, May 14, 1940, item 4; L-papers.
202. Löwenherz to Engel in re: Brunner 2 and Grevenik at the IKG, May 20, 1940, item 2; and to IKG Legal Department, item 9; L-papers.
203. AN *Vorsprache* Löwenherz at Eichmann in Berlin, June 12, 1940, item 8; L-papers.
204. AN *Vorsprache* Murmelstein at Eichmann, Apr. 4, 1940, item 2; L-papers.
205. AN *Vorsprache* Engel at Brunner 2, Apr. 16, 1940; L-papers.
206. AN June 12, 1940, ibid.
207. AN *Vorsprache* Löwenherz, Edelstein, Weidmann, Eppstein at Eichmann at RSHA Berlin, July 3, 1940, item 1; L-papers.
208. AN *Vorsprache* Löwenherz at Brunner 1, Sep. 19, 1940, item 1; L-papers.
209. AN telephone Kuchmann to Löwenherz, Oct. 9, 1940; L-papers.
210. AN *Vorsprache* Löwenherz at Brunner 1, Oct. 17, 1940, item 5; L-papers.
211. AN *Vorsprache* Löwenherz at Brunner 1, Oct. 31, 1940, item 5; L-papers.
212. AN *Vorsprache* Murmelstein at Brunner 1, Nov. 27, 1940, item 6; L-papers.
213. AN *Vorsprache* Löwenherz at Brunner 1, May 21, 1941, item 5; L-papers.
214. AN *Vorsprache* Murmelstein at Brunner 1, Aug. 8, 1941, item 4c; L-papers.
215. *Begründung für die niedrigere Entlohnung ist auch darin gegeben, dass kein geprüftes, sondern nur kurzerhand ungeschultes Personal Verwendung findet.*
216. AN Brunner 2 accompanied by SS Ostuf. [Sergeant Major] Grevenik at Löwenherz, May 20, 1940,. item 6; L-papers.
217. AN Löwenherz and Storfer at Brunner 1, May 23, 1940, item 3; L-papers.
218. AN Dannecker's telephone order to Murmelstein, June 6, 1940; L-papers.
219. AN *Vorsprache* Murmelstein at Brunner 1, June 20, 1940; L-papers.
220. Ibid.
221. AN Brunner 1 telephone to Murmelstein, July 5, 1940, item 1; L-papers.
222. AN *Vorsprache* Murmelstein at Brunner 1, June 20, 1940; L-papers.
223. Ibid. Addendum by telephone.
224. AN *Vorsprache* Löwenherz at Brunner 1, July 25, 1940, item 4; L-papers.
225. AN *Vorsprache* Murmelstein at Brunner 1, June 20, 1940; L-papers.
226. AN Inspection Ebner and Guenther at IKG, Nov. 25, 1940; item 4. AN Murmelstein at Brunner 1, item 10. Both L-papers.
227. AN *Vorsprache* Murmelstein at Brunner 1, June 20, 1940; L-papers.
228. AN Brunner 1 telephone at Murmelstein, item 2; L-papers.

229. AN *Vorsprache* Löwenherz at Brunner 1, July 10, 1940, item 1; L-papers.
230. AN *Vorsprache* Löwenherz at Brunner 1, July 15, 1940, item 7; L-papers.
231. AN *Vorsprache* Löwenherz at Brunner 1, Dec. 11, 1940, item 4; L-papers.
232. AN *Vorsprsche* Murmelstein at Brunner 1, Aug. 20, 1940, item 3; L-papers.
233. AN *Vorsprache* Löwenherz at Brunner 1, Dec. 29, 1940, item 5; L-papers.
234. Ibid.
235. AN *Vorsprache* Löwenherz at Eichmann at RSHA Berlin, June 12, 1940, item 1; L-papers.
236. AN June 24, 1940; L-papers.
237. AN *Vorsprache* Löwenherz at Brunner 1, June 26, 1940, item 3c; L-papers.
238. AN *Vorsprache* Edelstein, Weidmann, Löwenherz, and Eppstein at Eichmann at RSHA Berlin, July 3, 1940, item 1.i,1; L-papers.
239. AN telephone call Löwenherz to Engel, July 3, 1940, item 1; L-papers.
240. AN *Vorsprache* Löwenherz at Brunner 1, July 15, 1940, item 6; L-papers.
241. AN *Vorsprache* Murmelstein at Brunner 1, Aug. 20, 1940, item 3 and addendum 3; L-papers.
242. AN *Vorsprache* Löwenherz at Eichmann at RSHA, Berlin, Sep. 4, 1940, item 2; L-papers.
243. AN "concerning the directives issued by State Counselor Dr. Ebner and [SS] Captain Guenther on the occasion of their inspection of the several offices of the IKG on Nov. 25, 1940," preamble and item 1; L-papers.
244. Ibid., item 2.
245. AN *Vorsprache* Löwenherz at Guenther, Nov. 26, 1940, item 2; L-papers.
246. AN *Vorsprache* Murmelstein at Brunner 1, Nov. 27, 1940, item 3; L-papers.
247. Ibid., item 3A.
248. Ibid., item 3.
249. AN *Vorsprache* Murmelstein at Brunner 1, Dec. 3, 1940, item 1; L-papers.
250. AN (dated Dec. 8) *Vorsprache* Löwenherz at Eichmann at RSHA Berlin, Dec. 5, 1940 (also present, Brunner 1), item 3; L-papers.
251. AN *Vorsprache* Nov. 27, 1940, item 3b; L-papers.
252. AN *Vorsprachen* Löwenherz at Brunner 1, July 16, 1940, item 2. Löwenherz at Brunner 1, July 23, 1940, item 2b. Murmelstein at Brunner 1, Aug.15, 1940, item 1b; all L-papers.
253. See, e.g., *Beschluss* no. 9571, "Beschluss-Buch 85." CA: A/W 88/80.
254. See CA: A/W 575.1.
255. *Gerichtliche Ankündigung*, Housar vs. Floch, Amtsgericht Josefstadt, Feb. 10, 1939. DÖW 4916. Floch was fortunate enough to be able to coordinate quitting his apartment with emigration to the United States, where a professorship of classics awaited him at Yeshiva University in New York. The container with his library of 8,000 volumes was less fortunate; it got as far as Trieste before disappearing without a trace.
256. M. Bormann, "Rundschreiben 139/39, Betrifft: Gesetz über Mietverhältnisse mit Juden," Munich, July 8, 1939. YV: 02/1130.
257. AN *Vorsprache* Löwenherz et al. at Eichmann in Berlin, Mar. 7, 1940, item 15; L-papers.
258. *Auszug aus der Denkschrift über Judenumsiedlung und Wohnungsbedarf in Wien* (extract from the memorandum in regard to relocation of Jews and housing needs in Vienna), Oct. 12, 1939, 1. DÖW 9379.
259. Tavs was mentioned above in Löwenherz's minutes of his *Vorsprache* at Eichmann. AN *Vorsprache* Löwenherz et al. at Eichmann in Berlin, Mar. 7, 1940, item 15; L-papers.
260. AN *Vorsprache* Prochnik at Brunner 2, Mar. 29, 1940; L-papers.
261. AN *Vorsprache* Löwenherz at Kuchmann, May 27, 1940; L-papers.
262. *Wohnungsamt* (Housing Bureau) to Gestapo, Vienna, Oct. 3, 1939. DÖW 9386.
263. "Der Stellvertretende Gauleiter [Scharitzer] an alle Kreisleiter," Vienna, June 25, 1940. DÖW 1000.
264. "Der Stellvertretende Gauleiter [Scharitzer]: Rundschreiben 174/40. Betrifft: Judenumsiedlung," Vienna, Sep. 24, 1940. YV: 030/17.
265. AN *Vorsprache* Löwenherz at Brunner 1, Oct. 1, 1940, item 7; L-papers.
266. AN *Vorsprache* Löwenherz at Brunner 1, Oct. 8, 1940, item 6; L-papers.
267. AN *Vorsprache* Löwenherz at Brunner 1, Nov. 19, 1940, item 2; L-papers.
268. AN *Vorsprache* Löwenherz at Dr. Wedel in the office of Dr. Tavs of the Housing Bureau, Nov. 25, 1940; L-papers.

269. AN *Vorsprache* Löwenherz at Eichmann in Berlin on Dec. 5, 1940, in the presence of Brunner, Dec. 8, 1940, item 7; L-papers.
270. Rafelsberger to Gritzbach, Vienna, Sep. 5, 1939. DÖW 9403.
271. Neubacher to Funk, Vienna, Sep. 5, 1939. DÖW 9402.
272. "Preparation," lit., making kosher or fit.
273. AN *Vorsprache* Löwenherz and Storfer at Eichmann, Jan. 26, 1940, item 9; L-papers.
274. AN *Vorsprache* Prochnik at Brunner 1, Feb. 2, 1940; L-papers.
275. That is, the "eastern march" of the Carolingian Empire.
276. See Botz, *Wien*, 255f.
277. German: *Leute.*
278. *Neues Wiener Tagblatt*, Vienna Mar. 25, 1938, 4, as cited in Botz, *Wien*, 255.
279. *The Jewish Chronicle*, London, Apr. 1, 1938, 19 and 42, as cited in Rosenkranz, *Verfolgung*, 23.
280. AN *Vorsprache* Löwenherz at Brunner 1, May 31, 1940, item 4; L-papers.
281. AN *Vorsprache* Prochnik at Brunner 1, June 8, 1940; L-papers.
282. AN *Vorsprache* Engel at Brunner 1, June 27, 1940, item 2; L-papers.
283. See "Mitteilung an die Amtsdirektion," July 25, 1940. CA: A/W 165, 6.
284. AN *Vorsprache* Löwenherz at Brunner 1, July 10, 1940, item 6; L-papers.
285. Letter from *Die nichtarische Arbeiterschaft der Firma 'Asdag'* (the non-Aryan workforce of the ASDAG Company) to IKG Vienna, dated Eisenerz, July 14, 1940. CA: A/W 272.
286. AN *Vorsprache* Löwenherz at Brunner 1, July 23, 1940, item 2a; L-papers.
287. AN *Vorsprache* Murmelstein at Brunner 1, Aug. 15, 1940, items 2a and addendum 2a; L-papers.
288. AN *Vorsprache*, May 30, 1940.
289. AN *Vorsprache,* July 10, 1941, item 2.
290. AN *Vorsprache*, June 26, 1940, item 5.
291. AN *Vorsprache*, July 10, 1940, item 4.
292. AN *Vorsprache* Löwenherz at Eichmann, Aug. 4, 1940, item 3; L-papers.
293. AN *Vorsprache* July 5, 1940, item 5; L-papers.
294. AN *Vorsprache* June 26, 1940, item 6; L-papers.
295. AN *Vorsprache* Löwenherz at Eichmann at RSHA Berlin, June 12, 1940, item 9; L-papers.
296. AN Löwenherz's report to Eichmann about his inspection of Jan. 16 and 17, 1940; L-papers.
297. AN *Vorsprache* Murmelstein at Brunner 1, Aug. 16, 1940, item 4; L-papers.
298. AN *Vorsprache* Löwenherz at Brunner 1, Oct. 8, 1940, item 10; L-papers.
299. AN *Vorsprache* Löwenherz at Brunner 1, Sep. 19, 1940, item 3; L-papers.
300. AN *Vorsprache* Löwenherz at Brunner 1, Sep. 19, 1940, item 9; L-papers.
301. AN *Vorsprache* Murmelstein at Brunner 1, Sep. 27, 1940, item 3; L-papers.
302. AN *Vorsprache* Murmelstein at Brunner 1, Nov. 27, 1940, item 2; L-papers.
303. AN *Vorsprache* Oct. 10, 1940; L-papers.
304. AN *Vorsprache* Löwenherz at Brunner 1, Sep. 19, 1940, item 6; L-papers.
305. AN *Vorsprache* Murmelstein at Brunner 1, Dec. 4, 1940, item 8; L-papers.
306. AN *Vorsprache* Murmelstein at Brunner 1, July 22, 1940, item 1; L-papers.
307. Copy for Löwenherz, dated Sep. 5, 1940, of AN by Hirsch, Aug. 30, 1940; L-papers.
308. AN *Vorsprache* Murmelstein at Brunner 1, Aug. 16, 1940, item 3; L-papers.
309. AN *Vorsprache* Murmelstein at Brunner 1, Mar. 20, 1941, item 1; L-papers.
310. AN *Vorsprache* Löwenherz at Brunner 1, Mar. 27, 1941, item 1; L-papers.
311. AN *Vorsprache* Löwenherz at Brunner 1, May 14, 1941, item 8; L-papers.
312. AN *Vorsprache* Murmelstein at Brunner 1, June 11, 1941, item 4; L-papers.
313. AN *Vorsprache* Löwenherz at Brunner 1, Dec. 29, 1941, item 1; L-papers.
314. AN *Vorsprache* Murmelstein at Brunner 1, Sep. 4, 1941, item 8; L-papers.
315. AN *Vorsprache* Löwenherz at Brunner 1, Oct. 2, 1941, item 4; L-papers.
316. AN *Vorsprache* Löwenherz at Brunner 1, Dec. 29, 1941, item 1; L-papers.
317. AN *Vorsprache* Löwenherz at Brunner 1, June 17, 1941, item c; L-papers.
318. AN *Vorsprache* Murmelstein at Brunner 1, Dec. 4, 1940; L-papers.

Chapter 9

1. *Jüdisches Nachrichtenblatt*, Feb. 2, 1940.
2. *Jüdisches Nachrichtenblatt*, May 13, 1940, l.
3. AN *Vorsprache* Murmelstein at Brunner 1, Apr. 12, 1940; L-papers.
4. "Outline of the General Situation of the Jews of Vienna (Special Report)," dated Geneva, Feb. 1, 1940. Joint Archive, file AJ. These figures also coincide with Löwenherz's information at that time.
5. Letter from Dr. Reich to L. Kohn, Dec. 31, 1940.
6. Letter from Dr. Reich to S. Stössel, Jan. 10, 1940.
7. AN Murmelstein at Brunner 1, Jan. 15, 1940. L-papers.
8. AN Löwenherz and Storfer at Brunner 1, May 4, 1940; L-papers.
9. Ibid.
10. M-tapes II, 10A; 175f.
11. Ibid.
12. AN *Vorsprache* Murmelstein at Brunner 1, Nov. 27, 1940; L-papers.
13. AN Löwenherz at Brunner, Dec. 8, 1940; L-papers.
14. We will speak in more detail about this transport, which got stuck in Yugoslavia, in our discussion of the Palestine transports and Kladovo.
15. Memorandum from Rolf Günther in Mährisch-Ostrau, Oct. 12, 1939. W-W.
16. AN *Vorsprache* Löwenherz at Rolf Günther, Sep. 11, 1939, item 1; L-papers.
17. As early as May 1939, i.e., a few weeks after the restrictions set down in the White Paper went into effect, the German embassy in Sofia (Bulgaria) forwarded to the Foreign Ministry in Berlin a report received from the German consulate in Burgas, the largest port of Bulgaria, that a transport of 300 Jews from Slovakia and Hungary had left Burgas on the Greek ship *Atios Nikola* on April 20. Aside from the fact that the transport was halted in Greek waters because of gross irregularities, the consulate filed the following noteworthy report: "Even though the mandatory authorities could not grant immigration permits, the [British], according to reliable reports, have tacitly tolerated illegal landings at unguarded parts of the coast. Among the passengers there are about 350 men, all of whom have served in the military, who, according to reliable remarks, constitute a welcome addition to the Jewish police troop. . . ." (Copy of report, dated April 28, 1939, by Consul Jakubowski, Burgas, to German Embassy, Sofia, which was forwarded on May 3, 1939, to Foreign Office, Berlin, where it was received May 6, 1939. In John Mendelsohn, *The Holocaust Vol. 6: Jewish Emigration 1938–1940, Rublee Negotiations and the Intergovernmental Committee* [New York/London: Garland, 1982], 214ff.)
18. AN *Vorsprache* Löwenherz and Rothenberg at Eichmann, Sep. 17, 1939, items 3, 4; L-papers.
19. AN *Vorsprache* Löwenherz, Rothenberg, and Storfer at Eichmann, Aug. 12, 1939, item 8; L-papers.
20. Ibid., items 11, 12. See also Bondy, "*Elder of the Jews*," 147ff.
21. Ibid., item 9.
22. AN *Vorsprache* Löwenherz at Rolf Günther, Oct. 10, 1939, item 3; L-papers.
23. AN telephone call Troper to Löwenherz, Oct. 12, 1939; L-papers.
24. AN *Vorsprache* Löwenherz and Engel at Brunner 1, Oct. 23, 1939, item 5; L-papers.
25. AN *Vorsprache* Löwenherz at Eichmann, Oct. 27, 1939, item 3; L-papers.
26. AN *Vorsprache* Löwenherz at Brunner 1, Oct. 28, 1939, item 9; L-papers.
27. AN *Vorsprache* Löwenherz, Murmelstein, Rothenberg, Grün at Rolf Günther, Nov. 8, 1939, item 4; L-papers.
28. AN *Vorsprache* Löwenherz, Murmelstein, Rothenberg, Storfer at Eichmann, Nov. 13, 1939, item 6. AN *Vorsprache* Löwenherz at Eichmann, Nov. 14, 1939, item 6; L-papers.
29. AN *Vorsprache* Löwenherz, Rothenberg, Storfer at Eichmann, Nov. 27, 1939, item 1; L-papers.
30. See AN *Vorsprache* Löwenherz at Eichmann, Dec. 2, 1939, item 6; L-papers.
31. Ibid.
32. AN *Vorsprache* Murmelstein at Gestapo, Dec. 11, 1939, and Murmelstein and Engel at Rolf Günther, Dec. 12, 1939; L-papers. We note that the originally stipulated fee of RM 1,200 per person seemed to have turned into RM 30,000 for 330 persons, that is, RM 91 per person.
33. AN *Vorsprache* Löwenherz at Eichmann in Berlin, Dec. 19, 1939, item 9; L-papers.
34. Ibid.
35. AN *Vorsprache* Löwenherz and Rothenberg at Eichmann in Berlin, Jan. 15, 1940, item 16; and AN *Vorsprache* Löwenherz and Storfer at Eichmann in Vienna, Jan. 26, 1940, item viii; L-papers.

36. AN *Vorsprache* Edelstein, Storfer, Murmelstein, Hirsch, Eppstein, and Lyon at Eichmann at RSHA Berlin; also present were Rolf Günther and Dannecker, Mar. 27, 1940; L-papers. This AN is a "corrected and supplemented" version as directed by Eichmann, when Löwenherz, Murmelstein, and Storfer reported to him in Vienna, Mar. 30, 1940.
37. Ibid., item 1.
38. Later developments suggested to Murmelstein that Edelstein, motivated by his agenda, was behind this.
39. Ibid.
40. AN *Vorsprache* Löwenherz, Murmelstein, and Storfer at Eichmann, Mar. 30, 1940, item 1; L-papers.
41. Ibid., item 6.
42. Storfer's "*Mitteilung* [communiqué] no. 54," Apr. 23, 1941, item 1. CA: A/W 2515.
43. See Gabriele Anderl and Walter Manoschek, "Die Geschichte des Kladovo Transports 1939 bis 1942/ The Story of the Kladovo Transport, 1939 to 1942" in *Kladovo: Eine Flucht nach Palästina/Escape to Palestine*, edited by Alisa Douer for the Jewish Museum Vienna, 2001, 11, 18.
44. Letter from the president and secretary general of Savez Jevrejskin Veroispovednin Opština to IKG Vienna, Belgrade, Jan. 18, 1940. CA: A/W 272.
45. M-tape I7A, 93.
46. Later, Moshe Sharett, the second prime minister of Israel.
47. See Bondy, "*Elder of the Jews*," 180ff.
48. Ibid., 183.
49. Ibid., 182.
50. Ibid., 186.
51. Ibid.
52. It is mind-boggling to reflect on what Edelstein thought he could permit himself to do.
53. AN *Vorsprache* Murmelstein at Brunner 1, Apr. 4, 1940, item 1; L-papers.
54. Storfer, *Mitteilung* [here: "report"] 54, Apr. 23, 1940, item "*Überweisung* £13,800." CA: A/W 2515.
55. Ibid.
56. Ibid.
57. Storfer, *Mitteilung* 56, Apr. 27, 1940, item ii. CA: A/W 2515.
58. *Mitteilung* 54, item 2.
59. *Mitteilung* 24, items 3 and 4.
60. Ibid., item 4.
61. *Mitteilung* 26, item 2.
62. *Mitteilung* 24, item 3.
63. *Mitteilung* 56, item 2.
64. Ibid.
65. Ibid., item 1.
66. Article: "'Illegal' Immigration," *Encyclopedia Judaica*, CD-ROM version.
67. *Mitteilung* 56, item 1.
68. AN *Vorsprache* Murmelstein and Storfer at Brunner 1, Apr. 26, 1940, item 1 and addendum; L-papers.
69. *Mitteilung* 56, item iii.
70. Ibid., item v.
71. Ibid., item vi.
72. AN *Vorsprache* Löwenherz and Storfer at Brunner 1, May 4, 1940, items 1 and 10; L-papers.
73. AN *Vorsprache* Löwenherz and Storfer at Brunner 1, May 23, 1940, item 1; L-papers.
74. Ibid.
75. AN *Vorsprache* Löwenherz at Eichmann in Berlin, June 12, 1940, item 4; L-papers.
76. AN *Vorsprache* Löwenherz, Storfer, Eppstein, and Hirsch at Dannecker at RSHA Berlin, June 13, 1940, item 1; L-papers.
77. Letter Storfer to Troper, July 10, 1940, first (unnumbered) item. Joint Archive file AJ. This is not the original letter but a somewhat awkward English translation.
78. Letter Löwenherz to Troper c/o Joseph Schwartz in Lisbon, July 8, 1940. Joint Archive file AJ.
79. Letter Storfer to Troper, July 10, 1940, items ii and iii.
80. Ibid., first (unnumbered) item.
81. Ibid., item iii.
82. Ibid., item iv.

83. Letter Löwenherz to Troper, July 8, 1940.
84. Cable Löwenherz to Troper in New York, July 23, 1940.
85. AN *Vorsprache* Murmelstein at Brunner 1, July 15, 1940, item 1; L-papers.
86. AN *Vorsprache* Löwenherz at Brunner 1, July 15, 1940, item 8; L-papers.
87. AN *Vorsprache* Murmelstein at Brunner 1, July 22, 1940, item 4; L-papers.
88. AN *Vorsprache* Löwenherz at Brunner 1, July 23, 1940, item 2d; L-papers.
89. As so many other people, Murmelstein thought that what Hannah Arendt meant by "banality" when she spoke of the banality of Eichmann's evil meant that he was stupid.
90. M-tape I-7B, 96–100 passim.
91. In fact, when Mussolini cleaned up the ancient Roman Forum and enclosed it with a protective wall, he had the wall near the Colosseum decorated with a map of the Roman Empire with the Mediterranean Sea pretentiously marked, as the ancient Romans did, as *mare nostrum* (our sea) and, incidentally, the Levant not as "Iudaea" or "Palaestina" or even "Syria" but simply as "Arabia," as any traveler can see to this day, a designation which was in its time what later times would call "politically correct."
92. AN *Vorsprache* Löwenherz at Eichmann at RSHA, Sep. 4, 1940, item 8; L-papers.
93. AN *Vorsprache* Löwenherz at Brunner 1, Oct. 17, 1940, item 6; L-papers.
94. AN *Vorsprache* Löwenherz at Brunner 1, Dec. 11, 1940, item 4; L-papers.
95. This region became independent at the fall of the Soviet Union at the end of the twentieth century, under the name of Moldavia (Moldova).
96. For the following see *Rundschreiben* (Circular) No. 25, Storfer to IKG Vienna, RV Berlin, IKG Prague, Synagogue Community Danzig, IKG Brünn (Brno), Special Transports Committee Berlin, and Overseas Transports Dept. Prague, dated Jan. 16, 1941, 3 pp. CA: A/W 2515. See Yehuda Slutsky, "'Illegal' Immigration." *Encyclopedia Judaica*, 8: 1248–1254; and Aharon Zwergbaum. "Patria," *Encyclopaedia Judaica*, 13:181.
97. Letter Prochnik in Berlin to Storfer, Jan. 16, 1941. CA: A/W 2518.5.
98. Note Storfer to Prochnik, Jan. 19, 1941. CA: A/W 2518.5.
99. Most of the information about the final fate of the Kladovo group comes from Anderl and Manoschek, "Geschichte des Kladovo Transports," 13–16, 19–22.
100. AN *Vorsprache* Murmelstein at Brunner 1, Apr. 12, 1940, item 3; L-papers.
101. AN *Vorsprache* Löwenherz and Storfer at Brunner 1, May 4, 1940, item 9; L-papers.
102. IKG in-house memorandum, no title ("*Die Beratung der Auswanderer . . .*"), no date (evidently mid-. June 1940, since there are references to "*Betrifft: Auswanderung . . .*" See next note.); L-papers.
103. "*Betrifft: Auswanderung nach Nord- und Südamerika über den Fernen Osten*" (In re: emigration to North and South America via the Far East), dated June 12, 1940, signed by Eppstein, Löwenherz, and Hirsch; L-papers.
104. AN *Vorsprache* Löwenherz, Eppstein, and Hirsch at Dannecker in Berlin, June 12, 1940, item 3; L-papers.
105. *Betrifft: Auswanderung* . . . , item II.1.
106. AN *Vorsprache* Löwenherz and Rothenberg at Eichmann in Berlin, Jan. 15, 1940, item A 13; L-papers.
107. Ibid., item A 11.
108. AN *Vorsprache* Löwenherz, Grün, and Storfer at Eichmann in Berlin, Mar. 7, 1940, item 9; L-papers.
109. AN Löwenherz at Eichmann in Berlin, June 12, 1940, item 5; L-papers.
110. *Betrifft: Auswanderung* . . . , item II.2.
111. AN Löwenherz to Engel, Murmelstein for their information, June 17, 1940; L-papers.
112. AN Eppstein, Hirsch, Löwenherz, and Storfer at Dannecker at RSHA Berlin, June 13, 1940, item 5; L-papers.
113. AN Murmelstein to IKG in-house, June 20, 1940; L-papers.
114. AN telephone call Löwenstein (Berlin) to Löwenherz, June 21, 1940; L-papers.
115. Löwenherz to *Zentralstelle* Berlin report "*Betrifft: Auswanderung über den Fernen Osten,*" Berlin, June 13, 1940; L-papers.
116. Prochnik Deposition, Prochnik court case 1954. DÖW 127.
117. Cf., for example, the testimony of Dr. Hella Klang, *Senatspräsidentenwitwe* (widow of the president of the senate): "My husband told me that Prochnik went around in boots like an SS man and also imitated the SS people in his behavior." Interrogation of Witnesses, 1954. DÖW 127.
118. Prochnik to IKG *Amtsdirektion* (Central Administration), Sep. 19, 1940. CA: A/W 2517.5.
119. Prochnik Deposition, 5.

120. Letters Prochnik to IKG *Amtsdirektion*, June 29 and July 1, 1940. CA: A/W 2517.10.
121. Letter Prochnik to IKG *Amtsdirektion*, July 22, 1940, CA: A/W 2517.10. In this letter Prochnik also mentioned that he had just received the Manchurian visa for Engel and that his seat on the plane was not in danger. Others, Prochnik said, were much worse off.
122. AN Prochnik in Berlin to IKG *Amtsdirektion*, July 28, 1940. CA: A/W 2517.10.
123. Ibid.
124. Letter Prochnik to Murmelstein, Berlin, July 9, 1940. CA: A/W 2517.5.
125. Letter Prochnik to *Amtsdirektion*, Berlin, Aug. 22, 1940. CA: A/W 2517.5.
126. Letter Prochnik to *Amtsdirektion*, Berlin, Sep. 14, 1940. CA: A/W 2517.5.
127. Letter Prochnik to Murmelstein, Berlin, Sep. 15, 1940. CA: A/W 2517.4.
128. Letter Murmelstein to Braun, RV Emigration Section, Apr. 17, 1941. CA: A/W 2520.
129. Letter Prochnik to *Amtsdirektion*, Berlin, May 6, 1941. CA: A/W 2520.
130. Letter Prochnik to Murmelstein, Berlin, Nov. 13, 1940. CA: A/W 2517.4.
131. AN Murmelstein in-house re: Prochnik report of Apr. 14, Apr. 17, 1941. CA: A/W 2523.3.
132. Letter Prochnik to *Amtsdirektion*, Berlin, May 6, 1941. CA: A/W 2520. See also the IKG in-house memorandum apparently prepared in Murmelstein's office based on Prochnik's report of May 6, initialed by Löwenherz, May 8, 1941. CA: A/W.
133. Prochnik to *Auswärtiges Amt* (Foreign Office), *Dezernat* (Section) D III, July 6, 1940. CA: A/W 2518.1.
134. Prochnik to Berlin *Zentralstelle*, Aug. 7, 1940. CA: A/W 2518.1.
135. Prochnik to Berlin *Zentralstelle* re: directive of Aug. 9, 1940. CA: A/W 2518.1.
136. Prochnik to *Amtsdirektion* re: Russian visa, Aug. 2, 1940. CA: A/W 2517.5.
137. Prochnik to IKG *Abfertigung* (Dispatching Section), Aug. 18, 1940. CA: A/W 2517.5.
138. Prochnik to IKG *Abfertigung*, Aug. 28, 1940. CA: A/W 2517.5.
139. Murmelstein for Löwenherz to Braun, RV Section Emigration, Sep. 9, 1940. CA: A/W 2517.4.
140. AN Murmelstein in-house, no date (Jan. 8 or 9, 1941). CA: A/W 2516.
141. AN Murmelstein to *Zentralstelle*, Aug. 22, 1941. CA: A/W, 2516.
142. AN to IKG in-house by Breuer, Aug. 12, 1940; L-papers. The memorandum states that he went to the consulate on August 12. However, in light of Murmelstein's telegram to Shanghai, that seems to be the date when the memorandum was typed and signed.
143. Letter M. Birman, Manager Far Eastern Jewish Central Information Bureau for Emigrants to IKG emigration section, Shanghai, Aug. 15, 1940. CA: A/W 2546.2.
144. Prochnik to IKG *Amtsdirektion*, reporting the contents of a telegram he had received from its head office in Moscow, Aug. 31, 1940. CA: A/W 2517.5.
145. Note Murmelstein to Prochnik, Sep. 17, 1940. CA: A/W 2517.4.
146. Lit. *Erstellung eines Depots*. IKG in-house record of Prochnik report of Oct. 5, item "*Japanisches Transit*," Oct. 7, 1940. CA: A/W 2523.1.
147. Ibid., item "*Storno* NYK-Line."
148. IKG *Devisen-Auskunftsstelle* to Prochnik, Nov. 15, 1940. CA: A/W 2517.2.
149. Letter Prochnik to IKG *Amtsdirektion*, Mar. 20, 1941. CA: A/W 2517.5.
150. Letter Prochnik to Hanover travel bureau of the Hamburg-America Line, no date. CA: A/W 2519.5.
151. Report (*Vertraulich*, i.e., "confidential") Prochnik to *Amtsdirektion*, Berlin, June 6, 1941.
152. Ibid. Items "Vladivostok-Shanghai" and "Tschunking."
153. IKG in-house memorandum re: Prochnik letter of June 25, item "Intourist." CA: A/W 2523.3.
154. Internal AN telephone call Eppstein and Löwenherz, June 19, 1940; L-papers.
155. AN (for IKG) Storfer "*Amerikafahrt von Piräus aus*" (Voyage to America from Piraeus), item 1, July 4, 1940; L-papers.
156. Internal AN, June 19, 1940.
157. AN Storfer, July 4, 1940, item 2.
158. AN *Vorsprache* Murmelstein at Brunner 1, Aug. 20, 1940, items 6 and addendum 6; L-papers.
159. AN telephone call Murmelstein and Prochnik Sep. 14, 1940. CA: A/W 2523.1.
160. Consulado de Portugal em Viena to IKG, Sep. 5, 1940. CA: A/W 2513.
161. Consulado de España en Viena to IKG, Sep. 10, 1940. CA: A/W 2513.
162. AN telephone call Murmelstein and Spanish Consulate, Sep. 14, 1940. CA: A/W 2523.5.
163. Prochnik's written deposition sent to the *Landesgericht für Strafsachen, Wien* (Provincial Criminal Court, Vienna), dated June 25, 1954, 5f. DÖW, Prochnik Dossier.

164. Storfer to Keppler at *Mitteleuropäisches Reisebüro*. Storfer to Löwenstein at *RV Hilfsverein*. Storfer to Zentralstelle Berlin. Storfer to Prochnik in Berlin. All dated Nov. 6, 1940. CA: A/W 2518.5.
165. *Mitteleuropäisches Reisebüro* to *Reichsführer SS/Zentralstelle für Jüdische Auswanderer* (*sic*), Nov. 6, 1940. CA: A/W 2518.5.
166. Prochnik in Berlin to Storfer in Vienna, Nov. 13, 1940; ibid.
167. M-tapes, II-7A.
168. Walter at *Jüdische Kultusvereinigung zu* Berlin letter to Prochnik in Vienna, Sep. 28, 1941; CA: A/W 2518.3.
169. Prochnik in Vienna letter to Walter in Berlin, Oct. 5, 1941. CA: A/W 2518.3.
170. Prochnik in Berlin memorandum to IKG *Abfertigung* (Transport Dispatching), July 27, 1941. CA: A/W 2517.3.
171. Ibid.
172. See Walter to Prochnik, Sep. 28. 1941.
173. Prochnik to MER, Oct. 7, 1941. CA: A/W 2512.2.
174. Prochnik in Berlin: memorandum to IKG *Abfertigung*, July 19, 1941. CA: A/W 2517.3.
175. Murmelstein to Prochnik, July 30, 1941. CA: A/W 2517.3.
176. Murmelstein to Prochnik, July 29, 1941. CA: A/W 2517.3.
177. Marcus and Harting to MER, Mar. 31, 1941.CA: A/W 2523.3.
178. See Prochnik in Berlin to Joint Lisbon, "*Erwirkung der portugiesischen Transitvisa für Auswanderer-transport 7, 24. 2. ab Berlin*" (Procurement of Portuguese Transit visas for Emigration Transport no. 7, Leaving Berlin Feb. 24 [1941]). CA: A/W 2517.6.
179. The quota year ran from July to June.
180. AN *Vorsprache* Löwenherz and Engel at Hohenthal, July 1, 1940, enclosures: Consulate Forms 14 and 15; L-papers.
181. Ibid.
182. Ibid.
183. Quoted in E. Reich, "Das Problem der Immigration nach USA," *Jüdisches Nachrichtenblatt*, Dec. 23, 1940, 1f.
184. Ibid., 1.
185. AN *Vorsprache* Murmelstein at Brunner 1, July 15,1940, item 2; L-papers.
186. AN *Vorsprache* Löwenherz at Brunner 1, Aug. 30, 1940, item 10; L-papers.
187. For the following see AN *Vorsprache* Löwenherz at Consul Guinn, Sep. 19, 1940; L-papers.
188. Letter Löwenherz to Troper, Oct. 3, 1940. Main copy: Joint Archive, file AJ; carbon copy: CA: A/W 2517.1. The translation into English was one of the last tasks performed by Dr. Margaret Feiler before her emigration.
189. AN *Vorsprache* Löwenherz at Eichmann at RSHA Berlin, in the presence of Brunner 1, Dec. 5, 1940, item 8; L-papers.
190. "Summary memoranda on conversations with our friends Messrs. X [Paul Meyerheim, Berlin] and X [Löwenherz] during the month of January, 1941" under cover of letter by Herbert Katzki, AJDC Lisbon to Troper, Jan. 23, 1941, 13. Joint Archive, file AJ. Katzki's report concerned the last meeting Löwenherz had with representatives of the Joint.
191. At the end of December 1940 Prochnik wrote to Löwenherz that the U.S. consulate in Berlin had increased the number of appointments for the end of January and that for this reason the *Reichsvereinigung* had booked sizable blocks of passages for February and March. Prochnik to Löwenherz, Dec. 22, 1940. CA: A/W 2523.4.
192. Ibid.
193. Ibid.
194. Wyman, *Paper Walls*, 114f.
195. Aside from being a canard designed to turn attention away from the military unpreparedness of the Allies, the accusation of Jews spying is one of a number of recurring manifestations of the unsavory anti-Semitic view of the Jews as untrustworthy evildoers. A case in point is one of the *Edicts of Toleration* issued by the enlightened Habsburg Emperor Joseph II. According to that edict, Jews had to draft all documents and keep all account books and all registries of circumcisions and births in the German language and not in Hebrew as heretofore. The reason? It was said that in the border regions with Prussia, then an enemy of the Habsburg Empire, Jews had used Hebrew for purposes of spying on behalf of Prussia; no doubt such allegations were made by people who could not read Hebrew. (See Karl Gutkas,

Kaiser Josef II: Eine Biographie [Wien: P. Zsolnay, 1989], 290.) In short, the Jew as spy has a history, which it would be worthy to bring to light by critical research.

196. Wyman, *Paper Walls*, 173.
197. Memorandum Long to Adolf A. Berle Jr. and James C. Dunn, June 26, 1940; quoted in Wyman, *Paper Walls*, 173.
198. Wyman, *Paper Walls*, 174, 266n.
199. Ibid., 175.
200. See "Memorandum re: Emigration Procedures in the Vienna *Kultusgemeinde*, based on information received from Dr. Margarete Feiler, formerly of Vienna," Jan. 4, 1941. Joint Archive, folder AJ 446.
201. "Incoming Cable" Jointfund Lisbon to Jointdisco, New York, Mar. 10, 1941. Ibid.
202. "Incoming Cable" Jacobson Blum, Budapest to Jointdisco, New York, Mar. 12, 1941. Ibid.
203. "Incoming Cable Wien," Mar. 5, 1941; transcript of German, and in-house translation, Mar. 6, 1941. Ibid.
204. Letter Leavitt to Walter Wanger, Mar. 21, 1941. Joint Archive, file AJ 440.
205. Circular by Joseph C. Hyman, April 8, 1941, 2. Ibid.
206. Leavitt to Wanger.
207. "Campaign," summary memorandum, 19.
208. Ibid.
209. "Personal Matters 3." Ibid.
210. Letter Leavitt to Wanger, Mar. 21, 1941. Joint Archive, file AJ 440.
211. Löwenherz's son hebraicized his last name and became a distinguished musicologist named Siegmund Levarie (1914–2010).
212. For the following quotations to the end of this chapter, see Josef Löwenherz to his son Siegmund in Chicago, Lisbon, Jan. 9, 1941; L-papers: Personal Correspondence.

Chapter 10

1. Summary memorandum on conversations with Messrs. X [Mayerheim] and Y [Löwenherz], 17, under cover of letter AJDC Lisbon (signed Herbert Katzki) to Troper, New York, Jan. 23, 1941. Joint Archive, file AJ.
2. AN *Vorsprache* Löwenherz and Storfer at Eichmann, Jan. 26, 1940, item III; L-papers.
3. Ibid., supplemental directives by Brunner 1 to Löwenherz, item 3.
4. Perhaps nothing can better epitomize Riesser's varied career than an impassioned passage in his address to the National Assembly, which had gathered at St. Paul's Church [*Pauluskirche*] in Frankfurt-on-Main in 1849 to write a constitution for a federal union of the many German states. Riesser, though a Jew, was one of the vice presidents of the Assembly, which, among other matters, considered the civil equality of the Jews. Many delegates balked at full emancipation; and at the last minute a motion was introduced proposing that, in consideration of its peculiar circumstances, the Israelite nation be subject to special legislation. This, of course, would have constituted a resumption of the old legal policy that had prevailed in Christian lands over the centuries of imposing on the Jewish resident a status different from that of a normal citizen of the nation. In his speech Riesser explained that Jews had long rejected the idea of being a separate nationality; however, if this illusion were to persist in the public mind, the only recourse left for Jews in order to be accepted in the German nation would be their conversion to Christianity. But that, Riesser argued, would be a mockery of both ethnicity [*Volkstum*] and religion: "One ought not to believe that it is possible to enact [such] special legislation without thereby tearing the whole fabric of freedom to shreds." And this argument carried the day; in the end the Assembly adopted the following clause in their attempt at a liberal constitution: "The enjoyment of civil rights and the rights of citizenship is neither conditional upon nor restricted by one's religious confession. Neither does it abrogate one's duties as citizen." See Wanda Kampmann, *Deutsche und Juden* (Heidelberg: Schneider, 1963), 207ff.
5. Benjamin Murmelstein, *Geschichte der Juden*, Vienna, 1938, 360.
6. Letter from *Auswertiges Amt* (Foreign Office) Section D-III to Legation Councilor [Franz] Rademacher, Berlin, Feb. 10, 1942. EICH 762.
7. Foreign Ministry Section D-III in-house memo, dated June 3, 1949. EICH 934.
8. AN *Vorsprache* Edelstein, Weidmann, Löwenherz, and Eppstein at Eichmann, later at Dannecker at RSHA Berlin, July 3, 1940, item 4; L-papers.

9. Greater Germany, Italy, France, the Netherlands, Belgium, Luxemburg, Norway, Denmark, the Protectorate, Hungary, Slovakia, and the part of Poland not under the control of the Soviet Union.
10. AN *Vorsprache*, July 3, 1940, op. cit., item 5.
11. The excerpt is taken from Murmelstein manuscript, chapter 3 "From Lublin via Madagascar to Theresienstadt," 87f. Our translation. [This statement appears to conflict with the following passage that originally followed this excerpt: "It is regrettable that we did not get to see Murmelstein's manuscript. In fact, we do not know whether it survived, and, if so, where to look for it." It is unclear what the relationship of the one is to the other. — Ed.]
12. The quotations to follow are from "Betrifft: Ansiedlung von Juden aus europäischen Ländern in zur Verfügung gestelltem Siedlungsraum ausserhalb Europas," under cover of letter to *Zentralstelle für jüdische Auswanderung*, Berlin, July 4, 1940, signed by Dr. Otto Israel Hirsch and Dr. Paul Israel Eppstein for *Reichsvereinigung der Juden in Deutschland*, Dr. Josef Israel Löwenherz for IKG Wien, Jakob Edelstein and Dr. Franz Weidmann for *Jüdische Kultusgemeinde* Prag; L-papers.
13. AN *Vorsprache* Löwenherz at Brunner 1, item 5; L-papers.
14. AN *Vorsprache* Löwenherz and Storfer at Eichmann, Jan. 26, 1940; addendum: telephone call with Brunner, item 2; L-papers.
15. Translating *Brauchtum* as rites and customs.
16. AN *Vorsprache* Murmelstein at Brunner 1, Sep. 30, 1940, copy to Gestapo; L-papers. At the *Vorsprache* Murmelstein requested permission to contribute the first item to a scientific publication in an unspecified foreign country, which was granted, provided that the treatment did not deal with the period subsequent to the seventeenth century, that the publication not be a newspaper, and that offprints be submitted to the *Zentralstelle*.
17. Murmelstein, "Polnische Gebiete als Ziel und Ursprung jüdischer Wanderung" (Polish regions as goal and origin of Jewish migration), ms., 13. Moser private archive.
18. Ibid., 16.
19. Ibid., 18f.
20. Walther Hofer, *Der Nationalsozialismus: Dokumente 1933–1945* (Frankfurt/Main: Fischer Bücherei, 1957), 29.
21. Ibid., 28.
22. Murmelstein, "Das Judentum in Polen" (Jewry in Poland), ms., 9. Moser private archive.
23. Ibid., 11.
24. Ibid.
25. Ibid., 11f.
26. Ibid., 19.
27. Ibid., 19f.
28. Ibid., 20.
29. About two-thirds of the population were ethnic Poles, one-eighth Ruthenians and Ukrainians, 9 percent Jews, 3 percent White Russians, and 2 percent Germans, with Lithuanians, Czechs, and others making up the rest.
30. Murmelstein, "Jewry in Poland," 30.
31. Ibid., 31.
32. Ibid., 34.
33. Ibid., 35.
34. Ibid.
35. Ibid., 33.
36. "Ursprung und Entwicklung der jüdischen Mundart" (Origin and development of the Jewish dialect), ms., 19. Moser private archive.
37. Hofer, *Der Nationalsozialismus*, 114. Our translation.
38. Arendt, *Eichmann in Jerusalem*, 211f.
39. Ibid., 22.
40. Shortly before the outbreak of the Second World War, the Institute, with its holdings of books and documents, was moved to New York, where it is known as the Institute of Jewish Research or by its Yiddish acronym YIVO.
41. Ibid., 24.
42. In fact, we have seen that the subsection of the Security Service dealing with Jews began as a group of highly unqualified men doing "research" and disseminating "information."

43. Lit.: "The Eternal Jew," the German expression for "The Wandering Jew," a legendary Christian invention.
44. "Das jüdische Tauchbad," ms., 1. Moser private archive.
45. Ibid. 6.
46. Ibid., 9.
47. Ibid.
48. "Die jüdische Beschneidung" (Jewish circumcision), ms., Moser private archive.
49. "Jüdische Totengebräuche" (Jewish death customs), ms., Moser private archive.
50. "Die jüdische Bestattung" (Jewish burial), ms., Moser private archive.
51. "Jewish death customs," 3.
52. "Jewish burial," 4.
53. In 1772 Olaf Tychsen, Professor of Oriental Languages, characterizing the Jewish practice of early burial as cruel and inhuman, urged Duke Frederick of Mecklenburg-Schwerin to forbid this practice. The duke did so in an edict, which was in conflict with the assurance that Jews may practice their religion freely. The Jews of Mecklenburg, fearing further infringements on the exercise of their religion, appealed to Mendelssohn for intercession. In a memorandum Mendelssohn suggested that in addition to the ascertainment of death traditional among Jews, the occurrence of death also be certified by a physician; this was found satisfactory by the duke, who rescinded the edict. However, writing to the Jewish Community that had approached him, Mendelssohn opined that it is not clear whether the Talmudic ruling of early burial is mandated by the Bible and that a three-day waiting period was not only reasonable but was in fact practiced in ancient times. Historically this has been understood as Mendelssohn's endorsement of later burial. Unbeknownst to Mendelssohn, the Jews of Mecklenburg-Schwerin had also consulted the great rabbinic authority Rabbi Jacob Emden of Altona, who in a *responsum* strongly upheld the strict rabbinic stance and subsequently chided Mendelssohn for his memorandum. See Alexander Altmann, *Moses Mendelssohn* (Philadelphia: The Jewish Publication Society, 1973), 288ff. It is this series of events that Murmelstein is referring to.
54. "Jewish burial," 4.
55. Ibid., 18.
56. Ibid., 11. In quoting the verse, Murmelstein wrote *lesen* (read) instead of *singen* (sing). The verse is from the poem "*Gedächnisfeier* (Ceremony of Remembrance)" in Heine's book of poetry *Romancero. Zweites Buch: Lamentationen/Lazarus*. In English this passage from Heine's poem reads:

    No mass is to be sung / and no *Kaddish* said,
    nothing said and nothing sung / at my time of death.

57. "Jewish death customs," 1.
58. Ibid., 12.
59. "Jewish burial," 18.
60. "Die jüdische Schlachtung (Jewish slaughter)," ms., 1. Moser private archive.
61. Murmelstein does not hesitate to take another swipe at the materialistic idolatry found among Jews no less than among others: "In the Jewish past there is not only the golden calf, which the Israelites are alleged to have erected in the wilderness, or its imitations at the time of the Kings. . . , but also the image of the wonder-working serpent and the different [emblematic] tribal beasts. . . ."
62. "Jewish slaughter," 6.
63. Murmelstein refers to Heinrich Cornill, *Das alte Testament und die Humanität* (Leipzig: J.C. Hinrich, 1895), 17.
64. "Jewish slaughter," 19.
65. Ibid., 17.
66. Ibid., 19. Murmelstein might have mentioned that during the First World War the quartermaster of the Imperial Austro-Hungarian army required that the troops be supplied with meat from animals slaughtered according to the Jewish method.
67. Ibid., 21.
68. Ibid., 21f.
69. "Tisch'a Beaw, der Tag jüdischer Wanderung," *Jüdisches Nachrichtenblatt*, Aug. 12, 1940, 1. YV.
70. Our literal translation of Murmelstein's words. The words he is citing have been variously translated, and Murmelstein is interpreting the original text to suit the audience and their circumstances. The first JPS (Jewish Publication Society) translation of this verse comes close to the sense Murmelstein gave it:

"Thus said the Lord of hosts: The fast of the fourth month and the fast of the fifth [i.e., Av], and the fast of the seventh, and the fast of the tenth, shall be to the house of Judah joy and gladness, and cheerful seasons; therefore love ye truth and peace." Zechariah 8:19 as per *The Holy Scriptures* (Philadelphia: Jewish Publication Society, 25th ed.), 5711–1951.

71. The quotations which follow are from *Jüdisches Nachrichtenblatt, Ausgabe Wien*, Dec. 23, 1940, 1. YV.
72. From Friedrich Schiller's poem "*Hoffnung* (Hope)."
73. *Jüdisches Nachrichtenblatt, Ausgabe Wien*, Nov. 1, 1940, 1. YV.
74. Ibid., Nov. 4, 1940, 1f.
75. Ibid., Nov. 8, 1940, 1f. YV.
76. Ibid., Nov. 11, 1940, 1f. YV.
77. For the following see AN *Vorsprache* Löwenherz at Kochanowski at the Reich Ministry for the People's Enlightenment and Propaganda (*Reichsministerium für Volksaufklärung*. . .) in Berlin, Sep. 5, 1940; L-papers. Letter from Emil Israel Reich to Kochanowski at *Reichsministerium für Volksaufklärung*. . . , dated Vienna, Sep. 7, 1940. CA: A/W 475.
78. See list *Pflichtexemplare* added to Letter Reich to Kochanowski, op. cit.
79. Most of the ninety-seven free copies went to various agencies of the IKG. Some went to the sister publications in Berlin and Prague, some to Jewish communities in Berlin and the Protectorate. It is worthy of note that two copies went to the Jewish Council of Elders in Warsaw, and one to the *Jüdische Zeitung* in Krakow. See list *Freiexemplare* added to Letter Reich to Kochanowski, op. cit. See also Reich's correspondence with Warsaw *Judenrat*, CA: A/W 494.1; and with Krakow *Gazeta Żydowska*, CA: A/W 494.2.
80. AN *Vorsprache* Löwenherz at Kochanowski, Berlin, Sep. 5, 1940, item 2; L-papers.
81. Ibid.
82. Letter Reich to Kochanowski.
83. Louis P. Lochner (ed. and trans.), *The Goebbels Diaries 1942–1943* (Garden City, NY: Doubleday & Co., 1948), 350f. Emphasis added.
84. See file within SD-Hauptamt of Kulturwalter Hinkel, NA roll, frames 2/935594ff, National Archives, College Park, Maryland.
85. *Aktennotiz*: Betrifft: Besprechung mit SS-Oberführer Hinkel, Berlin, Oct. 27, 1938, signed by Hagen, II 112; NA roll, frames 2/935671-3.
86. Letter Hagen to Hinkel, Apr. 30, 1938, Betr.: Briefe von Juden aus Österreich, NA roll, frame 2/935613.
87. Letter Hinkel to Hagen, May 12, 1938, Betr.: Briefe von Juden aus Österreich, NA roll, frame 2/935614.
88. Letter Siegmund Stössel to Reich, Jan. 7, 1940; letter Reich to Stössel, Jan. 10, 1940. CA: A/W 495.2.
89. Letter Olga Hacker to Reich, May 13, 1941; letter Reich to Hacker, May 14, 1941. CA: A/W 495.2.
90. Letter Prochnik to Reich, Dec. 8, 1940. CA: A/W 495.2.
91. Letter Reich to Prochnik, Dec. 23, 1940. CA: A/W 495.2.
92. Letter Reich to Frankl, Mar. 4, 1942. Letter Reich to Siegmund Ortony, Jul. 27, 1941. CA: A/W 495.2.
93. Cf. CA: A/W 624.18. Also Wies, *Totenbuch Theresienstadt I: Deportierte aus Österreich* (Vienna: Jüdisches Komitee für Österreich, 1971); Moser, *Judenverfolgung*, 46.
94. Rudolf Beck in *Nachrichtenblatt* 86 (Oct. 25, 1940).
95. Ibid.
96. Quoted in letter Löwenherz to Troper, Jan. 23, 1940. Joint Archive, file AJ 414.
97. Letter Löwenherz to *Schriftleitung* . . . *Nachrichtenblatt*, Jan. 24, 1940. CA: A/W 272.
98. Letter Löwenherz to Reich, Jan. 24, 1940. CA: A/W 272.
99. Letter of Seligsohn at *Reichsvereinigung* (Berlin) to Reich, Apr. 4, 1940, enclosing Treguboff's letter of Feb. 8, 1940. CA: A/W 495.2.
100. Letter Reich to *Reichsvereinigung*, Apr. 12, 1940. CA: A/W 495.2.
101. *Das Problem der Immigration nach USA* [The problem of immigration to the USA]. YV.
102. See "Die Bevorzugten-Immigration nach den USA [preference-immigration to the USA]," *Jüdisches Nachrichtenblatt*, Vienna edition, Jan. 3, 1941. YV.
103. Letter Max to Murmelstein, Oct. 16, 1939. CA: P 151(7).
104. Löwenherz to Troper, Sep. 25, 1940. CA: A/W 181.1.
105. Summary memoranda on conversations with . . . Y [Löwenherz] during the month of January 1941, 19, enclosed in Memorandum Katzki (Lisbon) to Troper (New York), Jan. 23, 1941. Joint Archive, file AJ.
106. Letter Löwenherz (in Berlin) to Ehrenpreis, Jan. 23, 1941. CA: A/W 181.1.
107. For the following quotations, see letter Löwenherz to Ehrenpreis, Feb. 10, 1941. CA: A/W 181.1.

108. *Maggid* means preacher. What Löwenherz means is that Murmelstein's sermons tended toward teaching, exposition, and interpretation rather than toward hortatory preaching.
109. Letter Friedmann to Ehrenpreis, Mar. 14, 1941. CA: A/W 181.1.
110. *Der jüdische Gottesdienst im Auftrag zusammengestellt von Dr. Benjamin Murmelstein* (The Jewish Divine Service compiled by Dr. Benjamin Murmelstein); henceforth: *Gottesdienst*.
111. Named after the first word of Deuteronomy 6:4: "Hear, o Israel, the Lord is our God, the Lord alone," which serves as the introduction to this lengthy prayer comprising biblical quotations.
112. If Murmelstein meant this as a reproach to the effect that God provides sustenance for all men, but it is man who deprives fellow man, then it was overly subtle.
113. *Gottesdienst*, 6.
114. Ibid., 2f.
115. Ibid., 6.
116. Ibid., 8.
117. Murmelstein, *Geschichte der Juden*, 365ff.
118. Rabbi Mannheimer was designated Preacher because the reactionary regime of Emperor Francis [Franz] I (brother of the more liberal Emperor Joseph II) did not grant official status to any clergy other than the Roman Catholic.
119. *Gottesdienst*, 10.
120. Ibid.
121. Ibid., 11.
122. Ibid., 11f. The quoted passage is a translation of Murmelstein's rendering of the fourteenth of the eighteen benedictions. It is it is taken from Lamentations 5:21.
123. Ibid., 12.
124. AN *Vorsprache* Löwenherz at Brunner 1, Sep. 19, 1940, item 3; L-papers.
125. AN *Vorsprache* Murmelstein at Brunner 1, Sep. 27, 1940; L-papers.
126. *Betrifft Jugendgottesdienst am Samstag* (Concerning the youth service on Saturday), den 12. Apr. 1941. CA: A/W 1329.
127. Ansprache gehalten von Dr. Benjamin Israel Murmelstein beim Gottesdienst am 2. June 1941 in Wien I. Seitenstettengasse 4, 3. Moser private archive.
128. Ibid., 4.
129. Oehler's draft of notice, with approval of Löwenherz and Murmelstein, Aug. 7, 1941. CA: A/W 1329.
130. Oehler to Tuchmann, Sep. 19, 1941. CA: A/W 1329.
131. AN by Oehler, May 9, 1941; CA: A/W 1329. Among those who would take one of these seats was one Menasche Mauthner, a minor functionary at the IKG.
132. AN *Vorsprache* Löwenherz at Kuchmann, Sep. 5, 1941; CA: A/W 1329.
133. Instruktion für die Funktionäre, Maskir-Andachten am Schowuaus 1941, Betrifft Jugendgottesdienst. . . ; CA: A/W 1329.
134. *Esrogim und Lulawim für Sukkos* (Etrogim and Lulavim for Sukkot) 1941; CA: A/W 1329.
135. *Niederschrift über das Ergebnis der Augenscheinsverhandlungen vom 6. Juni 1941* (Record of the results of the inspection and ensuing negotiations). CA: A/W 1516.
136. See *Tätigkeitsbericht* attached to Feldsberg to Moses, Aug. 12, 1941. CA: A/W 1515.
137. *Tätigkeitsbericht*, Aug. 15, 1941. CA: A/W 1515.
138. Ibid.
139. Ibid.
140. *Tätigkeitsbericht*, Aug. 20, 1941. CA: A/W 1515.
141. *Tätigkeitsbericht*, July 17, 1940. CA: A/W 1515.
142. Peter Wiernik, "Ben-Ze'eb, Judah Löb," *The Jewish Encyclopedia* 2: 681f.
143. Max Seligsohn, "Obornik (Obernik), Meïr," *The Jewish Encyclopedia* 9: 371.
144. Henrietta Szold, "Arnstein, Fanny (Fögele) von," *The Jewish Encyclopedia* 2: 133. See also Meir Lamed, "Arnstein (Arnsteiner)," *Encyclopedia Judaica* 3: 488–491.
145. Gotthard Deutsch, "Horowitz, Lazar (Eleazar)," *The Jewish Encyclopedia* 6: 466f. See also *Tätigkeitsbericht* attached to Feldsberg to Moses, Dec. 24, 1941. CA: A/W 1515.
146. See *Tätigkeitsberichte* attached to Feldsberg to Moses, Dec. 24, 1941 and Jan. 3, 1942. CA: A/W 1515.
147. It was an orientation that at the end of the century would become known in the United States as the movement of Conservative Judaism, which was actually influenced by Mannheimer's blend of traditional Orthodoxy and modern Reform.

Glossary

Abfertigung (Ger.) Dispatching section/department
Abriegelung (Ger.) Bolting shut
Achtzehngebet (Ger.) The Eighteen Prayer; see also *'Amidah*; *Shemoneh 'esreh*
Agudas Jisroel (Ashkenazi Heb. for *Agudat Yisrael*) Union of Israel, an orthodox Jewish organization founded in 1912; also spelled in an anglicized manner as *Agudath Israel*
Aktennotiz(-en) (AN) (Ger.) Memorandum(-a)
Aliyah (Heb.) Jewish immigration to Palestine/Israel; literally, "going up"
Aliyah Bet (Heb.) Illegal immigration of Jews to British Mandatory Palestine during 1934–1948
Allgemeine Stiftung für jüdische Fürsorge in Wien (Ger.) General Foundation for Jewish Welfare in Vienna
Altersghetto (Ger.) A ghetto for the old
Ältestenrat(-räte) (Ger.) Council(s) of (Jewish) Elders appointed by the Nazis
Altreich (Ger.) The old Reich, that is, Germany without its conquests
'Amidah (Heb.) The Standing Prayer; see also *Shemoneh 'esreh*
Amtsdirektion (Ger.) Central office/administration of the IKG
Amtsdirektor (Ger.) Director of the Board
Anordnung (Ger.) Directive
Anschluss (Ger.) The absorption of Austria into the German Reich on March 12, 1938
Anstände (Ger.) Complaints
Arbeitsdienst (Ger.) Labor service
Arbeitseinsatz (Ger.) Labor force
Arbeitskammer (Ger.) Labor Bureau
Aufbaufonds (Ger.) The fund for reconstruction
Aufbauumlage (Ger.) Reconstruction charge
Auflage (Ger.) Surcharge
Aufsichtsbehörde (Ger.) Supervisory authority
Auftrag (Ger.) Assignment, commission
Ausgereiste (Ger.) People who had departed from the country presumably on their own volition
Ausgewanderte (Ger.) Emigrants, expatriates
Auswanderung (Ger.) Emigration
Auswanderungsabgabe (Ger.) The amount that emigrants had to pay from their remaining assets to receive their passports
Auswanderungsabteilung (Ger.) Emigration section
Auswärtiges Amt (Ger.) Foreign Office

Baurat (Ger.) Building councilor
Begründung (Ger.) Justification
Beirat (Ger.) Executive council
Beschlagnahme (Ger.) Confiscation
Beschluss/Beschluß (Ger.) Executive decision
Beschlussbuch (Ger.) Ledger of administrative decisions

Besprechung (Ger.) Discussion
Betar (Heb.) Revisionist Zionist organization
Blitzkrieg (Ger.) Lightning war
Blockälteste (Ger.) The block chief in a concentration camp
Blockwart (Ger.) Block superintendent; a Nazi responsible for supervising an area of the city
Brauchtum (Ger.) Rites and customs
Brigadeführer (Ger.) Major General
Brunnenvergiftung (Ger.) Well poisoning

Chevra Kadisha (Aram.) Jewish burial society; literally, "holy society"
Chutzpah (Heb.) Nerve, gall
Comité voor bijzondere joodsche belangen (Dutch) Committee for Special Jewish Concerns

Das schwarze Korps (Ger.) Weekly newspaper of SS; literally, "the black corps"
Der Stürmer (Ger.) The vulgar and graphic anti-Semitic weekly published in newspaper format in Nuremberg by Julius Streicher, the *Gauleiter* of Franconia
Deutsche Arbeitsfront (DAF) (Ger.) German Labor Front
Deutsche Reichsbahn (Ger.) German Reich Railway
Devisen (Ger.) Foreign exchange, foreign currency
Devisenabteilung (Ger.) Foreign Exchange Section
Devisenstelle Wien (Ger.) The Vienna branch of the German exchange office
Devisenzentrale (Ger.) The German agency that governed foreign exchange
Dezernat (Ger.) Section, department
Dienstanweisung (Ger.) Service directive, instructions
Donnerwetter (Ger.) Thunderstorm
Drashot (Heb.) Sermonettes
Dybbuk (Heb.) A creature/person inhabited by the tormented soul of one who has died

Eikha (Heb.) The biblical Book of Lamentations
Eingabe (Ger.) Statement/application/report
Einsatzgruppen (Ger.) Mobile killing task forces
Emigration involontaire (Fr.) Involuntary emigration
Endlösung (Ger.) Final solution
Endziel (Ger.) Ultimate goal
Eretz Yisrael (Heb.) The Land of Israel
Erfassung (Ger.) Laying hold
Erwerbsleben (Ger.) Economic life
Etrog(im) (Heb.) Citron(s), a symbol of the festival of Sukkot (September/October)

Fernplan (Ger.) Long-range plan
Frau (Ger.) Mrs. or Ms.
Friedhof (Ger.) Cemetery
Führerbefehl (Ger.) Order from the leader (i.e., Adolf Hitler)
Führerprinzip (Ger.) Leadership principle
Fürst Bischof (Ger.) Prince-bishop, sovereign bishop

Gabelfrühstück (Ger.) Second breakfast
Gau (Ger.) Region/district/county
Gauleiter (Ger.) Regional party leader
Gauwirtschaftsamt (Ger.) Regional economic agency
Gedächnisfeier (Ger.) Ceremony of Remembrance

Gesellschaft der Musikfreunde (Ger.) Society of the Friends of Music
Glaubensjude(n) (Ger.) Jew(s) by faith
Glaubensjüdin (Ger.) Jew by faith (fem.)
Gleichschaltung (Ger.) Alignment (political)
Gottesdienst (Ger.) Divine service
Goy(-im) (Heb.) Gentile(s)
Greis(e) (Ger.) Old person(s)
Greuelgeschichten (Ger.) Horror stories, malicious rumors of atrocities
Greuelpropaganda (Ger.) Horror propaganda
Grundbefindlichkeit (Ger.) The fundamental state of being in which we find ourselves
Gruppenführer (Ger.) Group Leader, a rank in the SS

Ha'avara (Heb.) Transfer
Haganah (Heb.) Defense; the pre-state Jewish paramilitary force
Hakhshara (Heb.) Preparation for immigration to Israel by training in manual labor
Halakhah (Heb.) Jewish religious law
Halutz(im) (Heb.) Pioneer(s); also *Chalutz(im)*
Hashomer Hatzair (Heb.) The Young Guard, a secular socialist/Zionist youth organization
Haskalah (Heb.) The Jewish Enlightenment
Hatikvah (Heb.) "The Hope," the Zionist anthem and later the national anthem of Israel
Hauptsturmführer (Ger.) A Nazi paramilitary rank roughly equivalent to captain
Hechalutz (Heb.) "The Pioneer," a Zionist youth organization preparing young people to immigrate to Israel/Palestine; also spelled *HeHalutz*
Herr (Ger.) Mister
Herrenlos (Ger.) Ownerless
Hilferuf (Ger.) Cry for help
Hilfsverein der deutschen Juden (Ger.) Aid Association of German Jews
Histadrut (Heb.) Labor Zionist organization
Hitachdut Olei Germania (Heb.) Organization of Immigrants/Zionists from Germany
Hofrat (Ger.) Court councilor, an honorific title dating back to the Habsburg monarchy

IKG Israelitische Kultusgemeinde Wien, Jewish Community of Vienna
Inbegriff (Ger.) Essence
Israelitische Kultusgemeinde (IKG) (Ger.) Jewish Community
Israelitisch-theologische Lehranstalt (Ger.) Jewish Theological Institute/Seminary of Vienna

Jause (Ger.) Afternoon coffee and cake
Jawohl (Ger.) Yes, of course
Jude(n) (Ger.) Jew(s)
Judenaktionen (Ger.) Actions against the Jews
Judenältester (Ger.) Jewish elder
Judenfrei (Ger.) Cleansed of Jews
Judenpolitik (Ger.) Jewish policy, i.e., policy regarding the Jews
Judenrat (s.)/**Judenräte** (pl.) (Ger.) Jewish Council(s)
Judenrein (Ger.) Free of Jews
Jüdische Ältestenräte (Ger.) The Councils of Jewish Elders
Jüdische Nachrichten (Ger.) Jewish News
Jüdische Pressezentrale Zürich (Ger.) Jewish Press Agency of Zurich, Switzerland
Jüdische Theologische Lehranstalt (Ger.) Jewish Theological Seminary
Jüdischer Hilfsverband für jüdische Kriegsopfer, Invaliden, Witwen und Waisen (Ger.) Jewish Association for the Aid of Jewish War Victims, Invalids, Widows and Orphans

Jüdischer Kulturbund (Ger.) Cultural Federation of German Jews
Jüdisches Nachrichtenblatt (Ger.) Jewish newspaper
Jüdische Rundschau (Ger.) Officially mandated Jewish newspaper in Berlin
Juniaktion (Ger.) "June action" that took place in Germany in 1938

Kaddish (Heb.) The prayer traditionally recited by mourners; it is actually a hymn of praise
Kalenderblätter (Ger.) Pages of a calendar
Kapitalistenzertifikate (Ger.) Capitalists' certificates
Karner (Ger.) Austrian dialect for a charnel house
Kaserne (Ger.) Barracks
Keren Hayesod (Heb.) The United Jewish Appeal
Keren Kayemeth LeIsrael (Heb.) The Jewish National Fund
Kompetenzenchaos (Ger.) Chaos of authority
Konto (Ger.) Account
Kontrolldienst (Ger.) Control duties
Kreisleiter (Ger.) Regional (Nazi) party leaders
Kreisleitung (Ger.) District (Nazi) party office
Kristallnacht (Ger.) The Nazi name for the Reich-wide pogrom against the Jews on November 9–10, 1938
Kultusgemeinde(-n) (Ger.) Jewish community(-ies), literally "religious community(-ies)"
Kultussteuer (Ger.) Religious tax/community dues

Lagebericht (Ger.) Situation report
Lager (Ger.) Camp
Landkommissar (Ger.) Territorial commissioner
Landsmannschaft(-en) (Ger.) Immigrant association(s)
Lehre (Ger.) Teaching
Leiter (Ger.) Leader, director
Leitstelle (Ger.) Headquarters
Lulav(-im) (Heb.) Branches tied together as a symbol of the festival of Sukkot (September/October)

Maggid (Heb.) Preacher
Maiaktion (Ger.) "May action" that took place in post-Anschluss Austria in 1938
Marrano (Sp.) A Christianized Jew, especially one who professed Christianity to avoid persecution; it was originally a pejorative term since it means "pig"
Matrikelamt (Ger.) Registry of births, marriages, deaths
Matzah(-ot) (Heb.) Matzah(s), unleavened bread
Melamed (Heb.) Teacher of traditional Jewish religious subjects
Meshugge (Yid.) Crazy, insane
Mikveh (mikva'ot) (Heb.) Jewish ritual bath(s)
Minyan(-im) (Heb.) Quorum(s) for traditional Jewish prayer (usually ten men)
Misrachi See *Mizrachi*
Mitteilung (Ger.) Communiqué, report
Mitteleuropäisches Reisebüro (MER) (Ger.) Central European Travel Bureau
Mitzvah (Heb.) Jewish religious commandment, by extension: a good deed
Mizrachi (Heb.) Religious Zionist organization; in German, spelled *Misrachi*
Mustertransport (Ger.) Transport that would function as model or pattern for the ones to follow

Nachlass (Ger.) Legacy, estate (literary)
Nahplan (Ger.) Immediate plan
Narodnyi Komissariat Vnutrennikh Del (NKVD) (Rus.) Soviet secret police

Nationalsozialistische Deutsche Arbeiterpartei (NSDAP) (Ger.) The National Socialist German Worker's Party; Nazi Party for short

Ne'ilah (Heb.) The concluding service of Yom Kippur, the Day of Atonement; the word refers to the imminent "closing" of the gates of repentance at the conclusion of the holiday

Nein (Ger.) No

Nichtglaubensjuden (Ger.) Jews not by faith, non-practicing Jews

Nichts übrig haben (Ger.) To have no concern or not to have anything left over

Oberdeutsch (Ger.) The southern German dialect

Oberführer (Ger.) SS rank equivalent to a Senior Colonel

Oberkommando der Wehrmacht (OKW) (Ger.) Supreme Command of the Wehrmacht

Oberscharführer (Ger.) Senior Sergeant

Obersenatsrat (Ger.) Chief magistrate

Obersturmbannführer (Ger.) Lieutenant Colonel

Obersturmführer (Ger.) Sergeant Major/First Lieutenant

Ordner (Ger.) Keeper of order

Ortsgruppenleiter (Ger.) Local party managers

Ostjuden (Ger.) Eastern Jews, used pejoratively to refer to Jews from Galicia (now southern Poland and Ukraine)

Ostmark (Ger.) The Eastern March (Territory) of the German Reich, that is, what had been Austria before the Anschluss

Palamt (Ger.) Abbreviation for Palästina-Amt, "Palestine Bureau"

Pfennig (Ger.) Cent, 1/100 of a Reichsmark

Pogrom (Rus.) Officially sanctioned persecution up to and including murder of helpless people; specifically, an action taken against Jews

Politische Bereitschaft (Ger.) Political task force

Pushke (Yid.) Box for charity contributions

Rassejuden (Ger.) Jews by race

Realgymnasium (Ger.) In Austria, a secondary school that emphasizes math, the natural sciences, and modern languages

Rechtsstaat (Ger.) A country ruled by law

Regierungsrat (Ger.) Councilor

Reichsbahn, Deutsche (Ger.) German National Railway

Reichsbank (Ger.) The Central Bank of Germany 1876–1945

Reichsbürger (Ger.) Citizens of the Reich

Reichsfluchtsteuer (Ger.) Reich flight tax, defection levy

Reichsführer SS (Ger.) National Leader of the SS, that is, Heinrich Himmler

Reichskommissar (Ger.) Reich Commissioner

Reichskulturkammer (Ger.) Reich Chamber of Culture

Reichskulturwalter (Ger.) Reich Superintendent of Cultural Affairs

Reichsprotektor (Ger.) Protector of the Reich, the official appointed over the Protectorate of Bohemia and Moravia

Reichssicherheitshauptamt (RSHA) (Ger.) Reich-headquarters of the SS, literally the Main Office for the Realm's Security

Reichsstatthalter (Ger.) Reich governor

Reichsstelle für jüdische Auswanderung (Ger.) Reich Center for Jewish Emigration

Reichstag (Ger.) German parliament

Reichsverband Jüdischer Kulturbünde (Ger.) National Association of Jewish Cultural Organizations

Reichsvereinigung (RV) (Ger.) Reich Association of Jewish Communities

Reichsvertretung der Deutschen Juden (Ger.) National Representation of German Jews
Reichswirtschaftsamt (Ger.) Reich Economics Office
Reichswirtschaftsministerium (RWM) (Ger.) Reich Ministry for Economics
Reichszentrale für die jüdische Auswanderung (Ger.) Reich Center for Jewish Emigration
Religionsgenossenschaft (Ger.) Religious body
Rosh Hashanah (Heb.) The Jewish New Year in September/October; literally, the head of the year
Responsum (Lat.) A rabbinic response to a question of interpretation of Jewish law
Rothschildspital (Ger.) Rothschild Hospital in Vienna
Rückwanderer (Ger.) Remigrants, that is, Jews who had emigrated to Italy but were forced to return to the Reich
Rundschreiben (Ger.) Circular

SA, Sturmabteilung (Ger.) "Storm Detachment," the original paramilitary wing of the Nazi Party, also known as the Brown Shirts; following the 1934 "Night of the Long Knives" they were overshadowed by the SS
Schmiergeld(er) (Ger.) Bribe(s)
Schutzbund (Ger.) Austrian socialist paramilitary organization
Schwärmerei (Ger.) Mystical ardor, enthusiasm
Schwerfällig (Ger.) Hard to budge
SD, Sicherheitsdienst (Ger.) Intelligence-gathering body of Nazi Party, separate from Gestapo
SD-Inland: Lebensgebiete (Ger.) Internal SD: Aspects of Life
Sephardim (Heb.) Sephardi Jews
Shema Yisrael (Heb.) "Hear, o Israel"—the beginning of Deuteronomy 6:4, which is the central Jewish declaration of faith
Shemoneh 'esreh (Heb.) The eighteen benedictions; see also *'Amidah*
Shtadlan (Heb./Yid.) Intercessor on behalf of the Jewish Community with the non-Jewish authorities
Shul (Yid.) A traditional term for a synagogue
Shulchan Arukh (Heb.) The most influential code of Jewish religious law, compiled by Joseph Caro in Safed, Israel, in the mid-sixteenth century
Sichtvermerk(e) (Ger.) The entry that was the final authorization for leaving Germany
Sippenforschung (Ger.) Research into bloodlines and descent
Sitzkrieg (Ger.) "Haunch-sitters" war, one in which there is little or no action
Sonderbevollmächtigter für das Vermögen (Ger.) Special Trustee for the Assets
Sopher (Heb.) Scribe
Sperrkonto(-i) (Ger.) Frozen account(s)
SS "Schutzstaffel" (Ger.) Hitler's bodyguards; later expanded to handle intelligence, security, policing, extermination
SS-Oberabschnitt Österreich (Ger.) SS Superior Regional Sector Austria
Staatsangehörige (Ger.) Nationals eligible for passport and liable for taxes
Staatspolizei (Ger.) State police (aka Stapo)
Staatsrat (Ger.) State Councilor
Staatssekretär (Ger.) Undersecretary
Stadtphysikus (Ger.) Municipal physician
Stände (Ger.) Estates or corporate associations
Ständestaat (Ger.) Corporate state
Stapo (Ger.) State police, that is, Staatspolizei
Stapoleitstelle(n) (Ger.) Regional state police headquarters
Statthalter (Ger.) Governor
Statthalterei (Ger.) The Nazi Party governor's (i.e., Bürckel's) office
Steuerunbedenklichkeitsbescheinigung (Ger.) Certificate of overall tax clearance
Steuerunbedenklichkeitserklärung (Ger.) Overall tax clearance

Stillhaltekommissar (Ger.) Receivership Commissioner for Jewish Organizations
Stimmungsbericht (Ger.) Mood report
Strassenbild (Ger.) Streetscape
Studentenverbindung (Ger.) Academic fraternity
Stylisieren (Ger.) Editorial skills
Sühneleistung (Ger.) Atonement

Tagesbericht (Ger.) Daily report
Tätigkeits- und Lage-Berichte (Ger.) Activity and situation reports
Tisha b'Av (Heb.) The ninth day of the Jewish month of Av, an annual fast day commemorating the destruction of the First and Second Temples in Jerusalem
Tschecho-Juden (Ger.) Czech (national) Jews
Tzedakah (Heb.) Charity, literally justice

Überfallswagen (Ger.) In Viennese dialect, an open police vehicle used for raids
Überholt (Ger.) Outdated
Umschichtung (Ger.) Regrouping
Umschulungskurse (Ger.) Retraining courses
Umschulungslager (Ger.) Retraining camps
Umsiedlung (Ger.) Relocation/resettlement
Unentbehrlich (Ger.) Indispensable, essential
Unliebsam (Ger.) Undesirable
Unternehmen (Ger.) Enterprise, business
Unterschiebung (Ger.) Imputation
Untersturmführer (Ger.) A rank in the SS equivalent to a Second Lieutenant

Vaad (Waad) Leumi (Heb.) National Council/Committee of Jewish organizations in pre-state Palestine
Verband der türkischen Israeliten [Sephardim] zu Wien (Ger.) Association of Sephardi Jews in Vienna
Verein (Ger.) Club
Vermögen (Ger.) Assets
Vermögensverkehrsstelle (Ger.) Governmental agency for the control of asset transfers
Vertrauensarzt (Ger.) Privy Physician
Vertraulich (Ger.) Confidential
Völkerwanderung (Ger.) Migration of peoples
Volksdeutsche Mittelstelle (Ger.) An aid organization for ethnic Germans
Volksgenosse(-n) (Ger.) Fellow countryman(-men) (of an ethnic persuasion)
Volkszorn (Ger.) Wrath of the people
Vorsprache (Ger.) Audience, visit (in the sense of a meeting)
Vorzeigegeld (Ger.) Money to be shown on arrival at a destination

Waffen-SS (Ger.) "Weapon SS," the armed wing of the SS and its members
Waisenhaus (Ger.) Orphanage
Wanderwillige (Ger.) Those willing to emigrate
Wehrwirtschaftsdienst (Ger.) An office concerned with military economy
Weisung(-en) (Ger.) Directive(s)
Weltanschaulich (Ger.) As determined by worldview
Weltfinanzjudentum (Ger.) International finance Jewry
Wesentlich (Ger.) Substantially
Westbahnhof (Ger.) The Western Railway Terminal of Vienna
Wirtschaftsministerium (Ger.) The Ministry for Economic Affairs

Wohnungsamt (Ger.) Housing Bureau

Yeshiva (Heb.) Traditional Jewish school for advanced religious learning
Yizkor (Heb.) A special service of remembrance taking place on certain Jewish holidays
Yom ha-zikkaron (Heb.) The Day of Remembrance

Zentralausschuss für Hilfe und Aufbau (Ger.) Central Committee for Aid and Reconstruction
Zentralfriedhof (Ger.) Central Cemetery
Zentralstelle(-n) (Ger.) Center(s) or central office(s)
Zentralstelle für jüdische Auswanderung (Ger.) Center for Jewish Emigration
Zimmerverbot (Ger.) Banishment from the office/room
Zionistische Rundschau (Ger.) Zionist Review
Zugereisten (Ger.) Those who immigrated, a designation for Jews from Poland who had immigrated to Vienna
Zwischenaufenthaltslager (Ger.) Transit camp

Bibliography

Adam, Uwe Dietrich. *Judenpolitik im dritten Reich*. Düsseldorf: Droste Verlag, 1972.

———. "Wie spontan war der Pogrom?" In *Der Judenpogrom 1938. Von der 'Reichskristallnacht' zum Völkermord*, ed. Walter H. Pehle. Frankfurt [Main]: Fischer, 1988.

Adler, H. G. *Theresienstadt. 1941–1945: Das Antlitz einer Zwangsgemeinschaft, Geschichte Soziologie Psychologie*. Tübingen: Mohr, 1955.

———. *Die verheimlichte Wahrheit: Theresienstädter Dokumente*. Tübingen: Mohr Siebeck, 1958.

Akten zur Deutschen Auswärtigen Politik 1918–1945, Series D, vol. 1. Baden-Baden/Göttingen, 1950ff. [*Documents on German Foreign Policy 1918–1945*, Part D, vol. 1. London, 1948ff.]

Altmann, Alexander. *Moses Mendelssohn*. Philadelphia: The Jewish Publication Society, 1973.

Anderl, Gabriele, and Walter Manoschek. "Die Geschichte des Kladovo Transports 1939 bis 1942 [The Story of the Kladovo Transport, 1939 to 1942]." In *Kladovo: Eine Flucht nach Palästina* [*Escape to Palestine*], ed. Alisa Douer. Vienna: Jewish Museum, 2001.

Arendt, Hannah. *Eichmann in Jerusalem: The Banality of Evil*. New York: Viking Press, 1963.

Arnberger, Heinz, Winfried R. Garscha, and Christa Meitterrutzner. *"Anschluss" 1938. Eine Dokumentation*. Wien: Österreichischer Bundesverlag, 1988.

Aronson, Shlomo. *Reinhard Heydrich und die Frühgeschichte von Gestapo und SD 1931–1935*. (diss. Freie Universität Berlin, 1967). Later published as *Reinhard Heydrich und die Frühgeschichte von Gestapo und SD*. Studien zur Zeitgeschichte. Stuttgart: Deutsche Verlags-Anstalt, 1971.

Barkai, Avraham. "Schicksalsjahr 1938." In *Der Judenpogrom 1938. Von der 'Reichskristallnacht' zum Völkermord*, ed. Walter H. Pehle. Frankfurt [Main]: Fischer, 1988.

Bentwich, Norman. *I Understand the Risks: The Story of the Refugees from Nazi Oppression Who Fought in the British Forces in the World War*. London: Gollancz, 1950.

———. *Wanderer in War 1939–45*. London: Gollancz, 1946.

Benz, Wolfgang."Der Rückfall in die Barbarei." In *Der Judenpogrom 1938. Von der 'Reichskristallnacht' zum Völkermord*, ed. Walter H. Pehle. Frankfurt [Main]: Fischer, 1988.

Böhm, Adolf. *Die zionistische Bewegung*. 2 vols. Berlin: Jüdischer Verlag, 1935–1937.

Bondy, Ruth. *"Elder of the Jews"—Jakob Edelstein of Theresienstadt*. Translated from the Hebrew by Evelyn Abel. New York: Grove Press, 1989.

Botz, Gerhard (and Karl R. Stadler). *Wien, vom "Anschluss" zum Krieg: nationalsozialistische Machtübernahme und politisch-soziale Umgestaltung am Beispiel der Stadt Wien 1938/39*. Wien / München: Jugend & Volk, 1978. [The text mentions works by Botz in two formats: *Wien* and *vom "Anschluss" zum Krieg*. While Gerhard Botz wrote a number of works with Wien in the title, my best guess is that all references are to this work.—Ed.]

Bracher, Karl Dietrich. *Die deutsche Diktatur: Entstehung, Struktur, Folgen des Nationalsozialismus*. Köln: Kiepenheuer & Witsch, 1969.

Bracher, Karl Dietrich, Wolfgang Schulz, and Gerhard Sauer, eds. *Die nationalsozialistische Machtergreifung: Studien zur Errichtung des totalitären Herrschaftssystems in Deutschland 1933/34. Vol. III, Die Mobilmachung der Gewalt*. Frankfurt [Main]/Köln: Ullstein, 1974.

Buchheim, Hans. "Befehl und Gehorsam." In *Anatomie des SS-Staates*, Vol. 1 , 3rd edition, ed. Hans Buchheim, Martin Broszat, Hans-Adolf Jacobsen, and Helmut Krausnick. München, 1982.

Buchheim, Hans, Martin Broszat, Hans-Adolf Jacobsen, and Helmut Krausnick, eds., *Anatomie des SS-Staates*, 3rd edition (München, 1982).

Bulletin of the Co-ordinating Committee for Refugees 3. London, April 1939.

Bullock, Alan. *Hitler, A Study in Tyranny*. New York: Harper & Row, 1964.

Churchill, Winston S. *The Gathering Storm*. Boston: Houghton Mifflin, 1948.

———. *History of the Second World War, Vol. 2: Their Finest Hour*. Boston: Houghton Mifflin, 1949.

Cohen, Roger. "U.S.-German Flare-Up over Vast Nazi Camp Archives," *New York Times*, February 20, 2006. http://www.nytimes.com/2006/02/20/world/europe/usgerman-flareup-over-vast-nazi-camp-archives.html.

Cornill, Heinrich. *Das alte Testament und die Humanität*. Leipzig: J. C. Hinrich, 1895.

Esh, Shaul. "Between Discrimination and Extermination." *Yad Vashem Studies* 2, 1958.

Faschismus-Getto-Massenmord, ed. Jüdisches Historisches Institut Warschau, Frankfurt/Main, 1962.

Fraenkel, Joseph, ed., *The Jews of Austria: Essays on Their Life, History and Destruction*. London: Vallentine, Mitchell, 1967.

Gold, Hugo. *Geschichte der Juden in Wien: Ein Gedenkbuch*. Tel Aviv: Olamenu, 1966.

Goshen, Ze'ev (Seev). "Eichmann und die Nisko-Aktion im Oktober 1939." *Vierteljahresheft für Zeitgeschichte*, Nr. 1/1981, 74–96.

Graml, Hermann. *Der 9. November 1938*. Bonn: Bundeszentrale für Heimatdienst, 1957.

———. *Reichskristallnacht: Antisemitismus und Judenverfolgung im Dritten Reich* (dtv 4519; Deutsche Geschichte der neusten Zeit. München: Deutscher Taschenbuch-Verlag, 1988).

Grenville, Anthony. "Charles Kapralik," *The Association of Jewish Refugees Journal*, December 2013. http://www.ajr.org.uk/index.cfm/section.journal/issue.Dec13/article=14001.

Grill, P. Severin. *Der Talmud und Schulchan Aruch: Eine theologische Studie für weitere Kreise.* Graz/Leipzig: U. Moser, 1934.

Gruenwald, Max. "The Beginning of the 'Reichsvertretung'." *Leo Baeck Institute Year Book* 1, 1956.

Gutkas, Karl. *Kaiser Josef II: Eine Biographie.* Wien: P. Zsolnay, 1989.

Hannak, Jacques. *Karl Renner und seine Zeit: Versuch einer Biographie.* Wien: Europa-Verlag, 1965.

Helmer, Oskar. *50 Jahre erlebte Geschichte.* Wien: Verlag der Wiener Volksbuchhandlung, 1957.

Hilberg, Raul. *The Destruction of the European Jews.* Chicago: Quadrangle Books, 1961.

Hoehne, Heinz. *The Order of the Death's Head: The Story of Hitler's S.S.* Translated by Richard H. Barry. New York: Penguin Books, 1971.

Hofer, Walther, ed. *Der Nationalsozialismus: Dokumente 1933–1945.* Frankfurt/Main: Fischer Bücherei, 1957.

The Holy Scriptures, 25th edition. Philadelphia: Jewish Publication Society, 5711–1951.

Jaffe, Benjamin, and Cecil Roth. "Bentwich." *Encyclopaedia Judaica*, vol. 3, 2nd edition. Ed. Michael Berenbaum and Fred Skolnik. Macmillan Reference USA, *Gale Virtual Reference Library*, 2007, p. 381.

Jaspers, Karl. *Schicksal und Wille: Autobiographische Schriften*, ed. Hans Saner. München: Piper, 1967.

Kampmann, Wanda, *Deutsche und Juden: Studien zur Geschichte der Deutschen Juden*. Heidelberg: Schneider, 1963.

Kochan, Lionel. *Pogrom: 10 November 1938.* London: A. Deutsch, 1957.

Kohut, Alexander, *Tosafot ha-arukh ha-shalem* (Publication of the Alexander Kohut Memorial Foundation, vol. 8; Vienna: Mosad Le Zicarohn Aleksander Kohut, 1937).

Kranzler, David. *Japanese, Nazis & Jews: The Jewish Refugee Community of Shanghai, 1939–1945*. New York: Yeshiva University Press, 1976.

Krausnick, Helmut. "Judenverfolgung." In *Anatomie des SS-Staates*, Vol. 2, 3rd edition. Ed. Hans Buchheim, Martin Broszat, Hans-Adolf Jacobsen, and Helmut Krausnick. München: Deutscher Taschenbuch Verlag, 1982.

Lamed, Meir. "Arnstein (Arnsteiner)." *Encyclopedia Judaica* 3, 488–91.

Laqueur, Walter. *A History of Zionism.* New York: Holt, Rinehart and Winston, 1972.

Lewy, Guenter. *The Catholic Church and Nazi Germany.* New York: McGraw-Hill, 1965.

Lochner, Louis P. (ed. and trans.). *The Goebbels Diaries 1942–1943*. Garden City, NY: Doubleday & Co., 1948.

Loewenberg, Peter. "The Kristallnacht as Degradation Ritual." *Simon Wiesenthal Center Annual* 2, 1985.

Maurer, Trude. "Abschiebung und Attentat." In *Der Judenpogrom 1938. Von der 'Reichskristallnacht' zum Völkermord*, ed. Walter H. Pehle. Frankfurt [Main]: Fischer, 1988.

Mendelsohn, John, ed. *The Holocaust: Selected Documents in 18 Volumes, Vol. 6: Jewish Emigration 1938–1940*. New York/London: Garland, 1982.

Morton, Frederic. *The Rothschilds: A Family Portrait*. New York: Atheneum, 1963.

Moser, Jonny. "Die Entrechtung der Juden im Dritten Reich." In *Der Judenpogrom 1938. Von der 'Reichskristallnacht' zum Völkermord*, ed. Walter H. Pehle. Frankfurt [Main]: Fischer, 1988.

———. *Die Judenverfolgung in Österreich 1938–1945*. Vienna/Frankfurt/Zurich: Europa-Verlag, 1966.

———. "Die Verfolgung der Juden." In *Widerstand und Verfolgung in Wien 1934–1945: Eine Dokumentation Vol. 3* (Dokumentationsarchiv des Österreichischen Widerstandes), ed. Wolfgang Neugebauer. Wien: Österreichischer Bundesverlag für Unterricht, Wissenschaft und Kunst, 1975.

Murmelstein, Benjamin. *Einige Fragen an Prof. Dr. P. Severin Grill, O. Cist., Verfasser der theolog. Studie "Der Talmud und Schulchan Aruch."* Wien: Union österreichischer Juden, 1935.

———. *Flavius Josephus*. Wien: Verlag Josef Belf, 1938.

———. *Geschichte der Juden: Des Volkes Weltwandern*. Wien: Verlag Josef Belf, 1938.

Neugebauer, Wolfgang, ed., *Widerstand und Verfolgung in Wien 1934–1945: Eine Dokumentation Vol. 3* (2nd edition; Dokumentationsarchiv des Österreichischen Widerstandes). Wien: Österreichischer Bundesverlag für Unterricht, Wissenschaft und Kunst, 1984.

Paul, Gerhard. *"Deutsche Mutter, heim zu Dir!" Warum es misslang, Hitler an der Saar zu schlagen: Der Saarkampf 1933–1935*. Köln: Bund-Verlag, 1984.

Pehle, Walter H., ed., *Der Judenpogrom 1938. Von der 'Reichskristallnacht' zum Völkermord*. Frankfurt [Main]: Fischer, 1988.

Perl, William R. *Operation Action: Rescue from the Holocaust*. New York: Ungar, 1978.

Prinz, Arthur. "The Role of the Gestapo in Obstructing and Promoting Jewish Emigration." *Yad Vashem Studies* 2, 1958.

Reich, E. "Das Problem der Immigration nach USA." *Jüdisches Nachrichtenblatt*, December 23, 1940, 1f.

Reimann, Viktor. *Innitzer: Kardinal zwischen Hitler und Rom*. Wien: Molden, 1967.

Rosenkranz, Herbert. "The Destruction of the Jewish Community in Austria 1938–45." In *The Jews of Austria: Essays on Their Life, History and Destruction*, ed. Josef Fraenkel. London: Vallentine, Mitchell, 1967.

———. *"Reichskristallnacht" 9. November 1938 in Österreich*. Wien: Europa Verlag, 1968.

———. *Verfolgung und Selbstbehauptung: Die Juden in Osterreich 1938–1945*. Wien/München: Herold, 1978.

Rosenstock, Werner. "Exodus 1933–1939, A Survey of Jewish Emigration from Germany." *Leo Baeck Institute Yearbook* 1, 1956.

Safrian, Hans, and Hans Witek. *Und keiner war dabei: Dokumente des alltäglichen Antisemitismus in Wien 1938*. Wien: Picus, 1988.

Seligsohn, Max. "Obornik (Obernik), Meïr." *The Jewish Encyclopedia* 9: 371.

Seraphim, Hans-Günther, ed. *Das politische Tagebuch Alfred Rosenbergs 1934/5 und 1939/40*. München: Deutscher Taschenbuch Verlag, 1964.

Slutsky, Yehuda. "'Illegal' Immigration." *Encyclopedia Judaica* 8: 1248–54.

Strauss, Herbert A. "Jewish Emigration from Germany, Nazi Policies and Jewish Responses." *Leo Baeck Institute Year Book* 25 (1980); *Leo Baeck Institute Year Book* 26 (1981).

Sulzer, Salomon. *Schir Zion*. Vienna: H. Engel, 1840 (1837).

Szold, Henrietta. "Arnstein, Fanny (Fögele) von." *The Jewish Encyclopedia* 2: 133.

Trunk, Isaiah. *Judenrat: The Jewish Councils in Eastern Europe under Nazi Occupation*. New York: Macmillan, 1972.

von Papen, Franz. *Der Wahrheit eine Gasse.* München: P. List, 1952, 491f. [*Memoir*, Translated by Brian Connell. New York: Dutton 1953 (1952)].

von Schuschnigg. Kurt. *Im Kampf gegen Hitler: Die Überwindung der Anschlussidee*. Wien: Amalthea, 1969.

von Weisl, Wolfgang. "Illegale Transporte." In *The Jews of Austria: Essays on Their Life, History and Destruction,* ed. Josef Fraenkel. London: Vallentine, Mitchell & Co.

Wagner, Dieter, and Gerhard Tomkowitz. *"Ein Volk, ein Reich, ein Führer!": Der Anschluss Österreichs, 1938.* München: Piper, 1968; in English: *Anschluss: The Week Hitler Seized Vienna*, trans. Geoffrey Strachan. New York/London: St. Martin's Press, 1971.

Wasserstein, Bernard. *Britain and the Jews of Europe 1939–1945.* London: Institute of Jewish Affairs / New York: Oxford University Press, 1979.

Weinzierl, Erika."Christen und Juden nach der NS-Machtergreifung in Österreich," In *Anschluß 1938: Protokoll des Symposiums in Wien am 14. und 15. März 1978.–Wien 1981*, 175–205. Veröffentlichungen der Wissenschaftlichen Kommission des Theodor-Körner-Stiftungsfonds und des Leopold-Kunschak-Preises zur Erforschung der österreichischen Geschichte der Jahre 1918 bis 1938, München: Oldenbourg, 1981.

———. *Zu wenig Gerechte: Österreicher und Judenverfolgung 1938–1945.* Graz: Styria, 1969.

Weis, Georg. *Totenbuch Theresienstadt 1: Deportierte aus Österreich.* Wien: Jüdisches Komitee für Theresienstadt, 1971.

Wiernik, Peter. "Ben-Ze'eb, Judah Löb." *The Jewish Encyclopedia* 2: 681f.

Wyman, David S. *Paper Walls: America and the Refugee Crisis 1938–1941.* Amherst: University of Massachusetts Press, 1968.

Yahil, Chaim. "Edelstein, Jacob." *Encyclopedia Judaica* 6: 365.

Zwergbaum, Aharon. "Patria." *Encyclopedia Judaica* 13:181.

Index

Page references in *italics* indicate photographs.

H

R

S

About the Authors

Leonard H. Ehrlich earned his doctorate degree at Yale University. From 1956 to 1991 he was professor of Philosophy, professor of Judaic Studies, and the founding director of the Judaic Studies Program (later Department of Judaic and Near Eastern Studies) at the University of Massachusetts at Amherst. His wife, **Edith Ehrlich née Schwarz**, earned her master's at Yale University and her doctorate at the University of Massachusetts. Both Leonard and Edith were born in Vienna, where they attended school together and whence they fled the Nazi occupation of Austria—Edith first to England on a *Kindertransport* and then to the United States, and Leonard directly to the United States. The two were eventually reunited and married when Leonard was drafted into the U.S. Army to serve as a frontline medic on the European front, in which capacity he was awarded the Silver Star and the Purple Heart. Following the war, Leonard and Edith took their undergraduate degrees at Roosevelt College (later University) in Chicago, before continuing their studies at the University of Basel, Switzerland. While pursuing degrees in Psychology there, the Ehrlichs became disciples of philosopher Karl Jaspers and changed the focus of their studies as a result. A contact established for them by Jaspers led them to return to the States to continue their studies at Yale. Over the ensuing decades, Leonard would become a leading scholar of twentieth-century continental — including Jewish — philosophy and the doyen of Jaspers studies, while Edith pursued a career as a teacher, translator, and researcher. Leonard and Edith Ehrlich would be inseparable partners, intellectual collaborators, and frequent coauthors for sixty-seven years, until their deaths in 2011 and 2015, respectively.

Carl S. Ehrlich earned his doctorate at Harvard University in Near Eastern Languages and Civilizations, specializing in Biblical and Ancient Near Eastern Studies. He is currently professor of History and of Humanities at York University in Toronto, where he also serves as director of the Israel and Golda Koschitzky Centre for Jewish Studies. Among his publications are the monograph *The Philistines in Transition: A History from ca. 1000–730 B.C.E.* (1996) and the edited collection *From an Antique Land: An Introduction to Ancient Near Eastern Literature* (2009).